MW01620822

JURISPRUDENCE AND PERSUASION: "YOU CAN'T ARGUE LIKE THAT"

A CASE-BASED APPROACH

■ ■ ■

Ralph G. Steinhardt
Professor of Law and International Affairs
Lobingier Professor of Comparative Law and Jurisprudence
The George Washington University

Benjamin Teich
Of the California Bar

AMERICAN CASEBOOK SERIES®

444 Cedar Street, Suite 700
St. Paul, MN 55101
1-877-888-1330

Printed in the United States of America

ISBN: 978-0-314-28127-2

PREFACE

In 1727, the great English poet and critic, Alexander Pope, published *The Art of Sinking in Poetry*, offering some vicious instruction in how *not* to write a poem. He did this not by developing a grand theory of poetry or a systematic school of criticism. He did it by parodying poets who had reached for the sublime and delivered the ridiculous. His advice drips with pointed personal references and irony, recommending for example that poets use grand language and absurd metaphors to glorify repulsive or meaningless things. Pope's essay had its limitations. It was a lousy way to make friends, and it comes across now as one long inside joke. Besides, tastes about poems vary and change, and what sounded ridiculous to a great poet of the eighteenth century may seem unexceptional to mere mortals in the twenty-first. On the other hand, the appeal of using actual examples to show how the language chosen to communicate an idea matters (and matters fundamentally) is not limited to poems or poets.

In fact, in some respects, this book is about "the art of sinking in law"—common forms of argument that should fail but don't always get what they deserve. Sometimes these arguments are about the nature of law generally and fall within the discipline of philosophy. They are arguments about jurisprudence. But sometimes the arguments are more earth-bound. They are made to win one particular case, on particular facts, under particular law. On the surface at least, these latter arguments are not philosophical at all. If they fall within any general discipline, it's advocacy. A prior generation would have recognized this art of persuasion as "rhetoric"—one of the seven original liberal arts taught at the medieval universities. The term has lost that original meaning and has come to mean something closer to verbiage, propaganda, or posturing. In this book, however, the term "rhetoric" is used without irony or deprecation. Understood as the art of argument, it is exactly what lawyers do. Honing it and keeping it respectable is in every law professor's job description.

This course offers a case-based approach to arguments about the nature of law, authority, and persuasion. In Part I, we examine some of the traditional and contemporary schools of jurisprudence (*e.g.*, natural law, positivism, law and economics, feminist legal theory, legal realism, and critical legal studies). In contrast to many jurisprudence texts, this book works primarily through decided cases and recurring forms of argument in court and then secondarily through the writings of philosophers and jurists. The unifying idea here is that every decided case has a philosophy within it, whether acknowledged or not. Each case at least implicitly reflects a judge's notion of his or her role and the propriety of relying on particular sources of law or axioms of inference. In Part II, a modern riff on rhetoric, we analyze certain identifiable types of legal arguments, including *inter alia* reasoning by default (*e.g.*, fictions, presumptions, and burdens), recurring fallacies (*e.g.*, begging the question, arguments *ad hominem*, asserting the consequent), and the nested problems of interpreting statutes and the common law. In Part III, we test what we know (or think we know) about theories of law by applying them in a particular setting: is international law really "law"? What is "property"?

Certain rules have guided this work. (i) If you're going to do philosophy, you have to have something to philosophize about. If for example, you want to develop a philosophy of science, it helps to know some science. If you want to develop a philosophy of law, it's helpful to have an understanding of law in the first place, including how particular cases are decided. You must be able to explain why a certain decision went the way it did before you can see a philosophical orientation within it and the uses to which that orientation (among others) might be put in future cases. We are in short looking for theory that can face the facts. (ii) The law is not an autonomous discipline and can be approached profitably from a number of perspectives—aesthetics, anthropology, literature—only some of which typically wend their way into the law school curriculum. (iii) Just because something is abstract doesn't mean that it has to be vague. And (iv) just because something is complex doesn't mean that it cannot be said simply.

Alexander Pope suffered many disabilities, but he had one big, unfair advantage. He was enough of a genius to transcend gossip and superiority even as he pointed out archetypes of failure. He left a literary legacy of beauty and humor and power. Our ambitions are modest: find the value in the humane arts of argument, even if the arguments in some of our examples sink before our eyes.

RALPH G. STEINHARDT

Washington, D.C.
March 2018

ACKNOWLEDGMENTS

I have many people to thank. Two people expressed faith in this book long before I felt it, and they kept the faith even when I lost it: Ben Teich, my former student and now my co-author, and Louis Higgins at West. Without them, this book would never have seen the light of day. Over the years, a virtual army of students brought a clear-eyed and intelligent enthusiasm to the manuscript and made it incomprehensibly better than it would otherwise have been. And every professor should be so lucky with their research assistants over the years. Julia Duke did especially brilliant and sustained work whipping the manuscript into proper form, and my deepest gratitude go to her and to Kate Bailey, Arin Brenner, Sarah Freuden, Scott Gilmore, Morgan Kelley, Janaat Majeed, Adriana Sarfarazi, Sahar Saqib, Jay Shah, Wendy Simon-Pearson, Stephen Walls, and Laura Withers. At the end of the day, this book has been a family project, and I dedicate it to the lights of my life—my wife, Donna Scarboro, and our children, Ruth and Tavi.

RGS

I want to thank my co-author, Professor Ralph Steinhardt, and the George Washington Law School for providing me with the unparalleled opportunity to transform my fledgling idea for a course into one of the most fantastic projects I've ever worked on in my life. I would also like to thank Professor Ira Lupu for his sage advice and my brother for his unwavering belief in me, in this and in all of my endeavors. Finally, I dedicate this book to my parents in hopes that it honors some of the principles which they encouraged me to live by: constant curiosity, pursuit of challenge, maintenance of perspective and self-reliance.

BT

PERMISSIONS

The authors gratefully acknowledge the permissions granted by the copyright holders to reprint portions of the following publications. All other materials in the book are original to the authors, in the public domain, or otherwise protected by the fair use doctrine under the laws of the United States.

Chapter 1

MARTHA C. NUSSBAUM, FROM DISGUST TO HUMANITY: SEXUAL ORIENTATION AND CONSTITUTIONAL LAW (2010)

LON FULLER, THE MORALITY OF LAW (1969)

JOHN FINNIS, NATURAL LAW AND NATURAL RIGHTS (1980)

Chapter 2

HANS KELSEN, GENERAL THEORY OF LAW AND STATE (1945)

H. L. A. HART, THE CONCEPT OF LAW (1962)

Chapter 3

Sanford Levinson, *Return of Legal Realism,* THE NATION (Jan. 8, 2001)

Herbert Wechsler, *Toward Neutral Principles of Constitutional Law*, 73 HARV. L. REV. 1 (1959)

Oliver Wendell Holmes, *The Path of the Law*, 10 HARV. L. REV. 457 (1897)

Karl N. Llewellyn, *Some Realism About Realism—Responding to Dean Pound*, 44 HARV. L. REV. 1222 (1931)

JEROME FRANK, LAW AND THE MODERN MIND (1930)

Felix S. Cohen, *Transcendental Nonsense and the Functional Approach*, 35 COLUM. L. REV. 809 (1935)

Joseph William Singer, *Legal Realism Now*, 76 CAL. L. REV. 465 (1988)

Thomas J. Miles & Cass R. Sunstein, *The New Legal Realism*, 75 U. CHI. L. REV. 831 (2008)

Chapter 4

Charles F. Sabel & William H. Simon, *Contextualizing Regimes: Institutionalization as a Response to the Limits of Interpretation and Policy Engineering*, 110 MICH. L. REV. 1265 (2012)

Robert Pear, "Justices' Ruling in Discrimination Case May Draw Quick Action by Obama," *New York Times* (January 4, 2009)

Michael Dorf, *Legal Indeterminacy and Institutional Design*, 78 N.Y.U. L. REV. 875 (2003)

WILLIAM ESKRIDGE AND PHILIP FRICKEY, EDS.. HART AND SACKS' THE LEGAL PROCESS: BASIC PROBLEMS IN THE MAKING AND APPLICATION OF LAW (1994)

Richard A. Posner, *What Has Pragmatism to Offer Law?*, 63 S. CAL. L. REV. 1653 (1990)

Chapter 5

Ronald Coase, *The Problem of Social Cost*, 3 J. LAW & ECON. 1 (1960)

Keith N. Hylton, *Calabresi and the Intellectual History of Law and Economics*, 64 MD. L. REV. 85 (2005)

Thomas F. Cotter, *Legal Pragmatism and the Law and Economics Movement*, 84 GEO. L.J. 2071 (1996)

Louis Kaplow & Steven Shavell, *Economic Analysis of Law*, 3 HANDBOOK OF PUBLIC ECONOMICS 1761 (A.J. Auerbach & M. Feldstein, 2002)

DANIEL H. PINK, DRIVE, THE SURPRISING TRUTH ABOUT WHAT MOTIVATES US (2009)

Christine Jolls, Cass R. Sunstein, & Richard Thaler, *A Behavioral Approach to Law and Economics*, 50 STAN. L. REV. 1471

Chapter 6

Jay M. Feinman & Peter Gabel, *Contract Law as Ideology*, in THE POLITICS OF LAW: A PROGRESSIVE CRITIQUE 373 (1990)

Clare Dalton, *An Essay in the Deconstruction of Contract Doctrine,* 94 YALE L.J. 997 (1985)

Roberto Unger, *The Critical Legal Studies Movement*, 96 HARV. L. REV. 561 (1983)

Chapter 7

Chisun Lee, "Counter 'Revolution:' FCC Dubs Feminist Lyrics 'Patently Offensive'," *The Village Voice* (19 June 2001)

DEBRAN ROWLAND, THE BOUNDARIES OF HER BODY: THE TROUBLING HISTORY OF WOMEN'S RIGHTS IN AMERICA 5 (2004)

Nadine Taub & Elizabeth M. Schneider, *Women's Subordination and the Rule of Law*, in THE POLITICS OF LAW: A PROGRESSIVE CRITIQUE 151 (1990)

Angela P. Harris, *Race and Essentialism in Feminist Legal Theory*, 42 STAN. L. REV. 581 (1990)

Chapter 8

Mari Matsuda & Charles R. Lawrence III, *Epilogue: Burning Crosses and the R.A.V. Case*, in WORDS THAT WOUND: CRITICAL RACE THEORY, ASSAULTIVE SPEECH, AND THE FIRST AMENDMENT 133 (1993)

Patricia Williams, *Spirit-Murdering the Messenger: The Discourse of Finger-Pointing as the Law's Response to Racism*, 42 U. MIAMI L. REV. 127 (1987)

W. Haywood Burns, *Law and Race in Early America*, in THE POLITICS OF LAW: A PROGRESSIVE CRITIQUE 115 (1990)

Paul Butler, *Racially Based Jury Nullification: Black Power in the Criminal Justice System*, 105 YALE L.J. 677 (1995)

Richard Delgado & Jean Stefancic, *Critical Perspectives on Police, Policing, and Mass Incarceration*, 104 GEO. L.J. 1531 (2016)

Chapter 9

W. WARD FEARNSIDE & WILLIAM B. HOLTHER, FALLACY: THE COUNTERFEIT OF ARGUMENT (1959)

Chapter 10

Laurence H. Tribe, *The Curvature of Constitutional Space: What Lawyers Can Learn from Modern Physics*, 103 HARV. L. REV. 1 (1989)

W. Bradley Wendel, *Explanation in Legal Scholarship: The Inferential Structure of Doctrinal Legal Analysis*, 96 CORNELL L. REV. 1035 (2011)

Alan M. Trammell & Derek E. Bambauer, *Personal Jurisdiction and the "Interwebs,"* 100 CORNELL L. REV. 1129 (2015)

Chapter 11

Peter J. Smith, *New Legal Fictions*, 95 GEO. L.J. 1435 (2007)

Chapter 12

Karl N. Llewellyn, *Remarks on the Theory of Appellate Decision and the Rules or Canons About How Statutes Are To Be Construed*, 3 VAND. L. REV. 395 (1950)

Stephen Breyer, *On the Uses of Legislative History in Interpreting Statutes*, 65 S. CAL. L. REV. 845 (1992)

RONALD DWORKIN, LAW'S EMPIRE (1986)

William N. Eskridge, Jr., *Dynamic Statutory Interpretation*, 35 U. PA. L. REV. 1479 (1987)

Amanda L. Tyler, *Continuity, Coherence, and the Canons*, 99 NW. U. L. REV. 1389 (2005)

Chapter 13

H.L.A. HART, THE CONCEPT OF LAW (1961)

Frederick Schauer, *Precedent*, 39 STAN. L. REV. 571 (1987)

Pierre Leval, *Judging Under the Constitution: Dicta About Dicta*, 81 N.Y.U. L. REV. 1249 (2006)

Chapter 14

Hans Kelsen, *The Pure Theory of Law and Analytical Jurisprudence*, 55 HARV. L. REV. 44 (1941)

MARY ELLEN O'CONNELL, THE POWER AND PURPOSE OF INTERNATIONAL LAW: INSIGHTS FROM THE THEORY AND PRACTICE OF ENFORCEMENT (2008)

Jack Goldsmith & Eric Posner, *The New International Law Scholarship*, 34 GA. J. INT'L & COMP. L. 463 (2006)

Roger Fisher, *Bringing Law to Bear on Governments*, 74 HARV. L. REV. 1130 (1961)

ABRAM CHAYES, THOMAS EHRLICH, & ANDREAS F. LOWENFELD,INTERNATIONAL LEGAL PROCESS: MATERIALS FOR AN INTRODUCTORY COURSE (1968)

Harold Koh, *Transnational Legal Process*, 75 NEB. L. REV. 181 (1996)

JOEL P. TRACHTMAN, THE ECONOMIC STRUCTURE OF INTERNATIONAL LAW (2008)

MOHAMMED BEDJAOUI, TOWARDS A NEW INTERNATIONAL ECONOMIC ORDER (1979)

MARTII KOSKENNIEMI, FROM APOLOGY TO UTOPIA: THE STRUCTURE OF INTERNATIONAL LAW ARGUMENT (2005)

Hilary Charlesworth, Christine Chinkin, & Shelley Wright, *Feminist Approaches to International Law*, 85 AMER. J. INT'L L. 613 (1991)

Makau Mutua, *Critical Race Theory and International Law: Convergence and Divergences*, 45 VILL. L. REV. 841 (2000)

W. Michael Reisman, Seigfried Wiessner & Andrew R. Willard, *The New Haven School: A Brief Introduction*, 32 YALE J. INT'L L. 575 (2007).

SUMMARY OF CONTENTS

PART I. PHILOSOPHIES OF LAW THROUGH THE CASES

PART II. RECURRING ARGUMENT TYPES THROUGH THE CASES

PART III. PERSPECTIVES TESTED

TABLE OF CONTENTS

PART III. PERSPECTIVES TESTED

TABLE OF CASES

The principal cases are in bold type.

JURISPRUDENCE AND PERSUASION: "YOU CAN'T ARGUE LIKE THAT"

A CASE-BASED APPROACH

PART I

PHILOSOPHIES OF LAW THROUGH THE CASES

■ ■ ■

CHAPTER ONE

LAW, JUSTICE, AND THE PROBLEM OF TASTE: ARGUMENTS FROM (AND ABOUT) NATURAL LAW

■ ■ ■

"Deep-seated preferences cannot be argued about—you cannot argue a man into liking a glass of beer. . . ."

— Oliver Wendell Holmes, Jr.

De gustibus non disputandum est ("There is no arguing about matters of taste.")

Orientation

One of the most persistent and provocative ways of thinking about the law is that it consists in principles of right and wrong that are independent from and superior to the law enacted by governments. By assertion, this higher law is inherent in nature and so is valid across time, cultures, religions, politics, and geography. It is not "at the mercy of the State"[1] or any other human choices. This natural law provides a standard of justice against which laws and cases can (or must) be judged. In his encapsulation of the natural law argument, for example, Augustine observed that "An unjust law is no law at all"—a clear subordination of human law to some higher moral law. In the modern era, not all natural law theorists are comfortable with the religious premises on which Augustine based his notion of justice, nor are they entirely sure what it means to say that an unjust law is "no law at all."[2] But the idea persists that the written or "positive" law of human beings can get in the way of moral decision-making and that an unjust law carries with it no moral obligation to obey. In short, at the heart of natural law theory, there exist certain norms that are by assertion permanent, grounded in nature, superior to the enacted or positive law, and accessible to human reason.

The nineteenth-century philosopher Jeremy Bentham famously referred to naturalism as "rhetorical nonsense—nonsense upon stilts," because he thought that justice was properly a matter of debate, not

---

1 JOHN CHIPMAN GRAY, NATURE AND SOURCES OF THE LAW 87 (1909).

2 *See, e.g.*, Jules L. Coleman, *The Architecture of Jurisprudence*, 121 YALE L.J. 2 (2011) ("If history is to be a guide, one cannot help but be struck by the fact that morally bad law is not merely conceptually possible but all too frequently realized.").

unchangeable or universal dogma. It became orthodox to separate law from morality, or more specifically to separate the existence of a law from its morality or justice. In the contemporary world of law and lawyers, it is certainly not uncommon to focus more on rules than on justice, and the effect on pedagogy, practice, and judging is profound: professors of law routinely ask their students to articulate the applicable rule in a case, rather than to assess its goodness. The justice of a rule may reflect something too idiosyncratic, too personal, too undiscussably taste-like—to be shared by other people, let alone enforceable as law. From that perspective, justice might be a political or religious concept but not necessarily a legal one. Similarly, in the courtroom, judges rarely agonize in print over a case in which justice may point in one direction and the applicable rules point in another. Instead, the rules will be identified and applied, while the "humane side of the question" must be addressed "not in the laws of [human beings], but in that higher law, the violation of which is condemned by the voice of conscience, whose sentence of punishment for the recreant act is swift and sure." *Union Pac. Ry. Co. v. Cappier*, 66 Kan. 649, 72 P. 281 (1903).

At a minimum, this discomfort with natural law argumentation reflects skepticism about morality and language. Specifically, from the critical perspective, to say that "stealing is *morally* wrong" is logically equivalent to saying "I really hate stealing" or "stealing—yuck." It is in short a report about the speaker's inner subjective feelings but says nothing objective or testable. By contrast, it is possible to come up with an apparently objective test for determining whether stealing is *legally* wrong: you look at the statute books or the enforcement practices of the police or the cases in which stealing is punished. Then, instead of some idiosyncratic notion of right and wrong, there is something empirical or objective to discuss and prove.

But nagging questions persist: is any rule really as depersonalized and determinative as it appears, and—equally important—*must* an argument about morality or justice or right and wrong devolve into an argument like whether spinach (or Holmes' "glass of beer") is delicious or not?

TRAITON V. TRAITON

23 Eng. Rep. 554 (1686)

[By the Lord Chancellor, in the English equity courts.] [*Summary*:] One differing with his mother settles his mansion-house on his brother, but first takes a bond from him in his sister's name that the brother should not permit his mother to come into the house. [*Held*:] Bond set aside in equity as an unnatural bond.

The heir [the eldest son, who owned the estate upon his father's death,] having had some difference with his mother, relating to the repairs of the mansion-house, he settles the estate upon his brother, but first takes a penal bond from him of £500 penalty in the name of the defendant his sister, that he should never suffer his mother to come into the house. . . .

The Court . . . decreed the bond to be delivered up and cancelled; *it being against the law of nature to prohibit a son to cherish his mother.*

It appears from the pleadings that the mother lived in the house several years, paying no rent and suffering it to run to decay, and that the heir fearing his mother would so continue to do after his death, and to make some provision for his sister (who had no portion), in case of such an event, took the bond from his brother as above stated.

The bond being in court was delivered in, and cancelled by the Register in open court, and afterwards delivered to the plaintiff.

NOTES AND QUESTIONS

1. *"Laws of nature" and the resolution of actual cases.* When the Lord Chancellor declares in *Traiton* that prohibiting a son "to cherish his mother" is against the law of nature, what kind of "law" is he talking about, and what authority can he draw upon to establish the existence of such a law? Is there *still* a law of nature along those lines, and how would you go about trying to prove that such a law exists or not?

2. *The institutional setting: law versus equity.* Courts of *equity*, like the Court of Chancery that decided *Traiton*, were common law courts that operated separately from courts of *law* and had their own procedures, their own remedies (*e.g.* injunctions and the rescission or specific performance of contracts), and their own doctrines (*e.g.* the "unclean hands" doctrine). They had jurisdiction when the remedy "at law"—usually money damages—was inadequate to compensate the plaintiff fully. Most relevant for our purposes. the equity courts were understood to be courts of conscience and were "allowed, indeed required, to bring ethical judgments and concepts—'humanity and policy,' 'conscience,' '[t]he equity of the case,' 'obvious principles of justice and equity,' 'gross injustice,' 'moral obligation,' and 'the substantial justice of the case'—to bear on the facts of each case, as part of their formal judicial role." John R. Kroger, *Supreme Court Equity, 1789–1835, and the History of American Judging*, 34 HOUS. L. REV. 1425, 1481 (1998). From that perspective, the Lord Chancellor in *Traiton* had the institutional prerogative to consult principles not necessarily found in statutes or precedent. These principles included maxims like "equity does not require an idle gesture;" and "equity aids the vigilant, not those who slumber on their rights;" and "equity delights to do justice and not by halves."

Not surprisingly perhaps, there is a political explanation for the separation of law courts and equity courts in England.[3] Nor is it surprising that one critique of the English Court of Chancery at the time was that a judge's sense of justice might not be shared by any one else and that the equity courts therefore essentially measured equity according to "a Chancellor's Foot."[4] But—thinking more abstractly about this institutional arrangement—what, if anything, does the separate, parallel existence of courts of conscience say about the limits of law?

3. *The merger of law and equity in the United States.* Under the U.S. Constitution, the Supreme Court has jurisdiction over cases both "in Law and Equity," Art. III, § 2, and it sat as a court of equity from 1790 to 1938, when a single system of federal civil procedure was adopted, merging equity and law. Law and equity have also been merged substantively in this country: the term "common law" includes non-statutory principles that originated in the decisions of the courts of equity. Does this merger suggest that a lawyer's arguments grounded in abstract justice or conscience are always as relevant as arguments based on the text of a statute or a contract or a will? Which arguments—justice or text or some amalgam of the two—prevailed in the following case?

RIGGS V. PALMER

115 N.Y. 506, 22 N.E. 188 (1889)

EARL, J. On the 13th day of August 1880, Francis B. Palmer made his last will and testament, in which he gave small legacies to his two daughters, Mrs. Riggs and Mrs. Preston, the plaintiffs in this action, and the remainder of his estate to his grandson, the defendant, Elmer E. Palmer, subject to the support of Susan Palmer, his mother, with a gift over to the two daughters, subject to the support of Mrs. Palmer, in case Elmer should survive him and die under age, unmarried and without any issue. The testator at the date of his will owned a farm and considerable personal property. He was a widower, and thereafter, in March 1882, he was married to Mrs. Bresee, with whom before his marriage he entered into an ante-nuptial contract in which it was agreed that, in lieu of dower and all other claims upon his estate in case she survived him, she should have her support upon his farm during her life, and such support was expressly charged upon the farm. At the date of the will, and, subsequently, to the

---

[3] *See, e.g.*, Kristin A. Collins, *"A Considerable Surgical Operation": Article III, Equity and Judge-Made Law in the Federal Courts*, 60 DUKE L.J. 249, 266–67 (2010) ("Despite equity's association with higher notions of justice and the chancellor's conscience, by the seventeenth century equity had developed a sullied reputation in some sectors. Especially among religious and political dissenters, the English Chancery Court was associated with royal prerogative, judicial overreaching, and standardless discretion. . . .")

[4] JOHN SELDEN, TABLE-TALK: BEING THE DISCOURSES OF JOHN SELDEN, ESQ. 44 (London, E. Smith 1689), cited *Id.*, at note 73.

death of the testator, Elmer lived with him as a member of his family, and at his death was sixteen years old. He knew of the provisions made in his favor in the will, and, that he might prevent his grandfather from revoking such provisions, which he had manifested some intention to do, and to obtain the speedy enjoyment and immediate possession of his property, he willfully murdered him by poisoning him. He now claims the property, and the sole question for our determination is, can he have it? The defendants say that the testator is dead; that his will was made in due form and has been admitted to probate, and that, therefore, it must have effect according to the letter of the law.

It is quite true that statutes regulating the making, proof and effect of wills, and the devolution of property, if literally construed, and if their force and effect can in no way and under no circumstances be controlled or modified, give this property to the murderer.

The purpose of those statutes was to enable testators to dispose of their estates to the objects of their bounty at death, and to carry into effect their final wishes legally expressed; and in considering and giving effect to them this purpose must be kept in view. It was the intention of the law-makers that the donees in a will should have the property given to them. But it never could have been their intention that a donee who murdered the testator to make the will operative should have any benefit under it. If such a case had been present to their minds, and it had been supposed necessary to make some provision of law to meet it, it cannot be doubted that they would have provided for it. It is a familiar canon of construction that a thing which is within the intention of the makers of a statute is as much within the statute as if it were within the letter; and a thing which is within the letter of the statute is not within the statute, unless it be within the intention of the makers. The writers of laws do not always express their intention perfectly, but either exceed it or fall short of it, so that judges are to collect it from probable or rational conjectures only, and this is called rational interpretation; and Rutherforth, in his *Institutes* (p. 407), says: "When we make use of rational interpretation, sometimes we restrain the meaning of the writer so as to take in less, and sometimes we extend or enlarge his meaning so as to take in more than his words express."

Such a construction ought to be put upon a statute as will best answer the intention which the makers had in view * * *. In Bacon's *Abridgment* (*Statutes* I, 5); Puffendorf (book 5, chapter 12), Rutherforth (pp. 422, 427), and in Smith's *Commentaries* (814), many cases are mentioned where it was held that matters embraced in the general words of statutes, nevertheless, were not within the statutes, because it could not have been the intention of the law-makers that they should be included. They were taken out of the statutes by an equitable construction, and it is said in Bacon: "By an equitable construction, a case not within the letter of the statute is sometimes holden to be within the meaning, because it is within the mischief for which a remedy is provided. The reason for such construction is that the law-makers could not set down every case in express terms. In order to form a right judgment whether a case be within the equity of a statute, it is a good way to suppose the law-maker present, and that you have asked him this question, did you intend to comprehend this case? Then you must give yourself such answer as you imagine he, being an upright and reasonable man, would have given. If this be that he did mean to comprehend it, you may safely hold the case to be within the equity of the statute; for while you do no more than he would have done, you do not act contrary to the statute, but in conformity thereto." In some cases the letter of a legislative act is restrained by an equitable construction; in others it is enlarged; in others the construction is contrary to the letter. The equitable construction which restrains the letter of a statute is defined by Aristotle, as frequently quoted, in this manner: *Aequitas est correctio legis generaliter latœ qua parti deficit* ["Equity is a corrective to the defective parts of general legal rules"]. If the law-makers could, as to this case, be consulted, would they say that they intended by their general language that the property of a testator or of an ancestor should pass to one who had taken his life for the express purpose of getting his property? In 1 Blackstone's *Commentaries* (91) the learned author, speaking of the construction of statutes, says: "If there arise out of them any absurd consequences manifestly contradictory to common reason, they are, with regard to those collateral consequences, void. * * * When some collateral matter arises out of the general words, and happen to be unreasonable, then the judges are in decency to conclude that the consequence was not foreseen by the parliament, and, therefore, they are at liberty to expound the statute by equity and only *quod hoc* disregard it;" and he gives as an illustration, if an act of parliament gives a man power to try all causes that arise within his manor of Dale, yet, if a cause should arise in which he himself is party, the act is construed not to extend to that because it is unreasonable that any man should determine his own quarrel.

There was a statute in Bologna that whoever drew blood in the streets should be severely punished, and yet it was held not to apply to the case of a barber who opened a vein in the street. It is commanded in the *Decalogue* that no work shall be done upon the Sabbath, and yet, giving the command a rational interpretation founded upon its design, the Infallible Judge held that it did not prohibit works of necessity, charity or benevolence on that day.

What could be more unreasonable than to suppose that it was the legislative intention in the general laws passed for the orderly, peaceable and just devolution of property, that they should have operation in favor of one who murdered his ancestor that he might speedily come into the possession of his estate? Such an intention is inconceivable. We need not, therefore, be much troubled by the general language contained in the laws.

Besides, all laws as well as all contracts may be controlled in their operation and effect by general, fundamental maxims of the common law. No one shall be permitted to profit by his own fraud, or to take advantage of his own wrong, or to found any claim upon his own iniquity, or to acquire property by his own crime. These maxims are dictated by public policy, have their foundation in universal law administered in all civilized countries, and have nowhere been superseded by statutes. They were applied in the decision of the case of the *New York Mutual Life Insurance Company v. Armstrong* (117 U. S. 591). There it was held that the person who procured a policy upon the life of another, payable at his death, and then murdered the assured to make the policy payable, could not recover thereon. Mr. Justice Field, writing the opinion, said: "Independently of any proof of the motives of Hunter in obtaining the policy, and even assuming that they were just and proper, he forfeited all rights under it when, to secure its immediate payment, he murdered the assured. It would be a reproach to the jurisprudence of the country if one could recover insurance money payable on the death of a party whose life he had feloniously taken. As well might he recover insurance money upon a building that he had willfully fired."

These maxims, without any statute giving them force or operation, frequently control the effect and nullify the language of wills. A will procured by fraud and deception, like any other instrument, may be decreed void and set aside, and so a particular portion of a will may be excluded from probate or held inoperative if induced by the fraud or undue influence of the person in whose favor it is. (*Allen v. M'Pherson*, 1 H. L. Cas. 191; *Harrison's Appeal*, 48 Conn. 202.) So a will may contain provisions which are immoral, irreligious or against public policy, and they will be held void.

Here there was no certainty that this murderer would survive the testator, or that the testator would not change his will, and there was no certainty that he would get this property if nature was allowed to take its course. He, therefore, murdered the testator expressly to vest himself with an estate. Under such circumstances, what law, human or divine, will allow him to take the estate and enjoy the fruits of his crime? The will spoke and became operative at the death of the testator. He caused that death, and thus by his crime made it speak and have operation. Shall it speak and operate in his favor? If he had met the testator and taken his property by force, he would have had no title to it. Shall he acquire title by murdering him? If he had gone to the testator's house and by force compelled him, or by fraud or undue influence had induced him to will him his property, the law would not allow him to hold it. But can he give effect and operation to a will by murder, and yet take the property? To answer these questions in the affirmative, it seems to me, would be a reproach to the jurisprudence of our state, and an offense against public policy.

Under the civil law evolved from the general principles of natural law and justice by many generations of jurisconsults, philosophers and statesmen, one cannot take property by inheritance or will from an ancestor or benefactor whom he has murdered. (Domat, part 2, book 1, tit. 1, § 3; Code Napoleon, § 727; Mackeldy's *Roman Law*, 530, 550.) In the Civil Code of Lower Canada the provisions on the subject in the Code Napoleon have been substantially copied. But, so far as I can find, in no country where the common law prevails has it been deemed important to enact a law to provide for such a case. Our revisers and law-makers were familiar with the civil law, and they did not deem it important to incorporate into our statutes its provisions upon this subject. This is not a *casus omissus*. It was evidently supposed that the maxims of the common law were sufficient to regulate such a case and that a specific enactment for that purpose was not needed.

For the same reasons the defendant Palmer cannot take any of this property as heir. Just before the murder he was not an heir, and it was not certain that he ever would be. He might have died before his grandfather, or might have been disinherited by him. He made himself an heir by the murder, and he seeks to take property as the fruit of his crime. What has before been said as to him as legatee applies to him with equal force as an heir. He cannot vest himself with title by crime.

My view of this case does not inflict upon Elmer any greater or other punishment for his crime than the law specifies. It takes from him no property, but simply holds that he shall not acquire property by his crime, and thus be rewarded for its commission. * * *

The judgment of the General Term and that entered upon the report of the referee should, therefore, be reversed and judgment should be entered as follows: That Elmer E. Palmer and the administrator be enjoined from using any of the personalty or real estate left by the testator for Elmer's benefit; that the devise and bequest in the will to Elmer be declared ineffective to pass the title to him; that by reason of the crime of murder committed upon the grandfather he is deprived of any interest in the estate left by him; that the plaintiffs are the true owners of the real and personal estate left by the testator, subject to the charge in favor of Elmer's mother and the widow of the testator, under the ante-nuptial agreement, and that the plaintiffs have costs in all the courts against Elmer.

GRAY, J., dissenting [emphasis added]. This appeal presents an extraordinary state of facts, and the case, in respect of them, I believe, is without precedent in this state. The respondent, a lad of sixteen years of age, being aware of the provisions in his grandfather's will, which constituted him the residuary legatee of the testator's estate, caused his death by poison in 1882. For this crime he was tried and was convicted of murder in the second degree, and at the time of the commencement of this action he was serving out his sentence in the state reformatory. This action was brought by two of the children of the testator for the purpose of having those provisions of the will in the respondent's favor canceled and annulled.

The appellants' argument for a reversal of the judgment, which dismissed their complaint, is that the respondent unlawfully prevented a revocation of the existing will, or a new will from being made, by his crime, and that he terminated the enjoyment by the testator of his property and effected his own succession to it by the same crime. They say that to permit the respondent to take the property willed to him would be to permit him to take advantage of his own wrong.

To sustain their position the appellants' counsel has submitted an able and elaborate brief, and, *if I believed that the decision of the question could be affected by considerations of an equitable nature*, I should not hesitate to assent to views which commend themselves to the conscience. But the matter does not lie within the domain of conscience. We are bound by the rigid rules of law, which have been established by the legislature, and within the limits of which the determination of this question is confined. The question we are dealing with is, whether a testamentary disposition can be altered, or a will revoked, after the testator's death, through an appeal to the courts, when the legislature has, by its enactments, prescribed exactly when and how wills may be made, altered and revoked, and, apparently, as it seems to me, when they have been fully complied with, has left no room for the exercise of an equitable jurisdiction by courts over such matters. Modern jurisprudence, in recognizing the right of the individual, under more or less restrictions, to dispose of his property after his death, subjects it to legislative control, both as to extent and as to mode of exercise. Complete freedom of testamentary disposition of one's property has not been and is not the universal rule; as we see from the provisions of the Napoleonic Code, from those systems of jurisprudence in other countries which are modeled upon the Roman law, and from the statutes of many of our states. To the statutory restraints, which are imposed upon the disposition of one's property by will, are added strict and systematic statutory rules for the execution, alteration and revocation of the will; which must be, at least, substantially, if not exactly, followed to insure validity and performance. The reason for the establishment of such rules, we may naturally assume, consists in the purpose to create those safeguards about these grave and important acts, which experience has demonstrated to be the wisest and surest. That freedom, which is permitted to be exercised in the testamentary disposition of one's estate by the laws of the state, is subject to its being exercised in conformity with the regulations of the statutes. The capacity and the power of the individual to dispose of his property after death, and the mode by which that power can be exercised, are matters of which the legislature has assumed the entire control, and has undertaken to regulate with comprehensive particularity.

The appellants' argument is not helped by reference to those rules of the civil law, or to those laws of other governments, by which the heir or legatee is excluded from benefit under the testament, if he has been convicted of killing, or attempting to kill, the testator. In the absence of such legislation here, the courts are not empowered to institute such a system of remedial justice. The deprivation of the heir of his testamentary succession by the Roman law, when guilty of such a crime, plainly, was intended to be in the nature of a punishment imposed upon him. The succession, in such a case of guilt, escheated to the exchequer. (See Domat's *Civil Law*, pt. 2, book 1, tit. 1, § 3.)

I concede that rules of law, which annul testamentary provision made for the benefit of those who have become unworthy of them, may be based on principles of equity and of natural justice. It is quite reasonable to suppose that a testator would revoke or alter his will, where his mind has been so angered and changed as to make him unwilling to have his will executed as it stood. But these principles only suggest sufficient reasons for the enactment of laws to meet such cases.

The statutes of this state have prescribed various ways in which a will may be altered or revoked; but the very provision, defining the modes of alteration and revocation, implies a prohibition of alteration or revocation in any other way. The words of the section of the statute are: "No will in writing, except in the cases hereinafter mentioned, nor any part thereof, shall be revoked or altered otherwise," etc. Where, therefore, none of the cases mentioned are met by the facts, and the revocation is not in the way described in the section, the will of the testator is unalterable. I think that a valid will must continue as a will always, unless revoked in the manner provided by the statutes. Mere intention to revoke a will does not have the effect of revocation. The intention to revoke is necessary to constitute the effective revocation of a will; but it must be demonstrated by one of the acts contemplated by the statute. As Woodworth, J., said in *Dan v. Brown* (4 Cow. 490): "Revocation is an act of the mind, which must be demonstrated by some outward and visible sign of revocation." The same learned judge said in that case: "The rule is that if the testator lets the will stand until he dies, it is his will; if he does not suffer it to do so, it is not his will." (*Goodright v. Glasier*, 4 Burr. 2512, 2514; *Pemberton v. Pemberton*, 13 Ves. 290.)

The finding of fact of the referee, that, presumably, the testator would have altered his will, had he known of his grandson's murderous intent, cannot affect the question. We may concede it to the fullest extent; but still the cardinal objection is undisposed of, that the making and the revocation of a will are purely matters of statutory regulation, by which the court is bound in the determination of questions relating to these acts. Two cases in this state and in Kentucky, at an early day, seem to me to be much in point. *Gains v. Gains* (2 Marshall, 190), was decided by the Kentucky Court of Appeals in 1820. It was there urged that the testator intended to have destroyed his will, and that he was forcibly prevented from doing so by the defendant in error or devisee, and it was insisted that the will, though not expressly, was thereby virtually revoked. The court held, as the act concerning wills prescribed the manner in which a will might be revoked, that as none of the acts evidencing revocation were done, the intention could not be substituted for the act. In that case the will was snatched away and forcibly retained.

In 1854, Surrogate Bradford, whose opinions are entitled to the highest consideration, decided the case of *Leaycraft v. Simmons* (3 Bradf. 35). In that case the testator, a man of eighty-nine years of age, desired to make a codicil to his will, in order to enlarge the provisions for his daughter. His son having the custody of the instrument, and the one to be prejudiced by the change, refused to produce the will, at testator's request, for the purpose of alteration. The learned surrogate refers to the provisions of the civil law for such and other cases of unworthy conduct in the heir or legatee, and says, "our statute has undertaken to prescribe the mode in which wills can be revoked (citing the statutory provision). This is the law by which I am governed in passing upon questions touching the revocation of wills. The whole of this subject is now regulated by statute, and a mere intention to revoke, however well authenticated, or however defeated, is not sufficient." And he held that the will must be admitted to probate. I may refer also to a case in the Pennsylvania courts. In that state the statute prescribed the mode for repealing or altering a will, and in *Clingan v. Mitcheltree* (31 Pa. State Rep. 25) the Supreme Court of the state held, where a will was kept from destruction by the fraud and misrepresentation of the devisee, that to declare it canceled as against the fraudulent party would be to enlarge the statute.

I cannot find any support for the argument that the respondent's succession to the property should be avoided because of his criminal act, when the laws are silent. Public policy does not demand it, for the demands of public policy are satisfied by the proper execution of the laws and the punishment of the crime. There has been no convention between the testator and his legatee, nor is there any such contractual element in such a disposition of property by a testator, as to impose or imply conditions in the legatee. The appellants' argument practically amounts to this: That as the legatee has been guilty of a crime, by the commission of which he is placed in a position to sooner receive the benefits of the testamentary provision, his rights to the property should be forfeited and he should be divested of his estate. To allow their argument to prevail would involve the diversion by the court of the testator's estate into the hands of persons, whom, possibly enough, for all we know, the testator might not have chosen or desired as its recipients. Practically the court is asked to make another will for the testator. The laws do not warrant this judicial action, and mere presumption would not be strong enough to sustain it.

But more than this, to concede appellants' views would involve the imposition of an additional punishment or penalty upon the respondent. What power or warrant have the courts to add to the respondent's penalties by depriving him of property? The law has punished him for his crime, and we may not say that it was an insufficient punishment. In the trial and punishment of the respondent the law has vindicated itself for the outrage which he committed, and further judicial utterance upon the subject of punishment or deprivation of rights is barred. We may not, in the language of the court in *People v. Thornton* (25 Hun, 456), "enhance the pains, penalties and forfeitures provided by law for the punishment of crime."

The judgment should be affirmed, with costs.

NOTES AND QUESTIONS

1. *Understanding the analysis in Riggs.* Early in his opinion, Judge Earl concedes that "[i]t is quite true that statutes regulating the making, proof and effect of wills, and the devolution of property, *if literally construed*, and if their force and effect can in no way and under no circumstances be controlled or modified, give this property to the murderer." Why isn't that the end of the analysis? What justifies his resort to principles beyond the literal terms of the relevant statutes?

To answer that question, it is essential to identify and assess the various arguments in Judge Earl's opinion and the authorities on which they rest.

(a) Consider for example the authorities he cites for the general proposition that a statute can or must be read "past its letter" and specifically that it must be interpreted in light of its purposes. These include Aristotle, Blackstone, Pufendorf—all famous philosophers or jurists but none of them qualifying as a controlling statute or case within Judge Earl's jurisdiction.

(b) Moving from the general interpretation of statutes to the principle that "[n]o one shall be permitted to profit by his own fraud, or to take advantage of his own wrong," he declares that "[t]hese maxims are dictated by public policy, have their foundation in universal law administered in all civilized countries, and have nowhere been superseded by statutes." He draws on a decision of the U.S. Supreme Court—*New York Mutual Life Ins. Co. v. Armstrong*—dealing with the proceeds of a life insurance policy.

(c) On the most specific articulation of the issue in the case, Judge Earl says that "[u]nder the civil law evolved from the *general principles of natural law and justice* by many generations of jurisconsults, philosophers and statesmen, one cannot take property by inheritance or will from an ancestor or benefactor whom he has murdered." The cited authorities include statutory enactments in Roman law, the Code Napoleon, and the "Civil Code of Lower

Canada," followed by his assurance that the principle was so well established and incorporated into the common law that "a specific enactment for that purpose was not needed." In other words, these general principles of natural law and justice constitute the basis for determining what the rule of law is in the case.

2. *Principles supporting an opposite result.* Consider Judge Earl's apparent certainty that "it could *never* have been [the law makers'] intention that a donee who murdered the testator to make the will operative should have any benefit under it." Why might you be skeptical of any argument based on a reconstructed or hypothetical conversation with a prior legislator? Besides, isn't it possible to articulate principles that would have upheld the title of the murderer in *Riggs*—that there are in effect respectable justice arguments on both sides of case?

Judge Benjamin Cardozo articulated two possibilities in favor of the opposite result: (i) "There was the principle of the binding force of a will disposing of the estate of a testator in conformity with law." (ii) "There was the principle that civil courts may not add to the pains and penalties of crimes." BENJAMIN N. CARDOZO, THE NATURE OF THE JUDICIAL PROCESS 41 (1921). What do you think accounts for the court's rejection of these alternative principles? According to Cardozo,

> in the end, the principle that was thought to be most fundamental, to represent the larger and deeper social interests, put its competitors to flight. . . . The murderer lost the legacy for which the murder was committed because the social interest served by refusing to permit the criminal to profit from his crime is greater than that served by the preservation and enforcement of legal rights of ownership.

Id. at 42–43. Especially if you agree with this "social interest" rationale for the result, how would you go about justifying your choice to one who disagreed?

3. *On the necessity of a statute having a "literal" meaning.* Do you share Judge Earl's certainty that the statute in *Riggs* has only one "literal" meaning? Stanley Fish, a literary critic, observed with respect to a poem that "[t]he objectivity of the text is an illusion and, moreover, a dangerous illusion, because it is so physically convincing. . . . A line of print is so obviously *there* . . . that it seems to be the sole repository of whatever value and meaning we associate with it." STANLEY E. FISH, IS THERE A TEXT FOR THIS CLASS: THE AUTHORITY OF INTERPRETIVE COMMUNITIES 43 (1980). Applying that perspective to the statute in *Riggs*, Fish argued that

> [n]o reading is the literal reading in the sense that it is available apart from any purpose whatsoever. If it is assumed that the purpose of probate is to ensure the orderly devolution of property at all costs, then the statute in this case will have the plain meaning urged by the defendant; but if it is assumed that no law ever operates in favor of someone who would profit by his crime, then the "same" statute will have a meaning that is different, but no less plain. In either case, the statute will have been literally construed, and what the court will

> have done is prefer one literal construction to another by invoking one purpose (assumed background) rather than another.

Id. at 280. Does it seem plausible (or helpful) that a statute has no literal meaning apart from, or prior to, its interpretation?

4. *Are Riggs-like "principles" distinct from natural law?* It is true that Judge Earl uses the rhetoric of natural law in resolving *Riggs*, invoking it by name, and the case is frequently interpreted as an illustration of how statutes might be applied in conformity with principles of justice that stand outside the law enacted by human beings. But consider the argument that the principle adopted by the majority in *Riggs*—that no one may benefit from his or her own wrong—is simply derived from prior decisions in other settings by other judges, rather than from some higher morality that might be identified as natural law.

For example, Ronald Dworkin—whose writing is excerpted in later chapters—argued that *Riggs* was symptomatic of legal reasoning whenever a statute or some other rule, standing alone, is an inadequate guide to the resolution of a case. Without embracing any universal or "natural" test of morality (or demanding that statutes be read in light of such a thing), Dworkin highlighted a variety of non-rule stuff that the Anglo-American legal system makes relevant to the judge's task. Among these non-rule standards, *principles* have particular salience, not because they are binding or control the result the way a rule would, but because they have authority and weight in practice. They may be grounded in "justice or fairness or some other dimension of morality," RONALD DWORKIN, TAKING RIGHTS SERIOUSLY 75 (1977), but their power lies in "a sense of appropriateness developed in the profession and the public over time. Their continued power depends on this sense of appropriateness being sustained." *Id.* at 40. Is this natural law refined and rebranded or something else entirely?

5. *When are arguments from natural law, justice, or conscience pragmatic?* It is sometimes assumed that the notion of universal, natural law is inherently more controversial than, say, the meaning of the words used in a statute or a will. To put the skepticism in its most stereotypical form: justice—like taste in beer—is idiosyncratic, cultures vary, social conventions change over time, religious beliefs are less common now than they used to be. The mark of post-modernism is that ideas are radically indeterminate. On the other hand, as the following case suggests, lawyers can sometimes *use* arguments from conscience successfully, without agonizing over its origins, its coherence, or its universality. In short, without making any systematic argument about natural law or its legitimacy or its accessibility, consider the possibility that arguments from conscience can be intensely pragmatic. If arguments of that type make a practical difference in the outcome of some decided cases, even if rarely, on what principle exactly should they be resisted?

ROCHIN V. CALIFORNIA

342 U.S. 165 (1952)

MR. JUSTICE FRANKFURTER delivered the opinion of the Court. Having "some information that [the petitioner here] was selling narcotics," three deputy sheriffs of the County of Los Angeles, on the morning of July 1, 1949, made for the two-story dwelling house in which Rochin lived with his mother, common-law wife, brothers and sisters. Finding the outside door open, they entered and then forced open the door to Rochin's room on the second floor. Inside they found petitioner sitting partly dressed on the side of the bed, upon which his wife was lying. On a "night stand" beside the bed the deputies spied two capsules. When asked "Whose stuff is this?" Rochin seized the capsules and put them in his mouth. A struggle ensued, in the course of which the three officers "jumped upon him" and attempted to extract the capsules. The force they applied proved unavailing against Rochin's resistance. He was handcuffed and taken to a hospital. At the direction of one of the officers a doctor forced an emetic solution through a tube into Rochin's stomach against his will. This "stomach pumping" produced vomiting. In the vomited matter were found two capsules which proved to contain morphine.

Rochin was brought to trial before a California Superior Court, sitting without a jury, on the charge of possessing "a preparation of morphine" in violation of the California Health and Safety Code 1947,§ 11500. Rochin was convicted and sentenced to sixty days' imprisonment. The chief evidence against him was the two capsules. They were admitted over petitioner's objection, although the means of obtaining them was frankly set forth in the testimony by one of the deputies, substantially as here narrated.

On appeal, the District Court of Appeal affirmed the conviction, despite the finding that the officer "were guilty of unlawfully breaking into and entering defendant's room and were guilty of unlawfully assaulting and battering defendant while in the room", and "were guilty of unlawfully assaulting, battering, torturing and falsely imprisoning the defendant at the alleged hospital." One of the three judges, while finding that "the record in this case reveals a shocking series of violations of constitutional rights", concurred only because he felt bound by decisions of his Supreme Court. These, he asserted, "have been looked upon by law enforcement officers as an encouragement, if not an invitation, to the commission of such lawless acts." The Supreme Court of California denied without opinion Rochin's petition for a hearing. Two justice dissented from this denial, and in doing so expressed themselves thus: "* * * a conviction which rests upon evidence of incriminating objects obtained from the body of the accused by physical abuse is as invalid as a conviction which rests upon a verbal confession extracted from him by such abuse. * * * Had the evidence forced from defendant's lips consisted of an oral confession that he illegally possessed a drug * * * he would have the protection of the rule of law which excludes coerced confessions from evidence. But because the evidence forced from his lips consisted of real objects the People of this state are permitted to base a conviction upon it. [We] find no valid ground of distinction between a verbal confession extracted by physical abuse and a confession wrested from defendant's body by physical abuse." This Court granted *certiorari*, because a serious question is raised as to the limitations which the Due Process Clause of the Fourteenth Amendment imposes on the conduct of criminal proceedings by the States. * * *

Regard for the requirements of the Due Process Clause "inescapably imposes upon this Court an exercise of judgment upon the whole course of the proceedings [resulting in a conviction] in order to ascertain whether they offend those canons of decency and fairness which express the notions of justice of English-speaking peoples even toward those charged with the most heinous offenses." *Malinski v. People of State of New York*, 324 U.S. at 416–417. These standards of justice are not authoritatively formulated anywhere as though they were specifics. Due process of law is a summarized constitutional guarantee of respect for those personal immunities which, as Mr. Justice Cardozo twice wrote for the Court, are "so rooted in the traditions and conscience of our people as to be ranked as fundamental", *Snyder v. Commonwealth of Massachusetts*, 291 U.S. 97, 105, or are "implicit in the concept of ordered liberty". *Palko v. State of Connecticut*, 302 U.S. 319, 325.

The Court's function in the observance of this settled conception of the Due Process Clause does not leave us without adequate guides in subjecting State criminal procedures to constitutional judgment. In dealing not with the machinery of government but with human rights, the absence of formal exactitude, or want of fixity of meaning, is not an unusual or even regrettable attribute of constitutional provisions. Words being symbols do not speak without a gloss. On the one hand the gloss may be the deposit of history, whereby a term gains technical content. Thus the requirements of the Sixth and Seventh Amendments for trial by jury in the federal courts have a rigid meaning. No changes or chances can alter the content of the verbal symbol of "jury"—a body of twelve men [*sic*] who must reach a unanimous conclusion if the verdict is to go against the defendant. On the other hand, the gloss of some of the verbal symbols of the Constitution does not give them a fixed technical content. It exacts a continuing process of application.

When the gloss has thus not been fixed but is a function of the process of judgment, the judgment is bound to fall differently at different times and differently at the same time through different judges. Even more specific provisions, such as the guaranty of freedom of speech and the detailed protection against unreasonable searches and seizures, have inevitably evoked as sharp divisions in this Court as the least specific and most comprehensive protection of liberties, the Due Process Clause.

The vague contours of the Due Process Clause do not leave judges at large. We may not draw on our merely personal and private notions and disregard the limits that bind judges in their judicial function. Even though the concept of due process of law is not final and fixed, these limits are derived from considerations that are fused in the whole nature of or judicial process. These are considerations deeply rooted in reason and in the compelling traditions of the legal profession. The Due Process Clause places upon this Court the duty of exercising a judgment, within the narrow confines of judicial power in reviewing State convictions, upon interests of society pushing in opposite directions.

Due process of law thus conceived is not to be derided as resort to a revival of "natural law." To believe that this judicial exercise of judgment could be avoided by freezing "due process of law" at some fixed stage of time or thought is to suggest that the most important aspect of constitutional adjudication is a function for inanimate machines and not for judges, for whom the independence safeguarded by Article III of the Constitution was designed and who are presumably guided by established standards of judicial behavior. * * * To practice the requisite detachment and to achieve sufficient objectivity no doubt demands of judges the habit of self-discipline and self-criticism, incertitude that one's own views are incontestable and alert tolerance toward views not shared. But these are precisely the presuppositions of our judicial process. They are precisely the qualities society has a right to expect from those entrusted with ultimate judicial power.

Restraints on our jurisdiction are self-imposed only in the sense that there is from our decisions no immediate appeal short of impeachment or constitutional amendment. But that does not make due process of law a matter of judicial caprice. The faculties of the Due Process Clause may be indefinite and vague, but the mode of their ascertainment is not self-willed. In each case "due process of law" requires an evaluation based on a disinterested inquiry pursued in the spirit of science, on a balanced order of facts exactly and fairly stated, on the detached consideration of conflicting claims, on a judgment not *ad hoc* and episodic but duly mindful of reconciling the needs both of continuity and of change in a progressive society.

Applying these general considerations to the circumstances of the present case, we are compelled to conclude that the proceedings by which this conviction was obtained do more than offend some fastidious squeamishness or private sentimentalism about combatting crime too energetically. This is conduct that shocks the conscience. Illegally breaking into the privacy of the petitioner, the struggle to open his mouth and remove what was there, the forcible extraction of his stomach's contents—

this course of proceeding by agents of government to obtain evidence is bound to offend even hardened sensibilities. They are methods too close to the rack and the screw to permit of constitutional differentiation.

It has long since ceased to be true that due process of law is heedless of the means by which otherwise relevant and credible evidence is obtained. This was not true even before the series of recent cases enforced the constitutional principle that the States may not base convictions upon confessions, however much verified, obtained by coercion. These decisions are not arbitrary exceptions to the comprehensive right of States to fashion their own rules of evidence for criminal trials. They are not sports in our constitutional law but applications of a general principle. They are only instances of the general requirement that States in their prosecutions respect certain decencies of civilized conduct. Due process of law, as a historic and generative principle, precludes defining, and thereby confining, these standards of conduct more precisely than to say that convictions cannot be brought about by methods that offend "a sense of justice." See Mr. Chief Justice Hughes, speaking for a unanimous Court in *Brown v. State of Mississippi*, 297 U.S. 278, 285–286. It would be a stultification of the responsibility which the course of constitutional history has cast upon this Court to hold that in order to convict a man the police cannot extract by force what is in his mind but can extract what is in his stomach.

* * * Use of involuntary verbal confessions in State criminal trials is constitutionally obnoxious not only because of their unreliability. They are inadmissible under the Due Process Clause even though statements contained in them may be independently established as true. Coerced confessions offend the community's sense of fair play and decency. So here, to sanction the brutal conduct which naturally enough was condemned by the court whose judgment is before us, would be to afford brutality the cloak of law. Nothing would be more calculated to discredit law and thereby to brutalize the temper of a society. * * *

On the facts of this case the conviction of the petitioner has been obtained by methods that offend the Due Process Clause. The judgment below must be reversed.

MR. JUSTICE BLACK, concurring. * * * What the majority hold is that the Due Process Clause empowers this Court to nullify any state law if its application "shocks the conscience", offends "a sense of justice" or runs counter to the "decencies of civilized conduct." The majority emphasize that these statements do not refer to their own consciences or to their senses of justice and decency. For we are told that "we may not draw on our merely personal and private notions"; our judgment must be grounded on "considerations deeply rooted in reason and in the compelling traditions of the legal profession." We are further admonished to measure the validity of state practices, not by our reason, or by the traditions of the legal profession, but by "the community's sense of fair play and decency' "; by the "traditions and conscience of our people"; or by "those canons of decency and fairness which express the notions of justice of English-speaking peoples". These canons are made necessary, it is said, because of "interests of society pushing in opposite directions."

If the Due Process Clause does vest this Court with such unlimited power to invalidate laws, I am still in doubt as to why we should consider only the notions of English-speaking peoples to determine what are immutable and fundamental principles of justice. Moreover, one may well ask what avenues of investigation are open to discover "canons" of conduct so universally favored that this Court should write them into the Constitution? All we are told is that the discovery must be made by an "evaluation based on a disinterested inquiry pursued in the spirit of science, on a balanced order of facts."

Some constitutional provisions are stated in absolute and unqualified language such, for illustration, as the First Amendment stating that no law shall be passed prohibiting the free exercise of religion or abridging the freedom of speech or press. Other constitutional provisions do require courts to choose between competing policies, such as the Fourth Amendment which, by its terms, necessitates a judicial decision as to what is an "unreasonable" search or seizure. There is, however, no express constitutional language granting judicial power to invalidate every state law of every kind deemed "unreasonable" or contrary to the Court's notion of civilized decencies; yet the constitutional philosophy used by the majority has, in the past, been used to deny a state the right to fix the price of gasoline, and even the right to prevent bakers from palming off smaller for larger loaves of bread.

These cases, and others, show the extent to which the evanescent standards of the majority's philosophy have been used to nullify state legislative programs passed to suppress evil economic practices. What paralyzing role this same philosophy will play in the future economic affairs of this country is impossible to predict. Of even graver concern, however, is the use of the philosophy to nullify the Bill of Rights. I long ago concluded that the accordion-like qualities of this philosophy must inevitably imperil all the individual liberty safeguards specifically enumerated in the Bill of Rights. Reflection and recent decisions of this Court sanctioning abridgment of the freedom of speech and press have strengthened this conclusion.

[The concurring opinion of JUSTICE DOUGLAS is omitted.]

NOTES AND QUESTIONS

1. *Natural law reasoning and the conscience of the Court.* In *Rochin*, the Supreme Court reverses a conviction on the ground that the conduct of the police "shocks the conscience." Specifically,

> [i]llegally breaking into the privacy of the petitioner, the struggle to open his mouth and remove what was there, the forcible ex-traction of his stomach's contents—this course of proceeding by agents of government to obtain evidence is bound to offend even hardened sensibilities. They are methods too close to the rack and the screw to permit of constitutional differentiation.

Whose conscience is the Court consulting? What connection is there between this conscience and natural law?

2. *Natural law limited to interpreting the Due Process Clause?* The Due Process Clause has been interpreted as a basic protection of fairness in a government's treatment of human beings, and so a "shock the conscience" test might be entirely predictable and defensible in a Due Process challenge to a criminal conviction, as in *Rochin*. Is a "shock the conscience" test equally available or meaningful in a separation of powers case testing, say, the power of the President to terminate a treaty (*Goldwater v. Carter*, 444 U.S. 996 (1979))? With respect to which other provisions of the Constitution would a "shock the conscience" test seem irrelevant? On the issue of bringing natural law argumentation into constitutional analysis generally, *see* HADLEY ARKES, BEYOND THE CONSTITUTION (1992).

3. *Natural law and the confirmation of Supreme Court justices.* During the confirmation hearings for Justice Clarence Thomas, the following exchange occurred between the nominee and then-Senator Joseph Biden, Chairman of the Senate Judiciary Committee:

> BIDEN: In a speech before the Federalist Society at the University of Virginia, you praised the first Justice [John] Harlan's opinion in *Plessy v. Ferguson*, and you said: "Implicit reliance on political first principles was implicit rather than explicit, as is generally appropriate for the Court's opinions. He gives us a foundation for interpreting not only cases involving race, but the entire Constitution in the scheme of protecting rights." You went on to say, "Harlan's opinion provides one of our best examples of natural law and higher law jurisprudence." Then you say, "The higher law background of the American government, whether explicitly appealed to or not, provides the only firm basis for a just and wise constitutional decision."
>
> Judge, what I would like to know is, I find it hard to understand how you can say what you are now saying, that natural law was only a—you were only talking about the philosophy in a general philosophic sense, and not how it informed or impacted upon constitutional interpretation.

> THOMAS: Well, let me attempt to clarify. That, in fact, though, was my approach. I was interested in the political theory standpoint. I was not interested in constitutional adjudication. I was not at the time adjudicating cases. But with respect to the background, I think that we can both agree that the founders of our country, or at least some of the drafters of our Constitution and our declaration, believed in natural rights. And my point was simply that in understanding overall our constitutional government, that it was important that we understood how they believed—or what they believed in natural law or natural rights.

"Thomas Spars With Committee Over Natural Law, Abortion." In CQ ALMANAC 1991, 47th ed., 17–E–22–E. Washington, DC: Congressional Quarterly, 1992.

Must someone committed to interpreting the Constitution in light of the original intent of the Founders embrace the natural law reasoning of the eighteenth century?

4. *"The interests of justice" principle and the "cellophane of subjectivity."* The "shock the conscience" test in *Rochin* (and its progeny) is not the only legal test with overtones of natural law reasoning. Some state courts have the power to reverse a criminal conviction in the "interests of justice" as part of their inherent supervisory powers. For example, in *State v. Beecroft*, 813 N.W.2d 814, 849 (2012), the Supreme Court of Minnesota had to consider whether the government was entitled to some advance warning that particular prosecutorial behaviors were contrary to the interests of justice:

> By its nature, our power to reverse a conviction in the interests of justice "provides, in effect, a 'safety valve' for the justice system." Henry W. McCarr & Jack S. Nordby, 9 *Minnesota Practice—Criminal Law & Procedure* § 47.57 (3d ed. 2001). Although a repeated pattern of prosecutorial misconduct may have been one basis for reversal in the past, we have never imposed a repeated behavior standard as a rigid threshold requirement on our ability to reverse in the interests of justice. Our authority to exercise our supervisory power over district courts must remain flexible based on the circumstances of each individual case. *See, e.g.[, State v.] Porter,* 526 N.W.2d [359 (Minn. 1995),] at 366 (reversing conviction based on prosecutorial misconduct resulting in prejudicial error and in the interests of justice). Simply put, the State is not always entitled to a "warning" before it realizes the consequences of violating established laws and rules and interfering with the fair administration of justice.

The court's admission that it is impossible to catalogue all forms of injustice ahead of time may seem like common sense, but, according to the dissent, a court's legitimate function is to apply law, not vague standards of morality:

> [A] leading treatise on Minnesota law accurately describes the power to reverse in the interests of justice as applying in a "very broad" kaleidoscope of circumstances and concludes that the standard for

> invoking the power cannot be "precisely described" or "defined." Henry W. McCarr & Jack S. Nordby, 9 *Minnesota Practice—Criminal Law & Procedure* § 47.57 (3d ed. 2001). As far as I can tell, there is no unifying or coherent standard defining the limits, if any, of our power to reverse prophylactically in the interests of justice. In one of the more helpful articulations of the power, we stated that we will reverse when "we are troubled by the unavoidable conclusion that justice [has] not [been] served." [*State v.*] *Windish*, 590 N.W.2d [311 (Minn. 1999),] at 319. But that articulation largely begs the question. How troubled must we be? Must we be unanimously troubled? My point is that it is difficult to understand, much less apply, a standard that turns on our sense of how "troubled" we are about the particular conduct or circumstances in a given case. *Cf. Cnty. of Sacramento v. Lewis*, 523 U.S. 833, 861 (1998) (Scalia, J., concurring) (disparaging the "shocks-the-conscience" test for substantive due-process claims as the "cellophane of subjectivity")."

Id., at 867–68 (Dietzen, J., dissenting).

5. *"Natural law" as an epithet.* In *Griswold v. Connecticut*, 381 U.S. 479 (1965), the Supreme Court invalidated a state law prohibiting the use of contraceptives by married couples on the ground that it infringes the right to marital privacy. Although no right by that name appears in the Constitution, the state law "cannot stand in light of the familiar principle, so often applied by this Court, that a 'governmental purpose to control or prevent activities constitutionally subject to state regulation may not be achieved by means which sweep unnecessarily broadly and thereby invade the area of protected freedoms.' " *Id.* at 485. In dissent, Justice Black observed, "[i]f these formulas based on 'natural justice,' or others which mean the same thing, are to prevail, they require judges to determine what is or is not constitutional on the basis of their own appraisal of what laws are unwise or unnecessary." *Id.* at 511–12. Are there sources of rights that are not explicitly identified in the Constitution but which are not solely the product of a judge's individual whims?

6. *Assessing the principal cases.* As you reflect on the analysis and the results in *Traiton*, *Riggs*, and *Rochin*, do they strike you as a highly respectable form of judicial reasoning—as though the mark of great judges is their ability to "do justice"—or as the very exemplar of gut-level, "taste"-based activism? Is there some middle ground between these two extremes?

Readings

1. Natural Law Arguments in Politics and the Arts

MARTIN LUTHER KING, JR., *LETTER FROM A BIRMINGHAM JAIL*

(16 April 1963)

My Dear Fellow Clergymen:

While confined here in the Birmingham city jail, I came across your recent statement calling my present activities "unwise and untimely." Seldom do I pause to answer criticism of my work and ideas. If I sought to answer all the criticisms that cross my desk, my secretaries would have little time for anything other than such correspondence in the course of the day, and I would have no time for constructive work. But since I feel that you are men of genuine good will and that your criticisms are sincerely set forth, I want to try to answer your statement in what I hope will be patient and reasonable terms.

I think I should indicate why I am here in Birmingham, since you have been influenced by the view which argues against "outsiders coming in." I have the honor of serving as president of the Southern Christian Leadership Conference, an organization operating in every southern state, with headquarters in Atlanta, Georgia. We have some eighty five affiliated organizations across the South, and one of them is the Alabama Christian Movement for Human Rights. Frequently we share staff, educational and financial resources with our affiliates. Several months ago the affiliate here in Birmingham asked us to be on call to engage in a nonviolent direct action program if such were deemed necessary. We readily consented, and when the hour came we lived up to our promise. So I, along with several members of my staff, am here because I was invited here. I am here because I have organizational ties here.

But more basically, I am in Birmingham because injustice is here. * * *

We have waited for more than 340 years for our constitutional and God given rights. The nations of Asia and Africa are moving with jetlike speed toward gaining political independence, but we still creep at horse and buggy pace toward gaining a cup of coffee at a lunch counter. Perhaps it is easy for those who have never felt the stinging darts of segregation to say, "Wait." But when you have seen vicious mobs lynch your mothers and fathers at will and drown your sisters and brothers at whim; when you have seen hate filled policemen curse, kick and even kill your black brothers and sisters; when you see the vast majority of your twenty million Negro brothers smothering in an airtight cage of poverty in the midst of an affluent society; when you suddenly find your tongue twisted and your speech stammering as you seek to explain to your six year old daughter why she can't go to the public amusement park that has just been advertised on television, and see tears welling up in her eyes when she is told that Funtown is closed to colored children, and see ominous clouds of inferiority beginning to form in her little mental sky, and see her beginning to distort her personality by developing an unconscious bitterness toward white people; when you have to concoct an answer for a five year old son who is asking: "Daddy, why do white people treat colored people so mean?"; when you take a cross county drive and find it necessary to sleep night after night in the uncomfortable corners of your automobile because no motel will accept you; when you are humiliated day in and day out by nagging signs reading "white" and "colored"; when your first name becomes "nigger," your middle name becomes "boy" (however old you are) and your last name becomes "John," and your wife and mother are never given the respected title "Mrs."; when you are harried by day and haunted by night by the fact that you are a Negro, living constantly at tiptoe stance, never quite knowing what to expect next, and are plagued with inner fears and outer resentments; when you are forever fighting a degenerating sense of "nobodiness"—then you will understand why we find it difficult to wait.

There comes a time when the cup of endurance runs over, and men are no longer willing to be plunged into the abyss of despair. I hope, sirs, you can understand our legitimate and unavoidable impatience. You express a great deal of anxiety over our willingness to break laws. This is certainly a legitimate concern. Since we so diligently urge people to obey the Supreme Court's decision of 1954 outlawing segregation in the public schools, at first glance it may seem rather paradoxical for us consciously to break laws. One may well ask: "How can you advocate breaking some laws and obeying others?" The answer lies in the fact that there are two types of laws: just and unjust. I would be the first to advocate obeying just laws. One has not only a legal but a moral responsibility to obey just laws. Conversely, one has a moral responsibility to disobey unjust laws. I would agree with St. Augustine that "an unjust law is no law at all."

Now, what is the difference between the two? How does one determine whether a law is just or unjust? A just law is a man made code that squares with the moral law or the law of God. An unjust law is a code that is out of harmony with the moral law. To put it in the terms of St. Thomas Aquinas: An unjust law is a human law that is not rooted in eternal law and natural law. Any law that uplifts human personality is just. Any law that degrades human personality is unjust. All segregation statutes are unjust because segregation distorts the soul and damages the personality. It gives the segregator a false sense of superiority and the segregated a false sense of inferiority. Segregation, to use the terminology of the Jewish philosopher Martin Buber, substitutes an "I-it" relationship for an "I-thou" relationship and ends up relegating persons to the status of things. Hence segregation is not only politically, economically and sociologically unsound, it is morally wrong and sinful. Paul Tillich has said that sin is separation. Is not segregation an existential expression of man's tragic separation, his awful estrangement, his terrible sinfulness? Thus it is that I can urge men to obey the 1954 decision of the Supreme Court, for it is morally right; and I can urge them to disobey segregation ordinances, for they are morally wrong.

Let us consider a more concrete example of just and unjust laws. An unjust law is a code that a numerical or power majority group compels a minority group to obey but does not make binding on itself. This is difference made legal. By the same token, a just law is a code that a majority compels a minority to follow and that it is willing to follow itself. This is sameness made legal. Let me give another explanation. A law is unjust if it is inflicted on a minority that, as a result of being denied the right to vote, had no part in enacting or devising the law. Who can say that the legislature of Alabama which set up that state's segregation laws was democratically elected? Throughout Alabama all sorts of devious methods are used to prevent Negroes from becoming registered voters, and there are some counties in which, even though Negroes constitute a majority of the population, not a single Negro is registered. Can any law enacted under such circumstances be considered democratically structured?

Sometimes a law is just on its face and unjust in its application. For instance, I have been arrested on a charge of parading without a permit. Now, there is nothing wrong in having an ordinance which requires a permit for a parade. But such an ordinance becomes unjust when it is used to maintain segregation and to deny citizens the First-Amendment privilege of peaceful assembly and protest.

I hope you are able to see the distinction I am trying to point out. In no sense do I advocate evading or defying the law, as would the rabid segregationist. That would lead to anarchy. One who breaks an unjust law must do so openly, lovingly, and with a willingness to accept the penalty. I submit that an individual who breaks a law that conscience tells him is unjust, and who willingly accepts the penalty of imprisonment in order to arouse the conscience of the community over its injustice, is in reality expressing the highest respect for law.

Of course, there is nothing new about this kind of civil disobedience. It was evidenced sublimely in the refusal of Shadrach, Meshach and Abednego to obey the laws of Nebuchadnezzar, on the ground that a higher moral law was at stake. It was practiced superbly by the early Christians, who were willing to face hungry lions and the excruciating pain of chopping blocks rather than submit to certain unjust laws of the Roman Empire. To a degree, academic freedom is a reality today because Socrates practiced civil disobedience. In our own nation, the Boston Tea Party represented a massive act of civil disobedience.

We should never forget that everything Adolf Hitler did in Germany was "legal" and everything the Hungarian freedom fighters did in Hungary was "illegal." It was "illegal" to aid and comfort a Jew in Hitler's Germany. Even so, I am sure that, had I lived in Germany at the time, I would have aided and comforted my Jewish brothers. If today I lived in a Communist country where certain principles dear to the Christian faith are suppressed, I would openly advocate disobeying that country's antireligious laws. * * *

Yours for the cause of Peace and Brotherhood,

Martin Luther King, Jr.

PLATO, *CRITO*

(360 B.C.E.)
(translated by Benjamin Jowett (1914))

[The *Crito* is Plato's dramatic portrayal of the last days of his teacher, Socrates, whom he described as "the wisest and most just of all men." In 399 B.C.E., Socrates was tried and convicted of impiety and corrupting the youth of Athens, for which he received the death penalty. In the following dialogue, Socrates' friend, Crito, has come to his jail cell to plead with him to escape. Socrates "explains" through a series of questions to Crito why he should not do so.]

Socrates: [Suppose] the laws and the government come and interrogate me: "Tell us, Socrates," they say; "what are you about? Are you going by an act of yours to overturn us—the laws and the whole State, as far as in you lies? Do you imagine that a State can subsist and not be overthrown, in which the decisions of law have no power, but are set aside and overthrown by individuals?" What will be our answer, Crito, to these and the like words? Anyone, and especially a clever rhetorician, will have a good deal to urge about the evil of setting aside the law which requires a sentence to be carried out; and we might reply, "Yes; but the State has injured us and given an unjust sentence." Suppose I say that?

Crito: Very good, Socrates.

Socrates: "And was that our agreement with you?" the law would say, "or were you to abide by the sentence of the State?" And if I were to express astonishment at their saying this, the law would probably add: "Answer, Socrates, instead of opening your eyes: you are in the habit of asking and answering questions. Tell us what complaint you have to make against us which justifies you in attempting to destroy us and the State? In the first place did we not bring you into existence? Your father married your mother by our aid and begat you. Say whether you have any objection to urge against those of us who regulate marriage?" None, I should reply. "Or against those of us who regulate the system of nurture and education of children in which you were trained? Were not the laws, who have the charge of this, right in commanding your father to train you in music and gymnastic?" Right, I should reply. "Well, then, since you were brought into the world and nurtured and educated by us, can you deny in the first place that you are our child and slave, as your fathers were before you? And if this is true you are not on equal terms with us; nor can you think that you have a right to do to us what we are doing to you. Would you have any right to strike or revile or do any other evil to a father or to your master, if you had one, when you have been struck or reviled by him, or received some other evil at his hands?—you would not say this? And because we think right to destroy you, do you think that you have any right to destroy us in return, and your country as far as in you lies? And will you, O professor of true virtue, say that you are justified in this? Has a philosopher like you failed to discover that our country is more to be valued and higher and holier far than mother or father or any ancestor, and more to be regarded in the eyes of the gods and of men of understanding? Also to be soothed, and gently and reverently entreated when angry, even more than a father, and if not persuaded, obeyed? And when we are punished by her, whether with imprisonment or stripes, the punishment is to be endured in silence; and if she leads us to wounds or death in battle, thither we follow as is right; neither may anyone yield or retreat or leave his rank, but whether in battle or in a court of law, or in any other place, he must do what his city and his country order him; or he must change their view of what is just: and if he may do no violence to his father or mother, much less may he do violence to his country." What answer shall we make to this, Crito? Do the laws speak truly, or do they not?

Crito: I think that they do.

Socrates: Then the laws will say: "Consider, Socrates, if this is true, that in your present attempt you are going to do us wrong. For, after having brought you into the world, and nurtured and educated you, and given you and every other citizen a share in every good that we had to give, we further proclaim and give the right to every Athenian, that if he does not like us when he has come of age and has seen the ways of the city, and made our acquaintance, he may go where he pleases and take his goods with him; and none of us laws will forbid him or interfere with him. Any of you who does not like us and the city, and who wants to go to a colony or to any other city, may go where he likes, and take his goods with him. But he who has experience of the manner in which we order justice and administer the State, and still remains, has entered into an implied contract that he will do as we command him. And he who disobeys us is, as we maintain, thrice wrong: first, because in disobeying us he is disobeying his parents; secondly, because we are the authors of his education; thirdly, because he has made an agreement with us that he will duly obey our commands; and he neither obeys them nor convinces us that our commands are wrong; and we do not rudely impose them, but give him the alternative of obeying or convincing us; that is what we offer and he does neither. These are the sort of accusations to which, as we were saying, you, Socrates, will be exposed if you accomplish your intentions; you, above all other Athenians." Suppose I ask, why is this? They will justly retort upon me that I above all other men have acknowledged the agreement. "There is clear proof," they will say, "Socrates, that we and the city were not displeasing to you. Of all Athenians you have been the most constant resident in the city, which, as you never leave, you may be supposed to love. For you never went out of the city either to see the games, except once when you went to the Isthmus, or to any other place unless when you were on military service; nor did you travel as other men do. Nor had you any curiosity to know other States or their laws: your affections did not go beyond us and our State; we were your especial favorites, and you acquiesced in our government of you; and this is the State in which you begat your children, which is a proof of your satisfaction. Moreover, you might, if you had liked, have fixed the penalty at banishment in the course of the trial. The State which refuses to let you go now would have let you go then. But you pretended that you preferred death to exile, and that you were not grieved at death. And now you have forgotten these fine sentiments, and pay no respect to us, the laws, of whom you are the destroyer; and are doing what only a miserable slave would do, running away and turning your back upon the compacts and agreements which you made as a citizen. And first of all answer this very question: Are we right in saying that you agreed to be governed according to us in deed, and not in word only? Is that true or not?" How shall we answer that, Crito? Must we not agree?

Crito: There is no help, Socrates.

Socrates: Then will they not say: "You, Socrates, are breaking the covenants and agreements which you made with us at your leisure, not in any haste or under any compulsion or deception, but having had seventy years to think of them, during which time you were at liberty to leave the city, if we were not to your mind, or if our covenants appeared to you to be unfair. You had your choice, and might have gone either to Lacedaemon or Crete, which you often praise for their good government, or to some other Hellenic or foreign State. Whereas you, above all other Athenians, seemed to be so fond of the State, or, in other words, of us her laws (for who would like a State that has no laws?), that you never stirred out of her: the halt, the blind, the maimed, were not more stationary in her than you were. And now you run away and forsake your agreements. Not so, Socrates, if you will take our advice; do not make yourself ridiculous by escaping out of the city.

"For just consider, if you transgress and err in this sort of way, what good will you do, either to yourself or to your friends? That your friends will be driven into exile and deprived of citizenship, or will lose their property, is tolerably certain; and you yourself, if you fly to one of the neighboring cities, as, for example, Thebes or Megara, both of which are well-governed cities, will come to them as an enemy, Socrates, and their government will be against you, and all patriotic citizens will cast an evil eye upon you as a subverter of the laws, and you will confirm in the minds of the judges the justice of their own condemnation of you. For he who is a corrupter of the laws is more than likely to be corrupter of the young and foolish portion of mankind. Will you then flee from well-ordered cities and virtuous men? And is existence worth having on these terms? Or will you go to them without shame, and talk to them, Socrates? And what will you say to them? What you say here about virtue and justice and institutions and laws being the best things among men? Would that be decent of you? Surely not. But if you go away from well-governed States to Crito's friends in Thessaly, where there is great disorder and license, they will be charmed to have the tale of your escape from prison, set off with ludicrous particulars of the manner in which you were wrapped in a goatskin or some other disguise, and metamorphosed as the fashion of runaways is—that is very likely; but will there be no one to remind you that in your old age you violated the most sacred laws from a miserable desire of a little more life? Perhaps not, if you keep them in a good temper; but if they are out of temper you will hear many degrading things; you will live, but how?—as the flatterer of all men, and the servant of all men; and doing what?—eating and drinking in Thessaly, having gone abroad in order that you may get a dinner. And where will be your fine sentiments about justice and virtue then? Say that you wish to live for the sake of your children, that you may bring them up and educate them—will you take them into Thessaly and deprive them of Athenian citizenship? Is that the benefit which you would confer upon them? Or are you under the impression that they will be better cared for and educated here if you are still alive, although absent from them; for that your friends will take care of them? Do you fancy that if you are an inhabitant of Thessaly they will take care of them, and if you are an inhabitant of the other world they will not take care of them? Nay; but if they who call themselves friends are truly friends, they surely will.

"Listen, then, Socrates, to us who have brought you up. Think not of life and children first, and of justice afterwards, but of justice first, that you may be justified before the princes of the world below. For neither will you nor any that belong to you be happier or holier or juster in this life, or happier in another, if you do as Crito bids. Now you depart in innocence, a sufferer and not a doer of evil; a victim, not of the laws, but of men. But if you go forth, returning evil for evil, and injury for injury, breaking the covenants and agreements which you have made with us, and wronging those whom you ought least to wrong, that is to say, yourself, your friends, your country, and us, we shall be angry with you while you live, and our brethren, the laws in the world below, will receive you as an enemy; for they will know that you have done your best to destroy us. Listen, then, to us and not to Crito."

This is the voice which I seem to hear murmuring in my ears, like the sound of the flute in the ears of the mystic; that voice, I say, is humming in my ears, and prevents me from hearing any other. And I know that anything more which you will say will be in vain. Yet speak, if you have anything to say.

Crito: I have nothing to say, Socrates.

Socrates: Then let me follow the intimations of the will of God.

HERMAN MELVILLE, *BILLY BUDD, SAILOR*

(1891)

[In his novella, *Billy Budd*, Herman Melville tells the story of the H.M.S. *Bellipotent*, a British man-of-war during the Napoleonic Wars. In a year when the British are threatened by the military ambitions of revolutionary France and rocked by two high-profile mutinies, Billy Budd is "impressed"—taken from the crew of a neutral vessel (christened *The Rights of Man*) and forced to serve in the British navy. Despite the hard conditions, Billy maintains a near-angelic simplicity, optimism, and charisma, and he becomes a favorite of the crew, but he is hated by a vicious and sadistic superior officer, the master-at-arms, John Claggart. In front of the captain, "Starry" Vere, Claggart falsely accuses Billy of conspiring to mutiny, and Billy, struck dumb, kills him at a blow. Captain Vere—a thoughtful man committed to the discipline of the naval code, which includes the death penalty for assaulting a superior officer—observes immediately "Struck dead by an angel of God! Yet the angel must hang!" Vere convenes a drumhead court martial and addresses the court:]

What he said was to this effect: "Hitherto I have been but the witness, little more; and I should hardly think now to take another tone, that of your coadjutor for the time, did I not perceive in you—at the crisis too—a troubled hesitancy, proceeding, I doubt not, from the clash of military duty with moral scruple—scruple vitalized by compassion. For the compassion, how can I otherwise than share it? But, mindful of paramount obligations, I strive against scruples that may tend to enervate decision. Not, gentlemen, that I hide from myself that the case is an exceptional one. Speculatively regarded, it well might be referred to a jury of casuists. But for us here, acting not as casuists or moralists, it is a case practical, and under martial law practically to be dealt with.

"But your scruples: do they move as in a dusk? Challenge them. Make them advance and declare themselves. Come now; do they import something like this: If, mindless of palliating circumstances, we are bound to regard the death of the master-at-arms as the prisoner's deed, then does that deed constitute a capital crime whereof the penalty is a mortal one. But in natural justice is nothing but the prisoner's overt act to be considered? How can we adjudge to summary and shameful death a fellow creature innocent before God, and whom we feel to be so? Does that state it aright? You sign sad assent. Well, I too feel that, the full force of that. It is Nature. But do these buttons that we wear attest that our allegiance is to Nature? No, to the King. Though the ocean, which is inviolate Nature primeval, though this be the element where we move and have our being as sailors, yet as the King's officers lies our duty in a sphere correspondingly natural? So little is that true, that in receiving our commissions we in the most important regards ceased to be natural free agents. When war is declared are we the commissioned fighters previously consulted? We fight at command. If our judgments approve the war, that is but coincidence. So in other particulars. So now. For suppose condemnation to follow these present proceedings. Would it be so much we ourselves that would condemn as it would be martial law operating through us? For that law and the rigor of it, we are not responsible. Our vowed responsibility is in this: That however pitilessly that law may operate in any instances, we nevertheless adhere to it and administer it.

"But the exceptional in the matter moves the hearts within you. Even so too is mine moved. But let not warm hearts betray heads that should be cool. Ashore in a criminal case, will an upright judge allow himself off the bench to be waylaid by some tender kinswoman of the accused seeking to touch him with her tearful plea? Well, the heart here, sometimes the feminine in man, is as that piteous woman, and hard though it be, she must here be ruled out."

He paused, earnestly studying them for a moment; then resumed.

"But something in your aspect seems to urge that it is not solely the heart that moves in you, but also the conscience, the private conscience. But tell me whether or not, occupying the position we do, private conscience should not yield to that imperial one formulated in the code under which alone we officially proceed?"

Here the three men [sitting as the court] moved in their seats, less convinced than agitated by the course of an argument troubling but the more the spontaneous conflict within.

Perceiving which, the speaker paused for a moment; then abruptly changing his tone, went on.

"To steady us a bit, let us recur to the facts. In wartime at sea a man-of-war's man strikes his superior in grade, and the blow kills. Apart from its effect the blow itself is, according to the Articles of War, a capital crime. Furthermore—"

"Ay, sir," emotionally broke in the officer of marines, "in one sense it was. But surely Budd purposed neither mutiny nor homicide."

"Surely not, my good man. And before a court less arbitrary and more merciful than a martial one, that plea would largely extenuate. * * * But how here? We proceed under the law of the Mutiny Act. In feature no child can resemble his father more than that Act resembles in spirit the thing from which it derives—War. In His Majesty's service—in this ship, indeed—there are Englishmen forced to fight for the King against their will. Against their conscience, for aught we know. Though as their fellow creatures some of us may appreciate their position, yet as navy officers what reck we of it? Still less recks the enemy. Our impressed men he would fain cut down in the same swath with our volunteers. As regards the enemy's naval conscripts, some of whom may even share our own abhorrence of the regicidal French Directory, it is the same on our side. War looks but to the frontage, the appearance. And the Mutiny Act, War's child, takes after the father. Budd's intent or non-intent is nothing to the purpose.

"But while, put to it by those anxieties in you which I cannot but respect, I only repeat myself—while thus strangely we prolong proceedings that should be summary—the enemy may be sighted and an engagement result. We must do; and one of two things must we do—condemn or let go."

"Can we not convict and yet mitigate the penalty?" asked the sailing master, here speaking, and falteringly, for the first.

"Gentlemen, were that clearly lawful for us under the circumstances, consider the consequences of such clemency. The people" (meaning the ship's company) "have native sense; most of them are familiar with our naval usage and tradition; and how would they take it? Even could you explain to them—which our official position forbids—they, long molded by arbitrary discipline, have not that kind of intelligent responsiveness that might qualify them to comprehend and discriminate. No, to the people the foretopman's deed, however it be worded in the announcement, will be plain homicide committed in a flagrant act of mutiny. What penalty for that should follow, they know. But it does not follow. Why? they will ruminate. You know what sailors are. Will they not revert to the recent outbreak at the Nore? Ay. They know the well-founded alarm—the panic it struck throughout England. Your clement sentence they would account pusillanimous. They would think that we flinch, that we are afraid of them—afraid of practicing a lawful rigor singularly demanded at this juncture, lest it should provoke new troubles. What shame to us such a conjecture on their part, and how deadly to discipline. You see then, whither, prompted by duty and the law, I steadfastly drive. But I beseech you, my friends, do not take me amiss. I feel as you do for this unfortunate boy. But did he know our hearts, I take him to be of that generous nature that he would feel even for us on whom in this military necessity so heavy a compulsion is laid."

With that, crossing the deck he resumed his place by the sashed porthole, tacitly leaving the three to come to a decision. On the cabin's opposite side the troubled court sat silent. Loyal lieges, plain and practical, though at bottom they dissented from some points Captain Vere had put to them, they were without the faculty, hardly had the inclination, to gainsay one whom they felt to be an earnest man, one too not less their superior in mind than in naval rank. But it is not improbable that even such of his words as were not without influence over them, less came home to them than his closing appeal to their instinct as sea officers: in the forethought he threw out as to the practical consequences to discipline, considering the unconfirmed tone of the fleet at the time, should a man-of-war's man's violent killing at sea of a superior in grade be allowed to pass for aught else than a capital crime demanding prompt infliction of the penalty.

Not unlikely they were brought to something more or less akin to that harassed frame of mind which in the year 1842 actuated the commander of the U.S. brig-of-war *Somers* to resolve, under the so-called Articles of War, Articles modeled upon the English Mutiny Act, to resolve upon the execution at sea of a midshipman and two sailors as mutineers designing the seizure of the brig. Which resolution was carried out though in a time of peace and within not many days' sail of home. An act vindicated by a naval court of inquiry subsequently convened ashore. History, and here cited without comment. True, the circumstances on board the *Somers* were different from those onboard the *Bellipotent*. But the urgency felt, well-warranted or otherwise, was much the same.

Says a writer whom few know, "Forty years after a battle it is easy for a noncombatant to reason about how it ought to have been fought. It is another thing personally and under fire to have to direct the fighting while involved in the obscuring smoke of it. Much so with respect to other emergencies involving considerations both practical and moral, and when it is imperative promptly to act. The greater the fog the more it imperils the steamer, and speed is put on though at the hazard of running somebody down. Little ween the snug card players in the cabin of the responsibilities of the sleepless man on the bridge." In brief, Billy Budd was formally convicted and sentenced to be hung at the yardarm in the early morning watch, it being now night.

MARTHA C. NUSSBAUM, FROM DISGUST TO HUMANITY: SEXUAL ORIENTATION AND CONSTITUTIONAL LAW

8–10 (2010)

How might widespread disgust toward a group help to justify laws that disadvantage that group? At first one might suppose that there is no connection, and I shall argue that this is in fact correct. Disgust, however, has been prominently defended as a legitimate, even a central, source for law. Before we think about why it might not be legitimate or reliable source, then, we ought to try to understand the arguments of its defenders.

The two most prominent defenders of disgust as a criterion for the legal regulation of conduct are Lord Patrick Devlin, a British lawyer, eventually a "Law Lord" who wrote influentially about disgust and the law in the 1950s and Leon Kass, an American bioethicist who is a professor at the University of Chicago and who was chair of the President's council on Bioethics from 2002–2005. The arguments of Devlin and Kass are rather different, but both conclude that widespread disgust at a practice is a sufficient reason to forbid that practice through law, even if it involves only consenting parties and does not violate the rights of the non-consenting. Devlin's central target was the proposed decriminalization of consenting same-sex sexual acts. Kass focuses on the prospect of human cloning, but he suggests that his strictures would apply to a wide range of other practices, including same-sex acts.

Devlin's well-known essays on public morality were written in opposition to the 1957 report of the Wolfenden Commission, which recommended abolishing legal penalties for consenting homosexual acts between adults. He agreed with the commission that personal liberty is an important social value that should not be curtailed in the absence of strong public interest. He argued, however, that any society that is going to survive needs an "established morality" that is broadly shared. The "loosening of moral bonds" is often a sign of social "disintegration." Society is therefore "justified in taking the same steps to preserve its moral code as it does to preserve its government and other essential institutions." To illustrate the idea of "disintegration," Devlin cites the dangers of widespread drunkenness and drug abuse. These "vices," he argued would prevent society from rallying to ward off enemy attack: "[a] nations of debauchees would not in 1940 have responded satisfactorily to Winston Churchill's call to blood and toil and sweat and tears." For Devlin, homosexuals are "debauchees"; they are "addicts," whose immersion in sex is incompatible with being a reliable citizen. (He never offered any argument to support his view that homosexuals are more addicted to sex than heterosexuals.) He concluded that homosexual acts are like drug use: both should be criminalized, because protection of a shared moral code is necessary in order to prevent a social shipwreck.

Not all threats to a society's moral code are sufficient to justify legal intervention, Devlin argued. We need a test to determine when the point has been reached beyond which society should not tolerate immoral conduct for the sake of liberty. Because Devlin viewed immorality as like an infection, weakening the body politic, he was unwilling to adopt John Stuart Mill's principle that only the imminent prospect of harm to others licenses restrictive laws * * *. Since Devlin was unwilling to look to harm as the test for legal regulability, he needed a different sort of criterion to identify when the point of regulability has been reached. Disgust, because it is a very intense form of disapproval, provides him with such a test. When an average member of society—Devlin calls this person "the man on the Clapham omnibus"—feels disgust at the thought of some behavior that does not directly affect him, we may conclude that this conduct is "a vice so abominable that its mere presence is an offence."

In other words, Devlin was not talking about cases in which disgust is elicited by an actual homosexual solicitation. Nor was he talking about public conduct, which might directly cause offense to its viewers. He was talking about what the Wolfenden Report proposed to decriminalize—private, consensual sex acts. He imagined that the man on the Clapham omnibus feels disgust at the mere thought that such acts were going on in his society. When such an intense reaction is present, we are entitled to restrict personal liberty by making laws against the conduct that provokes it. The reason for the restriction is not paternalistic, for the sake of "improving" the lives of those living "badly." It is, rather, self-protective: society defends itself by punishing those who violate conventional moral norms.

Leon Kass's argument is different from Devlin's. Devlin was a Burkean conservative: he relied on disgust because it seemed to him to be an expression of deep-seated social conventions. Like Devlin, Kass dislikes the Millian idea that people should be free to choose their own conduct, so long as it does no harm to others. He calls this a world "in which everything is held to be permissible so long as it is freely done, in which our given human nature no longer commands respect." Unlike Devlin, however, Kass has no particular respect for convention as such. But he believes that disgust is a reliable warning sign, steering us away from atrocity. It is unclear how he thinks this mechanism works, but the most likely reading is that he believes human nature to be purposively designed (perhaps by God) in such a way that its visceral responses give us important information about what is good for us. Disgust thus contains a "wisdom" that lies beneath all rational argument. It "revolts against the excesses of human willfulness, warning us not to transgress what is unspeakably profound."

NOTES AND QUESTIONS

1. *Natural law arguments for some purposes, not all.* Cicero observed in *De Legibus* that humans "are born for Justice, and that right is based, *not upon opinions, but upon Nature*." The framers of the Declaration of Independence were certainly fluent in the language of natural law, referring to the rights of human beings "endowed by their Creator." In his *Letter from a Birmingham Jail*, Martin Luther King, Jr., linked his strategy of civil disobedience to the

natural law argument that an unjust law carries no obligation to obey it. And much of literature across history and cultures turns on the dramatic tension between what the human law requires and what the human sense of justice (or the "natural order of things") requires. Socrates' reasoning in *Crito*—personifying the laws of Athens and giving them voice—and Captain Vere's monologue in *Billy Budd* are especially explicit examples.

(a) Is there a reason that natural law arguments might work better for revolutionaries, artists, and visionaries than they do for lawyers and judges?

(b) As between the two jailhouse "reasonings"—King's *Letter* and Plato's *Crito*—which do you find more persuasive? Are they addressing the same problem or the same type of audience?

2. *Convention and natural law.* Drawing on Professor Nussbaum's analysis of disgust in the history of discrimination against gay people, how would you articulate the difference if any between natural law and the conventional morality of the majority in a society?

3. *Confronting skepticism.* If you are generally skeptical about objective moral truths or their universality or their basis in reason, how do you respond to the suggestion from Professor Michael Moore, who invites the skeptic to "take whatever skeptical question you direct to morals and ask it of scientific fact. If such skepticism does not make you doubt the existence of oak trees and the like, then it should not make you skeptical of moral entities and qualities such as rights, obligations, and goodness." Michael S. Moore, *Remembrance of Things Past*, 74. S. CAL. L. REV. 239, 246 (2000).

4. *Natural law and the obligation to disobey an immoral law.* Does the natural law position *necessarily* imply a moral obligation to obey just laws and disobey unjust laws? That is, does the fact that a law is properly enacted give rise to an obligation to follow it, or does the obligation to follow the law depend on its content? *See* Joel Feinberg, *Civil Disobedience in the Modern World*, 2 HUMANITIES IN SOCIETY 37 (1979) ("Why should [we] have any respect or duty of fidelity toward a statute with a wicked or stupid content just because it was passed into law by a bunch of men (possibly very wicked men like the Nazi legislators) according to the accepted recipes for making law?"). *See also* Robert P. George, *Natural Law*, 31 HARV. J.L. & PUB. POL'Y 171, 192, 194 (2008):

> Natural law theorists through the ages have taken note of the distinction between the systemic validity of a proposition of law, the property of belonging to a legal system, and the law's moral validity and bindingness as a matter of conscience. These theorists have had no difficulty accepting the central thesis of what we today call legal positivism—that is, that the existence and content of the positive law depends on social facts and not on its moral merits. Indeed, it is hard to see how one would otherwise make sense of the locution "a law that is not just." * * * [L]aws that due to their injustice damage rather than serve the common good, lack the central justifying quality of law. Their law-creating power (and the duties they purport to impose)

is thus weakened or defeated. Unjust laws are, Aquinas says, "not so much laws as acts of violence."

5. *A comparative perspective: natural law-like structures in a variety of cultures.* The proposition that justice and law are intrinsically related recurs in disparate cultures, from the *dharma* of Hinduism and Buddhism, to the Confucian ideal of *li,* to structures of Islamic and Jewish law. *See, e.g.*, REBECCA REDWOOD FRENCH, MARK A. NATHAN EDS., BUDDHISM AND LAW: AN INTRODUCTION (2014); CHUNG-YING CHENG, NEW DIMENSIONS OF CONFUCIAN AND NEO-CONFUCIAN PHILOSOPHY (1991); ANVER M. EMON, MATTHEW LEVERING, AND DAVID NOVAK, NATURAL LAW: A JEWISH, CHRISTIAN, AND ISLAMIC TRIALOGUE (2014).

Perhaps what is natural and universal and accessible to reason is not the substantive content of natural law but the human instinct towards fairness and the recognition that the law made by governments—the "positive" law—can obstruct or delay justice, which is neither created nor defined by the actions of government. From that perspective, confronting the tension between the enacted law and justice is part of the human condition and a defining challenge for lawyers and judges trying in good faith to apply the rule of law.

6. *The minimum content of natural law.* Philosophers and lawyers have struggled to define what natural law requires, and especially whether there is some minimum content of natural law. Consider the observation of Russell Hittinger, *Varieties of Minimalist Natural Law Theory*, 34 AMER. J. JURIS. 133 (1989) (footnotes omitted):

> To his book ETHICS AFTER BABEL, Jeffrey Stout appends a lexicon of terminology used in the guild of moral philosophers. Under "natural law," which includes "the moral law," and "realm of values," the entry is as follows: "fancy names for all the moral truths, known and unknown, that can be formulated in all the possible moral vocabularies." This is not very helpful, which, of course, is Stout's point. Recourse to natural law language, he writes, is really an appeal to "further beliefs not currently in question."
>
> One of the most persistent criticisms of natural law discourse is that it is difficult to sort out whether the term natural law is used only as an emblematic circumlocution for "beliefs not currently in question," or whether it expresses something philosophically substantive—that is, something that might constructively guide inquiry about matters of law and morals. Some of our best legal theorists * * * make precisely this argument. It's not a bad one. After all, if natural law or natural rights discourse represents only what its various advocates take to be basically good, morally valuable, or unquestionably true, then the discourse is a rhetoric of exhortation rather than a mode of discovery about what ought to be valued. * * *

Id. One famous philosopher of law, H.L.A. Hart (1907–1992), frames the issue like this:

> Reflection on some very obvious generalizations—indeed truisms—concerning human nature and the world in which men live, show that as long as those hold good, there are certain rules of conduct which any social organization must contain if it is viable. Such rules do in fact constitute a common element in the law and conventional morality of all societies, which have progressed to the point where these are distinguished as different forms of social control. * * * Such universally recognized principles of conduct which have a basis in elementary truths concerning human beings, their natural environment, and aims, may be considered the minimum content of Natural Law, in contrast with the more grandiose and more challengeable constructions which have often been proffered under that name.

H.L.A. HART, THE CONCEPT OF LAW 192–93 (2d ed. 1994). If you temporarily suspend whatever skepticism you might bring to the project, what would you identify as the essential "elementary truths concerning human beings, their natural environment, and aims?" To what extent does your list resemble what follows?

---

2. The Philosophical Argument from (or for) Natural Law

THOMAS HOBBES, *LEVIATHAN*

(1651)

[Thomas Hobbes (1588–1679) defined natural law as "a precept, or general rule, found out by reason, by which a man is forbidden to do that which is destructive of his life, or takes away the means of preserving the same; and to omit that by which he thinks it may best be preserved." He identified nineteen such precepts or general rules, based on a conception of human life in a state of pre-social nature that was "solitary, poor, nasty, brutish, and short."]

1. The first Law of nature is that every man ought to endeavour peace, as far as he has hope of obtaining it; and when he cannot obtain it, that he may seek and use all helps and advantages of war.

2. The second Law of nature is that a man be willing, when others are so too, as far forth, as for peace, and defence of himself he shall think it necessary, to lay down this right to all things; and be contented with so much liberty against other men, as he would allow other men against himself.

3. The third Law is that men perform their covenants made. In this law of nature consisteth the fountain and original of justice . . . when a covenant is made, then to break it is unjust and the definition of injustice

is no other than the not performance of covenant. And whatsoever is not unjust is just.

4. The fourth Law is that a man which receiveth benefit from another of mere grace, endeavour that he which giveth it, have no reasonable cause to repent him of his good will. Breach of this law is called ingratitude.

5. The fifth Law is complaisance: that every man strive to accommodate himself to the rest. The observers of this law may be called sociable; the contrary, stubborn, insociable, forward [*sic*], intractable.

6. The sixth Law is that upon caution of the future time, a man ought to pardon the offences past of them that repenting, desire it.

7. The seventh Law is that in revenges, men look not at the greatness of the evil past, but the greatness of the good to follow.

8. The eighth Law is that no man by deed, word, countenance, or gesture, declare hatred or contempt of another. The breach of which law is commonly called contumely.

9. The ninth Law is that every man acknowledge another for his equal by nature. The breach of this precept is pride.

10. The tenth law is that at the entrance into the conditions of peace, no man require to reserve to himself any right, which he is not content should be reserved to every one of the rest. The breach of this precept is arrogance, and observers of the precept are called modest.

11. The eleventh law is that if a man be trusted to judge between man and man, that he deal equally between them.

12. The twelfth law is that such things as cannot be divided, be enjoyed in common, if it can be; and if the quantity of the thing permit, without stint; otherwise proportionably [*sic*] to the number of them that have right.

13. The thirteenth law is the entire right, or else * * * the first possession (in the case of alternating use), of a thing that can neither be divided nor enjoyed in common should be determined by lottery.

14. The fourteenth law is that those things which cannot be enjoyed in common, nor divided, ought to be adjudged to the first possessor; and in some cases to the first born, as acquired by lot.

15. The fifteenth law is that all men that mediate peace be allowed safe conduct.

16. The sixteenth law is that they that are at controversie [*sic*], submit their Right to the judgement of an Arbitrator.

17. The seventeenth law is that no man is a fit Arbitrator in his own cause.

18. The eighteenth law is that no man should serve as a judge in a case if greater profit, or honour, or pleasure apparently ariseth [for him] out of the victory of one party, than of the other.

19. The nineteenth law is that in a disagreement of fact, the judge should not give more weight to the testimony of one party than another, and absent other evidence, should give credit to the testimony of other witnesses.

ARISTOTLE, *RHETORIC*

(4th Century, B.C.E.)
Book I, Chapter 13

It will now be well to make a complete classification of just and unjust actions. We may begin by observing that they have been defined relatively to two kinds of law, and also relatively to two classes of persons. By the two kinds of law I mean particular law and universal law. Particular law is that which each community lays down and applies to its own members: this is partly written and partly unwritten. Universal law is the law of Nature. For there really is, as every one to some extent divines, a natural justice and injustice that is binding on all men, even on those who have no association or covenant with each other. It is this that Sophocles' Antigone clearly means when she says that the burial of Polyneices was a just act in spite of the prohibition: she means that it was just by nature.

Not of today or yesterday it is,

But lives eternal: none can date its birth.

And so Empedocles, when he bids us kill no living creature, says that doing this is not just for some people while unjust for others,

Nay, but, an all-embracing law, through the realms of the sky

Unbroken it stretcheth, and over the earth's immensity.

THOMAS AQUINAS, *SUMMA THEOLOGICA**

(1265–1274)

[In the following excerpt, Aquinas structures the argument in a peculiar and formal way. He begins each section by asking a particular question, then presenting the argument he intends to reject ("Objection 1, 2, *etc.*"), followed by his initial argument ("I answer that") and his refinements ("Reply objection 1, 2, *etc.*"). The authorities he cites would be easily

* [From THE BASIC WRITINGS OF SAINT THOMAS AQUINAS (Anton C. Pegis, ed. 1945), Vol. II 742–53,773–80,784–85,791–95.]

recognized by his contemporaries, especially books of the Bible, "the Philosopher" (Aristotle), "the Jurist" (Cicero), and Isidore of Saville, among others. As you read the excerpt, we suggest that you keep a running catalogue of the essential characteristics of natural law according to Aquinas.]

ON THE VARIOUS KINDS OF LAW

WHETHER THERE IS AN ETERNAL LAW?

Objection 1. It would seem that there is no eternal law. For every law is imposed on someone. But there was not someone from eternity on whom a law could be imposed, since God alone was from eternity. Therefore no law is eternal.

Obj. 2. Further, promulgation is essential to law. But promulgation could not be from eternity, because there was no one to whom it could be promulgated from eternity. Therefore no law can be eternal.

Obj. 3. Further, law implies order to an end. But nothing ordained to an end is eternal, for the last end alone is eternal. Therefore no law is eternal. On the contrary, Augustine says: That law which is the supreme Reason cannot be understood to be otherwise than unchangeable and eternal.

I answer that, * * * law is nothing else but a dictate of practical reason emanating from the ruler who governs a perfect community. Now it is evident, granted that the world is ruled by divine providence * * * that the whole community of the universe is governed by the divine reason. Therefore the very notion of the government of things in God, the ruler of the universe, has the nature of a law. And since the divine reason's conception of things is not subject to time, but is eternal, according to *Prov. viii. 23*, therefore it is that this kind of law must be called eternal.

Reply Obj. 1. Those things that do not exist in themselves exist in God, inasmuch as they are known and preordained by Him, according to *Rom. iv. 17*: Who calls those things that are not, as those that are. Accordingly, the eternal concept of the divine law bears the character of an eternal law in so far as it is ordained by God to the government of things foreknown by Him.

Reply Obj. 2. Promulgation is made by word of mouth or in writing, and in both ways the eternal law is promulgated, because both the divine Word and the writing of the Book of Life are eternal. But the promulgation cannot be from eternity on the part of the creature that hears or reads.

Reply Obj. 3. Law implies order to the end actively, namely, in so far as it directs certain things to the end; but not passively, that is to say, the law itself is not ordained to the end, except accidentally, in a governor whose end is extrinsic to him, and to which end his law must needs be ordained. But the end of the divine government is God Himself, and His law is not something other than Himself. Therefore the eternal law is not ordained to another end.

WHETHER THERE IS IN US A NATURAL LAW?

Objection 1. It would seem that there is no natural law in us. For man is governed sufficiently by the eternal law, since Augustine says that the eternal law is that by which it is right that all things should be most orderly. But nature does not abound in superfluities as neither does she fail in necessaries. Therefore man has no natural law.

Obj. 2. Further, by the law man is directed, in his acts, to the end, as was stated above. But the directing of human acts to their end is not a function of nature, as is the case in irrational creatures, which act for an end solely by their natural appetite; whereas man acts for an end by his reason and will. Therefore man has no natural law.

Obj. 3. Further, the more a man is free, the less is he under the law. But man is freer than all the animals because of his free choice, with which he is endowed in distinction from all other animals. Since, therefore, other animals are not subject to a natural law, neither is man subject to a natural law. On the contrary, the Gloss on *Rom ii. 14* (When the Gentiles, who have not the law, do by nature those things that are of the law) comments as follows: Although they have no written law, yet they have the natural law, whereby each one knows, and is conscious of; what is good and what is evil.

I answer that, * * * law, being a rule and measure, can be in a person in two ways: in one way, as in him that rules and measures; in another way, as in that which is ruled and measured, since a thing is ruled and measured in so far as it partakes of the rule or measure. Therefore, since all things subject to divine providence are ruled and measured by the eternal law, as was stated above, it is evident that all things partake in some way in the eternal law, in so far as, namely, from its being imprinted on them, they derive their respective inclinations to their proper acts and ends. Now among all others, the rational creature is subject to divine providence in a more excellent way, in so far as it itself partakes of a share of providence, by being provident both for itself and for others. Therefore it has a share of the eternal reason, whereby it has a natural inclination to its proper act and end; and this participation of the eternal law in the rational creature is called the natural law. Hence the Psalmist, after saying (*Ps. iv. 6*): Offer up the sacrifice of justice, as though someone asked what the works of justice are, adds: Many say, Who showeth us good things? in answer to which question he says: The light of Thy countenance, O Lord, is signed upon us. He thus implies that the light of natural reason, whereby we discern what is good and what is evil, which is the function of the natural law, is nothing else than an imprint on us of the divine light. It is therefore evident that the natural law is nothing else than the rational creature's participation of the eternal law.

Reply Obj. 1. This argument would hold if the natural law were something different from the eternal law; whereas it is nothing but a participation thereof, as we have stated above.

Reply Obj. 2. Every act of reason and will in us is based on that which is according to nature, as was stated above. For every act of reasoning is based on principles that are known naturally, and every act of appetite in respect of the means is derived from the natural appetite in respect of the last end. Accordingly, the first direction of our acts to their end must needs be through the natural law.

Reply Obj. 3. Even irrational animals partake in their own way of the eternal reason, just as the rational creature does. But because the rational creature partakes thereof in an intellectual and rational manner, therefore the participation of the eternal law in the rational creature is properly called a law, since a law is something pertaining to reason, as was stated above. Irrational creatures, however, do not partake thereof in a rational manner, and therefore there is no participation of the eternal law in them, except by way of likeness.

WHETHER THERE IS A HUMAN LAW?

Objection 1. It would seem that there is not a human law. For the natural law is a participation of the eternal law, as was stated above. Now through the eternal law all things are most orderly, as Augustine states. Therefore the natural law suffices for the ordering of all human affairs. Consequently there is no need for a human law.

Obj. 2. Further, law has the character of a measure, as was stated above. But human reason is not a measure of things, but vice versa, as is stated in *Metaph. x.* Therefore no law can emanate from the human reason.

Obj. 3. Further, a measure should be most certain, as is stated in *Metaph. x.* But the dictates of the human reason in matters of conduct are uncertain, according to *Wis. ix. 14*: The thoughts of mortal men are fearful, and our counsels uncertain. Therefore no law can emanate from the human reason. On the contrary, Augustine distinguishes two kinds of law, the one eternal, the other temporal, which he calls human.

I answer that, * * * a law is a dictate of the practical reason. Now it is to be observed that the same procedure takes place in the practical and in the speculative reason, for each proceeds from principles to conclusions, as was stated above. Accordingly, we conclude that, just as in the speculative reason, from naturally known indemonstrable principles we draw the conclusions of the various sciences, the knowledge of which is not imparted to us by nature, but acquired by the efforts of reason, so too it is that from the precepts of the natural law, as from common and indemonstrable principles, the human reason needs to proceed to the more particular determination of certain matters. These particular determinations, devised by human reason, are called human laws, provided that the other essential conditions of law be observed, as was stated above. Therefore Tully says in his *Rhetoric* that justice has its source in nature; thence certain things came into custom by reason of their utility; afterwards these things which emanated from nature, and were approved by custom, were sanctioned by fear and reverence for the law.

Reply Obj. 1. The human reason cannot have a full participation of the dictate of the divine reason, but according to its own mode, and imperfectly. Consequently, just as on the part of the speculative reason, by a natural participation of divine wisdom, there is in us the knowledge of certain common principles, but not a proper knowledge of each single truth, such as that contained in the divine wisdom, so, too, on the part of the practical reason, man has a natural participation of the eternal law, according to certain common principles, but not as regards the particular determinations of individual cases, which are, however, contained in the eternal law. Hence the need for human reason to proceed further to sanction them by law.

Reply Obj. 2. Human reason is not, of itself, the rule of things. But the principles impressed on it by nature are the general rules and measures of all things relating to human conduct, of which the natural reason is the rule and measure, although it is not the measure of things that are from nature.

Reply Obj. 3. The practical reason is concerned with operable matters, which are singular and contingent, but not with necessary things, with which the speculative reason is concerned. Therefore human laws cannot have that inerrancy that belongs to the demonstrated conclusions of the sciences. Nor is it necessary for every measure to be altogether unerring and certain, but according as it is possible in its own particular genus. * * *

THE NATURAL LAW

* * *

WHETHER THE NATURAL LAW IS THE SAME IN ALL MEN?

Objection 1. It would seem that the natural law is not the same in all. For it is stated in the Decretals that the natural law is that which is contained in the Law and the Gospel. But this is not common to all men, because, as it is written (*Rom.* x. 16), all do not obey the Gospel Therefore the natural law is not the same in all men.

Obj. 2. Further, things which are according to the law are said to be just, as is stated in *Ethics* v. But it is stated in the same book that nothing is so just for all as not to be subject to change in regard to some men. Therefore even the natural law is not the same in all men.

Obj. 3. Further, as was stated above, to the natural law belongs everything to which a man is inclined according to his nature. Now different men are naturally inclined to different things, some to the desire of pleasures, other to the desire of honors, and other men to other things. Therefore, there is not one natural law for all. On the contrary, Isidore says: The natural law is common to all nations.

I answer that, As we have stated above, to the natural law belong those things to which a man is inclined naturally; and among these it is proper to man to be inclined to act according to reason. Now it belongs to the reason to proceed from what is common to what is proper, as is stated in *Physics* i. The speculative reason, however, is differently situated, in this matter, from the practical reason. For, since the speculative reason is concerned chiefly with necessary things, which cannot be otherwise than they are, its proper conclusions, like the universal principles, contain the truth without fail. The practical reason, on the other hand, is concerned with contingent matters, which is the domain of human actions; and, consequently, although there is necessity in the common principles, the more we descend towards the particular, the more frequently we encounter defects. Accordingly, then, in speculative matters truth is the same in all men, both as to principles and as to conclusions; although the truth is not known to all as regards the conclusions, but only as regards the principles which are called common notions. But in matters of action, truth or practical rectitude is not the same for all as to what is particular, but only as to the common principles; and where there is the same rectitude in relation to particulars, it is not equally known to all.

It is therefore evident that, as regards the common principles whether of speculative or of practical reason, truth or rectitude is the same for all, and is equally known by all. But as to the proper conclusions of the speculative reason, the truth is the same for all, but it is not equally known to all. Thus, it is true for all that the three angles of a triangle are together equal to two right angles, although it is not known to all. But as to the proper conclusions of the practical reason, neither is the truth or rectitude the same for all, nor where it is the same, is it equally known by all. Thus, it is right and true for all to act according to reason, and from this principle it follows, as a proper conclusion, that goods entrusted to another should be restored to their owner. Now this is true for the majority of cases. But it may happen in a particular case that it would be injurious, and therefore unreasonable, to restore goods held in trust; for instance, if they are claimed for the purpose of fighting against one's country. And this principle will be found to fail the more, according as we descend further towards the particular, for example, if one were to say that goods held in trust should be restored with such and such a guarantee, or in such and such a way; because the greater the number of conditions added, the greater the number of ways in which the principle may fail, so that it be not right to restore or not to restore.

Consequently, we must say that the natural law, as to the first common principles, is the same for all, both as to rectitude and as to knowledge. But as to certain more particular aspects, which are conclusions, as it were, of those common principles, it is the same for all in the majority of cases, both as to rectitude and as to knowledge; and yet in some few cases, it may fail, both as to rectitude, by reason of certain obstacles (just as natures subject to generation and corruption fail in some few cases because of some obstacle), and as to knowledge, since in some the reason is perverted by passion, or evil habit, or an evil disposition of nature. Thus at one time theft, although it is expressly contrary to the natural law, was not considered wrong among the Germans, as Julius Caesar relates.

Reply Obj. 1. The meaning of the sentence quoted is not that whatever is contained in the Law and the Gospel belongs to the natural law, since they contain many things that are above nature; but that whatever belongs to the natural law is fully contained in them. Therefore Gratian, after saying that the natural law is what is contained in the Law and the Gospel, adds at once, by way of example, by which everyone is commanded to do to others as he would be done by.

Reply Obj. 2. The saying of the Philosopher is to be understood of things that are naturally just, not as common principles, but as conclusions drawn from them, having rectitude in the majority of cases, but failing in a few.

Reply Obj. 3. Just as in man reason rules and commands the other powers, so all the natural inclinations belonging to the other powers must needs be directed according to reason. Therefore it is universally right for all men that all their inclinations should be directed according to reason.

WHETHER THE NATURAL LAW CAN BE CHANGED?

Objection 1. It would seem that the natural law can be changed. For in *Ecclus.* xvii. 9 (He gave them instructions, and the law of life) the Gloss says: He wished the law of the letter to be written, in order to correct the law of nature. But that which is corrected is changed. Therefore the natural law can be changed.

Obj. 2. Further, the slaying of the innocent, adultery and theft are against the natural law. But we find these things changed by God: as when God commanded Abraham to slay his innocent son (*Gen.* xxii. 2); and when He ordered the Jews to borrow and purloin the vessels of the Egyptians (*Exod.* xii. 35); and when He commanded Osee to take to himself a wife of fornications (*Osee* i. 2). Therefore the natural law can be changed.

Obj. 3. Further, Isidore says that the possession of all things in common, and universal freedom, are matters of natural law. But these things are seen to be changed by human laws. Therefore it seems that the natural law is subject to change.

On the contrary, it is said in the Decretals [letters of the Pope regarding decisions on the ecclesiastical law of the Catholic Church], the natural law dates from the creation of the rational creature. It does not vary according to time, but remains unchangeable.

I answer that, A change in the natural law may be understood in two ways. First, by way of addition. In this sense, nothing hinders the natural law from being changed, since many things for the benefit of human life have been added over and above the natural law, both by the divine law and by human laws.

Secondly, a change in the natural law may be understood by way of subtraction, so that what previously was according to the natural law, ceases to be so. In this sense, the natural law is altogether unchangeable in its first principles. But in its secondary principles, which, as we have said, are certain detailed proximate conclusions drawn from the first principles, the natural law is not changed so that what it prescribes be not right in most cases. But it may be changed in some particular cases of rare occurrence, through some special causes hindering the observance of such precepts, as was stated above.

Reply Obj. 1. The written law is said to be given for the correction of the natural law, either because it supplies what was wanting to the natural law, or because the natural law was so perverted in the hearts of some men, as to certain matters, that they esteemed those things good which are naturally evil; which perversion stood in need of correction.

Reply Obj. 2. All men alike, both guilty and innocent, die the death of nature; which death of nature is inflicted by the power of God because of original sin, according to I *Kings* ii. 6: The Lord killeth and maketh alive. Consequently, by the command of God, death can be inflicted on any man, guilty or innocent, without any injustice whatever. In like manner, adultery is intercourse with another's wife; who is allotted to him by the law emanating from God. Consequently intercourse with any woman, by the command of God, is neither adultery nor fornication. The same applies to theft, which is the taking of another's property. For whatever is taken by the command of God, to Whom all things belong, is not taken against the will of its owner, whereas it is in this that theft consists. Nor is it only in human things that whatever is commanded by God is right; but also in natural things, what ever is done by God is, in some way, natural, as was stated in the First Part.

Reply Obj. 3. A thing is said to belong to the natural law in two ways. First, because nature inclines thereto: *e.g.*, that one should not do harm to another. Secondly, because nature did not bring with it the contrary. Thus, we might say that for man to be naked is of the natural law, because nature did not give him clothes, but art invented them. In this sense, the possession of all things in common and universal freedom are said to be of the natural law, because, namely, the distinction of possessions and slavery were not brought in by nature, but devised by human reason for the benefit of human life. Accordingly, the law of nature was not changed in this respect, except by addition. * * *

HUMAN LAW

WHETHER EVERY HUMAN LAW IS DERIVED FROM THE NATURAL LAW?

Objection 1. It would seem that not every human law is derived from the natural law. For the Philosopher says that the legal just is that which originally was a matter of indifference. But those things which arise from the natural law are not matters of indifference. Therefore the enactments of human laws are not all derived from the natural law.

Obj. 2. Further, positive law is divided against natural law, as is stated by Isidore and the Philosopher. But those things which flow as conclusions from the common principles of the natural law belong to the natural law, as was stated above. Therefore that which is established by human law is not derived from the natural law.

Obj. 3. Further, the law of nature is the same for all, since the Philosopher says that the natural just is that which is equally valid everywhere. If therefore human laws were derived from the natural law, it would follow that they too are the same for all; which is clearly false.

Obj. 4. Further, it is possible to give a reason for things which are derived from the natural law. But it is not possible to give the reason for all the legal enactments of the lawgivers, as the Jurist says. Therefore not all human laws are derived from the natural law.

On the contrary, Tully says: Things which emanated from nature, and were approved by custom, were sanctioned by fear and reverence for the laws.

I answer that, As Augustine says, that which is not just seems to be no law at all. Hence the force of a law depends on the extent of its justice. Now in human affairs a thing is said to be just from being right, according to the rule of reason. But the first rule of reason is the law of nature, as is clear from what has been stated above. Consequently, every human law has just so much of the nature of law as it is derived from the law of nature. But if in any point it departs from the law of nature, it is no longer a law but a perversion of law.

But it must be noted that something may be derived from the natural law in two ways: first, as a conclusion from principles; secondly, by way of a determination of certain common notions. The first way is like to that by which, in the sciences, demonstrated conclusions are drawn from the principles; while the second is likened to that whereby, in the arts, common forms are determined to some particular. Thus, the craftsman needs to determine the common form of a house to the shape of this or that particular house. Some things are therefore derived from the common principles of the natural law by way of conclusions: *e.g.*, that one must not kill may be derived as a conclusion from the principle that one should do harm to no man; while some are derived therefrom by way of determination: *e.g.*, the law of nature has it that the evil-doer should be punished, but that he be punished in this or that way is a determination of the law of nature.

Accordingly, both modes of derivation are found in the human law. But those things which are derived in the first way are contained in human law, not as emanating therefrom exclusively, but as having some force from the natural law also. But those things which are derived in the second way have no other force than that of human law.

Reply Obj. 1. The Philosopher is speaking of those enactments which are by way of determination or specification of the precepts of the natural law.

Reply Obj. 2. This argument holds for those things that are derived from the natural law by way of conclusion.

Reply Obj. 3. The common principles of the natural law cannot be applied to all men in the same way because of the great variety of human affairs; and hence arises the diversity of positive laws among various people.

Reply Obj. 4. These words of the Jurist are to be understood as referring to the decisions of rulers in determining particular points of the natural law; and to these determinations the judgment of expert and prudent men is related as to its principles, in so far, namely, as they see at once what is the best thing to decide. Hence the Philosopher says that, in such matters, we ought to pay as much attention to the undemonstrated sayings and opinions of persons who surpass us in experience, age and prudence, as to their demonstrations. * * *

WHETHER HUMAN LAW BINDS A MAN IN CONSCIENCE?

Objection 1. It would seem that human law does not bind a man in conscience. For an inferior power cannot impose its law on the judgment of a higher power. But the power of man, which frames human law, is beneath the divine power. Therefore human law cannot impose its precept on a divine judgment, such as is the judgment of conscience.

Obj. 2. Further, the judgment of conscience depends chiefly on the commandments of God. But sometimes God's commandments are made void by human laws, according to *Matt.* xv. 6: You have made void the commandment of God for your tradition. Therefore human law does not bind a man in conscience.

Obj. 3. Further, human laws often bring loss of character and injury on man, according to *Isa.* x. 1, 2: Woe to them that make wicked laws, and when they write, write injustice; to oppress the poor in judgment, and do violence to the cause of the humble of My people. But it is lawful for anyone to avoid oppression and violence. Therefore human laws do not bind man in conscience.

On the contrary, it is written (I *Pet.* ii. 19): This is thanksworthy, if for conscience * * * a man endure sorrows, suffering wrongfully.

I answer that, laws framed by man are either just or unjust. If they be just, they have the power of binding in conscience from the eternal law whence they are derived, according to *Prov.* viii. 15: By Me kings reign, and lawgivers decree just things. Now laws are said to be just, both from the end (when, namely, they are ordained to the common good), from their author (that is to say, when the law that is made does not exceed the power of the lawgiver), and from their form (when, namely, burdens are laid on the subjects according to an equality of proportion and with a view to the common good). For, since one man is a part of the community, each man, in all that he is and has, belongs to the community; just as a part, in all that it is belongs to the whole. So, too, nature inflicts a loss on the part in order to save the whole; so that for this reason such laws as these, which impose proportionate burdens, are just and binding in conscience, and are legal laws.

On the other hand, laws may be unjust in two ways: first, by being contrary to human good, through being opposed to the things mentioned above: either in respect of the ends, as when as authority imposes on his subjects burdensome laws, conducive, not to the common good, but rather to his own cupidity or vainglory; or in respect of the author, as when a man makes a law that goes beyond the power committed to him; or in respect of the form, as when burdens are imposed unequally on the community, although with a view to the common good. Such are acts of violence rather than laws, because, as Augustine says, a law that is not just seems to be no law at all. Therefore, such laws do not bind in conscience, except perhaps in order to avoid scandal or disturbance, for which cause a man should even yield his right, according to *Matt.* v. 40, 41: If a man * * * take away thy coat, let go thy cloak also unto him; and whosoever will force thee one mile, go with him other two.

Secondly, laws may be unjust through being opposed to the divine good. Such are the laws of tyrants inducing to idolatry, or to anything else contrary to the divine law. Laws of this kind must in no way be observed, because, as is stated in *Acts* v. 29, we ought to obey God rather than men.

Reply Obj. 1. As the Apostle says (*Rom.* xiii. 1, 2), all human power is from God . . . therefore he that resisteth the power, in matters that are within its scope, resisteth the ordinance of God; so that he becomes guilty in conscience.

Reply Obj. 2. This argument is true of laws that are contrary to the commandments of God, which is beyond the scope of [human] power. Therefore in such matters human law should not be obeyed.

Reply Obj. 3. This argument is true of a law that inflicts an unjust burden on its subjects. Furthermore, the power that man holds from God does not extend to this. Hence neither in such matters is man bound to obey the law, provided he avoid giving scandal or inflicting a more grievous injury. * * *

LON FULLER, THE MORALITY OF LAW

(REV. ED. 1969)

[Aquinas makes the explicit connection between natural law and religion, specifically the tenets, texts, and history of Roman Catholicism. At the time he produced the *Summa Theologica*, he could be certain that virtually all of his readers across Europe shared his religious commitments. After the Reformation, the Enlightenment, the Industrial Revolution, and the rise of scientific materialism, a self-described natural law theorist in the twentieth century, like Lon Fuller, confronted a radically different intellectual melieu. As you read the following excerpt, consider how a philosophy of law traceable to the ancients might morph under the influence of Christianity, and then morph again in a dramatically more pluralistic world.]

Chapter II: The Morality that Makes Law Possible

* * * [T]he attempt to create and maintain a system of legal rules may miscarry in at least eight ways; there are in this enterprise, if you will, eight distinct routes to disaster. The first and most obvious lies in a failure to achieve rules at all, so that every issue must be decided on an ad hoc basis. The other routes are: (2) a failure to publicize, or at least to make available to the affected party, the rules he is expected to observe; (3) the abuse of retroactive legislation, which not only cannot itself guide action, but undercuts the integrity of rules prospective in effect, since *it* puts them under the threat of retrospective change; (4) a failure to make rules understandable; (5) the enactment of contradictory rules or (6) rules that require conduct beyond the powers of the affected party; (7) introducing such frequent changes in the rules that the subject cannot orient his action by them and finally (8) a failure of congruence between the rules as announced and their actual administration.

A total failure in any one of these eight directions does not simply result in a bad system of law; it results in something that is not properly called a legal system at all, except perhaps in the * * * sense in which a void contract can still be said to be one kind of contract. Certainly there can be no rational ground for asserting that a man can have a moral obligation to obey a legal rule that does not exist, or is kept secret from him, or that came into existence only after he had acted, or was unintelligible, or was contradicted by another rule of the same system, or commanded the impossible, or changed every minute. It may not be impossible for a man to obey a rule that is disregarded by those charged with its administration, but at some point obedience becomes futile—as futile, in fact, as casting a vote that will never be counted. * * * [T]here is a kind of reciprocity between government and the citizen with respect to the observance of rules. * * * Government says to the citizen in effect, "These are the rules we expect you to follow. If you follow them, you have our assurance that they are the rules that will be applied to your conduct." When this bond of reciprocity is finally and completely ruptured by government nothing is left on which to ground the citizen's duty to observe the rules.

The citizen's predicament becomes more difficult when, though there is no total failure in any direction, there is a general and drastic deterioration in legality such as occurred in Germany under Hitler. * * * A situation begin to develop for example in which though some laws are published, others including the most important, are not. Though most laws are prospective in effect so free a use is made of retrospective legislation that no law is immune to change ex post facto if it suits the convenience of those in power. For the trial of criminal cases concerned with loyalty to the regime, special military tribunals are established and these tribunals disregard whenever it suits their convenience, the rules that are supposed to control their decisions. Increasingly the principal object of government seems to be, not that of giving the citizen rules by which to shape his conduct, but to frighten him into impotence. As such a situation develops, the problem faced by the citizen is not so simple as that of a voter who knows with certainty that his ballot will not be counted. It is more like that of the voter who knows that the odds are against his ballot being counted at all, and that if it is counted, there is a good chance that it will be counted for the side against which he actually voted. A citizen in this predicament has to decide for himself whether to stay with the system and cast his ballot as a kind of symbolic act expressing the hope of a better day. So it was with the German citizen under Hitler faced with deciding whether he had an obligation to obey such portions of the laws as the Nazi terror had left intact.

In situations like these there can be no simple principle by which to test the citizen's obligation of fidelity to law, any more than there can be such a principle for testing his right to engage in a general revolution. One thing is, however, clear. A mere respect for constituted authority must not be confused with fidelity to law. * * *

The Aspiration toward Perfection in Legality

So far we have been concerned to trace out eight routes to failure in the enterprise of creating law. Corresponding to these are eight kinds of legal excellence toward which a system of rules may strive. What appear at the lowest level as indispensable conditions for the existence of law at all, become, as we ascend the scale of achievement, increasingly demanding challenges to human capacity. At the height of the ascent we are tempted to imagine a utopia of legality in which all rules are perfectly clear, consistent with one another, known to every citizen, and never retroactive. In this utopia the rules remain constant through time, demand only what is possible, and are scrupulously observed by courts, police, and everyone else charged with their administration. For reasons that I shall advance shortly, this utopia, in which all eight of the principles of legality are realized to perfection, is not actually a useful target for guiding the impulse toward legality; the goal of perfection is much more complex.

Nevertheless it does suggest eight distinct standards by which excellence in legality may be tested. In expounding in my first chapter the distinction between the morality of duty and that of aspiration I spoke of an imaginary scale that starts at the bottom with the most obvious and essential moral duties and ascends upward to the highest achievements open to man. I also spoke of an invisible pointer as marking the dividing line where the pressure of duty leaves off and the challenge of excellence begins. The inner morality of law, it should now be clear, presents all of these aspects. It too embraces a morality of duty and a morality of aspiration. It too confronts us with the problem of knowing where to draw the boundary below which men will be condemned for failure, but can expect no praise for success, and above which they will be admired for success and at worst pitied for the lack of it.

* * * [I]t becomes essential to consider certain distinctive qualities of the inner morality of law. In what may be called the basic morality of social life, duties that run toward other persons generally (as contrasted with those running toward specific individuals) normally require only forbearances, or as we say, are negative in nature: Do not kill, do not injure, do not deceive, do not defame, and the like. Such duties lend themselves with a minimum of difficulty to formalized definition. That is to say, whether we are concerned with legal or moral duties, we are able to develop standards which designate with some precision though it is never complete-the kind of conduct that is to be avoided.

The demands of the inner morality of the law, however, though they concern a relationship with persons generally, demand more than forbearances; they are, as we loosely say, affirmative in nature: make the law known, make it coherent and clear, see that your decisions as an official are guided by it, etc. To meet these demands human energies must be directed toward specific kinds of achievement and not merely warned away from harmful acts.

Because of the affirmative and creative quality of its demands, the inner morality of law lends itself badly to realization through duties, whether they be moral or legal. No matter how desirable a direction of human effort may appear to be, if we assert there is a duty to pursue it, we shall confront the responsibility of defining at what point that duty has been violated. It is easy to assert that the legislator has a moral duty to make his laws clear and understandable. But this remains at best an exhortation unless we are prepared to define the degree of clarity he must attain in order to discharge his duty. The notion of subjecting clarity to quantitative measure presents obvious difficulties. We may content ourselves, of course, by saying that the legislator has at least a moral duty to try to be clear. But this only postpones the difficulty, for in some situations nothing can be more baffling than to attempt to measure how vigorously a man intended to do that which he has failed to do. In the morality of law, in any event, good intentions are of little avail * * *. All of this adds up to the conclusion that the inner morality of law is condemned to remain largely a morality of aspiration and not of duty. Its primary appeal must be to a sense of trusteeship and to the pride of the craftsman.

NOTES AND QUESTIONS

1. *Fuller's version of natural law.* This brief passage from Professor Fuller's book is a small part of a sustained argument about the requirements of a legal system, something he calls "the morality that makes law possible" or the "internal morality of law." He identifies eight principles and, using the conceptual machinery of natural law, describes them as preconditions for legality: (1) the rules must be in general terms, so that issues are not "decided on an *ad hoc* basis;" (2) the rules must be publicized or effectively communicated so that those affected will know what's required of them; (3) legislation must generally be prospective only, and whatever retroactive legislation exists cannot be "abused;" (4) the rules must be expressed in terms that are understandable; (5) the rules may not contradict one another or require inconsistent conduct; (6) the rules may not require conduct that is impossible to perform; (7) the rules cannot be changed so frequently that those affected by the rules "cannot orient[their] action by them; and (8) there must be congruence between the rules as announced and as administered or applied. Understanding that Aquinas and Fuller are both natural law theorists, separated by seven centuries of drastic change, what are the essential similarities and differences between them?

2. *What if a legal system flunks Fuller's tests?* The consequence of a system failing to meet any one of Fuller's criteria is that it cannot achieve the purpose of law, namely securing some measure of order through rules. As Fuller says: "A total failure in any one of these eight directions does not simply result in a bad system of law; it results in something that is not properly called a legal system at all." In many respects this is a strategic reformulation of natural law, because, instead of assessing the justice of a particular rule or result in a case, Fuller considers its pedigree within a system that satisfies the eight principles. How does that conception of the relationship between morality and the law compare with your understanding of natural law?

3. *One critique of Fuller.* H.L.A. Hart criticized Fuller for confusing morality with efficacy (or efficiency for a purpose):

> [T]he author's insistence on classifying these principles of legality as a "morality" is a source of confusion both for him and his readers. . . . [T]he crucial objection to the designation of these principles of good legal craftsmanship as morality, in spite of the qualification "inner," is that it perpetrates a confusion between two notions that it is vital to hold apart: the notions of purposive activity and morality. Poisoning is no doubt a purposive activity, and reflections on its purpose may show that it has its internal principles. ("Avoid poisons however lethal if they cause the victim to vomit". * * *) But to call these principles of the poisoner's art "the morality of poisoning" would simply blur the distinction between the notion of efficiency for a purpose and those final judgments about activities and purposes with which morality in its various forms is concerned.

H. L. A. Hart, *Review of* The Morality of Law, 78 HARVARD L. REV. 1281, 1285–86 (1965). In other words, in Hart's view, even if the eight principles are preconditions for the existence of law or of an effective legal system, that does not by itself establish the necessary conceptual connection between law and morality that is one hallmark of natural law theories.

4. *Testing Fuller's approach*. Can you imagine immoral laws that emerge from a legal system that fully satisfies Fuller's eight principles? How confident are you that the U.S. legal system satisfies the eight principles? Is it a defense of Fuller's insights to suggest that there is value in creating a rubric for aspiration or a set of criteria for critiquing a particular legal system or some of its rules?

JOHN FINNIS, NATURAL LAW AND NATURAL RIGHTS

(1980)

III. A BASIC FORM OF GOOD: KNOWLEDGE

III.1 AN EXAMPLE

Neither this chapter nor the next makes or presupposes any moral judgments. Rather, these two chapters concern the evaluative substratum of all moral judgments. That is to say, they concern the acts of practical understanding in which we grasp the basic values of human existence and thus, too, the basic principles of all practical reasoning.

The purpose of this chapter, in particular, is to illustrate (i) what I mean by "basic value" and "basic practical principle", (ii) how such values and principles enter into any consideration of good reasons for action and any full description of human conduct, and (iii) the sense in which such basic values are obvious ("self-evident") and even unquestionable. For this purpose, I discuss only one basic value, leaving to the next chapter the identification of the other forms of human good that, so far as I can see, are likewise irreducibly basic.

The example of a basic value to be examined now is: knowledge. Perhaps it would be more accurate to call it "speculative knowledge", using the term "speculative" here, not to make the Aristotelian distinction between the *theoretike* and the *praktike*, but to distinguish knowledge as sought for its own sake from knowledge as sought only instrumentally, *i.e.* as useful in the pursuit of some other objective, such as survival, power, popularity, or a money-saving cup of coffee. Now "knowledge", unlike "belief", is an achievement-word; there are true beliefs and false beliefs, but knowledge is of truth. So one could speak of truth as the basic good with which we are here concerned, for one can just as easily speak of "truth for its own sake" as of "knowledge for its own sake". In any event, truth is not a mysterious abstract entity; we want the truth when we want the judgments in which we affirm or deny propositions to be true judgments, or (what comes to the same) want the propositions affirmed or denied, or to be affirmed or denied, to be true propositions. So, to complete the explanation of what is meant by the knowledge under discussion here, as distinct from instrumental knowledge, I can add that the distinction I am drawing is not between one set of propositions and another. It is not a distinction between fields of knowledge. Any proposition, whatever its subject-matter, can be inquired into (with a view to affirming or denying it) in either of the two distinct ways, (i) instrumentally or (ii) out of curiosity, the pure desire to know, to find out the truth about it simply out of an interest in or concern for truth and a desire to avoid ignorance or error as such.

This chapter, then, is an invitation to reflect on one form of human activity, the activity of trying to find out, to understand, and to judge matters correctly. This is not, perhaps, the easiest activity to understand; but it has the advantage of being the activity which the reader himself is actually engaged in. But if it seems too abstruse and tricky to try to understand this form of activity reflexively (*i.e.* by reflecting on one's attempt to understand and assess the truth of this chapter itself), one can reflect on any other exercise of curiosity. One could consider, for example, the wide-ranging effort of historical inquiry involved in discovering the actual intentions of the principal authors of the Statute of Uses (1536) or of the Fourteenth Amendment of the US Constitution (1866). Or something more humble (like weighing the truth of some gossipy rumour), or more "scientific"—it makes no difference, for present purposes. * * *

III.4 THE SELF-EVIDENCE OF THE GOOD OF KNOWLEDGE

Is it not the case that knowledge is really a good, an aspect of authentic human flourishing, and that the principle which expresses its value formulates a real (intelligent) reason for action? It seems clear that such indeed is the case, and that there are no sufficient reasons for doubting it to be so. The good of knowledge is self-evident, obvious. It cannot be demonstrated, but equally it needs no demonstration.

This is not to say that everyone actually does recognize the value of knowledge, or that there are no pre-conditions for recognizing that value. The principle that truth (and knowledge) is worth pursuing is not somehow innate, inscribed on the mind at birth. On the contrary, the value of truth becomes obvious only to one who has experienced the urge to question, who has grasped the connection between question and answer, who understands that knowledge is constituted by correct answers to particular questions, and who is aware of the possibility of further questions and of other questioners who like himself could enjoy the advantage of attaining correct answers. A new-born child, for example, has presumably not had any such set of felt inclinations, memories, understandings, and (in short) experiences.

In asking oneself whether knowledge is indeed a value (for its own sake: thus, a basic value), one should not be deflected by the fact that one's inclination to seek truth has psychological roots. It may well be that at an early stage in the life of the mind the urge to know is scarcely differentiated from other urges, such as the sexual drive. This early lack of differentiation may be never wholly surmounted, so that the one urge remains capable not only of deflecting but also of reinforcing the other. Such facts, interesting and important as they may be in some contexts, are not relevant to the question "Is knowledge indeed a good, objectively worth pursuing?". In considering the question: "Is the psychologist's opinion that curiosity is a form of sexuality a true or at least a warranted opinion?", it is relevant to attend to the coherence of the psychologist's hypothesis, to the pertinence of his evidence, to the soundness of his inferences. But it is not relevant to ask whether the psychologist's opinion emerged in his psyche at the call of his sexuality or as a reflection of his organic constitution or under the influence of any other such sub-rational cause. The soundness of an answer to a particular question is never established or disconfirmed by the answer to the entirely different question of what are the physical, biological, and psychological pre-conditions and concomitants of the raising of that question (or any question) and of the proposing of that answer (or any answer). And all this holds true of the answer "Yes, obviously" to the question "Is knowledge worth having?".

Just as we should not appeal to causes, pre-conditions, and concomitants in order to raise an illegitimate doubt about the self-evidence of the value of knowledge, so we should not seek a deduction or inference of that value from facts. If one is to go beyond the felt urge of curiosity to an understanding grasp of the value of knowledge, one certainly must know at least the fact that some questions can be answered. Moreover, one certainly will be assisted if one also knows such facts as that answers tend to hang together in systems that tend to be illuminating over as wide a range as the data which stimulate one's questions. But one who, thus knowing the possibility of attaining truth, is enabled thereby to grasp the value of that possible object and attainment is not inferring the value from the possibility. No such inference is possible. No value can be deduced or otherwise inferred from a fact or set of facts.

Nor can one validly infer the value of knowledge from the fact (if fact it be) that "all men desire to know". The universality of a desire is not a sufficient basis for inferring that the object of that desire is really desirable, objectively good. Nor is such a basis afforded by the fact that the desire or inclination manifests, or is part of, a deep structure shaping the human mind, or by the fact that the desire, or the structure, is ineradicable, or by the fact that in whole or part the desire is (or is not) common to all animals, or by the fact that it is (or is not) peculiar to human beings.

Nor would it be logically decisive to establish that all human persons not only desire to know (have the urge of curiosity) but also affirm the value of knowledge and respect and pursue it in their lives. (Conversely, the fact that not all men pursue or admit to pursuing or even give lip-service to the value of knowledge does not give sufficient ground for denying or rejecting that value.) To know that and how other persons have valued knowledge is relevant, for it serves as a disclosure or intimation or reminder of the range of opportunities open to one. The life and death of a Socrates, and the disciplined, exact, profound, and illuminating investigations of a Plato (or a Galileo or a Maitland), reveal an aspect of human possibility only vaguely prefigured by one's own relatively feeble or fickle curiosity. * * * But to say that knowledge must be a real value, because intelligent men, or great men, or mature men have regarded it as a value and as an aspect of their own flourishing, is not to make what could be called an inference. For one's assessment of a person as flourishing, mature, great, or, in the relevant respect, intelligent is made possible only by one's own underived understanding that what that person is and does is really good (in the relevant respects). The "premises" of the apparent inference thus rests on its "conclusion".

But is there not something fishy about appeal to self-evidence? Do modern sciences and other theoretical disciplines rest on self-evident concepts or principles? Or is it not rather the case that appeal to allegedly self-evident principles is a relic of the discredited Aristotelian conception of axiomatized sciences of nature?

A proper discussion of self-evidence would have to be embarrassingly complex, not only because almost every controverted question in epistemology is here brought to a focus, but also because the modern conception of an axiom is not the conception taken for granted by Aristotle and Aquinas. For the axioms of, say, modern geometries are not selected, as those of Euclid apparently were, for their purported self-evidence, but rather for their capacity to generate a system of theorems, proofs, etc. which is consistent and complete. We may observe in passing that appeal to self-evidence does seem to be made (though without much advertisement) in a modern geometry (i) in establishing the meaning of at least some of the 'primitive' terms employed to formulate the axioms and theorems (e.g., in Hilbert's or Veblen's postulates for Euclidean geometry, the term "between", as in "C is between A and B"); (ii) in generating the theorems and proofs, by employing as inference rules a logic which (as geometers rather freely admit) is imported into geometry without too much scrutiny; (iii) at some point in the assessment of consistency, and (iv) at some point in the assessment of completeness. Still, someone may ask whether a modern pure geometry is intended to state truths or to amount to knowledge at all. So, leaving that question to one side, it may be more pertinent to observe that the natural sciences (not to mention the historical sciences, and the disciplined common sense of forensic assessment of evidence) certainly rest, implicitly but thoroughly, on the principles of elementary formal logic (though those principles are far from exhausting the rational principles on which the elaboration of such sciences and disciplines proceeds).

It may be still more helpful, for the purposes of this brief reflection on self-evidence, to consider some of the principles or norms of sound judgment in every empirical discipline. * * * But reflection on what it means to say that the principles or norms of sound empirical judgment are self-evident will help to eliminate some misunderstandings of what it means to say that the substantive principles of practical reasonableness are self-evident. In particular, it will help to show that the self-evidence of a principle entails neither (a) that it is formulated reflectively or at all explicitly by those who are guided by it, nor (b) that when it is so formulated by somebody his formulation will invariably be found to be accurate or acceptably refined and sufficiently qualified, nor (c) that it is arrived at, even only implicitly, without experience of the field to which it relates.

There are indeed many principles of sound empirical judgment or, more generally, of rationality in theoretical inquiries. One such principle is that the principles of logic, for example the forms of deductive inference, are to be used and adhered to in all one's thinking, even though no non-circular proof of their validity is possible (since any proof would employ them). Another is that an adequate reason why anything is so rather than otherwise is to be expected, unless one has a reason not to expect such a reason[.] * * * A third is that self-defeating theses are to be abandoned[.] * * * A fourth is that phenomena are to be regarded as real unless there is some reason to distinguish between appearance and reality. A fifth is that a full description of data is to be preferred to partial descriptions, and that an account or explanation of phenomena is not to be accepted if it requires or postulates something inconsistent with the data for which it is supposed to account. A sixth is that a method of interpretation which is successful is to be relied upon in further similar cases until contrary reason appears. A seventh is that theoretical accounts which are simple, predictively successful, and explanatorily powerful are to be accepted in preference to other accounts. And there are many others. * * *

Such principles of theoretical rationality are not demonstrable, for they are presupposed or deployed in anything that we would count as a demonstration. They do not describe the world. But although they cannot be verified by opening one's eyes and taking a look, they are obvious—obviously valid to anyone who has experience of inquiry into matters of fact or of theoretical (including historical and philosophical) judgment; they do not stand in need of demonstration. They are objective; their validity is not a matter of convention, nor is it relative to anybody's individual purposes. They can be meaningfully denied, for they are not principles of logic conformity to which is essential if one is to mean anything. But to defy them is to disqualify oneself from the pursuit of knowledge, and to deny them is as straightforwardly unreasonable as anything can be. In all these respects, the principles of theoretical rationality are self-evident. And it is in these respects, that we are asserting that the basic practical principle that knowledge is a good to be pursued is self-evident.

Nowadays, any claim that something is self-evident is commonly misunderstood by philosophers. They think that any such claim either asserts or presupposes that the criterion of the truth of the allegedly self-evident principle, proposition, or fact is one's feeling of certitude about it. This is indeed a misunderstanding. Self-evident principles such as those I have been discussing are not validated by feelings. On the contrary, they are themselves the criteria whereby we discriminate between feelings, and discount some of our feelings (including feelings of certitude), however intense, as irrational or unwarranted, misleading or delusive. * * *

III.6 SCEPTICISM ABOUT THIS BASIC VALUE IS INDEFENSIBLE

In the case of the basic values and practical principles to be identified in the next chapter, the discussion of their self-evidence and objectivity would have to rest at this point. But in the case of the basic value of knowledge we can go one step further. We can show that any argument raised by the sceptic is going to be self-defeating. To show this is not to show that the basic value of knowledge is self-evident or objective; it is only to show that counter-arguments are invalid. But to make even this limited defensive point, in relation to only one basic value, may help to undermine sceptical doubts about all and any of the basic principles of practical reasoning.

Some propositions refute themselves either because they are directly self-contradictory or because they logically entail their contradictory: for example, "I know that I know nothing"; "It can be proved that nothing can be proved"; "All propositions are false".

Then again, there are some statements whose occurrence happens to refute their content. An example of this pragmatic self-refutation is afforded by someone singing "I am not singing". Here there is what we may call performative inconsistency, that is, inconsistency between what is asserted by a statement and facts that are given in and by the making of the statement.

Thirdly, there are propositions which cannot be coherently asserted, because they are inevitably falsified by any assertion of them. The proposition "I am not singing" is not such a proposition, for it can be asserted in writing. But the proposition "I do not exist" is inevitably falsified by an assertion of it. Another example of this operational self-refutation is "No one can put words (or other symbols) together to form a sentence". Operationally self-refuting propositions are not logically incoherent. Nor are they meaningless or empty or semantically paradoxical, as are "This sentence is false" or "This provision shall come into effect on 1st January" (where "this sentence" or "this provision" in each case is not a colloquial reference to some other sentence or norm but is self-referential and fails to establish any definite reference). Operationally self-refuting propositions have a quite definite reference and so can be (and inevitably are) false. They have a type of performative inconsistency; that is, they are inconsistent with the facts that are given in and by any assertion of them. An operationally self-refuting proposition cannot be coherently asserted, for it contradicts either the proposition that someone is asserting it or some proposition entailed by the proposition that someone is asserting it.

The sceptical assertion that knowledge is not a good is operationally self-refuting. For one who makes such an assertion, intending it as a serious contribution to rational discussion, is implicitly committed to the proposition that he believes his assertion is worth making, and worth making qua true; he thus is committed to the proposition that he believes that truth is a good worth pursuing or knowing. But the sense of his original assertion was precisely that truth is not a good worth pursuing or knowing. Thus he is implicitly committed to formally contradictory beliefs.

One can certainly toy with the notion that knowledge is not a good worth pursuing. But the fact that to assert this (whether to an audience, or as the judgment concluding one's own inner cogitations) would be operationally self-refuting should persuade the sceptic to cut short idle doubting. Self-defeating positions should be abandoned. The sceptic, on this as on other matters, can maintain coherence by asserting nothing; but coherence is not the only requirement of rationality.

A judgment or belief is objective if it is correct. A proposition is objective if one is warranted in asserting it, whether because there is sufficient evidence for it, or compelling grounds, or because (to one who has the experience and intelligence to understand the terms in which it is expressed) it is obvious or self-evidently correct. And if a proposition seems to be correct and could never be coherently denied, we are certainly justified in affirming it and in considering that what we are affirming is indeed objectively the case (in the relevant sense of "what is the case"). But all this is true of the proposition we have been considering, viz. that knowledge is a good to be pursued. We do not thereby directly demonstrate that knowledge is a good to be pursued; that principle remains indemonstrable, self-evident. What we demonstrate is simply that it is presupposed in all demonstrations, indeed in all serious assertions, whatsoever, and has as much title to be called "objective" as any other proposition whose contradictory is inevitably falsified by the act of asserting it. * * *

IV.2 THE BASIC FORMS OF HUMAN GOOD: A PRACTICAL REFLECTION

It is now time to revert, from the descriptive or "speculative" findings of anthropology and psychology, to the critical and essentially practical discipline in which each reader must ask himself: What are the basic aspects of my well-being? Here each one of us, however extensive his knowledge of the interests of other people and other cultures, is alone with his own intelligent grasp of the indemonstrable (because self-evident) first principles of his own practical reasoning. From one's capacity to grasp intelligently the basic forms of good as "to-be-pursued" one gets one's ability, in the descriptive disciplines of history and anthropology, to sympathetically (though not uncritically) see the point of actions, life-styles, characters, and cultures that one would not choose for oneself. And one's speculative knowledge of other people's interests and achievements does not leave unaffected one's practical understanding of the forms of good that lie open to one's choice. But there is no inference from fact to value. At this point in our discourse (or private meditation), inference and proof are left behind (or left until later), and the proper form of discourse is: "[XYZ] is a good, in itself, don't you think?".

Remember: by "good", "basic good", "value", "well-being", *etc.* I do not yet mean "moral good", *etc.*

What, then, are the basic forms of good for us?

A. *Life*

A first basic value, corresponding to the drive for self-preservation, is the value of life. The term "life" here signifies every aspect of the vitality (*vita*, life) which puts a human being in good shape for self-determination. Hence, life here includes bodily (including cerebral) health, and freedom from the pain that betokens organic malfunctioning or injury. And the recognition, pursuit, and realization of this basic human purpose (or internally related group of purposes) are as various as the crafty struggle and prayer of a man overboard seeking to stay afloat until his ship turns back for him; the teamwork of surgeons and the whole network of supporting staff, ancillary services, medical schools, etc.; road safety laws and programmes; famine relief expeditions; farming and rearing and fishing; food marketing; the resuscitation of suicides; watching out as one steps off the kerb [*sic*].* * *

Perhaps we should include in this category the transmission of life by procreation of children. Certainly it is tempting to treat procreation as a distinct, irreducibly basic value, corresponding to the inclination to mate/reproduce/rear. But while there are good reasons for distinguishing the urge to copulate from both the urge to self-preservation and the maternal or paternal instincts, the analytical situation is different when we shift from the level of urges/instincts/drives to the level of intelligently grasped forms of good. There may be said to be one drive (say, to copulate) and one physical release for that drive (or a range of such physical forms); but as a human action, pursuit and realization of value, sexual intercourse may be play, and/or expression of love or friendship, and/or an effort to procreate. So, likewise, we need not be analytically content with an anthropological convention which treats sexuality, mating, and family life as a single category or unit of investigation; nor with an ethical judgment that treats the family, and the procreation and education of children, as an indistinguishable cluster of moral responsibilities. We can distinguish the desire and decision to have a child, simply for the sake of bearing a child, from the desire and decision to cherish and to educate the child. The former desire and decision is a pursuit of the good of life, in this case life-in-its-transmission; the latter desires and decisions are aspects of the pursuit of the distinct basic values of sociability (or friendship) and truth (truth-in-its-communication), running alongside the continued pursuit of the value of life that is involved in simply keeping the child alive and well until it can fend for itself.

B. Knowledge

The second basic value * * * is knowledge, considered as desirable for its own sake, not merely instrumentally.

C. Play

The third basic aspect of human well-being is play. A certain sort of moralist analysing human goods may overlook this basic value, but an anthropologist will not fail to observe this large and irreducible element in human culture. More importantly, each one of us can see the point of engaging in performances which have no point beyond the performance itself, enjoyed for its own sake. The performance may be solitary or social, intellectual or physical, strenuous or relaxed, highly structured or relatively informal, conventional or *ad hoc* in its pattern * * *. An element of play can enter into any human activity, even the drafting of enactments, but is always analytically distinguishable from its "serious" context; and some activities, enterprises, and institutions are entirely or primarily pure play. Play, then, has and is its own value.

D. Aesthetic experience

The fourth basic component in our flourishing is aesthetic experience. Many forms of play, such as dance or song or football, are the matrix or occasion of aesthetic experience. But beauty is not an indispensable element of play. Moreover, beautiful form can be found and enjoyed in nature. Aesthetic experience, unlike play, need not involve an action of one's own; what is sought after and valued for its own sake may simply be the beautiful form "outside" one, and the "inner" experience of appreciation of its beauty. But often enough the valued experience is found in the creation and/or active appreciation of some work of significant and satisfying form.

E. Sociability (friendship)

Fifthly, there is the value of that sociability which in its weakest form is realized by a minimum of peace and harmony amongst men, and which ranges through the forms of human community to its strongest form in the flowering of full friendship. Some of the collaboration between one person and another is no more than instrumental to the realization by each of his own individual purposes. But friendship involves acting for the sake of one's friend's purposes, one's friend's well-being. To be in a relationship of friendship with at least one other person is a fundamental form of good, is it not?

Friendship and, to a lesser degree, the other forms of sociability are of special significance for the theme of this book, and so are more amply discussed later. * * *

F. Practical reasonableness

Sixthly, there is the basic good of being able to bring one's own intelligence to bear effectively (in practical reasoning that issues in action) on the problems of choosing one's actions and lifestyle and shaping one's own character. Negatively, this involves that one has a measure of effective freedom; positively, it involves that one seeks to bring an intelligent and reasonable order into one's own actions and habits and practical attitudes. This order in turn has (i) an internal aspect, as when one strives to bring one's emotions and dispositions into the harmony of an inner peace of mind that is not merely the product of drugs or indoctrination nor merely passive in its orientation; and (ii) an external aspect, as when one strives to make one's actions (which are external in that they change states of affairs in the world and often enough affect the relations between persons) authentic, that is to say, genuine realizations of one's own freely ordered evaluations, preferences, hopes, and self-determination. This value is thus complex, involving freedom and reason, integrity and authenticity. But it has a sufficient unity to be treated as one; and for a label I choose "practical reasonableness". * * *

G. "Religion"

Seventhly, and finally in this list, there is the value of what, since Cicero, we summarily and lamely call "religion". For, as there is the order of means to ends, and the pursuit of life, truth, play, and aesthetic experience in some individually selected order of priorities and pattern of specialization, and the order that can be brought into human relations through collaboration, community, and friendship, and the order that is to be brought into one's character and activity through inner integrity and outer authenticity, so, finally there arise such questions as: (a) How are all these orders, which have their immediate origin in human initiative and pass away in death, related to the lasting order of the whole cosmos and to the origin, if any, of that order? (b) Is it not perhaps the case that human freedom, in which one rises above the determinism of instinct and impulse to an intelligent grasp of worthwhile forms of good, and through which one shapes and masters one's environment but also one's own character, is itself somehow subordinate to something which makes that human freedom, human intelligence, and human mastery possible (not just 'originally' but from moment to moment) and which is free, intelligent, and sovereign in a way (and over a range) no human being can be?

Misgivings may be aroused by the notion that one of the basic human values is the establishment and maintenance of proper relationships between oneself (and the orders one can create and maintain) and the divine. For there are, always, those who doubt or deny that the universal order-of-things has any origin beyond the "origins" known to the natural sciences, and who answer question (b) negatively. But is it reasonable to deny that it is, at any rate, peculiarly important to have thought reasonably and (where possible) correctly about these questions of the origins of cosmic order and of human freedom and reason—whatever the answer to those questions turns out to be, and even if the answers have to be agnostic or negative? And does not that importance in large part consist in this: that if there is a transcendent origin of the universal order-of-things and of human freedom and reason, then one's life and actions are in fundamental disorder if they are not brought, as best one can, into some sort of harmony with whatever can be known or surmised about that transcendent other and its lasting order? More important for us than the ubiquity of expressions of religious concerns, in all human cultures, is the question: Does not one's own sense of "responsibility", in choosing what one is to be and do, amount to a concern that is not reducible to the concern to live, play, procreate, relate to others, and be intelligent? Does not even a Sartre, taking as his *point de depart* that God does not exist (and that therefore "everything is permitted"), none the less appreciate that he is "responsible"—obliged to act with freedom and authenticity, and to will the liberty of other persons equally with his own—in choosing what he is to be; and all this, because, prior to any choice of his, "man" is and is-to-be free? And is this not a recognition (however residual) of, and concern about, an order of things "beyond" each and every man? And so, without wishing to beg any question, may we not for convenience call that concern, which is concern for a good consisting in an irreducibly distinct form of order, "religious"? * * *

NOTES AND QUESTIONS

1. *"Rescuing" natural law I.* What is the "nature" from which Finnis draws his "goods," and how does it differ from the "nature" relied upon by Aristotle or Aquinas or Hobbes? Why do you suppose Finnis puts the word "religion" in quotation marks? In this connection, compare the observation of Sir Edward Coke in *Calvin's Case* (1608), almost 400 years before Finnis published his book: "The law of nature is that which God at the time of creation of the nature of man infused into his heart, for his preservation and direction."

2. *"Rescuing" natural law II.* Perhaps natural law theories of law are weakest when they are broadest, which accounts in part for the attraction of articulating the *minimum* content of natural law. Consider the observations of Yves Simon:

> For a number of years we have been witnessing a tendency * * * to assume that natural law decides, with the universality proper to the necessity of essences, incomparably more issues than it is actually able to decide. There is a tendency to treat in terms of natural law questions which call for treatment in terms of prudence. * * * People are quick to realize what is weak, or dishonest, in pretending to decide by the axioms of natural law, or by airtight deduction from these axioms, questions that really cannot be solved except by the obscure methods of prudence, and they gladly extend to all theory of natural law the contempt that they rightly feel toward such sophistry. Thus, whereas an ideological current marked by relativistic and evolutionistic beliefs may cause a situation strongly unfavorable to the theory of natural law, ideological currents expressive of an eagerness to believe that some things are right and some things wrong by nature may cause another kind of difficulty and call for a supplement of wisdom on our part.

YVES R. SIMON, THE TRADITION OF NATURAL LAW: A PHILOSOPHER'S REFLECTIONS 23–4 (Vukan ed. 1998). In the preface to Simon's book, Russell Hittinger sounds a similar warning about the misunderstanding and abuse of natural law thinking: "in our time and culture, natural law is invoked as a response to the breakdown of tradition, to moral relativism and nihilism, to various species of utilitarianism, and to legal positivism. *It is expected to be an all-purpose antidote to the estrangements of modernity.* Called upon to remediate more than reasonably can be expected, natural law is liable to descend into ideology." *Ibid., at xxiii* (emphasis added). What are the best arguments (or principles) for distinguishing between natural law and ideology?

3. *Cataloging the self-evident goods.* What is your assessment of Finnis's list of self-evident goods? Do you think it is exhaustive? Do you agree that all of the goods listed there are *self-evident* goods? Finnis argues for example that knowledge is a self-evident good: "It cannot be demonstrated, but equally needs no demonstration." He claims that any argument against that proposition raised by a skeptic is self-defeating. Are you convinced? Is it learned (or just lazy) to doubt that anything related to law or morality can be self-evident?

4. *The law is not an autonomous discipline.* Do you think that Finnis's appeal to social sciences (anthropology in particular) makes his argument more or less convincing? Why do you think he decided to use social scientific evidence to bolster his argument?

5. *Natural law and the "ethical brain."* Suppose it could be demonstrated empirically that the human brain is hard-wired to think ethically. *See, e.g.*, MICHAEL S. GAZZANIGA, THE ETHICAL BRAIN: THE SCIENCE OF OUR MORAL DILEMMAS (2005). What are the best arguments for rigorously training that ethical instinct out of lawyers-to-be? Consider in this connection the observations of Professor Duncan Kennedy:

> The first step toward this sense of irrelevance of [natural justice] is the opposition in the first year curriculum between the technical, boring, difficult, obscure legal case, and the occasional case with outrageous facts and a piggish judicial opinion endorsing or tolerating the outrage. The first kind of case—call it a cold case—is a challenge to interest, understanding, even to wakefulness. It can be on any subject, so long as it is of no political or moral or emotional significance. Just to understand what happened and what's being said about it, you have to learn a lot of new terms a little potted legal history, and lots of rules, none of which is carefully explained by the casebook or the teacher. It is difficult to figure out why the case is there in the first place, difficult to figure out whether one has grasped it, and difficult to anticipate what the teacher will ask and what one should respond. The other kind of case usually involves a sympathetic plaintiff, say an Appalachian farm family, and an unsympathetic defendant, say a coal company. On first reading, it appears that the coal company has screwed the farm family, say by renting their land for strip mining, with a promise to restore it to its original condition once the coal has been extracted, and then reneging on the promise. And the case should include a judicial opinion awarding a meaningless couple of hundred dollars to the farm family, rather than making the coal company do the restoration work. The point of the class discussion will be that your initial reaction of outrage is naïve, non-legal, irrelevant to what you're supposed to be learning, and maybe substantively wrong into the bargain. There are good reasons for the awful result, when you take a legal and logical view, as opposed to a knee-jerk passionate view, and if you can't muster those reasons, maybe you aren't cut out to be a lawyer.

DUNCAN KENNEDY, LEGAL EDUCATION AND THE REPRODUCTION OF HIERARCHY 22–23 (2004).

6. *"Hume's Fork:" the is-ought problem.* The eighteenth-century philosopher, David Hume (1711–1776) argued that we cannot logically derive an "ought" statement from an "is" statement. It is in other words fundamentally fallacious to conclude that one *ought* to do something from what *is* as a matter of fact. Consider his observation that

> [i]n every system of morality, which I have hitherto met with, I have always remark'd, that the author proceeds for some time in the ordinary ways of reasoning, and establishes the being of a God, or makes observations concerning human affairs; when all of a sudden I am surpriz'd to find, that instead of the usual copulations of propositions, is, and is not, I meet with no proposition that is not connected with an ought, or an ought not. This change is imperceptible; but is however, of the last consequence. For as this ought, or ought not, expresses some new relation or affirmation, 'tis necessary that it shou'd be observ'd and explain'd; and at the same time that a reason should be given; for what seems altogether inconceivable, how this new relation can be a deduction from others, which are entirely different from it.

A TREATISE OF HUMAN NATURE 469 (1739). Consider how Hume's observation can be used as a powerful shorthand critique of natural law argumentation.

After Hume, natural law theories must grapple with how to get an "ought" statement from an "is" statement. If Finnis is saying that the basic forms are human flourishing are what "is," what does he think "ought" to be? How does he get from his "is" to his "ought?"

7. *The more definite the law, the more widespread the lawlessness.* As the readings and cases in this chapter suggest, one way to approach natural law thinking is to imagine circumstances in which the enacted or positive law gets in the way of moral decision-making. Joseph Needham offers this cautionary tale from ancient China:

> The inhabitants of the State of Chin were forced to contribute 480 catties of iron to make cauldrons on which the penal laws were inscribed * * * Confucius said "I fear that Chino is going to destruction. * * * Now the people will study the laws on the cauldrons and be content with that; they will have no respect for men of high rank."

JOSEPH NEEDHAM, SCIENCE AND CIVILISATION IN CHINA 522 (1956). For a more contemporary example of the assertion that fixating on the literal terms of the law can lead to greater lawlessness, consider the criminalization of "insider trading." In general terms, a publicly-traded company's officers and directors (among others) cannot trade in the stock of that company on the basis of material non-public information about that company, but there has been considerable controversy over what qualifies as "material" or "public" information and who besides directors and officers might qualify as "insiders."

In the past, calls for a statutory definition of "insider trading" have sometimes been resisted on the grounds that the more precise definition would amount to "roadmap for fraud." *See, e.g.*, Stuart J. Kaswell, *An Insider's View of the Insider Trading and Securities Fraud Enforcement Act of 1988*, 45 BUS. LAW. 145, 150 (1989).

8. *Grappling with the concept of justice as something other than a reflection of religious convictions or individual judgment and taste.* The political and moral philosopher John Rawls (1921–2002), popularized a thought-experiment as a way of coming to grips with the concept of justice. Justice is clearly central to natural law-based arguments *within* specific cases (as in *Trainton*) and *about* the law generally, but it remains elusive and is almost never taught explicitly in American law schools.

In A THEORY OF JUSTICE (1971), Rawls imagined an "original position," in which individuals, prior to entering into a society, stand behind a "veil of ignorance." They do not know what their personal characteristics are in the society-to-be (like their age, or gender, or social status), nor do they know what their individual conception of the good life will be. "[N]or does [the individual] know his fortune in the distribution of natural assets and abilities, his intelligence and strength, and the like." *Id.* at 137. The veil of ignorance also blocks knowledge of how the government will be organized and how resources will be distributed within the society.

The objective of the exercise is to identify those principles of justice that these individuals will rationally choose in light of radical, shared indeterminacy. In Rawls' words:

> The idea of the original position is to set up a fair procedure so that any principles agreed to will be just. * * * Somehow we must nullify the effects of specific contingencies which put men at odds and tempt them to exploit social and natural circumstances to their own advantage * * *. As far as possible, then, the only particular facts which the parties know is that their society is subject to the circumstances of justice and whatever this implies.

In ways that have challenged philosophers and lawyers for decades, Rawls simulates the deliberations behind the veil of ignorance as "a natural guide to intuition" about the concept of justice. Because Rawls conceives of justice in the rational ordering of society rather than as an aspect or consequence of a literal state of nature, he is not readily classified as a natural law philosopher. To the contrary, for him the state of nature is simply not an idea with moral significance. *See, e.g.*, JOHN RAWLS, POLITICAL LIBERALISM 278–80 (1993).

But you can use the thought-experiment of an original position and a veil of ignorance to articulate in general terms the principles of justice against which the positive laws of any legal system might be judged. What principles emerge from this process for you? What is the legal or moral status of a law that violates one or more of those principles, and who or what gets to answer that question?

CHAPTER TWO

AVOIDING THE PROBLEM OF "TASTE" IN LAW: LEGAL POSITIVISM

■ ■ ■

"There are few judges . . . today who do not begin a consideration of their typical problems with some formula designed to cause all moral ideals to disappear and to produce an issue purified for the procedure of positive empirical science. But the ideals have generally retired to hats from which later wonders will magically arise."

— Felix Cohen

"[T]he logical method and form flatter that longing for certainty and for repose which is in every human mind. But certainty generally is illusion, and repose is not the destiny of man. Behind the logical form lies a judgment as to the relative worth and importance of competing legislative grounds, often in inarticulate and unconscious judgment, it is true, and yet the very root and nerve of the whole proceeding."

— Oliver Wendell Holmes, Jr.

Orientation

After the Reformation and the Enlightenment, natural law arguments began to fall on conspicuously hard times. Statements about justice or morality—especially the suggestion that these notions were universal, unchangeable, and accessible to reason—were considered essentially unverifiable, and, for that reason, they amounted to a kind of nonsense. One jurisprudential response was to try to immunize "law" from these varying and idiosyncratic perceptions of goodness or rightness, to separate what the law *is* from what the law *ought* to be. In other words, the rules were one thing, and their underlying morality or virtue was another. Under that approach, abstract notions of justice added little or nothing to a successful account of the law or legal practice. Instead, a somewhat more empirical understanding of law could be embraced, one that looked to effectiveness or pedigree rather than justice in determining what the law is or requires. Lawyers and judges were to be concerned with the rules as they are, leaving moral and policy judgments to someone else, like legislators or revolutionaries or saints.

That emphasis on rules as a social fact and the willingness to separate law from morality brings us to *legal positivism*. There are many ways to frame this "separability theme" of legal positivism, not all of which are consistent with one another. For example, one of the fathers of legal positivism, John Austin, writing in apparent opposition to Augustine's observation that "an unjust law is no law at all," declared that

> [t]he existence of law is one thing; its merit or demerit is another. Whether it be or be not is one enquiry; whether it be or be not conformable to an assumed standard, is a different enquiry. A law, which actually exists, is a law, though we happen to dislike it, or though it vary from the text, by which we regulate our approbation and disapprobation.

JOHN AUSTIN, THE PROVINCE OF JURISPRUDENCE DETERMINED (1832), Lecture V. It is possible of course that Austin was taking Augustine's observation too literally, attributing to the natural law theorists a level of detachment and naivete that they never embraced. Augustine's observation might be taken as a rationale for not obeying an unjust law or as a reason not to consider it valid, rather than as some bizarre assertion that the unjust law does not actually exist.

Suppose however that the positivists' essential claim was not about whether an unjust law "exists" but whether moral considerations were relevant in determining what the law requires: "from the fact that a legal solution is morally objectionable it does not follow that it is legally mistaken."[1] On that understanding, if you were advising a client or making an argument to a judge or deciding a case yourself, your analysis of the law would not—and perhaps should not—be influenced by your personal sense of right and wrong. *See Union Pac. Ry. Co. v. Cappier*, *infra*.

Yet another possibility would be to frame the separation of law from morality by considering the source of the law: an assertion that "there exists at least one conceptually possible legal system in which the criteria of validity are exclusively source- or pedigree-based."[2] At a minimum, these latter terms—"source" and "pedigree"—refer to the legislative sovereign within a legal system: once that sovereign has been identified, the rules that emanate properly from it are valid, whether they are moral or not. This "pedigree theme" reinforces the legal positivists' separation of a law's validity from its merits.[3] John Gardner has given voice to the argument:

---

[1] Fernando Atria, *Legal Reasoning and Legal Theory Revisited*, 18 LAW & PHIL. 537, 547 (1999). Professor Jules Coleman offers a refined formulation of positivism's separability theme, expressed as a logical premise, namely as an assertion that either of two propositions must be true: "(a) The concept of immoral law is coherent; or (b) Sentences asserting that a particular legal requirement or directive is immoral do not—for that reason alone—constitute contradictions." Jules L. Coleman, *The Architecture of Jurisprudence*, 121 YALE L.J. 2, 9 (2011).

[2] Kenneth Einar Himma, *Inclusive Legal Positivism*, in THE OXFORD HANDBOOK OF JURISPRUDENCE AND PHILOSOPHY OF LAW 125, 136 (Jules Coleman & Scott Shapiro eds., 2002).

[3] *See e.g.*, RONALD DWORKIN, TAKING RIGHTS SERIOUSLY 17 (1977) (the positivistic criteria of legal validity are concerned "not with content but with the manner in which they were adopted or developed"); Joseph Raz, *Authority, Law and Morality*, 68 MONIST 295, 297–316 (1985).

> In any legal system, whether a given norm is legally valid, and hence whether it forms part of the law of that system, depends on its sources, not its merits* * *. It says, to be more exact, that in any legal system, a norm is valid as a norm of that system solely in virtue of the fact that at some relevant time and place some relevant agent or agents announced it, practiced it, invoked it, enforced it, endorsed it, or otherwise engaged with it.[4]

It is clearly not child's play to determine what the sovereign is and how we would go about recognizing which of its declarations are law. Austin considered law to be nothing more or less than an order backed by a threat of sanction, the so-called "gunman model" of law. As shown below, more modern positivists like Hans Kelsen and H.L.A. Hart have tried to refine that conception without linking the validity of law to its virtue. But difficulties remain, which is why Gardner in the paragraph just quoted understandably uses broad terms like "relevant agent or agents" and whether—in his catchall phrase—the agent or agents "engaged" with the norm. In this chapter, you will encounter different positivists' attempts to define and characterize the sovereign, but at a minimum—whatever analysis they pursue—the criteria of a norm's validity cannot be found in the individual moral faculties of the sovereign's human subjects.

To the separability and pedigree themes we might add a theme of "neutrality" and "minimal discretion." Legal positivism is sometimes portrayed as a conception of the law under which the mark of a proper legal decision is that it is both neutral and compelled: *neutral* because it purports to take the received rule and apply it to the facts without bias or political motivation, and *compelled* as in a syllogism[5] or a Euclidian proof in geometry. This is a formalism with considerable power in the popular and professional mind. The epithet "judicial activism" is generally attached to a decision with which one disagrees most profoundly, and it stings because it is illegitimate for judges to let their individual preferences interfere with their resolution of cases. The emphasis is on rules, especially the text of rules; discretion is minimized; and the preferred interpretive technique is literalism. In other words, if there is ambiguity in a rule, the judges should be as literal and as apolitical as possible. *See McBoyle v. United States*, *infra*. Whether formalism (a theory of adjudication) is a necessary part of positivism (a theory of law)—or could work equally well with other theories

---

[4] John Gardner, *Legal Positivism: 5½ Myths*, 46 AM. J. JURIS. 199–200 (2001). *See also* Anthony Sebok, *Misunderstanding Positivism*, 93 MICH. L. REV. 2054 (1995).

[5] A syllogism is a form of deductive reasoning consisting of a major and a minor premise and a conclusion. For example: "(i) All human beings are mortal (the major premise). (ii) Socrates is a human being (the minor premise). Therefore (iii) Socrates is mortal (the conclusion)." If the result in a case is to be compelled like a syllogism, (i) the applicable rule in the case would function as the major premise (*e.g.*, "all contracts in restraint of trade are illegal"), (ii) the facts of the case would function as the minor premise ("the contract between A and B is in restraint of trade"), and the decision would necessarily follow ("therefore the contract between A and B is illegal").

of law—is a question worth keeping in mind as you consider the cases and materials in this and subsequent chapters.

The positivists' separability of law and morality does not mean that there is no relation whatsoever between these two modes of thinking (as for example when someone criticizes an existing law for being immoral or notes the overlap between the law as written and some religious tradition), but it does mean that there is no *necessary* relation between them.[6] Determining whether this is an accurate, meaningful, and honoring conception of law is the purpose of the materials that follow, starting with cases in which some positivist argument apparently prevails.

A. SEPARATING LAW FROM MORALITY

UNION PAC. RY. CO. V. CAPPIER

66 Kan. 649, 72 P. 281 (1903)

SMITH, J. (emphasis added). This was an action brought by Adeline Cappier, the mother of Irvin Ezelle, to recover damages resulting to her by reason of the loss of her son, who was run over by a car of [appellant], and died from the injuries received. The trial court, at the close of the evidence introduced to support a recovery by plaintiff below, held that no careless act of the railway company's servants in the operation of the car was shown, and refused to permit the case to be considered by the jury on the allegations and attempted proof of such negligence. The petition, however, contained an averment that the injured person had one leg and an arm cut off by the car wheels, and that the servants of the railway company failed to call a surgeon, or to render him any assistance after the accident, but permitted him to remain by the side of the tracks and bleed to death. Under this charge of negligence a recovery was had.

While attempting to cross the railway tracks, Ezelle was struck by a moving freight car pushed by an engine. A yardmaster in charge of the switching operations was riding on the end of the car nearest to the deceased, and gave warning by shouting to him. The warning was either too late, or no heed was given to it. The engine was stopped. After the injured man was clear of the track, the yardmaster signaled the engineer to move ahead, fearing, as he testified, that a passenger train then about due would come upon them. The locomotive and car went forward over a bridge, where the general yardmaster was informed of the accident, and an ambulance was telephoned for. The yardmaster then went back where the

---

[6] H.L.A. Hart, *Positivism and the Separation of Law and Morals, in* ESSAYS IN JURISPRUDENCE AND PHILOSOPHY (1983); H.L.A. HART, THE CONCEPT OF LAW 185 (2d ed. 1994); Joseph Raz, THE AUTHORITY OF LAW 38–39 (1979). *But see* Brian Leiter, *Positivism, Formalism, Realism*, 99 COLUM. L. REV. 1138, 1142–44 (1999).

injured man was lying, and found three Union Pacific switchmen binding up the wounded limbs and doing what they could to stop the flow of blood. The ambulance arrived about 30 minutes later, and Ezelle was taken to a hospital, where he died a few hours afterwards.

In answer to particular questions of fact, the jury found that the accident occurred at 5:35 p.m.; that immediately one of the railway employees telephoned to police headquarters for help for the injured man; that the ambulance started at 6:05 p.m., and reached the nearest hospital with Ezelle at 6:20 p.m., where he received proper medical and surgical treatment. Judgment against the railway company was based on the following question and answer: "Q. Did not defendant's employees bind up Ezelle's wounds, and try to stop the flow of blood, as soon as they could after the accident happened? A. No." The lack of diligence in the respect stated was intended, no doubt, to apply to the yardmaster, engineer, and fireman in charge of the car and engine. These facts bring us to a consideration of their legal duty toward the injured man after his condition became known. Counsel for [Cappier] quote the language found in BEACH ON CONTRIBUTORY NEGLIGENCE (3d Ed.) § 215, as follows:

> Under certain circumstances, the railroad may owe a duty to a trespasser after the injury. When a trespasser has been run down, it is the plain duty of the railway company to render whatever service is possible to mitigate the severity of the injury. The train that has occasioned the harm must be stopped, and the injured person looked after, and, when it seems necessary, removed to a place of safety, and carefully nursed, until other relief can be brought to the disabled person.

The principal authority cited in support of this doctrine is *Northern Central Railway Co. v. State*, 29 Md. 420 [(1868)]. The court in that case first held that there was evidence enough to justify the jury in finding that the operatives of the train were negligent in running it too fast over a road crossing without sounding the whistle, and that the number of brakemen was insufficient to check its speed. Such negligence was held sufficient to uphold the verdict, and would seem to be all that was necessary to be said. The court, however, proceeded to state that, from whatever cause the collision occurred, it was the duty of the servants of the company, when the man was found on the pilot of the engine in a helpless and insensible condition, to remove him, and to do it with proper regard to his safety and the laws of humanity. In that case, the injured person was taken in charge by the servants of the railway company, and, being apparently dead, without notice to his family, or sending for a physician to ascertain his condition, he was moved to defendant's warehouse, laid on a plank, and locked up for the night. The next morning, when the warehouse was opened, it was found that during the night the man had revived from his stunned condition, and moved some paces from the spot where he had been laid, and was found in a stooping posture, dead, but still warm, having died from hemorrhage of the arteries of one leg which was crushed at and above the knee. It had been proposed to place him in the defendant's station house, which was a comfortable building, but the telegraph operator objected, and directed him to be taken into the warehouse, a place used for the deposit of old barrels and other rubbish.

The Maryland case does not support what is so broadly stated in BEACH ON CONTRIBUTORY NEGLIGENCE. It is cited by Judge Cooley, in his work on Torts, in a note to a chapter devoted to the negligence of bailees, indicating that the learned author understood the reasoning of the decision to apply where the duty began after the railway employees had taken charge of the injured person. After the trespasser on the track of a railway company has been injured in collision with a train, and the servants of the company have assumed to take charge of him, the duty, no doubt, arises to exercise such care in his treatment as the circumstances will allow. We are unable, however, to approve the doctrine that when the acts of a trespasser himself result in his injury, where his own negligent conduct is alone the cause, those in charge of the instrument which inflicted the hurt, being innocent of wrongdoing, are nevertheless blamable in law if they neglect to administer to the sufferings of him whose wounds we might say were self-imposed.

With the humane side of the question courts are not concerned. It is the omission or negligent discharge of legal duties only which come within the sphere of judicial cognizance. For withholding relief from the suffering, for failure to respond to the calls of worthy charity, or for faltering in the bestowment of brotherly love on the unfortunate, penalties are found not in the laws of men, but in that higher law, the violation of which is condemned by the voice of conscience, whose sentence of punishment for the recreant act is swift and sure. In the law of contracts it is now well understood that a promise founded on a moral obligation will not be enforced in the courts. Bishop states that some of the older authorities recognize a moral obligation as valid, and says: "Such a doctrine, carried to its legitimate results, would release the tribunals from the duty to administer the law of the land, and put in the place of law the varying ideas of morals which the changing incumbents of the bench might from time to time entertain." BISHOP ON CONTRACTS, § 44.

Ezelle's injuries were inflicted, as the court below held, without the fault of the yardmaster, engineer, or fireman in charge of the car and locomotive. The railway company was no more responsible than it would have been had the deceased been run down by the cars of another railroad company on a track parallel with that of plaintiff in error. If no duty was imposed on the servants of defendant below to take charge of and care for the wounded man in such a case, how could a duty arise under the circumstances of the case at bar? In BARROWS ON NEGLIGENCE, it is said:

> The duty must be owing from the defendant to the plaintiff, otherwise there can be no negligence, so far as the plaintiff is concerned. * * * And the duty must be owing to plaintiff in an individual capacity, and not merely as one of the general public. This excludes from actionable negligence all failures to observe the obligations imposed by charity, gratitude, generosity, and the kindred virtues. The moral law would obligate an attempt to rescue a person in a perilous position—as a drowning child—but the law of the land does not require it, no matter how little personal risk it might involve, provided that the person who declines to act is not responsible for the peril.

See Kenney v. The Hannibal & St. Joseph Railroad Company, 70 Mo. 252–257 [(1879)]. In the several cases cited in the brief of counsel for [appellee] to sustain the judgment of the trial court it will be found that the negligence on which recoveries were based occurred after the time when the person injured was in the custody and care of those who were at fault in failing to give him proper treatment.

The judgment of the court below will be reversed, with directions to enter judgment on the findings of the jury in favor of the railway company. All the Justices concurring.

MILLS V. WYMAN

20 Mass. 207 (Mass. 1825)

[In this case, Levi Wyman, the defendant's 25-year-old son, returned from a voyage at sea and suddenly became sick. "Being poor and in distress," he was taken care of by strangers, including Daniel Mills, who for more than two weeks gave him care and board. Wyman's father, the defendant, then wrote to Mills, promising to pay him for the expenses he had incurred. The father never made good on this promise, and the plaintiff sued for breach of contract. The lower court ruled that the "contract" was unenforceable because there was no consideration from the plaintiff for the father's promise. Under common law rules, both parties to a contract must offer something of value ("consideration") before the contract is enforceable. Whatever value the plaintiff brought to the transaction did not go to the father at the time it was tendered. Plaintiff appealed.]

PARKER, C. J. * * * The rule that a mere verbal promise, without any consideration, cannot be enforced by action, is universal in its application, and cannot be departed from to suit particular cases in which a refusal to perform such a promise may be disgraceful.

The promise declared on in this case appears to have been made without any legal consideration. The kindness and services towards the sick son of the defendant were not bestowed at his request. The son was in no respect under the care of the defendant. He was twenty-five years old, and had long left his father's family. On his return from a foreign country, he fell sick among strangers, and the plaintiff acted the part of the good Samaritan, giving him shelter and comfort until he died. The defendant, his father, on being informed of this event, influenced by a transient feeling of gratitude, promises in writing to pay the plaintiff for the expenses he had incurred. But he has determined to break this promise, and is willing to have his case appear on record as a strong example of particular injustice sometimes necessarily resulting from the operation of general rules.

* * * What a man ought to do, generally he ought to be made to do, whether he promise or refuse. But the law of society has left most of such obligations to the interior forum, as the tribunal of conscience has been aptly called. Is there not a moral obligation upon every son who has become affluent by means of the education and advantages bestowed upon him by his father, to relieve that father from pecuniary embarrassment, to promote his comfort and happiness, and even to share with him his riches, if thereby he will be made happy? And yet such a son may, with impunity, leave such a father in any degree of penury above that which will expose the community in which he dwells, to the danger of being obliged to preserve him from absolute want. Is not a wealthy father under strong moral obligation to advance the interest of an obedient, well-disposed son, to furnish him with the means of acquiring and maintaining a becoming rank in life, to rescue him from the horrors of debt incurred by misfortune? Yet the law will uphold him in any degree of parsimony, short of that which would reduce his son to the necessity of seeking public charity.

Without doubt there are great interests of society which justify withholding the coercive arm of the law from these duties of imperfect obligation, as they are called; imperfect, not because they are less binding upon the conscience than those which are called perfect, but because the wisdom of the social law does not impose sanctions upon them.

A deliberate promise, in writing, made freely and without any mistake, one which may lead the party to whom it is made into contracts and expenses, cannot be broken without a violation of moral duty. But if there was nothing paid or promised for it, the law, perhaps wisely, leaves the execution of it to the conscience of him who makes it. It is only when the party making the promise gains something, or he to whom it is made loses something, that the law gives the promise validity. * * *

These principles are deduced from the general current of decided cases upon the subject, as well as from the known maxims of the common law. The general position, that moral obligation is a sufficient consideration for an express promise, is to be limited in its application, to cases where at some time or other a good or valuable consideration has existed. * * *

For the foregoing reasons we are all of opinion that the [plaintiff's case must be dismissed and that the plaintiff must pay the defendant's court costs.]

NOTES AND QUESTIONS

1. *Cappier, Mills, and the lawyerly instinct to separate law from morality.* Why would the justices in *Cappier* feel compelled to observe that "with the *humane* side of the question courts are not concerned." What is gained and what is lost in such a view of the law and the judges' role? *Mills* invites a similar reflection: Chief Justice Parker observes that, "[w]ithout doubt there are great interests of society which justify withholding the coercive arm of the law from these duties of imperfect obligation, as they are called; imperfect, not because they are less binding upon the conscience than those which are called perfect, but because the wisdom of the social law does not impose sanctions upon them." What "great interests of society" are there in not imposing sanctions on violations of conscience, whether in a tort case like *Cappier* or a contract case like *Mills*?

2. *Imagining an opposite result in Cappier.* The decision in *Cappier* was unanimous and may for that reason trigger the conclusion that the result was inevitable or obvious. But consider the specific facts of the case (especially what various employees of the railroad did after the accident) and the authorities cited by the Kansas Supreme Court. What arguments consistent with those rules might justify the opposite result and serve the "humane side of the question" at the same time? In other words, is there an argument that the court in *Cappier* was more of a participant in articulating the applicable rule than it acknowledged?

3. *Uncovering implicit moral positions.* In his dissent in *Baker v. Carr*, 369 U.S. 186, 267 (1962), Justice Felix Frankfurter noted that when courts engage issues "strongly entangled in popular feeling," the judicial function is impaired. What is the operative (if implicit) moral principle behind the decision to ignore the humane or moral side of a question?

4. *The argument from inevitability.* Consider the possibility that deciding not to decide a case on moral grounds is itself a moral decision. Does it follow that moral decisions are unavoidable in legal cases, and, if so, why resist making them?

UNITED STATES V. CALLEY

1973 WL 14894, 48 C.M.R. 19 (1973)

QUINN, J. First Lieutenant Calley stands convicted of the premeditated murder of 22 infants, children, women, and old men, and of assault with intent to murder a child of about 2 years of age. All the killings and the assault took place on March 16, 1968, in the area of the village of My Lai in the Republic of South Vietnam. The Army Court of Military Review affirmed the findings of guilty and the sentence, which, as reduced by the convening authority, includes dismissal and confinement at hard labor for 20 years. The accused petitioned this Court for further review. * * *

[T]he accused contends that the evidence is insufficient to establish his guilt beyond a reasonable doubt. Summarized, the pertinent evidence is as follows: Lieutenant Calley was a platoon leader in C Company, a unit that was part of an organization known as Task Force Barker, whose mission was to subdue and drive out the enemy in an area in the Republic of Vietnam known popularly as Pinkville. Before March 16, 1968, this area, which included the village of My Lai 4, was a Viet Cong stronghold. C Company had operated in the area several times. Each time the unit had entered the area it suffered casualties by sniper fire, machine gun fire, mines, and other forms of attack. Lieutenant Calley had accompanied his platoon on some of the incursions.

On March 15, 1968, a memorial service for members of the company killed in the area during the preceding weeks was held. After the service Captain Ernest L. Medina, the commanding officer of C Company, briefed the company on a mission in the Pinkville area set for the next day. C Company was to serve as the main attack formation for Task Force Barker. In that role it would assault and neutralize My Lai 4, 5, and 6 and then mass for an assault on My Lai 1. Intelligence reports indicated that the unit would be opposed by a veteran enemy battalion, and that all civilians would be absent from the area. The objective was to destroy the enemy. Disagreement exists as to the instructions on the specifics of destruction.

Captain Medina testified that he instructed his troops that they were to destroy My Lai 4 by "burning the hootches, to kill the livestock, to close the wells and to destroy the food crops." Asked if women and children were to be killed, Medina said he replied in the negative, adding that, "You must use common sense. If they have a weapon and are trying to engage you, then you can shoot back, but you must use common sense." However, Lieutenant Calley testified that Captain Medina informed the troops they were to kill every living thing—men, women, children, and animals—and under no circumstances were they to leave any Vietnamese behind them as they passed through the villages en route to their final objective. Other witnesses gave more or less support to both versions of the briefing.

On March 16, 1968, the operation began with interdicting fire. C Company was then brought to the area by helicopters. Lieutenant Calley's platoon was on the first lift. This platoon formed a defense perimeter until the remainder of the force was landed. The unit received no hostile fire from the village.

Calley's platoon passed the approaches to the village with his men firing heavily. Entering the village, the platoon encountered only unarmed, unresisting men, women, and children. The villagers, including infants held in their mothers' arms, were assembled and moved in separate groups to collection points. Calley testified that during this time he was radioed twice by Captain Medina, who demanded to know what was delaying the platoon. On being told that a large number of villagers had been detained, Calley said Medina ordered him to "waste them." Calley further testified that he obeyed the orders because he had been taught the doctrine of obedience throughout his military career. Medina denied that he gave any such order.

One of the collection points for the villagers was in the southern part of the village. There, Private First Class Paul D. Meadlo guarded a group of between 30 to 40 old men, women, and children. Lieutenant Calley approached Meadlo and told him, "You know what to do," and left. He returned shortly and asked Meadlo why the people were not yet dead. Meadlo replied he did not know that Calley had meant that they should be killed. Calley declared that he wanted them dead. He and Meadlo then opened fire on the group, until all but a few children fell. Calley then personally shot these children. He expended 4 or 5 magazines from his M-16 rifle in the incident.

Lieutenant Calley and Meadlo moved from this point to an irrigation ditch on the east side of My Lai 4. There, they encountered another group of civilians being held by several soldiers. Meadlo estimated that this group contained from 75 to 100 persons. Calley stated, "We got another job to do, Meadlo," and he ordered the group into the ditch. When all were in the ditch, Calley and Meadlo opened fire on them. Although ordered by Calley to shoot, Private First Class James J. Dursi refused to join in the killings, and Specialist Four Robert E. Maples refused to give his machine gun to Calley for use in the killings. Lieutenant Calley admitted that he fired into the ditch, with the muzzle of his weapon within 5 feet of people in it. He expended between 10 to 15 magazines of ammunition on this occasion.

With his radio operator, Private Charles Sledge, Calley moved to the north end of the ditch. There, he found an elderly Vietnamese monk, whom he interrogated. Calley struck the man with his rifle butt and then shot him in the head. Other testimony indicates that immediately afterwards a young child was observed running toward the village. Calley seized him by the arm, threw him into the ditch, and fired at him. Calley admitted interrogating and striking the monk, but denied shooting him. He also denied the incident involving the child.

Appellate defense counsel contend that the evidence is insufficient to establish the accused's guilt. They do not dispute Calley's participation in the homicides, but they argue that he did not act with the malice or *mens rea* essential to a conviction of murder; that the orders he received to kill everyone in the village were not palpably illegal; that he was acting in ignorance of the laws of war; that since he was told that only "the enemy" would be in the village, his honest belief that there were no innocent civilians in the village exonerates him of criminal responsibility for their deaths; and, finally, that his actions were in the heat of passion caused by reasonable provocation.

In assessing the sufficiency of the evidence to support findings of guilty, we cannot reevaluate the credibility of the witnesses or resolve conflicts in their testimony and thus decide anew whether the accused's guilt was established beyond a reasonable doubt. Our function is more limited; it is to determine whether the record contains enough evidence for the triers of the facts to find beyond a reasonable doubt each element of the offenses involved. * * *

The testimony of Meadlo and others provided the court members with ample evidence from which to find that Lieutenant Calley directed and personally participated in the intentional killing of men, women, and children, who were unarmed and in the custody of armed soldiers of C Company. If the prosecution's witnesses are believed, there is also ample evidence to support a finding that the accused deliberately shot the Vietnamese monk whom he interrogated, and that he seized, threw into a ditch, and fired on a child with the intent to kill.

Enemy prisoners are not subject to summary execution by their captors. Military law has long held that the killing of an unresisting prisoner is murder. WINTHROP'S MILITARY LAW AND PRECEDENTS, 2d ed., 1920 Reprint, at 788–91. While it is lawful to kill an enemy "in the heat and exercise of war," yet "to kill such an enemy after he has laid down his arms . . . is murder." DIGEST OF OPINIONS OF THE JUDGE ADVOCATES GENERAL OF THE ARMY, 1912, at 1074–75 n. 3.

Conceding for the purposes of this assignment of error that Calley believed the villagers were part of "the enemy," the uncontradicted evidence is that they were under the control of armed soldiers and were offering no resistance. In his testimony, Calley admitted he was aware of the requirement that prisoners be treated with respect. He also admitted he knew that the normal practice was to interrogate villagers, release those who could satisfactorily account for themselves, and evacuate the suspect among them for further examination. Instead of proceeding in the usual way, Calley executed all, without regard to age, condition, or possibility of suspicion. On the evidence, the court-martial could reasonably find Calley guilty of the offenses before us.

At trial, Calley's principal defense was that he acted in execution of Captain Medina's order to kill everyone in My Lai 4. Appellate defense counsel urge this defense as the most important factor in assessment of the legal sufficiency of the evidence. The argument, however, is inapplicable to whether the evidence is legally sufficient. Captain Medina denied that he issued any such order, either during the previous day's briefing or on the date the killings were carried out. Resolution of the conflict between his testimony and that of the accused was for the triers of the facts. *United States v. Guerra*, 13 USCMA 463, 32 CMR 463 (1963). The general findings of guilty, with exceptions as to the number of persons killed, does not indicate whether the court members found that Captain Medina did not issue the alleged order to kill, or whether, if he did, the court members believed that the accused knew the order was illegal. For the purpose of the legal sufficiency of the evidence, the record supports the findings of guilty.

* * * [A]ppellate defense counsel assert gross deficiencies in the military judge's instructions to the court members. Only two assertions merit discussion. One contention is that the judge should have, but did not, advise the court members of the necessity to find the existence of "malice aforethought" in connection with the murder charges; the second allegation is that the defense of compliance with superior orders was not properly submitted to the court members. * * * [The Court found first that the judge's jury "instructions comported fully with requirements of existing law for the offense of premeditated murder, and neither statute nor judicial precedent requires that reference also be made to the pre-Code concept of malice."]

We turn to the contention that the judge erred in his submission of the defense of superior orders to the court. After fairly summarizing the evidence, the judge gave the following instructions pertinent to the issue:

> The killing of resisting or fleeing enemy forces is generally recognized as a justifiable act of war, and you may consider any such killings justifiable in this case. The law attempts to protect those persons not actually engaged in warfare, however; and limits the circumstances under which their lives may be taken.
>
> Both combatants captured by and noncombatants detained by the opposing force, regardless of their loyalties, political views, or prior acts, have the right to be treated as prisoners until released, confined, or executed, in accordance with law and established procedures, by competent authority sitting in judgment of such detained or captured individuals. Summary execution of detainees or prisoners is forbidden by law. Further, it's clear under the evidence presented in this case, that hostile acts or support of the enemy North Vietnamese or Viet Cong forces by inhabitants of My Lai (4) at some time prior to 16 March 1968, would not justify the summary execution of all or a part of the occupants of My Lai (4) on 16 March, nor would hostile acts committed that day, if, following the hostility, the belligerents surrendered or were captured by our forces. I therefore instruct you, as a matter of law, that if unresisting human beings were

killed at My Lai (4) while within the effective custody and control of our military forces, their deaths cannot be considered justified, and any order to kill such people would be, as a matter of law, an illegal order. Thus, if you find that Lieutenant Calley received an order directing him to kill unresisting Vietnamese within his control or within the control of his troops, that order would be an illegal order.

A determination that an order is illegal does not, of itself, assign criminal responsibility to the person following the order for acts done in compliance with it. Soldiers are taught to follow orders, and special attention is given to obedience of orders on the battlefield. Military effectiveness depends upon obedience to orders. On the other hand, the obedience of a soldier is not the obedience of an automaton. A soldier is a reasoning agent, obliged to respond, not as a machine, but as a person. The law takes these factors into account in assessing criminal responsibility for acts done in compliance with illegal orders.

The acts of a subordinate done in compliance with an unlawful order given him by his superior are excused and impose no criminal liability upon him unless the superior's order is one which a man of ordinary sense and understanding would, under the circumstances, know to be unlawful, or if the order in question is actually known to the accused to be unlawful.

* * *

In determining what orders, if any, Lieutenant Calley acted under, if you find him to have acted, you should consider all of the matters which he has testified reached him and which you can infer from other evidence that he saw and heard. Then, unless you find beyond a reasonable doubt that he was not acting under orders directing him in substance and effect to kill unresisting occupants of My Lai (4), you must determine whether Lieutenant Calley actually knew those orders to be unlawful.

* * * In determining whether or not Lieutenant Calley had knowledge of the unlawfulness of any order found by you to have been given, you may consider all relevant facts and circumstances, including Lieutenant Calley's rank; educational background; OCS schooling; other training while in the Army, including basic training, and his training in Hawaii and Vietnam; his experience on prior operations involving contact with hostile and friendly Vietnamese; his age; and any other evidence tending to prove or disprove that on 16 March 1968, Lieutenant Calley knew the order was unlawful. If you find beyond a reasonable doubt, on the basis of all the evidence, that Lieutenant Calley actually knew the

order under which he asserts he operated was unlawful, the fact that the order was given operates as no defense.

Unless you find beyond reasonable doubt that the accused acted with actual knowledge that the order was unlawful, you must proceed to determine whether, under the circumstances, a man of ordinary sense and understanding would have known the order was unlawful. Your deliberations on this question do not focus on Lieutenant Calley and the manner in which he perceived the legality of the order found to have been given him. The standard is that of a man of ordinary sense and understanding under the circum-stances.

Think back to the events of 15 and 16 March 1968. . . . Then determine, in light of all the surrounding circumstances, whether the order, which to reach this point you will have found him to be operating in accordance with, is one which a man of ordinary sense and understanding would know to be unlawful. Apply this to each charged act which you have found Lieutenant Calley to have committed. Unless you are satisfied from the evidence, beyond a reasonable doubt, that a man of ordinary sense and understanding would have known the order to be unlawful, you must acquit Lieutenant Calley for committing acts done in accordance with the order.

Appellate defense counsel contend that these instructions are prejudicially erroneous in that they require the court members to determine that Lieutenant Calley knew that an order to kill human beings in the circumstances under which he killed was illegal by the standard of whether "a man of ordinary sense and understanding" would know the order was illegal. They urge us to adopt as the governing test whether the order is so palpably or manifestly illegal that a person of "the commonest understanding" would be aware of its illegality. They maintain the standard stated by the judge is too strict and unjust; that it confronts members of the armed forces who are not persons of ordinary sense and understanding with the dilemma of choosing between the penalty of death for disobedience of an order in time of war on the one hand and the equally serious punishment for obedience on the other. Some thoughtful commentators on military law have presented much the same argument.[1]

The "ordinary sense and understanding" standard is set forth in the present Manual for Courts-Martial, United States, 1969 (Rev), and was the

1 In the words of one author: "If the standard of reasonableness continues to be applied, we run the unacceptable risk of applying serious punishment to one whose only crime is the slowness of his wit or his stupidity. The soldier, who honestly believes that he must obey an order to kill and is punished for it, is convicted not of murder but of simple negligence." FINKELSTEIN, DUTY TO OBEY AS A DEFENSE, March 9, 1970 (unpublished essay, Army War College). See also L. NORENE, OBEDIENCE TO ORDERS AS A DEFENSE TO A CRIMINAL ACT, March 1971 (unpublished thesis presented to The Judge Advocate General's School, U.S. Army).

standard accepted by this Court in *United States v Schultz*, 18 USCMA 133, 39 CMR 133 (1969) and *United States v Keenan*, 18 USCMA 108, 39 CMR 108 (1969). It appeared as early as 1917. Manual for Courts-Martial, U.S. Army, 1917, paragraph 442. Apparently, it originated in a quotation from F. WHARTON, HOMICIDE § 485 (3d ed. 1907). Wharton's authority is *Riggs v State*, 3 Coldwell 85, 91 American Decisions 272, 273 (Tenn 1866), in which the court approved a charge to the jury as follows:

> [I]n its substance being clearly illegal, so that a man of ordinary sense and understanding would know as soon as he heard the order read or given that such order was illegal, would afford a private no protection for a crime committed under such order. * * *

Colonel William Winthrop, the leading American commentator on military law, notes:

> But for the inferior to assume to determine the question of the lawfulness of an order given him by a superior would of itself, as a general rule, amount to insubordination, and such an assumption carried into practice would subvert military discipline. Where the order is apparently regular and lawful on its face, he is not to go behind it to satisfy himself that his superior has proceeded with authority, but is to obey it according to its terms, the only exceptions recognized to the rule of obedience being cases of orders so manifestly beyond the legal power or discretion of the commander as to admit of no rational doubt of their unlawfulness. . . .
>
> Except in such instances of palpable illegality, which must be of rare occurrence, the inferior should presume that the order was lawful and authorized and obey it accordingly, and in obeying it can scarcely fail to be held justified by a military court.

WINTHROP'S MILITARY LAW AND PRECEDENTS, 2d ed., 1920 Reprint, at 296–297 (footnotes omitted) (emphasis added).

In the stress of combat, a member of the armed forces cannot reasonably be expected to make a refined legal judgment and be held criminally responsible if he guesses wrong on a question as to which there may be considerable disagreement. But there is no disagreement as to the illegality of the order to kill in this case. For 100 years, it has been a settled rule of American law that even in war the summary killing of an enemy, who has submitted to, and is under, effective physical control, is murder. Appellate defense counsel acknowledge that rule of law and its continued viability, but they say that Lieutenant Calley should not be held accountable for the men, women and children he killed because the court-martial could have found that he was a person of "commonest understanding" and such a person might not know what our law provides; that his captain had ordered him to kill these unarmed and submissive people and he only carried out that order as a good disciplined soldier should.

Whether Lieutenant Calley was the most ignorant person in the United States Army in Vietnam, or the most intelligent, he must be presumed to know that he could not kill the people involved here. The United States Supreme Court has pointed out that "[t]he rule that 'ignorance of the law will not excuse' [a positive act that constitutes a crime] . . . is deep in our law." *Lambert v California*, 355 U.S. 225, 228 (1957). An order to kill infants and unarmed civilians who were so demonstrably incapable of resistance to the armed might of a military force as were those killed by Lieutenant Calley is, in my opinion, so palpably illegal that whatever conceptional [*sic*] difference there may be between a person of "commonest understanding" and a person of "common understanding," that difference could not have had any "impact on a court of lay members receiving the respective wordings in instructions," as appellate defense counsel contend. In my judgment, there is no possibility of prejudice to Lieutenant Calley in the trial judge's reliance upon the established standard of excuse of criminal conduct, rather than the standard of "commonest understanding" presented by the defense, or by the new variable test postulated in the dissent, which, with the inclusion of such factors for consideration as grade and experience, would appear to exact a higher standard of understanding from Lieutenant Calley than that of the person of ordinary understanding.

In summary, as reflected in the record, the judge was capable and fair, and dedicated to assuring the accused a trial on the merits as provided by law; his instructions on all issues were comprehensive and correct. Lieutenant Calley was given every consideration to which he was entitled, and perhaps more. We are impressed with the absence of bias or prejudice on the part of the court members. They were instructed to determine the truth according to the law and this they did with due deliberation and full consideration of the evidence. Their findings of guilty represent the truth of the facts as they determined them to be and there is substantial evidence to support those findings. No mistakes of procedure cast doubt upon them.

Consequently, the decision of the Court of Military Review is affirmed.

NOTES AND QUESTIONS

1. *The prosecution of William Calley.* The military operates under a system that requires immediate and unquestioning obedience to the order of superiors. From that perspective, the separability theme of positivism prevails: the existence of the superior's order is one thing and its justice is another. But according to the court in *Calley*, what is the test for whether an order is illegal, and what is the source of the knowledge that a particular order is illegal? Has

a natural law sensibility worked its way back into the most rigidly positivist legal system in American society?

2. *The laws of war*. The so-called "Martens Clause" has been considered an essential aspect of the law of war for over a century, having first appeared in the preamble to the 1899 Hague Convention (II) with respect to the laws and customs of war on land:

> Until a more complete code of the laws of war is issued, the High Contracting Parties think it right to declare that in cases not included in the Regulations adopted by them, populations and belligerents remain under the protection and empire of the principles of international law, as they result from the usages established between civilized nations, from the laws of humanity and the requirements of the public conscience.

One possible interpretation of the Martens Clause is that treaties relating to the laws of armed conflict are never complete, and the Clause assures that conduct not explicitly or literally prohibited by the multiple law-of-war treaties is not for that reason alone permitted. An even broader interpretation is that, in the process of determining a state's legal obligations, resort must be had not merely to applicable treaties and the general principles of international law but also "the requirements of the public conscience." As a result, it's not always feasible to offer a definitive, complete, and exhaustive list of states' and combatants' obligations under international humanitarian law, even if the core norms are fairly well-understood, internalized, and enforced in a variety of domestic and international institutions. *See* Chapter 14, *infra*. Is the Martens Clause a challenge to any pristine separation of positive law—in this case a treaty obligation—and morality?

B. POSITIVISM AND THE PROBLEM OF DISCRETION IN INTERPRETING AND APPLYING A RULE

MCBOYLE V. UNITED STATES

283 U.S. 25 (1931)

MR. JUSTICE HOLMES delivered the opinion of the Court. The petitioner was convicted of transporting from Ottawa, Illinois, to Guymon, Oklahoma, an airplane that he knew to have been stolen, and was sentenced to serve three years' imprisonment and to pay a fine of $2,000. The judgment was affirmed by the Circuit Court of Appeals for the Tenth Circuit. A writ of certiorari was granted by this Court on the question whether the National Motor Vehicle Theft Act applies to aircraft. Act of October 29, 1919, c. 89, 41 Stat. 324, U. S. Code, title 18, s 408 (18 USCA s 408). That Act provides:

> Sec. 2. That when used in this Act: (a) The term "motor vehicle" shall include an automobile, automobile truck, automobile wagon, motor cycle, or any other self-propelled vehicle not designed for running on rails. * * *
>
> Sec. 3. That whoever shall transport or cause to be transported in interstate or foreign commerce a motor vehicle, knowing the same to have been stolen, shall be punished by a fine of not more than $5,000, or by imprisonment of not more than five years, or both.

Section 2 defines the motor vehicles of which the transportation in interstate commerce is punished in Section 3. The question is the meaning of the word "vehicle" in the phrase "any other self-propelled vehicle not designed for running on rails." No doubt etymologically it is possible to use the word to signify a conveyance working on land, water or air, and sometimes legislation extends the use in that direction, *e. g.*, land and air, water being separately provided for, in the Tariff Act, 42 Stat. 858. But in everyday speech "vehicle" calls up the picture of a thing moving on land. Thus in Rev. St. s 4 (1 USCA s 4) intended [*sic*], the Government suggests, rather to enlarge than to restrict the definition, vehicle includes every contrivance capable of being used "as a means of transportation on land." And this is repeated, expressly excluding aircraft, in the Tariff Act, June 17, 1930, § 401(b), 46 Stat. 590, 708 (19 USCA § 1401). So here, the phrase under discussion calls up the popular picture. For after including automobile truck, automobile wagon and motor cycle, the words "any other self-propelled vehicle not designed for running on rails" still indicate that a vehicle in the popular sense, that is a vehicle running on land is the theme. It is a vehicle that runs, not something, not commonly called a vehicle, that flies. Airplanes were well known in 1919 when this statute was passed, but it is admitted that they were not mentioned in the reports or in the debates in Congress. It is impossible to read words that so carefully enumerate the different forms of motor vehicles and have no reference of any kind to aircraft, as including airplanes under a term that usage more and more precisely confines to a different class. The counsel for the petitioner have shown that the phraseology of the statute as to motor vehicles follows that of earlier statutes of Connecticut, Delaware, Ohio, Michigan and Missouri, not to mention the late Regulations of Traffic for the District of Columbia, none of which can be supposed to leave the earth.

Although it is not likely that a criminal will carefully consider the text of the law before he murders or steals, it is reasonable that a fair warning should be given to the world in language that the common world will understand, of what the law intends to do if a certain line is passed. To make the warning fair, so far as possible the line should be clear. When a rule of conduct is laid down in words that evoke in the common mind only the picture of vehicles moving on land, the statute should not be extended to aircraft simply because it may seem to us that a similar policy applies, or upon the speculation that if the legislature had thought of it, very likely broader words would have been used. *United States v. Bhagat Singh Thind*, 261 U. S. 204, 209. Judgment reversed.

NOTES AND QUESTIONS

1. *Testing positivism's fixation on rules and the minimization of discretion.* How should positivists account for the non-determinate, open-textured quality of law, especially when a statute is being interpreted as in *McBoyle*? Is it an adequate answer that the necessity of filling gaps—like whether a "plane" is a "vehicle"—is the rare case and that it's a mistake to base an entire philosophy of law on a rare or aberrant experience?

2. *Finding the better generalization.* Even if rough systematizations of the law are possible (*see, e.g.* the American Law Institute's RESTATEMENTS of various subjects in the law), what is the role of discretion and interpretation in a system so dominated by rules? Is the better generalization (a) that the law is overwhelmingly constrained by rules, with discretion as an occasional necessity, or (b) that the law is actually characterized by a systematic discretion with rules as a kind of window dressing for the judges' irreducibly personal decision-making? What difference does this difference make?

3. *Positivism and judging.* Consider the opening statement of John C. Roberts, Jr., Chief Justice of the United States, in his confirmation hearings before the Senate Judiciary Committee (2005):

> Judges and justices are servants of the law, not the other way around. Judges are like umpires. Umpires don't make the rules; they apply them. The role of an umpire and a judge is critical. They make sure everybody plays by the rules. But it is a limited role. Nobody ever went to a ball game to see the umpire * * *.

What are the virtues and what are the vices of Justice Roberts' umpire analogy?

4. *Distinguishing positivism from formalism.* As noted in the introduction to this chapter, there is a nice philosophical question whether formalism—which is a theory of adjudication that emphasizes judicial minimalism—is a necessary part of positivism—which is a theory of law—or not. William Eskridge offers a concise definition of formalism:

> Formalism posits that judicial interpreters can and should be tightly constrained by the objectively determinable meaning of a statute; if unelected judges exercise much discretion in these cases, democratic governance is threatened.

William Eskridge, Jr., *The New Textualism*, 37 UCLA L. REV. 621, 646 (1990). On the issue of the relationship between positivism and formalism, *compare* ANTHONY SEBOK, LEGAL POSITIVISM IN AMERICAN JURISPRUDENCE (1998), *with*

Brian Leiter, *Positivism, Formalism, Realism*, 99 COLUM. L. REV. 1138 (1999) (reviewing Professor Sebok's book).

5. *Hard cases*. Justice Oliver Wendell Holmes, Jr., is often credited with the observation that "hard cases make bad law." *Northern Securities Co. v. United States*, 193 U.S. 197 (1904). What is meant by "hard cases," and, if the positivists' emphasis on the rules aspect of the law is justified, why would there be *any* hard cases? Maybe "hard" is a label attached to a particular case by a judge when she or he is prepared to ignore some received or established rule, or to treat contradictory rules as equals, or to conclude that no settled rule resolves the case one way or the other. Conceived in these ways, how characteristic of the law generally are hard cases? *See generally*, Ronald Dworkin, *Hard Cases*, 88 HARV. L. REV. 1057 (1975).

6. *The empirical attack on positivism*. The neutrality and determinism of rules came to be less plausible with the rise of the West Reporting System in the early twentieth century, because it became impossible to maintain empirically that courts faced with the same facts reached the same conclusions. The idea that law was not some simple determinate thing also connected well with the demise of certainty in other disciplines in the early twentieth century, like physics (with the rise of quantum mechanics and the Heisenberg Uncertainty Principle) and mathematics (with the emergence of non-Euclidian geometries and Godel's proof of incompleteness in arithmetic). *See* Morris R. Cohen, *The Subject Matter of Formal Logic*, 15 J. PHIL. 688 (1918) (we "are wrong in claiming absolute logical necessity for material principles such as Euclid's geometries, Newton's mechanics, or Christian ethics").

7. *Positivism and democratic pluralism*. Consider the possibility that one rationale for positivism is that it serves pluralistic values and offers a means of resolving conflict. As Jeremy Waldron observes, "[t]he separation of law and morality, and the refusal to associate the concept of law with any particular moral theory or social or political program is not just an abstract thesis in jurisprudence. It reflects the reality of almost every developed legal system—that lawmaking takes place in a context of moral disagreement and political competition, and that almost every modern legal system operates politically under the auspices of a multi-party state." Jeremy Waldron, *"Transcendental Nonsense" and System in the Law*, 100 COLUM. L. REV. 16, 42 (2000) (footnote omitted). Professor Waldron continues:

> Any identification of law with morality, therefore, would be not only theoretically tendentious, but politically poisonous, as each party would accuse the other of abandoning the rule of law simply by virtue of its attempt to implement its own program. Legal positivism is a jurisprudence ready-made for the multi-party situation, the situation in which different moralities and ideologies compete for possession of the commanding heights; other legal philosophies, which deny the separation of law and morality, either have to regard some of the parties in modern political competition as anti-legal or else water down the moral content that they associate with the concept of law to some rather agreeably anodyne values.... [O]n the positivist

> account, law and the apparatus of lawmaking are understood in terms that are hospitable to various parties and ideologies (each of which, if it had the world to itself, would inject a different substantive content into the concept of law).

Id. at 42–43 (footnote omitted). *See also* TOM CAMPBELL, PRESCRIPTIVE LEGAL POSITIVISM: LAW, RIGHTS AND DEMOCRACY (2004). Is there hypocrisy or purity in the position that one argument for positivism is grounded in a moral commitment to the political ideal of pluralism?

8. *A connection to logical positivism.* "Positivism" has many different meanings, and self-described positivists can and do disagree with one another. *See, e.g.*, Robin West, *Three Positivisms*, 78 B.U. L. REV. 791 (1998); Jules L. Coleman & Brian Leiter, *Legal Positivism*, *in* A COMPANION TO PHILOSOPHY OF LAW AND LEGAL THEORY 241 (Dennis Paterson ed., 1996). But there is a rough historical and thematic connection between *legal* positivism and *logical* positivism, a philosophical movement of the early twentieth century which tried to identify and delegitimate language that lacked empirically-verifiable meaning. *See generally* RUDOLF CARNAP, THE LOGICAL STRUCTURE OF THE WORLD (Rolf A. George trans., 1968); ALFRED J. AYER, LANGUAGE, TRUTH, AND LOGIC (1936). To oversimplify the connection considerably: so long as moral statements about the meaning or status of a norm were unverifiable (or so long as there were no agreed-upon and verifiable principle for assessing the validity of such statements), they would be nonsense—what Felix Cohen memorably described as mere "word juggling."

Readings

JOHN AUSTIN, *THE PROVINCE OF JURISPRUDENCE DETERMINED*

(1832)
Excerpts from Lectures I and VI

LECTURE I

The matter of jurisprudence is positive law: law, simply and strictly so called: or law set by political superiors to political inferiors. But positive law (or law, simply and strictly so called) is often confounded with objects to which it is related by resemblance, and with objects to which it is related in the way of analogy: with objects which are also signified, properly and improperly, by the large and vague expression law. To obviate the difficulties springing from that confusion, I begin my projected Course with determining the province of jurisprudence, or with distinguishing the matter of jurisprudence from those various related objects: trying to define the subject of which I intend to treat, before I endeavour to analyse its numerous and complicated parts.

A law, in the most general and comprehensive acceptation in which the term, in its literal meaning, is employed, may be said to be a rule laid down for the guidance of an intelligent being by an intelligent being having power over him. Under this definition are concluded, and without impropriety, several species. It is necessary to define accurately the line of demarcation which separates these species from one another, as much mistiness and intricacy has been infused into the science of jurisprudence by their being confounded or not clearly distinguished. In the comprehensive sense above indicated, or in the largest meaning which it has, without extension by metaphor or analogy, the term law embraces the following objects: Laws set by God to his human creatures, and laws set by men to men.

The whole or a portion of the laws set by God to men is frequently styled the law of nature, or natural law: being, in truth, the only natural law of which it is possible to speak without a metaphor, or without a blending of objects which ought to be distinguished broadly. But, rejecting the appellation Law of Nature as ambiguous and misleading, I name those laws or rules, as considered collectively or in a mass, the Divine law, or the law of God.

Laws set by men to men are of two leading or principal classes: classes which are often blended, although they differ extremely; and which, for that reason, should be severed precisely, and opposed distinctly and conspicuously.

Of the laws or rules set by men to men, some are established by *political* superiors, sovereign and subject: by persons exercising supreme and subordinate government, in independent nations, or independent political societies. The aggregate of the rules thus established, or some aggregate forming a portion of that aggregate, is the appropriate matter of jurisprudence, general or particular. To the aggregate of the rules thus established, or to some aggregate forming a portion of that aggregate, the term law, as used simply and strictly, is exclusively applied. But, as contradistinguished to *natural law*, or to the law of nature (meaning, by those expressions, the law of God), the aggregate of the rules, established by political superiors, is frequently styled *positive* law, or law existing by position. * * *

Having suggested the purpose of my attempt to determine the province of jurisprudence: to distinguish positive law, the appropriate matter of jurisprudence, from the various objects to which it is related by resemblance, and to which it is related, nearly or remotely, by a strong or slender analogy: I shall now state the essentials of a law or rule (taken with the largest signification which can be given to the term properly).

Every law or rule * * * is a command. Or, rather, laws or rules, properly so called, are a species of commands.

Now, since the term command comprises the term law, the first is the simpler as well as the larger of the two. But, simple as it is, it admits of explanation. And, since it is the key to the sciences of jurisprudence and morals, its meaning should be analysed with precision.

Accordingly, I shall endeavour, in the first instance, to analyse the meaning of "command": an analysis which I fear, will task the patience of my hearers, but which they will bear with cheerfulness, or, at least, with resignation, if they consider the difficulty of performing it. * * *

If you express or intimate a wish that I shall do or forbear from some act, and if you will visit me with an evil in case I comply not with your wish, the expression or intimation of your wish is a command. A command is distinguished from other significations of desire, not by the style in which the desire is signified, but by the power and the purpose of the party commanding to inflict an evil or pain in case the desire be disregarded. If you cannot or will not harm me in case I comply not with your wish, the expression of your wish is not a command, although you utter your wish in imperative phrase. If you are able and willing to harm me in case I comply not with your wish, the expression of your wish amounts to a command, although you are prompted by a spirit of courtesy to utter it in the shape of a request. * * *

A command, then, is a signification of desire. But a command is distinguished from other significations of desire by this peculiarity: that the party to whom it is directed is liable to evil from the other, in case he comply not with the desire.

Being liable to evil from you if I comply not with a wish which you signify, I am bound or obliged by your command, or I lie under a duty to obey it. If, in spite of that evil in prospect, I comply not with the wish which you signify, I am said to disobey your command, or to violate the duty which it imposes. Command and duty are, therefore, correlative terms: the meaning denoted by each being implied or supposed by the other. Or (changing the expression) wherever a duty lies, a command has been signified; and whenever a command is signified, a duty is imposed.

Concisely expressed, the meaning of the correlative expressions is this: He who will inflict an evil in case his desire be disregarded, utters a command by expressing or intimating his desire. He who is liable to the evil in case he disregard the desire, is bound or obliged by the command.

The evil which will probably be incurred in case a command be disobeyed or (to use an equivalent expression) in case a duty be broken, is frequently called a sanction, or an enforcement of obedience. Or (varying the phrase) the command or the duty is said to be sanctioned or enforced by the chance of incurring the evil. Considered as thus abstracted from the command and the duty which it enforces, the evil to be incurred by disobedience is frequently styled a punishment. But, as punishments, strictly so called, are only a class of sanctions, the term is too narrow to express the meaning adequately. * * *

The truth is, that the magnitude of the eventual evil, and the magnitude of the chance of incurring it, are foreign to the matter in question. The greater the eventual evil, and the greater the chance of incurring it, the greater is the efficacy of the command, and the greater is the strength of the obligation: Or (substituting expressions exactly equivalent), the greater is the chance that the command will be obeyed, and that the duty will not be broken. But where there is the smallest chance of incurring the smallest evil, the expression of a wish amounts to a command, and, therefore, imposes a duty. The sanction, if you will, is feeble or insufficient; but still there is a sanction, arid, therefore, a duty and a command.

By some celebrated writers (by Locke, Bentham, and, I think, Paley), the term sanction, or enforcement of obedience, is applied to conditional good as well as to conditional evil: to reward as to punishment. But, with all my habitual veneration for the names of Locke and Bentham, I think that this extension of the term is pregnant with confusion and perplexity.

Rewards are, indisputably, motives to comply with the wishes of others. But to talk of commands and duties as sanctioned or enforced by rewards, or to talk of rewards as obliging or constraining to obedience, is surely a wide departure from the established meaning of the terms.

If you expressed a desire that I should render a service, and if you proffered a reward as the motive or inducement to render it, you would scarcely be said to command the service, nor should I, in ordinary language, be obliged to render it. In ordinary language, you would promise me a reward, on condition of my rendering the service, whilst I might be incited or persuaded to render it by the hope of obtaining the reward. Again: If a law hold out a reward as an inducement to do some act, an eventual right is conferred, and not an obligation imposed, upon those who shall act accordingly: The imperative part of the law being addressed or directed to the party whom it requires to render the reward.

In short, I am determined or inclined to comply with the wish of another, by the fear of disadvantage or evil. I am also determined or inclined to comply with the wish of another, by the hope of advantage or good. But it is only by the chance of incurring evil, that I am bound or obliged to compliance. It is only by conditional evil, that duties are sanctioned or enforced. It is the power and the purpose of inflicting eventual evil, and not the power and the purpose of imparting eventual good, which gives to the expression of a wish the name of a command.

If we put reward into the import of the term sanction, we must engage in a toilsome struggle with the current of ordinary speech; and shall often slide unconsciously, notwithstanding our efforts to the contrary, into the narrower and customary meaning.

It appears, then, from what has been premised, that the ideas or notions comprehended by the term command are the following. 1. A wish or desire conceived by a rational being, that another rational being shall do or forbear. 2. An evil to proceed from the former, and to be incurred by the latter, in case the latter comply not with the wish. 3. An expression or intimation of the wish by words or other signs. * * *

When I am talking directly of the chance of incurring the evil, or (changing the expression) of the liability or obnoxiousness to the evil, I employ the term *duty*, or the term *obligation*: The liability or obnoxiousness to the evil being put foremost, and the rest of the complex notion being signified implicitly.

When I am talking immediately of the evil itself, I employ the term *sanction*, or a term of the like import: The evil to be incurred being signified directly; whilst the obnoxiousness to that evil, with the expression or intimation of the wish, are indicated indirectly or obliquely. * * *

Commands are of two species. Some are laws or rules. The others have not acquired an appropriate name, nor does language afford an expression which will mark them briefly and precisely. I must, therefore, note them as well as I can by the ambiguous and inexpressive name of "occasional or particular commands".

The term *laws* or *rules* being not unfrequently applied to occasional or particular commands, it is hardly possible to describe a line of separation which shall consist in every respect with established forms of speech. But the distinction between laws and particular commands may, I think, be stated in the following manner.

By every command, the party to whom it is directed is obliged to do or to forbear.

Now where it obliges generally to acts or forbearances of a class, a command is a law or rule. But where it obliges to a specific act or forbearance, or to acts or forbearances which it determines specifically or individually, a command is occasional or particular. In other words, a class or description of acts is determined by a law or rule, and acts of that class or description are enjoined or forbidden generally. But where a command is occasional or particular, the act or acts, which the command enjoins or forbids, are assigned or determined by their specific or individual natures as well as by the class or description to which they belong. * * *

To conclude with an example which best illustrates the distinction, and which shows the importance of the distinction most conspicuously, judicial commands are commonly occasional or particular, although the commands which they are calculated to enforce are commonly laws or rules.

For instance, the lawgiver commands that thieves shall be hanged. A specific theft and a specified thief being given, the judge commands that the thief shall be hanged, agreeably to the command of the lawgiver.

Now the lawgiver determines a class or description of acts; prohibits acts of the class generally and indefinitely; and commands, with the like generality, that punishment shall follow transgression. *The command of the lawgiver is, therefore, a law or rule.* But the command of the judge is occasional or particular. For he orders a specific punishment, as the consequence of a specific offence.

According to the line of separation which I have now attempted to describe, a law and a particular command are distinguished thus: Acts or forbearances of a class are enjoined generally by the former. Acts determined specifically are enjoined or forbidden by the latter. * * *

It appears, from what has been premised, that a law, properly so called, may be defined in the following manner. A law is a command which obliges a person or persons. But, as contradistinguished or opposed to an occasional or particular command, a law is a command which obliges a person or persons, and obliges generally to acts or forbearances of a class. In language more popular but less distinct and precise, a law is a command which obliges a person or persons to a course of conduct. Laws and other commands are said to proceed from superiors, and to bind or oblige inferiors. I will, therefore, analyse the meaning of those correlative expressions; and will try to strip them of a certain mystery, by which that simple meaning appears to be obscured.

Superiority is often synonymous with precedence or excellence. We talk of superiors in rank; of superiors in wealth; of superiors in virtue: comparing certain persons with certain other persons; and meaning that the former precede or excel the latter in rank, in wealth, or in virtue.

But, taken with the meaning wherein I here understand it, the term superiority signifies *might*: the power of affecting others with evil or pain, and of forcing them, through fear of that evil, to fashion their conduct to one's wishes.

For example, God is emphatically the superior of Man. For his power of affecting us with pain, and of forcing us to comply with his will, is unbounded and resistless. To a limited extent, the sovereign One or Number is the superior of the subject or citizen: the master, of the slave or servant: the father, of the child.

In short, whoever can oblige another to comply with his wishes, is the superior of that other, so far as the ability reaches: The party who is obnoxious to the impending evil, being, to that same extent, the inferior.

The might or superiority of God, is simple or absolute. But in all or most cases of human superiority, the relation of superior and inferior, and the relation of inferior and superior, are reciprocal. Or (changing the expression) the party who is the superior as viewed from one aspect, is the inferior as viewed from another.

For example, to an indefinite, though limited extent, the monarch is the superior of the governed: his power being commonly sufficient to enforce compliance with his will. But the governed, collectively or in mass, are also the superior of the monarch: who is checked in the abuse of his might by his fear of exciting their anger; and of rousing to active resistance the might which slumbers in the multitude.

A member of a sovereign assembly is the superior of the judge: the judge being bound by the law which proceeds from that sovereign body. But, in his character of citizen or subject, he is the inferior of the judge: the judge being the minister of the law, and armed with the power of enforcing it.

It appears, then, that the term *superiority* (like the terms duty and sanction) is implied by the term *command.* For superiority is the power of enforcing compliance with a wish: and the expression or intimation of a wish, with the power and the purpose of enforcing it, are the constituent elements of a command.

"That laws emanate from superiors" is, therefore, an identical proposition. For the meaning which it affects to impart is contained in its subject.

If I mark the peculiar source of a given law, or if I mark the peculiar source of laws of a given class, it is possible that I am saying something which may instruct the hearer. But to affirm of laws universally "that they flow from superiors", or to affirm of laws universally "that inferiors are bound to obey them," is the merest tautology and trifling.

Like most of the leading terms in the sciences of jurisprudence and morals, the term *laws* is extremely ambiguous. Taken with the largest signification which can be given to the term properly, laws are a species of commands. But the term is improperly applied to various objects which have nothing of the imperative character: to objects which are not commands; and which, therefore, are not laws, properly so called.

Accordingly, the proposition "that laws are commands" must be taken with limitations. Or, rather, we must distinguish the various meanings of the term laws; and must restrict the proposition to that class of objects which is embraced by the largest signification that can be given to the term properly.

I have already indicated, and shall hereafter more fully describe, the objects improperly termed laws, which are not within the province of jurisprudence (being either rules enforced by opinion and closely analogous to laws properly so called, or being laws so called by a metaphorical application of the term merely). There are other objects improperly termed laws (not being commands) which yet may properly be included within the province of jurisprudence. These I shall endeavour to articularize:

1. Acts on the part of legislatures to explain positive law, can scarcely be called laws, in the proper signification of the term. Working no change in the actual duties of the governed, but simply declaring what those duties are, they properly are acts of interpretation by legislative authority. Or, to borrow an expression from the writers on the Roman Law, they are acts of authentic interpretation.

But, this notwithstanding, they are frequently styled laws; declaratory laws, or declaratory statutes. They must, therefore, be noted as forming an exception to the proposition "that laws are a species of commands." It often, indeed, happens (as I shall show in the proper place), that laws declaratory in name are imperative in effect: Legislative, like judicial interpretation, being frequently deceptive; and establishing new law, under guise of expounding the old.

2. Laws to repeal laws, and to release from existing duties, must also be excepted from the proposition "that laws are a species of commands." In so far as they release from duties imposed by existing laws, they are not commands, but revocations of commands. They authorize or permit the parties, to whom the repeal extends, to do or to forbear from acts which they were commanded to forbear from or to do. And, considered with regard to this, their immediate or direct purpose, they are often named permissive laws; or, more briefly and more properly, permissions.

Remotely and indirectly, indeed, permissive laws are often or always imperative. For the parties released from duties are restored to liberties or rights: and duties answering those rights are, therefore, created or revived. * * *

3. Imperfect laws, or laws of imperfect obligation, must also be excepted from the proposition "that laws are a species of commands".

An imperfect law (with the sense wherein the term is used by the Roman jurists) is a law which wants a sanction, and which, therefore, is not binding. A law declaring that certain acts are crimes, but annexing no punishment to the commission of acts of the class, is the simplest and most obvious example.

Though the author of an imperfect law signifies a desire, he manifests no purpose of enforcing compliance with the desire. But where there is not a purpose of enforcing compliance with the desire, the expression of a desire is not a command. Consequently, an imperfect law is not so properly a law, as counsel, or exhortation, addressed by a superior to inferiors.

Examples of imperfect laws are cited by the Roman jurists. But with us in England, laws professedly imperative are always (I believe) perfect or obligatory. Where the English legislature affects to command, the English tribunals not unreasonably presume that the legislature exacts obedience. And, if no specific sanction be annexed to a given law, a sanction is supplied by the courts of justice, agreeably to a general maxim which obtains in cases of the kind.

The imperfect laws, of which I am now speaking, are laws which are imperfect, in the sense of the Roman jurists: that is to say, laws which speak the desires of political superiors, but which their authors (by oversight or design) have not provided with sanctions. Many of the writers on morals, and on the so called law of nature, have annexed a different meaning to the term imperfect. Speaking of imperfect obligations, they commonly mean duties which are not legal: duties imposed by commands of God, or duties imposed by positive morality, as contradistinguished to duties imposed by positive law. An imperfect obligation, in the sense of the Roman jurists, is exactly equivalent to no obligation at all. For the term imperfect denotes simply, that the law wants the sanction appropriate to laws of the kind. An imperfect obligation, in the other meaning of the expression, is a religious or a moral obligation. The term imperfect does not denote that the law imposing the duty wants the appropriate sanction. It denotes that the law imposing the duty is not a law established by a political superior: that it wants that perfect, or that surer or more cogent sanction, which is imparted by the sovereign or state.

I believe that I have now reviewed all the classes of objects, to which the term laws is improperly applied. The laws (improperly so called) which I have here lastly enumerated, are (I think) the only laws which are not commands, and which yet may be properly included within the province of jurisprudence. But though these, with the so called laws set by opinion and the objects metaphorically termed laws, are the only laws which really are not commands, there are certain laws (properly so called) which may seem not imperative. Accordingly, I will subjoin a few remarks upon laws of this dubious character.

1. There are laws, it may be said, which merely create rights: And, seeing that every command imposes a duty, laws of this nature are not imperative. But * * * there are no laws merely creating rights. There are laws, it is true, which merely create duties: duties not correlating with correlating rights, and which, therefore may be styled absolute. But every law, really conferring a right, imposes expressly or tacitly a relative duty, or a duty correlating with the right. If it specify the remedy to be given, in case the right shall be infringed, it imposes the relative duty expressly. If the remedy to be given be not specified, it refers tacitly to pre-existing law, and clothes the right which it purports to create with a remedy provided by that law. Every law, really conferring a right, is, therefore, imperative: as

imperative, as if its only purpose were the creation of a duty, or as if the relative duty, which it inevitably imposes, were merely absolute.

The meanings of the term *right*, are various and perplexed; taken with its proper meaning, it comprises ideas which are numerous and complicated; and the searching and extensive analysis, which the term, therefore, requires, would occupy more room than could be given to it in the present lecture. It is not, however, necessary, that the analysis should be performed here. I purpose, in my earlier lectures, to determine the province of jurisprudence; or to distinguish the laws established by political superiors, from the various laws, proper and improper, with which they are frequently confounded. And this I may accomplish exactly enough, without a nice inquiry into the import of the term *right*.

2. According to an opinion which I must notice incidentally here, * * * customary laws must be excepted from the proposition "that laws are a species of command."

By many of the admirers of customary laws (and, especially, of their German admirers), they are thought to oblige legally (independently of the sovereign or state), because the citizens or subjects have observed or kept them. Agreeably to this opinion, they are not the creatures of the sovereign or state, although the sovereign or state may abolish them at pleasure. Agreeably to this opinion, they are positive law (or law, strictly so called), inasmuch as they are enforced by the courts of justice: But, that notwithstanding, they exist as positive law by the spontaneous adoption of the governed, and not by position or establishment on the part of political superiors. Consequently, customary laws, considered as positive law, are not commands. And, consequently, customary laws, considered as positive law, are not laws or rules properly so called.

An opinion less mysterious, but somewhat allied to this, is not uncommonly held by the adverse party: by the party which is strongly opposed to customary law; and to all law made judicially, or in the way of judicial legislation. According to the latter opinion, all judge-made law, or all judge-made law established by subject judges, is purely the creature of the judges by whom it is established immediately. To impute it to the sovereign legislature, or to suppose that it speaks the will of the sovereign legislature, is one of the foolish or knavish fictions with which lawyers, in every age and nation, have perplexed and darkened the simplest and clearest truths.

I think it will appear, on a moment's reflection, that each of these opinions is groundless: that customary law is imperative, in the proper signification of the term; and that all judge-made law is the creature of the sovereign or state.

At its origin, a custom is a rule of conduct which the governed observe spontaneously, or not in pursuance of a law set by a political superior. The custom is transmuted into positive law, when it is adopted as such by the courts of justice, and when the judicial decisions fashioned upon it are enforced by the power of the state. But before it is adopted by the courts, and clothed with the legal sanction, it is merely a rule of positive morality: a rule generally observed by the citizens or subjects; but deriving the only force, which it can be said to possess, from the general disapprobation falling on those who transgress it.

Now when judges transmute a custom into a legal rule (or make a legal rule not suggested by a custom), the legal rule which they establish is established by the sovereign legislature. A subordinate or subject judge is merely a minister. The portion of the sovereign power which lies at his disposition is merely delegated. The rules which he makes derive their legal force from authority given by the state: an authority which the state may confer expressly, but which it commonly imparts in the way of acquiescence. For, since the state may reverse the rules which he makes, and yet permits him to enforce them by the power of the political community, its sovereign will "that his rules shall obtain as law" is clearly evinced by its conduct, though not by its express declaration.

The admirers of customary law love to trick out their idol with mysterious and imposing attributes. But to those who can see the difference between positive law and morality, there is nothing of mystery about it. Considered as rules of positive morality, customary laws arise from the consent of the governed, and not from the position or establishment of political superiors. But, considered as moral rules turned into positive laws, customary laws are established by the state: established by the state directly, when the customs are promulgated in its statutes; established by the state circuitously, when the customs are adopted by its tribunals.

The opinion of the party which abhors judge-made laws, springs from their inadequate conception of the nature of commands.

Like other significations of desire, a command is express or tacit. If the desire be signified by words (written or spoken), the command is express. If the desire be signified by conduct (or by any signs of desire which are not words), the command is tacit.

Now when customs are turned into legal rules by decisions of subject judges, the legal rules which emerge from the customs are tacit commands of the sovereign legislature. The state, which is able to abolish, permits its ministers to enforce them: and it, therefore, signifies its pleasure, by that its voluntary acquiescence, "that they shall serve as a law to the governed."

My present purpose is merely this: to prove that the positive law styled customary (and all positive law made judicially) is established by the state directly or circuitously, and, therefore, is imperative. I am far from disputing, that law made judicially (or in the way of improper legislation) and law made by statute (or in the properly legislative manner) are distinguished by weighty differences. I shall inquire, in future lectures, what those differences are; and why subject judges, who are properly ministers of the law, have commonly shared with the sovereign in the business of making it.

I assume, then, that the only laws which are not imperative, and which belong to the subject-matter of jurisprudence, are the following: 1. Declaratory laws, or laws explaining the import of existing positive law. 2. Laws abrogating or repealing existing positive law. 3. Imperfect laws, or laws of imperfect obligation (with the sense wherein the expression is used by the Roman jurists).

But the space occupied in the science by these improper laws is comparatively narrow and insignificant. Accordingly, although I shall take them into account so often as I refer to them directly, I shall throw them out of account on other occasions. Or (changing the expression) I shall limit the term law to laws which are imperative, unless I extend it expressly to laws which are not.

LECTURE VI

* * * The superiority which is styled sovereignty, and the independent political society which sovereignty implies, is distinguished from other superiority, and from other society, by the following marks or characters: 1. The bulk of the given society are in a habit of obedience or submission to a determinate and common superior: let that common superior be a certain individual person or a certain body or aggregate of individual persons. 2. That certain individual, or that certain body of individuals, is not in a habit of obedience to a determinate human superior. Laws (improperly so called) which opinion sets or imposes, may permanently affect the conduct of that certain individual or body. To express or tacit commands of other determinate parties, that certain individual or body may yield occasional submission. But there is no determinate person, or determinate aggregate of persons, to whose commands, express or tacit, that certain individual or body renders habitual obedience.

Or the notions of sovereignty and independent political society may be expressed concisely thus. If a determinate human superior, not in a habit of obedience to a like superior, receive habitual obedience from the bulk of a given society, that determinate superior is sovereign in that society, and the society (including the superior) is a society political and independent.

To that determinate superior, the other members of the society are subject: or on that determinate superior, to other members of the society are dependent. The position of its other members towards that determinate superior, is a state of subjection, or a state of dependence. The mutual relation which subsists between that superior and them, may be styled the relation of sovereign and subject, or the relation of sovereignty and subjection.

Hence it follows, that it is only through an ellipsis, or an abridged form of expression, that the society is styled independent. The party truly independent (independent, that is to say, of a determinate human superior), is not the society, but the sovereign portion of the society: that certain member of the society, or that certain body of its members, to whose commands, expressed or intimated, the generality or bulk of its members render habitual obedience. Upon that certain person, or certain body of persons, the other members of the society are dependent: or to that certain person, or certain body of persons, the other members of the society are subject. By "an independent political society," or "an independent and sovereign nation," we mean a political society consisting of a sovereign and subjects, as opposed to a political society which is merely subordinate: that is to say, which is merely a limb or member of another political society, and which therefore consists entirely of persons in a state of subjection.

In order that a given society may form a society political and independent, the two distinguishing marks which I have mentioned above must unite. The generality of the given society must be in the habit of obedience to a determinate and common superior: whilst that determinate persons, or determinate body of persons must not be habitually obedient to a determinate person or body. It is the union of that positive, with this negative mark, which renders that given society (including that certain superior) a society political and independent.

To show that the union of those marks renders a given society a society political and independent, I call your attention to the following positions and examples.

1. In order that a given society may form a society political, the generality or bulk of its members must be in a habit of obedience to a determinate and common superior.

In case the generality of its members obey a determinate superior, but the obedience be rare or transient and not habitual or permanent, the relation of sovereignty and subjection is not created thereby between that certain superior and the members of that given society. In other words, that determinate superior and the members of that given society do not become thereby an independent political society. Whether that given society be political and independent or not, it is not an independent political society whereof that certain superior is the sovereign portion.

For example: In 1815 the allied armies occupied France; and so long as the allied armies occupied France, the commands of the allied sovereigns were obeyed by the French government, and, through the French government, by the French people generally. But since the commands and the obedience were comparatively rare and transient, they were not sufficient to constitute the relation of sovereignty and subjection between the allied sovereigns and the members of the invaded nation. In spite of those commands, and in spite of that obedience, the French government was sovereign or independent. Or in spite of those commands, and in spite of that obedience, the French government and its subjects were an independent political society whereof the allied sovereigns were not the sovereign portion.

Now if the French nation, before the obedience to those sovereigns, had been an independent society in a state of nature or anarchy, it would not have been changed by the obedience into a society political. And it would not have been changed by the obedience into a society political, because the obedience was not habitual. For, inasmuch as the obedience was not habitual, it was not changed by the obedience from a society political and independent, into a society political but subordinate. A given society, therefore, is not a society political, unless the generality of its members be in a habit of obedience to a determinate and common superior.

Again: A feeble state holds its independence precariously, or at the will of the powerful states to whose aggressions it is obnoxious. And since it is obnoxious to their aggressions, it and the bulk of its subjects render obedience to commands which they occasionally express or intimate. Such, for instance, is the position of the Saxon government and its subjects in respect of the conspiring sovereigns who form the Holy Alliance. But since the commands and the obedience are comparatively few and rare, they are not sufficient to constitute the relation of sovereignty and subjection between the powerful states and the feeble state with its subjects. In spite of those commands, and in spite of that obedience, the feeble state is sovereign or independent. Or in spite of those commands, and in spite of that obedience, the feeble state and its subjects are an independent political society whereof the powerful states are not the sovereign portion. Although the powerful states are permanently superior, and although the feeble state is permanently inferior, there is neither a habit of command on the part of the former, nor a habit of obedience on the part of the latter. Although the latter is unable to defend and maintain its independence, the latter is independent of the former in fact or practice.

From the example now adduced, as from the example adduced before, we may draw the following inference: that a given society is not a society political, unless the generality of its members be in a habit of obedience to a determinate and common superior. By the obedience to the powerful states, the feeble state and its subjects are not changed from an independent, into a sub ordinate political society. And they are not changed by the obedience into a subordinate political society, because the obedience is not habitual. Consequently, if they were a natural society (setting that obedience aside), they would not be changed by that obedience into a society political.

2. In order that a given society may form a society political, habitual obedience must be rendered, by the generality or bulk of its members, to a determinate and common superior. In other words, habitual obedience must be rendered, by the generality or bulk of its members, to one and the same determinate person, or determinate body of persons.

Unless habitual obedience be rendered by the bulk of its members, and be rendered by the bulk of its members to one and the same superior, the given society is either in a state of nature, or is split into two or more independent political societies.

For example: In case a given society be torn by intestine war, and in case the conflicting parties be nearly balanced, the given society is in one of the two positions which I have now supposed. As there is no common superior to which the bulk of its members render habitual obedience, it is not a political society single or undivided. If the bulk of each of the parties be in a habit of obedience to its head, the given society is broken into two or more societies, which, perhaps, may be styled independent political societies. If the bulk of each of the parties be not in that habit of obedience, the given society is simply or absolutely in a state of nature or anarchy. It is either resolved or broken into its individual elements, or into numerous societies of an extremely limited size: of a size so extremely limited, that they could hardly be styled societies independent and political. For, as I shall show hereafter, a given independent society would hardly be styled political, in case it fell short of a number which cannot be fixed with precision, but which may be called considerable, or not extremely minute.

3. In order that a given society may form a society political, the generality or bulk of its members must habitually obey a superior determinate as well as common.

On this position I shall not insist here. For I have shown sufficiently in my fifth lecture, that no indeterminate party can command expressly or tacitly, or can receive obedience or submission: that no indeterminate body is capable of corporate conduct, or is capable, as a body, of positive or negative deportment.

4. It appears from what has preceded, that, in order that a given society may form a society political, the bulk of its members must be in a habit of obedience to a certain and common superior. But, in order that the given society may form a society political and independent, that certain superior must not be habitually obedient to a determinate human superior.

The given society may form a society political and independent, although that certain superior be habitually affected by laws which opinion sets or imposes. The given society may form a society political and independent, although that certain superior render occasional submission to commands of determinate parties. But the society is not independent, although it may be political, in case that certain superior habitually obey the commands of a certain person or body.

Let us suppose, for example, that a viceroy obeys habitually the author of his delegated powers. And, to render the example complete, let us suppose that the viceroy receives habitual obedience from the generality or bulk of the persons who inhabit his province. Now though he commands habitually within the limits of his province, and receives habitual obedience from the generality or bulk of its inhabitants, the viceroy is not sovereign within the limits of his province, nor are he and its inhabitants an independent political society. The viceroy, and (through the viceroy) the generality or bulk of its inhabitants, are habitually obedient or submissive to the sovereign of a larger society. He and the inhabitants of his province are therefore in a state of subjection to the sovereign of that larger society. He and the inhabitants of his province are a society political but subordinate, or form a political society which is merely a limb of another.

NOTES AND QUESTIONS

1. *First things first.* How does Austin define "law?" What other terms must he define in order to define "law?" How does Austin distinguish natural law from positive law? Looking back at the text of Austin's Lecture I, what exactly is wrong with natural law as far as Austin is concerned?

2. *More first things first.* According to Austin, why might customary law and judge-made law be a challenge to the legal positivist's account of law, and what is his response to the challenge?

3. *Pushing back.* Can you think of examples of laws that don't fit the "order backed by threat" model? How is the First Amendment guarantee of free speech an "order backed by a threat?" How is hypothetical legislation requiring two witnesses on a will an "order backed by a threat?" Is international law "law" under Austin's model?

4. *"Gunmen" and legitimacy.* Assuming that the excerpt above from *The Province of Jurisprudence Determined* is representative of Austin's thought generally, does he offer any notion of what makes a sovereign "legitimate?" Is that a problem, or is that not within "the province of jurisprudence?"

5. *Assessing the claimed advantages of empiricism.* Is Austin describing what law is, or what law ought to be? In your mind, does this make positivism superior to natural law theories?

6. *"Rescuing" positivism.* As you read the following excerpts from two more modern positivists, Hans Kelsen and H.L.A. Hart, consider how each refines Austin's gunman model of law. Even if they do not embrace natural law arguments, what critique of Austin do they find compelling?

HANS KELSEN, *GENERAL THEORY OF LAW AND STATE*

(1945)

* * * A. The Unity of a Normative Order

a. The Reason of Validity: The Basic Norm [Grundnorm]

The legal order is a system of norms. The question then arises: What is it that makes a system out of a multitude of norms? When does a norm belong to a certain system of norms, an order? This question is in close connection with the question as to the reason of validity of a norm.

In order to answer this question, we must first clarify the grounds on which we assign validity to a norm. When we assume the truth of a statement about reality, it is because the statement corresponds to reality, because our experience confirms it. The statement "A physical body expands when heated" is true, because we have repeatedly and without exception observed that physical bodies expand when they are heated. A norm is not a statement about reality and is therefore incapable of being "true" or "false," in the sense determined above. A norm is either valid or non-valid. Of the two statements: "You shall assist a fellowman in need," and "You shall lie whenever you find it useful," only the first, not the second, is considered to express a valid norm. What is the reason?

The reason for the validity of a norm is not, like the test of the truth of an "is" statement, its conformity to reality. * * * [A] norm is not valid because it is efficacious. The question why something ought to occur can never be answered by an assertion to the effect that something occurs, but only by an assertion that something ought to occur. In the language of daily life, it is true, we frequently justify a norm by referring to a fact. We say, for instance: "You shall not kill because God has forbidden it in one of the Ten Commandments"; or a mother says to her child: "You ought to go to school because your father has ordered it." However, in these statements the fact that God has issued a command or the fact that the father has ordered the child to do something is only apparently the reason for the validity of the norms in question. The true reason is norms tacitly presupposed because taken for granted. The reason for the validity of the norm, You shall not kill, is the general norm, You shall obey the commands of God. The reason for the validity of the norm, You ought to go to school, is the general norm, Children ought to obey their father. If these norms are not presupposed, the references to the facts concerned are not answers to the questions why we shall not kill, why the child ought to go to school. The fact that somebody commands something is, in itself, no reason for the statement that one ought to behave in conformity with the command, no reason for considering the command as a valid norm, no reason for the validity of the norm the contents of which corresponds to the command. The reason for the validity of a norm is always a[nother] norm, not a fact. The quest for the reason of validity of a norm leads back, not to reality, but to another norm from which the first norm is derivable in a sense that will be investigated later. Let us, for the present, discuss a concrete example. We accept the statement "You shall assist a fellowman in need," as a valid norm because it follows from the statement "You shall love your neighbor." This statement we accept as a valid norm, either because it appears to us as an ultimate norm whose validity is self-evident, or—for instance—Christ has bidden that you shall love your neighbor, and we postulate as an ultimate valid norm the statement "You shall obey the commandments of Christ."

The statement "You shall lie whenever you find it useful," we do not accept as a valid norm, because it is neither derivable from another valid norm nor is it in itself an ultimate, self-evidently valid norm.

A norm the validity of which cannot be derived from a superior norm we call a "basic" norm. All norms whose validity may be traced back to one and the same basic norm form a system of norms, or an order. This basic norm constitutes, as a common source, the bond between all the different norms of which an order consists. That a norm belongs to a certain system of norms, to a certain normative order, can be tested only by ascertaining that it derives its validity from the basic norm constituting the order. Whereas an "is" statement is true because it agrees with the reality of sensuous experience, an "ought" statement is a valid norm only if it belongs to such a valid system of norms, if it can be derived from a basic norm presupposed as valid. The ground of truth of an "is" statement is its conformity to the reality of our experience; the reason for the validity of a norm is a presupposition, a norm presupposed to be an ultimately valid, that is, a basic norm. The quest for the reason of validity of a norm is not—like the quest for the cause of an effect—a *regressus ad infinitum* [an infinite regress]; it is terminated by a highest norm which is the last reason of validity within the normative system, whereas a last or first cause has no place within a system of natural reality.

b. The Static System of Norms

According to the nature of the basic norm, we may distinguish between two different types of orders or normative systems: static and dynamic systems. Within an order of the first kind the norms are "valid" and that means, we assume that the individuals whose behavior is regulated by the norms "ought" to behave as the norms prescribe, by virtue of their contents: Their contents have an immediately evident quality that guarantees their validity, or, in other terms: the norms are valid because of their inherent appeal. This quality the norms have because they are derivable from a specific basic norm as the particular is derivable from the general. The binding force of the basic norm is itself self-evident, or at least presumed to be so. Such norms as "You must not lie," "You must not deceive," "You shall keep your promise," follow from a general norm prescribing truthfulness. From the norm "You shall love your neighbor" one may deduce such norms as "You must not hurt your neighbor," "You shall help him in need," and so on. If one asks why one has to love one's neighbor, perhaps the answer will be found in some still more general norm, let us say the postulate that one has to live "in harmony with the universe." If that is the most general norm of whose validity we are convinced, we will consider it as the ultimate norm. Its obligatory nature may appear so obvious that one does not feel any need to ask for the reason of its validity. Perhaps one may also succeed in deducing the principle of truthfulness and its consequences from this "harmony" postulate. One would then have reached a norm on which a whole system of morality could be based. However, we are not interested here in the question of what specific norm lies at the basis of such and such a system of morality. It is essential only that the various norms of any such system are implicated by the basic norm as the particular is implied by the general, and that, therefore, all the particular norms of such a system are obtainable by means of an intellectual operation, viz., by the inference from the general to the particular. Such a system is of a static nature.

c. The Dynamic System of Norms

The derivation of a particular norm may, however, be carried out also in another way. A child, asking why it must not lie, might be given the answer that its father has forbidden it to lie. If the child should further ask why it has to obey its father, the reply would perhaps be that God has commanded that it obey its parents. Should the child put the question why one has to obey the commands of God, the only answer would be that this is a norm beyond which one cannot look for a more ultimate norm. That norm is the basic norm providing the foundation for a system of dynamic character. Its various norms cannot be obtained from the basic norm by any intellectual operation. The basic norm merely establishes a certain authority, which may well in turn vest norm-creating power in some other authorities. The norms of a dynamic system have to be created through acts of will by those individuals who have been authorized to create norms by some higher norm. This authorization is a delegation. Norm creating power is delegated from one authority to another authority; the former is the higher, the latter the lower authority. The basic norm of a dynamic system is the fundamental rule according to which the norms of the system are to be created. A norm forms part of a dynamic system if it has been created in a way that is—in the last analysis—determined by the basic norm. A norm thus belongs to the religious system just given by way of example if it is created by God or originates in an authority having its power from God, "delegated" by God.

B. The Law as a Dynamic System of Norms

a. The Positivity of Law

The system of norms we call a legal order is a system of the dynamic kind. Legal norms are not valid because they themselves or the basic norm have a content the binding force of which is self-evident. They are not valid because of their inherent appeal. Legal norms may have any kind of content. There is no kind of human behavior that, because of its nature, could not be made into a legal duty corresponding to a legal right. The validity of a legal norm cannot be questioned on the ground that its contents are incompatible with some moral or political value. A norm is a valid legal norm by virtue of the fact that it has been created according to a definite rule and by virtue thereof only. The basic norm of a legal order is the postulated ultimate rule according to which the norms of this order are established and annulled, receive and lose their validity. The statement "Any man who manufactures or sells alcoholic liquors as beverages shall be punished" is a valid legal norm if it belongs to a certain legal order. This it does if this norm has been created in a definite way ultimately determined by the basic norm of that legal order, and if it has not again been nullified in a definite way, ultimately determined by the same basic norm. The basic norm may, for instance, be such that a norm belongs to the system provided that it has been decreed by the parliament or created by custom or established by the courts, and has not been abolished by a decision of the parliament or through custom or a contrary court practice. The statement mentioned above is no valid legal norm if it does not belong to a valid legal order—it may be that no such norm has been created in the way ultimately determined by the basic norm, or it may be that, although a norm has been created in that way, it has been repealed in a way ultimately determined by the basic norm.

Law is always positive law, and its positivity lies in the fact that it is created and annulled by acts of human beings, thus being independent of morality and similar norm systems. This constitutes the difference between positive law and natural law, which, like morality, is deduced from a presumably self-evident basic norm which is considered to be the expression of the "will of nature" or of "pure reason." The basic norm of a positive legal order is nothing but the fundamental rule according to which the various norms of the order are to be created. It qualifies a certain event as the initial event in the creation of the various legal norms. It is the starting point of a norm-creating process and, thus, has an entirely dynamic character. The particular norms of the legal order cannot be logically deduced from this basic norm, as can the norm "Help your neighbor when he needs your help" from the norm "Love your neighbor." They are to be created by a special act of will, not concluded from a premise by an intellectual operation.

b. *Customary and Statutory Law*

Legal norms are created in many different ways: general norms through custom or legislation, individual norms through judicial and administrative acts or legal transactions. Law is always created by an act that deliberately aims at creating law, except in the case when law has its origin in custom, that is to say, in a generally observed course of conduct, during which the acting individuals do not consciously aim at creating law; but they must regard their acts as in conformity with a binding norm and not as a matter of arbitrary choice. This is the requirement of so-called *opinio juris sive necessitates* [an opinion of law or necessity]. The usual interpretation of this requirement is that the individuals constituting by their conduct the law-creating custom must regard their acts as determined by a legal rule; they must believe that they perform a legal duty or exercise a legal right. This doctrine is not correct. It implies that the individuals concerned must act in error: since the legal rule which is created by their conduct cannot yet determine this conduct, at least not as a legal rule. They may erroneously believe themselves to be bound by a rule of law, but this error is not necessary to constitute a law-creating custom. It is sufficient that the acting individuals consider themselves bound by any norm whatever.

We shall distinguish between statutory and customary law as the two fundamental types of law. By statutory law we shall understand law created in a way other than by custom, namely, by legislative, judicial, or administrative acts or by legal transactions, especially by contracts and (international) treaties.

C. The Basic Norm of a Legal Order

a. The Basic Norm and the Constitution

The derivation of the norms of a legal order from the basic norm of that order is performed by showing that the particular norms have been created in accordance with the basic norm. To the question why a certain act of coercion—*e.g.,* the fact that one individual deprives another individual of his freedom by putting him in jail—is a legal act, the answer is: because it has been prescribed by an individual norm, a judicial decision. To the question why this individual norm is valid as part of a definite legal order, the answer is: because it has been created in conformity with a criminal statute. This statute, finally, receives its validity from the constitution, since it has been established by the competent organ in the way the constitution prescribes.

If we ask why the constitution is valid, perhaps we come upon an older constitution. Ultimately we reach some constitution that is the first historically and that was laid down by an individual usurper or by some kind of assembly. The validity of this first constitution is the last presupposition, the final postulate, upon which the validity of all the norms of our legal order depends. It is postulated that one ought to behave as the individual, or the individuals, who laid down the first constitution have ordained. This is the basic norm of the legal order under consideration. The document which embodies the first constitution is a real constitution, a binding norm, only on the condition that the basic norm is presupposed to be valid. Only upon this presupposition are the declarations of those to whom the constitution confers norm-creating power binding norms. It is this presupposition that enables us to distinguish between individuals who are legal authorities and other individuals whom we do not regard as such, between acts of human beings which create legal norms and acts which have no such effect. All these legal norms belong to one and the same legal order because their validity can be traced back—directly or indirectly—to the first constitution. That the first constitution is a binding legal norm is presupposed, and the formulation of the presupposition is the basic norm of this legal order. The basic norm of a religious norm system says that one ought to behave as God and the authorities instituted by Him command. Similarly, the basic norm of a legal order prescribes that one ought to behave as the "fathers" of the constitution and the individuals—directly or indirectly—authorized by the constitution command. Expressed in the form of a legal norm: coercive acts ought to be carried out only under the conditions and in the way determined by the "fathers" of the constitution or the organs delegated by them. This is, schematically formulated, the basic norm of the legal order of a single State, the basic norm of a national legal order. It is to the national legal order that we have here limited our attention. Later, we shall consider what bearing the assumption of an international law has upon the question of the basic norm of national law.

b. The Specific Function of the Basic Norm

That a norm of the kind just mentioned is the basic norm of the national legal order does not imply that it is impossible to go beyond that norm. Certainly one may ask why one has to respect the first constitution as a binding norm. The answer might be that the fathers of the first constitution were empowered by God. The characteristic of so called legal positivism is, however, that it dispenses with any such religious justification of the legal order. The ultimate hypothesis of positivism is the norm authorizing the historically first legislator. The whole function of this basic norm is to confer law-creating power on the act of the first legislator and on all the other acts based on the first act. To interpret these acts of human beings as legal acts and their products as binding norms, and that means to interpret the empirical material which presents itself as law as such, is possible only on the condition that the basic norm is presupposed as a valid norm. The basic norm is only the necessary presupposition of any positivistic interpretation of the legal material.

The basic norm is not created in a legal procedure by a law-creating organ. It is not—as a positive legal norm is—valid because it is created in a certain way by a legal act, but it is valid because it is presupposed to be valid; and it is presupposed to be valid because without this presupposition no human act could be interpreted as a legal, especially as a norm-creating, act.

By formulating the basic norm, we do not introduce into the science of law any new method. We merely make explicit what all jurists, mostly unconsciously, assume when they consider positive law as a system of valid norms and not only as a complex of facts, and at the same time repudiate any natural law from which positive law would receive its validity. That the basic norm really exists in the juristic consciousness is the result of a simple analysis of actual juristic statements. The basic norm is the answer to the question: how—and that means under what condition—are all these juristic statements concerning legal norms, legal duties, legal rights, and so on, possible?

c. The Principle of Legitimacy

The validity of legal norms may be limited in time, and it is important to notice that the end as well as the beginning of this validity is determined only by the order to which they belong. They remain valid as long as they have not been invalidated in the way which the legal order itself determines. This is the principle of legitimacy.

This principle, however, holds only under certain conditions. It fails to hold in the case of a revolution, this word understood in the most general sense, so that it also covers the so called coup d'Etat. A revolution, in this wide sense, occurs whenever the legal order of a community is nullified and replaced by a new order in an illegitimate way, that is in a way not prescribed by the first order itself. It is in this context irrelevant whether or not this replacement is effected through a violent uprising against those individuals who so far have been the "legitimate" organs competent to create and amend the legal order. It is equally irrelevant whether the replacement is effected through a movement emanating from the mass of the people, or through action from those in government positions. From a juristic point of view, the decisive criterion of a revolution is that the order in force is overthrown and replaced by a new order in a way which the former had not itself anticipated. Usually, the new men whom a revolution brings to power annul only the constitution and certain laws of paramount political significance, putting other norms in their place. A great part of the old legal order "remains" valid also within the frame of the new order. But the phrase "they remain valid," does not give an adequate description of the phenomenon. It is only the contents of these norms that remain the same, not the reason of their validity. They are no longer valid by virtue of having been created in the way the old constitution prescribed. That constitution is no longer in force; it is replaced by a new constitution which is not the result of a constitutional alteration of the former. If laws which were introduced under the old constitution "continue to be valid" under the new constitution, this is possible only because validity has expressly or tacitly been vested in them by the new constitution. * * * The new order "receives," i.e., adopts, norms from the old order; this means that the new order gives validity to (puts into force) norms which have the same content as norms of the old order. "Reception" is an abbreviated procedure of law-creation. The laws which, in the ordinary inaccurate parlance, continue to be valid are, from a juristic viewpoint, new laws whose import coincides with that of the old laws. They are not identical with the old laws, because the reason for their validity is different. The reason for their validity is the new, not the old, constitution, and between the two continuity holds neither from the point of view of the one nor from that of the other. Thus, it is never the constitution merely but always the entire legal order that is changed by a revolution.

This shows that all norms of the old order have been deprived of their validity by revolution and not according to the principle of legitimacy. And they have been so deprived not only de facto but also de jure. No jurist would maintain that even after a successful revolution the old constitution and the laws based thereupon remain in force, on the ground that they have not been nullified in a manner anticipated by the old order itself. Every jurist will presume that the old order—to which no political reality any longer corresponds—has ceased to be valid, and that all norms, which are valid within the new order, receive their validity exclusively from the new constitution. It follows that, from this juristic point of view, the norms of the old order can no longer be recognized as valid norms.

d. Change of the Basic Norm

It is just the phenomenon of revolution which clearly shows the significance of the basic norm. Suppose that a group of individuals attempt to seize power by force, in order to remove the legitimate government in a hitherto monarchic State, and to introduce a republican form of government. If they succeed, if the old order ceases, and the new order begins to be efficacious, because the individuals whose behavior the new order regulates actually behave, by and large, in conformity with the new order, then this order is considered as a valid order. It is now according to this new order that the actual behavior of individuals is interpreted as legal or illegal. But this means that a new basic norm is presupposed. It is no longer the norm according to which the old monarchical constitution is valid, but a norm according to which the new republican constitution is valid, a norm endowing the revolutionary government with legal authority. If the revolutionaries fail, if the order they have tried to establish remains inefficacious, then, on the other hand, their undertaking is interpreted, not as a legal, a law-creating act, as the establishment of a constitution, but as an illegal act, as the crime of treason, and this according to the old monarchic constitution and its specific basic norm.

e. The Principle of Effectiveness

If we attempt to make explicit the presupposition on which these juristic considerations rest, we find that the norms of the old order are regarded as devoid of validity because the old constitution and, therefore, the legal norms based on this constitution, the old legal order as a whole, has lost its efficacy; because the actual behavior of men does no longer conform to this old legal order. Every single norm loses its validity when the total legal order to which it belongs loses its efficacy as a whole. The efficacy of the entire legal order is a necessary condition for the validity of every single norm of the order. * * * The efficacy of the total legal order is a condition, not the reason for the validity of its constituent norms. These norms are valid not because the total order is efficacious, but because they are created in a constitutional way. They are valid, however, only on the condition that the total order is efficacious; they cease to be valid, not only when they are annulled in a constitutional way, but also when the total order ceases to be efficacious. It cannot be maintained that, legally, men have to behave in conformity with a certain norm, if the total legal order, of which that norm is an integral part, has lost its efficacy. The principle of legitimacy is restricted by the principle of effectiveness. * * *

The relation between validity and efficacy thus appears to be the following: A norm is a valid legal norm if (a) it has been created in a way provided for by the legal order to which it belongs, and (b) if it has not been annulled either in a way provided for by that legal order or by way of *desuetudo* or by the fact that the legal order as a whole has lost its efficacy.

g. The "Ought" and the "Is"

The basic norm of a national legal order is not the arbitrary product of juristic imagination. Its content is determined by facts. The function of the basic norm is to make possible the normative interpretation of certain facts, and that means, the interpretation of facts as the creation and application of valid norms. Legal norms, as we pointed out, are considered to be valid only if they belong to an order which is by and large efficacious. Therefore, the content of a basic norm is determined by the facts through which an order is created and applied, to which the behavior of the individuals regulated by this order, by and large, conforms. The basic norm of any positive legal order confers legal authority only upon facts by which an order is created and applied which is on the whole effective. It is not required that the actual behavior of individuals be in absolute conformity with the order. On the contrary, a certain antagonism between the normative order and the actual human behavior to which the norms of the order refer must be possible. Without such a possibility, a normative order would be completely meaningless. What necessarily happens under the laws of nature does not have to be prescribed by norms: The basic norm of a social order to which the actual behavior of the individuals always and without any exception conforms would run as follows: Men ought to behave as they actually behave, or: You ought to do what you actually do. Such an order would be as meaningless as an order with which human behavior would in no way conform, but always and in every respect contradict. Therefore, a normative order loses its validity when reality no longer corresponds to it, at least to a certain degree. The validity of a legal order is thus dependent upon its agreement with reality, upon its "efficacy." The relationship which exists between the validity and efficacy of a legal order—it is, so to speak, the tension between the "ought" and the "is"—can be determined only by an upper and a lower borderline. The agreement must neither exceed a certain maximum nor fall below a certain minimum.

h. Law and Power (Right and Might)

Seeing that the validity of a legal order is thus dependent upon its efficacy, one may be misled into identifying the two phenomena, by defining the validity of law as its efficacy, by describing the law by "is" and not by "ought" statements. Attempts of this kind have very often been made and they have always failed. For, if the validity of law is identified with any natural fact, it is impossible to comprehend the specific sense in which law is directed towards reality and thus stands over against reality. Only if law and natural reality, the system of legal norms and the actual behavior of men, the "ought" and the "is," are two different realms, may reality conform with or contradict law, can human behavior be characterized as legal or illegal.

The efficacy of law belongs to the realm of reality and is often called the power of law. If for efficacy we substitute power, then the problem of validity, and efficacy is transformed into the more common problem of "right and might." And then the solution here presented is merely the precise statement of the old truth that though law cannot exist without power, still law and power, right and might, are not the same. Law is, according to the theory here presented, a specific order or organization of power.

i. The Principle of Effectiveness as Positive Legal Norm (International and National Law)

The principle that a legal order must be efficacious in order to be valid is, in itself, a positive norm. It is the principle of effectiveness belonging to international law. According to this principle of international law, an actually established authority is the legitimate government, the coercive order enacted by this government is the legal order, and the community constituted by this order is a State in the sense of international law, insofar as this order is, on the whole, efficacious. From the standpoint of international law, the constitution of a State is valid only if the legal order established on the basis of this constitution is, on the whole, efficacious. It is this general principle of effectiveness, a positive norm of international law, which, applied to the concrete circumstances of an individual national legal order, provides the individual basic norm of this national legal order. Thus, the basic norms of the different national legal orders are themselves based on a general norm of the international legal order. If we conceive of international law as a legal order to which all the States (and that means all the national legal orders) are subordinated, then the basic norm of a national legal order is not a mere presupposition of juristic thinking, but a positive legal norm, a norm of international law applied to the legal order of a concrete State. Assuming the primacy of international law over national law, the problem of the basic norm shifts from the national to the international legal order. Then the only true basic norm, a norm which is not created by a legal procedure but presupposed by juristic thinking, is the basic norm of international law.

j. Validity and Efficacy

That the validity of a legal order depends upon its efficacy does not imply, as pointed out, that the validity of a single norm depends upon its efficacy. The single legal norm remains valid as long as it is part of a valid order. The question whether an individual norm is valid is answered by recourse to the first constitution. If this is valid, then all norms which have been created in a constitutional way are valid, too. The principle of effectiveness embodied in international law refers immediately only to the first constitution of a national legal order, and therefore to this order only as a whole.

The principle of effectiveness may, however, be adopted to a certain extent also by national law, and thus within a national legal order the validity of a single norm may be made dependent upon its efficacy. Such is the case when a legal norm may lose its validity by *desuetudo*.

D. The Static and the Dynamic Concept of Law

If one looks upon the legal order from the dynamic point of view, as it has been expounded here, it seems possible to define the concept of law in a way quite different from that in which we have tried to define it in this theory. It seems especially possible to ignore the element of coercion in defining the concept of law.

It is a fact that the legislator can enact commandments without considering it necessary to attach a criminal or civil sanction to their violation. If such norms are also called legal norms, it is because they were created by an authority which, according to the constitution, is competent to create law. They are law because they issue from a law-creating authority. According to this concept, law is anything that has come about in the way the constitution prescribes for the creation of law. This dynamic concept differs from the concept of law defined as a coercive norm. According to the dynamic concept, law is something created by a certain process, and everything created in this way is law. This dynamic concept, however, is only apparently a concept of law. It contains no answer to the question of what is the essence of law, what is the criterion by which law can be distinguished from other social norms. This dynamic concept furnishes an answer only to the question whether or not and why a certain norm belongs to a system of valid legal norms, forms a part of a certain legal order. And the answer is, a norm belongs to a certain legal order if it is created in accordance with a procedure prescribed by the constitution fundamental to this legal order.

It must, however, be noted that not only a norm, i.e., a command regulating human behavior, can be created in the way prescribed by the constitution for the creation of law. An important stage in the law-creating process is the procedure by which general norms are created, that is, the procedure of legislation. The constitution may organize this procedure of legislation in the following ways: two corresponding resolutions of both houses of parliament, the consent of the chief of State, and publication in an official journal. This means that a specific form of law-creation is established. It is then possible to clothe in this form any subject, for instance, a recognition of the merits of a statesman. The form of a law—a declaration voted by parliament, consented to by the chief of State, published in the official journal—is chosen in order to give to a certain subject, here to the expression of the nation's gratitude, the character of a solemn act. The solemn recognition of the merits of a statesman is by no means a norm, even if it appears as the content of a legislative act, even if it has the form of a law. The law as the product of the legislative procedure, a statute in the formal sense of the term, is a document containing words, sentences; and that which is expressed by these sentences need not necessarily be a norm. As a matter of fact, many a law—in this formal sense of the term—contains not only legal norms, but also certain elements which are of no specific legal, i.e. normative, character, such as, purely theoretical views concerning certain matters, the motives of the legislator, political ideologies contained in references such as "justice" or "the will of God," etc., etc. All these are legally irrelevant contents of the statute, or, more generally, legally irrelevant products of the law-creating process. The law-creating process includes not only the process of legislation, but also the procedure of the judicial and administrative authorities. Even judgments of the courts very often contain legally irrelevant elements. If by the term "law" is meant something pertaining to a certain legal order, then law is anything which has been created according to the procedure prescribed by the constitution fundamental to this order. This does not mean, however, that everything which has been created according to this procedure is law in the sense of a legal norm. It is a legal norm only if it purports to regulate human behavior, and if it regulates human behavior by providing an act of coercion as sanction.

NOTES AND QUESTIONS

1. *The (relatively) new and improved positivism.* Consider how Kelsen tried to refine the gunman or command model offered by John Austin. How exactly does his conception of the Basic Norm ("*grundnorm*") improve the over-simplification of Austin's conception?

2. *Kelsen's "ought."* Consider the possibility of distinguishing two kinds of "ought" statements: a subjective or moral "ought" (as in "We ought not steal

our neighbor's tractor.") from an objective or empirical "ought" (as in "That 8:15 train from New Orleans ought to be here any minute."). What is the basis for the second meaning of the word "ought," and how if at all does it help in understanding Kelsen's analysis?

3. *Identifying the grundnorm.* What is the *grundnorm* in the United States? How do you know?

4. *International law as a test case.* You may recall that Austin would not consider international law "law" because there is no single sovereign with authority to compel governments to obey its commands. Is Kelsen similarly skeptical that international law cannot qualify as "law"? Why not?

H. L. A. HART, *THE CONCEPT OF LAW*

(1962)

V. Law as the Union of Primary and Secondary Rules

1. *A Fresh Start*

In the last three chapters we have seen that, at various crucial points, the simple model of law as the sovereign's coercive orders failed to reproduce some of the salient features of a legal system. To demonstrate this, we did not find it necessary to invoke (as earlier critics have done) international law or primitive law which some may regard as disputable or borderline examples of law; instead we pointed to certain familiar features of municipal law in a modern state, and showed that these were either distorted or altogether unrepresented in this over-simple theory.

The main ways in which the theory failed are instructive enough to merit a second summary. First, it became clear that though of all the varieties of law, a criminal statute, forbidding or enjoining certain actions under penalty, most resembles orders backed by threats given by one person to others, such a statute nonetheless differs from such orders in the important respect that it commonly applies to those who enact it and not merely to others. Secondly, there are other varieties of law, notably those conferring legal powers to adjudicate or legislate (public powers) or to create or vary legal relations (private powers) which cannot, without absurdity, be construed as orders backed by threats. Thirdly, there are legal rules which differ from orders in their mode of origin, because they are not brought into being by anything analogous to explicit prescription. Finally, the analysis of law in terms of the sovereign, habitually obeyed and necessarily exempt from all legal limitation, failed to account for the continuity of legislative authority characteristic of a modern legal system, and the sovereign, person or persons could not be identified with either the electorate or the legislature of a modern state.

It will be recalled that in thus criticizing the conception of law as the sovereign's coercive orders we considered also a number of ancillary devices which were brought in at the cost of corrupting the primitive simplicity of the theory to rescue it from its difficulties. But these too failed. One device, the notion of a tacit order, seemed to have no application to the complex actualities of a modern legal system, but only to very much simpler situations like that of a general who deliberately refrains from interfering with orders given by his subordinates. Other devices, such as that of treating power-conferring rules as mere fragments of rules imposing duties, or treating all rules as directed only to officials, distort the ways in which these are spoken of, thought of, and actually used in social life. This had no better claim to our assent than the theory that all the rules of a game are "really" directions to the umpire and the scorer. The device, designed to reconcile the self-binding character of legislation with the theory that a statute is an order given to others, was to distinguish the legislators acting in their official capacity, as one person ordering others who include themselves in their private capacities. This device, impeccable in itself, involved supplementing the theory with something it does not contain: this is the notion of a rule defining what must be done to legislate; for it is only in conforming with such a rule that legislators have an official capacity and a separate personality to be contrasted with themselves as private individuals.

The last three chapters are therefore the record of a failure and there is plainly need for a fresh start. Yet the failure is an instructive one, worth the detailed consideration we have given it, because at each point where the theory failed to fit the facts it was possible to see at least in outline why it was bound to fail and what is required for a better account. The root cause of failure is that the elements out of which the theory was constructed, viz. the ideas of orders, obedience, habits, and threats, do not include, and cannot by their combination yield, the idea of a rule, without which we cannot hope to elucidate even the most elementary forms of law. It is true that the idea of a rule is by no means a simple one: we have already seen in Chapter III the need, if we are to do justice to the complexity of a legal system, to discriminate between two different though related types. Under rules of the one type, which may well be considered the basic or primary type, human beings are required to do or abstain from certain actions, whether they wish to or not. Rules of the other type are in a sense parasitic upon or secondary to the first; for they provide that human beings may by doing or saying certain things introduce new rules of the primary type, extinguish or modify old ones, or in various ways determine their incidence or control their operations. Rules of the first type impose duties; rules of the second type confer powers, public or private. Rules of the first type concern actions involving physical movement or changes; rules of the second type provide for operations which lead not merely to physical movement or change, but to the creation or variation of duties or obligations.

We have already given some preliminary analysis of what is involved in the assertion that rules of these two types exist among a given social group, and in this chapter we shall not only carry this analysis a little farther but we shall make the general claim that in the combination of these two types of rule there lies what Austin wrongly claimed to have found in the notion of coercive orders, namely, "the key to the science of jurisprudence". We shall not indeed claim that wherever the word "law" is "properly" used this combination of primary and secondary rules is to be found; for it is clear that the diverse range of cases of which the word "law" is used are not linked by any such simple uniformity, but by less direct relations—often of analogy of either form or content to a central case. What we shall attempt to show, in this and the succeeding chapters, is that most of the features of law which have proved most perplexing and have both provoked and eluded the search for definition can best be rendered clear, if these two types of rule and the interplay between them are understood. We accord this union of elements a central place because of their explanatory power in elucidating the concepts that constitute the framework of legal thought. The justification for the use of the word "law" for a range of apparently heterogeneous cases is a secondary matter which can be undertaken when the central elements have been grasped.

2. The Idea of Obligation

It will be recalled that the theory of law as coercive orders, notwithstanding its errors, started from the perfectly correct appreciation of the fact that where there is law, there human conduct is made in some sense non-optional or obligatory. In choosing this starting-point the theory was well inspired, and in building up a new account of law in terms of the interplay of primary and secondary rules we too shall start from the same idea. It is, however, here, at this crucial first step, that we have perhaps most to learn from the theory's errors.

Let us recall the gunman situation. A orders B to hand over his money and threatens to shoot him if he does not comply. According to the theory of coercive orders this situation illustrates the notion of obligation or duty in general. Legal obligation is to be found in this situation writ large; A must be the sovereign habitually obeyed and the orders must be general, prescribing courses of conduct not single actions. The plausibility of the claim that the gunman situation displays the meaning of obligation lies in the fact that it is certainly one in which we would say that B, if he obeyed, was "obliged" to hand over his money. It is, however, equally certain that we should misdescribe the situation if we said, on these facts, that B "had an obligation" or a "duty" to hand over the money. So from the start it is clear that we need something else for an understanding of the idea of obligation. There is a difference, yet to be explained, between the assertion that someone was obliged to do something and the assertion that he had an obligation to do it. The first is often a statement about the beliefs and motives with which an action is done: B was obliged to hand over his money may simply mean, as it does in the gunman case, that he believed that some harm or other unpleasant consequences would befall him if he did not hand it over and he handed it over to avoid those consequences. In such cases the prospect of what would happen to the agent if he disobeyed has rendered something he would otherwise have preferred to have done (keep the money) less eligible.

Two further elements slightly complicate the elucidation of the notion of being obliged to do something. It seems clear that we should not think of B as obliged to hand over the money if the threatened harm was, according to common judgments, trivial in comparison with the disadvantage or serious consequences, either for B or for others, of complying with the orders, as it would be, for example, if A merely threatened to pinch B. Nor perhaps should we say that B was obliged, if there were no reasonable grounds for thinking that A could or would probably implement his threat of relatively serious harm. Yet, though such references to common judgments of comparative harm and reasonable estimates of likelihood, are implicit in this notion, the statement that a person was obliged to obey someone is, in the main, a psychological one referring to the beliefs and motives with which an action was done. But the statement that someone had an obligation to do something is of a very different type and there are many signs of this difference. Thus not only is it the case that the facts about B's action and his beliefs and motives in the gunman case, though sufficient to warrant the statement that B was obliged to hand over his purse, are not sufficient to warrant the statement that he had an obligation to do this; it is also the case that facts of this sort, *i.e.* facts about beliefs and motives, are not necessary for the truth of a statement that a person had an obligation to do something. Thus the statement that a person had an obligation, e.g. to tell the truth or report for military service, remains true even if he believed (reasonably or unreasonably) that he would never be found out and had nothing to fear from disobedience. Moreover, whereas the statement that he had this obligation is quite independent of the question whether or not he in fact reported for service, the statement that someone was obliged to do something, normally carries the implication that he actually did it.

Some theorists, Austin among them, seeing perhaps the general irrelevance of the person's beliefs, fears, and motives to the question whether he had an obligation to do something, have defined this notion not in terms of these subjective facts, but in terms of the chance or likelihood that the person having the obligation will suffer a punishment or "evil" at the hands of others in the event of disobedience. This, in effect, treats statements of obligation not as psychological statements but as predictions or assessments of chances of incurring punishment or evil. To many later theorists this has appeared as a revelation, bringing down to earth an elusive notion and restating it in the same clear, hard, empirical terms as are used in science. It has, indeed, been accepted sometimes as the only alternative to metaphysical conceptions of obligation or duty as invisible objects mysteriously existing "above" or "behind" the world of ordinary, observable facts. But there are many reasons for rejecting this interpretation of statements of obligation as predictions, and it is not, in fact, the only alternative to obscure metaphysics.

The fundamental objection is that the predictive interpretation obscures the fact that, where rules exist, deviations from them are not merely grounds for a prediction that hostile reactions will follow or that a court will apply sanctions to those who break them, but are also a reason or justification for such reaction and for applying the sanctions. * * *

There is, however, a second, simpler, objection to the predictive interpretation of obligation. If it were true that the statement that a person had an obligation meant that he was likely to suffer in the event of disobedience, it would be a contradiction to say that he had an obligation, e.g. to report for military service but that, owing to the fact that he had escaped from the jurisdiction, or had successfully bribed the police or the court, there was not the slightest chance of his being caught or made to suffer. In fact, there is no contradiction in saying this, and such statements are often made and understood.

It is, of course, true that in a normal legal system, where sanctions are exacted for a high proportion of offences, an offender usually runs a risk of punishment; so, usually the statement that a person has an obligation and the statement that he is likely to suffer for disobedience will both be true together. Indeed, the connexion between these two statements is somewhat stronger than this: at least in a municipal system it may well be true that, unless in general sanctions were likely to be exacted from offenders, there would be little or no point in making particular statements about a person's obligations. In this sense, such statements may be said to presuppose belief in the continued normal operation of the system of sanctions much as the statement "he is out" in cricket presupposes, though it does not assert, that players, umpire, and scorer will probably take the usual steps. Nonetheless, it is crucial for the understanding of the idea of obligation to see that in individual cases the statement that a person has an obligation under some rule and the prediction that he is likely to suffer for disobedience may diverge.

It is clear that obligation is not to be found in the gunman situation, though the simpler notion of being obliged to do something may well be defined in the elements present there. To understand the general idea of obligation as a necessary preliminary to understanding it in its legal form, we must turn to a different social situation which, unlike the gunman situation, includes the existence of social rules; for this situation contributes to the meaning of the statement that a person has an obligation in two ways. First, the existence of such rules, making certain types of behaviour a standard, is the normal, though unstated, background or proper context for such a statement; and, secondly, the distinctive function of such statement is to apply such a general rule to a particular person by calling attention to the fact that his case falls under it. We have already seen in Chapter IV that there is involved in the existence of any social rules a combination of regular conduct with a distinctive attitude to that conduct as a standard. We have also seen the main ways in which these differ from mere social habits, and how the varied normative vocabulary ("ought", "must", "should") is used to draw attention to the standard and to deviations from it, and to formulate the demands, criticisms, or acknowledgements which may be based on it. Of this class of normative words the words "obligation" and "duty" form an important sub-class, carrying with them certain implications not usually present in the others. Hence, though a grasp of the elements generally differentiating social rules from mere habits is certainly indispensable for understanding the notion of obligation or duty, it is not sufficient by itself.

The statement that someone has or is under an obligation does indeed imply the existence of a rule; yet it is not always the case that where rules exist the standard of behaviour required by them is conceived of in terms of obligation. "He ought to have" and "He had an obligation to" are not always interchangeable expressions, even though they are alike in carrying an implicit reference to existing standards of conduct or are used in drawing conclusions in particular case from a general rule. Rules of etiquette or correct speech are certainly rules: they are more than convergent habits or regularities of behaviour; they are taught and efforts are made to maintain them; they are used in criticizing our own and other people's behaviour in the characteristic normative vocabulary. "You ought to take your hat off", "It is wrong to say 'you was' ". But to use in connexion with rules of this kind the words "obligation" or "duty" would be misleading and not merely stylistically odd. It would misdescribe a social situation; for though the line separating rules of obligation from others is at points a vague one, yet the main rationale of the distinction is fairly clear.

Rules are conceived and spoken of as imposing obligations when the general demand for conformity is insistent and the social pressure brought to bear upon those who deviate or threaten to deviate is great. Such rules may be wholly customary in origin: there may be no centrally organized system of punishments for breach of the rules; the social pressure may take only the form of a general diffused hostile or critical reaction which may stop short of physical sanctions. It may be limited to verbal manifestations of disapproval or of appeals to the individuals' respect for the rule violated; it may depend heavily on the operation of feelings of shame, remorse, and guilt. When the pressure is of this last-mentioned kind we may be inclined to classify the rules as part of the morality of the social group and the obligation under the rules as moral obligation. Conversely, when physical sanctions are prominent or usual among the forms of pressure, even though these are neither closely defined nor administered by officials but are left to the community at large, we shall be inclined to classify the rules as a primitive or rudimentary form of law. We may, of course, find both these types of serious social pressure behind what is, in an obvious sense, the same rule of conduct; sometimes this may occur with no indication that one of them is peculiarly appropriate as primary and the other secondary, and then the question whether we are confronted with a rule of morality or rudimentary law may not be susceptible of an answer. But for the moment the possibility of drawing the line between law and morals need not detain us. What is important is that the insistence on importance or seriousness of social pressure behind the rules is the primary factor determining whether they are thought of as giving rise to obligations.

Two other characteristics of obligation go naturally together with this primary one. The rules supported by this serious pressure are thought important because they are believed to be necessary to the maintenance of social life or some highly prized feature of it. Characteristically, rules so obviously essential as those which restrict the free use of violence are thought of in terms of obligation. So too rules which require honesty or truth or require the keeping of promises, or specify what is to be done by one who performs a distinctive role or function in the social group are thought of in terms of either "obligation" or perhaps more often "duty". Secondly, it is generally recognized that the conduct required by these rules may, while benefiting others, conflict with what the person who owes the duty may wish to do. Hence obligations and duties are thought of as characteristically involving sacrifice or renunciation, and the standing possibility of conflict between obligation or duty and interest is, in all societies, among the truisms of both the lawyer and the moralist.

The figure of a bond binding the person obligated, which is buried in the word "obligation", and the similar notion of a debt latent in the word "duty" are explicable in terms of these three factors, which distinguish rules of obligation or duty from other rules. In this figure, which haunts much legal thought, the social pressure appears as a chain binding those who have obligations so that they are not free to do what they want. The other end of the chain is sometimes held by the group or their official representatives, who insist on performance or exact the penalty: sometimes it is entrusted by the group to a private individual who may choose whether or not to insist on performance or its equivalent in value to him. The first situation typifies the duties or obligations of criminal law and the second those of civil law where we think of private individuals having rights correlative to the obligations.

Natural and perhaps illuminating though these figures or metaphors are, we must not allow them to trap us into a misleading conception of obligation as essentially consisting in some feeling of pressure or compulsion experienced by those who have obligations. The fact that rules of obligation are generally supported by serious social pressure does not entail that to have an obligation under the rules is to experience feelings of compulsion or pressure. Hence there is no contradiction in saying of some hardened swindler, and it may often be true, that he had an obligation to pay the rent but felt no pressure to pay when he made off without doing so. To feel obliged and to have an obligation are different though frequently concomitant things. To identify them would be one way of misinterpreting, in terms of psychological feelings, the important internal aspect of rules to which we drew attention in [an earlier chapter].

Indeed, the internal aspect of rules is something to which we must again refer before we can dispose finally of the claims of the predictive theory. For an advocate of that theory may well ask why, if social pressure is so important a feature of rules of obligation, we are yet so concerned to stress the inadequacies of the predictive theory; for it gives this very feature a central place by defining obligation in terms of the likelihood that threatened punishment or hostile reaction will follow deviation from certain lines of conduct. The difference may seem slight between the analysis of a statement of obligation as a prediction, or assessment of the chances, of hostile reaction to deviation, and our own contention that though this statement presupposes a background in which deviations from rules are generally met by hostile reactions, yet its characteristic use is not to predict this but to say that a person's case falls under such a rule. In fact, however, this difference is not a slight one. Indeed, until its importance is grasped, we cannot properly understand the whole distinctive style of human thought, speech, and action which is involved in the existence of rules and which constitutes the normative structure of society.

The following contrast again in terms of the "internal" and "external" aspect of rules may serve to mark what gives this distinction its great importance for the understanding not only of law but of the structure of any society. When a social group has certain rules of conduct, this fact affords an opportunity for many closely related yet different kinds of assertion; for it is possible to be concerned with the rules, either merely as an observer who does not himself accept them, or as a member of the group which accepts and uses them as guides to conduct. We may call these respectively the "external" and the "internal points of view". Statements made from the external point of view may themselves be of different kinds. For the observer may, without accepting the rules himself, assert that the group accepts the rules, and thus may from outside refer to the way in which they are concerned with them from the internal point of view. But whatever the rules are, whether they are those of games, like chess or cricket, or moral or legal rules, we can if we choose occupy the position of an observer who does not even refer in this way to the internal point of view of the group. Such an observer is content merely to record the regularities of observable behaviour in which conformity with the rules partly consists and those further regularities, in the form of the hostile reaction, reproofs, or punishments, with which deviations from the rules are met. After a time the external observer may, on the basis of the regularities observed, correlate deviation with hostile reaction, and be able to predict with a fair measure of success, and to assess the chances that a deviation from the group's normal behaviour will meet with hostile reaction or punishment. Such knowledge may not only reveal much about the group, but might enable him to live among them without unpleasant consequences which would attend one who attempted to do so without such knowledge.

If, however, the observer really keeps austerely to this extreme external point of view and does not give any account of the manner in which members of the group who accept the rules view their own regular behaviour, his description of their life cannot be in terms of rules at all, and so not in the terms of the rule-dependent notions of obligation or duty. Instead, it will be in terms of observable regularities of conduct, predictions, probabilities, and signs. For such an observer, deviations by a member of the group from normal conduct will be a sign that hostile reaction is likely to follow, and nothing more. His view will be like the view of one who, having observed the working of a traffic signal in a busy street for some time, limits himself to saying that when the light turns red there is a high probability that the traffic will stop. He treats the light merely as a natural sign that people will behave in certain ways, as clouds are a sign that rain will come. In so doing he will miss out a whole dimension of the social life of those whom he is watching, since for them the red light is not merely a sign that others will stop: they look upon it as a signal for them to stop, and so a reason for stopping in conformity to rules which make stopping when the light is red a standard of behaviour and an obligation. To mention this is to bring into the account the way in which the group regards its own behaviour. It is to refer to the internal aspect of rules seen from their internal point of view.

The external point of view may very nearly reproduce the way in which the rules function in the lives of certain members of the group, namely those who reject its rules and are only concerned with them when and because they judge that unpleasant consequences are likely to follow violation. Their point of view will need for its expression, "I was obliged to do it", "I am likely to suffer for it if", "You will probably suffer for it if . . .", "They will do that to you if . . .". But they will not need forms of expression like "I had an obligation" or "You have an obligation" for these are required only by those who see their own and other persons' conduct from the internal point of view. What the external point of view, which limits itself to the observable regularities of behaviour, cannot reproduce is the way in which the rules function as rules in the lives of those who normally are the majority of society. These are the officials, lawyers, or private persons who use them, in one situation after another, as guides to the conduct of social life, as the basis for claims, demands, admissions, criticism, or punishment, viz., in all the familiar transactions of life according to rules. For them the violation of a rule is not merely a basis for the prediction that a hostile reaction will follow but a reason for hostility.

At any given moment the life of any society which lives by rules, legal or not, is likely to consist in a tension between those who, on the one hand, accept and voluntarily co-operate in maintaining the rules, and so see their own and other persons' behaviour in terms of the rules, and those who, on the other hand, reject the rules and attend to them only from the external point of view as a sign of possible punishment. One of the difficulties facing any legal theory anxious to do justice to the complexity of the facts is to remember the presence of both these points of view and not to define one of them out of existence. Perhaps all our criticisms of the predictive theory of obligation may be best summarized as the accusation that this is what it does to the internal aspect of obligatory rules.

3. The Elements of Law

It is, of course, possible to imagine a society without a legislature, courts or officials of any kind. Indeed, there are many studies of primitive communities which not only claim that this possibility is realized but depict in detail the life of a society where the only means of social control is that general attitude of the group towards its own standard modes of behaviour in terms of which we have characterized rules of obligation. A social structure of this kind is often referred to as one of "custom"; but we shall not use this term, because it often implies that the customary rules are very old and supported with less social pressure than other rules. To avoid these implications we shall refer to such a social structure as one of primary rules of obligation. If a society is to live by such primary rules alone, there are certain conditions which, granted a few of the most obvious truisms about human nature and the world we live in, must clearly be satisfied. The first of these conditions is that the rules must contain in some form restrictions on the free use of violence, theft, and deception to which human beings are tempted but which they must, in general, repress, if they are to coexist in close proximity to each other. Such rules are in fact always found in the primitive societies of which we have knowledge, together with a variety of others imposing on individuals various positive duties to perform services or make contributions to the common life. Secondly, though such a society may exhibit the tension, already described, between those who accept the rules and those who reject the rules except where fear of social pressure induces them to conform, it is plain that the latter cannot be more than a minority, if so loosely organized a society of persons, approximately equal in physical strength, is to endure: for otherwise those who reject the rules would have too little social pressure to fear. This too is confirmed by what we know of primitive communities where, though there are dissidents and malefactors, the majority live by the rules seen from the internal point of view.

More important for our present purpose is the following consideration. It is plain that only a small community closely knit by ties of kinship, common sentiment, and belief, and placed in a stable environment, could live successfully by such a regime of unofficial rules. In any other conditions such a simple form of social control must prove defective and will require supplementation in different ways. In the first place, the rules by which the group lives will not form a system, but will simply be a set of separate standards, without any identifying or common mark, except of course that they are the rules which a particular group of human beings accepts. They will in this respect resemble our own rules of etiquette. Hence if doubts arise as to what the rules are or as to the precise scope of some given rule, there will be no procedure for settling this doubt, either by reference to an authoritative text or to an official whose declarations on this point are authoritative. For, plainly, such a procedure and the acknowledgement of either authoritative text or persons involve the existence of rules of a type different from the rules of obligation or duty which *ex hypothesi* [by hypothesis] are all that the group has. This defect in the simple social structure of primary rules we may call its uncertainty.

A second defect is the static character of the rules. The only mode of change in the rules known to such a society will be the slow process of growth, whereby courses of conduct once thought optional become first habitual or usual, and then obligatory, and the converse process of decay, when deviations, once severely dealt with, are first tolerated and then pass unnoticed. There will be no means, in such a society, of deliberately adapting the rules to changing circumstances, either by eliminating old rules or introducing new ones: for, again, the possibility of doing this presupposes the existence of rules of a different type from the primary rules of obligation by which alone the society lives. In an extreme case the rules may be static in a more drastic sense. This, though never perhaps fully realized in any actual community, is worth considering because the remedy for it is something very characteristic of law. In this extreme case, not only would there be no way of deliberately changing the general rules, but the obligations which arise under the rules in particular cases could not be varied or modified by the deliberate choice of any individual. Each individual would simply have fixed obligations or duties to do or abstain from doing certain things. It might indeed very often be the case that others would benefit from the performance of these obligations; yet if there are only primary rules of obligation they would have no power to release those bound from performance or to transfer to others the benefits which would accrue from performance. For such operations of release or transfer create changes in the initial positions of individuals under the primary rules of obligation, and for these operations to be possible there must be rules of a sort different from the primary rules.

The third defect of this simple form of social life is the inefficiency of the diffuse social pressure by which the rules are maintained. Disputes as to whether an admitted rule has or has not been violated will always occur and will, in any but the smallest societies, continue interminably, if there is no agency specially empowered to ascertain finally, and authoritatively, the fact of violation. Lack of such final and authoritative determinations is to be distinguished from another weakness associated with it. This is the fact that punishments for violations of the rules, and other forms of social pressure involving physical effort or the use of force, are not administered by a special agency but are left to the individuals affected or to the group at large. It is obvious that the waste of time involved in the group's unorganized efforts to catch and punish offenders, and the smouldering vendettas which may result from self help in the absence of an official monopoly of "sanctions", may be serious. The history of law does, however, strongly suggest that the lack of official agencies to determine authoritatively the fact of violation of the rules is a much more serious defect; for many societies have remedies for this defect long before the other.

The remedy for each of these three main defects in this simplest form of social structure consists in supplementing the primary rules of obligation with secondary rules which are rules of a different kind. The introduction of the remedy for each defect might, in itself, be considered a step from the pre-legal into the legal world; since each remedy brings with it many elements that permeate law: certainly all three remedies together are enough to convert the regime of primary rules into what is indisputably a legal system. We shall consider in turn each of these remedies and show why law may most illuminatingly be characterized as a union of primary rules of obligation with such secondary rules. Before we do this, however, the following general points should be noted. Though the remedies consist in the introduction of rules which are certainly different from each other, as well as from the primary rules of obligation which they supplement, they have important features in common and are connected in various ways. Thus they may all be said to be on a different level from the primary rules, for they are all about such rules; in the sense that while primary rules are concerned with the actions that individuals must or must not do, these secondary rules are all concerned with the primary rules themselves. They specify the ways in which the primary rules may be conclusively ascertained, introduced, eliminated, varied, and the fact of their violation conclusively determined.

The simplest form of remedy for the uncertainty of the regime of primary rules is the introduction of what we shall call a "rule of recognition". This will specify some feature or features possession of which by a suggested rule is taken as a conclusive affirmative indication that it is a rule of the group to be supported by the social pressure it exerts. The existence of such a rule of recognition may take any of a huge variety of forms, simple or complex. It may, as in the early law of many societies, be no more than that an authoritative list or text of the rules is to be found in a written document or carved on some public monument. No doubt as a matter of history this step from the pre-legal to the legal may be accomplished in distinguishable stages, of which the first is the mere reduction to writing of hitherto unwritten rules. This is not itself the crucial step, though it is a very important one: what is crucial is the acknowledgement of reference to the writing or inscription as authoritative, i.e. as the proper way of disposing of doubts as to the existence of the rule. Where there is such an acknowledgement there is a very simple form of secondary rule: a rule for conclusive identification of the primary rules of obligation.

In a developed legal system the rules of recognition are of course more complex; instead of identifying rules exclusively by reference to a text or list they do so by reference to some general characteristic possessed by the primary rules. This may be the fact of their having been enacted by a specific body, or their long customary practice, or their relation to judicial decisions. Moreover, where more than one of such general characteristics are treated as identifying criteria, provision may be made for their possible conflict by their arrangement in an order of superiority, as by the common subordination of custom or precedent to statute, the latter being a "superior source" of law. Such complexity may make the rules of recognition in a modern legal system seem very different from the simple acceptance of an authoritative text: yet even in this simplest form, such a rule brings with it many elements distinctive of law. By providing an authoritative mark it introduces, although in embryonic form, the idea of a legal system: for the rules are now not just a discrete unconnected set but are, in a simple way, unified. Further, in the simple operation of identifying a given rule as possessing the required feature of being an item on an authoritative list of rules we have the germ of the idea of legal validity.

The remedy for the static quality of the regime of primary rules consists in the introduction of what we shall call "rules of change". The simplest form of such a rule is that which empowers an individual or body of persons to introduce new primary rules for the conduct of the life of the group, or of some class within it, and to eliminate old rules. As we have already argued in Chapter IV it is in terms of such a rule, and not in terms of orders backed by threats, that the ideas of legislative enactment and repeal are to be understood. Such rules of change may be very simple or very complex: the powers conferred may be unrestricted or limited in various ways: and the rules may, besides specifying the persons who are to legislate, define in more or less rigid terms the procedure to be followed in legislation. Plainly, there will be a very close connexion between the rules of change and the rules of recognition: for where the former exists the latter will necessarily incorporate a reference to legislation as an identifying feature of the rules, though it need not refer to all the details of procedure involved in legislation. Usually some official certificate or official copy will, under the rules of recognition, be taken as a sufficient proof of due enactment. Of course if there is a social structure so simple that the only "source of law" is legislation, the rule of recognition will simply specify enactment as the unique identifying mark or criterion of validity of the rules. This will be the case for example in the imaginary kingdom of Rex I * * *: there the rule of recognition would simply be that whatever Rex I enacts is law.

We have already described in some detail the rules which confer on individuals power to vary their initial positions under the primary rules. Without such private power-conferring rules society would lack some of the chief amenities which law confers upon it. For the operations which these rules make possible are the making of wills, contracts, transfers of property, and many other voluntarily created structures of rights and duties which typify life under law, though of course an elementary form of power-conferring rule also underlies the moral institution of a promise. The kinship of these rules with the rules of change involved in the notion of legislation is clear, and as recent theory such as Kelsen's has shown, many of the features which puzzle us in the institutions of contract or property are clarified by thinking of the operations of making a contract or transferring property as the exercise of limited legislative powers by individuals.

The third supplement to the simple regime of primary rules, intended to remedy the inefficiency of its diffused social pressure, consists of secondary rules empowering individuals to make authoritative determinations of the question whether, on a particular occasion, a primary rule has been broken. The minimal form of adjudication consists in such determinations, and we shall call the secondary rules which confer the power to make them "rules of adjudication". Besides identifying the individuals who are to adjudicate, such rules will also define the procedure to be followed. Like the other secondary rules these are on a different level from the primary rules: though they may be reinforced by further rules imposing duties on judges to adjudicate, they do not impose duties but confer judicial powers and a special status on judicial declarations about the breach of obligations. Again these rules, like the other secondary rules, define a group of important legal concepts: in this case the concepts of judge or court, jurisdiction and judgment. Besides these resemblances to the other secondary rules, rules of adjudication have intimate connexions with them. Indeed, a system which has rules of adjudication is necessarily also committed to a rule of recognition of an elementary and imperfect sort. This is so because, if courts are empowered to make authoritative determinations of the fact that a rule has been broken, these cannot avoid being taken as authoritative determinations of what the rules are. So the rule which confers jurisdiction will also be a rule of recognition, identifying the primary rules through the judgments of the courts and these judgments will become a "source" of law. It is true that this form of rule of recognition, inseparable from the minimum form of jurisdiction, will be very imperfect. Unlike an authoritative text or a statute book, judgments may not be couched in general terms and their use as authoritative guides to the rules depends on a somewhat shaky inference from particular decisions, and the reliability of this must fluctuate both with the skill of the interpreter and the consistency of the judges.

It need hardly be said that in few legal systems are judicial powers confined to authoritative determinations of the fact of violation of the primary rules. Most systems have, after some delay, seen the advantages of further centralization of social pressure; and have partially prohibited the use of physical punishments or violent self help by private individuals. Instead they have supplemented the primary rules of obligation by further secondary rules, specifying or at least limiting the penalties for violation, and have conferred upon judges, where they have ascertained the fact of violation, the exclusive power to direct the application of penalties by other officials. These secondary rules provide the centralized official "sanctions" of the system.

If we stand back and consider the structure which has resulted from the combination of primary rules of obligation with the secondary rules of recognition, change and adjudication, it is plain that we have here not only the heart of a legal system, but a most powerful tool for the analysis of much that has puzzled both the jurist and the political theorist.

Not only are the specifically legal concepts with which the lawyer is professionally concerned, such as those of obligation and rights, validity and source of law, legislation and jurisdiction, and sanction, best elucidated in terms of this combination of elements. The concepts (which bestride both law and political theory) of the state, of authority, and of an official require a similar analysis if the obscurity which still lingers about them is to be dissipated. The reason why an analysis in these terms of primary and secondary rules has this explanatory power is not far to seek. Most of the obscurities and distortions surrounding legal and political concepts arise from the fact that these essentially involve reference to what we have called the internal point of view: the view of those who do not merely record and predict behaviour conforming to rules, but use the rules as standards for the appraisal of their own and others' behaviour. This requires more detailed attention in the analysis of legal and political concepts than it has usually received. Under the simple regime of primary rules the internal point of view is manifested in its simplest form, in the use of those rules as the basis of criticism, and as the justification of demands for conformity, social pressure, and punishment. Reference to this most elementary manifestation of the internal point of view is required for the analysis of the basic concepts of obligation and duty. With the addition to the system of secondary rules, the range of what is said and done from the internal point of view is much extended and diversified. With this extension comes a whole set of new concepts and they demand a reference to the internal point of view for their analysis. These include the notions of legislation, jurisdiction, validity and, generally, of legal powers, private and public. There is a constant pull towards an analysis of these in the terms of ordinary or "scientific", fact-stating or predictive discourse. But this can only reproduce their external aspect: to do justice to their distinctive, internal aspect we need to see the different ways in which the law-making operations of the legislator, the adjudication of a court, the exercise of private or official powers, and other "acts-in-the-law" are related to secondary rules.

[Elsewhere] we shall show how the ideas of the validity of law and sources of law, and the truths latent among the errors of the doctrines of sovereignty may be rephrased and clarified in terms of rules of recognition. But we shall conclude this chapter with a warning: though the combination of primary and secondary rules merits, because it explains many aspects of law, the central place assigned to it, this cannot by itself illuminate every problem. The union of primary and secondary rules is at the centre of a legal system; but it is not the whole, and as we move away from the centre we shall have to accommodate, in ways indicated in later chapters, elements of a different character. * * *

NOTES AND QUESTIONS

1. *Hart and Austin.* Arguably, one of the reasons that contemporary legal reasoning is so dominated by legal positivism is that Hart's critique of Austin's gunman model saved positivism from its own reductionism. What exactly did Hart think was wrong with Austin's view, and how did he build on Kelsen to create a model with more power and nuance?

2. *The rule of recognition.* According to Hart, the basis for any legal system is its "rule of recognition," its ultimate rule, which "provides criteria for the assessment of the validity of other rules" but which cannot be validated by reference to any other rule. H.L.A. HART, THE CONCEPT OF LAW 107 (2d ed. 1994). How does the rule of recognition work in Hart's account of law, and how should judges deal with it? How does it differ from Kelsen's idea of the *grundnorm*? Is it in principle possible for a society to have more than one rule of recognition? *See* JOSEPH RAZ, PRACTICAL REASON AND NORMS 146–48 (1990).

3. *Primary and secondary rules.* (a) Try to define in your own words what Hart means by primary and secondary rules. Is it correct to distinguish between primary and secondary rules on the ground that primary rules are directed at citizens and others while secondary rules are directed at government actors? Can you think of some examples of U.S. laws that would be considered primary or secondary? (b) Why is the "union" between primary and secondary rules so important in Hart's view?

4. *The justice of treating likes alike*. In Book V of the NICOMACHEAN ETHICS, Aristotle argued that justice consisted in treating like cases alike. It has become common to argue that that principle—sometimes articulated as coherence or integrity—is an essential feature of the rule of law ideal. *See, e.g.*, JOHN RAWLS, A THEORY OF JUSTICE, § 38 (1971); RONALD DWORKIN, LAW'S EMPIRE 225–75 (1986). The question then arises: is a law just or moral simply by virtue of being a norm of general application? As Professor Gardner observes:

> Hart agreed with those who say that all laws have a redeeming merit which comes of their very nature as laws. However, he did not trace this redeeming merit of all laws to their positivity. He traced it instead to the fact that, in his view, laws are not merely norms but rules, *i.e.* norms capable of repeated application from case to case. This fact of their normative generality, he thought, means that wherever laws go a kind of justice (and hence a kind of merit) automatically follows, for the correct re-application of any law entails that like cases are treated alike.

John Gardner, *Legal Positivism: 5½ Myths*, 46 AM. J. JURIS. 199, 201–06 (2001), at 205–6. Does this suggest that any simple version of the separability theme must be more a caricature than a portrait of the law?

5. *The separability theme reconsidered*. Ever since H.L.A. Hart expressly articulated the "separation of law and morals," H.L.A. Hart, *Positivism and the Separation of Law and Morals*, 71 HARV. L. REV. 593 (1958), some of the most highly respected philosophers of law have struggled with the meaning—even the phraseology—of that idea. *See* Leslie Green, *Positivism and the Inseparability of Law and Morals*, 83 N.Y.U. L. REV. 1035, 1038 (2008):

> Jules Coleman described the separability thesis as undeniable and therefore useless as a demarcation line in legal theory: "We cannot usefully characterize legal positivism in terms of the separability thesis, once it is understood properly, because virtually no one—positivist or not—rejects it." [*citing* Jules Coleman, THE PRACTICE OF PRINCIPLE 152 (2001).] John Gardner, on the other hand, maintained that the separability thesis cannot characterize positivism for the opposite reason: It is "absurd and no legal philosopher of note has ever endorsed it." [*citing* John Gardner, *Legal Positivism: 5½ Myths*, 46 AM. J. JURIS. 199, 223 (2001).] Amid such cacophony, it is perhaps unsurprising that some onlookers found the thesis "hopelessly ambiguous" and the half-century of debate about the separability of law and morals "entirely pointless." [*citing* Klaus Füßer, *Farewell to 'Legal Positivism': The Separation Thesis Unraveling*, *in* THE AUTONOMY OF LAW 119, 120 (Robert P. George ed., 1996).]

Given this level of disagreement, perhaps the best advice would be to give fair notice of what you mean by "separability" before you try to say anything about it. What we know as an empirical minimum is that judges rarely frame out an opinion and advocates rarely advance an argument in explicit and exclusive reliance on their moral instincts or conclusions.

6. *Questioning neutrality*. Is it plausible to think that rules of law can be articulated and applied neutrally and in good faith? Professor Morton Horowitz offers multiple examples of legal doctrines emerging (or being reformulated) to protect the railroads and other infant industries in TRANSFORMATION OF AMERICAN LAW 1780–1860 74–78 (1977) (addressing the common law of nuisance). The next chapter, dealing with American legal realism, suggests that the formal and determinist aspects of positivism are illusory and unworthy of a learned profession.

CHAPTER THREE

SCRAPPING NATURAL LAW *AND* POSITIVISM: LEGAL REALISM AS A STRATEGY FOR RESISTING BOTH THEOLOGY LITE AND THE PRETENSE OF DETERMINACY

■ ■ ■

"The process of judging, so the psychologists tell us, seldom begins with a premise from which a conclusion is subsequently worked out. Judging begins rather the other way around—with a conclusion more or less vaguely formed; a [person] ordinarily starts with such a conclusion [and] afterwards tries to find premises which will substantiate it."

— Jerome Frank

"Within the law, I say, therefore, rules guide, but they do not control decision. There is no precedent the judge may not at his need either file down to razor thinness or expand into a bludgeon. Why should you expect the ethics of the game to be different from the game itself?"

— Karl Llewellyn

"Equity, like all of us, prefers the rich and good-looking."

— Eugene Volokh

Orientation

If the essence of *natural law theory* is that a universal justice gives meaning to the law, and if the essence of *legal positivism* is that rules can be applied in an apolitical and deterministic way to resolve disputes, the essence of *legal realism* is that those other two approaches are a waste of time, a distraction from the gritty, human business of resolving cases. There are multiple strands to American legal realism—not all of them consistent with one another—and some of its original proponents denied that it was (or was intended to be) a systematic or coherent philosophy of law. But it was at a minimum skeptical: skeptical that any notion of justice could be universal in its acceptance; skeptical that rules were determinate and neutral; skeptical that judges were as constrained by rules as they said they were; skeptical that the law was any less open-textured or depersonalized than politics or ethics; skeptical that the law was best conceived as an autonomous discipline, with little or nothing to learn from anthropology and other social sciences; skeptical that facts were hard realities rather than contingent versions of the truth. If American legal realism had a positive agenda, it was typically as a call to judicial responsibility and open premises in decision-making, though one distinguished historian has suggested that "[f]or many purposes, it is best to see Legal Realism as simply a continuation of the reformist agenda of early-twentieth-century Progressivism." MORTON J. HORWITZ, THE TRANSFORMATION OF AMERICAN LAW, 1870–1960, at 169 (1992). Indeed, whatever their views of judging and the nature of law may have been, the politics of the American legal realists trended towards the New Deal reforms of Franklin Roosevelt.

It can be difficult to know how seriously to take some of American legal realism's more corrosive observations: perhaps it will help as you read the following materials to think of realism as a revealing caricature rather than as a photograph of the judicial process. From that perspective, the realists' fixation on the power of judges to *make* law in the process of *finding* it has become so widely accepted as to seem obvious, with lawyers, academics, and law students routinely ascribing the result in a case to the personal disposition of the judge. Skepticism is so powerful that it is sometimes said that we are all Realists now. But what can you miss about the judicial process if you reduce it to the judge's personal idiosyncracies? What do you miss about "law" generally if you focus only on cases and *judicial* decision-making? And in the end, as Professor Joseph Singer asks, "if we are all realists, why are some of the insights of the realists so controversial? Why is it still so explosive to claim that law is a form of politics?"

BUSH V. GORE

531 U.S. 98 (2000)

PER CURIAM.

I

On December 8, 2000, the Supreme Court of Florida ordered that the Circuit Court of Leon County[, Florida] tabulate by hand 9,000 ballots in Miami-Dade County. It also ordered the inclusion in the certified vote totals of 215 votes identified in Palm Beach County and 168 votes identified in Miami-Dade County for Vice President Albert Gore, Jr., and Senator Joseph Lieberman, Democratic Candidates for President and Vice President. The Supreme Court noted that petitioner, Governor George W. Bush asserted that the net gain for Vice President Gore in Palm Beach County was 176 votes, and directed the Circuit Court to resolve that dispute on remand. The court further held that relief would require manual recounts in all Florida counties where so-called "undervotes" had not been subject to manual tabulation. The court ordered all manual recounts to begin at once. Governor Bush and Richard Cheney, Republican Candidates for the Presidency and Vice Presidency, filed an emergency application for a stay of this mandate. On December 9, we granted the application, treated the application as a petition for a writ of *certiorari*, and granted *certiorari*.

The proceedings leading to the present controversy are discussed in some detail in our opinion in *Bush v. Palm Beach County Canvassing Bd.* (*per curiam*) (*Bush I*). On November 8, 2000, the day following the Presidential election, the Florida Division of Elections reported that petitioner, Governor Bush, had received 2,909,135 votes, and respondent, Vice President Gore, had received 2,907,351 votes, a margin of 1,784 for Governor Bush. Because Governor Bush's margin of victory was less than "one-half of a percent . . . of the votes cast," an automatic machine recount was conducted under § 102.141(4) of the [state] election code, the results of which showed Governor Bush still winning the race but by a diminished margin. Vice President Gore then sought manual recounts in Volusia, Palm Beach, Broward, and Miami-Dade Counties, pursuant to Florida's election protest provisions. Fla. Stat. § 102.166 (2000). A dispute arose concerning the deadline for local county canvassing boards to submit their returns to the Secretary of State (Secretary). The Secretary declined to waive the November 14 deadline imposed by statute. The Florida Supreme Court, however, set the deadline at November 26. We granted *certiorari* and vacated the Florida Supreme Court's decision, finding considerable uncertainty as to the grounds on which it was based. *Bush I*. On December 11, the Florida Supreme Court issued a decision on remand reinstating that date.

On November 26, the Florida Elections Canvassing Commission certified the results of the election and declared Governor Bush the winner of Florida's 25 electoral votes. On November 27, Vice President Gore, pursuant to Florida's contest provisions, filed a complaint in Leon County Circuit Court contesting the certification. He sought relief pursuant to § 102.168(3)(c), which provides that "receipt of a number of illegal votes or rejection of a number of legal votes sufficient to change or place in doubt the result of the election" shall be grounds for a contest. The Circuit Court denied relief, stating that Vice President Gore failed to meet his burden of proof. He appealed to the First District Court of Appeal, which certified the matter to the Florida Supreme Court.

Accepting jurisdiction, the Florida Supreme Court affirmed in part and reversed in part. The court held that the Circuit Court had been correct to reject Vice President Gore's challenge to the results certified in Nassau County and his challenge to the Palm Beach County Canvassing Board's determination that 3,300 ballots cast in that county were not, in the statutory phrase, "legal votes."

The Supreme Court held that Vice President Gore had satisfied his burden of proof under § 102.168(3)(c) with respect to his challenge to Miami-Dade County's failure to tabulate, by manual count, 9,000 ballots on which the machines had failed to detect a vote for President ("undervotes"). Noting the closeness of the election, the Court explained that "on this record, there can be no question that there are legal votes within the 9,000 uncounted votes sufficient to place the results of this election in doubt." A "legal vote," as determined by the Supreme Court, is "one in which there is a 'clear indication of the intent of the voter.'" The court therefore ordered a hand recount of the 9,000 ballots in Miami-Dade County. Observing that the contest provisions vest broad discretion in the circuit judge to "provide any relief appropriate under such circumstances," the Supreme Court further held that the Circuit Court could order "the Supervisor of Elections and the Canvassing Boards, as well as the necessary public officials, in all counties that have not conducted a manual recount or tabulation of the undervotes . . . to do so forthwith, said tabulation to take place in the individual counties where the ballots are located." * * *

The petition presents the following questions: whether the Florida Supreme Court established new standards for resolving Presidential election contests, thereby violating Art. II, § 1, cl. 2, of the United States Constitution and failing to comply with 3 U.S.C. § 5,[1] and whether the use of standardless manual recounts violates the Equal Protection and Due Process Clauses. With respect to the equal protection question, we find a violation of the Equal Protection Clause.

---

1 [3 U.S.C. § 5 is part of the statutory regime governing the Electoral College, which technically elects the President of the United States under the Constitution. Section 5 creates a "safe harbor" for the method chosen by each State for selecting its electors to the College and provides as follows:

> *Determination of controversy as to appointment of electors.* If any State shall have provided, by laws enacted prior to the day fixed for the appointment of the electors, for its final determination of any controversy or contest concerning the appointment of all or any of the electors of such State, by judicial or other methods or procedures, and such determination shall have been made at least six days before the time fixed for the meeting of the electors, such determination made pursuant to such law so existing on said day, and made at least six days prior to said time of meeting of the electors, shall be conclusive, and shall govern in the counting of the electoral votes as provided in the Constitution, and as hereinafter regulated, so far as the ascertainment of the electors appointed by such State is concerned.

In the case at hand, the Electoral College was scheduled to meet on December 18, 2000; therefore, the "safe harbor" deadline in Section 5 was December 12, 2000, one day after oral arguments in this case and the day the decision was announced.]

II

A

The closeness of this election, and the multitude of legal challenges which have followed in its wake, have brought into sharp focus a common, if heretofore unnoticed, phenomenon. Nationwide statistics reveal that an estimated 2% of ballots cast do not register a vote for President for whatever reason, including deliberately choosing no candidate at all or some voter error, such as voting for two candidates or insufficiently marking a ballot. * * * In certifying election results, the votes eligible for inclusion in the certification are the votes meeting the properly established legal requirements. This case has shown that punch card balloting machines can produce an unfortunate number of ballots which are not punched in a clean, complete way by the voter. After the current counting, it is likely legislative bodies nationwide will examine ways to improve the mechanisms and machinery for voting.

B

The individual citizen has no federal constitutional right to vote for electors for the President of the United States unless and until the state legislature chooses a statewide election as the means to implement its power to appoint members of the Electoral College. U.S. Const., Art. II, § 1. This is the source for the statement in *McPherson v. Blacker*, 146 U.S. 1, 35 (1892), that the State legislature's power to select the manner for appointing electors is plenary; it may, if it so chooses, select the electors itself, which indeed was the manner used by State legislatures in several States for many years after the Framing of our Constitution. History has now favored the voter, and in each of the several States the citizens themselves vote for Presidential electors. When the state legislature vests the right to vote for President in its people, the right to vote as the legislature has prescribed is fundamental; and one source of its fundamental nature lies in the equal weight accorded to each vote and the equal dignity owed to each voter. * * *

The right to vote is protected in more than the initial allocation of the franchise. Equal protection applies as well to the manner of its exercise. Having once granted the right to vote on equal terms, the State may not, by later arbitrary and disparate treatment, value one person's vote over that of another. *See, e.g., Harper v. Virginia Bd. of Elections*, 383 U.S. 663, 665 (1966) ("Once the franchise is granted to the electorate, lines may not be drawn which are inconsistent with the Equal Protection Clause of the Fourteenth Amendment"). It must be remembered that "the right of suffrage can be denied by a debasement or dilution of the weight of a citizen's vote just as effectively as by wholly prohibiting the free exercise of the franchise." *Reynolds v. Sims*, 377 U.S. 533, 555 (1964).

There is no difference between the two sides of the present controversy on these basic propositions. Respondents say that the very purpose of vindicating the right to vote justifies the recount procedures now at issue. The question before us, however, is whether the recount procedures the Florida Supreme Court has adopted are consistent with its obligation to avoid arbitrary and disparate treatment of the members of its electorate.

Much of the controversy seems to revolve around ballot cards designed to be perforated by a stylus but which, either through error or deliberate omission, have not been perforated with sufficient precision for a machine to count them. In some cases a piece of the card—a chad—is hanging, say by two corners. In other cases there is no separation at all, just an indentation.

The Florida Supreme Court has ordered that the intent of the voter be discerned from such ballots. For purposes of resolving the equal protection challenge, it is not necessary to decide whether the Florida Supreme Court had the authority under the legislative scheme for resolving election disputes to define what a legal vote is and to mandate a manual recount implementing that definition. The recount mechanisms implemented in response to the decisions of the Florida Supreme Court do not satisfy the minimum requirement for non-arbitrary treatment of voters necessary to secure the fundamental right. Florida's basic command for the count of legally cast votes is to consider the "intent of the voter." *Gore v. Harris*, 779 So. 2d at 270 (slip op., at 39). This is unobjectionable as an abstract proposition and a starting principle. The problem inheres in the absence of specific standards to ensure its equal application. The formulation of uniform rules to determine intent based on these recurring circumstances is practicable and, we conclude, necessary.

The law does not refrain from searching for the intent of the actor in a multitude of circumstances; and in some cases the general command to ascertain intent is not susceptible to much further refinement. In this instance, however, the question is not whether to believe a witness but how to interpret the marks or holes or scratches on an inanimate object, a piece of cardboard or paper which, it is said, might not have registered as a vote during the machine count. The factfinder confronts a thing, not a person. The search for intent can be confined by specific rules designed to ensure uniform treatment.

The want of those rules here has led to unequal evaluation of ballots in various respects. *See Gore v. Harris*, 779 So. 2d at 270 (Wells, C. J., dissenting) ("Should a county canvassing board count or not count a 'dimpled chad' where the voter is able to successfully dislodge the chad in every other contest on that ballot? Here, the county canvassing boards disagree"). As seems to have been acknowledged at oral argument, the standards for accepting or rejecting contested ballots might vary not only from county to county but indeed within a single county from one recount team to another.

The record provides some examples. A monitor in Miami-Dade County testified at trial that he observed that three members of the county canvassing board applied different standards in defining a legal vote. * * * And testimony at trial also revealed that at least one county changed its evaluative standards during the counting process. Palm Beach County, for example, began the process with a 1990 guideline which precluded counting completely attached chads, switched to a rule that considered a vote to be legal if any light could be seen through a chad, changed back to the 1990 rule, and then abandoned any pretense of a *per se* rule, only to have a court order that the county consider dimpled chads legal. This is not a process with sufficient guarantees of equal treatment.

An early case in our one person, one vote jurisprudence arose when a State accorded arbitrary and disparate treatment to voters in its different counties. *Gray v. Sanders*, 372 U.S. 368 (1963). The Court found a constitutional violation. We relied on these principles in the context of the Presidential selection process in *Moore v. Ogilvie*, 394 U.S. 814 (1969), where we invalidated a county-based procedure that diluted the influence of citizens in larger counties in the nominating process. There we observed that "the idea that one group can be granted greater voting strength than another is hostile to the one man, one vote basis of our representative government."

The State Supreme Court ratified this uneven treatment. It mandated that the recount totals from two counties, Miami-Dade and Palm Beach, be included in the certified total. The court also appeared to hold *sub silentio* that the recount totals from Broward County, which were not completed until after the original November 14 certification by the Secretary of State, were to be considered part of the new certified vote totals even though the county certification was not contested by Vice President Gore. Yet each of the counties used varying standards to determine what was a legal vote. Broward County used a more forgiving standard than Palm Beach County, and uncovered almost three times as many new votes, a result markedly disproportionate to the difference in population between the counties.

In addition, the recounts in these three counties were not limited to so-called undervotes but extended to all of the ballots. The distinction has real consequences. A manual recount of all ballots identifies not only those ballots which show no vote but also those which contain more than one, the so-called overvotes. Neither category will be counted by the machine. This is not a trivial concern. At oral argument, respondents estimated there are as many as 110,000 overvotes statewide. As a result, the citizen whose ballot was not read by a machine because he failed to vote for a candidate in a way readable by a machine may still have his vote counted in a manual recount; on the other hand, the citizen who marks two candidates in a way discernable by the machine will not have the same opportunity to have his vote count, even if a manual examination of the ballot would reveal the requisite indicia of intent. Furthermore, the citizen who marks two candidates, only one of which is discernable by the machine, will have his vote counted even though it should have been read as an invalid ballot. The State Supreme Court's inclusion of vote counts based on these variant standards exemplifies concerns with the remedial processes that were under way. * * *

The recount process, in its features here described, is inconsistent with the minimum procedures necessary to protect the fundamental right of each voter in the special instance of a statewide recount under the authority of a single state judicial officer. Our consideration is limited to the present circumstances, for the problem of equal protection in election processes generally presents many complexities. * * *

Upon due consideration of the difficulties identified to this point, it is obvious that the recount cannot be conducted in compliance with the requirements of equal protection and due process without substantial additional work. It would require not only the adoption (after opportunity for argument) of adequate statewide standards for determining what is a legal vote, and practicable procedures to implement them, but also orderly judicial review of any disputed matters that might arise. In addition, the Secretary of State has advised that the recount of only a portion of the ballots requires that the vote tabulation equipment be used to screen out undervotes, a function for which the machines were not designed. If a recount of overvotes were also required, perhaps even a second screening would be necessary. Use of the equipment for this purpose, and any new software developed for it, would have to be evaluated for accuracy by the Secretary of State * * *.

The Supreme Court of Florida has said that the legislature intended the State's electors to "participate fully in the federal electoral process," as provided in 3 U.S.C. § 5. 779 So. 2d at 270. That [state] statute, in turn, requires that any controversy or contest that is designed to lead to a conclusive selection of electors be completed by December 12. That date is upon us, and there is no recount procedure in place under the State Supreme Court's order that comports with minimal constitutional standards. Because it is evident that any recount seeking to meet the December 12 date will be unconstitutional for the reasons we have discussed, we reverse the judgment of the Supreme Court of Florida ordering a recount to proceed.

Seven Justices of the Court agree that there are constitutional problems with the recount ordered by the Florida Supreme Court that demand a remedy. The only disagreement is as to the remedy. Because the Florida Supreme Court has said that the Florida Legislature intended to obtain the safe-harbor benefits of 3 U.S.C. § 5, Justice Breyer's proposed remedy—remanding to the Florida Supreme Court for its ordering of a constitutionally proper contest until December 18—contemplates action in violation of the Florida election code, and hence could not be part of an "appropriate" order authorized by [the Florida statute]. * * *

None are more conscious of the vital limits on judicial authority than are the members of this Court, and none stand more in admiration of the Constitution's design to leave the selection of the President to the people, through their legislatures, and to the political sphere. When contending parties invoke the process of the courts, however, it becomes our unsought responsibility to resolve the federal and constitutional issues the judicial system has been forced to confront. The judgment of the Supreme Court of Florida is reversed, and the case is remanded for further proceedings not inconsistent with this opinion.

CHIEF JUSTICE REHNQUIST, with whom JUSTICE SCALIA and JUSTICE THOMAS join, concurring. We join the *per curiam* opinion. We write separately because we believe there are additional grounds that require us to reverse the Florida Supreme Court's decision.

I

We deal here not with an ordinary election, but with an election for the President of the United States. * * * In most cases, comity and respect for federalism compel us to defer to the decisions of state courts on issues of state law. That practice reflects our understanding that the decisions of state courts are definitive pronouncements of the will of the States as sovereigns. Of course, in ordinary cases, the distribution of powers among the branches of a State's government raises no questions of federal constitutional law, subject to the requirement that the government be republican in character. See U.S. Const., Art. IV, § 4. But there are a few exceptional cases in which the Constitution imposes a duty or confers a power on a particular branch of a State's government. This is one of them. Article II, § 1, cl. 2, provides that "each State shall appoint, in such Manner as the Legislature thereof may direct," electors for President and Vice President. Thus, the text of the election law itself, and not just its interpretation by the courts of the States, takes on independent significance.

In *McPherson v. Blacker*, 146 U.S. 1 (1892), we explained that Art. II, § 1, cl. 2, "conveys the broadest power of determination" and "leaves it to the legislature exclusively to define the method" of appointment. A significant departure from the legislative scheme for appointing Presidential electors presents a federal constitutional question.

Title 3 U.S.C. § 5 informs our application of Art. II, § 1, cl. 2, to the Florida statutory scheme, which, as the Florida Supreme Court acknowledged, took that statute into account. Section 5 provides that the State's selection of electors "shall be conclusive, and shall govern in the counting of the electoral votes" if the electors are chosen under laws enacted prior to election day, and if the selection process is completed six days prior to the meeting of the electoral college. As we noted in *Bush v. Palm Beach County Canvassing Bd.*:

> Since § 5 contains a principle of federal law that would assure finality of the State's determination if made pursuant to a state law in effect before the election, a legislative wish to take advantage of the 'safe harbor' would counsel against any construction of the Election Code that Congress might deem to be a change in the law."

If we are to respect the legislature's Article II powers, therefore, we must ensure that post-election state-court actions do not frustrate the legislative desire to attain the "safe harbor" provided by § 5.

In Florida, the legislature has chosen to hold state-wide elections to appoint the State's 25 electors. Importantly, the legislature has delegated the authority to run the elections and to oversee election disputes to the Secretary of State (Secretary), and to state circuit courts. Isolated sections of the code may well admit of more than one interpretation, but the general coherence of the legislative scheme may not be altered by judicial interpretation so as to wholly change the statutorily provided apportionment of responsibility among these various bodies. In any election but a Presidential election, the Florida Supreme Court can give as little or as much deference to Florida's executives as it chooses, so far as Article II is concerned, and this Court will have no cause to question the court's actions. But, with respect to a Presidential election, the court must be both mindful of the legislature's role under Article II in choosing the manner of appointing electors and deferential to those bodies expressly empowered by the legislature to carry out its constitutional mandate.

In order to determine whether a state court has infringed upon the legislature's authority, we necessarily must examine the law of the State as it existed prior to the action of the court. Though we generally defer to state courts on the interpretation of state law—see, *e.g., Mullaney v. Wilbur*, 421 U.S. 684 (1975)—there are of course areas in which the Constitution requires this Court to undertake an independent, if still deferential, analysis of state law. * * *

[In] *Bouie v. City of Columbia*, 378 U.S. 347 (1964), * * * the state court had held, contrary to precedent, that the state trespass law applied to black sit-in demonstrators who had consent to enter private property but were then asked to leave. * * * [W]e concluded that the South Carolina Supreme Court's interpretation of a state penal statute had impermissibly broadened the scope of that statute beyond what a fair reading provided, in violation of due process. What we would do in the present case is precisely parallel: Hold that the Florida Supreme Court's interpretation of the Florida election laws impermissibly distorted them beyond what a fair reading required, in violation of Article II. * * *

II

Acting pursuant to its constitutional grant of authority, the Florida Legislature has created a detailed, if not perfectly crafted, statutory scheme that provides for appointment of Presidential electors by direct election. Under the statute, "votes cast for the actual candidates for President and Vice President shall be counted as votes cast for the presidential electors supporting such candidates." The legislature has designated the Secretary of State as the "chief election officer," with the responsibility to "obtain and maintain uniformity in the application, operation, and interpretation of the election laws." The state legislature has delegated to county canvassing boards the duties of administering elections. Those boards are responsible for providing results to the state Elections Canvassing Commission, comprising the Governor, the Secretary of State, and the Director of the Division of Elections. Cf. *Boardman v. Esteva*, 323 So. 2d 259, 268, n. 5 (1975) ("The election process . . . is committed to the executive branch of government through duly designated officials all charged with specific duties . . . . [The] judgments [of these officials] are entitled to be regarded by the courts as presumptively correct . . ."). After the election has taken place, the canvassing boards receive returns from precincts, count the votes, and in the event that a candidate was defeated by .05% or less, conduct a mandatory recount. The county canvassing boards must file certified election returns with the Department of State by 5 p.m. on the seventh day following the election. § 102.112(1). The Elections Canvassing Commission must then certify the results of the election. § 102.111(1).

The state legislature has also provided mechanisms both for protesting election returns and for contesting certified election results. * * *

III

The scope and nature of the remedy ordered by the Florida Supreme Court jeopardizes the "legislative wish" to take advantage of the safe harbor provided by 3 U.S.C. § 5. December 12, 2000, is the last date for a final determination of the Florida electors that will satisfy § 5. Yet in the late afternoon of December 8th—four days before this deadline—the Supreme Court of Florida ordered recounts of tens of thousands of so-called "undervotes" spread through 64 of the State's 67 counties. This was done in a search for elusive—perhaps delusive—certainty as to the exact count of 6 million votes. But no one claims that these ballots have not previously been tabulated; they were initially read by voting machines at the time of the election, and thereafter reread by virtue of Florida's automatic recount provision. No one claims there was any fraud in the election. The Supreme Court of Florida ordered this additional recount under the provision of the election code giving the circuit judge the authority to provide relief that is "appropriate under such circumstances."

Surely when the Florida Legislature empowered the courts of the State to grant "appropriate" relief, it must have meant relief that would have become final by the cutoff date of 3 U.S.C. § 5. In light of the inevitable legal challenges and ensuing appeals to the Supreme Court of Florida and petitions for certiorari to this Court, the entire recounting process could not possibly be completed by that date. Whereas the majority in the Supreme Court of Florida stated its confidence that "the remaining undervotes in these counties can be [counted] within the required time frame," 607 So. 2d at 509, n. 22 (slip op., at 38, n. 22), it made no assertion that the seemingly inevitable appeals could be disposed of in that time. Although the Florida Supreme Court has on occasion taken over a year to resolve disputes over local elections, it has heard and decided the appeals in the present case with great promptness. But the federal deadlines for the Presidential election simply do not permit even such a shortened process. * * *

Given all these factors, and in light of the legislative intent identified by the Florida Supreme Court to bring Florida within the "safe harbor" provision of 3 U.S.C. § 5, the remedy prescribed by the Supreme Court of Florida cannot be deemed an "appropriate" one as of December 8. It significantly departed from the statutory framework in place on November 7, and authorized open-ended further proceedings which could not be completed by December 12, thereby preventing a final determination by that date. For these reasons, in addition to those given in the *per curiam*, we would reverse.

JUSTICE STEVENS, with whom JUSTICE GINSBURG and JUSTICE BREYER join, dissenting. The Constitution assigns to the States the primary responsibility for determining the manner of selecting the Presidential electors. See Art. II, § 1, cl. 2. When questions arise about the meaning of state laws, including election laws, it is our settled practice to accept the opinions of the highest courts of the States as providing the final answers. On rare occasions, however, either federal statutes or the Federal Constitution may require federal judicial intervention in state elections. This is not such an occasion.

The federal questions that ultimately emerged in this case are not substantial. Article II provides that "each State shall appoint, in such Manner as the Legislature thereof may direct, a Number of Electors." It does not create state legislatures out of whole cloth, but rather takes them as they come—as creatures born of, and constrained by, their state constitutions. Lest there be any doubt, we stated over 100 years ago in *McPherson v. Blacker*, 146 U.S. 1, 25 (1892), that "what is forbidden or required to be done by a State" in the Article II context "is forbidden or required of the legislative power under state constitutions as they exist." In the same vein, we also observed that "the [State's] legislative power is the supreme authority except as limited by the constitution of the State." The legislative power in Florida is subject to judicial review pursuant to Article V of the Florida Constitution, and nothing in Article II of the Federal Constitution frees the state legislature from the constraints in the state constitution that created it. Moreover, the Florida Legislature's own decision to employ a unitary code for all elections indicates that it intended the Florida Supreme Court to play the same role in Presidential elections that it has historically played in resolving electoral disputes. The Florida Supreme Court's exercise of appellate jurisdiction therefore was wholly consistent with, and indeed contemplated by, the grant of authority in Article II.

It hardly needs stating that Congress, pursuant to 3 U.S.C. § 5, did not impose any affirmative duties upon the States that their governmental branches could "violate." Rather, § 5 provides a safe harbor for States to select electors in contested elections "by judicial or other methods" established by laws prior to the election day. Section 5, like Article II, assumes the involvement of the state judiciary in interpreting state election laws and resolving election disputes under those laws. Neither § 5 nor Article II grants federal judges any special authority to substitute their views for those of the state judiciary on matters of state law.

Nor are petitioners correct in asserting that the failure of the Florida Supreme Court to specify in detail the precise manner in which the "intent of the voter," Fla. Stat. § 101.5614(5) (Supp. 2001), is to be determined rises to the level of a constitutional violation. We found such a violation when individual votes within the same State were weighted unequally, *see, e.g., Reynolds v. Sims*, 377 U.S. 533, 568 (1964), but we have never before called into question the substantive standard by which a State determines that a vote has been legally cast. And there is no reason to think that the guidance provided to the fact-finders, specifically the various canvassing boards, by the "intent of the voter" standard is any less sufficient—or will lead to results any less uniform—than, for example, the "beyond a reasonable doubt" standard employed everyday by ordinary citizens in courtrooms across this country.

Admittedly, the use of differing substandards for determining voter intent in different counties employing similar voting systems may raise serious concerns. Those concerns are alleviated—if not eliminated—by the fact that a single impartial magistrate will ultimately adjudicate all objections arising from the recount process. Of course, as a general matter, "the interpretation of constitutional principles must not be too literal. We must remember that the machinery of government would not work if it were not allowed a little play in its joints." *Bain Peanut Co. of Tex. v. Pinson*, 282 U.S. 499, 501 (1931) (Holmes, J.). If it were otherwise, Florida's decision to leave to each county the determination of what balloting system to employ—despite enormous differences in accuracy—might run afoul of equal protection. So, too, might the similar decisions of the vast majority of state legislatures to delegate to local authorities certain decisions with respect to voting systems and ballot design.

Even assuming that aspects of the remedial scheme might ultimately be found to violate the Equal Protection Clause, I could not subscribe to the majority's disposition of the case. As the majority explicitly holds, once a state legislature determines to select electors through a popular vote, the right to have one's vote counted is of constitutional stature. As the majority further acknowledges, Florida law holds that all ballots that reveal the intent of the voter constitute valid votes. Recognizing these principles, the majority nonetheless orders the termination of the contest proceeding before all such votes have been tabulated. Under their own reasoning, the appropriate course of action would be to remand to allow more specific procedures for implementing the legislature's uniform general standard to be established.

In the interest of finality, however, the majority effectively orders the disenfranchisement of an unknown number of voters whose ballots reveal their intent—and are therefore legal votes under state law—but were for some reason rejected by ballot-counting machines. It does so on the basis of the deadlines set forth in Title 3 of the United States Code. But, as I have already noted, those provisions merely provide rules of decision for Congress to follow when selecting among conflicting slates of electors. They do not prohibit a State from counting what the majority concedes to be legal votes until a bona fide winner is determined. Indeed, in 1960, Hawaii appointed two slates of electors and Congress chose to count the one appointed on January 4, 1961, well after the Title 3 deadlines. Thus, nothing prevents the majority, even if it properly found an equal protection violation, from ordering relief appropriate to remedy that violation without depriving Florida voters of their right to have their votes counted. As the majority notes, "[a] desire for speed is not a general excuse for ignoring equal protection guarantees."

Finally, neither in this case, nor in its earlier opinion in *Palm Beach County Canvassing Bd. v. Harris*, 772 So. 2d 1273 (Fla., Nov. 21, 2000), did the Florida Supreme Court make any substantive change in Florida electoral law. Its decisions were rooted in long-established precedent and were consistent with the relevant statutory provisions, taken as a whole. It did what courts do—it decided the case before it in light of the legislature's intent to leave no legally cast vote uncounted. In so doing, it relied on the sufficiency of the general "intent of the voter" standard articulated by the state legislature, coupled with a procedure for ultimate review by an impartial judge, to resolve the concern about disparate evaluations of contested ballots. If we assume—as I do—that the members of that court and the judges who would have carried out its mandate are impartial, its decision does not even raise a colorable federal question.

What must underlie petitioners' entire federal assault on the Florida election procedures is an unstated lack of confidence in the impartiality and capacity of the state judges who would make the critical decisions if the vote count were to proceed. Otherwise, their position is wholly without merit. The endorsement of that position by the majority of this Court can only lend credence to the most cynical appraisal of the work of judges throughout the land. It is confidence in the men and women who administer the judicial system that is the true backbone of the rule of law. Time will one day heal the wound to that confidence that will be inflicted by today's decision. One thing, however, is certain. Although we may never know with complete certainty the identity of the winner of this year's Presidential election, the identity of the loser is perfectly clear. It is the Nation's confidence in the judge as an impartial guardian of the rule of law. I respectfully dissent.

* * *

JUSTICE BREYER, with whom JUSTICE STEVENS and JUSTICE GINSBURG join except as to Part IA-1, and with whom JUSTICE SOUTER joins as to Part I, dissenting. The Court was wrong to take this case. It was wrong to grant a stay. It should now vacate that stay and permit the Florida Supreme Court to decide whether the recount should resume.

I

The political implications of this case for the country are momentous. But the federal legal questions presented, with one exception, are insubstantial.

A

1

The majority raises three Equal Protection problems with the Florida Supreme Court's recount order: first, the failure to include overvotes in the manual recount; second, the fact that all ballots, rather than simply the undervotes, were recounted in some, but not all, counties; and third, the absence of a uniform, specific standard to guide the recounts. As far as the first issue is concerned, petitioners presented no evidence, to this Court or to any Florida court, that a manual recount of overvotes would identify additional legal votes. The same is true of the second, and, in addition, the majority's reasoning would seem to invalidate any state provision for a manual recount of individual counties in a statewide election.

The majority's third concern does implicate principles of fundamental fairness. The majority concludes that the Equal Protection Clause requires that a manual recount be governed not only by the uniform general standard of the "clear intent of the voter," but also by uniform subsidiary standards (for example, a uniform determination whether indented, but not perforated, "undervotes" should count). The opinion points out that the Florida Supreme Court ordered the inclusion of Broward County's undercounted "legal votes" even though those votes included ballots that were not perforated but simply "dimpled," while newly recounted ballots from other counties will likely include only votes determined to be "legal" on the basis of a stricter standard. In light of our previous remand, the Florida Supreme Court may have been reluctant to adopt a more specific standard than that provided for by the legislature for fear of exceeding its authority under Article II. However, since the use of different standards could favor one or the other of the candidates, since time was, and is, too short to permit the lower courts to iron out significant differences through ordinary judicial review, and since the relevant distinction was embodied in the order of the State's highest court, I agree that, in these very special circumstances, basic principles of fairness may well have counseled the adoption of a uniform standard to address the problem. In light of the majority's disposition, I need not decide whether, or the extent to which, as a remedial matter, the Constitution would place limits upon the content of the uniform standard.

2

Nonetheless, there is no justification for the majority's remedy, which is simply to reverse the lower court and halt the recount entirely. An appropriate remedy would be, instead, to remand this case with instructions that, even at this late date, would permit the Florida Supreme Court to require recounting all undercounted votes in Florida, including those from Broward, Volusia, Palm Beach, and Miami-Dade Counties, whether or not previously recounted prior to the end of the protest period, and to do so in accordance with a single-uniform substandard.

The majority justifies stopping the recount entirely on the ground that there is no more time. In particular, the majority relies on the lack of time for the Secretary to review and approve equipment needed to separate undervotes. But the majority reaches this conclusion in the absence of any record evidence that the recount could not have been completed in the time allowed by the Florida Supreme Court. The majority finds facts outside of the record on matters that state courts are in a far better position to address. Of course, it is too late for any such recount to take place by December 12, the date by which election disputes must be decided if a State is to take advantage of the safe harbor provisions of 3 U.S.C. § 5. Whether there is time to conduct a recount prior to December 18, when the electors are scheduled to meet, is a matter for the state courts to determine. And whether, under Florida law, Florida could or could not take further action is obviously a matter for Florida courts, not this Court, to decide.

By halting the manual recount, and thus ensuring that the uncounted legal votes will not be counted under any standard, this Court crafts a remedy out of proportion to the asserted harm. And that remedy harms the very fairness interests the Court is attempting to protect. The manual recount would itself redress a problem of unequal treatment of ballots. As Justice Stevens points out, the ballots of voters in counties that use punchcard systems are more likely to be disqualified than those in counties using optical-scanning systems. According to recent news reports, variations in the undervote rate are even more pronounced. See Fessenden, *No-Vote Rates Higher in Punch Card Count*, N. Y. TIMES, Dec. 1, 2000, p. A29 (reporting that 0.3% of ballots cast in 30 Florida counties using optical-scanning systems registered no Presidential vote, in comparison to 1.53% in the 15 counties using Votomatic punch card ballots). Thus, in a system that allows counties to use different types of voting systems, voters already arrive at the polls with an unequal chance that their votes will be counted. I do not see how the fact that this results from counties' selection of different voting machines rather than a court order makes the outcome any more fair. Nor do I understand why the Florida Supreme Court's recount order, which helps to redress this inequity, must be entirely prohibited based on a deficiency that could easily be remedied.

B

The remainder of petitioners' claims, which are the focus of the Chief Justice's concurrence, raise no significant federal questions. I cannot agree that the Chief Justice's unusual review of state law in this case is justified by reference either to Art. II, § 1, or to 3 U.S.C. § 5. Moreover, even were such review proper, the conclusion that the Florida Supreme Court's decision contravenes federal law is untenable.

While conceding that, in most cases, "comity and respect for federalism compel us to defer to the decisions of state courts on issues of state law," the concurrence relies on some combination of Art. II, § 1, and 3 U.S.C. § 5 to justify the majority's conclusion that this case is one of the few in which we may lay that fundamental principle aside. The concurrence's primary foundation for this conclusion rests on an appeal to plain text: Art. II, § 1's grant of the power to appoint Presidential electors to the State "Legislature." But neither the text of Article II itself nor the only case the concurrence cites that interprets Article II, *McPherson v. Blacker*, 146 U.S. 1 (1892), leads to the conclusion that Article II grants unlimited power to the legislature, devoid of any state constitutional limitations, to select the manner of appointing electors. Nor, as Justice Stevens points out, have we interpreted the Federal constitutional provision most analogous to Art. II, § 1—Art. I, § 4—in the strained manner put forth in the concurrence.

The concurrence's treatment of § 5 as "informing" its interpretation of Article II, § 1, cl. 2, is no more convincing. The Chief Justice contends that our opinion in *Bush v. Palm Beach County Canvassing Bd.* (*Bush I*), in which we stated that "a legislative wish to take advantage of [§ 5] would counsel against" a construction of Florida law that Congress might deem to be a change in law * * * now means that this Court "must ensure that post-election state court actions do not frustrate the legislative desire to attain the 'safe harbor' provided by § 5." However, § 5 is part of the rules that govern Congress' recognition of slates of electors. Nowhere in *Bush I* did we establish that this Court had the authority to enforce § 5. Nor did we suggest that the permissive "counsel against" could be transformed into the mandatory "must ensure." And nowhere did we intimate, as the concurrence does here, that a state court decision that threatens the safe harbor provision of § 5 does so in violation of Article II. The concurrence's logic turns the presumption that legislatures would wish to take advantage of § 5's "safe harbor" provision into a mandate that trumps other statutory provisions and overrides the intent that the legislature did express.

But, in any event, the concurrence, having conducted its review, now reaches the wrong conclusion. It says that "the Florida Supreme Court's interpretation of the Florida election laws impermissibly distorted them beyond what a fair reading required, in violation of Article II." But what precisely is the distortion? Apparently, it has three elements. First, the Florida court, in its earlier opinion, changed the election certification date from November 14 to November 26. Second, the Florida court ordered a manual recount of "undercounted" ballots that could not have been fully completed by the December 12 "safe harbor" deadline. Third, the Florida court, in the opinion now under review, failed to give adequate deference to the determinations of canvassing boards and the Secretary.

To characterize the first element as a "distortion," however, requires the concurrence to second-guess the way in which the state court resolved a plain conflict in the language of different statutes. *Compare* Fla. Stat. § 102.166 (2001) (foreseeing manual recounts during the protest period) with § 102.111 (setting what is arguably too short a deadline for manual recounts to be conducted); compare § 102.112(1) (stating that the Secretary "may" ignore late returns) with § 102.111(1) (stating that the Secretary "shall" ignore late returns). In any event, that issue no longer has any practical importance and cannot justify the reversal of the different Florida court decision before us now.

To characterize the second element as a "distortion" requires the concurrence to overlook the fact that the inability of the Florida courts to conduct the recount on time is, in significant part, a problem of the Court's own making. The Florida Supreme Court thought that the recount could be completed on time, and, within hours, the Florida Circuit Court was moving in an orderly fashion to meet the deadline. This Court improvidently entered a stay. As a result, we will never know whether the recount could have been completed.

Nor can one characterize the third element as "impermissible distorting" once one understands that there are two sides to the opinion's argument that the Florida Supreme Court "virtually eliminated the Secretary's discretion." *Ante*, at 9 (Rehnquist, C. J., concurring). The

Florida statute in question was amended in 1999 to provide that the "grounds for contesting an election" include the "rejection of a number of legal votes sufficient to . . . place in doubt the result of the election." Fla. Stat. §§ 102.168(3), (3)(c) (2000). And the parties have argued about the proper meaning of the statute's term "legal vote." The Secretary has claimed that a "legal vote" is a vote "properly executed in accordance with the instructions provided to all registered voters." *Brief for Respondent Harris et al.* 10. On that interpretation, punchcard ballots for which the machines cannot register a vote are not "legal" votes. *Id.*, at 14. The Florida Supreme Court did not accept her definition. But it had a reason. Its reason was that a different provision of Florida election laws (a provision that addresses damaged or defective ballots) says that no vote shall be disregarded "if there is a clear indication of the intent of the voter as determined by the canvassing board" (adding that ballots should not be counted "if it is impossible to determine the elector's choice"). Fla. Stat. § 101.5614(5) (2000). Given this statutory language, certain roughly analogous judicial precedent, e.g., *Darby v. State ex rel. McCollough*, 75 So. 411 (Fla. 1917) (*per curiam*), and somewhat similar determinations by courts throughout the Nation, the Florida Supreme Court concluded that the term "legal vote" means a vote recorded on a ballot that clearly reflects what the voter intended. *Gore v. Harris*, 779 So. 2d 270 (2000) (slip op., at 19). That conclusion differs from the conclusion of the Secretary. But nothing in Florida law requires the Florida Supreme Court to accept as determinative the Secretary's view on such a matter. Nor can one say that the Court's ultimate determination is so unreasonable as to amount to a constitutionally "impermissible distortion" of Florida law.

The Florida Supreme Court, applying this definition, decided, on the basis of the record, that respondents had shown that the ballots undercounted by the voting machines contained enough "legal votes" to place "the results" of the election "in doubt." Since only a few hundred votes separated the candidates, and since the "undercounted" ballots numbered tens of thousands, it is difficult to see how anyone could find this conclusion unreasonable—however strict the standard used to measure the voter's "clear intent." Nor did this conclusion "strip" canvassing boards of their discretion. The boards retain their traditional discretionary authority during the protest period. And during the contest period, as the court stated, "the Canvassing Board's actions [during the protest period] may constitute evidence that a ballot does or does not qualify as a legal vote." *Id.* at 13. Whether a local county canvassing board's discretionary judgment during the protest period not to conduct a manual recount will be set aside during a contest period depends upon whether a candidate provides additional evidence that the rejected votes contain enough "legal votes" to place the outcome of the race in doubt. To limit the local canvassing board's discretion in this way is not to eliminate that discretion. At the least, one could reasonably so believe.

The statute goes on to provide the Florida circuit judge with authority to "fashion such orders as he or she deems necessary to ensure that each allegation . . . is *investigated, examined, or checked,* . . . and to provide any relief appropriate." Fla. Stat. § 102.168(8) (2000) (emphasis added). The Florida Supreme Court did just that. One might reasonably disagree with the Florida Supreme Court's interpretation of these, or other, words in the statute. But I do not see how one could call its plain language interpretation of a 1999 statutory change so misguided as no longer to qualify as judicial interpretation or as a usurpation of the authority of the State legislature. Indeed, other state courts have interpreted roughly similar state statutes in similar ways. *See, e.g., In re Election of U.S. Representative for Second Congressional Dist.*, 231 Conn. 602, 621 (1994) ("Whatever the process used to vote and to count votes, differences in technology should not furnish a basis for disregarding the bedrock principle that the purpose of the voting process is to ascertain the intent of the voters"); Brown v. Carr, 130 W. Va. 455, 460, 43 S.E.2d 401, 404–405 (1947) ("Whether a ballot shall be counted . . . depends on the intent of the voter . . . . Courts decry any resort to technical rules in reaching a conclusion as to the intent of the voter"). I repeat, where is the "impermissible" distortion?

II

Despite the reminder that this case involves "an election for the President of the United States," *ante*, at 1 (Rehnquist, C. J., concurring), no preeminent legal concern, or practical concern related to legal questions, required this Court to hear this case, let alone to issue a stay that stopped Florida's recount process in its tracks. With one exception, petitioners' claims do not ask us to vindicate a constitutional provision designed to protect a basic human right. *See, e.g., Brown v. Board of Education*, 347 U.S. 483 (1954). Petitioners invoke fundamental fairness, namely, the need for procedural fairness, including finality. But with the one "equal protection" exception, they rely upon law that focuses, not upon that basic need, but upon the constitutional allocation of power. Respondents invoke a competing fundamental consideration—the need to determine the voter's true intent. But they look to state law, not to federal constitutional law, to protect that interest. Neither side claims electoral fraud, dishonesty, or the like. And the more fundamental equal protection claim might have been left to the state court to resolve if and when it was discovered to have mattered. It could still be resolved through a remand conditioned upon issuance of a uniform standard; it does not require reversing the Florida Supreme Court.

Of course, the selection of the President is of fundamental national importance. But that importance is political, not legal. And this Court should resist the temptation unnecessarily to resolve tangential legal disputes, where doing so threatens to determine the outcome of the election.

The Constitution and federal statutes themselves make clear that restraint is appropriate. They set forth a road map of how to resolve disputes about electors, even after an election as close as this one. That road map foresees resolution of electoral disputes by state courts. See 3 U.S.C. § 5 (providing that, where a "State shall have provided, by laws enacted prior to [election day], for its final determination of any controversy or contest concerning the appointment of . . . electors . . . by *judicial* or other methods," the subsequently chosen electors enter a safe harbor free from congressional challenge). But it nowhere provides for involvement by the United States Supreme Court.

To the contrary, the Twelfth Amendment commits to Congress the authority and responsibility to count electoral votes. A federal statute, the Electoral Count Act, enacted after the close 1876 Hayes-Tilden Presidential election, specifies that, after States have tried to resolve disputes (through "judicial" or other means), Congress is the body primarily authorized to resolve remaining disputes. *See* Electoral Count Act of 1887, 24 Stat. 373, 3 U.S.C. §§ 5, 6, and 15. * * *

The Act goes on to set out rules for the congressional determination of disputes about those votes. If, for example, a state submits a single slate of electors, Congress must count those votes unless both Houses agree that the votes "have not been . . . regularly given." 3 U.S.C. § 15. If, as occurred in 1876, one or more states submits two sets of electors, then Congress must determine whether a slate has entered the safe harbor of § 5, in which case its votes will have "conclusive" effect. *Ibid.* If, as also occurred in 1876, there is controversy about "which of two or more of such State authorities . . . is the lawful tribunal" authorized to appoint electors, then each House shall determine separately which votes are "supported by the decision of such State so authorized by its law." Ibid. If the two Houses of Congress agree, the votes they have approved will be counted. If they disagree, then "the votes of the electors whose appointment shall have been certified by the executive of the State, under the seal thereof, shall be counted." Ibid.

Given this detailed, comprehensive scheme for counting electoral votes, there is no reason to believe that federal law either foresees or requires resolution of such a political issue by this Court. Nor, for that matter, is there any reason to that think the Constitution's Framers would have reached a different conclusion. Madison, at least, believed that allowing the judiciary to choose the presidential electors "was out of the question." Madison, July 25, 1787 (*reprinted in* 5 ELLIOT'S DEBATES ON THE FEDERAL CONSTITUTION 363 (2d ed. 1876)).

The decision by both the Constitution's Framers and the 1886 Congress to minimize this Court's role in resolving close federal presidential elections is as wise as it is clear. However awkward or difficult it may be for Congress to resolve difficult electoral disputes, Congress, being a political body, expresses the people's will far more accurately than does an unelected Court. And the people's will is what elections are about.

Moreover, Congress was fully aware of the danger that would arise should it ask judges, unarmed with appropriate legal standards, to resolve a hotly contested Presidential election contest. Just after the 1876 Presidential election, Florida, South Carolina, and Louisiana each sent two slates of electors to Washington. Without these States, Tilden, the Democrat, had 184 electoral votes, one short of the number required to win the Presidency. With those States, Hayes, his Republican opponent, would have had 185. In order to choose between the two slates of electors, Congress decided to appoint an electoral commission composed of five Senators, five Representatives, and five Supreme Court Justices. Initially the Commission was to be evenly divided between Republicans and Democrats, with Justice David Davis, an Independent, to possess the decisive vote. However, when at the last minute the Illinois Legislature elected Justice Davis to the United States Senate, the final position on the Commission was filled by Supreme Court Justice Joseph P. Bradley.

The Commission divided along partisan lines, and the responsibility to cast the deciding vote fell to Justice Bradley. He decided to accept the votes by the Republican electors, and thereby awarded the Presidency to Hayes.

Justice Bradley immediately became the subject of vociferous attacks. Bradley was accused of accepting bribes, of being captured by railroad interests, and of an eleventh-hour change in position after a night in which his house "was surrounded by the carriages" of Republican partisans and railroad officials. C. WOODWARD, REUNION AND REACTION 159–160 (1966). Many years later, Professor Bickel concluded that Bradley was honest and impartial. He thought that " 'the great question' for Bradley was, in fact, whether Congress was entitled to go behind election returns or had to accept them as certified by state authorities," an "issue of principle." THE LEAST DANGEROUS BRANCH 185 (1962). Nonetheless, Bickel points out, the legal question upon which Justice Bradley's decision turned was not very important in the contemporaneous political context. He says that "in the circumstances the issue of principle was trivial, it was overwhelmed by all that hung in the balance, and it should not have been decisive."

For present purposes, the relevance of this history lies in the fact that the participation in the work of the electoral commission by five Justices, including Justice Bradley, did not lend that process legitimacy. Nor did it assure the public that the process had worked fairly, guided by the law. Rather, it simply embroiled Members of the Court in partisan conflict, thereby undermining respect for the judicial process. And the Congress that later enacted the Electoral Count Act knew it.

This history may help to explain why I think it not only legally wrong, but also most unfortunate, for the Court simply to have terminated the Florida recount. Those who caution judicial restraint in resolving political disputes have described the quintessential case for that restraint as a case marked, among other things, by the "strangeness of the issue," its "intractability to principled resolution," its "sheer momentousness, . . . which tends to unbalance judicial judgment," and "the inner vulnerability, the self-doubt of an institution which is electorally irresponsible and has no earth to draw strength from." Bickel, *supra*, at 184. Those characteristics mark this case.

At the same time, as I have said, the Court is not acting to vindicate a fundamental constitutional principle, such as the need to protect a basic human liberty. No other strong reason to act is present. Congressional statutes tend to obviate the need. And, above all, in this highly politicized matter, the appearance of a split decision runs the risk of undermining the public's confidence in the Court itself. That confidence is a public treasure. It has been built slowly over many years, some of which were marked by a Civil War and the tragedy of segregation. It is a vitally necessary ingredient of any successful effort to protect basic liberty and, indeed, the rule of law itself. We run no risk of returning to the days when a President (responding to this Court's efforts to protect the Cherokee Indians) might have said, "John Marshall has made his decision; now let him enforce it!" Loth, CHIEF JUSTICE JOHN MARSHALL AND THE GROWTH OF THE AMERICAN REPUBLIC 365 (1948). But we do risk a self-inflicted wound—a wound that may harm not just the Court, but the Nation.

I fear that in order to bring this agonizingly long election process to a definitive conclusion, we have not adequately attended to that necessary "check upon our own exercise of power," "our own sense of self-restraint." *United States v. Butler*, 297 U.S. 1, 79 (1936) (Stone, J., dissenting). Justice Brandeis once said of the Court, "The most important thing we do is not doing." Bickel, *supra*, at 71. What it does today, the Court should have left undone. I would repair the damage done as best we now can, by permitting the Florida recount to continue under uniform standards. I respectfully dissent.

SANFORD LEVINSON, *RETURN OF LEGAL REALISM*

THE NATION
(Jan. 8, 2001)

The most enduring debate among twentieth-century legal analysts has been that between "legal realists" and those who believe in a reasonably strong version of "the rule of law." Though legal realism was often caricatured as reducing law to what the judge ate for breakfast, what it was really about was attacking the notion of the majestic impersonality of the judge, who was above politics. As Felix Frankfurter once put it, "as judges we are neither Jew nor Gentile, neither Catholic nor agnostic [and, presumably, neither Democrat nor Republican]. We owe equal attachment to the Constitution and are equally bound by our judicial obligations." Such claims were derided by realists like Yale law professor Fred Rodell, who viewed judges as no more than politicians in robes using legalistic mumbo-jumbo to write their politics into law. The argument has proceeded apace into the twenty-first century.

Almost everyone has accepted what might be termed a "soft" legal realism, one articulated by Frankfurter himself when he wrote in 1930 that "the controlling conceptions of the justices are their 'idealized political pictures' of the existing social order." Thus it is a commonplace to refer to "conservative" and "liberal" wings of the Supreme Court as a shorthand reference to two quite different pictures painted by the two sides in cases involving race relations, the autonomy of states, the death penalty and the like. Though judges are "political," the politics are "high" rather than "low"; that is, decisions are based on ideology rather than a simple desire to help out one's political friends in the short run.

Thus the legal attack on racial gerrymandering led by "conservative" judges probably favors the interests of the Democratic Party, while its defense by "liberal" judges probably enhances the power of the Republican Party (because it "packs" overwhelmingly Democratic black voters into relatively few Congressional districts). Ideology seems to be a better explanation of the two positions than a desire to maximize the interests of one or the other party.

The Court's decision in *Bush v. Gore*, however, seems an exercise in low rather than high politics. How can one take seriously the majority's claims that their award of the presidency to Bush is based on their deep concern for safeguarding the fundamental values of equality? This majority has been infamous in recent years for relentlessly defending states' rights against the invocation of national legal or constitutional norms. *Bush v. Gore* is all too easily explainable as the decision by five conservative Republicans—at least two of whom are eager to retire and be replaced by Republicans nominated by a Republican President—to assure the triumph of a fellow Republican who might not become President if Florida were left to its own legal process.

Of course, a consistent realist might point to tension between the generally nationalist, equality-protecting positions taken by the dissenters and their esteem in *Bush v. Gore* for state autonomy and, concomitantly, for the different standards being applied in various county recounts. It is decidedly "unrealist" to denounce one group of judges as behaving politically while praising another for simply following the "rule of law." Rodell or any other hard-core realist would deride any praise of the Florida

Supreme Court for its wisdom in construing the Florida statutes. Those judges, too, could easily be depicted as Democratic partisans manipulating the law to serve their political favorite, Al Gore.

Few Americans, however, and almost no law professors, embrace such a complete legal realism, even if they rightly accept its "softer," more ideologically oriented version. Full-scale realism leaves one without the ability to argue that legal arguments can be assessed by their conformity to norms that can be invoked, by judges and others, to discipline the vagaries of political choice. But a strong critique of the Court's opinion that presupposes that it indeed violated basic norms and "descended" into raw politics would violate the premise of an unabashedly "political" realism.

That "hard" realism has nihilistic overtones might explain why we resist it so strongly, but it does not constitute a genuine refutation of the position. It is a sign of the truly unprecedented nature of *Bush v. Gore* that many liberal law professors, who have spent much of their career asserting the reality of the rule of law (and of the Supreme Court as what Ronald Dworkin terms "the forum of principle," even if they sometimes disagree with particular principles enunciated by the Court), find themselves wondering if they can continue to do so. *Bush v. Gore* may have superficially resolved a short-run political crisis, but it has triggered the deepest intellectual crisis—at least for people who profess to take the law seriously—in decades.

NOTES AND QUESTIONS

1. *Taking realism seriously.* As noted, American legal realism is sometimes reduced to the aphorism that the result in a case depends on what the judge had for breakfast. *See* [Judge] Alex Kozinski, *What I Ate for Breakfast and Other Mysteries of Judicial Decision*, in JUDGES ON JUDGING 55 (O'Brien, ed. 1997). That radically oversimplifies Legal Realism, but one question persists: Can judges or advocates actually afford to be "realists"? After all, as an advocate you presumably cannot go into court and say, "Your Honor, you're a Republican, my client is a Republican too," and then sit down. What looks like hip analysis outside the courtroom may be shoddy advocacy within it, and a judge who justified her decisions on explicitly political grounds would likely be removed from office in a hurry. Does that mean that realism offers a seductive way of accounting for a tiny portion of cases, especially the highest-profile decisions, but offers an implausible account for the overwhelming majority of run-of-the-mill cases? Perhaps American legal realism is like Vitamin A: a little is essential for life, but too much of it is toxic. *Compare* Michael C. Dorf, *Is There a Distinction Between Law and Politics? Yes, and the Bush v. Gore Decision Proves It* (Dec. 27, 2000), at http://writ.news.findlaw.com/dorf/20001227.html ("If law were just politics, it would be meaningless to criticize a judicial decision as political, and all the Court's decisions would seem

equally 'political' to observers."). Is this why Sanford Levinson distinguishes between "hard" and "soft" realism?

2. *Bush v. Gore in context.* The political and academic reaction to *Bush v. Gore* was (and to some extent remains) explosive.

> Few cases in the Supreme Court's 200-plus year history have more deeply tested its institutional legitimacy than *Bush v. Gore*. In that historic decision, the Supreme Court intervened in the most closely contested presidential election of all time—a virtual dead heat—and essentially called the election by blocking a recount of votes in Florida. As a result, victory went to George W. Bush, who had lost the popular vote but, by virtue of his exceedingly narrow and hotly disputed victory before recount in Florida, had managed to eke out an Electoral College majority.

David Cole, *The Liberal Legacy of* Bush v. Gore, 94 GEO. L.J. 1427, 1427 (2006). On January 13, 2001, roughly one month after the decision was announced, over 500 law professors from more than 100 law schools took out a full-page advertisement in the *New York Times* arguing that the members of the Court had acted as "political proponents for candidate Bush, not as judges." *554 Law Professors Say*, N.Y. TIMES, Jan. 13, 2001, at A7. Professor David Strauss suggests that the U.S. Supreme Court acted to prevent judicial engineering of the election at the state level:

> What explains this extraordinary behavior by the Supreme Court? The most plausible hypothesis, I believe, is that several members of the United States Supreme Court were convinced that the Florida Supreme Court would try to give the election to Vice President Gore and would act improperly if necessary to accomplish that objective. The governing intuition was that the Florida Supreme Court had to be stopped from doing this. The majority's actions in the litigation show a relentless search for some reason that could be put forward to justify a decision reversing the Florida Supreme Court. The outcome was a foregone conclusion.

David A. Strauss, Bush v. Gore: *What Were They Thinking?*, 68 U. CHI. L. REV. 737,738 (2001).

Defenders of the decision, though less numerous, were forceful arguing that the Court's action was well-grounded in principle and precedent. *See, e.g.*, Nelson Lund, *The Unbearable Rightness of* Bush v. Gore, 23 CARDOZO L. REV. 1219 (2002); Ronald D. Rotunda, *Yet Another Article on* Bush v. Gore, 64 OHIO ST. L.J. 283 (2003). Justice Breyer himself noted in a public presentation that the basis for the case "isn't ideology and it isn't politics." Linda Greenhouse, *Election Case a Test and a Trauma for Supreme Court Justices*, N.Y. TIMES, Feb. 20, 2001, at A1.

3. *Distinguishing pretext from text.* In deciding whether you agree with Sanford Levinson's assessment of the decision or not, outline the legal arguments that distinguish the various concurrences in *Bush v. Gore* (*e.g.*, the circumstances under which the Supreme Court defers to state court

determinations of state law, the impact of equal protection considerations, the proper remedy), and consider whether any of them seem pretextual. (i) Does your analysis correlate with your own political preferences? (ii) Does the following chart, listing the justices that decided *Bush v. Gore*, support or undermine your conclusions? And if it is helpful, would it be equally helpful to know the political backgrounds of the judges on the Florida Supreme Court?

Justice	**Nominated by President (Year)**	**President's Party**
Rehnquist	Richard Nixon (1971)	Republican
Stevens	Gerald Ford (1975)	Republican
O'Connor	Ronald Reagan (1981)	Republican
Scalia	Ronald Reagan (1986)	Republican
Kennedy	Ronald Reagan (1987)	Republican
Souter	George H.W. Bush (1990)	Republican
Thomas	George H.W. Bush (1991)	Republican
Ginsburg	Bill Clinton (1993)	Democrat
Breyer	Bill Clinton (1994)	Democrat

4. *Beware any jurisprudence based exclusively on controversial Supreme Court cases.* Given that presidents appoint members of the Supreme Court and the Senate confirms them (or not), it cannot be terribly surprising that some turning points in the Supreme Court's jurisprudence can be criticized by the losers as "political," especially if they are decided by a closely divided court. From among the multiple examples of this phenomenon, consider the academic response to treatment by the Burger Court (1969–1986) of Warren Court (1953–1969) precedents in the field of criminal procedure. *See, e.g.*, Henry Monaghan, *Taking Supreme Court Opinions Seriously*, 39 MD. L. REV. 1, 3 (1979) ("[S]tare decisis has no weight when the constitutional law on a particular subject seems, to a majority of the Court, to be in need of correction."); G.R. Stone, *The Miranda Doctrine in the Burger Court*, 1977 SUP. CT. REV. 99, 169 ("In its unyielding determination to reach the desired result, the [Burger] Court has too often resorted to distortion of the record, disregard of the precedents, and an unwillingness honestly to explain or to justify its conclusions."); Note, Miranda *and the State Constitution: State Courts Take a Stand*, 39 VAND. L. REV. 1693, 1699 (1986) ("Few commentators * * * would disagree with charges * * * that the [Burger] Court's holdings on the constitutionality of law enforcement practices have departed from the spirit, if not the letter, of Warren Court precedents.").

(a) Why might it be reductionistic to base a jurisprudential approach to American law on the reality that politics affect the appointment and decision-making of Supreme Court justices?

(b) Even if those "turning point" decisions are in some measure political, are they for that reason alone illegitimate?

5. *Beware any jurisprudence based exclusively on the American common law.* There was a school of "Scandinavian Legal Realism" in the first third of the twentieth century, but it pre-dated the analysis of adjudication that gave American legal realism its unique identity. Scandinavian Legal Realism dealt more with "the distorting influence of metaphysics upon legal thinking," Jes Bjarup, *The Philosophy of Scandinavian Legal Realism*, 18 RATIO JURIS 1 (2005), than with how judges do or should decide the cases before them. It was theory in the service of supporting a scientific knowledge of law, *id.*, rather than denying that such knowledge is even a possibility.

But the question arises: how generalizable is American legal realism to other legal cultures and systems? The common law significantly empowers judges and lawyers, with the result that outside observers consider it a system in name only. Chaos (or, less dramatically, the inability accurately to predict actual results in cases) is not "law" to those in the code-based civil law tradition. Does a completely different conception of judging and lawyering undermine the generalizability of American legal realism? Is it necessary to understand comparative law in order to offer a compelling account of law generally?

6. *Separation of powers concerns.* In THE NATURE OF THE JUDICIAL PROCESS (1921), Benjamin Cardozo argued that the law is a powerful but malleable notion that allows (indeed requires) judges to give content to deliberately open-textured words in statutes or constitutions, and in the process to justify the outcome they wish. Does that effectively convert judges into an arm of the legislature, or is there a less pathological view of the two branches' distinct functions?

Consider the fact that terms like "restraint of trade" or "equal protection" are not self-defining and necessarily require interpretation: the legislature (or the framers of a Constitution) cannot possibly anticipate every problem that might arise in the future, so they must rely on a judiciary obliged to explain itself to the public whenever it applies the old words to new situations. No other branch of government has quite the same burden of explicit, public justification. The law as it is being drafted or promulgated goes through an intensely political drama. The American legal realists are suggesting among other things that the law as adopted does not necessarily stop being political at the moment of its enactment, as though a curtain came down on a political drama to be replaced by some determinate, bloodless process.

7. *Legal realism from the opposite end of the American political spectrum?* Consider the following case, which, like *Bush v. Gore*, marked a turning point in the political history of the United States. Is there any argument that it justifies the realists' skepticism?

BROWN V. BOARD OF EDUCATION

347 U.S. 483 (1954)

MR. CHIEF JUSTICE WARREN delivered the opinion of the Court. These cases come to us from the States of Kansas, South Carolina, Virginia, and Delaware. They are premised on different facts and different local conditions, but a common legal question justifies their consideration together in this consolidated opinion. * * * In each of the cases, minors of the Negro race, through their legal representatives, seek the aid of the courts in obtaining admission to the public schools of their community on a non-segregated basis. In each instance, they have been denied admission to schools attended by white children under laws requiring or permitting segregation according to race. This segregation was alleged to deprive the plaintiffs of the equal protection of the laws under the Fourteenth Amendment. In each of the cases other than the Delaware case, a three-judge federal district court denied relief to the plaintiffs on the so-called "separate but equal" doctrine announced by this Court in *Plessy v. Ferguson*, 163 U.S. 537 [(1896)]. Under that doctrine, equality of treatment is accorded when the races are provided substantially equal facilities, even though these facilities be separate. In the Delaware case, the Supreme Court of Delaware adhered to that doctrine, but ordered that the plaintiffs be admitted to the white schools because of their superiority to the Negro schools.

The plaintiffs contend that segregated public schools are not "equal" and cannot be made "equal," and that hence they are deprived of the equal protection of the laws. Because of the obvious importance of the question presented, the Court took jurisdiction. Argument was heard in the 1952 Term, and reargument was heard this Term on certain questions propounded by the Court.

Reargument was largely devoted to the circumstances surrounding the adoption of the Fourteenth Amendment in 1868. It covered exhaustively consideration of the Amendment in Congress, ratification by the states, then existing practices in racial segregation, and the views of proponents and opponents of the Amendment. This discussion and our own investigation convince us that, although these sources cast some light, it is not enough to resolve the problem with which we are faced. At best, they are inconclusive. The most avid proponents of the post-War Amendments undoubtedly intended them to remove all legal distinctions among "all persons born or naturalized in the United States." Their opponents, just as certainly, were antagonistic to both the letter and the spirit of the Amendments and wished them to have the most limited effect. What others in Congress and the state legislatures had in mind cannot be determined with any degree of certainty.

An additional reason for the inconclusive nature of the Amendment's history, with respect to segregated schools, is the status of public education at that time.[4] In the South, the movement toward free common schools, supported by general taxation, had not yet taken hold. Education of white children was largely in the hands of private groups. Education of Negroes was almost nonexistent, and practically all of the race were illiterate. In fact, any education of Negroes was forbidden by law in some states. Today, in contrast, many Negroes have achieved outstanding success in the arts and sciences as well as in the business and professional world. It is true that public school education at the time of the Amendment had advanced further in the North, but the effect of the Amendment on Northern States was generally ignored in the congressional debates. Even in the North, the conditions of public education did not approximate those existing today. The curriculum was usually rudimentary; ungraded schools were common in rural areas; the school term was but three months a year in many states; and compulsory school attendance was virtually unknown. As a consequence, it is not surprising that there should be so little in the history of the Fourteenth Amendment relating to its intended effect on public education.

In the first cases in this Court construing the Fourteenth Amendment, decided shortly after its adoption, the Court interpreted it as proscribing all state-imposed discriminations against the Negro race.[5] The doctrine of "separate but equal" did not make its appearance in this court until 1896 in the case of *Plessy v. Ferguson*, *supra*, involving not education but

[4] For a general study of the development of public education prior to the Amendment, *see* BUTTS AND CREMIN, A HISTORY OF EDUCATION IN AMERICAN CULTURE (1953), Pts. I, II: CUBBERLEY, PUBLIC EDUCATION IN THE UNITED STATES (1934 ed.), cc. II-XII. School practices current at the time of the adoption of the Fourteenth Amendment are described in BUTTS AND CREMIN, *supra*, at 269–275; CUBBERLEY, *supra*, at 288–339, 408–431; KNIGHT, PUBLIC EDUCATION IN THE SOUTH (1922), cc. VIII, IX. See also H. Ex. Doc. No. 315, 41st Cong., 2d Sess. (1871). Although the demand for free public schools followed substantially the same pattern in both the North and the South, the development in the South did not begin to gain momentum until about 1850, some twenty years after that in the North. The reasons for the somewhat slower development in the South (*e.g.*, the rural character of the South and the different regional attitudes toward state assistance) are well explained in CUBBERLEY, *supra*, at 408–423. In the country as a whole, but particularly in the South, the War virtually stopped all progress in public education. Id., at 427–428. The low status of Negro education in all sections of the country, both before and immediately after the War, is described in BEALE, A HISTORY OF FREEDOM OF TEACHING IN AMERICAN SCHOOLS (1941), 112–132, 175–195. Compulsory school attendance laws were not generally adopted until after the ratification of the Fourteenth Amendment, and it was not until 1918 that such laws were in force in all the states. CUBBERLEY, supra, at 563–565.

[5] *In re Slaughter-House Cases*, 1873, 16 Wall. 36, 67–72; *Strauder v. West Virginia*, 1880, 100 U.S. 303, 307–308. "It ordains that no State shall deprive any person of life, liberty, or property, without due process of law, or deny to any person within its jurisdiction the equal protection of the laws. What is this but declaring that the law in the States shall be the same for the black as for the white; that all persons, whether colored or white, shall stand equal before the laws of the States, and, in regard to the colored race, for whose protection the amendment was primarily designed, that no discrimination shall be made against them by law because of their color? The words of the amendment, it is true, are prohibitory, but they contain a necessary implication of a positive immunity, or right, most valuable to the colored race, the right to exemption from unfriendly legislation against them distinctively as colored, exemption from legal discriminations, implying inferiority in civil society, lessening the security of their enjoyment of the rights which others enjoy, and discriminations which are steps towards reducing them to the condition of a subject race." *See also State of Virginia v. Rives*, 1879, 100 U.S. 313, 318; *Ex parte Virginia*, 1879, 100 U.S. 339, 344–345.

transportation.[6] American courts have since labored with the doctrine for over half a century. In this Court, there have been six cases involving the 'separate but equal' doctrine in the field of public education. In *Cumming v. Board of Education of Richmond County*, 175 U.S. 528, and *Gong Lum v. Rice*, 275 U.S. 78, the validity of the doctrine itself was not challenged.[8] In more recent cases, all on the graduate school level, inequality was found in that specific benefits enjoyed by white students were denied to Negro students of the same educational qualifications. *State of Missouri ex rel. Gaines v. Canada*, 305 U.S. 337; *Sipuel v. Board of Regents of University of Oklahoma*, 332 U.S. 631; *Sweatt v. Painter*, 339 U.S. 629; *McLaurin v. Oklahoma State Regents*, 339 U.S. 637. In none of these cases was it necessary to reexamine the doctrine to grant relief to the Negro plaintiff. And in *Sweatt v. Painter, supra*, the Court expressly reserved decision on the question whether *Plessy v. Ferguson* should be held inapplicable to public education.

In the instant cases, that question is directly presented. Here, unlike *Sweatt v. Painter*, there are findings below that the Negro and white schools involved have been equalized, or are being equalized, with respect to buildings, curricula, qualifications and salaries of teachers, and other "tangible" factors.[9] Our decision, therefore, cannot turn on merely a comparison of these tangible factors in the Negro and white schools involved in each of the cases. We must look instead to the effect of segregation itself on public education.

In approaching this problem, we cannot turn the clock back to 1868 when the Amendment was adopted, or even to 1896 when *Plessy v. Ferguson* was written. We must consider public education in the light of its full development and its present place in American life throughout the Nation. Only in this way can it be determined if segregation in public schools deprives these plaintiffs of the equal protection of the laws.

---

[6] The doctrine apparently originated in *Roberts v. City of Boston*, 1850, 5 Cush. 198, 59 Mass. 198, 206, upholding school segregation against attack as being violative of a state constitutional guarantee of equality. Segregation in Boston public schools was eliminated in 1855. Mass. Acts 1855, c. 256. But elsewhere in the North segregation in public education has persisted in some communities until recent years. It is apparent that such segregation has long been a nationwide problem, not merely one of sectional concern.

[8] In the *Cumming* case, Negro taxpayers sought an injunction requiring the defendant school board to discontinue the operation of a high school for white children until the board resumed operation of a high school for Negro children. Similarly, in the *Gong Lum* case, the plaintiff, a child of Chinese descent, contended only that state authorities had misapplied the doctrine by classifying him with Negro children and requiring him to attend a Negro school.

[9] In the Kansas case, the court below found substantial equality as to all such factors. 98 F.Supp. 797, 798. In the South Carolina case, the court below found that the defendants were proceeding 'promptly and in good faith to comply with the court's decree.' 103 F.Supp. 920, 921. In the Virginia case, the court below noted that the equalization program was already 'afoot and progressing,' 103 F. Supp. 337, 341; since then, we have been advised, in the Virginia Attorney General's brief on reargument, that the program has now been completed. In the Delaware case, the court below similarly noted that the state's equalization program was well under way. 91 A.2d 137, 139.

Today, education is perhaps the most important function of state and local governments. Compulsory school attendance laws and the great expenditures for education both demonstrate our recognition of the importance of education to our democratic society. It is required in the performance of our most basic public responsibilities, even service in the armed forces. It is the very foundation of good citizenship. Today it is a principal instrument in awakening the child to cultural values, in preparing him for later professional training, and in helping him to adjust normally to his environment. In these days, it is doubtful that any child may reasonably be expected to succeed in life if he is denied the opportunity of an education. Such an opportunity, where the state has undertaken to provide it, is a right which must be made available to all on equal terms.

We come then to the question presented: Does segregation of children in public schools solely on the basis of race, even though the physical facilities and other "tangible" factors may be equal, deprive the children of the minority group of equal educational opportunities? We believe that it does.

In *Sweatt v. Painter, supra*, in finding that a segregated law school for Negroes could not provide them equal educational opportunities, this Court relied in large part on "those qualities which are incapable of objective measurement but which make for greatness in a law school." In *McLaurin v. Oklahoma State Regents, supra* the Court, in requiring that a Negro admitted to a white graduate school be treated like all other students, again resorted to intangible considerations: '* * * his ability to study, to engage in discussions and exchange views with other students, and, in general, to learn his profession.' Such considerations apply with added force to children in grade and high schools. To separate them from others of similar age and qualifications solely because of their race generates a feeling of inferiority as to their status in the community that may affect their hearts and minds in a way unlikely ever to be undone. The effect of this separation on their educational opportunities was well stated by a finding in the Kansas case by a court which nevertheless felt compelled to rule against the Negro plaintiffs:

> Segregation of white and colored children in public schools has a detrimental effect upon the colored children. The impact is greater when it has the sanction of the law; for the policy of separating the races is usually interpreted as denoting the inferiority of the negro group. A sense of inferiority affects the motivation of a child to learn. Segregation with the sanction of law, therefore, has a tendency to [retard] the educational and mental development of Negro children and to deprive them of some of the benefits they would receive in a racial[ly] integrated school system.[10]

[10] A similar finding was made in the Delaware case: 'I conclude from the testimony that in our Delaware society, State-imposed segregation in education itself results in the Negro children,

Whatever may have been the extent of psychological knowledge at the time of *Plessy v. Ferguson*, this finding is amply supported by modern authority.[11] Any language in *Plessy v. Ferguson* contrary to this finding is rejected.

We conclude that in the field of public education the doctrine of "separate but equal" has no place. Separate educational facilities are inherently unequal. Therefore, we hold that the plaintiffs and others similarly situated for whom the actions have been brought are, by reason of the segregation complained of, deprived of the equal protection of the laws guaranteed by the Fourteenth Amendment. This disposition makes unnecessary any discussion whether such segregation also violates the Due Process Clause of the Fourteenth Amendment.

Because these are class actions, because of the wide applicability of this decision, and because of the great variety of local conditions, the formulation of decrees in these cases presents problems of considerable complexity. On reargument, the consideration of appropriate relief was necessarily subordinated to the primary question—the constitutionality of segregation in public education. We have now announced that such segregation is a denial of the equal protection of the laws. In order that we may have the full assistance of the parties in formulating decrees, the cases will be restored to the docket, and the parties are requested to present further argument on Questions 4 and 5 previously propounded by the Court for the reargument this Term.[13] * * * It is so ordered.

---

as a class, receiving educational opportunities which are substantially inferior to those available to white children otherwise similarly situated.' 87 A.2d 862, 865.

[11] K. B. Clark, Effect of Prejudice and Discrimination on Personality Development (Midcentury White House Conference on Children and Youth, 1950); Witmer and Kotinsky, Personality in the Making (1952), c. VI; Deutscher and Chein, *The Psychological Effects of Enforced Segregation: A Survey of Social Science Opinion*, 26 J. Psychol. 259 (1948); Chein, *What are the Psychological Effects of Segregation Under Conditions of Equal Facilities?*, 3 Int. J. Opinion and Attitude Res. 229 (1949); Brameld, Educational Costs, in Discrimination and National Welfare (MacIver, ed., 1949), 44–48; Frazier, The Negro in the United States (1949), 674–681. And *see generally* Myrdal, An American Dilemma (1944).

[13] "4. Assuming it is decided that segregation in public schools violates the Fourteenth Amendment

"(a) would a decree necessarily follow providing that, within the limits set by normal geographic school districting, Negro children should forthwith be admitted to schools of their choice, or

"(b) may this Court, in the exercise of its equity powers, permit an effective gradual adjustment to be brought about from existing segregated systems to a system not based on color distinctions?

"5. On the assumption on which questions 4(a) and (b) are based, and assuming further that this Court will exercise its equity powers to the end described in question 4(b),

"(a) should this Court formulate detailed decrees in these cases;

"(b) if so, what specific issues should the decrees reach;

"(c) should this Court appoint a special master to hear evidence with a view to recommending specific terms for such decrees;

"(d) should this Court remand to the courts of first instance with directions to frame decrees in these cases, and if so what general directions should the decrees of this Court

---

HERBERT WECHSLER, *TOWARD NEUTRAL PRINCIPLES OF CONSTITUTIONAL LAW*

73 HARV. L. REV. 1, 31–35 (1959)

* * * I come to the school decision [*Brown v. Board of Education*], which for one of my persuasion stirs the deepest conflict I experience in testing the thesis I propose. * * * The problem for me, I hardly need to say, is not that the Court departed from its earlier decisions holding or implying that the equality of public educational facilities demanded by the Constitution could be met by separate schools. I stand with the long tradition of the Court that previous decisions must be subject to reexamination when a case against their reasoning is made. Nor is the problem that the Court disturbed the settled patterns of a portion of the country; even that must be accepted as a lesser evil than nullification of the Constitution. Nor is it that history does not confirm that an agreed purpose of the fourteenth amendment was to forbid separate schools or that there is important evidence that many thought the contrary; the words are general and leave room for expanding content as time passes and conditions change. Nor is it that the Court may have miscalculated the extent to which its judgment would be honored or accepted; it is not a prophet of the strength of our national commitment to respect the judgments of the courts. Nor is it even that the Court did not remit the issue to the Congress, acting under the enforcement clause of the amendment. * * *

The problem inheres strictly in the reasoning of the opinion, an opinion which is often read with less fidelity by those who praise it than by those by whom it is condemned. The Court did not declare, as many wish it had, that the fourteenth amendment forbids all racial lines in legislation, though subsequent *per curiam* decisions may * * * now go that far. Rather, as Judge Hand observed, the separate-but-equal formula was not overruled "in form" but was held to have "no place" in public education on the ground that segregated schools are "inherently unequal," with deleterious effects upon the colored children in implying their inferiority, effects which retard their educational and mental development. So, indeed, the district court had found as a fact in the Kansas case, a finding which the Supreme Court embraced, citing some further "modern authority" in its support.

Does the validity of the decision turn then on the sufficiency of evidence or of judicial notice to sustain a finding that the separation harms the Negro children who may be involved? There were, indeed, some witnesses who expressed that opinion in the Kansas case, as there were

---

include and what procedures should the courts of first instance follow in arriving at the specific terms of more detailed decrees?"

also witnesses in the companion Virginia case, * * * whose view was to the contrary. Much depended on the question that the witness had in mind, which rarely was explicit. Was he comparing the position of the Negro child in a segregated school with his position in an integrated school where he was happily accepted and regarded by the whites; or was he comparing his position under separation with that under integration where the whites were hostile to his presence and found ways to make their feelings known? And if the harm that segregation worked was relevant, what of the benefits that it entailed: sense of security, the absence of hostility? Were they irrelevant? Moreover, was the finding in Topeka applicable without more to Clarendon County, South Carolina, with 2,799 colored students and only 295 whites? Suppose that more Negroes in a community preferred separation than opposed it? Would that be relevant to whether they were hurt or aided by segregation as opposed to integration? Their fates would be governed by the change of system quite as fully as those of the students who complained.

I find it hard to think the judgment really turned upon the facts. Rather, it seems to me, it must have rested on the view that racial segregation is, in principle, a denial of equality to the minority against whom it is directed; that is, the group that is not dominant politically and, therefore, does not make the choice involved. For many who support the Court's decision this assuredly is the decisive ground. But this position also presents problems. Does it not involve an inquiry into the motive of the legislature, which is generally foreclosed to the courts? Is it alternatively defensible to make the measure of validity of legislation the way it is interpreted by those who are affected by it? In the context of a charge that segregation *with equal facilities* is a denial of equality, is there not a point in *Plessy* in the statement that if "enforced separation stamps the colored race with a badge of inferiority" it is solely because its members choose "to put that construction upon it"? [(quoting from *Plessy v. Ferguson*, 163 U.S. 537, 551 (1896))]. Does enforced separation of the sexes discriminate against females merely because it may be the females who resent it and it is imposed by judgments predominantly male? Is a prohibition of miscegenation a discrimination against the colored member of the couple who would like to marry?

For me, assuming equal facilities, the question posed by state-enforced segregation is not one of discrimination at all. Its human and its constitutional dimensions lie entirely elsewhere, in the denial by the state of freedom to associate, a denial that impinges in the same way on any groups or races that may be involved. I think, and I hope not without foundation, that the Southern white also pays heavily for segregation, not only in the sense of guilt that he must carry but also in the benefits he is denied. In the days when I was joined with Charles H. Houston in a litigation in the Supreme Court, before the present building was constructed, he did not suffer more than I in knowing that we had to go to

Union Station to lunch together during the recess. Does not the problem of miscegenation show most clearly that it is the freedom of association that at bottom is involved, the only case, I may add, where it is implicit in the situation that association is desired by the only individuals involved? * * *

But if the freedom of association is denied by segregation, integration forces an association upon those for whom it is unpleasant or repugnant. Is this not the heart of the issue involved, a conflict in human claims of high dimension, not unlike many others that involve the highest freedoms * * *. Given a situation where the state must practically choose between denying the association to those individuals who wish it or imposing it on those who would avoid it, is there a basis in neutral principles for holding that the Constitution demands that the claims for association should prevail? I should like to think there is, but I confess that I have not yet written the opinion. To write it is for me the challenge of the school-segregation cases.

Having said what I have said, I certainly should add that I offer no comfort to anyone who claims legitimacy in defiance of the courts. This is the ultimate negation of all neutral principles, to take the benefits accorded by the constitutional system, including the national market and common defense, while denying it allegiance when a special burden is imposed. That certainly is the antithesis of law.

I am confident I have said much with which you disagree—both in my basic premises and in conclusions I have drawn. The most that I can hope is that the effort be considered worthy of a rostrum dedicated to the memory of Mr. Justice Holmes. Transcending all the lessons that he teaches through the years, the most important one for me has come to this: Those of us to whom it is not given to "live greatly in the law" are surely called upon to fail in the attempt.

NOTES AND QUESTIONS

1. *Narrowing the point of disagreement*. According to Wechsler, in what respect was *Brown not* based on neutral principles? If you wanted to push back on Wechsler's critique, would it matter that *Brown*—unlike *Bush v. Gore*—was a unanimous decision or that it is now generally viewed in retrospect as one of the Supreme Court's finest decisions?

2. *Legal realism and legal reform of the marketplace*. Many of the Legal Realists considered law to be a legitimate form of social engineering, and they brought their skepticism to bear in order to support reformist, progressive policy programs. Karl Llewellyn for example, whose work is excerpted below, was instrumental in the drafting of the Uniform Commercial Code, now considered one of the backbones of establishment legal practice. Many of the

programs in the New Deal grew out of the analysis of legal realists on law faculties across the country:

> The legal realists criticized the idea of a self-regulating market system which was immune from state involvement or control. They challenged the classical period's careful distinction between public and private spheres. The realists asserted that state and society could not be completely separated either logically or experientially. Once the state had been created, it altered (or was intended to alter) the distribution of power and wealth in society. Indeed, the whole purpose of legal rights was to impose collective limits on individuals' freedom of action in order to protect the interests of others. Moreover, even by failing to intervene in 'private' transactions, the state effectively altered contract relations; it delegated to the more powerful party the freedom to exercise her superior power or knowledge over the weaker party. Thus, the state determined the distribution of power and wealth in society both when it acted to limit freedom and when it failed to limit the freedom of some to dominate others.
>
> From this perspective, a free market system could not be distinguished in a significant sense from a regulatory system. All market systems distribute power, and thus constitute regulatory systems. The rules in force have the effect of privileging the interests of some persons over the interests of others. It is impossible for a legal system not to so distribute power and wealth. Any definition of property and contract rights necessarily requires the state to determine the character of relations among citizens in the marketplace. For the realists, the important questions were not how to define the limits of state power or the boundaries of a private realm beyond state power, but instead, whose interests market regulations should protect, and what distribution of power the rules in force should foster.

Joseph Singer, *Legal Realism Now,* 76 CAL. L. REV. 465, 482 (1988).

3. *Legal realism and totalitarianism*. Some scholars have argued that the relativism at the core of American legal realism was connected at least coincidentally to the rise of fascism and totalitarianism in the world in the 1930's. The critique rested on an asserted link to these broad political developments from realism's precepts that law was essentially a "marker" for power, that there was no necessary moral content to law, and that rules were largely illusory. *See, e.g.*, Neil Duxbury, *Jerome Frank and the Legacy of Legal Realism*, 18 J.L. & SOC'Y 175, 179 (1991) ("Quite simply, realists suddenly found themselves charged with offering an apologia for totalitarianism.")

> By denying any relationships between law and moral principles, [critics] argued, Realism was "prepar[ing] the intellectual ground for a tendency toward totalitarianism." In the face of this attack, some Realists, including Llewellyn and Frank, sought to modify their early

> views on the place of moral values in the law. By 1940 Llewellyn was "ready to do open penance" for suggesting that "the heart and core of Jurisprudence" could be determined empirically; it was related to ethical values and purposes. Frank ultimately came to affirm "the fundamental principles of Natural Law" as the basis of modern civilization.

G. Edward White, *From Sociological Jurisprudence to Realism: Jurisprudence and Social Change in Early Twentieth-Century America*, 58 VA. L. REV. 999, 1027 (1972) (citations omitted). *See generally*, WILLIAM ESKRIDGE ET AL., HART & SACKS' THE LEGAL PROCESS: BASIC PROBLEMS IN THE MAKING AND APPLICATION OF LAW (1994), at lxv.

Another, perhaps less feverish account would see in American legal realism the jurisprudential expression of a then-decades old radical change in the assumptions about the knowability of the world generally. Objectivity and determinism were under attack across the intellectual landscape, especially in physics with the Heisenberg Uncertainty Principle, in mathematics with Godel's incompleteness theorems, and across the arts. The rise of totalitarianism in short—to the extent that it had roots in any coherent intellectual "school" at all—was almost entirely separate from the jurisprudential fashion surrounding progressive and reformist energy in the United States.

4. *Fact skepticism versus rule skepticism*. In order to appreciate some of the distinctions among the different streams of American legal realism, it is important to distinguish fact skepticism from rule skepticism. In general terms, *fact skepticism* advances fundamental doubt about the ability of any judge or jury to determine the facts that are material to the resolution of disputes. Instead, the finder-of-fact sifts through various, sometimes contradictory accounts, and determines what happened for purposes of the case. That is a functional truth—"truthiness"—rather than a complete understanding of precisely what happened. From this perspective, the law in a case turns on a prevailing narrative offered by opposing advocates zealously representing their clients' interests, rather than on hard facts as might be established outside the courtroom. Indeed, this skepticism is a direct and systematic challenge to the very idea of hard facts, even as its proponents acknowledge the institutional necessity of some "black box," a way to determine what happened sufficiently to resolve the case. A fact skeptic conceives of the judging function in radically expansive ways and traces the resolution of a case to the power of a judge to resolve it by finding facts, sometimes simultaneously with, but not necessarily prior to, finding an applicable rule. The applicable rule after all will probably determine which facts are pertinent to find in the first place.

By contrast, *rule skepticism* is a form of doubt that judges are meaningfully constrained by legal rules when they resolve disputed cases. Advocates and judges alike are able to draw on competing rules requiring different, maybe even opposite results, and both sets of rules can be articulated with sufficient precision and pedigree to satisfy whatever demands there might be for consistency and authority. The picking of a dispositive rule in any given case is determined by some amalgam of reason, hunches, predispositions, intuitions, and other factors they do not teach you (or teach you about) in law school. From that perspective, rule-based justifications are always and irreducibly personal and inferential, even if they are expressed in seemingly deductive and historical terms.

Thinking now as a rule- or fact-skeptic, what is the argument that American legal realism offers an attractive if not compelling account of *Bush v. Gore* and/or *Brown v. Board of Education*?

Readings

OLIVER WENDELL HOLMES, *PATH OF THE LAW*

10 HARV. L. REV. 457, 459–461 (1897)

* * * If you want to know the law and nothing else, you must look at it as a bad man, who cares only for the material consequences which such knowledge enables him to predict, not as a good one, who finds his reasons for conduct, whether inside the law or outside of it, in the vaguer sanctions of conscience. * * * Take the fundamental question, What constitutes the law? You will find some text writers telling you that it is something different from what is decided by the courts of Massachusetts or England, that it is a system of reason, that it is a deduction from principles of ethics or admitted axioms or what not, which may or may not coincide with the decisions. But if we take the view of our friend the bad man we shall find that he does not care two straws for the axioms or deductions, but that he does want to know what the Massachusetts or English courts are likely to do in fact. I am much of his mind. *The prophecies of what the courts will do in fact, and nothing more pretentious, are what I mean by the law.*

KARL N. LLEWELLYN, *SOME REALISM ABOUT REALISM—RESPONDING TO DEAN POUND*

44 HARV. L. REV. 1222, 1233–1238 (1931)

* * * One thing is clear. There is no school of realists. There is no likelihood that there will be such a school. There is no group with an official or accepted, or even with an emerging creed. There is no abnegation of independent striking out. We hope that there may never be. New recruits acquire tools and stimulus, not masters, nor over-mastering ideas. Old recruits diverge in interests from each other. They are related, says [Jerome] Frank, only in their negations, and in their skepticisms, and in their curiosity.

There is, however, a *movement* in thought and work about law. The movement, the method of attack, is wider than the number of its adherents. It includes some or much work of many men who would scorn ascription to its banner. * * * Men more or less interstimulated—but no more than all of them have been stimulated by the orthodox tradition, or by that ferment at the opening of the century in which Dean Pound took a leading part. Individual men, working and thinking over law and its place in society. Their differences in point of view, in interest, in emphasis, in field of work, are huge. They differ among themselves well-nigh as much as any of them differs from, say, Langdell. Their number grows. Their work finds acceptance.

What one does find as he observes them is twofold. First (and to be expected) certain points of departure are common to them all. Second (and this, when one can find neither school nor striking likenesses among individuals, is startling) a cross-relevance, a complementing, an interlocking of their varied results "as if they were guided by an invisible hand." A third thing may be mentioned in passing: a fighting faith in their methods of attack on legal problems; but in these last years the battle with the facts has proved so much more exciting than any battle with traditionalism that the fighting faith had come * * * to manifest itself chiefly in enthusiastic labor to get on.

But as with a description of an economic order, tone and color of description must vary with the point of view of the reporter. No other one of the men would set the picture up as I shall. * * * Each man, of necessity, orients the whole to his own main interest of the moment—as I shall orient the whole to mine: the workings of case-law in appellate courts. Maps of the United States prepared respectively by a political geographer and a student of climate would show some resemblance; each would show a coherent picture; but neither's map would give much satisfaction to the other. So here. I speak for myself of that movement which in its sum is realism; I do not speak of "the realists"; still less do I speak *for* the participants or any of them. And I shall endeavor to keep in mind as I go that the justification for grouping these men together lies not in that they are *alike* in belief or work, but in that from certain common points of departure they have branched into lines of work which seem to be building themselves into a whole, a whole planned by none, foreseen by none, and (it may well be) not yet adequately grasped by any.

The common points of departure are several.

(1) The conception of law in flux, of moving law, and of judicial creation of law.

(2) The conception of law as a means to social ends and not as an end in itself; so that any part needs constantly to be examined for its purpose, and for its effect, and to be judged in the light of both and of their relation to each other.

(3) The conception of society in flux, and in flux typically faster than the law, so that the probability is always given that any portion of law needs reexamination to determine how far it fits the society it purports to serve.

(4) The *temporary* divorce of Is and Ought for purposes of study. By this I mean that whereas value judgments must always be appealed to in order to set objectives for inquiry, yet during the inquiry itself into what Is, the observation, the description, and the establishment of relations between the things described are to remain *as largely as possible* uncontaminated by the desires of the observer or by what he wishes might be or thinks ought (ethically) to be. More particularly, this involves during the study of what courts are doing the effort to disregard the question what they ought to do. Such divorce of Is and Ought is, of course, not conceived as permanent. To men who begin with a suspicion that change is needed, a permanent divorce would be impossible. The argument is simply that no judgment of what Ought to be done in the future with respect to any part of law can be intelligently made without knowing objectively, as far as possible, what that part of law is now doing. And realists believe that experience shows the intrusion of Ought-spectacles *during the investigation of the facts* to make it very difficult to see what is being done. On the Ought side this means an insistence on informed evaluations instead of armchair speculations. Its full implications on the side of Is-investigation can be appreciated only when one follows the contributions to objective description in business law and practice made by realists whose social philosophy rejects many of the accepted foundations of the existing economic order. * * *

(5) Distrust of traditional legal rules and concepts insofar as they purport to *describe* what either courts or people are actually doing. Hence the constant emphasis on rules as "generalized predictions of what courts will do." This is much more widespread as yet than its counterpart: the careful severance of rules *for* doing (precepts) from rules *of* doing (practices).

(6) Hand in hand with this distrust of traditional rules (on the descriptive side) goes a distrust of the theory that traditional prescriptive rule-formulations are *the* heavily operative factor in producing court decisions. This involves the tentative adoption of the theory of rationalization for the study of opinions. It will be noted that "distrust" in this and the preceding point is not at all equivalent to "negation in any given instance."

(7) The belief in the worthwhileness of grouping cases and legal situations into narrower categories than has been the practice in the past. This is connected with the distrust of verbally simple rules—which so often cover dissimilar and non-simple fact situations (dissimilarity being tested partly by the way cases come out, and partly by the observer's judgment as

to how they ought to come out; but a realist tries to indicate explicitly which criterion he is applying).

(8) An insistence on evaluation of any part of law in terms of its effects, and an insistence on the worthwhileness of trying to find these effects.

(9) Insistence on *sustained and programmatic attack* on the problems of law along any of these lines. None of the ideas set forth in this list is new. Each can be matched from somewhere; each can be matched from recent orthodox work in law. New twists and combinations do appear here and there. What is as novel as it is vital is for a goodly number of men to pick up ideas which have been expressed and dropped, used for an hour and dropped, played with from time to time and dropped—to pick up such idea and set about *consistently, persistently, insistently to carry them through.* Grant that the idea or point of view is familiar—the results of steady, sustained, systematic work with it are not familiar. Not hit-or-miss stuff, not the insight which flashes and is forgotten, but sustained effort to force an old insight into its full bearing, to exploit it to the point where it laps over upon an apparently inconsistent insight, to explore their bearing on each other by the test of fact. This urge, in law, is quite new enough over the last decades to excuse a touch of frenzy among the locust-eaters.[37] * * *

Bound, as all "innovators" are, by prior thinking, these innovating "realists" brought their batteries to bear in first instance on the work of appellate courts. Still wholly within the tradition of our law, they strove to improve on that tradition.

(a) An early and fruitful line of attack borrowed from psychology the concept of *rationalization* already mentioned. To recanvass the opinions, viewing them no longer as mirroring the process of deciding cases, but rather as trained lawyers' arguments made by the judges (after the decision has been reached), intended to make the decision seem plausible, legally decent, legally right, to make it seem, indeed, legally inevitable—this was to open up new vision. It was assumed that the deductive logic of opinions need by no means be either a *description* of the process of decision, or an *explanation* of how the decision was reached. Indeed over-enthusiasm has at times assumed that the logic of the opinion *could* be neither; and similar over-enthusiasm, perceiving case after case in which the opinion is clearly almost valueless as an indication of how that case came to decision, has worked at times almost as if the opinion were equally valueless in predicting what a later court will do.

But the line of inquiry via rationalization has come close to demonstrating that in any case doubtful enough to make litigation

---

[37] Since everyone who reads the manuscript in this sad age finds this allusion blind, but I still like it, I insert the passage: ". . . Preaching in the wilderness of Judea, And saying, Repent ye . . . . And the same John had his raiment of camel's hair, and a leathern girdle about his loins; *and his meat was locusts* and wild honey." Matthew III, 1, 2, 4.

respectable the available authoritative premises—*i.e.*, premises legitimate and impeccable under the traditional legal techniques—are at least two, and that the two are mutually contradictory as applied to the case in hand. Which opens the question of what made the court select the one available premise rather than the other. And which raises the greatest of doubts as to *how far* that supposed certainty in decision which derives merely from the presence of accepted rules really goes.

(b) A second line of attack has been to discriminate among rules with reference to their relative significance. Too much is written and thought about "law" and "rules," lump-wise. Which part of law? Which rule? Iron rules of policy, and rules "in the absence of agreement"; rules which keep a case from the jury, and rules as to the etiquette of instructions necessary to make a verdict stick—if one can get it; rules "of pure decision" for hospital cases, and rules which counsellors rely on in their counselling; rules which affect many (and which many, and how?) and rules which affect few. Such discriminations affect the traditional law curriculum, the traditional organization of law books and, above all, the orientation of study: to drive into the most important fields of ignorance.

(c) A further line of attack on the apparent conflict and uncertainty among the decisions in appellate courts has been to seek more understandable statement of them by grouping the facts in new—and typically but not always narrower—categories. The search is for correlations of fact-situation and outcome which (aided by common sense) may reveal *when* courts seize on one rather than another of the available competing premises. One may even stumble on the trail of *why* they do. Perhaps, *e.g.*, third party beneficiary difficulties simply fail to get applied to promises to make provision for dependents; perhaps the preexisting duty rule goes by the board when the agreement is one for a marriage-settlement. Perhaps, indeed, contracts in what we may broadly call family relations do not work out in general as they do in business. If so, the rules—viewed as statements of the course of judicial behavior—as *predictions* of what will happen—need to be restated. Sometimes it is a question of carving out hitherto unnoticed exceptions. But sometimes the results force the worker to reclassify an area altogether. Typically, as stated, the classes of situations which result are narrower, much narrower than the traditional classes. The process is in essence the orthodox technique of making distinctions, and reformulating—but undertaken systematically; exploited consciously, instead of being reserved until facts which refuse to be twisted by "interpretation" force action. The departure from orthodox procedure lies chiefly in distrust of, instead of search for, the widest sweep of generalization words permit. Not that such sweeping generalizations are not desired—*if they can be made so as to state what judges do.*

All of these three earliest lines of attack converge to a single conclusion: *there is less possibility of accurate prediction of what courts will* *do than the traditional rules would lead us to suppose* (and what possibility there is must be found in good measure outside these same traditional rules). The particular kind of certainty that men have thus far thought to find in law is in good measure an illusion. Realistic workers have sometimes insisted on this truth so hard that they have been thought pleased with it. (The danger lies close, for one thinking indiscriminately of Is and Ought, to suspect announcements of fact to reflect preferences, ethically normative judgments, on the part of those who do the announcing.) * * *

The immediate result of the preliminary work thus far described has been a further, varied series of endeavors; *the focussing of conscious attack on discovering the factors thus far unpredictable, in good part with a view to their control.* Not wholly with a view to such elimination; part of the conscious attack is directed to finding where and when and how far *un*certainty has value. Much of what has been taken as insistence on the exclusive significance of the particular (with supposed implicit denial of the existence of valid or apposite generalizations) represents in fact a clearing of the ground for such attack. Close study of particular unpredictables may lessen unpredictability. It may increase the value of what remains. It certainly makes clearer what the present situation is. * * *

(i) There is the question of the personality of the judge. (Little has as yet been attempted in study of the jury; Frank, *Law and the Modern Mind*, makes a beginning.) Within this field, again, attempts diverge. Some have attempted study of the particular judge—a line that will certainly lead to inquiry into his social conditioning. Some have attempted to bring various psychological hypotheses to bear. All that has become clear is that our government is not a government; of laws, but one of laws through men.

(ii) There has been some attempt to work out the varieties of interaction between the traditional concepts (the judge's "legal" equipment for thinking, seeing, judging) and the fact-pressures of the cases. This is a question not—as above—of getting at results on particular facts, but of studying the effect, *e.g.*, of a series of cases in which the facts either press successively in the one direction, or alternate in their pressures and counteract each other. Closely related in substance, but wholly diverse in both method and aim, is study of the machinery by which fact-pressures can under our procedure be brought to bear upon the court.

(iii) First efforts have been made to capitalize the wealth of our reported cases to make large-scale quantitative studies of facts and outcome; the hope has been that these might develop lines of prediction more sure, or at least capable of adding further certainty to the predictions based as hitherto on intensive study of smaller bodies of cases. * * *

(iv) Repeated effort has been made to work with the cases of single states, to see how far additional predictability might thus be gained.

(v) Study has been attempted of "substantive rules" in the particular light of the available remedial procedure; the hope being to discover in the court's unmentioned knowledge of the immediate consequences of this rule or that, in the case at hand, a motivation for decision which cuts deeper than any shown by the opinion. Related, but distinct, is the reassertion of the fundamental quality of remedy, and the general approach to restating "what the law is" (on the side of prediction) in terms not of rights, but of what can be done: Not only "no remedy, no right," but "precisely as much right as remedy."

(vi) The set-up of men's ways and practices and ideas on the subject matter of the controversy has been studied, in the hope that this might yield a further or even final basis for prediction. The work here ranges from more or less indefinite reference to custom (the historical school), or mores * * *, through rough or more careful canvasses of business practice and ideology * * * to painstaking and detailed studies in which practice is much more considered than is any prevailing set of ideas about what the practices are * * * or—even—to studies in which the concept of "practice" is itself broken up into behavior-sequences presented with careful note of the degree of their frequency and recurrence, and in which all reference to the actor's own ideas is deprecated or excluded * * *. While grouped here together, under one formula, these workers show differences in degree and manner of interest in the background-ways which range from one pole to the other. * * * This is not one "school"; here alone are the germs of many "schools."

(vii) Another line of attack, hardly begun, is that on the effect of the lawyer on the outcome of cases, as an element in prediction. The lawyer *in litigation* has been the subject thus far only of desultory comment. Groping approach has been made to the counsellor as field general, in the business field: in drafting, and in counselling (and so in the building of practices and professional understandings which influence court action later), and in the strategy of presenting cases in favorable series, settling the unfavorable cases, etc. * * *

Is it not obvious that—if this be realism—realism is a mass of trends in legal work and thinking? (1) They have their common core, present to some extent wherever realistic work is done: recognition of law as means; recognition of change in society that may call for change in law; interest in what happens; interest in effects; recognition of the need for effort toward keeping perception of the facts uncolored by one's views on Ought; a distrust of the received set of rules and concepts as adequate indications of what is happening in the courts; a drive toward narrowing the categories of description. (2) They have grown out of the study of the action of appellate courts, and that study still remains their potent stimulus. Uncertainty in the action of such courts is one main problem: to find the why of it; to find means to reduce it, where it needs reduction; to find where it needs reduction, where expansion. (3) But into the work of lower courts, of administrative bodies, of legislatures, of the life which lies before and behind law, the ferment of investigation spreads.

JEROME FRANK, LAW AND THE MODERN MIND

(1930)

CHAPTER XII: THE JUDGING PROCESS AND THE JUDGE'S PERSONALITY

The process of judging, so the psychologists tell us, seldom begins with a premise from which a conclusion is subsequently worked out. Judging begins rather the other way around—with a conclusion more or less vaguely formed; a man ordinarily starts with such a conclusion afterwards tries to find premises which will substantiate it. If he cannot, to his satisfaction, find proper arguments to link up his conclusion with premises which he finds acceptable, he will, unless he is arbitrary or mad, reject the conclusion and seek another.

In the case of the lawyer who is to present a case to a court, the dominance in his thinking of the conclusion over the premises is moderately obvious. He is a partisan working on behalf of his client. The conclusion is, therefore, not a matter of choice except within narrow limits. He must, that is if he is to be successful, begin with a conclusion which will insure his client's winning the law-suit. He then assembles the facts in such a fashion that he can work back from this result he desires to some major premise which he thinks the court will be willing to accept. The precedents, rules, principles and standards to which he will call the court's attention constitute this premise.

While "the dominance of the conclusion" in the case of the lawyer is clear, it is less so in the case of the judge. For the respectable and traditional descriptions of the judicial judging process admit no such backward-working explanation. In theory, the judge begins with some rule or principle of law as his premise, applies this premise to the facts, and thus arrives at his decision.

Now, since the judge is a human being and since no human being in his normal thinking processes arrives at decisions (except in dealing with a limited number of simple situations) by the route of any such syllogistic reasoning, it is fair to assume that the judge, merely by putting on the judicial ermine, will not acquire so artificial a method of reasoning. Judicial judgments, like other judgments, doubtless, in most cases, are worked out backward from conclusions tentatively formulated. * * *

But the conception that judges work back from conclusions to principles is so heretical that it seldom finds expression. Daily, judges, in connection with their decisions, deliver so-called opinions in which they purport to set forth the bases of their conclusions. Yet you will study these opinions in vain to discover anything remotely resembling a statement of the actual judging process. They are written in conformity with the time-honored theory. They picture the judge applying rules and principles to the facts, that is, taking some rule or principle (usually derived from opinions in earlier cases) as his major premise, employing the facts of the case as the minor premise, and then coming to his judgment by processes of pure reasoning.

Now and again some judge, more clear-witted and outspoken than his fellows, describes (when off the bench) his methods in more homely terms. Recently Judge Hutcheson essayed such an honest report of the judicial process. He tells us that after canvassing all the available material at his command and duly cogitating on it, he gives his imagination play,

> and brooding over the cause, waits for the feeling, the hunch—that intuitive flash of understanding that makes the jump-spark connection between question and decision and at the point where the path is darkest for the judicial feet, sets its light along the way. In feeling or "hunching" out his decisions, the judge acts not differently from but precisely as the lawyers do in working on their cases, with only this exception, that the lawyer, in having a predetermined destination in view,—to win the law-suit for his client—looks for and regards only those hunches which keep him in the path that he has chosen, while the judge, being merely on his way with a roving commission to find the just solution, will follow his hunch wherever it leads him. * * *

And Judge Hutcheson adds:

> I must premise that I speak now of the judgment or decision, the solution itself, as opposed to the apologia for that decision; the decree, as opposed to the logomachy, the effusion of the judge by which that decree is explained or excused. * * * The judge really decides by feeling and not by judgment, by hunching and not by ratiocination, such ratiocination appearing only in the opinion. The vital motivating impulse for the decision is an intuitive sense of what is right or wrong in the particular case; and the astute judge, having so decided, enlists his every faculty and belabors his laggard mind, not only to justify that intuition to himself, but to make it pass muster with his critics. Accordingly, he passes in review all of the rules, principles, legal categories, and concepts which he may find useful, directly or by an analogy, so as to select from them [those] which in his opinion will justify his desired result.

We may accept this as an approximately correct description of how all judges do their thinking. But see the consequences. If the law consists of the decisions of the judges and if those decisions are based on the judge's hunches, then the way in which the judge gets his hunches is the key to the judicial process. Whatever produces the judge's hunches makes the law.

What, then, are the hunch-producers? What are the stimuli which make a judge feel that he should try to justify one conclusion rather than another?

The rules and principles of law are one class of such stimuli. But there are many others, concealed or unrevealed, not frequently considered in discussions of the character or nature of law. To the infrequent extent that these other stimuli have been considered at all, they have been usually referred to as "the political, economic and moral prejudices of the judge." A moment's reflection would, indeed, induce any open-minded person to admit that factors of such character must be operating in the mind of the judge. * * *

The judge's decision is determined by a hunch arrived at long after the event on the basis of his reaction to fallible testimony. It is, in every sense of the word, ex post facto. It is fantastic, then, to say that usually men can warrantably act in reliance upon "established" law. Their inability to do so may be deplorable. But mature persons must face the truth, however unpleasant.

Why such resistance to the truth? Why has there been little investigation of the actualities of the judging process? If we are right in assuming that the very subject-matter of the law activates childish emotional attitudes, we can perhaps find an answer to these questions.

It is a marked characteristic of the young child, writes Piaget,[2] that he does very little thinking about his thinking. He encounters extreme difficulty if asked to give an account of the "how" of his mental processes. He cannot reflect on his own reasoning. If you ask him to state how he reached a conclusion, he is unable to recover his own reasoning processes, but instead invents an artificial account which will somehow seem to lead to the result. He cannot correctly explain what he did to find this result." Instead of giving a retrospect he starts from the result he has obtained as though he had known it in advance and then gives a more or less elaborate method for finding it again. * * * He starts from his conclusion and argues towards the premises as though he had known from the first whither those premises would lead him.

Once more these difficulties find their explanation in the child's relative unawareness of his self, of his incapacity for dealing with his own thoughts as subjective. For this obtuseness produces in the child an overconfidence in his own ideas, a lack of skepticism as to the subjectivity of his own beliefs. As a consequence, the child is singularly non-introspective. He has, according to Piaget, no curiosity about the motives

2 [*See* J. PIAGET, JUDGMENT AND REASONING IN THE CHILD 141–42 (1928).]

that guide his thinking. His whole attitude towards his own thinking is the antithesis of any introspective habit of watching himself think, of alertness in detecting the motives which push him in the direction of any given conclusion. The child, that is, does not take his own motives into account. They are ignored and never considered as a constituent of thinking.

It would not be surprising, then, to find that, in dealing, with a subject-matter which stimulates childish emotional attitudes, the inclination towards a critical analysis of the motives which lie behind thinking is not very vigorous. If we view the law as such a subject-matter, we have a key to our puzzle. Lawyers are constantly looking into the motives and biases of clients and witnesses, but are peculiarly reluctant to look into the motives and biases of judges. Yet such inquisitiveness, deliberately cultivated, is at the very core of intelligent dealing with the law. That it is virtually non-existent is perhaps due to the survival of childish resistance to introspection with reference to thinking about law. * * *

CHAPTER XIII: MECHANISTIC LAW; RULES; DISCRETION; THE IDEAL JUDGE

* * * It is sometimes asserted that to deny that law consists of rules is to deny the existence of legal rules. That is specious reasoning. To deny that a cow consists of grass is not to deny the reality of grass or that the cow eats it. So while rules are not the only factor in the making of law, *i.e.* decisions, that is not to say there are no rules. Water is not hydrogen; an ear of corn is not a plow; a song recital does not consist of vocal cords; a journey is not a railroad train. Yet hydrogen is an ingredient of water, a plow aids in the development of corn, vocal cords are necessary to a song recital, a railroad train may be a means of taking a journey, and hydrogen, plows, vocal cords and railroad trains are real. No less are legal rules.

If we are to learn the law by observing the conduct of judges, then we shall want to take legal principles into account, for they are among the causative factors affecting such conduct. But if we are not to be befogged by words we will not assume that the "principles of law" are similar to the "principles of biology." The principles of biology are based directly on the biologist's description of the conduct of animal organisms; the principles of law are often only remotely related to judicial conduct. Accurately to describe that conduct requires close watching of many other factors.

What lies back of the prevalent obsessive interest in legal rules we have already seen; it is naively expressed in the utterance of a well-known law teacher: "The law is a normative science and the investigator of this science has more interest in perfecting his generalization as a part of a unified and coherent whole than in observing the application and misapplication of a legal technique," a statement which is reminiscent of the spectator of Racine's comedy who wished to laugh according to the rules. By narrowing the observed data of the so-called science of law, certainty and predictability can seemingly be guaranteed, whereas such a guaranty is impossible if one is required to observe the "application and misapplication of a legal technique." But, alas, this latter is precisely the task of the lawyer.

The unwisdom of confining attention to rules and principles can perhaps be made more clear by such questions as these: Will these rules and principles suffice as the sole or chief bases of predicting future decisions? Are they the only mode of describing all future probabilities for the purpose of predicting future decisions? Do they, in other words, constitute sufficient explanations of past decisions or causes or indications of the course of future decisions? Are they adequate as records of what has heretofore happened in the courts and of what will happen? To what extent are they helpful as histories of past law or as guides to the law that is to come?

An answer to these questions must lead to a vision of law as something more than rules and principles, must lead us again to the opinion that the personality of the judge is the pivotal factor. Where, then, is the hope for complete uniformity, certainty, continuity in law? It is gone except to the extent that the personalities of all judges will be substantially alike, to the extent that the judges will all have substantially identical mental and emotional habits. * * *

It is sometimes said that part of the judge's function is to pick out the relevant facts. Not infrequently this means that in writing his opinion he stresses (to himself as well as to those who will read the opinion) those facts which are relevant to his conclusion—in other words, he unconsciously selects those facts which, in combination with the rules of law which he considers to be pertinent, will make "logical" his decision. A judge, eager to give a decision which will square with his sense of what is fair, but unwilling to break with the traditional rules, will often view the evidence in such a way that the "facts" reported by him, combined with those traditional rules, will justify the result which he announces.

If this were done deliberately, one might call it dishonest, but should remember that with judges this process is usually unconscious and that, however unwise it may be, upright men in other fields employ it, and sometimes knowingly. * * *

Surely here again we are confronting mythical thinking. All judges exercise discretion, individualize abstract rules, make law. Shall the process be concealed or disclosed? The fact is, and every lawyer knows it, that those judges who are most lawless, or most swayed by the "perverting influences of their emotional natures," or most dishonest, are often the very judges who use most meticulously the language of compelling mechanical logic, who elaborately wrap about themselves the pretense of merely discovering and carrying out existing rules, who sedulously avoid any indications that they individualize cases. If every judicial opinion contained a clear exposition of all the actual grounds of the decision, the tyrants, the bigots and the dishonest men on the bench would lose their disguises and become known for what they are.

It is time that we gave up the notion that indirection and evasion are necessary to legal technique and that in law we shall better achieve our ends if lawyers and judges remain half-ignorant, not only of these ends, but of the means of achieving them.

No, the pretense that judges are without the power to exercise an immense amount of discretion and to individualize controversies, does not relieve us of those evils which result from the abuse of that judicial power. On the contrary, it increases the evils. The honest, well-trained judge with the completest possible knowledge of the character of his powers and of his own prejudices and weaknesses is the best guaranty of justice. Efforts to eliminate the personality of the judge are doomed to failure. The correct course is to recognize the necessary existence of this personal element and to act accordingly. * * *

Is it not absurd to keep alive the artificial, orthodox tradition of the "ideal judge?" The rational alternative is to recognize that judges are fallible human beings. We need to see that biases and prejudices and conditions of attention affect the judge's reasoning as they do the reasoning of ordinary men. Our law schools must become, in part, schools of psychology applied to law in all its phases. In law schools, in law offices and law courts there must be explicit recognition of the meaning of the phrase "human nature in law." The study of human nature in law * * * may not only deepen our knowledge of legal institutions but open an unworked mine of judicial wisdom.

FELIX S. COHEN, *TRANSCENDENTAL NONSENSE AND THE FUNCTIONAL APPROACH*

35 COLUM. L. REV. 809, 812–14, 828–29, 833 (1935)

Logicians sometimes talk as if the only function of language were to convey ideas. But anthropologists know better and assure us that "language is primarily a pre-rational function."[10] Certain words and phrases are useful for the purpose of releasing pent-up emotions, or putting babies to sleep, or inducing certain emotions and attitudes in a political or a judicial audience. The law is not a science but a practical activity, and myths may impress the imagination and memory where more exact discourse would leave minds cold. * * *

[A]lthough judges and lawyers need not be legal scientists, it is of some practical importance that they should recognize that the traditional language of argument and opinion neither explains nor justifies court

[10] Sapir, LANGUAGE (1921) 14.

decisions. When the vivid fictions and metaphors of traditional jurisprudence are thought of as reasons for decisions, rather than poetical or mnemonic devices for formulating decisions reached on other grounds, then the author, as well as the reader, of the opinion or argument, is apt to forget the social forces which mold the law and the social ideals by which the law is to be judged. Thus it is that the most intelligent judges in America can deal with a concrete practical problem of procedural law and corporate responsibility without any appreciation of the economic, social, and ethical issues which it involves.

2. *When is a Corporation?*

The field of corporation law offers many illuminating examples of the traditional supernatural approach to practical legal problems. In the famous *Coronado* case,[11] the question was presented to the United States Supreme Court, whether employers whose business had been injured in the course of a strike could recover a judgment against a labor union which had "encouraged" the strike, or whether suit could be brought only against particular individuals charged with committing or inducing the injury. So far as appears from the printed record, counsel for the union defendants did not attempt to show that labor unions would be seriously handicapped by the imposition of financial responsibility for damage done in strikes, that it would be impossible for labor unions to control agents provocateurs, and that labor unions served a very important function in modern industrial society which would be seriously endangered by the type of liability in question. Instead of offering any such argument to support the claim of the labor union to legal immunity for the torts of its members, counsel for the union advanced the metaphysical argument that a labor union, being an unincorporated association, is not a person and, therefore, cannot be subject to tort liability. This is a very ancient and respectable argument in procedural law. Pope Innocent IV used it in the middle of the Thirteenth Century to prove that the treasuries of religious bodies could not be subject to tort liability. Unfortunately, the argument that a labor union is not a person is one of those arguments that remain true only so long as they are believed. When the court rejected the argument and held the union liable, the union became a person—to the extent of being suable as a legal entity—and the argument ceased to be true. The Supreme Court argued, "A labor union can be sued because it is, in essential aspects, a person, a quasi-corporation." The realist will say, "A labor union is a person or quasi-corporation because it can be sued; to call something a person in law, is merely to state, in metaphorical language, that it can be sued."

There is a significant difference between these two ways of describing the situation. If we say that a court acts in a certain way "because a labor union is a person," we appear to justify the court's action, and to justify that action, moreover, in transcendental terms, by asserting something

---

[11] *United Mine Workers of America v. Coronado Coal Co.*, 259 U.S. 344 (1922). * * *

that sounds like a proposition but which can not be confirmed or refuted by positive evidence or by ethical argument. If, on the other hand, we say that a labor union is a person "because the courts allow it to be sued," we recognize that the action of the courts has not been justified at all, and that the question of whether the action of the courts is justifiable calls for an answer in non-legal terms. To justify or criticize legal rules in purely legal terms is always to argue in a vicious circle.[14] * * *

6. *The Nature of Legal Nonsense*

[I]n every field of law we should find the same habit of ignoring practical questions of value or of positive fact and taking refuge in "legal problems" which can always be answered by manipulating legal concepts in certain approved ways. In every field of law we should find peculiar concepts which are not defined either in terms of empirical fact or in terms of ethics but which are used to answer empirical and ethical questions alike, and thus bar the way to intelligent investigation of social fact and social policy. Corporate entity, property rights, fair value, and due process are such concepts. So too are title, contract, conspiracy, malice, proximate cause, and all the rest of the magic "solving words" of traditional jurisprudence. Legal arguments couched in these terms are necessarily circular, since these terms are themselves creations of law, and such arguments add precisely as much to our knowledge as Moliere's physician's discovery that opium puts men to sleep because it contains a dormitive principle. Now the proposition that opium puts men to sleep because it contains a dormitive principle is scientifically useful if "dormitive principle" is defined physically or chemically. Otherwise it serves only to obstruct the path of understanding with the pretense of knowledge. So, too, the proposition that a law is unconstitutional because it deprives persons of property without due process of law would be scientifically useful if "property" and "due process" were defined in non-legal terms; otherwise such a statement simply obstructs study of the relevant facts. If the foregoing instances of legal reasoning are typical, we may summarize the basic assumptions of traditional legal theory in the following terms: Legal concepts (for example, corporations or property rights) are supernatural entities which do not have a verifiable existence except to the eyes of faith. Rules of law, which refer to these legal concepts, are not descriptions of empirical social facts (such as the customs of men or the customs of judges) nor yet statements of moral ideals, but are rather theorems in an independent system. It follows that a legal argument can never be refuted by a moral principle nor yet by any empirical fact. Jurisprudence, then, as an autonomous system of legal concepts, rules, and arguments, must be independent both of ethics and of such positive sciences as economics or

[14] *Cf.* Roguin, LA REGLE DU DROIT (1889): "Nothing is more fallacious than to believe that one may give an account of the law by means of the law itself."

psychology. In effect, it is a special branch of the science of transcendental nonsense.

II. THE FUNCTIONAL METHOD

That something is radically wrong with our traditional legal thought-ways has long been recognized. Holmes, Gray, Pound, Brooks Adams, M. R. Cohen, T. R. Powell, Cook, Oliphant, Moore, Radin, Llewellyn, Yntema, Frank, and other leaders of modern legal thought in America, are in fundamental agreement in their disrespect for "mechanical jurisprudence," for legal magic and word-jugglery.[32] But mutual agreement is less apparent when we come to the question of what to do: How are we going to get out of this tangle? How are we going to substitute a realistic, rational, scientific account of legal happenings for the classical theological jurisprudence of concepts? * * *

Attempts to answer this question have made persistent use of the phrase "functional approach." Unfortunately, this phrase has often been used with as little meaning as any of the magical legal concepts against which it is directed. Many who use the term "functional" intend no more than the vague connotation which the word "practical" conveys to the "practical" man. . . . I shall use the term rather to designate certain principles or tendencies which appear most clearly in modern physical and mathematical science and in modern philosophy. For it is well to note that the problem of eliminating supernatural terms and meaningless questions and redefining concepts and problems in terms of verifiable realities is not a problem peculiar to law. It is a problem which has been faced in the last two or three centuries, and more especially in the last four or five decades, by philosophy, mathematics, and physics, as well as by psychology, economics, anthropology, and doubtless other sciences as well. * * *

Fundamentally there are only two significant questions in the field of law. One is, "How do courts actually decide cases of a given kind?" The other is, "How ought they to decide cases of a given kind?" Unless a legal "problem" can be subsumed under one of these forms, it is not a meaningful question and any answer to it must be nonsense. * * *

---

[32] See Holmes, *The Path of the Law* (1897) 10 HARV. L. REV. 457, COLLECTED LEGAL PAPERS (1920) 167; Gray, NATURE AND SOURCES OF THE LAW (1909) Ch. 4–5; Pound, *Law in Books and Law in Action* (1910) 44 AM. L. REV. 12; Pound, *Mechanical Jurisprudence* (1908) 8 COLUM. L. REV. 605; Brooks Adams, LAW UNDER INEQUALITY: MONOPOLY, IN CENTRALIZATION AND THE LAW (1906) Lecture 2; M. R. Cohen, *The Process of Judicial Legislation*, (1914) 48 AM. L. REV. 161, LAW AND THE SOCIAL ORDER (1933) 112; T. R. Powell, *The Judiciality of Minimum Wage Legislation*, (1924) 37 HARV. L. REV. 545; Cook, *Logical and Legal Bases of the Conflict of Laws* (1924) 33 YALE L. J. 457; Oliphant, *A Return to Stare Decisis* (1928) 6 AM. L. REV. 215; U. Moore, *Rational Basis of Legal Institutions* (1923) 23 COLUM. L. REV. 609; M. Radin, *Case Law and Stare Decisis: Concerning Präjudizienrecht in Amerika* (1933) 33 COLUM. L. REV. 199; Llewellyn, *A Realistic Jurisprudence—The Next Step* (1930) 30 COLUM. L. REV. 431; Llewellyn, *Some Realism about Realism: Responding to Dean Pound* (1931) 44 HARV. L. REV. 1222; Yntema, *The Hornbook Method and the Conflict of Laws* (1928) 37 YALE L. J. 468; Frank, LAW AND THE MODERN MIND (1930).

In brief, Holmes and, one should add, Hohfeld,[53] have offered a logical basis for the redefinition of every legal concept in empirical terms, *i.e.* in terms of judicial decisions. The ghost-world of supernatural legal entities to whom courts delegate the moral responsibility of deciding cases vanishes; in its place we see legal concepts as patterns of judicial behavior, behavior which affects human lives for better or worse and is therefore subject to moral criticism. Of the functional method in legal science, one may say, as Russell has said of the method in contemporary philosophy, "Our procedure here is precisely analogous to that which has swept away from the philosophy of mathematics the useless menagerie of metaphysical monsters with which it used to be infested."[54]* * *

The age of the classical jurists is over, I think. The "Restatement of the Law" by the American Law Institute is the last long-drawn-out gasp of a dying tradition. The more intelligent of our younger law teachers and students are not interested in "restating" the dogmas of legal theology. There will, of course, be imitators and followers of the classical jurists, in the years ahead. But I think that the really creative legal thinkers of the future will not devote themselves, in the manner of Williston, Wigmore, and their fellow masters, to the taxonomy of legal concepts and to the systematic explication of principles of "justice" and "reason," buttressed by "correct" cases. Creative legal thought will more and more look behind the pretty array of "correct" cases to the actual facts of judicial behavior, will make increasing use of statistical methods in the scientific description and prediction of judicial behavior, will more and more seek to map the hidden springs of judicial decision and to weigh the social forces which are represented on the bench. And on the critical side, I think that creative legal thought will more and more look behind the traditionally accepted principles of "justice" and "reason" to appraise in ethical terms the social values at stake in any choice between two precedents.

JOSEPH WILLIAM SINGER, *LEGAL REALISM NOW*

76 CAL. L. REV. 465, 496–503 (1988)

2. Legal Reasoning

a. Formalism

Legal reasoning in both treatises and judicial opinions during the preclassical era was characterized by what Karl Llewellyn called the "Grand Style." It consisted of a mixture of argumentation techniques based on implied intent, morality, policy, precedent, and liberality. The legal community understood the law to impose moral obligations on citizens.

[53] *See* Hohfeld, FUNDAMENTAL LEGAL CONCEPTIONS (1919).

[54] Russell, [MYSTICISM AND LOGIC (1918) 155].

Lawyers were experts in using reason to identify such moral obligations, and in shaping the law to advance the general welfare. The goal of legal rules was not only to induce citizens to live up to their moral obligations, but also to attain commercial convenience. Judges and scholars also appealed to precedent, both because it was the source of the law and because it reflected established community standards regarding morality and social policy. At the same time, judges modernized many rules or interpreted them "liberally" to fit current ideas about morality and policy. This complex collection of reasoning techniques required judges to engage in grand theorizing about the proper goals of the legal system, the fair and customary obligations of citizens in social relationships, the proper limits on free contract, and the meaning and mutability of precedent.

In contrast, the classical era was the era of formalism. Formalism, sometimes called "mechanical jurisprudence," has been used in many different ways. I will note several different aspects of legal reasoning generally associated with formalism. First, the classical thinkers like Langdell, Williston, and Beale believed that the entire legal system could be reduced to a very small number of general principles. For example, the basic principle of contract law is that contracts protect the will of the parties; the basic principle of tort law is liability for fault; the basic policy of the estate system is promoting the alienability of land. Lawyers could discern these principles and policies by induction from appellate cases.

Second, the classical theorists believed that these general principles contained legal concepts that could be rigidly separated. Distinctions between concepts were analogized to boundary lines between two pieces of property; either you are on my property or you are on your property—there is no gray area. Either there is a contract with all its attendant legal obligations or there is no contract and there are no affirmative obligations; either a state has personal jurisdiction or it does not; either you have acted unreasonably or you have acted reasonably. Our current view of concepts as shading into each other was almost completely absent in this period.

Third, lawyers used these general principles composed of rigidly defined concepts to generate specific legal conclusions by a logical, objective, and scientific process of deduction. Highly abstract concepts were thought to be operative, or capable of generating specific consequences by their very nature. For example, John Austin used the concept of "law" to determine that there could be no liability without fault. His reasoning went like this: Law is defined as commands of the sovereign to do or refrain from doing an act; the goal of law, so defined, is to affect behavior by imposing sanctions for disobedience; and sanctions can induce people not to intentionally harm others and to act reasonably. But people cannot refrain from inadvertently harming others unless they do nothing. Strict liability imposes a legal obligation on someone who, by definition, was not intentionally or unreasonably posing a risk of harm to others. Any sanction for harm so inflicted could not influence that person's behavior; it therefore serves no purpose. Thus, anyone who favors the rule of law must object to liability in the absence of fault.

The *Coppage v. Kansas* [236 U.S. 1 (1915)] decision contains similar deductive reasoning. The Court there held that a statute outlawing "yellow dog"[107] contracts unconstitutionally interfered with liberty and property in violation of the fourteenth amendment. The Kansas legislature had sought to prohibit employers from insisting that employees promise not to join a union as a condition of accepting employment. According to the legislature, this condition by the employer constituted an act of coercion.[108] The Court, however, interpreted the rights of "liberty" and "property" protected by the Constitution to include the right of freedom of contract. The right to make contracts meant both that voluntary contracts would be enforced in accordance with their terms, and that the legislature possessed no power to outlaw contracts voluntarily adopted. According to Justice Pitney's majority opinion, the fact that employers possess greater bargaining power than employees was not inherently coercive. Indeed, he considered employment contracts to be "entirely devoid of any element of coercion, compulsion, duress, or undue influence." Nor could reasonable persons differ about the meaning of "voluntariness" or "duress." The Court deduced the meaning of these concepts from the concept of "free will." Agreements were considered voluntary absent "actual or implied coercion or duress, such as might overcome the will of the employee." This definition of "duress" actually came from the common law and did not include coercion resulting from unequal bargaining power. By deducing a definition of "coercion" or "duress" from the concept of "will" and identifying that definition with the constitutional principle of liberty of contract, the Court treated its decision as a logical question about the inherent meaning of established law. This meant that the legislature could not, "by designating as "coercion" conduct which is not such in truth, render criminal any normal and essentially innocent exercise of personal liberty or of property rights." To outlaw such a contract would interfere with the liberty of both employers and employees to agree on terms that are mutually advantageous. The legislature's attempt to define as coercion that which was not "actual coercion" was a sham attempt to redistribute property rights and limit liberty in the guise of promoting liberty.

Finally, formalism included a commitment to objective standards. This commitment signified a willingness to ignore the actual intent of the

---

107 Yellow dog contracts are agreements in which employees promise, as a condition of employment, that they will not join a union.

108 The statute made it "unlawful for any individual or member of any firm, or any agent, officer or employé of any company or corporation, to coerce, require, demand or influence any person or persons to enter into any agreement, either written or verbal, not to join or become or remain a member of any labor organization or association, as a condition of such person or persons securing employment, or continuing in the employment of such individual, firm, or corporation." 236 U.S. at 6 (quoting 1903 Kan. Sess. Law, ch. 222, § 1).

parties, their particular characteristics, abilities, and needs, and the social context in which the event or transaction occurred. In tort law, negligence was defined by a reasonable person standard, not by how one expected the specific defendant to act. In contract law, obligations imposed by mutual agreement were judged by objective manifestations of assent rather than by seeking to determine the parties' actual intent.

In summary, the classical era started with the notion of a self-regulating market system, a private sphere insulated from government interference, influence, and control. It then added the belief in a formalistic method of legal reasoning. Roscoe Pound called formalism "mechanical jurisprudence" because the classical lawyers had a tendency to apply their general principles relentlessly—regardless of the underlying policies or the consequences of these policies in specific cases. Judicial method was seen as scientific, apolitical, principled, objective, logical, and rational. Legal argument was pervaded with a sense of certainty. This sense of certainty, coupled with a commitment to the self-regulating market ideal, allowed classical judges to nullify hundreds of pieces of regulatory legislation to protect "property," "freedom of contract," and "liberty." They seldom recognized that these same concepts could be used to justify market regulation of exactly the sort that was being struck down. Nor did they recognize that their own definitions of property and contract embodied forms of government regulation and involvement in the market system. The legal realists made it their task to instruct classical lawyers on these points.

b. Legal Realism As Pragmatism

[T]he legal realists' approach to legal reasoning * * * assumes new significance, * * * when viewed in conjunction with the critique of the self-regulating market. The realists criticized formalism largely, although not entirely, in the context of developing arguments about the role that law played in the market. In so doing, the legal realists sought to base legal reasoning on pragmatism. Pragmatic legal reasoning—what Llewellyn called "Grand Style judging"—encompassed four broad propositions.

First, the realists argued that it is impossible to induce a unique set of legal rules from existing precedents. Llewellyn argued that it is always possible to generate both broad and narrow holdings from cases, and to construct competing lines of precedent on either side of every controversial issue of law. Felix Cohen further argued that every case was different from every other in some respect, and that judges had no alternative but to engage in ethical inquiry to determine those differences between the case at hand and the prior case that mattered.

Second, the realists argued against conceptualism. As Holmes noted in his dissent in *Lochner v. New York* [198 U.S. 45 (1905).]: "General propositions do not decide concrete cases. The decision will depend on a judgment or intuition more subtle than any articulate major premise."

According to the realists, the *Coppage* Court was irrational to suggest that the kind of coercion employees experience when required to desist from union membership as a condition of employment is not coercion "in truth." Coercion and freedom are relative concepts, shading into each other on a spectrum, not a rigid on/off distinction. Different sorts of coercion can also be distinguished qualitatively. Moreover, the definition of concepts like "coercion" is not a purely logical, deductive process; rather defining illegitimate coercion requires judgments about the relative importance of competing values.

By arguing against the practice of deducing rules from abstractions, the realists hoped to focus attention on the facts of specific cases and to understand the development of the law in terms of situation-types. Further, they hoped to lower the overall level of abstraction in legal reasoning by relating concepts like freedom of contract and duress to value choices. Concepts are not self-defining, nor can they be defined by logical deduction from general propositions, such as "contract law protects the will of the parties." Concepts can only be given meaning by reference to considerations of policy and morality. For example, to distinguish between freedom and duress sensibly, one must keep in mind (1) that contracts defined as "voluntary" will be enforced in accordance with their terms, and those defined as involuntary will be regulated; (2) the different consequences of enforcing or not enforcing contracts entered into under the circumstances of the case; (3) the competing interests of the parties; (4) the competing values of protecting individuals from coercion by other market actors and protecting market actors from regulation by the state; (5) the competing needs for predictability and regularity of law, and; (6) the need to shape law to achieve social justice and social welfare. Concentrating on factors such as these would allow judges to address more honestly the values at stake in defining a contract as sufficiently voluntary to enforce.

Third, the realists argued that judges should make law based on a thorough understanding of contemporary social reality. Judges should not make value judgments in the abstract about the substantive content of the law. Rather, they should closely examine the social context in which those affected by legal rules operate. Understanding this social context would enable judges to adjudicate disputes through "situation-sense," meaning the ability to fit the law to social practice and to satisfy the felt needs of society to achieve a "satisfying working result." For example, in drafting the Uniform Commercial Code, Llewellyn hoped to formulate legal rules that would take into account the social context in which commercial transactions took place. One goal was to protect the legitimate expectations of the parties by learning from experts about the customary practices of the trade.

Finally, the realists argued against formalistic, mechanical application of rigid rules regardless of their social consequences. Judges should apply rules in light of their purposes, looking to the goals of the rules and their social effects. Moreover, they should also change or modernize rules to respond to changing social values and circumstances. As Holmes argued in *The Path of the Law*:

> The language of judicial decision is mainly the language of logic. And the logical method and form flatter that longing for certainty and for repose which is in every human mind. But certainty generally is illusion, and repose is not the destiny of man. Behind the logical form lies a judgment as to the relative worth and importance of competing legislative grounds, often an inarticulate and unconscious judgment, it is true, and yet the very root and nerve of the whole proceeding. * * * *
>
> I think that the judges themselves have failed adequately to recognize their duty of weighing considerations of social advantage. The duty is inevitable, and the result of the often proclaimed judicial aversion to deal with such considerations is simply to leave the very ground and foundation of judgments inarticulate, and often unconscious . . .. I cannot but believe that if the training of lawyers led them habitually to consider more definitely and explicitly the social advantage on which the rule they lay down must be justified, they sometimes would hesitate where now they are confident, and see that really they were taking sides upon debatable and often burning questions.[126]

In ruling on such "burning questions," the realists wanted judges to balance pragmatically competing interests in light of competing policies, principles, and values. Judges must (1) identify a range of alternative legal solutions to any legal problem; (2) predict the consequences of deciding one way rather than another; (3) articulate the competing interests, values, and policies involved in the case and see how they conflict with one another; (4) compare the relative advantages of alternative approaches, including the social consequences of different alternative rules and the values that would be protected; and finally (5) make a choice designed, as Felix Cohen said, to "promot[e] the good life of those whom it affects."

The realists' proposals for legal reasoning have a characteristic quality of ambivalence. This ambivalence revolves around the issue of whether judges make or find law. On one hand, the realists seemed to embrace wholeheartedly the idea that judges make law. The realists argued that judges choose between conflicting lines of precedent; they choose between broad and narrow interpretations of cases; they formulate rules by determining the purposes and policies that the legal rules should achieve; they seek to adjudicate disputes in a way that will have desirable social consequences; they make ethical value choices. On the other hand, the

[126] Holmes, *The Path of the Law*, *supra*, at 465–68.

realists often made it seem as if judges could make these policy and precedential judgments without injecting personal political commitments into their decision-making. Realist scholars often argued that the legislature was the appropriate policymaking branch to which judges should defer; they often relied on custom (such as customary practices of the trade) to determine what was appropriate social conduct; they assumed conventional or consensual community norms for adjudicating disputes; they assumed a shared sense of what constituted the "public interest"; they assumed that experts (both commercial and administrative) could identify the most efficient means of implementing these shared goals; they had a sense that social science could tell us what rules work well; they relied on the metaphor of balancing interests which makes it seem as if controversial legal questions could be answered by a process of weighing (counting, observing, *finding*) rather than a process of judgment.

This ambivalence about the judicial role has survived to the present day. The question of whether judges make or find law troubles legal theorists to no end. We accept both the realist insight that judges exercise judgment (they make law) and the realist insight that judges are substantially constrained in that process by the social and institutional context in which they act (they find law). Confusion about how to understand the relation between these two insights is the most pronounced characteristic of the current state of legal theory. * * *

THOMAS J. MILES & CASS R. SUNSTEIN, *THE NEW LEGAL REALISM*

75 U. CHI. L. REV. 831 (2008)

In 1931, Karl Llewellyn attempted to capture the empirical goals of the legal realists by referring to early "efforts to capitalize the wealth of our reported cases to make large-scale quantitative studies of facts and outcome." Llewellyn emphasized "the hope that these might develop lines of prediction more sure, or at least capable of adding further certainty to the predictions based as hitherto on intensive study of smaller bodies of cases." But Llewellyn added, with apparent embarrassment: "I know of no published results."

We are in the midst of a flowering of "large-scale quantitative studies of facts and outcome," with numerous published results. The relevant studies have produced a New Legal Realism—an effort to understand the sources of judicial decisions on the basis of testable hypotheses and large data sets.[4] * * *

---

[4] We are hardly the only people to use this term. As best we can determine, the term "New Legal Realism" first appears in Frank B. Cross, *Political Science and the New Legal Realism: A Case of Unfortunate Interdisciplinary Ignorance*, 92 NW. U. L. REV. 251 (1997). Cross's

I. Law and Politics

A. *From Old to New Realism*

Llewellyn wrote in reaction to the formalist view that law, as expressed in statutes and precedents, determined the outcomes of particular cases.[6] He believed that, much of the time, existing law did not compel particular outcomes, in the sense that the available sources would not require a rational and fair-minded judge to reach only one result. And at times, the law itself was contradictory: "[I]n any case doubtful enough to make litigation respectable[,] the available authoritative premises are at least two, and [ ] the two are mutually contradictory as applied to the case at hand." For Llewellyn, the indeterminacy, sometimes even incoherence, of law meant that "the personality of the judge" must to some degree explain case outcomes. In his view, "our government is not a government of laws, but one of laws through men."

To modern readers, Llewellyn's suggestions are far too crude. The personality of the judge surely can matter, but what, exactly, is meant by "personality"? More fundamentally, whether ours is "a government of laws," and what it means for a system to be "one of laws through men," are partly empirical questions.[10]

Empirical work on judicial behavior is not, of course, a new endeavor. An entire subfield of political science, known as "law and politics," has contributed a large and valuable empirical literature investigating the influence of ideology on judicial outcomes.[11] Some early contributions to this literature treat the influence of law (the legal model) as an empirical hypothesis, opposed to a competing hypothesis involving the influence of judicial ideology (the attitudinal model). These studies often reject the legal model in favor of the attitudinal model. More recently, political scientists have given greater attention to the institutional context of judicial decision-making by positing and testing models of strategic behavior.

For their part, legal academics took little notice of "law and politics" political science. Perhaps they did so because the empirical methodology

---

understanding of the New Legal Realism is close to ours. A great deal of other work, some of it much broader, has also claimed that mantle. * * * For a helpful overview with varied work, see New Legal Realism, http://www.newlegalrealism.org (visited Apr 16, 2008).

[6] See Brian Leiter, *American Legal Realism*, in Martin P. Golding and William A. Edmundson, eds., THE BLACKWELL GUIDE TO THE PHILOSOPHY OF LAW AND LEGAL THEORY 50, 51–52 (Blackwell 2005).

[10] We say "partly" because some conceptual and normative analysis is necessary to establish what, exactly, will be tested, and how to evaluate what is found.

[11] See, for example, Lee Epstein and Jeffrey A. Segal, ADVICE AND CONSENT: THE POLITICS OF JUDICIAL APPOINTMENTS 117–41 (Oxford 2005) (analyzing judicial decisions since 1953 to conclude that the ideological association between presidents and their appointees' voting records is stronger with respect to Supreme Court justices than courts of appeals judges); Jeffrey A. Segal and Harold J. Spaeth, THE SUPREME COURT AND THE ATTITUDINAL MODEL REVISITED 2 (Cambridge 2002) (arguing that American history is replete with "egregious" examples of partisan judicial policymaking).

was unfamiliar and different from their own.[13] But recently, the appetite for empirical work in general has grown rapidly among law professors, and empirical research within law schools has become so prevalent as to constitute its own subgenre of legal scholarship, "empirical legal studies."[14] In view of the importance of judicial decisions as a source of law and their centrality to both teaching and scholarship in law schools, it is unsurprising that much of the burgeoning empirical legal scholarship focuses directly on judicial rulings and their sources.

We believe that much of the emerging empirical work on judicial behavior is best understood as a new generation of legal realism.[16] The New Legal Realists are conducting what Llewellyn and his peers only envisioned—"large-scale quantitative studies of facts and outcome" that assess the influence of the judicial personality on legal outcomes. We suspect that the new realist studies of judicial behavior will erode the distinctions between "law and politics" political science and "empirical legal studies." Through its conferences and professional journals, economic analysis of law has long drawn contributions from both law faculties and economics departments. We hope, and are willing to predict, that the New Legal Realism will increasingly bring together scholarly efforts of both

---

[13] See Barry Friedman, *Taking Law Seriously*, 4 PERSPECTIVES ON POLIT. 261, 261 (2006) (arguing that political science literature on judicial behavior "has not received nearly the attention it deserves" because it has ignored normative implications, overlooked the actual operation of legal institutions and actors, and failed to acknowledge the limitations of its data).

[14] The most revealing developments here include the emergence of a new journal devoted solely to empirical studies, with the (unsurprising but descriptive) name, Journal of Empirical Legal Studies, and a new professional organization, The Society for Empirical Legal Studies. The causes of the renewed interest in empirical studies among law schools are intriguing and well worth sustained attention. We speculate that important factors in this change include the decline in the costs of computing and data gathering, the increasing presence on law faculties of people with postgraduate training in both law and social sciences, and the prevailing sense in certain interdisciplinary fields, particularly economic analysis of law, that empirical work rather than abstract theory now presents the greatest opportunities for contribution. These changes have likely mitigated or even eliminated some of the professional disadvantages of conducting empirical research. See Peter H. Schuck, *Why Don't Law Professors Do More Empirical Research?*, 39 J. LEGAL EDUC. 323, 331–33 (1989) (listing reasons why empirical research runs counter to careerist objectives of legal academics, particularly untenured ones).

[16] We emphasize that others have used the phrase "New Legal Realism" to describe a broader set of interdisciplinary inquiries not limited to judicial decision-making. See, for example, the illuminating discussions in Stewart Macaulay, *The New versus the Old Legal Realism: "Things Ain't What They Used to Be,"* 2005 WIS. L. REV. 365, 385–86 (describing the New Legal Realism as involving "the law in action, the gap between the law in the books and the actual practices of legal officials and the public in cases of disputes"); Howard Erlanger, et al., *Is It Time for a New Legal Realism?,* 2005 WIS. L. REV. 335, 337 ("[N]ew legal realist scholars bring together legal theory and empirical research to build a stronger foundation for understanding law and formulating legal policy."). It would certainly be possible to understand the form of realism we discuss here as a subpart of a broader conception of the New Legal Realism.

In contrast, still others label recent studies of judicial behavior as a part of "the new legal empiricism." See, for example, Michael Heise, *The Past, Present, and Future of Empirical Legal Scholarship: Judicial Decision Making and the New Empiricism*, 2002 U. ILL. L. REV. 819, 822 (noting the "recent reemergence of legal empiricism, or what Professor James Lindgren has labeled 'the new empiricism' ").

lawyers and political scientists; economists will play a substantial and probably growing role as well.

A distinguishing feature of the New Legal Realism is the close examination of reported cases in order to understand how judicial "personality," understood in testable ways, influences legal outcomes, and how legal institutions constrain or unleash these influences. These inquires represent an effort to test certain intuitive ideas about the indeterminacy of law, and to implement the (old-style) realist call for empirical study of how different judges decide cases by responding to the "stimulus" of each case. Political science has devoted much attention to the Supreme Court, a sensible choice given the Court's importance. But the New Legal Realism tends to focus on lower federal courts because the random assignment of judges to cases is a sort of natural experiment that permits plausible causal inferences about the effect of judicial characteristics on outcomes.

B. The Standard Pattern

The New Legal Realists are beginning to make progress on these questions because of increasing agreement about how to measure relevant aspects of the "personality of the judge" and the features of each case. What Llewellyn termed "personality," the New Legal Realists have taken to mean the observable, personal characteristics of judges, such as their political affiliations, demographics, and prior professional experience. The goal is to develop testable hypotheses—and then to test them. Much more can and will be done, but much has been done already.

To date, the characteristics of the cases most commonly examined by the New Legal Realists are the types of litigants, the nature of their claims, and the procedural posture of the dispute. The New Legal Realism also seeks to capture the institutional context of judicial behavior; the New Legal Realists are interested in social influences, and especially collegial influences, on judicial votes. Dimensions of the institutional setting include whether a judge renders her decision while presiding alone or as a member of a panel, and if as a member of a panel, whether the co-panelists have similar characteristics. An important stimulus—and sometimes an important constraint—is the law itself. Some legal scholars play up the role of legal constraints[19] while others emphasize what they see as the decisive role of the values or commitments of particular judges.[20] Some of the old-

---

[19] Within the New Legal Realism, this is the tendency in, for example, Frank B. Cross, *Decision-Making in the U.S. Circuit Courts of Appeals*, 91 CAL. L. REV. 1457, 1514 (2003) (concluding that legal precedent plays a larger role in judicial decision-making than do judges' political ideologies, their desire to strategically limit external reactions to their decisions, or the self-interested behavior of the litigants).

[20] Within the New Legal Realism, this is the tendency in, for example, [Richard L.] Revesz, [*Environmental Regulation, Ideology, and the D.C. Circuit*, 83 VA. L. REV. 1717, 1727 (1997), at] 1766–67 (construing data to argue that judges' ideological views will affect their decisions unless they are sufficiently tempered by a strategic motivation to avoid higher court review). * * *

style realists could be read to adopt the latter position, but they rested content with impressions and anecdotes, not with any kind of systematic study. By contrast, the New Legal Realists take these claims about legal reasoning as hypotheses, which can and should be tested. They want to know when and how law is indeterminate and thus exactly when and how "the personality of the judge" matters for outcomes.

To date, the question that has received the most attention from the New Legal Realists is the influence of a judge's political ideology or attitudes.[22] This question holds perennial interest because judicial ideology—usually proxied by the party of the appointing president—often appears influential in constitutional decisions, and it is a recurrent, even dominant, theme of media coverage of the Supreme Court. But do Republican appointees systematically differ from Democratic appointees? In what domains? It is reasonable to speculate that in ideologically contested domains—involving, for example, environmental protection, labor law, immigration, sex discrimination, abortion, and campaign finance law—the two sets of appointees will vote very differently. If so, how much do they differ? Does the party affiliation of the appointing president matter as much as it seems to in the domain of politics? Do the relevant differences persist in less ideologically contested domains?

If party effects can be found, does the institutional setting of decision-making matter as well? Much of the New Legal Realism has focused on federal appellate decisions. In federal circuit courts, judges sit on three-member panels, and the New Legal Realists have investigated whether the presence of a judge's colleagues on a panel influences her decision-making. It is reasonable to speculate that when Democratic appointees sit on three-judge panels consisting exclusively of Democratic appointees, their voting patterns will be unusually "liberal"—and that when Democratic appointees sit on three-judge panels with two Republican appointees, their voting patterns will be unusually "conservative." (Whether a decision counts as "liberal" or "conservative" can be assessed by standard if admittedly crude judgments, such as whether a disabled person or a woman wins in a discrimination case, or whether a restriction on abortion is upheld or struck down.) It is even reasonable to speculate that it might be possible to do pretty well in predicting judicial votes, in some areas, by asking about the

---

[22] This issue is explored in many places. See generally, for example, William Landes and Richard A. Posner, *Judicial Behavior: A Statistical Study* (unpublished manuscript, 2007) (discussing whether a judge's political voting behavior changes over her term of office and whether it depends on the ideological makeup of other judges on the court); Thomas J. Miles and Cass R. Sunstein, *Do Judges Makes Regulatory Policy? An Empirical Investigation of Chevron*, 73 U. CHI. L. REV. 823 (2006) (concluding, after empirical analysis, that judicial political ideology affects the application of Chevron deference); Cass R. Sunstein, et al., ARE JUDGES POLITICAL? AN EMPIRICAL ANALYSIS OF THE FEDERAL JUDICIARY (Brookings 2006) (analyzing the effects of the political party of the appointing president on judicial panel voting in a variety of cases); Cross, 92 NW. U. L. REV. 251 (cited in note [14, *supra*]. The issue is also investigated in Jaya Ramji-Nogales, Andrew I. Schoenholtz, and Phillip G. Schrag, *Refugee Roulette: Disparities in Asylum Adjudication*, 60 STAN. L. REV. 295, 369, 371, 410 (2007) (finding that political affiliation sometimes plays a role in federal court of appeals judges' review of asylum cases).

political affiliation of the appointing president—and perhaps equally well by asking about the political affiliation of the president who appointed the two other judges on the panel. New Legal Realists describe the impact of the colleagues on an appellate panel on a judge's own votes as "peer effects" or "panel effects."

A good deal of evidence on these questions has recently emerged. * * * Results of this kind have been found in so many diverse areas that they might fairly be described as the "standard Pattern of Judicial Voting," at least in ideologically contested cases. In the Standard Pattern, the political affiliation of the appointing president greatly matters to judicial votes. The observed panel effects are commonly interpreted as two behavioral responses. The first is ideological dampening: Republican appointees show fairly liberal voting patterns when sitting with two Democratic appointees; and Democratic appointees show fairly conservative voting patterns when sitting with two Republican appointees. The second is ideological amplification: Republican appointees show especially conservative voting patterns when sitting with two Republican appointees; and Democratic appointees show especially liberal voting patterns when sitting with two Democratic appointees.

Ideological dampening seems to be a kind of conformity effect, reminiscent of empirical findings to the effect that isolated people typically yield when confronted with the unanimous views of others. Both Republican and Democratic appointees appear to show a conformity effect by issuing a kind of "collegial concurrence." Ideological amplification seems to be a form of group polarization, reminiscent of empirical findings to the effect that like-minded people, engaged in deliberation with one another, end up at more extreme points in line with their pre-deliberation tendencies. In the context of judicial behavior, the underlying mechanisms remain imprecisely understood, but at least it can be said that members of unified panels typically show more extreme voting patterns, in a way that fits with the general phenomenon of group polarization.

Importantly, the Standard Pattern is not universal. Republican appointees and Democratic appointees do not differ in their voting patterns in some areas in which significant differences might well be expected; examples include criminal appeals, property rights, congressional power under the Commerce Clause, and standing to sue.[28] Perhaps the law imposes a great deal of discipline in these domains, so that ideological differences cannot emerge; perhaps Republican and Democratic appointees do not much disagree in such areas. Moreover, panel effects are not present in the important domains of abortion and capital punishment. In those domains, judges apparently vote their convictions and are not influenced, at least in their conclusions, by the other judges on the panel. A natural explanation is that here, judicial judgments are entrenched, and hence

[28] Sunstein, et al., ARE JUDGES POLITICAL? at 48–49 (cited in note [23]).

judges are not much affected by the votes and arguments of those of a different political party. (Notably, judges of the notoriously divided Sixth Circuit show essentially no panel influences. Republican appointees on that court are unaffected by Democratic appointees, and vice versa; the Sixth Circuit is the only court of appeals to show that pattern in that data.) In the domain of asylum cases, Republican and Democratic appointees show very different voting patterns on the Sixth Circuit and the Ninth Circuit, but not on the Third Circuit, suggesting that ideological differences may exist, or break out, in some places but not in others.

Other New Legal Realist work has begun to investigate the role of other aspects of a judge's background, particularly the judge's demographic characteristics, such as race and sex. These results mirror the findings for partisanship or ideology in two ways. First, just as with partisanship, these characteristics have been found to influence a judge's own vote as well as those of other judges on the panel. Second, these judicial characteristics matter in certain legal contexts but not in others.

For example, a significant finding is that in sex discrimination cases, a judge's sex matters: female judges are more likely to vote in favor of plaintiffs, and male judges are more likely to vote in favor of plaintiffs if a female judge is sitting on the panel. In sexual harassment cases, there is a clear gender effect. However, a judge's race does not exert a meaningful influence in employment discrimination cases, an area where one might predict race would be particularly salient. In contrast, race matters in voting rights cases; African American judges are more likely to vote in favor of plaintiffs, and white judges are more likely to vote in favor of plaintiffs if an African American judge is sitting on the panel.[34] (Another way to put these points is that white judges are less likely than African American judges to vote in favor of plaintiffs, and white judges are even less likely to vote in favor of plaintiffs if no African American judge is sitting on the panel.) Interestingly, a judge's sex does not matter in voting rights cases. * * *

C. *Limitations and Unanswered Questions*

Notwithstanding several advances in understanding judicial behavior, the New Legal Realism continues to have important limitations, and a great deal remains to be done. Some of these limitations involve data gathering. Others are conceptual and normative.

Most of the relevant studies are limited to published judicial opinions. Such opinions may well be un-representative of the typical case, and if courts are more likely to publish difficult and controversial opinions, the estimates from published opinions will likely overstate the actual effects of judicial ideology and other characteristics. A great deal might be learned

[34] See Adam B. Cox and Thomas J. Miles, *Judging the Voting Rights Act*, 108 COLUM. L. REV. 1, 29–37 (2008).

by incorporating unpublished opinions into the analysis. But to the extent that an objective of the New Legal Realism is to understand the impact of judicial personality on law, rather than quotidian decisions lacking precedential value, published cases are relevant subjects of analysis. A special problem here is that publication practices are not uniform across circuits, and hence cross-circuit comparisons may be unreliable if unpublished opinions are excluded.

It also remains true that the current findings provide only fragments of the overall puzzle. We know something, for example, about judicial behavior in EPA and NLRB cases between 1996 and 2006. But it would be much better to know about judicial behavior in a broader range of administrative law cases in that period, including, for example, cases involving the SEC, the OSHA, the FCC, and the FTC. It would be better still to be able to learn as well about cases from 1986 to 1996, and 1976 to 1986, and even 1946 to 1976. To what extent is the Standard Pattern found across agencies and across time? Even in the domain of administrative law, no one has explored the effects of party affiliation on purely procedural challenges to agency decisions. Suppose, for example, agency decisions are challenged for failure to comply with the procedural requirements of the Administrative Procedure Act. Do Republican appointees show different voting patterns from Democratic appointees? Are the former more likely to accept a procedural challenge from (say) companies complaining about environmental regulation, and the latter from (say) the Sierra Club and the Natural Resources Defense Council? We suspect so, but we lack data.

Studies of race, sex, and disability discrimination cases remain badly incomplete, limited as they are to relatively brief periods of time. Many areas of law remain entirely unstudied in the standard terms, including, for example, antitrust, intellectual property, and bankruptcy. It would be useful to know in which areas of law and under what circumstances the judicial personality has the greatest (and the least) influence on decisions.

In addition, we continue to know only a small amount about what might be learned with respect to the effects of key aspects of judicial background on judicial voting. What is the impact of age or of number of years on the bench? Of service as (for example) a prosecutor or a corporate lawyer? Of religious background? (An especially intriguing question: are judges of certain religious backgrounds likely to rule differently in abortion cases, sex discrimination cases, and religion cases than are judges of other religions or of no religion?) How do sex and race affect behavior in multiple areas of the law? Are female appointees more likely to be pro-choice? In these domains, we glimpse only the tip of the iceberg.

Still more troubling is the fact that much of the New Legal Realism remains largely atheoretical. Our work in administrative law is vulnerable to just this criticism; our inquiry is simply whether judicial ideology matters to judicial votes in the context of *Chevron U.S.A. Inc. v. NRDC*[41] and arbitrariness review cases. Though we have referred to the potential role of conformity effects and group polarization, the mechanisms generating panel effects remain inadequately understood. An exception to the absence of behavioral theory is the literature that employs rational choice models to predict how the possibility of review by higher courts, such as *en banc* review of a panel's decision, may influence a judge's decision. A core prediction of these analyses is that the risk of reversal by an unfriendly overseeing court may induce a judge to alter her vote or the legal basis of her decision.

A particular advantage of these models is that they generate (and test) predictions about a judge's strategic choice of the grounds for a decision. In so doing, they move beyond the focus on mere votes and come closer to Llewellyn's vision of studying the effect of judicial personality on legal reasoning in appellate decisions.[44] Even in the absence of explicit rational choice models, other researchers have begun to consider the application of particular legal doctrines, rather than a judge's votes, as a unit of analysis.[45] We think that a great deal might be learned by examining opinions, not just votes, though the coding problems are far more serious for the former than for the latter.

In addition, the implications of the Standard Pattern for (old-style) legal realism and its opponents are not so clear. Are the observed impacts of judicial ideology large or small? Committed realists, emphasizing the importance of political judgments, will want to declare a clear victory. They will stress the evident disagreement, in many domains, between Republican and Democratic appointees—and thus point to the plain impact of political convictions on judicial decisions. But on the data as it stands, judicial policy preferences are only part of the picture. In most domains, the division between Republican and Democratic appointees, while significant, is far from huge; the law, as such, seems to be having a constraining effect. In review of agency decisions for arbitrariness, for example, both Democratic and Republican appointees vote in favor of

---

41 467 U.S. 837 (1984).

44 See, for example, Stephen J. Choi and Mitu Gulati, *Bias in Judicial Citations: A Window into the Behavior of Judges?*, 37 J. LEGAL STUD. 87 (2009) (reporting that federal judges are more likely to cite judges of their own political party, particularly in high-stakes litigation, and that judges are more likely to cite judges who cite them back); Michael Abramowicz and Emerson H. Tiller, *Judicial Citation to Legislative History: Contextual Theory and Empirical Analysis* 2 (Northwestern University Law and Economics Research Paper No 05–11, May 2005) (reporting that the more judges of one political party on a circuit court or on a panel, the higher the rate of legislative history citations to legislators of that party, irrespective of the party of the judge authoring the opinion).

45 See, for example, Cox and Miles, 108 COLUM. L. REV. at 18–25 (examining how judicial ideology correlates with the application of multifactor tests in voting rights decisions); Mark J. Richards and Herbert M. Kritzer, *Jurisprudential Regimes in Supreme Court Decision Making*, 96 AM. POLIT. SCI. REV. 305, 305 (2002) (developing a test for "jurisprudential regimes" that define relevant factors or set standards of review for subsequent decisions).

validation most of the time, regardless of whether the outcome is liberal or conservative. * * *

NOTES AND QUESTIONS

1. *Varieties of legal realism.* One of the best accounts of American legal realism in its various forms is Brian Leiter, *American Legal Realism*, in Martin P. Golding and William A. Edmundson, eds., THE BLACKWELL GUIDE TO THE PHILOSOPHY OF LAW AND LEGAL THEORY 50 (2005); Brian Leiter, *In Praise of Realism (and Against "Nonsense" Jurisprudence)*, 100 GEO. L.J. 865 (2012). *See also* Brian Leiter, *American Legal Realism,* U. of Texas Law Public Law Research Paper No. 42 which summarizes the various "wings" of realism:

> [My] reading emphasizes the commitment of all the Realists to a core descriptive claim about adjudication (judges respond primarily to the underlying facts of the cases, rather than to legal rules and reasons); shows how the Realists divide in to two camps over the correct interpretation of this "core" claim (the Idiosyncrasy Wing of Frank, and the Sociological Wing of Llewellyn, Oliphant, Moore, Green, and the vast majority of Realists); demonstrates the connection of the Sociological Wing of Realism to the Realist project of law reform, including the work of the American Law Institute; examines and distinguishes the Realist arguments for the indeterminacy of law from Critical Legal Studies arguments; and shows how the Realists lay the foundation for the program of a "naturalized" jurisprudence, in opposition to the dominant "conceptual" jurisprudence of Anglophone legal philosophy. The revisionary reading also debunks certain popular myths about Legal Realism, like the following: the Realists believed "what the judge ate for breakfast determines the decision"; a critique of the public/private distinction was a central part of Realist jurisprudence; and the Realists were committed to an incoherent form of rule-skepticism.

Some are not convinced that the various strands of legal realism can be reconciled in any way. *See, e.g.*, William Twining, *Talk About Realism*, 69 N.Y.U. L. REV. 329 (1985); John Henry Schlegel, *The Ten Thousand Dollar Question*, 41 STAN. L. REV. 435 (1989), at 464 (legal realism "is just a name. Like 'chicken soup', it means what we choose to call it.")

2. *Realism, the practice of law, and professional ethics.* Professor David Wilkins has observed that

> [l]egal realism has dominated American legal education for over half a century. Despite this prominence, discussions about realism have generally been confined to either the abstract realm of legal theory or the often bitter debate over judicial interpretation. Curiously neglected has been any systematic investigation of the effect of core realist insights on traditional understandings of the lawyer's role.

> This neglect is unfortunate. By failing to explore the implications of the realist critique for prevailing assumptions about the relationship among lawyers, clients, and the legal system, the traditional model of legal ethics masks the extent to which lawyers inevitably exercise discretionary power over the substantive content of legal rules. As a result, the model fails to address how this power should be exercised in a manner consistent with the lawyer's public responsibilities as an officer of the legal system.

David Wilkins, *Legal Realism for Lawyers*, 104 HARV. L. REV. 468 (1990), at 469–70. If legal realism is a convincing account of the law, how should that affect the lawyer's dual roles as zealous representative of a client and as an " 'officer of the court' with a separate duty of loyalty to the fair and efficient administration of justice"? *Id.*, at 471.

3. *"When you open your jurisprudence museum, please put legal realism on the first floor with the other old things."* What of American legal realism—with its roots in the Depression and Franklin Roosevelt's New Deal—survives into the twenty-first century? At a minimum, as shown in later chapters, the realists' axiom that the law is characteristically indeterminate spun out a variety of more radical approaches, including critical legal studies, feminist jurisprudence, and critical race theory. *See* Thomas C. Grey, *Modern American Legal Thought*, 106 YALE L. J. 493 (1996); Herbert Hovenkamp, *Knowledge About Welfare: Legal Realism and the Separation of Law and Economics,* 84 MINN. L. REV. 84 (April 2000). Its fixation on how the law actually works finds its contemporary manifestation in the massive number and breadth of empirical studies of doctrine and its effects, judicial decision-making, alternative dispute resolution, and the power structures—both patent and hidden—that infuse the law, as Miles and Sunstein suggest. *See, e.g.*, Donald Braman & Dan M. Kahan, *Legal Realism as Psychological and Cultural (Not Political) Realism*, in HOW LAW KNOWS 93, 94 (Austin Sarat *et al.* eds., 2007). *See generally* Michael Heise, *The Past, Present, and Future of Empirical Legal Scholarship: Judicial Decision Making and the New Empiricism*, 2002 U. ILL. L. REV. 819. Hundreds of articles have been published since 2000 claiming the mantle of the "new legal realism." There's even a "New Legal Realism Project," which is specifically "developing a sophisticated interdisciplinary approach for translating social science into legal settings." Howard Erlanger, et al., *Foreword: New Legal Realism Symposium: Is It Time for a New Legal Realism*, 2005 WIS. L. REV. 335 (2005).

If we give the title "new legal realism" to any contemporary attack on formalism or determinacy in legal decision-making and legal scholarship, it may have evolved into a particularly virulent form in the aftermath of the global economic crisis early in the twenty-first century. The Law and Economics approach to law, explored in Chapter 5, *infra,* became quite powerful in the late twentieth century, both in courtrooms and in the academy, and there is a strong argument that "[e]ach of the varieties of new legal realism defines itself in part in opposition to the assumptions of neoclassical law and economics' theory of judging, its theory of the individual and the state, and its approach to legal scholarship." Victoria Nourse & Gregory Shaffer, *Varieties of New Legal Realism: Can A New World Order Prompt A New Legal Theory,?* 95 CORNELL L. REV. 61, 65–66 (2009):

> By neoclassical law and economics, we refer to the "straightforward application of microeconomic (or price-theoretic) analysis to the law," often associated with the "Chicago school," and with Judge [Richard] Posner [of the University of Chicago and the Seventh Circuit Court of Appeals] as its early leading and path-breaking advocate. Neoclassical law-and-economics theory builds from the premise that individuals act as rational preference-maximizers who respond to incentives and views law as a price that shapes such incentives. The theory combines such positive vision, often rigidly applied for the sake of parsimonious models, with the normative claim that legal rules should be evaluated in terms of outcome efficiency, defined by Judge Posner to mean "wealth maximization" or Kaldor-Hicks efficiency, such that all other concerns (including distributive implications) are bracketed or ignored. The theory prescribes that policymakers should accordingly rely predominantly on market mechanisms. * * *
>
> We emphasize that the new realism is not a movement against economics. That would be silly, as economics is a vast, rich, and evolving field that has a broad array of competing movements. Many of the scholars attacking the assumptions of neoclassical law and economics and its formalism are economists, and there are economists working in each of the three variants of new legal realism. * * *
>
> We offer a taxonomy of work aspiring to a new legal realism. First, [there are] *behavioral approaches*: studies that borrow from other scholarly disciplines, in particular behavioral economics and political science, to reach conclusions about law-as-behavior—in one case, law viewed as reflective of behavior and, in particular, of judges' politics; in the other case, law viewed as progressively shaping behavior by considering individuals' rational and irrational predispositions. Second, [there are] *contextual approaches*: empirical work that includes studies engaged in bottom-up, participatory forms of empiricism (what we dub "action studies"), based on philosophical pragmatism's premise that one cannot know one's ends until one assesses means because one's means open up new understandings of ends. Third, [there are] *institutional approaches*: studies focusing on the power of institutions and institutional choices to determine our policies and shape our very ideas of self, society, and the state.

Id., at 65–66, 68–70.

Each of the following chapters in Part I of this book deals with various approaches to law as *reactions* to legal realism. That is an intellectual and a pragmatic legacy that justifies understanding realism in its various forms, warts and all.

CHAPTER FOUR

POST-REALIST APPROACHES TO LAW AND OBLIGATION (I): THE LEGAL PROCESS SCHOOL AND CONTEMPORARY PRAGMATISM

■ ■ ■

"The legal process school sought to absorb and temper the insights of Legal Realism after the triumph of the New Deal. Its most important concession to Realism was its recognition that doctrinal formalism was incapable of eliminating discretion in the law. The task was instead to harness and channel that discretion through institutional arrangements."

— Morton Horowitz

"[D]ecisions which are the duly arrived at result of duly established procedures . . . ought to be accepted as binding upon the whole society unless and until they are duly changed."

— Henry Hart & Albert Sacks

Orientation

If taken seriously and systematically, legal realism required lawyers to rethink their work from top to bottom. The realists had debunked the idea that law was a deductive and autonomous science. They had exposed a deep vein of formalism and word-worship in the practice, teaching, and conceptualization of the law. They had attacked and sometimes ridiculed the traditional law school exercise in the extraction of "doctrine" from cases, long attributed to Christopher Columbus Langdell (whom Jerome Frank memorably called a "brilliant neurotic.") In the aftermath of the realists' critique, a natural question arose: is there a way to teach effective lawyering without reducing "law [to] nothing but politics and whimsy?"[1]

One response was the "Legal Process" school, which offered law students an opportunity to understand the organic interplay among institutions that create or apply law instead of requiring them to deduce rules of law from one judicial opinion after another. The "Legal Process" school focused not on adjudication in isolation but on the relationships

---

[1] William Eskridge and Philip Frickey, eds., HART AND SACKS' THE LEGAL PROCESS: BASIC PROBLEMS IN THE MAKING AND APPLICATION OF LAW (1994), at xci.

among judicial, legislative, and executive powers, each of which offered levers of influence that lawyers and policy-makers might pull as needed. By shifting focus from dry cases to illustrative problems in law and society, the Legal Process movement—without cynicism or irony—exposed the non-doctrinal aspects of the law in operation, including the role of reasoned discretion in judging, the roles of different branches and levels of government in resolving disputes, and the role of advocates in finding and deploying the available, sometimes contradictory authorities.

If this was philosophy at all, it was a philosophy of the law's process—and the legitimating role that rule-of-law procedures play in a pluralistic democracy—instead of the law's doctrinal substance or its essential nature. "[W]ithin the [Legal Process] framework, ascertaining *the proper allocation of authority* is the very point of law and thus also the master skill of legal policymakers, lawyers, and ultimately judges."[2]

The illustrative problem in this chapter—dealing with pay equity between men and women—suggests that this approach may be easier to experience than it is to describe in the abstract. That's consistent with the classic articulation of the Legal Process movement, which, unlike other schools of jurisprudence, appeared in a couple of casebooks intended for classroom use. Oddly enough, the dominant Legal Process casebook was used by generations of law students in manuscript form, because its authors never completed or published it. Henry M. Hart & Albert Sacks, THE LEGAL PROCESS: BASIC PROBLEMS IN THE MAKING AND APPLICATION OF LAW (tent. ed. 1958) ("*Hart & Sacks*");[3] Henry M. Hart & Herbert Wechsler, THE FEDERAL COURTS AND THE FEDERAL SYSTEM (1953). *Hart & Sacks* opens with the "Case of the Spoiled Cantaloupes," a seemingly pedestrian case involving the interstate shipment of perishable agricultural goods (cantaloupes apparently being inexplicably more comical to law professors than, say, okra or soy beans or even sorghum). The case study, described in greater detail below, offers the elements for an extended fugue on the role of commercial practices in the resolution of disputes, the power and limits of contract law, the interplay of public and private actors, the art of statutory interpretation, the workings of the administrative state, and the ideal relationship between courts and regulatory agencies. Readers and

---

[2] Michael Dorf, *Legal Indeterminacy and Institutional Design*, 78 N.Y.U. L. REV. 875, 923 (2003) (emphasis added). *See also* David Kennedy & William W. Fisher, *Introduction to Henry M. Hart, Jr., and Albert M. Sacks, The Legal Process: Basic Problems in the Making and Application of Law, in* THE CANON OF AMERICAN LEGAL THOUGHT (David Kennedy & William W. Fisher III eds., 2006) at 245 ("[t]he role of law in the broadest sense is to set, monitor, and enforce the procedural arrangements determining who does what.").

[3] In 1994, almost four decades after the classic 1958 version of THE LEGAL PROCESS, two highly-respected scholars published an edited version of the materials, including a masterful overview of the materials, their effects, and their limitations. William Eskridge and Philip Frickey, eds., *Hart and Sacks' The Legal Process: Basic Problems in the Making and Application of Law* (1994). The *Henry* Hart who co-authored *Hart & Sacks* is to be distinguished from the *H.L.A.* Hart who wrote THE CONCEPT OF LAW and other seminal works of legal positivism (see Chapter 2, *supra*).

students are cast as problem-solvers, not as archeologists digging up nuggets of doctrine in its inert form. Like the other problems in *Hart & Sacks*, the Spoiled Cantaloupes Case illustrates the authors' essential point about the law in operation:

> [K]nowledge consists, not in doctrine, not in propositional statements stored away in the brain; but in the capacity to solve problems as they are actually presented in life; the capacity to see all the implications * * * of the action to be taken; the capacity to bring to bear in the taking of decisions the maximum of the available experience of mankind.[4]

By promoting access to the raw material of law in all its variety, the Legal Process school may have been more realistic than the Realists were.

The fundamental, related themes to watch for in this chapter include at a minimum:

(i) *"Institutional settlement" of disputes and public policy debates.* Although not the first to stress institutional competence in the resolution of legal and social problems, Hart and Sacks did make "the principle of institutional settlement" central to the very idea of law.[5]

> The lawyer's business in any given institutional system is to help in seeing that the principle of institutional settlement operates not merely as a principle of necessity but as a principle of justice. This means attention to the constant improvement of all of the procedures which depend upon the principle in the effort to assure that they yield decisions which are not merely preferable to the chaos of no decision but are calculated as well as may be affirmatively to advance the larger purposes of the society.[6]

In other words, "institutional settlement" in the Legal Process school is not just a descriptive claim about how the law works in the real world. It is also a normative claim about how the law should work ideally. *Hart & Sacks* endorses a preference—grounded in then-dominant insights from political science—for a pluralistic democratic process as a vehicle for orderly, rational, and dynamic improvements in public policy. All citizens in society should obey the decisions "which are the duly arrived at result of duly established procedures" until those decisions are changed.

The assertion that such a system actually exists and works rested on a classically liberal idealization of American society:

> Basic in the American system is the assumption that every normal person counts one in determining the objectives of primary

---

4 *Id.* at lxxvi (quoting a letter dated 15 October 1941, from Henry M. Hart, Jr. to John H. Williams, then the Dean of the Harvard Graduate School of Public Administration).

5 *Hart & Sacks,* at 4.

6 *Id.* at 6.

> control. * * * Basic also, in the structure of this system, is the reflection of this assumption in the equal distribution of personal capacity to be [the] subject of primary liberties, duties, and powers, and to exercise rights of action and defend actions in vindication of them. * * * Given these basic equalities, it follows that every normal member of the society has the same personal capacity to exercise private powers, and thereby to command the backing of society for his own personal arrangements. Every such member has the same personal capacity to be the subject of duties and to exercise liberties. In principle, every such member is supposed to have the same personal capacity in the political processes of the system, both as a potential office holder and as a unit, counting one, in the ultimate institutional procedure of the election.[7]

From that perspective, Legal Process was an expression of its time, the jurisprudential equivalent of the poodle skirt or cars with fins. But fashions change, and the civic faith in the neutrality and expertise of administrative agencies, which had characterized the New Deal era, and the virtues of a largely passive, technocratic Supreme Court, had no permanent shelf-life. In Elizabeth Mensch's words, the Legal Process School "rested on the complacent, simplistic assumption that American society consisted of happy, private actors maximizing their valid human wants while sharing their profound belief in institutional competencies. That may have reflected the mind-set of many in the 1950s, but by the end of the 1960s it seemed oddly out of touch with reality."[8]

In short, Legal Process began to lose its descriptive bite as the courts (especially the Warren Court (1953–1969)) became "activist" in interpreting the due process and equal protection clauses of the Constitution *inter alia* and as a new understanding of the administrative state came to predominate, one characterized not by neutrality and expertise but by "agency capture" in which the regulated effectively control the regulator. Simultaneously, Legal Process lost its normative bite as the conventional consensus of the 1950s dissolved into the restive ideological diversity of the 1960s. But good ideas tend to get absorbed and transcended with the passage of time, and one good question—explored near the end of this chapter—is "what remains in the Legal Process tradition that is of contemporary value?"

(ii) *The power of "reasoned elaboration" by the courts acting within a restricted zone of competence.* In contrast to the caricature that the result in a case depends on what the judge had for breakfast, the Legal Process

---

7 *Id.* at 309.

8 Elizabeth Mensch, *Mainstream Legal Thought*, *in* THE POLITICS OF LAW: A PROGRESSIVE CRITIQUE (David Kairys ed., 1982), at 30.

school suggested that the "permitted scope of discretion"[9]—though obviously broad—was constrained by the obligation of judges to explain their decisions rationally and to avoid the kinds of judgments properly left to legislative and executive bodies. Hart and Sacks seem agnostic on the question of whether there are objectively "right" answers to legal questions, but the fact that decisions can be rationally criticized suggests that randomness is neither expected nor acceptable. Instead, they argue that analysts should consider "not only . . . the rightness or wrongness of the particular result but . . . the validity of the process by which the court arrived at it."[10] It is a mistake to assume that Hart and Sacks single-handedly replaced the "judge's breakfast" theory of adjudication with the light of pure reason, but they did swing the pendulum back from the reductionism of the realists towards a system that valued process and rationality in an adjudicative system that was irreducibly dependent on discretion. Invoking an image from the work of Lon Fuller, Hart and Sacks stressed the ability of the common law "to work itself pure,"[11] to bend the arc of the common law away from personality or ideology or policy and towards reason and justice and the maximization of social good.

In the specialized setting of statutory interpretation, Hart and Sacks enjoined the courts to understand that all law is purposive and that part of the judges' craft is construing ambiguous statutes so as to effectuate their purpose, *i.e.* to understand and redress the problem to which the statute was the supposed solution. "The purpose of the statute must always be treated as including not only an immediate purpose or group of related purposes but also a larger and subtler purpose as to how the particular statute is to be fitted into the legal system as a whole."[12] Unobjectionable as this approach may seem, subsequent accounts of legislation have suggested that statutes characteristically reflect not some general public interest but the interests of particular private groups bargaining in a largely obscure legislative environment. The "public choice" literature[13]

---

[9] *Hart & Sacks, supra,* at 164. *See also* G. Edward White, *The Evolution of Reasoned Elaboration: Jurisprudential Criticism and Social Change* 59 VA. L. REV. 279, 285 (1973) ("In emphasizing the disingenuous aspects of the use of precedent, rule, and doctrine, the Realists had made too simplistic an appraisal of the function of the rationalization process in judicial opinions. They had failed to grant due respect to the fact that a judge's use of these devices was itself constrained by the expectations of others.").

[10] *Id.* at 1148.

[11] *Id.* at 100. In his detailed account of the Legal Process school, Professor Neil Duxbury points out that the image can be found in an eighteenth-century decision of Lord Mansfield: "A statute can seldom take in all cases, therefore *the common law that works itself pure* by rules drawn from the fountain of justice is for this reason superior to an Act of Parliament." *Omychund v. Barker*, 26 Eng. Rep. 15, 33 (1744) (emphasis added). *See* NEIL DUXBURY, PATTERNS OF AMERICAN JURISPRUDENCE 261 (1995).

[12] *Hart & Sacks, supra,* at 1414.

[13] *See, e.g.*, Daniel A. Farber & Philip P. Frickey, *Legislative Intent and Public Choice*, 74 VA. L. REV. 423 (1988). *See also* Richard A. Posner, *What Has Pragmatism to Offer Law?*, 63 S. CAL. L. REV. 1653, 1665 (1990) ("[C]omplicating the interpretive picture in general is our current understanding of the legislative process, a more critical understanding than reigned when [ ] the legal realists and the realists' successors in the legal process school wrote. We no longer think of

(described in Chapter 5, *infra*) suggests that there is something deeply naïve in the Legal Process presumption that the public and private purposes of legislation converge or that the maximization of social good is even plausible as a purpose of modern legislation.

(iii) *The distinction between—and the relation between—public and private institutions*. One common way to misunderstand the Legal Process school is to treat it exclusively as an account of American public law. With the rise of New Deal bureaucracies, it would have been strange for Hart and Sacks to ignore the impact of rule-making and adjudications by government agencies. But "in pursuit of the ultimate goal of maximizing the satisfactions of valid human wants," they also observed that "the law finds many a tool besides force that suits its purpose."[14] And, in keeping with their effort to identify those "tools," Hart and Sacks identified relationships between public and private institutions, even as they distinguished between them. In some cases, the law frames out large zones for private arrangements among citizens, where the use of "self-applying regulation" allows them to order and rationalize their conduct. "Overwhelmingly the greater part of the general body of the law is self-applying, including almost the whole of the law of contracts, torts, property, crimes, and the like. Under such a scheme of control, only the troublesome cases come before officials, and these only after the event."[15] In the laissez-faire system Hart and Sacks preferred, the private ordering enabled by this form of law is the hallmark of an efficient system that maximizes liberty under the rule of law. But Hart and Sacks are concerned "as much with the shortcomings of the common law [ ] as with its merits,"[16] and, when private ordering fails, public regulation is justified. Figuring out where that tipping point is in any given case will keep rational policy-makers and judges busy. At best perhaps, Hart and Sacks propose "to lay a foundation for an understanding of the frequent need for one of the more sophisticated types of administered regulation or non-regulatory control."[17]

(iv) *Law as a purposive enterprise, with social improvement as its object*. There is a long philosophical tradition of responding to skepticism with pragmatism, countering metaphysical abstractions with assertions grounded in empirical experience. The pragmatic Legal Process response to the realists' rule skepticism began by asking what law is *for*, echoing some instrumentalist views of the law that had emerged earlier in the twentieth century but with the twist that law would be viewed as a "policy

statutes as typically, let alone invariably, the product of well-meaning efforts to maximize the public interest by legislators who are devoted to the public interest and who are the faithful representatives of constituents who share the same devotion.").

[14] *Hart & Sacks*, *supra*, at 881.

[15] *Id.* at 133.

[16] *Id.* at 366.

[17] *Id.*

instrument *with a particular institutional structure*."[18] Hart and Sacks argued that

> law is essential to the satisfaction of basic human wants and needs and to the advancement of humankind. Law is or ought to be goal-oriented, rational, and dynamic. Starting with this vision, Hart and Sacks worked out an architecture for thinking about a dynamic public law that was nonetheless accountable to the rule of law in a democracy. Their synthesis emphasized the purposiveness of law, *the coordination of institutions each operating within their fields of competence,* and the legitimizing role of procedure. Developed modestly (and always "tentatively") within the medium of teaching materials, these ideas caught on like a prairie brushfire.[19]

Whether or not this understanding literally converted law into a social "science,"[20] using the law as it is to improve social conditions was part of the rational exercise of discretion—sometimes by the courts but always in accordance with statutes and "neutral principles." Herbert Wechsler, *Toward Neutral Principles of Constitutional Law*, 73 HARV. L REV. 1, 19 (1959) ("A principled decision [ ] is one that rests on reasons with respect to all the issues in the case, reasons that in their generality and their neutrality transcend any immediate result that is involved.") The fact that one goal—neutrality—might be inconsistent with another—improving society by, say, enforcing racial or gender equality—became acutely obvious in the decade after *Hart & Sacks* was published. The question now is whether there is anything of value for the contemporary practice, pedagogy, and conceptualization of law in this decades-old, pragmatic, and generally unacknowledged framework.

A. THE LEGAL PROCESS APPROACH DESCRIBED: "THE CASE OF THE SPOILED CANTALOUPES"

Generations of law students were introduced to the Legal Process school through a famous case study, designed to show a variety of actors and ideas at work in the resolution of the legal issues that arose from a shipment of rotten fruit. Because the problem presented was approached from a variety of angles and in a variety of institutional settings, this case *study* differed fundamentally from the case *method*, developed by

---

18 David Kennedy & William W. Fisher III, *Introduction to Henry M. Hart, Jr., and Albert M. Sacks, The Legal Process: Basic Problems in the Making and Application of Law*, *in* THE CANON OF AMERICAN LEGAL THOUGHT 243, 245 (David Kennedy & William W. Fisher III eds., 2006).

19 William Eskridge and Philip Frickey, eds., HART AND SACKS' THE LEGAL PROCESS: BASIC PROBLEMS IN THE MAKING AND APPLICATION OF LAW (1994), at liii (emphasis added).

20 *Hart & Sacks, supra*, at 2, 198 (observing that law is "a pervasive aspect of social science.").

Christopher Columbus Landgell over a century ago and inflicted on law students ever since. To appreciate the lessons of the foundational case study (without replicating the case itself), consider the following description and be prepared to take those lessons into the case study of pay inequity between men and women.

CHARLES F. SABEL & WILLIAM H. SIMON, *CONTEXTUALIZING REGIMES: INSTITUTIONALIZATION AS A RESPONSE TO THE LIMITS OF INTERPRETATION AND POLICY ENGINEERING*

110 MICH. L. REV. 1265, 1274–77 (2012) (emphasis added)

The first and longest of the case studies featured in [*Hart & Sacks*] was "The Case of the Spoiled Cantaloupes." In 1943, through a series of telegrams, a Chicago broker sold a railroad carload of cantaloupes en route from Yuma, Arizona, to a Springfield, Massachusetts, wholesaler specifying "rolling acceptance final." When the cantaloupes arrived in Springfield, they were extensively spoiled and did not satisfy the contractual specification of "U.S. No. 1 cantaloupes." The spoilage resulted from Cladosporium Rot, a disease "of field origin" that was latent but perhaps not observable at the time of shipment.[29] The wholesaler sent a notice of rejection[, paid no part of the contract price,] and abandoned the cantaloupes at the loading dock in Springfield, from where the railroad eventually disposed of them for salvage value. The broker sued [the wholesaler] for the contract price.[30]

Hart and Sacks entitle this chapter "The Significance of an Institutional System." Their most general and basic point is that the case cannot be effectively resolved by doctrine as taught in law schools and elaborated in treatises, but requires a set of institutions configured to the industry. This lesson rests on a series of more specific ones.

First, there is the realist lesson of *the indeterminacy of doctrine*. Hart and Sacks show that the general law of sales is ambiguous as to whether, in this situation, the seller's shipment of non-conforming goods permits the buyer to reject the goods, instead of accepting and claiming damages for their reduced value. They proceed to point out that, if we had concluded that there was a right to reject, there would remain the question of whether a rejecting buyer has a duty to assist the seller by disposing of the spoiled goods. And after those questions are answered, a court might still have to answer the further question of whether the buyer's failure to salvage or his wrongful rejection leads to offsetting damages or a complete forfeiture of

---

[29] *Id.*, [Henry M. Hart, Jr. & Albert M. Sacks, THE LEGAL PROCESS (William N. Eskridge & Philip P. Frickey eds., Found. Press tent. ed. 1958)], at 10–11.

[30] *Id.* at 45–46.

his defense.[31] The resources of general contract law are inadequate to resolve these questions.

A second lesson is *the importance of context*. The cantaloupes dispute is not simply a contract case; it is a case about the interstate exchange of perishable agricultural products. Assessment must take account of "[t]he practices, attitudes, and expectations . . . of members of the industry."[32] In particular, it must pay attention to "the rejection evil." When prices fall, buyers may seek to escape their commitments by seizing minor nonconformities as excuses to reject. Small shippers may have limited ability to dispose of rejected goods or to pursue litigation in distant locales. What is needed in this context is "a better means of preventing abuses from occurring, and of discouraging unscrupulous dealers from taking advantage of reluctance to litigate."[33] Such considerations encourage us to consider whether interpretations that give broad latitude to reject or that do not penalize failure to salvage may exacerbate the rejection problem.

The third lesson Hart and Sacks draw is *the need to adapt to new circumstances*.[34] This case was eventually resolved in favor of the seller. Hart and Sacks approve of that decision, but they conclude by noting later cases in which courts plausibly decided not to apply the forfeiture result. In these later cases, it appeared that the seller misrepresented the condition of the goods or unilaterally altered the terms of the sale after the goods had shipped. Hart and Sacks portray these decisions sympathetically, suggesting that to apply the forfeiture rule where there was evidence of opportunism on the seller's part would shift the balance of vulnerability too far toward the buyer.

These lessons lead to a final one—*the importance of institutional structure*.[35] The courts and other actors with responsibility for resolving the dispute need to understand that they and the dispute are embedded in structures of roles and responsibilities. A regime has developed in response to the distinctive problems of interstate trade in perishable fruits and vegetables. The preeminent player is the United States Department of Agriculture, and the normative keystone is the Perishable Agricultural Commodities Act ("PACA"), which makes it a violation of federal law for "any dealer to reject or fail to deliver . . . without reasonable cause any perishable agricultural commodity" in an interstate transaction.[36] Congress enacted the statute in 1930 in part as a response to "the rejection

---

31 *See id.* at 11.

32 *Id.* at 9.

33 *Id.* at 40.

34 *Id.* at 64–66.

35 *See* Michael C. Dorf, *Legal Indeterminacy and Institutional Design*, 78 N.Y.U. L. REV. 875 (2003) (discussing and applying Hart and Sacks's institutionalism to questions of public law indeterminacy). * * *

36 Hart & Sacks, *supra*, at 33–34.

evil."[37] The Act instructs the Secretary of Agriculture to operate an arbitration process that reduces the cost of adjudicating claims and to administer a licensing scheme designed to screen irresponsible buyers and sellers from the industry.[38]

Another important element of the regime is a set of regulations promulgated by the Department to guide the interpretation of undefined contract terms like "U.S. No. 1 cantaloupes" and "rolling acceptance final." ("U.S. No. 1 cantaloupes" requires, among other things, that not more than one percent of the shipment be "affected by soft rot," while "rolling acceptance final" entails, among other things, that the buyer "has no right of rejection on arrival.")[39] In addition, the Department operates an inspection service at major shipping terminals that makes it feasible to prove the condition of goods at pertinent times.[40]

Although extensive, the Department's activities are part of a still larger structure. State commercial law continues to play a background role, filling the interstices of federal authority. Private industry associations facilitate enforcement of the Secretary's orders by publicizing noncompliance and mobilizing informal industry pressures against repeat offenders. Moreover, industry groups play an important role in the Department's formulation of its regulations on default contract terms. The Department actively consults trade associations and, in some cases, it incorporates norms they have previously enacted for their members.[41]

Hart and Sacks are centrally concerned with the relation of courts to contextualizing regimes, and especially to agencies. The cantaloupes case came to the courts in an action for review of a decision by a Department of Agriculture hearing officer in a PACA arbitration.[42] Treating the case in terms of the general law of sales, the district court held that the buyer could offset the reduction in value caused by the cantaloupes' nonconformity against the seller's claim for the purchase price. However, this decision was ultimately reversed by the appellate court on the ground that the buyer had forfeited his defense by failing to salvage.

Hart and Sacks defend the forfeiture resolution as the response developed for this situation by the Department of Agriculture, [which] they deem and think the courts should defer to as the institutional actor best qualified to address it. Yet, they suggest deference should be conditioned on the agency providing a clear, minimally plausible explanation of its decision. Moreover, they point to cases where the courts could properly take the lead role instead of deferring to the Secretary. They approve of

---

37 *Id.* at 40.

38 *Id.* at 33–34.

39 *Id.* at 18 n.10 (discussing several since-repealed provisions of 7 C.F.R.).

40 *Id.* at 11.

41 *Id.* at 41–42, 44.

42 *Id.* at 47–53.

decisions in which the courts overrule the Secretary in order to protect buyers from seller fraud or sharp practice, suggesting (debatably) that the courts' expertise is superior in matters involving basic fairness.[43]

B. THE LEGAL PROCESS APPROACH EXEMPLIFIED: STATUTES OF LIMITATIONS AND THE PROBLEM OF EQUAL PAY FOR WOMEN AND MEN

The Spoiled Cantaloupes Case was the very exemplar of the Legal Process School, and the prior excerpt from Professors Sabel and Simon's article reflects its inner workings and suggests its significance for generations of law students. In an effort to replicate the same Legal Process experience with the raw materials of a more contemporary case study, we now offer a range of authorities, in a variety of institutional settings, touching on the problem of equal pay for women and men. A reminder: as noted in the introduction to this chapter, the themes to look for in these materials are: (i) "institutional settlement" of disputes and public policy debates; (ii) the power of "reasoned elaboration" by the courts acting within a restricted zone of competence; (iii) the distinction between—and the relation between—public and private institutions; (iv) law as a purposive enterprise, with social improvement as its object.

The Federal Statutory Background

The Civil Rights Act of 1964, Title VII (as amended) ("Title VII"):

42 U.S.C. § 2000e–2(a)(1)

> It shall be an unlawful employment practice for an employer . . . to discriminate against any individual with respect to his compensation, terms, conditions, or privileges of employment, because of such individual's race, color, religion, sex, or national origin. . . .

42 U.S.C. § 2000e–5(e)(1)

> A charge under this section shall be filed within one hundred and eighty days after the alleged unlawful employment practice occurred.

42 U.S.C. § 2000e–2(h)

> It shall not be an unlawful employment practice for an employer to apply different standards of compensation . . . provided that

---

[43] *Id.* at 63–64.

such differences are not the result of an intention to discriminate because of race, color, religion, sex, or national origin.

The Equal Pay Act ("EPA"):

29 U.S.C. § 206(d)

(d) Prohibition of sex discrimination

(1) No employer having employees subject to any provisions of this section shall discriminate, within any establishment in which such employees are employed, between employees on the basis of sex by paying wages to employees in such establishment at a rate less than the rate at which he pays wages to employees of the opposite sex in such establishment for equal work on jobs the performance of which requires equal skill, effort, and responsibility, and which are performed under similar working conditions, except where such payment is made pursuant to (i) a seniority system; (ii) a merit system; (iii) a system which measures earnings by quantity or quality of production; or (iv) a differential based on any other factor other than sex: Provided, That an employer who is paying a wage rate differential in violation of this subsection shall not, in order to comply with the provisions of this subsection, reduce the wage rate of any employee.

(2) No labor organization, or its agents, representing employees of an employer having employees subject to any provisions of this section shall cause or attempt to cause such an employer to discriminate against an employee in violation of paragraph (1) of this subsection.

(3) For purposes of administration and enforcement, any amounts owing to any employee which have been withheld in violation of this subsection shall be deemed to be unpaid minimum wages or unpaid overtime compensation under this chapter.

(4) As used in this subsection, the term "labor organization" means any organization of any kind, or any agency or employee representation committee or plan, in which employees participate and which exists for the purpose, in whole or in part, of dealing with employers concerning grievances, labor disputes, wages, rates of pay, hours of employment, or conditions of work.

The Administrative Process

U.S. EQUAL EMPLOYMENT OPPORTUNITY COMMISSION
CODE OF FEDERAL REGULATIONS
TITLE 29: LABOR
PART 1601—PROCEDURAL REGULATIONS
SUBPART B—PROCEDURE FOR THE PREVENTION OF UNLAWFUL EMPLOYMENT PRACTICES

29 C.F.R. § 1601.1: Purpose.

The regulations set forth in this part contain the procedures established by the Equal Employment Opportunity Commission for carrying out its responsibilities in the administration and enforcement of title VII of the Civil Rights Act of 1964 * * *. Based on its experience in the enforcement of title VII, the Americans with Disabilities Act, and the Genetic Information Nondiscrimination Act, and upon its evaluation of suggestions and petitions for amendments submitted by interested persons, the Commission may from time to time amend and revise these procedures.

29 C.F.R. § 1601.7: Charges by or on behalf of persons claiming to be aggrieved.

(a) A charge that any person has engaged in or is engaging in an unlawful employment practice within the meaning of title VII, * * * may be made by or on behalf of any person claiming to be aggrieved. A charge on behalf of a person claiming to be aggrieved may be made by any person, agency, or organization. The written charge need not identify by name the person on whose behalf it is made. The person making the charge, however, must provide the Commission with the name, address and telephone number of the person on whose behalf the charge is made. During the Commission investigation, Commission personnel shall verify the authorization of such charge by the person on whose behalf the charge is made. Any such person may request that the Commission shall keep his or her identity confidential. However, such request for confidentiality shall not prevent the Commission from disclosing the identity to Federal, State or local agencies that have agreed to keep such information confidential. * * *

29 C.F.R. § 1601.9: Form of charge.

A charge shall be in writing and signed and shall be verified.

29 C.F.R. § 1601.12: Contents of charge; amendment of charge.

(a) Each charge should contain the following:

(1) The full name, address and telephone number of the person making the charge except as provided in § 1601.7;

(2) The full name and address of the person against whom the charge is made, if known (hereinafter referred to as the respondent);

(3) A clear and concise statement of the facts, including pertinent dates, constituting the alleged unlawful employment practices * * *;

(4) If known, the approximate number of employees of the respondent employer or the approximate number of members of the respondent labor organization, as the case may be; and

(5) A statement disclosing whether proceedings involving the alleged unlawful employment practice have been commenced before a State or local agency charged with the enforcement of fair employment practice laws and, if so, the date of such commencement and the name of the agency.

(b) Notwithstanding the provisions of paragraph (a) of this section, a charge is sufficient when the Commission receives from the person making the charge a written statement sufficiently precise to identify the parties, and to describe generally the action or practices complained of. A charge may be amended to cure technical defects or omissions, including failure to verify the charge, or to clarify and amplify allegations made therein. Such amendments and amendments alleging additional acts which constitute unlawful employment practices related to or growing out of the subject matter of the original charge will relate back to the date the charge was first received. * * *

The Supreme Court Speaks

LEDBETTER V. GOODYEAR TIRE & RUBBER CO.

550 U.S. 618 (2007)

JUSTICE ALITO delivered the opinion of the Court. * * * Petitioner Lilly Ledbetter (Ledbetter) worked for respondent Goodyear Tire & Rubber Company (Goodyear) at its Gadsden, Alabama, plant from 1979 until 1998. During much of this time, salaried employees at the plant were given or denied raises based on their supervisors' evaluation of their performance. In March 1998, Ledbetter submitted a questionnaire to the [U.S. Equal Employment Opportunity Commission (EEOC)] alleging certain acts of sex discrimination, and in July of that year she filed a formal EEOC charge. After taking early retirement in November 1998, Ledbetter commenced this action, in which she asserted, among other claims, a Title VII pay discrimination claim and a claim under the Equal Pay Act of 1963 (EPA), 29 U.S.C. § 206(d).

The District Court granted summary judgment in favor of Goodyear on several of Ledbetter's claims, including her EPA claim, but allowed others, including her Title VII pay discrimination claim, to proceed to trial. In support of this latter claim, Ledbetter introduced evidence that during the course of her employment several supervisors had given her poor evaluations because of her sex, that as a result of these evaluations her pay was not increased as much as it would have been if she had been evaluated fairly, and that these past pay decisions continued to affect the amount of her pay throughout her employment. Toward the end of her time with Goodyear, she was being paid significantly less than any of her male colleagues. Goodyear maintained that the evaluations had been nondiscriminatory, but the jury found for Ledbetter and awarded her backpay and damages.

On appeal, Goodyear contended that Ledbetter's pay discrimination claim was time barred with respect to all pay decisions made prior to September 26, 1997—that is, 180 days before the filing of her EEOC questionnaire. And Goodyear argued that no discriminatory act relating to Ledbetter's pay occurred after that date.

The Court of Appeals for the Eleventh Circuit reversed, holding that a Title VII pay discrimination claim cannot be based on any pay decision that occurred prior to the last pay decision that affected the employee's pay during the EEOC charging period. The Court of Appeals then concluded that there was insufficient evidence to prove that Goodyear had acted with discriminatory intent in making the only two pay decisions that occurred within that time span, namely, a decision made in 1997 to deny Ledbetter a raise and a similar decision made in 1998.

Ledbetter filed a petition for a writ of *certiorari* * * * [seeking] review of the following question:

> Whether and under what circumstances a plaintiff may bring an action under Title VII of the Civil Rights Act of 1964 alleging illegal pay discrimination when the disparate pay is received during the statutory limitations period, but is the result of intentionally discriminatory pay decisions that occurred outside the limitations period.

In light of disagreement among the Courts of Appeals as to the proper application of the limitations period in Title VII disparate-treatment pay cases, *compare* [the Eleventh Circuit's decision below in this case,] 421 F.3d 1169 with [*Forsyth v. Federation Employment & Guidance Serv.,* 409 F.3d 565 (C.A.2 2005) ("Any paycheck given within the [charge-filing] period . . . would be actionable, even if based on a discriminatory pay scale set up outside of the statutory period") and] *Shea v. Rice,* 409 F.3d 448 (C.A.D.C. 2005) [("[An] employer commit[s] a separate unlawful employment practice each time he pa[ys] one employee less than another for a discriminatory reason.")], we granted *certiorari*.

II

Title VII of the Civil Rights Act of 1964 makes it an "unlawful employment practice" to discriminate "against any individual with respect to his compensation . . . because of such individual's . . . sex." 42 U.S.C. § 2000e–2(a)(1). An individual wishing to challenge an employment practice under this provision must first file a charge with the EEOC. § 2000e–5(e)(1). Such a charge must be filed within a specified period (either 180 or 300 days, depending on the State) "after the alleged unlawful employment practice occurred," *ibid.*, and if the employee does not submit a timely EEOC charge, the employee may not challenge that practice in court, § 2000e–5(f)(1).

In addressing the issue whether an EEOC charge was filed on time, we have stressed the need to identify with care the specific employment practice that is at issue. [*National Railroad Passenger Corporation v. Morgan*, 536 U.S. 101 (2002), at 110–111]. Ledbetter points to two different employment practices as possible candidates. Primarily, she urges us to focus on the paychecks that were issued to her during the EEOC charging period (the 180-day period preceding the filing of her EEOC questionnaire), each of which, she contends, was a separate act of discrimination. Alternatively, Ledbetter directs us to the 1998 decision denying her a raise, and she argues that this decision was "unlawful because it carried forward intentionally discriminatory disparities from prior years." Both of these arguments fail because they would require us in effect to jettison the defining element of the legal claim on which her Title VII recovery was based.

Ledbetter asserted disparate treatment, the central element of which is discriminatory intent. * * * However, Ledbetter does not assert that the relevant Goodyear decision-makers acted with actual discriminatory intent either when they issued her checks during the EEOC charging period or when they denied her a raise in 1998. Rather, she argues that the paychecks were unlawful because they would have been larger if she had been evaluated in a nondiscriminatory manner *prior to* the EEOC charging period. Similarly, she maintains that the 1998 decision was unlawful because it "carried forward" the effects of prior, uncharged discrimination decisions. * * *

In *United Air Lines, Inc. v. Evans,* 431 U.S. 553 (1977), we rejected an argument that is basically the same as Ledbetter's. Evans was forced to resign because the airline refused to employ married flight attendants, but she did not file an EEOC charge regarding her termination. Some years later, the airline rehired her but treated her as a new employee for seniority purposes. Evans then sued, arguing that, while any suit based on the original discrimination was time barred, the airline's refusal to give her credit for her prior service gave "present effect to [its] past illegal act and therefore perpetuate[d] the consequences of forbidden discrimination." *Id.*, at 557.

We agreed with Evans that the airline's "seniority system [did] indeed have a continuing impact on her pay and fringe benefits," but we noted that "the critical question [was] whether any present *violation* exist[ed]." We concluded that the continuing effects of the precharging period discrimination did not make out a present violation. As Justice STEVENS wrote for the Court:

> United was entitled to treat [Evans' termination] as lawful after respondent failed to file a charge of discrimination within the 90 days then allowed by § 706(d). A discriminatory act which is not made the basis for a timely charge . . . is merely an unfortunate event in history which has no present legal consequences.

It would be difficult to speak to the point more directly.

Equally instructive is *Delaware State College v. Ricks,* 449 U.S. 250 (1980), which concerned a college professor, Ricks, who alleged that he had been discharged because of national origin. In March 1974, Ricks was denied tenure, but he was given a final, nonrenewable 1-year contract that expired on June 30, 1975. Ricks delayed filing a charge with the EEOC until April 1975, but he argued that the EEOC charging period ran from the date of his actual termination rather than from the date when tenure was denied. In rejecting this argument, we recognized that "one of the *effects* of the denial of tenure," namely, his ultimate termination, "did not occur until later." But because Ricks failed to identify any specific discriminatory act "that continued until, or occurred at the time of, the actual termination of his employment," we held that the EEOC charging period ran from "the time the tenure decision was made and communicated to Ricks."

This same approach dictated the outcome in *Lorance v. AT & T Technologies, Inc.,* 490 U.S. 900 (1989), which grew out of a change in the way in which seniority was calculated under a collective-bargaining agreement. Before 1979, all employees at the plant in question accrued seniority based simply on years of employment at the plant. In 1979, a new agreement made seniority for workers in the more highly paid (and traditionally male) position of "tester" depend on time spent in that position alone and not in other positions in the plant. Several years later, when female testers were laid off due to low seniority as calculated under the new provision, they filed an EEOC charge alleging that the 1979 scheme had been adopted with discriminatory intent, namely, to protect incumbent male testers when women with substantial plant seniority began to move into the traditionally male tester positions.

We held that the plaintiffs' EEOC charge was not timely because it was not filed within the specified period after the adoption in 1979 of the new seniority rule. We noted that the plaintiffs had not alleged that the new seniority rule treated men and women differently or that the rule had been applied in a discriminatory manner. Rather, their complaint was that the rule was adopted originally with discriminatory intent. And as in *Evans* and *Ricks,* we held that the EEOC charging period ran from the time when the discrete act of alleged intentional discrimination occurred, not from the date when the effects of this practice were felt. We stated:

> Because the claimed invalidity of the facially nondiscriminatory and neutrally applied tester seniority system is wholly dependent on the alleged illegality of signing the underlying agreement, it is the date of that signing which governs the limitations period. *Id.,* at 911.[2]

Our most recent decision in this area confirms this understanding. In *Morgan,* we explained that the statutory term "employment practice" generally refers to "a discrete act or single 'occurrence' " that takes place at a particular point in time. We pointed to "termination, failure to promote, denial of transfer, [and] refusal to hire" as examples of such "discrete" acts, and we held that a Title VII plaintiff "can only file a charge to cover discrete acts that 'occurred' within the appropriate time period."

The instruction provided by *Evans, Ricks, Lorance,* and *Morgan* is clear. The EEOC charging period is triggered when a discrete unlawful practice takes place. A new violation does not occur, and a new charging period does not commence, upon the occurrence of subsequent nondiscriminatory acts that entail adverse effects resulting from the past discrimination. But of course, if an employer engages in a series of acts each of which is intentionally discriminatory, then a fresh violation takes place when each act is committed.

Ledbetter's arguments here—that the paychecks that she received during the charging period and the 1998 raise denial each violated Title VII and triggered a new EEOC charging period—cannot be reconciled with *Evans, Ricks, Lorance,* and *Morgan.* Ledbetter, as noted, makes no claim that intentionally discriminatory conduct occurred during the charging period or that discriminatory decisions that occurred prior to that period were not communicated to her. Instead, she argues simply that Goodyear's

---

[2] After *Lorance,* Congress amended Title VII to cover the specific situation involved in that case. See 42 U.S.C. § 2000e–5(e)(2) (allowing for Title VII liability arising from an intentionally discriminatory seniority system both at the time of its adoption and at the time of its application). The dissent attaches great significance to this amendment, suggesting that it shows that *Lorance* was wrongly reasoned as an initial matter. However, the very legislative history cited by the dissent explains that this amendment and the other 1991 Title VII amendments " '*expand[ed]* the scope of relevant civil rights statutes in order to provide adequate protection to victims of discrimination.' " For present purposes, what is most important about the amendment in question is that it applied only to the adoption of a discriminatory seniority system, not to other types of employment discrimination. *Evans* and *Ricks,* upon which *Lorance* relied, and which employed identical reasoning, were left in place, and these decisions are more than sufficient to support our holding today.

conduct during the charging period gave present effect to discriminatory conduct outside of that period. But current effects alone cannot breathe life into prior, uncharged discrimination; as we held in *Evans,* such effects in themselves have "no present legal consequences." Ledbetter should have filed an EEOC charge within 180 days after each allegedly discriminatory pay decision was made and communicated to her. She did not do so, and the paychecks that were issued to her during the 180 days prior to the filing of her EEOC charge do not provide a basis for overcoming that prior failure. * * *

Ledbetter's attempt to take the intent associated with the prior pay decisions and shift it to the 1998 pay decision is unsound. It would shift intent from one act (the act that consummates the discriminatory employment practice) to a later act that was not performed with bias or discriminatory motive. The effect of this shift would be to impose liability in the absence of the requisite intent.

Our cases recognize this point. In *Evans,* for example, we did not take the airline's discriminatory intent in 1968, when it discharged the plaintiff because of her sex, and attach that intent to its later act of neutrally applying its seniority rules. Similarly, in *Ricks,* we did not take the discriminatory intent that the college allegedly possessed when it denied Ricks tenure and attach that intent to its subsequent act of terminating his employment when his nonrenewable contract ran out. On the contrary, we held that "the only alleged discrimination occurred—and the filing limitations periods therefore commenced—at the time the tenure decision was made and communicated to Ricks." * * *

Statutes of limitations serve a policy of repose. They "represent a pervasive legislative judgment that it is unjust to fail to put the adversary on notice to defend within a specified period of time and that 'the right to be free of stale claims in time comes to prevail over the right to prosecute them.'" *United States v. Kubrick,* 444 U.S. 111, 117 (1979).

The EEOC filing deadline "protect[s] employers from the burden of defending claims arising from employment decisions that are long past." *Ricks, supra,* at 256–257. Certainly, the 180-day EEOC charging deadline is short by any measure, but "[b]y choosing what are obviously quite short deadlines, Congress clearly intended to encourage the prompt processing of all charges of employment discrimination." [Mohasco Corp. v. Silver, 447 U.S. 807 (1980)], at 825. This short deadline reflects Congress' strong preference for the prompt resolution of employment discrimination allegations through voluntary conciliation and cooperation. [*Occidental Life Ins. Co. of Cal. v. EEOC,* 432 U.S. 355 (1977),] at 367–368. * * *

III

A

In advancing her two theories Ledbetter does not seriously contest the logic of *Evans, Ricks, Lorance,* and *Morgan* as set out above, but rather argues that our decision in *Bazemore v. Friday,* 478 U.S. 385 (1986) *(per curiam),* requires different treatment of her claim because it relates to pay. Ledbetter focuses specifically on our statement that "[e]ach week's paycheck that delivers less to a black than to a similarly situated white is a wrong actionable under Title VII." *Id.,* at 395. She argues that in *Bazemore* we adopted a "paycheck accrual rule" under which each paycheck, even if not accompanied by discriminatory intent, triggers a new EEOC charging period during which the complainant may properly challenge any prior discriminatory conduct that impacted the amount of that paycheck, no matter how long ago the discrimination occurred. On this reading, *Bazemore* dispensed with the need to prove actual discriminatory intent in pay cases and, without giving any hint that it was doing so, repudiated the very different approach taken previously in *Evans* and *Ricks*. Ledbetter's interpretation is unsound. * * *

Bazemore stands for the proposition that an employer violates Title VII and triggers a new EEOC charging period whenever the employer issues paychecks using a discriminatory pay structure. But a new Title VII violation does not occur and a new charging period is not triggered when an employer issues paychecks pursuant to a system that is "facially nondiscriminatory and neutrally applied." *Lorance,* 490 U.S., at 911. The fact that precharging period discrimination adversely affects the calculation of a neutral factor (like seniority) that is used in determining future pay does not mean that each new paycheck constitutes a new violation and restarts the EEOC charging period.

Because Ledbetter has not adduced evidence that Goodyear initially adopted its performance-based pay system in order to discriminate on the basis of sex or that it later applied this system to her within the charging period with any discriminatory animus, *Bazemore* is of no help to her. Rather, all Ledbetter has alleged is that Goodyear's agents discriminated against her individually in the past and that this discrimination reduced the amount of later paychecks. Because Ledbetter did not file timely EEOC charges relating to her employer's discriminatory pay decisions in the past, she cannot maintain a suit based on that past discrimination at this time. * * *

IV

In addition to the arguments previously discussed, Ledbetter relies largely on analogies to other statutory regimes and on extra-statutory policy arguments to support her "paycheck accrual rule."

A

Ledbetter places significant weight on the EPA, which was enacted contemporaneously with Title VII and prohibits paying unequal wages for equal work because of sex. 29 U.S.C. § 206(d). Stating that "the lower courts routinely hear [EPA] claims challenging pay disparities that first arose outside the limitations period," Ledbetter suggests that we should hold that Title VII is violated each time an employee receives a paycheck that reflects past discrimination.

The simple answer to this argument is that the EPA and Title VII are not the same. In particular, the EPA does not require the filing of a charge with the EEOC or proof of intentional discrimination. See § 206(d)(1) (asking only whether the alleged inequality resulted from "any other factor other than sex"). Ledbetter originally asserted an EPA claim, but that claim was dismissed by the District Court and is not before us. If Ledbetter had pursued her EPA claim, she would not face the Title VII obstacles that she now confronts. * * *

B

Ledbetter, finally, makes a variety of policy arguments in favor of giving the alleged victims of pay discrimination more time before they are required to file a charge with the EEOC. Among other things, she claims that pay discrimination is harder to detect than other forms of employment discrimination.

We are not in a position to evaluate Ledbetter's policy arguments, and it is not our prerogative to change the way in which Title VII balances the interests of aggrieved employees against the interest in encouraging the "prompt processing of all charges of employment discrimination," *Mohasco,* 447 U.S., at 825, and the interest in repose.

Ledbetter's policy arguments for giving special treatment to pay claims find no support in the statute and are inconsistent with our precedents. We apply the statute as written, and this means that any unlawful employment practice, including those involving compensation, must be presented to the EEOC within the period prescribed by statute. For these reasons, the judgment of the Court of Appeals for the Eleventh Circuit is affirmed.

JUSTICE GINSBURG, with whom JUSTICE STEVENS, JUSTICE SOUTER, and JUSTICE BREYER join, dissenting. Lilly Ledbetter was a supervisor at Goodyear Tire & Rubber's plant in Gadsden, Alabama, from 1979 until her retirement in 1998. For most of those years, she worked as an area manager, a position largely occupied by men. Initially, Ledbetter's salary was in line with the salaries of men performing substantially similar work. Over time, however, her pay slipped in comparison to the pay of male area managers with equal or less seniority. By the end of 1997, Ledbetter was the only woman working as an area manager and the pay discrepancy between Ledbetter and her 15 male counterparts was stark: Ledbetter was paid $3,727 per month; the lowest paid male area manager received $4,286 per month, the highest paid, $5,236.

Ledbetter launched charges of discrimination before the Equal Employment Opportunity Commission (EEOC) in March 1998. Her formal administrative complaint specified that, in violation of Title VII, Goodyear paid her a discriminatorily low salary because of her sex. *See* 42 U.S.C. § 2000e–2(a)(1) (rendering it unlawful for an employer "to discriminate against any individual with respect to [her] compensation . . . because of such individual's . . . sex"). That charge was eventually tried to a jury, which found it "more likely than not that [Goodyear] paid [Ledbetter] a[n] unequal salary because of her sex." In accord with the jury's liability determination, the District Court entered judgment for Ledbetter for backpay and damages, plus counsel fees and costs.

The Court of Appeals for the Eleventh Circuit reversed. Relying on Goodyear's system of annual merit-based raises, the court held that Ledbetter's claim, in relevant part, was time barred. 421 F.3d, at 1171, 1182–1183. Title VII provides that a charge of discrimination "shall be filed within [180] days after the alleged unlawful employment practice occurred." 42 U.S.C. § 2000e–5(e)(1). Ledbetter charged, and proved at trial, that within the 180-day period, her pay was substantially less than the pay of men doing the same work. Further, she introduced evidence sufficient to establish that discrimination against female managers at the Gadsden plant, not performance inadequacies on her part, accounted for the pay differential. That evidence was unavailing, the Eleventh Circuit held, and the Court today agrees, because it was incumbent on Ledbetter to file charges year by year, each time Goodyear failed to increase her salary commensurate with the salaries of male peers. Any annual pay decision not contested immediately (within 180 days), the Court affirms, becomes grandfathered, a *fait accompli* beyond the province of Title VII ever to repair.

The Court's insistence on immediate contest overlooks common characteristics of pay discrimination. Pay disparities often occur, as they did in Ledbetter's case, in small increments; cause to suspect that discrimination is at work develops only over time. Comparative pay information, moreover, is often hidden from the employee's view. Employers may keep under wraps the pay differentials maintained among supervisors, no less the reasons for those differentials. Small initial discrepancies may not be seen as meet for a federal case, particularly when the employee, trying to succeed in a nontraditional environment, is averse to making waves.

Pay disparities are thus significantly different from adverse actions "such as termination, failure to promote, . . . or refusal to hire," all involving fully communicated discrete acts, "easy to identify" as discriminatory. *See National Railroad Passenger Corporation v. Morgan,* 536 U.S. 101, 114 (2002). It is only when the disparity becomes apparent and sizable, *e.g.*, through future raises calculated as a percentage of current salaries, that an employee in Ledbetter's situation is likely to comprehend her plight and, therefore, to complain. Her initial readiness to give her employer the benefit of the doubt should not preclude her from later challenging the then current and continuing payment of a wage depressed on account of her sex.

On questions of time under Title VII, we have identified as the critical inquiries: "What constitutes an 'unlawful employment practice' and when has that practice 'occurred'?" *Id.,* at 110. Our precedent suggests, and lower courts have overwhelmingly held, that the unlawful practice is the *current payment* of salaries infected by gender-based (or race-based) discrimination—a practice that occurs whenever a paycheck delivers less to a woman than to a similarly situated man.

I

Title VII proscribes as an "unlawful employment practice" discrimination "against any individual with respect to his compensation . . . because of such individual's race, color, religion, sex, or national origin." 42 U.S.C. § 2000e–2(a)(1). An individual seeking to challenge an employment practice under this proscription must file a charge with the EEOC within 180 days "after the alleged unlawful employment practice occurred." § 2000e–5(e)(1).

Ledbetter's petition presents a question important to the sound application of Title VII: What activity qualifies as an unlawful employment practice in cases of discrimination with respect to compensation. One answer identifies the pay-setting decision, and that decision alone, as the unlawful practice. Under this view, each particular salary-setting decision is discrete from prior and subsequent decisions, and must be challenged within 180 days on pain of forfeiture. Another response counts both the pay-setting decision and the actual payment of a discriminatory wage as unlawful practices. Under this approach, each payment of a wage or salary infected by sex-based discrimination constitutes an unlawful employment practice; prior decisions, outside the 180-day charge-filing period, are not themselves actionable, but they are relevant in determining the lawfulness of conduct within the period. The Court adopts the first view, but the second is more faithful to precedent, more in tune with the realities of the workplace, and more respectful of Title VII's remedial purpose.

A

In *Bazemore,* we unanimously held that an employer, the North Carolina Agricultural Extension Service, committed an unlawful employment practice each time it paid black employees less than similarly situated white employees. Before 1965, the Extension Service was divided into two branches: a white branch and a "Negro branch." Employees in the "Negro branch" were paid less than their white counterparts. In response to the Civil Rights Act of 1964, which included Title VII, the State merged the two branches into a single organization, made adjustments to reduce the salary disparity, and began giving annual raises based on nondiscriminatory factors. Nonetheless, "some pre-existing salary disparities continued to linger on." We rejected the Court of Appeals' conclusion that the plaintiffs could not prevail because the lingering disparities were simply a continuing effect of a decision lawfully made prior to the effective date of Title VII. Rather, we reasoned, "[e]ach week's paycheck that delivers less to a black than to a similarly situated white is a wrong actionable under Title VII." Paychecks perpetuating past discrimination, we thus recognized, are actionable not simply because they are "related" to a decision made outside the charge-filing period, but because they discriminate anew each time they issue.

Subsequently, in *Morgan,* we set apart, for purposes of Title VII's timely filing requirement, unlawful employment actions of two kinds: "discrete acts" that are "easy to identify" as discriminatory, and acts that recur and are cumulative in impact. See *id.,* at 110, 113–115 ("[A] [d]iscrete ac[t] such as termination, failure to promote, denial of transfer, or refusal to hire," *id.,* at 114, we explained, " 'occur[s]' on the day that it 'happen[s].' A party, therefore, must file a charge within . . . 180 . . . days of the date of the act or lose the ability to recover for it." *Id.*, at 110; see *id.*, at 113 ("[D]iscrete discriminatory acts are not actionable if time barred, even when they are related to acts alleged in timely filed charges. Each discrete discriminatory act starts a new clock for filing charges alleging that act.").

"[D]ifferent in kind from discrete acts," we made clear, are "claims . . . based on the cumulative effect of individual acts." *Id.,* at 115. The *Morgan* decision placed hostile work environment claims in that category. "Their very nature involves repeated conduct." *Ibid.* "The unlawful employment practice" in hostile work environment claims "cannot be said to occur on any particular day. It occurs over a series of days or perhaps years and, in direct contrast to discrete acts, a single act of harassment may not be actionable on its own." *Ibid.* The persistence of the discriminatory conduct both indicates that management should have known of its existence and produces a cognizable harm. *Ibid.* Because the very nature of the hostile work environment claim involves repeated conduct,

> [i]t does not matter, for purposes of the statute, that some of the component acts of the hostile work environment fall outside the statutory time period. Provided that an act contributing to the claim occurs within the filing period, the entire time period of the hostile environment may be considered by a court for the purposes of determining liability. *Id.*, at 117.

Consequently, although the unlawful conduct began in the past, "a charge may be filed at a later date and still encompass the whole." *Ibid.*

Pay disparities, of the kind Ledbetter experienced, have a closer kinship to hostile work environment claims than to charges of a single episode of discrimination. Ledbetter's claim, resembling Morgan's, rested not on one particular paycheck, but on "the cumulative effect of individual acts." See *id.*, at 115. She charged insidious discrimination building up slowly but steadily. Initially in line with the salaries of men performing substantially the same work, Ledbetter's salary fell 15 to 40 percent behind her male counterparts only after successive evaluations and percentage-based pay adjustments. Over time, she alleged and proved, the repetition of pay decisions undervaluing her work gave rise to the current discrimination of which she complained. Though component acts fell outside the charge-filing period, with each new paycheck, Goodyear contributed incrementally to the accumulating harm.[2]

B

The realities of the workplace reveal why the discrimination with respect to compensation that Ledbetter suffered does not fit within the category of singular discrete acts "easy to identify." A worker knows immediately if she is denied a promotion or transfer, if she is fired or refused employment. And promotions, transfers, hirings, and firings are generally public events, known to co-workers. When an employer makes a decision of such open and definitive character, an employee can immediately seek out an explanation and evaluate it for pretext. Compensation disparities, in contrast, are often hidden from sight. It is not unusual, decisions in point illustrate, for management to decline to publish employee pay levels, or for employees to keep private their own salaries. Tellingly, as the record in this case bears out, Goodyear kept salaries confidential; employees had only limited access to information regarding their colleagues' earnings.

The problem of concealed pay discrimination is particularly acute where the disparity arises not because the female employee is flatly denied a raise but because male counterparts are given larger raises. Having received a pay increase, the female employee is unlikely to discern at once that she has experienced an adverse employment decision. She may have little reason even to suspect discrimination until a pattern develops incrementally and she ultimately becomes aware of the disparity. Even if an employee suspects that the reason for a comparatively low raise is not performance but sex (or another protected ground), the amount involved

---

[2] *National Railroad Passenger Corporation v. Morgan,* 536 U.S. 101, 117 (2002), the Court emphasizes, required that "an act contributing to the claim occu[r] within the [charge-]filing period." Here, each paycheck within the filing period compounded the discrimination Ledbetter encountered, and thus contributed to the "actionable wrong," *i.e.*, the succession of acts composing the pattern of discriminatory pay, of which she complained.

may seem too small, or the employer's intent too ambiguous, to make the issue immediately actionable—or winnable. * * *

C

In light of the significant differences between pay disparities and discrete employment decisions of the type identified in *Morgan,* the cases on which the Court relies hold no sway. *Evans* and *Ricks* both involved a single, immediately identifiable act of discrimination: in *Evans,* a constructive discharge, in *Ricks,* a denial of tenure. In each case, the employee filed charges well after the discrete discriminatory act occurred: When United Airlines forced Evans to resign because of its policy barring married female flight attendants, she filed no charge; only four years later, when Evans was rehired, did she allege that the airline's former no-marriage rule was unlawful and therefore should not operate to deny her seniority credit for her prior service. Similarly, when Delaware State College denied Ricks tenure, he did not object until his terminal contract came to an end, one year later. No repetitive, cumulative discriminatory employment practice was at issue in either case. * * *

Lorance is also inapposite, for, in this Court's view, it too involved a one-time discrete act: the adoption of a new seniority system that "had its genesis in sex discrimination." *See* 490 U.S., at 902, 905. The Court's extensive reliance on *Lorance,* moreover, is perplexing for that decision is no longer effective: In the 1991 Civil Rights Act, Congress superseded *Lorance's* holding. § 112, 105 Stat. 1079 (codified as amended at 42 U.S.C. § 2000e–5(e)(2)). Repudiating our judgment that a facially neutral seniority system adopted with discriminatory intent must be challenged immediately, Congress provided:

> "For purposes of this section, an unlawful employment practice occurs . . . when the seniority system is adopted, when an individual becomes subject to the seniority system, or when a person aggrieved is injured by the application of the seniority system or provision of the system."

Ibid.

Congress thus agreed with the dissenters in *Lorance* that "the harsh reality of [that] decision" was "glaringly at odds with the purposes of Title VII." 490 U.S., at 914 (opinion of Marshall, J.). See also § 3, 105 Stat. 1071 (1991 Civil Rights Act was designed "to respond to recent decisions of the Supreme Court by expanding the scope of relevant civil rights statutes in order to provide adequate protection to victims of discrimination"). True, § 112 of the 1991 Civil Rights Act directly addressed only seniority systems. But Congress made clear (1) its view that this Court had unduly *contracted* the scope of protection afforded by Title VII and other civil rights statutes, and (2) its aim to generalize the ruling in *Bazemore.* As the Senate Report accompanying the proposed Civil Rights Act of 1990, the precursor to the 1991 Act, explained:

> Where, as was alleged in *Lorance,* an employer adopts a rule or decision with an unlawful discriminatory motive, each application of that rule or decision is a new violation of the law. In *Bazemore* . . ., for example, . . . the Supreme Court properly held that each application of th[e] racially motivated salary structure, *i.e.,* each new paycheck, constituted a distinct violation of Title VII. Section 7(a)(2) generalizes the result correctly reached in *Bazemore.*" Civil Rights Act of 1990, S.Rep. No. 101–315, p. 54 (1990).

See also 137 Cong. Rec. 29046, 29047 (1991) (Sponsors' Interpretative Memorandum) ("This legislation should be interpreted as disapproving the extension of *[Lorance]* to contexts outside of seniority systems."). * * *

Until today, in the more than 15 years since Congress amended Title VII, the Court had not once relied upon *Lorance.* It is mistaken to do so now. Just as Congress' "goals in enacting Title VII . . . never included conferring absolute immunity on discriminatorily adopted seniority systems that survive their first [180] days," 490 U.S., at 914 (Marshall, J., dissenting), Congress never intended to immunize forever discriminatory pay differentials unchallenged within 180 days of their adoption. This assessment gains weight when one comprehends that even a relatively minor pay disparity will expand exponentially over an employee's working life if raises are set as a percentage of prior pay. * * *

D

In tune with the realities of wage discrimination, the Courts of Appeals have overwhelmingly judged as a present violation the payment of wages infected by discrimination: Each paycheck less than the amount payable had the employer adhered to a nondiscriminatory compensation regime, courts have held, constitutes a cognizable harm. * * *

Similarly in line with the real-world characteristics of pay discrimination, the EEOC—the federal agency responsible for enforcing Title VII, see, *e.g.,* 42 U.S.C. §§ 2000e–5(f), 2000e–12(a)—has interpreted the Act to permit employees to challenge disparate pay each time it is received. The EEOC's Compliance Manual provides that "[r]epeated occurrences of the same discriminatory employment action, such as discriminatory paychecks, can be challenged as long as one discriminatory act occurred within the charge filing period." 2 *EEOC Compliance Manual* § 2–IV–C(1)(a), p. 605:0024, and n. 183 (2006); cf. *id.*, § 10–III, p. 633:0002 Title VII requires an employer to eliminate pay disparities attributable to a discriminatory system, even if that system has been discontinued).

The EEOC has given effect to its interpretation in a series of administrative decisions. See *Albritton v. Potter,* No. 01A44063, 2004 WL 2983682, *2 (EEOC Office of Fed. Operations, Dec. 17, 2004) (although disparity arose and employee became aware of the disparity outside the charge-filing period, claim was not time barred because "[e]ach paycheck that complainant receives which is less than that of similarly situated employees outside of her protected classes could support a claim under Title VII if discrimination is found to be the reason for the pay discrepancy." And in this very case, the EEOC urged the Eleventh Circuit to recognize that Ledbetter's failure to challenge any particular pay-setting decision when that decision was made "does not deprive her of the right to seek relief for discriminatory paychecks she received in 1997 and 1998." *Brief of EEOC in Support of Petition for Rehearing and Suggestion for Rehearing En Banc*, in No. 03–15264–GG (CA11), p. 14 (hereinafter EEOC Brief).[6]

II

The Court asserts that treating pay discrimination as a discrete act, limited to each particular pay-setting decision, is necessary to "protec[t] employers from the burden of defending claims arising from employment decisions that are long past." But the discrimination of which Ledbetter complained is *not* long past. As she alleged, and as the jury found, Goodyear continued to treat Ledbetter differently because of sex each pay period, with mounting harm. Allowing employees to challenge discrimination "that extend[s] over long periods of time," into the charge-filing period, we have previously explained, "does not leave employers defenseless" against unreasonable or prejudicial delay. *Morgan,* 536 U.S., at 121. Employers disadvantaged by such delay may raise various defenses. Doctrines such as "waiver, estoppel, and equitable tolling" "allow us to honor Title VII's remedial purpose without negating the particular purpose of the filing requirement, to give prompt notice to the employer." *Id.*, at 121 (quoting *Zipes v. Trans World Airlines, Inc.,* 455 U.S. 385, 398 (1982)); *see* 536 U.S., at 121 (defense of laches may be invoked to block an employee's suit "if he unreasonably delays in filing [charges] and as a result harms the defendant"); EEOC Brief 15 ("[I]f Ledbetter unreasonably delayed challenging an earlier decision, and that delay significantly impaired Goodyear's ability to defend itself . . . Goodyear can raise a defense of laches . . . .").

In a last-ditch argument, the Court asserts that this dissent would allow a plaintiff to sue on a single decision made 20 years ago "even if the employee had full knowledge of all the circumstances relating to the . . . decision at the time it was made." It suffices to point out that the defenses

[6] The Court dismisses the EEOC's considerable "experience and informed judgment," *Firefighters v. Cleveland,* 478 U.S. 501, 518 (1986), as unworthy of any deference in this case. But the EEOC's interpretations mirror workplace realities and merit at least respectful attention. In any event, the level of deference due the EEOC here is an academic question, for the agency's conclusion that Ledbetter's claim is not time barred is the best reading of the statute even if the Court "were interpreting [Title VII] from scratch." See *Edelman v. Lynchburg College,* 535 U.S. 106, 114 (2002).

just noted would make such a suit foolhardy. No sensible judge would tolerate such inexcusable neglect. See *Morgan,* 536 U.S., at 121 ("In such cases, the federal courts have the discretionary power . . . to locate a just result in light of the circumstances peculiar to the case.").

Ledbetter, the Court observes, dropped an alternative remedy she could have pursued: Had she persisted in pressing her claim under the Equal Pay Act of 1963 (EPA), 77 Stat. 56, 29 U.S.C. § 206(d), she would not have encountered a time bar.[8] Notably, the EPA provides no relief when the pay discrimination charged is based on race, religion, national origin, age, or disability. Thus, in truncating the Title VII rule this Court announced in *Bazemore,* the Court does not disarm female workers from achieving redress for unequal pay, but it does impede racial and other minorities from gaining similar relief.[9]

Furthermore, the difference between the EPA's prohibition against paying unequal wages and Title VII's ban on discrimination with regard to compensation is not as large as the Court's opinion might suggest. The key distinction is that Title VII requires a showing of intent. In practical effect, "if the trier of fact is in equipoise about whether the wage differential is motivated by gender discrimination," Title VII compels a verdict for the employer, while the EPA compels a verdict for the plaintiff. 2 C. Sullivan, M. Zimmer, & R. White, EMPLOYMENT DISCRIMINATION: LAW AND PRACTICE § 7.08[F][3], p. 532 (3d ed. 2002). In this case, Ledbetter carried the burden of persuading the jury that the pay disparity she suffered was attributable to intentional sex discrimination.

III

To show how far the Court has strayed from interpretation of Title VII with fidelity to the Act's core purpose, I return to the evidence Ledbetter presented at trial. Ledbetter proved to the jury the following: She was a member of a protected class; she performed work substantially equal to work of the dominant class (men); she was compensated less for that work; and the disparity was attributable to gender-based discrimination.

Specifically, Ledbetter's evidence demonstrated that her current pay was discriminatorily low due to a long series of decisions reflecting Goodyear's pervasive discrimination against women managers in general and Ledbetter in particular. Ledbetter's former supervisor, for example,

---

[8] Under the EPA, which is subject to the Fair Labor Standards Act's time prescriptions, a claim charging denial of equal pay accrues anew with each paycheck. 1 B. Lindemann & P. Grossman, EMPLOYMENT DISCRIMINATION LAW 529 (3d ed.1996); cf. 29 U.S.C. § 255(a) (prescribing a two-year statute of limitations for violations generally, but a three-year limitation period for willful violations).

[9] For example, under today's decision, if a black supervisor initially received the same salary as his white colleagues, but annually received smaller raises, there would be no right to sue under Title VII outside the 180-day window following each annual salary change, however strong the cumulative evidence of discrimination might be. The Court would thus force plaintiffs, in many cases, to sue too soon to prevail, while cutting them off as time barred once the pay differential is large enough to enable them to mount a winnable case.

admitted to the jury that Ledbetter's pay, during a particular one-year period, fell below Goodyear's minimum threshold for her position. Although Goodyear claimed the pay disparity was due to poor performance, the supervisor acknowledged that Ledbetter received a "Top Performance Award" in 1996. The jury also heard testimony that another supervisor—who evaluated Ledbetter in 1997 and whose evaluation led to her most recent raise denial—was openly biased against women. And two women who had previously worked as managers at the plant told the jury they had been subject to pervasive discrimination and were paid less than their male counterparts. One was paid less than the men she supervised. Ledbetter herself testified about the discriminatory animus conveyed to her by plant officials. Toward the end of her career, for instance, the plant manager told Ledbetter that the "plant did not need women, that [women] didn't help it, [and] caused problems." After weighing all the evidence, the jury found for Ledbetter, concluding that the pay disparity was due to intentional discrimination.

Yet, under the Court's decision, the discrimination Ledbetter proved is not redressable under Title VII. Each and every pay decision she did not immediately challenge wiped the slate clean. Consideration may not be given to the cumulative effect of a series of decisions that, together, set her pay well below that of every male area manager. Knowingly carrying past pay discrimination forward must be treated as lawful conduct. Ledbetter may not be compensated for the lower pay she was in fact receiving when she complained to the EEOC. Nor, were she still employed by Goodyear, could she gain, on the proof she presented at trial, injunctive relief requiring, prospectively, her receipt of the same compensation men receive for substantially similar work. The Court's approbation of these consequences is totally at odds with the robust protection against workplace discrimination Congress intended Title VII to secure. See, *e.g., Teamsters v. United States,* 431 U.S., at 348 ("The primary purpose of Title VII was to assure equality of employment opportunities and to eliminate . . . discriminatory practices and devices . . . ."; *Albemarle Paper Co. v. Moody,* 422 U.S. 405, 418 (1975) ("It is . . . the purpose of Title VII to make persons whole for injuries suffered on account of unlawful employment discrimination.").

This is not the first time the Court has ordered a cramped interpretation of Title VII, incompatible with the statute's broad remedial purpose. See also *Wards Cove Packing Co. v. Atonio,* 490 U.S. 642 (1989) (superseded in part by the Civil Rights Act of 1991); *Price Waterhouse v. Hopkins,* 490 U.S. 228 (1989) (plurality opinion) (same); 1 B. Lindemann & P. Grossman, EMPLOYMENT DISCRIMINATION LAW 2 (3d ed. 1996) ("A spate of Court decisions in the late 1980s drew congressional fire and resulted in demands for legislative change[,]" culminating in the 1991 Civil Rights Act (footnote omitted)). Once again, the ball is in Congress' court. As in 1991, the Legislature may act to correct this Court's parsimonious reading of Title VII.

For the reasons stated, I would hold that Ledbetter's claim is not time barred and would reverse the Eleventh Circuit's judgment.

In the Media and in the Political Realm

ROBERT PEAR, "JUSTICES' RULING IN DISCRIMINATION CASE MAY DRAW QUICK ACTION BY OBAMA"

New York Times (January 4, 2009)

WASHINGTON—President-elect Barack Obama and Democrats in Congress are planning swift action to overturn a Supreme Court decision that made it much harder for people to challenge discrimination in employment, education, housing and other fields. The decision, involving a woman named Lilly M. Ledbetter, who had accused her employer of sex-based pay discrimination, was issued in May 2007. Since then, courts around the country have gone far beyond the facts of that case and cited it as a reason for rejecting lawsuits claiming discrimination based on race, sex, age and disability. In some cases, after initially ruling for employees, judges have reversed themselves and ruled in favor of employers. The judges said they had to switch because of the Supreme Court decision.

Ms. Ledbetter, who worked at a Goodyear tire plant in Gadsden, Ala., for 19 years, spoke at the Democratic National Convention in August, campaigned for Mr. Obama and made a television commercial for him. She became a hero to many Democrats, their answer to "Joe the Plumber." As a senator, Mr. Obama was a co-sponsor of a bill to overturn the Supreme Court decision. In the final presidential debate, he said he would appoint judges who understood the struggles of "real-world folks" like Ms. Ledbetter.

The legislation would essentially relax the statute of limitations under various civil rights laws, giving people more time to file charges. President Bush threatened to veto the bill, but Mr. Obama is eager to sign it. "Obama said he would see me in the White House when he signs the bill," Ms. Ledbetter said in an interview.

Mr. Obama describes the bill as part of a broader effort by his incoming administration to "update the social contract," reinvigorate civil rights and close the pay gap between men and women. At issue in the Ledbetter case was the deadline for filing charges under Title VII of the Civil Rights Act of 1964. The Supreme Court did not deny that Ms. Ledbetter had suffered discrimination, but said she should have filed her claim within 180 days of "the alleged unlawful employment practice"—the initial decision to pay her less than men performing similar work. The Supreme Court rejected the argument that each paycheck was a violation of the law. Writing for the majority, Justice Samuel A. Alito Jr. said the statute of limitations must be strictly interpreted to protect employers against "stale claims" and "tardy lawsuits."

In a dissenting opinion, Justice Ruth Bader Ginsburg said Ms. Ledbetter's pay fell behind that of men because of "a long series of decisions reflecting Goodyear's pervasive discrimination against women managers in general and Ledbetter in particular." Justice Ginsburg invited Congress to correct the court's "cramped interpretation" of the law.

That is exactly what Speaker Nancy Pelosi and other Democrats say they plan to do. Their bill states that a violation occurs each time a person receives a paycheck resulting from "a discriminatory compensation decision." The House passed a similar bill, 225 to 199, in July 2007. In the Senate, supporters fell three votes short of the 60 needed to overcome a filibuster, but they will almost surely be able to clear that hurdle in the new Congress.

The United States Chamber of Commerce opposes the bill, saying it "would lead to an explosion of litigation" against employers. Under the bill, "it is possible that claims could be filed decades after an allegedly discriminatory act occurred," said R. Bruce Josten, executive vice president of the chamber.

In the last 19 months, federal judges have cited the *Ledbetter* decision in more than 300 cases involving not only Title VII, but also the Age Discrimination in Employment Act; the Fair Housing Act; a law known as Title IX, which bars sex discrimination in schools and colleges; and even the Eighth Amendment to the Constitution, which protects prisoners' rights. Lower-court judges have been influenced by two particular aspects of the *Ledbetter* decision. The Supreme Court drew a sharp distinction between "discrete acts" of discrimination and the continuing effects of past violations. Employers, it said, do not necessarily violate the law when their recent actions have no discriminatory purpose, but perpetuate the adverse effects of pay decisions made in the past.

The *Ledbetter* precedent has stymied a wide range of civil rights plaintiffs. In March 2007, Judge Paul L. Friedman of the Federal District Court here allowed employees at the Federal Aviation Administration to challenge the agency's pay scales as biased against older workers. A year later he reversed himself and ruled for the government, saying, "The import of *Ledbetter* for this case is clear." F.A.A. employees cannot sue on the theory that each paycheck constitutes "a discrete act of discrimination," the judge said.

The United States Court of Appeals for the Seventh Circuit reached a similar conclusion in a lawsuit by blacks who had applied unsuccessfully for jobs as firefighters in Chicago. Judge Richard A. Posner cited the *Ledbetter* case in rejecting their contention that they were victims of a "continuing violation" of the civil rights law. The United States Court of Appeals for the Ninth Circuit extended this logic to a housing discrimination case in Idaho. The ruling significantly limits the ability of plaintiffs to enforce their rights under the Fair Housing Act. The Idaho plaintiff, Noll Garcia, uses a wheelchair. He said his apartment violated federal standards because it was not readily accessible. Under the law, he had two years to challenge a "discriminatory housing practice" in court. Chief Judge Alex Kozinski, writing for the majority, said this two-year period began when construction of the building was complete. Mr. Garcia lost out because he filed suit in 2003—within two years of renting the apartment, but 10 years after it was built. Three dissenting judges said the decision showed how "statutes of limitations have been twisted by courts to limit the scope and thrust of civil rights laws."

A federal district judge in Sacramento also relied on the *Ledbetter* case in rejecting claims by female wrestlers who said they had been denied athletic opportunities at the University of California, Davis. The women missed the deadline for filing suit—one year after the last "discrete act" of discrimination—and cannot breathe new life into their claims by pointing to the continuing effects of prior discriminatory decisions, the court said.

Congress and the courts have been tussling over the scope of civil rights for more than a century. In 1883, the Supreme Court struck down a law that barred racial discrimination by hotels, theaters and railroads, saying Congress had exceeded its power. In 1988 and 1991, Congress expanded civil rights protections that had been curtailed by the Supreme Court. In September, Congress repudiated several Supreme Court decisions that had undercut the Americans With Disabilities Act. "There's a historic pattern of the court's being hostile to civil rights statutes and Congress stepping in to overturn those narrow court rulings," said Deborah L. Brake, a law professor at the University of Pittsburgh.

Congress and the President Respond

Public Law 111–2

111th Congress

An Act

To amend title VII of the Civil Rights Act of 1964 and the Age Discrimination in Employment Act of 1967, and to modify the operation of the Americans with Disabilities Act of 1990 * * *, to clarify that a discriminatory compensation decision or other practice that is unlawful under such Acts occurs each time compensation is paid pursuant to the discriminatory compensation decision or other practice, and for other purposes.

Be it enacted by the Senate and House of Representatives of the United States of America in Congress assembled,

SECTION 1. SHORT TITLE.

This Act may be cited as the "Lilly Ledbetter Fair Pay Act of 2009".

SEC. 2. FINDINGS.

Congress finds the following:

(1) The Supreme Court in *Ledbetter v. Goodyear Tire & Rubber Co.*, 550 U.S. 618 (2007), significantly impairs statutory protections against discrimination in compensation that Congress established and that have been bedrock principles of American law for decades. The *Ledbetter* decision undermines those statutory protections by unduly restricting the time period in which victims of discrimination can challenge and recover for discriminatory compensation decisions or other practices, contrary to the intent of Congress.

(2) The limitation imposed by the Court on the filing of discriminatory compensation claims ignores the reality of wage discrimination and is at odds with the robust application of the civil rights laws that Congress intended.

(3) With regard to any charge of discrimination under any law, nothing in this Act is intended to preclude or limit an aggrieved person's right to introduce evidence of an unlawful employment practice that has occurred outside the time for filing a charge of discrimination. * * *

SEC. 3. DISCRIMINATION IN COMPENSATION BECAUSE OF RACE, COLOR, RELIGION, SEX, OR NATIONAL ORIGIN.

Section 706(e) of the Civil Rights Act of 1964 (42 U.S.C. 2000e–5(e)) is amended by adding at the end the following:

"(3)(A) For purposes of this section, an unlawful employment practice occurs, with respect to discrimination in compensation in violation of this title, when a discriminatory compensation decision or other practice is adopted, when an individual becomes subject to a discriminatory compensation decision or other practice, or when an individual is affected by application of a discriminatory compensation decision or other practice, including each time wages, benefits, or other compensation is paid, resulting in whole or in part from such a decision or other practice. * * *"

SEC. 6. EFFECTIVE DATE.

This Act, and the amendments made by this Act, take effect as if enacted on May 28, 2007 and apply to all claims of discrimination in compensation under title VII of the Civil Rights Act of 1964 (42 U.S.C. 2000e et seq.), the Age Discrimination in Employment Act of 1967 (29 U.S.C. 621 et seq.), title I and section 503 of the Americans with Disabilities Act of 1990, and sections 501 and 504 of the Rehabilitation Act of 1973, that are pending on or after that date.

Approved by Congress and Signed by the President of the United States: January 29, 2009

One Part of the Aftermath

ALEXANDER V. SETON HALL UNIVERSITY

204 N.J. 219, 8 A.3d 198 (2010)

JUSTICE LA VECCHIA. In this appeal, we review the timeliness of a wage discrimination complaint, brought under New Jersey's Law Against Discrimination (LAD), N.J.S.A. 10:5–1 to –49, which the courts below dismissed based on a statute of limitations application that incorporated the reasoning of *Ledbetter v. Goodyear Tire & Rubber Co.*, 550 U.S. 618 (2007) (establishing framework for analyzing accrual and timeliness in Title VII wage discrimination claims).

Plaintiffs, three female tenured professors at Seton Hall University, filed this 2007 action claiming that they were paid unequal wages in comparison to younger and/or male employees. Their complaint sought damages back to their respective dates of initial hire. The University moved to dismiss based on timeliness grounds. The motion court declared that its analysis would be controlled by the *Ledbetter* decision, and held that any and all disparate wages paid to plaintiffs, including those paid within the two-year period immediately prior to the complaint's filing, were simply the result of allegedly intentional discriminatory pay decisions that occurred outside of the limitations period. The trial court's final order of dismissal was affirmed on appeal.

We granted plaintiffs' petition for certification, recognizing that this appeal would afford us the opportunity to address whether New Jersey's LAD jurisprudence would be enhanced by importation of the Supreme Court's *Ledbetter* analysis. We now conclude that there is no necessary or beneficial purpose to be drawn from adoption of the *Ledbetter* approach.

Our holding today reaffirms that in New Jersey the payment of unequal wages on the discriminatory basis of age or sex is proscribed by the LAD, and each payment of such discriminatory wages constitutes an actionable wrong that is remediable under the LAD. The two-year statute of limitations applies to such violations by merely cutting off the untimely portion of such claims. Thus, the statute of limitations' operation results in limiting the damages recoverable for past discriminatory compensation. Case law in this state has long approached issues concerning the timeliness of LAD actions in wage claims in such a manner, and no persuasive reason has been advanced to supplant that established state law. We hold that plaintiffs' complaint was timely in respect of the allegedly discriminatory wages they received during the two years immediately prior to the filing of their complaint. We therefore reverse and remand for reinstatement of plaintiffs' timely claims of wage dis-crimination.

I.

On July 27, 2007, Paula Alexander, Joan Coll, and Cheryl Thompson-Sard, all veteran professors, filed a complaint against their employer, Seton Hall University, and certain school officials (defendants are collectively referred to as "the University"). Plaintiffs alleged LAD violations on the basis of age and gender, specifically, discriminatory discrepancies between their salaries and those earned by younger employees and male employees. As this case was decided below on the basis of a motion to dismiss filed by defendants, we recite the facts in a light most favorable to plaintiffs.

The catalyst for plaintiffs' pursuit of this claim was a 2004–2005 annual report ("Report"), compiled by the University, which detailed the salaries of its full-time faculty members by "College," "Gender," "Rank," and "Salary." Although the Report was not generally available to the faculty, plaintiffs obtained a copy in August of 2005. The Report revealed that higher salaries were paid to newer, younger faculty members as compared to those paid to longer-term, older faculty members. A gender-based pattern of disparate compensation was also apparent. The plaintiffs, each over sixty years in age and boasting at least nineteen years of service to the University, claim that the discrimination permeates several University departments.

Paula Alexander is an Associate Professor in the Stillman School of Business ("Business School"), Management Department. She was hired in 1976, and received tenure in 1981 when she was promoted to Associate Professor. In 2004–2005, Alexander earned $79,000 after twenty-four years of service at the Associate Professorship level. The Report revealed that two female Associate Professors, considerably younger and newer to the University than Alexander, were each earning approximately $50,000 a year more than she was. The following year, the University hired a young male Assistant Professor for the Business School at a salary of $105,000 per annum, as compared to Alexander's $87,000 for that year.

Joan Coll is a Full Professor in the Business School, Management Department. She was hired in 1981, and since 1994 has held the position of Full Professor, the University's highest rank. The 2004–2005 Report revealed that Coll was earning approximately $20,000 a year less than the male Full Professors in the Business School. Upon reviewing the Report, both Alexander and Coll requested an internal adjustment to bring their salaries in line with those of comparable younger professors and male professors. Those requests were denied.

Cheryl Thompson-Sard is an Associate Professor in the College of Education and Human Services, Department of Professional Psychology and Family Therapy. She was hired in 1987 and promoted to the rank of Associate Professor with tenure in 1992. Thompson-Sard's claims are based on averages, calculated from the Report, indicating that male Associate Professors in the College of Education earned approximately $15,000 more per year than their female counterparts.

The matter proceeded on the basis of the University's motion to dismiss for failure to file timely. [The lower court, citing *Ledbetter*, ultimately dismissed the complaints as untimely.] * * * Plaintiffs appealed, framing their argument in terms of the "continuing violation" doctrine common to workplace harassment claims. * * * [A panel of the state court of appeals affirmed.] Influenced by recent federal case law on the subject of wage discrimination claims, specifically the United States Supreme Court's decision in *Ledbetter*, the panel concluded that the continuing violation doctrine had no applicability in a wage discrimination setting. Rather, citing *Ledbetter*, it held that "a pay-setting decision is a discrete act sufficient to trigger the limitations period." *Id.* at 584.[2] Consequently, the panel determined that plaintiffs' complaint was untimely because no discriminatory pay-setting decision had occurred during the statute of limitations period. *Id.* at 586–87 (concluding that receipt of disparate paycheck, without showing discriminatory animus tied to same, is "merely the effect of discriminatory acts that occurred outside the [charging] period and, therefore, did not support a timely cause of action".

II.

* * * The University views the LAD violation that has been alleged as one that, to the extent it arose, accrued as a discrete act of discriminatory animus when the wage was established. Plaintiffs, on the other hand, argue that through operation of the continuing violation doctrine that has been used in workplace harassment claims, each paycheck that perpetuates a discriminatory wage continues the original LAD violation

[2] Although the panel debated whether to follow the policy adopted in *Ledbetter*, it concluded that the State Legislature's failure to adopt a post-*Ledbetter* LAD amendment, similar in kind to that codified on the federal level, was indicative of a legislative preference for the federal jurisprudential approach in LAD claims. *Alexander, supra*, 410 *N.J.Super.* at 588, 983 A.2d 1128. *See* Lilly Ledbetter Fair Pay Act of 2009, 42 U.S.C.A. § 2000e–5(e)(3)(B) (amending Title VII and allowing recovery of back pay for up to two years preceding filing of Title VII charge notwithstanding that original discriminatory compensation decision was made outside time frame for charge's filing).

and sweeps in all prior and current discriminatory, disparate paychecks. Based on that argument, plaintiffs maintain that they are entitled to equitable relief from the two-year statute of limitations. * * *

III.

Plaintiffs' cause of action seeks the vindication of a major public policy of this state, which assures, as enshrined in the LAD, that

> persons shall have the opportunity to obtain employment . . . without discrimination because of race, creed, color, national origin, ancestry, age, marital status, affectional or sexual orientation, familial status, disability, nationality, sex, gender identity or expression . . ., subject only to conditions and limitations applicable alike to all persons. This opportunity is recognized as and declared to be a civil right.

N.J.S.A. 10:5–4.

The Legislature committed firmly to its purpose, declaring plainly the state's public interest in eliminating practices of discrimination:

> [P]ractices of discrimination against any of its inhabitants, because of race, creed, color, national origin, ancestry, age, sex, affectional or sexual orientation, marital status, familial status, liability for [military] service . . ., or nationality, are matters of concern to the government of the State, and . . . such discrimination threatens not only the rights and proper privileges of the inhabitants of the State but menaces the institutions and foundation of a free democratic State[.]

N.J.S.A. 10:5–3.

Without doubt, the LAD "unequivocally expresses a legislative intent to prohibit discrimination in all aspects of the employment relationship, including hiring and firing, compensation, the terms and conditions of employment, and retirement." *Nini v. Mercer County Cmty. Coll.*, 202 N.J. 98, 106–07, 995 A.2d 1094 (2010). Those commands provide the force underlying the frequent case law refrain that "the clear public policy of this State is to eradicate invidious discrimination from the workplace." *Craig v. Suburban Cablevision, Inc.,* 140 N.J. 623, 630 (1995) (*citing Fuchilla v. Layman*, 109 N.J. 319, 334–35, *cert. denied*, 488 U.S. 826 (1988)).

It is equally well settled that LAD claims are subject to the two-year statute of limitations contained in N.J.S.A. 2A:14–2(a) ("Every action at law for an injury to the person caused by the wrongful act, neglect or default of any person within this State shall be commenced within two years next after the cause of any such action shall have accrued[.]"). Determining when the limitation period begins to run depends on when the cause of action accrued, which in turn is affected by the type of conduct a plaintiff alleges to have violated the LAD.

Generally stated, discrete acts of discrimination, such as termination or a punitive retaliatory act, are usually readily known when they occur and thus easily identified in respect of timing. Hence, their treatment for timeliness purposes is straightforward: "A discrete retaliatory or discriminatory act occurs on the day that it happens." *Roa v. Roa*, 200 N.J. 555, 567 (2010). Discriminatory termination and other similar abrupt, singular adverse employment actions that are attributable to invidious discrimination, prohibited by the LAD, generally are immediately known injuries, whose two-year statute of limitations period commences on the day they occur. *Id.* at 569.[3]

However, when the complained-of conduct constitutes "a series of separate acts that collectively constitute one unlawful employment practice[,]" the entire claim may be timely if filed within two years of "the date on which the last component act occurred." *Id.* at 567. The "continuing violation" doctrine, recognized under federal Title VII law as an appropriate equitable exception to the strict application of a statute of limitations, provided the analytic framework that has been used in the assessment of a LAD hostile workplace environment claim.

This Court's decision in *Shepherd v. Hunterdon Developmental Center*, 174 N.J. 1 (2002), specifically adopted the federal continuing violation equitable doctrine to determine the accrual date of a cause of action in a hostile workplace course-of-conduct claim. *Id.* at 18–19 (embracing analysis advanced in *Nat'l R.R. Passenger Corp. v. Morgan*, 536 U.S. 101 (2002)). We turned to the equitable doctrine for assistance in addressing the thorny factual circumstances of an ongoing workplace harassment claim that involved alleged incidents of both discrete and non-discrete acts of discriminatory workplace hostility. *Shepherd*, 174 N.J. at 21 (citing *Morgan*, 536 U.S. at 116). *Morgan* had clarified the distinction between discrete acts of discrimination and hostile work environment claims, stating that hostile work environment claims by "[t]heir very nature involve[ ] repeated conduct" of varying types and that "[s]uch claims are based on the cumulative effect of individual acts." *Morgan*, 536 U.S. at 115. Recognizing the beneficial effect of adopting *Morgan*'s approach to such difficult hostile work environment scenarios where an employee may be subjected to ongoing indignities, we held in *Shepherd*, that "a victim's knowledge of a claim is insufficient to start the limitations clock so long as the defendant continues the series of non-discrete acts on which the claim as a whole is based." 174 N.J. at 22. Stated differently, knowledge of hostility and of ongoing acts consistent with that hostility in such a setting is insufficient to trigger the limitation timeframe within which a LAD cause of action must be filed.

---

[3] That is not to preclude application of the discovery rule, where discriminatory animus is concealed and therefore the LAD-violation aspect to the injury may not be discoverable until a later time.

Roa further clarified the point, explaining that "the continuing violation theory was developed to allow for the aggregation of acts, each of which, in itself, might not have alerted the employee of the existence of a claim, but which together show a pattern of discrimination." *Roa*, 200 N.J. at 569. However, we warned that "[w]hat the doctrine does not permit is the aggregation of discrete discriminatory acts for the purposes of reviving an untimely act of discrimination that the victim knew or should have known was actionable." *Ibid.*

With that backdrop in mind, we turn to the question of the timeliness of plaintiffs' claim.

IV.

A.

Plaintiffs seek to have the continuing violation equitable doctrine, which is used in hostile workplace and similar discrimination-claim settings, sweep in as timely the entirety of the period during which they claim they were paid discriminatory wages. Specifically, they argue that the most current periods of discriminatory pay (*i.e.*, the allegedly discriminatory disparate wages paid within two years of the filing of the complaint) should have the effect of sweeping in, and including as timely, all prior periods of discriminatory disparate pay (dating back to their dates of initial hire, which for one occurred in 1976), as may occur in hostile work environment claims.

That approach to assessment of the timeliness of a wage discrimination claim was rebuffed in respect of Title VII wage claims by the holding in *Ledbetter*, which "reject[ed] the suggestion that an employment practice committed with no improper purpose and no discriminatory intent is rendered unlawful nonetheless because it gives some effect to an intentional discriminatory act that occurred outside the charging period." 550 U.S. at 632. * * *

It is noteworthy that the majority holding in *Ledbetter* no longer reflects federal policy. In response to the decision, Congress adopted the Lilly Ledbetter Fair Pay Act of 2009 (FPA), amending Title VII. The FPA clarifies that an unlawful act occurs "each time wages, benefits, or other compensation [are] paid" resulting from an earlier discriminatory practice. 42 U.S.C.A. § 2000e–5(e)(3)(A). Further, the FPA allows for

> recovery of back pay for up to two years preceding the filing of the charge, where the unlawful employment practices that have occurred during the charge filing period are similar or related to the unlawful employment practices with regard to discrimination in compensation that occurred outside the time for filing a charge.

42 U.S.C.A. § 2000e–5(e)(3)(B).

Thus, although the FPA changed *Ledbetter's* ruling, the modification was not as drastic as the present plaintiffs would have the law be. Under the FPA, although each new payment of discriminatory wages constitutes a separate act in respect of the cause of action, the effect of the two-year statute of limitations remains: the limitations period will allow for the inclusion of only the periods of unequal wages that occurred within two years of the filing of the discrimination charge. Thus, regardless of the length of time a plaintiff has been subjected to discriminatory pay, the back-pay recovery for a claim based solely on wage discrimination will be limited to a cut-off date of two years before the filing of the discrimination charge.

The courts below succumbed to the draw of aligning our LAD jurisprudence to that which was developing under federal case law for wage discrimination claims. We do not see the allure of that congruity, not in respect of the case as it presents itself now, or as it stood prior to the time Congress altered the federal landscape.

B.

Our state law jurisprudence has a developed approach to discriminatory wage claims. Prior decisions had treated the payment of discriminatory wages as the dissent in *Ledbetter* would have held: wage disparity based on invidious, proscribed discrimination is a violation of the LAD for which a remedy is available so long as the discriminatory wage continues. *See Decker v. Bd. of Educ. of Elizabeth*, 153 N.J.Super. 470 (App.Div. 1977), *certif. denied*, 75 N.J. 612 (1978) (treating each pay period as unlawful act under LAD); *see also Terry v. Mercer County Bd. of Chosen Freeholders*, 173 N.J.Super. 249, 253 (App.Div. 1980) (same), *mod. on other grounds*, 86 N.J. 141 (1981).

In *Decker*, the Appellate Division reviewed the claim of a female cook, who alleged wage discrimination under the LAD based on the disparity between her salary and that of a male employee performing the same function. In affirming the judgment in favor of plaintiff, the panel asserted that each pay period constituted a new violation of the LAD in the wage discrimination setting. The Appellate Division reasserted this principle in *Terry*, 173 N.J.Super. at 253. In *Terry*, plaintiffs were female supervisors who claimed that they were paid less than their male counterparts, in violation of the LAD. Again, the Appellate Division determined that the payment of unequal wages is an unlawful employment practice under the LAD and remains so as long as disparate payment persists. Consistent with the LAD's strong promise to eliminate discrimination from the workplace, the *Decker* and *Terry* decisions reflect the public policy of this state to treat each issuance of a pay check that reflects discriminatory treatment toward a protected group as an actionable wrong under the LAD. Accordingly, we reject the alternative approach taken by the *Ledbetter* majority, despite the principled arguments of defendant and reasoning by the lower courts. That said, we also reject plaintiffs' attempt to convert the references to the continuing nature of the wrongs in *Decker* and *Terry* into something more binding in respect of modern limitations-tolling jurisprudence, specifically the "continuing violation" doctrine. * * *

In sum, we reject the sea change that would be effected were we to adopt the *Ledbetter* majority approach to wage discrimination claims under our LAD. In light of settled prior case law that treated payment of unequal wages in violation of our anti-discrimination law as a series of actionable wrongs under the LAD, which are subject to the two-year statute of limitations, we see no persuasive reason for adopting the Ledbetter majority's restrictive approach to the vindication of a plaintiff's right to relief under the LAD for wage discrimination. Although we have turned for guidance to federal Title VII law when navigating new, uncharted paths as novel LAD issues have arisen, *see, e.g.*, *Carmona v. Resorts Int'l Hotel, Inc.*, 189 N.J. 354, 370 (2007) (stating, "we have frequently looked to case law under Title VII . . . for guidance in developing standards to govern the resolution of LAD claims" (citation omitted)); *Lehmann v. Toys 'R' Us, Inc.*, 132 N.J. 587, 600 (1993) (calling federal Title VII precedent "a key source of interpretive authority" when construing LAD (citation omitted)); in the present matter, federal guidance is not necessary to settle any complicated legal issue under our LAD.

Under this state's prior precedent, the statutory violation for which plaintiffs seek vindication is not untimely in respect of the allegedly discriminatory wages that have been paid to them as recently as during the two years that immediately preceded the filing of their complaint. That no affirmative act, beyond continued payment of allegedly discriminatory disparate wages, occurred during that two-year period does not bar plaintiffs' right to seek fulfillment of the LAD's promise of a discrimination-free workplace, and its specific prohibition against payment of wages on a discriminatory basis. Finally, we add that any attraction attributable to neatly aligning our jurisprudence with case law developing for Title VII is undermined by the congressional reaction repudiating the Ledbetter decision. It would be an odd step to bring this state's jurisprudence into conformity with case law that has been rendered obsolete.

We hold that the payment of wages on a discriminatory basis proscribed by the LAD is, and remains, an actionable violation of our state's anti-discrimination law as long as the wage remains tainted by the original discriminatory action. Each payment of such discriminatory wages thus constitutes a renewed separable and actionable wrong that is remediable under the LAD. The two-year statute of limitations applies to such violations, cutting off the untimely portion and, as a result, operating as a limit on the back period for which a plaintiff may seek recovery under the LAD. We further hold that plaintiffs' complaint was timely in respect of the allegedly discriminatory wages paid during the two years immediately prior to the filing of their complaint. We therefore reverse and remand for reinstatement of plaintiffs' timely claims of wage discrimination. * * *

A Reality Check

JACQUELINE A. BERRIEN, CHAIR, U.S. EQUAL EMPLOYMENT OPPORTUNITY COMMISSION, *STATEMENT ON EQUAL PAY DAY*

17 April 2012

Today is Equal Pay Day, which is the annual recognition of the date on which a woman's average earnings equal a man's average earnings in the prior year. Despite almost 50 years of enforcement of the Equal Pay Act and Title VII of the Civil Rights Act of 1964, wage disparities between men and women have not yet been eliminated.

When President John F. Kennedy signed the Equal Pay Act in 1963, he said that it "affirms our determination that when women enter the labor force, they will find equality in their pay envelope." At that time, women accounted for less than 35% of the labor force and their median pay was approximately 58.9% of men's.

Today, women are nearly half of the workforce, and their wages have risen to roughly 78% of those of men. While the pay gap has narrowed, it persists for every age group and in every job category, including those dominated by women. This is true whether women hold advanced degrees or a high school diploma. The gap is particularly severe for women of color: African-American women receive 61 cents and Hispanic or Latina women earn just 52 cents for every dollar earned by men. * * *

NOTES AND QUESTIONS

1. *Identifying the relevant institutions involved in "institutional settlement."* Judging from the materials on pay equity and the statute of limitations, how many sovereigns are there in the United States? Who (or what) makes the anti-discrimination law in the United States?

2. *Statutory interpretation through the lens of the Legal Process school (I): deferring to the policy decisions of the legislature and finding the purpose of a statute.* In the Legal Process school, the integrity of adjudication (and of the judiciary generally) is linked to the judges' willingness to defer to the legislature on matters requiring policy judgment and their ability to unearth a statute's essential purpose. The U.S. Court of Appeals for the Ninth Circuit, quoting *Hart & Sacks*, observed that,

> [i]n determining the more immediate purpose which ought to be attributed to a statute, and to any subordinate provision of it which may be involved, a court should try to put itself in imagination in the position of the legislature which enacted the measure. . . . It should assume, unless the contrary unmistakably appears, that the legislature was made up of reasonable persons pursuing reasonable purposes reasonably. . . . The court should then proceed to [ask] . . . Why would reasonable men, confronted with the law as it was, have enacted this new law to replace it? . . . . The most reliable guides to an answer will be found in the instances of unquestioned application of the statute. Even in the case of a new statute there almost invariably are such instances, in which, because of the perfect fit of words and context, the meaning seems unmistakable. . . . What is crucial here is the realization that law is being made, and that law is not supposed to be irrational.

Pakootas v. Teck Cominco Metals, Ltd., 646 F.3d 1214, 1224 (9th Cir. 2011) (citing HENRY M. HART, JR. & ALBERT M. SACKS, THE LEGAL PROCESS 1378 (William N. Eskridge, Jr. & Philip P. Frickey eds., 1994) (1958); HENRY M. HART JR. & ALBERT M. SACKS, THE LEGAL PROCESS 1414–15 (tent. ed. 1958)). In what respects, if any, is the extraction of a purpose from a piece of legislation more constrained than the extraction of a doctrine from a case?

3. *Statutory interpretation through the lens of the Legal Process school (II): law as an ongoing "conversation" between the courts and the legislature*. In *Ledbetter*, the majority and the dissent both recognize the continuing interplay between Congress and the Court on the proper scope and remedial power of the nation's anti-discrimination laws. According to the majority:

> After *Lorance*, Congress amended Title VII to cover the specific situation involved in that case. See 42 U.S.C. § 2000e–5(e)(2) (allowing for Title VII liability arising from an intentionally discriminatory seniority system both at the time of its adoption and at the time of its application). The dissent attaches great significance to this amendment, suggesting that it shows that *Lorance* was wrongly reasoned as an initial matter. * * * For present purposes, what is most important about the amendment in question is that it applied only to the adoption of a discriminatory seniority system, not to other types of employment discrimination. *Evans* and *Ricks*, upon which *Lorance* relied, and which employed identical reasoning, were left in place, and these decisions are more than sufficient to support our holding today.

The dissent offered a contrasting perspective:

> This is not the first time the Court has ordered a cramped interpretation of Title VII, incompatible with the statute's broad remedial purpose. *See also Wards Cove Packing Co. v. Atonio*, 490 U.S. 642 (1989) (superseded in part by the Civil Rights Act of 1991); *Price Waterhouse v. Hopkins*, 490 U.S. 228 (1989) (plurality opinion)

> (same); 1 B. Lindemann & P. Grossman, EMPLOYMENT DISCRIMINATION LAW 2 (3d ed. 1996) ("A spate of Court decisions in the late 1980s drew congressional fire and resulted in demands for legislative change[,]" culminating in the 1991 Civil Rights Act). Once again, the ball is in Congress' court. As in 1991, the Legislature may act to correct this Court's parsimonious reading of Title VII.

With the passage of the Lilly Ledbetter Act, *supra*, Congress evidently accepted the dissent's invitation to "correct" the Court. Does this suggest that "institutional settlement" is always in principle just a temporary truce? Maybe the law, like any piece of art according to Leonardo de Vinci, is never finished, only abandoned.

4. *Statutory interpretation through the lens of the Legal Process school (III): when should the courts defer to the expertise of administrative agencies?* Part of the drill in Legal Process thinking is exploring the appropriate relationship between the courts and other organs of government, including administrative agencies like the Equal Employment Opportunity Commission. The principle at work here is not that an agency's administrative regulations or interpretations are on a par with federal legislation, but the specialized expertise of the agency, developed under a delegation of authority from Congress, can in certain circumstances assist in the interpretation of an ambiguous statute. In *Chevron U.S.A., Inc. v. Natural Res. Def. Council, Inc.*, 467 U.S. 837, 865–66 (1984), for example, the Supreme Court held that, where an agency-administered statute is ambiguous, the courts should defer to an agency's "reasonable" construction of that statute.

From that perspective, consider this observation of the *Ledbetter* majority and contrast it with the dissent's treatment of the same point. The majority points out that

> Ledbetter argues that the EEOC's endorsement of her approach in its COMPLIANCE MANUAL and in administrative adjudications merits deference. But we have previously declined to extend *Chevron U.S.A. Inc. v. Natural Resources Defense Council, Inc.,* 467 U.S. 837 (1984), deference to the COMPLIANCE MANUAL, *Morgan, supra*, at 111, n. 6, and similarly decline to defer to the EEOC's adjudicatory positions. The EEOC's views in question are based on its misreading of *Bazemore*. Agencies have no special claim to deference in their interpretation of our decisions. *Reno v. Bossier Parish School Bd.*, 528 U.S. 320, 336, n. 5. Nor do we see reasonable ambiguity in the statute itself, which makes no distinction between compensation and other sorts of claims and which clearly requires that discrete employment actions alleged to be unlawful be motivated "because of such individual's . . . sex." 42 U.S.C. § 2000e–2(a)(1).

The dissent by contrast observes:

> The Court dismisses the EEOC's considerable "experience and informed judgment," *Firefighters v. Cleveland*, 478 U.S. 501, 518 (1986) (internal quotation marks omitted), as unworthy of any

> deference in this case. But the EEOC's interpretations mirror workplace realities and merit at least respectful attention. In any event, the level of deference due the EEOC here is an academic question, for the agency's conclusion that Ledbetter's claim is not time barred is the best reading of the statute even if the Court "were interpreting [Title VII] from scratch." *See Edelman v. Lynchburg College*, 535 U.S. 106, 114 (2002).

What does the dissent mean by "at least respectful attention," and how does the dissent know that the majority did not give "at least respectful attention"—whatever that is—to the agency's position? Note also that the dissent finds the agency's relevant expertise in the EEOC's Brief in Support of Petition for Rehearing and Suggestion for Rehearing En Banc. Why might the court treat an agency's formal regulations differently from its litigation documents?

Stepping back, which of these two conclusions—the majority's or the dissent's—do you find more persuasive? Notice that your conclusion may depend on your agreement with one characterization of the issue or another: the majority viewed the issue as a matter of interpreting Supreme Court *precedent*, as to which the EEOC has no particular expertise. The dissent views the issue as an interpretation of a *statute* that lies within the agency's expertise, especially its understanding of the "realities of the workplace." The Legal Process school would treat the characterization of the issue as an essential step in the "institutional settlement" of the case, but it offers no criteria for conclusively characterizing the issue one way or the other. A defensible characterization or framing of the issue is an essential tool for the advocates. Using it is a skill that can be learned and practiced. *See* Chapter 11, *infra*.

5. *"Reasoned elaboration" and the role of precedent in Ledbetter*. Legal Process scholars were concerned about the tendency of the Vinson Court (1946–1953) to dispose of cases through summary procedures and *per curiam* opinions "that quite frankly fail to build the bridge between the authorities [the justices] cite and the results they decree." Alexander Bickel & Harry Wellington, *Legislative Purpose and the Judicial Process: The Lincoln Mills Case*, 71 HARV. L. REV. 1, 3 (1957). The putative solution to that problem was *reasoned elaboration,* which required "first, that judges give reasons for their decisions; second, that the reasons be set forth in a detailed and coherent manner; third, that they exemplify what [Henry] Hart called "the maturing of collective thought"; and fourth, that the Court adequately demonstrate that its decisions, in the area of constitutional law, were vehicles for the expression of the ultimate social preferences of contemporary society." G. Edward White, *The Evolution of Reasoned Elaboration: Jurisprudential Criticism and Social Change*, 59 VA. L. REV. 279, 286 (1973).

Ledbetter argued that "each paycheck that offers a woman less pay than a similarly situated man because of her sex is a separate violation of Title VII with its own limitations period, regardless of whether the paycheck simply implements a prior discriminatory decision made outside the limitations period." Is the majority clearly right that Supreme Court precedents (*e.g.*,

Evans, Ricks, Lorance, Morgan and *Bazemore*) "foreclose" this argument? Which opinion—the majority or the dissent—seems to show greater fidelity to the holdings of those cases?

It's worth noting in passing that the majority and dissent analyze the same cases and draw opposing lessons from them. Do these contrasting displays of "reasoned elaboration" (a) exemplify and justify or (b) refine and supercede the realists' skepticism about the possibility of extracting doctrine from precedent?

6. *Supremacy, federalism, and "institutional settlement."* Federal statutes are the "supreme law of the land" under the Supremacy Clause of the Constitution. At one point in *Seton Hall*, the New Jersey Supreme Court frames the issue before it as "whether New Jersey's LAD jurisprudence would be *enhanced* by importation of the Supreme Court's *Ledbetter* analysis" and concludes "that there is no necessary or *beneficial purpose* to be drawn from adoption of the *Ledbetter* approach." Why exactly is it appropriate (and lawful) for the New Jersey Supreme Court to follow an independent path on the statute-of-limitations issues in *Seton Hall*? What does that tell lawyers about the prospects for "institutional settlement?"

7. *Making law through institutional inaction.* An essential part of the "institutional settlement" ideal was the obligation of each institution to stay in its own lane and respect the prerogatives of other authoritative decision-makers. That separation-of-powers ideal translated into an adversarial principle for savvy lawyers, who could blunt an opponent's otherwise winning argument on the merits by challenging the propriety of submitting the issue to a particular institution in the first place.

To make this more concrete, consider the various doctrines of abstention governing the judiciary—doctrines under which the courts are ruled (or rule themselves) out of bounds in the resolution of certain issues. Among these abstention doctrines, some preserve the power of state courts, to the exclusion of federal courts, over certain issues of state law. *See, e.g., Railroad Commission v. Pullman Co.*, 312 U.S. 496 (1941) (resolution of certain state constitutional questions); *Burford v. Sun Oil Co.*, 319 U.S. 315 (1943) (allowing a federal court to dismiss a case if it presents "difficult questions of state law bearing on policy problems of substantial public import whose importance transcends the result in the case then at bar," or if its adjudication in a federal forum "would be disruptive of state efforts to establish a coherent policy with respect to a matter of substantial public concern.") The vertical separation of powers between federal and state authorities is obviously served by these doctrines of judicial diffidence.

No less important are the horizontal separation-of-powers concerns behind the deference shown by courts to the executive branch and Congress, which can take a variety of forms. (i) For example, courts will defer to an administrative agency's interpretation of an ambiguous regulatory statute if the agency's interpretation is merely "reasonable." *Chevron U.S.A., Inc. v. Natural Resources Defense Council*, 467 U.S. 837 (1984). To put that in Legal

Process terms, the Supreme Court has determined that federal agencies, not the judiciary, are generally empowered to resolve ambiguities as necessary in order to interpret and exercise the authority delegated to the agency by Congress. (ii) Similarly, the court has articulated a political question doctrine, under which some questions are simply not justiciable (or appropriate for judicial resolution). The doctrine is narrow and obviously doesn't prevent the courts from resolving politically-charged cases, but it does prevent the courts from hearing cases directly raising issues the resolution of which is "textually-committed" by the Constitution to Congress or the executive branch or where there are no "judicially-manageable" standards to guide the court's decision. *Baker v. Carr*, 369 U.S. 186 (1962). *See also Nixon v. United States*, 506 U.S. 224 (1993) (lawsuit challenging Congressional impeachment procedures presents non-justiciable political question); *Oetjen v. Central Leather Co.*, 246 U.S. 297 (1918) (legal challenge to foreign affairs decisions by the executive branch presents non-justiciable political question).

Armed with the insights of the Legal Process school, how does the refusal of the court to decide an issue contribute to the "institutional settlement" of that issue? *See generally,* Louis Henkin, *Is There a "Political Question" Doctrine?*, 85 YALE L. J. 597 (1976). What law, if any, emerges in a case when these "passive virtues" are exercised?" *See generally* Alexander M. Bickel, *Foreword: The Passive Virtues*, 75 HARV. L. REV. 40 (1961–1962). Is this a philosophy of law or a philosophy of adjudication?

8. *Law as a proxy for arguments over institutional prerogative.* Sometimes identifying the right institution to resolve a dispute depends on how a legal issue is framed in the first place. This can make the characterization of the issue part of a bitter struggle between institutions of great power. Consider the following legal/political struggle over the status of the seceded states during and after the American Civil War:

> Lincoln never deviated from the theory that secession was illegal and southern states therefore remained in the Union. Rebels had temporarily taken over their governments; the task of reconstruction was to return "loyal" officials to power. At one level all Republicans subscribed to this theory of indestructible states in an indissoluble Union; to believe otherwise would stultify their war aims. But at another level, no one could deny that the southern states had gone out of the Union and had formed a new government with all the attributes of a nation. A few radical Republicans led by Thaddeus Stevens boldly insisted that they had therefore ceased to exist as legal states. When invaded and controlled by the Union army they became "conquered provinces" subject to the conqueror's will. But most Republicans were unwilling to go this far. Instead, many of them subscribed to one variant or another of a theory that by attempting the treasonable act of secession, southern states had committed "state suicide" (Charles Sumner's phrase) or had "forfeited" their rights as states and reverted to the condition of territories.

> Discussion of these theories consumed much time and energy in Congress. Disliking "pernicious abstraction," Lincoln expressed impatience with this "merely metaphysical question" whether "the seceded States, so called, are in the Union or out of it." Everyone agreed, he said, that they were "out of their proper practical relation with the Union; and that the sole object of the government . . . is to again get them into that proper practical relation." What Lincoln well understood, but did not acknowledge, was that the "metaphysical question" of reconstruction theories concealed a power struggle between Congress and the Executive over control of the process. *If the southern states had reverted to the status of territories, Congress had the right to frame the terms of their readmission under its constitutional authority to govern territories and admit new states. If, on the other hand, the states were indestructible and secession was the act of individuals, the president had the power to prescribe the terms of restoration under his constitutional authority to suppress insurrection and to grant pardons and amnesty.*

JAMES MCPHERSON, BATTLE CRY OF FREEDOM: THE CIVIL WAR ERA 699–700 (2003) (emphasis added).

9. *Procedural fetishism.* Legal Process is not entirely descriptive, with a powerful status quo bias, but it offers a peculiar connection between what is and what ought to be. As noted above, Hart and Sacks observe that "decisions which are the duly arrived at result of duly established procedures [ ] *ought* to be accepted as binding upon the whole society unless and until they are duly changed." Elsewhere Henry Hart described "[t]he *moral* claims of settled law in a constitutional democracy." Henry Hart, *Holmes' Positivism—An Addendum*, 64 HARV. L. REV. 929, 937 (1951) (emphasis added). Does that mean that something is moral or just so long as the right American procedures are followed?

10. *Now what?* According to the statement of Jacqueline A. Berrien, Chair of the U.S. Equal Employment Opportunity Commission, *supra*, gender equity remains a serious problem in the American workplace: "While the pay gap has narrowed, it persists for every age group and in every job category, including those dominated by women [and] is particularly severe for women of color." In Legal Process terms, what is the right legal strategy now for closing that gap?

Readings

MICHAEL DORF, *LEGAL INDETERMINACY AND INSTITUTIONAL DESIGN*

78 N.Y.U. L. REV. 875, 920–935 (2003)

There is * * * an account of law, indeed a whole school of thought, that purports to show how the legal process constrains judicial discretion within tolerable bounds even while permitting the effectuation of the law's human ends. I refer, of course, to the Legal Process School. For Hart and Sacks, the purpose of judges, indeed of law itself, is to allocate decision-making authority among competing institutions. In those cases that fall within the courts' own circumscribed domain of ultimate decision-making, the Legal Process view treats the distinctive comparative advantage of the judiciary as its ability—using the defining tools of legal craft—to render decisions according to principle rather than discretion or subjective policy judgment.[170] * * *

In the opening pages of THE LEGAL PROCESS, (Henry) Hart and Sacks write of the procedures used by every modern society to allocate decision-making authority: "Implicit in every such system of procedures is the central idea of law—an idea which can be described as the principle of institutional settlement."[181] That principle means simply "that decisions which are the duly arrived at result of duly established procedures . . . ought to be accepted as binding upon the whole society unless and until they are duly changed."[182]

It is not much of an overstatement to say that the principle of institutional settlement performs the same role in THE LEGAL PROCESS as the rule of recognition performs in [H.L.A. Hart's] THE CONCEPT OF LAW [see Chapter 2, *supra*]. Each grounds the authority of law in social acceptance of a master rule or principle allocating authority among various institutional actors. The rule of law is, in each account, the submission to duly constituted authority.[183]

---

170 See Hart & Sacks, *supra*, at 143–44 (contrasting exercise of discretion by judiciary with that by executive officials). Herbert Wechsler, who collaborated with Henry Hart on what is in many ways the companion text to *The Legal Process*, THE FEDERAL COURTS AND THE FEDERAL SYSTEM (1st ed. 1950), famously referred to such principles as "neutral." *See* Herbert Wechsler, *Toward Neutral Principles of Constitutional Law*, 73 HARV. L. REV. 1, 17 (1959) (arguing that Constitution should be interpreted "so far as possible . . . by standards that transcend the case at hand"). Although the Hart and Sacks materials consistently advance a view of law that is deeply proceduralist, they do not insist on the neutrality of the principles the courts employ. See Hart & Sacks, at 144 (conceding that judicial decision-making involves value judgments).

181 Hart & Sacks, *supra*, at 4.

182 *Id.*

183 It is nonetheless a bit of an overstatement to equate Hart's rule of recognition with the principle of institutional settlement in Hart and Sacks. For the rule of recognition is a social fact that may be good or bad—recall that Hart wants to give a sociological, i.e., descriptive, account of law—whereas Hart and Sacks defend the principle of institutional settlement in normative terms. Accordingly, I do not claim that Hart and Sacks were positivists. See Brian Leiter, *Positivism,*

Whereas H.L.A. Hart insists on the existence of a rule of recognition, in THE LEGAL PROCESS Hart and Sacks offer guidance on how in any given setting, one moves from the general principle of institutional settlement to deciding which institutional actor has authority to make a decision in some particular case, and whether that actor's decision falls within the bounds of its authority. The answer, understandably, is complex, but at bottom it amounts to legal craft.

The first step in the Hart and Sacks conception of legal craft is an awareness of the problem-solving limitations of the judiciary. Thus, the punch line of the case study with which THE LEGAL PROCESS opens—the case of the spoiled cantaloupes—is a judicial decision to defer to agency decision-making, even though the court plainly would have chosen a different outcome if reviewing the case *de novo*.[184] But deference is not the end of the story, for courts must decide to which institution to defer in any given case—legislature or administrative agency; federal, state, or local body; public or private actor—and sometimes they must decide not to defer, especially when there is some defect in the decision-making process employed by the entity seeking deference.

Accordingly, as the academic literature generally acknowledges, within the Hart and Sacks framework, ascertaining the proper allocation of authority is the very point of law and thus also the master skill of legal policymakers, lawyers, and ultimately judges.[185] Yet strikingly, THE LEGAL PROCESS materials nowhere state the meta-principle of institutional allocation of decision-making authority. As Eskridge and Frickey note, "[l]egal process thinkers had no theory of law's 'professional culture' that suggested how it constrains judges."[186] But this was not a careless omission

Formalism, Realism, 99 COLUM. L. REV. 1138, 1155–58 (1999) (reviewing Anthony J. Sebok, LEGAL POSITIVISM IN AMERICAN JURISPRUDENCE (1998)) (challenging Sebok's claim that Hart and Sacks held positivist commitments).

[184] *See* Hart & Sacks, *supra*, at 57–58 (reproducing *L. Gillarde Co. v. Joseph Martinelli & Co.*, 169 F.2d 60 (1st Cir. 1948)). We know the court would have reached a different result if left to its own devices because it in fact did just that in *L. Gillarde Co. v. Joseph Martinelli & Co.*, 168 F.2d 276 (1st Cir. 1948), reproduced in Hart & Sacks, *supra*, at 53–56, before reversing itself in response to a submission by the Federal Department of Agriculture in connection with a petition for rehearing.

[185] *See, e.g.*, [William N. Eskridge, Jr. & Philip P. Frickey, *An Historical and Critical Introduction to THE LEGAL PROCESS*], in Hart & Sacks, *supra*, at li, cxvii, at xciii ("Where private ordering does not work well enough, Hart and Sacks contemplate an interaction between private and public institutions, with their roles allocated according to their relative 'competence' to handle the matter . . . [and] through the choice of rules versus standards."); Carl Landauer, *Deliberating Speed: Totalitarian Anxieties and Postwar Legal Thought*, 12 YALE J.L. & HUMAN. 171, 214 (2000) (describing Hart and Sacks view of law as "a system of allocation"); John F. Manning, *Constitutional Structure and Judicial Deference to Agency Interpretations of Agency Rules*, 96 Colum. L. Rev. 612, 636–37 (1996) (referring to "the relatively subjective Hart and Sacks methodology [of] determin[ing] a 'reasonable' allocation of interpretive authority"). The same point has been made with respect to other classic texts of the Legal Process School. *See, e.g.*, Richard H. Fallon, Jr., *Reflections on the Hart and Wechsler Paradigm*, 47 VAND. L. REV. 953, 962 (1994) ("As defined by Hart and Wechsler, the central, organizing question of Federal Courts doctrine involves allocations of authority. . . .").

[186] Eskridge & Frickey, *supra*, at cxx.

by Hart and Sacks. Instead of providing a theory, their materials exemplify a method. Only by absorbing the lessons of all 1380 pages of the published edition, which Hart and Sacks themselves still regarded as tentative, can aspiring lawyers/policymakers/judges begin to acquire the subtle, tacit knowledge that enables them to play their chosen roles.

Thus, to return to our main theme, the discretion of a judge who has learned the lessons of THE LEGAL PROCESS will be safely bounded. * * * [B]y encompassing allocational decisions within the lawyer's toolbox, THE LEGAL PROCESS appears to make good on H.L.A. Hart's claim that the law's areas of open texture are manageably small.

The problem, conventional wisdom holds, is that the Hart and Sacks method does not work. From the right, public choice theory [*see* Chapter 5, *infra*] challenged the central premise of the Hart and Sacks approach to statutory interpretation—that there is such a thing as a legislative purpose beyond the compromises among the competing goals of competing interest groups who sought or fought the legislation in question.[187] From the left, within a decade after its publication, THE LEGAL PROCESS was attacked as hopelessly naïve in its assumption that American law could be deemed fair on procedural grounds without attention to how, in both substance and procedure, it systematically favored the interests of the strong over the weak [see the various critical schools explored in Chapters 6, 7, & 8, *infra*]. The upshot of both the right and left critiques was that The Legal Process approach functioned only so long as there was a broad consensus about social goals—as there arguably was in the decade and a half after the Second World War—but could not deal with the fractious world that followed.[189]

That, at any rate, is the more or less conventional narrative. Yet these criticisms are ultimately unfair to the Hart and Sacks project. Most prominently, their method does not assume consensus. Quite the opposite, as scholars whose primary focus was private law, Hart and Sacks were well aware of both the ubiquity of conflict and the diversity of interests in human affairs. They understood that law must accommodate the often competing interests of producers, distributors, wholesalers, retailers, and consumers, taking account of the parallel competition among federal, state, and local regulators acting through legislative, executive, administrative,

---

[187] *See, e.g.*, Frank H. Easterbrook, *Statutes' Domains*, 50 U. CHI. L. REV. 533, 540 (1983) ("Almost all statutes are compromises, and the cornerstone of many a compromise is the decision, usually unexpressed, to leave certain issues unresolved."); William M. Landes & Richard A. Posner, *The Independent Judiciary in an Interest-Group Perspective*, 18 J.L. & ECON. 875, 877 (1975) (describing "the economists' version of the interest-group theory of government").

[189] *See* Jerold S. Auerbach, UNEQUAL JUSTICE: LAWYERS AND SOCIAL CHANGE IN MODERN AMERICA 260 (1976) (describing THE LEGAL PROCESS as "perfectly attuned to the end-of-ideology politics of the Cold War"); Eskridge & Frickey, *supra* at cxviii-cxxv (describing end of consensus in 1960s and rise of scarcity theory of economics in 1970s as fostering public choice theory of politics, "the most serious challenge to the legal process approach"). Because Eskridge and Frickey see the Hart and Sacks method as dependent upon consensus, they view its revival in the 1980s as reflecting a movement back towards moderation in public life. *See id.* at cxxv–cxxvi.

and judicial channels. The whole idea of understanding law as a system for allocating authority reflects the centrality of conflict in the Hart and Sacks view.

To be sure, right-wing critics of the regulatory state can object that the Hart and Sacks method makes the unrealistic assumption of panoptic knowledge on the part of the regulator, and there is considerable truth in this criticism. Their New Deal faith in the expertise of administrators as neutral scientists has not worn well. Yet even here, the criticism goes too far. For one thing, Hart and Sacks saw the domain of regulation as small, generally preferring private ordering in the first instance.[191]

In addition, it is hardly clear that the solutions proposed by the right are preferable to those proposed by Hart and Sacks. Hart and Sacks generally believed that effective regulation requires intimate familiarity with and accommodation of the practices of the regulated actors.[192] In private law, this translated into an approach that is something like that of the Uniform Commercial Code (U.C.C.), which gives primacy to merchant practice.[193] In public law, it meant purposivism in statutory interpretation.[194]

By contrast, in both domains, the right now urges formalism. In private law, formalism is proposed as a means of providing economic actors with clear end-game rules that reduce uncertainty and promote efficiency.[195] The best developed and most careful such account is given by

---

[191] *See* Hart & Sacks, *supra*, at 161 (restating "[t]he thesis that private ordering is the primary process of social adjustment, in the dynamics of a legal system").

[192] *See, e.g., id.* at 118 ("A cardinal principle in dealing with every type of legal arrangement is to keep steadily in view the kinds of people to whom the directions of the arrangement in question are initially addressed—who the people are, in other words, who are expected to act or refrain from acting in accordance with the arrangement if it works successfully, and under what circumstances they are to act."); *see also id.* at 119 ("Directions have to be understood in the light of the circumstances in which they are given, and one of the most significant of all the circumstances is the position of the person who is supposed to carry out the direction.").

[193] *See* U.C.C. §§ 1–205, 2–202, 2–316, 2–504, 2–723 (2000) (prescribing deference to "courses of dealing" and "usages of trade" in various contexts).

[194] *See* Hart & Sacks, *supra*, at 1121 (asking rhetorically whether "the enactment of every statute is, of necessity, a purposive act [such] that no statute can be properly interpreted without considering the purpose which ought to be attributed to it").

[195] *See* Omri Ben-Shahar, *The Tentative Case Against Flexibility in Commercial Law*, 66 U. CHI. L. REV. 781, 785 (1999) (suggesting "that the type of flexibility that the Code potentially promotes is one that often makes contractual parties worse off"); Lisa Bernstein, *The Questionable Empirical Basis of Article 2's Incorporation Strategy: A Preliminary Study*, 66 U. CHI. L. REV. 710, 770 (1999) (arguing that because "relationship-creating and relationship-preserving norms are likely to differ in content and structure from the optimal endgame norms for a tribunal to apply in the event of a dispute, . . . merchants do not want either their relationship-specific courses of performance and courses of dealing or their every-day customary practices . . . written into the law" (footnotes omitted)); Jody S. Kraus, *Legal Design and the Evolution of Commercial Norms*, 26 J. LEGAL STUD. 377, 406–08 (1997) (arguing that although "the average efficiency of the practices identified by commercial norms will increase over time," there is "no basis for inferring that commercial practices will be even nearly optimal on average"); Eric A. Posner, *Law, Economics, and Inefficient Norms*, 144 U. PA. L. REV. 1697, 1698 (1996) (criticizing "the view that the norms of closely knit groups are efficient" and arguing for laws that differ from custom on ground "that under a variety of plausible conditions, the state—in particular, its legislatures and courts—

Lisa Bernstein, who grounds her tentative proposals in empirical studies of merchant practices regarding various commodities.[196] Whether her findings apply to the special-purpose goods that account for an increasing proportion of economic activity in a world of flexible production remains to be seen. In any event, even if the work of Bernstein and others calls into question Karl Llewellyn's assumptions in drafting the U.C.C., it leaves the Hart and Sacks approach largely intact, for they saw the law's role as largely facilitating private transactions—and, perhaps in contrast to Llewellyn, they had no objection to enforcing formal rules in circumstances where such enforcement had demonstrable benefits.[197]

In public law, the right urges formalism as a means of, among other things, disciplining legislators. For example, Justice Scalia's crusade against the use of legislative history in statutory interpretation [*see* Chapter 12, *infra*] aims at reforming legislative practices that, he and his fellow travelers say, enable interest groups to obtain the benefits of legislation without the full measure of legislative enactment.[198] Yet it hardly follows that courts, in the name of respect for the decisions of the elected branches, are the appropriate institution to discipline the legislative process. Symbolism aside, legislative practices, to say nothing of the administrative practices that also fall within the purview of judicial canons of construction, are complex and refractory. It is for just this reason that so much of the Hart and Sacks material addresses matters of institutional detail. Even with a strong inclination to defer to the appropriate institutional settlement, a judge operating within the Hart and Sacks paradigm attempts to learn the details of the legislative process that produced a statute, the administrative process that produced a rulemaking or adjudication pursuant to that statute, and the sphere of

---

produces rules that are more efficient than group norms and, furthermore, that help correct the deficiencies of group norms").

[196] *See* Lisa Bernstein, *Merchant Law in a Merchant Court: Rethinking the Code's Search for Immanent Business Norms*, 144 U. PA. L. REV. 1765, 1769–70 (1996) (grain and feed); Lisa Bernstein, *Opting Out of the Legal System: Extralegal Contractual Relations in the Diamond Industry*, 21 J. LEGAL STUD. 115, 115 (1992) (diamonds); Bernstein, *supra*, at 715 (hay, grain and feed, textiles, and silk).

[197] *See* Hart & Sacks, *supra*, at 139 ("Innumerable legal rules do manage th[e] miracle of successful operation in many if not most of their applications."). I say "perhaps in contrast to Llewellyn" because although Llewellyn was a well-known rule-skeptic, *see, e.g.*, Karl N. Llewellyn, *Remarks on the Theory of Appellate Decision and the Rules or Canons About How Statutes Are to Be Construed*, 3 VAND. L. REV. 395, 401 (1950) (making famous argument that "there are two opposing canons [of statutory construction] on almost every point"), the U.C.C. does include a goodly number of rules, notwithstanding its preference for industry practice.

[198] *See* [Antonin] Scalia, [*Common-Law Courts in a Civil-Law System: The Role of United States Federal Courts in Interpreting the Constitution and Laws*, *in* A MATTER OF INTERPRETATION: FEDERAL COURTS AND THE LAW (Amy Gutmann ed., 1997),] at 34 ("[T]he more courts have relied upon legislative history, the less worthy of reliance it has become. . . . One of the routine tasks of the Washington lawyer-lobbyist is to draft language that sympathetic legislators can recite in a prewritten 'floor debate'—or, even better, insert into a committee report."); John F. Manning, *Textualism as a Nondelegation Doctrine*, 97 COLUM. L. REV. 673, 687–88 (1997) (noting that textualist judges like Justice Scalia believe that "once legislators become aware that legislative history influences courts, they and their agents (the staff) will try to achieve desired outcomes through the lower-cost mechanism of legislative history" (footnote omitted)).

primary activity (such as the trade in fresh cantaloupes) regulated. It may turn out that in certain contexts, application of this method will lead an astute judge or legislator to favor formalism, but for Hart and Sacks, that is always because of particulars, rather than a general commitment to formalism.

If the right has not proved the superiority of a thoroughgoing formalism over the Hart and Sacks approach, neither has the left advanced its own program. And that is largely because * * * the left has no program—in the sense of an approach to adjudication that faithfully seeks to render adjudication legitimate. Duncan Kennedy's A CRITIQUE OF ADJUDICATION[202] is instructive. * * * Ultimately, however, Kennedy can propose only three options: One can passively lament; one can pretend to accept the law's claims to autonomy while surreptitiously advancing a particular ideological agenda; or one can struggle to bring the law's deep ambiguity into the open. This counsel of despair is hardly an alternative to the Hart and Sacks method, even if one thinks (as I do not) that it thoroughly discredits that method.

The great strength of the Hart and Sacks approach, which enables it to withstand attacks from both the right and the left, is its emphasis on the law as a vehicle for coordinating the activities of actors with diverse interests and skills. Hart and Sacks anticipated a time—our own—when one of the master skills of the lawyer would be coordinating the activities of and cooperating with others, including many non-lawyers. In this sense, they partially anticipated a new, emerging conception of a professional, for THE LEGAL PROCESS was meant as a sophisticated training device for aspiring legal professionals. In the traditional conception, professionals bring to bear highly specialized skills on highly specialized problems; in the new model envisioned here, professionals (including lawyers) are generalists, whose principal skill is their ability to collaborate across disciplinary boundaries to solve problems. But Hart and Sacks only just barely hinted at this new role * * *.

Hart and Sacks assumed that the sorts of conflict that law was needed to resolve would occur principally along economic lines: management versus labor, producer versus consumer, and so forth. When new lines of conflict emerged—most prominently in the form of the Civil Rights movement and successor rights movements—it became clear that deference to one or another existing institutional settlement would pit substantive justice against the notion of a circumscribed judicial role. Issues of racial inequality had, of course, been central to the entire American experience, but it was not until the Warren Court that the vindication of the fundamental rights of citizens (other than property rights) came to be understood as a basic function of courts.

---

[202] Duncan Kennedy, A CRITIQUE OF ADJUDICATION: FIN DE SIÈCLE (1997).

On these questions, however, THE LEGAL PROCESS was at best silent. The 1958 materials make no mention of *Brown v. Board of Education*, decided just four years earlier. And on the question of apportionment, which was soon to become the second great front of the Warren Court's assault on judicial passivity, Hart and Sacks strongly implied that courts should do nothing about patently undemocratic legislatures.[211]

The conventional account of Hart and Sacks faults them on this score for defining legal legitimacy in solely procedural terms, a move, it is said, characteristic of the post-World War II era. In this account, Legal Process School thinkers wanted to retain the modernist legacy of legal realism, while at the same time distancing their sociological jurisprudence from Nazism, fascism, and communist totalitarianism. The solution was a sharp distinction between is and ought, between procedure and substance.[212] On this view, Hart and Sacks could not condemn racial apartheid on substantive grounds; thus, Henry Hart's collaborator Herbert Wechsler was left unsuccessfully trying to muster the energy to justify *Brown* in terms of a right of association.[213]

There is some truth to this line of analysis and criticism. The Hart and Sacks materials were rooted in the assumptions of their age. But at the same time, the criticism rests on something of a mischaracterization of THE LEGAL PROCESS. Hart and Sacks were well aware that judgments about procedural fairness rested upon and implicated substantive value judgments, as, for example, their embrace of purposivism in statutory interpretation clearly reflects. Where they went wrong was their assumption—perhaps reasonable in its time—that America had generated all of the institutions necessary to resolve the conflicts likely to emerge, or at worst, that the needed institutions could be found among the menu of arrangements throughout the world. What Hart and Sacks did not contemplate was the possibility of new sorts of public institutions whose

---

211 *See* Hart & Sacks, *supra*, at 672–86. Although Hart and Sacks do not formally endorse a position, their rhetorical questions suggest, to this reader at least, a disposition similar to Justice Frankfurter's:

> Is there any escape from the conclusion that the composition of a state legislature is a constitutional problem in the elementary sense of having to do with the basic structure of the body politic? Does it not then follow that the problem is appropriate for solution only by the basic process of constitution making? Should a people who lack the political wisdom to establish a sound constitution for themselves expect to be able to shuffle off their deficiencies simply by running for help to the Magi on the bench?

Id. at 686.

212 *See* Gary Peller, *Neutral Principles in the 1950's*, 21 U. MICH. J.L. REFORM 561, 566–86 (1988) (noting that Legal Process School thinkers "chang[ed] the focus for critical evaluation from the substance to the process").

213 *See* Herbert Wechsler, *Toward Neutral Principles of Constitutional Law*, 73 HARV. L. REV. 1 (1959), at 31–35 ("Given a situation where the state must practically choose between denying the association to those individuals who wish it or imposing it on those who would avoid it, is there a basis in neutral principles for holding that the Constitution demands [the latter]? I should like to think there is, but I confess that I have not yet written the opinion.").

job it would be, not to resolve legal ambiguity, but to foster continual deliberation and experimentation. * * *

WILLIAM ESKRIDGE AND PHILIP FRICKEY, EDS., HART AND SACKS' THE LEGAL PROCESS: BASIC PROBLEMS IN THE MAKING AND APPLICATION OF LAW

cxxiv *et seq.*
(1994)

The Legal Process has enjoyed an unusually robust afterlife. What is its future? As long as statutory interpretation remains a fruitful field of scholarship, Hart and Sacks will and should be read and studied. As long as American government is procedurally complex, involves interacting institutions, and affects our lives pervasively, THE LEGAL PROCESS will be instructive. Although the government does not regulate delivery of perishable foods today as it did in the 1940s, the "Case of the Spoiled Cantaloupes" remains a pedagogical classic for its still-fresh illumination of how state procedures, private actions, and unforeseen developments interact in human affairs. * * *

Intellectual developments in the 1990s suggest that THE LEGAL PROCESS may not only remain relevant to public law discussions, but may offer fresh lessons. For example, positive theories of political institutions are finding their way into public law scholarship. These theories not only suggest more sophisticated ways of thinking about institutions' different competencies and about the dynamics of their relationships—in other words, better ways of doing Hart and Sacks analysis—but they have also introduced Hart and Sacks to a new audience of political scientists and their camp followers in legal academe. Positive political theorists such as these view Hart and Sacks as an attractive normative countervision to the law-as-deals or law-as-text visions of law popular among some judges. Indeed, this is a possibly enduring value of THE LEGAL PROCESS, especially its statutory interpretation chapter. While legal process is, as Duncan Kennedy wrote twenty years ago, a "utopian" or romantic vision of law, it is one that is attractive to a polity burned by the 1980s' cynical bonfire of the vanities.

Finally, the biggest change in American public law—multi-culturalism—might well contribute to the continuing relevance of THE LEGAL PROCESS. Values and assumptions in law are more contested today than they were in the 1950s, and we think this has been useful as well as inevitable. The very sharpness of the contest, however, generates social pressure toward a mediating position. That is, after periods of ideological disagreement, centrism—a moderation that seeks change without disruption, accommodation without great cost—tends to make a comeback in American public law. Hart and Sacks staked out thoughtful strategies for centrism: dialogue among diverse points of view, postponement of issues until agreement can be reached, deliberation and openness to new facts and points of view, a search for common ground and a willingness to approach issues from a different angle, and creation of structures for working out disagreements. Considered this way, legal process thought is related to similar ideas derived from feminism, pragmatism, literature, hermeneutics, and other schools of jurisprudence.

That legal process theory, forged in the consensus of the fifties and shattered in the dissonance that followed, remains vital for the more diverse legal community of the nineties is surely one of the larger ironies we have suggested. The staying power of legal process indicates that much of what Henry Hart and Albert Sacks captured in THE LEGAL PROCESS is deeply rooted in the collective American legal psyche. They probably never conceived of their "tentative" edition as a bequest to later generations, but it has proved to be a legacy worth preserving. They surely never imagined that their 1958 edition, their last collaborated version, would ever be published in its incomplete form, much less over a third of a century later. In a story replete with ironies, this last one may be the strangest of all. Nonetheless, it preserves for posterity the fascinating work of two remarkable men who sought to capture between covers "the legal process" in its entirety. That their reach ultimately exceeded their grasp does nothing to diminish the value of their product, not merely as a brilliant encapsulation of the sophisticated jurisprudence of its time, but also as an inspiration for succeeding generations of legal scholars and their students.

Are the Legal Process School and Its Contemporary Variants "Pragmatic?"

RICHARD A. POSNER, *WHAT HAS PRAGMATISM TO OFFER LAW?*

63 S. CAL. L. REV. 1653 (1990)

[P]ragmatism has three "essential" elements. * * * The first is a distrust of metaphysical entities ("reality," "truth," "nature," etc.) viewed as warrants for certitude whether in epistemology, ethics, or politics. The second is an insistence that propositions be tested by their consequences, by the difference they make-and if they make none, set aside. The third is an insistence on judging our projects, whether scientific, ethical, political, or legal, by their conformity to social or other human needs rather than to "objective," "impersonal" criteria. These elements in turn imply an outlook that is progressive (in the sense of forward-looking), secular, and experimental, and that is commonsensical without making a fetish of common sense-for common sense is a repository of prejudice and ignorance as well as a fount of wisdom. R.W. Sleeper has helpfully summarized the pragmatic outlook in describing Dewey's philosophy as "a philosophy rooted in common sense and dedicated to the transformation of culture, to the resolution of the conflicts that divide us."[19] Also apt is Cornel West's description of the "common denominator" of pragmatism as "a future-oriented instrumentalism that tries to deploy thought as a weapon to enable more effective action."[20] * * *

The pragmatic outlook can help us maintain a properly critical stance toward mysterious entities that seem to play a large role in many areas of law, particularly tort and criminal law. Such entities as mind, intent, free will, and causation are constantly invoked in debates over civil and criminal liability. Tested by the pragmatic criterion of practical consequence, these entities are remarkably elusive. Even if they exist, law has no practical means of locating them and in fact ignores them on any but the most superficial verbal level. Judges and juries do not, as a precondition to finding that a killing was intentional, peer into the defendant's mind in quest of the required intent. They look at the evidence of what the defendant did and try to infer from it whether the deed involved advance planning or other indicia of high probability of success, whether there was concealment of evidence or other indicia of likely escape, and whether the circumstances of the crime argue a likelihood of repetition-all considerations that go to dangerousness rather than to intent or free will. The legal fact-finder follows this approach because the social concern behind criminal punishment is a concern with dangerousness rather than with mental states (evil or otherwise), and because the methods of litigation do not enable the fact-finder to probe beneath dangerousness into mental or spiritual strata so elusive they may not even exist.

Similarly, while interested in consequences and therefore implicitly in causality, the law does not make a fetish of "causation." It does not commit itself to any side of the age-old philosophical controversy over causation, but instead elides the issue by basing judgments of liability on social, rather than philosophical, considerations. People who have caused no harm at all because their plans were interrupted are regularly punished for attempt and conspiracy; persons may be held liable in tort law when their acts were neither a necessary nor a sufficient condition of the harm that ensued (as where two defendants, acting independently, simultaneously inflict the harm, and only one is sued); and persons whose acts "caused" injury in an uncontroversial sense may be excused from liability because the harm was an unforeseeable consequence of the act. The principle of legal liability can be redescribed without reference to metaphysical entities such as mind and causation. This redescription is an important part of the

---

19 R. Sleeper, THE NECESSITY OF PRAGMATISM: JOHN DEWEY'S CONCEPTION OF PHILOSOPHY 8–9 (1986).

20 C. West, [THE AMERICAN EVASION OF PHILOSOPHY: A GENEALOGY OF PRAGMATISM (1989)], at 5.

project of a pragmatic jurisprudence, although it will not please those for whom law's semantic level is its most interesting and important. * * *

Pragmatism remains a powerful antidote to formalism, which is enjoying a resurgence in the Supreme Court. Legal formalism is the idea that legal questions can be answered by inquiry into the relation between concepts and hence without need for more than a superficial examination of their relation to the world of fact. It is, therefore, anti-pragmatic as well as anti-empirical. It asks not, What works?, but instead, What rules and outcomes have a proper pedigree in the form of a chain of logical links to an indisputably authoritative source of law, such as the text of the United States Constitution? Those rules and outcomes are correct and the rest incorrect. Formalism is the domain of the logician, the casuist, the Thomist, the Talmudist. * * *

The main choices in "interpretive" theory that the new learning allows are either some version of strict construction or a pragmatic approach in which, recognizing the difficult and problematic nature of statutory interpretation, judges use consequences to guide their decisions, always bearing in mind that the relevant consequences include systemic ones such as debasing the currency of statutory language by straying too far from it.

Mention of systemic concerns should help demolish the canard that legal pragmatism implies the suppression of such concerns in favor of doing shortsighted substantive justice between the parties to the particular case. The relevant consequences to the pragmatist are long run as well as short run, systemic as well as individual, the importance of stability and predictability as well as the importance of justice to the individual parties, and the importance of maintaining language as a reliable method of communication as well as the importance of interpreting statutes and constitutional provisions freely in order to make them speak intelligently to circumstances not envisaged by their drafters. * * *

Pragmatism has implications, some already sketched under the rubrics of formalism and interpretation, for the theory of adjudication—of what judges do and should do. Although professional discourse has always been predominantly formalist, most American judges have been practicing pragmatists, in part because the materials for decision in American law have always been so various and conflicting that formalism was an unworkable ideal.

NOTES AND QUESTIONS

1. *An unacknowledged dependency on myth?* At the end of the day, we can understand the Legal Process school as more method than theory, but to what extent, if any, does it rely on a defective (or naïve) notion of representative democracy and social consensus? *See* Gary Peller, *Neutral Principles in the*

1950's, 21 U. MICH. J. L. REF. 561 (1988); Neil Duxbury, *Faith in Reason: The Process Tradition in American Jurisprudence*, 15 CARDOZO L. REV. 601 (1993).

2. *The courts as protectors of the constitutionally-defined democratic process.* Consider a handful of examples of the Supreme Court protecting (or purporting to protect) the electoral process in the United States:

(i) In *United States v. Carolene Prods. Co.*, 304 U.S. 144, 152 n.4 (1938), the Supreme Court made it clear that the judiciary was constitutionally authorized to protect "discrete and insular minorities" from any prejudice that "tends seriously to curtail the operation of those political processes ordinarily to be relied upon to protect minorities, and which may call for a correspondingly more searching judicial inquiry."

(ii) In *Reynolds v. Sims*, 377 U.S. 533 (1964), the Supreme Court invalidated a state's plan for apportioning seats in the state legislature under the Equal Protection Clause, noting that the districts were irrational and violated the one-person-one vote principle of representation.

(iii) In *Harper v. Virginia State Bd. of Elections,* 383 U.S. 663 (1966), the Court invalidated poll taxes on the ground that "[w]ealth, like race, creed, or color, is not germane to one's ability to participate intelligently in electoral process, [ ] and to introduce wealth or payment of a fee as a measure of a voter's qualifications is to introduce a capricious or irrelevant factor."

(iv) In *Bush v. Gore*, 531 U.S. 98 (2000), the Court ruled that, in the unprecedentedly-close presidential election of 2000, the manual recounts of ballots in the state of Florida, ordered by the Florida Supreme Court, violated the Equal Protection Clause because the Florida court had defined no specific standards to implement its order to discern the "intent of the voter." (Surprisingly perhaps, the proper remedy was not to remand the case to the Florida Supreme Court for the articulation of such standards.)

(v) In *Citizens United v. Federal Election Com'n*, 558 U.S. 310 (2010), the Court ruled that the First Amendment prohibits the government from suppressing political speech on the basis of the speaker's corporate identity and that a federal statute barring independent corporate expenditures for electioneering communications violates the First Amendment.

Is it fair to say that the Legal Process premium on "institutional settlement" requires that each of these decisions be treated with equal respect? In the process of answering that question, define what you mean by "equal" and "respect."

3. *Pragmatism.* Pragmatism has a long and complicated history in philosophy generally and in legal philosophy specifically. It is clear that different authors mean different things by the word "pragmatism," although

Judge Posner attempts to identify some common elements in the excerpt above. The recent renaissance of pragmatism as a respectable account of law (along with its debt to the success and failures of the Legal Process school) can be traced in a variety of scholarly writings. *See especially* John C.P. Goldberg, *Introduction: Pragmatism and Private Law*, 125 HARV. L. REV. 1640 (2012); Dmitri N. Shalin, *Legal Pragmatism, An Ideal Speech Situation, and the Fully Embodied Democratic Process*, 5 NEV. L. REV. 432 (2004–2005); Steven D., Smith, *The Pursuit of Pragmatism*, 100 YALE L. J. 409 (1990); Margaret Jane Radin, *The Pragmatist and the Feminist*, 63 S. CAL. L. REV. 1699 (1990); Daniel Farber, *Legal Pragmatism and the Constitution*, 72 MINN. L. REV. 1331 (1988). *See generally* RICHARD RORTY, CONTINGENCY, IRONY, AND SOLIDARITY (1989).

4. *Thinking across jurisprudential schools*. It might be valuable at this point to track some specific similarities between Legal Process and the schools of jurisprudence explored earlier in this book. Professor Edward Rubin has offered helpful generalizations about Legal Process which may remind you of the natural law theories, positivism, and legal realism. Edward L. Rubin, *The New Legal Process, the Synthesis of Discourse, and the Microanalysis of Institutions*, 109 HARV. L. REV. 1393 (1996). Which of those three labels arguably attaches to which of the following summaries?

> (a) "The legal process school thus reconstituted the prior separation between law and politics, not by positing transcendent legal principles, but by identifying a separate and politically established legal realm in which reasoned argument prevails." *Id.* at 1396.
>
> (b) "[T]he legal process movement * * * began by acknowledging * * * that all law is derived from political decisions. Thus, a theory of law must operate within a narrower ambit than the formalists claimed; there are no substantive legal principles that transcend the political process and that can be invoked to invalidate political decisions." *Id.* at 1395–1396.
>
> (c) "Legal process theorists accepted the prevailing notion that government institutions act rationally to achieve their goals. The question they asked about these institutions involved their legitimacy: that is, whether their actions correspond with the common good." *Id.* at 1397.

5. *Thinking ahead*. Are there now institutions for the resolution of legal disputes that either did not exist at all or that operated in a much more constrained form in the 1950's? What would a twenty-first century version of Legal Process include in its list of relevant institutions or regimes for lawyers to understand?

CHAPTER FIVE

POST-REALIST APPROACHES TO LAW AND OBLIGATION (II): LAW AND ECONOMICS

■ ■ ■

"The basis of an economic approach to law is the assumption that the people involved with the legal system act as rational maximizers of their satisfactions."

— Richard Posner

"Economic analysis has had greater success than any other discipline as a colonizer of legal scholarship."

— Carol Rose

"Your law is but the will of your class exalted into statutes, a will which acquires its content from the material conditions of the existence of your class."

— Karl Marx

Orientation

What kind of jurisprudence can survive the corrosive skepticism of American legal realism? The Realists had demonstrated (at least to their own satisfaction) that law is constantly in flux and that individual judges play an unacknowledged but dominant creative role in its development. In their view, the notion that neutral rules actually determine results in contested cases is a fiction bordering on a delusion, with serious consequences for the practice of law and for society at large. If "we are all Realists now" as suggested in Chapter 3, is it plausible that some underlying unity or cohesion actually gives an understandable structure to law? And, if so, how different will that orderliness be from the much-disparaged, allegedly-universal, accessible-to-reason unity of natural law?

One post-Realist response to the challenge has been "law and economics" ("L&E") or more precisely the economic approach to law. Historically, law and economics have been analyzed together since ancient times, and the Marxist critique of law predates the contemporary law and economics movement by a century. But modern L&E theorists draw heavily on the Realists' insight that the law is not an autonomous discipline—that it should draw from other disciplines—in this case the essential claim of neoclassical economics that human beings rationally maximize their satisfactions.

In a continuing demonstration of the truth in George Bernard Shaw's observation that all professions are conspiracies against the laity, some people are put off by the systematics, the graphs, and the jargon of law and economics theory, but its essence is not beyond mortal comprehension. To the contrary: in simple terms, the theoretical foundation is *efficiency*. Admittedly, "efficiency" can be defined and measured in various ways, but for current purposes the law is efficient to the extent that it recognizes a right in the party that would value it the most, *i.e.,* who would at least metaphorically be willing to pay the most for it. As Richard Posner—perhaps the leading contemporary exponent of the economic approach to law—has suggested: "[t]he common law method is to allocate responsibilities between people engaged in interacting activities in such a way as to maximize the joint value, or, what amounts to the same thing, minimize the joint costs of the activities. It may do this by redefining a property right, by devising a new rule of liability, or by recognizing a contract right, but nothing fundamental turns on which device is used. . . ." RICHARD POSNER, ECONOMIC ANALYSIS OF LAW 98 (1972). At a minimum, the law and economics theorists are advancing both a descriptive and a prescriptive claim: that the common law *is* efficient in fact and that judges *should* decide cases so as to maximize efficiency.

Second, law and economics theorists emphasize that markets are inherently more efficient than courts and therefore that the legal system should channel transactions into the marketplace. The bedrock assumption is that these consensual transactions create value for the people involved and for society at large (assuming at least that the transaction doesn't add its own costs that exceed the value created). If markets are impossible, the courts should try to mimic the market and reconstruct what the parties—as rational maximizers of their own satisfactions—would have wanted if a market did exist. These premises bring with them certain conclusions with respect to legislation as well: that part of law and economics called *public choice theory* emphasizes that judge-made rules are better than legislation in achieving efficiency, because common law rules are not infected by the rent-seeking and other political pitfalls of the legislative process.

A third aspect of law and economics theory is its understanding of incentives and their effect on people's or companies' rational behavior. For example, in tort cases, damages not only compensate the injured party, they create incentives for rational actors to take efficient (*i.e.*, cost-justified) precautions to avoid the damage in the first place. *See Carroll Towing* and *Spano, infra.* Similarly in property law, the legal system should define property rights unambiguously, and the right should be assigned to the party that values it the most. On the other hand, if these rights can be exchanged, the initial assignment of the right may be less important: the

Coase Theorem, a crucial building-block in the economic approach to law, states that if there are no obstacles to transactions between the parties (*i.e.*, no transaction costs), and if the rights themselves are clear and transferable, then bargaining will ensure an efficient outcome regardless of the initial allocation of property rights. The rights will in effect "gravitate" toward the use that is most highly valued. *See Ploof v. Putnam, infra.* R.H. Coase, *The Problem of Social Cost*, 3 J. LAW & ECON. 1 (1960). There are also particular areas of the law, like antitrust, where the law and economics approach has particular power, *see Syufy Enterprises, infra*, but the broadest claims of the school make it applicable to the law generally, regardless of subject matter.

There are also certain characteristic methodological tools within the law and economics school: statistical and empirical proofs predominate, as does game theory (especially in the analysis of parties' negotiation and litigation behavior). There are also echoes of utilitarianism, the ethical philosophy from the 1800's that found the rightness of an act in the greatest good for the greatest number, what Jeremy Bentham referred to as the "felicific calculus of pains and pleasures." The object of the following materials is to acquaint you with the form of argument in economic analyses of the law and to invite you to identify the ethical, institutional, psychological, and empirical assumptions on which they rest.

Tort Law: Negligence

UNITED STATES V. CARROLL TOWING CO.

159 F.2d 169 (2d Cir. 1947)

L. HAND, CIRCUIT JUDGE. These appeals concern the sinking of the barge, "Anna C," on January 4, 1944, off Pier 51, North River. [The Conners Company owned the barge "Anna C," which on the day of the accident was tied up to a pier along with several other barges. The tugboat "Carroll," owned by the Carroll Towing Company and chartered by Grace Lines, moved one of the other barges, as a result of which the "Anna C" broke loose, drifted downriver and collided with a tanker. In the accident, the tanker's propeller pierced the bottom of the "Anna C," which sank, taking its cargo of flour—shipped for the government of the United States—to the bottom. Conners had no employee one on board the "Anna C" at the time (known as a "bargee"). Under applicable law, the defendants would be excused from paying part of the damages if they could demonstrate that Conner's negligence contributed to the loss. The question for current purposes is whether Conners' failure to have a bargee on board the "Anna C" constituted negligence or not.]

We cannot [ ] excuse the Conners Company for the bargee's failure to care for the barge, and we think that this prevents full recovery. * * * We do not [ ] attribute it as in any degree a fault of the "Anna C" that the flotilla broke adrift. Hence she may recover in full against the Carroll Company and the Grace Line for any injury she suffered from the contact with the tanker's propeller, which we shall speak of as the "collision damages." On the other hand, if the bargee had been on board, and had done his duty to his employer, he would have gone below at once, examined the injury, and called for help from the "Carroll" and the Grace Line tug. Moreover, it is clear that these tugs could have kept the barge afloat, until they had safely beached her, and saved her cargo. This would have avoided what we shall call the "sinking damages." Thus, if it was a failure in the Conner Company's proper care of its own barge, for the bargee to be absent, the company can recover only one third of the "sinking" damages from the Carroll Company and one third from the Grace Line. For this reason the question arises whether a barge owner is slack in the care of his barge if the bargee is absent. * * *

It appears [ ] that there is no general rule to determine when the absence of a bargee or other attendant will make the owner of the barge liable for injuries to other vessels if she breaks away from her moorings. However, in any cases where he would be so liable for injuries to others obviously he must reduce his damages proportionately, if the injury is to his own barge. It becomes apparent why there can be no such general rule, when we consider the grounds for such a liability. Since there are occasions when every vessel will break from her moorings, and since, if she does, she becomes a menace to those about her; the owner's duty, as in other similar situations, to provide against resulting injuries is a function of three variables: (1) The probability that she will break away; (2) the gravity of the resulting injury, if she does; (3) the burden of adequate precautions. Possibly it serves to bring this notion into relief to state it in algebraic terms: if the probability be called P; the injury, L; and the burden, B; liability depends upon whether B is less than L multiplied by P: *i.e.*, whether $B < PL$. Applied to the situation at bar, the likelihood that a barge will break from her fasts and the damage she will do, vary with the place and time; for example, if a storm threatens, the danger is greater; so it is, if she is in a crowded harbor where moored barges are constantly being shifted about. On the other hand, the barge must not be the bargee's prison, even though he lives aboard; he must go ashore at times. We need not say whether, even in such crowded waters as New York Harbor a bargee must be aboard at night at all; it may be that the custom is otherwise, [ ] and that, if so, the situation is one where custom should control. We leave that question open; but we hold that it is not in all cases a sufficient answer to a bargee's absence without excuse, during working hours, that he has properly made fast his barge to a pier, when he leaves her. In the case at bar the bargee left at five o'clock in the afternoon of January 3rd, and the flotilla broke away at about two o'clock in the afternoon of the following day, twenty-one hours afterwards. The bargee had been away all the time, and we hold that his fabricated story was affirmative evidence that he had no excuse for his absence. At the locus in quo—especially during the short January days and in the full tide of war activity—barges were being constantly "drilled" in and out. Certainly it was not beyond reasonable expectation that, with the inevitable haste and bustle, the work might not be done with adequate care. In such circumstances we hold—and it is all that we do hold—that it was a fair requirement that the Conners Company should have a bargee aboard (unless he had some excuse for his absence), during the working hours of daylight. * * *

[The Court declared that the Connors Company must bear part of the liability for the "sinking damages."]

Tort Law: Strict Liability

SPANO V. PERINI CORPORATION ET AL.

25 N.Y.2d 11, 250 N.E.2d 31 (1969)

FULD, CHIEF JUDGE. The principal question posed on this appeal is whether a person who has sustained property damage caused by blasting on nearby property can maintain an action for damages without a showing that the blaster was negligent. Since 1893, when this court decided the case of *Booth v. Rome, W. & O. T. R. R. Co.* (140 N. Y. 267), it has been the law of this State that proof of negligence was required unless the blast was accompanied by an actual physical invasion of the damaged property—for example, by rocks or other material being cast upon the premises. We are now asked to reconsider that rule.

The plaintiff Spano is the owner of a garage in Brooklyn which was wrecked by a blast occurring on November 27, 1962. There was then in that garage, for repairs, an automobile owned by the plaintiff Davis which he also claims was damaged by the blasting. Each of the plaintiffs brought suit against the two defendants who, as joint venturers, were engaged in constructing a tunnel in the vicinity pursuant to a contract with the City of New York. * * * The two cases were tried together, without a jury, in the Civil Court of the City of New York, New York County, and judgments were rendered in favor of the plaintiffs. The judgments were reversed by the Appellate Term and the Appellate Division affirmed that order, granting leave to appeal to this court.

It is undisputed that, on the day in question (November 27, 1962), the defendants had set off a total of 194 sticks of dynamite at a construction site which was only 125 feet away from the damaged premises. Although both plaintiffs alleged negligence in their complaints, no attempt was made to show that the defendants had failed to exercise reasonable care or to take necessary precautions when they were blasting. Instead, they chose to rely, upon the trial, solely on the principle of absolute liability either on a tort theory or on the basis of their being third-party beneficiaries of the defendants' contract with the city. At the close of the plaintiff Spano's case, when defendants' attorney moved to dismiss the action on the ground, among others, that no negligence had been proved, the trial judge expressed the view that the defendants could be held liable even though they were not shown to have been careless. The case then proceeded, with evidence being introduced solely on the question of damages and proximate cause. Following the trial, the court awarded damages of some $4,400 to Spano and of $329 to Davis.

On appeal, a divided Appellate Term reversed that judgment, declaring that it deemed itself concluded by the established rule in this State requiring proof of negligence. Justice Markowitz, who dissented, urged that the *Booth* case should no longer be considered controlling precedent. The Appellate Division affirmed; it called attention to a decision in the Third Department (*Thomas v. Hendrickson Bros.*, 30 A.D. 2d 730, 731), in which the court observed that "[i]f *Booth* is to be overruled, 'the announcement thereof should come from the authoritative source and not in the form of interpretation or prediction by an intermediate appellate court' ".

In our view, the time has come for this court to make that "announcement" and declare that one who engages in blasting must assume responsibility, and be liable without fault, for any injury he causes to neighboring property.

The concept of absolute liability in blasting cases is hardly a novel one. The overwhelming majority of American jurisdictions have adopted such a rule. * * * Indeed, this court itself, several years ago, noted that a change in our law would "conform to the more widely (indeed almost universally) approved doctrine that a blaster is absolutely liable for any damages he causes, with or without trespass". (*Schlansky v. Augustus V. Riegel, Inc.,* 9 N.Y. 2d 493, 496.)

We need not rely solely, however, upon out-of-state decisions in order to attain our result. Not only has the rationale of the *Booth* case been overwhelmingly rejected elsewhere but it appears to be fundamentally inconsistent with earlier cases in our own court which had held, long before *Booth* was decided, that a party was absolutely liable for damages to neighboring property caused by explosions. In [*Hay v. Cohoes Co.*, 2 N.Y. 159], for example, the defendant was engaged in blasting an excavation for a canal and the force of the blasts caused large quantities of earth and stones to be thrown against the plaintiff's house, knocking down his stoop and part of his chimney. The court held the defendant *absolutely* liable for the damage caused, stating:

> It is an elementary principle in reference to private rights, that every individual is entitled to the undisturbed possession and lawful enjoyment of his own property. The mode of enjoyment is necessarily limited by the rights of others—otherwise it might be made destructive of their rights altogether. Hence the maxim *sic utere tuo, &c.* The defendants had the right to dig the canal. The plaintiff the right to the undisturbed possession of his property. If these rights conflict, the former must yield to the latter, as the more important of the two, since, upon grounds of public policy, it is better that one man should surrender a particular use of his land, than that another should be deprived of the beneficial use of his property altogether, which might be the consequence if the privilege of the former should be wholly unrestricted. The case before us illustrates this principle. For if the defendants in excavating their canal, in itself a lawful use of their land, could, in the manner mentioned by the witnesses, demolish the stoop of the plaintiff with impunity, they might, for the same purpose, on the exercise of reasonable care, demolish his house, and thus deprive him of all use of his property.

Although the court in *Booth* drew a distinction between a situation—such as was presented in the *Hay* case—where there was "a physical invasion" of, or trespass on, the plaintiff's property and one in which the damage was caused by "setting the air in motion, or in some other unexplained way", it is clear that the court, in the earlier cases, was not concerned with the particular manner by which the damage was caused but by the simple fact that any explosion in a built-up area was likely to cause damage. Thus, in *Heeg v. Licht (*80 N.Y. 579), the court held that there should be absolute liability where the damage was caused by the accidental explosion of stored gunpowder, even in the absence of a physical trespass:

> The defendant had erected a building and stored materials therein, which from their character were liable to and actually did explode, causing injury to the plaintiff. The fact that the explosion took place tends to establish that the magazine was dangerous and liable to cause damage to the property of persons residing in the vicinity. * * * The fact that the magazine was liable to such a contingency, which could not be guarded against or averted by the greatest degree of care and vigilance, evinces its dangerous character, * * * In such a case, the rule which exonerates a party engaged in a lawful business, when free from negligence, has no application.

Such reasoning should, we venture, have led to the conclusion that the *intentional* setting off of explosives—that is, blasting—in an area in which it was likely to cause harm to neighboring property similarly results in absolute liability. However, the court in the *Booth* case rejected such an extension of the rule for the reason that "[to] exclude the defendant from blasting to adapt its lot to the contemplated uses, at the instance of the plaintiff, would not be a compromise between conflicting rights, but an extinguishment of the right of the one for the benefit of the other". The court expanded on this by stating, "This sacrifice, we think, the law does not exact. Public policy is promoted by the building up of towns and cities and the improvement of property. Any unnecessary restraint on freedom of action of a property owner hinders this."

This rationale cannot withstand analysis. The plaintiff in *Booth* was not seeking, as the court implied, to "exclude the defendant from blasting" and thus prevent desirable improvements to the latter's property. Rather, he was merely seeking compensation for the damage which was inflicted upon his own property as a result of that blasting. The question, in other words, was not *whether* it was lawful or proper to engage in blasting but *who* should bear the cost of any resulting damage—the person who engaged in the dangerous activity or the innocent neighbor injured thereby. Viewed in such a light, it clearly appears that *Booth* was wrongly decided and should be forthrightly overruled.

In more recent cases, our court has already gone far toward mitigating the harsh effect of the rule laid down in the *Booth* case. Thus, we have held that negligence can properly be inferred from the mere fact that a blast has caused extensive damage, even where the plaintiff is unable to show "the method of blasting or the strength of the charges or the character of the soil or rock." (*Schlansky v. Augustus V. Riegel, Inc.*, 9 N.Y.2d 493, 497, *supra*). But, even under this liberal interpretation of *Booth*, it would still remain possible for a defendant who engages in blasting operations—which he realizes are likely to cause injury—to avoid liability by showing that he exercised reasonable care. Since blasting involves a substantial risk of harm no matter the degree of care exercised, we perceive no reason for ever permitting a person who engages in such an activity to impose this risk upon nearby persons or property without assuming responsibility therefor.

Indeed, the defendants devote but brief argument in defense of the *Booth* rule. The principal thrust of their argument is directed not to the requisite standard of care to be used but, rather, to the sufficiency of the plaintiffs' pleadings and the proof adduced on the issue of causation.

As to the sufficiency of the pleadings, we need but point out that both Spano's and Davis's complaints alleged that the defendants engaged in blasting operations which resulted in damage to their respective property. Thus, they contained adequate "notice of the transactions * * * intended to be proved and the material elements of [the] cause of action." The fact that, in Davis's case, these allegations were subsumed in a cause of action for negligence is immaterial, since the inclusion of unnecessary additional allegations does not affect the sufficiency of a complaint.

There remains, then, only the matter of proof on the issue of causation. Although the evidence adduced by the plaintiffs on this question was entirely circumstantial, it may not be said that it was insufficient as a matter of law. The plaintiffs' principal witness was a contractor who had leased a portion of the premises from Spano. It was his testimony that there was no damage on or to the premises prior to November 27; that he had heard an explosion at about noon on that day while he was working some three blocks away and that, when he returned a few hours later, the building "was cracked in the wall * * * the window broke, and the cement floor all pop up." In addition, an insurance adjuster, an expert with wide experience in handling explosion claims, who inspected the damage to Davis's car, testified that the damage was evidently "caused by a concussion of one form or another." The defendants' expert attributed the damage to another cause—poor maintenance and building deterioration—but, admittedly, the defendants were engaged in blasting operations in the area at the time and, as the Appellate Term expressly found, the inference that this was the cause of the damage could properly be drawn. Even though the proof was not insufficient as a matter of law, however, the Appellate Division affirmed on the sole ground that no negligence had been proven against the defendants and thus had no occasion to consider the question whether, in fact, the blasting caused the damage. That being so, we must remit the case to the Appellate Division so that it may pass upon the weight of the evidence.

NOTES AND QUESTIONS

1. *Carroll Towing and the "Hand Formula."* In Judge Hand's view, the law of negligence can be understood through a deceptively simple formula: a party will be found to be liable for negligence and therefore liable for at least some part of the resulting damages if B<PL, where "B" is the burden of precaution, meaning the cost of avoiding the accident in the first place; "P" is the probability that the accident will occur; and "L" is the cost of the accident if it does occur.

> [U]nder this principle, I must compensate you for your losses if the safety device [that would have prevented the accident] would have cost me less than the "discounted" cost of the accident, that is, the cost discounted by the chance that it might not occur even without the device. But I need not compensate you if the cost of installing the device would have been higher than the discounted cost of the accident.

RONALD DWORKIN, LAW'S EMPIRE 276 (1986). In other words, "when the costs of preventing an accident are less than the expected loss (properly discounted by the probability of an accident occurring,) it is negligent not to take precautionary measures." DAVID BARNES & LYNN STOUT, CASES AND

MATERIALS ON LAW AND ECONOMICS 95 (1992). To begin to understand the economic approach to law, start by noticing how the rule and the result in *Carroll Towing* follow from an apparent quantification of costs, benefits, and probabilities. *Cf.* JULES L. COLEMAN, RISKS AND WRONGS 6–12 (1992) (rejecting the market paradigm for torts but incorporating some insights of economic analysis).

2. *Things that make you go "hmmmm."* If existing liability rules create an incentive for efficient behavior, why would people ever be negligent in the first place? Could it be because they are not rational, or is something else going on?

3. *One shorthand summary of negligence law.* Consider the following comment to Section 283 of RESTATEMENT (SECOND) OF TORTS: "Where a defendant's negligence is to be determined, the 'reasonable [person]' is a [person] who is reasonably 'considerate' of the safety of others and does not look primarily at his own advantage." Is that formulation consistent with the Hand Formula or not? Trick Question Alert: which is easier for a court to apply? If you were lawyer arguing a negligence case to a jury, which formulation would you prefer to argue about?

4. *Generalizing the Hand Formula.* Negligence and strict liability are two very different categories of tort liability, but, after reading *Spano v. Perini Corp.,* is it possible to view the imposition of strict liability as a specialized application of the Hand Formula? How might it help to identify the cheapest cost-avoider, as in cases involving blasting? *See also Greenman v. Yuba Power Products, Inc.*, 59 Cal. 2d 57, 377 P.2d 897 (Cal. 1963).

5. *Efficiency of the common law hypothesis.* One premise of the economic approach to law is that the common law (*i.e.*, judge-made law) evolves from the effort to produce "efficient" outcomes. One school argues that this evolution occurs because parties are more likely to litigate inefficient rules than efficient rules. *See, e.g.*, Paul H. Rubin, *Why is the Common Law Efficient?*, 6 J. LEG. STUDIES 51 (1977); George L. Priest, *The Common Law Process and the Selection of Efficient Rules,* 6 J. LEG. STUDIES 65 (1977). The inefficient rules impose greater costs on the parties than the efficient rules, raising the stakes in the dispute, and increasing in turn the likelihood of repeat litigation. Because in this view the inefficient rules are litigated more frequently, their "survival rate" is lower. Over time, it is the repeat litigators, with their utility-maximizing decisions and strategies, and not the judges' effort to maximize efficiency, that make the common law evolve towards efficiency: the law's equivalent of natural selection.

6. *Externalities and the law's treatment of economic side effects.* For our purposes, an externality is any consequence of an activity by an individual or firm that is felt by some unrelated third party. In *Spano*, prior to the litigation, the Perini Corporation's blasting activities imposed a cost on Spano that was not reflected in the cost of its goods or services. Similarly, in the standard illustration of environmental degradation, the cost of a factory's air pollution is imposed on the community and, in the absence of regulation or lawsuit, is

not reflected in the cost of the goods produced at the factory. You could consider the result in *Spano* as the court's effort to "internalize the externalities," forcing Perini to pay the costs of its damage to Spano. (i) Assuming that Perini (or the factory owner in the pollution case) pays compensatory damages, who or what ends up footing the bill? Then what? (ii) Should the law be as vigilant about forcing compensation for positive externalities, as it is with respect to negative externalities like those in *Spano*? Suppose an apple farmer alters her operations in ways that inadvertently but positively affect her neighbor's bee-keeping operations, making them more profitable. That too is an externality. Should the apple farmer be able to use the law to extract "compensation" from the bee-keeper, based perhaps on a share of the increased profits? If not, why not?

7. *Pareto Optimality and the problem of defining "efficiency."* What exactly do law and economics theorists mean when they say that a case result or a legal doctrine are "efficient?" One recurring definition turns on the notion of "Pareto Optimality," named after the Italian economist, Vilfredo Pareto (1848–1923): *efficiency exists when conditions are such that no member of society can be made better off without hurting someone else*. Benefit to all has been maximized, and so-called "Pareto optimality" has been achieved, because any increase in benefit to one would come at the expense of hurting another. In other words, "[a] given economic arrangement is efficient if there can be no arrangement which will leave someone better off without worsening the position of others." RICHARD MUSGRAVE & PEGGY MUSGRAVE, PUBLIC FINANCE IN THEORY AND PRACTICE 67 (2nd ed. 1976). That arrangement is sometimes described as being at the "Pareto frontier."

Pareto Optimality can be useful in comparing various policies dealing with everything from health care to patent protection, rent control to marginal tax rates, environmental regulation to public education. It can also be used more generally as a rationale for free market enthusiasm:

> Exchanges among knowledgeable, rational persons in a free market are generally Pareto superior; rational individuals do not strike bargains with one another unless each perceives it to be in his or her own interest to do so. A successful exchange between such parties is, therefore, one in which the value to each of what he or she relinquishes is perceived as less than the value of what each receives in return.

JULES L. COLEMAN, MARKETS, MORALS, AND THE LAW 101 (1998).

The concept of Pareto Optimality has been refined in ways that may be helpful when dealing with cases at law, where there is the possibility of compensatory damages. Specifically, economists recognize the concept of "Kaldor-Hicks optimality," which refers to Pareto improvements made possible when the winners can in principle compensate the losers for their losses: even if no compensation is actually paid, the winners have won more than the losers have lost.

As you think about what should go into the decision of cases, are you concerned that Pareto and Kaldor-Hicks Optimality leaves something important out of the analysis? When is fidelity to text or fairness to the parties "efficient" according to these standards?

8. *Distinguishing the prescriptive claims from the descriptive claims*. It is true that judges and advocates do not routinely couch their arguments and conclusions in predominantly economic terms. But supporters of the economic approach to law suggest that common law rules have in fact arisen out of arguments that are essentially economic in nature, giving them a deep coherence or unity. J.W. HARRIS, LEGAL PHILOSOPHIES 43 (1980). For example, Richard Posner has argued

> that a society which aims at maximizing wealth, unlike a society which aims at maximizing utility (happiness), will produce an ethically attractive combination of happiness, of rights (to liberty and property), and of sharing with the less fortunate members of society.... [T]he same considerations which ma[k]e wealth maximization an ethically attractive norm in common law adjudication might help to explain why it has played an important role in shaping the substantive rules and procedures of the common law.

Richard A. Posner, *The Ethical and Political Basis of the Efficiency Norm in Common Law Adjudication*, 8 HOFSTRA L. REV. 487, 487 (1980) (citations omitted). (i) What do you make of Posner's distinction between maximizing wealth and maximizing utility or happiness? (i) How do you think that distinction connects to the distinction between Pareto Optimality and Kaldor-Hicks optimality, laid out in note 7, *supra*? (iii) What assumptions—empirical, analytical, and moral—underlie Posner's position? (iv) How exactly are these assumptions different from the natural law theories?

9. *Defenses*. It is one thing to understand the rough cost-benefit analysis at work in *Carroll Towing* as a way of determining when negligence liability will be imposed. Must defenses to negligence liability (like contributory negligence, assumption of the risk, or the last clear chance doctrine) *also* pass the *Carroll Towing* test? In other words, is the defendant the only party in a position to adopt precautions, and, if not, how should that affect the computation of the value of B?

10. *The cost-benefit approach to contracts: "efficient breach."* Is it possible to extend the Hand Formula on negligence to contractual obligations? In *Lake River Corp. v. Carborundum Co.*, 769 F.2d 1284, 1289 (7th Cir. 1985) (Posner, J.), the court had to consider the enforceability of a contractual provision for liquidated damages:

> Suppose a breach would cost the promisee $12,000 in actual damages but would yield the promisor $20,000 in additional profits. Then there would be a net social gain from breach. After being fully compensated for his loss the promisee would be no worse off than if the contract had been performed, while the promisor would be better off by $8,000.

> But now suppose the contract contains a penalty clause under which the promisor if he breaks his promise must pay the promisee $25,000. The promisor will be discouraged from breaking the contract, since $25,000, the penalty, is greater than $20,000, the profits of the breach; and a transaction that would have increased value will be forgone.
>
> On this view, since compensatory damages should be sufficient to deter inefficient breaches (that is, breaches that cost the victim more than the gain to the contract breaker), penal damages could have no effect other than to deter some efficient breaches. But this overlooks the * * * point that the willingness to agree to a penalty clause is a way of making the promisor and his promise credible and may therefore be essential to inducing some value-maximizing contracts to be made. It also overlooks the more important point that the parties (always assuming they are fully competent) will, in deciding whether to include a penalty clause in their contract, weigh the gains against the costs—costs that include the possibility of discouraging an efficient breach somewhere down the road—and will include the clause only if the benefits exceed those costs as well as all other costs.

Does the concept of an efficient breach mean that it's not illegal to break your promises?

Property Law

PLOOF V. PUTNAM

81 Vt. 471, 71 A. 188 (1908)

MUNSON, J. It is alleged as the ground of recovery that on the 13th day of November, 1904, the defendant was the owner of a certain island in Lake Champlain, and of a certain dock attached thereto, which island and dock were then in charge of the defendant's servant; that the plaintiff was then possessed of and sailing upon said lake a certain loaded sloop, on which were the plaintiff and his wife and two minor children; that there then arose a sudden and violent tempest, whereby the sloop and the property and persons therein were placed in great danger of destruction; that to save these from destruction or injury the plaintiff was compelled to, and did, moor the sloop to defendant's dock; that the defendant by his servant unmoored the sloop, whereupon it was driven upon the shore by the tempest, without the plaintiff's fault; and that the sloop and its contents were thereby destroyed, and the plaintiff and his wife and children cast into the lake and upon the shore, receiving injuries.

This claim is set forth in two counts; one in trespass, charging that the defendant by his servant with force and arms willfully and designedly unmoored the sloop; the other in case, alleging that it was the duty of the defendant by his servant to permit the plaintiff to moor his sloop to the dock, and to permit it to remain so moored during the continuance of the tempest, but that the defendant by his servant, in disregard of this duty, negligently, carelessly and wrongfully unmoored the sloop. Both counts are demurred to generally.

There are many cases in the books which hold that necessity, and an inability to control movements inaugurated in the proper exercise of a strict right, will justify entries upon land and interferences with personal property that would otherwise have been trespasses. A reference to a few of these will be sufficient to illustrate the doctrine.

In *Miller v. Fandrye*, Poph. 161, trespass was brought for chasing sheep, and the defendant pleaded that the sheep were trespassing upon his land, and that he with a little dog chased them out, and that as soon as the sheep were off his land he called in the dog. It was argued that, although the defendant might lawfully drive the sheep from his own ground with a dog, he had no right to pursue them into the next ground. But the court considered that the defendant might drive the sheep from his land with a dog, and that the nature of a dog is such that he cannot be withdrawn in an instant, and that as the defendant had done his best to recall the dog trespass would not lie.

In trespass of cattle taken in A, defendant pleaded that he was seized of C, and found the cattle there damage feasant, and chased them toward the pound, and that they escaped from him and went into A, and he presently retook them; and this was held a good plea. 21 Edw. IV. 64; Vin. Ab. Trespass, H. a 4 pl. 19. If one have a way over the land of another for his beasts to pass, and the beasts, being properly driven, feed the grass by morsels in passing, or run out of the way and are promptly pursued and brought back, trespass will not lie. *See* Vin. Ab. Trespass, K. a. pl. 1.

A traveller on a highway, who finds it obstructed from a sudden and temporary cause, may pass upon the adjoining land without becoming a trespasser, because of the necessity. * * * An entry upon land to save goods which are in danger of being lost or destroyed by water or fire is not a trespass. * * * In *Proctor v. Adams*, 113 Mass. 376, the defendant went upon the plaintiff's beach for the purpose of saving and restoring to the lawful owner a boat which had been driven ashore and was in danger of being carried off by the sea; and it was held no trespass.

This doctrine of necessity applies with special force to the preservation of human life. One assaulted and in peril of his life may run through the close of another to escape from his assailant. 37 Hen. VII, pl. 26. One may sacrifice the personal property of another to save his life or the lives of his fellows. In *Mouse's Case*, 12 Coke 63, the defendant was sued for taking and carrying away the plaintiff's casket and its contents. It appeared that the ferryman of Gravesend took forty-seven passengers into his barge to pass to London, among whom were the plaintiff and defendant; and the barge being upon the water a great tempest happened, and a strong wind, so that the barge and all the passengers were in danger of being lost if certain ponderous things were not cast out, and the defendant thereupon cast out the plaintiff's casket. It was resolved that in case of necessity, to save the lives of the passengers, it was lawful for the defendant, being a passenger, to cast the plaintiff's casket out of the barge; that if the ferryman surcharge the barge the owner shall have his remedy upon the surcharge against the ferryman, but that if there be no surcharge, and the danger accrue only by the act of God, as by tempest, without fault of the ferryman, every one ought to bear his loss, to safeguard the life of a man.

It is clear that an entry upon the land of another may be justified by necessity, and that the declaration before us discloses a necessity for mooring the sloop. But the defendant questions the sufficiency of the counts because they do not negative the existence of natural objects to which the plaintiff could have moored with equal safety. The allegations are, in substance, that the stress of a sudden and violent tempest compelled the plaintiff to moor to defendant's dock to save his sloop and the people in it. The averment of necessity is complete, for it covers not only the necessity of mooring, but the necessity of mooring to the dock; and the details of the situation which created this necessity, whatever the legal requirements regarding them, are matters of proof and need not be alleged. It is certain that the rule suggested cannot be held applicable irrespective of circumstance, and the question must be left for adjudication upon proceedings had with reference to the evidence or the charge. * * * [The court held that plaintiff was allowed to recover.]

NOTES AND QUESTIONS

1. *Replicating an imaginary market.* How might you analyze *Ploof* as an example of a court trying to mimic a market where none exists or existed? Does the law—like the property doctrines in *Ploof* or the tort doctrines in *Carroll Towing* and *Spano*—in effect create and enforce a mythical contract between strangers, after the fact but replicating what they would rationally have agreed to if they had known what was about to happen?

2. *The Coase Theorem.* Ronald Coase won the Nobel Prize in 1991 for what the Nobel Committee described as "his discovery and clarification of the significance of transaction costs and property rights for the institutional structure and functioning of the economy." The importance of Coase's article, *The Problem of Social Cost*, 3 J. LAW & ECON. 1 (1960), might be inferred from the fact that it is one of the most frequently cited articles in the history of legal scholarship, even though its author was not a lawyer. In Coase's words, *The Problem of Social Cost* was concerned "with those actions of business firms which have harmful effects on others." He continued:

> The standard example is that of a factory the smoke from which has harmful effects on those occupying neighbouring properties. The economic analysis of such a situation has usually proceeded in terms of a divergence between the private and social product of the factory, in which economists have largely followed the treatment of Pigou in THE ECONOMICS OF WELFARE. The conclusions to which this kind of analysis seems to have led most economists is that it would be desirable to make the owner of the factory liable for the damage caused to those injured by the smoke, or alternatively, to place a tax on the factory owner varying with the amount of smoke produced and equivalent in money terms to the damage it would cause, or finally, to exclude the factory from residential districts (and presumably from other areas in which the emission of smoke would have harmful effects on others). It is my contention that the suggested courses of action are inappropriate, in that they lead to results which are not necessarily, or even usually, desirable. * * *
>
> The traditional approach has tended to obscure the nature of the choice that has to be made. The question is commonly thought of as one in which A inflicts harm on B and what has to be decided is: how should we restrain A? But this is wrong. We are dealing with a problem of a reciprocal nature. To avoid the harm to B would inflict harm on A. The real question that has to be decided is: should A be allowed to harm B or should B be allowed to harm A? The problem is to avoid the more serious harm.

Id. at 1–2.

Although the Coase Theorem can be articulated in a number of ways, at base it states—as noted above—that if there are no obstacles to transactions between the parties (*i.e.*, no transaction costs), and if the rights themselves are clear and transferable, then bargaining within the market will ensure an efficient outcome regardless of the initial allocation of property rights. The initial (or *ex ante*) assignment of property rights as a matter of law will generally be irrelevant to overall welfare, because—in the absence of transaction costs—the market will determine the ultimate allocation of legal entitlements based on their relative value to the different parties involved. In Professor Coase's words:

> It is always possible to modify by transactions in the market the initial legal delimitation of rights. And, of course, if such market transactions are costless, such a rearrangement of rights will *always* take place if it would lead to an increase in the value of production.

Id. at 15 (emphasis supplied). As noted by Professor, later Judge Guido Calabresi, "*The Problem of Social Cost* emphasized the possible benefits of markets. It pointed out that when transaction costs were not prohibitive, people would enter into transactions creating markets, not only to get around 'inefficient' hierarchical or command structures, but also to fill the vacuum left by the absence of preexisting market or command relationships." Guido

Calabresi, *The Pointlessness of Pareto: Carrying Coase Further*, 100 YALE L.J. 1211, 121 (1991).

Admittedly, assuming that there are no transaction costs is a little like quenching your thirst by assuming a bottle of water, but Coase was careful to identify the transaction costs that actually do arise (*e.g.*, incomplete information, the inability to communicate at all or in a timely way, ambiguity in the underlying rights) and their efficiency implications. In short, Coase was highlighting, not minimizing, the reality of transaction costs in society; indeed, *Ploof* invites you to think through what happens when there *are* obstacles or costs to bargaining. (i) Does it mean for example that the initial allocation of property rights now *is* relevant? (ii) In what sense can lawyers be viewed as "transaction cost engineers?" Ronald Gilson, *Value Creation by Business Lawyers: Legal Skills and Asset Pricing*, 94 YALE L.J. 239, 243 (1984).

In coming to understand the law-and-economics rationale for the result in *Ploof*, would it help to know (assuming that it's true) that the dock and the boat cost exactly the same amount of money? Would it help to know (assuming that it's true) that Putman, the dock owner, was rich and Ploof, the boat owner, was not? Is something other than monetary value at stake in the case?

3. *The economic approach to property law and "the tragedy of the commons."* Law and economics scholars have attempted to demonstrate that, in market economies at least, property rights are generally defined and enforced efficiently. They have determined that the genetic markers of efficient property rights are universality (in that everything is owned), exclusivity (in that each thing is owned by one actor), and transferability (property and rights in property can be exchanged). What happens though when property rights are inefficient, and why might that matter to advocates for more environmental protection?

To get a handle on that problem, consider the "tragedy of the commons," as developed by Professor Garrett Hardin:

> Picture a pasture open to all. It is to be expected that each herdsman will try to keep as many cattle as possible on the commons. Such an arrangement may work reasonably satisfactorily for centuries because tribal wars, poaching, and disease keep the numbers of both man and beast well below the carrying capacity of the land. Finally, however, comes the day of reckoning, that is, the day when the long-desired goal of social stability becomes a reality. At this point, the inherent logic of the commons remorselessly generates tragedy. * * *
>
> Adding together the component partial utilities, the rational herdsman concludes that the only sensible course for him to pursue is to add another animal to his herd. And another; and another. . . But this is the conclusion reached by each and every rational herdsman sharing a commons. Therein is the tragedy. Each man is locked into a system that compels him to increase his herd without limit—in a world that is limited. Ruin is the destination toward which

> all men rush, each pursuing his own best interest in a society that believes in the freedom of the commons. Freedom in a commons brings ruin to all.

Garrett Hardin, *The Tragedy of the Commons*, 162 SCIENCE 1243 (13 December 1968). Over 2500 years ago, the Greek historian, Thucydides, observed similar effects of individuals pursuing their own interests to the detriment of the common good:

> [T]hey devote a very small fraction of time to the consideration of any public object, most of it to the prosecution of their own objects. Meanwhile each fancies that no harm will come to his neglect, that it is the business of somebody else to look after this or that for him; and so, by the same notion being entertained by all separately, the common cause imperceptibly decays.

I HISTORY OF THE PELOPONNESIAN WAR 141 (Crawley, trans. 1910). In short, the tragedy of the commons is the dilemma that arises whenever multiple individuals, acting independently and rationally in their own self-interest, necessarily deplete a shared limited resource, even when that result is in no individual's long-term self-interest. As one example of the "tyranny of small decisions," the tragedy of the commons has sometimes been used to argue for government regulation of otherwise legally-protected private action.

The "tragedy" analysis has been criticized over the years, especially its postulate that independence and greed are *either* inevitable even up to the point that the common resource is destroyed *or* controllable only by regulatory interference. Examples of spontaneous cooperation in the long-term protection of a shared resource are not impossible to find; indeed, they take many forms. But the "tragedy of the commons" does raise a pointed question for our purposes: what legal doctrines or concepts can you imagine to avoid or minimize the damage to the "commons?" In other words, what legal rights, concepts, burdens, or privileges—and what systems of enforcement—can you devise to minimize the impact of this dilemma? Can you use those approaches to imagine legal responses to global climate change?

4. *Property rights as deprivations.* Pierre-Joseph Proudhon (1809–1865), a French philosopher and politician, famously observed that "property is theft." What does that mean? Theft from whom? Are there circumstances under which you would view the rigid protection of intellectual property rights on the internet as a form of theft?

Statutory Law: Antitrust

UNITED STATES V. SYUFY ENTERPRISES

903 F.2d 659 (9th Cir. 1991)

KOZINSKI, CIRCUIT JUDGE. Suspect that giant film distributors like Columbia, Paramount and Twentieth Century-Fox had fallen prey to Raymond Syufy, the canny operator of a chain of Las Vegas, Nevada, movie theatres, the United States Department of Justice brought this civil antitrust action to force Syufy to disgorge the theatres he had purchased in 1982–84 from his former competitors. The case is unusual in a number of respects: The Department of Justice concedes that moviegoers in Las Vegas suffered no direct injury as a result of the allegedly illegal transactions; nor does the record reflect complaints from Syufy's bought-out competitors, as the sales were made at fair prices and not precipitated by any monkey business; and the supposedly oppressed movie companies have weighed in on Syufy's side. The Justice Department nevertheless remains intent on rescuing this platoon of Goliaths from a single David.

After extensive discovery and an 8½ day trial, the learned district judge entered comprehensive findings of fact and conclusions of law, holding for Syufy. He found, *inter alia*, that Syufy's actions did not injure competition because there are no barriers to entry—others could and did enter the market—and that Syufy therefore did not have the power to control prices or exclude the competition. While Justice raises a multitude of issues in its appeal, these key findings of the district court present the greatest hurdle it must overcome. * * *

Gone are the days when a movie ticket cost a dime, popcorn a nickel and theatres had a single screen: This is the age of the multiplex. With more than 300 new films released every year—each potentially the next *Batman* or *E.T.*—many successful theatres today run a different film on each of their six, twelve or eighteen screens. The multiplex offers something for everyone: Moviegoers can choose from a wider selection of films; theatre operators are able to balance profits and losses from blockbusters and flops, and to reduce manpower by consolidating concession islands; the producers, of course, like having the extra screens on which to display their wares.

Raymond Syufy understood the formula well. In 1981, he entered the Las Vegas market with a splash by opening a six-screen theatre. Newly constructed and luxuriously furnished, it put existing facilities to shame. Syufy's entry into the Las Vegas market caused a stir, precipitating a titanic bidding war.[1] Soon, theatres in Las Vegas were paying some of the

---

[1] Film distributors do not hand out prints for free; they sell exhibition licenses. These licenses normally specify a percentage of weekly house receipts, known as license fees, payable by the theatre owner to the distributor. Where more than one theatre in a given area volunteers to pay the license fee for a particular film, the distributor has several options: It can license the film

highest license fees in the nation, while distributors sat back and watched the easy money roll in.

It is the nature of free enterprise that fierce, no holds barred competition will drive out the least effective participants in the market, providing the most efficient allocation of productive resources. And so it was in the Las Vegas movie market in 1982. After a hard fought battle among several contenders, Syufy gained the upper hand. Two of his rivals, Mann Theatres and Plitt Theatres, saw their future as rocky and decided to sell out to Syufy. While Mann and Plitt are major exhibitors nationwide, neither had a large presence in Las Vegas. Mann operated two indoor theatres with a total of three screens; Plitt operated a single theatre with three screens. Things were relatively quiet until September 1984; in September, Syufy entered into earnest negotiations with Cragin Industries, his largest remaining competitor. Cragin sold out to Syufy midway through October, leaving Roberts Company, a small exhibitor of mostly second-run films, as Syufy's only competitor for first-run films in Las Vegas.

It is these three transactions—Syufy's purchases of the Mann, Plitt and Cragin theatres—that the Justice Department claims amount to antitrust violations.[3] As government counsel explained at oral argument, the thrust of its case is that "you may not get monopoly power by buying out your competitors." * * *

Competition is the driving force behind our free enterprise system. Unlike centrally planned economies, where decisions about production and allocation are made by government bureaucrats who ostensibly see the big picture and know to do the right thing, capitalism relies on decentralized planning—millions of producers and consumers making hundreds of millions of individual decisions each year—to determine what and how much will be produced. Competition plays the key role in this process: It imposes an essential discipline on producers and sellers of goods to provide the consumer with a better product at a lower cost; it drives out inefficient and marginal producers, releasing resources to higher-valued uses; it

---

to more than one theatre in the area; it can award the film to a particular theatre with which it has an ongoing relationship; or it can let them all bid for exclusive exhibition rights. Where the distributor adopts the competitive bidding approach, as virtually all distributors did in Las Vegas prior to October 1984, the high bid usually includes a guarantee—a minimum fee payable to the distributor even if the film bombs.

As bidding in Las Vegas grew more fierce, guarantee amounts went over the top. Too often, the bids were so high that theatre owners ran up substantial losses. The industry refers to these as busted guarantees, meaning that because the film did less business than was expected, the theatre was trapped into paying the higher guarantee amount instead of the percentage of box office it had negotiated. Occasionally, guarantees in Las Vegas were so high that they exceeded the gate at a particular theatre.

[3] Specifically, the government's complaint alleges monopolization and/or attempted monopolization of a part of commerce in violation of Section 2 of the Sherman Act, 15 U.S.C. § 2 (1988), and substantial lessening of competition by acquisition within a line of commerce in violation of Section 7 of the Clayton Act, 15 U.S.C. § 18 (1988).

promotes diversity, giving consumers choices to fit a wide array of personal preferences; it avoids permanent concentrations of economic power, as even the largest firm can lose market share to a feistier and hungrier rival. If, as the metaphor goes, a market economy is governed by an invisible hand, competition is surely the brass knuckles by which it enforces its decisions.

When competition is impaired, producers may be able to reap monopoly profits, denying consumers many of the benefits of a free market. It is a simple but important truth, therefore, that our antitrust laws are designed to protect the integrity of the market system by assuring that competition reigns freely. While much has been said and written about the antitrust laws during the last century of their existence, ultimately the court must resolve a practical question in every monopolization case: Is this the type of situation where market forces are likely to cure the perceived problem within a reasonable period of time? Or, have barriers been erected to constrain the normal operation of the market, so that the problem is not likely to be self-correcting? In the latter situation, it might well be necessary for a court to correct the market imbalance; in the former, a court ought to exercise extreme caution because judicial intervention in a competitive situation can itself upset the balance of market forces, bringing about the very ills the antitrust laws were meant to prevent. *See* R. Coase, *The Firm, The Market, and the Law* 117–19 (1988); R. Posner, *Economic Analysis of Law* 324–25, 338–39 (3d ed. 1986).

It is with these observations in mind that we turn to the case before us. Perhaps the most remarkable aspect of this case is that the accused monopolist is a relatively tiny regional entrepreneur while the alleged victims are humongous national corporations with considerable market power of their own. While this is not dispositive—it is conceivable that a little big man may be able to exercise monopoly power locally against large national entities—chances are it is not without significance. Common sense suggests, and experience teaches, that monopoly power is far more easily exercised by larger, economically more powerful entities against smaller, economically punier ones, than vice versa.

Also of significance is the government's concession that Syufy was only a monopsonist, not a monopolist.[4] Thus, the government argues that Syufy had market power, but that it exercised this power only against its suppliers (film distributors), not against its consumers (moviegoers). This is consistent with the record, which demonstrates that Syufy always treated moviegoers fairly: The movie tickets, popcorn, nuts and the Seven-Ups cost about the same in Las Vegas as in other, comparable markets. While it is theoretically possible to have a middleman who is a monopolist upstream but not downstream, this is a somewhat counterintuitive

[4] Monopsony is defined as a "market situation in which there is a single buyer or a group of buyers making joint decisions. Monopsony and monopsony power are the equivalent on the buying side of monopoly and monopoly power on the selling side." R. Lipsey, P. Steiner & D. Purvis, ECONOMICS 976 (7th ed. 1984).

scenario. Why, if he truly had significant market power, would Raymond Syufy have chosen to take advantage of the big movie distributors while giving a fair shake to ordinary people? And why do the distributors, the alleged victims of the monopolization scheme, think that Raymond Syufy is the best thing that ever happened to the Las Vegas movie market?

The answers to these questions are significant because, like all antitrust cases, this one must make economic sense. * * * Keeping in mind that competition, not government intervention, is the touchstone of a healthy, vigorous economy, we proceed to examine whether the district court erred in concluding that Syufy does not, in fact, hold monopoly power. There is universal agreement that monopoly power is the power to exclude competition or control prices. *United States v. E. I. du Pont de Nemours & Co.*, 351 U.S. 377, 391 (1956). * * * The district court determined that Syufy possessed neither power. As the government's case stands or falls with these propositions, the parties have devoted much of their analysis to these findings. So do we.

1. Power to Exclude Competition

It is true, of course, that when Syufy acquired Mann's, Plitt's and Cragin's theatres he temporarily diminished the number of competitors in the Las Vegas first-run film market. But this does not necessarily indicate foul play; many legitimate market arrangements diminish the number of competitors. It would be odd if they did not, as the nature of competition is to make winners and losers.[5] If there are no significant barriers to entry, however, eliminating competitors will not enable the survivors to reap a monopoly profit; any attempt to raise prices above the competitive level will lure into the market new competitors able and willing to offer their commercial goods or personal services for less. *See Metro Mobile CTS, Inc. v. New Vector Commun., Inc.*, 892 F.2d 62 (9th Cir. 1989).

Time after time, we have recognized this basic fact of economic life:

> A high market share, though it may ordinarily raise an inference of monopoly power, will not do so in a market with low entry barriers or other evidence of a defendant's inability to control prices or exclude competitors.

Oahu Gas Serv., Inc. v. Pacific Resources, Inc., 838 F.2d 360, 366 (9th Cir.), *cert. denied*, 488 U.S. 870 (1988) (citation omitted). *See also Hunt-Wesson Foods, Inc. v. Ragu Foods, Inc.*, 627 F.2d 919, 924 (9th Cir. 1980), *cert. denied*, 450 U.S. 921 (1981) ("Blind reliance upon market share, divorced from commercial reality, [can] give a misleading picture of a firm's actual

[5] *See* 3 P. Areeda & D. Turner, ANTITRUST LAW para. 608e, at 20–21 (1978); L. Sullivan, HANDBOOK OF THE LAW OF ANTITRUST § 34, at 96 (1977). Given this reality, it would be perverse to expect rivals engaged in head on competition to act like best friends; indeed, it would be cause for suspicion if they did.

ability to control prices or exclude competition.").[6] There is nothing magic about this proposition; it is simple common sense, embodied in the Antitrust Division's own Merger Guidelines:

> If entry into a market is so easy that existing competitors could not succeed in raising price for any significant period of time, the Department is unlikely to challenge mergers in that market.

Antitrust Policies and Guidelines, U.S. Dep't of Justice, Merger Guidelines § 3.3, reprinted in 4 Trade Reg. Rep. (CCH) P 13,103 at 20,562 (1988).

The district court, after taking testimony from a dozen and a half witnesses and examining innumerable graphs, charts, statistics and other exhibits, found that there were no barriers to entry in the Las Vegas movie market. Our function is narrow: we must determine whether that finding is clearly erroneous. Our review of the record discloses that the district court's finding is amply supported by the record.

We bypass as surplusage the hundreds of pages of expert and lay testimony that support the district court's finding, and focus instead only on a single—to our minds conclusive—item. Immediately after Syufy bought out the last of his three competitors in October 1984, he was riding high, having captured 100% of the first-run film market in Las Vegas. But this utopia proved to be only a mirage. That same month, a major movie distributor, Orion, stopped doing business with Syufy, sending all of its first-run films to Roberts Company, a dark horse competitor previously relegated to the second-run market.[7] Roberts Company took this as an invitation to step into the major league and, against all odds, began giving Syufy serious competition in the first-run market. Fighting fire with fire, Roberts opened three multiplexes within a 13-month period, each having six or more screens. By December 1986, Roberts was operating 28 screens, trading places with Syufy, who had only 23. At the same time, Roberts was displaying a healthy portion of all first-run films. In fact, Roberts got

---

[6] We have previously held that a district court acts within the legitimate scope of its discretion in determining that evidence of a high market share establishes a prima facie antitrust violation, shifting to the defendant the burden of rebutting the prima facie violation. *See California v. American Stores Co.*, 872 F.2d 837, 842 (9th Cir. 1989), *reversed on other grounds*, 495 U.S. 271 (1990). The converse is not true, however; evidence of a high market share does not require a district court to conclude that there is an antitrust violation. In fact, such a conclusion normally should not be drawn where the evidence also indicates that there is no barrier to entry into the relevant market. *See Oahu Gas Serv., Inc. v. Pacific Resources, Inc.*, 838 F.2d 360, 366 (9th Cir.), *cert. denied*, 488 U.S. 870 (1988); *accord American Stores*, 872 F.2d at 842 ("An absence of entry barriers into a market constrains anticompetitive conduct, irrespective of the market's degree of concentration."). The explanation is simple; where entry barriers are low, market share does not accurately reflect the party's market power. * * *

[7] Second-run films are the same as first-run films, only older. When a film is initially released for public exhibition, it is in its first run. Once public demand for the film has fallen off (but usually before it is reduced to a dead calm), the first-run theatre will ship it out to make room for something more recent. The film may then open elsewhere in the same area, usually at a lower ticket price, this being the film's second run.

exclusive exhibition rights to many of its films, meaning that Syufy could not show them at all.

By the end of 1987, Roberts was showing a larger percentage of first-run films than was the Redrock multiplex at the time Syufy bought it. Roberts then sold its theatres to United Artists, the largest theatre chain in the country, and Syufy continued losing ground. It all boils down to this: Syufy's acquisitions did not short circuit the operation of the natural market forces; Las Vegas' first-run film market was more competitive when this case came to trial than before Syufy bought out Mann, Plitt and Cragin.

The Justice Department correctly points out that Syufy still has a large market share, but attributes far too much importance to this fact. In evaluating monopoly power, it is not market share that counts, but the ability to *maintain* market share. Syufy seems unable to do this. In 1985, Syufy managed to lock up exclusive exhibition rights to 91% of all the first-run films in Las Vegas. By the first quarter of 1988, that percentage had fallen to 39%; United Artists had exclusive rights to another 25%, with the remaining 36% being played on both Syufy and UA screens.

Syufy's share of box office receipts also dropped off, albeit less precipitously. In 1985, Syufy raked in 93% of the gross box office from first-run films in Las Vegas. By the first quarter of 1988, that figure had fallen to 75%. The government insists that 75% is still a large number, and we are hard-pressed to disagree; but that's not the point. The antitrust laws do not require that rivals compete in a dead heat, only that neither is unfairly kept from doing his personal best. Accordingly, the government would do better to plot these points on a graph and observe the pattern they form than to focus narrowly on Syufy's market share at a particular time. The numbers reveal that Roberts/UA has steadily been eating away at Syufy's market share: In two and a half years, Syufy's percentage of exclusive exhibition rights dropped 52% and its percentage of box office receipts dropped 18%. During the same period, Roberts/UA's newly opened theatres evolved from absolute beginners, barely staying alive, into a big business. [ ]

The government concedes that there are no structural barriers to entry into the market: Syufy does not operate a bank or similar enterprise where entry is limited by government regulation or licensing requirements. Nor is this the type of industry, like heavy manufacturing or mining, which requires onerous front-end investments that might deter competition from all but the hardiest and most financially secure investors. *See* R. Posner, *supra* p. 663, at 290. Nor do we have here a business dependent on a scarce commodity, control over which might give the incumbent a substantial structural advantage. Nor is there a network of exclusive contracts or distribution arrangements designed to lock out potential competitors. To the contrary, the record discloses a rough-and-tumble industry, marked by easy market access, fluid relationships with distributors, an ample and continuous supply of product, and a healthy and growing demand. It would be difficult to design a market less susceptible to monopolization.

Confronted with this record and the district court's clear findings, the government trots out a shopworn argument we had thought long abandoned: that efficient, aggressive competition is itself a structural barrier to entry. According to the government, competitors will be deterred from entering the market because they could not hope to turn a profit competing against Syufy. In the words of government counsel:

> There is no legal barrier. There is no law that says you can't come into this market, it's not that kind of barrier. . . . But, the fact of mere possibility in the literal sense, is not the appropriate test. Entry, after all, must, to be effective to dissipate the monopoly power that Syufy has, entry must hold some reasonable prospect of profitability for the entrant, or else the entrant will say, as Mann Theatres said . . . this is not an attractive market to enter. There will be shelter. And the reason is very clear. You have to compete effectively in this market. And witness after witness testified you would need to build anywhere from 12 to 24 theatres, which is a very expensive and time consuming proposition. *And, you would then find yourself in a bidding war against Syufy.*

Tr. of Oral Arg. at 5 (emphasis added).

The notion that the supplier of a good or service can monopolize the market simply by being efficient reached high tide in the law 44 years ago in Judge Learned Hand's opinion in *United States v. Aluminum Co. of Am.*, 148 F.2d 416 (2d Cir. 1945).[14] In the intervening decades the wisdom of this notion has been questioned by just about everyone who has taken a close look at it. * * * It has been soundly repudiated by the Second Circuit. *See Berkey Photo, Inc. v. Eastman Kodak Co.,* 603 F.2d 263, 273–74 (2d Cir. 1979), *cert. denied,* 444 U.S. 1093 (1980).

---

[14] In *Alcoa*, Judge Hand concluded that defendant corporation violated the antitrust laws simply by making all the right moves, in particular, by filling the demand of which it was the creator:

> True, it stimulated demand and opened new uses for the metal, but not without making sure that it could supply what it had evoked. . . . "Alcoa" avows it as evidence of the skill, energy and initiative with which it has always conducted its business; as a reason why, having won its way by fair means, it should be commended, and not dismembered. . . . We may assume that all it claims for itself is true. . . . [But] it was not inevitable that it should always anticipate increases in the demand for ingot and be prepared to supply them. Nothing compelled it to keep doubling and redoubling its capacity before others entered the field. It insists that it never excluded competitors; but we can think of no more effective exclusion than progressively to embrace each new opportunity as it opened, and to face every newcomer with new capacity already geared into a great organization, having the advantage of experience, trade connections and the elite of personnel. . . . That was to "monopolize" that market, however innocently it otherwise proceeded.

148 F.2d at 430–32.

The argument government counsel presses here is a close variant of *Alcoa*: The government is not claiming that Syufy monopolized the market by being too efficient, but that Syufy's effectiveness as a competitor creates a structural barrier to entry, rendering illicit Syufy's acquisition of its competitors' screens. We hasten to sever this new branch that the government has caused to sprout from the moribund *Alcoa* trunk.

It can't be said often enough that the antitrust laws protect competition, *not* competitors. As we noted earlier, competition is essential to the effective operation of the free market because it encourages efficiency, promotes consumer satisfaction and prevents the accumulation of monopoly profits. When a producer is shielded from competition, he is likely to provide lesser service at a higher price; the victim is the consumer who gets a raw deal. This is the evil the antitrust laws are meant to avert. But when a producer deters competitors by supplying a better product at a lower price, when he eschews monopoly profits, when he operates his business so as to meet consumer demand and increase consumer satisfaction, the goals of competition are served, even if no actual competitors see fit to enter the market at a particular time. While the successful competitor should not be raised above the law, neither should he be held down by law.

The Supreme Court has accordingly distanced itself from the *Alcoa* legacy, taking care to distinguish unlawful monopoly power from "growth or development as a consequence of a superior product, business acumen, or historic accident," *United States v. Grinnell Corp.*, 384 U.S. 563, 571 (1966), which are off limits to the enforcer of our antitrust laws. If a dominant supplier acts consistent with a competitive market—out of fear perhaps that potential competitors are ready and able to step in—the purpose of the antitrust laws is amply served. We make it clear today, if it was not before, that an efficient, vigorous, aggressive competitor is not the villain antitrust laws are aimed at eliminating. Fostering an environment where businesses fight it out using the weapon of efficiency and consumer goodwill is what the antitrust laws are meant to champion. * * *

But we need not rely on theory alone in rejecting the government's argument. The record here conclusively demonstrates that neither acquiring the screens of his competitors nor working hard at better serving the public gave Syufy deliverance from competition. Immediately following the disappearance of Mann, Plitt and Cragin, Roberts took up the challenge, aggressively competing with Syufy for first-run films—and with considerable success. United Artists, with substantial resources at its disposal and nationwide experience in running movie theatres, considered the market sufficiently open that it bought out Roberts in 1987. We see no indication that competition suffered in the Las Vegas movie market as a result of Syufy's challenged acquisitions.[15] The district court certainly had ample basis in the record for its finding that Syufy lacked the power to exclude competitors. Indeed, on this voluminous record we are hard-pressed to see how the district court could have come to the other conclusion.

2. Power to Control Prices

The crux of the Justice Department's case is that Syufy, top gun in the Las Vegas movie market, had the power to push around Hollywood's biggest players, dictating to them what prices they could charge for their movies. The district court found otherwise. This finding too has substantial support in the record.

Perhaps the most telling evidence of Syufy's inability to set prices came from movie distributors, Syufy's supposed victims. At the trial, distributors uniformly proclaimed their satisfaction with the way the Las Vegas first-run film market operates; none complained about the license fees paid by Syufy. Columbia's President of Domestic Distribution testified that "Syufy paid a fair amount of film rental" that compared favorably with other markets. A representative of Buena Vista, a division of Disney, testified that Syufy had never refused to accept its standard terms. Particularly damaging to the government's case was the testimony of the former head of distribution for MGM/UA that his company "never had any difficulty . . . in acquiring the terms that we thought were reasonable," explaining that the license fees Syufy paid "were comparable or better than any place in the United States. And in most cases better." Indeed, few if any of the distributors were willing to say anything to support the government's claim.

The documentary evidence bears out this testimony. Syufy has at all times paid license fees far in excess of the national average, even higher than those paid by exhibitors in Los Angeles, the Mecca of Moviedom. In fact, Syufy paid a higher percentage of his gross receipts to distributors in 1987 and 1988 than he did during the intensely competitive period just before he acquired Cragin's Redrock. [ ]

While successful, Syufy is in no position to put the squeeze on distributors. The one time he tried there was an immediate backlash. In

---

[15] The government points out that the interiors of United Artists' theatres were not as luxurious as those of Syufy. We have no clue what sinister inference the government would have us draw from this fact. As the district court noted, "No one stopped United Artists from remodeling Roberts' theatres after it acquired them. As the largest exhibitor in the nation, it certainly has the resources to do so." Competitors need not provide a perfectly undifferentiated product in order to be competitive; it is a strength of our free market economy that competitors often provide products that cater to the varied tastes and preferences of consumers. Syufy made a business decision to invest in luxury theatres while Roberts and United Artists apparently decided to dispose of their profits in some other fashions. It remains to be seen which strategy will ultimately prevail. Indeed, it is not a winner take all situation; in a free market, any number can play and any number can win. We therefore agree with the district court's refusal to conclude that this difference in business strategies was an indication of market failure.

1984, about seven days after allegedly acquiring its monopoly, Syufy informed Orion Releasing Group that he had cold feet about *The Cotton Club* and would not honor the large guarantees he had contracted for, only to see his gambit backfire. Orion sued Syufy for breach of contract, licensed the film to Roberts and cut Syufy off cold turkey. To this day, Orion refuses to play its films in any Syufy theatre, in Las Vegas or elsewhere. Accordingly, Syufy lost the opportunity to exhibit top moneymakers like *Robocop*, *Platoon*, *Hannah and Her Sisters* and *No Way Out*.[17] The district court found no evidence that Orion considered Roberts/UA's theatres a less than adequate substitute for Syufy's.

Because he needs plenty of first-run films to fill his many screens (22 at the time of trial; 34 now), Syufy is vulnerable. Distributors like Orion have substantial leverage over Syufy and they know it. One witness, the President of Domestic Distribution for Columbia, testified at length about the power he and other distributors wield over Syufy:

> . . . [W]ith Syufy having 23 first-run screens, he could not get into a two and a half percent fight with Columbia; he had so many mouths to feed in those theatres, that he was more or less compelled to pay national suggested terms for films.
>
> . . . .
>
> . . . He could have tried [to dictate terms], but he wouldn't have gotten away with it, your Honor. He was very vulnerable. My point is that he was very vulnerable in that market. He could not—he needed the flow of product to fill those screens, and to take on—to get into a fight with the distributor over terms, or film rentals paid to a distributor, would create an attitude where we could sell [to] his opposition and he'd be egregiously hurt.
>
> . . . .
>
> . . . He was his own competition, your Honor. He had created such a large amount of screens that he was—he was himself—he was himself vulnerable. As I described before, if he would have pressed, and if he would have come to Jimmie Spitz and said, "I'm not going to pay you this percentage for the film," I would have said, "Fine, Ray, we'll stay out of the marketplace." He couldn't afford—he has to—he has to have film in his theatres. And that's the leverage that this company had with Mr. Syufy.

RT 5:714–16 (testimony of James Spitz).

After hours of such testimony, the judge quite rightly concluded that Syufy did not have the power to control license fees. This evidence,

[17] The list of Orion films that played exclusively at Roberts theaters also includes such popular fare as *Amadeus*, *Back to School*, *Bull Durham*, *Colors*, *Hoosiers*, *Married to the Mob*, *Radio Days* and the unforgettable *Throw Momma From the Train*.

moreover, reveals the trap in the oft made assumption that, by virtue of being a leviathan, a company will automatically have the power to wield a big stick with which to push around suppliers, customers and competitors. While size no doubt provides significant business advantages, it can also have very substantial drawbacks, such as increased management costs and other diseconomies of scale.

More fundamentally, in a free economy the market itself imposes a tough enough discipline on all market actors, large and small. Every supplier of goods and services is integrated into an endless chain of supply and demand relationships, making it dependent on the efficiency and goodwill of upstream suppliers, as well as the patronage of customers. Absent structural constraints that keep competition from performing its levelling function, few businesses can dictate terms to customers or suppliers with impunity. It's risky business even to try. As Syufy learned in dealing with Orion and his other suppliers, a larger company often is more vulnerable to a squeeze play than a smaller one. It is for that reason that neither size nor market share alone suffice to establish a monopoly. Without the power to exclude competition, large companies that try to throw their weight around may find themselves sitting ducks for leaner, hungrier competitors. Or, as Syufy saw, the tactic may boomerang, causing big trouble with suppliers.

On this record, we have no basis for overturning the district court's finding that Syufy lacked the power to set the prices he paid his suppliers. As with the district court's finding as to Syufy's power to exclude competition, we believe the record here lent itself to only one sensible conclusion. [ ]

It is a tribute to the state of competition in America that the Antitrust Division of the Department of Justice has found no worthier target than this paper tiger on which to expend limited taxpayer resources. Yet we cannot help but wonder whether bringing a lawsuit like this, and pursuing it doggedly through 27 months of pretrial proceedings, about two weeks of trial and now the full distance on appeal, really serves the interests of free competition.

The record here demonstrates in graphic detail that Syufy's entry into the Las Vegas first-run movie market resulted in a vast improvement for movie distributors and consumers alike. By all accounts, Raymond Syufy's theatres are among the finest built and best run in the nation, making him somewhat of a local hero. At the same time, movie distributors have nothing but praise for Syufy, as his being there has invigorated theatre attendance in Las Vegas, substantially driving up their revenues. As is often the case when a vigorous competitor enters the market, more complacent theatre operators were eliminated, but there was no credible evidence that Syufy did anything improper to drive them out. Indeed, by buying them out, Syufy may well have helped cushion the losses they would have suffered had they been required to sell the theatres at fire sale prices or leave them abandoned.

What then was the problem the government sought to solve by bringing this lawsuit? At oral argument, the lawyer for the government explained it thus:

> [B]asically if you drive down by anti-competitive conduct the price at which theatre owners buy film licenses, then there will be less film[s] ultimately produced, because there will be a distortion in the natural market in the competitive forces, and people who go to movies like you and me would ultimately have less choice.

Tr. of Oral Arg. at 9. It is, we suppose, not out of the question that what Raymond Syufy and other local theatre operators do in their respective markets could stem the avalanche of movies that comes to us out of Hollywood every year. Yet movie distributors are not exactly a powerless lot, likely to surrender the first time they are presented with hard choices by a theatre operator; nor are they reluctant to precipitate a showdown when they believe their rights are being infringed. And, as we have seen, the market has its own fail-safe mechanisms. Where the government inserts an antitrust enforcement action into this type of situation, there is a real danger of stifling competition and creativity in the marketplace.

It is well known that some of the most insuperable barriers in the great race of competition are the result of government regulation. Regulation often helps entrench existing businesses by placing new entrants at a competitive disadvantage. It is perhaps less well appreciated that litigation itself can be a form of regulation; lawsuits brought by the government impose significant costs on enterprises that are sued, and create significant disincentives for those that are not.

In this case, the government was suspicious because Syufy bought out the movie theatres of his retreating competitors. But, in a competitive market, buying out competitors is not merely permissible, it contributes to market stability and promotes the efficient allocation of resources. The fact is, a relentless, growing competitor is frequently the most logical buyer of a business that is declining. For competitors in a free market to fear buying each other out lest they be hit with the expense and misery of an antitrust enforcement action amounts to a burden only slightly less palpable than a direct governmental prohibition against such a purchase. In a free enterprise system decisions such as these should be made by market actors responding to market forces, not by government bureaucrats pursuing their notions of how the market should operate. Personal initiative, not government control, is the fountainhead of progress in a capitalist economy.

The judgment of the district court is affirmed.

NOTES AND QUESTIONS

1. *Syufy Enterprises and ~~the humorous side of~~ economics.* One theme in the law and economics school is the effect of legal rules—in legislation or the common law—on behavior to correct market failures. (a) Judging from *Syufy Enterprises*, what are the economic indicators (or symptoms) of a monopolized market? (b) How does Judge Kozinski's analysis of the antitrust statute reflect the law and economics approach? (c) Is there any reason to think that Congress in adopting the antitrust law was necessarily motivated by exclusively economic considerations?

2. *The law and economics approach to legislation: public choice and Arrow's Impossibility Theorem.* Law and economics theorists generally express a preference for judge-made law over statutes, on the ground that legislative decision-making tends to be channeled and constrained by self-interested or "rent-seeking" conduct on the part of those interests most affected by the proposed legislation. In other words, instead of idealizing legislators as dispassionate sages—listening fairly to representatives from across their constituencies, balancing the various policy possibilities, and choosing rationally among them—public choice theory starts from the presumption that concentrated interests have counter-majoritarian interests and power over the legislative process itself. In effect, it demonstrates that the legislative process is a profoundly failed market.

> * * * Public choice theorists typically treat legislation as an economic transaction in which interest groups form the demand side, and legislators form the supply side. On the whole, this branch of public choice theory demonstrates that the market for legislation is a badly functioning one. That is, the market systematically yields too few laws that provide "public goods" (*i.e.*, laws that contribute to the overall efficiency of society by providing a collective benefit that would probably not arise from individuals acting separately). And it systematically yields too many laws that are "rent-seeking" (*i.e.*, laws that distribute resources to a designated group without any contribution to society's overall efficiency).
>
> The demand for legislation is determined by the incidence and activity of interest groups. The optimistic pluralists believed that interest groups would form in response to true disturbances in the social environment and, hence, normally would press legitimate grievances and would bring a variety of socioeconomic perspectives into the subsequent political debates. Public choice theory suggests, however, that interest groups form more selectively and, therefore, that the demand for legislation is highly biased. * * *
>
> Optimistic pluralists paid little attention to the incentive structures of elected representatives and generally just assumed that the representatives' policy choices represented some kind of amalgam of constituency preferences and reasonable judgment. Public choice theorists, however, suggest that representatives' supply of legislation

> is driven by a desire to avoid controversy and, hence, is skewed toward non-decision and rent-seeking.

William N. Eskridge, Jr., *Politics Without Romance: Implications of Public Choice Theory for Statutory Interpretation*, 74 VA. L. REV. 275 (1988), at 285–86, 287–88. From this perspective, "democracy markets" are notoriously unstable.

Adding to the difficulty of using statutes to implement majority will is the difficulty of actually determining what the majority wants when there are multiple possible outcomes and multiple criteria guiding legislators' (or voters') judgment. Beginning with Professor Kenneth J. Arrow's seminal article, *A Difficulty in the Concept of Social Welfare,* 58 J. POL. ECON. 328 (1950), a rich and complicated literature has explored the implausibility of basing legislative decisions on the purported will of the majority.

> * * * According to Kenneth Arrow's impossibility theorem, any method of collective choice that meets certain plausible constraints will be unable to guarantee a transitive collective ranking of preferences. A simple example helps to illustrate: imagine that three legislators, A, B, and C, are tasked with choosing between three options, x, y, and z, by majority vote. A prefers x to y to z, B prefers y to z to x, and C prefers z to x to y. The legislature first votes x against y, and x prevails by a 2–1 vote. Next, they vote the victor, x, against z; z defeats x 2–1. But if the legislature then decides to resurrect y and see how it fares against z, y beats z 2–1. So while the body as a whole prefers z to x and x to y, it also prefers y to z. The collective ranking of preferences is intransitive.
>
> The implications of this intransitivity for the coherence ideal are fatal. Normative coherence demands that the body of legal rules to which it applies function harmoniously to advance a single, consistent ranking of values. The ranking, to be a ranking, must be transitive. Arrow's theorem shows that a legislature is perpetually at risk of failing to meet this constraint. In our simplified example above, the legislature's choice between x, y, and z will be determined by the agenda: whoever dictates the order in which the votes occur and the point at which voting stops in fact dictates the legislature's choice. This means that a series of legislative choices between x, y, and z made by the same legislators, but following different procedural pathways, will result in different, inconsistent rankings of the three values. Where these conditions hold, coherence is conceptually impossible.

John David Ohlendorf, *Against Coherence in Statutory Interpretation*, 90 NOTRE DAME L. REV. 735, 771 (2014). *See also* Mark Klock, *Is It "The Will of the People" or a Broken Arrow? Collective Preferences, Out-of-the-Money Options, Bush v. Gore, and Arguments for Quashing Post-Balloting Litigation Absent Specific Allegations of Fraud*, 57 U. MIAMI L. REV. 1, 14 (2002) ("The paradox of voting—the fact that election results need not map into social preferences and social preferences need not be transitive—was formally proven by Professor Arrow about fifty years ago. While variations and refinements on the proof have been presented, the conclusions have withstood rigorous scrutiny over the test of time.")

If you were trying to implement laws that promote economic efficiency, why might the public choice perspective tilt you towards judge-made law?

Readings

Adam Smith (1723–1790) is generally considered the father of classical economics, especially its organizing principle that individuals' self-interest in a competitive free market is the means to a more generalized economic well-being. The idea is often captured in the metaphor of the "invisible hand," which appears in Smith's THE WEALTH OF NATIONS (1776):

> [B]y directing [domestic] industry in such a manner as its produce may be of greatest value, [an individual] intends only his own gain, and he is in this, as in many other cases, led by an *invisible hand* to promote an end which was no part of his intention. . . . By pursuing his own interest he frequently promotes that of the society more effectually than when he really intends to promote it.

Id. at book IV, chap. 2, para. 9. In context, Smith is addressing a narrow question of the economic value of domestic goods as opposed to imports, but the metaphor of the invisible hand has been deployed more generally as a shorthand explanation for the conviction that social welfare is maximized when individual self-interest is pursued in a competitive free market. Framed that way, the connection of Adam Smith to conventional law and economics is easy to see, which is why we begin these readings with him. On the other hand, the genius of Adam Smith is not easily cabined: his conception of bounded rationality—the range of behavioral drivers beyond pure reason—anticipated by almost 250 years a profound refinement of conventional law and economics, grounded in human behavior in its infinite, sometimes mindless variety.

ADAM SMITH, THE THEORY OF THE MORAL SENTIMENTS

(1759)

Part I, Section I, Chapter I, Paragraph 1

How selfish soever man may be supposed, there are evidently some principles in his nature which interest him in the fortune of others and render their happiness necessary to him though he derives nothing from it except the pleasure of seeing it. Of this kind is pity or compassion, the emotion we feel for the misery of others, when we either see it, or are made to conceive it in a very lively manner. That we often derive sorrow from the sorrow of others, is a matter of fact too obvious to require any instances to prove it; for this sentiment like all the other original passions of human nature, is by no means confined to the virtuous and humane, though they perhaps may feel it with the most exquisite sensibility. The greatest ruffian, the most hardened violator of the laws of society, is not altogether without it. * * *

Part VII, Chapter II, Paragraphs 16–18

The habits of economy, industry, discretion, attention, and application of thought, are generally supposed to be cultivated from self-interested motives, and at the same time are apprehended to be very praise-worthy qualities, which deserve the esteem and approbation of everybody. The mixture of a selfish motive, it is true, seems often to sully the beauty of those actions which ought to arise from a benevolent affection. The cause of this, however, is not that self-love can never be the motive of a virtuous action, but that the benevolent principle appears in this particular case to want its due degree of strength, and to be altogether unsuitable to its object. The character, therefore, seems evidently imperfect, and upon the whole to deserve blame rather than praise. The mixture of a benevolent motive in an action to which self-love alone ought to be sufficient to prompt us, is not so apt indeed to diminish our sense of its propriety, or of the virtue of the person who performs it. We are not ready to suspect any person of being defective in selfishness. This is by no means the weak side of human nature, or the failing of which we are apt to be suspicious. If we could really believe, however, of any man, that, was it not from a regard to his family and friends, he would not take that proper care of his health, his life, or his fortune, to which self-preservation alone ought to be sufficient to prompt him, it would undoubtedly be a failing, though one of those amiable failings, which render a person rather the object of pity than of contempt or hatred. It would still, however, somewhat diminish the dignity and respectableness of his character. Carelessness and want of economy are universally disapproved of, not, however, as proceeding from a want of benevolence, but from a want of the proper attention to the objects of self-interest.

Though the standard by which casuists frequently determine what is right or wrong in human conduct, be its tendency to the welfare or disorder of society, it does not follow that a regard to the welfare of society should be the sole virtuous motive of action, but only that, in any competition, it ought to cast the balance against all other motives.

Benevolence may, perhaps, be the sole principle of action in the Deity, and there are several, not improbable, arguments which tend to persuade us that it is so. It is not easy to conceive what other motive an independent and all-perfect Being, who stands in need of nothing external, and whose happiness is complete in himself, can act from. But whatever may be the case with the Deity, so imperfect a creature as man, the support of whose existence requires so many things external to him, must often act from many other motives. The condition of human nature were peculiarly hard, if those affections, which, by the very nature of our being, ought frequently to influence our conduct, could upon no occasion appear virtuous, or deserve esteem and commendation from anybody.

RONALD COASE, *THE PROBLEM OF SOCIAL COST*

3 J. LAW & ECON. 1 (1960) (emphasis added)

* * * The traditional approach [to the problem of social costs] has tended to obscure the nature of the choice that has to be made. The question is commonly thought of as one in which A inflicts harm on B and what has to be decided is: how should we restrain A? But this is wrong. We are dealing with a problem of a reciprocal nature. To avoid the harm to B would inflict harm on A. The real question that has to be decided is: should A be allowed to harm B or should B be allowed to harm A? The problem is to avoid the more serious harm. I instanced in [a] previous article the case of a confectioner the noise and vibrations from whose machinery disturbed a doctor in his work. To avoid harming the doctor would inflict harm on the confectioner. The problem posed by this case was essentially whether it was worthwhile, as a result of restricting the methods of production which could be used by the confectioner, to secure more doctoring at the cost of a reduced supply of confectionery products. Another example is afforded by the problem of straying cattle which destroy crops on neighbouring land. If it is inevitable that some cattle will stray, an increase in the supply of meat can only be obtained at the expense of a decrease in the supply of crops. The nature of the choice is clear: meat or crops. What answer should be given is, of course, not clear unless we know the value of what is obtained as well as the value of what is sacrificed to obtain it. * * *

The harmful effects of the activities of a business can assume a wide variety of forms. An early English case concerned a building which, by obstructing currents of air, hindered the operation of a windmill. A recent case in Florida concerned a building which cast a shadow on the cabana, swimming pool and sunbathing areas of a neighbouring hotel. The problem of straying cattle and the damaging of crops [ ] is in fact but one example of a problem which arises in many different guises. * * *

Judges have to decide on legal liability but this should not confuse economists about the nature of the economic problem involved. In the case of the cattle and the crops, it is true that there would be no crop damage without the cattle. It is equally true that there would be no crop damage without the crops. The doctor's work would not have been disturbed if the confectioner had not worked his machinery; but the machinery would have disturbed no one if the doctor had not set up his consulting room in that particular place. * * * If we are to discuss the problem in terms of causation, both parties cause the damage. If we are to attain an optimum allocation of resources, it is therefore desirable that both parties should take the harmful effect (the nuisance) into account in deciding on their course of action. It is one of the beauties of a smoothly operating pricing system that [ ] the fall in the value of production due to the harmful effect would be a cost for both parties.

Bass v. Gregory[12] will serve as an excellent final illustration of the problem. The plaintiffs were the owners and tenant of a public house called the Jolly Anglers. The defendant was the owner of some cottages and a yard adjoining the Jolly Anglers. Under the public house was a cellar excavated in the rock. From the cellar, a hole or shaft had been cut into an old well situated in the defendant's yard. The well therefore became the ventilating shaft for the cellar. The cellar "had been used for a particular purpose in the process of brewing, which, without ventilation, could not be carried on." The cause of the action was that the defendant removed a grating from the mouth of the well, "so as to stop or prevent the free passage of air from [the] cellar upwards through the well. . . ." What caused the defendant to take this step is not clear from the report of the case. Perhaps "the air . . . impregnated by the brewing operations" which "passed up the well and out into the open air" was offensive to him. At any rate, he preferred to have the well in his yard stopped up. The court had first to determine whether the owners of the public house could have a legal right to a current of air. If they were to have such a right, this case would have to be distinguished from *Bryant v. Lefever*[1]. This, however, presented no difficulty. In this case, the current of air was confined to "a strictly defined channel." In the case of *Bryant v. Lefever*, what was involved was "the general current of air common to all mankind." The judge therefore held that the owners of the public house could have the right to a current of air whereas the owner of the private house in *Bryant v. Lefever* could not. An economist might be tempted to add "but the air moved all the same." However, all that had been decided at this stage of the argument was that there could be a legal right, not that the owners of the public house possessed it. But evidence showed that the shaft from the cellar to the well had existed for over forty years and that the use of the well as a ventilating shaft must have been known to the owners of the yard since the air, when it emerged, smelt of the brewing operations. The judge therefore held that the public house had such a right by the "doctrine of lost grant." This doctrine states "that if a legal right is proved to have existed and been exercised for a number of years the law ought to presume that it had a legal

12 25 Q.B.D. 481 (1890).

1 [4 C.P.D. 172 (1878–1879.]

origin." So the owner of the cottages and yard had to unstop the well and endure the smell.

The reasoning employed by the courts in determining legal rights will often seem strange to an economist because many of the factors on which the decision turns are, to an economist, irrelevant. Because of this, situations which are, from an economic point of view, identical will be treated quite differently by the courts. The economic problem in all cases of harmful effects is how to maximise the value of production. In the case of *Bass v. Gregory* fresh air was drawn in through the well which facilitated the production of beer but foul air was expelled through the well which made life in the adjoining houses less pleasant. The economic problem was to decide which to choose: a lower cost of beer and worsened amenities in adjoining houses or a higher cost of beer and improved amenities. In deciding this question, the "doctrine of lost grant" is about as relevant as the colour of the judge's eyes. But it has to be remembered that the immediate question faced by the courts is not what shall be done by whom but who has the legal right to do what. It is always possible to modify by transactions on the market the initial legal delimitation of rights. *And, of course, if such market transactions are costless, such a rearrangement of rights will always take place if it would lead to an increase in the value of production.*

KEITH N. HYLTON, *CALABRESI AND THE INTELLECTUAL HISTORY OF LAW AND ECONOMICS*

64 MD. L. REV. 85 (2005)

* * *

I. A Bird's-Eye View of the Intellectual History of Law and Economics

Law and economics views law from an instrumentalist perspective. That is a perspective that seeks to determine the function of law and the manner in which it solves the social problems thrown before it. [Jeremy] Bentham is the most obvious source that comes to mind for this approach. Bentham's core contribution to legal theory was a rejection of the view that law should be understood as emanating from or growing out of some set of *a priori* fundamental rights.[4] [William] Blackstone had led students to think of the law in this way, and Bentham, as one of those students, seemed to have staked his career on overturning this view.[5] He succeeded; though

---

4 E.g., JEREMY BENTHAM, A COMMENT ON THE COMMENTARIES: A CRITICISM OF WILLIAM BLACKSTONE'S COMMENTARIES ON THE LAWS OF ENGLAND 35–44 (photo. reprint 1979) (Charles Warren Everett ed., 1928) (1776) [hereinafter A COMMENT ON THE COMMENTARIES].

5 See, e.g., RICHARD A. POSNER, THE ECONOMICS OF JUSTICE 32–33 (1983) [hereinafter ECONOMICS OF JUSTICE].

Blackstone was a more complicated thinker than Bentham's early caricature suggests.

Blackstone himself incorporated instrumentalist reasoning in parts of his COMMENTARIES.[6] His volume on criminal law both refers to and shows the influence of [Cesare] Beccaria's utilitarian writing on punishment.[7] Taking the sum of his views as a theorist, Blackstone presents a muddled picture. He comes across as utilitarian in his treatment of criminal law, and a promoter of nonconsequentialist, fundamental-rights theory in other parts of the COMMENTARIES; especially when he discusses the most basic protections provided by the common law—of life, liberty, and property.[8]

As I have suggested, the instrumentalist or functionalist approach to law typically identified with Bentham makes some appearances in the theoretical literature that predates Bentham. * * * Beccaria's theory that punishment should be set at a level that wipes out the expected gains of the criminal actor, and not above that level, formed the basis of his influential critique of criminal law enforcement published in 1764.[9] Beccaria's critique served as the chief source of theoretical insights for Blackstone's treatment of criminal law, and also likely served as the chief inspiration for Bentham's work on criminal law. While Blackstone provided a negative inspiration for Bentham, a figure that Bentham would caricature, ridicule, and hold up as an example of all that is wrong with legal theory, Beccaria provided a positive inspiration.

Almost at the same time as Beccaria was writing, Adam Smith gave lectures on jurisprudence to a class at Glasgow University.[12] Smith's lectures, seldom discussed in the law and economics literature, provide really the first sustained treatment of law from an economic perspective. Smith provides especially detailed discussions of property and criminal law. His lectures on criminal law [ ] argue that criminal penalties tend to be inversely related to the probability of detection. Smith's work has never received the attention showered on Bentham, which I find puzzling.

Immediately before Beccaria and Smith, one finds Hume's discussion of property and norms, which treats property law as the result of an implicit contract that develops over time within a society.[15] * * * Before Hume, one finds Hobbes's discussion of the common law. Hobbes argued

---

[6] See 4 WILLIAM BLACKSTONE, COMMENTARIES ON THE LAWS OF ENGLAND 14–19 (photo. reprint 1979) (1769) (discussing the deterrence value of criminal punishment).

[7] See, e.g., 4 id. at 17 (describing Beccaria's "ingenious" writing on punishment).

[8] See, e.g., 1 Blackstone, *supra*, at 117–41 (discussing the "absolute rights of individuals"). Another reason Blackstone's perspective as a theorist is unclear is that he shows influences from Hobbes in parts of his discussion. His perspective may be closer to utilitarian than is commonly recognized.

[9] CESARE BECCARIA, ON CRIMES AND PUNISHMENTS 62–64 (Henry Paolucci trans., Bobbs-Merrill Educ. Publ'g 1978) (1764).

[12] ADAM SMITH, LECTURES ON JURISPRUDENCE (R.L. Meek et al. eds., Oxford Univ. Press 1978) (1762–66).

[15] DAVID HUME, A TREATISE OF HUMAN NATURE 484–516 (Prometheus Books 1992) (1739).

that the king should have a strong hand in interpreting the law, and, more importantly, suggested that the law's purpose is to maximize social welfare.[16]

Although Bentham is generally viewed as the source of instrumentalism in legal theory, I think the starting point is Hobbes. For at the core of instrumentalism is a notion that the law's purpose should be understood from the perspective of what an economist would call a social planner or what a philosopher might call a Platonic philosopher-king. Hobbes is probably the fundamental source for the argument that law should not be understood or justified only on its own terms, or, equivalently, rejecting the notion that law can only be understood or justified by a lawyer steeped in the intricacies of legal opinions and terminology. Law and economics practitioners make this argument frequently today; the first wave of legal realists, including Holmes, made the argument several generations ago.[17] Bentham preceded the realists by roughly one hundred years. All of them are partly in debt to Hobbes.

* * * The starting point for instrumentalism in law is the notion of detachment: that the law should be justifiable to a detached spectator who is not committed to maintaining some set of perceived logical connections among various legal doctrines. Once that notion is accepted, we have the groundwork set for all instrumentalist theories of law. * * *

[In Bentham's work,] we see a purposive and goal-oriented marriage of instrumentalism and utilitarianism * * *. After Bentham, roughly one hundred years passed before Holmes wrote THE COMMON LAW,[19] presenting a largely utilitarian justification for the law. But there are big differences from Bentham's approach. Holmes backs away from the detachment of Hobbes and Bentham: he wants us to understand the law and its internal logic. Holmes backs away from the role of independent critic or censor. He sets out to justify the law as it is.

Following Holmes, we find another long dry spell up to the roughly simultaneous publications of [Guido] Calabresi's COSTS[2] and Becker's article[3] on crime.[20] There are interesting similarities between the two

---

16 THOMAS HOBBES, A DIALOGUE BETWEEN A PHILOSOPHER AND A STUDENT OF THE COMMON LAWS OF ENGLAND 57–71 (Joseph Cropsey ed., Univ. of Chi. Press 1971) (1681).

17 See O.W. Holmes, *The Path of the Law*, 10 HARV. L. REV. 457 (1897).

19 O.W. HOLMES, JR., THE COMMON LAW (1881).

2 [GUIDO CALABRESI, THE COSTS OF ACCIDENTS: A LEGAL AND ECONOMIC ANALYSIS (1970) [hereinafter THE COSTS OF ACCIDENTS].]

3 [Gary S. Becker, *Crime and Punishment: An Economic Approach*, 76 J. POL. ECON. 169 (1968).]

20 I refer to this period as a dry spell only because there does not appear to be anything as ambitious in scope as we see at the endpoints (Holmes on one end, Calabresi on the other). However, there were novel and important contributions to law and economics over this period. The best known is that of Ronald Coase. See R.H. Coase, *The Problem of Social Cost*, 3 J.L. & ECON. 1 (1960) (setting out the "Coase Theorem," which holds that if transaction costs are low, individuals will bargain their way to an efficient arrangement, whatever the liability rule). While the Coase Theorem has become perhaps the key starting point for any economic analysis of law, I have not

works. Both Becker and Calabresi step comfortably into the role of detachment, following the tradition of Hobbes and Bentham. Neither thinks it is important for his reader to understand the law from the perspective of a specialist in the common law. * * *

Indeed, one could describe the personality reflected in Calabresi's COSTS as one of hyper-detachment. The book describes itself as a "legal and economic analysis," which it most assuredly is. But Calabresi takes a position of detachment from both the law and the economics. He prefaces his economic remarks in several parts of the book with comments such as "an economist would say," to remind us that he does not necessarily agree with them. He tells us early on that economics is good for solving certain problems, but not all problems, especially those involving basic questions of identity or morality. In spite of this, he conducts an economic analysis that appears to be on the highest level of sophistication that one could imagine for the topic at hand. * * * Calabresi shows a far greater awareness of the machinery of law and government, and the limits of human rationality, than even the best economists would have brought to the task.

Calabresi's book and Becker's article are thoroughly in the tradition of Bentham. Like Bentham, both Calabresi and Becker apply utilitarianism in an effort to promote sweeping reforms of vast areas of the law. In Calabresi's case, his ultimate goal is to replace the "fault system" (or negligence regime) of tort law with a "mixed system" that relies heavily on strict liability for injury-causing activities. Becker, on the other hand, aims to change the goal of criminal punishment from completely deterring criminal acts to internalizing costs to offenders. Both reforms are so ambitious that neither author seriously could have expected to see them implemented within his lifetime.

* * * Calabresi's approach would have replaced the core of tort doctrine with simpler, more direct liability rules that, on a statistical basis, would have loaded liability on the most appropriate actors (the cheapest cost avoiders). Becker's approach would have resulted in a Bentham-like revolution in an indirect manner. By changing the system of penalties to ones based on cost-internalization, it would no longer be necessary under Becker's regime to know whether you had violated the law. If we could calculate the external costs of your actions accurately, we could impose those costs on you, and the law, whatever it says, would eventually whither away—like law under Marxism.

The next development following Calabresi and Becker was the publication of the first edition of Richard Posner's ECONOMIC ANALYSIS OF

---

focused on it here because it is not associated with a broad school of thought in law and economics. The best known are those of Aaron Director, probably the founder of Chicago School antitrust analysis, and Ward Bowman. The institutional and labor economics of John R. Commons is another important contribution.

LAW.[28] Just as Holmes bought into utilitarianism but rejected the reform efforts of Bentham, Posner bought into economic analysis and rejected the reform efforts of Calabresi and Becker. Like Holmes, Posner defended the law as it is. However, Posner is much more explicit in his adoption of economic theory than Holmes. Posner claims that the common law aims to maximize wealth. Wealth maximization is distinguishable from utilitarianism, largely in the sense that wealth maximization makes no effort to take into account differences in individual preferences, except in so far as those differences are expressed in the market through prices. * * *

IV. Rationality in the Law and Economics Literature

* * * Becker and Calabresi represent a fork in the road in the development of the rationality assumption in the law and economics literature. Becker presents a model in which criminals are rational actors.[58] It makes sense in Becker's model, to reduce the probability of capture to near zero and increase the fine to near infinity, because this maintains a high expected penalty and at the same time saves the state the costs of frequent enforcement efforts. This is the sort of prescription that could only come from a model that assumes a strong form of rationality. Studies of behavior and psychology—e.g., those of B.F. Skinner—suggest, contrary to Becker's model of deterrence, that people learn best through frequent rewards or penalties in connection to desired or undesired acts.[59]

Calabresi, on the other hand, allows for less than perfect rationality and the need for the state to act paternalistically at times. In particular, Calabresi describes four important deviations from the strong form of rationality. First, people may not have enough information to make rational decisions. Second, even if given sufficient information, they may suffer from an optimism bias—a belief that bad things will happen only to other people. Third, they may be judgment-proof, so that an increase in the amount of liability in excess of their assets has no marginal effect on their incentives for care. Fourth, and most interestingly, people are likely to do poorly in comparing short-term benefits and long-term costs—a problem Calabresi describes in terms of the Faustian bargain. Part of the problem may be free-riding, or a version of the familiar Prisoner's Dilemma. Knowing that society will not want to see me suffer in my old age, I may not save today, expecting society to help me out when I reach poverty in my later years. This is perfectly rational behavior at an individual level, but irrational on an aggregate level. Another part of the problem is time-inconsistency in preferences. Looking at his overall preferences, Ulysses

---

28 RICHARD A. POSNER, ECONOMIC ANALYSIS OF LAW (1972) [hereinafter ECONOMIC ANALYSIS, 1st ed.].

58 Becker, *supra*, at 176 (assuming that "a person commits an offense if the expected utility to him exceeds the utility that he could get by using his time and other resources at other activities").

59 B.F. SKINNER, SCIENCE AND HUMAN BEHAVIOR (1953).

knows that he should pay no attention to the Sirens. However, at the point at which he hears their song, he can only see clearly the part of his preference map directly in front of him. Because our preferences are dependent upon the perspective from which we view them, we may rationally choose to take actions in the short run that are welfare-reducing in the long run.

* * * Becker assumes rationality in its strongest form. His argument that deterrence could be maintained under a program that reduces the frequency of punishment while increasing its severity assumed a degree of rationality that had never received support from behavioral studies in the social sciences. Famous studies by Skinner and others that long predated Becker's paper suggested that people do not behave as rationally as Becker's model assumed. Calabresi, in contrast, assumes a weak form of rationality: that men are basically rational subject to some pretty consistent deviations.

From this fork in the road, with Becker adopting strong-form rationality and Calabresi a weak form, the law and economics literature seems to have taken Becker's path. Posner, whose name is virtually synonymous with the Chicago School, adhered to Becker's approach to rationality, and the strong-rationality assumption has since become a defining characteristic of Chicago School law and economics.

It should be clear that things did not need to go this way. There is nothing special about the strong-form rationality assumption that makes it a necessary feature of the economic analysis of law. The scholars, largely Chicago School, who immediately followed Becker and Calabresi could have chosen to follow Calabresi's example rather than Becker's. If that path had been followed, there would be far less criticism of law and economics. The behavioral law and economics school, still in its infancy, would have been old by now.

It should also be clear that Calabresi's description of weak rationality, remarkable in its clarity, anticipated the behavioral law and economics school by a generation. The behavioral school has identified an expanding list of deviations from strong-form rationality: over-optimism,[66] framing effects,[67] endowment effects,[68] ignorance of baseline probabilities,[69] and

---

[66] See, e.g., Linda Babcock & George Loewenstein, *Explaining Bargaining Impasse: The Role of Self-Serving Biases*, 11 J. Econ. Persp. 109, 110 (1997) (exploring the tendency "to conflate what is fair with what benefits oneself").

[67] See, e.g., Jeffrey J. Rachlinski, *Gains, Losses, and the Psychology of Litigation*, 70 S. CAL. L. REV. 113, 118 (1996) (studying how the framing effect, the fact that "the structure of many choices lures people into making decisions that are suboptimal," influences decisions in litigation).

[68] See, e.g., Richard Thaler, THE WINNER'S CURSE: PARADOXES AND ANOMALIES OF ECONOMIC LIFE 63 (1992) (describing the endowment effect "as the fact that people often demand much more to give up an object than they would be willing to pay to acquire it").

[69] See, e.g., Amos Tversky & Daniel Kahneman, *Judgment Under Uncertainty: Heuristics and Biases*, 185 SCI. 1124, 1124 (1974) (arguing that "people rely on a limited number of heuristic

others.[70] The behavioral literature has expanded * * * far beyond where it stood when Calabresi wrote COSTS * * *. Still, in the end, it appears that the behavioral school's message leaves us in the same position that Calabresi did, viewing men as weakly rational—*i.e.,* rational, subject to some pretty consistent deviations.

Calabresi's analysis shows that the behavioralist position is not a critique of a deep flaw in law and economics. It is a reaction to a particular strong-form version of rationality that emerged with Becker and the Chicago School. Economic analysis of law can easily incorporate the behavioralist position, as we observe in COSTS. The question is whether it would be desirable, as a general matter, to incorporate the behavioralist view in economic analysis of law. * * *

Now let us reconsider the standard analysis of bargaining under transaction costs in the context of Calabresi's "spongy bumpers" hypothetical:

> Suppose car-pedestrian accidents currently cost $100. Suppose also that if cars had spongy bumpers the total accident costs would only be $10. Suppose finally that spongy bumpers cost $50 more than the present bumpers. Assuming no transaction costs, spongy bumpers would become established regardless of who was held responsible for car-pedestrian accidents. If car manufacturers were held liable they would prefer to spend $50 for the new bumpers plus $10 in accident damages, instead of $100 for accident damages. If pedestrians were held responsible and could foresee the costs, they would prefer to bribe car manufacturers $50 to put in spongy bumpers and bear $10 in damages, rather than bear $100 in damages. Exactly the same result would occur if an arbitrary third party, *e.g.*, television manufacturers, were held liable initially; they too could lessen costs to themselves by bribing car manufacturers to put in spongy bumpers.[77]

Calabresi is careful to note in his hypothetical that all parties involved know the costs at issue and the technological alternatives. He then shows that if you add transaction costs to this hypothetical, you find that the lowest cost outcome may not result. For example, it may be too expensive for pedestrians to bribe manufacturers to install spongy bumpers. One question Calabresi does not take up in this hypothetical is why car manufacturers would not simply install the spongy bumpers and raise the price of a car by a sufficient amount to cover the cost. Perhaps car

---

principles which reduce the complex task of assessing probabilities and predicting values to simpler judgmental operations" that "sometimes . . . lead to severe and systematic errors").

70 See, e.g., Robert H. Frank et al., *Does Studying Economics Inhibit Cooperation?*, 7 J. ECON. PERSP. 159, 159 (1993) (concluding that "exposure to the self-interest model [of economics] . . . encourage[s] self-interested behavior"); David Laibson, *Golden Eggs and Hyperbolic Discounting*, 112 Q.J. ECON. 443 (1997) (discussing hyperbolic discounting of future payoffs).

77 [The Costs of Accidents, *supra*, at 136.]

consumers are too uninformed to know the value of spongy bumpers, or perhaps they would not receive a sufficient reduction in insurance rates, or perhaps pedestrians sue so infrequently that drivers bear too little of the costs of car-pedestrian accidents to put significant design-reform pressure on manufacturers. These are all potential problems with "market deterrence" (liability-based deterrence) * * *. Let us assume that one of these is true in order to continue with the hypothetical.

Now alter Calabresi's hypothetical slightly: assume that there are no transaction costs and that pedestrians (and television manufacturers) are not aware of the spongy bumpers alternative. Suppose, in addition, that liability falls on pedestrians. Since spongy bumpers would allow pedestrians to avoid $100 in losses, they clearly would be willing to pay at least $50 to have them installed. In a Coasean bargaining game, the result would be that the manufacturer reveals the availability of spongy bumpers as a technological alternative, and pedestrians bribe the manufacturer to have them installed. The manufacturer should be willing to reveal the availability of spongy bumpers because he will be able to collect a bribe from pedestrians that more than compensates for the cost of installing them.

Suppose, however, that pedestrians, as a group, * * * would much prefer to impose their desired result rather than pay for it in a Coasean bargain. Once the manufacturer reveals the availability of spongy bumpers as a technological alternative, the pedestrians would seek to impose it. They might petition the legislature to have a law passed requiring spongy bumpers on all cars. Car manufacturers, anticipating the danger, would never reveal the safer alternative.

This version of the spongy bumpers hypothetical * * * involves the threat of expropriation as a type of transaction cost. Indeed, one could say that transaction costs are of three types: basic bargaining costs, *i.e.*, the costs of meeting to bargain; information costs, *i.e.*, the costs associated with asymmetric information; and opportunism costs, *i.e.*, the costs connected to the threat of expropriation. The point of this discussion, however, is to show that one's approach to rationality has important implications for the possibility of Coasean bargaining. Calabresi's assumption of weak rationality immediately introduces obstacles to Coasean bargaining, even in settings in which basic bargaining costs are zero.

THOMAS F. COTTER, *LEGAL PRAGMATISM AND THE LAW AND ECONOMICS MOVEMENT*

84 GEO. L.J. 2071, 2102–2129 (1996)

B. DO LAW AND ECONOMICS SCHOLARS PRIVILEGE EFFICIENCY OVER EQUITY?

Although no one professes to believe that efficiency should be the legal policymaker's *only* goal, many law and economics scholars *do* share a belief that may not seem significantly different: namely, that legal rules should be used to achieve efficiency but not distributional equity. To understand what this means, consider the following example, which will be commonplace to readers who are familiar with the Coase Theorem.

Suppose that a factory manufactures some product that generates a profit of $1000 over the relevant time period; in the course of the manufacturing process, however, the factory emits smoke that causes the value of a neighboring landowner's property to drop from $1500 to $1000. There are three ways to prevent the neighbor's property from declining in value. First, the factory can install a smoke scrubber at a cost of $200. Second, the neighbor can install a fan that blows the smoke away at a cost of $100. Third, the factory can cease manufacture altogether, at a cost of $1000. With respect to aggregate wealth, then, there are four possible outcomes: (1) if the factory continues to emit smoke and nothing else changes, aggregate wealth will be $2000; (2) if the scrubber is installed, aggregate wealth will be $2300; (3) if the fan is installed, aggregate wealth will be $2400; and (4) if the factory ceases production, aggregate wealth will be $1500.

The Coase Theorem posits that, if transaction costs are zero, the wealth-maximizing outcome will result—the neighbor will install the fan—regardless of whether the neighbor has the right to enjoin the factory owner or the factory owner has the right to pollute. The analysis is straightforward. If the factory has the right to pollute, the neighbor will voluntarily install the fan, because by installing the fan (as opposed to tolerating the smoke) the neighbor is better off in the amount of $400. If instead the neighbor has the right to enjoin the factory, the factory will be better off paying the neighbor a fee (between $100 and $200) to install the fan; this will leave the factory at least as well off as it would be under the second-best solution (installing the scrubber). Either way the fan will be installed.

Several things may prevent, or at least hinder, the efficient result from occurring. For one thing, in the real world the parties will incur transaction costs, including the cost of getting together, of acquiring the relevant information, and so on. These costs are likely to be particularly significant if there are *multiple* property owners facing an aggregate loss of only $500.

Another potential obstacle is strategic behavior;[145] for example, if the neighbor has the right to enjoin the factory, the parties may waste time and resources haggling over the price the factory will pay the owner to install the fan, thereby eating up some of the aggregate profit to be derived from the transaction. At the margin this squabbling may prevent the transaction from going forward. Or the parties may be constrained by bounded rationality,[147] social norms that discourage bargaining in situations like this, or other obstacles.

Deciding which legal rule to adopt will depend (in part) on which social goal or goals the legal policymaker deems important. If the relevant goal is wealth maximization, the policymaker should pick a rule that minimizes the effect of transaction costs and other bargaining obstacles; generally speaking, there are three such rules to consider. First, the policymaker may assign the right to the party who, in the absence of transaction costs, would have purchased the right if it initially had been assigned to the other party. This mimic-the-market approach requires the court to determine which use—in this instance, factory or clean air—is more highly valued, and is the approach actually used in nuisance cases. A second strategy would be to assign the applicable right to the party who can facilitate an exchange at lower cost; for example, if a transfer of rights from neighbor to factory owner would generate transaction costs of $300 while a transfer of rights from factory owner to neighbor would generate costs of only $200, the policymaker would assign the right to the factory owner. A third strategy would be to minimize transaction costs and other obstacles by, for example, promulgating rules that reduce the incidence of strategic behavior.

If the applicable social goal, however, is some form of distributional equity, the outcome may be different. For example, suppose that the relevant goal is to minimize disparities in wealth, and that neighboring landowners generally are less wealthy than factory owners. Under this criterion, the better result is to assign the neighbor a right to enjoin the factory, because this result is more likely to result in the favored distribution: the rich factory owner, rather than the poor neighbor, will incur the cost of abating the pollution. If transaction costs and other bargaining obstacles are absent, assigning the neighbor a right to enjoin will also produce an efficient result—as would assigning the factory owner a right to pollute.

---

[145] Strategic behavior occurs when "what one individual is prepared to do depends on his assessment of what others are likely to do." JEFFRIE G. MURPHY & JULES L. COLEMAN, PHILOSOPHY OF LAW: AN INTRODUCTION TO JURISPRUDENCE 200 (rev. ed. 1990)[.]

[147] "Bounded rationality" means that "[t]he capacity of the human mind for formulating and solving complex problems is very small compared with the size of the problems whose solution is required for objectively rational behavior in the real world . . . ." HERBERT A. SIMON, MODELS OF MAN 198 (1957).

But in the real world the equitable result may depart from the efficient result. To illustrate, suppose that the only way to abate or reduce the pollution would be to shut down the factory (neither scrubbers nor fans are an option); that instead of one neighbor facing a potential $500 loss if the pollution is not abated there are five hundred neighbors each facing an individual loss of $1; and that aggregate transaction costs are $750. Under these circumstances, assigning the factory owner a right to pollute is wealth maximizing (aggregate wealth is $2000). Assigning the neighbors a right to enjoin will not be wealth maximizing—transaction costs will preclude selling the factory a right to pollute and aggregate wealth will be only $1500—but the neighbors will be better off, in the amount of $500, than they would have been if the factory had been assigned a right to pollute. Thus, it is possible in this and other cases that the choice of an equity goal will lead to a result that is not wealth maximizing; equity will be gained only at the cost of efficiency. The mainstream economists' tenet that legal rules should be used to promote efficiency but not distributional equity may seem to leave law and economics scholars vulnerable to the charge of foundationalism: what justification can there be for the *a priori* rejection of distributional equity as a social goal? Scholars who adhere to the mainstream view respond, however, that they are not (necessarily) rejecting distributional equity as a social goal; instead, their position is that equity can be attained more effectively if the courts and legislature adopt efficient legal rules, and the legislature then taxes the well-off and redistributes some portion of the resulting tax revenues to the poor (a "tax-and-transfer" policy). The basic idea is that aggregate wealth will increase by some increment "X" if the policymaker adopts the efficient rule, rather than a rule that promotes equity at the cost of efficiency. It can be mathematically demonstrated that the state can (1) impose a tax that captures this increment and (2) redistribute the increment to make everyone better off than he would be under the "equitable" rule. To put it another way, the efficient rule increases the size of the pie—thereby creating more wealth that can be taxed and redistributed to the poor—than does a legal rule that seeks to redistribute to the poor in the first instance. * * *

Of course, one might [argue] that the courts should not take it upon themselves to accomplish what the people presumably have chosen not to accomplish through their elected representatives. But this is a somewhat facile response. For one thing, public choice theory suggests that if the gains from the adoption of an efficient rule would be concentrated among a handful of small, well-financed, or well-organized groups, those groups are likely to exercise disproportionate influence to defeat any proposed legislative redistribution. Alternatively, as Guido Calabresi has argued, even if the legislature *does* respond to majoritarian pressure "the link between majoritarianism . . . and just distribution is by no means clear. Valid philosophical notions of justice may have more impact, for example, on judges than on legislators."[168] Of course, none of this suggests that courts should simply do whatever they wish whenever they wish to do it; there are good reasons for deferring to legislative judgments, and much of the time we expect courts to defer to them. But sometimes there are good reasons *not* to defer—particularly when, because of legislative inactivity, it may be unclear whether the legislature has made an antidistributive "judgment" at all. A preference for deferring to legislative judgments provides no basis for rejecting court-sponsored distributional policies altogether. * * *

2. The Values Embedded in the Paradigm

In this subsection, I focus on three interrelated values that are embedded in the economic paradigm, and I discuss the consequences of according these values a foundational status in relation to other competing values that the paradigm cannot detect. The three values are: (1) the satisfaction of currently existing preferences; (2) the satisfaction of preferences that are supported by wealth over preferences that are not; and (3) the use of a single metric to measure and compare competing preferences.

The satisfaction of currently existing preferences follows from the economists' assumption that preferences are exogenous. This assumption simplifies the analysis and may be adequate for many purposes; even if the economic analyst (like the pragmatist) believes that individual preferences are largely a product of one's environment, she may conclude that the assumption of exogeneity will not materially alter the predictive power of her model, as long as the model deals with the short run and preference transformation is a long-run phenomenon. But for the legal policymaker who needs to consider the long-run consequences of various legal rules, the assumption of exogenous preferences may be highly inadequate. Certainly there is reason to believe that at least some legal rules—for example, rules prohibiting racial and sexual discrimination in employment and providing greater rights for the disabled—have been moderately successful at modifying individual attitudes and preferences, albeit not overnight. By obscuring such preference-altering phenomena, the economic paradigm introduces two distortions. First, it reduces the predictive power of the model in various ways (e.g., by predicting that attitudes towards groups that have been victimized by discrimination will never change). Second, it can lead the policymaker to ignore the possibility that efforts to change preferences, through for example, education and the inculcation of civic virtue, may lead to greater aggregate satisfaction or well-being in the long run. * * *

A second assumption embedded in the economic paradigm is that the only preferences that count are those that have been revealed through

---

[168] Guido Calabresi, *The Pointlessness of Pareto*, 100 YALE L.J. 1211, 1224 n.36 (1991) * * *.

offers to pay or offers to accept. For the economist, this concept of "revealed preferences" is a way of coping with the fact that individual preferences are not directly observable or measurable; we cannot just peek inside someone's brain to determine how intensely he likes or dislikes Corn Flakes, or whether he prefers Corn Flakes to Shredded Wheat. Because direct observation is impossible, the economist proposes as a surrogate the observation of consumer behavior. For example, if we observe someone purchasing a box of Shredded Wheat for $3 instead of a box of Corn Flakes for $2.50, we can infer by his willingness to pay that he prefers the $3 box of Shredded Wheat to the $2.50 box of Corn Flakes. A consumer's observable behavior is assumed to reveal his preferences, to the extent his willingness to pay or willingness to accept payment embodies those preferences.

For business firms in need of a rational method for setting supply and price, revealed preferences may well be a very useful tool. Firms tend to be interested only in those preferences that are backed by willingness to pay, because preferences that are not so backed cannot add to their profitability. As with exogenous preferences, however, the use of revealed preferences to formulate legal policy presents several serious problems. First, the relationship between choice and willingness to pay (or accept) is often unclear; * * * sometimes preferences may be unstable, or nontransitive, or may concern other preferences, or may not fit the model for a variety of reasons. Sunstein notes, for example, that people sometimes appear to have different private and public preferences; I may not give much to private charities, and yet I may prefer that government use a portion of what I pay in taxes to distribute benefits to the poor. Or I may not be very interested in visiting national parks or attending the opera, yet still value having the government partially finance these amenities through tax revenues. * * *

A second problem arising from revealed preference theory is that, even if choice accurately mirrors willingness to pay, willingness to pay is necessarily a function of ability to pay; this implies that agents who have the means to reveal their preferences will be satisfied, while the preferences of those who do not will remain unrevealed and unsatisfied. To cite the obvious example, suppose that a rich man and a poor man both need a liver transplant; without a transplant, both will die within a month, though with a transplant each stands a fifty-percent chance of surviving for another five years. If society allocates health care based on revealed preferences, the policymaker will perceive the rich man as having a more intense preference for the liver and will allocate it to him. This creates two problems. The first is that allocating "goods" such as organs on the basis of wealth conflicts with many people's moral beliefs or intuitions. The second is that, even from a utilitarian standpoint, allocating the liver to the rich man may not increase aggregate social well-being. It may be the case that the poor man has a more intense desire to live than the rich man, or that the poor man's family needs his meager earning power more than the wealthy family needs the rich man's. And yet if only dollar-votes count, the rich man (who has many more such votes) gets the liver; social "wealth," as defined by ability to pay, is maximized, but social utility decreases. In short, the use of revealed-preference theory leads the policymaker to ignore various phenomena that otherwise might be relevant to social well-being.

A third obscuring aspect of the conventional paradigm is the assumption of commensurability. To illustrate, suppose that a consumer drives to the grocery store to buy one box of Shredded Wheat and one box of Corn Flakes for his personal consumption, but that he then discovers that the store is out of Shredded Wheat. Conventional analysis assumes that a package of zero boxes of Shredded Wheat and some boxes of Corn Flakes (two? three? ten?) will make the consumer as well off as he would be with one box of each. In other words, his preferences for different types of cereal are commensurable; at some point, the consumer will consider himself as well off, or even better off, with a different combination of commensurable goods. The conventional paradigm assumes that all preferences can be expressed in a common currency and measured along a unitary metric, and thus that any commodity can be traded off for some number of other commodities.

For the legal policymaker, the problem is that some preferences do not seem to be interchangeable with other preferences, or at least not easily so. Jeffrey Harrison provides an example of a voter who (1) intensely wishes that his friend, a prostitute, would stop engaging in prostitution; and (2) strongly believes that the law should permit people to do what they want with their bodies. Although the friend has agreed to give up prostitution if a ballot initiative outlawing the practice passes, the voter cannot bring himself to vote for the initiative, because his belief in personal autonomy takes lexical preference even over his intense concern for his friend. Sunstein suggests another example, of a lawyer who has agreed to have lunch with a friend but by mid-morning has become very busy and would like to cancel. Should the lawyer offer the friend a cash payment as compensation for agreeing to forgo the lunch? The obvious answer is no—even though the friend might be willing to accept the money if the offer were high enough—because to make such an offer would be inconsistent with the way that people value their friends. Thus, Sunstein argues that "[i]ncommensurability occurs when the relevant goods cannot be aligned along a single metric without doing violence to our considered judgments about how these goods are best characterized." * * *

The preceding illustrations demonstrate some of the ways in which economic analysis privileges quantifiable and measurable phenomena over the non-quantifiable and the unmeasurable. The question thus arises whether the economic paradigm necessarily obscures more than it illuminates, or whether it can be adapted to the purposes of practical reason. * * *

LOUIS KAPLOW & STEVEN SHAVELL, *ECONOMIC ANALYSIS OF LAW*

3 HANDBOOK OF PUBLIC ECONOMICS 1761–65
(A.J. Auerbach & M. Feldstein, 2002)

Many observers, and particularly non-economists, view economic analysis of law with skepticism. In this section, we briefly note some of the most common criticisms.

[1.] Positive analysis

It is often claimed that individuals and firms do not respond to legal rules as rational maximizers of their well-being. Sometimes this criticism of the conventional economic approach verges on an outright rejection of the use of models. Such an extreme view reflects a failure to appreciate the role of simplifying assumptions, and, accordingly, it can be largely dismissed. Frequently, however, the criticism is limited to particular contexts. For example, it is often asserted that decisions to commit crimes are not governed by economists' usual assumptions. Ultimately, such criticisms raise questions that can only be answered by empirical investigation.

It is also suggested that, in predicting individuals' behavior, certain standard assumptions should be modified. For example, in predicting compliance with a law, the assumption that preferences be taken as given would be inappropriate if a legal rule would change people's preferences, as some say was the case with civil rights laws. In addition, laws may frame individuals' understanding of problems, which could affect their probability assessments or willingness to pay. * * * The emerging field of behavioral economics and work in various disciplines that address social norms is beginning to examine these sorts of issues.

[2.] Normative analysis

[2(a).] *Distribution of income.* A frequent criticism of economic analysis of law concerns its focus on efficiency, to the exclusion of the distribution of income. The claim of critics is that legal rules—such as the choice between strict liability and negligence to govern automobile-pedestrian accidents—should be selected in a manner that reflects their effects on the rich and the poor.

There is not a good reason, however, to employ legal rules to accomplish redistributive objectives given the general alternative of achieving sought-after redistribution through the income tax and transfer programs. Such direct methods of redistribution tend to be superior to redistribution through the choice of legal rules: selecting legal rules other than those that are most efficient in order to effect redistribution is itself costly, and it also will distort individuals' labor-leisure decision in the same manner as does the income tax.

Moreover, it is difficult to redistribute income systematically through the choice of legal rules. In the first place, many individuals are never involved in litigation. Also, for those who are, there is substantial income heterogeneity both among plaintiffs and among defendants. Additionally, in contractual contexts, the choice of a legal rule often will not have any effect on distribution because contract terms, notably, the price, will adjust so that any agreement into which parties enter will continue to reflect the initial bargaining power of each party.

[2(b).] *Victim compensation.* Another major criticism of economic analysis of law is that it usually emphasizes the effects of legal rules on behavior, but not the compensation of victims—which, some believe, is the main purpose of private law. Economic analysis does not, though, ignore victim compensation per se; victim compensation is relevant to social welfare if victims are risk averse. However, as we have discussed, if victims can obtain insurance, as is often possible, then the legal system need not be relied on to provide compensation. Moreover, providing compensation through legal rules tends to be significantly more expensive than doing so through insurance.

[2(c).] *Concerns for fairness.* An additional source of criticism is that the welfare-economic approach slights important concerns about fairness, justice, and rights. Some of these notions refer implicitly to the appropriateness of the distribution of income and, accordingly, are encompassed by our preceding remarks. Also, to some degree, the notions are motivated by instrumental concerns. For example, the attraction of just punishment must inhere in part in its deterrent effect, and the appeal of obeying contractual promises must rest in part on the beneficial effect this has on production and exchange. To this extent, critics' concerns are already taken into account in standard welfare economic analysis.

However, many who advance ideas of fairness and cognate notions do not regard them merely as some sort of proxy for attaining instrumental objectives. Instead, they believe that satisfying the notions is intrinsically valuable. This view too can be partially reconciled with economists' conception of social welfare: if individuals have a taste for a legal rule or institution because they regard it as fair, that should be credited in the determination of social welfare, just as any taste should. (Note that, in this case, the importance of fairness is converted from a philosophical issue to an empirical question about individuals' tastes.)

But many uphold the view that notions of fairness are important as ethical principles in themselves, without regard to any possible relationship the principles may have to individuals' welfare. This opinion is, of course, the subject of longstanding debate among moral philosophers.[202] Some readers (along with us) may be skeptical of normative views that are not grounded in individuals' well-being because embracing such views entails a willingness to sacrifice individuals' well-being. Indeed, consistently pursuing any non-welfarist principle will sometimes result in everyone being made worse off. Nevertheless, it is clear that such views will be reflected in criticism of economic analysis of law for the foreseeable future.

[3.] Purported efficiency of judge-made law

Also criticized is the contention of some economically-oriented academics * * * that judge-made law tends to be efficient (in contrast to legislation, which is said to reflect the influence of special interest groups). Instead, critics believe that the judge-made law is guided by notions of fairness, justice, and rights, and thus will not necessarily be efficient. Several observations about these competing views may be made. First, one would certainly expect legal rules to promote efficiency, at least in a very approximate sense, for that is consistent with many notions of fairness and with common sense. But second, one would not expect that legal rules would be efficient in a detailed sense for a variety of reasons. Third, we note that judge-made law is peculiar to "common-law" countries, those of the former British Commonwealth, yet common law legal rules are not markedly different from those in the civil-law countries of Continental Europe, which rely more on statutes and less on judicial development than common-law countries. Moreover, to the extent that legal rules in common-law and civil-law systems differ, it is hardly clear that the typical civil-law rules are less efficient. Finally, it should be emphasized that the economic efficiency thesis is a particular descriptive claim about the law, and its validity does not bear on the power of economics to predict behavior in response to legal rules or on the merits of normative economic analysis of law.

The Challenge of Behavioral Economics

DANIEL H. PINK, DRIVE, THE SURPRISING TRUTH ABOUT WHAT MOTIVATES US

24–5 (2009)

When I took my first economics course back in the early 1980s, our professor—a brilliant lecturer with a Patton-like stage presence—offered an important clarification before she'd chalked her first indifference curve

---

[202] We note, however, that much of the philosophical debate is about what principles should guide personal behavior in everyday life, which may not be applicable to the determination of what principles should guide social policy. * * *

on the blackboard. Economics, she explained, wasn't the study of money. It was the study of behavior. In the course of a day, each of us was constantly figuring the cost and benefits of our actions and then deciding how to act. Economists studied what people did, rather than what we said, because we did what was best for us. We were rational calculators of our economic self-interest.

When I studied law a few years later, a similar idea reappeared. The newly ascendant field of "law and economics" held that precisely because we were such awesome self-interest calculators, laws and regulations often impeded, rather than permitted, sensible and just outcomes. I survived law school in no small part because I discovered the talismanic phrase and offered it on exams: "In a world of perfect information and low transaction costs, the parties will bargain to a wealth-maximizing result."

Then, about a decade later, came a curious turn of events that made me question much of what I'd worked hard, and taken on enormous debt, to learn. In 2002, the Nobel Foundation awarded its prize in economics to a guy who wasn't even an economist. And they gave him the field's highest honor largely for revealing that we weren't always rational calculators of our economic self-interest and that the parties often didn't bargain to a wealth-maximizing result. Daniel Kahneman, an American psychologist who won the Nobel Prize in economics that year for work he'd done with Israeli Amos Tversky, helped force a change in how we think about what we do. * * *

Kahneman and others in the field of behavioral economics agreed with my professor that economics was the study of human economic behavior. They just believed that we'd placed too much emphasis on the economic and not enough on the human. That hyperrational calculator-brained person wasn't real. He was a convenient fiction.

CHRISTINE JOLLS, CASS R. SUNSTEIN, AND RICHARD THALER, *A BEHAVIORAL APPROACH TO LAW AND ECONOMICS*

50 STANFORD L. REV. 1471, 1473–74, 1476, 1545–47 (1998)

* * * Objections to the rational actor model in law and economics are almost as old as the field itself. Early skeptics about the economic analysis of law were quick to marshal arguments from psychology and other social sciences to undermine its claims. But in law, challenges to the rational actor assumption by those who sympathize with the basic objectives of economic analysis have been much less common. The absence of sustained and comprehensive economic analysis of legal rules from a perspective informed by insights about actual human behavior makes for a significant contrast with many other fields of economics, where such "behavioral"

analysis has become relatively common. This is especially odd since law is a domain where behavioral analysis would appear to be particularly promising in light of the fact that nonmarket behavior is frequently involved.

Our goal in this article is to advance an approach to the economic analysis of law that is informed by a more accurate conception of choice, one that reflects a better understanding of human behavior and its wellsprings. We build on and attempt to generalize earlier work in law outlining behavioral findings by taking the two logical next steps: proposing a systematic framework for a behavioral approach to economic analysis of law, and using behavioral insights to develop specific models and approaches addressing topics of abiding interest in law and economics. The analysis of these specific topics is preliminary and often in the nature of a proposal for a research agenda; we touch on a wide range of issues in an effort to show the potential uses of behavioral insights. The unifying idea in our analysis is that behavioral economics allows us to model and predict behavior relevant to law with the tools of traditional economic analysis, but with more accurate assumptions about human behavior, and more accurate predictions and prescriptions about law. * * *

I. FOUNDATIONS: WHAT IS "BEHAVIORAL LAW AND ECONOMICS"?

In order to identify, in a general way, the defining features of behavioral law and economics, it is useful first to understand the defining features of law and economics. As we understand it, this approach to the law posits that legal rules are best analyzed and understood in light of standard economic principles. Gary Becker offers a typical account of those principles: "[A]ll human behavior can be viewed as involving participants who [1] maximize their utility [2] from a stable set of preferences and [3] accumulate an optimal amount of information and other inputs in a variety of markets."[5] The task of law and economics is to determine the implications of such rational maximizing behavior in and out of markets, and its legal implications for markets and other institutions. Although some of Becker's particular applications of the economic approach might be thought of as contentious, that general approach underlies a wide range of work in the economic analysis of law. What then is the task of behavioral law and economics? How does it differ from standard law and economics? These are the questions we address below.

A. *Homo Economicus* and Real People

The task of behavioral law and economics, simply stated, is to explore the implications of actual (not hypothesized) human behavior for the law. How do "real people" differ from *homo economicus*? We will describe the differences by stressing three important "bounds" on human behavior,

---

5 GARY S. BECKER, THE ECONOMIC APPROACH TO HUMAN BEHAVIOR 14 (1976).

bounds that draw into question the central ideas of utility maximization, stable preferences, rational expectations, and optimal processing of information. People can be said to display bounded rationality, bounded willpower, and bounded self-interest. All three bounds are well documented in the literature of other social sciences, but they are relatively unexplored in economics (although, as we noted at the outset, this has begun to change). Each of these bounds represents a significant way in which most people depart from the standard economic model. While there are instances in which more than one bound comes into play, at this stage we think it is best to conceive of them as separate modeling problems. Nonetheless, each of the three bounds points to systematic (rather than random or arbitrary) departures from conventional economic models, and thus each of the three bears on generating sound predictions and prescriptions for law. They also provide the foundations for new and sometimes quite formal models of behavior.

1. *Bounded rationality*. Bounded rationality, an idea first introduced by Herbert Simon, refers to the obvious fact that human cognitive abilities are not infinite. We have limited computational skills and seriously flawed memories. People can respond sensibly to these failings; thus it might be said that people sometimes respond rationally to their own cognitive limitations, minimizing the sum of decision costs and error costs. To deal with limited memories we make lists. To deal with limited brain power and time we use mental shortcuts and rules of thumb. But even with these remedies, and in some cases because of these remedies, human behavior differs in systematic ways from that predicted by the standard economic model of unbounded rationality. Even when the use of mental shortcuts is rational, it can produce predictable mistakes. The departures from the standard model can be divided into two categories: judgment and decision-making. Actual judgments show systematic departures from models of unbiased forecasts, and actual decisions often violate the axioms of expected utility theory.

A major source of differences between actual judgments and unbiased forecasts is the use of rules of thumb. As stressed in the path-breaking work of Daniel Kahneman and Amos Tversky, rules of thumb such as the availability heuristic—in which the frequency of some event is estimated by judging how easy it is to recall other instances of this type (how "available" such instances are)—lead us to erroneous conclusions. People tend to conclude, for example, that the probability of an event (such as a car accident) is greater if they have recently witnessed an occurrence of that event than if they have not. What is especially important in the work of Kahneman and Tversky is that it shows that shortcuts and rules of thumb are predictable. While the heuristics are useful on average (which explains how they become adopted), they lead to errors in particular circumstances. This means that someone using such a rule of thumb may be behaving rationally in the sense of economizing on thinking time, but such a person will nonetheless make forecasts that are different from those that emerge from the standard rational-choice model. * * *

2. *Bounded willpower.* In addition to bounded rationality, people often display bounded willpower. This term refers to the fact that human beings often take actions that they know to be in conflict with their own long-term interests. Most smokers say they would prefer not to smoke, and many pay money to join a program or obtain a drug that will help them quit. As with bounded rationality, many people recognize that they have bounded willpower and take steps to mitigate its effects. They join a pension plan or "Christmas Club" (a special savings arrangement under which funds can be withdrawn only around the holidays) to prevent under-saving, and they don't keep tempting desserts around the house when trying to diet. In some cases they may vote for or support governmental policies, such as social security, to eliminate any temptation to succumb to the desire for immediate rewards. Thus, the demand for and supply of law may reflect people's understanding of their own (or others') bounded willpower; consider "cooling off" periods for certain sales and programs that facilitate or even require saving.

3. *Bounded self-interest.* Finally, we use the term bounded self-interest to refer to an important fact about the utility function of most people: They care, or act as if they care, about others, even strangers, in some circumstances. (Thus, we are not questioning here the idea of utility maximization, but rather the common assumptions about what that entails.) Our notion is distinct from simple altruism, which conventional economics has emphasized in areas such as bequest decisions. Self-interest is bounded in a much broader range of settings than conventional economics assumes, and the bound operates in ways different from what the conventional understanding suggests. In many market and bargaining settings (as opposed to non-market settings such as bequest decisions), people care about being treated fairly and want to treat others fairly if those others are themselves behaving fairly. As a result of these concerns, the agents in a behavioral economic model are both nicer and (when they are not treated fairly) more spiteful than the agents postulated by neoclassical theory. * * *

B. Testable Predictions

Behavioral and conventional law and economics do not differ solely in their assumptions about human behavior. They also differ, in testable ways, in their predictions about how law (as well as other forces) affects behavior. To make these differences more concrete, consider [one of] the three "fundamental principles of economics" set forth by Richard Posner in his ECONOMIC ANALYSIS OF LAW, in a discussion that is, on these points, quite conventional. (Posner's discussion represents an application of the basic economic methodology set forth by Becker above.) To what extent would an account based on behavioral law and economics offer different "fundamental principles"? * * *

[One] fundamental principle of conventional law and economics is that "resources tend to gravitate toward their most valuable uses" as markets drive out any unexploited profit opportunities. When combined with the notion that opportunity and out-of-pocket costs are equated [ ], this yields the Coase theorem—the idea that initial assignments of entitlements will not affect the ultimate allocation of resources so long as transaction costs are zero. Many economists and economically oriented lawyers think of the Coase theorem as a tautology; if there were really no transaction costs (and no wealth effects), and if an alternative allocation of resources would make some agents better off and none worse off, then of course the agents would move to that allocation. Careful empirical study, however, shows that the Coase theorem is not a tautology; indeed, it can lead to inaccurate predictions. That is, even when transaction costs and wealth effects are known to be zero, initial entitlements alter the final allocation of resources. These results are predicted by behavioral economics, which emphasizes the difference between opportunity and out-of-pocket costs.

Consider the following set of experiments conducted to test the Coase theorem; let us offer an interpretation geared to the particular context of economic analysis of law. The subjects were forty-four students taking an advanced undergraduate course in law and economics at Cornell University. Half the students were endowed with tokens. Each student (whether or not endowed with a token) was assigned a personal token value, the price at which a token could be redeemed for cash at the end of the experiment; these assigned values induce supply and demand curves for the tokens. Markets were conducted for tokens. Those without tokens could buy one, while those with tokens could sell. Those with tokens should (and do) sell their tokens if offered more than their assigned value; those without tokens should (and do) buy tokens if they can get one at a price below their assigned value. These token markets are a complete victory of economic theory. The equilibrium price was always exactly what the theory would predict, and the tokens did in fact flow to those who valued them most.

However, life is generally not about tokens redeemable for cash. Thus another experiment was conducted, identical to the first except that now half the students were given Cornell coffee mugs instead of tokens. Here behavioral analysis generates a prediction distinct from standard economic analysis: Because people do not equate opportunity and out-of-pocket costs for goods whose values are not solely exogenously defined (as they were in the case of the tokens), those endowed with mugs should be reluctant to part with them even at prices they would not have considered paying to acquire a mug had they not received one.

Was this prediction correct? Yes. Markets were conducted and mugs bought and sold. Unlike the case of the tokens, the assignment of property rights had a pronounced effect on the final allocation of mugs. The students who were assigned mugs had a strong tendency to keep them. Whereas the Coase theorem would have predicted that about half the mugs would trade (since transaction costs had been shown to be essentially zero in the token experiments, and mugs were randomly distributed), instead only fifteen percent of the mugs traded. And those who were endowed with mugs asked more than twice as much to give up a mug as those who didn't get a mug were willing to pay. This result did not change if the markets were repeated. This effect is generally referred to as the "endowment effect"; it is a manifestation of the broader phenomenon of "loss aversion"—the idea that losses are weighted more heavily than gains—which in turn is a central building block of Kahneman and Tversky's prospect theory.

What are we to make of these findings? There are at least three important lessons. First, markets are indeed robust institutions. Even naive subjects participating at low stakes produce outcomes indistinguishable from those predicted by the theory when trading for tokens. Second, when agents must determine their own values (as with the mugs), outcomes can diverge substantially from those predicted by economic theory. Third, these departures will not be obvious outside an experiment, even when they exist and have considerable importance. That is, even in the mugs markets, there was trading; there was just not as much trading as the theory would predict. These lessons can be applied to other markets; we offer some examples below.

The foregoing discussion illustrates the point [that the] difference between conventional and behavioral law and economics is not just a difference in the validity of the assumptions about human behavior. While the assumptions of unbounded rationality, willpower, and self-interest are unrealistic, the force of behavioral economics comes from the difference in its predictions (for example, fewer trades for mugs than for tokens). In this sense, our analysis is consistent with the precept originally proposed by Milton Friedman: Economics should not be judged on whether the assumptions are realistic or valid, but rather on the quality of its predictions. * * *

B. Bargaining Around Court Orders

1. *Coasian prediction.* As noted above, an important aspect of law and economics is the Coase theorem, which says that the assignment of a legal entitlement will not influence the ultimate allocation of that entitlement when transaction costs and wealth effects are zero. A straightforward application of this idea is that when a court enters a judgment, whether in the form of an injunction or a damage award, the parties are likely to bargain to a different outcome if that outcome is preferable to what the court did and the transaction costs and wealth

effects are small. (Thus, for instance, if the court enters a prohibitively high damage award but the activity in question is efficient, the parties should bargain for a lower damage level, since this would increase the surplus to be shared between them.) To whom an entitlement is allocated after litigation, and how it is protected (by a property rule or a liability rule), are irrelevant to the ultimate allocation of the entitlement in these circumstances.

2. *Behavioral analysis.* Influenced by behavioral economics, many legal commentators have observed that in light of the endowment effect ([ ] an instance of bounded rationality), the assignment of a legal entitlement may well affect the outcome of bargaining, even when transaction costs (as conventionally defined) and wealth effects are zero. This conclusion is suggested by the mugs experiments described [above], as well as by a substantial body of other evidence on the endowment effect. The mugs results were obtained in circumstances that were the most favorable to the predictions of the conventional theory. Transaction costs were zero and the sort of emotional attachments that can grow over time in the real world were absent. Mug owners had become mug owners just minutes before the markets were run. Compare that with a homeowner who has been endowed with the right to have her homestead protected from noxious fumes being emitted nearby.

Although the endowment effect suggests generally that the assignment of a legal entitlement may affect the outcome of bargaining, such an effect is especially likely when the entitlement is in the form of a court order obtained after legal proceedings between opposing parties (our focus here). This is so for several reasons.

First, the process of going through litigation may strengthen the endowment effect. Experimental evidence suggests that there is an especially strong endowment effect when a party believes that he has earned the entitlement or that he particularly deserves it. Of course someone who has received a court judgment in his favor will believe that he has earned it. Such a person may also believe strongly that this outcome is fair, based on the self-serving bias * * *.

Bounded self-interest, and specifically the [possibility of] acrimony [between the parties], provide an additional reason we might expect less bargaining in real world settings than in law and economics texts. Even if there are financial gains from making a deal, it is difficult to bargain without communication, and litigants are often not on speaking terms by the end of a protracted trial. Even if communication is possible, bargains are unlikely to be struck when both sides take pleasure in making the other side worse off; in such circumstances it can be difficult to reach agreements on settlements even if they would substantially improve the lot of both parties. For all of these reasons, behavioral research suggests that injunctions and damage awards may stick even with low transaction costs (as conventionally defined).

Note that another way of phrasing this conclusion is that the concept of transaction costs is broader than conventional analysis assumes. The costs of a transaction include not only the conventionally recognized ones (for example, the cost of assembling all of the relevant parties), but also costs such as the discomfort or displeasure of dealing with an adversary. If "transaction costs" are defined in this broader way, then, for the reasons given above, they will very often be substantial in the case of bargaining around court orders; hence, deals are unlikely to occur. This observation illustrates an important general point. Once the behavioral analysis is understood, it can often be incorporated into economic analyses using standard concepts such as transaction costs. This should not be taken to imply, however, that the behavioral analysis is superfluous. Under the usual account, transaction costs would have been assumed to be zero as long as the two sides could easily negotiate.

It is of course true that most cases settle, so that those which do not, and which thus produce court orders, may be atypical in some respects. But that does not mean they are unimportant objects of study for purposes of positive analysis. With conventional law and economics, behavioral analysis is concerned with the fact (and the consequences of the fact) that some cases proceed to trial.

Although our focus in this section is on positive analysis, there is also a tricky normative issue: When people fail to reach bargains that would be reached in the absence of endowment effects and spiteful behavior, is there any problem from the standpoint of efficiency? On one view, the answer is no; if the parties do not contract around a court-ordered outcome for these reasons, then the outcome must be efficient (even if another, different outcome—favoring the other side—would also have been efficient). An underlying question, however, is whether spite ought to count in the efficiency calculus. Some of the most prominent utilitarian philosophers believe that it should not.

3. *Evidence.* Conventional economic theory and behavioral analysis thus generate distinct predictions about what happens after trials. These theories can therefore be tested with empirical evidence. What happens once a court judgment has been entered? How often do the parties bargain to a different outcome? Consider the set of cases where the court has assigned an entitlement to the party who values it less. In these circumstances, the standard theory would predict contracting around the court order whenever transaction costs (as conventionally defined) and wealth effects are small. (The possibility of asymmetric information is discussed below in connection with the existing empirical findings.) The behavioral theory predicts that even in such cases, there will often be no

recontracting. Since it is unlikely that court orders are, across the board, uniquely efficient, it should be possible to test these differing predictions.

Even without this detailed type of information, data gathered by Ward Farnsworth suggest that there is much less post-trial bargaining than the economic model would predict. Farnsworth interviewed attorneys from approximately twenty nuisance cases in which injunctive relief was sought and either granted or denied after full litigation before a judge. In not a single case of those Farnsworth studied did parties even attempt to contract around the court order, even when transaction costs were low, and even when an objective third party might think that there was considerable room for mutually advantageous deals. Conventional analysis might attribute failures to reach an ultimate agreement to asymmetric information; but under such analysis it is difficult to explain the complete failure even to negotiate. It is also interesting to note that the lawyers interviewed said that the parties would not have reached a contractual solution if the opposite result had been reached. (This last point also means that the no-bargaining result cannot be explained by supposing that the court orders entered were uniquely efficient.)

The lawyers' explanations for these results are behavioral in character. Once people have received a court judgment, they are unwilling to negotiate with the opposing party, partly because of an unwillingness by victorious plaintiffs to confer advantages upon their opponents. Having invested a great deal of resources in pursuing the case all the way to court and through a trial, victors perceive themselves as having a special right to the legally endorsed status quo, and they are unlikely to give that right up, especially to their opponent, for all, or most, of the tea in China. Their investment in the entitlement gives it a distinctive character. Bargains are unlikely in the extreme; the plaintiff and the defendant tend not even to think about them. These tendencies are reinforced (according to the lawyers in Farnsworth's study) by the presence of acrimony between the parties; thus acrimony combines with the endowment effect to produce an absence of negotiation.

Here, as elsewhere in this article, our emphasis is on whether empirical evidence exists to test the predictions of the conventional and behavioral economic accounts, and, if more evidence would be helpful, what sort of study might be most useful. It is frequently remarked that law and economics is primarily theoretical or analytic, and rarely empirical. Victory is often declared based on a dataless model. We think that before victory can be declared for either conventional or behavioral law and economics, the fit of the theory with the available evidence must be assessed. For behavioral analysis, it is not enough to build a model consistent with behavior observed in an experimental setting (such as behavior in the ultimatum game or the mugs experiments); the model must be compared and tested against what we observe in the world. A good aspiration for both conventional and behavioral approaches is careful empirical work that provides reasonably definitive conclusions about predictive failures and successes.

The empirical data and future empirical research discussed in this section concern behavior after a court has entered a judgment. Of course, most cases settle before trial, and so it is also important to ask to what degree bargaining is likely to be successful prior to this point. This is a separate question; bargaining may be more likely in that setting because neither side has yet been endowed through a court judgment with a clear entitlement. On the other hand, self-serving bias and conditions of acrimony (as well as the background force of the "ordinary" endowment effect) may still preclude successful bargaining. * * *

IV. PRESCRIPTIONS

A. Negligence Determinations and Other Determinations of Fact or Law

1. Background.

Frequently juries are called upon to determine the probability of an event that ended up occurring; a prominent example is the negligence standard, which (in the formulation favored by the economic analysis of law) requires jurors to assess the costs and benefits of the defendant's course of action from an ex ante perspective, and thus to determine the probability that harm would end up coming of that action. These determinations are made with the "benefit" of hindsight; jurors know at the time they make their decision that the event in question did in fact occur. Jurors' determinations are thus likely to be afflicted by "hindsight bias"—the tendency of decision-makers to attach an excessively high probability to an event simply because it ended up occurring.

Hindsight bias has been observed in a large number of studies, including studies of "expert" actors such as physicians, who, when asked to assess the probabilities of alternative diagnoses, given a set of symptoms, offer significantly different estimates depending on what they are told the actual diagnosis turned out to be. Hindsight bias also appears to occur in the specific context of negligence determinations. In the negligence studies, subjects in the role of jurors—armed with knowledge that harm had in fact occurred—were found to attach significantly higher probabilities to harm than subjects in the role of ex ante decision-makers—those not informed of the occurrence of harm. This is a straightforward prediction of the many prior studies on hindsight bias. Although the negligence studies asked for individual rather than group probabilities (raising the question whether group interaction on an actual jury could dispel hindsight bias), other studies have found hindsight bias in group as well as individual settings.

Hindsight bias will lead juries making negligence determinations to find defendants liable more frequently than if cost-benefit analysis were done correctly—that is, on an ex ante basis. Thus, plaintiffs will win cases they deserve to lose. This prediction is consistent with the frequently expressed (though difficult to verify) view that the tort system imposes too much liability.

A threshold issue raised by the hindsight-bias account of negligence determinations is whether hindsight bias is simply a countervailing weight to a tendency on the part of defendants to underestimate the likelihood of being sanctioned. A common feature of human behavior is over-optimism: People tend to think that bad events are far less likely to happen to them than to others. Thus, most people think that their probability of a bad outcome is far less than others' probability, although of course this cannot be true for more than half the population. If defendants exhibit such over-optimism, then they will be under-deterred by a correct application of the negligence standard; overestimation of the probability of harm based on hindsight bias might then be a desirable countervailing factor. We think that defendant over-optimism is likely to be a much smaller factor for firms than for individual defendants, since firms that make systematic errors in judgment will be at a competitive disadvantage. And for individuals, the role of over-optimism is likely to vary significantly with context. In a case in which the threat of being found liable is highly salient, individuals may tend to overestimate the likelihood of being sanctioned, for reasons discussed in connection with our account of Superfund above. Hindsight bias, in contrast, seems to be an across-the-board phenomenon; it has been observed in a wide range of contexts across many studies and is likely to be present whenever a jury makes a negligence determination.

It is also possible that the occurrence of harm itself provides genuine information about the probability of harm; this fact has led some to consider the possibility of an "ex post negligence" standard, under which negligence is assessed based on the information available ex post, rather than *ex ante*. (However, if prospective defendants cannot easily ascertain (*ex ante*) the information that will be available *ex post*, then an *ex post* approach may be inefficient. But, even apart from situations in which the fact of harm provides new information about the probability of harm, hindsight bias suggests that decision-makers will weigh the fact of harm heavily in assessing its probability.

The findings on hindsight bias provide new empirical support for the old idea that such bias may distort negligence determinations. Despite the vast law and economics literature in the area of torts, no attention seems to have been paid to the potentially significant implications of hindsight bias for achieving optimal deterrence—the goal posited by that literature, and the goal on which we focus here. (Thus, we accept this goal for purposes of our prescriptive analysis; we do not necessarily endorse this goal from a normative perspective.) Law and economics scholars generally approve of the use of the negligence standard for achieving the goal of optimal deterrence; the negligence standard, if applied in an error-free fashion, leads to an efficient level of precaution (although other standards will as well; note that these other standards may be worse or better along other dimensions, such as encouraging victim precautions and inducing optimal activity levels). These scholars have also analyzed reasons that legal rules, including the negligence standard, may be imperfectly applied, but they do not offer any clear prescriptions for addressing this problem, since as they see it, the problem does not have a clear direction; either under-deterrence or over-deterrence relative to correct application of the cost-benefit standard is possible. In contrast, we can offer clear prescriptions because the hindsight bias points in only one direction: over-deterrence (again relative to what correct cost-benefit analysis would produce).

In fact the law in areas such as patent law already takes clear steps to address the problems caused by hindsight bias. * * * But in the area of tort law the existing responses are partial and incomplete at best. Hindsight bias seems to be so deeply ingrained in the tort system that even when it is called to a court's attention, it may be difficult for the court (never mind a juror) to recognize or address it. A colorful example is provided by litigation in which one of the present authors (Thaler) was an expert witness. The litigation involved whether investment decisions involving $100 million in assets had been made in a negligent fashion. Although the court explicitly recognized that "[c]ase law . . . ties [this determination] to the circumstances extant at the time in question, rather than as they may appear in hindsight," the court characterized as "very imaginative" defendant's offer of testimony that "a decision based on information known at the time the decision was made can be evaluated as good or bad without regard to the outcome. In that way the evaluation is not biased by hindsight."[161] Although the judge was very active throughout the trial, he never suggested that the expert testimony offered by the plaintiff, which focused almost exclusively on the fact that the portfolio had lost money (rather than on the reasonableness of the investment decisions at the time they were made), was off-target or irrelevant. While the court ultimately accepted the "imaginative" argument of the defendant and ruled in his favor, its evident surprise at the nature of the argument suggests the pervasiveness of hindsight-based thinking in the tort system.

How might the law respond to hindsight bias in tort cases? An obvious response is the use of jury instructions that inform jurors of the bias and tell them to focus on the *ex ante* situation. Unfortunately, such debiasing techniques appear either to have no effect on decisions or to reduce hindsight bias by only a limited degree, leaving a significant gap between *ex post* and *ex ante* decisionmaking.[162] * * *

---

[161] Johnson v. Johnson, 515 A.2d 255, 266–67 & n.17 (N.J. Super. 1986).

[162] *See, e.g.*, Martin F. Davies, *Reduction of Hindsight Bias by Restoration of Foresight Perspective: Effectiveness of Foresight-Encoding and Hindsight-Retrieval Strategies*, 40 ORG.

CONCLUSION

We do not doubt that replacing the simple maximizing model of economics with a more complicated psychological treatment comes at some cost. Solving optimization problems is usually easier than describing actual behavior. It has been said (we believe by Herbert Simon) that economics makes things hard on agents, but easy on economists; behavioral economics, we suggest, does the opposite. We recapitulate here some of the reasons we think the enriched model is worth the trouble for those interested in the economic analysis of law.

1. Some of the predictions of the standard model are simply wrong. For example, people can be both more spiteful and more cooperative than traditional analysis predicts, and this matters a great deal to law. It is also important to know that even in a world without transaction costs and wealth effects, the assignment of property rights alters the ultimate allocation of those rights, and that this may be particularly true for certain forms of property-rights assignment (such as court orders). These features of the world matter greatly for making predictions and formulating policy.

2. In other cases economics makes no predictions (or incorrect predictions of no effect). Prominent in this category are the effects of presentation; since economic theory assumes that choices are invariant to the manner in which a problem is framed, it falsely predicts that the language of a media account or advertisement has no effect on behavior, holding the information content constant. In contrast, it is well established that people react differently to potential outcomes depending on whether they are perceived as foregone gains or out-of-pocket costs (losses), and that they are likely to think, mistakenly, that salient events are more common than equally prevalent but more subtle ones. These points bear on the supply of and the demand for law, and on the behavior of agents in their interactions with the legal system.

3. Standard economic theories of the content of law are based on an unduly limited range of potential explanations, namely optimal (or second-best) rules set by judges and rent-seeking legislation determined by self-interested log-rolling. Behavioral economics offers other sources of potential explanation—most prominently, perceptions of fairness. We have tried to show that many laws which are seemingly inefficient and do not benefit powerful interest groups may be explained on grounds of judgments about right and wrong.

4. A behavioral approach to law and economics offers a host of novel prescriptions regarding how to make the legal system work better. Some stem from the improved predictions mentioned in point 2 above. Cognitive difficulties and motivational distortions undermine or alter conventional

BEHAV. & HUM. DECISION PROCESSES 40, 61–64 (1987); Baruch Fischhoff, *Perceived Informativeness of Facts*, 3 J. EXPERIMENTAL PSYCHOL. 349, 354–56 (1977); * * *.

economic prescriptions about the jury's role, most notably in the context of assessing negligence and making other determinations of fact or law. We have taken some preliminary steps in suggesting ways to reduce the costs of some of these problems.

5. A behavioral approach to law and economics produces new questions about possible mistakes by private and public actors. On the one hand, it raises serious doubts about the reflexive anti-paternalism of some economic analysis of law. On the other hand, it raises equivalent questions about whether even well-motivated public officials will be able to offer appropriate responses to private mistakes and confusion.

We hope that this article will encourage others to continue the inquiry and research, both theoretical and empirical, that will be needed to flesh out the behavioral approach for which we have argued here. This approach will use traditional economic tools, enhanced by a better understanding of human behavior. Thirty years from now, we hope that there will be no such thing as behavioral economics. Instead we hope that economists and economically oriented lawyers will simply incorporate the useful findings of other social sciences, and in so doing, transform economics into behavioral economics, and economic analysis of law into one of its most important branches.

NOTES AND QUESTIONS

1. *Varieties of economics.* How would you articulate the differences between conventional law and economics on one hand and behavioral law and economics on the other?

2. *Varieties of (ir)rationality and the power of games.* Law and economics theorists have used the tools of neo-classical economics and game theory to model human behavior and to predict the effects of actual (or proposed) legal rules on people's behavior. Games can be used to illustrate Coasean bargains, or to manipulate transaction costs (by for example providing or withholding information from the players or by allowing them to play a game repeatedly and learn its lessons), or to illustrate the value of competition or cooperation as strategies for maximizing utility or wealth. And because many of these games can actually be played out in experimental settings, hypotheses can be tested empirically and refined in ways that most other approaches to law cannot.

For example, in the excerpt above, Professors Jolls, Sunstein, and Thaler show *inter alia* how the Endowment Effect distorts otherwise rational pricing, drawing on the mugs-and-chocolate game. *See also* Leaf Van Boven, George Loewenstein & David Dunning, *Mispredicting the Endowment Effect: Underestimation of Owners' Selling Prices by Buyer's Agents*, 51 J. ECON. BEHAV. & ORG. 351, 351 (2003) (endowment effect described as is "among the most robust phenomena in the emerging field of behavioral economics.") That the Endowment Effect may have its basis in evolutionary biology presumably makes it even more salient to behavioral law and economics and potentially more useful to lawyers constructing settlement offers or trying to renegotiate contracts. Owen D. Jones & Sarah F. Brosnan, *Law, Biology, and Property: A New Theory of the Endowment Effect,* 49 WM. & MARY L. REV. 1935 (2008) (confirming the endowment effect in chimpanzees).

Psychologists, biologists, and economists have identified other "irrationalities" which affect human behavior in predictable and testable ways and which the various approaches to law might be expected to take into account. These phenomena include—among many others—the "bandwagon effect," which induces people to do things simply because other people do them; the "framing effect," which leads people to reach conclusions depending on how data are presented; "over-optimism," a cognitive bias that leads people to underestimate the risks to themselves compared to other people; "availability bias," which is the tendency to accept an illusory correlation or to judge a probability on the basis of how easily examples come to mind (*e.g.*, shark attacks and winning the lottery); "path dependency," the limits imposed by past practices or decisions to constrain current decisions, even if better alternatives are available and past circumstances are irrelevant (*e.g.*, the QWERTY layout in typewriters still being used on computer keyboards); the "cultural cognition of risk," which is the tendency of a human being to perceive risks in ways that are congenial to his or her values; and "confirmation bias," the human tendency to interpret information in ways that confirm that person's preconceptions. It is entirely rational to conclude that human beings are not rational.

Consider how the following famous games illustrate the logic and limits of law and economics in both its conventional and behavioral forms.

(a) *"I cut, you choose:" rational self-interest that maximizes satisfaction.* In the simplest form of this game, two people (usually five-year-old children or their grown-up equivalents) will share a cake. To ensure that neither one feels cheated, they decide to divide the cake by allowing one person to cut the cake and allowing the other person to choose first between the two pieces. Each party can assure that he or she gets at least half of the cake regardless of what the other person does and no matter what their subjective tastes or desires are. In the absence of altruism, generosity, or indifference, the cutter knows that he or she gets second choice and so tries to cut the cake precisely in half, and the final distribution of cake slices will be equitable and envy-free for all concerned. The game can be extended to other scarce resources, desirable and undesirable, including real estate, broadcast frequencies, and chores. The game gets considerably more complicated when there are multiple players (and not just two), or if the resource to be divided is not homogeneous (like a cake that is half chocolate and half vanilla), or if the various players put very different values on the resource (or parts of it), or if at least one of the players is motivated by something other than self-interest (like affection for the other player).

(b) *"The Ultimatum Game:" bounded rationality, the power of fairness, and spite*. In the Ultimatum Game, two players will split a sum of money. One player is designated as the Proposer, who makes an offer as to how the money will be divided, and the other player, designated the Responder, can either accept or reject the offer, but no negotiation is allowed. If the Proposer's offer is accepted, the money is split accordingly, but, if the offer is rejected, then neither player gets anything. The typical economic prediction—based on rational self-interest—is that the Proposer will offer the smallest amount of money to the Responder, who will rationally accept it, because—no matter how small it is—it's better than the nothing that will follow from rejecting the offer. A vast range of empirical research shows something that is inexplicable if the economic model were an accurate predictor of human behavior. It turns out that Proposers routinely offer around 50% of the money and that low (*i.e.*, rational) offers around 20% of the sum are rejected about half the time, suggesting that something statistically significant motivates Proposers to make an "irrationally" generous offer (*see e.g.*, the excerpt from Adam Smith's THEORY OF THE MORAL SENTIMENTS, *supra*) and motivates Responders to refuse financial betterment. What are your predictions about how gender differences and physical attractiveness affect the behavior of the players? *See, e.g.,* Sara J. Solnicka & Maurice E. Schweitzerb, *The Influence of Physical Attractiveness and Gender on Ultimatum Game Decisions*, 79 DECISION PROCESSES 199 (1999).

(c) *"The Prisoner's Dilemma:" rationality under conditions of limited information and limited altruism*. Perhaps the most popular and provocative game in the law and economics literature is the Prisoner's Dilemma. *See generally* WILLIAM POUNDSTONE, PRISONER'S DILEMMA (1992). In its formalized version, the thought experiment is attributed to A.W. Tucker:

> Two men, charged with a joint violation of law, are held separately by the police. Each is told that
>
> (1) if one confesses and the other does not, the former will be given a reward of one unit and the latter will be fined two units,
>
> (2) if both confess, each will be fined one unit.
>
> At the same time each has reason to believe that
>
> (3) if neither confesses both will go clear.[4]

To make this somewhat more concrete, stipulate explicitly that the prisoners—A and B—cannot communicate with one another and will not be able to find out what the other has decided to do until after both have made their decisions. Stipulate further that the prosecutors do not have enough evidence to convict A and B on the principal charge but hope to both sentenced to one year in prison on a lesser charge. Their offer to the prisoners is stark: modifying Tucker's original formulation, assume that, (i) if A and B betray one another,

---

[4] A.W. Tucker, *A Two-Person Dilemma: The Prisoner's Dilemma* (1950), *reprinted in* Philip D. Straffin, Jr., *The Mathematics of Tucker: A Sampler*, 14 TWO-YEAR COLL. MATHEMATICS J. 228 (1983).

both will serve two years in prison; (ii) if A betrays B and B remains silent, A will go free and B will serve three years in prison and *vice versa*; (iii) if A and B both remain silent, each will serve one year on a lesser charge. Portraying the dilemma graphically, it might look like this:

	Prisoner B stays silent ("Cooperates" with A)	Prisoner B betrays A ("Defects" from A)
Prisoner A stays silent ("Cooperates" with B)	A and B serve one year each on the lesser charge	A serves 3 years. B goes free.
Prisoner A betrays B ("Defects" from B)	A goes free. B serves 3 years.	A and B serve 2 years each

With no assurance of loyalty or altruism, no opportunity to communicate with one another, and no chance to run the game more than once to learn from it, it has long been assumed that each prisoner will rationally decide to betray the other: no matter which decision B makes, A is better off singing like the proverbial canary. And in the process of pursuing their rational self-interest, both will be worse off. "What the Prisoner's Dilemma captures so well is the tension between the advantages of selfishness in the short run versus the need to elicit cooperation from the other player in the longer run. The very simplicity of the Prisoner's Dilemma is highly valuable in helping us to discover and appreciate the deep consequences of the fundamental processes in dealing with this tension." ROBERT AXELROD, THE COMPLEXITY OF COOPERATION: AGENT BASED MODELS OF COMPETITION AND COLLABORATION 6 (1997).

In contrast to judges with cases to decide,[5] law professors have used the Prisoner's Dilemma to describe their analyses of the law, especially as a metaphor for collective action problems; indeed, "legal scholars are nearly obsessed with the Prisoners' Dilemma, mentioning the game in a staggering number of law review articles (over three thousand [as of 2009]), while virtually ignoring other equally simple games offering equally sharp insights into legal problems. Richard H. McAdams, *Beyond the Prisoners' Dilemma: Coordination, Game Theory, and Law*, 82 S. CAL. L. REV. 209, 210–11 (2009).

3. *Explaining the ban on certain kinds of markets*. From the economic standpoint of allowing transactions to assure that a resource flows toward those who value it the most, why is it generally illegal to scalp tickets to a popular concert? Why is it illegal to sell your vote in an election? Why is it legal to donate a kidney but generally not to sell one? Why can't a pregnant woman lawfully sell her baby to the highest bidder? Should we consider plea bargaining in criminal cases to occur within a "market?" *See, e.g.*, Frank H. Easterbrook, *Plea Bargaining as Compromise*, 101 YALE L.J. 1969, 1975 (1992). What if anything do banned markets have in common? *See generally* MICHAEL J. SANDEL, WHAT MONEY CAN'T BUY: THE MORAL LIMITS OF MARKETS

---

[5] A Westlaw search in mid-2015 revealed that exactly two courts—one federal and one state—had referred to the Prisoner's Dilemma since 2000.

(2012) ("The most fateful change that unfolded during the past three decades was not an increase in greed. It was the expansion of markets, and of market values, into spheres of life where they don't belong. To contend with this condition, we need to do more than inveigh against greed; we need to rethink the role that markets should play in our society. We need to have a public debate about what it means to keep markets in their place.").

4. *The Hand Formula through the lens of behavioral economics.* How might the reality of "hindsight bias" compromise the simplicity and rationality of the Hand Formula for determining liability for negligence, as laid out in *Carroll Towing*? If Jolls *et al.* are correct that jury instructions alone are not enough to undo hindsight bias and that over-deterrence (*i.e.* over-compensation to plaintiffs) is the result, is the solution simply to *withhold* information from the jury about what actually happened in a negligence case, and force the jury to make the cost-benefit analysis *ex ante*, at the time of the company's decision-making, not *ex post*, after the injury? To make the problem more concrete, consider this hypothetical:

> Suppose that a food-processing company is claimed to have decided in a negligent fashion to use a particular chemical in its production process; imagine that the chemical ended up causing cancer in a small number of residents who live near the company's plant. The company claims that not using the cancer-causing (as it turned out) chemical would have carried significant risks to residents in terms of bacterial contamination. We know that if jurors are told that the chemical was used and ended up causing cancer, they will be likely to overestimate the probability of harm from the chemical and, thus, hold the food-processing company liable even if liability is not in fact justified under an unbiased application of the cost-benefit standard. (Indeed, in this context the effects of hindsight bias may be exacerbated by the fact that the choice made by the defendant is an act of commission, rather than (as would have been the case had the chemical not been used) an act of omission.

Christine Jolls, Cass R. Sunstein, and Richard Thaler, *A Behavioral Approach to Law and Economics*, 50 STAN. L. REV. 1471, 1527 (1998).

As the judge in this hypothetical case against the food-processing company, would you keep the jury ignorant of the injury at the liability phase of the trial, recognizing that it would be relevant at the damage phase only after liability was established? Would you instead offer a jury instruction on hindsight bias? On what rationale might you give the jury all the relevant and admissible evidence about injuries and let the jury decide—in the black box of its deliberations—how to assess the evidence? As an alternative way to counteract hindsight bias, would it make sense to alter the standard of evidence, so that liability would be established—not by a mere preponderance of the evidence (a 51% likelihood)—but by an overwhelming preponderance of the evidence (say, a 75% likelihood)? *Id.* at 1529–1532.

5. *Neuroscience and behavioral economics*. The structure and operation of the human brain has moved from the preserve of doctors and neuroscientists to become a proper concern for lawyers and philosophers of law. *See e.g.*, Owen D. Jones, Joshua W. Buckholtz, Jeffrey D. Schall, & Rene Marquis, *Brain Imaging for Legal Thinkers: A Guide for the Perplexed*, 2009 STAN. TECH. L. REV. 5, ¶ 13. Brain imaging has also been used to expand the conception of what qualifies as rational. "Standard economic models of human decision-making (such as utility theory) have typically minimized or ignored the influence of emotions on people's decision-making behavior, idealizing the decision-maker as a perfectly rational cognitive machine. However, in recent years this assumption has been challenged by behavioral economists, who have identified additional psychological and emotional factors that influence decision-making, and recently researchers have begun using neuroimaging to examine behavior in economic games." Alan G. Sanfey, *et al.*, *The Neural Basis of Economic Decision-Making in the Ultimatum Game*, 300 SCIENCE 1755 (2003).

6. *Distributional equity and the wealth gap*. Does law and economics theory offer grounds for challenging the cause and the fairness of the initial distribution of wealth in a society? From what perspective does that matter? As you reflect on the strengths and weaknesses of the economic approach to law—especially in comparison to other schools of jurisprudence—it may be helpful to appreciate what might be viewed as its minimal claim. *See* DAVID FREIDMAN, LAWS ORDER: WHAT ECONOMICS HAS TO DO WITH THE LAW AND WHY IT MATTERS 8 (2005):

> You live in a state where the most severe criminal punishment is life imprisonment. Someone proposes that since armed robbery is a very serious crime, armed robbers should get a life sentence. A constitutional lawyer asks whether that is consistent with the prohibition on cruel and unusual punishment. A legal philosopher asks whether it is just. An economist points out that if punishment for armed robbery and for armed robbery plus murder are the same, the additional punishment for murder is zero—and asks whether you really want to make it in the interest of robbers to murder their victims.

Does it seem realistic to think either that murderous robbers consult the law before committing their crimes or that they just throw a murder into a robbery because the *law* creates an "interest" in killing somebody?

CHAPTER SIX

POST-REALIST APPROACHES TO LAW AND OBLIGATION (III): CRITICAL LEGAL STUDIES

■ ■ ■

"The conflicting tendencies within law constantly suggest alternative schemes of human association. The focused disputes of legal doctrine repeatedly threaten to escalate into struggles over the basic imaginative structure of social existence."

— Roberto Unger

"Ideals without technique are a mess. But technique without ideals is a menace."

— Karl Llewellyn

Orientation

It is one thing to argue that legal doctrine can be indeterminate or contradictory, as the Legal Realists had concluded. It is quite another to argue that the law is systematically and inevitably incoherent. It is yet another to suggest that there is actually a structure to the incoherence—a *reason* that there are contradictions in the rules of law. The loose school of thought gathered under the rubric of "critical legal studies" (or CLS) holds that the incoherence in doctrine is actually intelligible: there is a structure to the incoherence of so-called settled law. The structure can be observed if we see the law as reflecting the irreconcilable ideological conflicts in our political life. In other words, indeterminacy or incoherence in the law is directly related to (indeed is caused by) indeterminacy in politics and in particular the irreconcilable ideologies that operate in society. In short, the law is incoherent precisely *because* legal doctrines reflect irreconcilably opposed conceptions of the just and the good. In David Kairys' words, "[v]irtually the entire spectrum of ideological conflict which fragments our political life, from far right to far left, is reproduced in the authoritative materials of the law." From this perspective, the "settled law" is a transitory outcome of ideological struggles, and in those struggles opposing normative conceptions get compromised, truncated, and adjusted as they fit themselves into the body of legal doctrine.

Of course, alleging this relationship and proving it are two different things, and part of the difficulty with critical legal theory is that much of it seems witheringly abstract and obscure (perhaps in some cases deliberately so). Drawing on French hermeneutics, deconstruction, cultural theory, story-telling, and wordplay, some CLS scholarship will strike the general reader as virtually impenetrable. But the idea that the rule of law ideal has a political tilt is striking, even revolutionary. It suggests that "fidelity to law" or the "rule of law ideal"—so central to conventional jurisprudence and legal practice—is simply implausible. From this perspective, the Legal Realists had not gone far enough. They may have demonstrated that the law cannot resolve disputes in some neutral and objective way, but they missed the fact that the dominant function of law is to provide a ritualized and false legitimacy for existing social and power relations. The dominant system of values has simply declared itself value-free: powerful, historically-contingent ideas and doctrines have become so entrenched as to be deemed "objective" or "neutral," in the same way that we become so accustomed to the smell of our own house that we wrongly think the house has no smell at all.

With some oversimplification, the central tenets of critical legal theory may be summarized (and should be hunted down in the materials that follow).

(i) Contradictions in the legal doctrine—principles and counter-principles—reflect deeper conflicts in our political ideologies and conceptions of social life. In this chapter, for example, we focus on the critical legal account of contracts law, but that must be understood as the merest representative sample of the CLS argument. Similar "arguments by escalation" can work in tort law, criminal labor law, constitutional law, and virtually every other field in the law school curriculum.

(ii) There is no such thing as legal reasoning as understood in the conventional narrative of law. Note that the critique is not that judges sometimes or aberrationally make mistakes in their legal reasoning, or that they dissemble by hiding their ideological preferences in the language of law and doctrine. The claim is more skeptical than that: it is that there is no such thing as a neutral methodology for reaching a result in any actual case. Any set of principles can logically yield competing or even contradictory results. "There is a distinctly legal and quite elaborate system of discourse and body of knowledge, replete with its own language and conventions of argumentation, logic, and even manners. . . . But in terms of a method or process for decision-making—for determining correct rules, facts, or results—*the law provides only a wide and conflicting variety of stylized rationalizations from which courts pick and choose.*"[1] The result may be mystification and legitimation, but it is not compelled.

(iii) The skepticism of the Legal Realists could be elevated from the level of specific fields of law—like statutory construction or torts—to the level of social theory; indeed, unlike the New Deal reform agenda of the Realists, the major objective of the CLS movement in its heyday was the political one of transforming law and legal education as part of a general attack on social inequality and alienation.

(iv) Despite the radical indeterminacy of doctrine (or perhaps because of it), particular groups, entities, and institutions benefit systematically from legal decisions, and it is the proper job of law students, lawyers, and law professors to expose the subsidy offered by doctrine to these centers of power. One provision of the Statement of Critical Legal Studies Conference, for example, said that its purpose was "to explore the manner in which legal doctrine and legal education and the practices of legal institutions work to buttress and support a pervasive system of oppressive, inegalitarian relations."[2]

(v) Among the most important, historically-contingent, politically-loaded legal constructs is the separation of the public realm from the private realm. In part, the claim is that so-called private law (like tort or contract) serves public functions. But there is also the more systemic critique that the law defines and preserves a realm of privacy in which some of the most dominant power relations in society are allowed to operate without regulation by the state through law. Rape within a marriage can be a legal impossibility for example only if the private realm of the family is effectively exempt from the reach of laws criminalizing nonconsensual sex.

It is a challenge to identify a common political agenda for action among the adherents to CLS. Doubtless they are as impatient with classical liberal, New Deal approaches as they are with any identifiably conservative program, and CLS has been criticized for failing to offer a movement-wide program of positive action. The cogency of that criticism depends on your answer to one basic question: do you expect every other school of jurisprudence to have some coherent political basis, implication, and aspiration?

---

1 David Kairys, *Introduction in* THE POLITICS OF LAW: A PROGRESSIVE CRITIQUE 4 (1990) (emphasis added).

2 PETER FITZPATRICK & ALAN HUNT, *Critical Legal Studies: An Introduction, in* CRITICAL LEGAL STUDIES 1–2 (Peter Fitzpatrick & Alan Hunt eds., 1987).

Critical Legal Studies and Contract Law

COPPAGE V. STATE OF KANSAS

236 U.S. 1 (1915)

MR. JUSTICE PITHEY delivered the opinion of the Court. In a local court in one of the counties of Kansas, [T.B. Coppage] was found guilty and adjudged to pay a fine, with imprisonment as the alternative, upon an information charging him with a violation of an act of the legislature of that state * * * [which] reads as follows:

> * * * Section 1. That it shall be unlawful for any individual or member of any firm, or any agent, officer, or employee of any company or corporation, to coerce, require, demand, or influence any person or persons to enter into any agreement, either written or verbal, not to join or become or remain a member of any labor organization or association, as a condition of such person or persons securing employment, or continuing in the employment of such individual, firm, or corporation.
>
> Section 2. Any individual or member of any firm, or any agent, officer, or employee of any company or corporation violating the provisions of this act, shall be deemed guilty of a misdemeanor, and upon conviction thereof shall be fined in a sum not less than $50, or imprisoned in the county jail not less than thirty days.

The judgment was affirmed by the supreme court of the state, two justices dissenting, and the case is brought here upon the ground that the statute, as construed and applied in this case, is in conflict with that provision of the 14th Amendment of the Constitution of the United States which declares that no state shall deprive any person of liberty or property without due process of law.

* * * Hedges was employed as a switchman by the St. Louis & San Francisco Railway Company, and was a member of a labor organization called the Switchmen's Union of North America. [Coppage] was employed by the railway company as superintendent, and as such he requested Hedges to sign an agreement [requiring Hedges to withdraw from the union while employed by the railroad company], * * * at the same time informing him that if he did not sign it he could not remain in the employ of the company. * * * Hedges refused to sign this, and refused to withdraw from the labor organization. Thereupon [Coppage], as such superintendent, discharged him from the service of the company.

At the outset, a few words should be said respecting the construction of the act. It uses the term "coerce," and some stress is laid upon this in the opinion of the Kansas supreme court. But, on this record, we have nothing to do with any question of actual or implied coercion or duress, such as might overcome the will of the employee by means unlawful without the act. In the case before us, the state court treated the term "coerce" as applying to the mere insistence by the employer, or its agent, upon its right to prescribe terms upon which alone it would consent to a continuance of the relationship of employer and employee. In this sense we must understand the statute to have been construed by the court, for in this sense it was enforced in the present case; there being no finding, nor any evidence to support a finding, that [Coppage] was guilty in any other sense. * * * There is neither finding nor evidence that the contract of employment was other than a general or indefinite hiring, such as is presumed to be terminable at the will of either party. * * * We have to deal, therefore, with a statute that, as construed and applied, makes it a criminal offense, punishable with fine or imprisonment, for an employer or his agent to merely prescribe, as a condition upon which one may secure certain employment or remain in such employment (the employment being terminable at will), that the employee shall enter into an agreement not to become or remain a member of any labor organization while so employed; the employee being subject to no incapacity or disability, but, on the contrary, free to exercise a voluntary choice.

In *Adair v. United States*, 208 U. S. 161 [(1908)], this court had to deal with a question not distinguishable in principle from the one now presented. Congress, in § 10 of an act [ ] entitled, "An Act Concerning Carriers Engaged in Interstate Commerce and Their Employees," had enacted

> that any employer subject to the provisions of this act, and any officer, agent, or receiver of such employer, who shall require any employee, or any person seeking employment, as a condition of such employment, to enter into an agreement, either written or verbal, not to become or remain a member of any labor corporation, association, or organization; or shall threaten any employee with loss of employment, or shall unjustly discriminate against any employee because of his membership in such a labor corporation, association, or organization . . . is hereby declared to be guilty of a misdemeanor, and, upon conviction thereof . . . shall be punished for each offense by a fine of not less than one hundred dollars and not more than one thousand dollars.

Adair was convicted upon an indictment charging that he, as agent of a common carrier subject to the provisions of the act, unjustly discriminated against a certain employee by discharging him from the employ of the carrier because of his membership in a labor organization. The court held that portion of the act upon which the conviction rested to be an invasion of the personal liberty as well as of the right of property guaranteed by the 5th Amendment, which declares that no person shall be deprived of liberty or property without due process of law. Speaking by Mr. Justice Harlan, the court said:

> While, as already suggested, the right of liberty and property guaranteed by the Constitution against deprivation without due process of law is subject to such reasonable restraints as the common good or the general welfare may require, it is not within the functions of government—at least, in the absence of contract between the parties—to compel any person in the course of his business and against his will to accept or retain the personal services of another, or to compel any person, against his will, to perform personal services for another. The right of a person to sell his labor upon such terms as he deems proper is, in its essence, the same as the right of the purchaser of labor to prescribe the conditions upon which he will accept such labor from the person offering to sell it. So the right of the employee to quit the service of the employer, for whatever reason, is the same as the right of the employer, for whatever reason, to dispense with the services of such employee. It was the legal right of the defendant Adair—however unwise such a course might have been—to discharge [the employee] because of his being a member of a labor organization, as it was the legal right of [the employee], if he saw fit to do so—however unwise such a course on his part might have been—to quit the service in which he was engaged, because the defendant employed some persons who were not members of a labor organization. In all such particulars the employer and the employee have equality of right, and any legislation that disturbs that equality is an arbitrary interference with the liberty of contract, which no government can legally justify in a free land.

Unless it is to be overruled, this decision is controlling upon the present controversy; for if Congress is prevented from arbitrary interference with the liberty of contract because of the "due process" provision of the 5th Amendment, it is too clear for argument that the states are prevented from the like interference by virtue of the corresponding clause of the 14th Amendment; and hence, if it be unconstitutional for Congress to deprive an employer of liberty or property for threatening an employee with loss of employment, or discriminating against him because of his membership in a labor organization, it is unconstitutional for a state to similarly punish an employer for requiring his employee, as a condition of securing or retaining employment, to agree not to become or remain a member of such an organization while so employed.

* * * The constitutional right of the employer to discharge an employee because of his membership in a labor union being granted, can the employer be compelled to resort to this extreme measure? May he not offer to the employee an option, such as was offered in the instant case, to

remain in the employment if he will retire from the union; to sever the former relationship only if he prefers the latter? Granted the equal freedom of both parties to the contract of employment, has not each party the right to stipulate upon what terms only he will consent to the inception, or to the continuance, of that relationship? And may he not insist upon an express agreement, instead of leaving the terms of the employment to be implied? Can the legislature in effect require either party at the beginning to act covertly; concealing essential terms of the employment-terms to which, perhaps, the other would not willingly consent-and revealing them only when it is proposed to insist upon them as a ground for terminating the relationship? Supposing an employer is unwilling to have in his employ one holding membership in a labor union, and has reason to suppose that the man may prefer membership in the union to the given employment without it-we ask, can the legislature oblige the employer in such case to refrain from dealing frankly at the outset? And is not the employer entitled to insist upon equal frankness in return? Approaching the matter from a somewhat different standpoint, is the employee's right to be free to join a labor union any more sacred, or more securely founded upon the Constitution, than his right to work for whom he will, or to be idle if he will? And does not the ordinary contract of employment include an insistence by the employer that the employee shall agree, as a condition of the employment, that he will not be idle and will not work for whom he pleases, but will serve his present employer, and him only, so long as the relation between them shall continue? Can the right of making contracts be enjoyed at all, except by parties coming together in an agreement that requires each party to forego, during the time and for the purpose covered by the agreement, any inconsistent exercise of his constitutional rights?

These queries answer themselves. The answers, as we think, lead to a single conclusion: Under constitutional freedom of contract, whatever either party has the right to treat as sufficient ground for terminating the employment, where there is no stipulation on the subject, he has the right to provide against by insisting that a stipulation respecting it shall be a *sine qua non* of the inception of the employment, or of its continuance if it be terminable at will. It follows that this case cannot be distinguished from *Adair v. United States*.

The decision in that case was reached as the result of elaborate argument and full consideration. The opinion states: "This question is admittedly one of importance, and has been examined with care and deliberation. And the court has reached a conclusion which, in its judgment, is consistent with both the words and spirit of the Constitution, and is sustained as well by sound reason." We are now asked, in effect, to overrule it; and in view of the importance of the issue we have reexamined the question from the standpoint of both reason and authority. As a result, we are constrained to reaffirm the doctrine there applied. Neither the doctrine nor this application of it is novel; we will endeavor to restate some of the grounds upon which it rests. The principle is fundamental and vital. Included in the right of personal liberty and the right of private property—partaking of the nature of each—is the right to make contracts for the acquisition of property. Chief among such contracts is that of personal employment, by which labor and other services are exchanged for money or other forms of property. If this right be struck down or arbitrarily interfered with, there is a substantial impairment of liberty in the long-established constitutional sense. The right is as essential to the laborer as to the capitalist, to the poor as to the rich; for the vast majority of persons have no other honest way to begin to acquire property, save by working for money.

An interference with this liberty so serious as that now under consideration, and so disturbing of equality of right, must be deemed to be arbitrary, unless it be supportable as a reasonable exercise of the police power of the state. But, notwithstanding the strong general presumption in favor of the validity of state laws, we do not think the statute in question, as construed and applied in this case, can be sustained as a legitimate exercise of that power. To avoid possible misunderstanding, we should here emphasize, what has been said before, that so far as its title or enacting clause expresses a purpose to deal with coercion, compulsion, duress, or other undue influence, we have no present concern with it, because nothing of that sort is involved in this case. * * * We do not mean to say, therefore, that a state may not properly exert its police power to prevent coercion on the part of employers towards employees, or *vice versa*. But, in this case, the Kansas court of last resort has held that Coppage, the plaintiff in error, is a criminal, punishable with fine or imprisonment under this statute, simply and merely because, while acting as the representative of the railroad company, and dealing with Hedges, an employee at will and a man of full age and understanding, subject to no restraint or disability, Coppage insisted that Hedges should freely choose whether he would leave the employ of the company or would agree to refrain from association with the union while so employed. This construction is, for all purposes of our jurisdiction, conclusive evidence that the state of Kansas intends by this legislation to punish conduct such as that of Coppage, although entirely devoid of any element of coercion, compulsion, duress, or undue influence, just as certainly as it intends to punish coercion and the like. But, when a party appeals to this court for the protection of rights secured to him by the Federal Constitution, the decision is not to depend upon the form of the state law, nor even upon its declared purpose, but rather upon its operation and effect as applied and enforced by the state; and upon these matters this court cannot, in the proper performance of its duty, yield its judgment to that of the state court. * * *

Laying aside, therefore, as immaterial for present purposes, so much of the statute as indicates a purpose to repress coercive practices, what possible relation has the residue of the act to the public health, safety, morals, or general welfare? None is suggested, and we are unable to conceive of any. The act, as the construction given to it by the state court shows, is intended to deprive employers of a part of their liberty of contract, to the corresponding advantage of the employed and the upbuilding of the labor organizations. But no attempt is made, or could reasonably be made, to sustain the purpose to strengthen these voluntary organizations, any more than other voluntary associations of persons, as a legitimate object for the exercise of the police power. They are not public institutions, charged by law with public or governmental duties, such as would render the maintenance of their membership a matter of direct concern to the general welfare. If they were, a different question would be presented.

As to the interest of the employed, it is said by the Kansas supreme court to be a matter of common knowledge that "employees, as a rule, are not financially able to be as independent in making contracts for the sale of their labor as are employers in making a contract of purchase thereof." No doubt, wherever the right of private property exists, there must and will be inequalities of fortune; and thus it naturally happens that parties negotiating about a contract are not equally unhampered by circumstances. This applies to all contracts, and not merely to that between employer and employee. Indeed, a little reflection will show that wherever the right of private property and the right of free contract coexist, each party when contracting is inevitably more or less influenced by the question whether he has much property, or little, or none; for the contract is made to the very end that each may gain something that he needs or desires more urgently than that which he proposes to give in exchange. And, since it is self-evident that, unless all things are held in common, some persons must have more property than others, it is from the nature of things impossible to uphold freedom of contract and the right of private property without at the same time recognizing as legitimate those inequalities of fortune that are the necessary result of the exercise of those rights. But the 14th Amendment, in declaring that a state shall not "deprive any person of life, liberty, or property without due process of law," gives to each of these an equal sanction; it recognizes "liberty" and "property" as coexistent human rights, and debars the states from any unwarranted interference with either. * * *

[A]n interference with the normal exercise of personal liberty and property rights is the primary object of the statute, and not an incident to the advancement of the general welfare. But, in our opinion, the 14th Amendment debars the states from striking down personal liberty or property rights, or materially restricting their normal exercise, excepting so far as may be incidentally necessary for the accomplishment of some other and paramount object, and one that concerns the public welfare. The mere restriction of liberty or of property rights cannot of itself be denominated "public welfare," and treated as a legitimate object of the police power; for such restriction is the very thing that is inhibited by the Amendment. * * *

Of course we do not intend to say, nor to intimate, anything inconsistent with the right of individuals to join labor unions, nor do we question the legitimacy of such organizations so long as they conform to the laws of the land as others are required to do. Conceding the full right of the individual to join the union, he has no inherent right to do this and still remain in the employ of one who is unwilling to employ a union man, any more than the same individual has a right to join the union without the consent of that organization. * * *

To ask a man to agree, in advance, to refrain from affiliation with the union while retaining a certain position of employment, is not to ask him to give up any part of his constitutional freedom. He is free to decline the employment on those terms, just as the employer may decline to offer employment on any other; for "it takes two to make a bargain." Having accepted employment on those terms, the man is still free to join the union when the period of employment expires; or, if employed at will, then at any time upon simply quitting the employment. And, if bound by his own agreement to refrain from joining during a stated period of employment, he is in no different situation from that which is necessarily incident to term contracts in general. For constitutional freedom of contract does not mean that a party is to be as free after making a contract as before; he is not free to break it without accountability. Freedom of contract, from the very nature of the thing, can be enjoyed only by being exercised; and each particular exercise of it involves making an engagement which, if fulfilled, prevents for the time any inconsistent course of conduct. * * *

Upon both principle and authority, therefore, we are constrained to hold that the Kansas act of March 13, 1903, as construed and applied so as to punish with fine or imprisonment an employer or his agent for merely prescribing, as a condition upon which one may secure employment under or remain in the service of such employer, that the employee shall enter into an agreement not to become or remain a member of any labor organization while so employed, is repugnant to the "due process" clause of the 14th Amendment, and therefore void. * * *

MR. JUSTICE HOLMES, dissenting. I think the judgment should be affirmed. In present conditions a workman not unnaturally may believe that only by belonging to a union can he secure a contract that shall be fair to him. If that belief, whether right or wrong, may be held by a reasonable man, it seems to me that it may be enforced by law in order to establish the equality of position between the parties in which liberty of contract begins. Whether in the long run it is wise for the workingmen to enact legislation of this sort is not my concern, but I am strongly of opinion that there is nothing in the Constitution of the United States to prevent it, and that *Adair v. United States*, and *Lochner v. New York*, 198 U. S. 45 [(1905)], should be overruled. I have stated my grounds in those cases and think it unnecessary to add others that I think exist. * * *

HOFFMAN V. RED OWL STORES, INC.

26 Wis.2d 683, 133 N.W.2d 267 (1965)

The complaint alleged that Lukowitz, as agent for Red Owl, represented to and agreed with plaintiffs that Red Owl would build a store building in Chilton and stock it with merchandise for Hoffman to operate in return for which plaintiffs were to put up and invest a total sum of $18,000; that in reliance upon the above mentioned agreement and representations plaintiffs sold their bakery building and business and their grocery store and business; also in reliance on the agreement and representations Hoffman purchased the building site in Chilton and rented a residence for himself and his family in Chilton; plaintiffs' actions in reliance on the representations and agreement disrupted their personal and business life; plaintiffs lost substantial amounts of income and expended large sums of money as expenses. Plaintiffs demanded recovery of damages for the breach of defendants' representations and agreements. * * * [After trial, a jury returned a verdict, awarding substantial damages to the Hoffmans, even though there was no final agreement between the parties on the details of the proposal.]

CURRIE, CHIEF JUSTICE. The instant appeal and cross-appeal present these questions: (1) Whether this court should recognize causes of action grounded on promissory estoppel as exemplified by sec. 90 of Restatement (First) of Contracts [(hereinafter "Restatement)]? [and] (2) Do the facts in this case make out a cause of action for promissory estoppel? * * *

Recognition of a Cause of Action Grounded on Promissory Estoppel

Sec. 90 of [the] Restatement provides:

> A promise which the promisor should reasonably expect to induce action or forbearance of a definite and substantial character on the part of the promisee and which does induce such action of forbearance is binding if injustice can be avoided only by enforcement of the promise.

The Wisconsin Annotations to [the] Restatement * * * stated:

> The Wisconsin cases do not seem to be in accord with this section of the Restatement. It is certain that no such proposition has ever been announced by the Wisconsin court and it is at least doubtful if it would be approved by the court.

Since 1933, the closest approach this court has made to adopting the rule of the Restatement occurred in the recent case of *Lazarus v. American Motors Corp.*, (1963), 21 Wis.2d 76, 85, wherein the court stated:

> We recognize that upon different facts it would be possible for a seller of steel to have altered his position so as to effectuate the equitable considerations inherent in sec. 90 of the Restatement.

While it was not necessary to the disposition of the *Lazarus* Case to adopt the promissory estoppel rule of the Restatement, we are squarely faced in the instant case with that issue. Not only did the trial court frame the special verdict on the theory of sec. 90 of [the] Restatement, but no other possible theory has been presented to or discovered by this court which would permit plaintiffs to recover. Of other remedies considered that of an action for fraud and deceit seemed to be the most comparable. An action at law for fraud, however, cannot be predicated on unfulfilled promises unless the promisor possessed the present intent not to perform. Here, there is no evidence that would support a finding that Lukowitz [a Red Owl employee] made any of the promises upon which plaintiffs' complaint is predicated, in bad faith with any present intent that they would not be fulfilled by Red Owl.

Many courts of other jurisdictions have seen fit over the years to adopt the principle of promissory estoppel, and the tendency in that direction continues. As Mr. Justice McFaddin, speaking in behalf of the Arkansas court, well stated, that the development of the law of promissory estoppel "is an attempt by the courts to keep remedies abreast of increased moral consciousness of honesty and fair representations in all business dealings." *Peoples National Bank of Little Rock v. Linebarger Construction Company* (1951), 219 Ark. 11. * * *

Because we deem the doctrine of promissory estoppel, as stated in sec. 90 of Restatement, 1 Contracts, is one which supplies a needed tool which courts may employ in a proper case to prevent injustice, we endorse and adopt it.

Applicability of Doctrine to Facts of this Case

The record here discloses a number of promises and assurances given to Hoffman by Lukowitz in behalf of Red Owl upon which plaintiffs relied and acted upon to their detriment.

Foremost were the promises that for the sum of $18,000 Red Owl would establish Hoffman in a store. After Hoffman had sold his grocery store and paid the $1,000 on the Chilton lot, the $18,000 figure was changed to $24,100. Then in November, 1961, Hoffman was assured that if the $24,100 figure were increased by $2,000 the deal would go through. Hoffman was induced to sell his grocery store fixtures and inventory in June, 1961, on the promise that he would be in his new store by fall. In November, plaintiffs sold their bakery building on the urging of defendants and on the assurance that this was the last step necessary to have the deal with Red Owl go through.

We determine that there was ample evidence to sustain the answers of the jury to the questions of the verdict with respect to the promissory representations made by Red Owl, Hoffman's reliance thereon in the exercise of ordinary care, and his fulfillment of the conditions required of him by the terms of the negotiations had with Red Owl.

There remains for consideration the question of law raised by defendants that agreement was never reached on essential factors necessary to establish a contract between Hoffman and Red Owl. Among these were the size, cost, design, and layout of the store building; and the terms of the lease with respect to rent, maintenance, renewal, and purchase options. This poses the question of whether the promise necessary to sustain a cause of action for promissory estoppel must embrace all essential details of a proposed transaction between promisor and promisee so as to be the equivalent of an offer that would result in a binding contract between the parties if the promisee were to accept the same.

Originally the doctrine of promissory estoppel was invoked as a substitute for consideration rendering a gratuitous promise enforceable as a contract. In other words, the acts of reliance by the promisee to his detriment provided a substitute for consideration. If promissory estoppel were to be limited to only those situations where the promise giving rise to the cause of action must be so definite with respect to all details that a contract would result were the promise supported by consideration, then the defendants' instant promises to Hoffman would not meet this test. However, sec. 90 of [the] Restatement does not impose the requirement that the promise giving rise to the cause of action must be so comprehensive in scope as to meet the requirements of an offer that would ripen into a contract if accepted by the promisee. Rather the conditions imposed are:

(1) Was the promise one which the promisor should reasonably expect to induce action or forbearance of a definite and substantial character on the part of the promisee?

(2) Did the promise induce such action or forbearance?

(3) Can injustice be avoided only by enforcement of the promise?

We deem it would be a mistake to regard an action grounded on promissory estoppel as the equivalent of a breach of contract action. * * * [I]t is desirable that fluidity in the application of the concept be maintained. While the first two of the above listed three requirements of promissory estoppel present issues of fact which ordinarily will be resolved by a jury, the third requirement, that the remedy can only be invoked where necessary to avoid injustice, is one that involves a policy decision by the court. Such a policy decision necessarily embraces an element of discretion.

We conclude that injustice would result here if plaintiffs were not granted some relief because of the failure of defendants to keep their promises which induced plaintiffs to act to their detriment. * * *

NOTES AND QUESTIONS

1. *Change and continuity*. The result in *Coppage* was overturned by the Supreme Court in *Phelps Dodge Corp. v. N.L.R.B.*, 313 U.S. 177 (1941), and there is today a statutory regime protecting membership in unions. But the freedom of contract principle—invoked so rigorously in *Coppage*—remains unchanged and fundamental. From a critical perspective, how might the freedom of contract principle work systematically to the detriment of the powerless? What assumptions did the Supreme Court make about the relative power of the company and Hedges in that case?

2. *Principles and counter-principles*. What is the holding in *Hoffman v. Red Owl Stores*? Is it possible to extrapolate from that holding a profoundly different view or conception of contracts from that expressed in *Coppage*? Another way to phrase the question would be: "is there any principle in *Red Owl* that an advocate might have used to support the opposite result in *Coppage*?"

JAY M. FEINMAN & PETER GABEL, *CONTRACT LAW AS IDEOLOGY*

THE POLITICS OF LAW: A PROGRESSIVE CRITIQUE 373–386
(David Kairys, ed., rev. ed. 1990)

In 1915 the United States Supreme Court struck down a Kansas statute that prevented employers from requiring their employees to quit or refrain from joining unions because the statute interfered with the "freedom of contract" protected by the Fourteenth Amendment to the Constitution. In *Coppage v. Kansas* the Court said:

> The principle is fundamental and vital. Included in the right of personal liberty and the right of private property—partaking of the nature of each—is the right to make contracts. . . . The right is as essential to the laborer as to the capitalist, to the poor as to the rich . . .

The right of freedom of contract expressed in this opinion conveys a sense of personal autonomy, projecting a free market in which laborer and capitalist, rich and poor can freely transact to get what they want, unfettered by the needs of others or the dictates of government. At the same time, the image also conveys a sense of social solidarity, suggesting that the market is an arena of mutual respect in which people can hammer out their collective destiny through firm handshakes enforceable in a court of law.

The view of contract in *Coppage v. Kansas* is now generally regarded as incomplete. Under modern contract law, "society may restrict the individual's freedom to contract. . . . At the very least, the state may strive to ensure that [people making contracts] do in fact bargain in acceptable ways and are not so powerful as to substitute coercion for bargain."[3] The principle of personal autonomy underlying freedom of contract has been supplemented by modern principles of cooperation and fairness to ameliorate the harshest aspects of market exchanges. The modern image of contract conveys a new sense of autonomy and solidarity, in which people are both free to act and protected from the most harmful consequences of their actions and the actions of others. * * *

Traditional freedom of contract and modern contract law [ ] express elements of people's authentic yearning for personal autonomy and social solidarity. However, the images also mask the extent to which the social order makes it difficult to achieve true autonomy and solidarity. The truth is that we live within social and economic hierarchies that often leave us feeling powerless, alienated from one another, and locked into the routines of everyday activities so that it is difficult to achieve increased personal power and freedom and genuine social connection and equality. And the truth also is that this impoverishment of our human possibilities can be overcome not by the implementation of an abstract legal principle or a political slogan but only by our own sustained efforts to transform these hierarchies, to take control over the whole of our lives, and to shape them toward the satisfaction of our real human needs. This sort of concrete, practical movement would embody the realization of the utopian content of images like these. However, the law denies the oppressive nature of the existing hierarchies, suggests instead that inequality, powerlessness, and alienation are consequences of what people have chosen through their own actions, and therefore retards the achievement of the utopian ideals.

The law is one of many vehicles for the development and transmission of ideological imagery. In order to understand the historical and present nature of the legal system, and of contract law as a part of this system, one must grasp the relationship between the utopian images transmitted through legal ideas and the socioeconomic context with which the images have been associated. This essay provides a brief introduction to a method for understanding this ideological power of law by tracing the history of contract law over the last two hundred years.

Contract Law in the Eighteenth Century

Eighteenth-century contract law would be barely recognizable to the modern lawyer. The core of eighteenth-century contract law was not the

---

[3] E. ALLAN FARNSWORTH, CONTRACTS 23 (Boston: Little, Brown, 1982).

enforcement of private agreements but the implementation of customary practices and traditional norms. Indeed, in his Commentaries on the Law of England, written in the 1760s, Sir William Blackstone did not consider contracts to be a separate body of law at all.

In part, contracts was that portion of the law of property concerning the transfer of title to specific things from one person to another—the process by which "my horse" became "your horse." Because of this present-oriented title theory, legal enforcement of an executory agreement (an agreement under which the parties promised to render their performances at some time in the future) was not generally available. Contract law also concerned customary obligations between people related to status, occupation, or social responsibilities. For example, a patient was "contractually" obligated by custom to pay for a physician's services whether or not he actually had promised to pay prior to the rendering of the services. In all types of contracts cases, the substantive fairness of the agreement or relation was subject to scrutiny by a lay jury applying community standards of justice. If a physician sued for his fee or a seller of goods for her price, the jury could decide that even an amount agreed to by the parties was excessive and inequitable, and so award a smaller sum instead.

Thus, eighteenth-century contract law did not encourage commercial exchange. The traditional image of the world presented by contract law regarded the enforcement of market transactions as often illegitimate, so a seller could never be guaranteed the price he or she had bargained for, and liability might be imposed in the absence of agreement when required by popular notions of fairness. Such a system could exist because the development of a system of production founded upon universal competition in national and world markets had not yet fully emerged, and the political worldview that justified the relatively static property relations of traditional, precapitalist society had not yet been entirely overturned.

Between the latter part of the eighteenth century and the middle of the nineteenth century, the economic and political relations that had been associated with eighteenth-century contract law were burst asunder. In this period the system of economic and social relations known as free-market capitalism achieved a full development begun several centuries earlier, and the political climate was explosively transformed in the service of those social and economic developments with the aid of violent revolutions in America and Western Europe. These changes dramatically transformed the life situations of people in Western society and brought about an equally dramatic transformation in contract law.

Contract Law in the Nineteenth Century

In the nineteenth century, the key changes in society were its split into capital-owning and non-owning classes, and the dissolution of traditional patterns of social relations. As to the first, the social and economic positions of those who owned capital in the form of land, money, and machinery, and those who, having been thrown off the land or out of their traditional crafts, owned only their minds and bodies, increasingly diverged. Business owners were driven irrespective of their personal will or greed to compete with one another for markets for their products and to extract, with the assistance of a developing mechanical technology, the greatest possible production from their workers at the lowest possible cost. Workers were forced to sell their labor power to owners for a wage in order to survive and thereby to subject much of their daily lives to the owners' control; at the same time, competition among them often drove wages down to bare survival levels.

The second great change in society was the dissolution of many of the traditional bonds among people that had characterized the social relations of earlier periods. The social meaning of work, property, and community were increasingly fragmented as socioeconomic processes that were characterized by competition and individual self-interest reorganized the social universe. Traditional social environments had hardly been idyllic and certainly embodied forms of alienation and class domination that ought not to be idealized. But the rise of capitalism—with its universal market in which people and things were everywhere made subject to the exigencies of money exchange—and the transformation of traditional society—a profound disruption of people's everyday experience in their homes, work, and social life—generated a dramatic and dislocating social upheaval. Within a short stretch of historical time, people experienced and were forced to adapt to the appearance of the factory and the slum, the rise of the industrial city, and a violent rupture of group life and feeling that crushed traditional forms of moral and community identity. While part of this transformation was an attempt to overturn the repressive aspects of a traditional, hierarchical society, it also created that blend of aggression, paranoia, and profound emotional isolation and anguish that is known romantically as the rugged individual.

How could people have been persuaded or forced to accept such massive disruptions in their lives? One vehicle of persuasion was the law of contracts, which generated a new ideological imagery that sought to give legitimacy to the new order. Contract law was one of many such forms of imagery in law, politics, religion, and other representations of social experience that concealed and denied the oppressive and alienating aspects of the new social and economic relations. Contract law denied the nature of the system by creating an imagery that made the oppression and alienation appear to be the consequences of what the people themselves desired.

Denial and legitimation were accomplished by representing reality in ideal terms, as if things were the way they were because the people wished them to be so. This representation was not the product of conspiratorial manipulation by power-mad lawyers and judges. Instead, the legal elites tended to identify with the structure of the social and economic order because of what they perceived to be their privileged position within it, and they expressed the legitimacy of that structure when arguing and deciding cases in their professional roles. During this period important members of the bench and bar associated themselves emotionally and intellectually with the new socioeconomic order and expressed in their professional activities the essential nature of the new system. In arguing and deciding cases, they fit the situation presented within that system to resolve the conflict represented by the dispute at issue. Those resolutions tended to legitimate the basic social relations, no matter how unjust, oppressive, and alienating they actually were. In the process of resolving many cases, legal concepts were built up that embodied the new social relations. The result was a system of contract law that appeared to shape economic affairs according to normative principles but that was, in fact, only a recast form of the underlying socioeconomic relations.

"Freedom of contract," later expressed in *Coppage v. Kansas*, was the legitimating image of classical contract law in the nineteenth century. It projected an ideal of free competition as the consequence of wholly voluntary interactions among many private persons, all of whom were in their nature free and equal to one another. From one point of view this was simple truth, for the practical meaning of the market system was that people conceived of as interchangeable productive units ("equality") had unfettered mobility ("freedom") in the market. From an ideological point of view, this ideal expressed the sense of personal freedom involved in the destruction of the traditional social order with its status relations and hierarchies, but it also constituted denial and apology. It did not take account of the practical limitations on market freedom and equality arising from class position or unequal distribution of wealth. It also ignored other meanings of freedom and equality having to do with the realization of human spirit and potential through work and community. The legitimation of the free market was achieved by seizing upon a narrow economic notion of freedom and equality, and fusing it in the public mind with the genuine meaning.

The legal consequences of this legitimating mystification were the separation of contract law from the law of property and the law of nonconsensual relations, the representation of all social relations as deriving from the free and voluntary association of individuals without coercion by the state, and the allocation of responsibility for the coercion worked by operation of the market to personal merit or luck. In an economy founded upon the accumulation of capital through exchange transactions occurring in a competitive market, the proper role of the state was conceived to be that of the relatively passive enforcer of the "free will" of the parties themselves, of their "freedom of contract." As a result, the nineteenth-century law of contracts consisted of a series of forms ostensibly designed solely to realize the will of free and equal parties, as that will was objectively manifested in agreements.

Some leading contracts cases taught to first-year law students illustrate the power and effects of this mystification. The rules for contract formation and performance were extensions of the principle of objectively manifested free will. A son and his wife worked for his father on the father's farm for some twenty-five years without pay, in the expectation that the father would will the farm to him on his death. When the father died without a will, the farm was divided among all his heirs. Could the son, like the eighteenth-century physician, recover in contract, if not for the farm, at least for the value of his services? No, because there was no clear expression of an agreement between father and son, without which the court would be invading the freedom of the parties if it imposed liability. On the other hand, where the parties had made a definite agreement, it bound them absolutely. Thus, a builder contracted to build a schoolhouse; the partly finished building was blown down by a windstorm; and after being rebuilt, it collapsed again due to soil conditions that could not be remedied. Was the builder liable for failure to build a third time? Indeed he was, for "where a party, by his own contract, creates a duty or charge upon himself, he is bound to make it good if he may, notwithstanding any accident by inevitable necessity."[9]

The most important and in some ways the most peculiar rules of classical contract law concerned the doctrine of "consideration," which grew out of the principles of freedom and equality. Since the market was the measure of all things, only those promises were enforceable that represented market transactions—those for which the person making the promise received something, a "consideration," in return. Thus, a promise to make a gift was not enforceable because it was gratuitous. Further, if a person offered to sell his house to another and agreed to give the other person until Friday to decide whether to buy or not, he could change his mind and revoke the promise because it was, like a gift, a gratuity." Conversely, when a bargain had been struck, it was firm, and the courts would not inquire into the "adequacy of consideration," *i.e.*, the fairness of the bargain. If a person promised to pay a large sum of money in return for a worthless piece of paper, the nineteenth-century court, unlike the eighteenth-century jury, would "protect" the exercise of free will between supposedly equal parties and bind him without weighing the substantive fairness of the transaction."

The results in these cases may seem unfair or irrational today, but to the judges of the time they were neither. The courts could not easily have intervened to protect a party or to remedy unfairness without violating the ideological image that the source of social obligation rests only upon the bargain that the parties themselves have evinced, not upon the

---

9 *School Trustees of Trenton v. Bennett*, 27 New Jersey Law Reports 513 (1859).

community's version of justice. This imagery, drawn as it was from the experience of competitive exchange and the privatization of the social order, served to deny the oppressive character of the market and the lack of real personal liberty experienced by people in their private and work lives. Most important, it served to deny that there was a system at all that was coercively shaping and constricting the social world, because the imagery made it appear that this world was simply the perpetual realization of an infinite number of free choices made by an infinite number of voluntary actors.

Contract Law in the Twentieth Century

Today judges applying contemporary contract law would probably reach different results in these cases. The son might receive a recovery for the value of the services conferred on the father. Liberalized doctrines of excuse for nonperformance might relieve the builder. In many circumstances, a "firm offer," such as the offer to sell the house upon acceptance before Friday, is binding without consideration; in other cases, the court might not enforce the offer but would at least compensate the buyer for expenses incurred in reliance on the offer. And, purportedly, courts today will in extreme cases correct any gross unfairness in a bargain.

Contemporary contract law views these cases differently not because twentieth-century judges are wiser or smarter than their nineteenth-century counterparts, or because a new and more equitable style of legal reasoning has somehow sprung into being through a progressive maturation of the judicial mind. The old rules disintegrated for the same reason they were conceived: there has been a transformation of social and economic life that has brought about a parallel transformation in the ideological imagery required to explain it.

The transformation from the nineteenth-century to the twentieth-century forms of American capitalism was the consequence of a variety of factors that can only be summarized here: competition among businesses produced ever larger concentrations of capital within fewer and fewer companies; workers organized in response to their collective dependence on these emerging monopolies and challenged in a revolutionary way the myths of freedom and equality; exploitation of the Third World, advancing technology, and efficient organization of production facilitated the partial assimilation of the American labor movement, allowing for the payment of higher wages while deflecting more radical labor demands; this increase in the level of wages, the use of part of the economic surplus for unemployment insurance, Social Security, and other types of welfare benefits, and the greater psychological control of consumer purchases through the mass media helped to alleviate the system's persistent tendency toward under-consumption. The basic requirement for understanding contemporary contract law is to look at the socioeconomic system thus produced and to observe its transposition, through the medium of law, into an imaginary construct that accommodates the progressive elements of the attack on classical law while ultimately securing the system's appearance of legitimacy.

The essential characteristic of contemporary capitalism is a shift toward greater integration and coordination in the economy and away from the unbridled competition of the free market. Coordination is accomplished first by very large corporations that are vertically and horizontally integrated (meaning there are relatively few "horizontal" corporations at the top of the major industries that own the capital that controls "vertically" production and distribution in each industry); and second, by a massive involvement of the state in regulating and stabilizing the system. In place of the unrestricted mobility of productive units that characterized the operation of the market in the nineteenth century, we now have integration, coordination, and cooperation to maintain systemic stability through more pervasive and efficient administration.

The rise of the coordinated economy has created a major problem for the law—how to transform the ideology of "freedom and equality" and its adjunct, "freedom of contract," into a new image that might retain the legitimating power of the older images while modifying them to conform more closely to the actual organization of daily life in the modern era. The method of addressing this problem has been to transform contract law into a relatively uniform code for business transactions that is predominantly defined not by the individualist principle of unregulated free competition but by the more collective principle of competition regulated by trade custom. Since most "trades" (whatever nostalgia for a bygone era that term may evoke) are actually integrated production networks subject to supervision by dominant firms, the modern law of contracts is able to retain the legitimating features of private agreement while effectuating the regulatory and stabilizing component that is a central principle of the contemporary economy.

The principle of regulated competition leads to different results in the kinds of cases mentioned earlier. The twentieth-century counterpart to the case of the son who could not recover from his father's estate because of the absence of an express promise is the 1965 Wisconsin case of *Hoffman v. Red Owl Stores*. The Hoffmans were small-town bakers who were induced to sell their bakery and move to a new town in reliance on the promises of an agent of the Red Owl supermarket chain that they would be granted a franchise, which never came. Under classical contract law, the Hoffmans would be without a remedy because the formal franchise contract had never been executed; in the twentieth century, however, the Wisconsin court discarded that restricted notion of agreement and held that they could recover because their reliance on the agent's representation had been commercially reasonable. The strict nineteenth-century requirement of bargain was rejected in favor of a broader standard of social obligation more expressive of the realities of the late-capitalist economy.

Hoffman v. Red Owl is a leading case for the principle that atomistic, concrete agreement is no longer the sole principle of contract law; people's tendency to act in reliance on less formal representations must be protected as well. It also illustrates the doctrine that private economic actors have a duty to act in "good faith." Both principles embody the ethic of cooperation and coordination reflective of the modern economy.

These principles apply in other cases also. The promise to keep open until Friday an offer to sell a house would now frequently be enforced because that is recognized as an appropriate and necessary way to do business today. In rare cases, courts can even be moved to inquire into the fairness of a bargain—into the adequacy of consideration—under the recently developed doctrine of unconscionability. While this doctrine has more theoretical significance than practical effect, sometimes consumers and other parties with little economic power can be protected from the more outrageous excesses of economic predators. In sum, people are conceived to be partners in a moral community where equity and the balancing of interests according to standards of fair dealing have supplanted the primitive era, when every moral tie was dissolved in "the icy waters of egotistical calculation."[17] And the state as passive enforcer of private transactions has become the state as active enforcer of the newly conceived notion of the general welfare.

Conclusion

* * * [T]his three-stage transformation of the economic and legal world [] shows how at each stage in our history the ideological imagery of contract law served to legitimate an oppressive socioeconomic reality by denying its oppressive character and representing it in imaginary terms.

This is a very different explanation of the role of contract law from liberal or leftist instrumental analyses, which suggest that particular rules of law or particular results "helped" capitalists by providing a framework for legal enforcement of market activity. Instrumental analyses of contract law confuse the role of direct force with the role of law in the development of sociohistorical processes. Social processes like "free-market capitalism" do not get "enforced" by "laws." Rather, these processes are accepted through social conditioning, through the collective internalization of practical norms that have their foundation in concrete socioeconomic reality. Since these norms are in part alienating and oppressive, the process of collective conditioning requires the constant threat of force and the occasional use of it. For example, if you fail to perform your part of a bargain, it may be the case that a sheriff with a gun will attach your bank

[17] KARL MARX AND FRIEDRICH ENGELS, THE COMMUNIST MANIFESTO (New York: Washington Square Press, 1964), p. 62.

account to pay the aggrieved party his or her damages. The occasional deployment of direct force serves to maintain the status quo as well as to get people to accept its legitimacy.

"The law" does not enforce anything, however, because the law is nothing but ideas and the images they signify. The law justifies the practical norms and thus contributes to the collective conditioning process. In addition, the law contributes to constituting and reconstituting the norms and the social reality that they represent, as occurred with the transformations among the historical epochs discussed above.

One important way that this justification process occurs is through judicial opinions. Judicial opinions "work" as ideology by a rhetorical process in which oppressive practical norms are encoded as "general rules" with ideological content; these "rules" then serve as the basis for a logic ("legal reasoning") that supposedly determines the outcome of the lawsuit. A key social function of the opinion, however, is not to be found in the outcome and the use of state power which may follow from it, but in the rhetorical structure of the opinion itself, in the legitimation and reconstitution of the practical norm that occurs through the application of it in the form of a "legal rule." That enforcement of bargains was much more likely to occur under nineteenth-century contract law than under eighteenth-century law is, of course, true; but this does not mean that the function of nineteenth-century contract law was to "enforce bargains." The reverse expresses the truth more accurately—that the enforcement of bargains functioned to permit the elaboration of contract law as legitimating ideology.

The central point to understand from this is that contract law today constitutes in large part an elaborate attempt to conceal what is going on in the world. Contemporary capitalism bears no more relation to the imagery of contemporary contract law than did nineteenth-century capitalism to the imagery of classical contract law. Contemporary capitalism is a coercive system of relationships that more or less corresponds to the brief description given here. The proof of this statement inheres in the situations we all face in our daily lives in the functional roles to which we are consigned: lawyer, secretary, student, tenant, welfare recipient, consumer of the products and services of Exxon, Citibank, and Sears. Despite the doctrines of reliance and good faith, large business corporations daily disappoint our expectations as to how they should behave. Despite the doctrine of unconscionability, unfairness is rampant in the marketplace. In this reality our narrow functional roles produce isolation, passivity, unconnectedness, and impotence. Contract law, like the other images constituted by capitalism, is a denial of these painful feelings and an apology for the system that produces them.

Most of the time the socioeconomic system operates without any need for law as such because people at every level have been imbued with its inevitability and necessity. When the system breaks down and conflicts arise, a legal case comes into being. This is the "moment" of legal ideology, the moment at which lawyers and judges in their narrow, functional roles seek to justify the normal functioning of the system by resolving the conflict through an idealized way of thinking about it.

But this also can be the moment for struggle against the narrow limits imposed in law on genuine values such as freedom, equality, moral community, and good faith.

We can see glimpses of that sort of struggle in the transformation from classical to modern contract law. Classical legal thought represented the world in its image of freedom of contract. Because of the socioeconomic transformation and because of their own perception of the falseness and injustice of that image, lawyers developed the modern image of contract, which includes more elements of interdependence, trust, and cooperation than did classical law. However, instead of holding out these ideals as a goal, in its legitimating function contract law presents them as standards of the marketplace that have been achieved.

The critical approach to law exposes the limits imposed on law by the ideological nature of the system and questions whether the legal system helps or hinders the actual realization of authentic values in a meaningful sense in everyday life. For example, consider the doctrine of reliance as the basis of enforcement of a promise exemplified in *Hoffman v. Red Owl*. The current doctrine is artificially constrained by focusing on a discrete promise and a discrete act of reliance, as when the Hoffmans sold their bakery specifically because they had been promised a Red Owl franchise. We might instead recognize that people rely in intangible ways on more diffuse promises and representations; indeed, some of the most important ways people rely on each other is expressed in the continuity of behavior within institutions that are important to their lives. Workers rely on their employers to treat them fairly in everyday events and to consider their interests when making decisions of major importance. Accordingly, contract law might prohibit an employer from firing a worker without good cause even in the absence of a specific contractual provision requiring the employer to do so, and it might even prohibit a company from closing a plant in one area without taking adequate account of the importance of its continued operations to the workers and to the local community.

Recently courts and legislatures have begun to recognize the power of these arguments, but in each of these instances, the power of legal ideology has constrained the recognition. In the plant closing situation, for example, workers at a U.S. Steel plant in Youngstown, Ohio, and their lawyers buttressed their political action and community organizing with legal claims that U.S. Steel was prohibited by contract law and property law from simply closing the plants that were the lifeblood of the community. Although the federal trial and appeals courts recognized the enormity of the situation and the power of the workers' arguments, they failed to provide a remedy because "the mechanism [to do so] . . . is not now in existence in the code of laws of our nation."[21] In fact, it was not the law that restrained the judges, but their own beliefs in the ideology of law. By recognizing the possibilities for social responsibility and solidarity which are immanent in the doctrine of reliance, they could have both provided the workers a remedy and transformed the ideology of contract law.

New developments in contract law such as these would have positive instrumental effects. But consistent with this essay's emphasis on the ideological role of contract law, their greater importance would be in exposing the legitimating function of traditional doctrines and providing a forum for peoples' struggle to achieve freedom, connection, and authenticity. The law's treatment of a worker's rights in his or her job is intimately connected with the economic and social power structures that define what it means to be a worker and an employer. Critically rethinking contract law permits us to expose the limits of the system and to explore the possibility of a different order of things.

Critical Legal Studies and the Public/Private Distinction

HERTZOG V. HERTZOG

29 Pa. 465 (1857)

This suit was brought by John Hertzog to recover from the estate of his father [George Hertzog] compensation for services rendered the latter in his lifetime, and for money lent. The plaintiff was twenty-one years of age about the year 1825, but continued to reside with his father, who was a farmer, and to labour for him on the farm, except one year that he was absent in Virginia, until 1842, when the plaintiff married and took his wife to his father's, where they continued for some time as he had done before. His father then put him on another farm which he owned, and some time afterwards the father and his wife moved into the same house with John, and continued to reside there until his death in 1849.

The testimony of Adam Stamm and Daniel Roderick was relied on to prove a contract or agreement on the part of George Hertzog to pay for the services of plaintiff. Adam Stamm, affirmed: "John laboured for his father; all worked together. The old man got the proceeds. I know the money from the grain went to pay for the farm—the old man said so. John's services worth $12 per month; the wife's worth $1 per week, beside attending to her

---

[21] *Local 1330, United Steel Workers v. United States Steel Corp.*, 631 F.2d 1264, 1266 (6th Cir. 1980). * * *

own family. I heard the old man say he would pay John for the labour he had done."

Daniel Roderick, sworn: "John Hertzog requested him to see his father about paying him for his work, which he had done and was doing, and stated that he had frequently spoken to the old man, his father, about it, and he had still put him off; he agreed to see him, and thinks it was in June, 1849. Coming from Duncan's Furnace, he spoke to the old man about paying John for his work. He said he intended to make John safe. John spoke to me in the spring of 1848; the old man died in August, 1849, I think."

The plaintiff also proved the services rendered by himself and by his wife, and by the declarations of the intestate that he had received from the plaintiff $500, money that belonged to the latter's wife, at the time of purchasing a farm in 1847. The court, after the defendant's points were presented, permitted the plaintiff to add to his declaration a count on a *quantum meruit*[.] * * * [The lower court awarded judgment to the son.]

The opinion of the court was delivered by LOWRIE, J.

> Express contracts are, where the terms of the agreement are openly uttered and avowed at the time of the making: as, to deliver an ox or ten loads of timber, or to pay a stated price for certain goods. Implied are such as reason and justice dictate; and which, therefore, the law presumes that every man undertakes to perform. As, if I employ a person to do any business for me, or perform any work, the law implies that I undertook and contracted to pay him as much as his labour deserves. If I take up wares of a tradesman without any agreement of price, the law concludes that I contracted to pay their real value.

This is the language of Blackstone, 2 COMMENTARIES 443, and it is open to some criticism. There is some looseness of thought in supposing that reason and justice ever dictate any contracts between parties, or impose such upon them. All true contracts grow out of the intentions of the parties to transactions, and are dictated only by their mutual and accordant wills. When this intention is expressed, we call the contract an express one. When it is not expressed, it may be inferred, implied, or presumed, from circumstances as really existing, and then the contract, thus ascertained, is called an implied one. The instances given by Blackstone are an illustration of this.

But it appears in another place, 3 COMMENTARIES 159–166, that Blackstone introduces this thought about reason and justice dictating contracts, in order to embrace, under his definition of an implied contract, another large class of relations, which involve no intention to contract at all, though they may be treated as if they did. Thus, whenever, not our variant notions of reason and justice, but the common sense and common justice of the country, and therefore the common law or statute law, impose upon any one a duty, irrespective of contract, and allow it to be enforced by a contract remedy, he calls this a case of implied contract. * * *

It is quite apparent, therefore, that radically different relations are classified under the same term, and this must often give rise to indistinctness of thought. And this was not at all necessary; for we have another well-authorized technical term exactly adapted to the office of making the true distinction. The latter class are merely constructive contracts, while the former are truly implied ones. In one case the contract is mere fiction, a form imposed in order to adapt the case to a given remedy; in the other it is a fact legitimately inferred. In one, the intention is disregarded; in the other, it is ascertained and enforced. In one, the duty defines the contract; in the other, the contract defines the duty.

We have, therefore, in law three classes of relations called contracts.

1. Constructive contracts, which are fictions of law adapted to enforce legal duties by actions of contract, where no proper contract exists, express or implied.

2. Implied contracts, which arise under circumstances which, according to the ordinary course of dealing and the common understanding of men, show a mutual intention to contract.

3. Express contracts, already sufficiently distinguished.

In the present case there is no pretence of a constructive contract, but only of a proper one, either express or implied. And it is scarcely insisted that the law would imply one in such a case as this; yet we may present the principle of the case the more clearly, by showing why it is not one of implied contract.

The law ordinarily presumes or implies a contract whenever this is necessary to account for other relations found to have existed between the parties.

Thus if a man is found to have done work for another, and there appears no known relation between them that accounts for such service, the law presumes a contract of hiring. But if a man's house takes fire, the law does not presume or imply a contract to pay his neighbours for their services in saving his property. The common principles of human conduct mark self-interest as the motive of action in the one case, and kindness in the other; and therefore, by common custom, compensation is mutually counted on in one case, and in the other not.

On the same principle the law presumes that the exclusive possession of land by a stranger to the title is adverse, unless there be some family or other relation that may account for it. And such a possession by one tenant in common is not presumed adverse to his co-tenants, because it is, *prima facie*, accounted for by the relation. And so of possession of land by a son of the owner. And in *Magaw's Case*, where an heir was in a foreign land at the time of a descent cast upon him, and his younger brother entered, he was presumed to have entered for the benefit of the heir. And one who enters as a tenant of the owner is not presumed to hold adversely even after his term has expired. In all such cases, if there is a relation adequate to account for the possession, the law accounts for it by that relation, unless the contrary be proved. A party who relies upon a contract must prove its existence; and this he does not do by merely proving a set of circumstances that can be accounted for by another relation appearing to exist between the parties. * * *

Every induction, inference, implication, or presumption in reasoning of any kind, is a logical conclusion derived from, and demanded by, certain data or ascertained circumstances. If such circumstances demand the conclusion of a contract to account for them, a contract is proved; if not, not. If we find, as ascertained circumstances, that a stranger has been in the employment of another, we immediately infer a contract of hiring, because the principles of individuality and self-interest, common to human nature, and therefore the customs of society, require this inference.

But if we find a son in the employment of his father, we do not infer a contract of hiring, because the principle of family affection is sufficient to account for the family association, and does not demand the inference of a contract. And besides this, the position of a son in a family is always esteemed better than that of a hired servant, and it is very rare for sons remaining in their father's family even after they arrive at age, to become mere hired servants. If they do not go to work or business on their own account, it is generally because they perceive no sufficient inducement to sever the family bond, and very often because they lack the energy and independence necessary for such a course; and very seldom because their father desires to use them as hired servants. Customarily no charges are made for boarding and clothing and pocket-money on one side, or for work on the other; but all is placed to the account of filial and parental duty and relationship.

Judging from the somewhat discordant testimony in the present case, this son remained in the employment of his father until he was about forty years old; for we take no account of his temporary absence. While living with his father, in 1842, he got married, and brought his wife to live with him in the house of his parents. Afterwards his father placed him on another farm of the father, and very soon followed him there, and they all lived together until the father's death in 1849. The farm was the father's, and it was managed by him and in his name, and the son worked on it under him. No accounts were kept between them, and the presumption is that the son and his family obtained their entire living from the father while they were residing with him.

Does the law, under the circumstances, presume that the parties mutually intended to be bound, as by contract, for the service and compensation of the son and his wife? It is not pretended that it does. But it is insisted that there are other circumstances besides these which, taken together, are evidence of an express contract for compensation in some form, and we are to examine this.

In this court it is insisted that the contract was that the farm should be worked for the joint benefit of the father and son, and that the profits were to be divided; but there is not a shadow of evidence of this. And moreover it is quite apparent that it was wages only that was claimed before the jury for the services of the son and his wife, and all the evidence and the charge point only in that direction. There was no kind of evidence of the annual products.

Have we then any evidence of an express contract of the father to pay his son for his work or that of his wife? We concede that, in a case of this kind, an express contract may be proved by indirect or circumstantial evidence. If the parties kept accounts between them, these might show it. Or it might be sufficient to show that money was periodically paid to the son as wages; or, if there be no creditors to object, that a settlement for wages was had, and a balance agreed upon. But there is nothing of the sort here.

The court told the jury that a contract of hiring might be inferred from the evidence of Stamm and Roderick. Yet these witnesses add nothing to the facts already recited, except that the father told them, shortly before his death, that he intended to pay his son for his work. This is no making of a contract or admission of one; but rather the contrary. It admits that the son deserved some reward from his father, but not that he had a contract for any.

And when the son asked Roderick to see the father about paying him for his work, he did not pretend that there was any contract, but only that he had often spoken to his father about getting pay, and had always been put off. All this makes it very apparent that it was a contract that was wanted, and not at all that one already existed; and the court was in error in saying it might be inferred, from such talk, that there was a contract of any kind between the parties.

The difficulty in trying causes of this kind often arises from juries supposing that, because they have the decision of the cause, therefore they may decide according to general principles of honesty and fairness, without reference to the law of the case. But this is a despotic power, and is lodged with no portion of this government.

Their verdict may, in fact, declare what is honest between the parties, and yet it may be a mere usurpation of power, and thus be an effort to correct one evil by a greater one. Citizens have a right to form connections on their own terms and to be judged accordingly. When parties claim by contract, the contract proved must be the rule by which their rights are to be decided. To judge them by any other rule is to interfere with the liberty of the citizen.

It is claimed that the son lent $500 of his wife's money to his father. The evidence of the fact and of its date is somewhat indistinct. Perhaps it was when the farm was bought. If the money was lent by her or her husband, or both, before the law of 1848 relating to married women, we think he might sue for it without joining his wife.

Judgment reversed and a new trial awarded.

NOTES AND QUESTIONS

1. *The family setting.* Is there a textual basis for concluding that a person who behaved similarly to John Hertzog but who was not related to George Hertzog by blood would actually have won this case?

2. *A critical understanding of Hertzog.* If it is true that the family setting of *Hertzog* is critical to the outcome of the case, what are the law's assumptions about the family? If you were writing on a clean slate, how would you justify such an approach?

3. *Public vs. private.* In what respect do the doctrines and categories of contract law—generally described as "private" law—have public consequences? In what sense are those consequences chosen? And by whom?

CLARE DALTON, *AN ESSAY IN THE DECONSTRUCTION OF CONTRACT DOCTRINE*

94 YALE L.J. 997, 1010–1039 (1985)

I. PUBLIC AND PRIVATE

The opposing ideas of public and private have traditionally dominated discourse about contract doctrine. The underlying notion has been that to the extent contract doctrine is "private," or controlled by the parties, it guarantees individual autonomy or freedom; to the extent it is "public," or controlled by the state, it infringes individual autonomy.

Since at least the mid-nineteenth century, the discourse of contract doctrine has tried to portray contract as essentially private and free.[26] At

---

[26] To borrow from Kessler:

> The freedom of contract dogma is the real hero or villain in the drama . . . but it prefers to remain in the safety of the background if possible, leaving the actual fighting to consideration and to the host of other satellites—all of which is very often confusion to the audience which vaguely senses the unreality of the atmosphere.

all times, nonetheless, traditional doctrine has uneasily recognized a public aspect of contract, viewing certain state interests as legitimate limitations on individual freedom. But this public aspect has traditionally been assigned a strictly supplemental role; indeed, a major concern of contract doctrine has been to suppress "publicness" by a series of doctrinal moves.

The public aspect of contract doctrine is suppressed differently in each area of that doctrine, and in each historical period. The method of suppression is generally either an artificial conflation of public and private, in which the public is represented as private, or an artificial separation of public from private, which distracts attention from the public element of the protected "private" arena by focusing attention on the demarcated (and limited) "public" arena.

The current mainstream treatment of quasi-contracts and implied contracts illustrates doctrine's techniques of separation and conflation. The prevailing position, represented by the Second Restatement, but also by cases and commentary from the 1850's to the present, is that quasi-contracts are not contracts at all, but constitute instead an exceptional imposition of obligation by the state in order to prevent unjust enrichment. An artificially sharp line of demarcation is therefore presented as separating quasi-contracts from implied-in-fact contracts, and public from private. But this position obscures the fact that the finding of contractual implication is guided in the so-called "private" sphere by the same considerations that dictate the imposition of quasi-contract. Any inquiry into a party's intent must confront the problem of knowledge—our ultimate inability to gain access to the subjective intent underlying any particular agreement. The indicia or manifestations of intent, discussed in detail in Part II, serve as substitutes for subjective intent. But in relying on this objective evidence, we move from the realm of the private to that of the public. Calling implied contracts based on party intention "private," and thereby ignoring the extent to which their content is shaped by external norms, conflates public with private.

This same pattern of separation and conflation characterizes the doctrines of duress and unconscionability. Like quasi-contract, they are presented in current doctrine as public supplements to the otherwise private law of contract, supplements necessary for policing the limits of fair bargain. The separation of duress and unconscionability from the main body of contract doctrine diverts attention from the fact that the entire doctrine of consideration reflects societal attitudes about which bargains are worthy of enforcement. But even as the technique of separation marks out duress and unconscionability as public exceptions to private contract doctrine, within duress and unconscionability doctrine public and private are conflated—the public grounds for disapproving bargains recast as

---

Kessler, *Contracts of Adhesion—Some Thoughts About Freedom of Contract*, 43 COLUM. L. REV. 629, 639 (1943).

evidence that there is no private bargain to be enforced. In this arena, the techniques of separation and conflation serve to camouflage critical issues of power—the power of the state to police private agreements, and the power of one private party over another. These issues lie not only at the heart of duress and unconscionability doctrine, but also at the heart of consideration doctrine, as Part III of this Article elaborates.

My analysis of public and private starts with a brief historical overview of the way these themes have been treated in contract doctrine since the nineteenth century. I then examine in greater detail the suppression of the public aspect of contract in doctrine's treatment of quasi-contract, and in the rules governing duress and unconscionability.

A. *A Brief History*

In the earlier part of the nineteenth century, a will theory of contract dominated the commentary and influenced judicial discussion. Contractual obligation was seen to arise from the will of the individual. This conception of contract was compatible with (and early cases appear sympathetic to) an emphasis on subjective intent: Judges were to examine the circumstances of a case to determine whether individuals had voluntarily willed themselves into positions of obligation. In the absence of a "meeting of the minds," there was no contract. This theory paid no particular attention to the potential conflict between a subjective intention and an objective expression of that intention.

The idea that contractual obligation has its *source* in the individual will persisted into the latter part of the nineteenth century, consistent with the pervasive individualism of that time and the general incorporation into law of notions of liberal political theory. Late nineteenth-century theorists like Holmes and Williston, however, began to make clear that the proper *measure* of contractual obligation was the formal expression of the will, the will objectified. Obligation should attach, they reasoned, not according to the subjective intention of the parties, but according to a reasonable interpretation of the parties' language and conduct. Enforcement of obligation could still be viewed as a neutral facilitation of intent, despite this shift, if the parties are imagined as selecting their language and conduct as accurate and appropriate signals of their intent. Thus, even in this objectified form, the will theory of contract was equated with the absence of state regulation: The parties governed themselves; better yet, each party governed himself.

The Realists made it impossible to believe any longer that contract is private in the sense suggested by this caricature. By insisting that the starting point of contract doctrine is the state's decision to intervene in a dispute, the Realists exposed the fiction of state neutrality. As Morris Cohen argued:

> [I]n enforcing contracts, the government does not merely allow two individuals to do what they have found pleasant in their eyes. Enforcement, in fact, puts the machinery of the law in the service of one party against the other. When that is worthwhile and how that should be done are important questions of public policy.

From this vantage point, the objectivist reliance on intent as the source of contractual obligation was a blatant abdication of responsibility, a failure to address and debate the substantive public policy issues involved in decisions about when and how courts should intervene in disputes between contracting parties.

At its most radical, the Realist critique portrays the "publicness" of contract as overshadowing its "privateness." According to Cohen, "[T]he law of contract may be viewed as a subsidiary branch of public law, as a body of rules according to which the sovereign power of the state will be exercised as between the parties to a more or less voluntary transaction." Thinking about contract from this perspective revealed that the state's interest in maintaining a free enterprise system—while policing its excesses—was at work in doctrines such as duress and consideration. Problems of power—the state's power over individuals, and the power of individuals over one another—came into focus.

This basic challenge to the "privateness" of contract, however, was accompanied by a continuing faith in the ability of courts to understand the agreements made by contracting parties. For example, the contract was felt to restrain the terms on which the court, if it chose to intervene, would favor one party over the other. In the hands of the Realists, then, a sensitivity to the problem of power was coupled, by and large, with an apparent lack of sensitivity to the problem of knowledge, and to the way in which power could be subtly exercised through the interpretation and construction of intention.[36]

In the decades since, the Realist challenge to the "privateness" of contract has been assimilated and defused, a process aided by the incomplete nature of the Realist assault. Thus our principal vision of contract law is still one of a neutral facilitator of private volition. We understand that contract law is concerned at the periphery with the imposition of social duties, that quasi-contract governs situations where obligation attaches even in the absence of agreement, that doctrines of duress and fraud deprive the contracting reprobate of benefits unfairly extorted. But we conceive the central arena to be an unproblematic enforcement of obligations voluntarily undertaken. We excise regulated and compulsory contracts from the corpus of contract doctrine altogether,

[36] Jerome Frank is an exception, in that he did consistently focus on the problematic relationship between subjective and objective in the area of contractual interpretation. On occasion, he stresses the vagaries of competing idiosyncratic subjectivities, as for example, in *Zell v. American Seating Co.*, 138 F.2d 641, 647 (2d Cir. 1943), *rev'd*, 322 U.S. 709 (1944) (*per curiam*)[.] * * *

and create special niches for them, as in labor law and utility regulation. Although we concede that the law of contract is the result of public decisions about what agreements to enforce, we insist that the overarching public decision is to respect and enforce private intention.

Thus, for better than a hundred years, contract doctrine and the commentary it has generated have been characterized by a concern with public imposition and private volition. In the remainder of this section, I explore in much more detail how the public-private dichotomy has influenced doctrine in both the area of the implied contract and in that of duress and unconscionability. I begin each story with some history, and end each by suggesting that our modern formulations do nothing more than give a new disguise to age-old problems.

B. The Implied Contract Story: Wrestling with the Problem of Knowledge

The implied-in-law or quasi-contract plays a crucial role in sustaining the notion that contract law is essentially private. The implied-in-law contract is portrayed as essentially non-contractual and public, in contrast to the implied-in-fact contract in which the private is dominant. In this account, the implied-in-fact contract is presented as kin to the express contract, the only difference being that the former is constituted by conduct and circumstance rather than words. An examination of how and when courts choose to impose quasi-contractual obligations, however, reveals the essential similarity between the decision and the supposedly dissimilar decision that a given situation evidences implied-in-fact contractual obligations. Thus, although the distinction between the two types of implied contracts accords with our experience—we intuitively know that being bound by one's word is different from being bound by an externally imposed obligation—the methods of legal argument used for over one hundred years to distinguish the two situations do not and cannot hold.

1. Hertzog—The Constructive Contract

Hertzog v. Hertzog,[38] decided by the Pennsylvania Supreme Court in 1857, is reputedly the first American case to distinguish the quasi-contract from the implied-in-fact contract. The themes and method of analysis present in Hertzog still reverberate in the treatment of implied contract found in the Second Restatement and in modern case law.

In *Hertzog*, an adult son lived and worked with his father until his father's death, at which point the son sued the estate for compensation for services rendered. The trial judge instructed the jury that John Hertzog could recover only if an employment contract existed between father and son. Two witnesses gave testimony that could be interpreted as evidence of such an agreement: One Stamm testified that he "heard the old man say he would pay John for the labour he had done," while one Roderick swore

[38] 29 Pa. 465 (1857). * * *

that the father "said he intended to make John safe." The jury found for John, and the defendant appealed, successfully.

Pennsylvania Supreme Court Justice Lowrie begins the opinion by distinguishing express, implied-in-fact, and implied-in-law contracts. In advancing this categorization, Lowrie particularly criticized Blackstone for failing to distinguish the implied-in-fact from the implied-in-law contract.

Blackstone had suggested that "[i]mplied [contracts] are such as reason and justice dictate; and which, therefore, the law presumes that every man undertakes to perform." Lowrie, true to his advanced understanding of the implications of the will theory of contract, observes, "There is some looseness of thought in supposing that reason and justice ever dictate any contracts between parties, or impose such upon them. All true contracts grow out of the intentions of the parties to transactions, and are dictated only by their mutual and accordant wills." The only "contracts" that reason and justice dictate, according to Lowrie, are "*constructive* contracts" in which the contract is "mere fiction," a form adopted solely to enforce a duty independent of intention. "In one," says Lowrie, "the duty defines the contract; in the other, the contract defines the duty."

Lowrie offers this definition of quasi-contract:

> [W]henever, not our variant notions of reason and justice, but the common sense and common justice of the country, and therefore the common law or statute law, impose upon any one a duty, irrespective of contract, and allow it to be enforced by a contract remedy, [this is] a case of [quasi-] contracts.

For Justice Lowrie, quasi-contract, unlike contract proper, reflects public norms. Public norms, however, require legitimation, and Lowrie offers two types—one positivist, the other dependent on natural law. The norms are "positively" binding because they are part of the body of common law or statute recognized as authoritative. They are "naturally" binding because they reflect "common sense and common justice." While Lowrie distinguishes these public obligations from obligations based on consent, he invokes consent to legitimize public norms: Consent underlies his distinction between "*variant* notions of reason and justice" and "*common* sense and *common* justice."

Lowrie avoids the need to devote more time and attention in *Hertzog* to quasi-contract by stating that "[i]n the present case there is no pretence of a constructive contract, but only of a proper one, either express or implied." The focus of the opinion, then, is on whether John Hertzog can demonstrate the existence of a contract by words spoken or by an account of the relationship and circumstances.

As to the express contract, Lowrie explicitly uses the parties' relationship and their circumstances to "frame" the words spoken in such a way that they become words of "non-contract" instead of contract:

> The court told the jury that a contract of hiring might be inferred from the evidence of Stamm and Roderick. Yet these witnesses add nothing to the facts already recited, except that the father told them, shortly before his death, that he intended to pay his son for his work. This is no making of a contract or admission of one; but rather the contrary. It admits that the son deserved some reward from his father, but not that he had a contract for any.

The father-son relationship clearly influences Lowrie's conclusion. *Hertzog* thus illustrates that words of intention are inconclusive until they are shaped by a judicial reading of the context in which they are uttered. Even the paradigmatically self-sufficient "express" contract, in which "the terms of the agreement are openly uttered and avowed at the time of the making," is invaded by "publicness" in its interpretation and enforcement.

In regard to the implied-in-fact contract, Lowrie says that "[t]he law ordinarily presumes or implies a contract whenever this is necessary to account for other relations found to have existed between the parties." In *Hertzog*, Lowrie's willingness to find an employment contract will therefore turn on whether the parties are related: He assumes that strangers assist one another only on the expectation of reward, whereas precisely the opposite is true of employment between intimates.

Lowrie thus bases his conclusion that no implied contract exists almost entirely upon "the customs of society" and commonly accepted notions about human nature in general and family relationships in particular. But his reliance on such customs and commonalities hopelessly undermines his distinction between contracts implied-in-fact and quasi-contracts. Lowrie's treatment of the absence of a contract proper could just as easily be read as an account of the absence of a quasi-contract. Plainly he has decided that common sense and common justice demand a finding that no contract exists here. The advantage of his contractual analysis is that it permits public considerations to be introduced as if they were private, without the elaborate scrutiny of their source and justification that a quasi-contractual analysis would require.

Lowrie's concluding ruminations about the jury's finding for the son ironically illustrate his obliviousness to the "publicness" of his analysis:

> The difficulty in trying causes of this kind often arises from juries supposing that, because they have the decision of the cause, therefore they may decide according to general principles of honesty and fairness, without reference to the law of the case. But this is a despotic power, and is lodged with no portion of this government.
>
> Their verdict may, in fact, declare what is honest between the parties, and yet it may be a mere usurpation of power, and thus be an effort to correct one evil by a greater one. Citizens have a

> right to form connexions on their own terms and to be judged accordingly. When parties claim by contract, the contract proved must be the rule by which they rights are to be decided. To judge them by any other rule is to interfere with the liberty of the citizen.

This moralizing might be more convincing if the judge had not just exercised, in the guise of fact-finding, the type of state power he now labels "despotic."

In resolving this dispute, then, Lowrie proves incapable of sustaining the distinction between public and private on which he places so much emphasis. He asserts that the intrusion of the state into the relationships of private individuals is generally undesirable. He suggests that in extreme circumstances such intrusion can be justified, provided we impose only those obligations grounded both in community standards and in positive promulgation. In normal circumstances, however, contract law is purely about the intentions of the parties. Disciplined and rational judges, aware of the limitations of their authority, are better equipped to discern these intentions than undisciplined and irrational juries who confuse their sense of what is fair and honest with what the parties had in mind. But when it comes to deciding the case, Lowrie uses standards that were neither explicitly adopted by the parties nor promulgated by the state. In determining that the relationship between the parties was not contractual, he invokes common understandings about the context of the agreement to transform words of agreement into evidence of non-contract. In so doing he avoids the problem of power by appearing to endorse the parties' own choice that their relationship be without legal consequence, and avoids the problem of knowledge by presenting his own normative interpretation of the situation as nothing more than a transparent reading of the parties' intentions.

2. *Since Hertzog—Plus Ca Change . . .*

By the first decades of this century, theorists had begun cautiously to explore the extent to which an objectified will theory required public intrusion on private volition. In 1920, for example, Costigan[61] suggested that quasi-contractual obligations could not be successfully separated from implied-in-fact obligations without recognizing that there were, in addition to "meeting-of-the-minds implied-in-fact contracts," those implied-in-fact contracts that were not based on meetings of minds. Costigan's prime example was the implied warranty, which he described in terms that would also apply to Lowrie's analysis of the absence of contract in *Hertzog*: "Implied warranties are founded upon the implied facts of general . . . experience and understanding—implied because people in general, and not necessarily the particular parties concerned, when acting understandingly

[61] Costigan, *Implied-in-Fact Contracts and Mutual Assent*, 33 HARV. L. REV. 376 (1920).

and fairly, normally agree upon such an assumed factual basis . . .." As the quotation suggests, Costigan explicitly recognizes that the actual intent of the parties is not the basis of the obligation in these cases. At the same time, rather than asserting explicitly the "public" interest in the imposition of such terms, he "privatizes" the imposition of obligation by reference to what other fair-minded people would intend under similar circumstances.

Costigan is left having to explain why his category of "no-meeting-of-the-minds" contracts are still contracts rather than quasi-contracts. To this end, he focuses initially on the remedy attached: Where the court awards a restitutionary measure, the action is quasi-contractual; where an expectation measure is awarded, the action is contractual. Costigan himself, however, later recognizes that this position is indefensible: He acknowledges that "the contractual right justifies the measure of damages, not the measure the right." Ultimately, then, he fails to demonstrate how these cases can be viewed as contractual without the parties' minds having met.

* * * [T]he Realist approach to contract involves a radical shift of emphasis from the private to the public aspects of enforcement. Predictably, then, when the Realist Cohen addresses the question of interpretation, he sees and describes its public face. He pinpoints the way in which judges, in the guise of interpretation, "decide the 'equities,' the rights and obligations of the parties . . . . These legal relations are determined by the courts and the jural system and not by the agreed will of the contesting parties."[68] Cohen also identifies how rules of interpretation serve as state regulation:

> When courts follow the same rules of interpretation in diverse cases, they are in effect enforcing uniformities of conduct. We may thus view the law of contract not only as a branch of public law but also as having a function somewhat parallel to that of the criminal law. Both serve to standardize conduct by penalizing departures from the legal norm.

Cohen laments that while the fictional nature of the will theory is at one level a commonplace, it is at the same time ignored, forgotten, or otherwise resisted—in part, because of the force of the traditional language. And indeed, the Realists did generally fail to explore the implications of the will theory's fictional basis. They tended to be much more concerned with problems of coercion and of relief from the bad bargain. The Realist focus was the public-private split as it implicates the problem of power, not the public-private split as it implicates the problem of knowledge. Since the line of inquiry initiated by those such as Costigan has been given only scant attention in the following decades, Cohen's criticism could be levelled with equal force today.

---

[68] Cohen[, *The Basis of Contract*, 46 HARV. L. REV. 553, 575–78 (1933)], at 577.

The position taken by the *Second Restatement* is essentially that of Justice Lowrie. The *Second Restatement* divides the universe of contracts along the private-public axis into express contracts, contracts implied-in-fact, and contracts implied-in-law or quasi-contracts. It defines the express contract as an agreement made up of words, either oral or written, and the implied-in-fact contract as one that a court infers wholly or partly from conduct or circumstances. Quasi-contracts, in contrast, are "public." And because they are not concerned with the intentions of the parties, they are not really contracts at all. * * * Like torts, quasi-contracts are "obligations created by law for reasons of justice." Their non-contractual nature is so essential that they are separated out for treatment in the *Restatement of Restitution*. Only that fact even alerts us that the "reasons of justice" that dictate the imposition of quasi-contractual obligations have to do with the idea of unjust enrichment.

At the same time, the *Second Restatement of Contracts* confesses that this analytically clear distinction between contract and quasi-contract does not always work in practice, that "in some cases the line between the two is indistinct." The *Restatement* attributes the potential for confusion to the difficulties of "Conduct as Manifestation of Assent." Except where formal requirements give words special significance as evidence of agreement, "there is no distinction in the effect of the promise whether it is expressed in writing, or orally, or in acts, or partly in one of these ways and partly in others." But conduct "is more uncertain and more dependent on its setting than are words." The uncertainty of conduct as evidence of agreement can make it unclear whether a particular relationship should be considered contractual or quasi-contractual.

This explanation allows the *Restatement* to save the express contract from involvement in potential confusion between public and private. Words that directly express the parties' intentions make state intrusion unnecessary. Only conduct, inherently more ambiguous and open-textured, threatens the public-private distinction by requiring the interpreter of fact to add his sense of the context to the acts of the parties in order to understand them.

As *Hertzog* demonstrates, however, the division between public and private cannot be so neatly made. Divining intention in order to find an implied-in-fact contract depends on understanding the societal background against which a relationship is formed: A knowledge of private thus requires a knowledge of public. Deciding that a social relationship requires the imposition of a quasi-contract depends on knowing which relationship the parties have entered: A knowledge of public thus requires a knowledge of private.

In failing to account successfully for the kinship of the implied-in-fact and quasi-contract, the *Restatement* is not an aberration in modern treatments. The note in Kessler and Gilmore's casebook introducing the topic of the implied contract also fails in this regard. The note begins by repeating the standard distinction between "genuine" contracts and the fictional quasi-contract, but warns that the "famous, plausible and innocent-looking" distinction raises "a host of troublesome questions." The next passage of the note is a spectacular account of how what is commonly conceived of as private in the realm of contract formation and interpretation is in fact public. In a short compass, Kessler and Gilmore suggest that in one sense all contracts, even express ones, are implied: that express contracts are possible only through "a regulation which is originally social"; that "environment" is crucial; that "official control becomes an integral part of the contract itself"; and that the courts' habit of presenting their enforcement task as one of "interpretation" obscures the "degree of control over private volition thus exercised."

Then, abruptly, the note introduces the concept of quasi-contract. Early in its treatment we are warned: "If it [quasi-contract] is unduly extended, private autonomy . . . will suffer erosion." The degree of erosion demonstrated in the interpretation of contracts proper was never explicitly presented as this kind of a threat, however, and it is not clear why the threat inheres in quasi-contract and not in contract.

At this point the very distinction about which the authors expressed doubt in their opening paragraphs is reintroduced as essential: Although the "borderline" may be "wavering and blurred," the boundary is "necessary," and "not to be ignored." The separation of quasi-contract and contract is vital, not just for the sake of private autonomy, but because of the different remedies attaching, even though in many situations the measure of recovery is the same. We are also warned that judges are not as good at recognizing the essentially different natures of these kinds of contracts as we will presumably be once we have digested the elaborate "guidance" the note provides.

There are manifold messages here. Kessler and Gilmore understand the world of contract to be more complicated and difficult than the standard division into implied-in-fact and implied-in-law would indicate. They fully and sympathetically present the problem of knowledge as it affects issues of interpretation. But this insight is not permitted to influence their treatment of the quasi-contract, which is still presented as the place where the real threat to privateness exists. In shoring up the distinction between real and quasi-contracts by referring to the remedies attached, Kessler and Gilmore repeat Costigan's mistake—unless their point is instead that we should draw this distinction in order to know what remedy is appropriate. This is different from Costigan's claim that the remedy given lets us know what kind of action we are dealing with, but it leaves us asking why we should base a choice of remedy on so weak a foundation. Kessler and Gilmore's final move of pinning the blame on judges deflects attention from the inadequacies of the conceptual scheme itself.

The inadequacies of Kessler and Gilmore's treatment echo those evident in the Second Restatement and in *Hertzog*. None of the accounts fully acknowledges the interrelationship of public and private. None adequately recognizes that public concerns and conceptions necessarily inform the judicial decision about whether to impose contractual obligations. None suggests that quasi-contractual obligation depends on prior understandings of the private relationship of the parties. Once these inter-relationships are understood, as the (failed) attempt to distinguish contract from quasi-contract allows us to understand them, the public-private dichotomy threatens to dissolve. * * *

D. Summary

In the implied contract story, we saw how public and private were confounded, how our understanding of implied-in-fact and express contracts requires us to draw on a fund of public information and values that influences our judgment of what we see. Similarly, our imposition of a public quasi-contractual obligation requires us to look for private signals from the parties about their conception of their relationship. Rather than banishing quasi-contract as a dangerous public exception to a private law of contract, therefore, we embraced its lesson that all contract is as public as it is private. * * *

The lessons of duress and unconscionability are similar. The efforts to incorporate these doctrines into the world of private contract through a focus on contractual "will," or to situate them as public exceptions to a rule that traditionally rejects interference in private exchanges, necessarily end in failure. Furthermore, the lessons of duress and unconscionability have the same direct bearing on consideration doctrine that the lessons of quasi-contract have on doctrines of contract formation and interpretation. These lessons reveal consideration doctrine to be as public as the doctrines of duress and unconscionability—as preoccupied with norms of fairness, as concerned to deny that preoccupation by recourse to identification of party will or intention.

NOTES AND QUESTIONS

1. *Dalton's thesis*. Drawing on cases and authorities like the Restatement and casebooks in contract law, Dalton attempts to show how a variety of contract doctrines and types give voice to an ideology that depends for its power on the separation of the public and private realm. What is the ideology?

2. *The public-private distinction and legitimation*. How do you respond to the argument that the most important function of the law is that it provides a false legitimacy for existing social and power relations and that it does this

by preserving an area of great power as largely immune from state power and labeling it "private"?

3. *A link to contract law.* As you reflect on the way that the public-private distinction works to legitimate power in the "private" realm, consider the continuing salience of the perspective in *Coppage*, supra, even if the result in *Coppage* has been overturned by statute:

> *Coppage* presented a classic defense for, and simultaneously exposed the vulnerability of, libertarian ideas about the legitimate exercise of governmental power. The argument presented is disarming because it does not deny the obvious point that bargaining power, measured by wealth among other things, influences when one might consent to an employment contract. But, by presenting the distribution of wealth as the outcome of the exercise of private rights to private property and the freedom of contract enjoyed by all, the image of unequal bargaining power is turned around (from the modern perspective) to be consistent with liberty rather than a threat to it. Accordingly, the resulting distribution of wealth is assigned to the private side of the public/private divide, and the Fourteenth Amendment "debars the states" from interference with either private property or free contract. The problematic character of a progressive income tax is explicable from this conception of liberty—if the distribution of wealth is rooted in private rights, then there is no basis for public redistribution.

Gary Peller, *Privilege*, 104 GEO. L.J. 883, 889 (2016).

4. *Chewing more than you've bitten off.* Are you convinced that the *Hertzog* case can stand the stress it's under in Dalton's analysis? Is there in short *less* here than meets the eye?

Readings

ROBERTO UNGER, *THE CRITICAL LEGAL STUDIES MOVEMENT*

96 HARV. L. REV. 561, 561–5 (1983)

I. Introduction: The Tradition of Leftist Movements in Legal Thought and Practice

The critical legal studies movement has undermined the central ideas of modern legal thought and put another conception of law in their place. This conception implies a view of society and informs a practice of politics.[1]

---

[1] [Editor's Note: In Professor Unger's break-through article, which runs some 112 pages, there is exactly one footnote. Bless him. Here it is:] Two main tendencies can be distinguished in the critical legal studies movement. One tendency sees past or contemporary doctrine as the expression of a particular vision of society while emphasizing the contradictory and manipulable

The ideas and activities of the movement respond to a familiar situation of constraint upon theoretical insight and transformative effort. This situation is exemplary: its dangers and opportunities reappear in many areas of contemporary politics and thought. Our response may, therefore, also have an exemplary character.

One of the most important obligations anybody has toward a movement in which he participates is to hold up before it what, to his mind, should represent its highest collective self-image. My version of this image of critical legal studies is more proposal than description. It may meet with little agreement among the critical legal scholars. But I have unequivocally preferred the risks of repudiation to those of indefinition. In this, if in nothing else, my statement will exemplify the spirit of our movement.

It may help to begin by placing critical legal studies within the tradition of leftist tendencies in modern legal thought and practice. Two overriding concerns have marked this tradition.

The first concern has been the critique of formalism and objectivism. Let me pause to define formalism and objectivism carefully, for these ideas will play an important role in later stages of my argument. By formalism I do not mean what the term is usually taken to describe: belief in the availability of a deductive or quasi-deductive method capable of giving determinate solutions to particular problems of legal choice. What I mean

---

character of doctrinal argument. Its immediate antecedents lie in antiformalist legal theories and structuralist approaches to cultural history. Examples include Kennedy, *The Structure of Blackstone's Commentaries*, 28 BUFFALO L. REV. 205 (1979), and Kelman, *Interpretive Construction in the Substantive Criminal Law*, 33 STAN. L. REV. 591 (1981). Another tendency grows out of the social theories of Marx and Weber and the mode of social and historical analysis that combines functionalist methods with radical aims. Its point of departure has been the thesis that law and legal doctrine reflect, confirm, and reshape the social divisions and hierarchies inherent in a type or stage of social organization such as "capitalism." But this thesis has been increasingly modified by the awareness that institutional types or stages lack the cohesive and foreordained character that received leftist theory attributes to them. *See* M. HORWITZ, THE TRANSFORMATION OF AMERICAN LAW, 1780–1860 (1977); Trubek, *Complexity and Contradiction in the Legal Order: Balbus and the Challenge of Critical Social Thought About Law*, 11 LAW & SOC'Y REV. 527 (1977). Many of the essays in THE POLITICS OF LAW: A PROGRESSIVE CRITIQUE (D. Kairys ed. 1982) also exemplify this perspective.

Both tendencies criticize the dominant style of legal doctrine and the legal theories that try to refine and preserve this style. Both repudiate in the course of this critique the attempt to impute current social arrangements to the requirements of industrial society, human nature, or moral order. Both have yet to take a clear position on the method, the content, and even the possibility of prescriptive and programmatic thought, perhaps because some of the assumptions inherited from the radical tradition make it hard to turn constructive proposals into more than statements of commitment or anticipations of history.

The significance of the contrast between these tendencies should not be overstated. The actual works often differ less than the abstract interpretations placed upon them. And many writings do not fall into either of the two groups mentioned. *See* Gordon, *Historicism in Legal Scholarship*, 90 YALE L.J. 1017 (1981); Parker, *The Past of Constitutional Theory—And Its Future*, 42 OHIO ST. L.J. 223 (1981); Simon, *The Ideology of Advocacy: Procedural Justice and Professional Ethics*, 1978 WIS. L. REV 29; Stone, *The Post-War Paradigm in American Labor Law*, 90 YALE L.J. 1509 (1981).

Though the view of critical legal studies presented here cannot be reconciled with much in the way these and other tendencies in the movement understand their own critical practice, I hope it remains faithful to a shared intention and direction.

by formalism in this context is a commitment to, and therefore also a belief in the possibility of, a method of legal justification that can be clearly contrasted to opened disputes about the basic terms of social life, disputes that people call ideological, philosophical, or visionary. Though such conflicts may not be entirely bereft of criteria, they fall far short of the rationality that the formalist claims for legal analysis. The formalism I have in mind characteristically invokes impersonal purposes, policies, and principles as an indispensable component of legal reasoning. Formalism in the conventional sense—the search for a method of deduction from a gapless system of rules—is merely the anomalous, limiting case of this jurisprudence.

You might add a second distinctive formalist thesis: that only through such a restrained, relatively apolitical method of analysis is legal doctrine possible. By legal doctrine or legal analysis, in turn, I mean a form of conceptual practice that combines two characteristics: the willingness to work from the institutionally defined materials of a given collective tradition and the claim to speak authoritatively within this tradition, to elaborate it from within in a way that is meant, at least ultimately, to affect the application of state power. Doctrine can exist—the formalist says or assumes—because of a contrast between the more determinate rationality of legal analysis and the less determinate rationality of ideological contests.

This thesis can be restated as the belief that lawmaking and law application differ fundamentally, as long as legislation is seen to be guided only by the looser rationality of ideological conflict. Lawmaking and law application diverge in both how they work and how their results may properly be justified. To be sure, law application may have an important creative element. But in the politics of lawmaking the appeal to principle and policy—when it exists at all—is supposed to be both more controversial in its foundations and more indeterminate in its implications than the corresponding features of legal analysis. Other modes of justification allegedly compensate for the diminished force and precision of the ideal element in lawmaking. Thus, legislative decisions may be validated as results of procedures that are themselves legitimate because they allow all interest groups to be represented and to compete for influence or, more ambitiously, because they enable the wills of citizens to count equally in choosing the laws that will govern them.

By objectivism I mean the belief that the authoritative legal materials—the system of statutes, cases, and accepted legal ideas—embody and sustain a defensible scheme of human association. They display, though always imperfectly, an intelligible moral order. Alternatively they show the results of practical constraints upon social life—constraints such as those of economic efficiency—that, taken together with constant human desires, have a normative force. The laws are not merely the outcome of contingent power struggles or of practical pressures lacking in rightful authority. * * *

1. *Contract Theory Disintegrated.* * * * The problems to be discussed include all those that present-day legal thought treats as issues of contract. The argument, however, reaches far beyond the scope of our still-reigning contract theory. For the applicability of this theory has been subject over time to several qualifications. First, there are the exclusions: whole areas of law, like family law, labor law, antitrust, corporate law, and perhaps even international law, that were once regarded as branches of unified contract theory but gradually came to be seen as requiring a specific set of categories unassimilable to that theory. Then there are the exceptions: bodies of law and social practice such as fiduciary relationships that come under an anomalous set of principles within the central area of contract. Finally, there are the repressions: problems like those of long-term contractual dealings that, though resistant to the solutions provided by a theory oriented primarily toward the one-shot, arm's-length, and low-trust transaction, are nevertheless more often dealt with by ad hoc deviations from the dominant rules and ideas than by clearly distinct norms. When you add up the exclusions, the exceptions, and the repressions, you begin to wonder in just what sense traditional contract theory dominates at all. It seems like an empire whose claimed or perceived authority vastly outreaches its actual power. Yet this theory continues to rule in at least one important sense: it compels all other modes of thought to define themselves negatively, by contrast to it. This intellectual dominance turns out to have important practical consequences.

A major objective of the following argument is to show how this whole field of problems can be grasped by a single, cohesive set of ideas. Thus, though its main concern is to contribute to the development of a prescriptive vision, it also claims to supply the conceptual instruments with which to understand contract and related fields more clearly and coherently. It wants to replace the contrast between the overbearing theory and the runaway exclusions, exceptions, and repressions with a view that can explain or justify different practical solutions for different practical problems within a continuous set of ideas. If this task can be accomplished, the proposed account will have beaten the received theory at its own game of persuasive generalization. As might be expected in the case of legal doctrine, new explanations come hand in hand with new evaluations: the same ideas that can effectively reunify and reorganize the entire realm of contract problems also help discredit the normative commitments of established thought.

Classical contract theory has always proved seductive to jurists in search of a legal calculus that could claim to generate the impersonal rules of free human interaction. For the same reason, it offers the most valuable challenge to a conception of doctrine that emphasizes the continuity of legal analysis with ideological conflict. The cost of the attempt to penetrate the inner defenses of a seemingly apolitical technique is greater complexity. Moreover, the earlier model dealt with an aspect of the gross institutional structure of society. This one must address a portion of the fine texture of social life and strive for the delicacy that the legal analysis of this texture demands.

My analysis of contract doctrine will pass through several stages. The first stage is the enumeration of dominant principles and counter-principles that inform this entire body of law. The second step is to examine specific points of controversy in the law that bring into focus an ambiguity in the relation between the principles and the counter-principles. Though the counter-principles may be seen as mere restraints upon the principles, they may also serve as points of departure for a different organizing conception of this whole area of law. The third stage generalizes this alternative conception by discussing the theory of the sources of obligation and the nature of entitlements that it implies. The fourth step tests and refines this alternative by applying it to problems other than those points of controversy that provided the occasion for its original formulation. The fifth and last stage of the argument is, in a sense, the first, because it offers retrospectively a more complete justification for the direction in which all the steps of the analysis move. But to understand internal development is to see why justification can be achieved little by little, through cumulative explication, generalization, and revision, rather than by deduction from already developed commitments. Taken as a whole, this exercise in critical doctrine exemplifies the most characteristic recourse of the subversive mind: to transform the deviant into the dominant for the sake of a vision that becomes clearer in the course of the transformation itself, a vision that ends up redefining what it began by promoting.

2. *Principle and Counter-principle: Freedom to Contract and Community.* The initial stage in this variant of deviationist doctrine is the effort to understand the better part of contract law and doctrine as an expression of a small number of opposing ideas: principles and counter-principles. These ideas connect the more concrete legal rules and standards to a set of background assumptions about the kinds of human association that can and should prevail in different areas of social life. The principles and counter-principles are more than artifacts of theoretical curiosity. They provisionally settle what would otherwise be pervasive ambiguities in the more concrete legal materials. But they themselves can be understood and justified only as expressions of background schemes of possible and desirable human association. For only this deeper context can offer guidance about the relative reach and the specific content of the opposing principles and counter-principles. Because the conventional methods of legal analysis are committed to the contrast between doctrine and ideology or philosophy, they almost invariably prefer to leave implicit the reference to the larger imaginative foundations of rules and principles.

Thus, I have argued, they gain a semblance of higher certainty at the cost of an arbitrary dogmatism.

But why should the controlling ideas come in the form of antagonistic principles and counter-principles? Such an opposition can alone generate a body of law and legal thought that applies different models of human association to distinct areas of social life. At a minimum the counter-principles keep the principles in place and prevent them from extending, imperialistically, to all social life. Once the crucial role of counter-principles has been recognized, the appeal to a larger vision of the possible and desirable models of human connection becomes inevitable. Because conventional analysis wants to avoid, if not the reality, at least the appearance of such an appeal, it also systematically downplays the counter-principles.

The structure of reigning ideas about contract and its adjacent fields can be stated with the greatest possible simplicity, in the form of only two pairs of principles and counter-principles. If we were concerned with a specific contract problem, many intermediate levels of generalization might be warranted.

The first principle is that of the freedom to enter or to refuse to enter into contracts. More specifically, it is the faculty of choosing your contract partners. It might be called, for short, the freedom to contract. The qualifications that the law of assignment imposes upon the doctrine of privity show that the principle of freedom of contract is marked by a certain complexity of meaning even when the currently dominant forms of market organization are taken for granted. In a system that treats the consolidated property right as the exemplary form of right itself and that conceives property in part as that which can be freely bought and sold in an impersonal market, restraints upon assignability must be limited. The law must treat contractual relations as if they were powerless to imprint a permanent character upon the tangible or intangible things (including the labor of other people) that these relations concern. Any way you look at it—from the perspective of the common meaning of freedom to contract, or the practical demands of the existing kinds of markets, or the actual behavior and motivations of economic agents—the interplay of the ideals of personality and impersonality, manifested respectively in doctrines of privity and assignability, represents less a conflict between the first principle and a counter-principle than a disharmony within that principle itself. This disharmony can be resolved by any number of practical compromises.

Other areas of law and doctrine, however, do circumscribe the principle of freedom to contract on behalf of an entirely different idea. They embody a counter-principle: that the freedom to choose the contract partner will not be allowed to work in ways that subvert the communal aspects of social life. To understand this counter-principle with greater precision, remember some of its manifestations.

One occurs in the area of compulsory contracts and of the legal situations analogous to them. Voluntary entrance into a course of dealing with another party may make a party liable for violating certain expectations to which the dealing gave rise (*e.g.*, precontractual liability or *culpa in contrahendo*). Or the occupancy of a status or the exercise of a profession (*e.g.*, medicine) may bring special responsibilities and justify special expectations. Whether liability in these cases is portrayed as contractual or delictual, it is based upon a network of personal interactions rather than upon either a fully articulated bargain or an exercise of direct governmental regulation.

A second example of the counter-principle appears in bodies of rule and doctrine that affirm an obligation to answer for another's justified reliance on one's own promises (promissory estoppel) and to make restitution for "unjust enrichment' " (quasi-contract). The protection of the reliance interest applies on its face to situations that a worked-out bilateral agreement cannot reach. Much of the law of restitution has the same character of compensating for violations of trust in a context of close dealing or exceptional defenselessness. Thus, both reliance and restitution rules may operate to prevent the principle of freedom to contract from tracing the limits of liability rigidly and narrowly that the fine texture of reciprocities is left entirely unprotected.

The most instructive application of the counter-principle lies, however, in a third area: the rules of contract law that discourage contract-making in noncommercial settings. These rules express a reluctance to allow contract law to intrude at all upon the world of family and friendship, lest by doing so it destroy their peculiar communal quality. Let us approach the issue indirectly, through the norms that govern the interpretation of the intent to contract. These norms about intent to contract elucidate more clearly than any others the boundaries of the principle of freedom to contract and the vision of human coexistence within and outside commerce that these boundaries imply.

The general first-level rule in contemporary Anglo-American contract law is that a declaration of intent to be legally bound may be unnecessary, although a declaration of intent not to be held at law may be effective. Those who devote themselves to self-interest in the harsh business world are presumed to want all the help they can get to avoid being done in by their contract partners. A second-level rule guides and qualifies the interpretation of the first-level one. Whenever possible a court construes intention in a manner that protects justified reliance and reads the parties out of a situation in which they stand at each other's mercy. Thus, if the bargain is one for separate deliveries over a long period and one party has seriously relied upon continued supply, the court may be expected to lean over backwards to interpret the exclusion of liability as narrowly as possible. A third-level rule limits the scope of both the first-level and second-level ones. As a qualification to the latter, it affirms that the impulse to interpret intent so as to avoid delivering one party into another's hands will be suppressed in noncommercial contexts. As a limitation upon the former, it reverses in family life or friendship the presumption of intent to be legally bound; an explicit assertion of intent will be required. " 'Social arrangements,' " it is said, are either rarely intended to have legal consequence or ought not to have such consequences. Intent should be construed accordingly. In one sense this third-level criterion is prior to the other two, for it determines the scope of their application. Its apparent justification lies in the attempt to defend private community against the disruptive intervention of the law and of the regime of rigidly defined rights and duties that the law would bring in its wake. Just why private community needs this defense is something that can be explained only after the vision that underlies the interplay between the principle of freedom to contract and its counter-principle has been made explicit.

Note that, while family bargains are disfavored, family gifts may be encouraged. Thus, common law consideration doctrine is riddled with exceptions, like the doctrine of meritorious consideration, designed to facilitate bounties within the family. The hostility toward donative transactions suspected of undermining family duties (*e.g.*, a married man's gift to his mistress) contrasts with the solicitude that may be shown toward intrafamilial donations (*e.g.*, a parent's gift to his child) when there are no competing inheritance or creditors' rights to protect. Just as classical contract theory depicts the bargain as the beneficial creature of anticommunal self-interest, it sees the gift as an instrument of either community-preserving generosity or community-destroying circumvention of the law.

The relation of principle and counterprinciple in contract law can be interpreted as an expression of two different views of how people can and should interact in the areas of social life touched by contract law: one crude and easy to criticize, the other more subtle and justifiable. The crude view is the one displayed most clearly by the rules that try to keep contract out of the realm of "social arrangements.' " It contrasts an ideal of private community, meant to be realized chiefly in the life of family and friendship, to the ideal of contractual freedom, addressed to the world of self-interested commerce. The social realm is pictured as rich in precisely the attributes that are thought to be almost wholly absent from the economic realm. The communal forms in which it abounds, islands of reciprocal loyalty and support, neither need much law nor are capable of tolerating it. For law in this conception is the regime of rigidly defined rights that demarcate areas for discretionary action.

The idea that there is an area of experience outside the serious world of work, in which communal relations flourish, can be made to justify the devolution of practical life to the harshest self-interest. The premises to this devolution recall the contrast between Venice and Belmont in *The Merchant of Venice*. In Venice people make contracts; in Belmont they exchange wedding rings. In Venice they are held together by combinations of interest; in Belmont by mutual affection. The wealth and power of Venice depend upon the willingness of its courts to hold men to their contracts. The charm of Belmont is to provide its inhabitants with a community in which contracts remain for the most part superfluous. Venice is tolerable because its citizens can flee occasionally to Belmont and appeal from Venetian justice to Belmontine mercy. But the very existence of Belmont presupposes the prosperity of Venice, from which the denizens of Belmont gain their means of livelihood. This is the form of life classical contract theory claims to describe and seeks to define—an existence separated into a sphere of trade supervised by the state and an area of private family and friendship largely though not wholly beyond the reach of contract. Each half of this life both denies the other and depends upon it. Each is at once the other's partner and its enemy.

The larger imaginative background to this contrast is a vision of social life that distinguishes more or less sharply among separate models of human connection. These models are meant to be realized in separate areas of social life: democracy for the state and citizenship, private community for family and friendship, and an amalgam of contract and impersonal technical hierarchy for the everyday world of work and exchange. The most remarkable feature of this vision is its exclusion of the more morally ambitious models of human connection from the prosaic activities and institutions that absorb most people most of the time. These models are democracy and private community. Their moral ambition consists in their promise of a partial reconciliation between the competing claims of self-assertion and attachment to other people—a reconciliation, in fact, between two competing sides of the experience of self-assertion itself. According to the logic of the vision, any attempt to extend these ideals beyond their proper realm of application into everyday life will meet with disaster. Not only will the extension fail, but the practical and psychological conditions that enable the higher ideals to flourish on their own ground may also be destroyed in the course of the attempt.

A closer look at the contrast of contract law to private community shows how this contrast depends upon empirical and normative assumptions that cannot be justified even in the light of the ruling social ideals and the current understandings of social fact. The prime instance of the ideal of private community is the family. There are two reasons classical contract theory has trouble with the family: one of them explicit, the other tacit though equally important. Like most well established ideological preconceptions, these reasons combine insight and illusion.

First, the family is supposed to depend upon a union of sentiments and a flexible give-and-take that contract law, with its fixed allocations of right and duty under rigid rules, would disrupt. The very process by which the members of a family cast their relationships in the language of formal entitlement would confirm and hasten the dissolution of the family. Communal life needs to maintain the lines of right and duty fluid in attention to an untrammeled trust. It must subordinate the jealous defense of individualistic prerogative to the promotion of shared purpose and the reinforcement of mutual involvement.

The other reason for separating the family, as the paradigmatic core of private community, from contract, as the denial of community, is generally left implicit. It does, however, prevent this conception of law and the family from being merely sentimental. The nineteenth century bourgeois family or its diluted successor constitutes a certain structure of power. Like all structures of power, it calls upon its members to accept the legitimacy of gross inequalities in the distribution of trust. In the most pristine versions, the husband had to be allowed wide powers of supervision and control over wife and children, as if discretion in their hands would endanger the family group. The fluidity of entitlements seems consistent with the maintenance and prosperity of the family only because there is an authority at the head capable of giving direction to the team.

Classical contract theory was born fighting against such a frankly personalistic and asymmetrical exercise of power. Family law may still be penetrated by notions of status and attentive to hierarchic distinctions among relatives. But the modern law of contract was built as the culminating expression of abstract universalism. It is hostile to personal authority as a source of order; it preaches equality in distrust. The mechanisms of egalitarian, self-interested bargaining and adjudication cannot be made to jibe with the illiberal blend of power and allegiance.

If you now put together these two elements of the dominant conception of family and law, you come to this result: the family is a structure of power, ennobled by sentiment. Both as sentiment and as power, it repudiates the rule of law. Were the family mere sentiment, it would disintegrate, for according to this outlook sentiment is precarious and formless. Were the family brute power, unsoftened by sentiment, it might not merit preservation. The redemptive union of authority and affection provides the alternative to legal or at least to contractual ordering. It supplies the master key to an understanding of what Belmont is supposed, or admitted, to be like in a world in which it can never pretend to be more than a satellite to Venice.

Note that the whole view of family beyond contract depends upon the interaction between an impoverished conception of community and a narrow view of law in general and of contract in particular. The conception of community defines communal life largely negatively, as the absence of conflict. The view of law exhibits the prudence of distrust. It insists upon clear-cut zones of discretionary entitlement within which the right-holder may be free to exercise his right as he wants and beyond which he has no claim to protection. The practical result of the polemical opposition of contract to community is to leave inadequately supported the subtle interdependencies of social life that flourish outside the narrow zone of recognized community. The practical result for private community itself is to renew the identification of the communal ideal with the personalistic authority and dependence that often characterize family life. This result explains the paradoxical fact that mutual responsibility may do better, legally and factually, in the pitiless world of deals than in the supposedly communal haven of family life. * * *

3. *Principle and Counter-principle: Freedom of Contract and Fairness.* Now consider a second pair of principles and counter-principles. The parties must be free to choose the terms of their agreement. Save in special cases, they will not be second-guessed by a court, not at least as long as they stay within the ground rules that define a regime of free contract. * * * Call this principle freedom of contract as distinguished from freedom to contract. Its boundaries are traced by the counter-principle that unfair bargains should not be enforced. Before the limits and manifestations of this counter-principle are probed, it may help to understand the central problem that this second pair of legal ideas must solve.

A regime of contract is just another legal name for a market. It ceases to exist when inequalities of power and knowledge accumulate to the point of turning a set of contractual relations into the outward form of a power order. The ability of the contracting parties to bargain on their own initiative and for their own account must be real. On the other hand, a commitment to cancel out every inequality of power or knowledge as soon as it arose would also undermine a contract system. Real markets are never just machines for instantaneous transactions among economic agents equally knowledgeable and equally able to await the next offer or to withdraw from current courses of dealing. Continued success in market transactions shows partly in the buildup of advantages of power or knowledge that enable their beneficiaries to do that much better in the next round of transactions. If everyone were quickly restored to a situation of equality within the market order, the method responsible for this restoration would be the true system of resource allocation. It would empty market transactions of much of their apparent significance.

At first these two boundaries—allowing the inequalities to accumulate unrestrictedly and correcting them as soon as they emerge—may seem to leave so large an intermediate space of solution that they hardly constrain the organization of a contract regime. There are any number of points within them at which the compromise between correction and allowance might be struck. The decision to draw the line at one place rather than another cannot itself be deduced from the abstract idea of a market. When, however, we combine the analysis of this tension with the thesis that the market lacks any inherent institutional structure, the joint result of the two ideas begins to look far more consequential. The distance between the boundaries does not remain constant as the institutional character of the market changes. Some market regimes, taken in their actual political and social settings, may regularly generate or incorporate so much inequality that the minimum of correction needed to prevent them from degenerating into power orders amounts to more than the maximum correction compatible with the autonomy of decentralized market decisions. * * * The real solution is then to change the institutional character of the market. In the absence of such a solution, attempts must be made to find moderating solutions, either by singling out the most serious problems for special treatment (*e.g.*, labor law) or by preferring vague slogans (*e.g.*, good faith, unconscionability) that can be used to support limited, ad hoc corrective interventions. Both of these responses have in common the capacity to limit the subversive impact of correction upon the central though shrinking and porous body of contract law. * * *

Consider the forms taken by the counter-principle of fairness in two of the obvious areas of its application: the law governing discharge for changed circumstances and mistake about basic assumptions and the law of duress, whose problems extend into labor law. In each of these settings, the fairness idea takes on a slightly different sense. Its inclusive sense is the sum of these and other loosely linked connotations.

One or both parties may attribute to something they exchange a quality it does not possess, or conversely they may ignore a quality it does have. An event supervenient to the making of an executory contract may change, perhaps radically, the relative value of the performances. In either case a discrepancy may emerge between the actual and the expected or imagined value. At what point does the distortion produced by the mistake about the present or the future justify a revision of the contract? To let the losses fall where they lay or ought to have lain at the moment of discharge might produce an outcome at least as arbitrary as the strict enforcement of the original agreement. Hence, if a revision is to take place at all, the real issue becomes whether and how to find an alternative distribution of profits and losses. Against correction you may argue that all contracts are guesses by which parties imagine how much things are likely to be worth to them in the future. The outer limit to this argument, however, lies in the assumptions made about the risks that the parties intended to assume. The problem arises constantly from an ambiguity in the expectancies that contract law is supposed to protect: the expectancy may be an interest either in a certain performance or in the exchange value that this performance embodies. Even when the performance consists in a payment of money, the ambiguity does not disappear. Money itself matters for its value in exchange, and this value may be subject to radical and unexpected dislocations.

The issue could be settled if the law saw the parties in every ordinary transaction as high-risk gamblers and abided relentlessly by the logic that things are worth only the values that parties place on them in particular transactions. But this the law refuses to do. To the objection that this refusal merely construes party intent rather than imposing an independent idea of fairness, there are two answers. First, given the impossibility of spelling out all the presuppositions of a transaction, intentions never could be enough. Second, in rejecting the extreme gambling idea, the law commits itself to the search for minimalist standards of equivalence that transcend the terms of particular transactions, standards needed both to tell when things have gone wrong and to set them right.

The tenacity with which the law conducts the search for such standards is all the more remarkable because it betrays a willingness to imagine how an alternatively organized market would have operated. The legal objectivist as naive economic theorist may claim that we are thus merely required to picture the workings of a more "perfect" market. But the critic of objectivism knows that more decentralized markets can be decentralized in different ways and with different effects. He sees that the selection of corrective standards already involves an implicit choice of one among indefinitely many conceivable more perfect markets, each with its distinctive institutional presuppositions. This imaginary market will then provide the criteria for completing, reforming, or replacing transactions in existing markets.

The counter-principle of fairness reappears in the rules and doctrines that police the bargaining process itself. An agreement will be enforced only if it results from an indispensable minimum of free and considered decision by all parties concerned. The obvious attraction of this tactic is that it seems to dispense with the need to second-guess the equivalence of the performances. It therefore minimizes the market-subverting effects of interventionist correction. Besides, it merely extends into contract law the same quest for neutral process that characterizes the traditional liberal case for established institutions and the ruling methods of liberal political philosophy. Here as elsewhere this search runs into trouble. The heart of the trouble lies in what must be done to reconcile the idealized bargaining picture with the existing institutional forms of the market economy. The attempted reconciliation ends up requiring—however sporadically and indirectly—the very policing of contract terms that the emphasis on bargaining procedures is meant to avoid. No branch of contract law presents these themes more clearly than the law of duress.

The modern Anglo-American doctrine of duress tends to cross each of the three frontiers that surround its traditional territory. It has developed on the border between aberrational and structural inequality—the case of the drowning man and the case of the poor one—in a way that casts doubt upon the very distinction between the two. It has shown a greater willingness to impose a standard of good faith upon the exercise of formal rights. It has demonstrated a more or less explicit concern with the rough equivalence of the performances, though it often treats the gross failure of equivalence as a mere trigger for stricter scrutiny of the bargaining process.

The most characteristic result of this multiple expansion has been the doctrine of economic duress with its key concept of equal bargaining power. According to this doctrine, a contract may be voidable for economic duress whenever a significant inequality of bargaining power exists between the parties. Gross inequalities of bargaining power, however, are all too common in the current forms of market economy, a fact shown not only by the dealings between individual consumers and large corporate enterprises, but also by the huge disparities of scale and market influence among enterprises themselves. Thus, the doctrine of economic duress must serve as a roving commission to correct the most egregious and overt forms of an omnipresent type of disparity. But the unproven assumption of the doctrine is that the amount of corrective intervention needed to keep a contractual regime from becoming a power order will not be so great that it destroys the vitality of decentralized decisionmaking through contract. If this assumption proved false, no compromise between correction and abstention could achieve its intended effect. The only solution would be the one that every such compromise is meant to avoid: the remaking of the institutional arrangements that define the market economy. The doctrinal manifestation of this problem is the vagueness of the concept of economic duress. The cost of preventing the revised duress doctrine from running wild and from correcting almost everything is to draw unstable, unjustified, and unjustifiable lines between the contracts that are voidable and those that are not. In the event, the law draws these lines by a strategy of studied indefinition, though it might just as well have done so—as it so often does elsewhere—through precise but makeshift distinctions.

In at least one area of social life, however, the equivocations of economic duress will not do: the relations between capital and labor. If labor were not allowed to organize and to bargain collectively, the disparity between the contract model and economic reality would remain immense and unmistakable in a central aspect of social life. It would then be clear that the only kind of correction capable of distinguishing contract from subjugation would be one that effectively abolished contract by policing all of the terms or correcting all of the outcomes. The solution has been to factor labor relations out of the central body of contract law and to enlist the method of "countervailing power": once workers are allowed to organize, they can face employers on equal terms. The institutionalized collective bargaining of labor and management can then reestablish the validity of the contract model. It can do so without threatening any deeper disruption and without even making it appear that the rest of the economic order is also an artifact of institutional invention and social warfare. But the limited solution faces two connected problems. These constitute the central issues of labor law doctrine.

The first problem could be called the paradox of procedural justice. Its specific doctrinal context in American labor law is the problem of the duty to bargain in good faith and of its relation to the administrative and judicial scrutiny of the substantive proposals made in the course of collective bargaining. The special, reconstructed market of capital and labor will not work unless both parties remain committed to it, unless they accept it as the basic institutional framework of their relation to each other. Unlike the general market and the general polity, it might be circumvented precisely because it is only a localized part of that surrounding order, constructed according to distinctive rules. The more powerful party—usually though not always the employer—will have the incentive to move outside it. The duty to bargain in good faith is the duty to take the special framework as the one that counts. But how is the performance of this duty to be assessed? If the court or administrative agency rests content with a show of compliance—a willingness to go through the motions of bargaining—the duty loses its force. The parties can then trust only to their power and guile. On the other hand, any more ambitious test of compliance seems to require that the National Labor Relations Board or the court pass judgment on the fairness of the proposals and counterproposals that the parties make to each other in the course of their negotiations. This requirement would involve the supervisory body in something perilously close to the substantive regulation of labor relations that the whole machinery of countervailing power is designed to avoid. Thus, the American Congress amended the National Labor Relations Act to overturn a line of administrative and judicial decisions that took the duty to bargain in good faith as a mandate to evaluate the content of party offers and counteroffers. Yet even after having had this view repudiated by the legislature, the National Labor Relations Board found more circumspect ways to reassert it. The paradox of procedural justice suggests why: as the institution most immediately responsible for supervising the integrity of the collective bargaining system as a corrective institutional framework, the Board had good reason not to give up. * * *

We can now take stock of the meanings accumulated by the counter-principle of fairness in the contexts of its application that have just been discussed. Fairness means not treating the parties, and not allowing them to treat each other, as pure gamblers unless they really see themselves this way and have the measure of equality that enables each to look out for himself. The parties must normally be deemed to act in a situation of limited and discriminate risks and to transact on presuppositions that can never be fully spelled out and whose relevant parts may be explicable only after the fact. The participants must insure each other against the mistakes and misfortunes that fall outside these boundaries. To this extent the second counter-principle intersects the first.

Fairness also means that inequality between the parties renders a contract suspect and, beyond a certain measure of disparity in power, invalid. In particular, unequal parties will not easily be read into a situation of mere gambling. When the limit of accepted and acceptable risks is reached or when the inequalities in the contractual relation begin to weaken the force of the contract model, the law will try to restore or invent a rough equivalence of performances or of participation in gains and losses. It may do so confusedly and covertly, but as long as the counter-principle remains alive it will do so nevertheless. Thus, the fairness idea turns out to connect a concern for rough equivalence in outcomes with a view of the defining features of contractual relationships.

The analysis of the interplay between the second principle and counter-principle reveals many permutations of a single central problem. The fairness correction must be focused and sporadic rather than pervasive if the regime of contract is not to be superseded by an overriding method of allocation. Yet in its limited and contract-preserving form, the correction becomes arbitrarily selective: for every situation corrected, there seems to exist another similar to it that is left untouched. This lesson is the same taught by the analysis of generality-correcting equal protection: a pattern of unjustifiable distinctions appears as the alternative to an overbearing and comprehensive intervention. There, in equal protection, this intervention would frustrate the constitutional plan by concentrating all real power in the hands of judges or other operators of doctrine. Here, in contract, it would liquidate the contractual regime while preserving its outward forms. Here, as there, the real solution is the transformation—including the transformation through doctrine—of the institutional framework of economic and political action.

The relation of the two counter-principles to the two principles can be represented in two different ways. The dominant view treats the existing institutional structure as given. It regards the imaginative scheme of models of possible and desirable human association, including the contrast of contract to community, as rigidly defined. On this view the counter-principles are anomalies. They prevent the principles from doing injustice in unusual if not extreme cases. The separation of equity and common law in Anglo-American legal history lent this approach institutional support. But if we start from the assumption that the underlying institutional and imaginative order can and should be changed, the counter-principles lose any stable, natural, and contained relation to the principles. They may even serve as the points of departure for a system of law and doctrine that reverses the traditional relationship and reduces the principles to a specialized role. * * *

VII. Conclusion: The Lessons of Incongruity

The chief objection to this view of the critical legal studies movement may be simply the formidable gap it suggests between the reach of our intellectual and political commitments and the many severe constraints upon our situation. We must still decide what to make of this gap.

First, there is the disproportion between our transformative goals and the established social peace. We have not sought in the deceptions of a social and legal theory that claims to trump politics consolation for our political disappointments. Surrounded by people who implicitly deny the transformability of arrangements whose contingency they also assert, we have refused to mistake the ramshackle settlements of this post-War age for the dispensations of moral providence or historical fate.

Then we face the contrast between the scope of our theoretical concerns and the relatively limited domain in which we pursue them. But every truly radical movement, radical both as leftist and as deep cutting, must reject the antithesis of the technical and the philosophical. It must insist upon seeing its theoretical program realized in particular disciplines and practices if that program is to be realized at all.

Finally, there is the disparity between our intentions and the archaic social form that they assume: a joint endeavor undertaken by discontented, factious intellectuals in the high style of nineteenth century bourgeois radicalism. For all who participate in such an undertaking, the disharmony between intent and presence must be a cause of rage. We neither suppress this rage nor allow it the last word, because we do not give the last word to the historical world we inhabit. We build with what we have and willingly pay the price for the inconformity of vision to circumstance.

The legal academy that we entered dallied in one more variant of the perennial effort to restate power and preconception as right. In and outside the law schools, most jurists looked with indifference and even disdain upon the legal theorists who, like the rights and principles or the law and economics schools, had volunteered to salvage and recreate the traditions of objectivism and formalism. These same unanxious skeptics, however, also rejected any alternative to the formalist and objectivist view. Having failed to persuade themselves of all but the most equivocal versions of the inherited creed, they nevertheless clung to its implications and brazenly advertised their own failure as the triumph of worldly wisdom over intellectual and political enthusiasm. History they degraded into the retrospective rationalization of events. Philosophy they abased into an inexhaustible compendium of excuses for the truncation of legal analysis. The social sciences they perverted into the source of argumentative ploys with which to give arbitrary though stylized policy discussions the blessing of a specious authority.

When we came, they were like a priesthood that had lost their faith and kept their jobs. They stood in tedious embarrassment before cold altars. But we turned away from those altars, and found the mind's opportunity in the heart's revenge.

NOTES AND QUESTIONS

1. *A self-styled Copernican revolution?* At one point in his essay, Unger observes, "[t]hough the counter-principles may be seen as mere restraints upon the principles, they may also serve as points of departure for a different organizing conception of this whole area of law." Who exactly might be tempted to view the counter-principles in this limited, pragmatic way, and what exactly does Unger mean by a "point of departure?" When Copernicus discovered that the earth was not the center of the universe, the observed cosmic data remained the same as they had for centuries (of course), but his new explanation fit the data, did it more simply, and inverted the received wisdom. What's the connection to Unger's project?

2. *"Deviationist doctrine."* Unger's so-called deviationist approach rests on a "conception of doctrine that emphasizes the continuity of legal analysis with ideological conflict." An essential part of his method requires him to identify pairs of principles-in-conflict in contract law. In Unger's examples, what are the principles in conflict, and how would you articulate the opposing ideologies that map onto them?

3. *CLS as a mode of argument.* Consider the following characterization of traditional legal reasoning:

> * * * [P]redominant legal theory claimed that reasoning proceeded syllogistically from rules and precedents that had been clearly defined historically and logically, through the particular facts of a case, to a clear decision. The function of a judge was to discover analytically the proper rules and precedents involved and to apply them to the case as first premises. Once he had done that, the judge could decide the case with certainty and uniformity.

EDWARD A. PURCELL, JR., THE CRISIS OF DEMOCRATIC THEORY 74–75 (1973). From what you've read in this chapter, how does the CLS mode of argument differ from the traditional approach?

4. *Connection to modern ethical thought.* In AFTER VIRTUE: A STUDY IN MORAL THEORY (3rd ed. 2007), Alisdair MacIntyre demonstrates that modern ethical thought is an amalgam of irreconcilable views about the good and human nature. Mere fragments of what were once coherent ethical views have wended their way into modern ethics and in the process have been transformed, truncated, and modified. The result is that modern ethical thought has come to consist of a logically incoherent body of ideas. What connection can you make from that observation to the essential insight of CLS?

5. *CLS, legal pedagogy, and the ritual slaying of the elders.* At the end of his essay, Unger says, "When we came, [the existing faculties of law] were like a priesthood that had lost their faith and kept their jobs. They stood in tedious embarrassment before cold altars. But we turned away from those altars, and found the mind's opportunity in the heart's revenge." As you can imagine, not everybody took this criticism well. Paul Carrington, then the dean of Duke University School of Law argued that the Crits had "an ethical duty to depart the law school, perhaps to seek a place elsewhere in the academy." Paul Carrington, *Of Law and the River*, 34 J. LEGAL EDUC. 222, 227 (1984), analogizing them to atheists teaching in a seminary: "Teaching cynicism may, and perhaps probably does, result in the learning of the skills of corruption: bribery and intimidation. In an honest effort to proclaim the need for revolution, nihilist teachers are more likely to train crooks than radicals." *Ibid.*

There is no doubt that CLS theorists viewed the legal academy as a training ground for the servants of hierarchy:

> Teachers teach nonsense when they persuade students that legal reasoning is distinct, as a *method* for reaching correct results, from ethical and political discourse in general (*i.e.*, from policy analysis). It is true that there is a distinctive lawyers' body of knowledge of the rules in force. It is true that there are distinctive lawyers' argumentative techniques for spotting gaps, conflicts, and ambiguities in the rules [ ]. But these are *only* argumentative techniques. There is never a "correct legal solution" that is other than the correct ethical and political solution to that legal problem. Put another way, everything taught, except the formal rules themselves and the argumentative techniques for manipulating them, is policy and nothing more. It follows that the classroom distinction between the unproblematic, legal case and the policy-oriented case is a mere artifact: each could as well be taught in the opposite way.

Duncan Kennedy, *Legal Education as Training for Hierarchy*, *in* THE POLITICS OF LAW: A PROGRESSIVE CRITIQUE 38, 45 (David Kairys, ed., 1990).

6. *Family resemblances.* How is CLS like Legal Realism, and where do the similarities stop?

7. *Now what?* Armed with the insights of critical legal theory, what should a lawyer be or do? As an associate at a big law firm, should you break the copier at strategic moments? Leak your corporate clients' misdeeds? Decline to laugh at the partners' jokes? On the other hand, what is the argument that a heightened sensitivity to textual ambiguity and the historical contingency of doctrine actually makes better lawyers?

8. *The positive political program (such as it is).* Do the insights of critical legal studies support or require a particular political structure or reform? If not, is that necessarily a problem? After all, you were asked in the introduction to this chapter whether you expect other schools of jurisprudence to have some coherent political basis, implication, and aspiration. And if you do insist on some connection between a philosophy of law and the structure of an ideal

society that it implies, what is the proper political arrangement in the CLS world?

One strong possibility (which finds textual support in much critical writing) is a radical departure from the New Deal liberalism that held many of the Realists together. *See* John Hasnas, *Back to the Future: From Critical Legal Studies Forward to Legal Realism, or How Not to Miss the Point of the Indeterminacy Argument*, 45 DUKE L.J. 84, 132 (1995) (*quoting* Gerald E. Frug, *Language as Power*, 84 COLUM. L. REV. 1881, 1895–96 (1984) (book review)) ("they see themselves as committed to the egalitarian creation of 'nonhierarchical communit[ies] of interest,' and thus, the empowerment of those oppressed by the current legal system."); Statement of Critical Legal Studies Conference, *quoted in* PETER FITZPATRICK & ALAN HUNT, *Critical Legal Studies: An Introduction, in* CRITICAL LEGAL STUDIES 1–2 (Peter Fitzpatrick & Alan Hunt eds., 1987) ("to explore the manner in which legal doctrine and legal education and the practices of legal institutions work to buttress and support a pervasive system of oppressive, inegalitarian relations"). *See generally* Peter Gabel and Paul Harris, *Building Power and Breaking Images: Critical Legal Theory and the Practice of Law*, 11 N.Y.U. REV. L. & SOC. CHANGE 369 (1982–83).

One possible interpretation of the inkblot—also with support in CLS scholarship—is that the critical approach echoes the Marxist and neo-Marxist critique of liberalism, namely that,

> in egalitarian orders, rights differentially empower different social groups, depending on their ability to enact the power that a right potentially entails. This is not to say that generically distributed rights offer nothing to those in the lower strata of such orders—the First Amendment offers something to all—but that, as countless critics have pointed out, the more social resources and the less social vulnerability one brings to the exercise of a right, the more power that exercise will reap, whether the right at issue is sexual freedom, private property, speech, or abortion. And still another conundrum of rights comes into play here. To the extent that rights such as private property rights are exercised not only against the state but against one another in economic arrangements in which some gain at the expense of others, universally distributed rights function not only as power but as deprivation: the right to private property is a vehicle for the accumulation of wealth through the production of another's poverty.

Wendy Brown, *Suffering the Paradoxes of Rights, in* LEFT LEGALISM/LEFT CRITIQUE 423 (Brown & Halley, eds. 2002). *See also* Richard Abel, *A Socialist Approach to Risk,* 41 MD. L. REV. 695, 718 (1982) ("Autonomy is not ensured by eliminating political restraints. That is the great myth of liberalism. Economic, social, and psychological constraints are just as important and often more powerful.")

On the other hand, as Professor Brian Leiter has pointed out, some parts of the critical project proceed in ways that Marx had specifically rejected:

> CLS writers [ ] locate the source of "indeterminacy" in law in one of two sources: either in general features of language itself (drawing here—not always accurately—on the semantic skepticism associated with Wittgenstein and Derrida); or in the existence of "contradictory" moral and political principles that they claim underlie the substantive law, understood at a suitable level of abstraction. [In the book under review, the author] recognizes this strand of CLS, which he aptly describes as claiming, ". . . that liberal consciousness is somehow a false or corrupted consciousness, that there exists within liberal thought—liberal legal thought included—a tension so fundamental, so irresolvable, that it must ultimately implode and make way for radical social transformation."
>
> * * * This strategy of argument signals the rather curious intellectual pedigree of CLS, a pedigree that [the author] does not appear to recognize. For what CLS has done in American legal thought is to revive a certain strategy of left-wing critique that dates back to the Left Young Hegelians of the 1830's in Germany. Seizing upon the Hegelian notion that *ideas* are the engine of historical change, the Left Hegelians sought to effect change by demonstrating that the prevailing conservative ideas were inherently contradictory and thus unstable. To resolve these contradictions, it would be necessary to change our ideas, and thus change the world.
>
> This strand of Hegelianism was a dead issue by the 1850's—in part because of Schopenhauer's devastating anti-Hegelian polemics, in part because of Marx's criticisms (about which more below), and in part because of the more general "materialistic" and "positivistic" turn in German intellectual life associated with Feuerbach and the so-called "German Materialists." It was not revived until 1922 when Georg Lukács re-introduced Left Hegelian themes into the Marxist tradition of social critique in *History and Class Consciousness*, especially in the central chapter on "The Antinomies of Bourgeois Thought." CLS, however, acquires the style of argument less from Lukács—though he is a favorite figure in the footnotes of CLS articles—than from Harvard Law School professor and CLS "founding father" Roberto Unger, whose 1975 book *Knowledge and Politics* is quite obviously a replay of the central arguments and themes of *History and Class Consciousness*.
>
> What is slightly ironic in this intellectual genealogy—one that most CLS writers seem only vaguely aware of—is that CLS should have revived precisely the tradition in left-wing thought that Marx had so viciously lampooned 150 years earlier! Indeed, with certain obvious emendations, we find Marx and Engels articulating (in *The German Ideology*) a critique one often hears, with some cause, of CLS:

> Since [the Crits] consider conceptions, thoughts, ideas, in fact all the products of consciousness . . . as the real chains of men . . . it is evident that [the Crits] have to fight only against these illusions of the consciousness. Since, according to their fantasy, the relationships of men, all their doings, their chains and their limitations are products of their consciousness, [the Crits] logically put to men the moral postulate of exchanging their present consciousness for human, critical or egoistic consciousness, and thus of removing their limitations. This demand to change consciousness amounts to a demand to interpret reality in another way, i.e., to recognize it by means of another interpretation. . . . They forget, however, that to these phrases [constituting the old interpretation] they are only opposing other phrases, and that they are in no way combating the real existing world when they are merely combating the phrases of this world.

Showing the right-wing professors that their ideas are incoherent and demanding that they change their ideas is politically irrelevant for Marx: it is, of course, “contradictions” in the material circumstances of life that are the real engine of historical change. What CLS has done is to revive precisely this discredited strand of critical theory—the critique of ideas or “consciousness”—in the legal domain. It is not obvious that these critiques are any more plausible or relevant now than they were in 1840.

Brian Leiter, *Is There an “American” Jurisprudence?: Review of NEIL DUXBURY, PATTERNS OF AMERICAN JURISPRUDENCE*, 17 OXFORD J. LEG. STUD. 367, 382–84 (Summer 1997),

9. *Obscurantism as a strategy?* Grounded in the discipline of semiotics and the French hermeneutic theory of Jacques Derrida, CLS writing is not necessarily for the faint-hearted (or the impatient). The opponents of CLS and its style always have parody at their fingertips:

> I (the “subject”) have (has) at various (“~~*different*~~”) times (“moments”) con(side)red (presup(posed)) writing (sharing “discourse” pertaining to) an article (“text”) “defining” (destroying) pomo (“postmodernist” and “legal postmodernist”) jargon (“signs”) for the “uninitiated” (unhip dullai[ ]rds). I was afraid it wouldn't be very “good”—and that it might even be “ ‘good’ ”—but took comfort from Richard Delgado's reassuring observation that Randall Kennedy's insistence on merit in legal scholarship was “potentially hostile to the idea of voice.”

Dennis W. Arrow, *Pomobabble: Postmodern Newspeak and Constitutional “Meaning” for the Uninitiated*, 96 MICH. L. REV. 461, 463–72 (1997) ([hilarious, self-referential] footnotes omitted). Why might the supporters of a radical re-imagination of the law require (or conclude that they require) new forms of scholarship and style? How do you respond to the argument that paradox or obscurantism is an essential first step towards enlightenment?

10. *Looking back in anger?* Like many of the other schools of jurisprudence explored in this book, CLS seems to have reached a generational highpoint and then passed into relative obscurity, at least in its original forms. CLS activity—measured through publishing, or faculty hiring, or "conferencing"—seems to have peaked two or three decades ago. Granting that some insights are powerful enough to survive fashions and the aging of the professoriate that articulated them, why might CLS be considered passé now?

CHAPTER SEVEN

POST-REALIST APPROACHES TO LAW AND OBLIGATION (IV): FEMINIST JURISPRUDENCE

■ ■ ■

"I myself have never been able to find out precisely what feminism is; I only know that people call me a feminist whenever I express sentiments that differentiate me from a doormat."

— Rebecca West

"Men feared witches and burned women."

— Louis Brandeis

Orientation

If the unifying theme of critical jurisprudence is that the law is a legitimating tool for power in society, feminist jurisprudence demonstrates with particularity that it works to perpetuate patriarchy and gender oppression. There are of course multiple varieties and generations of feminist thought and no single school of feminist legal theory, but at a minimum feminist jurisprudence draws on the lived experience of women and girls to expose the gendered components of supposedly neutral laws and practices. This demonstration can be accomplished in a number of ways. One stream of analysis focuses on gender inequality in particular substantive areas of law, like employment law (*e.g.*, sexual harassment and unequal pay), criminal law (*e.g.*, rape and domestic violence), and family law (*e.g.*, the distribution of assets in divorce and the valuing of the wife's work inside and outside the home), among others. Another technique more broadly demonstrates that law's presence in the "public" realm and its absence in the "private" realm systematically perpetuate male supremacy and the submission of women. Yet another resists fixating on inequality and discrimination, because that treats maleness as the norm, which systematically distorts the law and undermines its alleged neutrality. The opening readings and cases in this chapter invite you to think through the power and the limits of the discrimination template in various settings, including equal protection, violence against women, and pornography. The subsequent readings broaden focus to explore the law's control of women's lives, their autonomy, and their sexuality.

One essential step in approaching feminist jurisprudence is understanding the legal significance of the fact that gender and sex are not the same things. The physiological differences between males and females may be broad biological realities along a spectrum, but gender is a social construction so fundamental as to be virtually beyond notice:

> Talking about gender for most people is the equivalent of fish talking about water. Gender is so much the routine ground of everyday activities that questioning its taken-far-granted assumptions and presuppositions is like thinking about whether the sun will come up. Gender is so pervasive that in our society we assume it is bred into our genes. Most people find it hard to believe that gender is constantly created and re-created out of human interaction, out of social life, and is the texture and order of that social life. Yet gender, like culture, is a human production that depends on everyone constantly "doing gender". . . . Gender signs and signals are so ubiquitous that we usually fail to note them—unless they are missing or ambiguous. Then we are uncomfortable until we have successfully placed the other person in a gender status; otherwise, we feel socially dislocated * * *.

Judith Lorber, *"Night to His Day": The Social Construction of Gender* in PARADOXES OF GENDER 13–14 (1994) (footnotes and citations omitted). One way to approach feminist jurisprudence is to think of it as an effort both to make the social construct of "female" more visible and to expose the law's role in defining, policing, and transforming it.

In whatever way it is approached, feminist jurisprudence in its various forms has triggered a variety of minimization strategies by its critics and opponents. One of the most prominent strategies is the suggestion that whatever gender discrimination existed at one time has largely been redressed. That is, it is easy to see patriarchy protected by law in the past, as when the Supreme Court upheld the Illinois Supreme Court's decision in 1873 to refuse Myra Bradwell admission to the Illinois bar because she was a woman.[1] It is apparently difficult for some contemporary observers to see gender-based discrimination or other forms of patriarchy in the law as it is today. A second strategy of minimization suggests that gender oppression in the law (or through the rule of law ideal) is limited to a few isolated substantive fields or cases or jurisdictions but is not characteristic of any modern legal system as a whole. A third critique uses the variety of feminist thought to suggest that the rubric "feminist jurisprudence" covers no single coherent philosophy of law. It is true that the important distinctions among varieties of feminism as a social, cultural, and

---

[1] *Bradwell v. Illinois*, 83 U.S. (16 Wall.) 130 (1873). In his concurring opinion in *Bradwell*, Justice Bradley wrote that "Man is, or should be, woman's protector and defender. The natural and proper timidity and delicacy which belongs to the female sex evidently unfits it for many of the occupations of civil life. . . . The paramount destiny and mission of woman are to fulfil[l] the noble and benign offices of wife and mother."

intellectual movement do not necessarily translate into different results or shades of argument in the decided cases or other material culture of the law. In this of course, feminist jurisprudence is not all that different from other broad rubrics, like the "natural law" theories explored in Chapter 1 or the "legal realism" explored in Chapter 3.

A. THE DISCRIMINATION TEMPLATE AND ITS LIMITATIONS

1. GENDER AND THE EQUAL PROTECTION CLAUSE

REED V. REED

404 U.S. 71 (1971)

MR. CHIEF JUSTICE BURGER **delivered the opinion for a unanimous Court.** Richard Lynn Reed, a minor, died intestate in Ada County, Idaho, on March 29, 1967. His adoptive parents, who had separated sometime prior to his death, are the parties to this appeal. Approximately seven months after Richard's death, his mother, appellant Sally Reed, filed a petition in the Probate Court of Ada County, seeking appointment as administratrix of her son's estate. Prior to the date set for a hearing on the mother's petition, appellee Cecil Reed, the father of the decedent, filed a competing petition seeking to have himself appointed administrator of the son's estate. The probate court held a joint hearing on the two petitions and thereafter ordered that letters of administration be issued to appellee Cecil Reed upon his taking the oath and filing the bond required by law. The court treated §§ 15–312 and 15–314 of the Idaho Code as the controlling statutes and read those sections as compelling a preference for Cecil Reed because he was a male.

Section 15–312 designates the persons who are entitled to administer the estate of one who dies intestate. In making these designations, that section lists 11 classes of persons who are so entitled and provides, in substance, that the order in which those classes are listed in the section shall be determinative of the relative rights of competing applicants for letters of administration. One of the 11 classes so enumerated is "[t]he father or mother" of the person dying intestate. Under this section then appellant and appellee, being members of the same entitlement class, would seem to have been equally entitled to administer their son's estate. Section 15–314 provides, however, that "(o)f several persons claiming and equally entitled (under § 15–312) to administer, males must be preferred to females, and relatives of the whole to those of the half blood."

In issuing its order, the probate court implicitly recognized the equality of entitlement of the two applicants under § 15–312 and noted that neither of the applicants was under any legal disability; the court ruled, however, that appellee, being a male, was to be preferred to the female appellant "by reason of Section 15–314 of the Idaho Code." In stating this conclusion, the probate judge gave no indication that he had attempted to determine the relative capabilities of the competing applicants to perform the functions incident to the administration of an estate. It seems clear the probate judge considered himself bound by statute to give preference to the male candidate over the female, each being otherwise "equally entitled."

Sally Reed appealed from the probate court order, and her appeal was treated by the District Court of the Fourth Judicial District of Idaho as a constitutional attack on § 15–314. In dealing with the attack, that court held that the challenged section violated the Equal Protection Clause of the Fourteenth Amendment and was, therefore, void; the matter was ordered "returned to the Probate Court for its determination of which of the two parties" was better qualified to administer the estate.

This order was never carried out, however, for Cecil Reed took a further appeal to the Idaho Supreme Court, which reversed the District Court and reinstated the original order naming the father administrator of the estate. In reaching this result, the Idaho Supreme Court first dealt with the governing statutory law and held that under § 15–312 "a father and mother are 'equally entitled' to letters of administration," but the preference given to males by § 15–314 is 'mandatory' and leaves no room for the exercise of a probate court's discretion in the appointment of administrators. Having thus definitively and authoritatively interpreted the statutory provisions involved, the Idaho Supreme Court then proceeded to examine, and reject, Sally Reed's contention that § 15–314 violates the Equal Protection Clause by giving a mandatory preference to males over females, without regard to their individual qualifications as potential estate administrators.

Sally Reed thereupon appealed for review by this Court * * *. Having examined the record and considered the briefs and oral arguments of the parties, we have concluded that the arbitrary preference established in favor of males by § 15–314 of the Idaho Code cannot stand in the face of the Fourteenth Amendment's command that no State deny the equal protection of the laws to any person within its jurisdiction.

Idaho does not, of course, deny letters of administration to women altogether. Indeed, under § 15–312, a woman whose spouse dies intestate has a preference over a son, father, brother, or any other male relative of the decedent. Moreover, we can judicially notice that in this country, presumably due to the greater longevity of women, a large proportion of estates, both intestate and under wills of decedents, are administered by surviving widows.

Section 15–314 is restricted in its operation to those situations where competing applications for letters of administration have been filed by both male and female members of the same entitlement class established by § 15–312. In such situations, § 15–314 provides that different treatment be accorded to the applicants on the basis of their sex; it thus establishes a classification subject to scrutiny under the Equal Protection Clause.

In applying that clause, this Court has consistently recognized that the Fourteenth Amendment does not deny to States the power to treat different classes of persons in different ways. The Equal Protection Clause of that amendment does, however, deny to States the power to legislate that different treatment be accorded to persons placed by a statute into different classes on the basis of criteria wholly unrelated to the objective of that statute. A classification "must be reasonable, not arbitrary, and must rest upon some ground of difference having a fair and substantial relation to the object of the legislation, so that all persons similarly circumstanced shall be treated alike." *Royster Guano Co. v. Virginia*, 253 U.S. 412, 415 (1920). The question presented by this case, then, is whether a difference in the sex of competing applicants for letters of administration bears a rational relationship to a state objective that is sought to be advanced by the operation of §§ 15–312 and 15–314.

In upholding the latter section, the Idaho Supreme Court concluded that its objective was to eliminate one area of controversy when two or more persons, equally entitled under § 15–312, seek letters of administration and thereby present the probate court "with the issue of which one should be named." The court also concluded that where such persons are not of the same sex, the elimination of females from consideration "is neither an illogical nor arbitrary method devised by the legislature to resolve an issue that would otherwise require a hearing as to the relative merits * * * of the two or more petitioning relatives * * *."

Clearly the objective of reducing the workload on probate courts by eliminating one class of contests is not without some legitimacy. The crucial question, however, is whether § 15–314 advances that objective in a manner consistent with the command of the Equal Protection Clause. We hold that it does not. To give a mandatory preference to members of either sex over members of the other, merely to accomplish the elimination of hearings on the merits, is to make the very kind of arbitrary legislative choice forbidden by the Equal Protection Clause of the Fourteenth Amendment; and whatever may be said as to the positive values of avoiding intra-family controversy, the choice in this context may not lawfully be mandated solely on the basis of sex.

We note finally that if § 15–314 is viewed merely as a modifying appendage to § 15–312 and as aimed at the same objective, its constitutionality is not thereby saved. The objective of § 15–312 clearly is to establish degrees of entitlement of various classes of persons in accordance with their varying degrees and kinds of relationship to the intestate. Regardless of their sex, persons within any one of the enumerated classes of that section are similarly situated with respect to that objective. By providing dissimilar treatment for men and women who are thus similarly situated, the challenged section violates the Equal Protection Clause. * * * Reversed and remanded.

CRAIG V. BOREN

429 U.S. 190 (1976)

MR. JUSTICE BRENNAN **delivered the opinion of the Court.** The interaction of two sections of an Oklahoma statute, §§ 241 and 245,[1] prohibits the sale of "non-intoxicating" 3.2% beer to males under the age of 21 and to females under the age of 18. The question to be decided is whether such a gender-based differential constitutes a denial to males 18–20 years of age of the equal protection of the laws in violation of the Fourteenth Amendment.

This action was brought in the District Court for the Western District of Oklahoma * * * by appellant Craig, a male then between 18 and 21 years of age, and by appellant Whitener, a licensed vendor of 3.2% beer. The complaint sought declaratory and injunctive relief against enforcement of the gender-based differential on the ground that it constituted invidious discrimination against males 18–20 years of age. A three-judge court * * * sustained the constitutionality of the statutory differential and dismissed the action. * * * We reverse. * * *

Before 1972, Oklahoma defined the commencement of civil majority at age 18 for females and age 21 for males. In contrast, females were held criminally responsible as adults at age 18 and males at age 16. After the Court of Appeals for the Tenth Circuit held in 1972, on the authority of *Reed v. Reed*, 404 U.S. 71 (1971), that the age distinction was unconstitutional for purposes of establishing criminal responsibility as adults, the Oklahoma Legislature fixed age 18 as applicable to both males and females. In 1972, 18 also was established as the age of majority for males and females in civil matters, except that §§ 241 and 245 of the 3.2% beer statute were simultaneously codified to create an exception to the gender-free rule.

Analysis may appropriately begin with the reminder that *Reed* emphasized that statutory classifications that distinguish between males

---

[1] Sections 241 and 245 provide in pertinent part:

§ 241. "It shall be unlawful for any person who holds a license to sell and dispense beer . . . to sell, barter or give to any minor any beverage containing more than one-half of one per cent of alcohol measured by volume and not more than three and two-tenths (3.2) per cent of alcohol measured by weight.

§ 245. "A 'minor,' for the purposes of Section . . . 241 . . . is defined as a female under the age of eighteen (18) years, and a male under the age of twenty-one (21) years."

and females are "subject to scrutiny under the Equal Protection Clause." To withstand constitutional challenge, previous cases establish that classifications by gender must serve important governmental objectives and must be substantially related to achievement of those objectives. Thus, in *Reed*, the objectives of "reducing the workload on probate courts" and "avoiding intra-family controversy," were deemed of insufficient importance to sustain use of an overt gender criterion in the appointment of administrators of intestate decedents' estates. Decisions following *Reed* similarly have rejected administrative ease and convenience as sufficiently important objectives to justify gender-based classifications. *See, e. g., Stanley v. Illinois*, 405 U.S. 645 (1972); *Frontiero v. Richardson*, 411 U.S. 677, 690 (1973); *cf. Schlesinger v. Ballard*, 419 U.S. 498, 506–507 (1975). And only two Terms ago, *Stanton v. Stanton*, 421 U.S. 7 (1975), expressly stating that *Reed v. Reed* was "controlling," held that *Reed* required invalidation of a Utah differential age-of-majority statute, notwithstanding the statute's coincidence with and furtherance of the State's purpose of fostering "old notions" of role typing and preparing boys for their expected performance in the economic and political worlds.

Reed v. Reed has also provided the underpinning for decisions that have invalidated statutes employing gender as an inaccurate proxy for other, more germane bases of classification. Hence, "archaic and overbroad" generalizations, *Schlesinger v. Ballard, supra*, 419 U.S., at 508, concerning the financial position of servicewomen, *Frontiero v. Richardson, supra*, 411 U.S., at 689 n. 23, and working women, *Weinberger v. Wiesenfeld*, 420 U.S. 636, 643, could not justify use of a gender line in determining eligibility for certain governmental entitlements. Similarly, increasingly outdated misconceptions concerning the role of females in the home rather than in the "marketplace and world of ideas" were rejected as loose-fitting characterizations incapable of supporting state statutory schemes that were premised upon their accuracy. *Stanton v. Stanton, supra*; *Taylor v. Louisiana*, 419 U.S. 522, 535 n. 17 (1975). In light of the weak congruence between gender and the characteristic or trait that gender purported to represent, it was necessary that the legislatures choose either to realign their substantive laws in a gender-neutral fashion, or to adopt procedures for identifying those instances where the sex-centered generalization actually comported with fact. * * *

We turn then to the question whether, under *Reed*, the difference between males and females with respect to the purchase of 3.2% beer warrants the differential in age drawn by the Oklahoma statute. We conclude that it does not. * * *

The District Court recognized that *Reed v. Reed* was controlling. In applying the teachings of that case, the court found the requisite important governmental objective in the traffic-safety goal proffered by the Oklahoma Attorney General. It then concluded that the statistics introduced by the appellees established that the gender-based distinction was substantially related to achievement of that goal. * * *

We accept for purposes of discussion the District Court's identification of the objective underlying §§ 241 and 245 as the enhancement of traffic safety. Clearly, the protection of public health and safety represents an important function of state and local governments. However, appellees' statistics in our view cannot support the conclusion that the gender-based distinction closely serves to achieve that objective and therefore the distinction cannot under *Reed* withstand equal protection challenge.

The appellees introduced a variety of statistical surveys. First, an analysis of arrest statistics for 1973 demonstrated that 18–20-year-old male arrests for "driving under the influence" and "drunkenness" substantially exceeded female arrests for that same age period. Similarly, youths aged 17–21 were found to be overrepresented among those killed or injured in traffic accidents, with males again numerically exceeding females in this regard. Third, a random roadside survey in Oklahoma City revealed that young males were more inclined to drive and drink beer than were their female counterparts. Fourth, Federal Bureau of Investigation nationwide statistics exhibited a notable increase in arrests for "driving under the influence." Finally, statistical evidence gathered in other jurisdictions, particularly Minnesota and Michigan, was offered to corroborate Oklahoma's experience by indicating the pervasiveness of youthful participation in motor vehicle accidents following the imbibing of alcohol. Conceding that "the case is not free from doubt," the District Court nonetheless concluded that this statistical showing substantiated "a rational basis for the legislative judgment underlying the challenged classification."

Even were this statistical evidence accepted as accurate, it nevertheless offers only a weak answer to the equal protection question presented here. The most focused and relevant of the statistical surveys, arrests of 18–20-year-olds for alcohol-related driving offenses, exemplifies the ultimate unpersuasiveness of this evidentiary record. Viewed in terms of the correlation between sex and the actual activity that Oklahoma seeks to regulate driving while under the influence of alcohol the statistics broadly establish that .18% of females and 2% of males in that age group were arrested for that offense. While such a disparity is not trivial in a statistical sense, it hardly can form the basis for employment of a gender line as a classifying device. Certainly if maleness is to serve as a proxy for drinking and driving, a correlation of 2% must be considered an unduly tenuous "fit." Indeed, prior cases have consistently rejected the use of sex as a decision-making factor even though the statutes in question certainly rested on far more predictive empirical relationships than this.

Moreover, the statistics exhibit a variety of other shortcomings that seriously impugn their value to equal protection analysis. Setting aside the obvious methodological problems, the surveys do not adequately justify the salient features of Oklahoma's gender-based traffic-safety law. None purports to measure the use and dangerousness of 3.2% beer as opposed to alcohol generally, a detail that is of particular importance since, in light of its low alcohol level, Oklahoma apparently considers the 3.2% beverage to be "non-intoxicating." Moreover, many of the studies, while graphically documenting the unfortunate increase in driving while under the influence of alcohol, make no effort to relate their findings to age-sex differentials as involved here. Indeed, the only survey that explicitly centered its attention upon young drivers and their use of beer albeit apparently not of the diluted 3.2% variety reached results that hardly can be viewed as impressive in justifying either a gender or age classification.

There is no reason to belabor this line of analysis. It is unrealistic to expect either members of the judiciary or state officials to be well versed in the rigors of experimental or statistical technique. But this merely illustrates that proving broad sociological propositions by statistics is a dubious business, and one that inevitably is in tension with the normative philosophy that underlies the Equal Protection Clause. Suffice to say that the showing offered by the appellees does not satisfy us that sex represents a legitimate, accurate proxy for the regulation of drinking and driving. In fact, when it is further recognized that Oklahoma's statute prohibits only the selling of 3.2% beer to young males and not their drinking the beverage once acquired (even after purchase by their 18–20-year-old female companions), the relationship between gender and traffic safety becomes far too tenuous to satisfy *Reed's* requirement that the gender-based difference be substantially related to achievement of the statutory objective.

J.E.B. v. ALABAMA *EX REL.* T.B.

511 U.S. 127 (1994)

JUSTICE BLACKMUN delivered the opinion of the Court. In *Batson v. Kentucky*, 476 U.S. 79 (1986), this Court held that the Equal Protection Clause of the Fourteenth Amendment governs the exercise of peremptory challenges by a prosecutor in a criminal trial. The Court explained that although a defendant has "no right to a 'petit jury composed in whole or in part of persons of his own race," the "defendant does have the right to be tried by a jury whose members are selected pursuant to nondiscriminatory criteria." Since *Batson*, we have reaffirmed repeatedly our commitment to jury selection procedures that are fair and nondiscriminatory. We have recognized that whether the trial is criminal or civil, potential jurors, as well as litigants, have an equal protection right to jury selection procedures that are free from state-sponsored group stereotypes rooted in, and reflective of, historical prejudice.

Although premised on equal protection principles that apply equally to gender discrimination, all our recent cases defining the scope of *Batson* involved alleged racial discrimination in the exercise of peremptory challenges. Today we are faced with the question whether the Equal Protection Clause forbids intentional discrimination on the basis of gender, just as it prohibits discrimination on the basis of race. We hold that gender, like race, is an unconstitutional proxy for juror competence and impartiality. * * *

On behalf of * * * T.B., the mother of a minor child, [the] State of Alabama filed a complaint for paternity and child support against petitioner J.E.B. in the District Court of Jackson County, Alabama. On October 21, 1991, the matter was called for trial and jury selection began. The trial court assembled a panel of 36 potential jurors, 12 males and 24 females. After the court excused three jurors for cause, only 10 of the remaining 33 jurors were male. The State then used 9 of its 10 peremptory strikes to remove male jurors; petitioner used all but one of his strikes to remove female jurors. As a result, all the selected jurors were female.

Before the jury was empaneled, petitioner objected to the State's peremptory challenges on the ground that they were exercised against male jurors solely on the basis of gender, in violation of the Equal Protection Clause of the Fourteenth Amendment. Petitioner argued that the logic and reasoning of *Batson v. Kentucky*, which prohibits peremptory strikes solely on the basis of race, similarly forbids intentional discrimination on the basis of gender. The court rejected petitioner's claim and empaneled the all-female jury. The jury found petitioner to be the father of the child, and the court entered an order directing him to pay child support. On post judgment motion, the court reaffirmed its ruling that *Batson* does not extend to gender-based peremptory challenges. The Alabama Court of Civil Appeals affirmed. The Supreme Court of Alabama denied [review].

We granted *certiorari* to resolve a question that has created a conflict of authority—whether the Equal Protection Clause forbids peremptory challenges on the basis of gender as well as on the basis of race. Today we reaffirm what, by now, should be axiomatic: Intentional discrimination on the basis of gender by state actors violates the Equal Protection Clause, particularly where, as here, the discrimination serves to ratify and perpetuate invidious, archaic, and overbroad stereotypes about the relative abilities of men and women. * * *

Discrimination on the basis of gender in the exercise of peremptory challenges is a relatively recent phenomenon. Gender-based peremptory strikes were hardly practicable during most of our country's existence, since, until the 20th century, women were completely excluded from jury service.[2] So well entrenched was this exclusion of women that in 1880 this Court, while finding that the exclusion of African-American men from juries violated the Fourteenth Amendment, expressed no doubt that a State "may confine the selection [of jurors] to males." *Strauder v. West Virginia*, 100 U.S., at 310.

Many States continued to exclude women from jury service well into the present century, despite the fact that women attained suffrage upon ratification of the Nineteenth Amendment in 1920. States that did permit women to serve on juries often erected other barriers, such as registration requirements and automatic exemptions, designed to deter women from exercising their right to jury service. *See, e.g., Fay v. New York*, 332 U.S., at 289 ("[I]n 15 of the 28 states which permitted women to serve [on juries in 1942], they might claim exemption because of their sex"); *Hoyt v. Florida*, 368 U.S. 57 (1961) (upholding affirmative registration statute that exempted women from mandatory jury service).

The prohibition of women on juries was derived from the English common law which, according to Blackstone, rightfully excluded women from juries under "the doctrine of *propter defectum sexus*, literally, the 'defect of sex.'" *United States v. De Gross*, 960 F.2d 1433, 1438 (CA9 1992) (*en banc*), *quoting* 2 W. Blackstone, Commentaries *362. In this country, supporters of the exclusion of women from juries tended to couch their objections in terms of the ostensible need to protect women from the ugliness and depravity of trials. Women were thought to be too fragile and virginal to withstand the polluted courtroom atmosphere. See *Bailey v. State*, 215 Ark. 53, 61, 219 S.W.2d 424, 428 (1949) ("Criminal court trials often involve testimony of the foulest kind, and they sometimes require consideration of indecent conduct, the use of filthy and loathsome words, references to intimate sex relationships, and other elements that would prove humiliating, embarrassing and degrading to a lady"); *In re Goodell*, 39 Wis. 232, 245–246 (1875) (endorsing statutory ineligibility of women for admission to the bar because "[r]everence for all womanhood would suffer in the public spectacle of women . . . so engaged"); *Bradwell v. State*, 16 Wall. 130, 141, 21 L.Ed. 442 (1873) (concurring opinion) ("[T]he civil law, as well as nature herself, has always recognized a wide difference in the respective spheres and destinies of man and woman. Man is, or should be, woman's protector and defender. The natural and proper timidity and delicacy which belongs to the female sex evidently unfits it for many of the occupations of civil life. . . . The paramount destiny and mission of woman are to fulfill[l] the noble and benign offices of wife and mother. This is the law of the Creator"). *Cf. Frontiero v. Richardson*, 411 U.S. 677, 684 (1973)

---

[2] There was one brief exception. Between 1870 and 1871, women were permitted to serve on juries in Wyoming Territory. They were no longer allowed on juries after a new chief justice who disfavored the practice was appointed in 1871.

(plurality opinion) (This "attitude of 'romantic paternalism' . . . put women, not on a pedestal, but in a cage").

This Court in *Ballard v. United States*, 329 U.S. 187 (1946), first questioned the fundamental fairness of denying women the right to serve on juries. Relying on its supervisory powers over the federal courts, it held that women may not be excluded from the venire in federal trials in States where women were eligible for jury service under local law. In response to the argument that women have no superior or unique perspective, such that defendants are denied a fair trial by virtue of their exclusion from jury panels, the Court explained:

> It is said . . . that an all male panel drawn from the various groups within a community will be as truly representative as if women were included. The thought is that the factors which tend to influence the action of women are the same as those which influence the action of men—personality, background, economic status—and not sex. Yet it is not enough to say that women when sitting as jurors neither act nor tend to act as a class. Men likewise do not act like a class. . . . The truth is that the two sexes are not fungible; a community made up exclusively of one is different from a community composed of both; the subtle interplay of influence one on the other is among the imponderables. To insulate the courtroom from either may not in a given case make an iota of difference. Yet a flavor, a distinct quality is lost if either sex is excluded.

Fifteen years later, however, the Court still was unwilling to translate its appreciation for the value of women's contribution to civic life into an enforceable right to equal treatment under state laws governing jury service. In *Hoyt v. Florida*, 368 U.S., at 61, the Court found it reasonable, "[d]espite the enlightened emancipation of women," to exempt women from mandatory jury service by statute, allowing women to serve on juries only if they volunteered to serve. The Court justified the differential exemption policy on the ground that women, unlike men, occupied a unique position "as the center of home and family life."

In 1975, the Court finally repudiated the reasoning of *Hoyt* and struck down, under the Sixth Amendment, an affirmative registration statute nearly identical to the one at issue in *Hoyt*. *See Taylor v. Louisiana*, 419 U.S. 522 (1975). We explained: "Restricting jury service to only special groups or excluding identifiable segments playing major roles in the community cannot be squared with the constitutional concept of jury trial." The diverse and representative character of the jury must be maintained " 'partly as assurance of a diffused impartiality and partly because sharing in the administration of justice is a phase of civic responsibility.' " *Id.*, at 530–531, *quoting Thiel v. Southern Pacific Co.*, 328 U.S. 217, 227 (1946) (Frankfurter, J., dissenting). * * *

Despite the heightened scrutiny afforded distinctions based on gender, respondent argues that gender discrimination in the selection of the petit jury should be permitted, though discrimination on the basis of race is not. Respondent suggests that "gender discrimination in this country . . . has never reached the level of discrimination" against African-Americans, and therefore gender discrimination, unlike racial discrimination, is tolerable in the courtroom.

While the prejudicial attitudes toward women in this country have not been identical to those held toward racial minorities, the similarities between the experiences of racial minorities and women, in some contexts, "overpower those differences." Note, "Beyond Batson: Eliminating Gender-Based Peremptory Challenges," 105 HARV.L.REV. 1920, 1921 (1992). As a plurality of this Court observed in *Frontiero v. Richardson*, 411 U.S., at 685:

> [T]hroughout much of the 19th century the position of women in our society was, in many respects, comparable to that of blacks under the pre-Civil War slave codes. Neither slaves nor women could hold office, serve on juries, or bring suit in their own names, and married women traditionally were denied the legal capacity to hold or convey property or to serve as legal guardians of their own children. . . . And although blacks were guaranteed the right to vote in 1870, women were denied even that right—which is itself 'preservative of other basic civil and political rights' until adoption of the Nineteenth Amendment half a century later. (Footnote omitted.)

Certainly, with respect to jury service, African-Americans and women share a history of total exclusion, a history which came to an end for women many years after the embarrassing chapter in our history came to an end for African-Americans.

We need not determine, however, whether women or racial minorities have suffered more at the hands of discriminatory state actors during the decades of our Nation's history. It is necessary only to acknowledge that "our Nation has had a long and unfortunate history of sex discrimination," *id.*, at 684, a history which warrants the heightened scrutiny we afford all gender-based classifications today. Under our equal protection jurisprudence, gender-based classifications require "an exceedingly persuasive justification" in order to survive constitutional scrutiny. Thus, the only question is whether discrimination on the basis of gender in jury selection substantially furthers the State's legitimate interest in achieving a fair and impartial trial. In making this assessment, we do not weigh the value of peremptory challenges as an institution against our asserted commitment to eradicate invidious discrimination from the courtroom. Instead, we consider whether peremptory challenges based on gender stereotypes provide substantial aid to a litigant's effort to secure a fair and impartial jury.

Far from proffering an exceptionally persuasive justification for its gender-based peremptory challenges, respondent maintains that its decision to strike virtually all the males from the jury in this case "may reasonably have been based upon the perception, supported by history, that men otherwise totally qualified to serve upon a jury in any case might be more sympathetic and receptive to the arguments of a man alleged in a paternity action to be the father of an out-of-wedlock child, while women equally qualified to serve upon a jury might be more sympathetic and receptive to the arguments of the complaining witness who bore the child."[9]

We shall not accept as a defense to gender-based peremptory challenges "the very stereotype the law condemns." Respondent's rationale, not unlike those regularly expressed for gender-based strikes, is reminiscent of the arguments advanced to justify the total exclusion of women from juries.[10] Respondent offers virtually no support for the conclusion that gender alone is an accurate predictor of juror's attitudes; yet it urges this Court to condone the same stereotypes that justified the wholesale exclusion of women from juries and the ballot box.[11] Respondent

---

[9] Respondent cites one study in support of its quasi-empirical claim that women and men may have different attitudes about certain issues justifying the use of gender as a proxy for bias. See R. Hastie, S. Penrod, & N. Pennington, INSIDE THE JURY 140 (1983). The authors conclude: "Neither student nor citizen judgments for typical criminal case materials have revealed differences between male and female verdict preferences. . . . The picture differs [only] for rape cases, where female jurors appear to be somewhat more conviction-prone than male jurors." The majority of studies suggest that gender plays no identifiable role in jurors' attitudes. *See, e.g.*, V. Hans & N. Vidmar, JUDGING THE JURY 76 (1986) ("[I]n the majority of studies there are no significant differences in the way men and women perceive and react to trials; yet a few studies find women more defense-oriented, while still others show women more favorable to the prosecutor"). Even in 1956, before women had a constitutional right to serve on juries, some commentators warned against using gender as a proxy for bias. See F. Busch, LAW AND TACTICS IN JURY TRIALS § 143, p. 207 (1949) ("In this age of general and specialized education, availed of generally by both men and women, it would appear unsound to base a peremptory challenge in any case upon the sole ground of sex. . .").

[10] A manual formerly used to instruct prosecutors in Dallas, Texas, provided the following advice: " 'I don't like women jurors because I can't trust them. They do, however, make the best jurors in cases involving crimes against children. It is possible that their "women's intuition" can help you if you can't win your case with the facts.' " Alschuler, "The Supreme Court and the Jury: Voir Dire, Peremptory Challenges, and the Review of Jury Verdicts," 56 U.CHI.L.REV. 153, 210 (1989). Another widely circulated trial manual speculated:

> If counsel is depending upon a clearly applicable rule of law and if he wants to avoid a verdict of 'intuition' or 'sympathy,' if his verdict in amount is to be proved by clearly demonstrated blackboard figures for example, generally he would want a male juror. [But] women . . . are desired jurors when plaintiff is a man. A woman juror may see a man impeached from the beginning of the case to the end, but there is at least the chance [with] the woman juror (particularly if the man happens to be handsome or appealing) [that] the plaintiff's derelictions in and out of court will be overlooked. A woman is inclined to forgive sin in the opposite sex; but definitely not her own.

3 M. Belli, MODERN TRIALS §§ 51.67 and 51.68, pp. 446–447 (2d ed. 1982).

[11] Even if a measure of truth can be found in some of the gender stereotypes used to justify gender-based peremptory challenges, that fact alone cannot support discrimination on the basis of gender in jury selection. We have made abundantly clear in past cases that gender classifications that rest on impermissible stereotypes violate the Equal Protection Clause, even when some

seems to assume that gross generalizations that would be deemed impermissible if made on the basis of race are somehow permissible when made on the basis of gender.

Discrimination in jury selection, whether based on race or on gender, causes harm to the litigants, the community, and the individual jurors who are wrongfully excluded from participation in the judicial process. The litigants are harmed by the risk that the prejudice that motivated the discriminatory selection of the jury will infect the entire proceedings. *See Edmonson*, 500 U.S., at 628 (discrimination in the courtroom "raises serious questions as to the fairness of the proceedings conducted there"). The community is harmed by the State's participation in the perpetuation of invidious group stereotypes and the inevitable loss of confidence in our judicial system that state-sanctioned discrimination in the courtroom engenders.

When state actors exercise peremptory challenges in reliance on gender stereotypes, they ratify and reinforce prejudicial views of the relative abilities of men and women. Because these stereotypes have wreaked injustice in so many other spheres of our country's public life, active discrimination by litigants on the basis of gender during jury selection "invites cynicism respecting the jury's neutrality and its obligation to adhere to the law." *Powers v. Ohio*, 499 U.S., at 412. The potential for cynicism is particularly acute in cases where gender-related issues are prominent, such as cases involving rape, sexual harassment, or paternity. Discriminatory use of peremptory challenges may create the impression that the judicial system has acquiesced in suppressing full participation by one gender or that the "deck has been stacked" in favor of one side. * * *

In view of these concerns, the Equal Protection Clause prohibits discrimination in jury selection on the basis of gender, or on the assumption that an individual will be biased in a particular case for no reason other than the fact that the person happens to be a woman or happens to be a man. As with race, the "core guarantee of equal protection, ensuring citizens that their State will not discriminate . . ., would be meaningless

---

statistical support can be conjured up for the generalization. *See, e.g., Weinberger v. Wiesenfeld*, 420 U.S. 636, 645 (1975) (holding unconstitutional a Social Security Act classification authorizing benefits to widows but not to widowers despite the fact that the justification for the differential treatment was "not entirely without empirical support"); *Craig v. Boren*, 429 U.S. 190, 201 (1976) (invalidating an Oklahoma law that established different drinking ages for men and women, although the evidence supporting the age differential was "not trivial in a statistical sense"). The generalization advanced by Alabama in support of its asserted right to discriminate on the basis of gender is, at the least, overbroad, and serves only to perpetuate the same "outmoded notions of the relative capabilities of men and women," *Cleburne v. Cleburne Living Center*, Inc., 473 U.S. 432, 441 (1985), that we have invalidated in other contexts. The Equal Protection Clause, as interpreted by decisions of this Court, acknowledges that a shred of truth may be contained in some stereotypes, but requires that state actors look beyond the surface before making judgments about people that are likely to stigmatize as well as to perpetuate historical patterns of discrimination.

were we to approve the exclusion of jurors on the basis of such assumptions, which arise solely from the jurors' [gender]." *Batson*, 476 U.S., at 97–98.

NOTES AND QUESTIONS

1. *Intermediate vs. strict scrutiny of gender classifications*. The courts have identified three levels of scrutiny whenever a law or government policy is challenged on the ground that it deprives someone of the "Equal Protection of the Laws" under the Fourteenth Amendment to the U.S. Constitution. Some classifications made by the government will be sustained by the court if they have a "rational basis." For example, a tax provision that requires wealthy people to pay more would not rest on a suspect classification, because a rational basis can be made for a progressive tax code. Of course, literally interpreted, "rational basis" could amount to no effective scrutiny at all, because it would suggest that a law or regulation would satisfy the Equal Protection requirement "if there is *any conceivable state of facts* that could provide a rational basis for the classification." *Federal Communications Commission v. Beach Communications, Inc.*, 508 U.S. 307 (1993) (emphasis supplied). At the opposite extreme is "strict scrutiny," under which a government classification will be upheld only if (1) justified by a "compelling government interest," like national security or complying with the Constitution; (2) the law or policy must be narrowly-tailored to achieve or further that interest, and be neither overbroad nor under-inclusive; and (3) the law or policy must be the "least restrictive means" for achieving or furthering that interest. Classifications by race, national origin, or religion are generally subject to strict scrutiny, which is frequently fatal. *But see Korematsu v. United States*, 323 U.S. 214 (1944) (sustaining the constitutionality of a government program to intern American citizens of Japanese descent during World War II).

Between these two extremes is the "intermediate scrutiny" standard, under which a government classification will be sustained only if it furthers an important government interest in a way that is substantially related to that interest. *Craig v. Boren*, *supra*, apparently determined that gender-based classifications were subject to the intermediate standard of judicial review. But, in *Mississippi University for Women v. Hogan*, 458 U.S. 718 (1982), the Supreme Court decided that the government is under an obligation to show an "exceedingly persuasive justification" for gender-based classifications, and the Court has sometimes preferred the term "exacting scrutiny" when referring to the intermediate level of Equal Protection analysis. Why would gender be treated differently from race or religion?

2. *Statistics and stereotypes*. Consider the role of statistics in *Reed*, *Craig*, and *J.E.B.* As a matter of law, how relevant are studies of gender differences under the Equal Protection Clause? What if there is a "shred of truth * * * in some stereotypes," as the Court said in the last footnote of *J.E.B.*? Does it matter which right or privilege is involved in the case? Can you imagine

an actual case in which the state might be able to defend a gender-based classification?

3. *Irony, inevitability, or consistency?* Considering the results in the cases excerpted above, which gender (assuming for the moment that there are only two) apparently benefits more from gender neutrality in the law? *See also Mississippi University for Women v. Hogan*, 458 U.S. 718 (1982) (state's female-only admissions policy of school of nursing struck down on equal protection grounds). *Compare United States v. Virginia*, 518 U.S. 515 (1996) (striking down the male-only admissions policy of the Virginia Military Institution on equal protection grounds). Are there strategic merits in advancing an equal protection argument on the assumption that men might benefit as well (or first)?

4. *Understanding the variety in gender discrimination.* Some forms of gender-based discrimination are obvious: disparities in earnings for equal work; the overrepresentation of men in management and leadership positions; limited occupational and professional choices for women or choices based on gender stereotypes, discrimination on the basis of pregnancy or appearance. It is also well-established that sexual harassment is a form of discrimination, whether in the form of *quid pro quo* harassment or the creation of a "hostile work environment." In *Meritor Savings Bank v. Vinson*, 477 U.S. 57 (1986), for example, the Supreme Court ruled that sexual harassment leading to noneconomic injury was a form of gender discrimination in violation of Title VII of the Civil Rights Act of 1964. According to the Court, in adopting Title VII, Congress intended to " 'to strike at the entire spectrum of disparate treatment of men and women' in employment," and plaintiffs could establish violations of the Act "by proving that discrimination based on sex has created a hostile or abusive work environment."

The following materials allow you to explore the question of whether gender-based discrimination adequately accounts as a matter of law for other problems that are symptomatic of patriarchy.

---

2. VIOLENCE AGAINST WOMEN AS DISCRIMINATION

The Convention on the Elimination of All Forms of Discrimination against Women ("CEDAW") was adopted in 1979 by the UN General Assembly. It is one of the most widely ratified treaties in the world, but many governments have modified their legal obligations by attaching reservations to their acceptance of the Convention. CEDAW defines discrimination against women as "any distinction, exclusion or restriction made on the basis of sex which has the effect or purpose of impairing or nullifying the recognition, enjoyment or exercise by women, irrespective of their marital status, on a basis of equality of men and women, of human rights and fundamental freedoms in the political, economic, social, cultural, civil or any other field." Governments that are parties to the Convention are obliged to adopt a variety of measures to end discrimination against women in all its forms. According to the Office of the United Nations High Commissioner for Human Rights,

> [t]he Convention provides the basis for realizing equality between women and men through ensuring women's equal access to, and equal opportunities in, political and public life—including the right to vote and to stand for election—as well as education, health and employment. States parties agree to take all appropriate measures, including legislation and temporary special measures, so that women can enjoy all their human rights and fundamental freedoms.

The Convention also creates a Committee to monitor States-party's compliance. In that capacity, the Committee receives periodic reports from governments on the measures they take to comply with the treaty. The Committee is also empowered to adopt so-called "general recommendations," which offer an authoritative interpretation of the provisions of the Convention, the reporting obligations of States-party, thematic issues, or the Committee's work methods. *See, e.g.*, General Recommendation 19, *infra*. Under an Optional Protocol to the Convention, the Committee is further empowered to hear individual complaints against parties to the Convention. *See e.g.*, *A.T. v. Hungary*, *infra*. The Committee has frequently addressed domestic violence as a form of discrimination.

UNITED NATIONS COMMITTEE ON THE ELIMINATION OF DISCRIMINATION AGAINST WOMEN, GENERAL RECOMMENDATION 19: *VIOLENCE AGAINST WOMEN*

U.N. Doc. A/47/38(SUPP), at 1–8 (1993)

1. Gender-based violence is a form of discrimination that seriously inhibits women's ability to enjoy rights and freedoms on a basis of equality with men. * * *

6. The Convention [on the Elimination of Discrimination Against Women] in article 1 defines discrimination against women. The definition of discrimination includes gender-based violence, that is, violence that is directed against a woman because she is a woman or that affects women disproportionately. It includes acts that inflict physical, mental or sexual harm or suffering, threats of such acts, coercion and other deprivations of liberty. Gender-based violence may breach specific provisions of the Convention, regardless of whether those provisions expressly mention violence.

7. Gender-based violence, which impairs or nullifies the enjoyment by women of human rights and fundamental freedoms under general

international law or under human rights conventions, is discrimination within the meaning of article 1 of the Convention. These rights and freedoms include:

(a) The right to life;

(b) The right not to be subject to torture or to cruel, inhuman or degrading treatment or punishment;

(c) The right to equal protection according to humanitarian norms in time of international or internal armed conflict;

(d) The right to liberty and security of person;

(e) The right to equal protection under the law;

(f) The right to equality in the family;

(g) The right to the highest standard attainable of physical and mental health;

(h) The right to just and favourable conditions of work.

8. The Convention applies to violence perpetrated by public authorities. Such acts of violence may breach that State's obligations under general international human rights law and under other conventions, in addition to breaching this Convention.

9. It is emphasized, however, that discrimination under the Convention is not restricted to action by or on behalf of Governments. For example, under article 2(e) the Convention calls on States parties to take all appropriate measures to eliminate discrimination against women by any person, organization or enterprise. Under general international law and specific human rights covenants, States may also be responsible for private acts if they fail to act with due diligence to prevent violations of rights or to investigate and punish acts of violence, and for providing compensation. * * *

11. Traditional attitudes by which women are regarded as subordinate to men or as having stereotyped roles perpetuate widespread practices involving violence or coercion, such as family violence and abuse, forced marriage, dowry deaths, acid attacks and female circumcision. Such prejudices and practices may justify gender-based violence as a form of protection or control of women. The effect of such violence on the physical and mental integrity of women is to deprive them the equal enjoyment, exercise and knowledge of human rights and fundamental freedoms. While this comment addresses mainly actual or threatened violence the underlying consequences of these forms of gender-based violence help to maintain women in subordinate roles and contribute to the low level of political participation and to their lower level of education, skills and work opportunities.

12. These attitudes also contribute to the propagation of pornography and the depiction and other commercial exploitation of women as sexual objects, rather than as individuals. This in turn contributes to gender-based violence. * * *

13. States parties are required by article 6 to take measures to suppress all forms of traffic in women and exploitation of the prostitution of women.

14. Poverty and unemployment increase opportunities for trafficking in women. In addition to established forms of trafficking there are new forms of sexual exploitation, such as sex tourism, the recruitment of domestic labour from developing countries to work in developed countries and organized marriages between women from developing countries and foreign nationals. These practices are incompatible with the equal enjoyment of rights by women and with respect for their rights and dignity. They put women at special risk of violence and abuse.

15. Poverty and unemployment force many women, including young girls, into prostitution. Prostitutes are especially vulnerable to violence because their status, which may be unlawful, tends to marginalize them. They need the equal protection of laws against rape and other forms of violence.

16. Wars, armed conflicts and the occupation of territories often lead to increased prostitution, trafficking in women and sexual assault of women, which require specific protective and punitive measures. * * *

17. Equality in employment can be seriously impaired when women are subjected to gender-specific violence, such as sexual harassment in the workplace.

18. Sexual harassment includes such unwelcome sexually determined behaviour as physical contact and advances, sexually coloured remarks, showing pornography and sexual demand, whether by words or actions. Such conduct can be humiliating and may constitute a health and safety problem; it is discriminatory when the woman has reasonable grounds to believe that her objection would disadvantage her in connection with her employment, including recruitment or promotion, or when it creates a hostile working environment. * * *

19. States parties are required by article 12 to take measures to ensure equal access to health care. Violence against women puts their health and lives at risk.

20. In some States there are traditional practices perpetuated by culture and tradition that are harmful to the health of women and children. These practices include dietary restrictions for pregnant women, preference for male children and female circumcision or genital mutilation. * * *

21. Rural women are at risk of gender-based violence because traditional attitudes regarding the subordinate role of women that persist in many rural communities. Girls from rural communities are at special risk of violence and sexual exploitation when they leave the rural community to seek employment in towns. * * *

22. Compulsory sterilization or abortion adversely affects women's physical and mental health, and infringes the right of women to decide on the number and spacing of their children.

23. Family violence is one of the most insidious forms of violence against women. It is prevalent in all societies. Within family relationships women of all ages are subjected to violence of all kinds, including battering, rape, other forms of sexual assault, mental and other forms of violence, which are perpetuated by traditional attitudes. Lack of economic independence forces many women to stay in violent relationships. The abrogation of their family responsibilities by men can be a form of violence, and coercion. These forms of violence put women's health at risk and impair their ability to participate in family life and public life on a basis of equality.

Specific recommendation

24. In light of these comments, the Committee on the Elimination of Discrimination against Women recommends that:

(a) States parties should take appropriate and effective measures to overcome all forms of gender-based violence, whether by public or private act;

(b) States parties should ensure that laws against family violence and abuse, rape, sexual assault and other gender-based violence give adequate protection to all women, and respect their integrity and dignity. Appropriate protective and support services should be provided for victims. Gender-sensitive training of judicial and law enforcement officers and other public officials is essential for the effective implementation of the Convention;

(c) States parties should encourage the compilation of statistics and research on the extent, causes and effects of violence, and on the effectiveness of measures to prevent and deal with violence;

(d) Effective measures should be taken to ensure that the media respect and promote respect for women;

(e) States parties in their reports should identify the nature and extent of attitudes, customs and practices that perpetuate violence against women and the kinds of violence that result. They should report on the measures that they have undertaken to overcome violence and the effect of those measures;

(f) Effective measures should be taken to overcome these attitudes and practices. States should introduce education and public information programmes to help eliminate prejudices that hinder women's equality;

(g) Specific preventive and punitive measures are necessary to overcome trafficking and sexual exploitation;

(h) States parties in their reports should describe the extent of all these problems and the measures, including penal provisions, preventive and rehabilitation measures that have been taken to protect women engaged in prostitution or subject to trafficking and other forms of sexual exploitation. The effectiveness of these measures should also be described;

(i) Effective complaints procedures and remedies, including compensation, should be provided;

(j) States parties should include in their reports information on sexual harassment, and on measures to protect women from sexual harassment and other forms of violence of coercion in the workplace;

(k) States parties should establish or support services for victims of family violence, rape, sexual assault and other forms of gender-based violence, including refuges, specially trained health workers, rehabilitation and counselling;

(*l*) States parties should take measures to overcome such practices and should take account of the Committee's recommendation on female circumcision * * * in reporting on health issues;

(m) States parties should ensure that measures are taken to prevent coercion in regard to fertility and reproduction, and to ensure that women are not forced to seek unsafe medical procedures such as illegal abortion because of lack of appropriate services in regard to fertility control;

(n) States parties in their reports should state the extent of these problems and should indicate the measures that have been taken and their effect;

(*o*) States parties should ensure that services for victims of violence are accessible to rural women and that where necessary special services are provided to isolated communities;

(p) Measures to protect them from violence should include training and employment opportunities and the monitoring of the employment conditions of domestic workers;

(q) States parties should report on the risks to rural women, the extent and nature of violence and abuse to which they are subject, their need for and access to support and other services and the effectiveness of measures to overcome violence;

(r) Measures that are necessary to overcome family violence should include:

(i) Criminal penalties where necessary and civil remedies in cases of domestic violence;

(ii) Legislation to remove the defence of honour in regard to the assault or murder of a female family member;

(iii) Services to ensure the safety and security of victims of family violence, including refuges, counselling and rehabilitation programmes;

(iv) Rehabilitation programmes for perpetrators of domestic violence;

(v) Support services for families where incest or sexual abuse has occurred;

(s) States parties should report on the extent of domestic violence and sexual abuse, and on the preventive, punitive and remedial measures that have been taken;

(t) States parties should take all legal and other measures that are necessary to provide effective protection of women against gender-based violence, including, *inter alia*:

(i) Effective legal measures, including penal sanctions, civil remedies and compensatory provisions to protect women against all kinds of violence, including *inter alia* violence and abuse in the family, sexual assault and sexual harassment in the workplace;

(ii) Preventive measures, including public information and education programmes to change attitudes concerning the roles and status of men and women;

(iii) Protective measures, including refuges, counselling, rehabilitation and support services for women who are the victims of violence or who are at risk of violence;

(u) States parties should report on all forms of gender-based violence, and such reports should include all available data on the incidence of each form of violence and on the effects of such violence on the women who are victims;

(v) The reports of States parties should include information on the legal, preventive and protective measures that have been taken to overcome violence against women, and on the effectiveness of such measures.

A.T. v. HUNGARY

United Nations Committee on the Elimination of Discrimination Against Women
CEDAW Communication No. 2/2003
U.N. Doc. CEDAW/C/32/D/2/2003 (2005)

* * * The author [A.T.] states that for the past four years she has been subjected to regular severe domestic violence and serious threats by her common law husband, L.F., father of her two children, one of whom is severely brain-damaged. Although L.F. allegedly possesses a firearm and has threatened to kill the author and rape the children, the author has not gone to a shelter, reportedly because no shelter in the country is equipped to take in a fully disabled child together with his mother and sister. The author also states that there are currently no protection orders or restraining orders available under Hungarian law.

In March 1999, L.F. moved out of the family apartment. His subsequent visits allegedly typically included battering and/or loud shouting, aggravated by his being in a drunken state. In March 2000, L.F. reportedly moved in with a new female partner and left the family home, taking most of the furniture and household items with him. The author claims that he did not pay child support for three years, which forced her to claim the support by going to the court and to the police, and that he has used this form of financial abuse as a violent tactic in addition to continuing to threaten her physically. Hoping to protect herself and the children, the author states that she changed the lock on the door of the family's apartment on 11 March 2000. On 14 and 26 March 2000, L.F. filled the lock with glue and on 28 March 2000, he kicked in a part of the door when the author refused to allow him to enter the apartment. The author further states that, on 27 July 2001, L.F. broke into the apartment using violence.

L.F. is said to have battered the author severely on several occasions, beginning in March 1998. Since then, 10 medical certificates have been issued in connection with separate incidents of severe physical violence, even after L.F. left the family residence, which, the author submits, constitute a continuum of violence. The most recent incident took place on 27 July 2001 when L.F. broke into the apartment and subjected the author to a severe beating, which necessitated her hospitalization.

The author states that there have been civil proceedings regarding L.F.'s access to the family's residence, a 2 and a half room apartment * * * jointly owned by L.F. and the author. * * * On 4 September 2003, the Budapest Regional Court * * * issued a final decision authorizing L.F. to return and use the apartment. The judges reportedly based their decision on the following grounds: (a) lack of substantiation of the claim that L.F. regularly battered the author; and (b) that L.F.'s right to the property, including possession, could not be restricted. Since that date, and on the basis of the earlier attacks and verbal threats by her former partner, the author claims that her physical integrity, physical and mental health and life have been at serious risk and that she lives in constant fear. * * *

The author states that she also initiated civil proceedings regarding division of the property, which have been suspended. She claims that L.F. refused her offer to be compensated for half of the value of the apartment and turn over ownership to her. * * *

The author states that there have been two ongoing criminal procedures against L.F. * * *. L.F. has not been detained at any time in this connection and that no action has been taken by the Hungarian authorities to protect the author from him. The author claims that, as a victim, she has not been privy to the court documents and, that, therefore, she cannot submit them to the Committee.

The author also submits that she has requested assistance in writing, in person and by phone, from the local child protection authorities, but that her requests have been to no avail since the authorities allegedly feel unable to do anything in such situations. * * *

The State party maintains that although the author did not make effective use of the domestic remedies available to her, and although some domestic proceedings are still pending, the State party does not wish to raise any preliminary objections as to the admissibility of the communication. At the same time, the State party admits that these remedies were not capable of providing immediate protection to the author from ill-treatment by her former partner. * * *

With regard to article 2 (a), (b), and (e), the Committee notes that the State party has admitted that the remedies pursued by the author were not capable of providing immediate protection to her against ill-treatment by her former partner and, furthermore, that legal and institutional arrangements in the State party are not yet ready to ensure the internationally expected, coordinated, comprehensive and effective protection and support for the victims of domestic violence. While appreciating the State party's efforts at instituting a comprehensive action programme against domestic violence and the legal and other measures envisioned, the Committee believes that these have yet to benefit the author and address her persistent situation of insecurity. The Committee further notes the State party's general assessment that domestic violence cases as such do not enjoy high priority in court proceedings. The Committee is of the opinion that the description provided of the proceedings resorted to in the present case, both the civil and criminal proceedings, coincides with this general assessment. Women's human rights to life and to physical and mental integrity cannot be superseded by other rights, including the right to property and the right to privacy. The Committee also takes note that the State party does not offer information as to the existence of alternative avenues that the author might have pursued that would have provided sufficient protection or security from the danger of continued violence. In this connection, the Committee recalls its concluding comments from August 2002 on the State party's combined fourth and fifth periodic report, which state "... [T]he Committee is concerned about the prevalence of violence against women and girls, including domestic violence. It is particularly concerned that no specific legislation has been enacted to combat domestic violence and sexual harassment and that no protection or exclusion orders or shelters exist for the immediate protection of women victims of domestic violence". Bearing this in mind, the Committee concludes that the obligations of the State party set out in article 2 (a), (b) and (e) of the Convention extend to the prevention of and protection from violence against women, which obligations in the present case, remain unfulfilled and constitute a violation of the author's human rights and fundamental freedoms, particularly her right to security of person.

The Committee * * * has stated on many occasions that traditional attitudes by which women are regarded as subordinate to men contribute to violence against them. The Committee recognized those very attitudes when it considered the combined fourth and fifth periodic report of Hungary in 2002. At that time it was concerned about the "persistence of entrenched traditional stereotypes regarding the role and responsibilities of women and men in the family . . .". In respect of the case now before the Committee, the facts of the communication reveal aspects of the relationships between the sexes and attitudes towards women that the Committee recognized vis-à-vis the country as a whole. For four years and continuing to the present day, the author has felt threatened by her former common law husband, the father of her two children. The author has been battered by this same man, her former common law husband. She has been unsuccessful, either through civil or criminal proceedings, to temporarily or permanently bar L. F. from the apartment where she and her children have continued to reside. The author could not have asked for a restraining or protection order since neither option currently exists in the State party. She has been unable to flee to a shelter because none are equipped to accept her together with her children, one of whom is fully disabled. None of these facts have been disputed by the State party and, considered together, they indicate that the rights of the author under * * * the Convention have been violated. * * *

[T]he Committee is of the view that the State party has failed to fulfil its obligations and has thereby violated the rights of the author under * * * the Convention on the Elimination of All Forms of Discrimination against Women, and makes the following recommendations to the State party:

I. Concerning the author of the communication

(a) Take immediate and effective measures to guarantee the physical and mental integrity of A. T. and her family;

(b) Ensure that A. T. is given a safe home in which to live with her children, receives appropriate child support and legal assistance as well as reparation proportionate to the physical and mental harm undergone and to the gravity of the violations of her rights;

II. General

(a) Respect, protect, promote and fulfil women's human rights, including their right to be free from all forms of domestic violence, including intimidation and threats of violence;

(b) Assure victims of domestic violence the maximum protection of the law by acting with due diligence to prevent and respond to such violence against women;

(c) Take all necessary measures to ensure that the national strategy for the prevention and effective treatment of violence within the family is promptly implemented and evaluated;

(d) Take all necessary measures to provide regular training on the Convention on the Elimination of All Forms of Discrimination against Women and the Optional Protocol thereto to judges, lawyers and law enforcement officials;

(e) Implement expeditiously and without delay the Committee's concluding comments of August 2002 on the combined fourth and fifth periodic report of Hungary in respect of violence against women and girls, in particular the Committee's recommendation that a specific law be introduced prohibiting domestic violence against women, which would provide for protection and exclusion orders as well as support services, including shelters;

(f) Investigate promptly, thoroughly, impartially and seriously all allegations of domestic violence and bring the offenders to justice in accordance with international standards;

(g) Provide victims of domestic violence with safe and prompt access to justice, including free legal aid where necessary, in order to ensure them available, effective and sufficient remedies and rehabilitation;

(h) Provide offenders with rehabilitation programmes and programmes on non-violent conflict resolution methods. * * *

NOTES AND QUESTIONS

1. *"When the only tool you have is a hammer, every problem looks like a nail."* Can every problem with patriarchy be viewed as a matter of discrimination or unequal treatment between/among the genders? If you were working to eradicate violence against women, would your first argument at law be that it constitutes acts of gender-based discrimination? What does the discrimination template miss or distort?

2. *Pornography as gender discrimination, women as men's speech.* In *American Booksellers Ass'n, Inc. v. Hudnut*, 771 F.2d 323 (7th Cir. 1985), the court had to assess the constitutionality of a municipal ordinance, adopted by the city of Indianapolis, which defined "pornography" as a practice that discriminates against women. "Pornography" refers to material that is not obscene (obscenity being entitled to no constitutional protection anyway) and which is the graphic sexually explicit subordination of women, whether in pictures or in words, that also includes one or more of the following:

> (1) Women are presented as sexual objects who enjoy pain or humiliation; or
>
> (2) Women are presented as sexual objects who experience sexual pleasure in being raped; or
>
> (3) Women are presented as sexual objects tied up or cut up or mutilated or bruised or physically hurt, or as dismembered or truncated or fragmented or severed into body parts; or
>
> (4) Women are presented as being penetrated by objects or animals; or
>
> (5) Women are presented in scenarios of degradation, injury, abasement, torture, shown as filthy or inferior, bleeding, bruised, or hurt in a context that makes these conditions sexual; or
>
> (6) Women are presented as sexual objects for domination, conquest, violation, exploitation, possession, or use, or through postures or positions of servility or submission or display.

Indianapolis Code § 16–3(q). According to the city council which adopted the legislation, "[p]ornography is central in creating and maintaining sex as a basis of discrimination. Pornography is a systematic practice of exploitation and subordination based on sex which differentially harms women. The bigotry and contempt it produces, with the acts of aggression it fosters, harm women's opportunities for equality and rights [of all kinds]." Indianapolis Code § 16–1(a)(2).

The Court, per Judge Easterbrook, ruled the Indianapolis ordinance unconstitutional even as it "accept[ed] the premises of this legislation. Depictions of subordination tend to perpetuate subordination. The subordinate status of women in turn leads to affront and lower pay at work, insult and injury at home, battery and rape on the streets. * * *" The Court continued:

Yet this simply demonstrates the power of pornography as speech. All of these unhappy effects depend on mental intermediation. Pornography affects how people see the world, their fellows, and social relations. If pornography is what pornography does, so is other speech. Hitler's orations affected how some Germans saw Jews. Communism is a world view, not simply a Manifesto by Marx and Engels or a set of speeches. Efforts to suppress communist speech in the United States were based on the belief that the public acceptability of such ideas would increase the likelihood of totalitarian government. Religions affect socialization in the most pervasive way. The opinion in *Wisconsin v. Yoder*, 406 U.S. 205 (1972), shows how a religion can dominate an entire approach to life, governing much more than the relation between the sexes. Many people believe that the existence of television, apart from the content of specific programs, leads to intellectual laziness, to a penchant for violence, to many other ills. The Alien and Sedition Acts passed during the administration of John Adams rested on a sincerely held belief that disrespect for the government leads to social collapse and revolution-a belief with support in the history of many nations. Most governments of the world act on this empirical regularity, suppressing critical speech. In the United States, however, the strength of the support for this belief is irrelevant. Seditious libel is protected speech unless the danger is not only grave but also imminent. *See New York Times Co. v. Sullivan*, 376 U.S. 254 (1964); *cf. Brandenburg v. Ohio, supra*; *New York Times Co. v. United States*, 403 U.S. 713 (1971).

Racial bigotry, anti-semitism, violence on television, reporters' biases—these and many more influence the culture and shape our socialization. None is directly answerable by more speech, unless that speech too finds its place in the popular culture. Yet all is protected as speech, however insidious. Any other answer leaves the government in control of all of the institutions of culture, the great censor and director of which thoughts are good for us.

Sexual responses often are unthinking responses, and the association of sexual arousal with the subordination of women therefore may have a substantial effect. But almost all cultural stimuli provoke unconscious responses. Religious ceremonies condition their participants. Teachers convey messages by selecting what not to cover; the implicit message about what is off limits or unthinkable may be more powerful than the messages for which they present rational argument. Television scripts contain unarticulated assumptions. People may be conditioned in subtle ways. If the fact that speech plays a role in a process of conditioning were enough to permit governmental regulation, that would be the end of freedom of speech.

In this connection, consider Professor Catherine MacKinnon's position on the problem of pornography:

> [P]ornography's protection fits perfectly with the power relations embedded in First Amendment structure and jurisprudence from the start. Pornography is exactly the speech of men that silences the speech of women. I take it seriously when Justice Douglas speaking on pornography and others preaching absolutism say that pornography has to be protected speech or else free expression will not mean what it has always meant in this country.

CATHERINE MACKINNON, FEMINISM UNMODIFIED: DISCOURSES ON LIFE AND LAW 208–9 (1987). The Supreme Court of Canada reached a conclusion consistent with Professor MacKinnon's position and opposite the result in *Hudnut. See R. v. Butler*, [1992] 1 S.C.R. 452.

The recurrent metaphor of the "marketplace of ideas"—which underlies much of First Amendment jurisprudence and *Hudnut* specifically—makes certain assumptions about society and the power relations within it. Like what? Are you convinced that pornography is another form of gender discrimination?

3. *Statutory interpretation*. In *Hudnut*, Judge Easterbrook expressed concern that the Indianapolis ordinance would ban certain works of art, including W.B. Yeats' poem, *Leda and the Swan*? The poem in its entirety:

> A sudden blow: the great wings beating still
>
> Above the staggering girl, her thighs caressed
>
> By the dark webs, her nape caught in his bill,
>
> He holds her helpless breast upon his breast.
>
> How can those terrified vague fingers push
>
> The feathered glory from her loosening thighs?
>
> And how can body, laid in that white rush,
>
> But feel the strange heart beating where it lies?
>
> A shudder in the loins engenders there
>
> The broken wall, the burning roof and tower
>
> And Agamemnon dead.
>
> Being so caught up,
>
> So mastered by the brute blood of the air,
>
> Did she put on his knowledge with his power
>
> Before the indifferent beak could let her drop?

What are the best arguments that the pornography ordinance does not reach this poem?

4. *Feminist opposition to anti-pornography laws.* Some feminists criticized the anti-pornography laws as a poor tactic in the war against the oppression of women and suggested that such laws could be used to stifle the freedom of speech and sexuality of women and sexual minorities:

CHISUN LEE, COUNTER 'REVOLUTION:' FCC DUBS FEMINIST LYRICS 'PATENTLY OFFENSIVE'

The Village Voice
(19 June 2001)

your revolution will not happen between
these thighs . . .
the real revolution
ain't about booty size . . .
and though we've lost Biggie Smalls
your Notorious revolution
will never allow you to lace no lyrical douche
in my bush . . .
your revolution will not be you
smackin' it up, flippin' it, or rubbin' it down
nor will it take you downtown or
humpin' around . . .
you will not be touching your lips to
my triple dip of
french vanilla butter pecan chocolate deluxe
or having Akinye's dream
a six-foot blowjob machine . . .
your revolution will not happen between
these thighs . . .
because the revolution, when it
finally comes, is gon' be real
—from "Your Revolution," by Sarah Jones

Feminist black performance artist Sarah Jones and less-than-politically-correct white rapper Eminem aren't an obvious pair. But the Federal Communications Commission has censored both artists by recently issuing $7000 indecency fines to radio stations for playing their songs.

Ironically, Jones's "Your Revolution" makes a powerful statement against indecency—in particular, the sexual exploitation of women in popular music. The song, originally a poem, pulls no punches in making its feminist critique, taking direct aim at famous hip-hop songs by artists including LL Cool J and Notorious B.I.G. by quoting and then denouncing some of their macho lyrics.

"The hip-hop game is very misogynistic," explains Deena Barnwell, a volunteer DJ at Portland's KBOO-FM radio. "I've been totally disrespected as a woman in this game. Jones's song is inspirational. It says it's cool, you can be in the hip-hop game, but you don't have to be no 'ho. There's nothing else out there besides this song that tells girls that. I feel like it's a personal responsibility for me as a B-girl to get it out there." So Barnwell played the track, and according to the FCC, a listener was offended by an October 20, 1999, airing.

Station manager Chris Merrick figured the song's empowerment message would easily exempt it from the FCC investigation, which beginning this February looked at about a half-dozen other hip-hop songs broadcast on KBOO. "We all had a very good feeling about this song," he says. According to its written guidelines, the aim of the largely listener-supported station is "filling needs that other media do not, providing programming to diverse communities and unserved or underserved groups."

In fact, the Jones song was the only one to make the FCC's final cut. "Our lawyer and I were both stunned," says Merrick, when they received the May 17 notice fining KBOO for airing indecent language at a time—between 6 a.m. and 10 p.m.—when children might have been listening. "The rap song, 'Your Revolution,'" the notice states, "contains unmistakable patently offensive sexual references. . . . [T]he sexual references appear to be designed to pander and shock. . . ." Merrick objects, "It's clearly not pandering. In fact, I thought it was antisexual."

The FCC's characterization of the song betrays a deep political and cultural ignorance, argues the station. "The contemporary social commentary in 'Your Revolution' is a relevant contextual consideration, but is not in itself dispositive," concludes the agency notice. KBOO lawyer John Crigler argues, "[The FCC] oversimplified the context. We said, you gotta listen to the song. You have to understand that the song itself, musically, is a critique, it's a feminist attack on macho values of typical rap music. And you don't get that unless you listen to something. The commission just said, no thanks, we don't want to consider that." Fearing further fines, KBOO management temporarily suspended Barnwell and then moved her show to after 10 p.m., when the FCC believes children will not be listening. Other programmers have also been warned of decency issues, but Crigler says the station will challenge the fine and the reasoning behind it in a July appeal.

Most troubling about the FCC finding to "Your Revolution" supporters is that it condemns precisely the elements of the song that make it such an effective protest in the first place. The feminist message would less likely grab listeners' attention if it did not use such familiar lyrics, according to DJ Barnwell. The original rhymes are offensive, says Jones, and they are especially troubling because they are so popular; that's why she highlighted and responded to them in a song of protest.

But the FCC has reinforced the very image of women as sexual teases that the song means to challenge, protests Jones. "Your Revolution" was inspired by her experience "as a black woman, growing up in a culture where women of color too often are perceived as somehow oversexed," she says. "I read these words—that I'm sexually pandering and intending to shock—and it was just so clear to me that they were attacking my freedom as a person, as a woman, and as a woman of color, to defend myself." The FCC enforcement bureau's John Winston refused to comment on the KBOO case.

Calling for stricter on-air decency standards, commissioner Susan Ness this April exhorted stations to monitor their programming more closely and broadcast "in a manner that celebrates rather than debases humankind."

For Hunter College student Veronica De La Rosa, Jones's song does just that. "Sometimes we listen but we don't actually hear. . . . Bringing out the famous rappers and their lyrics allowed me to see that they are viewing women as sex objects," she writes in a class essay. "Jones tells us women that we don't have to allow these lyrics to be true, because 'Your revolution will not happen between these thighs.' "

B. CONTROLLING WOMEN'S SEXUALITY AND AUTONOMY

STATE V. SMITH

85 N.J. 193, 426 A.2d 38 (1981)

Since the enactment in New Jersey of the new Code of Criminal Justice, no person can claim that a sexual assault committed after the effective date of the Code, September 1, 1979, is exempt from prosecution because the accused and victim were husband and wife. The Criminal Code expressly excludes marriage to the victim as a defense against prosecution of sexual crimes. N.J.S.A. 2C:14–5(b). The criminal acts alleged in this case, however, occurred before the effective date of the Code. The issue before the Court is whether a defendant can be charged with and convicted of raping his wife under the former statute, N.J.S.A. 2A:138–1. We hold that, at least under the circumstances of this case, he can.

I

The State alleges that on October 1, 1975, defendant Albert Smith broke into the apartment of his estranged wife, Alfreda Smith, and repeatedly beat and raped her. On that date the accused and victim were legally married. They had been married for seven years but had lived separately for approximately one year. The separation may have followed another violent incident involving defendant and his wife in September 1974. Although the record is not clear on this point, Alfreda Smith testified that she and the defendant appeared before a judge, who ordered the defendant to leave the marital home. Counsel have informed this Court that the existence of such an order cannot be verified because it would have been issued six years ago and sound recordings of oral Municipal Court orders are kept for only three years. Therefore, we must assume that no judicial orders recognizing separation or restraining contact existed at the time of the alleged criminal acts. It also appears from the record that the parties had not entered into a formal agreement setting down the terms of their separation, nor had either filed a complaint for divorce.

At the time of the alleged incident on October 1, 1975, defendant and his wife lived in different cities. The State accuses defendant of arriving at his wife's apartment at about 2:30 a. m., breaking through two doors to get inside, and once there threatening, choking and striking her. According to the State, over a period of a few hours he repeatedly beat her, forced her to have sexual intercourse and committed various other atrocities against her person. As a result of these alleged attacks, Alfreda Smith required medical care at a hospital.

After hearing testimony * * *, the Essex County Grand Jury returned an indictment charging defendant with four separate counts atrocious assault and battery, private lewdness, impairing the morals of a minor, and rape. Defendant moved to dismiss the rape charge on the ground that he was legally married to the victim at the time of the incident. The trial judge reluctantly granted the motion. He believed that the common law included a marital exemption from the crime of rape, which was implicitly incorporated into this State's statutory definition of rape from early Revolutionary times to the present. Although the trial judge expressed unequivocal disapproval of such an anachronistic rule of law, he considered it the prerogative of the Legislature to change it.

The State appealed the dismissal of the rape count to the Appellate Division, which affirmed the judgment of the trial court, stating:

> There is ample reasonable cause to believe that the common law rule excluding a husband from a statute condemning rape has heretofore obtained in New Jersey if for no other reason than

> because the rule did exist at common law and has not been abrogated here by legislation or judicial decision.

The appellate court did not agree with the trial judge that it was beyond a trial court's authority to change such a rule of law. Nevertheless, it declined to make a change here because the new rule could not be applied retroactively to this defendant and the Legislature had already changed the law for future acts of marital rape by enactment of N.J.S.A. 2C:14–5(b) as part of the Criminal Code.

We granted the State's petition for certification to consider the reach of our former rape statute.

II

The rape statute under which defendant was charged provided in part:

> Any person who has carnal knowledge of a woman forcibly against her will . . . is guilty of a high misdemeanor and shall be punished by a fine of not more than $5,000, or by imprisonment for not more than 30 years, or both . . . . (N.J.S.A. 2A:138–1 (repealed))

The State argues that the statute covered the conduct of a husband against his wife because it applied to "any person."

This argument, although superficially appealing, does not resolve the issue before the Court. The marital exemption, if it existed, may have acted as a defense by negating some element of the crime. Thus the statute may well have applied to "any person," but a husband's forcible sexual intercourse with his wife was not rape because it did not include all three elements of the crime carnal knowledge, force, and lack of consent, *see State v. Heyer*, 89 N.J.L. 187, 98 A. 413 (E & A 1916). Similarly, the reference to "any person" could be construed not to include infants; insane persons, who lack the necessary state of mind to form an intent to rape; or women, at least as the principal actor. Thus, our inquiry must go beyond the "plain meaning" of the statute, the language of which alone does not reveal whether a husband was exempt from the charge of raping his wife.

Defendant, by contrast, contends that a marital exemption had always been part of this State's criminal law of rape until enactment of the new Criminal Code. Yet he is unable to cite any statutory or judicial authority from this State to support his position. In fact, prior to the decisions of the courts below, the only case in New Jersey that considered whether a marital exemption from rape existed under N.J.S.A. 2A:138–1 expressly declined to decide the issue. Nevertheless, defendant contends that the exemption was a rule of English common law which was incorporated into New Jersey's first rape statute in 1796 and remained unchanged throughout the time that N.J.S.A. 2A:138–1 was in effect.

The first State Constitution of New Jersey provided for a limited incorporation of English common and statutory law in existence at that time by providing:

> That the common law of England, as well as so much of the statute law, as have been heretofore practiced in this colony, shall still remain in force, until they shall be altered by a future law of the legislature; such parts only excepted, as are repugnant to the rights and privileges contained in this charter. . . . (N.J.Const. (1776), Art. XXII)

Thus, English common law as of 1776 became part of this State's law after the Revolution subject to change by the Legislature or except where in conflict with the State Constitution. The 1844 Constitution likewise kept in force laws then in effect. N.J. Const. (1844), Art. X, § 1. Finally, our current State Constitution states:

> All law, statutory and otherwise, all rules and regulations of administrative bodies and all rules of courts in force at the time this Constitution or any Article thereof takes effect shall remain in full force until they expire or are superseded, altered or repealed by this Constitution or otherwise. (N.J. Const. (1947), Art. XI, § 1, par. 3)

The result of these successive constitutional provisions is that certain centuries-old rules of law may still be the law in this State. The question in this case is whether a marital exemption from rape was, at the time of defendant's conduct, one such rule. To answer that question, we must first consider whether there actually existed a marital exemption rule under pre-Revolutionary common law.

A

Sir Matthew Hale, a seventeenth century English jurist, wrote a treatise on English law which is invariably cited as authority for the rule. Hale discussed the crime of rape and possible defenses, stating:

> But the husband cannot be guilty of a rape committed by himself upon his lawful wife, for by their mutual matrimonial consent and contract the wife hath given up herself in this kind unto her husband, which she cannot retract.

Hale cited no authority for this proposition and we have found none in earlier writers. Thus the marital exemption rule expressly adopted by many of our sister states has its source in a bare, extra-judicial declaration made some 300 years ago. Such a declaration cannot itself be considered a definitive and binding statement of the common law, although legal commentators have often restated the rule since the time of Hale without evaluating its merits.

The common law which was adopted as the law of this State in 1776 consisted of the underlying reasons and policies that justified particular rules of law as well as the legal rules themselves. "It is the principles of the common law which (this State has) adopted generally, and not necessarily the decisions of the English courts in exposition of the common law." *Heise v. Earle*, 134 N.J.Eq. 393, 402, 35 A.2d 880 (E & A 1944). English judicial opinions are only "evidence of what is common law." *Id.* Therefore, it is even clearer that extra-judicial discussions should not always be considered accurate expositions of the common law. In the absence of case law in this State or in England before the Revolution, we are more wary than the lower courts here of accepting Hale's rule as part of the common law.

We need not decide, however, the broad question of whether a marital exemption existed under English common law. The narrower question here is whether such a marital exemption, even if it existed, would have applied inflexibly for as long as a marriage continued to exist in the legal sense. We think not.

We believe that Hale's statements concerning the common law of spousal rape derived from the nature of marriage at a particular time in history. Hale stated the rule in terms of an implied matrimonial consent to intercourse which the wife could not retract. This reasoning may have been persuasive during Hale's time, when marriages were effectively permanent, ending only by death or an act of Parliament. Since the matrimonial vow itself was not retractable, Hale may have believed that neither was the implied consent to conjugal rights. Consequently, he stated the rule in absolute terms, as if it were applicable without exception to all marriage relationships. In the years since Hale's formulation of the rule, attitudes towards the permanency of marriage have changed and divorce has become far easier to obtain. The rule, formulated under vastly different conditions, need not prevail when those conditions have changed.

Even in pre-Revolutionary England, matrimonial law permitted a wife to live apart from her husband. Judicial separation, sometimes called divorce *a mensa et thoro*, was available, and courts would also enforce mutual separation agreements. In *Rex v. Lister*, 1 Strange 477, 93 Eng.Rep. 645 (1721), the court released a wife from confinement by her husband after he had forcibly seized her and carried her away during a time when they were living separately pursuant to a mutual agreement. The court held that only "where the wife will make an undue use of her liberty, either by squandering away the husband's estate, or going into lewd company; it is lawful for the husband, in order to preserve his honour and estate, to lay such a wife under a restraint." 93 Eng.Rep. at 646. If a wife had a right to live separately from her husband, it follows that she also had a right to refuse sexual intercourse with him at least while they were separated. Therefore, it would appear that Hale's rule was subject to an exception even in pre-Revolutionary England.

To summarize our view of the marital exemption under English common law, we think that the existence of the rule is not as obvious as the lower courts here or courts in other jurisdictions have believed. The rule may simply not have been applicable to revocable marriages, which exist today as a result of changes in divorce laws. The fact that many jurisdictions have mechanically applied the rule, without evaluating its merits under changed conditions, does not mean that such blind application was part of the "principles of the common law" adopted in this State. Without deciding whether an exemption existed in any situations at all, we think that it was not meant to exist during the entire legal duration of a marriage. Therefore, we decline to apply mechanically a rule whose existence is in some doubt and which may never have been intended to apply to the factual situation presented by this case.

B

Having determined that the common law did not include an absolute marital exemption from prosecution for rape under all conditions, we next consider what rule of exemption, if any, did exist as the law in this State at the time of these alleged criminal acts.

The inquiry must begin with enactment of the State's first rape statute in 1796. That statute provided in part:

> That any person who shall have carnal knowledge of a woman, forcibly and against her will, . . . shall, on conviction, be adjudged guilty of a high misdemeanor. . . . (L. 1796, An Act for the Punishment of Crimes, § 8)

This statutory language is almost identical to N.J.S.A. 2A:138–1, the applicable statute in this case. The definition of forcible rape seems to have come directly from Blackstone's eighteenth century definition. See 4 BLACKSTONE, COMMENTARIES *210 ("rape, *raptus mulierum*, or the carnal knowledge of a woman forcibly and against her will"). Although discussing other statements by Hale, Blackstone never mentions a marital exemption. Thus, we do not know whether the 1796 Legislature intended to incorporate implicitly any form of a marital exemption within the statutory definition of rape. However, we need not answer that question for the purposes of this case. Our concern here is whether a marital exemption, even if it existed in this State, covered defendant's conduct.

We have previously concluded that the common law spousal exemption was not absolute or mechanically applicable to all legal marriages. We have also concluded that the enactment of a rape statute in this State did not clarify the existence or extent of such a rule. Nevertheless, we will assume for the purpose of our inquiry that some form of a marital exemption did exist in eighteenth century New Jersey and next consider whether that exemption was the rule in 1975, when defendant allegedly raped his wife.

A common law rule of marital exemption was probably based on three major justifications, which might have constituted the common law principles adopted in this State. The first of these, the notion that a woman was the property of her husband or father, *see* S. BROWNMILLER, AGAINST OUR WILL 18–28 (1975), was never valid in this country. Rape laws may originally have protected a woman's chastity and therefore her value to her father or husband. In this State, however, rape statutes have always aimed to protect the safety and personal liberty of women. Thus, the common law "principle" that a wife is her husband's chattel does not support the view that our rape statute included a marital exemption.

Second, the common law once included the concept that a husband and wife were one person, that after marriage a man and woman no longer retained separate legal existence. As a result of this concept, some have argued that a husband could not be convicted of, in effect, raping himself. This argument does not take into account how, in spite of marital unity, a husband could always be convicted of other crimes upon his wife, such as assault and battery.

Furthermore, even if the argument had validity at one time, the "principle" of marital unity was discarded in this State long before the commission of defendant's alleged crime. See N.J.S.A. 37:2–1 to –30 (Married Woman's Acts, enacted in the nineteenth and early twentieth centuries, giving married women rights to sue and be sued, own property, and enter contracts separately from their husbands); *Immer v. Risko*, 56 N.J. 482, 267 A.2d 481 (1970) (abolition of spousal tort immunity); *King v. Greene*, 30 N.J. 395, 153 A.2d 49 (1959) (alienability of wife's interest in property held in tenancy by the entirety); *In re Lawrence*, 133 N.J. Super. 408, 336 A.2d 80 (App.Div.1975) (wife not compelled to assume husband's surname); *State v. Pittman*, 124 N.J. Super. 334, 306 A.2d 500 (Law Div.1973) (indictment of husband and wife for conspiracy). If the concept of marital unity was the basis for the marital exemption, the statutes and cases cited above, all part of our laws before October 1975, changed the common law and eliminated this basis for the exemption.

The third and most prevalent justification for the exemption rule is the one utilized by Hale himself that upon entering the marriage contract a wife consents to sexual intercourse with her husband. This irrevocable consent negates the third essential element of the crime of rape, lack of consent. We cannot say with certainty whether such a rationale was justified even in the seventeenth century.

More importantly, this implied consent rationale, besides being offensive to our valued ideals of personal liberty, is not sound where the marriage itself is not irrevocable. If a wife can exercise a legal right to separate from her husband and eventually terminate the marriage "contract," may she not also revoke a "term" of that contract, namely, consent to intercourse? Just as a husband has no right to imprison his wife because of her marriage vow to him, he has no right to force sexual relations upon her against her will. If her repeated refusals are a "breach" of the marriage "contract," his remedy is in a matrimonial court, not in violent or forceful self-help.

Changes in divorce laws have significantly affected judicial and legislative construction of marital exemption rules. Some jurisdictions have recognized that consent to intercourse does not automatically continue until a marriage is officially at an end. They have refused to exempt husbands from the charge of rape where a judicial decree of separation has been entered, where a spouse has filed for divorce or separate maintenance, or where the spouses are simply living apart.

Since the common law exemption supposedly operated by negating an essential element of the crime—lack of consent—it could not be applied where marital consent to sexual intercourse could be legally revoked. By 1975 our matrimonial laws recognized the right of a wife to withdraw consent prior to the dissolution of a marriage and even prior to a formal judicial order of separation.

This conclusion is consistent with those cases or statutes which have refused to apply the exemption rule after a judicial decree of separation has been issued. Such cases have reasoned that a legal process which originally created the marital state has stepped in to terminate it. But the wife could not rely on her unilateral decision outside the legal process to mark the end of the marriage, for unless she could allege and prove proper grounds, a court would probably decline to terminate the marriage. The legal setting in this State is different. Since the advent of the no-fault ground for divorce, any spouse may make a unilateral decision to end the marriage. By separating from her husband and living apart for 18 months, a wife is entitled to a divorce without further proof of proper grounds. The corollary of this right is that a wife can refuse sexual intercourse with her husband during the period of separation. If a wife has a right to refuse intercourse, or deny consent, then a husband's forceful carnal knowledge of his wife clearly includes all three essential elements of the crime of rape. He cannot defend by asserting that there was no lack of consent because he was still legally married to the victim.

Our no-fault divorce law has existed since 1971, several years before the parties here separated and before the alleged acts of defendant. Defendant cannot claim that in 1975 his wife consented to have sexual intercourse with him although they were living separately. Whether or not any other husband could have based a defense on such implied consent—a proposition that we doubt seriously but do not decide—this husband could not.

With none of the three major common law justifications viable under our laws at the time of defendant's conduct, it would be irrational to believe that a common law marital exemption for rape endured in this State while other laws had changed so dramatically. The "principles of the common law" incorporated into our laws by our successive Constitutions, and supposedly justifying a marital exemption had been abrogated by subsequent legislative and judicial actions. With their demise, no justification remained at this late date for believing that a rigid marital exemption rule based on those principles would be retained. Therefore, we hold that this State did not have a marital exemption rule for rape in 1975 that would have applied to this defendant and prevented his indictment and conviction on the charge of raping his wife.

III

In the criminal context, the Due Process Clause of the Fourteenth Amendment requires that an accused have had fair warning at the time of his alleged crime that his conduct might be proscribed by a particular statute. *Bouie v. Columbia*, 378 U.S. 347, 351 (1964). Defendant contends, and the Appellate Division agreed, that any change in this State's rule of marital exemption for rape could not be applied retroactively to him consistently with due process.

This due process argument assumes that at the time of defendant's acts the law of this State would have exempted him from prosecution for rape. We have held, however, that no rule of law would have exempted this defendant from the charge of raping his estranged wife. Our holding does not deprive defendant "of any defense available according to law at the time when the act was committed," *Beazell v. Ohio*, 269 U.S. 167, 169 (1925). At least under the circumstances of this case, the defense was not available when defendant committed the acts.

We have not changed a common law rule clearly in existence at the time of defendant's acts. Instead, our decision today is a first judicial application of a rule. * * * [T]here is no violation of due process when a court merely applies for the first time a rule which has developed under existing principles and laws, instead of changing a previously stated rule that clearly applied to defendant's acts at the time of their commission. * * *

[I]n a more general sense, defendant had ample notice and fair warning that the people of this State would no longer tolerate a husband's violent sexual assault of his wife. The personal liberty of women and the recognition of them as independent citizens under the law had developed beyond question through legislative and judicial actions over more than a century. The right of women to make their own choices regarding reproduction and sexual conduct was also apparent under the abortion and contraception cases. *Roe v. Wade*, 410 U.S. 113 (1973); *Doe v. Bolton*, 410 U.S. 179 (1973). No person in this State in 1975 could justifiably claim that a man had a legal right to impose his sexual will forcefully and violently on a woman, even if it was his wife, over her unmistakable objection.

We hold that defendant had fair warning that his conduct might lead to conviction for rape, and that his conviction under N.J.S.A. 2A:138–1 would not deprive him of due process.

CONCLUSION

The enactment of the new Criminal Code has made it unnecessary for this Court to discuss at length all the inequities of a medieval rule that denies some women protection against sexual attack and treats them as sexual property of their husbands. Under N.J.S.A. 2C:14–5(b) married men or women, whether living with or separately from their spouses, will not be able to force their sexual wills upon their spouses without incurring the severe penalties attached to our laws proscribing sexual assault.

But neither was the law of this State under the former rape statute as blind to personal liberty and privacy as defendant would have this Court believe. A man separated from his wife and perhaps one not separated could not invoke an outdated and doubtful rule to avoid prosecution for rape simply because he was still legally married to his victim. The judgment of the Appellate Division is reversed and the rape count of the indictment against defendant is reinstated.

NOTES AND QUESTIONS

1. *The public-private distinction exemplified.* It is obvious how Hale's articulation of the old common law rule—and its rationale—preserves patriarchy. How does it demonstrate that the orthodox distinction between the public and the private realm exemplifies and enforces patriarchy? Consider Professor MacKinnon's succinct summation of the position: "Those domains in which women are distinctively subordinated are assumed by the Constitution to be the domain of freedom." CATHERINE MACKINNON, FEMINISM UNMODIFIED: DISCOURSES ON LIFE AND LAW 207 (1987).

2. *Interpreting Smith, perpetuating the prospect of control.* Is the law after *Smith* that the husband and wife must be separated before a charge of marital rape can be sustained? If so, does that mean that a man living with his wife cannot as a matter of law rape his wife?

IN RE FAUZIYA KASINGA

Board of Immigration Appeals
U.S. Department of Justice
Int. Dec. 3278 (1996)

This is a timely appeal by the applicant from a decision of an Immigration Judge dated August 25, 1995. The Immigration Judge found the applicant excludable as an intending immigrant, denied her applications for asylum and withholding of deportation, and ordered her excluded and deported from the United States. Upon reviewing the appellate record anew ("de novo review"), we will sustain the applicant's appeal, grant asylum, and order her admitted to the United States as an asylee.

A fundamental issue before us is whether the practice of female genital mutilation ("FGM") can be the basis for a grant of asylum under section 208 of the Immigration and Nationality Act, 8 U.S.C. § 1158 (1994). [Under U.S. law, an applicant may be granted refugee status if he or she

> is outside any country of such person's nationality or, in the case of a person having no nationality, is outside any country in which such person last habitually resided, and who is unable or unwilling to return to, and is unable or unwilling to avail himself or herself of the protection of, that country because of persecution or a well-founded fear of persecution on account of race, religion, nationality, membership in a particular social group, or political opinion.] * * *

We make seven major findings in the applicant's case. * * * First, the record before us reflects that the applicant is a credible witness. Second, FGM, as practiced by the Tchamba-Kunsuntu Tribe of Togo and documented in the record, constitutes persecution. Third, the applicant is a member of a social group consisting of young women of the Tchamba-Kunsuntu Tribe who have not had FGM, as practiced by that tribe, and who oppose the practice. Fourth, the applicant has a well-founded fear of persecution. Fifth, the persecution the applicant fears is "on account of" her social group. Sixth, the applicant's fear of persecution is country-wide. Seventh, and finally, the applicant is eligible for and should be granted asylum in the exercise of discretion. * * *

I. CREDIBILITY

A. The Applicant's Testimony

The applicant is a 19-year-old native and citizen of Togo. She attended 2 years of high school. She is a member of the Tchamba-Kunsuntu Tribe of northern Togo. She testified that young women of her tribe normally undergo FGM at age 15. However, she did not because she initially was protected from FGM by her influential, but now deceased, father. The applicant stated that upon her father's death in 1993, under tribal custom her aunt, her father's sister, became the primary authority figure in the family. The applicant's mother was driven from the family home, left Togo, and went to live with her family in Benin. The applicant testified that she does not currently know her mother's exact whereabouts.

The applicant further testified that her aunt forced her into a polygamous marriage in October 1994, when she was 17. The husband selected by her aunt was 45 years old and had three other wives at the time of marriage. The applicant testified that, under tribal custom, her aunt and her husband planned to force her to submit to FGM before the marriage was consummated.

The applicant testified that she feared imminent mutilation. With the help of her older sister, she fled Togo for Ghana. However, she was afraid that her aunt and her husband would locate her there. Consequently, using money from her mother, the applicant embarked for Germany by airplane. Upon arrival in Germany, the applicant testified that she was somewhat disoriented and spent several hours wandering around the airport looking for fellow Africans who might help her. Finally, she struck up a conversation, in English, with a German woman. After hearing the applicant's story, the woman offered to give the applicant temporary shelter in her home until the applicant decided what to do next. For the next 2 months, the applicant slept in the woman's living room, while performing cooking and cleaning duties.

The applicant further stated that in December 1994, while on her way to a shopping center, she met a young Nigerian man. He was the first person from Africa she had spoken to since arriving in Germany. They struck up a conversation, during which the applicant told the man about her situation. He offered to sell the applicant his sister's British passport so that she could seek asylum in the United States, where she has an aunt, an uncle, and a cousin. The applicant followed the man's suggestion, purchasing the passport and the ticket with money given to her by her sister.

The applicant did not attempt a fraudulent entry into the United States. Rather, upon arrival at Newark International Airport on December 17, 1994, she immediately requested asylum. She remained in detention by the Immigration and Naturalization Service ("INS") until April 1996.

The applicant testified that the Togolese police and the Government of Togo were aware of FGM and would take no steps to protect her from the practice. She further testified that her aunt had reported her to the Togolese police. Upon return, she would be taken back to her husband by the police and forced to undergo FGM. She testified at several points that there would be nobody to protect her from FGM in Togo. In her testimony, the applicant referred to letters in the record from her mother. Those letters confirmed that the Togolese police were looking for the applicant and that the applicant's father's family wanted her to undergo FGM.

The applicant testified that she could not find protection anywhere in Togo. She stated that Togo is a very small country and her husband and aunt, with the help of the police, could locate her anywhere she went. She also stated that her husband is well known in Togo and is a friend of the police. On cross-examination she stated that it would not be possible for her to live with another tribe in Togo.

The applicant also testified that the Togolese police could locate her in Ghana. She indicated that she did not seek asylum in Germany because she could not speak German and therefore could not continue her education there. She stated that she did not have relatives in Germany as she does in the United States.

B. Background Information

1. The Asylum Application

The applicant's written asylum application was filed on April 18, 1995, while she was in INS detention. That application is consistent with the above testimony in all material respects.

A number of documents are attached to the applicant's asylum application. First, there are copies of two letters, dated December 27, 1994, and December 30, 1994, respectively, signed by the applicant's mother. The letters are in English. One letter confirms that the applicant's father's family wishes to have the applicant marry an older man and be subjected to FGM. That letter further confirms that the applicant's mother gave the applicant money to assist her escape. The other letter confirms that the Togolese police were looking for the applicant following her escape in October 1994.

The applicant testified that 1) her mother cannot write English; 2) the letters were prepared by the applicant's sister, at her mother's request; and 3) the letters are signed by the applicant's mother.

A translated copy of the applicant's marriage certificate also is appended to the asylum application. That document, dated October 7, 1994, is signed by the applicant's husband, but not by the applicant. * * *

2. Applicant's Other Exhibits

The applicant's prior counsel also offered a letter dated August 24, 1995, from Charles Piot, Assistant Professor of Cultural Anthropology at Duke University. That letter 1) states that it was written at counsel's request, on the basis of information furnished by counsel; 2) briefly describes Professor Piot's qualifications as a cultural anthropologist who spent 3 years doing research in Northern Togo in the 1980s; and 3) offers the opinion that a woman of the Tchamba people probably would be expected by her husband to have undergone a clitoridectomy (a type of FGM) prior to marriage. The Immigration Judge admitted the Piot letter into evidence.

The Immigration Judge noted that the weight given the letter would be affected by the inability of the INS to cross-examine Professor Piot. However, the Immigration Judge also stated that he "would accept the applicant on her word, that the tribe requires the circumcision [FGM] prior to marriage." * * *

3. Group Exhibit 4

The applicant's prior counsel also filed a lengthy pre-hearing brief accompanied by extensive documentation. That documentation included information on the practice of FGM, its harmful effects on women, its lack of legitimate justification, and its condemnation by the international community. The documentation also confirmed the generally poor human rights situation in Togo, particularly for women. * * *

4. Description of FGM

According to the applicant's testimony, the FGM practiced by her tribe, the Tchamba-Kunsuntu, is of an extreme type involving cutting the genitalia with knives, extensive bleeding, and a 40-day recovery period. The background materials confirm that the FGM practiced in some African countries, such as Togo, is of an extreme nature causing permanent damage, and not just a minor form of genital ritual. See, e.g., NAHID TOUBIA, FEMALE GENITAL MUTILATION: A CALL FOR GLOBAL ACTION 9, 24–25 (Gloria Jacobs ed., Women Ink. 1993).

The record material establishes that FGM in its extreme forms is a practice in which portions of the female genitalia are cut away. In some cases, the vagina is sutured partially closed. This practice clearly inflicts harm or suffering upon the girl or woman who undergoes it. FGM is extremely painful and at least temporarily incapacitating. It permanently disfigures the female genitalia. FGM exposes the girl or woman to the risk of serious, potentially life-threatening complications. These include, among others, bleeding, infection, urine retention, stress, shock, psychological trauma, and damage to the urethra and anus. It can result in permanent loss of genital sensation and can adversely affect sexual and erotic functions. *See generally* * * * INS Resource Information Center, Alert Series—Women—Female Genital Mutilation, Ref. No. AL/NGA/94.001 (July 1994) [hereinafter FGM Alert].

The FGM Alert, compiled and distributed by the INS Resource Information Center, notes that "few African countries have officially condemned female genital mutilation and still fewer have enacted legislation against the practice." Further, according to the FGM Alert, even in those few African countries where legislative efforts have been made, they are usually ineffective to protect women against FGM. The FGM Alert notes that "it remains practically true that [African] women have little legal recourse and may face threats to their freedom, threats or acts of physical violence, or social ostracization for refusing to undergo this harmful traditional practice or attempting to protect their female children." Togo is not listed in the FGM Alert as among the African countries that have made even minimal efforts to protect women from FGM.

The record also contains a May 26, 1995, memorandum from Phyllis Coven, Office of International Affairs, INS, which is addressed to all INS Asylum Officers and sets forth guidelines for adjudicating women's asylum claims. Those guidelines state that "rape . . ., sexual abuse and domestic violence, infanticide and genital mutilation are forms of mistreatment primarily directed at girls and women and they may serve as evidence of past persecution on account of one or more of the five grounds."

5. State Department Reports on Conditions in Togo

The record also contains two reports compiled by the United States Department of State. The first of these, dated January 31, 1994, 1) confirms that FGM is practiced by some ethnic groups in Togo; 2) notes that while some reports indicate that the practice may be diminishing, an expert indicates that as many as 50% of Togolese females may have been mutilated; and 3) notes that various acts of violence against women occur in Togo with little police intervention. Committees on Foreign Affairs and Foreign Relations, 103d Cong., 2d Sess., Country Report on Human Rights Practices for 1993 (Joint Comm. Print 1994) [hereinafter 1993 Country Reports].

The second Department of State Report on Togo, prepared by the Bureau of Democracy, Human Rights and Labor, is dated April 1995. Bureau of Democracy, Human Rights and Labor, U.S. Dep't of State, Togo—Profile of Asylum Claims & Country Conditions (April 1995) [hereinafter Profile]. While not specifically addressing FGM, that report states that the President of Togo has a poor human rights record and confirms that the government's military and security forces have been involved in serious human rights abuses. * * *

D. The Applicant's Credibility

We have conducted an independent review of the applicant's credibility. We note that the Immigration Judge's adverse credibility determination was based on a perceived lack of "rationality," "persuasiveness," and "consistency." The Immigration Judge did not rely on the applicant's demeanor. We, like the Immigration Judge, can determine from the record whether the applicant's testimony is "rational, plausible, and consistent."

We find that the applicant's testimony in support of her asylum application is plausible, detailed, and internally consistent. It is consistent with her asylum application and with the substantial background information in the record. The latter includes information from the Department of State and the INS Resource Information Center.

The applicant is a 19-year-old woman, who was a 17-year-old high school student at the time the events in question occurred. The applicant's father had died, she was separated from her mother, and she was under the control of an unsympathetic aunt. Her arrival in the United States followed flight from her homeland and a lonely journey of thousands of miles that took her through a strange country. Her testimony followed more than 8 months of continuous INS detention, in several facilities, one of which was closed by a riot.

We specifically reject the Immigration Judge's findings that the applicant's failure to know the present whereabouts of her mother; her claim to have avoided FGM through her father's efforts; the incident involving the German woman; or the incident with the Nigerian man were irrational, unpersuasive, or inconsistent. Each of those matters was adequately and reasonably explained by the applicant during her testimony and each of them reasonably could have happened to a teenage girl in the applicant's situation. Her testimony on these points was not impeached by the INS through cross-examination.

For the foregoing reasons, on the basis of the record before us, we find the applicant to be a credible witness.

II. FGM AS PERSECUTION

For the purposes of this case, we adopt the description of FGM drawn from the record and summarized [above]. We agree with the parties that this level of harm can constitute "persecution" within the meaning of section 101(a)(42)(A) of the Act, 8 U.S.C. § 1101(a)(42)(A) (1994). While a number of descriptions of persecution have been formulated in our past decisions, we have recognized that persecution can consist of the infliction of harm or suffering by a government, or persons a government is unwilling or unable to control, to overcome a characteristic of the victim. The "seeking to overcome" formulation has its antecedents in concepts of persecution that predate the Refugee Act of 1980, Pub. L. No. 96–212, 94 Stat. 102.

As observed by the INS, many of our past cases involved actors who had a subjective intent to punish their victims. However, this subjective "punitive" or "malignant" intent is not required for harm to constitute persecution. Our characterization of FGM as persecution is consistent with our past definitions of that term. * * *

III. SOCIAL GROUP

To be a basis for a grant of asylum, persecution must relate to one of five categories described in section 101(a)(42)(A) of the Act. The parties agree that the relevant category in this case is "particular social group." Each party has advanced several formulations of the "particular social group" at issue in this case. However, each party urges the Board to adopt only that definition of social group necessary to decide this individual case.

In the context of this case, we find the particular social group to be the following: young women of the Tchamba-Kunsuntu Tribe who have not had FGM, as practiced by that tribe, and who oppose the practice. This is very similar to the formulations suggested by the parties. The defined social group meets the test we set forth in [prior cases * * * finding that identifiable shared ties of kinship warrant characterization as a social group. It also is consistent with the law of the United States Court of Appeals for the Third Circuit, where this case arose. *Fatin v. INS*, 12 F.3d 1233, 1241 (3d Cir. 1993) (stating that Iranian women who refuse to conform to the Iranian Government's gender-specific laws and social norms may well satisfy the [legal] definition).

In accordance with [BIA precedent], the particular social group is defined by common characteristics that members of the group either cannot change, or should not be required to change because such characteristics are fundamental to their individual identities. The characteristics of being a "young woman" and a "member of the Tchamba-Kunsuntu Tribe" cannot be changed. The characteristic of having intact genitalia is one that is so fundamental to the individual identity of a young woman that she should not be required to change it.

IV. WELL-FOUNDED FEAR

The burden of proof is upon an applicant for asylum to establish that a "reasonable person" in her circumstances would fear persecution upon return to Togo. The applicant has met this burden through a combination of her credible testimony and the introduction of documentary evidence and background information that supports her claim.

V. "ON ACCOUNT OF"

To be eligible for asylum, the applicant must establish that her well-founded fear of persecution is "on account of" one of the five grounds specified in the Act, here, her membership in a "particular social group." *See, e.g., Matter of H-* (holding that harm or abuse because of clan membership constitutes persecution on account of social group). Both parties have advanced, and the background materials support, the proposition that there is no legitimate reason for FGM. Group Exhibit 4 contains materials showing that the practice has been condemned by such groups as the United Nations, the International Federation of Gynecology and Obstetrics, the Council on Scientific Affairs, the World Health Organization, the International Medical Association, and the American Medical Association.

Record materials state that FGM "has been used to control woman's sexuality," FGM Alert, supra, at 4. It also is characterized as a form of "sexual oppression" that is "based on the manipulation of women's sexuality in order to assure male dominance and exploitation." Toubia, *supra*, at 42 (quoting Raqiya Haji Dualeh Abdalla, Somali Women's Democratic Organization). During oral argument before us, the INS General Counsel agreed with the latter characterization. He also stated that the practice is a "severe bodily invasion" that should be regarded as meeting the asylum standard even if done with "subjectively benign intent".

We agree with the parties that, as described and documented in this record, FGM is practiced, at least in some significant part, to overcome sexual characteristics of young women of the tribe who have not been, and do not wish to be, subjected to FGM. We therefore find that the persecution the applicant fears in Togo is "on account of" her status as a member of the defined social group.

VI. COUNTRY-WIDE PERSECUTION

The INS suggests, in its brief and at oral argument, that a remand is necessary because the applicant has not established that she would be unable to avoid FGM by moving to some other part of Togo. As we found in Part I of our opinion, the applicant presented credible testimony that her husband is a well-known individual who is a friend of the police in Togo. She testified that her aunt and her husband were looking for her and that there could be no refuge for her because Togo is a small country and the police would not protect her.

The applicant's testimony is consistent with the background information in the record. That information confirms that 1) FGM is widely practiced in Togo; 2) acts of violence and abuse against women in Togo are tolerated by the police; 3) the Government of Togo has a poor human rights record; and 4) most African women can expect little governmental protection from FGM. See 1993 Country Reports, supra; Profile, supra; FGM Alert, supra, at 6–7. We also take notice that Togo is a small country of approximately 22,000 square miles, slightly smaller than West Virginia.

Neither in its briefs nor at oral argument did the INS raise any claim of "new evidence" that might show changed country conditions. We assume that if the INS had any new documentation showing that the applicant could find safety from FGM elsewhere in Togo, it would have offered that evidence in support of its motion to remand.

For the foregoing reasons, we find that this record adequately supports the applicant's claim that she has a country-wide fear of persecution in Togo.

VII. DISCRETION

We have determined that the applicant is eligible for asylum because she has a well-founded fear of persecution on account of her membership in a particular social group in Togo. A grant of asylum to an eligible applicant is discretionary. The final issue is whether the applicant merits a favorable exercise of discretion. The danger of persecution will outweigh all but the most egregious adverse factors. The type of persecution feared by the applicant is very severe.

To the extent that the Immigration Judge suggested that the applicant had a legal obligation to seek refuge in Ghana or Germany, the record does not support such a conclusion. The applicant offered credible reasons for not seeking refuge in either of those countries in her particular circumstances. The applicant purchased someone else's passport and used it to come to the United States. However, upon arrival, she did not attempt to use the false passport to enter. She told the immigration inspector the truth.

We have weighed the favorable and adverse factors and are satisfied that discretion should be exercised in favor of the applicant. Therefore, we will grant asylum to the applicant. * * *

IX. SUMMARY AND CONCLUSION

The applicant has a well-founded fear of persecution in the form of FGM if returned to Togo. The persecution she fears is on account of her membership in a particular social group consisting of young women of the Tchamba-Kunsuntu Tribe who have not had FGM, as practiced by that tribe, and who oppose the practice. Her fear of persecution is country-wide. We exercise our discretion in her favor, and we grant her asylum. Therefore, we sustain the applicant's appeal, grant her asylum, and order her admitted to the United States. * * *

NOTES AND QUESTIONS

1. *Culture and the state.* Does or should the law distinguish between (i) norms imposed by a culture and tolerated by the state and (ii) norms imposed by the state in legal form? Looking again at the description of FGM in Togo, is there an argument that FGM is actually matriarchal rather than patriarchal in that culture, or is there a different interpretation?

2. *State control of sexuality.* The *Smith* and *Kasinga* cases primarily involve control of female sexuality, and that issue is not remote in time or place: as of this writing for example, there is a split among the federal circuit courts of appeal on the legality of state laws restricting access to sex toys, especially those of particular interest to women, as obscenity. *Compare Reliable Consultants, Inc. v. Earle*, 517 F.3d 738 (5th Cir. 2008) *with Williams v. Attorney Gen. of Ala.*, 378 F.3d 1232 (11th Cir. 2004), *cert. denied sub nom. Williams v. King*, 543 U.S. 1152 (2005).

3. *Defining "social group."* The Refugee Act of 1980 applies to those who face persecution on account of their membership in a "social group." The 1951 Refugee Treaty, on which the Refugee Act was based, used the phrase "social group" as a synonym for "caste," with the economic and religious overtones of that classification. What is the "social group" in *Kasinga*?

4. *Women's bodies as cultural markers.* Women in France have been banned from wearing veils on the ground that the veil is contrary to French

culture and is oppressive to women. "A nearly all male legislature under the guise of public safety and protecting women's dignity will deny a minority the right to choose how to dress." Ronald P. Sokol, "Veiled Arguments," *New York Times* (14 July 2010). Does not allowing women to wear what they choose and proscribing the ways they can exhibit their bodies stop oppression of women or perpetuate it?

5. *Does a woman lose the expectation of privacy if she wears a skirt in public?* Consider the following news report from the Associated Press (12 March 2008):

> **Court Drops Case of 'Peeping Tom' in Target; Says Victim Was Not in Private Place**
>
> OKLAHOMA CITY—A man accused of using a camera to take pictures under the skirt of an unsuspecting 16-year-old girl at a Tulsa store did not commit a crime, a state appeals court has ruled. The state Court of Criminal Appeals voted 4–1 in favor of Riccardo Gino Ferrante, who was arrested in 2006 for situating a camera underneath the girl's skirt at a Target store and taking photographs. Ferrante, now 34, was charged under a "Peeping Tom" statute that requires the victim to be "in a place where there is a right to a reasonable expectation of privacy." Testimony indicated he followed the girl, knelt down behind her and placed the camera under her skirt.
>
> In January 2007, Tulsa County District Judge Tom Gillert ordered Ferrante's felony charge dismissed. That was based upon a determination that "the person photographed was not in a place where she had a reasonable expectation of privacy," according to the appellate ruling issued last week. The District Attorney's Office had appealed Gillert's ruling to the Court of Criminal Appeals.
>
> "We agree with the district court's analysis," stated the opinion written by Appeals Judge Charles Johnson, with Judges Charles Chapel, David Lewis and Arlene Johnson concurring. In a dissent, Appeals Judge Gary Lumpkin wrote that "what this decision does is state to women who desire to wear dresses that there is no expectation of privacy as to what they have covered with their dress. * * * In other words, it is open season for peeping Toms in public places who want to look under a woman's dress," Lumpkin wrote. He said he found the majority's finding of no reasonable expectation of privacy "interesting and disturbing." * * *

6. *Abortion rights and autonomy.* It is not possible to address the law's recognition of and limitation on the autonomy of women without considering abortion rights. In *Roe v. Wade*, 410 U.S. 113 (1973), the Supreme Court decided that the right to privacy under the due process clause of the 14th Amendment protected a woman's right to have an abortion, but, as the pregnancy progressed into the second and third trimesters, that right had to be balanced against the state's potential interests in protecting prenatal life

and protecting women's health. Subsequent cases generally confirmed the essence of *Roe v. Wade*, including the privacy right at issue, even as certain state limitations were sustained. The debate continues, as the following materials suggest.

DEBRAN ROWLAND, THE BOUNDARIES OF HER BODY: THE TROUBLING HISTORY OF WOMEN'S RIGHTS IN AMERICA 5

(2004)

Through the eyes of America's early lawmakers, women were meant—by God, Darwinian invention, or man-made invention—to serve mankind. "In a relatively primitive society based mainly on agriculture and animal husbandry, security and wealth do not depend primarily on technical or rational factors," notes essayist Erich Fromm. "It's nature's productive force—that is, the fertility of the soil, the effects of water and sunlight—that plays the decisive role in human life and death. The crux of the economy is the mysterious power of nature giving birth out of itself to ever new products essential for human life. Who possesses this mysterious power of natural productiveness? Only woman."

Women had—and have—the mysterious power to give birth to "themselves"—and to men—which has been held through time and memoria to be their societal mission. Therefore, although the oft-stated goals of the Mayflower Compact and the Constitutional Convention were "justice and "equality", the rule of law laid down during this time would limit the rights and choices of women in every aspect of life for the next three centuries. Indeed, it was not until the 1960s, for instance, that the notion of personal privacy was extended to women, allowing women to make certain choices about their bodies.

Prior to that, female reproduction and a body that could nurture life was largely deemed public property, certainly public enough that the state would have a say in a woman's decisions regarding reproduction. Women, lawmakers argued well into the twentieth century, were obligated to reproduce. . . .

GONZALES V. CARHART

550 U.S. 124 (2007)

[Editors' note. In *Stenberg v. Carhart*, 530 U.S. 914 (2000), the Supreme Court decided that Nebraska's "partial birth abortion" statute violated the federal Constitution, as interpreted in *Planned Parenthood of Southeastern Pa. v. Casey*, 505 U.S. 833 (1992) and *Roe v. Wade*, 410 U.S. 113 (1973). In the aftermath of *Stenberg*, Congress passed the Partial-Birth Abortion Ban

Act of 2003, 18 U.S.C. § 1531 (2000 ed., Supp. IV), which prohibited "intact" dilation and evacuation (D & E), a surgical method of ending fetal life in the later stages of pregnancy. In separate actions, certain physicians and abortion-rights advocacy groups sued the Attorney General of the United States, challenging the constitutionality of the Act. In *Gonzales v. Carhart*, the Supreme Court, *per* Justice Kennedy, held that the Act's prohibition of D & E procedures was not void for vagueness and did not impose an undue burden on women seeking late-term, but pre-viability, abortions. The majority also ruled that the Act furthered a legitimate congressional purpose—specifically "protecting the life of a fetus that might become a life"—and that the absence of a health exception did not render the Act unconstitutional on its face.]

JUSTICES GINSBURG, STEVENS, SOUTER, and BREYER, dissenting. Today's decision is alarming. It refuses to take *Casey* and *Stenberg* seriously. It tolerates, indeed applauds, federal intervention to ban nationwide a procedure found necessary and proper in certain cases by the American College of Obstetricians and Gynecologists. It blurs the line, firmly drawn in *Casey*, between pre-viability and post-viability abortions. And, for the first time since *Roe*, the Court blesses a prohibition with no exception safeguarding a woman's health. . . .

The Court offers flimsy and transparent justifications for upholding a nationwide ban on intact D & E *sans* any exception to safeguard a woman's health. Today's ruling, the Court declares, advances "a premise central to [*Casey's*] conclusion"—*i.e.,* the Government's "legitimate and substantial interest in preserving and promoting fetal life." ("[W]e must determine whether the Act furthers the legitimate interest of the Government in protecting the life of the fetus that may become a child."). But the Act scarcely furthers that interest: The law saves not a single fetus from destruction, for it targets only a *method* of performing abortion. And surely the statute was not designed to protect the lives or health of pregnant women. cf. *Casey,* 505 U.S., at 846, (recognizing along with the State's legitimate interest in the life of the fetus, its "legitimate interes[t] . . . in protecting the *health of the woman*" (emphasis added)). In short, the Court upholds a law that, while doing nothing to "preserv[e] . . . fetal life," bars a woman from choosing intact D & E although her doctor "reasonably believes [that procedure] will best protect [her]," *Stenberg,* 530 U.S., at 946, (Stevens, J., concurring).

As another reason for upholding the ban, the Court emphasizes that the Act does not proscribe the non-intact D & E procedure. But why not, one might ask. Non-intact D & E could equally be characterized as "brutal," [as in the majority opinion,] *ante,* at 1633, involving as it does "tear[ing] [a fetus] apart" and "ripp[ing] off" its limbs, [as in the majority opinion,] *ante,* at 1620–1621, 1621–1622. "[T]he notion that either of these two equally gruesome procedures . . . is more akin to infanticide than the other, or that the State furthers any legitimate interest by banning one but not the other, is simply irrational." *Stenberg,* 530 U.S., at 946–47 (Stevens, J., concurring).

Delivery of an intact, albeit non-viable, fetus warrants special condemnation, the Court maintains, because a fetus that is not dismembered resembles an infant. But so, too, does a fetus delivered intact after it is terminated by injection a day or two before the surgical evacuation, or a fetus delivered through medical induction or cesarean. Yet, the availability of those procedures—along with D & E by dismemberment—the Court says, saves the ban on intact D & E from a declaration of unconstitutionality. Never mind that the procedures deemed acceptable might put a woman's health at greater risk.

Ultimately, the Court admits that "moral concerns" are at work, concerns that could yield prohibitions on any abortion. *See* [the majority opinion,] *ante,* at 1633–1634 ("Congress could . . . conclude that the type of abortion proscribed by the Act requires specific regulation because it implicates additional ethical and moral concerns that justify a special prohibition."). Notably, the concerns expressed are untethered to any ground genuinely serving the Government's interest in preserving life. By allowing such concerns to carry the day and case, overriding fundamental rights, the Court dishonors our precedent. See, *e.g., Casey,* 505 U.S., at 850 ("Some of us as individuals find abortion offensive to our most basic principles of morality, but that cannot control our decision. Our obligation is to define the liberty of all, not to mandate our own moral code."); *Lawrence v. Texas,* 539 U.S. 558, 571 (2003) (Though "[f]or many persons [objections to homosexual conduct] are not trivial concerns but profound and deep convictions accepted as ethical and moral principles," the power of the State may not be used "to enforce these views on the whole society through operation of the criminal law." (citing *Casey,* 505 U.S., at 850).

Revealing in this regard, the Court invokes an antiabortion shibboleth for which it concededly has no reliable evidence: Women who have abortions come to regret their choices, and consequently suffer from "[s]evere depression and loss of esteem."[7] Because of women's fragile

[7] The Court is surely correct that, for most women, abortion is a painfully difficult decision. But "neither the weight of the scientific evidence to date nor the observable reality of 33 years of legal abortion in the United States comports with the idea that having an abortion is any more dangerous to a woman's long-term mental health than delivering and parenting a child that she did not intend to have. . . ." Cohen, *Abortion and Mental Health: Myths and Realities,* 9 GUTTMACHER POLICY REV. 8 (2006); *see generally* Bazelon, *Is There a Post-Abortion Syndrome?,* N.Y. TIMES MAGAZINE, Jan. 21, 2007, p. 40. See also, *e.g.,* American Psychological Association, APA BRIEFING PAPER ON THE IMPACT OF ABORTION (2005) (rejecting theory of a post-abortion syndrome and stating that "[a]ccess to legal abortion to terminate an unwanted pregnancy is vital to safeguard both the physical and mental health of women"); Schmiege & Russo, *Depression and Unwanted First Pregnancy: Longitudinal Cohort Study,* 331 BRITISH MEDICAL J. 1303 (2005) (finding no credible evidence that choosing to terminate an unwanted first pregnancy contributes to risk of subsequent depression); Gilchrist, Hannaford, Frank, & Kay, *Termination of Pregnancy and Psychiatric Morbidity,* 167 BRITISH J. OF PSYCHIATRY 243, 247–248 (1995) (finding, in a cohort of more than 13,000 women, that the rate of psychiatric disorder was no higher among women who

emotional state and because of the "bond of love the mother has for her child," the Court worries, doctors may withhold information about the nature of the intact D & E procedure.[8] The solution the Court approves, then, is *not* to require doctors to inform women, accurately and adequately, of the different procedures and their attendant risks. Cf. *Casey,* 505 U.S., at 873 (plurality opinion) ("States are free to enact laws to provide a reasonable framework for a woman to make a decision that has such profound and lasting meaning."). Instead, the Court deprives women of the right to make an autonomous choice, even at the expense of their safety.[9]

This way of thinking reflects ancient notions about women's place in the family and under the Constitution—ideas that have long since been discredited. Compare, *e.g., Muller v. Oregon,* 208 U.S. 412, 422–423 (1908) ("protective" legislation imposing hours-of-work limitations on women only held permissible in view of women's "physical structure and a proper discharge of her maternal functio[n]"); *Bradwell v. State,* 16 Wall. 130, 141, 21 L.Ed. 442 (1873) (Bradley, J., concurring) ("Man is, or should be, woman's protector and defender. The natural and proper timidity and delicacy which belongs to the female sex evidently unfits it for many of the occupations of civil life. . . . The paramount destiny and mission of woman

---

terminated pregnancy than among those who carried pregnancy to term); Stotland, *The Myth of the Abortion Trauma Syndrome*, 268 JAMA 2078, 2079 (1992) ("Scientific studies indicate that legal abortion results in fewer deleterious sequelae for women compared with other possible outcomes of unwanted pregnancy. There is no evidence of an abortion trauma syndrome."); American Psychological Association, Council Policy Manual: (N)(I)(3), Public Interest (1989) (declaring assertions about widespread severe negative psychological effects of abortion to be "without fact"). *But see* Cougle, Reardon, & Coleman, *Generalized Anxiety Following Unintended Pregnancies Resolved Through Childbirth and Abortion: A Cohort Study of the 1995 National Survey of Family Growth*, 19 J. ANXIETY DISORDERS 137, 142 (2005) (advancing theory of a post-abortion syndrome but acknowledging that "no causal relationship between pregnancy outcome and anxiety could be determined" from study); Reardon et al., *Psychiatric Admissions of Low-Income Women Following Abortion and Childbirth*, 168 CANADIAN MEDICAL ASSN. J. 1253, 1255–1256 (May 13, 2003) (concluding that psychiatric admission rates were higher for women who had an abortion compared with women who delivered); cf. Major, *Psychological Implications of Abortion—Highly Charged and Rife with Misleading Research*, 168 CANADIAN MEDICAL ASSN. J. 1257, 1258 (May 13, 2003) (critiquing Reardon study for failing to control for a host of differences between women in the delivery and abortion samples).

[8] Notwithstanding the "bond of love" women often have with their children, see ante, at 1633–1634, not all pregnancies, this Court has recognized, are wanted, or even the product of consensual activity. See *Casey*, 505 U.S., at 891 ("[O]n an average day in the United States, nearly 11,000 women are severely assaulted by their male partners. Many of these incidents involve sexual assault.").

[9] Eliminating or reducing women's reproductive choices is manifestly not a means of protecting them. When safe abortion procedures cease to be an option, many women seek other means to end unwanted or coerced pregnancies. See, e.g., World Health Organization, UNSAFE ABORTION: GLOBAL AND REGIONAL ESTIMATES OF THE INCIDENCE OF UNSAFE ABORTION AND ASSOCIATED MORTALITY IN 2000, pp. 3, 16 (4th ed. 2004) ("Restrictive legislation is associated with a high incidence of unsafe abortion" worldwide; unsafe abortion represents 13 percent of all "maternal" deaths); Henshaw, *Unintended Pregnancy and Abortion: A Public Health Perspective*, in A CLINICIAN'S GUIDE TO MEDICAL AND SURGICAL ABORTION 11, 19 (M. Paul, E. Lichtenberg, L. Borgatta, D. Grimes, & P. Stubblefield eds. 1999) ("Before legalization, large numbers of women in the United States died from unsafe abortions."); H. Boonstra, R. Gold, C. Richards, & L. Finer, ABORTION IN WOMEN'S LIVES 13, and fig. 2.2 (2006) ("as late as 1965, illegal abortion still accounted for an estimated . . . 17% of all officially reported pregnancy-related deaths"; "[d]eaths from abortion declined dramatically after legalization").

are to fulfil[l] the noble and benign offices of wife and mother."), with *United States v. Virginia,* 518 U.S. 515, 533 (1996) (State may not rely on "overbroad generalizations" about the "talents, capacities, or preferences" of women; "[s]uch judgments have . . . impeded . . . women's progress toward full citizenship stature throughout our Nation's history"); *Califano v. Goldfarb,* 430 U.S. 199, 207 (1977) (gender-based Social Security classification rejected because it rested on "archaic and overbroad generalizations" "such as assumptions as to [women's] dependency" (internal quotation marks omitted)).

Though today's majority may regard women's feelings on the matter as "self-evident," *ante,* at 1634, this Court has repeatedly confirmed that "[t]he destiny of the woman must be shaped . . . on her own conception of her spiritual imperatives and her place in society," *Casey,* 505 U.S., at 852. See also *id.*, at 877 (plurality opinion) ("[M]eans chosen by the State to further the interest in potential life must be calculated to inform the woman's free choice, not hinder it."). . .

Readings

NADINE TAUB AND ELIZABETH M. SCHNEIDER, *WOMEN'S SUBORDINATION AND THE ROLE OF LAW*

THE POLITICS OF LAW: A PROGRESSIVE CRITIQUE 151–176 (1990)

The Anglo-American legal tradition purports to value equality, by which it means, at a minimum, equal application of the law to all persons. Nevertheless, throughout this country's history, women have been denied the most basic rights of citizenship, allowed only limited participation in the marketplace, and otherwise denied access to power, dignity, and respect. Women have instead been largely occupied with providing the personal and household services necessary to sustain family life.

The work women perform in the domestic sphere is barely acknowledged, let alone valued. Institutional arrangements that preclude women's economic and sexual autonomy ensure that this work will be done primarily by women. Often, though not always, these institutions are expressed in legal form.

This chapter explores two aspects of the law's role in maintaining women in an inferior status. It first considers the way the law has furthered male dominance by explicitly excluding women from the public sphere and by refusing to regulate the domestic sphere to which they are thus confined. It then examines the way the law has legitimized sex discrimination through the articulation of an ideology that justifies differential treatment on the basis of perceived differences between men and women.

THE LEGAL ORDER AND THE PUBLIC/PRIVATE SPLIT

Excluded in the past from the public sphere of marketplace and government, women have been consigned to a private realm to carry on their primary responsibilities, *i.e.*, bearing and rearing children, and providing men with a refuge from the pressures of the capitalist world. This separation of society into the male public sphere and the female private sphere was most pronounced during the nineteenth century, when production moved out of the home. But even today, women's opportunities in the public sphere are limited by their obligations in the private domestic sphere.

Men dominate both the public sphere and the private sphere. Male control in the public sphere has often been consolidated explicitly by legal means. The law, however, is in large part absent from the private sphere, and that absence itself has contributed to male dominance and female subservience. In discussing the role of law in relation to this public/private split, this section first reviews the legal means by which women have been excluded from the public sphere, and then considers the law's absence from the private sphere and how that absence furthers male dominance.

Legal Exclusion from the Public Sphere

The most obvious exclusion of women from public life was the denial of the franchise. Although in colonial times unmarried, propertied women were technically entitled to vote on local issues, all state constitutions that were adopted after the War of Independence, with the temporary exception of New Jersey's, barred women from voting. This initial exclusion gained even greater significance in the 1820s and 1830s, when the franchise was extended to virtually every white male regardless of property holdings. Even after the Civil War, when black men gained the right to vote, women of all races continued to be denied the ballot. The Nineteenth Amendment, giving women the vote, finally became law in 1920 after what has been described as "a century of struggle."

The amendment's passage, however, did not mean that women were automatically accorded the rights and duties that generally accompanied elector status. For example, the exclusion of women from jury duty was upheld as late as 1961, when the Supreme Court explicitly rejected the equal-protection claim of a woman accused of murdering her husband. The Court found Florida's exclusion of women who did not voluntarily register for jury service "reasonable, since:

> Despite the enlightened emancipation of women from the restrictions and protections of bygone years, and their entry into many parts of community life formerly considered to be reserved

to men, woman is still regarded as the center of home and family life.[5]

* * * Women have likewise been excluded from full participation in the economy. Under English common law, not only were they barred from certain professions (such as law), but, once married, they were reduced to legal nonentities unable to sell, sue, or contract without the approval of their husbands or other male relatives. Although these disabilities were initially rigidified by codification of laws, which began in the 1820s, they were gradually lifted in the middle and latter part of the nineteenth century. Starting in the 1840s, various states passed laws that gave women the right to hold certain property in their own name. Subsequent legislation, enacted over the following half-century, afforded them the right to conduct business and retain their own earnings. The enactments were, however, repeatedly subjected to restrictive judicial interpretations that continued to confirm male dominance in business matters.

Even as women moved into the paid labor force, they were limited in their work opportunities and earning power by the ideological glorification of their domestic role reflected in the law. Women have been consistently excluded from certain occupational choices and denied equal earning power by statute and other governmental action. * * *

Legislation denying women the right to determine whether and when they will bear children has also served to exclude women from the public sphere. Beginning in the 1870s, legislative restrictions began to reinforce and supplement existing religious and cultural constraints on birth control. The Comstock Law forbidding obscene material (expressly including contraceptive devices) in the United States mail was invalidated in 1938,[16] while the Supreme Court did not invalidate state restrictions on the marital use of contraceptives until 1965[17] and their distribution to single persons until 1972.[18] Similarly, in the middle and late nineteenth century, most states enacted criminal statutes against abortion, although the procedure, at least in the pre-"quickening" stage, had not been a crime at the common law. While a number of these statutes were liberalized in the 1960s, criminal sanctions remained in force until they were invalidated by the 1973 Supreme Court decisions.[20] Since then, provisions have been upheld that exclude abortion from Medicaid coverage and require the parents of many minors to be notified. And in 1989, the Supreme Court once again signaled to the states that they would uphold restrictions on abortion.[22]

---

5 Hoyt v. Florida, 368 U.S. 57, 61 (1961). * * *

16 United States v. Nicholas, 97 F. 2d 510 (2d Cir. 1938). * * *

17 Griswold v. Connecticut, 381 U.S. 479 (1965).

18 Eisenstadt v. Baird, 405 U.S. 438 (1972).

20 [Roe v. Wade, 410 U.S. 113 (1973)]; Doe v. Bolton, 410 U.S. 179 (1973).

22 Webster v. Reproductive Services, 109 S. Ct. 3040 (1989).

The Absence of Law in the Private Sphere

While sex-based exclusionary laws have joined with other institutional and ideological constraints to directly limit women's participation in the public sphere, the legal order has operated more subtly in relation to the private sphere to which women have been relegated. On the one hand, the legal constraints against women retaining their earnings and conveying property—whose remnants endured well into the twentieth century—meant that married women could have legal relations with the outside world only through their husbands. In this sense, the law may be viewed as directing male domination in the private sphere. On the other hand, the law has been conspicuously absent from the private sphere itself. Despite the fundamental similarity of conflicts in the private sphere to legally cognizable disputes in the public sphere, the law generally refuses to interfere in ongoing family relationships. For example, the essence of the marital relation as a legal matter is the exchange of the man's obligation to support the women for her household and sexual services. Yet contract law, which purports to enforce promissory obligations between individuals, is not available during the marriage to enforce either the underlying support obligation or other agreements by the parties to a marriage to matters not involving property. * * * And while premarital property agreements will be enforced on divorce, courts' enormous discretion in awarding support and distributing property makes it highly unlikely that these decisions will reflect the parties' conduct during the marriage in regard to either the underlying support obligation or other agreements. It is as if in regulating the beginning and the end of a business partnership the law disregarded the events that transpired during the partnership and refused to enforce any agreements between the partners as to how they would behave.

Similarly, tort law, which is generally concerned with injuries inflicted on individuals, has traditionally been held inapplicable to injuries inflicted by one family member on another. Under the doctrines of interspousal and parent-child immunity, courts have consistently denied recoveries for injuries that would be compensable but for the fact that they occurred in the private realm. In the same way, criminal law declined to punish intentional injuries to family members. Common law and statutory definitions of rape in many states continue to carve out a special exception for a husband's forced intercourse with his wife. Wife beating was initially omitted from the definition of criminal assault on the ground that a husband had the right to chastise his wife. Even today, after courts have explicitly rejected the definitional exception and its rationale, judges, prosecutors, and police officers decline to enforce assault laws in the family context.

While in recent years, there has been some modification of these doctrines, the idea that law is inappropriate in the private sphere persists.

A modern example of this phenomenon is the idea that family disputes are best suited for mediation rather than more formal legal proceedings.

The state's failure to regulate the domestic sphere is now often justified on the ground that the law should not interfere with emotional relationships involved in the family realm because it is too heavy-handed. Indeed, the recognition of a familial privacy right in the early twentieth century has given this rationale a constitutional dimension. The importance of this concern, however, is undercut by the fact that the same result was previously justified by legal fictions, such as the woman's civil death on marriage. More importantly, the argument misconstrues the point at which the law is invoked. Legal relief is sought when family harmony has already been disrupted. Family members, like business associates, can be expected to forgo legal claims until they are convinced that harmonious relations are no longer possible. Equally important, the argument reflects and reinforces powerful myths about the nature of family relations. It is not true that women perform personal and household services purely for love. The family is the locus of fundamental economic exchanges, as well as important emotional ties.

Isolating women in a sphere divorced from the legal order contributes directly to their inferior status by denying them the legal relief that they seek to improve their situations and by sanctioning conduct of the men who control their lives. * * *

But beyond its direct, instrumental impact, the insulation of women's world from the legal order also conveys an important ideological message to the rest of society. Although this need not be the case in all societies, in our society the law's absence devalues women and their functions: women simply are not sufficiently important to merit legal regulation. This message is clearly communicated when particular relief is withheld. By declining to punish a man for inflicting injuries on his wife, for example, the law implies she is his property and he is free to control her as he sees fit. Women's work is discredited when the law refuses to enforce the man's obligation to support his wife, since it implies she makes no contribution worthy of support. Similarly, when courts decline to enforce contracts that seek to limit or specify the extent of the wife's services, the law implies that household work is not real work in the way that the type of work subject to contract in the public sphere is real work. These are important messages, for denying women's humanity and the value of her traditional work are key ideological components in maintaining woman's subordinate status. The message of women's inferiority is compounded by the totality of the law's absence from the private realm. In our society, law is for business and other important things. The fact that the law in general has so little bearing on women's day-to-day concerns reflects and underscores their insignificance. Thus, the legal order's overall contribution to the devaluation of women is greater than the sum of the negative messages conveyed by individual legal doctrines.

Finally, isolating women in a world where the law refuses to intrude further obscures the discrepancy between women's actual situation and our nominal commitment to equality. Like other collective ideals, the equality norm is expressed predominantly in legal form. Because the law as a whole is removed from women's world, the equality norm is perceived as having very limited application to women. In this way, people are encouraged to favor equality in the public sphere of government and business (*e.g.*, "equal pay for equal work") while denigrating the need for any real change in social roles ("I'm not a woman's libber"). The law can thus purport to guarantee equality while simultaneously denying it.

In short, the law plays a powerful role, though certainly not an exclusive role, in shaping and maintaining women's subordination. The law has operated directly and explicitly to prevent women from attaining self-support and influence in the public sphere, thereby reinforcing their dependence on men. At the same time, its continued absence from the private sphere to which women are relegated not only leaves individual women without formal remedies but also devalues and discredits them as a group. * * *

ANGELA P. HARRIS, *RACE AND ESSENTIALISM IN FEMINIST LEGAL THEORY*

42 STAN. L. REV. 581 (1990)

In this article, I discuss some of the writings of feminist legal theorists Catharine MacKinnon and Robin West. I argue that their work, though powerful and brilliant in many ways, relies on what I call gender essentialism—the notion that a unitary, "essential" women's experience can be isolated and described independently of race, class, sexual orientation, and other realities of experience. The result of this tendency toward gender essentialism, I argue, is not only that some voices are silenced in order to privilege others (for this is an inevitable result of categorization, which is necessary both for human communication and political movement), but that the voices that are silenced turn out to be the same voices silenced by the mainstream legal voice of "We the People"—among them, the voices of black women.

This result troubles me for two reasons. First, the obvious one: As a black woman, in my opinion the experience of black women is too often ignored both in feminist theory and in legal theory, and gender essentialism in feminist legal theory does nothing to address this problem. A second and less obvious reason for my criticism of gender essentialism is that, in my view, contemporary legal theory needs less abstraction and not simply a different sort of abstraction. To be fully subversive, the methodology of feminist legal theory should challenge not only law's content but its tendency to privilege the abstract and unitary voice, and this gender essentialism also fails to do.

In accordance with my belief that legal theory, including feminist legal theory, is in need of less abstraction, in this article I destabilize and subvert the unity of MacKinnon's and West's "woman" by introducing the voices of black women, especially as represented in literature. Before I begin, however, I want to make three cautionary points to the reader. First, my argument should not be read to accuse either MacKinnon or West of "racism" in the sense of personal antipathy to black people. Both writers are steadfastly anti-racist, which in a sense is my point. Just as law itself, in trying to speak for all persons, ends up silencing those without power, feminist legal theory is in danger of silencing those who have traditionally been kept from speaking, or who have been ignored when they spoke, including black women. The first step toward avoiding this danger is to give up the dream of gender essentialism.

Second, in using a racial critique to attack gender essentialism in feminist legal theory, my aim is not to establish a new essentialism in its place based on the essential experience of black women. Nor should my focus on black women be taken to mean that other women are not silenced either by the mainstream culture or by feminist legal theory. Accordingly, I invite the critique and subversion of my own generalizations.

Third and finally, I do not mean in this article to suggest that either feminism or legal theory should adopt the voice of [one] for whom every experience is unique and no categories or generalizations exist at all. Even a jurisprudence based on multiple consciousness must categorize; without categorization each individual is * * * isolated * * *, and there can be no moral responsibility or social change. My suggestion is only that we make our categories explicitly tentative, relational, and unstable, and that to do so is all the more important in a discipline like law, where abstraction and "frozen" categories are the norm. * * *

The need for multiple consciousness in feminist movement—a social movement encompassing law, literature, and everything in between—has long been apparent. Since the beginning of the feminist movement in the United States, black women have been arguing that their experience calls into question the notion of a unitary "women's experience."[19] In the first

---

[19] For example, in 1851, Sojourner Truth told the audience at the woman's rights convention in Akron, Ohio:

> That man over there says women need to be helped into carriages, and lifted over ditches, and to have the best place everywhere. Nobody ever helps me into carriages, or over mud-puddles, or gives me any best place! And ain't I a woman? Look at me! Look at my arm! I have ploughed, and planted, and gathered into barns, and no man could head me! And ain't I a woman? I could work as much and eat as much as a man—when I could get it—and bear the lash as well! And ain't I a woman? I have borne thirteen children, and seen

wave of the feminist movement, black women's[20] realization that the white leaders of the suffrage movement intended to take neither issues of racial oppression nor black women themselves seriously was instrumental in destroying or preventing political alliances between black and white women within the movement.[21] In the second wave, black women are again speaking loudly and persistently,[22] and at many levels our voices have begun to be heard. Feminists have adopted the notion of multiple consciousness as appropriate to describe a world in which people are not oppressed only or primarily on the basis of gender, but on the bases of race, class, sexual orientation, and other categories in inextricable webs. Moreover, multiple consciousness is implicit in the precepts of feminism itself. In Christine Littleton's words, "[f]eminist method starts with the very radical act of taking women seriously, believing that what we say about ourselves and our experience is important and valid, even when (or perhaps especially when) it has little or no relationship to what has been or is being said about us."[24] If a unitary "women's experience" or "feminism" must be distilled, feminists must ignore many women's voices.[25]

> them most all sold off to slavery, and when I cried out with my mother's grief, none but Jesus heard me! And ain't I a woman?

Address by Sojourner Truth (1851), reprinted in BLACK WOMEN IN NINETEENTH-CENTURY AMERICAN LIFE: THEIR WORDS, THEIR THOUGHTS, THEIR FEELINGS 234, 235 (B.J. Loewenberg & R. Bogin eds.1976).

20 I use "black" rather than "African-American" because some people of color who do not have African heritage and/or are not Americans nevertheless identify themselves as black, and in this essay I am more interested in stressing issues of culture than of nationality or genetics. I use "black" rather than "Black" because it is my contention in this essay that race and gender issues are inextricably intertwined, and to capitalize "Black" and not "Woman" would imply a privileging of race with which I do not agree.

21 For a discussion of white racism in the suffrage movement, see Angela Y. Davis, WOMEN, RACE AND CLASS 110–26 (1981); Paula Giddings, WHEN AND WHERE I ENTER: THE IMPACT OF BLACK WOMEN ON RACE AND SEX IN AMERICA 159–70 (1984).

22 See, e.g., A. Davis, *supra*; bell hooks, AIN'T I A WOMAN? BLACK WOMEN AND FEMINISM (1981) [hereinafter b. hooks, AIN'T I A WOMAN?]; bell hooks, FEMINIST THEORY: FROM MARGIN TO CENTER (1984) [hereinafter b. hooks, FEMINIST THEORY]; bell hooks, TALKING BACK: THINKING FEMINIST, THINKING BLACK (1989) [hereinafter b. hooks, TALKING BACK]; Gloria I. Joseph & Jill Lewis, COMMON DIFFERENCES: CONFLICTS IN BLACK AND WHITE FEMINIST PERSPECTIVES (1981); THIS BRIDGE CALLED MY BACK: WRITINGS BY RADICAL WOMEN OF COLOR (C. Moraga & G. Anzaldua 2d ed. 1983) [Hereinafter THIS BRIDGE CALLED MY BACK]; Hazel V. Carby, *White Woman Listen! Black Feminism and the Boundaries of Sisterhood* in THE EMPIRE STRIKES BACK: RACE AND RACISM IN 70S BRITAIN 212 (Centre for Contemporary Cultural Studies ed., 1982); Martia C. Lugones & Elizabeth v. Spelman, Have We Got A Theory for You! Feminist Theory, Cultural Imperialism and the demand for "The Woman's Voice," 66 WOMEN'S STUD. INT'L F. 573 (1983).

24 Christine A. Littleton, *Feminist Jurisprudence: The Difference Method Makes (Book Review)*, 41 STAN. L. REV. 751, 764 (1989). MacKinnon's definition of feminist method is the practice of "believing women's accounts of sexual use and abuse by men." Catharine A. MacKinnon, *Introduction: The Art of the Impossible*, in FEMINISM UNMODIFIED 1, 5 (1987). Littleton argues that MacKinnon's major contribution to feminist jurisprudence has been "more methodological than programmatic." Littleton, supra, at 753–54. In Littleton's view, "the essence of MacKinnon's view on 'feminisms' comes down to a single choice: feminist method or not." Id. at 752–53.

25 See Jane Flax, *Postmodernism and Gender Relations in Feminist Theory*, 12 SIGNS 621, 633 (1987):

> [W]ithin feminist theory a search for a defining theme of the whole or a feminist viewpoint may require the suppression of the important and discomforting voices of persons with

In feminist legal theory, however, the move away from univocal toward multivocal theories of women's experience and feminism has been slower than in other areas. In feminist legal theory, the pull of the second voice, the voice of abstract categorization, is still powerfully strong: "We the People" seems in danger of being replaced by "We the Women." And in feminist legal theory, as in the dominant culture, it is mostly white, straight, and socio-economically privileged people who claim to speak for all of us.[26] Not surprisingly, the story they tell about "women," despite its claim to universality, seems to black women to be peculiar to women who are white, straight, and socio-economically privileged—a phenomenon Adrienne Rich terms "white solipsism."[27]

Elizabeth Spelman notes:

> [T]he real problem has been how feminist theory has confused the condition of one group of women with the condition of all. . . . A measure of the depth of white middle-class privilege is that the apparently straightforward and logical points and axioms at the heart of much of feminist theory guarantee the direction of its attention to the concerns of white middle-class women.[28]

The notion that there is a monolithic "women's experience" that can be described independent of other facets of experience like race, class, and sexual orientation is one I refer to in this essay as "gender essentialism."[29] A corollary to gender essentialism is "racial essentialism"—the belief that there is a monolithic "Black Experience," or "Chicano Experience." The

---

> experiences unlike our own. The suppression of these voices seems to be a necessary condition for the (apparent) authority, coherence, and universality of our own.

Elizabeth Spelman sees this as "the paradox at the heart of feminism: Any attempt to talk about all women in terms of something we have in common undermines attempts to talk about the differences among us, and vice versa." Elizabeth V. Spelman, INESSENTIAL WOMAN: PROBLEMS OF EXCLUSION IN FEMINIST THOUGHT 3 (1988).

[26] *See, e.g.,* Catharine A. MacKinnon, *On Collaboration*, in FEMINISM UNMODIFIED, *supra*, at 198, 204 ("I am here to speak for those, particularly women and children, upon whose silence the law, including the law of the First Amendment, has been built.").

[27] Rich defines white solipsism as the tendency to "think, imagine, and speak as if whiteness described the world." Adrienne Rich, *Disloyal to Civilization: Feminism, Racism, Gynephobia*, in ON LIES, SECRETS, AND SILENCE 275, 299 (1979).

[28] E. Spelman, *supra*, at 4.

[29] Elizabeth Spelman lists five propositions which I consider to be associated with gender essentialism:

> 1. Women can be talked about "as women."
>
> 2. Women are oppressed "as women."
>
> 3. Gender can be isolated from other elements of identity that bear on one's social, economic, and political position such as race, class, ethnicity; hence sexism can be isolated from racism, classism, etc.
>
> 4. Women's situation can be contrasted to men's.
>
> 5. Relations between men and women can be compared to relations between other oppressor/oppressed groups (whites and Blacks, Christians and Jews, rich and poor, etc.), and hence it is possible to compare the situation of women to the situation of Blacks, Jews, the poor, etc.

Id. at 165.

source of gender and racial essentialism (and all other essentialisms, for the list of categories could be infinitely multiplied) is the second voice, the voice that claims to speak for all. The result of essentialism is to reduce the lives of people who experience multiple forms of oppression to addition problems: "racism + sexism = straight black women's experience," or "racism + sexism + homophobia = black lesbian experience."[30] Thus, in an essentialist world, black women's experience will always be forcibly fragmented before being subjected to analysis, as those who are "only interested in race" and those who are "only interested in gender" take their separate slices of our lives.

Moreover, feminist essentialism paves the way for unconscious racism. Spelman puts it this way:

> [T]hose who produce the "story of woman" want to make sure they appear in it. The best way to ensure that is to be the storyteller and hence to be in a position to decide which of all the many facts about women's lives ought to go into the story, which ought to be left out. Essentialism works well in behalf of these aims, aims that subvert the very process by which women might come to see where and how they wish to make common cause. For essentialism invites me to take what I understand to be true of me "as a woman" for some golden nugget of womanness all women have as women; and it makes the participation of other women inessential to the production of the story. How lovely: the many turn out to be one, and the one that they are is me.[31]

In a racist society like this one, the storytellers are usually white, and so "woman" turns out to be "white woman."

Why, in the face of challenges from "different" women and from feminist method itself, is feminist essentialism so persistent and pervasive? I think the reasons are several. Essentialism is intellectually convenient, and to a certain extent cognitively ingrained. Essentialism also carries with it important emotional and political payoffs. Finally, essentialism often appears (especially to white women) as the only alternative to chaos, mindless pluralism (the Funes trap), and the end of the feminist movement. In my view, however, as long as feminists, like theorists in the dominant culture, continue to search for gender and racial essences, black women will never be anything more than a crossroads

---

[30] See Deborah K. King, *Multiple Jeopardy, Multiple Consciousness: The Context of a Black Feminist Ideology*, 14 SIGNS 42, 51 (1988) ("To reduce this complex of negotiations to an addition problem (racism + sexism = black women's experience) is to define the issues, and indeed black womanhood itself, within the structural terms developed by Europeans and especially white males to privilege their race and their sex unilaterally."); see also E. Spelman, *supra* at 114–32 (chapter entitled "Gender & Race: The Ampersand Problem in Feminist Thought"); Barbara Smith, *Notes for Yet Another Paper on Black Feminism, or Will the Real Enemy Please Stand Up?*, 5 CONDITIONS 123, 123 (1979) (the effect of multiple oppression is "not merely arithmetic").

[31] E. Spelman, *supra*, at 159.

between two kinds of domination, or at the bottom of a hierarchy of oppressions; we will always be required to choose pieces of ourselves to present as wholeness. * * *

NOTES AND QUESTIONS

1. *The Equal Rights Amendment.* The proposed Equal Rights Amendment ("ERA") provides in its entirety:

> Section 1. Equality of rights under the law shall not be denied or abridged by the United States or by any state on account of sex.
>
> Section 2. The Congress shall have the power to enforce, by appropriate legislation, the provisions of this article.
>
> Section 3. This amendment shall take effect two years after the date of ratification.

The ERA, drafted principally by Alice Paul, was introduced in every session of Congress from 1923 to 1972, when it was approved and sent to the states for ratification. The proposing clause included a seven-year time limit, subsequently extended to 30 June 1982. At that date, the ERA had been ratified by 35 states, three states short of the number required for ratification. Fewer than half the states have an ERA in their constitutions. What accounts for this state of affairs?

2. *Gender stereotyping and the legal challenge to prohibitions of same-sex marriage.* By referendum in 2008, the State of California adopted Proposition 8, which prohibited same-sex marriages. In striking down Proposition 8, Judge Vaughn Walker decided that:

> [t]he evidence shows that the tradition of restricting an individual's choice of spouse based on gender does not rationally further a state interest despite its "ancient lineage." Instead, the evidence shows that the tradition of gender restrictions arose when spouses were legally required to adhere to specific gender roles. California has eliminated all legally-mandated gender roles except the requirement that a marriage consist of one man and one woman. Proposition 8 thus enshrines in the California Constitution a gender restriction that the evidence shows to be nothing more than an artifact of a foregone notion that men and women fulfill different roles in civic life. The tradition of restricting marriage to opposite-sex couples does not further any state interest. Rather, the evidence shows that Proposition 8 harms the state's interest in equality, because it mandates that men and women be treated differently based only on antiquated and discredited notions of gender.

Perry v. Schwarzenegger, 704 F. Supp. 2d 921, 998 (N.D. Cal. 2010). After considerable procedural twists, the Supreme Court ruled that the proponents of Proposition 8 had no standing to challenge the District Court's disposition.

Hollingsworth v. Perry, 133 S. Ct. 2652 (June 26, 2013) (No. 12–144). Two years later, in June 2015, the U.S. Supreme Court ruled that the Fourteenth Amendment requires a state to license a marriage between two people of the same sex. *Obergefell v. Hodges*, 576 U.S. ___ (2015) (the fundamental liberties protected by the Fourteenth Amendment "extend to certain personal choices central to individual dignity and autonomy, including intimate choices defining personal identity and beliefs.") After *Obergefell*, legal challenges to other orientation-based forms of discrimination remain, especially *inter alia* in housing, employment, and exposure to violence.

3. *Feminist jurisprudences.* Not all feminist theory necessarily connects to law, and the varieties of feminist theory (*e.g.,* liberal feminism, cultural feminism, radical feminism, "maternal" feminism, democratic feminism *inter alia*) do not necessarily translate into different approaches to cases with a gendered component. Feminist jurisprudence itself has evolved over time, changing its strategies and theories, as well as the issues to which it speaks. From a focus on equality and non-discrimination, some contemporary feminist jurisprudence has rejected the essentialism of difference between the sexes, and attempts to include those women who have been historically left out of the feminist movement—women of color, queer women, transgender people, women with disabilities, women in lower socioeconomic classes. Postmodernist feminist theory focuses on intersectionality: the way that race, class, gender, and other social factors affect women under the law. And some feminist legal theory departs from critical legal studies by accepting the possibility that legal rights are not inherently meaningless or corrupted. *Compare* MARTHA MINOW, MAKING ALL THE DIFFERENCE: INCLUSION, EXCLUSION, AND AMERICAN LAW (1991); Mary Joe Frug, POSTMODERN LEGAL FEMINISM (1992); PATRICIA WILLIAMS, THE ALCHEMY OF RACE AND RIGHTS (1992); and NANCY LEVIT & ROBERT R. M. VERCHICK, FEMINIST LEGAL THEORY: A PRIMER (2006).

CHAPTER EIGHT

POST-REALIST APPROACHES TO LAW AND OBLIGATION (VI): CRITICAL RACE THEORY

■ ■ ■

"[T]he histories of the African, Asian, Latin, and Native American people in the United States are replete with examples of the law and the legal process as the means by which the generalized racism in the society was made particular and converted into standards and policies of social control."

— W. Haywood Burns

"What is logical to the oppressor isn't logical to the oppressed. And what is reason to the oppressor isn't reason to the oppressed. The black people in this country are beginning to realize that what sounds reasonable to those who exploit us doesn't sound reasonable to us. There just has to be a new system of reason and logic devised by us who are at the bottom, if we want to get some results in this struggle that is called 'the Negro revolution.' "

— Malcolm X

Orientation

The core premise of Critical Race Theory ("CRT") is that the history of law and the history of racism in the United States are intimately connected. Consistent with other "critical" schools like feminist jurisprudence and critical legal studies, CRT aims to demonstrate that even apparently neutral principles and idealizations like the rule of law can mask power, specifically racism and racial inequality. As the cases in this chapter suggest, the neutrality in principle of equal protection or freedom of speech or the rights of private property is *characteristically* compromised in application in ways that disadvantage people of color. Drawing on the history of white supremacy and privilege in multiple forms, CRT exposes the disconnect between the liberal orthodoxy that race is or ought to be irrelevant in the law *versus* the historical reality that the law has been a dominant vehicle for enforcing racial inequality in the United States. So for example, whatever initial progress may have been made in the early days of the civil rights movement, legislative reform efforts—like the antidiscrimination laws of the United States—have not been allowed to work in ways that reorder the racial status quo. To the contrary, reform has been incremental and done a better job of defusing demands for racial justice than meeting them. In the end, CRT goes considerably further than observing and tagging white supremacy in American law, building on the anthropological truth that "race" itself names not some biological reality but a social construct—a construct created, projected, and protected by the law and legal practice. In grounding its legal analysis on such insights from disciplines other than law, CRT stands in the mainstream of post-Realist jurisprudence.

One way to misunderstand CRT is to think of it as some highlight reel of famously racist decisions by American courts in the past. *See, e.g.*, *Dred Scott v. Sanford*, 19 How. 393 (1857) ("[T]hey [the black race] had for more than a century before [the adoption of the Constitution] been regarded as beings of an inferior order, and altogether unfit to associate with the white race, either in social or political relations; and so far inferior, that they had no rights which the white man was bound to respect. . . ."); *Plessy v. Ferguson*, 163 U.S. 537 (1896) (establishing the "separate but equal" doctrine that institutionalized segregation and racial oppression, observing that "[i]f one race be inferior to the other socially, the Constitution of the United States cannot put them upon the same plane"); *Korematsu v. United States*, 323 U.S. 214 (1944) (authorizing the exclusion of American citizens of Japanese descent from vast areas on the Pacific coast, including their homes). The fact that each of these decisions has been overturned or repudiated might be over-interpreted as a sign that race now plays no role in American law. By contrast, Critical Race Theory tracks out the legal component of *continuing* forms of white supremacy: "racism has contributed to all contemporary manifestations of group advantage and disadvantage along racial lines, including differences in income, imprisonment, health, housing, education, political representation, and military service." MARI MATSUDA AND CHARLES R. LAWRENCE III, *Introduction*, WORDS THAT WOUND: CRITICAL RACE THEORY, ASSAULTIVE SPEECH, AND THE FIRST AMENDMENT 6 (1993).

As shown in this chapter, the scholarly strategy generally associated with CRT includes not only doctrinal analysis but also story-telling and other forms of narrative that privilege the experiential knowledge of people of color. Predictably perhaps, not everyone is impressed. Richard Posner, a leading law-and-economics theorist, has "label[ed] critical race theorists and postmodernists the 'lunatic core' of 'radical legal egalitarianism.'* * * What is most arresting about critical race theory is that * * * it turns its back on the Western tradition of rational inquiry, forswearing analysis for narrative." Richard A. Posner, *The Skin Trade*, NEW REPUBLIC (Oct. 13 1997).

A different way of misunderstanding CRT, is to limit it to the American experience. Other countries with different racial histories may also find that their law, in principle or in application, systematically disadvantages one group. International law can also be forced to reveal the racist elements of its history. For example, international law long protected the title of a state to territory it "discovered." If Spain discovered an island in the Pacific for example, international law generally protected its title until it might be displaced by some other state, generally some other European imperial state. The legal move required to protect title by discovery was the pretense that these lands were empty, uninhabited at the time they were "discovered." They were, as the latinism runs, *terra nullius*, that is "land belonging to no one." But these territories were often inhabited by indigenous peoples, with organized forms of government and culture. These peoples were not in the club of nations giving voice to international norms, and so their interests—indeed their legal existence—were largely invisible. Perhaps the latinism should have been translated as "land belonging to no one who looks like us," but it hardly seems radical now to recognize that the notion of *terra nullius* could be understood as an apparently neutral doctrine which operated in fact to mask the displacement of racially-identifiable peoples. Thinking about legal doctrine and how it perpetuates racial inequality—whether in the United States or not—is the genetic marker of critical race theory.

In many ways, CRT departs from critical legal studies and other post-modern critiques of rights discourse. Professors Richard Delgado and Patricia Williams among others have suggested that rights may have more meaning than the Crits realized. After all, the intellectual target of critical legal studies was liberalism and its methods, not racism and its effects, and so its assessment of American civil rights law has an air of Olympian detachment about it. CLS, with its deconstruction of rights and of formalism generally, discounts the occasional advantages of formality and rights to outsider groups. In Professor Kimberlé Crenshaw's words, "Rights have been important. They may have legitimated racial inequality, but they have also been the means by which oppressed groups have secured both entry as formal equals into the dominant order and the survival of their movement in the face of private and state repression." Kimberlé Williams Crenshaw, *Race, Reform, and Retrenchment: Transformation and Legitimation in Antidiscrimination Law*, 101 HARV. L. REV. 1331, 1384–85 (1988). What is the proper response when rights and the law generally do not adequately protect against inequality, expropriation, and oppression? How different is the right response when the law—for all its apparent neutrality—actually provides the architecture of discrimination?

MCCLESKEY V. KEMP

481 U.S. 279 (1987)

JUSTICE POWELL delivered the opinion of the Court. * * * McCleskey, a black man, was convicted of two counts of armed robbery and one count of murder in the Superior Court of Fulton County, Georgia, on October 12, 1978. McCleskey's convictions arose out of the robbery of a furniture store and the killing of a white police officer during the course of the robbery. The evidence at trial indicated that McCleskey and three accomplices planned and carried out the robbery. All four were armed. McCleskey entered the front of the store while the other three entered the rear. McCleskey secured the front of the store by rounding up the customers and forcing them to lie face down on the floor. The other three rounded up the employees in the rear and tied them up with tape. The manager was forced at gunpoint to turn over the store receipts, his watch, and $6. During the course of the robbery, a police officer, answering a silent alarm, entered the store through the front door. As he was walking down the center aisle of the store, two shots were fired. Both struck the officer. One hit him in the face and killed him.

Several weeks later, McCleskey was arrested in connection with an unrelated offense. He confessed that he had participated in the furniture store robbery, but denied that he had shot the police officer. At trial, the State introduced evidence that at least one of the bullets that struck the officer was fired from a .38 caliber Rossi revolver. This description matched the description of the gun that McCleskey had carried during the robbery. The State also introduced the testimony of two witnesses who had heard McCleskey admit to the shooting.

The jury convicted McCleskey of murder. At the penalty hearing, the jury heard arguments as to the appropriate sentence. Under Georgia law, the jury could not consider imposing the death penalty unless it found beyond a reasonable doubt that the murder was accompanied by one of the statutory aggravating circumstances. The jury in this case found two aggravating circumstances to exist beyond a reasonable doubt: the murder was committed during the course of an armed robbery; and the murder was committed upon a peace officer engaged in the performance of his duties. In making its decision whether to impose the death sentence, the jury considered the mitigating and aggravating circumstances of McCleskey's conduct. McCleskey offered no mitigating evidence. The jury recommended that he be sentenced to death on the murder charge and to consecutive life sentences on the armed robbery charges. The court followed the jury's recommendation and sentenced McCleskey to death.

On appeal, the Supreme Court of Georgia affirmed the convictions and the sentences. * * * McCleskey [ultimately] filed a petition for a writ of habeas corpus in the Federal District Court for the Northern District of Georgia. [He claimed] that the Georgia capital sentencing process is administered in a racially discriminatory manner in violation of the Eighth and Fourteenth Amendments to the United States Constitution. In support of his claim, McCleskey proffered a statistical study performed by Professors David C. Baldus, Charles Pulaski, and George Woodworth (the

Baldus study) that purports to show a disparity in the imposition of the death sentence in Georgia based on the race of the murder victim and, to a lesser extent, the race of the defendant. The Baldus study is actually two sophisticated statistical studies that examine over 2,000 murder cases that occurred in Georgia during the 1970's. The raw numbers collected by Professor Baldus indicate that defendants charged with killing white persons received the death penalty in 11% of the cases, but defendants charged with killing blacks received the death penalty in only 1% of the cases. The raw numbers also indicate a reverse racial disparity according to the race of the defendant: 4% of the black defendants received the death penalty, as opposed to 7% of the white defendants.

Baldus also divided the cases according to the combination of the race of the defendant and the race of the victim. He found that the death penalty was assessed in 22% of the cases involving black defendants and white victims; 8% of the cases involving white defendants and white victims; 1% of the cases involving black defendants and black victims; and 3% of the cases involving white defendants and black victims. Similarly, Baldus found that prosecutors sought the death penalty in 70% of the cases involving black defendants and white victims; 32% of the cases involving white defendants and white victims; 15% of the cases involving black defendants and black victims; and 19% of the cases involving white defendants and black victims.

Baldus subjected his data to an extensive analysis, taking account of 230 variables that could have explained the disparities on nonracial grounds. One of his models concludes that, even after taking account of 39 nonracial variables, defendants charged with killing white victims were 4.3 times as likely to receive a death sentence as defendants charged with killing blacks. According to this model, black defendants were 1.1 times as likely to receive a death sentence as other defendants. Thus, the Baldus study indicates that black defendants, such as McCleskey, who kill white victims have the greatest likelihood of receiving the death penalty.[5]

The District Court held an extensive evidentiary hearing on McCleskey's petition. * * * It concluded that McCleskey's "statistics do not demonstrate a *prima facie* case in support of the contention that the death penalty was imposed upon him because of his race, because of the race of the victim, or because of any Eighth Amendment concern." As to

5 Baldus' 230—variable model divided cases into eight different ranges, according to the estimated aggravation level of the offense. Baldus argued in his testimony to the District Court that the effects of racial bias were most striking in the midrange cases. "[W]hen the cases become tremendously aggravated so that everybody would agree that if we're going to have a death sentence, these are the cases that should get it, the race effects go away. It's only in the midrange of cases where the decision makers have a real choice as to what to do. If there's room for the exercise of discretion, then the [racial] factors begin to play a role." Under this model, Baldus found that 14.4% of the black-victim midrange cases received the death penalty, and 34.4% of the white-victim cases received the death penalty. According to Baldus, the facts of McCleskey's case placed it within the midrange.

McCleskey's Fourteenth Amendment claim, the court found that the methodology of the Baldus study was flawed in several respects. Because of these defects, the court held that the Baldus study "fail[ed] to contribute anything of value" to McCleskey's claim. Accordingly, the court denied the petition insofar as it was based upon the Baldus study.

The Court of Appeals for the Eleventh Circuit, sitting *en banc*, carefully reviewed the District Court's decision on McCleskey's claim. 753 F.2d 877 (1985). It assumed the validity of the study itself and addressed the merits of McCleskey's Eighth and Fourteenth Amendment claims. That is, the court assumed that the study "showed that systematic and substantial disparities existed in the penalties imposed upon homicide defendants in Georgia based on race of the homicide victim, that the disparities existed at a less substantial rate in death sentencing based on race of defendants, and that the factors of race of the victim and defendant were at work in Fulton County." *Id.*, at 895. Even assuming the study's validity, the Court of Appeals found the statistics "insufficient to demonstrate discriminatory intent or unconstitutional discrimination in the Fourteenth Amendment context, [and] insufficient to show irrationality, arbitrariness and capriciousness under any kind of Eighth Amendment analysis." * * *

The Court of Appeals affirmed the denial by the District Court of McCleskey's petition for a writ of habeas corpus insofar as the petition was based upon the Baldus study, with three judges dissenting as to McCleskey's claims based on the Baldus study. We granted *certiorari* and now affirm.

II

McCleskey's first claim is that the Georgia capital punishment statute violates the Equal Protection Clause of the Fourteenth Amendment.[7] He argues that race has infected the administration of Georgia's statute in two ways: persons who murder whites are more likely to be sentenced to death than persons who murder blacks, and black murderers are more likely to be sentenced to death than white murderers. As a black defendant who killed a white victim, McCleskey claims that the Baldus study demonstrates that he was discriminated against because of his race and because of the race of his victim. In its broadest form, McCleskey's claim of discrimination extends to every actor in the Georgia capital sentencing process, from the prosecutor who sought the death penalty and the jury

[7] Although the District Court rejected the findings of the Baldus study as flawed, the Court of Appeals assumed that the study is valid and reached the constitutional issues. Accordingly, those issues are before us. As did the Court of Appeals, we assume the study is valid statistically without reviewing the factual findings of the District Court. Our assumption that the Baldus study is statistically valid does not include the assumption that the study shows that racial considerations actually enter into any sentencing decisions in Georgia. Even a sophisticated multiple-regression analysis such as the Baldus study can only demonstrate a risk that the factor of race entered into some capital sentencing decisions and a necessarily lesser risk that race entered into any particular sentencing decision.

that imposed the sentence, to the State itself that enacted the capital punishment statute and allows it to remain in effect despite its allegedly discriminatory application. We agree with the Court of Appeals, and every other court that has considered such a challenge, that this claim must fail.

A

Our analysis begins with the basic principle that a defendant who alleges an equal protection violation has the burden of proving "the existence of purposeful discrimination." *Whitus v. Georgia*, 385 U.S. 545, 550 (1967).[10] A corollary to this principle is that a criminal defendant must prove that the purposeful discrimination "had a discriminatory effect" on him. *Wayte v. United States*, 470 U.S. 598, 608 (1985). Thus, to prevail under the Equal Protection Clause, McCleskey must prove that the decision-makers in *his* case acted with discriminatory purpose. He offers no evidence specific to his own case that would support an inference that racial considerations played a part in his sentence. Instead, he relies solely on the Baldus study.[11] McCleskey argues that the Baldus study compels an inference that his sentence rests on purposeful discrimination. McCleskey's claim that these statistics are sufficient proof of discrimination, without regard to the facts of a particular case, would extend to all capital cases in Georgia, at least where the victim was white and the defendant is black.

The Court has accepted statistics as proof of intent to discriminate in certain limited contexts. First, this Court has accepted statistical disparities as proof of an equal protection violation in the selection of the jury venire in a particular district. Although statistical proof normally must present a "stark" pattern to be accepted as the sole proof of discriminatory intent under the Constitution,[12] *Arlington Heights v. Metropolitan Housing Dev. Corp.*, 429 U.S. 252, 266 (1977), "[b]ecause of the nature of the jury-selection task, . . . we have permitted a finding of constitutional violation even when the statistical pattern does not

---

[10] *See Arlington Heights v. Metropolitan Housing Dev. Corp., supra*, 429 U.S., at 265; *Washington v. Davis*, 426 U.S. 229, 240 (1976).

[11] McCleskey's expert testified:

"Models that are developed talk about the effect on the average. They do not depict the experience of a single individual. What they say, for example, [is] that on the average, the race of the victim, if it is white, increases on the average the probability . . . (that) the death sentence would be given. "Whether in a given case that is the answer, it cannot be determined from statistics." 580 F.Supp., at 372.

[12] *Gomillion v. Lightfoot*, 364 U.S. 339 (1960), and *Yick Wo v. Hopkins*, 118 U.S. 356 (1886), are examples of those rare cases in which a statistical pattern of discriminatory impact demonstrated a constitutional violation. In *Gomillion*, a state legislature violated the Fifteenth Amendment by altering the boundaries of a particular city "from a square to an uncouth twenty-eight-sided figure." The alterations excluded 395 of 400 black voters without excluding a single white voter. In *Yick Wo*, an ordinance prohibited operation of 310 laundries that were housed in wooden buildings, but allowed such laundries to resume operations if the operator secured a permit from the government. When laundry operators applied for permits to resume operation, all but one of the white applicants received permits, but none of the over 200 Chinese applicants were successful. In those cases, the Court found the statistical disparities "to warrant and require" a "conclusion [that was] irresistible, tantamount for all practical purposes to a mathematical demonstration" that the State acted with a discriminatory purpose.

approach [such] extremes." *Id.*, at 266, n. 13.[13] Second, this Court has accepted statistics in the form of multiple-regression analysis to prove statutory violations under Title VII of the Civil Rights Act of 1964. *Bazemore v. Friday*, 478 U.S. 385, 400–401 (1986) (opinion of Brennan, J., concurring in part).

But the nature of the capital sentencing decision, and the relationship of the statistics to that decision, are fundamentally different from the corresponding elements in the venire-selection or Title VII cases. Most importantly, each particular decision to impose the death penalty is made by a petit jury selected from a properly constituted venire. Each jury is unique in its composition, and the Constitution requires that its decision rest on consideration of innumerable factors that vary according to the characteristics of the individual defendant and the facts of the particular capital offense. Thus, the application of an inference drawn from the general statistics to a specific decision in a trial and sentencing simply is not comparable to the application of an inference drawn from general statistics to a specific venire-selection or Title VII case. In those cases, the statistics relate to fewer entities, and fewer variables are relevant to the challenged decisions.[15]

Another important difference between the cases in which we have accepted statistics as proof of discriminatory intent and this case is that, in the venire-selection and Title VII contexts, the decision-maker has an opportunity to explain the statistical disparity. Here, the State has no practical opportunity to rebut the Baldus study. "[C]ontrolling considerations of . . . public policy," *McDonald v. Pless*, 238 U.S. 264, 267 (1915), dictate that jurors "cannot be called . . . to testify to the motives and influences that led to their verdict." *Chicago, B. & Q.R. Co. v. Babcock*, 204 U.S. 585, 593 (1907). Similarly, the policy considerations behind a prosecutor's traditionally "wide discretion" suggest the impropriety of our

---

[13] *See, e.g., Castaneda v. Partida*, 430 U.S. 482, 495 (1977) (2-to-1 disparity between Mexican-Americans in county population and those summoned for grand jury duty); *Turner v. Fouche*, 396 U.S. 346, 359 (1970) (1.6-to-1 disparity between blacks in county population and those on grand jury lists); *Whitus v. Georgia*, 385 U.S. 545, 552 (1967) (3-to-1 disparity between eligible blacks in county and blacks on grand jury venire).

[15] We refer here not to the number of entities involved in any particular decision, but to the number of entities whose decisions necessarily are reflected in a statistical display such as the Baldus study. The decisions of a jury commission or of an employer over time are fairly attributable to the commission or the employer. Therefore, an unexplained statistical discrepancy can be said to indicate a consistent policy of the decision-maker. The Baldus study seeks to deduce a state "policy" by studying the combined effects of the decisions of hundreds of juries that are unique in their composition. It is incomparably more difficult to deduce a consistent policy by studying the decisions of these many unique entities. It is also questionable whether any consistent policy can be derived by studying the decisions of prosecutors. The District Attorney is elected by the voters in a particular county. *See* Ga. Const., Art. 6, § 8, ¶ 1. Since decisions whether to prosecute and what to charge necessarily are individualized and involve infinite factual variations, coordination among district attorney offices across a State would be relatively meaningless. Thus, any inference from statewide statistics to a prosecutorial "policy" is of doubtful relevance. Moreover, the statistics in Fulton County alone represent the disposition of far fewer cases than the statewide statistics. Even assuming the statistical validity of the Baldus study as a whole, the weight to be given the results gleaned from this small sample is limited.

requiring prosecutors to defend their decisions to seek death penalties, "often years after they were made." *See Imbler v. Pachtman*, 424 U.S. 409, 425–426 (1976).[18] Moreover, absent far stronger proof, it is unnecessary to seek such a rebuttal, because a legitimate and unchallenged explanation for the decision is apparent from the record: McCleskey committed an act for which the United States Constitution and Georgia laws permit imposition of the death penalty.

Finally, McCleskey's statistical proffer must be viewed in the context of his challenge. McCleskey challenges decisions at the heart of the State's criminal justice system. "[O]ne of society's most basic tasks is that of protecting the lives of its citizens and one of the most basic ways in which it achieves the task is through criminal laws against murder." *Gregg v. Georgia*, 428 U.S. 153, 226 (1976) (White, J., concurring). Implementation of these laws necessarily requires discretionary judgments. Because discretion is essential to the criminal justice process, we would demand exceptionally clear proof before we would infer that the discretion has been abused. The unique nature of the decisions at issue in this case also counsels against adopting such an inference from the disparities indicated by the Baldus study. Accordingly, we hold that the Baldus study is clearly insufficient to support an inference that any of the decision-makers in McCleskey's case acted with discriminatory purpose.

B

McCleskey also suggests that the Baldus study proves that the State as a whole has acted with a discriminatory purpose. He appears to argue that the State has violated the Equal Protection Clause by adopting the capital punishment statute and allowing it to remain in force despite its allegedly discriminatory application. But " '[d]iscriminatory purpose' . . . implies more than intent as volition or intent as awareness of consequences. It implies that the decision-maker, in this case a state legislature, selected or reaffirmed a particular course of action at least in part 'because of,' not merely 'in spite of,' its adverse effects upon an identifiable group." *Personnel Administrator of Massachusetts v. Feeney*, 442 U.S. 256, 279 (1979). For this claim to prevail, McCleskey would have to prove that the Georgia Legislature enacted or maintained the death penalty statute because of an anticipated racially discriminatory effect. In *Gregg v. Georgia*, *supra*, this Court found that the Georgia capital sentencing system could operate in a fair and neutral manner. There was

[18] Although *Imbler* was decided in the context of damages actions under 42 U.S.C. § 1983 brought against prosecutors, the considerations that led the Court to hold that a prosecutor should not be required to explain his decisions apply in this case as well: "[I]f the prosecutor could be made to answer in court each time . . . a person charged him with wrongdoing, his energy and attention would be diverted from the pressing duty of enforcing the criminal law." 424 U.S., at 425. Our refusal to require that the prosecutor provide an explanation for his decisions in this case is completely consistent with this Court's longstanding precedents that hold that a prosecutor need not explain his decisions unless the criminal defendant presents a *prima facie* case of unconstitutional conduct with respect to his case.

no evidence then, and there is none now, that the Georgia Legislature enacted the capital punishment statute to further a racially discriminatory purpose.[20]

Nor has McCleskey demonstrated that the legislature maintains the capital punishment statute because of the racially disproportionate impact suggested by the Baldus study. As legislatures necessarily have wide discretion in the choice of criminal laws and penalties, and as there were legitimate reasons for the Georgia Legislature to adopt and maintain capital punishment, we will not infer a discriminatory purpose on the part of the State of Georgia. Accordingly, we reject McCleskey's equal protection claims. * * * [The Court's analysis of McCleskey's claims under the Eighth Amendment is omitted.]

* * * McCleskey's arguments are best presented to the legislative bodies. It is not the responsibility—or indeed even the right—of this Court to determine the appropriate punishment for particular crimes. It is the legislatures, the elected representatives of the people, that are "constituted to respond to the will and consequently the moral values of the people." *Furman v. Georgia*, 408 U.S., at 383 (Burger, C.J., dissenting). Legislatures also are better qualified to weigh and "evaluate the results of statistical studies in terms of their own local conditions and with a flexibility of approach that is not available to the courts," *Gregg v. Georgia*, *supra*, 428 U.S., at 186. Capital punishment is now the law in more than two-thirds of our States. It is the ultimate duty of courts to determine on a case-by-case basis whether these laws are applied consistently with the Constitution. Despite McCleskey's wide-ranging arguments that basically challenge the validity of capital punishment in our multiracial society, the only question before us is whether in his case the law of Georgia was properly applied. We agree with the District Court and the Court of Appeals for the Eleventh Circuit that this was carefully and correctly done in this case. * * *

JUSTICE BLACKMUN, with whom JUSTICE MARSHALL and JUSTICE STEVENS join, and with whom JUSTICE BRENNAN joins * * *, dissenting. The Court today sanctions the execution of a man despite his presentation of evidence that establishes a constitutionally intolerable level of racially based discrimination leading to the imposition of his death sentence. I am disappointed with the Court's action not only because of its denial of constitutional guarantees to petitioner McCleskey individually,

[20] McCleskey relies on "historical evidence" to support his claim of purposeful discrimination by the State. This evidence focuses on Georgia laws in force during and just after the Civil War. Of course, the "historical background of the decision is one evidentiary source" for proof of intentional discrimination. *Arlington Heights v. Metropolitan Housing Dev. Corp.*, 429 U.S., at 267. But unless historical evidence is reasonably contemporaneous with the challenged decision, it has little probative value. *Cf. Hunter v. Underwood*, 471 U.S. 222, 228–233 (1985) (relying on legislative history to demonstrate discriminatory motivation behind state statute). Although the history of racial discrimination in this country is undeniable, we cannot accept official actions taken long ago as evidence of current intent.

but also because of its departure from what seems to me to be well-developed constitutional jurisprudence. * * *

McCleskey's case raises concerns that are central not only to the principles underlying the Eighth Amendment, but also to the principles underlying the Fourteenth Amendment. Analysis of his case in terms of the Fourteenth Amendment is consistent with this Court's recognition that racial discrimination is fundamentally at odds with our constitutional guarantee of equal protection. The protections afforded by the Fourteenth Amendment are not left at the courtroom door. Nor is equal protection denied to persons convicted of crimes. The Court in the past has found that racial discrimination within the criminal justice system is particularly abhorrent: "Discrimination on the basis of race, odious in all aspects, is especially pernicious in the administration of justice." *Rose v. Mitchell*, 443 U.S. 545, 555 (1979). Disparate enforcement of criminal sanctions "destroys the appearance of justice and thereby casts doubt on the integrity of the judicial process." *Id.*, at 555–556. And only last Term Justice Powell, writing for the Court, noted: "Discrimination within the judicial system is most pernicious because it is 'a stimulant to that race prejudice which is an impediment to securing to [black citizens] that equal justice which the law aims to secure to all others.' " *Batson v. Kentucky*, 476 U.S. 79, 87–88 (1986), quoting *Strauder v. West Virginia*, 100 U.S. (10 Otto) 303, 308 (1880).

Moreover, the legislative history of the Fourteenth Amendment reminds us that discriminatory enforcement of States' criminal laws was a matter of great concern for the drafters. In the introductory remarks to its Report to Congress, the Joint Committee on Reconstruction, which reported out the Joint Resolution proposing the Fourteenth Amendment, specifically noted: "This deep-seated prejudice against color . . . leads to acts of cruelty, oppression, and murder, which the local authorities are at no pains to prevent or punish." H.R. Joint Comm.Rep. No. 30, 39th Cong., 1st Sess., p. XVII (1866). Witnesses who testified before the Committee presented accounts of criminal acts of violence against black persons that were not prosecuted despite evidence as to the identity of the perpetrators.[2]

[2] *See, e.g.*, H.R. Joint Comm.Rep. No. 30, 39th Cong., 1st Sess., pt. II, p. 25 (1866) (testimony of George Tucker, Virginia attorney) ("They have not any idea of prosecuting white men for offenses against colored people; they do not appreciate the idea"); *id.*, at 209 (testimony of Dexter H. Clapp) ("Of the thousand cases of murder, robbery, and maltreatment of freedmen that have come before me, . . . I have never yet known a single case in which the local authorities or police or citizens made any attempt or exhibited any inclination to redress any of these wrongs or to protect such persons"); *id.*, at 213 (testimony of J.A. Campbell) (although identities of men suspected of killing two blacks [were] known, no arrest or trial had occurred); *id.*, pt. III, p. 141 (testimony of Brev. Maj. Gen. Wager Swayne) ("I have not known, after six months' residence at the capital of the State, a single instance of a white man being convicted and hung or sent to the penitentiary for crime against a negro, while many cases of crime warranting such punishment have been reported to me"); *id.*, pt. IV, p. 75 (testimony of Maj. Gen. George A. Custer) ("[I]t is of weekly, if not of daily, occurrence that freedmen are murdered. . . . [S]ometimes it is not known who the perpetrators are; but when that is known no action is taken against them. I believe a white man has never been hung for murder in Texas, although it is the law").

I

A

The Court today seems to give a new meaning to our recognition that death is different. Rather than requiring "a correspondingly greater degree of scrutiny of the capital sentencing determination," *California v. Ramos*, 463 U.S. 992, 998–999 (1983), the Court relies on the very fact that this is a case involving capital punishment to apply a *lesser* standard of scrutiny under the Equal Protection Clause. The Court concludes that "legitimate" explanations outweigh McCleskey's claim that his death sentence reflected a constitutionally impermissible risk of racial discrimination. The Court explains that McCleskey's evidence is too weak to require rebuttal "because a legitimate and unchallenged explanation for the decision is apparent from the record: McCleskey committed an act for which the United States Constitution and Georgia laws permit imposition of the death penalty." The Court states that it will not infer a discriminatory purpose on the part of the state legislature because "there were legitimate reasons for the Georgia Legislature to adopt and maintain capital punishment."

The Court's assertion that the fact of McCleskey's conviction undermines his constitutional claim is inconsistent with a long and unbroken line of this Court's case law. The Court on numerous occasions during the past century has recognized that an otherwise legitimate basis for a conviction does not outweigh an equal protection violation. In cases where racial discrimination in the administration of the criminal justice system is established, it has held that setting aside the conviction is the appropriate remedy. * * * The Court has maintained a *per se* reversal rule rejecting application of harmless-error analysis in cases involving racial discrimination that "strikes at the fundamental values of our judicial system and our society as a whole." *Rose v. Mitchell*, 443 U.S., at 556. We have noted that a conviction "in no way suggests that the discrimination did not impermissibly infect" earlier phases of the criminal prosecution "and, consequently, the nature or very existence of the proceedings to come." *Vasquez v. Hillery*, 474 U.S., at 263. Hence, McCleskey's conviction and the imposition of his death sentence by the jury do not suggest that discrimination did not impermissibly infect the earlier steps in the prosecution of his case, such as the prosecutor's decision to seek the death penalty.

In *Brown v. Board of Education*, 347 U.S. 483 (1954), this Court held that, despite the fact that the legislative history of the Fourteenth Amendment indicated that Congress did *not* view racial discrimination in public education as a specific target, the Amendment nevertheless prohibited such discrimination. The Court today holds that even though the Fourteenth Amendment *was* aimed specifically at eradicating discrimination in the enforcement of criminal sanctions, allegations of such discrimination supported by substantial evidence are *not* constitutionally cognizable. *But see Batson v. Kentucky*, 476 U.S. 79, 85 (1986) (allegations of racially discriminatory exercise of peremptory challenges by prosecutor subject to review under Fourteenth Amendment because "[e]xclusion of black citizens from service as jurors constitutes a primary example of the evil the Fourteenth Amendment was designed to cure").

The Court's reliance on legitimate interests underlying the Georgia Legislature's enactment of its capital punishment statute is likewise inappropriate. Although that reasoning may be relevant in a case involving a facial challenge to the constitutionality of a statute, it has no relevance in a case dealing with a challenge to the Georgia capital sentencing system as applied in McCleskey's case. In *Batson v. Kentucky*, *supra*, we rejected such reasoning: "The Constitution requires . . . that we look beyond the face of the statute . . . and also consider challenged selection practices to afford 'protection against action of the State through its administrative officers in effecting the prohibited discrimination.' " * * * McCleskey presented evidence of numerous decisions impermissibly affected by racial factors over a significant number of cases. The exhaustive evidence presented in this case certainly demands an inquiry into the prosecutor's actions.

The Court's assertion that, because of the necessity of discretion in the criminal justice system, it "would demand exceptionally clear proof," before inferring abuse of that discretion thus misses the point of the constitutional challenge in this case. Its conclusory statement that "the capacity of prosecutorial discretion to provide individualized justice is 'firmly entrenched in American law,' " is likewise not helpful. The issue in this case is the extent to which the constitutional guarantee of equal protection limits the discretion in the Georgia capital sentencing system. As the Court concedes, discretionary authority can be discriminatory authority. Prosecutorial decisions may not be " 'deliberately based upon an unjustifiable standard such as race, religion, or other arbitrary classification.' " *Bordenkircher v. Hayes*, 434 U.S. 357, 364 (1978), *quoting Oyler v. Boles*, 368 U.S. 448, 456 (1962). Judicial scrutiny is particularly appropriate in McCleskey's case because "[m]ore subtle, less consciously held racial attitudes could also influence" the decisions in the Georgia capital sentencing system. *Turner v. Murray*, 476 U.S. 28, 35 (1986) * * *. The Court's rejection of McCleskey's equal protection claims is a far cry from the "sensitive inquiry" mandated by the Constitution. * * *

NOTES AND QUESTIONS

1. *One equal-protection hypothetical in the aftermath of McCleskey.* Section 1 of the Fourteenth Amendment to the Constitution provides that

> All persons born or naturalized in the United States, and subject to the jurisdiction thereof, are citizens of the United States and of the State wherein they reside. No State shall make or enforce any law which shall abridge the privileges or immunities of citizens of the United States; nor shall any State deprive any person of life, liberty, or property, without due process of law; *nor deny to any person within its jurisdiction the equal protection of the laws.* (emphasis added)

McCleskey advanced two different equal-protection arguments, one based on the race of the defendant and—more forcefully—one based on the race of the victim. *See* Transcript of Oral Argument at 16, *McCleskey v. Kemp*, 107 S. Ct. 1756 (1987) (No. 84–6811) ("[R]ace of defendant discrimination exists * * * but it's not as pervasive. It really is more of a subdivision of the cases in Georgia. But the race of victim discrimination . . . is statewide, and in all the cases."). Obviously, neither equal-protection argument prevailed, but, focusing only the latter, suppose there were a statute in Georgia that penalized the killing of white people more seriously than the killing of black people. There is no doubt that the statute would be struck down as a violation of the Equal Protection Clause of the Fourteenth Amendment, because it explicitly valued ("protected") white lives more than African-American lives. Why exactly is the *McCleskey* case resolved differently?

2. *The interior dynamics of the Supreme Court.* After the death of Justice Thurgood Marshall, his papers were made available by the Library of Congress. Included in those papers was a memorandum from Justice Antonin Scalia to his Supreme Court colleagues, dated January 6, 1987, dealing specifically with the Court's deliberations in *McCleskey*. The memorandum is short and provides in its entirety:

> Re: NO. 84–6811—*McCleskey v. Kemp*
>
> MEMORANDUM TO THE CONFERENCE:
>
> I plan to join Lewis's opinion in this case, with two reservations. I disagree with the argument that the inferences that can be drawn from the Baldus study are weakened by the fact that each jury and each trial is unique, or by the large number of variables at issue. And I do not share the view, implicit in the opinion, that an effect of racial factors upon sentencing, if it could only be shown by sufficiently strong statistical evidence, would require reversal. Since it is my view that the unconscious operation of irrational sympathies and antipathies, including racial, upon jury decisions and (hence) prosecutorial decisions is real, acknowledged in the decisions of this court, and ineradicable, I cannot honestly say that all I need is more proof. I expect to write separately to make these points, but not until I see the dissent.

See Erwin Chemerinsky, *Eliminating Discrimination in Administering the Death Penalty: The Need for the Racial Justice Act*, 35 SANTA CLARA L. REV. 519, 528 (1995). Parse each of Justice Scalia's sentences carefully. Is he saying that the Baldus study is valid but that even stronger evidence of discrimination would not make out a violation of the Equal Protection Clause? Has the Court left us with the perversity that the death penalty in Georgia is demonstrably imposed in a racially disproportionate way that cannot be fixed and therefore will not be fixed?

3. *"The New Jim Crow."* Consider the following analysis of the burden of proof that the Supreme Court has imposed on those claiming that they are victims of racial discrimination in the criminal justice system:

> In *McCleskey v. Kemp* and *United States v. Armstrong*, [517 U.S. 456 (1996)], the Supreme Court made clear that only evidence of conscious, intentional racial bias—the sort of bias that is nearly impossible to prove these days in the absence of an admission—is deemed sufficient. No matter how impressive the statistical evidence, no matter how severe the racial disparities and racial impacts might be, the Supreme Court is not interested. The Court has, as a practical matter, closed the door to claims of racial bias in the criminal justice system. It has immunized the new caste system from judicial scrutiny for racial bias, much as it once rallied to legitimate and protect slavery and Jim Crow.

Michelle Alexander, *The New Jim Crow*, 9 OHIO ST. J. CRIM. L. 7, 19 (2011). The suggestion that the criminal justice system in the United States has created a racial caste system on a par with Jim Crow-era segregation laws is inconsistent with the "post-racial" narrative that draws on the election of Barack Obama and the successes of many individual African-Americans. But Professor Alexander argues:

> What has changed since the collapse of Jim Crow has less to do with the basic structure of our society than the language we use to justify it. In the era of colorblindness, it is no longer socially permissible to use race, explicitly, as a justification for discrimination, exclusion, and social contempt. So we don't. Rather than rely on race, we use our criminal justice system to label people of color "criminals" and then engage in all the practices we supposedly left behind. Today it is perfectly legal to discriminate against criminals in nearly all the ways it was once legal to discriminate against African Americans. Once you're labeled a felon, the old forms of discrimination—employment discrimination, housing discrimination, denial of the right to vote, and exclusion from jury service—are suddenly legal. As a criminal, you have scarcely more rights, and arguably less respect, than a black man living in Alabama at the height of Jim Crow. We have not ended racial caste in America; we have merely redesigned it.

MICHELLE ALEXANDER, THE NEW JIM CROW: MASS INCARCERATION IN THE AGE OF COLORBLINDNESS 2 (2010). The argument that the greater incarceration rates simply reflect greater rates of criminal behavior or drug use is not supported by the crime statistics published by the Department of Justice: crime rates have varied since the 1980's, but the incarceration rates have skyrocketed. *Id.* Felony disenfranchisement, discrimination in housing and employment, exclusion from juries and other discrepancies are not the same as Jim Crow segregation laws, just as the Jim Crow laws were not the same as slavery, but the family resemblance—and the role of law in each setting—is not to be minimized. *See also* Sheila A. Bedi, *The Constructed Identities of Asian and African Americans: A Story of Two Races and the Criminal Justice System*, 19 HARV. BLACKLETTER L.J. 181 (2003).

4. *"Driving While Black:" the Equal Protection Clause "versus" the Fourth Amendment prohibition on unreasonable searches and seizures*. The Fourth Amendment to the Constitution guarantees "[t]he right of the people to be secure in their persons, houses, papers, and effects, against unreasonable searches and seizures." When the police stop an automobile and temporarily detain individuals during that stop, a seizure within the meaning of the Fourth Amendment has occurred. The stop is therefore subject to the constitutional requirement that it not be "unreasonable" under the circumstances, and, "[a]s a general matter, the decision to stop an automobile is reasonable where the police have probable cause to believe that a traffic violation has occurred." *Whren v. United States*, 517 U.S. 806, 810 (1996) (citing *inter alia Delaware v. Prouse*, 440 U.S. 648, 659 (1979). Efforts to challenge racial profiling—traffic stops for "Driving While Black"—have been made difficult by the courts' unwillingness to consider officer motives (and Equal Protection concerns generally) in the context of a Fourth Amendment suppression motion.

> We think [prior decisions] foreclose any argument that the constitutional reasonableness of traffic stops depends on the actual motivations of the individual officers involved. We of course agree with petitioners that the Constitution prohibits selective enforcement of the law based on considerations such as race. But the constitutional basis for objecting to intentionally discriminatory application of laws is the Equal Protection Clause, not the Fourth Amendment. Subjective intentions play no role in ordinary, probable-cause Fourth Amendment analysis.

Whren, 517 U.S. at 813. Can you articulate a neutral principle to justify the separation of Fourth Amendment reasonableness analysis from Fourteenth Amendment equal protection analysis?

5. *Capital sentencing as a public good. McCleskey* might support an argument to abolish the death penalty altogether, on the ground that the system of capital punishment is discriminatory (as Baldus found and the Supreme Court assumed (see footnote 2, *supra*) and cannot be fixed because we cannot locate the discriminatory intent if any. Professor Randall Kennedy, without supporting the abolition of the death penalty, has criticized *McCleskey* "as an instance of racial inequality in the provision of public goods. Whereas other cases have involved the racially unequal provision of street lights, sidewalks, and sewers, *McCleskey* involves racial inequality in the provision of a peculiar sort of public good—capital sentencing." Randall L. Kennedy, *McCleskey v. Kemp: Race, Capital Punishment, and the Supreme Court*, 101 HARV. L. REV. 1388, 1394 (1988), at 1394. Does that imply that the proper response to the racial inequality uncovered in the Baldus study is to execute more defendants, regardless of race, whose victims were black?

6. *Does the meaning of equal protection vary with context?* Precedent in other areas of the law, including employment discrimination, establishes that a racially disparate effect can qualify as *prima facie* evidence of racial discrimination. *See, e.g., Griggs v. Duke Power Co.*, 401 U.S. 424, 431 (1971) (Title VII of Civil Rights Act of 1964 "proscribes not only overt discrimination

but also practices that are fair in form, but discriminatory in operation"). According to the majority in *McCleskey*, why is the death penalty so different as to require those challenging it to prove more than racially-disparate effects? Are you persuaded?

7. *Interest convergence: when is an iconic decision not what it seems?* Will white people support civil rights only when it is in their self-interest to do so? Consider the following observation by Professor Richard Delgado, one of the founders of CRT:

> In 1980, Derrick Bell startled the legal world when he posited, in an article entitled *Brown v. Board of Education and the Interest Convergence Dilemma*, [93 HARV. L. REV. 518 (1980),] that this groundbreaking decision arrived when it did, not because of a belated spasm of conscience on the part of the Supreme Court, but because of a fortuitous combination of material and sociopolitical circumstances. The NAACP Legal Defense and Education Fund, Bell pointed out, had been litigating school desegregation cases throughout the South for decades and achieving, at most, narrow victories. Yet the skies opened in 1954 when the Supreme Court, in a unanimous decision, appeared to grant the organization everything it wanted.
>
> Why just then? Based on fragmentary evidence coupled with some highly astute intuition, Bell posited that America's need to burnish its image in the eyes of the international community set the stage for the breakthrough decision. At the time, the United States was competing with its Soviet adversaries for the loyalties of the uncommitted Third World, much of which was black, brown, or Asian. Every time the world press featured front-page stories and photographs of lynchings and Jim Crow treatment in the South, our Cold War rivals made capital at our expense.
>
> Thus, it behooved America's establishment to arrange a spectacular victory for African Americans as a way to improve our competitive position *vis-à-vis* the Soviet bloc. In addition, the country was then absorbing back into its civilian population tens of thousands of black servicemen and women who had served in World War II and Korea. Having for the first time experienced an environment where a person of color might advance more readily than in civilian life and having risked their lives in the defense of democracy, these men and women were unlikely to return meekly to lives of menial labor and deference to whites. For the first time in years, domestic unrest loomed.

Richard Delgado, *Liberal McCarthyism and the Origins of Critical Race Theory*, 94 IOWA L. REV. 1505, 1506–7 (2009).

8. *Law outside "explicitly racialized contexts."* It is easy enough to see race in *McCleskey*, which challenged race-based discrimination in the imposition of the death penalty. That is an example of what Professor Naomi Cahn has called an "explicitly racialized context." Naomi R. Cahn,

Representing Race Outside of Explicitly Racialized Contexts, 95 MICH. L. REV. 965 (1997). But a more complete understanding of the CRT project requires the recognition—the seeing—of race in areas of the law conventionally considered race-neutral. Consider, for example, tax: critical tax scholars expose implicit but structural discrimination in the Internal Revenue Code by tracking out the race-based effects of facially neutral tax provisions and policy. *See, e.g.*, Dorothy A. Brown, *Teaching Civil Rights Through the Basic Tax Course*, 54 ST. LOUIS U. L.J. 809 (2010); Beverly I. Moran & William Whitford, *A Black Critique of the Internal Revenue Code*, [1996] WIS. L. REV. 751, 757–58 (arguing that factors other than income contribute to the differential impact of certain tax provisions on African-American taxpayers). As the following cases suggest, other parts of the law with a reputation for neutrality might deserve another, searching look.

R.A.V. v. CITY OF ST. PAUL, MINNESOTA

505 U.S. 377 (1992)

JUSTICE SCALIA **delivered the opinion of the Court.** In the predawn hours of June 21, 1990, petitioner and several other teenagers allegedly assembled a crudely made cross by taping together broken chair legs. They then allegedly burned the cross inside the fenced yard of a black family that lived across the street from the house where petitioner was staying. Although this conduct could have been punished under any of a number of laws,[1] one of the two provisions under which respondent city of St. Paul chose to charge petitioner (then a juvenile) was the St. Paul Bias—Motivated Crime Ordinance, St. Paul, Minn., Legis.Code § 292.02 (1990), which provides:

> Whoever places on public or private property a symbol, object, appellation, characterization or graffiti, including, but not limited to, a burning cross or Nazi swastika, which one knows or has reasonable grounds to know arouses anger, alarm or resentment in others on the basis of race, color, creed, religion or gender commits disorderly conduct and shall be guilty of a misdemeanor.

Petitioner moved to dismiss this count on the ground that the St. Paul ordinance was substantially overbroad and impermissibly content based and therefore facially invalid under the First Amendment. The trial court granted this motion, but the Minnesota Supreme Court reversed. That court rejected petitioner's overbreadth claim because, as construed in prior Minnesota cases, *see, e.g.*, *In re Welfare of S.L.J.*, 263 N.W.2d 412

---

[1] The conduct might have violated Minnesota statutes carrying significant penalties. *See, e.g.*, Minn.Stat. § 609.713(1) (1987) (providing for up to five years in prison for terroristic threats); § 609.563 (arson) (providing for up to five years and a $10,000 fine, depending on the value of the property intended to be damaged); § 609.595 (Supp.1992) (criminal damage to property) (providing for up to one year and a $3,000 fine, depending upon the extent of the damage to the property).

(Minn.1978), the modifying phrase "arouses anger, alarm or resentment in others" limited the reach of the ordinance to conduct that amounts to "fighting words," *i.e.,* "conduct that itself inflicts injury or tends to incite immediate violence . . .," *In re Welfare of R.A.V.*, 464 N.W.2d 507, 510 (Minn.1991) (citing *Chaplinsky v. New Hampshire*, 315 U.S. 568, 572 (1942)), and therefore the ordinance reached only expression "that the first amendment does not protect," 464 N.W.2d, at 511. The court also concluded that the ordinance was not impermissibly content based because, in its view, "the ordinance is a narrowly tailored means toward accomplishing the compelling governmental interest in protecting the community against bias-motivated threats to public safety and order." We granted *certiorari.*

I

In construing the St. Paul ordinance, we are bound by the construction given to it by the Minnesota court. Accordingly, we accept the Minnesota Supreme Court's authoritative statement that the ordinance reaches only those expressions that constitute "fighting words" within the meaning of *Chaplinsky*. 464 N.W.2d, at 510–511. Petitioner and his *amici* urge us to modify the scope of the *Chaplinsky* formulation, thereby invalidating the ordinance as "substantially overbroad," *Broadrick v. Oklahoma*, 413 U.S. 601, 610 (1973). We find it unnecessary to consider this issue. Assuming, *arguendo,* that all of the expression reached by the ordinance is proscribable under the "fighting words" doctrine, we nonetheless conclude that the ordinance is facially unconstitutional in that it prohibits otherwise permitted speech solely on the basis of the subjects the speech addresses.

The First Amendment generally prevents government from proscribing speech, *see, e.g., Cantwell v. Connecticut,* 310 U.S. 296, 309–311 (1940), or even expressive conduct, *see, e.g., Texas v. Johnson,* 491 U.S. 397, 406 (1989), because of disapproval of the ideas expressed. Content-based regulations are presumptively invalid. *Simon & Schuster, Inc. v. Members of N.Y. State Crime Victims Bd.*, 502 U.S. 105, 115 (1991); *Consolidated Edison Co. of N.Y. v. Public Serv. Comm'n of N.Y.*, 447 U.S. 530, 536 (1980); *Police Dept. of Chicago v. Mosley*, 408 U.S. 92, 95 (1972). From 1791 to the present, however, our society, like other free but civilized societies, has permitted restrictions upon the content of speech in a few limited areas, which are "of such slight social value as a step to truth that any benefit that may be derived from them is clearly outweighed by the social interest in order and morality." *Chaplinsky, supra*, 315 U.S., at 572. We have recognized that "the freedom of speech" referred to by the First Amendment does not include a freedom to disregard these traditional limitations. *See, e.g., Roth v. United States,* 354 U.S. 476 (1957) (obscenity); *Beauharnais v. Illinois*, 343 U.S. 250 (1952) (defamation); *Chaplinsky v. New Hampshire*, *supra* ("fighting' words"). Our decisions since the 1960's have narrowed the scope of the traditional categorical exceptions for defamation, *see New York Times Co. v. Sullivan,* 376 U.S. 254; *Gertz v.*

Robert Welch, Inc., 418 U.S. 323 (1974); *see generally Milkovich v. Lorain Journal Co.*, 497 U.S. 1, 13–17 (1990), and for obscenity, *see Miller v. California*, 413 U.S. 15 (1973), but a limited categorical approach has remained an important part of our First Amendment jurisprudence.

We have sometimes said that these categories of expression are "not within the area of constitutionally protected speech," *Roth, supra*; *Beauharnais, supra*, 343 U.S., at 266; *Chaplinsky, supra*, 315 U.S., at 571–572; or that the "protection of the First Amendment does not extend" to them, *Bose Corp. v. Consumers Union of United States, Inc.*, 466 U.S. 485, 504 (1984); *Sable Communications of Cal., Inc. v. FCC*, 492 U.S. 115, 124 (1989). Such statements must be taken in context, however, and are no more literally true than is the occasionally repeated shorthand characterizing obscenity "as not being speech at all," Sunstein, *Pornography and the First Amendment*, 1986 DUKE L.J. 589, 615, n. 146. What they mean is that these areas of speech can, consistently with the First Amendment, be regulated *because of their constitutionally proscribable content* (obscenity, defamation, etc.)—not that they are categories of speech entirely invisible to the Constitution, so that they may be made the vehicles for content discrimination unrelated to their distinctively proscribable content. Thus, the government may proscribe libel; but it may not make the further content discrimination of proscribing *only* libel critical of the government. We recently acknowledged this distinction in *Ferber,* 458 U.S., at 763, where, in upholding New York's child pornography law, we expressly recognized that there was no "question here of censoring a particular literary theme. . . ." *See also id.*, at 775 (O'Connor, J., concurring) ("As drafted, New York's statute does not attempt to suppress the communication of particular ideas").

Our cases surely do not establish the proposition that the First Amendment imposes no obstacle whatsoever to regulation of particular instances of such proscribable expression, so that the government "may regulate [them] freely," *post* (White, J., concurring in judgment). That would mean that a city council could enact an ordinance prohibiting only those legally obscene works that contain criticism of the city government or, indeed, that do not include endorsement of the city government. Such a simplistic, all-or-nothing-at-all approach to First Amendment protection is at odds with common sense and with our jurisprudence as well. It is not true that "fighting words" have at most a "*de minimis*" expressive content, *ibid.,* or that their content is *in all respects* "worthless and undeserving of constitutional protection," *post,* at 2553; sometimes they are quite expressive indeed. We have not said that they constitute "*no* part of the expression of ideas," but only that they constitute "no *essential* part of any exposition of ideas." *Chaplinsky, supra,* 315 U.S., at 572 (emphasis added).

The proposition that a particular instance of speech can be proscribable on the basis of one feature (*e.g.,* obscenity) but not on the basis of another (*e.g.,* opposition to the city government) is commonplace and has found application in many contexts. We have long held, for example, that nonverbal expressive activity can be banned because of the action it entails, but not because of the ideas it expresses—so that burning a flag in violation of an ordinance against outdoor fires could be punishable, whereas burning a flag in violation of an ordinance against dishonoring the flag is not. *See Johnson*, 491 U.S., at 406–407. Similarly, we have upheld reasonable "time, place, or manner" restrictions, but only if they are "justified without reference to the content of the regulated speech." *Ward v. Rock Against Racism*, 491 U.S. 781, 791 (1989); *see also Clark v. Community for Creative Non-Violence*, 468 U.S. 288, 298 (1984) (noting that the *O'Brien* test differs little from the standard applied to time, place, or manner restrictions). And just as the power to proscribe particular speech on the basis of a noncontent element (*e.g.*, noise) does not entail the power to proscribe the same speech on the basis of a content element; so also, the power to proscribe it on the basis of *one* content element (*e.g.*, obscenity) does not entail the power to proscribe it on the basis of *other* content elements.

In other words, the exclusion of "fighting words" from the scope of the First Amendment simply means that, for purposes of that Amendment, the unprotected features of the words are, despite their verbal character, essentially a "nonspeech" element of communication. Fighting words are thus analogous to a noisy sound truck: Each is, as Justice Frankfurter recognized, a "mode of speech," *Niemotko v. Maryland*, 340 U.S. 268, 282 (1951) (opinion concurring in result); both can be used to convey an idea; but neither has, in and of itself, a claim upon the First Amendment. As with the sound truck, however, so also with fighting words: The government may not regulate use based on hostility—or favoritism—towards the underlying message expressed. *Compare Frisby v. Schultz*, 487 U.S. 474 (1988) (upholding, against facial challenge, a content-neutral ban on targeted residential picketing), *with Carey v. Brown*, 447 U.S. 455 (1980) (invalidating a ban on residential picketing that exempted labor picketing).

The concurrences describe us as setting forth a new First Amendment principle that prohibition of constitutionally proscribable speech cannot be "underinclusiv[e]"—a First Amendment "absolutism" whereby "[w]ithin a particular 'proscribable' category of expression, . . . a government must either proscribe *all* speech or no speech at all." That easy target is of the concurrences' own invention. In our view, the First Amendment imposes not an "underinclusiveness" limitation but a "content discrimination" limitation upon a State's prohibition of proscribable speech. There is no problem whatever, for example, with a State's prohibiting obscenity (and other forms of proscribable expression) only in certain media or markets, for although that prohibition would be "underinclusive," it would not discriminate on the basis of content. *See, e.g., Sable Communications,* 492 U.S., at 124–126 (upholding 47 U.S.C. § 223(b)(1), which prohibits obscene *telephone* communications).

Even the prohibition against content discrimination that we assert the First Amendment requires is not absolute. It applies differently in the context of proscribable speech than in the area of fully protected speech. The rationale of the general prohibition, after all, is that content discrimination "raises the specter that the Government may effectively drive certain ideas or viewpoints from the marketplace," *Simon & Schuster*, 502 U.S., at 116; *Leathers v. Medlock*, 499 U.S. 439, 448 (1991); *FCC v. League of Women Voters of Cal.*, 468 U.S. 364, 383–384 (1984); *Consolidated Edison Co.*, 447 U.S., at 536; *Police Dept. of Chicago v. Mosley*, 408 U.S., at 95–98. But content discrimination among various instances of a class of proscribable speech often does not pose this threat.

When the basis for the content discrimination consists entirely of the very reason the entire class of speech at issue is proscribable, no significant danger of idea or viewpoint discrimination exists. Such a reason, having been adjudged neutral enough to support exclusion of the entire class of speech from First Amendment protection, is also neutral enough to form the basis of distinction within the class. To illustrate: A State might choose to prohibit only that obscenity which is the most patently offensive *in its prurience—i.e.,* that which involves the most lascivious displays of sexual activity. But it may not prohibit, for example, only that obscenity which includes offensive *political* messages. *See Kucharek v. Hanaway*, 902 F.2d 513, 517 (CA7 1990), *cert. denied*, 498 U.S. 1041 (1991). And the Federal Government can criminalize only those threats of violence that are directed against the President, *see* 18 U.S.C. § 871—since the reasons why threats of violence are outside the First Amendment (protecting individuals from the fear of violence, from the disruption that fear engenders, and from the possibility that the threatened violence will occur) have special force when applied to the person of the President. *See Watts v. United States*, 394 U.S. 705, 707 (1969) (upholding the facial validity of § 871 because of the "overwhelmin[g] interest in protecting the safety of [the] Chief Executive and in allowing him to perform his duties without interference from threats of physical violence"). But the Federal Government may not criminalize only those threats against the President that mention his policy on aid to inner cities. And to take a final example, a State may choose to regulate price advertising in one industry but not in others, because the risk of fraud (one of the characteristics of commercial speech that justifies depriving it of full First Amendment protection, *see Virginia State Bd. of Pharmacy v. Virginia Citizens Consumer Council, Inc.*, 425 U.S. 748, 771–772 (1976)) is in its view greater there. *Cf. Morales v. Trans World Airlines, Inc.*, 504 U.S. 374 (1992) (state regulation of airline advertising); *Ohralik v. Ohio State Bar Assn.*, 436 U.S. 447 (1978) (state regulation of lawyer advertising). But a State may not prohibit only that commercial advertising that depicts men in a demeaning fashion.

Another valid basis for according differential treatment to even a content-defined subclass of proscribable speech is that the subclass happens to be associated with particular "secondary effects" of the speech, so that the regulation is "*justified* without reference to the content of the . . . speech," *Renton v. Playtime Theatres, Inc.*, 475 U.S. 41, 48 (1986). A State could, for example, permit all obscene live performances except those involving minors. Moreover, since words can in some circumstances violate laws directed not against speech but against conduct (a law against treason, for example, is violated by telling the enemy the Nation's defense secrets), a particular content-based subcategory of a proscribable class of speech can be swept up incidentally within the reach of a statute directed at conduct rather than speech. Thus, for example, sexually derogatory "fighting words," among other words, may produce a violation of Title VII's general prohibition against sexual discrimination in employment practices, 42 U.S.C. § 2000e–2; 29 CFR § 1604.11 (1991). Where the government does not target conduct on the basis of its expressive content, acts are not shielded from regulation merely because they express a discriminatory idea or philosophy.

These bases for distinction refute the proposition that the selectivity of the restriction is "even arguably 'conditioned upon the sovereign's agreement with what a speaker may intend to say.' " *Metromedia, Inc. v. San Diego*, 453 U.S. 490 (1981) (Stevens, J., dissenting in part). There may be other such bases as well. Indeed, to validate such selectivity (where totally proscribable speech is at issue) it may not even be necessary to identify any particular "neutral" basis, so long as the nature of the content discrimination is such that there is no realistic possibility that official suppression of ideas is afoot. (We cannot think of any First Amendment interest that would stand in the way of a State's prohibiting only those obscene motion pictures with blue-eyed actresses.) Save for that limitation, the regulation of "fighting words," like the regulation of noisy speech, may address some offensive instances and leave other, equally offensive, instances alone. * * *

II

Applying these principles to the St. Paul ordinance, we conclude that, even as narrowly construed by the Minnesota Supreme Court, the ordinance is facially unconstitutional. Although the phrase in the ordinance, "arouses anger, alarm or resentment in others," has been limited by the Minnesota Supreme Court's construction to reach only those symbols or displays that amount to "fighting words," the remaining, unmodified terms make clear that the ordinance applies only to "fighting words" that insult, or provoke violence, "on the basis of race, color, creed, religion or gender." Displays containing abusive invective, no matter how vicious or severe, are permissible unless they are addressed to one of the specified disfavored topics. Those who wish to use "fighting words" in connection with other ideas-to express hostility, for example, on the basis of political affiliation, union membership, or homosexuality-are not covered. The First Amendment does not permit St. Paul to impose special prohibitions on those speakers who express views on disfavored subjects. *See Simon & Schuster,* 502 U.S., at 116; *Arkansas Writers' Project, Inc. v. Ragland,* 481 U.S. 221, 229–230 (1987).

In its practical operation, moreover, the ordinance goes even beyond mere content discrimination, to actual viewpoint discrimination. Displays containing some words—odious racial epithets, for example—would be prohibited to proponents of all views. But "fighting words" that do not themselves invoke race, color, creed, religion, or gender-aspersions upon a person's mother, for example-would seemingly be usable *ad libitum* in the placards of those arguing *in favor* of racial, color, *etc.*, tolerance and equality, but could not be used by those speakers' opponents. One could hold up a sign saying, for example, that all "anti-Catholic bigots" are misbegotten; but not that all "papists" are, for that would insult and provoke violence "on the basis of religion." St. Paul has no such authority to license one side of a debate to fight freestyle, while requiring the other to follow Marquis of Queensberry rules.

What we have here, it must be emphasized, is not a prohibition of fighting words that are directed at certain persons or groups (which would be *facially* valid if it met the requirements of the Equal Protection Clause); but rather, a prohibition of fighting words that contain (as the Minnesota Supreme Court repeatedly emphasized) messages of "bias-motivated" hatred and in particular, as applied to this case, messages "based on virulent notions of racial supremacy." 464 N.W.2d, at 508, 511. One must wholeheartedly agree with the Minnesota Supreme Court that "[i]t is the responsibility, even the obligation, of diverse communities to confront such notions in whatever form they appear," *id.,* at 508, but the manner of that confrontation cannot consist of selective limitations upon speech. St. Paul's brief asserts that a general "fighting words" law would not meet the city's needs because only a content-specific measure can communicate to minority groups that the "group hatred" aspect of such speech "is not condoned by the majority." The point of the First Amendment is that majority preferences must be expressed in some fashion other than silencing speech on the basis of its content.

Despite the fact that the Minnesota Supreme Court and St. Paul acknowledge that the ordinance is directed at expression of group hatred, Justice Stevens suggests that this "fundamentally misreads" the ordinance. It is directed, he claims, not to speech of a particular content, but to particular "injur[ies]" that are "qualitatively different" from other injuries. This is wordplay. What makes the anger, fear, sense of dishonor, *etc.*, produced by violation of this ordinance distinct from the anger, fear, sense of dishonor, *etc.*, produced by other fighting words is nothing other than the fact that it is caused by a distinctive idea, conveyed by a distinctive message. The First Amendment cannot be evaded that easily.

It is obvious that the symbols which will arouse "anger, alarm or resentment in others on the basis of race, color, creed, religion or gender" are those symbols that communicate a message of hostility based on one of these characteristics. St. Paul concedes in its brief that the ordinance applies only to "racial, religious, or gender-specific symbols" such as "a burning cross, Nazi swastika or other instrumentality of like import." Indeed, St. Paul argued in the Juvenile Court that "[t]he burning of a cross does express a message and it is, in fact, the content of that message which the St. Paul Ordinance attempts to legislate."

The content-based discrimination reflected in the St. Paul ordinance comes within neither any of the specific exceptions to the First Amendment prohibition we discussed earlier nor a more general exception for content discrimination that does not threaten censorship of ideas. It assuredly does not fall within the exception for content discrimination based on the very reasons why the particular class of speech at issue (here, fighting words) is proscribable. As explained earlier, the reason why fighting words are categorically excluded from the protection of the First Amendment is not that their content communicates any particular idea, but that their content embodies a particularly intolerable (and socially unnecessary) *mode* of expressing *whatever* idea the speaker wishes to convey. St. Paul has not singled out an especially offensive mode of expression—it has not, for example, selected for prohibition only those fighting words that communicate ideas in a threatening (as opposed to a merely obnoxious) manner. Rather, it has proscribed fighting words of whatever manner that communicate messages of racial, gender, or religious intolerance. Selectivity of this sort creates the possibility that the city is seeking to handicap the expression of particular ideas. That possibility would alone be enough to render the ordinance presumptively invalid, but St. Paul's comments and concessions in this case elevate the possibility to a certainty.

St. Paul argues that the ordinance comes within another of the specific exceptions we mentioned, the one that allows content discrimination aimed only at the "secondary effects" of the speech, *see Renton v. Playtime Theatres, Inc.*, 475 U.S. 41 (1986). According to St. Paul, the ordinance is intended, "not to impact on [*sic*] the right of free expression of the accused," but rather to "protect against the victimization of a person or persons who are particularly vulnerable because of their membership in a group that historically has been discriminated against." Even assuming that an ordinance that completely proscribes, rather than merely regulates, a specified category of speech can ever be considered to be directed only to the secondary effects of such speech, it is clear that the St. Paul ordinance is not directed to secondary effects within the meaning of *Renton*. As we said in *Boos v. Barry*, 485 U.S. 312 (1988), "Listeners' reactions to speech are not the type of 'secondary effects' we referred to in *Renton*. "The emotive impact of speech on its audience is not a 'secondary effect.' " *Id.*

It hardly needs discussion that the ordinance does not fall within some more general exception permitting *all* selectivity that for any reason is beyond the suspicion of official suppression of ideas. The statements of St. Paul in this very case afford ample basis for, if not full confirmation of, that suspicion.

Finally, St. Paul and its *amici* defend the conclusion of the Minnesota Supreme Court that, even if the ordinance regulates expression based on hostility towards its protected ideological content, this discrimination is nonetheless justified because it is narrowly tailored to serve compelling state interests. Specifically, they assert that the ordinance helps to ensure the basic human rights of members of groups that have historically been subjected to discrimination, including the right of such group members to live in peace where they wish. We do not doubt that these interests are compelling, and that the ordinance can be said to promote them. But the "danger of censorship" presented by a facially content-based statute, *Leathers v. Medlock*, 499 U.S., at 448, requires that that weapon be employed only where it is "*necessary* to serve the asserted [compelling] interest," *Burson v. Freeman*, 504 U.S. 191, 199 (1992) (plurality opinion); *Perry Ed. Assn. v. Perry Local Educators' Assn.*, 460 U.S. 37, 45 (1983). The existence of adequate content-neutral alternatives thus "undercut[s] significantly" any defense of such a statute, *Boos v. Barry, supra*, 485 U.S., at 329, casting considerable doubt on the government's protestations that "the asserted justification is in fact an accurate description of the purpose and effect of the law," *Burson, supra*, 504 U.S., at 213 (Kennedy, J., concurring). *See Boos, supra,* 485 U.S., at 324–329; cf. *Minneapolis Star & Tribune Co. v. Minnesota Comm'r of Revenue*, 460 U.S. 575, 586–587 (1983). The dispositive question in this case, therefore, is whether content discrimination is reasonably necessary to achieve St. Paul's compelling interests; it plainly is not. An ordinance not limited to the favored topics, for example, would have precisely the same beneficial effect. In fact the only interest distinctively served by the content limitation is that of displaying the city council's special hostility towards the particular biases thus singled out. That is precisely what the First Amendment forbids. The politicians of St. Paul are entitled to express that hostility—but not through the means of imposing unique limitations upon speakers who (however benightedly) disagree. * * *

Let there be no mistake about our belief that burning a cross in someone's front yard is reprehensible. But St. Paul has sufficient means at its disposal to prevent such behavior without adding the First Amendment to the fire. The judgment of the Minnesota Supreme Court is reversed, and the case is remanded for proceedings not inconsistent with this opinion.

MARI MATSUDA AND CHARLES R. LAWRENCE III, *EPILOGUE: BURNING CROSSES AND THE R.A.V. CASE*

WORDS THAT WOUND: CRITICAL RACE THEORY, ASSAULTIVE SPEECH, AND THE FIRST AMENDMENT 133–6 (1993)

In the early morning hours of June 21, 1990, long after they had put their five children to bed, Russ and Laura Jones were awakened by voices outside their house. Russ got up, went to his bedroom window, and peered into the dark. "I saw a glow," he recalled. There, in the middle of his yard, was a burning cross. The Joneses are African Americans. In the spring of 1990 they had moved into their four-bedroom, three-bathroom dream house in St. Paul, Minnesota. They were the only Black family on the block. Two weeks after they had settled into their predominantly white neighborhood, the tires on both of their cars were slashed. A few weeks later one of their car windows was shattered, and a group of teenagers walked past their house and shouted "nigger" at their nine-year-old son. And now this burning cross. Russ Jones did not have to guess at the meaning of this symbol of racial hatred. There is no Black person in America who has not learned the significance of this instrument of persecution and intimidation, who has not had emblazoned on his or her mind the image of Black men's scorched bodies hanging from trees.

The assailant who burned the makeshift cross in the fenced yard of the Jones home was identified and prosecuted under a local hate crime ordinance. * * *[T]he defendant claimed the assaultive act was protected by the first amendment: Burning a cross is political speech, and any ordinance directed against such speech is thus unconstitutional. The Minnesota Supreme Court rejected this argument. Citing Mari Matsuda's work, the court found:

> Burning a cross in the yard of an African American family's home is deplorable conduct that the City of St. Paul may without question prohibit. The burning cross is itself an unmistakable symbol of violence and hatred based on virulent notions of racial supremacy. It is the responsibility, even the obligation, of diverse communities to confront such notions in whatever form they appear.

The Minnesota judges thus adopted a perspective urged by critical race theorists. They looked to history and context to understand the effect of a cross burning. Unlike ordinary trespassing or littering on someone's front lawn, the burning cross is inextricably tied to violence, to lynching, and to exclusion. Crosses burn to warn newcomers out of segregated neighborhoods, to silence whites who speak up in favor of racial tolerance, to draw upon and promote the fear that began with the nightriders of the Reconstruction era and continues to this day in the rituals of skinheads, Klansmen, and local thugs. Attackers use this symbol precisely because of the extreme and concrete distress it causes. Their aim is to cause harm, to silence and to exclude. As with death threats and fraud, the goal of cross burning is accomplished through speech. * * * [H]owever, ending the analysis at the determination that hate speech *is* speech is simplistic and doctrinally unworkable. It is also an affirmative harm to those whose injury goes unredressed by law.

In a climate of media attention focused on right-wing claims that a powerful "politically correct movement" was overrunning the nation, disempowering and silencing conservative white men, the Supreme Court of the United States agreed in June 1991 to review the Minnesota cross-burning case. Critical race theorists were immediately concerned that the Reagan-Bush Court took on the case in order to further dismantle civil rights gains. We were thus not surprised at Justice Antonin Scalia's opinion declaring the anti-cross-burning ordinance unconstitutional. Local governments, Scalia held, may prohibit littering or arson on peoples' lawns, but they may not single out racially motivated acts, such as cross burning, for criminalization. The decision thus limits the ability to treat the racist assault of cross burning as a particularly serious crime.

Justice Scalia's opinion in the *R.A.V.* case * * * was a clear example of exactly the kind of legal analysis [we] intend[ ] to counter. It is completely ahistorical and acontextual. The Jones family's terror at finding a cross burning in their yard in the middle of the night is nowhere described. We are told that a "crudely made cross" was burned in the yard of a Black family, but we are told nothing about that family or the hostility they experienced upon moving into the neighborhood. The Ku Klux Klan, lynching, nightriders, the Reconstruction, continuing patterns of hate crimes and racial violence in this country are never mentioned. Hate crime statistics and social science evidence showing increasing use of burning crosses and swastikas to harass ethnic and religious minorities are not mentioned. The many reported cases in which state and federal courts have struggled to protect schoolchildren, voters, homeowners, workers, and other citizens from ethnic intimidation by cross burners are neither discussed nor cited. In effect, the opinion proceeds as though we know nothing about the origins of the practice of cross burning or about the meaning that a burning cross carries both for those who use it and those whom it terrorizes.

What we do learn from the opinion is that cross burning is not a "majority preference" and that the ordinance reflects inappropriate "special hostility" against "particular biases." The cross burners are portrayed as an unpopular minority that the Supreme Court must defend against the power of the state. The injury to the Jones family is appropriated and the cross burner is cast as the injured victim. The reality of ongoing racism and exclusion is erased and bigotry is redefined as majoritarian condemnation of racist views. The powerful impact of the burning cross—the assault, the terror—is also inverted. The power is replaced in the hands of those who oppose racism. The powerful antiracists have captured the state and will use the state to oppress powerless racists. As a final element to this upside-down story, the Reagan-Bush judges are cast as the defenders of the down-trodden, the courageous upholders of the bill of rights.

This inverted story will no doubt surprise the many local lawmakers and law-enforcement officials who are struggling daily to keep the lid on the pressure cooker of racial animosity. Hate crime ordinances came about not because local legislators were bent on oppressing a tiny minority of unpopular racists, but because hate crimes had reached such an epidemic proportion that no one concerned with keeping the peace could ignore them. Civil rights organizations struggled mightily to raise public consciousness about the prevalence of hate crimes and to show how the targets of hate crimes were disempowered, silenced, and disenfranchised. None of this is mentioned in the Scalia opinion, however. Instead, local legislators dealing responsibly with local problems are painted as group-think imposers of orthodoxy.

Concurring Justices Byron White, Harry Blackmun, Sandra Day O'Connor, and John Paul Stevens would also overturn the St. Paul ordinance for over-breadth, but they would not prohibit all local efforts to prevent cross burnings and other forms of bigoted intimidation. Two of these Justices condemn the Scalia opinion for turning first amendment doctrine "on its head." While the critique is intended as a doctrinal one,' for the Scalia opinion both misstates and revises existing doctrine in confusing and astonishing ways, it also echoes the political critique made by critical race theorists. Judges from Oliver Wendell Holmes to Harry Blackmun have not had to be radicals to recognize the simple truth that doing justice requires more than manipulating doctrine in a vacuum. The concurring opinions explicitly discuss the harm of cross burnings and respect the determination of local lawmakers that the threat to society from burning crosses is greater than the threat from burning trash.

Where does the *R.A.V.* decision leave us? It provides little guidance for legislators, school administrators, and community activists who are attempting to deal with the racism that—Supreme Court erasures notwithstanding—still plagues our neighborhoods and institutions. The *R.A.V* decision will not outlive the problem of racism, and, indeed, its incoherence and illogic are unlikely to withstand the test of even a few years' time. We urge those concerned about racism to continue their creative efforts to respond to assaultive speech, guided by the reality of racism's concrete harms. This requires listening carefully to the stories of families who spend the night imprisoned by fear while crosses burn and linking that to the broad gulfs that separate, still, the life chances of haves and have-nots in America. As critical race theorists, we do not separate cross burning from police brutality nor epithets from infant mortality rates. We believe there are systems of culture, of privilege, and of power that intertwine in complex ways to tell a sad and continuing story of insider/outsider. We choose to see and to struggle against a world made by burning crosses.

* * * The first amendment goal of maximizing public discourse is not attained in a marketplace of ideas distorted by coercion and privilege. Burning crosses do not bring to the table more ideas for discussion, and the Court's failure to see this is part of a long history of not seeing what folks on the bottom see. We hold faith that a critical view of law can reconstruct the first amendment to bring the voices of the least to the places of power. In arguing against existing law, we argue not against law but for a legal world worthy of democracy's name.

NOTES AND QUESTIONS

1. *Liberal versus critical jurisprudence*. On the basis of the *R.A.V.* decision and the Matsuda/Lawrence critique, how would you articulate the essential difference between the liberal and the CRT approaches to freedom of speech?

2. *Cross-burning as protected speech*. In *Virginia v. Black*, 538 U.S. 343 (2003), the Supreme Court considered a statute in Virginia which banned cross burning with "an intent to intimidate a person or group of persons." It held that Virginia could, "consistent with the First Amendment, [ ] ban cross burning carried out with the intent to intimidate, [but] the provision in the Virginia statute treating any cross burning as *prima facie* evidence of intent to intimidate renders the statute unconstitutional in its current form." *Id.* at 348. Evidently, "threats of intimidation" are proscribable in a way that the Ku Klux Klan's "messages of shared ideology" are protected. Does that decision confirm or complicate the CRT perspective as you understand it?

3. *Foreign and international approaches to hate speech*. The United States is considerably more tolerant of hate speech than other democracies, especially those in which "personal dignity" or group rights are at least as protected as individual free speech. *See generally* Michel Rosenfeld, *Hate Speech in Comparative Jurisprudence: A Comparative Analysis*, 24 CARDOZO L. REV. 1523 (2003); Sionaidh Douglas-Scott, *The Hatefulness of Protected Speech: A Comparison of the American and European Approaches*, 7 WM. & MARY BILL RTS. J. 305 (1999); Kevin Boyle, *Hate Speech—The United States Versus the Rest of the World*, 53 ME. L. REV. 487 (2001). Of many possible examples, consider the Canadian Supreme Court's disposition of *The Queen v. Keegstra*, [1990] 3 S.C.R. 697, decided two years before *R.A.V.* In *Keegstra,* the Canadian court sustained the constitutionality of certain hate speech legislation, and the Chief Justice looked explicitly at the more tolerant jurisprudence of the First Amendment, observing:

> Though I have found the American experience tremendously helpful in coming to my own conclusions regarding this appeal, and by no

> means reject the whole of the First Amendment doctrine, in a number of respects I am [ ] dubious as to the applicability of this doctrine in the context of a challenge to hate propaganda legislation. . . . [T]he special role given equality and multiculturalism in the Canadian Constitution necessitates a departure from the view, reasonably prevalent in America at present, that the suppression of hate propaganda is incompatible with guarantee of free expression.

Keegstra, [1990] 3 S.C.R. at 743 (Dickson, C.J.).

BISHOP V. TOYS "R" US

414 F. Supp. 2d 385 (S.D.N.Y. 2006)

CASTEL, DISTRICT JUDGE. Plaintiff alleges that, on July 3, 2004, after purchasing a doll set for his daughter at a Toys "R" Us store in the Bronx, a store security guard demanded that he present a receipt before exiting the store. He declined to do so, and was then allegedly detained and assaulted by store and security personnel until such time as plaintiff himself summoned the police. He presented his sales receipt to the police and was thereupon "freed" from the store. Plaintiff alleges that the motivating factor in his treatment at the hands of Toys "R" Us and its employees and agents was that he is African-American and/or the fact that the store was located in a predominantly African-American neighborhood. He has thus brought suit against defendants alleging violations of his civil rights under 42 U.S.C. §§ 1981, 1982, and 1983. He has also asserted a host of state law claims, ranging from false imprisonment to intentional infliction of emotional distress.

Defendants, after filing answers to plaintiff's amended complaint, have moved for judgment on the pleadings pursuant to Rule 12(c), Fed.R.Civ.P., and/or dismissal pursuant to Rule 12(h)(3), Fed.R.Civ.P. Rule 12(h)(3) provides that "[w]henever it appears by suggestion of the parties or otherwise that the court lacks jurisdiction of the subject matter, the court shall dismiss the action." For the reasons set forth below, defendants' motions are granted in part and denied in part.

* * * Judgment on the pleadings should be granted only if " 'it appears beyond doubt that the plaintiff can prove no set of facts in support of his claim which would entitle him to relief.' This standard is applied with particular strictness when the plaintiff complains of a civil rights violation." *Sheppard v. Beerman*, 18 F.3d 147, 150 (2d Cir.), *cert. denied*, 513 U.S. 816 (1994) (*quoting Conley v. Gibson*, 355 U.S. 41, 45–46 (1957). Moreover, as plaintiff is proceeding *pro se*, his pleadings are to be read liberally, and interpreted to "raise the strongest arguments that they suggest." *Jorgensen v. Epic/Sony Records*, 351 F.3d 46, 50 (2d Cir. 2003).

Where a plaintiff brings claims premised on federal statutes, a district court has jurisdiction, and a motion to dismiss based on lack of subject matter jurisdiction is properly denied unless the allegations are "frivolous on their face," and the alleged federal question is "so plainly insubstantial as to be devoid of any merits and thus [does] not present[ ] any issue worthy of adjudication." *Nowak v. Iron-workers Local 6 Pension Fund*, 81 F.3d 1182, 1189, 1190 (2d Cir.1996). Plaintiff's allegations are not entirely frivolous. Thus, defendants' Rule 12(h)(3) motion is denied. I will, however, consider, in the context of defendants' 12(c) motion, whether plaintiff's amended complaint adequately states a claim under each of the applicable civil rights statutes, with both the notice pleading standard and the liberal reading afforded pro se complaints in mind. [ ]

Section 1981 Claims

Section 1981(a) provides that, "[a]ll persons within the jurisdiction of the United States shall have the same right in every State and Territory to make and enforce contracts, to sue, be parties, give evidence, and to the full and equal benefit of all laws and proceedings for the security of persons and property as is enjoyed by white citizens, and shall be subject to like punishment, pains, penalties, taxes, licenses, and exactions of every kind, and no other." 42 U.S.C. § 1981(a).

To survive a motion to dismiss (or, in this case, a motion for judgment on the pleadings), a plaintiff bringing a claim under section 1981 must allege the following three elements: "(1) the plaintiff is a member of a racial minority; (2) an intent to discriminate on the basis of race by the defendant; and (3) the discrimination concerned one or more of the activities enumerated in the statute. . . ." *Mian v. Donaldson, Lufkin & Jenrette Sec. Corp.*, 7 F.3d 1085, 1087 (2d Cir.1993) (*per curiam*). Defendants do not contest that plaintiff has adequately pled the first element, as the amended complaint clearly alleges that he is African-American. They do, however, contend that plaintiff's complaint is insufficient with regard to its allegations of intentional discrimination and that it does not adequately allege that any discrimination concerned one of the statute's enumerated activities.

Courts are instructed to be "cautious of summary adjudication" when issues of discriminatory intent are involved. *Hicks v. IBM*, 44 F.Supp.2d 593, 598 (S.D.N.Y.1999) (*citing Schwapp v. Town of Avon*, 118 F.3d 106, 110 (2d Cir.1997)). However, in pleading intentional racial discrimination, a plaintiff may not rely on "naked assertions" of discrimination, but rather "must specifically allege the events claimed to constitute intentional discrimination as well as circumstances giving rise to a plausible inference of racially discriminatory intent." *Yusuf v. Vassar Coll.*, 35 F.3d 709, 713–14 (2d Cir.1994).

Here, plaintiff's complaint contains detailed allegations of specific conduct which, if proven at trial, could give rise to an inference of discrimination. Plaintiff alleges that he was "stopped and detained by Defendant McDaniel for no other reason than being an African American." While this allegation alone might be too conclusory to support a section 1981 claim, plaintiff goes on to describe in detail the events that occurred as he attempted to leave the store. He alleges that he was "assaulted, battered, [and] visited with use of excessive force, as McDaniel physically forced [plaintiff] back into Toys 'R' Us store [*sic*]. . . ." In fact, he alleges that McDaniel chased him "in a wild manner like a runaway freight train and blocked [plaintiff's] path with his body," and then "shoved" him back into the store. He alleges that he repeatedly asked McDaniel, as well as defendant House, if he was free to leave the store, and was told that he was not.

Plaintiff alleges that McDaniel explained his demand for plaintiff's receipt as based on a "store policy." He also alleges that McDaniel elaborated, saying, "This is the Bronx, not the suburbs and black people steal more than whites." Plaintiff further alleges that, while he was still in the vicinity of the store exit, two white women carrying Toys "R" Us shopping bags exited the store, walking past McDaniel, and were not asked to show their receipts.

At the pleading stage, such allegations are sufficient to support a section 1981 claim. Where plaintiffs "allege that they are African-Americans, describe defendants' actions in detail, and allege that defendants selected them for maltreatment 'solely because of their color,' " they have done all that is necessary to withstand a motion to dismiss. *Phillip v. Univ. of Rochester*, 316 F.3d 291, 298 (2d Cir.2003). Plaintiff's allegations that he was subjected to racial epithets during the alleged detention and assault, and that white customers were not subjected to the same scrutiny on the way out of the store easily meet this standard. *See, e.g., Straker v. Metro. Transit Auth.*, 2005 WL 3287445 at *2–*3 (E.D.N.Y. Dec. 5, 2005) (citing *Phillip* and denying motion to dismiss where plaintiff alleged he was African-American, described what defendants did to him, alleged such actions were taken because of racial animus, and alleged that white co-workers were treated differently); *Hicks*, 44 F.Supp.2d at 598 (racially motivated comments sufficient to sustain a section 1981 claim against a 12(b)(6) motion); *Perry v. Burger King Corp.*, 924 F. Supp. 548, 551–52 (S.D.N.Y. 1996) (allegations sufficient to sustain section 1981 claim where employees made "racially-based offensive comments" and plaintiff observed white patrons using restroom to which he was denied access).

Thus the question remains as to whether plaintiff has adequately pled that the alleged discrimination concerned one of the activities enumerated in section 1981(a). Plaintiff alleges that defendants' actions impaired both his right to "make and enforce contracts" and his right to "the full and equal benefit of all laws and proceedings for the security of persons and property."

Defendants contend that plaintiff has failed to sufficiently plead impairment of either right.

Section 1981(b), which provides the definition of "make and enforce contracts" for purposes of the statute, was enacted as part of the Civil Rights Act of 1991, in response to the Supreme Court's 1989 decision in *Patterson v. McLean Credit Union*, 491 U.S. 164 (1989).[4] In *Patterson*, prior to the enactment of section 1981(b), the Court construed "make and enforce contracts" as not encompassing conduct occurring after the formation of a contract. Section 1981, the Court held, "covers only conduct at the initial formation of the contract and conduct which impairs the right to enforce contract obligations through legal process."

Congress amended section 1981 to include sub-sections (b) and (c), and thereby "to embrace all aspects of the contractual relationship, including contract terminations, [so] enlarg[ing] the category of conduct that is subject to § 1981 liability." *Rivers v. Roadway Express, Inc.*, 511 U.S. 298, 303 (1994). Even so, courts that have addressed section 1981 claims in the context of retail transactions have held that after a purchase is completed, "there is no continuing contractual relationship. Instead, the relationship is based on a single discrete transaction—the purchase of goods." *Arguello*, 330 F.3d at 360; *see also e.g., Youngblood v. Hy-Vee Food Stores, Inc.*, 266 F.3d 851, 854 (8th Cir. 2001) ("While there is scant precedent, courts that have addressed the issue have concluded that once the purchase is completed, no contractual relationship remains.") *cert. denied* 535 U.S. 1017 (2002); *Garrett v. Tandy Corp.*, 295 F.3d 94, 101 (1st Cir. 2002) (dismissing section 1981 claim where "the appellant fully consummated the contract while he was in the store (i.e., he completed the purchase of a book, a telephone, and some batteries) and thereafter retained the items he acquired"); *Nevin v. Citibank, N.A.*, 107 F.Supp.2d 333, 349 (S.D.N.Y. 2000) (granting summary judgment on section 1981 claim where "[p]laintiff purchased everything she desired at both the Lord & Taylor and Charisma stores"); *Rogers v. Elliott*, 135 F.Supp.2d 1312, 1315 (N.D. Ga.2001) ("Virtually all federal courts that have analyzed Section 1981 claims in the retail merchandise context have required the plaintiff to show that he was actually prevented from making a purchase."); *cf. Williams v. Cloverland Farms Dairy, Inc.*, 78 F.Supp.2d 479, 485 (D. Md.1999) (summary judgment denied where plaintiff was delayed in ability to complete purchase); *Perry*, 924 F.Supp. at 552 (section 1981 contract rights may be implicated by denial of bathroom use subsequent to purchase in a fast food restaurant).

Here, plaintiff alleges that the detention and assault occurred only after he had completed his purchase of the doll set and was attempting to

---

[4] Section 1981(b) provides that, "[f]or purposes of this section, the term 'make and enforce contracts' includes the making, performance, modification, and termination of contracts, and the enjoyment of all benefits, privileges, terms, and conditions of the contractual relationship."

exit the store. Thus, the contractual relationship between he and Toys "R" Us had ended, and none of defendants' actions interfered with his right to "make" or "enforce" that contract. Plaintiff seeks to escape this conclusion by arguing that his contractual rights were indeed implicated because his sales receipt noted the store's return policy, pursuant to which he was allegedly entitled to return his merchandise for a refund within 90 days of purchase. He alleges that his potential exercise of his rights under the return policy, as well as his "future and potential opportunities to engage in contractual relations" with Toys "R" Us were "chilled," as the July 3, 2004 encounter has led him to fear that he may be subject to similar treatment should he return to the store in the future.

However, "[a] claim for interference with the right to make and enforce a contract must allege the actual loss of a contract interest, not merely the possible loss of future contract opportunities." *Morris v. Office Max, Inc.*, 89 F.3d 411, 414–15 (7th Cir.1996). * * * While plaintiff alleges that he had the right to return the doll set, nowhere does he allege that he attempted to do so and his attempt was somehow thwarted. Indeed, he does not allege an intention to return the goods. True, he claims that because of defendants' actions on July 3, 2004, he would be loath to return to the store in the future, even had the doll set eventually proven to be defective or otherwise unsatisfactory. But, "[t]he naked assertion that a party might have elected to return a previously purchased product had he believed the environment to be more welcoming is simply too ephemeral a hook from which to hang a cause of action under 42 U.S.C. § 1981."

Plaintiff has not adequately pled a cause of action under section 1981 for interference with his right to "make and enforce contracts."

Apart from the "make and enforce contracts" provision, the statute also prohibits interference with the right "to the full and equal benefit of all laws and proceedings for the security of persons and property." 42 U.S.C. § 1981(a). Contrary to the holdings of some of its sister Circuits, [ ] the Second Circuit has made clear that there is no state action requirement to invoke the equal benefit clause of the section. *Phillip*, 316 F.3d at 295–96. Rather, plaintiffs must 1) allege racial animus, which, as discussed above, plaintiff here has done; 2) identify a relevant "law or proceeding for the security of persons and property;" and 3) allege that defendants deprived them of the "full and equal benefit" thereof. *Phillip*, 316 F.3d at 298.

The court in *Phillip* expressly avoided any "attempt to define the universe of laws and proceedings for the security of persons and property, believing this task best resolved case by case." There have been few cases to date construing the "equal benefit" provision.

Judge Dearie's opinion in *Pierre* [*v. J.C. Penney Co.*, 340 F.Supp.2d 308, 310 (E.D.N.Y. 2004),] deals with a factual situation similar to that presented by the instant action. Plaintiff in that case alleged that after she left a J.C. Penney store in Queens without making a purchase, she was approached on the street by store security guards. The guards accused her of shoplifting and forced her to return to the store, where she alleged that she was verbally and physically abused. Though a search of the plaintiff revealed no stolen merchandise, she was detained for nearly three hours, during which time the guards sought to have her sign a false confession, which she refused to do. The store never called the police or filed any form of complaint against plaintiff, though plaintiff filed a police complaint against the store. Plaintiff brought suit alleging, *inter alia*, violation of her rights under the "equal benefit" clause of section 1981.

The plaintiff had not alleged a nexus to a state legal proceeding, but Judge Dearie went on to consider whether plaintiff had adequately alleged a nexus to a state law for the protection of persons and property. Plaintiff's complaint in Pierre alleged that defendants had violated, *inter alia*, state laws prohibiting assault, battery, and false imprisonment. The court held that such laws qualified as those "intended for the security of persons." Thus, defendants' motion to dismiss was denied.

Here, the facts alleged by plaintiff track the allegations in *Pierre,* though plaintiff did, in fact, make a purchase, and the duration of his detention was shorter. Plaintiff also alleges that defendants acted in violation of state laws intended for the security of persons and property, by, *inter alia*, their alleged false imprisonment, false arrest, assault, battery, trespass to chattels, and violations of state civil rights laws. Beyond the *ipse dixit* denial that they interfered with plaintiff's full and equal benefit rights, defendants fail entirely to address this aspect of plaintiff's section 1981 claims in their motion papers.

As noted, defendants' briefing on the "equal benefit" claim has been wholly inadequate. Under the liberal pleading standard espoused by the Supreme Court [ ], this Court cannot conclude that "it appears beyond doubt that the plaintiff can prove no set of facts in support of his claim which would entitle him to relief." *Conley*, 355 U.S. at 45–46. Defendants' motion to dismiss plaintiff's section 1981 claim is denied to the extent he relies on the "equal benefit" clause. [ ] The Court remains open to reconsideration of its preliminary assessment of the viability of the "equal benefit" claim after the parties have had an opportunity to conduct discovery, the purported nexus to state law is in sharper focus and defendants adequately brief the issue.

Section 1982 Claim

Section 1982 provides that, "[a]ll citizens of the United States shall have the same right, in every State and Territory, as is enjoyed by white citizens thereof to inherit, purchase, lease, sell, hold, and convey real and personal property." 42 U.S.C. § 1982. Though the statute has been interpreted broadly, a plaintiff, to state a claim, must allege interference with some right involving real or personal property. Plaintiff here, according to his opposition papers, apparently asserts that defendants interfered with his "fundamental right to travel freely within the United States of America," and that this constitutes deprivation of a property interest.

The right to interstate travel has long been recognized as fundamental, but it does not constitute the sort of interest in real or personal property that is protected by section 1982. As discussed above in connection with plaintiff's section 1981 claims, he was not prevented from making any purchases at the store. *Cf. Burgin v. Toys-R-Us-Nytex, Inc.*, 1999 WL 454302 at *4 (W.D.N.Y. June 30, 1999) (claim stated under section 1982 where cashier refused to complete sale, returned money already tendered, and had plaintiff escorted from store); *Shen v. A & P Food Stores*, 1995 WL 728416 at *2–*3 (E.D.N.Y. Nov. 21, 1995) (claim stated under section 1982 where employees refused to sell apple juice to plaintiffs). In retail cases alleging violations of both the contracts clause of section 1981 and section 1982, the two claims are often considered together, and the conclusion that plaintiff has not pled that he was denied the right to enter into a contract counsels in favor of dismissal of the section 1982 claim.

Plaintiff relies heavily on the Second Circuit's decision in *Olzman v. Lake Hills Swim Club, Inc.*, 495 F.2d 1333 (2d Cir.1974). In *Olzman*, the court held that a section 1982 claim could be premised on a rule change at a swim club, which would have had the effect of denying black children the right to use the club's facilities as guests. The court held that it was "reasonable to characterize the freedom of blacks to come and go as guests of a swim club member as sufficiently pertaining to a condition of property to be a right capable of being held under § 1982." The court recognized that status as a guest would not normally be considered a property right, but also acknowledged that when a black child was invited by a member, he attained certain rights to the "property" of the club, which rights were protectable.

Here, it is doubtful that plaintiff could claim any interest in the "property" of the store, but even assuming he could, he has not alleged that he was denied access to the store. Even interpreting plaintiff's complaint liberally, he has failed to identify a cognizable interest in real or personal property.

Defendants' motion for judgment on the pleadings as to plaintiff's section 1982 claim is granted.

Section 1983 Claims

Defendants contend that plaintiff has not adequately alleged the requisite state action under section 1983. "In order to state a claim under § 1983, a plaintiff must allege that he was injured by either a state actor or a private party acting under color of state law." *Ciambriello v. County of Nassau*, 292 F.3d 307, 323 (2d Cir.2002).

For a private individual or entity to be deemed to have been acting under color of state law, the allegedly unconstitutional conduct of which plaintiff complains must be "fairly attributable to the state." *Tancredi v. Metro. Life Ins. Co.*, 316 F.3d 308, 312 (2d Cir.), *cert. denied*, 539 U.S. 942 (2003). For this to be the case, there must be "such a close nexus between the State and the challenged action that seemingly private behavior may be fairly treated as that of the State itself." *Id.* Such a nexus is found "where the state exercises coercive power over, is entwined in [the] management or control of, or provides significant encouragement, either overt or covert to, a private actor, or where the private actor operates as a willful participant in joint activity with the State or its agents, is controlled by an agency of the State, has been delegated a public function by the state or is entwined with governmental policies." *Id.* at 313.

The acts of a store security guard generally do not constitute state action for purposes of section 1983. In his complaint, however, plaintiff alleges, upon information and belief, that defendant McDaniel has been sworn in as a "special patrolman" by the City and/or the State of New York, and was thus a "quasi-peace officer act[ing] under color of law." A "special patrol-man" may be appointed by the Commissioner of the NYPD, "to do special duty at any place in the city," and "shall possess the powers and discharge all the duties of the [police] force, applicable to regular members of the force." NYC ADMIN. CODEE § 14–106(c).

In *Rojas v. Alexander's Dept. Store, Inc.*, 654 F.Supp. 856, 858 (E.D.N.Y.1986), the court held that an allegation that a store security officer is also a "special patrolman" under the City Administrative Code suffices to render him a "government official subject to section 1983 liability." *Id.* (citing *Williams v. United States*, 341 U.S. 97 (1951)); *see also Temple v. Albert*, 719 F.Supp. 265, 267 (S.D.N.Y.1989) ("Special Patrolmen acting pursuant to a statutory grant of police power are sufficiently controlled by the state to be properly characterized as acting under color of state law.") Defendants, in their opposition papers, dispute that McDaniel is a "special patrolman" within the meaning of the Administrative Code, and instead aver that he is "an active Deputy Sheriff of the City of New York."

While the plaintiff's allegation is thin, and may ultimately prove to be untrue, it is sufficient, at the pleading stage, to withstand McDaniel's motion to dismiss for lack of alleged state action. * * *

As regards the potential liability of defendants other than McDaniel under section 1983, defendants are correct that liability may not be found based on a theory of *respondeat superior*. However, plaintiff has alleged that the constitutional violations by McDaniel were part and parcel of a Toys "R" Us policy to select minorities for increased (and unjustified) scrutiny. He also alleges that McDaniel's actions were carried out "at the direction of" both Toys "R" Us and Metro One and/or pursuant to contracts between Toys "R" Us and one or more of Metro One, McDaniel, House and Nieves.

Assuming the truth of the allegation as to McDaniel's "special patrolman" status, plaintiff's complaint, liberally construed, can be said to include allegations that "the institution is the driving force behind the constitutional violation," *Temple*, 719 F.Supp. at 268, and/or that the other defendants conspired with McDaniel to violate plaintiff's constitutional rights. *See Ciambriello*, 292 F.3d at 324–25 (section 1983 conspiracy requires pleading "(1) an agreement between a state actor and a private party; (2) to act in concert to inflict an unconstitutional injury; and (3) an overt act done in furtherance of that goal causing damages").

Defendants' motions for judgment on the pleadings as to plaintiff's claim under section 1983 are denied. * * *

PATRICIA WILLIAMS, *SPIRIT-MURDERING THE MESSENGER: THE DISCOURSE OF FINGERPOINTING AS THE LAW'S RESPONSE TO RACISM*

42 U. MIAMI L. REV. 127, 127–29 (1987)

Buzzers are big in New York City. Favored particularly by smaller stores and boutiques, merchants throughout the city have installed them as screening devices to reduce the incidence of robbery. When the buzzer sounds, if the face at the door looks "desirable," the door is unlocked. If the face is that of an "undesirable," the door stays locked. Predictably, the issue of undesirability has revealed itself to be primarily a racial determination. Although the buzzer system was controversial at first, even civil rights organizations have backed down in the face of arguments that the system is a "necessary evil,"[1] that it is a "mere inconvenience" compared to the risks of being murdered,[2] that discrimination is not as bad as assault,[3] and that in any event, it is not all blacks who are barred, just "17-year-old black males wearing running shoes and hooded sweatshirts."[4]

Two Saturdays before Christmas, I saw a sweater that I wanted to purchase for my mother. I pressed my brown face to the store window and my finger to the buzzer, seeking admittance. A narrow-eyed white youth who looked barely seventeen, wearing tennis sneakers and feasting on bubble gum, glared at me, evaluating me for signs that would pit me

---

1 Gross, *When 'By Appointment' Means Keep Out*, N.Y. TIMES, Dec. 17, 1986, at B1, col. 3.

2 *Id.*

3 Letter to the Editor from Michael Levin and Marguerita Levin, N.Y. TIMES, Jan. 11, 1987, at E32, col. 3 [hereinafter Letter to the Editor].

4 *Id.*

against the limits of his social understanding. After about five seconds, he mouthed, "We're closed," and blew pink rubber at me. It was one o'clock in the afternoon. There were several white people in the store who appeared to be shopping for things for *their* mothers.

I was enraged. At that moment I literally wanted to break all of the windows in the store and *take* lots of sweaters for my mother. In the flicker of his judgmental grey eyes, that saleschild had reduced my brightly sentimental, joy-to-the-world, pre-Christmas spree to a shambles. He had snuffed my sense of humanitarian catholicity, and there was nothing I could do to snuff his, without simply making a spectacle of myself.

I am still struck by the structure of power that drove me into such a blizzard of rage. There was almost nothing I could do, short of physically intruding upon him, that would humiliate him the way he humiliated me. No words, no gestures, no prejudices of my own would make a bit of difference to him. His refusal to let me into the store was an outward manifestation of his never having let someone like me into the realm of his reality. He had no connection, no compassion, no remorse, no reference to me, and no desire to acknowledge me even at the estranged level of arm's length transactor. He saw me only as one who would take his money and therefore could not conceive that I was there to give him money.

In this weird ontological imbalance, I realized that buying something in that store was like bestowing a gift: the gift of my commerce. In the wake of my outrage, I wanted to take back the gift of my appreciation, which my peering in the window must have appeared to be. I wanted to take it back in the form of unappreciation, disrespect, and defilement. I wanted to work so hard at wishing he could feel what I felt that he would never again mistake my *hatred* for some sort of plaintive wish to be included. I was quite willing to disenfranchise myself in the heat of my need to revoke the flattery of my purchasing power. I was willing to boycott this particular store, random white-owned businesses, and anyone who blew bubble gum in my face again.

My rage was admittedly diffuse, even self-destructive, but it was symmetrical. The perhaps loose-ended but utter propriety of that rage is no doubt lost not just to the young man who barred me, but to those who appreciate my being barred only as an abstract precaution, and who approve of those who would bar, even as they deny that *they* would bar *me*.

The violence of my desire to have burst into that store is probably quite apparent to the reader. I wonder if the violence and the exclusionary hatred are equally apparent in the repeated public urging that blacks put themselves in the shoes of white store owners,[5] and that, in effect, blacks look into the mirror of frightened whites faces to the reality of their

[5] Gross, *supra.*

undesirability; and that then blacks would "just as surely conclude that [they] would not let [themselves] in under similar circumstances."[6]

NOTES AND QUESTIONS

1. *CRT, Toys "R" Us, and the interpretation of statutes designed to stop discrimination.* In contrast to *McCleskey* and *R.A.V.*, which address constitutional rights, the *Toys "R" Us* case deals with statutory rights. The central statute is Section 1981, Reconstruction-era legislation, which *inter alia* guarantees to all people within the United States the same right "as is enjoyed by white citizens" to "make and enforce contracts." In the months after Lee's surrender at Appomattox in 1865, Congress had become concerned that white people in the South were effectively recreating conditions of slavery for newly-freed African Americans. Senator Lyman Trumbull of Illinois introduced a bill to "grant to the Freedmen basic economic rights—to make and enforce contracts, to sue and be sued, and to purchase and lease property." Congress adopted the Civil Rights Act of 1866 under its power to enforce the Thirteenth Amendment's prohibition of slavery and involuntary servitude, effectively extending the Thirteenth Amendment into the domain of private relationships within the marketplace. In her article, Professor Williams encapsulates the special scrutiny African-Americans undergo in retail outlets across the country. What does it say about the role of race in American jurisprudence that a civil rights statute designed to prevent discrimination in economic relationships is largely interpreted in a way to deny the possibility of a remedy to Mr. Bishop?

2. *Thinking beyond black and white.* It is a mistake to assume that CRT is limited to the experience of African-Americans. As shown in the readings below, the approach has expanded (or fragmented) into a variety of subspecialties, including LatCrit, Asian Crit, TribalCrit, and Critical Race Feminism, each of which grows out of the particular experience of particular groups in American society and none of which fits into the dominant black-white dichotomy. *See, e.g.*, Juan F. Perea, *The Black/White Binary Paradigm of Race: The "Normal Science" of American Racial Thought*, 85 CALIF. L. REV. 1213 (1997); Ian F. Haney López, *Race, Ethnicity, Erasure: The Salience of Race to LatCrit Theory*, 85 CALIF. L. REV. 1143 (1997); Richard Delgado, *Centennial Reflections on the California Law Review's Scholarship on Race: The Structure of Civil Rights Thought*, 100 CAL. L. REV. 431 (2012).

The application of CRT to the experience of Native Americans for example reveals that racism has played a systematic role in the mistreatment of indigenous peoples but that colonization—its law, its processes, its mindset—is no less powerful. For these purposes, colonization may be defined as "the process by which a people exploit and/or annex the lands and resources of

---

[6] Letter to the Editor, *supra*. The fact that some blacks might agree with the store owners, shows that some of us have learned too well the lessons of privatized self-hatred and rationalized away the fullness of our public, participatory selves.

another without their consent and unilaterally expand political power over them" R. O. Porter, *The Decolonization of Indigenous Government*, *in* FOR INDIGENOUS EYES ONLY: A DECOLONIZATION HANDBOOK 108 (W. A. Wilson & M. Yellow Bird, eds., 2005).

In Professor Robert Williams' words, the

> "European-derived law of colonization was inescapably and irredeemably racist in its discriminatory application to the New World's indigenous peoples and their tribal systems of self-government. The cultural racism of Europeans * * * denied the idea that indigenous tribal peoples should be in control of their own destinies, and imposed upon them instead a legal regime of alien domination that refused recognition of their fundamental human rights of self-determination."

Robert A. Williams, Jr., *Columbus's Legacy as an Instrument of Racial Discrimination Against Indigenous Peoples' Rights of Self-Determination*, 8 ARIZ. J. INT'L & COMP. L., no. 2, 51, 51 (1991).

There is even precedent for considering "Indian-ness" a political and not a racial classification at all. *See Morton v. Mancari*, 417 U.S. 535 (1974). "The [*Mancari*] Court upheld the preference [in employment of Native Americans], holding that the preference did not constitute racial or ethnic discrimination, but was a political classification reflecting the relationship between the federal government and recognized Indian tribes." William C. Canby, Jr., *The Concept of Equality in Indian Law*, 85 WASH. L. REV. 13, 16 (2010). *See also Artichoke Joe's Cal. Grand Casino v. Norton*, 353 F.3d 712, 734 (9th Cir. 2003) ("Our early discussions of *Mancari* suggested that, so long as a federal statute evinced a rational relationship to Congress's trust obligations toward the Indians, it involved political classification, so rational-basis review was appropriate."); Nell Jessup Newton, *Federal Power Over Indians: Its Sources, Scope, and Limitations*, 132 U. PA. L. REV. 195 (1984); Robert A. Williams Jr., *The Algebra of Federal Indian Law: The Hard Trail of Decolonizing and Americanizing the White Man's Indian Jurisprudence*, [1986] WIS. L. REV. 219; Jessica Jones, *Cherokee by Blood and the Freedmen Debate: The Conflict of Minority Group Rights in a Liberal State*, 22 NAT'L BLACK L.J. 1 (2009).

3. *The power and limits of parable*. In his short story, *Space Traders*, Derrick Bell—one of the founders of CRT—imagines alien invaders who come to the United States and offer the nation all the material and technical resources it needs to solve its financial, social, and environmental problems. But in exchange, the aliens demand every African-American, whose fate will be unknown. In the story, the United States makes the deal. Judge Alex Kozinski responds in *Bending the Law*:

> The radical multiculturalists' views raise insuperable barriers to mutual understanding. Consider the *Space Traders* story. How does one have a meaningful dialogue with Derrick Bell? Because his thesis is utterly untestable, one quickly reaches a dead end after either accepting or rejecting his assertion that white Americans would

> cheerfully sell all blacks to the aliens. The story is also a poke in the eye of American Jews, particularly those who risked life and limb by actively participating in the civil rights protests of the 1960's. Bell clearly implies that this was done out of tawdry self-interest. Perhaps most galling is Bell's insensitivity in making the symbol of Jewish hypocrisy the little girl who perished in the Holocaust—as close to a saint as Jews have. A Jewish professor who invoked the name of Rosa Parks so derisively would be bitterly condemned—and rightly so.

Alex Kozinski, *Bending the Law*, N.Y. TIMES, Nov. 2, 1997. *Cf.* Gloria Ladson-Billings foreword to *Critical Race Theory in Education: All God's Children Got a Song* vii (2006) ("CRT never makes claims of objectivity or rationality.").

4. *The right strategy: "affirmative action" and its limitations.* One powerful strain of CRT resists assimilationist strategies as a way of integrating minorities into the larger society. The critique is that those strategies effectively maintain the status quo, "colorizing" the institutions without making meaningful change. They might also note that the antidiscrimination statutes do not work exclusively for the benefit of racial minorities.

In *Ricci v. DeStefano*, 557 U.S. 557 (2009), the city government of New Haven, Connecticut, refused to certify the results of a promotional examination for firefighters, because it feared that doing so could have a disparate impact on minorities, especially African-Americans, and that the city would face liability under the federal antidiscrimination statutes. The test had been developed specifically so as not to discriminate on the basis of race, but the results were racially disproportionate. Petitioners, a group of white and Hispanic firefighters who had passed the test, challenged the city's decision, but the lower courts ruled in favor of the city. The Supreme Court reversed, 5–4, concluding that the city's action violated federal anti-discrimination law. In prior cases, the Court had ruled that certain government actions to remedy past racial discrimination—actions that were themselves based on race—are constitutional only where there is a "strong basis in evidence" that the remedial actions were necessary. *See, e.g., Watson v. Fort Worth Bank & Trust*, 487 U.S. 977 (1988); *Richmond v. J.A. Croson Co.*, 488 U.S. 469 (1989). In this case, the city could be liable for disparate-impact discrimination only if the exams at issue were not job related and consistent with business necessity, or if there existed an equally valid, less discriminatory alternative that served the City's needs but that the city refused to adopt. Neither of those conditions was satisfied. *See* Justin Driver, *Recognizing Race*, 112 COLUM. L. REV. 404, 409 (2012) (addressing *Ricci* and observing that "judges often appear to make poor decisions regarding racial recognition: Courts not only recognize race when they should avoid doing so, but courts also fail to recognize race when they should.").

What are the right alternatives?

Readings

W. HAYWOOD BURNS, *LAW AND RACE IN EARLY AMERICA*

THE POLITICS OF LAW: A PROGRESSIVE CRITIQUE 115–9
(David Kairys ed., 1990)

In 1855 white men sitting in the Kansas legislature, duly elected by other white men, passed a law that sentenced white men convicted of rape of a white woman to up to five years in prison, while the penalty for a black man convicted of the same offense was castration, the costs of the procedure to be rendered by the desexed. The penalty of sexual mutilation appears at many points in the annals of American jurisprudence, Kansas in 1855 being but one of the more recent examples. What is special about the sentence of castration is that where it was in force, it was almost universally reserved for blacks (and, in some cases, Indians).

Apart from what this example reveals about the sexual psychopathology of white America, or at least of those in power, it graphically demonstrates the working of law in a racist society. The nexus between law and racism cannot be much more direct than this. Indeed, the histories of the African, Asian, Latin, and Native American people in the United States are replete with examples of the law and the legal process as the means by which the generalized racism in the society was made particular and converted into standards and policies of social control. Going beyond the Kansas example cited, a systematic analysis of racism and law provides keen insight into the operations of both.

In early-seventeenth-century colonial America, blacks and whites often existed and toiled side by side in various degrees of bondage. Though there were gradations of unfreedom, there was, at first, no clearly defined status of "slave." As the century drew to a close, however, the social reality and objective conditions changed sufficiently for the members of the colonial legislatures to recognize officially that the situations of the black person in bondage and the white person in bondage were diverging, with that of the black person becoming more debased. "Free choice" was hardly an issue for either whites or blacks who came in bondage to the New World. Still, there was a considerable difference in being, for example, an Irish indentured servant and a kidnapped African arriving in chains after the unspeakable horrors of the Middle Passage. There are vast differences between a societally enforced discrimination and an entire legal order founded explicitly on racism—a world of difference between "Irish need not apply," as reprehensible as that was, and statutory denial of legal personality, of humanity.

Black people were severed from much of their culture, language, kindred, religion, and all communication with the Old World of their fathers and mothers, from which they had been torn. The ugly sentiments of white racial superiority were beginning to sprout and rear their heads above the native soil. These facts, coupled with a growing understanding of the tremendous economic advantage to be gained from the long-term exploitation of black labor, brought about a social consensus (among whites) that sought to permanently relegate black people to the lowest stratum in a vertical relationship of white over black. This consensus found expressions and implementation in the form of laws passed in colonial legislatures that made slavery for black people both a lifetime condition and a hereditary condition. Thus, through the operation of law, in this case legislated societal racism, the institution of American chattel slavery was created and perpetuated.

With the advent of the detailed and oppressive colonial slave codes of the early eighteenth century, law played a consistent role throughout the period, up to and including the American Revolution. The Revolution, of course, produced a golden opportunity to do business other than as usual. It was, after all, a revolution fought in the name of liberty and egalitarian principles. It was an opportunity that was nonetheless missed or, perhaps better said, rejected. The revolution of Jefferson, Washington, and Madison was never intended to embrace the ebony throngs of captured and enslaved people in their white midsts. It was too much for the eighteenth-century white American mind to view these captured and enslaved people fully as people. It was too much for the Founding Fathers and the economic interests they represented to tamper with that amount of property—even for those who on moral, philosophical, or religious grounds opposed slavery.

Thus, the birth of the new order in the establishment of the Republic brought with it no new day for the African on American soil. In erecting the new state, black people were still consigned to be the hewers of wood, the drawers of water, for there enshrined in the fundamental law of the land, the new Constitution itself was the guaranteed continuation of the slave trade; the guaranteed return of fugitive slaves; and the counting of black persons as three-fifths human beings for purposes of taxation and political representation.

The pre-Revolutionary slave codes were more than ample models for the post-Revolutionary slave codes, which continued their detailed, oppressive harshness into the nineteenth century and into the new and expanding nation. The nineteenth-century slave codes provide an excellent example of law and state operating to impose a given social order. The slave codes legislated and regulated in minute detail every aspect of the life of a slave and of black/white interaction; assured white-over-black dominance; and made black people into virtual nonpersons, refusing to recognize any right of family, free movement, choice, and legal capacity to bring a suit or to testify where the interest of a white person was involved. This legal structure defining a black person's place in society was reinforced by statutes requiring cruel and brutal sanctions for any black man or woman who forgot his or her place and stepped, or even tried to step, out of it.

Even in the so-called Free States there was ample borrowing from the statutory schemes of the slavocracy to enforce a societal (white) view of the black person's rightful station in life. Thus, northern states systematically resorted to legislative devices to impose their collective view on the lives of "free" blacks, restricting them in employment, education, the franchise, legal personality, and public accommodation.

The legal issue of the status of black people in pre-Civil War America came to a head in 1857 in the case of *Dred Scott v. Sanford*[, 60 U.S. (19 How.) 393 (1857)]. It proved to be one of the most important judicial decisions in the history of the black experience with the law. In that case, Dred Scott, a slave who had been taken to a free territory by his master, attempted to sue for his freedom based upon the theory that residence in a free state had made him free. As Mr. Chief Justice Taney put it, "The question is simply this: Can a negro, whose ancestors were imported into this country, and sold as slaves, become a member of the political community formed and brought into existence by the Constitution of the United States, and as such become entitled to all the rights, and privileges, and immunities, guaranteed by that instrument to the citizen . . .?"

The Court's answer was, simply, "No." In ruling that Dred Scott, and by extension, any other black person, could not be a citizen under the Constitution, Taney went back to the founding of the Republic, examining what he declared was the public view of the black race at that point and tracing its history through time: ". . . [T]he public history of every European nation displays it in a manner too plain to be mistaken. [T]hey (the black race) had for more than a century before been regarded as beings of an inferior order, and altogether unfit to associate with the white race, either in social or political relations; and so far inferior, that they had no rights which the white man was bound to respect. . . ." This ringing Taney dictum dashed the hopes of black people and abolitionists who had looked to the courts to resolve one of the most troubling questions of racial justice of the day. The majority's decision and its view of black people as inferior brought down a rain of criticism on the Court from the North and caused cries of joy to rise from below the Mason-Dixon line. It also set the stage for the oncoming War between the States.

Logically, the Civil War should have made a decided difference in this racial legal dynamic. It did not, for though slavery itself was destroyed by this cataclysmic confrontation, the racism and economic exploitation undergirding slavery remained very much intact. Thus, even after the Emancipation Proclamation, after the war and the Thirteenth Amendment, the South set out to win the peace, despite having lost the war. The states of the South, where well over 90 percent of the nation's black people then lived, countered the emancipation by putting in place a series of laws known as the Black Codes, designed to approximate as closely as possible, in view of the legal abolition of slavery, a white-over-black, master/servant society. This legal order governed movement, marriage, work relations, and most major aspects of the freedperson's life.

In fact, there are many ways in which the Black Codes very much resembled the pre-Civil War slave codes. Laws were instituted against vagabonds to curtail black men from moving away from the land. Sharecropping and the convict-lease laws were designed to keep the former slaves on the land. Unlike other statutes, the vagabond- and convict-leasing statutes were not racial in their terms; however, their purpose and effect were entirely clear. The southern economy was predicated upon a large, exploited black labor force; and except for the brief and bright interregnum of Reconstruction, the law and the state throughout the last years of the nineteenth century and the early years of the twentieth operated to preserve the old order and to wring maximum advantage from white hegemony over an oppressed and economically ravaged black populace.

It was the law as well that played a crucial role in "the strange career of Jim Crow." In an uneven and nonsystematic way, culture and mores had provided for a separation of the races in many aspects of American life. For most of the nation's history, that was not even much of an issue because the presence of slavery took care of any need for social definition. However, during the late 1800s, states began to systematically codify separation of the races, *requiring* segregation literally from the hospital where one was born to the cemetery where one was laid to rest. Segregation no longer was open to local option, custom, and usage but was the state's legal order of the day. These developments occurred at the same point in time that an increasingly conservative Supreme Court was narrowing its interpretation of the Thirteenth, Fourteenth, and Fifteenth Amendments—the Civil War amendments. These trends culminated in the *Plessy v. Ferguson* decision of the Supreme Court in 1896, [163 U.S. 537 (1896)], in which "separate but equal" was approved as the law of the land, and the seal of approval of the nation's highest court was placed upon our own American brand of apartheid.

The use of the legal system to create and protect a racially segregated society was coincident with government's manipulation of the law to disenfranchise black citizens. Beginning with the Mississippi constitutional convention of 1890, revising the state's constitution through a series of legal stratagems and artifices—and greatly aided by the extralegal depredations of lynch law—black people were stripped of the ballot and any real semblance of black political power. The poll tax, the literacy test, and the Grandfather Clause were legal devices employed in the service of this racist cause to desired effect.

As a result of state uses of the law in this fashion, black Americans entered the twentieth century segregated, sundered from full and free participation in American life, and politically powerless to do much about it. This situation largely obtained through this century, with minor indications of change and advancement from time to time but with no real major breakthrough in the wall of apartheid and powerlessness until the Supreme Court decision in *Brown v. Board of Education*[, 347 U.S. 483 (1954)].

Brown and the struggle that followed in its wake—much of which involved use of the law to support and effect positive social change—obviously represent a highly significant advance in black Americans' quest for liberation. It would be an analytical mistake of considerable proportion, however, to view *Brown* as the end of explicitly racist legislation and court decisions, and the advent of civil rights laws as indicative of the end of the relationship among racism and the law and the state. For all our gains, America remains a country deeply infected by racism. Though this racism may not be as explicit or as obvious as it was in earlier times, it is present and no less real. Indeed, the last decade has seen a resurgence of racism in its most virulent as well as sophisticated forms.

PAUL BUTLER, *RACIALLY BASED JURY NULLIFICATION: BLACK POWER IN THE CRIMINAL JUSTICE SYSTEM*

105 YALE L. J. 677 (1995)

* * * I was a Special Assistant United States Attorney in the District of Columbia in 1990. I prosecuted people accused of misdemeanor crimes, mainly the drug and gun cases that overwhelm the local courts of most American cities. As a federal prosecutor, I represented the United States of America and used that power to put people, mainly African-American men, in prison. I am also an African-American man. While at the U.S. Attorney's office, I made two discoveries that profoundly changed the way I viewed my work as a prosecutor and my responsibilities as a black person.

The first discovery occurred during a training session for new Assistants conducted by experienced prosecutors. We rookies were informed that we would lose many of our cases, despite having persuaded a jury beyond a reasonable doubt that the defendant was guilty. We would lose because some black jurors would refuse to convict black defendants who they knew were guilty.

The second discovery was related to the first, but was even more unsettling. It occurred during the trial of Marion Barry, then the second-term mayor of the District of Columbia. Barry was being prosecuted by my office for drug possession and perjury. I learned, to my surprise, that some of my fellow African-American prosecutors hoped that the mayor would be acquitted, despite the fact that he was obviously guilty of at least one of the charges—he had smoked cocaine on FBI videotape. These black prosecutors wanted their office to lose its case because they believed that the prosecution of Barry was racist.

Federal prosecutors in the nation's capital hear many rumors about prominent officials engaging in illegal conduct, including drug use. Some African-American prosecutors wondered why, of all those people, the government chose to "set up" the most famous black politician in Washington, D.C. They also asked themselves why, if crack is so dangerous, the FBI had allowed the mayor to smoke it. Some members of the predominantly black jury must have had similar concerns: They convicted the mayor of only one count of a fourteen-count indictment, despite the trial judge's assessment that he had " 'never seen a stronger government case'." Some African-American prosecutors thought that the jury, in rendering its verdict, jabbed its black thumb in the face of a racist prosecution, and that idea made those prosecutors glad.

As such reactions suggest, lawyers and judges increasingly perceive that some African-American jurors vote to acquit black defendants for racial reasons,[ ] a decision sometimes expressed as the juror's desire not to send yet another black man to jail. This Essay examines the question of what role race should play in black jurors' decisions to acquit defendants in criminal cases. Specifically, I consider trials that include both African-American defendants and African-American jurors. I argue that the race of a black defendant is sometimes a legally and morally appropriate factor for jurors to consider in reaching a verdict of not guilty or for an individual juror to consider in refusing to vote for conviction.[9]

My thesis is that, for pragmatic and political reasons, the black community is better off when some nonviolent lawbreakers remain in the community rather than go to prison. The decision as to what kind of conduct by African-Americans ought to be punished is better made by African-Americans themselves, based on the costs and benefits to their community, than by the traditional criminal justice process, which is controlled by white lawmakers and white law enforcers. Legally, the doctrine of jury nullification gives the power to make this decision to African-American jurors who sit in judgment of African-American defendants. Considering the costs of law enforcement to the black community and the failure of white lawmakers to devise significant non-incarcerative responses to black antisocial conduct, it is the moral responsibility of black jurors to emancipate some guilty black outlaws.

* * * [In this Essay,] I describe racial critiques of the criminal justice system. I then examine the evolution of the doctrine of jury nullification and suggest, in light of this doctrine, that racial considerations by African-

[9] An acquittal on this basis would be jury nullification. Although most American jurisdictions require a unanimous verdict, and a single juror's vote for acquittal would not itself free the defendant, such a vote would prevent conviction. The prosecution would then have the option of either retrying the case or dismissing it.

American jurors are legally and morally right. [I also] propose a framework for analysis of the kind of criminal cases involving black defendants in which jury nullification is appropriate, and considers some of the concerns that implementation of the proposal raises.

My goal is the subversion of American criminal justice, at least as it now exists. Through jury nullification, I want to dismantle the master's house with the master's tools.[ ] My intent, however, is not purely destructive; this project is also constructive, because I hope that the destruction of the status quo will not lead to anarchy, but rather to the implementation of certain non-criminal ways of addressing antisocial conduct. Criminal conduct among African-Americans is often a predictable reaction to oppression. Sometimes black crime is a symptom of internalized white supremacy; other times it is a reasonable response to the racial and economic subordination every African-American faces every day. Punishing black people for the fruits of racism is wrong if that punishment is premised on the idea that it is the black criminal's "just deserts." Hence, the new paradigm of justice that I suggest [ ] rejects punishment for the sake of retribution and endorses it, with qualifications, for the ends of deterrence and incapacitation.

In a sense, this Essay simply may argue for the return of rehabilitation as the purpose of American criminal justice, but a rehabilitation that begins with the white-supremacist beliefs that poison the minds of us all—you, me, and the black criminal. I wish that black people had the power to end racial oppression right now. African-Americans can prevent the application of one particularly destructive instrument of white supremacy—American criminal justice—to some African-American people, and this they can do immediately. I hope that this Essay makes the case for why and how they should. * * *

II. "JUSTICE OUTSIDE THE FORMAL RULES OF LAW"[71]

Why would a black juror vote to let a guilty person go free? Assuming that the juror is a rational actor, she must believe that she and her community are, in some way, better off with the defendant out of prison than in prison. But how could any rational person believe that about a criminal? The following section describes racial critiques of the American criminal justice system. I then examine the evolution of the doctrine of jury nullification and argue that its practice by African-Americans is, in many cases, consistent with the Anglo-American tradition and, moreover, is legally and morally right.

---

[71] *United States v. Dougherty*, 473 F.2d 1113, 1137 (D.C. Cir. 1972) (describing scope of interests served by jury system).

A. *The Criminal Law and African-Americans: Justice or "Just us"?*[72]

Imagine a country in which more than half of the young male citizens are under the supervision of the criminal justice system, either awaiting trial, in prison, or on probation or parole. Imagine a country in which two-thirds of the men can anticipate being arrested before they reach age thirty. Imagine a country in which there are more young men in prison than in college. Now give the citizens of the country the key to the prison. Should they use it?

Such a country bears some resemblance to a police state. When we criticize a police state, we think that the problem lies not with the citizens of the state, but rather with the form of government or law, or with the powerful elites and petty bureaucrats whose interests the state serves. Similarly, racial critics of American criminal justice locate the problem not so much with the black prisoners as with the state and its actors and beneficiaries. As evidence, they cite their own experiences and other people's stories, African-American history, understanding gained from social science research on the power and pervasiveness of white supremacy, and ugly statistics like those in the preceding paragraph.

For analytical purposes, I will create a false dichotomy among racial critics by dividing them into two camps: liberal critics and radical critics. Those are not names that the critics have given themselves or that they would necessarily accept, and there would undoubtedly be disagreement within each camp and theoretical overlap between the camps. Nonetheless, for the purposes of a brief explication of racial critiques, my oversimplification may be useful.

1. *The Liberal Critique*

According to this critique, American criminal justice is racist because it is controlled primarily by white people, who are unable to escape the culture's dominant message of white supremacy, and who are therefore inevitably, even if unintentionally, prejudiced. These white actors include legislators, police, prosecutors, judges, and jurors. They exercise their discretion to make and enforce the criminal law in a discriminatory fashion.[ ] Sometimes the discrimination is overt, as in the case of Mark Fuhrman, the police officer in the O.J. Simpson case who, in interviews, used racist language and boasted of his own brutality, and sometimes it is unintentional, as with a hypothetical white juror who invariably credits the testimony of a white witness over that of a black witness. * * *

2. *The Radical Critique*

The radical critique does not discount the role of discrimination in accounting for some of the racial disparity in crime rates, but it also does

---

[72] "Just us" is a familiar pun in the African-American community. *See, e.g.*, Henry L. Gates, Jr., *Thirteen Ways Of Looking At A Black Man,* NEW YORKER, Oct. 23, 1995, at 56, 58 ("As older blacks like to repeat, 'When white folks say "justice," they mean "just us." ' ").

not, in contrast to the liberal critique, attribute all or even most of the differential to police and prosecutor prejudice. The radical critique offers a more fundamental, structural explanation. It suggests that criminal law is racist because, like other American law, it is an instrument of white supremacy. Law is made by white elites to protect their interests and, especially, to preserve the economic status quo, which benefits those elites at the expense of blacks, among others. Due to discrimination and segregation, the majority of African-Americans receive few meaningful educational and employment opportunities and, accordingly, are unable to succeed, at least in the terms of the capitalist ideal. Some property crimes committed by blacks may be understood as an inevitable result of the tension between the dominant societal message equating possession of material resources with success and happiness and the power of white supremacy to prevent most African-Americans from acquiring "enough" of those resources in a legal manner. "Black-on-black" violent crime, and even "victimless" crime like drug offenses, can be attributed to internalized racism, which causes some African-Americans to devalue black lives—either those of others or their own. * * *

I am persuaded by the radical critique when I wonder about the roots of the ugly truth that blacks commit many crimes at substantially higher rates than whites. Most white Americans, especially liberals, would publicly offer an environmental, as opposed to genetic, explanation for this fact. They would probably concede that racism, historical and current, plays a major role in creating an environment that breeds criminal conduct. From this premise, the radical critic deduces that but for the (racist) environment, the African-American criminal would not be a criminal. In other words, racism creates and sustains the criminal breeding ground, which produces the black criminal. Thus, when many African-Americans are locked up, it is because of a situation that white supremacy created.

Obviously, most blacks are not criminals, even if every black is exposed to racism. To the radical critics, however, the law-abiding conduct of the majority of African-Americans does not mean that racism does not create black criminals. Not everyone exposed to a virus will become sick, but that does not mean that the virus does not cause the illness of the people who do.

The radical racial critique of criminal justice is premised as much on the criminal law's *effect* as on its intent. The system is discriminatory, in part, because of the disparate impact law enforcement has on the black community. This unjust effect is measured in terms of the costs to the black community of having so many African-Americans, particularly males, incarcerated or otherwise involved in the criminal justice system. These costs are social and economic, and include the perceived dearth of men "eligible" for marriage, the large percentage of black children who live in female-headed households, the lack of male "role models" for black children, especially boys, the absence of wealth in the black community, and the large unemployment rate among black men.

3. *Examples of Racism in Criminal Justice*

Examples commonly cited by both liberal and radical critics as evidence of racism in criminal justice include: the Scottsboro case; the history of the criminalization of drug use; past and contemporary administration of the death penalty; the use of imagery linking crime to race in the 1988 presidential campaign and other political campaigns; the beating of Rodney King and the acquittal of his police assailants; disparities between punishments for white-collar crimes and punishments for other crimes; more severe penalties for crack cocaine users than for powder cocaine users; * * *; police corruption scandals in minority neighborhoods in New York and Philadelphia; the O.J. Simpson case, including the extraordinary public and media fascination with it, the racist police officer who was the prosecution's star witness, and the response of many white people to the jury's verdict of acquittal; and, cited most frequently, the extraordinary rate of incarceration of African-American men. * * *

African-American jurors who endorse these critiques are in a unique position to act on their beliefs when they sit in judgment of a black defendant. As jurors, they have the power to convict the defendant or to set him free. May the responsible exercise of that power include voting to free a black defendant who the juror believes is guilty? The next section suggests that, based on legal doctrine concerning the role of juries in general, and the role of black jurors in particular, the answer to this question is "yes."

B. *Jury Nullification*

When a jury disregards evidence presented at trial and acquits an otherwise guilty defendant, because the jury objects to the law that the defendant violated or to the application of the law to that defendant, it has practiced jury nullification. In this section, I describe the evolution of this doctrine and consider its applicability to African-Americans. * * * In light of judicial rulings in these areas, I argue that it is both lawful and morally right that black jurors consider race in reaching verdicts in criminal cases.

1. *What Is Jury Nullification?*

Jury nullification occurs when a jury acquits a defendant who it believes is guilty of the crime with which he is charged. In finding the defendant not guilty, the jury refuses to be bound by the facts of the case or the judge's instructions regarding the law. Instead, the jury votes its conscience.

In the United States, the doctrine of jury nullification originally was based on the common law idea that the function of a jury was, broadly, to decide justice, which included judging the law as well as the facts. If jurors believed that applying a law would lead to an unjust conviction, they were not compelled to convict someone who had broken that law. * * * Thus, even when a trial judge thinks that a jury's acquittal directly contradicts the evidence, the jury's verdict must be accepted as final. The jurors, in judging the law, function as an important and necessary check on government power.

2. *A Brief History*

The prerogative of juries to nullify has been part of English and American law for centuries. In 1670, the landmark decision in *Bushell's Case*[126] established the right of juries under English common law to nullify on the basis of an objection to the law the defendant had violated. Two members of an unpopular minority group—the Quakers—were prosecuted for unlawful assembly and disturbance of the peace. At trial, the defendants, William Penn and William Mead, admitted that they had assembled a large crowd on the streets of London. Upon that admission, the judge asked the men if they wished to plead guilty. Penn replied that the issue was not " 'whether I am guilty of this Indictment but whether this Indictment be legal,' " and argued that the jurors should go "behind" the law and use their consciences to decide whether he was guilty. The judge disagreed, and he instructed the jurors that the defendants' admissions compelled a guilty verdict. After extended deliberation, however, the jurors found both defendants not guilty. The judge then fined the jurors for rendering a decision contrary to the evidence and to his instructions. When one juror, Bushell, refused to pay his fine, the issue reached the Court of Common Pleas, which held that jurors in criminal cases could not be punished for voting to acquit, even when the trial judge believed that the verdict contradicted the evidence. * * *

This decision "changed the course of jury history."[130] It is unclear why the jurors acquitted Penn and Mead, but their act has been viewed in near mythological terms. Bushell and his fellow jurors have come to be seen as representing the best ideals of democracy because they "rebuffed the tyranny of the judiciary and vindicated their own true historical and moral purpose."[131]

American colonial law incorporated the common law prerogative of jurors to vote according to their consciences after the British government began prosecuting American revolutionaries for political crimes. The best known of these cases involved John Peter Zenger, who was accused of seditious libel for publishing statements critical of British colonial rule in

---

[126] 124 Eng. Rep. 1006 (C.P. 1670).

[130] [Jeffrey Abramson, WE, THE JURY: THE JURY SYSTEM AND THE IDEAL OF DEMOCRACY 72 (1994).]

[131] Thomas A. Green, VERDICT ACCORDING TO CONSCIENCE: PERSPECTIVES ON THE ENGLISH CRIMINAL TRIAL JURY, 1200–1800, at 225–26 (1985).

North America. In seditious libel cases, English law required that the judge determine whether the statements made by the defendant were libelous; the jury was not supposed to question the judge's finding on this issue. At trial, Zenger's attorney told the jury that it should ignore the judge's instructions that Zenger's remarks were libelous because the jury " 'ha[d] the right beyond all dispute to determine both the law and the facts.' " The lawyer then echoed the language of *Bushell's Case,* arguing that the jurors had " 'to see with their eyes, to hear with their own ears, and to make use of their own consciences and understandings, in judging of the lives, liberties or estates of their fellow subjects.' " Famously, the jury acquitted Zenger, and another case entered the canon as a shining example of the benefits of the jury system.

After Zenger's trial, the notion that juries should decide "justice," as opposed to simply applying the law to the facts, became relatively settled in American jurisprudence. In addition to pointing to political prosecutions of white American revolutionaries like Zenger, modern courts and legal historians often cite with approval nullification in trials of defendants "guilty" of helping to free black slaves. In these cases, Northern jurors with abolitionist sentiments used their power as jurors to subvert federal law that supported slavery. In *United States v. Morris,*[138] for example, three defendants were accused of aiding and abetting a runaway slave's escape to Canada. The defense attorney told the jury that, because it was hearing a criminal case, it had the right to judge the law, and if it believed that the Fugitive Slave Act was unconstitutional, it was bound to disregard any contrary instructions given by the judge. The defendants were acquitted, and the government dropped the charges against five other people accused of the same crime. Another success story entered the canon. * * *

The idea that jury nullification undermines the rule of law is the most common criticism of the doctrine. The concern is that the meaning of self-government is threatened when twelve individuals on a jury in essence remake the criminal law after it has already been made in accordance with traditional democratic principles. Another critique of African-American jurors engaging in racially based jury nullification is that the practice by black jurors is distinct from the historically approved cases because the black jurors are not so much "judging" the law as preventing its application to members of their own race. The reader should recognize that these are moral, not legal, critiques because, as discussed above, the legal prerogative of any juror to acquit is well established. In the next section, I respond to these moral critiques.

C. *The Moral Case for Jury Nullification by African-Americans*

Any juror legally may vote for nullification in any case, but, certainly, jurors should not do so without some principled basis. The reason that some

[138] 26 F. Cas. 1323 (C.C.D. Mass. 1851) (No. 15,815).

historical examples of nullification are viewed approvingly is that most of us now believe that the jurors in those cases did the morally right thing; it would have been unconscionable, for example, to punish those slaves who committed the crime of escaping to the North for their freedom. It is true that nullification later would be used as a means of racial subordination by some Southern jurors, but that does not mean that nullification in the approved cases was wrong. It only means that those Southern jurors erred in their calculus of justice. I distinguish racially based nullification by African-Americans from recent right-wing proposals for jury nullification on the ground that the former is sometimes morally right and the latter is not.

The question of how to assign the power of moral choice is a difficult one. Yet we should not allow that difficulty to obscure the fact that legal resolutions involve moral decisions, judgments of right and wrong. The fullness of time permits us to judge the fugitive slave case differently than the Southern pro-white-violence case. One day we will be able to distinguish between racially based nullification and that proposed by certain right-wing activist groups. We should remember that the morality of the historically approved cases was not so clear when those brave jurors acted. After all, the fugitive slave law was enacted through the democratic process, and those jurors who disregarded it subverted the rule of law. Presumably, they were harshly criticized by those whose interests the slave law protected. Then, as now, it is difficult to see the picture when you are inside the frame.

* * * I [next] explain why African-Americans have the moral right to practice nullification in particular cases. I do so by responding to the traditional moral critiques of jury nullification.

1. *African-Americans and the "Betrayal" of Democracy*

There is no question that jury nullification is subversive of the rule of law. It appears to be the antithesis of the view that courts apply settled, standing laws and do not "dispense justice in some *ad hoc*, case-by-case basis."[159] To borrow a phrase from the D.C. Circuit, jury nullification "betrays rather than furthers the assumptions of viable democracy."[160] Because the Double Jeopardy Clause makes this power part-and-parcel of the jury system, the issue becomes whether black jurors have any moral right to "betray democracy" in this sense. I believe that they do for two reasons that I borrow from the jurisprudence of legal realism and critical race theory: First, the idea of "the rule of law" is more mythological than real, and second, "democracy," as practiced in the United States, has betrayed African-Americans far more than they could ever betray it. Explication of these theories has consumed legal scholars for years, and is

[159] Michael S. Moore, *A Natural Law Theory of Interpretation,* 58 S. CAL. L. REV. 277, 313 (1985).

[160] United States v. Dougherty, 473 F.2d 1113, 1136 (D.C. Cir. 1972).

well beyond the scope of this Essay. I describe the theories below not to persuade the reader of their rightness, but rather to make the case that a reasonable juror might hold such beliefs, and thus be morally justified in subverting democracy through nullification.

2. *The Rule of Law as Myth*

The idea that "any result can be derived from the preexisting legal doctrine" either in every case or many cases,[161] is a fundamental principle of legal realism (and, now, critical legal theory). The argument, in brief, is that law is indeterminate and incapable of neutral interpretation.[ ] When judges "decide" cases, they "choose" legal principles to determine particular outcomes. Even if a judge wants to be neutral, she cannot, because, ultimately, she is vulnerable to an array of personal and cultural biases and influences; she is only human. In an implicit endorsement of the doctrine of jury nullification, legal realists also suggest that, even if neutrality were possible, it would not be desirable, because no general principle of law can lead to justice in every case.[ ]

It is difficult for an African-American knowledgeable of the history of her people in the United States not to profess, at minimum, sympathy for legal realism.[164] Most blacks are aware of countless historical examples in which African-Americans were not afforded the benefit of the rule of law: Think, for example, of the existence of slavery in a republic purportedly dedicated to the proposition that all men are created equal, or the law's support of state-sponsored segregation even after the Fourteenth Amendment guaranteed blacks equal protection. That the rule of law ultimately corrected some of the large holes in the American fabric is evidence more of its malleability than of its virtue; the rule of law had, in the first instance, justified the holes. * * *

If the rule of law is a myth, or at least is not applicable to African-Americans, the criticism that jury nullification undermines it loses force. The black juror is simply another actor in the system, using her power to fashion a particular outcome; the juror's act of nullification—like the act of the citizen who dials 911 to report Ricky but not Bob, or the police officer who arrests Lisa but not Mary, or the prosecutor who charges Kwame but not Brad, or the judge who finds that Nancy was illegally entrapped but Verna was not—exposes the indeterminacy of law, but does not create it.

3. *The Moral Obligation to Disobey Unjust Laws*

For the reader who is unwilling to concede the mythology of the rule of law, I offer another response to the concern about violating it. Assuming, for the purposes of argument, that the rule of law exists, there still is no

161 *See* Lawrence B. Solum, *On the Indeterminacy Crisis: Critiquing Critical Dogma,* 54 U. CHI. L. REV. 462, 470 (1987) (describing "indeterminacy thesis").

164 *See* A. Leon Higginbotham, Jr., IN THE MATTER OF COLOR: RACE AND THE AMERICAN LEGAL PROCESS 3–16 (1978) (describing discrimination by legal system against African-Americans throughout American history and consequent skepticism towards equality of "rule of law").

moral obligation to follow an unjust law.[ ] This principle is familiar to many African-Americans who practiced civil disobedience during the civil rights protests of the 1950s and 1960s. Indeed, Martin Luther King suggested that morality requires that unjust laws not be obeyed. As I state above, the difficulty of determining which laws are unjust should not obscure the need to make that determination. * * *

4. *Democratic Domination*

Related to the "undermining the law" critique is the charge that jury nullification is antidemocratic. * * * A jury that nullifies "betrays rather than furthers the assumptions of viable democracy." In a sense, the argument suggests that the jurors are not playing fair: The citizenry made the rules, so the jurors, as citizens, ought to follow them.

What does "viable democracy" assume about the power of an unpopular minority group to make the laws that affect them? It assumes that the group has the power to influence legislation. The American majority-rule electoral system is premised on the hope that the majority will not tyrannize the minority, but rather represent the minority's interests. Indeed, in creating the Constitution, the Framers attempted to guard against the oppression of the minority by the majority.[ ] Unfortunately, these attempts were expressed more in theory than in actual constitutional guarantees, a point made by some legal scholars, particularly critical race theorists.

* * *

If African-Americans believe that democratic domination exists, * * * they should not back away from lawful self-help measures, like jury nullification, on the ground that the self-help is antidemocratic. African-Americans are not a numerical majority in any of the fifty states, which are the primary sources of criminal law. In addition, they are not even proportionally represented in the U.S. House of Representatives or in the Senate. As a result, African-Americans wield little influence over criminal law, state or federal. African-Americans should embrace the antidemocratic nature of jury nullification because it provides them with the power to determine justice in a way that majority rule does not. * * *

III. A PROPOSAL FOR RACIALLY BASED JURY NULLIFICATION

To allow African-American jurors to exercise their responsibility in a principled way, I make the following proposal: African-American jurors should approach their work cognizant of its political nature and their prerogative to exercise their power in the best interests of the black community. In every case, the juror should be guided by her view of what is "just." For the reasons stated in the preceding parts of this Essay, I have more faith in the average black juror's idea of justice than I do in the idea that is embodied in the "rule of law."

A. *A Framework for Criminal Justice in the Black Community*

In cases involving violent *malum in se* crimes like murder, rape, and assault, jurors should consider the case strictly on the evidence presented, and, if they have no reasonable doubt that the defendant is guilty, they should convict. For nonviolent *malum in se* crimes such as theft or perjury, nullification is an option that the juror should consider, although there should be no presumption in favor of it. A juror might vote for acquittal, for example, when a poor woman steals from Tiffany's, but not when the same woman steals from her next-door neighbor. Finally, in cases involving nonviolent, *malum prohibitum* offenses, including "victimless" crimes like narcotics offenses, there should be a presumption in favor of nullification.

This approach seeks to incorporate the most persuasive arguments of both the racial critics and the law enforcement enthusiasts. If my model is faithfully executed, the result would be that fewer black people would go to prison; to that extent, the proposal ameliorates one of the most severe consequences of law enforcement in the African-American community. At the same time, the proposal, by punishing violent offenses and certain others, preserves any protection against harmful conduct that the law may offer potential victims. If the experienced prosecutors at the U.S. Attorney's Office are correct, some violent offenders currently receive the benefit of jury nullification, doubtless from a misguided, if well-intentioned, attempt by racial critics to make a political point. Under my proposal, violent lawbreakers would go to prison.

In the language of criminal law, the proposal adopts utilitarian justifications for punishment: deterrence and isolation. To that extent, it accepts the law enforcement enthusiasts' faith in the possibility that law can prevent crime. The proposal does not, however, judge the lawbreakers as harshly as the enthusiasts would judge them. Rather, the proposal assumes that, regardless of the reasons for their antisocial conduct, people who are violent should be separated from the community, for the sake of the nonviolent. The proposal's justifications for the separation are that the community is protected from the offender for the duration of the sentence and that the threat of punishment may discourage future offenses and offenders. I am confident that balancing the social costs and benefits of incarceration would not lead black jurors to release violent criminals simply because of race. While I confess agnosticism about whether the law can deter antisocial conduct, I am unwilling to experiment by abandoning any punishment premised on deterrence.

Of the remaining traditional justifications for punishment, the proposal eschews the retributive or "just deserts" theory for two reasons. First, I am persuaded by racial and other critiques of the unfairness of punishing people for "negative" reactions to racist, oppressive conditions. In fact, I sympathize with people who react "negatively" to the countless manifestations of white supremacy that black people experience daily.

While my proposal does not "excuse" all antisocial conduct, it will not punish such conduct on the premise that the intent to engage in it is "evil." The antisocial conduct is no more evil than the conditions that cause it, and, accordingly, the "just deserts" of a black offender are impossible to know. And even if just deserts were susceptible to accurate measure, I would reject the idea of punishment for retribution's sake.

My argument here is that the consequences are too severe: African-Americans cannot afford to lock up other African-Americans simply on account of anger. There is too little bang for the buck. Black people have a community that needs building, and children who need rescuing, and as long as a person will not hurt anyone, the community needs him there to help. Assuming that he actually will help is a gamble, but not a reckless one, for the "just" African-American community will not leave the lawbreaker be: It will, for example, encourage his education and provide his health care (including narcotics dependency treatment) and, if necessary, sue him for child support. In other words, the proposal demands of African-Americans responsible self-help outside of the criminal courtroom as well as inside it. When the community is richer, perhaps then it can afford anger.

The final traditional justification for punishment, rehabilitation, can be dealt with summarily. If rehabilitation were a meaningful option in American criminal justice, I would not endorse nullification in any case. It would be counterproductive, for utilitarian reasons: The community is better off with the antisocial person cured than sick. Unfortunately, however, rehabilitation is no longer an objective of criminal law in the United States,[215] and prison appears to have an antirehabilitative effect. For this reason, unless a juror is provided with a specific, compelling reason to believe that a conviction would result in some useful treatment for an offender, she should not use her vote to achieve this end, because almost certainly it will not occur.

* * *

C. *Some Political and Procedural Concerns*

1. *What if White People Start Nullifying Too?*

One concern is that whites will nullify in cases of white-on-black crime. The best response to this concern is that often white people do nullify in those cases. The white jurors who acquitted the police officers who beat up Rodney King are a good example. There is no reason why my proposal should cause white jurors to acquit white defendants who are guilty of violence against blacks any more frequently. My model assumes that black

[215] *See* Sanford H. Kadish & Stephen J. Schulhofer, CRIMINAL LAW AND ITS PROCESSES 155 (5th ed. 1989) ("[T]he rehabilitative ideal had great influence on American penology and corrections policies. In recent years, however, its influence has gone into eclipse . . . .") * * *.

violence against whites would be punished by black jurors; I hope that white jurors would do the same in cases involving white defendants. * * *

2. *How Do You Control Anarchy?*

Why would a juror who is willing to ignore a law created through the democratic process be inclined to follow my proposal? There is no guarantee that she would. But when we consider that black jurors are already nullifying on the basis of race because they do not want to send another black man to prison, we recognize that these jurors are willing to use their power in a politically conscious manner. Many black people have concerns about their participation in the criminal justice system as jurors and might be willing to engage in some organized political conduct, not unlike the civil disobedience that African-Americans practiced in the South in the 1950s and 1960s. It appears that some black jurors now excuse some conduct—like murder—that they should not excuse. My proposal, however, provides a principled structure for the exercise of the black juror's vote. I am not encouraging anarchy. Instead, I am reminding black jurors of their privilege to serve a higher calling than law: justice. I am suggesting a framework for what justice means in the African-American community. * * *

I hope that all African-American jurors will follow my proposal, and I am encouraged by the success of other grass-roots campaigns, like the famous Montgomery bus boycott, aimed at eliminating racial oppression. I note, however, that even with limited participation by African-Americans, my proposal could have a significant impact. In most American jurisdictions, jury verdicts in criminal cases must be unanimous. One juror could prevent the conviction of a defendant. The prosecution would then have to retry the case, and risk facing another African-American juror with emancipation tendencies. I hope that there are enough of us out there, fed up with prison as the answer to black desperation and white supremacy, to cause retrial after retrial, until, finally, the United States "retries" its idea of justice. * * *

NOTES AND QUESTIONS

1. *Confronting the idea of race-based jury nullification.* Try to identify the themes and techniques of Critical Race Theory that are at work in Professor Butler's analysis and proposal. What does he mean when he says that he "want[s] to dismantle the master's house with the master's tools?" Does that suggest a power and utility in the law that distinguishes CRT from critical legal studies?

2. *The legitimating role of black jurors.* One objection to the idea of targeted race-based jury nullification is that it violates the ideal of equality under the law. But, if that ideal is systematically inaccessible to people on the

basis of race, what is the justification for requiring those most injured by the discrimination to respect that ideal anyway? Consider in this connection the role of black jurors in assuring that the legal system is perceived to be fair. The Supreme Court has repeatedly emphasized this symbolic function, but it portrays the legal system in a way that is potentially directly contrary to a black juror's experience or judgment or will. On that basis, Professor Butler offers the following hypothetical:

> Let us assume that there is a black defendant who, the evidence suggests, is guilty of the crime with which he has been charged, and a black juror who thinks that there are too many black men in prison. The black juror has two choices: She can vote for conviction, thus sending another black man to prison and implicitly allowing her presence to support public confidence in the system that puts him there, or she can vote "not guilty," thereby acquitting the defendant, or at least causing a mistrial. In choosing the latter, the juror makes a decision not to be a passive symbol of support for a system for which she has no respect. Rather than signaling her displeasure with the system by breaching "community peace," the black juror invokes the political nature of her role in the criminal justice system and votes "no." In a sense, the black juror engages in an act of civil disobedience, except that her choice is better than civil disobedience because it is lawful. Is the black juror's race-conscious act moral? Absolutely. It would be farcical for her to be the sole color-blind actor in the criminal process, *especially when it is her blackness that advertises the system's fairness.*

Id. at 714 (emphasis added). Whether you agree with Professor Butler's proposal or not (and taking your own experience of race into account), what is the result when you conduct this thought-experiment for yourself?

3. *Jury instructions on jury nullification.* In *Sparf v. United* States, 156 U.S. 51 (1895), the Supreme Court formally protected the jury's power of nullification on the ground that an acquittal is unreviewable, but the Court did not endorse a requirement that judges inform juries of this prerogative. As a consequence, in most jurisdictions, defendants in criminal cases do not have a right to a jury instruction on this matter. *See, e.g., United States v. Dougherty*, 473 F.2d 1113, 1176 (D.C. Cir. 1972) ("what makes for health as an occasional medicine would be disastrous as a daily diet."). (a) What is the best rationale for preserving this discrepancy? Are you persuaded? (b) Not only is a criminal defendant not entitled to have the jurors instructed on their power of nullification, a criminal defense lawyer may violate the rules of professional conduct by telling them about it and arguing explicitly for nullification. *See, e.g., People v. Williams*, 25 Cal. 4th 441, 448, 21 P.3d 1209, 1212, 106 Cal. Rptr. 2d 295, 298 (2001) (counsel's jury nullification argument in closing considered a violation of the state's Rules of Professional Conduct). Realistically then, how would jurors *ever* become aware of their lawful prerogative and its sometimes proud history?

4. *Black Lives Matter: the racial architecture of American criminal law and policing.* The #BlackLivesMatter movement, organized in 2012 by Patrisse Cullors, Opal Tometi, and Alicia Garza, arose in response to the extrajudicial killings of African-Americans in encounters with police and vigilantes. Its focus rapidly expanded to highlight the full range of ways that Black lives are devalued in American law and society. One jurisprudential connection to Critical Race Theory would expose how existing law protects discriminatory practices without offering commensurate means to stop or remedy them. In Professor Butler's words,

> many of the problems identified by critics are not actually problems, but are instead integral features of policing and punishment in the United States. *They are how the system is supposed to work.* This is why some reforms efforts are doomed. They are trying to fix a system that is not actually broken. The most far-reaching racial subordination stems not from illegal police misconduct, but rather from legal police conduct.

Paul Butler, *The System Is Working the Way It Is Supposed To: The Limits of Criminal Justice Reform*, 104 GEO. L.J. 1419, 1425 (2016) (emphasis added). To prove the point, he analyzes Supreme Court cases protecting police practices with disproportionate impact on people of color including a "super power to kill," *Scott v. Harris*, 550 U.S. 372 (2007); a "super power to racially profile," *Whren v. United States*, 517 U.S. 806 (1996); and a "super power to arrest," *Atwater v. City of Lago Vista*, 532 U.S. 318 (2001). *Id.* at 1452–57. After *McCleskey*, *supra*, why should it matter that the impact of these "super power" decisions falls predominantly on African-Americans?

RICHARD DELGADO & JEAN STEFANCIC, *CRITICAL PERSPECTIVES ON POLICE, POLICING, AND MASS INCARCERATION*

104 GEO. L.J. 1531, 1537–39 (2016)

* * *

a. Many Jim Crows: Considering the Experience of Nonblack Minority Groups

Identifying parallels in the experience of nonblack groups would have been fairly simple * * *. For example, consider spatial relocation as a control device. Imprisonment removes African-Americans—particularly young men, often for drug offenses—from the street, the voting rolls, and the job market, thus reducing competition with whites over jobs, political power, and the distribution of genes in the next generation.[ ] Police stops and arrests of black males are, of course, a means of increasing their incarceration rate.[40]

An even greater percentage of the U.S. population (17.4 versus 13.2 percent for African-Americans in 2014),[ ] Latinos are also marginalized and disadvantaged, although in ways different from those haunting blacks. Statistics show that Latinos have low average family income, school completion rates, and access to health care.[42] They are, however, by and large a law-abiding group,[43] whose percentage of the U.S. prison population (just over fifteen) is slightly lower than their share of the overall population.[ ] Many are undocumented and hail from small villages that are socially cohesive;[45] they are thus strongly motivated to avoid coming to the attention of the authorities while working hard to support themselves and their families and to send a little money to relatives back home.[ ] The criminal justice system is therefore not a ready avenue for controlling their numbers and patterns of settlement. Instead, our system employs immigration quotas, detention, and deportation to achieve these ends.[47]

Imprisonment, then, removes blacks from the American mainstream, whereas deportations and their specter accomplish the same for Latinos.[ ] Even the resulting numbers are similar for both mechanisms.[ ] That these two mechanisms determine the fates of two large groups of near-equal size suggests that they have much the same social purpose—namely, control.

History reveals a similar pattern for Native Americans. The Discovery Doctrine[50] and, a few decades later, the Trail of Tears,[51] the Dawes Act,[52] and relocation to reservations[53] removed them from land and opportunities

---

[40] *See* Eisha Jain, *Arrests as Regulation*, 67 STAN. L. REV. 809, 817 (2015) * * *.

[42] *See, e.g.*, Anna Brown & Eileen Patten, *Statistical Portrait of Hispanics in the United States, 2012*, Pew Res. Ctr. (Apr. 29, 2014), [https://perma.cc/MCN4-57DJ].

[43] Communities with a high immigrant population almost invariably exhibit lower rates of crime than ones with high native populations. *See* John M. MacDonald & Robert J. Sampson, Opinion, *Don't Shut the Golden Door*, N.Y. Times (June 19, 2012), http://www.nytimes.com/2012/06/20/opinion/the-beneficial-impact-of-immigrants.html [http://perma.cc/Q3PK-TVHB].

[45] *See generally* RODOLFO F. ACUÑA, CORRIDORS OF MIGRATION: THE ODYSSEY OF MEXICAN LABORERS, 1600–1933 (2008) (noting that Mexican immigrants from a given village or family tend to follow the same pattern of migration in succeeding waves of migration).

[47] *See Barack Obama, Deporter-in-Chief*, Economist (Feb. 8, 2014), [https://perma.cc/6FD8-PRF9] (noting that the "deportation machine" tears families apart and "costs more than all other federal criminal law-enforcement areas combined"); Julia Preston, *Judge Orders Release of Immigrant Children Detained by U.S.*, N.Y. Times (July 25, 2015), http://www.nytimes.com/2015/07/26/us/detained-immigrant-children-judge-dolly-gee-ruling.html [https://perma.cc/8H8J-BN3Z] (explaining that Homeland Security officials initially detained immigrant families "to send a message to others in Central America to deter them from coming to the United States illegally").

[50] *See* Johnson v. M'Intosh, 21 U.S. 543, 567–68, 572–73 (1823) (declaring that European colonizers divided up the new lands and, to minimize conflict, tacitly agreed to a policy of granting control to those who arrived in a region first).

[51] *See* JUAN F. PEREA ET AL., RACE AND RACES: CASES AND RESOURCES FOR A DIVERSE AMERICA 207–13 (3d ed. 2015).

[52] *See id.* at 223–25, 852, 1051–53.

[53] *See id.* at 243–45.

that whites coveted. For Asians, Chinese Exclusion,[54] alien land laws,[55] and wartime removal of Japanese-Americans[56] achieved much the same. For Muslims and Middle Eastern people, close surveillance, profiling, and demands for immigration restriction send the message that they are unwelcome.[57] History, then, discloses five groups—blacks, Latinos, Native Americans, Asians, and Muslims—removed from the principal arenas of American life: one to large prisons, a second to foreign countries, a third to reservations located far from where their ancestors were buried, a fourth to wartime concentration camps, and a fifth barred entirely, but each dispossessed of heritage, freedom of movement, and opportunity to participate in American life.

Sometimes, examining the experience of a single group through a microscope enables one to discern important patterns. [In THE NEW JIM CROW: MASS INCARCERATION IN THE AGE OF COLORBLINDNESS, Michelle] Alexander shows how society employed slavery, the Black Codes, Jim Crow, and imprisonment to control blacks as the needs of the majority group shifted.[ ] At other times, however, looking at matters through a wider lens—a telescope rather than a microscope—brings broader patterns into view. Reviewing similarities among the experiences of each of the major groups of color could have brought to light common features calling for redress on a broader scale.

NOTES AND QUESTIONS

1. *"Crimmigration."* The LatCrit version of CRT exposes the legal component of race-based discrimination against Latino populations, with particular emphasis on the use of the criminal immigration ("crimmigration") system to detain, remove, and deport them.

> While America describes itself as the "nation of immigrants,"[ ] membership in America's "imagined community"[ ] has been directly correlated to white superiority.[ ] For centuries, immigration policy has been responsible for shaping our nation's composition.[ ] Through its laws of exclusion and inclusion, individuals are categorized and separated into "desirable" and "undesirable" groups, excluding the undesirables, while admitting the desirables into the social and

---

54 *See id.* at 395–400.

55 *See Terrace v. Thompson*, 263 U.S. 197, 222–24 (1923) (upholding a Washington state measure that effectively barred the Japanese from owning or leasing farms). *See generally* Jean Stefancic, *Terrace v. Thomson and the Legacy of Manifest Destiny*, 12 NEV. L. REV. 532 (2012) (reviewing the background of *Terrace*).

56 *See, e.g., Hirabayashi v. United States*, 320 U.S. 81, 93–114 (1943) (upholding wartime curfew); *Korematsu v. United States*, 323 U.S. 214, 217–19 (1944) (upholding wartime removal and detention).

57 *See* Wajahat Ali, *The Muslim Drill*, N.Y. Times (Dec. 9, 2015), http://www.nytimes.com/2015/12/09/opinion/the-muslim-drill.html [https://perma.cc/SF4C-6TP2].

> territorial fabric of the nation as members and citizens.[ ] Historically, categories of "undesirables" have included ethnicity, national origin, and race.[ ] * * *
>
> Despite its creation through race-neutral laws, crimmigration enforces racial politics as well as organizes and constructs racial identities through the laws and procedures it institutes and uses for detection, arrest, detention, and surveillance.[ ] Through the label of the "criminal alien," the law legitimates the exclusion and exploitation of Latinos, thereby, ensuring their subordination and marginal status.

Yolanda Vazquez, *Constructing Crimmigration: Latino Subordination in a "Post-Racial World,"* 76 OHIO ST. L.J. 599, 617–18, 650 (2015).

2. *Intersectionality*. It is a mistake to assess CRT as though it looked at the world through the single lens of race or ethnicity. To the contrary, it embraces "intersectionality," examining how certain grounds of oppression—like race, sex, national origin, sexual orientation, and class—reinforce one another. *See* KIMBERLÉ WILLIAMS CRENSHAW; MARI MATSUDA; RICHARD DELGADO; AND JEAN STEFANCIC, CRITICAL RACE THEORY: AN INTRODUCTION 51 (2001); Kimberlé Crenshaw, *Mapping the Margins: Intersectionality, Identity Politics, and Violence against Women of Color*, 43 STAN. L. REV. 1241, 1244 (1991) (arguing that people can experience discrimination in a variety of ways depending on their multiple identities). Nor does CRT concede that race exists independently of, or prior to, the law. The two are intrinsically related: "[R]ace itself is made meaningful by law, and law writ large is a reflection of racial-classification systems, racial ideology, and racial inequality." Laura E. Gomez, *Looking for Race in All the Wrong Places*, 46 LAW & SOC'Y REV. 221, 231 (2012).

3. *Scholarship, pedagogy, service*. From your perspective, which part of a law professor's job description, if any, requires her or him to avoid social activism? *See* Robert A. Williams Jr., *Vampires Anonymous and Critical Race Practice*, 95 MICH. L. REV. 741 (1997).

PART II

RECURRING ARGUMENT TYPES THROUGH THE CASES

■ ■ ■

CHAPTER NINE

"YOU CAN'T ARGUE LIKE THAT:" FAMOUS FALLACIES

■ ■ ■

"Logic takes care of itself; all we have to do is to look and see how it does it."

— Ludwig Wittgenstein

"Logic is neither an art nor a science but a dodge."

— Stendhal

"It would be a very good thing if every trick could receive some short and obviously appropriate name, so that when a man used this or that particular trick, he could at once be reproved for it."

— Arthur Schopenhauer

Orientation

It is a truth universally acknowledged that logic is the most powerful analytical system ever devised by human beings. We know this because every great civilization emerged *after* the development of formal logic, and, when civilizations have fallen, it is because they departed from a cultural commitment to logical thought. Some of the richest people in the world have argued that every schoolchild should be taught logic. Besides, everybody knows that geometry is better than philosophy because geometrical arguments can be proved logically, using accepted axioms and defined modes of inference. Without logic you can't make any sense at all, and, frankly, if you don't understand this point, you just haven't thought about it very deeply. We hope you agree with us, because we've put a lot of effort into writing just this one paragraph. . . .

Regrettably, there are many ways to be wrong, a handful of which are illustrated in every sentence in the preceding paragraph. There are for example errors of fact ("the *Dred Scott* decision is important because it established the principle of one-person-one-vote in American electoral law"), errors of interpretation ("*The Wizard of Oz* is actually a parable about the perils of home schooling"), and errors of language ("The statute as written would never pass constitutional mustard"). In this chapter, we focus on particular errors of logic—fallacies that have been recognized as formally fatal to an argument. It turns out that the common practices of inferring causation after the fact or generalizing from too few data or attacking the person who makes an argument rather than the argument itself or asserting the truth of a proposition because a rich person said it have been recognized as fallacies since ancient times. They have even been given names.

You might think of the materials that follow as arguments about arguments. Each case offers a specialized illustration of *non sequiturs*, *i.e.* conclusions that for one well-identified and abstract reason or another do not follow from the premises. Needless to say, the fact that an argument is fallacious doesn't mean that advocates don't make it or that courts don't incorporate it into their opinions. To the contrary, every famous fallacy discussed in this chapter appears in briefs and decided cases; indeed, as shown in some of the cases that follow, sometimes lawyers are required by their professional ethical obligations to make arguments that the logician must disparage or dismiss. The purpose here is both to sharpen the ability to hunt down the fallacy and to understand the limits of logic or formal reasoning in the first place, to appreciate the cryptic truth in Oliver Wendell Holmes' observation that "the life of the law has not been logic; it has been experience."

Post hoc, ergo propter hoc

Literally translated, the phrase *post hoc, ergo propter hoc* means "after this, therefore because of this" and refers to the fallacy of improperly inferring causation after the fact. Causation is not directly perceptible and generally involves some measure of inference, but it remains fallacious to infer causation from a merely chronological sequence. Consider for example the argument "you should drop out of college because it obviously worked for Bill Gates." Maybe someone should drop out of college, and maybe Bill Gates himself would look back fondly on his decision to drop out, but it is as fallacious to attribute his success to that decision as it would be to attribute his success to the fact that his parents owned a garage. In short, though proving causation is notoriously difficult and open, not just any technique will do.

Logic (and law) are considerably better at naming and shaming the improper ways to prove causation than they are at identifying which techniques work. The law—especially the law of evidence—is filled with examples of courts warning the members of a jury to watch out for *post hoc* inferences and other fallacious conclusions. But advocates sometimes persist, always at their peril, whether there's a jury in the case or not.

FEDERAL TRADE COMMISSION V. QT, INC.

512 F.3d 858 (7th Cir. 2008)

Wired Magazine recently put the Q-Ray Ionized Bracelet on its list of the top ten Snake-Oil Gadgets. * * * The Federal Trade Commission has an even less honorable title for the bracelet's promotional campaign: fraud. In this action under 15 U.S.C. §§ 45(a), 52, 53, a magistrate judge, presiding by the parties' consent, concluded after a bench trial that the bracelet's promotion has been thoroughly dishonest. The court enjoined the promotional claims and required defendants to disgorge some $16 million (plus interest) for the FTC to distribute to consumers who have been taken in.

According to the district court's findings, almost everything that defendants have said about the bracelet is false. Here are some highlights:

- Defendants promoted the bracelet as a miraculous cure for chronic pain, but it has no therapeutic effect.
- Defendants told consumers that claims of "immediate, significant or complete pain relief" had been "test-proven"; they hadn't.
- The bracelet does not emit "Q-Rays" (there are no such things) and is not ionized (the bracelet is an electric conductor, and any net charge dissipates swiftly). The bracelet's chief promoter chose these labels because they are simple and easily remembered—and because Polaroid Corp. blocked him from calling the bangle "polarized".
- The bracelet is touted as "enhancing the flow of bio-energy" or "balancing the flow of positive and negative energies"; these empty phrases have no connection to any medical or scientific effect. Every other claim made about the mechanism of the bracelet's therapeutic effect likewise is techno-babble.
- Defendants represented that the therapeutic effect wears off in a year or two, despite knowing that the bracelet's properties do not change. This assertion is designed to lead customers to buy new bracelets. Likewise the false statement that the bracelet has a "memory cycle specific to each individual wearer" so that only the bracelet's original wearer can experience pain relief is designed to increase sales by eliminating the second-hand market and "explaining" the otherwise-embarrassing fact that the buyer's friends and neighbors can't perceive any effect.

- Even statements about the bracelet's physical composition are false. It is sold in "gold" and "silver" varieties but is made of brass.

The magistrate judge did not commit a clear error, or abuse his discretion, in concluding that the defendants set out to bilk unsophisticated persons who found themselves in pain from arthritis and other chronic conditions.

Defendants maintain that the magistrate judge subjected their statements to an excessively rigorous standard of proof. Some passages in the opinion could be read to imply that any statement about a product's therapeutic effects must be deemed false unless the claim has been verified in a placebo-controlled, double-blind study: that is, a study in which some persons are given the product whose effects are being investigated while others are given a placebo (with the allocation made at random), and neither the person who distributes the product nor the person who measures the effects knows which received the real product. Such studies are expensive, not only because of the need for placebos and keeping the experimenters in the dark, but also because they require large numbers of participants to achieve statistically significant results. Defendants observe that requiring vendors to bear such heavy costs may keep useful products off the market (this has been a problem for drugs that are subject to the FDA's testing protocols) and prevent vendors from making truthful statements that will help consumers locate products that will do them good.

Nothing in the Federal Trade Commission Act, the foundation of this litigation, requires placebo-controlled, double-blind studies. The Act forbids false and misleading statements, and a statement that is plausible but has not been tested in the most reliable way cannot be condemned out of hand. The burden is on the Commission to prove that the statements are false. * * * Think about the seller of an adhesive bandage treated with a disinfectant such as iodine. The seller does not need to conduct tests before asserting that this product reduces the risk of infection from cuts. The bandage keeps foreign materials out of the cuts and kills some bacteria. It may be debatable *how much* the risk of infection falls, but the direction of the effect would be known, and the claim could not be condemned as false. Placebo-controlled, double-blind testing is not a legal requirement for consumer products.

But how could this conclusion assist defendants? In our example the therapeutic claim is based on scientific principles. For the Q-Ray Ionized Bracelet, by contrast, all statements about how the product works—Q-Rays, ionization, enhancing the flow of bio-energy, and the like—are blather. Defendants might as well have said: "Beneficent creatures from the 17th Dimension use this bracelet as a beacon to locate people who need pain relief, and whisk them off to their homeworld every night to provide help in ways unknown to our science."

Although it is true, as Arthur C. Clarke said, that "[a]ny sufficiently advanced technology is indistinguishable from magic" by those who don't understand its principles ("Profiles of the Future" (1961)), a person who promotes a product that contemporary technology does not understand must establish that this "magic" actually works. Proof is what separates an effect new to science from a swindle. Defendants themselves told customers that the bracelet's efficacy had been "test-proven"; that statement was misleading unless a reliable test had been used and statistically significant results achieved. A placebo-controlled, double-blind study is the best test; something less may do (for there is no point in spending $1 million to verify a claim worth only $10,000 if true); but defendants have no proof of the Q-Ray Ionized Bracelet's efficacy. The "tests" on which they relied were bunk. (We need not repeat the magistrate judge's exhaustive evaluation of this subject.) What remain are testimonials, which are not a form of proof because most testimonials represent a logical fallacy: *post hoc ergo propter hoc*. (A person who experiences a reduction in pain after donning the bracelet may have enjoyed the same reduction without it. That's why the "testimonial" of someone who keeps elephants off the streets of a large city by snapping his fingers is the basis of a joke rather than proof of cause and effect.)

To this defendants respond that one study shows that the Q-Ray Ionized Bracelet *does* reduce pain. This study, which the district court's opinion describes in detail, compared the effects of "active" and "inactive" bracelets (defendants told the experimenter which was which), with the "inactive" bracelet serving as a control. The study found that both "active" and "inactive" bracelets had a modest—and identical—effect on patients' reported levels of pain. In other words, the Q-Ray Ionized Bracelet exhibits the placebo effect. Like a sugar pill, it alleviates symptoms even though there is no apparent medical reason. The placebo effect is well established. * * * Defendants insist that the placebo effect vindicates their claims, even though they are false—indeed, especially *because* they are false, as the placebo effect depends on deceit. Tell the patient that the pill contains nothing but sugar, and there is no pain relief; tell him (falsely) that it contains a powerful analgesic, and the perceived level of pain falls. A product that confers this benefit cannot be excluded from the market, defendants insist, just because they told the lies necessary to bring the effect about.

Yet the Federal Trade Commission Act condemns material falsehoods in promoting consumer products; the statute lacks an exception for "beneficial deceit." We appreciate the possibility that a vague claim—along the lines of "this bracelet will reduce your pain without the side effects of drugs"—could be rendered true by the placebo effect. To this extent we are skeptical about language in *FTC v. Pantron I Corp.*, 33 F.3d 1088 (9th Cir. 1994), suggesting that placebo effects always are worthless to consumers. But our defendants advanced claims beyond those that could be supported by a placebo effect. They made statements about Q-Rays, ionization, and bio-energy that they knew to be poppycock; they stated that the bracelet remembers its first owner and won't work for anyone else; the list is extensive.

One important reason for requiring truth is so that competition in the market will lead to appropriate prices. Selling brass as gold harms consumers independent of any effect on pain. Since the placebo effect can be obtained from sugar pills, charging $200 for a device that is represented as a miracle cure but works no better than a dummy pill is a form of fraud. That's not all. A placebo is necessary when scientists are searching for the marginal effect of a new drug or device, but once the study is over a reputable professional will recommend whatever works best.

Medicine aims to do *better* than the placebo effect, which any medieval physician could achieve by draining off a little of the patient's blood. If no one knows how to cure or ameliorate a given condition, then a placebo is the best thing going. Far better a placebo that causes no harm (the Q-Ray Ionized Bracelet is inert) than the sort of nostrums peddled from the back of a wagon 100 years ago and based on alcohol, opium, and wormwood. But if a condition responds to treatment, then selling a placebo as if it had therapeutic effect directly injures the consumer.

Physicians know how to treat pain. Why pay $200 for a Q-Ray Ionized Bracelet when you can get relief from an aspirin tablet that costs 1¢? Some painful conditions do not respond to analgesics (or the stronger drugs in the pharmacopeia) or to surgery, but it does not follow that a placebo at any price is better. Deceit such as the tall tales that defendants told about the Q-Ray Ionized Bracelet will lead some consumers to avoid treatments that cost less and do more; the lies will lead others to pay too much for pain relief or otherwise interfere with the matching of remedies to medical conditions. That's why the placebo effect cannot justify fraud in promoting a product. * * *

Affirming the Consequent

Something may be a *sufficient* but not a *necessary* condition for something else to be true. Consider this syllogism:

A. If it rained during the night, the sidewalk is wet in the morning.

B. The sidewalk is wet this morning.

C. Therefore, it must have rained last night.

This is fallacious, even though both A and B may be true, because many things could make a sidewalk wet, like snow that melted, a lawn sprinkler badly aimed, or an errant pet. You cannot logically conclude from the fact that the sidewalk is wet that it must have rained last night. Rain is a sufficient but not a necessary precondition for making the sidewalk wet. Similarly, you don't have to be Aristotle to figure out that it's wrong to say "Pneumonia makes you cough; therefore, if you cough, you have pneumonia," as even the Texas Court of Criminal Appeals has recognized. *Paulson v. State*, 28 S.W.3d 570, 572 (Tex. Crim. App. 2000).

This logical mistake has a name—"affirming the consequent"—and typically takes the form, "if A, then B. B, therefore A." Problematic reasoning of this sort is common, even if the name of the fallacy—and its formal existence—are not commonly known. Courts routinely use and explain the fallacy to demonstrate the correctness of their analyses. For example, in *Stewart Foods v. Broecker*, 64 F.3d 141, 145 (4th Cir. 1995), a commercial debt case, the court found reversible error explicitly on this ground:

> The district court's reasoning was logically flawed. The district court noted that, under [the relevant statutory provisions,] the rejection of an executory contract creates a general unsecured claim. From this premise, the district court erroneously inferred that the existence of a general unsecured claim must imply the rejection of an executory contract. [Note 3]
>
> Note 3. This type of inference is an example of affirming the consequent, a classic form of invalid reasoning. Consider the following syllogism: (1) If A is true, then B is true. (2) B is true. (3) Therefore, A is also true. The conclusion that A is true does not logically follow from the premises. The district court's reasoning roughly reduces to the following syllogism: (1) If a debtor rejects a contract, then a general unsecured claim exists. (2) A general unsecured claim exists. (3) Therefore, the debtor must have rejected a contract. The district court's conclusion does not follow from its premises.

Notice from this passage that you don't actually need to know what an "unsecured claim" is as a matter of law to know that the district court's analysis—as described—is fallacious.

Advocates (and not just lower courts) periodically make this syllogistic mistake. In *United States v. Carlson*, 67 M.J. 693 (N-M.C.C.A. 2009), for example, the accused had been convicted in a court-martial of several violations including forcible sodomy. The United States Navy-Marine Corps Court of Criminal Appeals denied a motion for retrial, concluding that new DNA evidence did not sufficiently impeach the blood analysis presented at trial by a Mr. Phillip Mills, who was a chemist at the U.S. Army Criminal Investigation Laboratory. The argument on appeal turned on whether there was cross-contamination among DNA samples.

> The general thrust of the appellant's argument is that all of the new evidence leads to the conclusion that Mr. Mills cannot be trusted and, if he cannot be trusted, the members [of the court-martial] would conclude cross-contamination is either likely, or at least could not be ruled out. We reject this argument for several reasons. First, it represents a flawed logical syllogism incorporating the fallacy of affirming the consequent. That syllogism is: (1) a forensic serology examiner who cross-contaminates samples did not follow the rules; (2) Mr. Mills did not follow the rules; so, (3) Mr. Mills cross-contaminated the samples. Even those not readily conversant in formal logic would perceive the fatal flaw inherent in this argument. We decline to accept it.

Id. at 699. For other case examples of the fallacy of affirming the consequent, *see e.g., Gilliam v. Nev. Power Co.,* 488 F.3d 1189, 1197 (9th Cir. 2007) (tax law); *United Tel. Co. v. Federal Commc'ns Comm.*, 559 F.2d 720, 725–26 (D.C. Cir. 1977) (administrative law); *Topliff v. Wal-Mart Stores E. LP*, 2007 U.S. Dist. LEXIS 20533 (N.D.N.Y Mar. 22, 2007) (tort law); *City of Green Ridge v. Kreisel*, 25 S.W.3d 559, 564 (Mo. Ct. App. 2000) (zoning law).[1]

Denying the Antecedent

"Denying the antecedent" is a fallacy in the form "if A, then B. Not A, therefore not B." Consider the following example, which may speak to law students in particular:

A. If I am in medical school, I have too much reading to do.

B. I am not in medical school.

C. Therefore, I do not have too much reading to do.

Again both A and B may be true, but C is a fallacious conclusion: many students have too much to read, whether they are in medical school or not. The example provided by one federal district court focused not on heavy reading assignments but on the Queen of England: "If Queen Elizabeth is an American citizen, then she is a human being. Queen Elizabeth is not an American citizen. Therefore, she is not a human being." *Northwest Steel*

---

[1] Notice how the logical relation changes if the argument takes the form: "*Only* if A, then B. B, therefore A." In this case, "A" is made a necessary condition for "B" by using the phrase "only if." As a result, the existence or truth of "B" now allows you logically to infer the existence or truth of "A." The following argument is therefore valid and is not an example of affirming the consequent: "*Only if* a court has subject matter jurisdiction is its judgment enforceable. The court's judgment in *Gilliam v. Nevada Power Company* is enforceable. Therefore, the court in *Gilliam* had subject matter jurisdiction."

Erection Co. v. Zurich Am. Ins. Co., 2008 U.S. Dist. LEXIS 4082, 3–4 (D. Neb. Jan. 18, 2008).

The consequences of committing this fallacy are not always trivial or amusing:

WILSON V. CLARK

372 F. App'x 745 (9th Cir. 2010)

Robert Alan Wilson appeals the denial of his federal habeas petition challenging his conviction [in state court] for violating California Penal Code § 69, resisting an executive officer.[*] Wilson argues that there was insufficient evidence that Officer Ellison was performing a lawful duty, an element of § 69, to sustain a conviction. We reverse the [federal] district court and grant Wilson's petition for habeas relief.

The state court decision denying Wilson's sufficiency of the evidence claim was unreasonable * * *. The state court's conclusion that Officer Ellison was performing a lawful duty merely because Officer Ellison did not use excessive force in detaining Wilson effectively reads the "lawful duty" element out of § 69 and is thus contrary to [Supreme Court precedent]. [Note 1] The state court's decision would find an arbitrary, malicious, or even knowingly illegal action by the officer to be "lawful." Moreover, the decision relies on both the formal fallacy of denying the antecedent—concluding that because Officer Ellison's action was not unlawful due to the use of excessive force, the action must have been lawful—and on an illogical application of § 69 to the privilege to use force against an officer who is using excessive force.

> Note 1. This error is particularly problematic because the defendant's use of force is an element of § 69. The state court's reasoning would find lawful *any* action by an officer, no matter how egregious, as long as the officer refrained from using excessive force.

Argumentum ad hominem

Arguments *ad hominem* ("against the person") oppose a claim or proposition by attacking the person who made it. For example, suppose a scientist argued that "Professor Tirebeiter's theory of subatomic

* Section 69 of the California Penal Code provides:

Every person who attempts, by means of any threat or violence, to deter or prevent an executive officer from performing any duty imposed upon such officer by law, or who knowingly resists, by the use of force or violence, such officer, in the performance of his duty, is punishable by a fine not exceeding ten thousand dollars ($10,000), or by imprisonment in the state prison, or in a county jail not exceeding one year, or by both such fine and imprisonment.

symmetries is wrong because he writes incredibly lame poetry in his spare time." The validity of an argument may depend on a number of contextual factors but is not generally a function of who makes it or what their politics are or how they spend their leisure time. There are various types or formulations of *ad hominem* arguments, including the fallacy of personal attack or an appeal to personal ridicule. IRVING M. COPI & CARL COHEN, INTRODUCTION TO LOGIC 122–23 (9th ed. 1994). Compare argument by association ("You know who else made that argument—Hitler.")

Although egregious examples of such arguments are easily found and rejected, the law sometimes not only allows *ad hominem* arguments but requires them as part of the lawyer's ethical obligation to represent his or her clients' interests zealously. For example, it may be essential in a particular case to question the credentials of an opponent's expert witness, or to demonstrate that the lead plaintiff in a class action is not an adequate representative of the class, or to impeach an opposing witness's credibility. Each of these in effect requires an attack on the person in narrowly-defined circumstances. On which side of the line is the following closing argument from the defense attacking the prosecution's tactics in a criminal case?

> I think that's one of the shabbiest and shoddiest things I've seen in this building in years, and I would like them and [one of the prosecutors] to get up here and explain to you why he tried to deceive you. . . . Let him explain that to you, and I'll sit here with the rest of us and listen to his explanation, listen to his explanation as to why he tried to pull a fast one in this court on you people to try to convict these people. Is it that desperate? Did they need his scalp so bad? What, are they going to put a headline in their office? Is it going to help them get a better job when they leave the U.S. Attorney's office, to try to deceive you?

United States v. Howard, 774 F.2d 838, 847 (7th Cir. 1985). Generally, what would you look for in differentiating the acceptable *ad hominem* from the unacceptable kind?

COOK INV. CO. V. HARVEY

1975 WL 394 (N.D. Ohio 1975)

This cause is before the court upon a motion by plaintiffs to certify this cause as a class action pursuant to Rule 23 Federal Rules of Civil Procedure. All concerned have extensively briefed the matter. * * * As a general proposition relating to all class actions, Rule 23(a) provides:

> One or more members of a class may sue or be sued as representative parties on behalf of all only if (1) the class is so numerous that joinder of all members is impracticable (2) there are questions of law or fact common to the class (3) the claims or defenses of the representative parties are typical of the claims or

defenses of the class, and (4) the representative parties will fairly and adequately protect the interests of the class.

Although defendants oppose the motion on the basis that all of these elements are lacking the court has concluded that an extended discussion of each is not necessary.

There can be little question that the proposed class is too numerous to permit joinder as a practical alternative. It appears that the proposed class * * * contains nearly 3,000 members. Defendants' contention that the class will have to be reduced to only those who can show actual reliance on the allegedly misleading proxy statements is plainly wrong [under Supreme Court precedent].

There further can be little question as to the existence of common questions of law and fact. Cases such as this one, which allege the use of a deceptive or fraudulent proxy statement in connection with a merger, are particularly susceptible to class action treatment. Commonality of claims is not undermined by any need to show reliance, as noted above. Proof that the statements were material also does not show lack of commonality either because, if the alleged misstatements are material to one member of the class, they probably are material to all.

And it should be clear from the foregoing that plaintiffs' claims are typical of the class claims. Whatever the class of stock held, there can be no question that the proxy solicitation and the other allegedly misleading communications are claimed to have violated the same legal interests.

Defendants' principal argument seems to be that the plaintiffs will not fairly and adequately protect the interests of the class. Although defendants have filed several briefs on this motion, the court has had considerable difficulty in discerning the nub of their argument that plaintiffs are not proper representatives of the class. Unfortunately the court feels constrained to concur with plaintiffs that many of defendants' contentions amount to an *argumentum ad hominem*. Although, by its very nature, an argument attacking a plaintiff as an inadequate representative of a class is something of an *argumentum ad hominem,* this kind of dialectic requires something more than mere "poisoning the well." Once a plaintiff has shown the requisite stake in the outcome and that counsel is competent to conduct class action litigation, it is incumbent upon those opposing the class action to show *how* a plaintiff will not adequately protect the interests of the class. Defendants herein have made several accusations, but they have not shown how these accusations even if true somehow disable the plaintiff Sachnoff from representing the class. The court thus finds it very distressing that so much verbiage sheds so little light on an issue.

Defendants contend, e.g., that plaintiff Sachnoff has shown only a "superficial interest" in this lawsuit, that he failed to show any interest in [a] previous [related] lawsuit, that he concealed * * * his status as a "market maker", and that he is related by blood to one of the counsel for plaintiffs who was also counsel in [that] case. Even assuming that all of these contentions are true it is difficult for this court to understand how they disable plaintiff Sachnoff from being the class representative in the face of his ownership of 100 shares of stock and plaintiffs' counsel's apparent expertise in class action litigation.

The court has concluded, therefore, that it is not necessary to discuss defendants' contentions in any more detail because their contentiousness on every tertiary detail has led this court to the belief that these are tactics of obfuscation and delay. * * *

"The Strawman"

By definition, strawman arguments distort another's argument into a less defensible position and attack only the latter. Consider an argument in this form: "My opponent supports the Nuclear Non-Proliferation Treaty, but I can't understand why he would want to leave the United States completely defenseless like that." The treaty in question may be good or bad, effective or ineffective, but it distorts the opponent's position to recharacterize it as advocating the complete disarmament of the United States. (Of course, if the advocate actually did argue for complete unilateral disarmament, it's no strawman to point that out.) The strategy behind deploying the strawman is transparent: it is easier to defeat an argument for complete disarmament than it is to defeat the argument against the treaty itself.

WASHINGTON COUNTY V. KIEPER

148 Wis.2d 953, 438 N.W.2d 597 (1989)

Washington County appeals from an order dismissing its complaint against Kevin Kieper for operating a motor vehicle after revocation of his driver's license (OAR), contrary to sec. 343.44(1), Stats. The trial court concluded that the dirt bike Kieper was operating when he was arrested was not a motor vehicle for purposes of the OAR statute. We conclude, based on secs. 340.01(35) and 340.01(32), Stats., that the complaint sufficiently alleges that the dirt bike in this case is a motor vehicle for purposes of the OAR statute. Accordingly, we reverse and remand for further proceedings on the complaint.

The relevant facts are undisputed. Kieper was operating a dirt bike on a county highway[ ] when he was cited for OAR. His license had been revoked a few weeks earlier. According to Kieper's affidavits, the dirt bike in question was an off-road, racing motorcycle that lacked lights, warning devices, a speed indicator and appropriate tires. The record contains neither pictures, nor a more specific description of the vehicle.

Kieper pled no contest to OAR, without consulting with an attorney. The trial court found him guilty and imposed a forfeiture. Thereafter, Kieper retained counsel and made a motion to vacate his plea. The trial court granted Kieper's request.

Kieper then moved the trial court to dismiss the complaint, arguing that the dirt bike was unlicensable by statute, and operating it did not require a driver's license.[ ] Therefore, Kieper reasoned that it is not a violation of the OAR statute to operate a dirt bike on a highway after revocation. The trial court agreed, and dismissed the complaint. The county appeals.

* * * Because the question on appeal is whether the facts alleged by the county constitute a cause of action under a specific statute, we look to the county's complaint. In so doing, we bear in mind that when testing the sufficiency of a complaint, the facts as pled and all reasonable inference therefrom are accepted as true.[ ] Whether a complaint states a cause of action is a question of law which we determine without deference to the trial court's ruling. *Garvey v. Buhler*, 146 Wis.2d 281, 290, 430 N.W.2d 616, 620 (Ct.App.1988).

The county's complaint alleged that Kieper violated the provisions of sec. 343.44(1), Stats., when he operated his Yamaha dirt bike on a county highway after his license had been revoked. Section 343.44(1) provides that "[n]o person whose operating privilege has been duly revoked or suspended pursuant to the laws of this state shall operate a motor vehicle upon any highway in this state during such suspension or revocation. . . ." Neither party disputes that the complaint stated facts which alleged that Kieper operated some type of vehicle on a highway after revocation. The dispute is whether the dirt bike constituted a "motor vehicle" within the meaning of sec. 343.44(1).

When it dismissed the county's complaint, the trial court in essence determined that the facts alleged in the complaint did not state a violation of sec. 343.44(1), Stats., because a dirt bike is not a motor vehicle for purposes of the OAR statute.

The county contends that this is error, and that a dirt bike is in fact a motor vehicle. In support, the county cites the definitions of motor vehicle and motorcycle given in the motor vehicle code. Section 340.01(35), Stats., defines "motor vehicle" as "a vehicle which is self propelled. . . ." Section 340.01(32), provides the following definition of "motorcycle":

> "Motorcycle" means a motor vehicle, excluding a tractor or an all-terrain vehicle, which is capable of speeds in excess of 30 miles per hour with a 150-pound rider on a dry, level, hard surface with

> no wind, with a power source as an integral part of the vehicle, and which meets the conditions under par. (a) or (b):
>
> (a) Type 1 is a motor vehicle which meets either of the following conditions:
>
> 1. Is designed and built with 2 wheels in tandem and a seat for the operator, and may be modified to have no more than 3 wheels by attaching a sidecar to one side of the wheels in tandem without changing the location of the power source.

A reasonable inference from the complaint's allegation that Kieper was operating a Yamaha dirt bike is that it was a self-propelled machine pursuant to sec. 340.01(35), Stats., thus a motor vehicle. In addition, a reasonable inference from the complaint's allegation is that Kieper's dirt bike qualifies as the "motorcycle motor vehicle" described in sec. 340.01(32)(a) with two wheels in tandem and a seat for the operator. We therefore conclude from the allegations in the complaint that the dirt bike Kieper was operating at the time of his arrest was a motor vehicle.

Kieper responds to the county's contentions with a classic "strawman" argument. The strawman is that a cause of action for OAR requires a showing that the vehicle is required to be registered and licensed. The strawman is then knocked down by Kieper's argument that a dirt bike, such as the one he was operating, does not require registration under secs. 341.10(5) and (6), Stats.

Regardless of the correctness of this argument, the flaw is that a complaint alleging an OAR violation can be actionable in certain situations even if the motor vehicle need not be registered. Section 343.44(1), Stats., merely requires that the defendant have operated a motor vehicle on a Wisconsin highway while his or her operating privileges are revoked. There is no requirement that a motor vehicle be eligible for registration in order for it to qualify as a motor vehicle. For example, a farm tractor is a motor vehicle. Secs. 340.01(35) and (16), Stats. Yet, a farm tractor, used in certain operations, need not be registered. Sec. 341.05(7), Stats. This registration exemption does not mean that one could operate a farm tractor upon a highway while intoxicated and escape responsibility under the drunk driving laws. The same is true with respect to the OAR laws.

Kieper makes a similar "strawman" argument when he notes that an operator of a dirt bike need not be licensed. It is correct that the unlicensed operation of a dirt bike off the public highways does not violate sec. 343.05(1)(a), Stats., requiring that operators be licensed. In addition, dirt bikes operated under such conditions need not be registered. Sec. 341.10(6), Stats. However, if such a dirt bike qualifies as a motor vehicle, and if an unlicensed driver operates such a dirt bike upon the public highways, the prohibitions of the driver licensing statutes properly come into play. So do the OAR laws. * * *

Argumentum ad ignorantiam

Argumentum ad ignorantiam or "arguing from ignorance" is the fallacy of asserting that, because a proposition has not been proven to be false, it must be true, or conversely that because a proposition has not been proven to be true, it must be false. The lack of conclusive proof may be cause for caution in reaching a conclusion, but it does not logically prove anything. So for example, if someone started from the premise that aliens have never been captured and argued on that basis that extraterrestrial intelligent life therefore does not exist, she would be committing the fallacy of *argumentum ad ignorantiam*: the fact that no alien has yet been captured on Earth (conspiracy theories aside) cannot prove that there is no extraterrestrial intelligent life anywhere else in the universe. In a phrase variously attributed to William Cowper and Charles Darwin, among others, "the absence of proof is not the proof of absence." *Compare with* the observation of then-Secretary of Defense, Donald Rumsfeld, after failing to find evidence of Saddam Hussein's weapons of mass destruction in Iraq—"the absence of evidence is not evidence of absence."

ALABAMA-TOMBIGBEE RIVERS COALITION V. KEMPTHORNE

477 F.3d 1250 (11th Cir. 2007)

Two fish, or not two fish? That is the question. More specifically, are the Alabama sturgeon and the shovelnose sturgeon separate species? The answer lies primarily in the field of taxonomy, which one observer has noted "is described sometimes as a science and sometimes as an art, but really it's a battle-ground." BILL BRYSON, A SHORT HISTORY OF NEARLY EVERYTHING 437 (2003). The battle over the Alabama sturgeon has been more like the Thirty Years War. A scientist first classified this small freshwater fish found in the Mobile River Basin of Alabama as endangered in 1976. Three decades and three trips to this Court later the fight over whether the Alabama sturgeon is an endangered species continues. On one side are various business interests, including the Alabama-Tombigbee Rivers Coalition, and on the other are the Fish and Wildlife Service ["the Service"] and several federal officials involved with it. * * *

The Alabama sturgeon was once so plentiful that it was captured commercially. At the end of the nineteenth century, an estimated 20,000 of the fish were caught commercially, but its numbers have declined drastically and it is now thought to reside only in small portions of the Alabama River channel in south Alabama and downstream to the mouth of the Tombigbee River. The historic decline of the species—if it is a species—is due to a combination of over-fishing, dam construction for power production, dredging and channeling to improve navigation in the Mobile River Basin, and declines in water and habitat quality resulting from river and land management practices. *Id.* The Service began to study the decline of the Alabama sturgeon in 1980, four years after a scientist first classified it as endangered. [In its Final Rule, the Service ultimately did list the Alabama sturgeon as an endangered species, and the Alabama-Tombigbee River Coalition, a group of industries and associations opposed to the listing, sued to get that administrative decision overturned. After many years of litigation, the government was awarded a summary judgment, and the Coalition appealed.] * * *

The Coalition's first argument in support of its contention that the Service failed to consider the best scientific data is that it used "the older, subjective method of morphological taxonomy" instead of "the modern, objective science of genetics," to classify the Alabama sturgeon as a separate species. Genetics is the superior science, according to the Coalition, and in its view "[a]ll reliable genetic evidence" confirms that the Alabama sturgeon and the more-abundant shovelnose sturgeon are "genetically identical." * * *

The Service believes that instead of relying on genetics alone, "[t]he most scientifically credible approach to making taxonomic determinations is to consider all available data involving as many different classes of characters as possible." The class of relevant characters "includes morphological, karyological (chromosomal), biochemical (including DNA analysis and other molecular genetic techniques), physiological, behavioral, ecological, and biogeographic characters." The Service argues that it did consider genetics, and simply concluded that the available genetic studies could not definitively resolve the taxonomic status of the Alabama sturgeon, and that the balance of the relevant data supported classifying the fish as its own species. * * *

The Coalition overstates its case when it asserts that "[a]ll reliable genetic evidence" confirms that the Alabama sturgeon and the shovelnose sturgeon are "identical." The two types of fish are not "genetically identical." If two complete samples of animal genetic material truly are identical, then they did not just come from the same species, they came from the same animal (or perhaps from a pair of twins). What the evidence tendered by the Coalition actually reveals is that when scientists have examined particular segments of the mitochondrial cytochrome *b* gene, a gene that scientists often test to help them distinguish between vertebrate species, they have found that the cytochrome *b* samples taken from those particular genetic segments of the Alabama sturgeon are very similar—not identical, but very similar—to those taken from shovelnose sturgeon.

At several points in the Final Rule, the agency addressed the significance of genetic testing. It found that the genetic evidence was much less lopsided—and much more consistent with other taxonomic indicators—than the Coalition suggests. * * * [One particular study by Fain *et al.*] found small but consistent differences between Alabama and shovelnose sturgeon, though the study concluded that these differences were too insignificant to support the use of cytochrome *b* testing in criminal prosecutions [under the Endangered Species Act]. * * * After addressing individually each type of genetic study in the administrative record, the Service expressed its general doubt that examination of genetic data could definitively resolve the Alabama sturgeon's taxonomic status. * * * The Service specifically questioned the value of cytochrome *b* studies. * * *

The Coalition emphasizes the fact that the cytochrome *b* genes of the Alabama sturgeon and the shovelnose sturgeon are very similar. As it points out, the Service uses cytochrome *b* testing to criminally prosecute defendants for violating federal species protection laws. According to the Fain report, examination of the cytochrome *b* gene can be used to positively identify fifteen of the world's twenty-seven sturgeon and paddlefish species. The implication the Coalition wishes us to draw is that if the Service considers cytochrome *b* testing to be conclusive enough for criminal prosecutions, it ought to be conclusive enough for rule-making as well.

This argument misapprehends both the conclusions of the Fain study and the role of cytochrome *b* testing in criminal trials. The Fain study did not conclude that the Alabama sturgeon is not a distinct species. * * * When the cytochrome *b* genes of two species of sturgeon vary significantly from one another, but their intraspecific variation, or variance among individual members of each species, is low, the gene provides a useful marker to distinguish between the two types of sturgeon. Under these conditions, scientists can use cytochrome *b* testing to debunk a criminal defendant's false claim that caviar taken from an endangered species of sturgeon came from another nonendangered species.

The Fain report also states that cytochrome *b* testing cannot be used to distinguish between caviar from Alabama sturgeon and caviar from shovelnose sturgeon with sufficient reliability to be useful for forensic identification. The Coalition argues that because cytochrome *b* testing cannot reliably prove that the Alabama sturgeon is a distinct species, it must not be. Holding a position of centrality in that argument is the idea that inconclusive results of difference are conclusive proof of sameness. The reasoning is a species of *argumentum ad ignorantiam*, a fancier, and hence less denigrating, way of describing "an argument from ignorance." An argument from ignorance is "the mistake that is committed whenever it is argued that a proposition is true simply on the basis that it has not been proved false, or that it is false because it has not been proved true." IRVING M. COPI & CARL COHEN, INTRODUCTION TO LOGIC 93 (8th ed. 1990). Our point is that difficulty in proving a proposition (particularly by only one method) does not prove its opposite.

Of course, an argument from ignorance is not always a fallacy. Under some circumstances, such as where a scientific inquiry produces a complete knowledge base, or where an experiment is certain to reveal a fact if that fact exists and it fails to do so, the lack of positive evidence can prove a negative—the absence of evidence can be conclusive evidence. But not here. Examining one mitochondrial DNA gene hardly provides scientists with a total picture of the entire Alabama sturgeon genome, which would be necessary for a complete knowledge base. There are a multitude of mitochondrial and nuclear genes in every species of animal. That one particular gene does not demonstrably vary between two species is not, by itself, exceptional. Humans and chimpanzees, in genetic terms, are nearly 99% identical, yet we generally have little difficulty distinguishing between the two species.

Differences in the cytochrome *b* gene often correlate with speciation in vertebrates, but the Service had a reasonable basis for believing that gene would not serve as an effective, species-differentiating genetic marker in this case. Biogeographic evidence indicates that the Alabama and shovelnose sturgeon diverged only within the past 10,000 years, an eyeblink in evolutionary terms, and speciation can outpace differentiation of the cytochrome *b* marker which would explain the absence of a detectable difference. The rule making record included evidence of other separate species of fish with very little genetic divergence in the cytochrome *b* gene.

The decreased utility of the cytochrome *b* marker in younger species, combined with some evidence of divergence at other genetic markers, creates substantial doubt about whether genetic typing can conclusively resolve the proper taxonomic classification of the Alabama sturgeon. At a minimum, it justifies the Service's decision to examine the entirety of the taxonomic record, rather than ending its analysis with the DNA results.

"The Slippery Slope"

Slippery slope arguments—much favored by law professors, harried parents, and high school administrators across the country—conclude that an action (or proposition) is wrong, not in itself but because it inevitably leads to increasingly unacceptable events (or arguments). For example:

> If the government restricts civilian ownership of high-powered assault weapons, it will eventually lead to restrictions on all weapons and the violation of other rights protected by the Constitution, leading to the creation of a fascist state.

Slippery slope arguments are attractive rhetorically and are commonly used as a rationale for not doing the right thing now because we cannot be trusted to make reasonable distinctions later. The slippery slope can be defeated by offering a principle of moderation or differentiation that distinguishes the particular argument at issue from the parade of horribles at the bottom of the slope. *Compare with reductio ad absurdum*. R. BORK, THE TEMPTING OF AMERICA 169 (1990) ("Judges and lawyers live on the slippery slope of analogies; they are not supposed to ski it to the bottom.").

Consider for example, *Thomas v. Benchmark Ins. Co.*, 140 P.3d 438 (Kan. App. 2006), in which an insurance company declined to pay a claim because the death and injuries caused by an automobile accident were the result of the insured's intentional acts. The contract had provided that "[t]his coverage does not apply to bodily injury caused intentionally by you or any family member." Specifically, the insured had driven in excess of 100 miles per hour, fleeing from police, when the accident occurred. The court ruled in favor of the insurance company:

> [T]he dissent asks these questions: "[I]f we conclude that intentionally speeding bars coverage here, will it always do so or just sometimes? If just sometimes, we must then ask at what level of a driver's intentional speed do we conclude that death and injury are a probable and foreseeable result that precludes coverage? . . . Would it be a speed of 40, 60, 70, 90, or 100 m.p.h.?"
>
> These questions suggest a slippery slope argument. The fallacy in the slippery slope is the assumption that once something gets started there is no stopping. Nevertheless, intentional act questions are decided on a case-by-case basis. Moreover, the type of conduct that is sufficiently volitional to bar coverage is highly fact-based. Consequently, this slippery slope argument is not logically relevant to the resolution of this case.

Id. at 419. Similarly, in *Gonzales v. O Centro Espirita Beneficente Uniao do Vegetal*, 546 U.S. 418 (2006), a religious sect, UDV, sought to enjoin the federal government's ban under the Controlled Substances Act, 21 U.S.C. § 801 *et seq.* (2000 ed. and Supp. I), of the sacramental use of a tea containing a powerful hallucinogen. The lower courts granted relief under the Religious Freedom Restoration Act of 1993, § 3(b), 42 U.S.C.A. § 2000bb–1(b) (RFRA). Among other things, RFRA prohibits the federal government from substantially burdening a person's exercise of religion, "even if the burden results from a rule of general applicability," except when the Government can "demonstrat[e] that application of the burden to the person—(1) [furthers] a compelling governmental interest; and (2) is the least restrictive means of furthering that . . . interest." *Id.* The government conceded that the sect's use of the tea was a *bona fide* religious practice, a form of communion, but there was also no doubt that the active ingredient in the tea was a prohibited substance—like cocaine or peyote. The government argued that an exception for the sect would radically undermine the government's "compelling governmental interest" in the uniform application of the nation's drug laws. Chief Justice Roberts, writing for a unanimous court, acknowledged that there was precedent for the proposition that the government could

> demonstrate a compelling interest in uniform application of a particular program by offering evidence that granting the requested religious accommodations would seriously compromise its ability to administer the program. [But h]ere the Government's argument for uniformity is different; it rests not so much on the particular statutory program at issue as on slippery-slope concerns that could be invoked in response to any RFRA claim for an exception to a generally applicable law. The Government's argument echoes the classic rejoinder of bureaucrats throughout history: If I make an exception for you, I'll have to make one for everybody, so no exceptions."

Id. at 435–36. The government's slippery slope argument went nowhere with any member of the Court, and UDV was allowed to continue its use of the tea.

Forewarned is forearmed: an argument may have apparent rhetorical power on the surface—and be a constant feature of the political and legal landscape—but that does not mean it's sound.

"Begging the Question" (*petitio principii*)

"Begging the question" is a logician's way of conveying that an argument assumes the very thing to be proved. The word "beg" in this setting does not mean asking for something or leading to something. It means trivializing or impoverishing the argument. For example, the statement that "lying is wrong, because we should always tell the truth" begs the question, because the validity of the conclusion ("lying is wrong") is assumed in the premise ("because we should always tell the truth."). *See* Jamie Whyte, CRIMES AGAINST LOGIC 108 (2005) ("The fallacy of begging the question consists in taking for granted precisely what is in dispute, in passing off as an argument what is really no more than an assertion of your position.")[2]

The overwhelming popular usage—that "begging the question" is the same as raising or inviting or even necessitating a question—is incorrect, and, like fingernails on a blackboard, it can irritate people who actually know what it means. *See* William Safire, *On Language: Take My Question Please!*, NEW YORK TIMES (July 26, 1998). It is wrong to say for example: "The students' destructive behavior during Spring Break begs the question:

---

[2] The fallacy of begging the question is related to but distinct from circular reasoning (*circulus in demonstrando*), which is "[t]he basing of two conclusions each upon the other. That the world is good follows from the known goodness of God; that God is good is known from the excellence of the world he has made." H.W. FOWLER, MODERN ENGLISH USAGE 599–600 (1926).

is there anything we can do about it?" The students' destructive behavior may force or invite us to think about the question of what to do about it, but it does not logically "beg" that question. Or consider two statements in isolation:

> (1) "The President's health care law may be constitutional as a matter of law, but that just begs the question whether it will actually improve people's health."
>
> (2) "To argue that the President's health care law is constitutional because it falls within the congressional taxing power laid out in the Constitution is to beg the question."

Which of these really is an example of begging the question and which is an example of the how that idea is misunderstood?

These examples of begging the question may suggest that it's relatively easy to spot when it happens, but that's not true:

> To beg the question is to assume the truth of what one seeks to prove, in the effort to prove it. That would seem to be a silly mistake, evident to all—but how silly or obvious the mistake is depends largely on the way in which the premisses [*sic*] of the argument are formulated. Their wording often obscures the fact that buried within one of the premisses [*sic*] assumed lies the conclusion itself. . . . Those who fall into this error often do not realize that they have assumed what they set out to prove. The fact of that assumption can be obscured by confusing and therefore unrecognized synonyms, or by a chain of intervening argument. Every petitio is a circular argument, but the circle that has been constructed may—if it is large or fuzzy—go quite undetected. . . . Powerful minds are sometimes snared by this fallacy. * * *

IRVING M. COPI & CARL COHEN, INTRODUCTION TO LOGIC 102 (8th ed., 1990). The accusation that an argument begs the question appears more frequently in Supreme Court dissents than in majority or plurality opinions. (Why might this be so?) For example, in *Gonzales v. Oregon*, 546 U.S. 243 (2006), the Supreme Court ruled that the Controlled Substances Act, *supra*, did not authorize the Attorney General of the United States to prohibit doctors from prescribing regulated drugs for use in physician-assisted suicide, as authorized by the Oregon Death With Dignity Act. In dissent, Justice Scalia wrote that

> [t]he Court concludes that the Attorney General lacked authority to declare assisted suicide *illicit* under the Controlled Substances Act (CSA), because the CSA is concerned only with "*illicit* drug dealing and trafficking," (emphasis added). This question-begging conclusion is obscured by a flurry of arguments that distort the

> statute and disregard settled principles of our interpretive jurisprudence.

546 U.S. at 275. Assuming without agreeing that Justice Scalia's description of the majority's approach in the first sentence is accurate, how exactly did the majority beg the question?

The fallacy of assuming the premise in the conclusion is illustrated by *Rosen v. Unilever, infra.*

Fallacies of Composition and Division

The fallacy of composition consists in the inference that a statement that is true of a part of something is necessarily true of the whole thing: "All atoms are invisible. I am made of atoms. Therefore I am invisible." The fallacy of division is the reverse of that and consists in assuming that something true of the whole must be true of each constituent part: "As a species, human beings are capable of language. Human beings are made of atoms. Therefore atoms are capable of speech." Plato's *Republic* tries to construct the institutions of the ideal state by reference to the characteristics of virtuous human beings. If Plato's argument is persuasive, that is despite the fallacy of composition at its heart.

ROSEN V. UNILEVER U.S., INC.

2010 WL 4807100 (N.D. Cal., May 3, 2010)

Amnon Rosen ("Plaintiff") brings this putative class action against Unilever United States, Inc. ("Defendant"), alleging violations of California Consumers Legal Remedies Act ("CLRA"), Unfair Competition Law ("UCL"), and False Advertising Law ("FAL"). Plaintiff alleges that Defendant has misrepresented the ingredients of its butter-substitute product through its advertising and product labeling. * * * In [its] Complaint, * * * Plaintiff alleges as follows:

> Plaintiff is a California citizen living in Santa Clara County. Defendant is an international consumer products company based in Englewood Cliff, New Jersey. Defendant produces the product "I Can't Believe It's Not Butter" ("ICBINB"). ICBINB is a "soft spread" that is often used as a substitute for butter in cooking. Between June 2004 and present day, Defendant used marketing, advertising, and labeling to misrepresent that ICBINB is nutritious, healthy to consume, and better than butter and similar products. The front and side of the ICBINB packaging states "Made With A Blend of Nutritious Oils." However, ICBINB contains partially hydrogenated oil. Partially hydrogenated oil is

> an artificial, manmade substance that has no nutritional value and is known to cause a number of health problems.

* * * Presently before the Court is Defendant's Motion to Dismiss. Pursuant to Federal Rule of Civil Procedure 12(b)(6), a complaint may be dismissed against a defendant for failure to state a claim upon which relief may be granted against that defendant. Dismissal may be based on either the lack of a cognizable legal theory or the absence of sufficient facts alleged under a cognizable legal theory. For purposes of evaluating a motion to dismiss, the court "must presume all factual allegations of the complaint to be true and draw all reasonable inferences in favor of the nonmoving party." Any existing ambiguities must be resolved in favor of the pleading. However, mere conclusions couched in factual allegations are not sufficient to state a cause of action. Courts may dismiss a case without leave to amend if the plaintiff is unable to cure the defect by amendment. * * * Defendant moves to dismiss Plaintiff's Complaint on multiple grounds. * * *

Here, Plaintiff alleges as follows:

> Defendant [is] misleading consumers about the nutritional and health qualities of its product. During the period from June 2004 to the present . . . Defendant made misleading statements that its Product was nutritious, healthy to consume, and, consequently, better than similar products such as butter.
>
> Defendant conveyed this message through a multi-million dollar advertising campaign . . . [and] stated prominently in bold-face type directly on the front and side of its Product containers that the Product was "Made with a Blend of Nutritious Oils." This message . . . is misleading and deceptive because Defendant's Product contains a highly unhealthy, non-nutritious oil known as partially hydrogenated oil.
>
> In combination with the misleading claims made on its packaging, Defendant has conducted multi-million dollar, widespread marketing campaigns to deceptively convey the message that its Product is nutritious and healthy. For instance, during the Class Period Defendant ran a marketing campaign entitled "Big Fat Truth" in which Defendant deceptively portrayed its Product as nutritious and healthy. As part of the "Big Fat Truth" marketing campaign, Defendant states on its website that "our soft spreads are a better nutrition option than butter because they are made with a blend of nutritious oils, including canola and soybean. . . ." Defendant also proclaims on its website that the Product is "made with nutritious plant oils like soybean and canola." These statements are deceptive and misleading given that ICBINB contains dangerous, non-nutritious, unhealthy partially hydrogenated oil.

(Complaint ¶¶ 1–4, 15.) * * *

Defendant moves to dismiss Plaintiff's Complaint for failure to state a claim. A complaint must plead "enough facts to state a claim for relief that is plausible on its face." *Bell Atl. Corp. v. Twombly,* 550 U.S. 544, 570 (2007). A claim is plausible on its face "when the plaintiff pleads factual content that allows the court to draw the reasonable inference that the defendant is liable for the misconduct alleged." *Ashcroft v. Iqbal,* 556 U.S. 662, 678 (2009). Thus, "for a complaint to survive a motion to dismiss, the non-conclusory "factual content," and reasonable inferences from that content, must be plausibly suggestive of a claim entitling the plaintiff to relief." *Moss v. U.S. Secret Serv.,* 572 F.3d 962, 969 (9th Cir. 2009).

In *Iqbal,* the Supreme Court set forth a two-pronged approach by which courts are to review the sufficiency of allegations in a complaint. First, a court reviews the complaint and discounts any allegations that amount to little more than "threadbare recitals of the elements of a cause of action, supported by mere conclusory statements." *Iqbal,* 556 U.S., at 678. Second, the court examines the remaining allegations to determine whether they "state a plausible claim for relief." *Id.* at 1950. A claim is plausible, as opposed to merely possible, if its factual content "allows the court to draw the reasonable inference that the defendant is liable for the misconduct alleged." *Id.* at 1949. In contrast, a complaint alleging facts that are "merely consistent with a defendant's liability, stops short of the line between possibility and plausibility of entitlement to relief." *Id.*

Here, Plaintiff's Complaint rests on the allegation that Defendant's use of the word "nutritious" with respect to the product is false and misleading. Plaintiff alleges that the statement "Made with a Blend of Nutritious Oils" is printed on the product label and is made in advertisements. In addition, Plaintiff alleges that Defendant advertises that the product is "a better nutrition option than butter." The gravamen of Plaintiff's allegations is that these statements are misleading because they imply that the product contains *only* nutritious oils. Plaintiff alleges that the product contains partially hydrogenated oil and that type of oil is "not nutritious or healthy." Therefore, Plaintiff alleges that the "nutrition" representations are false or misleading. In substance, Plaintiff alleges that the content of the blend of ingredients in the product remove it from being in the category of nutritious products. The implausibility of Plaintiff's allegations can more readily be seen if the allegation are expressed as a categorical syllogism:[8]

> *For the representation "blend of nutritious oils" to be true, all constituent oils must be nutritious. One of the constituent oils in*

---

[8] A "categorical syllogism" is one in which the conclusion follows from the relationship between the concepts in the premises and their membership in certain categories. *See, e.g.*, Aylett v. Secretary of HUD, 54 F.3d 1560, 1567–68 (10th Cir. 1995).

the product [partially hydrogenated oil] is not nutritious. Therefore, the product representation is false.

Applying the first prong of *Iqbal* to Plaintiff's claim, the Court finds that Plaintiff's major premise (that all constituent oils must be nutritious in order for the blend to be nutritious) is merely a conclusion. If essential elements of a claim are supported by a conclusion, the complaint is plausible only if the conclusion is supported by allegations of fact elsewhere in the complaint. Here, Plaintiff does not allege any facts with respect to what a "blend" must contain in order to be "nutritious." Furthermore, since Plaintiff concedes that some of the oils in the blend are nutritious, Plaintiff fails to allege any facts to support the conclusion that the nutritious nature of the "blend of nutritious oils" is negated because a partially hydrogenated oil is blended with them.

Similarly, Plaintiff's minor premise (that partially hydrogenated oil is not nutritious) is a mere conclusion that lacks factual support. Plaintiff's allegation that partially hydrogenated oil is not nutritious is devoid of any allegations of facts to support that allegation. Moreover, this unsupported conclusion is contrary to [Federal Food, Drug, and Cosmetic Act] regulations that define trans fat as a "nutrient" whose quantity is required to appear on food labels. It thus appears that Plaintiff is not able to allege truthfully that partially hydrogenated oil is not a nutrient.

Applying the second prong of *Iqbal,* even if the Court assumes the truth of Plaintiff's premise that partially hydrogenated oil is not a nutrient, and examines the relationship between that premise and the allegedly false representations, the Court finds an implausible legal theory. Plaintiff's reasoning is that the inclusion of partially hydrogenated oil in the blend makes the "nutritious" representations false and misleading. Plaintiff commits three logical fallacies: *petitio principii* (begging the question), "fallacy of composition" and the "fallacy of division."

The fallacy of *petitio principii* or begging the question, is committed when one attempts to establish a basis for a conclusion by constructing a premise that assumes that the conclusion has already been established. Plaintiff incorporates this fallacy in his major premise: *For the representation "blend of nutritious oils" to be true, all constituent oils must be nutritious*. The premise that every constituent oil must be nutritious in order to truthfully represent that the blend of oils is nutritious is alleged by Plaintiff without ever establishing its truth. Then, in the conclusion (*Therefore, the product representation is false*) this unsupported premise is used to support the very conclusion that is assumed in the premise.

The "fallacy of composition" is committed when one reasons from the properties of a "part" to the properties of the "whole." The fallacy is sometimes referred to as "the whole is nothing more than the sum of its parts." The reasoning is fallacious because things joined together may have different properties as a whole than they do separately. Here, Plaintiff's allegations are based on the premise that the use of a non-nutritious oil, irrespective of amount, in a blend of otherwise nutritious oils makes the "blend" non-nutritious. Besides the lack of any facts to support this transformation, it does not logically follow from the fact that one oil in a blend does not have the nutritional properties of other nutritious oils, that the blend is rendered devoid of being nutritious.

The "fallacy of division" is the reverse of the fallacy of composition. It is committed when one argues that what is true of a whole must also be true of its parts. To reason that since a blend of oils is represented as being nutritious, if partially hydrogenated oil is part of the blend, it must also be nutritious commits the fallacy of division. Inherent in Plaintiff's allegations is the fallacious reasoning that in order to be a part of what is represented to be a "blend of nutritious oils," partially hydrogenated oil must have the same characteristics of the other oils in the blend.

Thus, even presuming the truthfulness of Plaintiff's allegations about the nature of partially hydrogenated oil, the Court concludes that the illogical relationships Plaintiff draws between the nature of partially hydrogenated oil and the representations Defendant makes about the blend of oils renders Plaintiff's complaint implausible on its face. *See Iqbal,* 129 S. Ct. at 1949 (citing *Twombly,* 550 U.S. at 570). Accordingly, the Court grants Defendant's Motion to Dismiss on the ground that Plaintiff fails to state facts constituting a plausible legal claim. Since the Court finds that there is no cure for the lack of logical tie discussed above, any amendment would be futile. * * *

The False Dilemma

The "False Dilemma" arises when an advocate claims that there are only a few (usually two) alternatives, when there are considerably more options in fact. The common argument-type "You're either with me or you're against me" is better as exhortation than as argument, because one could agree with the speaker and "be with [him]" in some matters and not in others. Truly accomplished propagandists understand this particular technique very well. Consider the following passage from Hitler's *Mein Kampf*:

> The task of propaganda is, for example, not a weighing of the various rights, but the exclusive emphasis of the one advocated by it. It has not to inquire objectively into the truth, so far as it favors the other sides, in order to represent it to the masses in doctrinary honesty, but it has to serve its own side continuously. . . . This feeling [of the masses] is not complicated, but very simple and conclusive. There are not many differentiations, but a positive or

> a negative, love or hate, right or wrong, truth or lie, but never half so and half so, or partially, etc.

Generally, the false dilemma arises in a case whenever an argument assumes that there are only two possible results, when there are actually several defensible outcomes. But sometimes, the false dilemma appears in the facts of the case. In *Atkinson v. Kirchoff Enterprises Inc.*, 181 Ga. App. 139, 351 (S.E.2d 477), for example, a customer sued a store owner for personal injuries she had suffered when she fell on construction debris in front of the store, on her way to Sears. The lower court granted summary judgment in favor of the store owner, and the customer appealed. The Georgia Court of Appeals reversed on the ground that there was a question of fact that precluded summary judgment, namely the relative knowledge of the store owner and the customer about the existence of a sharp object in the debris and the danger posed by that debris. The dissent smelled a false dilemma:

> By appellant's own admission, there was no pressing reason, no emergency, which required her to visit Sears on that day and at that time. Nor does the record support appellant's argument that there was coercion prompting which path she was required to take to reach her destination. Appellant's automobile was parked nearby, enabling her to drive to Sears; appellant could have exited appellee's store by means of the other main exit and approached Sears from the opposite side; or appellant could have "picked" her way between the cars parked between the sidewalk and the street, assuming there was not enough space at the rear of the cars in the parking spaces to walk behind them without stepping on the trafficked street itself. Or, as the special concurrence suggests, appellant could have postponed her visit to Sears to a more propitious time.
>
> By the characterization of the decision appellant faced as a choice between walking in a heavily trafficked road or traversing the building debris, appellant and the special concurring members of the Court seek to represent appellant as having been placed between the horns of a dilemma. It is a false dilemma, unwarranted by the facts, and thus constitutes a material fallacy to appellant's argument. Rather than indicating a decision coerced by circumstances, appellant's actions indicate that her decision to visit Sears by traversing appellee's debris-covered sidewalk was made strictly as a matter of personal convenience, not necessity. Appellant chose to hazard the danger of the building debris because it was more convenient to her than the more time-consuming alternatives available.

Id. at 144–45.

Fallacies of Interrogation

Declarative arguments are not the only things that can be fallacious. Questions themselves can be fallacious, especially to the extent that they have compound elements within them. The "Fallacies of Interrogation" refer to questions that either (a) contain multiple parts, each of which may require separate treatment, as in "Did you conspire with the defendant to rob the bank and drive the getaway car?;" or (b) requires acceptance of an implicit and unrelated presupposition, as in the classic example, "Have you stopped beating your wife?" The federal rules of civil procedure and of evidence govern depositions during discovery and direct and cross-examination at trial, and questions posed to witnesses that commit these fallacies of interrogation are objectionable, and the lawyer posing them may be required to reframe them so as to remove the multiplicity and ambiguity.

UNITED STATES V. EDDY

737 F.2d 564 (6th Cir. 1984)

Terrance Alan Eddy appeals his conviction for perjury pursuant to 18 U.S.C. § 1623(a):

> Whoever under oath . . . in any proceeding before . . . any court of the United States knowingly makes any false material declaration . . . shall be fined not more than $10,000 or imprisoned not more than five years, or both.

* * * The statements which were the basis of the perjury indictment were made in a hearing in chambers where the United States sought to prove that Eddy had used an Ohio State University College of Medicine diploma and an Ohio State University college transcript in efforts to enlist as a physician in the United States Navy. * * *

Here, Eddy argues the United States failed to prove that his declarations were false. In response it is argued that Eddy's claims that his declarations were literally true provide no protection from a perjury conviction because the falsity of the statements and the questions were sufficiently clear to withstand a vagueness challenge.

We address first the argument by Eddy that his testimony was the literal truth. In *Bronston v. United States*, 409 U.S. 352 (1973), the Court held a witness may not be convicted of "perjury for an answer, under oath, that is literally true but not responsive to the question asked and arguably misleading by negative implication." The Court noted that it is the "lawyer's responsibility to recognize [evasive testimony] and to bring the witness back to the mark, to flush out the whole truth with the tools of adversary examination." Also rejected was the claim that a perjury conviction could be founded upon an attempt by a witness to mislead his examiner.

> A jury should not be permitted to engage in conjecture whether an unresponsive answer, true and complete on its face, was intended to mislead or divert the examiner; the state of mind of the witness is relevant only to the extent that it bears on whether "he does not believe [his answer] to be true."

Bronston, 409 U.S. at 359. The Court dismissed the contention that the perjury statute could be broadly construed to apply to a situation where a witness makes "affirmative statements of one fact that in context constituted denials by negative implication of a related fact." It noted the perjury statute was not intended to cover unresponsive testimony that is untrue only by "negative implication," despite the misleading nature of such testimony. "It does not matter that the unresponsive answer is stated in the affirmative, thereby implying the negative of the question actually imposed." 409 U.S. at 362. Where a witness initially succeeds in avoiding direct answers to an examiner's questions, it is the questioner's burden "to pin the witness down to the specific object" of his inquiry.

Although *Bronston* dealt with a conviction under 18 U.S.C. § 1621, its reasoning has been extended to 18 U.S.C. § 1623, the provision involved here. As the Third Circuit has noted, in perjury cases, "[n]o guessing is tolerated [in the drafting of a perjury indictment] and the indictment must set out the allegedly perjurious statements and the objective truth in stark contrast so that the claim of falsity is clear to all who read the charge." *United States v. Tonelli*, [577 F.2d 194 (3d Cir. 1978)], at 195. In order to sustain a perjury conviction, the questions and answers which support the conviction must demonstrate both that the defendant was fully aware of the actual meaning behind the examiner's questions and that the defendant knew his answers were not the truth. *Bronston, supra*, 409 U.S. at 358–59. "Once a defendant raises the affirmative defense of his belief in the truth of a statement, the burden is on the government to disprove this belief beyond a reasonable doubt." *United States v. Stassi*, 443 F.Supp. 661, 666–67 (D.N.J. 1977). Vague and ambiguous questions are not acceptable.

Count I of the indictment charges that Eddy's declarations were false because he did contact the Navy Recruiting District in Jacksonville, Florida, claiming to be a doctor, and "did submit a diploma from the Ohio State University College of Medicine and [an] official college transcript." Eddy, however, argues he spoke the literal truth because, though he concedes contacting the Navy, he maintains that he did not submit an "official" medical diploma or an "official" college transcript. He claims that the documents he submitted were novelty items not meant to be taken seriously. Therefore, according to Eddy, his negative response to the prosecutor's questions were the literal truth. Indeed, the record supports

Eddy's claims. At the suppression hearing in question, the following exchange occurred between Eddy and the prosecutor concerning Eddy's activities in Florida in trying to join the Navy.

> PROSECUTOR: Are you the same Terrance Alan Eddy who, on March 20, 1981, contacted the Navy Medical Programs Recruiter for the Navy Recruiting District of Jacksonville, Florida, claiming to be a doctor graduated from the Ohio State University of Medicine and expressing a desire to join the Navy as a doctor; and as proof of your credentials submitted a diploma from the Ohio State University College of Medicine and official college transcript?
>
> THE COURT: Do you want to confer with Mr. Johnson [Eddy's trial counsel]?
>
> DEFENDANT: No, sir.
>
> PROSECUTOR: That's on or about March 20, 1981.
>
> DEFENDANT: My attempt to join the Navy, yes, but conferring myself as a physician, no.
>
> PROSECUTOR: Your Honor, may I ask with regard to his understanding of that question?
>
> THE COURT: Yes, sir. Repeat that.
>
> PROSECUTOR: Mr. Eddy, do you understand what I asked you?
>
> DEFENDANT: (Nodded his head)
>
> PROSECUTOR: Okay, I will repeat the question. Are you the same Terrance Alan Eddy that on or about March 20, 1981, contacted the Navy Medical Programs Recruiter for the Navy Recruiting District of Jacksonville, Florida, claiming to be a doctor graduated from the Ohio State University School of Medicine and expressing a desire to join the Navy as a doctor; and as proof of your credentials, provided a diploma from the Ohio State University College of Medicine and an official college transcript?
>
> DEFENDANT: (There was no response.)
>
> THE COURT: If you want to confer with Mr. Johnson, sir, the Court will give you an opportunity.
>
> DEFENDANT: No, sir. It's a loaded question.
>
> THE COURT: Yes, sir.
>
> DEFENDANT: The reason being I applied to the Navy but not as a physician. I went, I wanted to go into the Navy.
>
> PROSECUTOR: Mr. Eddy, you understand my question?
>
> THE COURT: Let him answer the question.

PROSECUTOR: I am sorry.

DEFENDANT: I wanted to go into the Navy into the medical program, but not as a doctor. I never told them I was a doctor. I told them I wanted to go into their medical program because I understood they had a very good program. I did not apply as a physician.

PROSECUTOR: Did you represent yourself as a physician?

DEFENDANT: Not unless they took it different than I did.

PROSECUTOR: Submit false documentation?

DEFENDANT: Do they have false documentation that I did?

PROSECUTOR: I asked you the question.

DEFENDANT: No, sir.

THE COURT: You didn't submit a diploma to them?

DEFENDANT: It is not my recollection, Your Honor.

THE COURT: Read specifically.

PROSECUTOR: Pardon me?

THE COURT: Read specifically the documentation he was supposed.

PROSECUTOR: The documentation I am talking about, if we are talking about the entire documentation that was submitted, a statement of personal history, a diploma from the Ohio State University College of Medicine, official college transcripts. Those are the pertinent documentation. There is other documentation that was submitted I will read the Court, if the Court would like to hear it.

THE COURT: That is sufficient. Do you understand the question, sir?

DEFENDANT: Yes, sir.

THE COURT: Do you desire to talk to Mr. Johnson, your attorney?

DEFENDANT: I am fine, sir.

THE COURT: Okay.

PROSECUTOR: One other question, Your Honor.

THE COURT: Wait just a moment.

DEFENDANT: I have one answer to that. You have brought in as your witness yourself, a registrar, I believe, from Ohio State University who has stated I am not a doctor and I am not certified

> as a physician. If I am not certified as a doctor, how would I have an official transcript?
>
> PROSECUTOR: Mr. Eddy, I simply asked you a question. You answered it.

As is evident from this dialogue, which occurred shortly before the testimony which was the basis of Count I of the perjury indictment, Eddy attempted to communicate that the documentation submitted to the Navy was falsified. Later it was admitted in the hearing that there was no evidence to rebut Eddy's claim that the documents were false. This admission resulted in the denial of the request to question Eddy, before the jury, concerning the questions which were the basis of Count I.

At the perjury trial, all witnesses agreed with Eddy's assertion that the documents he presented were not authentic. The Assistant United States Attorney in conceding this fact at a bench conference during the trial, stated:

> I don't think there is any doubt that the testimony adduced at trial has shown in fact that was not an actual OSU diploma and those are not actual copies of OSU transcripts. I obviously concede that. But the questions were asked at trial, the questions were asked at trial based upon the best available information to the United States at the time. I don't think that the fact that the evidence has developed that those were not an actual diploma and not an actual transcript is enough to support a motion for a judgment of acquittal.

Thus, it is undisputed that Eddy did not submit an "official" Ohio State University diploma and a genuine university transcript during his meetings with naval recruiters. Hence, Eddy's negative responses to the prosecutor's questions were the literal truth "in light of the meaning that he, not his interrogator, attributed to the questions and answers," *United States v. Cook*, 497 F.2d at 773 (emphasis in original), and therefore, could not support a perjury conviction. *Bronston*, 409 U.S. at 359; *see also United States v. Wall*, 371 F.2d at 400 ("[T]he essence of the crime of perjury . . . is the belief of the witness concerning the veracity of his testimony.") It is no answer to argue that Eddy's testimony was unresponsive or intentionally misleading. An "intent to mislead" or "perjury by implication" is insufficient to support a perjury conviction. *Bronston*, 409 U.S. at 359; *United States v. Slawik*, 548 F.2d 75, 83–84 (3d Cir.1977). "[I]f the prosecutor never asks the critical question and never presses for an unequivocal answer the defendant may not be convicted of false swearing." *Slawik, supra*, 548 F.2d at 84.

Nor can Eddy's conviction be upheld because, as the United States contends, Eddy understood, or should have understood, the import behind the prosecutor's questions. "Precise questioning is imperative as a predicate for the offense of perjury." *Bronston*, 409 U.S. at 362. If the Assistant United States Attorney sought to inquire about Eddy's submitting false documents, the burden was on the United States, and not the witness, to be concise and to the point. The perjury statute was not intended to extend situations where "a wily witness succeeds in derailing the questioner—so long as the witness speaks the literal truth. The burden is on the questioner to pin the witness down to the specific object of the questioner's inquiry." *Bronston*, 409 U.S. at 360.

We also reject the argument that, when a witness is confronted with ambiguous questions, it is for the jury to decide whether the witness has committed perjury. *Bronston* discredited this type of jury conjecture which is now contended should be permissible. A contrary rule would allow a jury to infer from a witness' unresponsive answer to a vague question that the witness knew his testimony to be false. In expressly rejecting this, *Bronston*, 409 U.S. at 358, the Court stated,

> Under the pressures and tensions of interrogation, it is not uncommon for the most earnest witnesses to give answers that are not entirely responsive. Sometimes the witness does not understand the question, or may in an excess of caution or apprehension read too much or too little into it. . . . It is the responsibility of the lawyer to probe; testimonial interrogation, and cross-examination in particular, is a probing, prying, pressing form of inquiry. If a witness evades, it is the lawyer's responsibility to recognize the evasion and to bring the witness back to the mark, to flush out the whole truth with the tools of adversary examination.

See also United States v. Tonelli, 577 F.2d at 200; *United States v. Slawik*, 548 F.2d at 84 (petit jury should not be permitted "to resolve not only ambiguity of the interrogator's question and the defendant's response, but also the ambiguity of the grand jury's understanding of both question and response.").

Similarly, Eddy's conviction under Count II of the indictment must also be reversed and the indictment dismissed. The testimony charged to have been perjured, and used as the basis for Count II also occurred during the suppression hearing during Eddy's original trial. At one point Eddy was asked if he had applied for staff privileges at a hospital, would he remember doing so. Eddy responded in the affirmative. The following question was then asked:

> PROSECUTOR: In that case, I would ask you the question again. Are you the same Terrance Alan Eddy who attempted to gain staff privileges at the Putnam County Community Hospital in Palatka, Florida, and in doing so showed credentials from the Ohio State University and a certificate from the Board of Medical Examiners from the State of Florida indicating that you were licensed to

practice medicine in that state? And I think we can take that to mean you represented yourself as a physician. Did you do that?

EDDY: Like I said, I don't remember going there. I don't remember doing this action. No, sir.

The indictment charges that Eddy's response was false because he "did make [an] application for staff privileges at the Putnam Community Hospital, Palatka, Florida, and in so doing, represented himself to be a physician, showed credentials from the State of Florida indicating that he was licensed to practice medicine in that state." As with the situations in *Slawik, supra*, 548 F.2d at 83, and *Tonelli, supra*, 577 F.2d at 198, the second count in Eddy's indictment fails to specify the alleged falsehood in his testimony. The indictment does not precisely allege what was false about Eddy's response. It cannot be determined whether Eddy testified falsely because (1) he failed to remember going to Florida when in fact there was sufficient proof that he had remembered going there, or because (2) he denied ever going to Florida when in fact he knew he had been there. If the former, there is no factual basis in the indictment or the record itself to demonstrate the untruthfulness of Eddy's declaration. Because the indictment does not allege that Eddy's failure to remember was perjurious, it will not be so assumed. *United States v. Brumley*, 560 F.2d 1268, 1277 (5th Cir. 1977). Nor is the latter interpretation appropriate in view of Eddy's equivocal response. Concededly, Eddy's answer was obscure, and may have misled the casual observer. Nevertheless, it was the Assistant United States Attorney's "responsibility to recognize [Eddy's] evasion and bring him back to the mark, to flush out the whole truth with the tools of adversary examination." *Bronston*, 409 U.S. at 359. This was not done. Here, the crucial question was hardly precise. In fact, it was a multiple question with at least four separate inquiries. Understandably, Eddy's answer reflected the same imprecision. "A charge of perjury, however, is not a substitute for careful questioning on the part of a prosecutor." *United States v. Tonelli, supra*, 577 F.2d at 198. In a perjury case, the defendant "may not be assumed into the penitentiary." *United States v. Brumley, supra*, 560 F.2d at 1277. Any reading of the charges found in Count II of the indictment leads one to believe that it has failed to set forth with sufficient clarity the precise falsehood alleged, the factual basis of that falsehood and the objective truth in "stark contrast so that the claim of falsity is clear to all who read the charge." *Tonelli*, 577 F.2d at 195. * * *

The declarations alleged to be perjurious in Count I of the indictment were in fact answers that were literally true. The declaration alleged to be perjurious in Count II was an obscure response to a multiple question which was inherently confusing and vague. In other words, the perjurious nature of Eddy's testimony was not manifest. This fact, combined with the knowledge that the initial criminal charges against Eddy resulted in the defendant's acquittal, leaves us convinced that there existed a "realistic likelihood of vindictiveness" in the institution of Eddy's perjury prosecution, and therefore, provides a second reason why his conviction under 18 U.S.C. § 1623 must be reversed.

Accordingly, the judgment of the district court is reversed and the indictment against Eddy is ordered dismissed.

Appeals to Motives

Arguments based on motives rather than reasons are famously fallacious. So for example the appeal to force or fear (*argumentum ad baculum* or "to [or by] the stick") is a fallacy, as in the argument that "You should agree with the President's war policy, or your children could die." Similarly, the appeal to pity (*argumentum ad misericordiam*) is not an argument, which is why it rarely convinces a teacher to change a grade if the student argues, "I deserve a really good grade on this project, because I've been working on it for three straight days. Have a heart." The appeal to popularity (*argumentum ad populum*), though ancient and familiar, has little to do with reason, as in the example "You should be in favor of legalizing pot, because the cool kids already support the idea." This also accounts for the inter-generational ineffectiveness of telling parents that "you should let me [fill in the blank] because everyone else is doing it."

The difference between a legitimate argument about fairness (or equity) and illegitimate arguments to pity can be difficult to discern. In the following case, one party's argument is rejected essentially because it is a mere *argumentum ad misericordiam*, but what would it have taken to frame her argument as a logically-valid and legally-compelling argument from fairness?

PETRACCA V. PETRACCA

706 So. 2d 904 (Fla. App. 1998)

The issue presented in this appeal is whether an agreement settling dissolution of marriage litigation is subject to a "fair and reasonable" determination by the trial judge under *Del Vecchio v. Del Vecchio,* 143 So.2d 17 (Fla.1962). We hold that it is not under the facts and circumstances of this case and affirm the trial judge on that issue. There is an ambiguity in the agreement, however, and so we remand the case to the trial court for resolution of the parties' actual intent as regards the subject provision.

Because the background for an agreement is usually indispensable to an understanding of it, we begin with the history of this litigation. Represented by experienced counsel, the wife filed this petition for dissolution of marriage in June 1994. The husband appeared through his own counsel shortly thereafter. From that point on, the battle raged. In the next two years the combatants filed nearly 70 substantive motions, including four attempts to have the husband held in contempt, and one appeal.

Many of these motions were directed to discovery, including one by the wife to have her expert inspect and value land, and another by the husband seeking to have her provide handwriting exemplars. The wife's pretrial witness list (filed some eight months before the settlement) names a CPA to testify (presumably as to the husband's financial interests). The case was set for trial on five separate occasions, the last scheduled to begin little more than two weeks from the day the parties announced a settlement on the record (apparently at a deposition). Thus even in this day of overheated divorce litigation, the battle in this case was fierce.

Turning to the settlement itself, the parties announced it before a court reporter whose transcribed notes are part of the record. After going through the terms of the settlement item by item, each counsel agreed on the specific provisions in the presence of the parties themselves. At that point each party's lawyer examined that party under oath to establish assent to the agreement. The wife testified as follows:

> COUNSEL: And you have participated and assisted in the negotiation which led to this settlement we just placed on the record. Correct?
>
> WIFE: Correct.
>
> COUNSEL: You understand the settlement?
>
> WIFE: Correct.
>
> COUNSEL: You intend to be bound by it?
>
> WIFE: Correct.
>
> COUNSEL: You entered into freely—you entered into it freely and voluntarily and after advice of counsel?
>
> WIFE: Yes.
>
> COUNSEL: You understand this is a complete and final resolution of this case?
>
> WIFE: What has been stated so far?
>
> COUNSEL: Yes.
>
> WIFE: Yes.

The significance of this testimony, of course, needs no comment.

Just two weeks after the settlement her original lawyer moved for leave to withdraw, citing irreconcilable differences. Soon a new lawyer appeared on her behalf and filed a motion to invalidate the agreement.

After first setting out what can be characterized only as allegations that the parties now dispute one of the settlement's terms, the wife then sets forth in great detail why her analysis of the disputed provision should be accepted. * * * Her version failing, she then appears to suggest that the whole thing should be called off. She argues that the absence of an agreement on the disputed provision can mean only the lack of an entire agreement between the parties. Her motion closes with the following:

> It must be remembered that the agreement should be subject to the approval of the Court, and if the agreement either plunges this petitioner into poverty, or leaves the parties in a position monitarily [sic] which would be completely inequitable, which is the case herein, the Court should dissaprove [sic] the agreement in its entirety!

The motion ends with a plea *ad misericordiam* to let her out of the bargain or rewrite it to suit her contended version of the parties' actual intent. It is this motion that, she argues, authorizes a judge to set aside a litigation settlement agreement reached just before trial and that requires an evidentiary hearing on the motion.

Her primary emphasis is on *Casto v. Casto,* 508 So.2d 330 (Fla.1987). That case, she argues, empowers judges to set aside a litigation settlement agreement that makes an "unfair or unreasonable provision for the [challenging] spouse." * * * [T]he court there confronted an agreement made just one year before the husband filed his action to dissolve the parties' 10-year marriage. She sought to have the agreement set aside on the grounds of duress and overreaching. She also alleged that she lacked adequate knowledge of his financial picture at the time of contracting, resulting in an unfair disposition of marital property. The court's opinion notes that "the husband did not advise the wife on the value of his assets," that the husband told her that unless she signed the agreement she would lose her house and furniture, and that she was deeply depressed the week before signing the agreement. The trial court set aside the agreement upon a finding that the wife was coerced into the agreement, that it was made without adequate knowledge of his assets, and without the assistance of competent counsel, and that it was unfair and inequitable to the wife. This court affirmed that decision.[3] * * *

The supreme court granted review to clarify the grounds on which a trial court could vacate or modify a postnuptial agreement in a later dissolution of marriage proceeding. The court began by stating that there are essentially two separate grounds for invalidating such agreements. The first ground deals with fraud, duress, coercion, misrepresentation, or over-

[3] In affirming our decision, the supreme court rejected any reliance on competent assistance of counsel as a ground for invalidating postnuptial agreements. The court noted that such a holding would be inconsistent with its previous holdings that a "complaining spouse need not have legal counsel for a valid agreement." * * *

reaching. The second ground—which we shall call unfairness—is the one relied upon by the wife in this case. It was explained by the court as follows:

> The second ground to vacate a settlement agreement contains multiple elements. Initially, the challenging spouse must establish that the agreement makes an unfair or unreasonable provision for that spouse, given the circumstances of the parties. *Del Vecchio*, 143 So.2d at 20. To establish that an agreement is unreasonable, the challenging spouse must present evidence of the parties' relative situations, including their respective ages, health, education, and financial status. With this basic information, a trial court may determine that the agreement, on its face, does not adequately provide for the challenging spouse and, consequently, is unreasonable. In making this determination, the trial court must find that the agreement is "disproportionate to the means" of the defending spouse. This finding requires some evidence in the record to establish a defending spouse's financial means. Additional evidence other than the basic financial information may be necessary to establish the unreasonableness of the agreement.
>
> Once the claiming spouse establishes that the agreement is unreasonable, a presumption arises that there was either concealment by the defending spouse or a presumed lack of knowledge by the challenging spouse of the defending spouse's finances at the time the agreement was reached. The burden then shifts to the defending spouse, who may rebut these presumptions by showing that there was either (a) a full, frank disclosure to the challenging spouse by the defending spouse before the signing of the agreement relative to the value of all the marital property and the income of the parties, or (b) a general and approximate knowledge by the challenging spouse of the character and extent of the marital property sufficient to obtain a value by reasonable means, as well as a general knowledge of the income of the parties. The test in this regard is the adequacy of the challenging spouse's knowledge at the time of the agreement and whether the challenging spouse is prejudiced by the lack of information.

508 So. 2d at 333. Critical to this case, the court stated an important qualification on its holding:

> As reflected by the above principles, the fact that one party to the agreement apparently made a bad bargain is not a sufficient ground, by itself, to vacate or modify a settlement agreement. The critical test in determining the validity of marital agreements is whether there was fraud or over-reaching on one side, or, assuming unreasonableness, whether the challenging spouse did not have adequate knowledge of the marital property and income

> of the parties at the time the agreement was reached. A bad fiscal bargain that appears unreasonable can be knowledgeably entered into for reasons other than insufficient knowledge of assets and income. There may be a desire to leave the marriage for reasons unrelated to the parties' fiscal position. If an agreement that is unreasonable is freely entered into, it is enforceable. Courts, however, must recognize that parties to a marriage are not dealing at arm's length, and, consequently, trial judges must carefully examine the circumstances to determine the validity of these agreements.

508 So. 2d at 334. * * *

As the court emphasized, "[i]f an agreement that is unreasonable is freely entered into, it is enforceable." The narrowness of this holding undoubtedly arises from its earlier decisions laying down an elementary principle from our common law: freedom to contract is fundamental, and the contracts of capable people are enforced by courts even when the bargain is difficult. * * * Obviously under Florida's common law, it is ordinarily not the province of judges to say whether a voluntary agreement is fair to one of the contracting parties. Courts are obligated to uphold even hard or bad bargains freely made without fraud or coercion, so long as they are not against public policy.

In order to be faithful to this primary contract law, it is critical to acknowledge the narrowness of the *Casto* holding * * *. Bad domestic bargains—meaning unfair or unreasonable property and monetary settlement agreements—are nevertheless enforceable so long as they are knowing, voluntary and not otherwise against public policy. *Casto* makes very clear to us that, unless a party can show the reasonable lack of sufficient knowledge of the parties' financial resources, there can be no judicial inquiry into the agreement's fairness.

Because *Casto* really turns on the adequacy of the knowledge of the challenging spouse as a predicate for an unreasonableness challenge, it is restricted to those circumstances in which the adequacy of knowledge might plausibly be raised. The adequacy of knowledge can be plausibly raised only when the agreement was reached by marital parties in conditions of mutual trust and confidence and who were, therefore, not dealing at arm's length.[6] The wife in this case attempts to imply that even when the parties are engaged in contested dissolution of marriage proceedings—when there has been ample opportunity for the party to make use of the procedural rules for discovery of financial resources—a party can still plausibly allege that the they were still dealing in mutual trust and

---

[6] *See Del Vecchio*, 143 So.2d at 21 ("The relationship between the parties to an antenuptial agreement is one of mutual trust and confidence. Since they do not deal at arm's length they must exercise a high degree of good faith and candor in all matters bearing upon the contract.").

confidence and not at arm's length or from inadequate knowledge of finances.

We are compelled by the supreme court holdings discussed above to reject the wife's argument. Once the parties are involved in full fledged litigation over dissolution property and support rights, they are necessarily dealing at arm's length and without the special fiduciary relationship of unestranged marital parties. * * * [T]here can be no question of the adequacy of knowledge when an adversarial party has had the opportunity of financial discovery under the applicable rules of procedure. The *Casto* line of cases, therefore, logically has no application when the challenging spouse has had the benefit of litigation discovery through independently chosen counsel to learn the full nature and extent of the finances of the other spouse. The very purpose of litigation discovery is to unearth the other party's assets and income. The law quite properly presumes that a litigation settlement made after discovery and just before trial was done with full knowledge by the challenging spouse.[7]

This litigation settlement presumption arises from the special treatment that courts give to voluntary settlements of lawsuits. Under the rule for consent judgments, an agreement settling litigation cannot be opened, changed or set aside without the assent of the parties in the absence of fraud, mutual mistake, or the actual lack of consent. The obvious intent behind the consent judgment rule is that it ought to be very difficult to unsettle an agreement settling litigation. Settlements of civil lawsuits merit the greatest protection from judges. * * * In short, it is the policy of this state to encourage settlements and enforce them whenever it is possible to do so.

In order to avoid an agreement settling a dissolution of marriage action in which the parties were adversaries, to be consistent with *Casto* and the common law the challenging spouse is similarly limited to showing fraud, misrepresentation in the discovery, or coercion. The supreme court's cases preclude judicial inquiry into the reasonableness of a litigation settlement to either party. The parties alone are competent to say what is reasonable to resolve a lawsuit and what is not. If parties choose to settle a case without fraud or coercion after adequate opportunity to engage in discovery—from which ample knowledge must be presumed—they should not be heard to assail the relative fairness of the bargain. If they agreed to the terms, it is presumptively and conclusively fair as a matter of law.

To allow this kind of "reasonableness" challenge to a litigation settlement agreement also threatens the likelihood of settlements in many cases and thus would require more trials on the merits. If one of the settling parties can have the court later inquire into its reasonableness and

[7] We note that the wife makes no suggestion, veiled or otherwise, that any of husband's discovery responses was false or intentionally misleading, and that she relied on such a false representation when she entered into the settlement agreement.

fairness, there would be little incentive for courts to encourage settlements. For it is undoubtedly true that, in deciding the reasonableness of a marital property settlement, the court is really trying the merits of the underlying dispute. If the trial judge is going to be called upon to decide what a fair division of property and support is anyway, settlement is a waste of time and the parties might just as well proceed directly to trial and have a judicial disposition.

* * * *Casto* makes clear that the reasonability or fairness of a pre-litigation settlement is open to question by a judge only when there is some reason to suppose from the relationship of mutual trust and confidence that the parties were not dealing at arm's length and that the agreement resulted from inadequate disclosure of financial resources. After resorting to litigation over marital property rights, neither party can be thought [to be] dealing as fiduciaries or inadequately informed as to financial affairs. * * *

It is clear to us that the wife in this case has made no allegation of fraud or coercion in her motion to invalidate the settlement agreement. A fair and reasonable agreement is what negotiating and bargaining are for, whether they occur in formal mediation or by informal settlement conferences just before trial. We must therefore leave the parties, as this trial judge did, with the bargain they struck. * * *

Tu quoque

The *tu quoque* ("you're another" or "you too") fallacy occurs when one opposes an argument because it is inconsistent with the speaker's prior actions or claims. A person may be inconsistent, even to the point of hypocrisy, but that by itself is not logically sufficient on the merits to refute the argument he or she now makes. So for example, suppose A said, "You really should stop smoking. Smoking ruins your health and makes your clothes smell bad." B responds: "You're argument is ridiculous on its face. You've been smoking for years." A may say one thing and do another (which is problematic), but the validity of A's argument—that smoking is bad for you—is logically independent of his or her individual behavior in the past. Similarly, to oppose an argument on the ground that the advocate doesn't really believe it may be true in its premise but irrelevant to the argument itself and may qualify as *ad hominem*.

So for example, *State v. Melone*, 2009 Ohio 6710 (Ohio Ct. App., Lake County Dec. 18, 2009), suggests a range of arguments *not* to make after a near-collision and confrontation with a police officer:

> Appellant contends that the near collision between his vehicle and Officer McNeely's cruiser was a result of the officer's failure to

> remain standing at the clearly marked stop line and yield the right-of-way, a violation of * * * Ohio's "Steady Red Indication" statute. Even assuming the officer failed to remain at a standing stop, appellant * * * had no right-of-way. Moreover, any improper maneuvering on the officer's part would not negate the illegality of appellant's actions. Appellant's point is an example of the classic "tu quoque" ("you're another") fallacy. As a matter of logic, the fact that another may be guilty of an accusation does not prove that the accuser is innocent. These points aside, Officer McNeely explained that her decision to move past the stop line was a result of her observation that, prior to driving directly at the curb cut, appellant actually began to turn right. The record established the officer did make a complete stop. She advanced beyond the stop line to initiate a right turn on red, a permissible maneuver at that intersection. Thus, the near-miss was precipitated by appellant's illegal driving, not the officer's alleged violation the steady red indication statute.

For other examples of the *tu quoque* fallacy, *see, e.g.*, *O'Grady v. Superior Court*, 139 Cal. App. 4th 1423, 1442 (Cal. App. 6th Dist. 2006) (fallacy committed by counsel for Apple, Inc.); *United States v. Camacho*, 353 F. Supp. 2d 524, 532–533 (S.D.N.Y. 2005); *Worthington v. Anderson*, 386 F.3d 1314, 1320 (10th Cir. 2004); *United States v. Rahman*, 861 F. Supp. 266, 279 (S.D.N.Y. 1994); *General Tire & Rubber Co. v. Jefferson Chemical Co.*, 497 F.2d 1283, 1285 (2d Cir. N.Y. 1974); *Laflin & Rand Powder Co. v. Tearney*, 30 Ill. App. 321, 323 (Ill. App. Ct. 1889).

The Naturalist Fallacy

David Hume is credited with identifying the fallacy that consists in deriving a normative or "ought" statement from a descriptive or "is" statement. History or science (description) and morality (normativity) are not necessarily related; indeed, the existence of some state of affairs is logically independent of its moral status. Suppose someone argued for example that the institution of slavery cannot be morally wrong, because it has existed in multiple cultures for centuries. The supposedly moral justification for slavery would be based on history, which deals with what was or is, and not with what is right. Hume used the naturalist fallacy as a way of criticizing natural rights theory, offering a profound skepticism that one could derive any moral system from the asserted nature of human beings. *See* Chapter 1, *supra*.

The Hasty Generalization ("The Fallacy of the Lonely Fact" or "The Fallacy of Converse Accident" or "Observational Selection")

"The Hasty Generalization" refers to the fallacy of deriving a conclusion from a sample that is too small or unrepresentative. So for example: "Everybody I know speaks English; therefore, everybody in the world speaks English." There may be logical disagreements in good faith about the quality and sufficiency of data, but the goal must be to assure that data actually prove what they are asserted to prove and that the generalizations based on data are not premature—that the speaker has not leapt to a conclusion. When referring to a generalization made from a single example it has been called the "fallacy of the lonely fact."

Awareness of the fallacy has been especially important in developing the law of evidence dealing with the admissibility of evidence of prior criminal acts. In *Jennings v. Commonwealth*, 20 Va.App. 9, 454 S.E.2d 752 (Va. App., 1995), for example, the court had to decide whether to admit evidence of the defendant's prior sex offences.

> Merely proving that a person has a propensity to commit acts or crimes similar to the charged offense does not, without more, logically justify an inference that the person committed that offense. Thus, it does not logically follow that because a person previously sodomized one or more children, subsequent contact with a child is for the purpose of sodomizing the child. The fallacy in this form of nondeductive reasoning is termed "hasty generalization."

Id., at 15–16. *See also State v. Boggs*, 38 Kan.App.2d 683, 170 P.3d 912 (Kan. App. 2007) ("[I]t does not logically follow that because a person previously smoked marijuana, the person's later proximity to an area where marijuana is located is for the purpose of possessing the marijuana. The fallacy in this form of nondeductive reasoning is termed "hasty generalization."). Expert testimony that rests on insufficient data are routinely excluded, *see, e.g., O'Conner v. Commonwealth Edison Co.*, 807 F.Supp. 1376 (C.D. Ill. 1992), and administrative agency actions are vulnerable to the extent that they rest on hasty generalizations, *see, e.g., Peerless of America, Inc. v. N.L.R.B*, 484 F.2d 1108 (7th Cir. 1973). *See generally* RUGGERO J. ALDISERT, LOGIC FOR LAWYERS: A GUIDE TO CLEAR LEGAL THINKING 191–92 (1989).

STATE V. SMITH

42 Kan. App. 2d 344, 212 P.3d 232, 233 (2009)

The issue before this court is whether the trial court abused its discretion in refusing to appoint Charles Smith [a defendant in a robbery prosecution] new counsel. Based on the lone assertion of Smith's attorney who refused to present potentially relevant defense evidence on Smith's behalf because he believed that a suspect shown in a crime surveillance video was Smith, the trial court developed a general rule covering all attorneys who could have represented Smith, thus committing the logical fallacy known as a hasty generalization. Just because Smith's attorney believed that the suspect shown in a crime video was the defendant, it does not follow that all attorneys would have viewed that video in the same way as Smith's attorney, especially when the assertion is based on the sense of sight. More important, this generalization theorizes that all attorneys would have refused to present potentially relevant evidence in Smith's defense. Accordingly, we reverse and remand for a new trial.

The False Analogy

Sometimes an advocate will assert that two things are similar and therefore share some property or characteristic. When the analogy works well the argument can be very powerful indeed, but an analogy ill-framed can also lead to illogical conclusions that are divorced from the merits of the argument.

> The argument by analogy is not necessarily a dishonest or crooked method of thought, although it is a dangerous one always requiring careful examination. . . . To an extraordinary extent, otherwise intelligent people become convinced of highly improbable things because they have heard them supported by an analogy whose unsoundness should be apparent to an imbecile."

ROBERT H. THOULESS, STRAIGHT AND CROOKED THINKING 146, 157 (1932). For example, an advocate—generally the dean of a law school—might argue that law faculties are like forests and should therefore be cleared periodically. There may be good arguments for getting rid of the institution of tenure or compelling radical, periodic turnover in law faculties, but whatever those good arguments might be, they have nothing to do with some lame analogy between faculties and forests. Stupid deans. *Compare reductio ad Hitlerum* and Godwin's Law: as an internet discussion thread becomes longer and more heated, the probability of a comparison involving Nazis or Hitler approaches one, *i.e.*, certainty. By tradition, whoever first invokes Hitler or the Nazis loses the argument then in progress.

HAGLUND V. PHILIP MORRIS, INC.

446 Mass. 741, 847 N.E.2d 315 (2006)

We determine in this case whether a cigarette manufacturer in a wrongful death action predicated on breach of the warranty of merchantability may assert as an affirmative defense that the decedent smoker's use of cigarettes was "unreasonable." See *Correia v. Firestone Tire and Rubber Co.*, 388 Mass. 342, 356 (1983) (in warranty liability action, "the user's negligence does not prevent recovery except when he unreasonably uses a product that he knows to be defective and dangerous") (*Correia* defense).

Following the death from lung cancer of her husband, Stephen C. Haglund (decedent), a long-time smoker, Brenda Haglund filed a wrongful death product liability action against Philip Morris Incorporated (Philip Morris) pursuant to G.L. c. 106, § 2–314(2)(c).[3] In denying all liability, Philip Morris asserted, among other things, that the decedent's decision to begin and continue smoking its cigarettes constituted "unreasonable use" pursuant to our holding in *Correia, supra*. The plaintiff moved for summary judgment to preclude assertion of the *Correia* defense, arguing that the *Correia* defense should, as a matter of law, be unavailable because a cigarette is an inherently dangerous product that causes injury when used for its ordinary purpose. The judge treated the summary judgment motion as a motion to strike, denied it, and dismissed the action *sua sponte*. The plaintiff appealed, and we granted her application for direct appellate review. * * *

We affirm the judge's denial of the motion to strike and reverse the judgment of dismissal. As we explain more fully below, the *Correia* defense presumes that the product at issue is, in normal circumstances, reasonably safe and capable of being reasonably safely used, and therefore that the consumer's unreasonable use of the product he knows to be defective and dangerous is appropriately penalized. Here, however, both Philip Morris and the plaintiff agree that cigarette smoking is inherently dangerous and that there is no such thing as a safe cigarette. Because no cigarette can be safely used for its ordinary purpose, smoking, there can be no non-unreasonable use of cigarettes. Thus the *Correia* defense, which serves to deter unreasonable use of products in a dangerous and defective state, will, in the usual course, be inapplicable.

However, we also agree with Philip Morris that, in certain conceivable scenarios, an individual consumer's behavior may be so overwhelmingly unreasonable in light of the consumer's knowledge about, for example, a specific medical condition from which he suffers, that the *Correia* defense may be invoked. The jury determines unreasonable use from the specific factual context of each case, and we are loathe to foreclose assertion of the defense as a matter of law in every cigarette-related product liability action. Because the plaintiff's motion for summary judgment on the *Correia* defense was brought early in the litigation, we reverse the judgment of dismissal to afford the parties the opportunity to develop more fully the evidence supporting their claims and defenses. * * *

---

[3] General Laws c. 106, § 2–314(2)(c), provides: "Goods to be merchantable must at least be such as . . . are fit for the ordinary purposes for which such goods are used."

The manufacture, marketing, and sale of cigarettes are, indisputably, legitimate, for-profit business enterprises. The United States Congress has declared the marketing of tobacco to be "one of the greatest basic industries of the United States." *Food & Drug Admin. v. Brown & Williamson Tobacco Corp.*, 529 U.S. 120, 137 (2000), quoting 7 U.S.C. § 1311(a). We may take judicial notice that, as a for-profit enterprise and a publicly traded company, Philip Morris seeks to manufacture, market, and sell cigarettes to the general adult public in a manner intended to attract and retain as many consumers as possible. Philip Morris does not dispute that its efforts to market and sell its cigarettes to the broad general adult public is anything other than robust.

At the same time, and as Philip Morris readily admits, cigarettes are a product that cannot be used safely for the "ordinary purposes" for which they are fit, namely, smoking. The record discloses two inherent dangers of smoking cigarettes that Philip Morris does not deny. First, cigarette smoking poses serious health risks. We have previously taken judicial notice of a report by the Surgeon General of the United States released in May, 2004, that "presents persuasive evidence that smoking [cigarettes] harms nearly every organ of the human body, causes many diseases and reduces the health of smokers in general." *Aspinall v. Philip Morris Co.*, 442 Mass. 381, 388 n. 16 (2004). *See Food & Drug Admin. v. Brown & Williamson Tobacco Corp.*, *supra* at 125, ("one of the most troubling public health problems facing our Nation today: the thousands of premature deaths that occur each year because of tobacco use"). Philip Morris concedes that "smoking causes serious disease, and there is no such thing as a safe cigarette."

The second danger of cigarette smoking is that the nicotine in cigarettes is addictive. An addiction is an "[h]abitual psychological and physiological dependence on a substance or practice which is beyond voluntary control." STEDMAN'S MEDICAL DICTIONARY 23 (25th ed. 1990). *See Food & Drug Admin. v. Brown & Williamson Tobacco Corp.*, supra at 138, *citing* United States Department of Health and Human Services, Public Health Service, The Health Consequences of Smoking: Nicotine Addiction 6–9, 145–239 (1988) ("concluding that tobacco products are addicting in much the same way as heroin and cocaine, and that nicotine is the drug that causes addiction"). A reasonable inference from Philip Morris's acknowledgment that the nicotine in cigarettes makes smoking addictive is that its product was consciously designed to induce cigarette dependency in the ordinary smoker, regardless whether any individual smoker becomes addicted to cigarettes.

Because the product cannot be used safely in its ordinary-use environment, cigarette merchandising is incompatible with the *Correia* defense in most circumstances. The purpose of our warranty laws, as we have shown, is to encourage safe products in the stream of commerce. The duty of the consumer is "to act reasonably with respect to a product which he knows to be defective and dangerous." *Correia v. Firestone Tire and Rubber Co.*, 388 Mass. 342, 355 (1983). But in the case of cigarette use, the consumer cannot fulfill that duty, because no non-unreasonable use of cigarettes, as they are currently designed, is possible. The social policy that animates the *Correia* defense—to encourage reasonable use of products by consumers—cannot be accomplished. The legislative intent of our warranty laws would be sidestepped were the manufacturer of cigarettes permitted routinely to escape all liability merely by proving that the plaintiff was an ordinary consumer who used its products in a manner readily foreseeable.

Philip Morris argues that consumers often elect to use products that may cause harm as a "byproduct" of normal use and for which the *Correia* defense presumptively is available. One can become addicted to the sugar in candy, it points out, or contract skin cancer by using suntan oil. Guns are dangerous; aspirin taken for a headache can reduce the tendency of blood to clot. These are false analogies. The fallacy in Philip Morris's argument is that in none of these examples, or others it offers, is any reasonable use of the product whatsoever foreclosed by the nature of the product itself. Sugar, suntan oil, guns, and aspirin are not inherently addictive to the general public or incapable of being used reasonably. The *Correia* defense is available for warranty claims for these products because the defense serves an actual purpose: to deter a consumer from knowingly using a product in a defective and dangerous (as opposed to its ordinary) condition. The consumer has a choice of using a product reasonably or unreasonably, and the defense penalizes the consumer for unreasonable use. It does not presume that the only safe use of a product is nonuse, a position urged on us by Philip Morris but which runs contrary to our entire scheme of commerce.

We have examined the numerous warranty cases cited to us by the parties in which the *Correia* defense was invoked and there is none where the defendant conceded that reasonable use of the product was impossible. * * *

Argumentum ad lazarum vel ad crumenam

Argumentum ad lazarum refers to the fallacy of supposing a conclusion is valid just because the argument is made by a poor person. Suppose a rebel commander in a civil war said at a press conference, "This war is justified, because I have to live in a shanty while the general who commands the government's troops lives in a mansion in the capital city." The argument could be valid to the extent that it grounds the rationale for the rebellion in that country's grinding economic inequality, but the poverty of the speaker is no assurance that his argument is valid. More familiar perhaps is the opposite argument, the fallacy *argumentum ad crumenam*, which supposes a conclusion valid because the argument is made by a wealthy person. If for example a candidate for President of the United States argued that her wealth alone prepared her for the office, one of the fallacies in the argument would be that it was *ad crumenam*. *Compare with* "if you're so smart, why aren't you rich?"

Fallacy of Flamboyance

The Fallacy of Flamboyance recognizes that an argument is not valid just because the speaker is especially eloquent or passionate or witty about it. As Bertrand Russell observed, "[t]o acquire immunity to eloquence is of the utmost importance to the citizens of a democracy." BERTRAND RUSSELL, POWER: A NEW SOCIAL ANALYSIS 314 (1938). On the other hand, much of a politician's or a trial lawyer's effectiveness would disappear if this fallacy were taken seriously. Learning to resist the seductive power of eloquence, or in any event to distinguish the power of an argument from the eloquence of its proponent, is notoriously difficult, and can be perverted into an attack on eloquence, as though a political candidate's eloquence were a weakness. *See, e.g.*, James Wood, *Verbage*, NEW YORKER ___ (Oct. 13, 2008).

"The Genetic Fallacy"

An attack on the origin of an argument or belief, rather than its substance and merit, constitutes the "genetic fallacy," that is "the fallacy of believing that the causal origin of a belief affects the truth or reasonableness of that belief." JEFFRIE G. MURPHY, EVOLUTION, MORALITY, AND THE MEANING OF LIFE 24 (1982). Suppose for example that an advocate argued that "The Prime Minister's argument for a surge of troops stems from his subconscious desire to kill his father and should therefore be rejected." It may be true that there is some psychological basis for the Prime Minister's decision, and there may be good arguments on the merits against the surge, but to oppose the policy because of the Freudian origins of the Prime Minister's decision is fallacious. (This example might also qualify as an example of arguments *ad hominem*.) Similarly, pundits and political candidates, when they discredit an idea simply by saying that it fits their opponents' worldview, commit the genetic fallacy. S. MORRIS ENGEL, WITH GOOD REASON: AN INTRODUCTION TO INFORMAL FALLACIES 194 (3d ed. 1986).

Ignoratio elenchi

Every magician knows that misdirection—drawing the eyes of the audience away from the real action—is essential to certain tricks. In rhetoric, misdirection or distraction can also qualify as the logical fallacy of *ignoratio elenchi* ("ignoring the disproof" or ignorance of what disproof looks like), also known as a red herring (or what certain devotees of the early twenty-first century television series *South Park* would recognize as the "Chewbacca Defense"). Essentially, it is the fallacy of proving or disproving something other than the proposition in question: if two issues are not related, arguing about one says nothing about the other. Anytime an advocate argues for a proposition that no-one denies, or against a proposition that no-one supports, there will be strong whiff of *ignoratio elenchi*.

To offer a ridiculous example, suppose in her closing statement, a trial attorney said "Members of the jury, you cannot convict my client of securities fraud. He's good to his mother and has a nice head of hair." A subtler form of this fallacy might take the form: "you should support the President's gun control bill, because we as a nation cannot afford to have so many weapons in circulation." The argument is technically fallacious, because you might agree that (A) the nation cannot afford so many weapons in circulation without agreeing that (B) the President's bill will reduce their number.

In *EEOC v. Franklin & Marshall College*, 775 F.2d 110 (3d Cir. 1985), the Equal Employment Opportunity Commission was investigating the claims of a college professor that he had been denied tenure on discriminatory grounds, specifically on grounds of nationality, in violation of Title VII. The issue in the case was whether certain EEOC subpoenas would be enforced or not. In dissenting from the decision that they were enforceable, Judge Aldisert wrote:

> The cited legislative history convincingly demonstrates that Congress intended Title VII to apply to universities and colleges. No one can argue to the contrary. The majority nonetheless rest their *ratio decidendi* entirely upon an analysis of the 1972 amendment to Title VII that eliminated the exemption for academic institutions. We are thus treated to a classic fallacy of irrelevance, or *ignoratio elenchi*. The error is made by attempting to prove something that has not been denied, to-wit that the 1972 amendment to Title VII took in institutions of higher learning. The question under consideration, however, is not whether Title VII was amended but whether, on the strength of a mere conclusory allegation of discrimination, the EEOC is permitted the kind of intrusion into the tenure review process it seeks here. I find no support in the legislative history for the proposition that Congress foresaw the possibility, much less intended, that a

> college instructor may, with a blunderbuss allegation of discriminatory treatment against Frenchmen, devoid of factual specificity, gain unfettered access to the confidential personnel files of all his colleagues. * * * At bottom always is the task of divining the intention of the legislature. Learned Hand has observed: "When a judge tries to find out what the government would have intended which it did not say, he puts into its mouth things which he thinks it ought to have said, and that is very close to substituting what he himself thinks right. . . . Nobody does this exactly right; great judges do it better than the rest of us. It is necessary that someone shall do it, if we are to realize the hope that we can collectively rule ourselves [citing L. HAND, THE SPIRIT OF LIBERTY 100, 109–110 (2d ed. 1954)]."

Id. at 120.

"Invincible Ignorance" (a.k.a. The Ostrich Syndrome)

It is a fallacy to persist in asserting one's position despite directly contradictory facts: "I don't care what the so-called experts say. Nothing they say can convince me that I'm wrong about the healthy effects of eating chocolate-covered bacon cheeseburgers on a glazed doughnut." The single word argument—"whatever"—offers another potent example.

"The Undistributed Middle"

It is fallacious to argue in the form "All A are B. All C are B. Therefore, all A are C." This is sometimes referred to as the Undistributed Middle, because the "middle" term—B—is not distributed—equally or at all—between A and C. So for example: "All men are human. All women are human. Therefore all men are women." Or "all maples are trees. All elms are trees. Therefore all maples are elms." It's so easy to see the fallacy in these examples that you may wonder how an advocate or a court could ever commit it. As usual, the invalidity is easier to see in the rear-view mirror, *i.e.* after the fact, than it is through the windshield, *i.e.* as it happens:

HERNANDEZ V. DENTON

861 F.2d 1421, 1438–39, 1440 (9th Cir. 1988)

(ALDISERT, J., concurring and dissenting).

[Hernandez brought civil rights complaints for mistreatment in prison, including multiple rapes by prison officials and inmates. These complaints were generally dismissed, and Hernandez appealed.] Suffice it to say, as an experienced student and researcher in prisoner civil rights petitions, I believe that these three appeals go beyond the pale of frivolity. They are sheer and utter nonsense. * * * Even assuming appellant's rape fantasy had some basis in rationality, his complaints are utterly devoid of any allegations establishing the personal involvement of any of the defendants. His contentions depend upon the following prosyllogisms and episyllogisms:

A.

Major Premise: Some needle marks are signs of drug injection.

Minor Premise: I awoke with some needle marks.

Conclusion: Therefore, I was drugged.

B.

Major Premise: One who is drugged can be raped without his knowledge.

Minor Premise: I was drugged.

Conclusion: Therefore, I was raped.

C.

Major Premise: Those correctional officials who are involved or knowledgeable of inmate rapes are liable.

Minor Premise: Defendants are correctional officials.

Conclusion: Therefore, defendants are liable.

Both fallacies of form and material fallacies inhere in each of these three arguments. Rules of syllogistic logic, first identified by Aristotle, and universally acknowledged by all logicians, are involved here.[2] Syllogism "A" represents the fallacy of the undistributed middle term:[3] In a formally valid categorical syllogism, the middle term must be distributed in at least one of the premises. If either the minor term or the major term is distributed in the conclusion, it must be distributed in the premise in which it originates.[4] Here, the middle term "needle marks" is undistributed in both the major and minor premises. It does not necessarily follow that all needle marks are evidence of drug ingestion simply because *some* are.

---

2 *See* I. Copi, *Introduction to Logic* 201–02, 217–18 (7th ed.) (1986); J. Cooley, *A Primer of Formal Logic* 306 (1942); J. Creighton, *An Introduction to Logic* 139 (1958); R. Eaton, *General Logic* 95 (1931); W. Jevon, *Elementary Lessons in Logic* 127 (1965); L. Stebbing, *A Modern Introduction to Logic* 88 (1948).

3 Copi, *supra,* at 219–20. The three terms of the categorical syllogism are "middle," "major," and "minor." A term is "distributed" if it refers to the whole of its class; if it refers to only part of its class, it is "undistributed."

4 "For the two terms of the conclusion really to be connected through the third, at least one of them must be related to the *whole* of the class designated by the third or middle term." Copi, *supra,* at 219.

Syllogism "B" discloses the formal fallacy of the illicit major term. Here, the major term in the syllogism ("raped") is undistributed in the major premise ("can be raped"), but distributed in the conclusion ("was raped"). The resulting fallacy is obvious. Hundreds of physical or mental consequences can possibly follow injection or ingestion of drugs; being raped is only one possible consequence. Syllogism "C" violates a fundamental rule of categorical syllogisms: "A valid standard-form categorical syllogism must contain exactly three terms, each of which is used in the same sense throughout the argument." Copi, *supra*, at 217. In this case, the middle term, "correctional officials," is used in a different sense in the minor premise than it is in the major premise, where it refers to "correctional officials who are involved or knowledgeable of inmate rapes." This syllogism also exhibits the fallacy of the undistributed middle. The middle term, "those correctional officials who are involved or knowledgeable of inmate rapes" is undistributed in the major premise. The term "correctional officials" is also undistributed in the minor premise because it refers only to the defendant-correctional officials, not the entire universe of correctional officials.

But even if Hernandez' arguments met the requirements of formal logical form, they would still contain fatal defects. The arguments contain material fallacies, that is, errors or evasions that appear only through an analysis of the meaning of the terms, rather than an analysis of the logical form. For example, each syllogism is a *non sequitur,* an argument exhibiting the lack of a logical connection. From the mix of pleaded facts—needle marks, fecal stains on a tee-shirt, sleeping later than usual on one occasion—any conclusion pinning liability on the defendants here is a paradigmatic *non sequitur*. * * *

I would affirm the judgment of the district court in all respects for the reasons stated herein. The grand purpose of prisoner civil rights petitions under section 1983 is to insure that the structured society within penal institutions possesses the minimum accoutrements of civilized order. It is to eliminate savage and barbarous treatment. It should not be prostituted by the hallucinations of a troubled man. And that is what we have here.

Fallacies of Ambiguity

Ambiguity assumes a virtually infinite number of forms, but some forms fall into recurring patterns:

> *Equivocation*: the same word is used but has at least two different meanings. Example: "A plane is a carpenter's tool. The F-16 is a plane. Therefore the F-16 is a carpenter's tool." Or: "Time flies like an arrow, but fruit flies like a banana."

Emphasis: emphasis is used to suggest a meaning other than the literal meaning of the proposition. Example: In a recommendation letter, the professor writes, "You'll be very lucky indeed if you can get this young man to work for you. Do not waste a moment reading his resume."

Amphiboly: A sentence can have two very different meanings. Example: "Last night I shot a burglar in my pajamas."

Readings

Twenty-four centuries ago, Aristotle identified thirteen fallacies and placed them in two separate categories. In the following excerpt, watch for the distinction between "linguistic" or "verbal" fallacies (ambiguity, amphiboly, equivocation, composition and division, accent, and form of expression (or figure of speech)) and "non-linguistic" or "material" fallacies (Accident, Affirming the Consequent, In a Certain Respect and Simply, Ignorance of Refutation, Begging the Question, False Cause, and Many (or Compound) Questions). Aside from the labels, what distinguishes these two broad categories?

ARISTOTLE, *ON SOPHISTICAL REFUTATIONS*

(translated by W. A. Pickard-Cambridge)

4

There are two styles of refutation: for some depend on the language used, while some are independent of language. Those ways of producing the false appearance of an argument which depend on language are six in number: they are ambiguity, amphiboly, combination, division of words, accent, form of expression. Of this we may assure ourselves both by induction, and by syllogistic proof based on this—and it may be on other assumptions as well—that this is the number of ways in which we might fail to mean the same thing by the same names or expressions.

Arguments such as the following depend upon ambiguity. "Those learn who know: for it is those who know their letters who learn the letters dictated to them." For to "learn" is ambiguous; it signifies both "to understand" by the use of knowledge, and also "to acquire knowledge." Again, "Evils are good: for what needs to be is good, and evils must needs be." For "what needs to be" has a double meaning: it means what is inevitable, as often is the case with evils, too (for evil of some kind is inevitable), while on the other hand we say of good things as well that they "need to be." Moreover, "The same man is both seated and standing and he is both sick and in health: for it is he who stood up who is standing, and he who is recovering who is in health: but it is the seated man who stood up, and the sick man who was recovering." For "The sick man does so and so," or "has so and so done to him" is not single in meaning: sometimes it means "the man who is sick or is seated now," sometimes "the man who was sick formerly." Of course, the man who was recovering was the sick man, who really was sick at the time: but the man who is in health is not sick at the same time: he is "the sick man" in the sense not that he is sick now, but that he was sick formerly.

Examples such as the following depend upon amphiboly: "I wish that you the enemy may capture." Also the thesis, "There must be knowledge of what one knows": for it is possible by this phrase to mean that knowledge belongs to both the knower and the known. Also, "There must be sight of what one sees: one sees the pillar: ergo the pillar has sight," Also, "What you profess to-be, that you profess to-be: you profess a stone to-be: ergo you profess-to-be a stone". Also, "Speaking of the silent is possible": for "speaking of the silent" also has a double meaning: it may mean that the speaker is silent or that the things of which he speaks are so.

There are three varieties of these ambiguities and amphibolies: (1) When either the expression or the name has strictly more than one meaning, *e.g. aetos* and the "dog"; (2) when by custom we use them so; (3) when words that have a simple sense taken alone have more than one meaning in combination; *e.g.* "knowing letters." For each word, both "knowing" and "letters," possibly has a single meaning: but both together have more than one—either that the letters themselves have knowledge or that someone else has it of them.

Amphiboly and ambiguity, then, depend on these modes of speech. Upon the combination of words there depend instances such as the following: "A man can walk while sitting, and can write while not writing." For the meaning is not the same if one divides the words and if one combines them in saying that "it is possible to walk-while-sitting" and write while not writing. The same applies to the latter phrase, too, if one combines the words "to write-while-not-writing:" for then it means that he has the power to write and not to write at once; whereas if one does not combine them, it means that when he is not writing he has the power to write. * * *

Upon division depend the propositions that 5 is 2 and 3, and odd, and that the greater is equal: for it is that amount and more besides. For the same phrase would not be thought always to have the same meaning when divided and when combined, *e.g.* "I made thee a slave once a free man", and "God-like Achilles left fifty [of] a hundred men."

An argument depending upon accent it is not easy to construct in unwritten discussion; in written discussions and in poetry it is easier. Thus (*e.g.*) some people emend Homer against those who criticize as unnatural his expression *to men ou kataputhetai ombro*. For they solve the difficulty by a change of accent, pronouncing the *ou* with an acuter accent. Also, in the passage about Agamemnon's dream, they say that Zeus did not himself say "We grant him the fulfilment of his prayer," but that he bade the dream grant it. Instances such as these, then, turn upon the accentuation.

Others come about owing to the form of expression used, when what is really different is expressed in the same form, *e.g.* a masculine thing by a feminine termination, or a feminine thing by a masculine, or a neuter by either a masculine or a feminine; or, again, when a quality is expressed by a termination proper to quantity or vice versa, or what is active by a passive word, or a state by an active word, and so forth with the other divisions previously" laid down. For it is possible to use an expression to denote what does not belong to the class of actions at all as though it did so belong. Thus (*e.g.*) "flourishing" is a word which in the form of its expression is like "cutting" or "building": yet the one denotes a certain quality—*i.e.* a certain condition—while the other denotes a certain action. In the same manner also in the other instances.

Refutations, then, that depend upon language are drawn from these common-place rules. Of fallacies, on the other hand, that are independent of language there are seven kinds:

(1) that which depends upon Accident;

(2) the use of an expression absolutely or not absolutely but with some qualification of respect or place, or time, or relation;

(3) that which depends upon ignorance of what "refutation" is;

(4) that which depends upon the consequent;

(5) that which depends upon assuming the original conclusion;

(6) stating as cause what is not the cause;

(7) the making of more than one question into one.

5

Fallacies, then, that depend on Accident occur whenever any attribute is claimed to belong in like manner to a thing and to its accident. For since the same thing has many accidents there is no necessity that all the same attributes should belong to all of a thing's predicates and to their subject as well. Thus (*e.g.*), "If Coriscus be different from "man, he is different from himself: for he is a man:" or "If he be different from Socrates, and Socrates be a man, then," they say, "he has admitted that Coriscus is different from a man, because it so happens (*accidit*) that the person from whom he said that he (Coriscus) is different is a man."

Those that depend on whether an expression is used absolutely or in a certain respect and not strictly, occur whenever an expression used in a particular sense is taken as though it were used absolutely, *e.g.* in the argument "If what is not is the object of an opinion, then what is not is:" for it is not the same thing "to be x" and "to be" absolutely. Or again, "What is, is not, if it is not a particular kind of being, *e.g.* if it is not a man." For it is not the same thing "not to be x" and "not to be" at all: it looks as if it were, because of the closeness of the expression, *i.e.* because "to be x" is but little different from "to be," and "not to be x" from "not to be." Likewise also with any argument that turns upon the point whether an expression is used in a certain respect or used absolutely. Thus *e.g.* "Suppose an Indian to be black all over, but white in respect of his teeth; then he is both white and not white." Or if both characters belong in a particular respect, then, they say, "contrary attributes belong at the same time." This kind of thing is in some cases easily seen by any one, *e.g.* suppose a man were to secure the statement that the Ethiopian is black, and were then to ask whether he is white in respect of his teeth; and then, if he be white in that respect, were to suppose at the conclusion of his questions that therefore he had proved dialectically that he was both white and not white. But in some cases it often passes undetected, *viz.* in all cases where, whenever a statement is made of something in a certain respect, it would be generally thought that the absolute statement follows as well; and also in all cases where it is not easy to see which of the attributes ought to be rendered strictly. A situation of this kind arises, where both the opposite attributes belong alike: for then there is general support for the view that one must agree absolutely to the assertion of both, or of neither: *e.g.* if a thing is half white and half black, is it white or black?

Other fallacies occur because the terms "proof" or "refutation" have not been defined, and because something is left out in their definition. For to refute is to contradict one and the same attribute—not merely the name, but the reality—and a name that is not merely synonymous but the same name—and to confute it from the propositions granted, necessarily, without including in the reckoning the original point to be proved, in the same respect and relation and manner and time in which it was asserted. A "false assertion" about anything has to be defined in the same way. Some people, however, omit some one of the said conditions and give a merely apparent refutation, showing (*e.g.*) that the same thing is both double and not double: for two is double of one, but not double of three. Or, it may be, they show that it is both double and not double of the same thing, but not that it is so in the same respect: for it is double in length but not double in breadth. Or, it may be, they show it to be both double and not double of the same thing and in the same respect and manner, but not that it is so at the same time: and therefore their refutation is merely apparent. One might, with some violence, bring this fallacy into the group of fallacies dependent on language as well.

Those that depend on the assumption of the original point to be proved, occur in the same way, and in as many ways, as it is possible to beg the original point; they appear to refute because men lack the power to keep their eyes at once upon what is the same and what is different.

The refutation which depends upon the consequent arises because people suppose that the relation of consequence is convertible. For whenever, suppose A is, B necessarily is, they then suppose also that if B is, A necessarily is. This is also the source of the deceptions that attend opinions based on sense-perception. For people often suppose bile to be honey because honey is attended by a yellow colour: also, since after rain the ground is wet in consequence, we suppose that if the ground is wet, it has been raining; whereas that does not necessarily follow. In rhetoric proofs from signs are based on consequences. For when rhetoricians wish to show that a man is an adulterer, they take hold of some consequence of an adulterous life, *viz.* that the man is smartly dressed, or that he is observed to wander about at night. There are, however, many people of whom these things are true, while the charge in question is untrue. It happens like this also in real reasoning; *e.g.* Melissus" argument, that the universe is eternal, assumes that the universe has not come to be (for from what is not nothing could possibly come to be) and that what has come to be has done so from a first beginning. If, therefore, the universe has not come to be, it has no first beginning, and is therefore eternal. But this does not necessarily follow: for even if what has come to be always has a first beginning, it does not also follow that what has a first beginning has come to be; any more than it follows that if a man in a fever be hot, a man who is hot must be in a fever.

The refutation which depends upon treating as cause what is not a cause, occurs whenever what is not a cause is inserted in the argument, as though the refutation depended upon it. This kind of thing happens in arguments that reason *ad impossible*: for in these we are bound to demolish one of the premisses. If, then, the false cause be reckoned in among the questions that are necessary to establish the resulting impossibility, it will often be thought that the refutation depends upon it, *e.g.* in the proof that the "soul" and "life" are not the same: for if coming-to-be be contrary to perishing, then a particular form of perishing will have a particular form of coming-to-be as its contrary: now death is a particular form of perishing and is contrary to life: life, therefore, is a coming to-be, and to live is to come-to-be. But this is impossible: accordingly, the "soul" and "life" are not the same. Now this is not proved: for the impossibility results all the same, even if one does not say that life is the same as the soul, but merely says that life is contrary to death, which is a form of perishing, and that perishing has "coming-to-be" as its contrary. Arguments of that kind, then, though not inconclusive absolutely, are inconclusive in relation to the proposed conclusion. Also even the questioners themselves often fail quite as much to see a point of that kind.

Such, then, are the arguments that depend upon the consequent and upon false cause. Those that depend upon the making of two questions into one occur whenever the plurality is undetected and a single answer is returned as if to a single question. Now, in some cases, it is easy to see that there is more than one, and that an answer is not to be given, e.g. "Does the earth consist of sea, or the sky?" But in some cases it is less easy, and then people treat the question as one, and either confess their defeat by failing to answer the question, or are exposed to an apparent refutation. Thus "Is A and is B a man?" "Yes." "Then if any one hits A and B, he will strike a man" (singular), "not men" (plural). Or again, where part is good and part bad, "is the whole good or bad?" For whichever he says, it is possible that he might be thought to expose himself to an apparent refutation or to make an apparently false statement: for to say that something is good which is not good, or not good which is good, is to make a false statement. Sometimes, however, additional premisses may actually give rise to a genuine refutation; *e.g.* suppose a man were to grant that the descriptions "white" and "naked" and "blind" apply to one thing and to a number of things in a like sense. For if "blind" describes a thing that cannot see though nature designed it to see, it will also describe things that cannot see though nature designed them to do so. Whenever, then, one thing can see while another cannot, they will either both be able to see or else both be blind; which is impossible.

6

The right way, then, is either to divide apparent proofs and refutations as above, or else to refer them all to ignorance of what "refutation" is, and make that our starting-point: for it is possible to analyse all the aforesaid modes of fallacy into breaches of the definition of a refutation. In the first place, we may see if they are inconclusive: for the conclusion ought to result from the premisses laid down, so as to compel us necessarily to state it and not merely to seem to compel us. Next we should also take the definition bit by bit, and try the fallacy thereby. For of the fallacies that consist in language, some depend upon a double meaning, *e.g.* ambiguity of words and of phrases, and the fallacy of like verbal forms (for we habitually speak of everything as though it were a particular substance)—while fallacies of combination and division and accent arise because the phrase in question or the term as altered is not the same as was intended. Even this, however, should be the same, just as the thing signified should be as well, if a refutation or proof is to be effected; *e.g.* if the point concerns a doublet, then you should draw the conclusion of a "doublet," not of a "cloak." For the former conclusion also would be true, but it has not been proved; we need a further question to show that "doublet" means the same thing, in order to satisfy anyone who asks why you think your point proved.

Fallacies that depend on Accident are clear cases of *ignoratio elenchi* when once "proof" has been defined. For the same definition ought to hold good of "refutation" too, except that a mention of "the contradictory" is here added: for a refutation is a proof of the contradictory. If, then, there is no proof as regards an accident of anything, there is no refutation. For supposing, when A and B are, C must necessarily be, and C is white, there is no necessity for it to be white on account of the syllogism. So, if the triangle has its angles equal to two right-angles, and it happens to be a figure, or the simplest element or starting point, it is not because it is a figure or a starting point or simplest element that it has this character. For the demonstration proves the point about it not qua figure or qua simplest element, but qua triangle. Likewise also in other cases. If, then, refutation is a proof, an argument which argued *per accidens* ["by chance"] could not be a refutation. It is, however, just in this that the experts and men of science generally suffer refutation at the hand of the unscientific: for the latter meet the scientists with reasonings constituted *per accidens*; and the scientists for lack of the power to draw distinctions either say "Yes" to their questions, or else people suppose them to have said "Yes," although they have not.

Those that depend upon whether something is said in a certain respect only or said absolutely, are clear cases of *ignoratio elenchi* because the affirmation and the denial are not concerned with the same point. For of "white in a certain respect" the negation is "not white in a certain respect," while of "white absolutely" it is "not white, absolutely. If, then, a man treats the admission that a thing is "white in a certain respect" as though it were said to be white absolutely, he does not effect a refutation, but merely appears to do so owing to ignorance of what refutation is.

The clearest cases of all, however, are those that were previously described" as depending upon the definition of a "refutation:" and this is also why they were called by that name. For the appearance of a refutation is produced because of the omission in the definition, and if we divide fallacies in the above manner, we ought to set "Defective definition" as a common mark upon them all.

Those that depend upon the assumption of the original point and upon stating as the cause what is not the cause, are clearly shown to be cases of *ignoratio elenchi* through the definition thereof. For the conclusion ought to come about "because these things are so", and this does not happen where the premisses are not causes of it: and again it should come about without taking into account the original point, and this is not the case with those arguments which depend upon begging the original point.

Those that depend upon the assumption of the original point and upon stating as the cause what is not the cause, are clearly shown to be cases of *ignoratio elenchi* through the definition thereof. For the conclusion ought to come about "because these things are so", and this does not happen where the premisses are not causes of it: and again it should come about without taking into account the original point, and this is not the case with those arguments which depend upon begging the original point.

Those that depend upon the consequent are a branch of Accident: for the consequent is an accident, only it differs from the accident in this, that you may secure an admission of the accident in the case of one thing only (*e.g.* the identity of a yellow thing and honey and of a white thing and swan), whereas the consequent always involves more than one thing: for we claim that things that are the same as one and the same thing are also the same as one another, and this is the ground of a refutation dependent on the consequent. It is, however, not always true, e.g. suppose that and B are the same as C *per accidens*; for both "snow" and the "swan" are the same as something white." Or again, as in Melissus' argument, a man assumes that to "have been generated" and to "have a beginning" are the same thing, or to "become equal" and to "assume the same magnitude." For because what has been generated has a beginning, he claims also that what has a beginning has been generated, and argues as though both what has been generated and what is finite were the same because each has a beginning. Likewise also in the case of things that are made equal he assumes that if things that assume one and the same magnitude become equal, then also things that become equal assume one magnitude: *i.e.* he assumes the consequent. Inasmuch, then, as a refutation depending on accident consists in ignorance of what a refutation is, clearly so also does a refutation depending on the consequent. We shall have further to examine this in another way as well.

Those fallacies that depend upon the making of several questions into one consist in our failure to dissect the definition of "proposition." For a proposition is a single statement about a single thing. For the same definition applies to "one single thing only" and to the "thing," simply, *e.g.* to "man" and to "one single man only" and likewise also in other cases. If, then, a "single proposition" be one which claims a single thing of a single thing, a "proposition," simply, will also be the putting of a question of that kind. Now since a proof starts from propositions and refutation is a proof, refutation, too, will start from propositions. If, then, a proposition is a single statement about a single thing, it is obvious that this fallacy too consists in ignorance of what a refutation is: for in it what is not a proposition appears to be one. If, then, the answerer has returned an answer as though to a single question, there will be a refutation; while if he has returned one not really but apparently, there will be an apparent refutation of his thesis. All the types of fallacy, then, fall under ignorance of what a refutation is, some of them because the contradiction, which is the distinctive mark of a refutation, is merely apparent, and the rest failing to conform to the definition of a proof.

W. WARD FEARNSIDE & WILLIAM B. HOLTHER, FALLACY: THE COUNTERFEIT OF ARGUMENT

(1959)

The famous pessimist Schopenhauer, in "The Art of Controversy," turns an experienced eye on "the art of getting the best of it in a dispute.

He allows that "unquestionably the safest plan is to be in the right to begin with," but sarcastically adds that "this in itself is not enough in the existing disposition of mankind, and, on the other hand, with the weakness of the human intellect, it is not altogether necessary."

It seems doubtful that the level of public discussion has much improved in our own day. Cogency, to be sure, is admired in the scientific laboratories, just as coherence and sensitivity are encouraged amongst our mathematicians and poets. In the committee rooms of Congress, in the editorials of the chain newspapers, on radio, TV, and billboards—in all of the noise and distraction in which we live our lives, only a child or a saint could expect truth to prevail simply because it is true. Truth has a chance when Noise and Distraction are on her side; otherwise she may be overcome. And these two can and do daily prevail without her or against her.

The triumph of rhetoric is like the spread of a virus infection. When an epidemic spreads through an area, it is said to prevail there, and local measures may be taken. But to say it prevails does not mean that everyone is infected. Some persons escape infection; others are immune. It is not necessary to labor the analogy in order to show that it would be a good idea if the community could somehow develop a serum against some forms of persuasion.

Few can hope to become immune to all the tricks of persuasion since, like viruses, there are too many of them. People are daily exposed to appeals to blind faith, self interest, fear, prejudice, fancy. [We] cannot discuss persuasion in all its variety and complexity, but [we] can attempt to describe and illustrate some of the most dangerous strains.

Logic is the defense against trickery. The kinds of argument with which logic deals are the reasonable ones. Mistakes are possible, even frequent, in applying the forms of logical argument, and these mistakes are regarded as fallacies, many of them having been noted as early as Aristotle. We shall wish to guard against them. But the most common fallacies today are of a very different sort. It is a small comfort to know that an argument is entirely logical, that it validly derives its conclusion from its premises, and that all the rules of the syllogism, or whatever, are observed to a nicety, if it turns out that the premises are frauds, snares, delusions. There are brilliant tricks for getting people to accept all sorts of false premises as true (some of these tricks have been spotted since the time of ancient Greece), and these tricks of argument are so prevalent that even when people realize that something is being pulled on them, they tend to let it pass. * * *

Arguments are a highly complicated human activity and cannot be successfully studied in a sort of vacuum, as if the language uttered and answered itself. Like Schopenhauer, we have just had some hard words for the general run of discussion. This discussion at least takes place in a world of activity and interest, is directed toward goals, and, if at all successful, takes shrewd account of human nature. It is an oversimplification to suggest a clear-cut opposition between argument on one side and persuasion on the other. The most blatant singing commercial usually contains some argument, some alleging of reasons and drawing of conclusions: buy this because it's so good. * * *

To find good standards [for argument], the best thing to do is to examine a model product. The field of science abounds in clear examples of sound reasoning. The very model of a convincing argument built on reliable evidence is a scientific argument. Let us look at these model arguments, the demonstrations of science, and we may see more clearly how some other arguments fall short.

The various physical sciences establish their general laws by working backwards, as it were, from observational sentences, sentences known to be true in experience. The laws can be considered as premises that lead to the observations as conclusions: if the laws are true, the observations have to be true, too. This is the backwards effect, since, after all, it is the observations that are known to be true—the laws are inferred from them. But in the demonstrations, the arguments in scientific writing, the observations are "derived" from the laws by a vigorous process of logical or mathematical proof.

The laws are so designed as to be perfectly inclusive; that is, no known observations contradict them. Moreover, no other plausible premises are known from which the observations could follow. The laws are economically drafted: each has as wide a scope as the facts allow, and two laws never stand where one would do. Finally, all scientific laws are consistent with one another.

In all cases new observations can be predicted, not mere duplications of previous data (such as laboratory experiments in school), but actually new experiments. When Einstein published his theory, in addition to taking into account all relevant past observations in a way no other theory had succeeded in doing, he was also able to predict further observations that would be logical consequences of the laws he had discovered. The observations were made as soon as feasible, for example those connected with the bending of light rays. They "confirmed" the laws, since they could not have been predicted as a consequence of any other intelligible hypothesis.

Why, in their arguments, do the scientists treat the laws as "premises"? Why, that is, do they want to express the observations as conclusions derivable from the laws? They want to know exactly where they stand. If only one predicted observation should contradict the "law," then the latter would become a discarded hypothesis. Moreover, though the observations are derived from the law, they do not prove the law true in turn, no matter how numerous they are. The so-called laws remain hypotheses.

What would it mean to "prove" a law? Until the time of David Hume it had been thought that there was a "necessary connection" between the law and the observations, the sort of relation that there is in geometry between the theorem and the postulates and axioms. Hume showed that in the case of empirical laws, one can always imagine the sun rising in the west, gravitation working in reverse, water freezing at 100° C. But where there is a necessary connection, the contrary case is inconceivable. I cannot conceive of a prime number between 7 and 11. I cannot conceive of my being both present and absent at the same time, in the literal sense of these words. I can say these things, but I cannot say them without contradiction. I can say that 8, or 9, or 10 is a prime number, but I cannot say so and mean by "prime number" or by "8," "9," "10" what mathematicians mean by them. On the other hand, there is no logical contradiction at all in speaking of water running uphill.

There is no mathematical certainty, but the probability that the laws of science hold is enormous. They may be regarded as generalizations with no exceptions. Moreover, these generalizations are much stronger than the sort of naive generalizations traditionally discussed by philosophers of science * * * or J. S. Mill's "All hyacinths are blue." The generalizations of science never stand isolated. Rather, they are interwoven into more and more complex statements, like a web drawn together at certain points. The web endures as a whole, the strength of each strand contributing to the strength of the others. The "induction" for a generalization of physical science is thus not a simple leap from positive instances, free from the occurrence of a negative instance, to an "all" statement. It is a moving from strand to strand in a tightly woven lattice. Everything known about the world, or nearly everything, supports what is known about any small part of it.

Though there cannot be certainty that every occurrence will conform to the laws, throughout all time and space, there is still perfect certainty that every known instance is derivable from them and, moreover, that a counter instance can not occur if the laws arc true. The absence of a counter or negative instance is a necessary condition for the truth of a given law. The presence of such an instance would be a sufficient condition for the falsification of the law. In this respect, it would seem that the given law is no better off than the generalization about hyacinths. Logically it is not, but practically it is * * *

The experimental conditions are so well defined that scientists know exactly how to test the laws. This is to say, they characteristically know what experimental or observational procedures to set up for finding the negative instance if it has the remotest probability of occurring. They don't have to sit around waiting for it to show itself,.

With the model of scientific law before us, what can we say about the principles and generalizations by which we must, in our every-day problems, attempt understanding and venture deeds?

A step-by-step comparison is hardly necessary. It is all too evident that ordinary life wisdom is a tissue of vague categories, where truth is relative to ignorance, which is vast, where procedures are clumsy and blind. Far from weaving a tight lattice of systematic investigations, individuals make isolated observations. Since man must understand so that he may move and act, he leaps to some hasty generalization and "induces" some broad principles from scraps of evidence.

The common man's hypotheses sometimes fail to survive their first test. As to the so-called laws, such as the laws of human conduct, they are often incapable of confirmation with the means at hand ("Democracy is the most efficient form of government," "A world state is the only check to world war"). Responsible persons wish to act on principle, so they affirm their generalizations on faith or pretend to believe in them while the crisis of action lasts.

This is the human predicament. It has been well expressed by I.A. Richards. (From PRACTICAL CRITICISM, New York: Harcourt, Brace & Company, 1929.)

> There are subjects—mathematics, physics and the descriptive sciences supply some of them—which can be discussed in terms of verifiable fact and precise hypothesis. There are other subjects—the concrete affairs of commerce, law, organization, and police work—which can be handled by rule of thumb and generally accepted convention. But in between is the vast corpus of problems, assumptions, adumbrations, fictions, prejudices, tenets; the sphere of random belief and hopeful guesses; the whole world, in brief, of abstract opinion and disputation about matters of feeling. To this world belongs everything about which civilized man cares most.

It is not always the case, of course, that people must understand and act at once, getting on with the evidence at hand. Sometimes they can wait for better evidence and continue to gather it. Sometimes, when action is forced on them, they act well and meet with signal success. What a man can always do is act in humility. He can learn to regard his hypotheses as tentative aids to understanding, rather than as eternal principles or absolute dogmas. When the pressure of events forces a man to take sides, to do what he can, he should recognize that he is engaging in a trial-and-error process, which, though he fail, may still afford rich experience for future guidance.

Even in the "sphere of random beliefs and hopeful guesses," there are some reasons better than others. All of the materials out of which the common man builds his arguments may be far from scientific standards, but some are considerably further than others. There are many occasions of error in the gathering and arranging of the evidence from which to build arguments. * * *

Making sure that the premises are true to the evidence is a problem of meaning: premises must mean no more than the evidence supporting them. Moreover, they must be intelligible and clear, for the conclusion will be vague or haphazard if the premises are—you cannot get out more at the end of an argument than goes in at the beginning. Casting the evidence into the form of cogent premises, with the language clear and intelligible, is also a problem of meaning. The whole process, then, of setting up true premises for an argument is a matter of meaning, of what is called "semantics." There are two fairly distinct problems:

a. is the evidence truly and fairly represented in the premises?

b. are the premises which represent the evidence clear and intelligible?

A simple example may make these necessary distinctions clear. If one wished to make an argument to show that certain forms of advertising are good for the consumer as well as for the business man, he would want to be sure that the general propositions he was advancing as premises represented the facts as they are, and that the classification of the kinds of advertising treated was clear and consistent. Could he assert that all advertising must, say, appeal to some real need of the consumer? Is the distinction (b) between, say, prestige sponsorship of a symphony orchestra and direct product pushing clearly drawn and easily applicable?

We shall first treat the problems of stating the facts right, of correctly representing the known situation in the premises. Here occur the familiar fallacies of hasty generalization, *post hoc* arguments, faulty analogies. After treating of these and related fallacies, [one can] turn to the problems of vague classifications, word magic, and the rest of the nightmare horde that haunt the semanticist.

NOTES AND QUESTIONS

1. *Categories of fallacies*. For millennia, philosophers have identified, named, and categorized fallacies. In addition to Aristotle's *Sophistici Elenchi*, excerpted above, the urge to systematize recurring bad arguments has occupied some of the best minds of the Middle Ages (Peter Abelard, *Logica Ingredientibus* (1121(?)); William of Ockham (he of "Ockham's Razor" fame)); the Renaissance (Francis Bacon, *Novum Organum* (1620); Thomas Browne, *Pseudodoxia Epidemica* (1658)); through the nineteenth century (Jeremy Bentham, *Book of Fallacies* (1824)); J.S. Mill, *A System of Logic, Ratiocinative and Inductive* (1843); Gottlob Frege, *Begriffsschrift* (1879)), and into modern

times, with the work of Alfred North Whitehead and Irving Copi. *See also* CHARLES HAMBLIN, FALLACIES (1970), RALPH H. JOHNSON & J. ANTHONY BLAIR, LOGICAL SELF-DEFENCE (1977), and T. EDWARD DAMER, ATTACKING FAULTY REASONING: A PRACTICAL GUIDE TO FALLACY-FREE ARGUMENTS (2008).

Assuming that the effort is worth the candle, look back over the fallacies in this chapter and consider what broad categories suggest themselves to you. Is it useful for example to distinguish among (i) fallacies as to the *premises* (*i.e.*, assuring that the material premises of the argument are sound), (ii) faulty *inferences* from valid premises, including appeals to non-reason, and (iii) fallacies of *meaning*. Which fallacies described above fall into which categories?

2. *Patronizing science.* Are you convinced by Fearnside and Holther's argument that science offers a model of logical reasoning to which other disciplines might aspire? In this connection, consider the meaning(s) and jurisprudential implications of Alfred North Whitehead's observation in *Science and the Modern World* 232 (1925): "In formal logic, a contradiction is the signal of defeat, but in the evolution of real knowledge it marks the first step in progress toward a victory."

3. *Patronizing law.* Samuel Butler once observed that "No mistake is more common and more fatuous than appealing to logic in cases which are beyond her jurisdiction." What is the argument that the law cannot and should not be reduced to logical inference? In this connection, consider additional examples of legal doctrine or practice that seem to require (or reward) argument-types that the logician would reject.

4. *"Jury rationality."* Are there circumstances in which the law embraces *institutions* that bring something other than logic and rationality to decision-making? Consider for example recent scholarship attacking the jury system by demonstrating how irrational jurors can be. *See, e.g.,* CASS SUNSTEIN ET AL., PUNITIVE DAMAGES: HOW JURIES DECIDE (2002). Precisely what value do juries add that might make the rationality costs worth paying?

5. *The "nightmare horde" of fallacies.* Over time, new fallacies have been discovered (or perhaps merely articulated and named). In 1856, for example John Ruskin coined the pathetic fallacy, in which human emotions or characteristics are attributed to objects or animals or nature. JOHN RUSKIN, III MODERN PAINTERS § 5 (1856). In 1890, William James identified what he called the psychologist's fallacy: "The great snare of the psychologist is the confusion of his own standpoint with that of the mental fact about which he is making his report. I shall hereafter call this the 'psychologist's fallacy' *par excellence.*" WILLIAM JAMES, 1 THE PRINCIPLES OF PSYCHOLOGY 196 (1890). In 1981, Stephen Jay Gould referred to the fallacy of reification, that is "our tendency to convert abstract concepts into entities." STEPHEN JAY GOULD, THE MISMEASURE OF MAN 24 (1981).

When Fearnside and Holther refer to the "nightmare horde," they might be taken to refer to the impossibility of cataloguing and dissecting all fallacies that operate in our lives. Which fallacy covers the assertion that all of the fallacies relevant to the law (and the practice of law) have been catalogued in this chapter?

CHAPTER TEN

STRUCTURES OF LEGAL ARGUMENT (I): FRAMING THE ISSUE

■ ■ ■

"On the question you ask depends the answer you get."

— Felix Frankfurter

"Give me a place to stand, and I will move the earth."

— Archimedes

"If you don't know where you're going, when you get there, you'll be lost."

— Yogi Berra

Orientation

The curriculum of a law school is not necessarily a lawyer's friend. Breaking the law down into digestible bits named "contracts" or "torts" or "trusts and estates" may be essential at the beginning of a professional education, but it's a trap after graduation. That's because the orthodox taxonomy of law hides the reality that no problem comes into a lawyer's office with a sign around its neck announcing that it is a "contracts" problem, or a "civil procedure" problem, or a "professional ethics" problem. In that world, the lawyerly skill consists first in being able to identify the analytical frame or paradigm that offers the lawful resolution best tailored to the client's interest. That in turn requires counsel to anticipate the frames that smart and professional opponents will use to get in the way.

This chapter exposes the process by analyzing a handful of cases in which the framing of the issue seems to compel a particular result. In every illustration, the paradigm that's chosen defines what is relevant for the advocates to argue and what is relevant for the judge to say in defending the result. In each case, it is also right (and necessary) to ask how contingent or determined the choice of frame really is. In some cases, the frame is so obvious or routine that neither the lawyers nor the judges are even aware of making a choice: they are all operating within a single box and making their arguments (or writing their opinions) within it. In a criminal case, for example, the prosecutor may argue that every element of the crime is satisfied beyond a reasonable doubt, and the defense may argue that the defendant was insane at the time the acts were committed.

The result in such a case obviously depends on which argument the jury buys after being instructed in the applicable law by the judge. Every actor operates within the box labeled "criminal law." But sometimes—and not infrequently—the controversy is more fundamental and turns on the advocates' ability to categorize the dispositive issue—as a matter of substance or procedure for example, or as a matter of fact or a matter of law, or as a tort or a contract. Either characterization may be defensible in hard cases, and it is an art to make one frame persuasive and the other misleading or wrong.

The history of science offers a limited but useful analogy. In *The Structure of Scientific Revolutions*, Thomas Kuhn argued that science is not a linear or steady process of accumulating scientific knowledge. Rather it is "a series of peaceful interludes punctuated by intellectually violent revolutions," in the course of which "one conceptual world view is replaced by another." These world views or "paradigms" define what is relevant for scientists to study, and their research tends to reinforce the archetype. They would be performing what Kuhn called "normal science." But "[f]rameworks must be lived with and explored before they can be broken," and every so often, a visionary scientist could account for the known data and explain whatever aberrations exist with a completely different world view—one that did not simply improve the old paradigm but supplanted it altogether. Kuhn offered examples from physics (the relativity and quantum theories of Einstein versus the mechanics of Newton); biology (the natural selection theories of Darwin versus the taxonomic or design-driven view of biology); astronomy (Ptolemy's theory that the sun revolves around the Earth versus the heliocentric view of Copernicus or Aristarchus).

According to Kuhn, these revolutions occur only after extended periods of tradition-bound normal science, during which the number of aberrations or unexplained data mount. As one critic of *The Structure of Scientific Revolutions* has summarized the position:

> in the period of normal science, scientists tend to agree about what phenomena are relevant and what constitutes an explanation of these phenomena, about what problems are worth solving and what is a solution of a problem. Near the end of a period of normal science a crisis occurs—experiments give results that don't fit existing theories, or internal contradictions are discovered in these theories. There is alarm and confusion. Strange ideas fill the scientific literature. Eventually there is a revolution. Scientists become converted to a new way of looking at nature, resulting eventually in a new period of normal science. The "paradigm" has shifted.

Steven Weinberg, *The Revolution that Didn't Happen*, 45 NEW YORK REVIEW OF BOOKS 48 (October 8, 1998).

Kuhn's ideas have not met with universal approval,[1] and he uses the term "paradigm" (or "common disciplinary matrix") so frequently that it seems to have multiple meanings. But it does offer a language for thinking about legal argumentation. As you read the following cases, which analytical frames or paradigms are in conflict, and how was the choice among them made and defended?

A. TORT VERSUS CONTRACT

LEVY V. DANIELS' U-DRIVE AUTO RENTING CO.

108 Conn. 333, 143 A. 163 (1928)

* * * The defendant, Daniels' U-Drive Auto Renting Company, Incorporated, rented in Hartford to Sack an automobile, which he operated, and in which Levy, the plaintiff, was a passenger. During the time the automobile was rented and operated, the defendant renting company was subject to section 21 of chapter 195 of the Public Acts of Connecticut, 1925, which provides:

> Any person renting or leasing to another any motor vehicle owned by him shall be liable for any damage to any person or property caused by the operation of such motor vehicle while so rented or leased.

While the plaintiff was a passenger, Sack brought the car to a stop on the main highway at Longmeadow, Mass., and negligently allowed it to stand directly in the path of automobiles proceeding southerly in the same direction his automobile was headed, without giving sufficient warning to automobiles approaching from his rear, and without having a tail light in operation, and when, due to inclement weather, the visibility was reduced to an exceedingly low degree. At this time the defendant Maginn negligently ran into and upon the rear end of the car Sack was operating, and threw plaintiff forcibly forward, causing him serious injuries. The specific acts of Maginn's negligence are set up at length in the complaint; it is not essential at this time to recite them. The plaintiff suffered his severe injuries in consequence of the concurrent negligence of both defendants.

The defendant [Daniels' U-Drive] demurred[2] to the complaint upon several grounds, upon only one of which the trial court rested its decision; namely, that the liability of the defendant must be determined by the law of Massachusetts, which did not impose upon persons renting automobiles

---

1 *See, e.g.*, Lakatos, *Falsification and the Methodology of Scientific Research Programmes* in CRITICISM AND THE GROWTH OF KNOWLEDGE (I. LAKATOS & A. MUSGRAVE EDS. 1970), at 91.

2 [Editor's Note: A demurrer is a response in a court proceeding in which the defendant does not dispute the truth of the allegation but claims it is not sufficient grounds to justify legal action.]

any such obligation as the Connecticut act did. This is the only ground of demurrer which was presented in the argument of the appeal. Since all of the grounds of demurrer were raised by the appeal, we have examined the others, and deem it sufficient in disposing of them to say that none is well taken.

It is the defendant's contention in support of this ground of demurrer that the action set forth in the complaint is one of tort, and, since Massachusetts has no statute like, or substantially like, the Connecticut act, it must be determined by the common law of that state, under which the plaintiff must prove, to prevail, the negligence of the defendant in renting a defective motor vehicle and in failing to disclose the defect. If this were the true theory of the complaint, the conclusion thus reached must have followed. "The *locus delicti* [place of the wrong] determined the existence of the cause of action." *Orr v. Ahern*, 107 Conn. 174, 176, 139 A. 691, 692. Under the law of Massachusetts, the plaintiff concededly would have a cause of action against Sack and Maginn for their tortious conduct in the operation of the cars they were driving. * * * His counsel, however, construe the complaint as one in its nature contractual. The [Connecticut] act makes him who rents or leases any motor vehicle to another liable for any damage to any person or property caused by the operation of the motor vehicle while so rented or leased. Liability for "damage caused by the operation of such motor vehicle" means caused by its tortious operation. This was undoubtedly the legislative intent * * *. The plaintiff concedes this to be the true construction of these words, and the defendant acquiesces in this construction.

The complaint alleges a tortious operation of the automobile rented to Sack by the defendant, causing the injuries to the plaintiff as alleged, and constituting an action *ex delicto*. The statute gives, in terms, the injured person a right of action against the defendant which rented the automobile to Sack, though the injury occurred in Massachusetts. It was a right which the statute gave directly, not derivatively, to the injured person as a consequence of the contract of hiring. The purpose of the statute was not primarily to give the injured person a right of recovery against the tortious operator of the car, but to protect the safety of the traffic upon highways by providing an incentive to him who rented motor vehicles to rent them to competent and careful operators, by making him liable for damage resulting from the tortious operation of the rented vehicles. The common law would not hold the defendant liable upon the facts recited in the complaint for the negligence of Sack in the operation of this automobile. The rental of motor vehicles to any but competent and careful operators, or to persons of unknown responsibility, would be liable to result in injury to the public upon or near highways, and this imminent danger justified, as a reasonable exercise of the police power, this statute, which requires all who engage in this business to become responsible for any injury inflicted upon the public by the tortious operation of the rented motor vehicle. * * *

Statutes of this character are so clearly within the reasonable exercise of the police power that we do not deem it necessary to fortify his opinion, or the opinion we have already expressed, by detailed reference to the cases.

The statute made the liability of the person renting motor vehicles a part of every contract of hiring a motor vehicle in Connecticut. A liability *ex delicto* ["from a wrong," in this case a tort] is created by the law of the place of the *delict*. A liability arising out of a contract depends upon the law of the place of contract, "unless the contract is to be performed or to have its beneficial operation and effect elsewhere, or it is made with reference to the law of another place." *Illustrated Postal Card & Novelty Co. v. Holt*, 85 Conn. 140, 143, 81 A. 1061, 1062. We will enforce rights of action on contracts arising in other jurisdictions unless these contravene our own law, or our own fundamental and important public policy imperatively requires their non-enforcement. It is a general rule, subject to the exceptions we have noted, that rights *ex contractu* ["from a contract"] may be enforced anywhere.

If the liability of this defendant under this statute is contractual, no question can arise as to the plaintiff's right to enforce this contract, provided the obligation imposed upon this defendant was for the "direct, sole and exclusive benefit" of the plaintiff. The contract was made in Connecticut; at the instant of its making the statute made a part of the contract of hiring the liability of the defendant which the plaintiff seeks to enforce. The law inserted in the contract this provision. The statute did not create the liability; it imposed it in case the defendant voluntarily rented the automobile. Whether the defendant entered into this contract of hiring was his own voluntary act; if he did he must accept the condition upon which the law permitted the making of the contract. The contract was for the "direct, sole, and exclusive benefit" of the plaintiff, who is alleged to have been injured through the tortious operation of the automobile rented by the defendant to Sack. The right of the plaintiff as a beneficiary of this contract to maintain this action is no longer an open question in this state. The contract was made for him and every other member of the public. That the beneficiary was undisturbed because each of the public was a beneficiary is of no consequence. His injury determines his identity and right of action. The assent of the beneficiary, if required, is manifested in his action upon the contract. The demurrer should have been overruled. * * *

NOTES AND QUESTIONS

1. *Characterization as a framing device*. In *Levy*, the lower court framed the case as a matter of tort law and applied the traditional rule that every substantive issue in such cases should generally be resolved by the law of the place where the tort—especially the injury—occurred, *i.e.*, Massachusetts. On

appeal, the Supreme Court of Connecticut framed the issue as one of contract and applied the traditional rule that every substantive issue in a contract case should generally be resolved by the law of the place where the contract was made, *i.e.* Connecticut. The case suggests that whichever party frames or categorizes the case more persuasively wins. What exactly guided the court in its choice of frames?

2. *"Normal" law and the theory of a case.* Paradigm shifts may be revolutionary in science, as Kuhn suggests, but *Levy* demonstrates that the choice of paradigms in the law can be dispositive even in routine cases with no drama or implications for the broader society.

At some point in every case, advocates have to develop and deploy a "theory of the case," defined as:

> A comprehensive and orderly mental arrangement of principles and facts, conceived and constructed for the purpose of securing a judgment or decree of a court in favor of a litigant; the particular line of reasoning of either party to a suit, the purpose being to bring together certain facts of the case in a logical sequence and to correlate them in a way that produces in the decision-maker's mind a definite result or conclusion favored by the advocate.

BLACK'S LAW DICTIONARY 1616 (9th ed.). This is not some broad "theory" of law at work: it is an effort to conceive of a particular, contested transaction in a coherent and compelling way. The overall narrative of the case has to make sense, evidence has to be collected tending to confirm the essential "truths" of the case from the client's perspective, inconvenient facts have to be anticipated and explained, and the relevant legal principles have to be articulated and their authority established.

3. *A patchwork quilt of applicable laws?* Is it defensible to have two different states' laws applying to a single case? In *Levy*, how would you go about determining which issues should be resolved under Massachusetts law and which should be resolved under Connecticut law? Is it sensible that this hybrid result should occur or not?

4. *Blatant result-orientation versus an analysis of state interests.* One critique of the result in *Levy* is that the Connecticut Supreme Court simply did not want a Connecticut business to escape liability under a Connecticut statute that would have applied if the accident had occurred a few minutes earlier on the Connecticut side of the border with Massachusetts. In that case, the traditional choice of law in tort—that the law of place of the injury controls all substantive matters—would have pointed towards Connecticut. Perhaps the Supreme Court wished to avoid awarding a windfall to the defendant just because it had the random good fortune to have rented a car that was in an accident in Massachusetts. The Court wanted a particular result, and it manufactured that result by treating an obvious tort case as a contract case.

But suppose we put off the frame of result orientation as an explanation of this case. Suppose instead that we defended the result by pointing out that the policies behind the Connecticut statute *would* be advanced on application to these facts (common domicile of the plaintiff and defendant in Connecticut, defendant plainly within the legislative reach of the Connecticut legislature and clearly the target of the legislation), while the policies behind the Massachusetts' rule of non-liability—whatever they are—*would not* be advanced be applying that rule to parties from Connecticut, whose relationship is centered entirely in Connecticut, and whose presence in Massachusetts is temporary and coincidental. Admittedly this state interest analysis is not in the court's opinion, but is it an attractive explanation of the result? After all, if law is an irreducibly purposeful discipline of social order, and a choice of law is necessary, why would you ever apply a statute in circumstances when its purposes were not advanced?

5. *Pushing back on the tort-contract distinction*. It is easy enough to see how characterizing *Levy* as a contract case yields one result, and characterizing it as a tort case yields an opposite result. In broad terms, it is also possible to define the respective spheres of operation for these two bodies of law. But what happens when these two paradigms clash or influence one another?

In THE DEATH OF CONTRACT (1974), Professor Grant Gilmore argued that tort liability doctrines, which do not generally rest on consent, was colonizing contract liability doctrines, which generally do. In Gilmore's analysis, contractual liability had been systematized by Christopher Columbus Langdell in the nineteenth-century around the organizing principle of the parties' bargain. The "bargain theory" explained a wide variety of rules that effectively *limited* contractual liability, which in turn reflected and supported the dominant free-market values of the time. *Id.* at 23–24, 36 (rules on consideration, the unenforceability of agreements to agree, the revocability of offers, the unenforceability of contract modifications, and the requirement of mutuality of obligations). The "death" of contract law consisted in the rise of contractual liability that turned on implicit conditions and the parties' circumstances—matters that had not been the subject of any bargain. So for example, Gilmore noted the rise of liability based on doctrines of good faith or detrimental reliance or unjust enrichment, which he argued are better conceived as tort or tort-like categories. They certainly cannot be forced to fit the bargain paradigm. *Id.* at 77–81, 85–93.

Academics have been reacting to THE DEATH OF CONTRACT for decades and not always favorably, but it offers a useful example of how doctrinal frameworks can morph over time, showing how one paradigm can affect others, and how aberrational decisions can mount in the law just as aberrational data can mount in the sciences, occasionally requiring the reconceptualization of entire fields of thought and practice.

B. PROCEDURE VERSUS SUBSTANCE

GRANT V. MCAULIFFE

41 Cal.2d 859, 264 P.2d 944 (1953)

On December 17, 1949, plaintiffs W. R. Grant and R. M. Manchester were riding west on United States Highway 66 in an automobile owned and driven by plaintiff D. O. Jensen. Defendant's decedent, W. W. Pullen, was driving his automobile east on the same highway. The two automobiles collided at a point approximately 15 miles east of Flagstaff, Arizona. Jensen's automobile was badly damaged, and Jensen, Grant, and Manchester suffered personal injuries. Nineteen days later, on January 5, 1950, Pullen died as a result of injuries received in the collision. Defendant McAuliffe was appointed administrator of his estate and letters testamentary were issued by the Superior Court of Plumas County. All three plaintiffs, as well as Pullen, were residents of California at the time of the collision. After the appointment of defendant, each plaintiff presented his claim for damages. Defendant rejected all three claims, and on December 14, 1950, each plaintiff filed an action against the estate of Pullen to recover damages for the injuries caused by the alleged negligence of the decedent. Defendant filed a general demurrer and a motion to abate each of the complaints. The trial court entered an order granting the motion in each case. Each plaintiff has appealed. The appeals are based on the same ground and have therefore been consolidated.

The basic question is whether plaintiffs' causes of action against Pullen survived his death and are maintainable against his estate. The statutes of this state provide that causes of action for negligent torts survive the death of the tortfeasor and can be maintained against the administrator or executor of his estate. Defendant contends, however, that the survival of a cause of action is a matter of substantive law, and that the courts of this state must apply the law of Arizona governing survival of causes of action. There is no provision for survival of causes of action in the statutes of Arizona, although there is a provision that in the event of the death of a party to a pending proceeding his personal representative can be substituted as a party to the action, if the cause of action survives. The Supreme Court of Arizona has held that if a tort action has not been commenced before the death of the tortfeasor a plea in abatement must be sustained.

Thus, the answer to the question whether the causes of action against Pullen survived and are maintainable against his estate depends on whether Arizona or California law applies. In actions on torts occurring abroad, the courts of this state determine the substantive matters inherent in the cause of action by adopting as their own the law of the place where the tortious acts occurred, unless it is contrary to the public policy of this state. * * * But the forum does not adopt as its own the procedural law of the place where the tortious acts occur. It must, therefore, be determined whether survival of causes of action is procedural or substantive for conflict of laws purposes.

This question is one of first impression in this state. The precedents in other jurisdictions are conflicting. In many cases [in other states] it has been held that the survival of a cause of action is a matter of substance and that the law of the place where the tortious acts occurred must be applied to determine the question. * * * The [First] Restatement of the Conflict of Laws, section 390, is in accord. It should be noted, however, that the majority of the foregoing cases were decided after drafts of the Restatement were first circulated in 1929. Before that time, it appears that the weight of authority was that survival of causes of action is procedural and governed by the domestic law of the forum. Many of the cases, decided both before and after the Restatement, holding that survival is substantive and must be determined by the law of the place where the tortious acts occurred, confused the problems involved in survival of causes of action with those involved in causes of action for wrongful death. A cause of action for wrongful death is statutory. It is a new cause of action vested in the widow or next of kin, and arises on the death of the injured person. Before his death, the injured person himself has a separate and distinct cause of action and, if it survives, the same cause of action can be enforced by the personal representative of the deceased against the tortfeasor. The survival statutes do not create a new cause of action, as do the wrongful death statutes. * * * They merely prevent the abatement of the cause of action of the injured person, and provide for its enforcement by or against the personal representative of the deceased. They are analogous to statutes of limitation, which are procedural for conflict of laws purposes and are governed by the domestic law of the forum. (*Biewend v. Biewend,* 17 Cal.2d 108, 114. Thus, a cause of action arising in another state, by the laws of which an action cannot be maintained thereon because of lapse of time, can be enforced in California by a citizen of this state, if he has held the cause of action from the time it accrued.

Defendant contends, however, that the characterization of survival of causes of action as substantive or procedural is foreclosed by *Cort v. Steen,* 36 Cal.2d 437, 442 [224 P.2d 723], where it was held that the California survival statutes were substantive and therefore did not apply retroactively. The problem in the present proceeding, however, is not whether the survival statutes apply retroactively, but whether they are substantive or procedural for purposes of conflict of laws. " 'Substance' and 'procedure' . . . are not legal concepts of invariable content" (*Black Diamond Steamship Corp. v. Stewart & Sons,* 336 U.S. 386, 397), and a statute or other rule of law will be characterized as substantive or procedural according to the nature of the problem for which a characterization must be made. * * *

Since we find no compelling weight of authority for either alternative, we are free to make a choice on the merits. We have concluded that survival of causes of action should be governed by the law of the forum. Survival is not an essential part of the cause of action itself but relates to the procedures available for the enforcement of the legal claim for damages. Basically the question is one of the administration of decedents' estates, which is a purely local proceeding. The problem here is whether the causes of action that these plaintiffs had against Pullen before his death survive as liabilities of his estate. Section 573 of the [California] Probate Code provides that "all actions founded . . . upon any liability for physical injury, death or injury to property, may be maintained by or against executors and administrators in all cases in which the cause of action . . . is one which would not abate upon the death of their respective testators or intestates. . . ." Civil Code, section 956, provides that "A thing in action arising out of a wrong which results in physical injury to the person . . . shall not abate by reason of the death of the wrongdoer . . .," and causes of action for damage to property are maintainable against executors and administrators under section 574 of the Probate Code. Decedent's estate is located in this state, and letters of administration were issued to defendant by the courts of this state. The responsibilities of defendant, as administrator of Pullen's estate, for injuries inflicted by Pullen before his death are governed by the laws of this state. This approach has been followed in a number of well-reasoned cases. It retains control of the administration of estates by the local Legislature and avoids the problems involved in determining the administrator's amenability to suit under the laws of other states. The common law doctrine *actio personalis moritur cum persona* ["a personal action dies with the person"] had its origin in a penal concept of tort liability. Today, tort liabilities of the sort involved in these actions are regarded as compensatory. When, as in the present case, all of the parties were residents of this state, and the estate of the deceased tortfeasor is being administered in this state, plaintiff's right to prosecute their causes of action is governed by the laws of this state relating to administration of estates.

The orders granting defendant's motions to abate are reversed, and the causes remanded for further proceedings.

SCHAUER, J., dissenting. In *Cort v. Steen* (1950), 36 Cal.2d 437, 442 [224 P.2d 723], this court held that under the doctrine of nonsurvivability the abatement of an action by the death of the injured person through the tortfeasor's act or otherwise, or by the death of the tortfeasor, abates the wrong as well; that the effect of a survival statute is to create a right or cause of action rather than to either continue an existing right or revive or extend a remedy theretofore accrued for the redress of an existing wrong; and that consequently a survival statute enacted after death of the tortfeasor did not apply to the tort or cause of action involved. And more recently, in *Estate of Arbulich* (1953), [257 P.2d 433], we recognized the rule that the burden of proof provisions of the Probate Code sections dealing with reciprocal inheritance rights are not merely procedural in nature, but, rather, are substantive statutes regulating succession, and that consequently such rights are to be determined by the law as it existed on the date of decedent's death.

Irreconcilably inconsistent with the cases cited in the preceding paragraph, the majority now hold that "Survival is not an essential part of the cause of action itself but relates to the procedures available for the enforcement of the legal claim for damages. Basically the question is one of the administration of decedents' estates, which is a purely local proceeding." If the above stated holding is to prevail, then for the sake of the law's integrity and clarity, and in fairness to lower courts and to counsel, the cited cases should be expressly overruled. But even more regrettable than the failure to either follow or unequivocally overrule the cited cases is the character of the "rule" which is now promulgated: the majority assert that henceforth "a statute or other rule of law will be characterized as substantive or procedural according to the nature of the problem for which a characterization must be made," thus suggesting that the court will no longer be bound to consistent enforcement or uniform application of "a statute or other rule of law" but will instead apply one "rule" or another as the untrammeled whimsy of the majority may from time to time dictate, "according to the nature of the problem" as they view it in a given case. This concept of the majority strikes deeply at what has been our proud boast that ours was a government of laws rather than of men.

Although any administration of an estate in the courts of this state is local in a procedural sense, the rights and claims both in favor of and against such an estate are substantive in nature, and vest irrevocably at the date of death. Since this court has clearly held that a right or cause of action created by a survival statute is likewise substantive, rather than procedural, we should hold, if we would follow the law, that the trial court properly granted defendant's motions to abate.

NOTES AND QUESTIONS

1. *Distinguishing substance from procedure.* If you were writing on a clean slate, what would be the genetic marker of a procedural rule, *i.e.*, the things that all such rules would have in common and that would distinguish them from substantive rules? By those criteria, is the survival statute in *Grant* procedural or substantive?

2. *Grant and the choice of frames.* What—if anything—justified the Court's characterization of the issues in the *Grant* case?

3. *Result-orientation and the analysis of state interests*. One possible interpretation of *Grant* is that the California court simply wanted to reach a particular result, and it did so by manipulating the label "procedural" and applying it to the administration of estates. But can the result be justified by tracking whether the policies behind the two laws in conflict would actually be advanced or not on the particular facts of the case?

C. MATTERS OF FACT VERSUS MATTERS OF LAW

The law frequently distinguishes between matters of law and matters of fact. The line may be difficult to draw in a particular case, and the definition of either is rarely articulated,[3] but the consequences of one designation or the other can be profound. In a jury trial for example, issues of fact are generally for the jury to resolve, and issues of law are resolved by the judge. On appeal, under Rule 52(a) of the Federal Rules of Civil Procedure, findings of fact at trial are subject to a highly deferential standard of review: they cannot be disturbed unless they are "clearly erroneous." By contrast, conclusions of law from the court below are subject on appeal to *de novo* review, meaning that the court of appeal can treat the issue afresh. Similarly, in administrative law, an executive agency's findings of fact are binding on a reviewing court so long as those findings are supported by "substantial evidence",[4] in light of the whole record.[5] By contrast, an agency's "legal determinations are reviewed *de novo*," although the reviewing court will "accord[ ] substantial deference to the agency's interpretation of the statutes and regulations it administers."[6]

What accounts for these institutional divisions of responsibility? How would you articulate the difference between these two frames of reference labeled "law" and "fact"? And suppose the issue is neither one nor the other but is a "mixed" question of law and fact. What standard of review is appropriate then? In *Salve Regina College v. Russell*, 499 U.S. 225, 233 (1991), the Supreme Court said that "deferential review of mixed questions of law and fact is warranted when it appears that the district court is

---

[3] Even when a court tries to define the difference between fact and law, its progress may be microscopic. Consider the effort by the Ninth Circuit Court of Appeals: "A finding of fact, to which the clearly erroneous rule applies, is a finding based on the 'fact-finding tribunal's experience with the mainsprings of human conduct.' A conclusion of law would be a conclusion based on [the] application of a legal standard." *Lundgren v. Freeman*, 307 F.2d 104, 115 (9th Cir. 1962), *citing Comm. Int. Rev. v. Duberstein*, 363 U.S. 278, 289 (1960). That formulation has been considered largely unworkable almost since its inception. *See, e.g.,* Stephen A. Weiner, *The Civil Nonjury Trial and the Law-Fact Distinction,* 55 CALIF.L.REV. 1020, 1054 (1967).

[4] *F.T.C. v. Indiana Fed'n of Dentists*, 476 U.S. 447, 454 (1986); *Universal Camera Corp. v. NLRB*, 340 U.S. 474, 477 (1951) (holding that court is bound by agency fact-finding if supported by "such relevant evidence as a reasonable mind might accept as adequate to support a conclusion.").

[5] 5 U.S.C. § 706.

[6] *Sara Lee Corp. v. Am. Bakers Ass'n Ret. Plan*, 512 F. Supp. 2d 32, 37 (D.D.C. 2007); *see Chevron U.S.A., Inc. v. Natural Resources Defense Council, Inc.*, 467 U.S. 837, 842–43 (1984).

'better positioned' than the appellate court to decide the issue in question or that probing appellate scrutiny will not contribute to the clarity of legal doctrine." Is that progress?

SAUL ORNELAS V. UNITED STATES

517 U.S. 690 (1996)

CHIEF JUSTICE REHNQUIST delivered the opinion of the Court. Petitioners each pleaded guilty to possession of cocaine with intent to distribute. They reserved their right to appeal the District Court's denial of their motion to suppress the cocaine found in their car. The District Court had found reasonable suspicion to stop and question petitioners as they entered their car, and probable cause to remove one of the interior panels where a package containing two kilograms of cocaine was found. The Court of Appeals opined that the findings of reasonable suspicion to stop, and probable cause to search, should be reviewed "deferentially," and "for clear error." We hold that the ultimate questions of reasonable suspicion and probable cause to make a warrantless search should be reviewed *de novo*.

The facts are not disputed. In the early morning of a December day in 1992, Detective Michael Pautz, a 20-year veteran of the Milwaukee County Sheriff's Department with 2 years specializing in drug enforcement, was conducting drug-interdiction surveillance in downtown Milwaukee. Pautz noticed a 1981 two-door Oldsmobile with California license plates in a motel parking lot. The car attracted Pautz's attention for two reasons: because older model, two-door General Motors cars are a favorite with drug couriers because it is easy to hide things in them; and because California is a "source State" for drugs. Detective Pautz radioed his dispatcher to inquire about the car's registration. The dispatcher informed Pautz that the owner was either Miguel Ledesma Ornelas or Miguel Ornelas Ledesma from San Jose, California; Pautz was unsure which name the dispatcher gave. Detective Pautz checked the motel registry and learned that an Ismael Ornelas accompanied by a second man had registered at 4 a.m., without reservations.

Pautz called for his partner, Donald Hurrle, a detective with approximately 25 years of law enforcement experience, assigned for the past 6 years to the drug enforcement unit. When Hurrle arrived at the scene, the officers contacted the local office of the Drug Enforcement Administration (DEA) and asked DEA personnel to run the names Miguel Ledesma Ornelas and Ismael Ornelas through the Narcotics and Dangerous Drugs Information System (NADDIS), a federal database of known and suspected drug traffickers. Both names appeared in NADDIS. The NADDIS report identified Miguel Ledesma Ornelas as a heroin dealer from El Centro, California, and Ismael Ornelas, Jr., as a cocaine dealer from Tucson, Arizona. The officers then summoned Deputy Luedke and the department's drug-sniffing dog, Merlin. Upon their arrival, Detective Pautz left for another assignment. Detective Hurrle informed Luedke of what they knew and together they waited.

Sometime later, petitioners emerged from the motel and got into the Oldsmobile. Detective Hurrle approached the car, identified himself as a police officer, and inquired whether they had any illegal drugs or contraband. Petitioners answered "No." Hurrle then asked for identification and was given two California driver's licenses bearing the names Saul Ornelas and Ismael Ornelas. Hurrle asked them if he could search the car and petitioners consented. The men appeared calm, but Ismael was shaking somewhat. Deputy Luedke, who over the past nine years had searched approximately 2,000 cars for narcotics, searched the Oldsmobile's interior. He noticed that a panel above the right rear passenger armrest felt somewhat loose and suspected that the panel might have been removed and contraband hidden inside. Luedke would testify later that a screw in the doorjam adjacent to the loose panel was rusty, which to him meant that the screw had been removed at some time. Luedke dismantled the panel and discovered two kilograms of cocaine. Petitioners were arrested.

Petitioners filed pretrial motions to suppress, alleging that the police officers violated their Fourth Amendment rights when the officers detained them in the parking lot and when Deputy Luedke searched inside the panel without a warrant. The Government conceded in the court below that when the officers approached petitioners in the parking lot, a reasonable person would not have felt free to leave, so the encounter was an investigatory stop. An investigatory stop is permissible under the Fourth Amendment if supported by reasonable suspicion, *Terry v. Ohio*, 392 U.S. 1 (1968), and a warrantless search of a car is valid if based on probable cause, *California v. Acevedo*, 500 U.S. 565, 569–570 (1991).

After conducting an evidentiary hearing, the Magistrate Judge concluded that the circumstances gave the officers reasonable suspicion, but not probable cause. The Magistrate found, as a finding of fact, that there was no rust on the screw and hence concluded that Deputy Luedke had an insufficient basis to conclude that drugs would be found within the panel. The Magistrate nonetheless recommended that the District Court deny the suppression motions because he thought, given the presence of the drug-sniffing dog, that the officers would have found the cocaine by lawful means eventually and therefore the drugs were admissible under the inevitable discovery doctrine. *See Nix v. Williams*, 467 U.S. 431 (1984).

The District Court adopted the Magistrate's recommendation with respect to reasonable suspicion, but not its reasoning as to probable cause. The District Court thought that the model, age, and source-State origin of the car, and the fact that two men traveling together checked into a motel at 4 o'clock in the morning without reservations, formed a drug-courier profile and that this profile together with the NADDIS reports gave rise to reasonable suspicion of drug-trafficking activity; in the court's view, reasonable suspicion became probable cause when Deputy Luedke found the loose panel. Accordingly, the court ruled that the cocaine need not be excluded.

The Court of Appeals reviewed deferentially the District Court's determinations of reasonable suspicion and probable cause; it would reverse only upon a finding of "clear error." The court found no clear error in the reasonable-suspicion analysis and affirmed that determination. With respect to the probable-cause finding, however, the court remanded the case for a determination on whether Luedke was credible when testifying about the loose panel. On remand, the Magistrate Judge expressly found the testimony credible. The District Court accepted the finding, and once again ruled that probable cause supported the search. The Seventh Circuit held that determination not clearly erroneous.

We granted *certiorari* to resolve the conflict among the Circuits over the applicable standard of appellate review[, "clear error" or "*de novo*".]

Articulating precisely what "reasonable suspicion" and "probable cause" mean is not possible. They are commonsense, nontechnical conceptions that deal with " 'the factual and practical considerations of everyday life on which reasonable and prudent men, not legal technicians, act.' " *Illinois v. Gates*, 462 U.S. 213, 231 (1983) (*quoting Brinegar v. United States*, 338 U.S. 160, 175 (1949)). As such, the standards are "not readily, or even usefully, reduced to a neat set of legal rules." We have described reasonable suspicion simply as "a particularized and objective basis" for suspecting the person stopped of criminal activity, *United States v. Cortez*, 449 U.S. 411, 417–418 (1981), and probable cause to search as existing where the known facts and circumstances are sufficient to warrant a man of reasonable prudence in the belief that contraband or evidence of a crime will be found, *see Brinegar, supra*, at 175–176; *Gates, supra*, at 238. We have cautioned that these two legal principles are not "finely-tuned standards," comparable to the standards of proof beyond a reasonable doubt or of proof by a preponderance of the evidence. They are instead fluid concepts that take their substantive content from the particular contexts in which the standards are being assessed. * * *

The principal components of a determination of reasonable suspicion or probable cause will be the events which occurred leading up to the stop or search, and then the decision whether these historical facts, viewed from the standpoint of an objectively reasonable police officer, amount to reasonable suspicion or to probable cause. The first part of the analysis involves only a determination of historical facts, but the second is a mixed question of law and fact: "[T]he historical facts are admitted or established, the rule of law is undisputed, and the issue is whether the facts satisfy the [relevant] statutory [or constitutional] standard, or to put it another way, whether the rule of law as applied to the established facts is or is not violated." *Pullman-Standard v. Swint*, 456 U.S. 273, 289, n. 19 (1982).

We think independent appellate review of these ultimate determinations of reasonable suspicion and probable cause is consistent with the position we have taken in past cases. We have never, when reviewing a probable-cause or reasonable-suspicion determination ourselves, expressly deferred to the trial court's determination. A policy of sweeping deference would permit, "[i]n the absence of any significant difference in the facts," "the Fourth Amendment's incidence [to] tur[n] on whether different trial judges draw general conclusions that the facts are sufficient or insufficient to constitute probable cause." *Brinegar, supra*, at 171. Such varied results would be inconsistent with the idea of a unitary system of law. This, if a matter-of-course, would be unacceptable.

In addition, the legal rules for probable cause and reasonable suspicion acquire content only through application. Independent review is therefore necessary if appellate courts are to maintain control of, and to clarify, the legal principles. *See Miller v. Fenton*, 474 U.S. 104, 114 (1985) (where the "relevant legal principle can be given meaning only through its application to the particular circumstances of a case, the Court has been reluctant to give the trier of fact's conclusions presumptive force and, in so doing, strip a federal appellate court of its primary function as an expositor of law").

Finally, *de novo* review tends to unify precedent and will come closer to providing law enforcement officers with a defined " 'set of rules which, in most instances, makes it possible to reach a correct determination beforehand as to whether an invasion of privacy is justified in the interest of law enforcement.' " *New York v. Belton*, 453 U.S. 454, 458 (1981); *see also Thompson v. Keohane*, 516 U.S. 99, 115 (1995) ("[T]he law declaration aspect of independent review potentially may guide police, unify precedent, and stabilize the law," and those effects "serve legitimate law enforcement interests"). * * *

The Court of Appeals, in adopting its deferential standard of review here, reasoned that *de novo* review for warrantless searches would be inconsistent with the " 'great deference' " paid when reviewing a decision to issue a warrant, *see Illinois v. Gates*, 462 U.S. 213 (1983). We cannot agree. The Fourth Amendment demonstrates a "strong preference for searches conducted pursuant to a warrant," *Gates, supra*, at 236, and the police are more likely to use the warrant process if the scrutiny applied to a magistrate's probable-cause determination to issue a warrant is less than that for warrantless searches. Were we to eliminate this distinction, we would eliminate the incentive.

We therefore hold that as a general matter determinations of reasonable suspicion and probable cause should be reviewed *de novo* on appeal. Having said this, we hasten to point out that a reviewing court should take care both to review findings of historical fact only for clear error and to give due weight to inferences drawn from those facts by resident judges and local law enforcement officers.

A trial judge views the facts of a particular case in light of the distinctive features and events of the community; likewise, a police officer views the facts through the lens of his police experience and expertise. The background facts provide a context for the historical facts, and when seen together yield inferences that deserve deference. For example, what may not amount to reasonable suspicion at a motel located alongside a transcontinental highway at the height of the summer tourist season may rise to that level in December in Milwaukee. That city is unlikely to have been an overnight stop selected at the last minute by a traveler coming from California to points east. The 85-mile width of Lake Michigan blocks any further eastward progress. And while the city's salubrious summer climate and seasonal attractions bring many tourists at that time of year, the same is not true in December. Milwaukee's average daily high temperature in that month is 31 degrees and its average daily low is 17 degrees; the percentage of possible sunshine is only 38 percent. It is a reasonable inference that a Californian stopping in Milwaukee in December is either there to transact business or to visit family or friends. The background facts, though rarely the subject of explicit findings, inform the judge's assessment of the historical facts.

In a similar vein, our cases have recognized that a police officer may draw inferences based on his own experience in deciding whether probable cause exists. To a layman the sort of loose panel below the back seat armrest in the automobile involved in this case may suggest only wear and tear, but to Officer Luedke, who had searched roughly 2,000 cars for narcotics, it suggested that drugs may be secreted inside the panel. An appeals court should give due weight to a trial court's finding that the officer was credible and the inference was reasonable.

We vacate the judgments and remand the case to the Court of Appeals to review *de novo* the District Court's determinations that the officer had reasonable suspicion and probable cause in this case.

JUSTICE SCALIA, dissenting. The Court today decides that a district court's determinations whether there was probable cause to justify a warrantless search and reasonable suspicion to make an investigatory stop should be reviewed *de novo*. We have in the past reviewed some mixed questions of law and fact on a *de novo* basis, and others on a deferential basis, depending upon essentially practical considerations. Because, with respect to the questions at issue here, the purpose of the determination and its extremely fact-bound nature will cause *de novo* review to have relatively little benefit, it is in my view unwise to require courts of appeals to undertake the searching inquiry that standard requires. I would affirm the judgment of the Court of Appeals.

As the Court recognizes, determinations of probable cause and reasonable suspicion involve a two-step process. First, a court must identify all of the relevant historical facts known to the officer at the time of the stop or search; and second, it must decide whether, under a standard of objective reasonableness, those facts would give rise to a reasonable suspicion justifying a stop or probable cause to search. Because this second step requires application of an objective legal standard to the facts, it is properly characterized as a mixed question of law and fact.

Merely labeling the issues "mixed questions," however, does not establish that they receive *de novo* review. While it is well settled that appellate courts "accep[t] findings of fact that are not 'clearly erroneous' but decid[e] questions of law *de novo*," *First Options of Chicago, Inc. v. Kaplan*, 514 U.S. 938, 948 (1995), there is no rigid rule with respect to mixed questions. We have said that "deferential review of mixed questions of law and fact is warranted when it appears that the district court is 'better positioned' than the appellate court to decide the issue in question or that probing appellate scrutiny will not contribute to the clarity of legal doctrine." *Salve Regina College v. Russell*, 499 U.S. 225, 233 (1991) (*citing Miller v. Fenton*, 474 U.S. 104, 114 (1985)). * * *

NOTES AND QUESTIONS

1. *Some first-order distinctions between fact and law.* Facts play different roles over the life cycle of a case. At the initial pleading stage, a plaintiff's complaint must contain a "short and plain statement of the claim showing that the pleader is entitled to relief." FEDERAL RULE OF CIVIL PROCEDURE 8(a)(2). The rule does not require "detailed factual allegations," but it does require "more than an unadorned, the-defendant-unlawfully-harmed-me accusation. * * * A pleading that offers 'labels and conclusions' or 'a formulaic recitation of the elements of a cause of action will not do. * * * Nor does a complaint suffice if it tenders "naked assertion[s]" devoid of "further factual enhancement." *Ashcroft v. Iqbal*, 556 U.S. 662, 677–78 (2009), *quoting Bell Atlantic Corp. v. Twombly*, 550 U.S. 544, 555–57 (2007).

In testing the legal sufficiency of a complaint, American courts must first accept all well-pleaded factual allegations as true, but "[t]hreadbare recitals of the elements of a cause of action, supported by mere conclusory statements, do not suffice." *Iqbal*, 556 U.S. at 678. Nor must the court "accept as true a legal conclusion couched as a factual allegation." *Id.* (quoting *Twombly*, 550 U.S. at 555). Second, once the well-pleaded factual allegations are taken as true at this early stage, the court must "determine whether they plausibly give rise to an entitlement to relief." *Id.* at 679.

> Determining whether a complaint states a plausible claim for relief will, as the Court of Appeals observed, be a context-specific task that requires the reviewing court to draw on its judicial experience and common sense. But where the well-pleaded facts do not permit the court to infer more than the *mere possibility* of misconduct, the complaint has alleged—but it has not "show[n]"—"that the pleader is entitled to relief." Fed. Rule Civ. Proc. 8(a)(2).

Id. (emphasis added).

At trial, different institutions have different responsibilities, so that, in a jury trial, the judge instructs on the law and the jury finds the facts and determines guilt or liability. On appeal, the lower court's findings of fact are entitled to a highly deferential standard of review: they have to be clearly erroneous, which is obviously difficult to prove. On the other hand, the lower court's conclusions of law are subject to *de novo* review, meaning that they are to be assessed anew, without any particular deference to the lower court's disposition: subject only to applicable precedent in the jurisdiction, the court of appeals can decide legal issues fresh.

Regrettably, nothing in the *Ornelas* litigation turns on the name of the drug-sniffing dog, but the case does reflect an essential adversarial turning point: portraying something as a matter of fact (as a way of keeping the appeals court at a distance and increasing the chances of affirmance) or portraying that something as a matter of law (as a way of getting the court of appeals into the weeds, unburdened by any standard of deference, and applying the *de novo* standard of review).

Why did the Supreme Court decide to review the court of appeals decision in *Ornelas*? What conflict among the various circuit courts of appeals did it have to resolve? How did it defend its decision to place determinations of "reasonable suspicion" and "probable cause" on one side of the law/fact line or the other?

2. *Facts and inferences.* Why does it merit attention as a matter of *law* that the average daily high temperature in Milwaukee in December is 31 degrees Farenheit as a matter of *fact*?

3. *The sustained, borderline-legislative effects of de novo review.* Why would Chief Justice Rehnquist conclude that "*de novo* review *tends to unify precedent*?" And what is the value of this unity, or to put the question somewhat adversarially, who specifically benefits from unifying precedent?

D. THE PUBLIC DOMAIN VERSUS THE PRIVATE DOMAIN

REPUBLIC OF ARGENTINA V. WELTOVER, INC.

504 U.S. 607 (1992)

This case requires us to decide whether the Republic of Argentina's default on certain bonds issued as part of a plan to stabilize its currency was an act taken "in connection with a commercial activity" that had a "direct effect in the United States" so as to subject Argentina to suit in an American court under the Foreign Sovereign Immunities Act of 1976, 28 U.S.C. § 1602 et seq.

I

Since Argentina's currency is not one of the mediums of exchange accepted on the international market, Argentine businesses engaging in foreign transactions must pay in United States dollars or some other internationally accepted currency. In the recent past, it was difficult for Argentine borrowers to obtain such funds, principally because of the instability of the Argentine currency. To address these problems, petitioners, the Republic of Argentina and its central bank, Banco Central (collectively Argentina), in 1981 instituted a foreign exchange insurance contract program (FEIC), under which Argentina effectively agreed to assume the risk of currency depreciation in cross-border transactions involving Argentine borrowers. This was accomplished by Argentina's agreeing to sell to domestic borrowers, in exchange for a contractually predetermined amount of local currency, the necessary United States dollars to repay their foreign debts when they matured, irrespective of intervening devaluations.

Unfortunately, Argentina did not possess sufficient reserves of United States dollars to cover the FEIC contracts as they became due in 1982. The Argentine Government thereupon adopted certain emergency measures, including refinancing of the FEIC-backed debts by issuing to the creditors government bonds. These bonds, called "Bonods," provide for payment of interest and principal in United States dollars; payment may be made through transfer on the London, Frankfurt, Zurich, or New York market, at the election of the creditor. Under this refinancing program, the foreign creditor had the option of either accepting the Bonods in satisfaction of the initial debt, thereby substituting the Argentine Government for the private debtor, or maintaining the debtor/creditor relationship with the private borrower and accepting the Argentine Government as guarantor.

When the Bonods began to mature in May 1986, Argentina concluded that it lacked sufficient foreign exchange to retire them. Pursuant to a Presidential Decree, Argentina unilaterally extended the time for payment and offered bondholders substitute instruments as a means of rescheduling the debts. Respondents, two Panamanian corporations and a Swiss bank who hold, collectively, $1.3 million of Bonods, refused to accept the rescheduling and insisted on full payment, specifying New York as the place where payment should be made. Argentina did not pay, and respondents then brought this breach-of-contract action in the United States District Court for the Southern District of New York, relying on the Foreign Sovereign Immunities Act of 1976 as the basis for jurisdiction. Petitioners moved to dismiss for lack of subject-matter jurisdiction, lack of personal jurisdiction, and *forum non conveniens*. The District Court denied these motions, 753 F. Supp. 1201 (S.D.N.Y.1991), and the Court of Appeals affirmed, 941 F.2d 145 (CA2 1991). We granted Argentina's petition for *certiorari*, which challenged the Court of Appeals' determination that, under the Act, Argentina was not immune from the jurisdiction of the federal courts in this case.

II

The Foreign Sovereign Immunities Act of 1976 (FSIA), 28 U.S.C. § 1602 et seq., establishes a comprehensive framework for determining whether a court in this country, state or federal, may exercise jurisdiction over a foreign state. Under the Act, a "foreign state shall be immune from the jurisdiction of the courts of the United States and of the States" unless one of several statutorily defined exceptions applies. § 1604. The FSIA thus provides the "sole basis" for obtaining jurisdiction over a foreign sovereign in the United States. *See Argentine Republic v. Amerada Hess Shipping Corp.*, 488 U.S. 428, 434–439 (1989). The most significant of the FSIA's exceptions—and the one at issue in this case—is the "commercial" exception of § 1605(a)(2), which provides that a foreign state is not immune from suit in any case

> in which the action is based upon a commercial activity carried on in the United States by the foreign state; or upon an act performed in the United States in connection with a commercial activity of the foreign state elsewhere; or upon an act outside the territory of the United States in connection with a commercial activity of the foreign state elsewhere and that act causes a direct effect in the United States.

§ 1605(a)(2). In the proceedings below, respondents relied only on the third clause of § 1605(a)(2) to establish jurisdiction, and our analysis is therefore limited to considering whether this lawsuit is (1) "based . . . upon an act outside the territory of the United States"; (2) that was taken "in connection with a commercial activity" of Argentina outside this country; and (3) that "cause[d] a direct effect in the United States."[1] The complaint in this case alleges only one cause of action on behalf of each of the

---

1 It is undisputed that both the Republic of Argentina and Banco Central are "foreign states" within the meaning of the FSIA. See 28 U.S.C. § 1603(a), (b) ("[F]oreign state" includes certain "agenc[ies] or instrumentalit[ies] of a foreign state").

respondents, *viz.,* a breach-of-contract claim based on Argentina's attempt to refinance the Bonods rather than to pay them according to their terms. The fact that the cause of action is in compliance with the first of the three requirements—that it is "based upon an act outside the territory of the United States" (presumably Argentina's unilateral extension)—is uncontested. The dispute pertains to whether the unilateral refinancing of the Bonods was taken "in connection with a commercial activity" of Argentina, and whether it had a "direct effect in the United States." We address these issues in turn.

A

Respondents and their amicus, the United States, contend that Argentina's issuance of, and continued liability under, the Bonods constitute a "commercial activity" and that the extension of the payment schedules was taken "in connection with" that activity. The latter point is obvious enough, and Argentina does not contest it; the key question is whether the activity is "commercial" under the FSIA.

The FSIA defines "commercial activity" to mean:

> "[E]ither a regular course of commercial conduct or a particular commercial transaction or act. The commercial character of an activity shall be determined by reference to the nature of the course of conduct or particular transaction or act, rather than by reference to its purpose." 28 U.S.C. § 1603(d).

This definition, however, leaves the critical term "commercial" largely undefined: The first sentence simply establishes that the commercial nature of an activity does not depend upon whether it is a single act or a regular course of conduct; and the second sentence merely specifies what element of the conduct determines commerciality (*i.e.*, nature rather than purpose), but still without saying what "commercial" means. Fortunately, however, the FSIA was not written on a clean slate. As we have noted, *see Verlinden B.V. v. Central Bank of Nigeria*, 461 U.S. 480, 486–489 (1983), the Act (and the commercial exception in particular) largely codifies the so-called "restrictive" theory of foreign sovereign immunity first endorsed by the State Department in 1952. The meaning of "commercial" is the meaning generally attached to that term under the restrictive theory at the time the statute was enacted.

This Court did not have occasion to discuss the scope or validity of the restrictive theory of sovereign immunity until our 1976 decision in *Alfred Dunhill of London, Inc. v. Republic of Cuba*, 425 U.S. 682. Although the Court there was evenly divided on the question whether the "commercial" exception that applied in the foreign-sovereign-immunity context also limited the availability of an act-of-state defense, there was little disagreement over the general scope of the exception. The plurality noted that, after the State Department endorsed the restrictive theory of foreign sovereign immunity in 1952, the lower courts consistently held that foreign sovereigns were not immune from the jurisdiction of American courts in cases "arising out of purely commercial transactions," *id.*, at 703; *citing, inter alia, Victory Transport, Inc. v. Comisaria General*, 336 F.2d 354 (CA2 1964), *cert. denied*, 381 U.S. 934 (1965), and *Petrol Shipping Corp. v. Kingdom of Greece*, 360 F.2d 103 (CA2), *cert. denied*, 385 U.S. 931 (1966). The plurality further recognized that the distinction between state sovereign acts, on the one hand, and state commercial and private acts, on the other, was not entirely novel to American law. *See* 425 U.S., at 695–696, *citing, inter alia, Parden v. Terminal Railway of Alabama Docks Dept.*, 377 U.S. 184, 189–190 (1964) (Eleventh Amendment immunity); *Bank of United States v. Planters' Bank of Georgia*, 9 Wheat. 904, 907–908 (1824) (same); *New York v. United States*, 326 U.S. 572, 579 (1946) (opinion of Frankfurter, J.) (tax immunity of States); and *South Carolina v. United States*, 199 U.S. 437, 461–463 (1905) (same). The plurality stated that the restrictive theory of foreign sovereign immunity would not bar a suit based upon a foreign state's participation in the marketplace in the manner of a private citizen or corporation. 425 U.S., at 698–705. A foreign state engaging in "commercial" activities "do[es] not exercise powers peculiar to sovereigns"; rather, it "exercise[s] only those powers that can also be exercised by private citizens." *Id.*, at 704. The dissenters did not disagree with this general description. Given that the FSIA was enacted less than six months after our decision in *Alfred Dunhill* was announced, we think the plurality's contemporaneous description of the then-prevailing restrictive theory of sovereign immunity is of significant assistance in construing the scope of the Act.

In accord with that description, we conclude that when a foreign government acts, not as regulator of a market, but in the manner of a private player within it, the foreign sovereign's actions are "commercial" within the meaning of the FSIA. Moreover, because the Act provides that the commercial character of an act is to be determined by reference to its "nature" rather than its "purpose," 28 U.S.C. § 1603(d), the question is not whether the foreign government is acting with a profit motive or instead with the aim of fulfilling uniquely sovereign objectives. Rather, the issue is whether the particular actions that the foreign state performs (whatever the motive behind them) are the type of actions by which a private party engages in "trade and traffic or commerce," BLACK'S LAW DICTIONARY 270 (6th ed. 1990). Thus, a foreign government's issuance of regulations limiting foreign currency exchange is a sovereign activity, because such authoritative control of commerce cannot be exercised by a private party; whereas a contract to buy army boots or even bullets is a "commercial" activity, because private companies can similarly use sales contracts to acquire goods.

The commercial character of the Bonods is confirmed by the fact that they are in almost all respects garden-variety debt instruments: They may be held by private parties; they are negotiable and may be traded on the international market (except in Argentina); and they promise a future stream of cash in-come. We recognize that, prior to the enactment of the FSIA, there was authority suggesting that the issuance of public debt instruments did not constitute a commercial activity. There is, however, nothing distinctive about the state's assumption of debt (other than perhaps its purpose) that would cause it always to be classified as *jure imperii* * * *. Because the FSIA has now clearly established that the "nature" governs, we perceive no basis for concluding that the issuance of debt should be treated as categorically different from other activities of foreign states.

Argentina contends that, although the FSIA bars consideration of "purpose," a court must nonetheless fully consider the context of a transaction in order to determine whether it is "commercial." Accordingly, Argentina claims that the Court of Appeals erred by defining the relevant conduct in what Argentina considers an overly generalized, acontextual manner and by essentially adopting a per se rule that all "issuance of debt instruments" is "commercial." *See* 941 F.2d, at 151 (" '[I]t is self-evident that issuing public debt is a commercial activity within the meaning of [the FSIA]' "), quoting *Shapiro v. Republic of Bolivia*, 930 F.2d 1013, 1018 (CA2 1991). We have no occasion to consider such a *per se* rule, because it seems to us that even in full context, there is nothing about the issuance of these Bonods (except perhaps its purpose) that is not analogous to a private commercial transaction.

Argentina points to the fact that the transactions in which the Bonods were issued did not have the ordinary commercial consequence of raising capital or financing acquisitions. Assuming for the sake of argument that this is not an example of judging the commerciality of a transaction by its purpose, the ready answer is that private parties regularly issue bonds, not just to raise capital or to finance purchases, but also to refinance debt. That is what Argentina did here: By virtue of the earlier FEIC contracts, Argentina was already obligated to supply the United States dollars needed to retire the FEIC-insured debts; the Bonods simply allowed Argentina to restructure its existing obligations. Argentina further asserts (without proof or even elaboration) that it "received consideration [for the Bonods] in no way commensurate with [their] value." Assuming that to be true, it makes no difference. Engaging in a commercial act does not require the receipt of fair value, or even compliance with the common-law requirements of consideration.

Argentina argues that the Bonods differ from ordinary debt instruments in that they "were created by the Argentine Government to fulfill its obligations under a foreign exchange program designed to address a domestic credit crisis, and as a component of a program designed to control that nation's critical shortage of foreign exchange." In this regard,

Argentina relies heavily on *De Sanchez v. Banco Central de Nicaragua*, 770 F.2d 1385 (1985), in which the Fifth Circuit took the view that "[o]ften, the essence of an act is defined by its purpose"; that unless "we can inquire into the purposes of such acts, we cannot determine their nature"; and that, in light of its purpose to control its reserves of foreign currency, Nicaragua's refusal to honor a check it had issued to cover a private bank debt was a sovereign act entitled to immunity. Indeed, Argentina asserts that the line between "nature" and "purpose" rests upon a "formalistic distinction [that] simply is neither useful nor warranted." We think this line of argument is squarely foreclosed by the language of the FSIA. However difficult it may be in some cases to separate "purpose" (i.e., the reason why the foreign state engages in the activity) from "nature" (i.e., the outward form of the conduct that the foreign state performs or agrees to perform), the statute unmistakably commands that to be done, 28 U.S.C. § 1603(d). We agree with the Court of Appeals, that it is irrelevant why Argentina participated in the bond market in the manner of a private actor; it matters only that it did so. * * *

We conclude that Argentina's issuance of the Bonods was a "commercial activity" under the FSIA; that its rescheduling of the maturity dates on those instruments was taken in connection with that commercial activity and had a "direct effect" in the United States; and that the District Court therefore properly asserted jurisdiction, under the FSIA, over the breach-of-contract claim based on that rescheduling. Accordingly, the judgment of the Court of Appeals is affirmed.

NOTES AND QUESTIONS

1. *The Foreign Sovereign Immunities Act of 1976 ("the FSIA").* In *Weltover*, the Supreme Court explained that the FSIA is the exclusive means of obtaining subject matter jurisdiction in any case filed in a U.S. court against a foreign sovereign or its agencies or instrumentalities. Foreign states are entitled to a rebuttable presumption of immunity, which can be overcome if the case falls within any of the statutory exceptions to immunity, including certain non-commercial torts in the United States and commercial activities with a nexus to the United States. The statute thus requires courts to distinguish a foreign sovereign's public or governmental acts, which are generally immunized, and its private or commercial acts, which are not. There is precious little guidance in the statute about making this critical distinction aside from the fact that "[t]he commercial character of an activity shall be determined by reference to the *nature* of the course of conduct or particular transaction or act, rather than by reference to its *purpose*." 28 U.S.C. 1603 (emphasis supplied). But that just postpones the inevitable: the "nature" of commercial and governmental activity is never identified.

One might have thought that a country's effort to protect its foreign currency reserves would qualify as a sovereign prerogative and not just a matter of playing in the marketplace. Is there something other than offering bond instruments that might have accomplished the same end without entering the market? Would those actions have been immunized?

2. *Identifying essentially governmental functions*. How confident are you that you can either (a) articulate a *principle* for distinguishing governmental activity from commercial activity or (b) articulate an authoritative *list* of functions that properly belong in one box or the other. Consider in this regard the analysis of the Supreme Court in *Garcia v. San Antonio Metropolitan Transit Authority*, 469 U.S. 528, 541–43 (1985), reviewing several precedents addressing the immunity of state actors from tax:

> If these tax-immunity cases had any common thread, it was in the attempt to distinguish between "governmental" and "proprietary" functions. To say that the distinction between "governmental" and "proprietary" proved to be stable, however, would be something of an overstatement. In 1911, for example, the Court declared that the provision of a municipal water supply "is no part of the essential governmental functions of a State." *Flint v. Stone Tracy Co.,* 220 U.S. 107. Twenty-six years later, without any intervening change in the applicable legal standards, the Court simply rejected its earlier position and decided that the provision of a municipal water supply *was* immune from federal taxation as an essential governmental function, even though municipal water-works long had been operated for profit by private industry. *Brush v. Commissioner,* 300 U.S., at 370–373. At the same time that the Court was holding a municipal water supply to be immune from federal taxes, it had held that a state-run commuter rail system was *not* immune. *Helvering v. Powers,* 293 U.S. 214 (1934). Justice Black, in *Helvering v. Gerhardt,* 304 U.S. 405, 427 (1938), was moved to observe:
>
> > "An implied constitutional distinction which taxes income of an officer of a state-operated transportation system and exempts income of the manager of a municipal water works system manifests the uncertainty created by the 'essential' and 'non-essential' test"
>
> (concurring opinion). It was this uncertainty and instability that led the Court shortly thereafter, in *New York v. United States,* 326 U.S. 572 (1946), unanimously to conclude that the distinction between "governmental" and "proprietary" functions was "untenable" and must be abandoned. *See id.*, at 583 (opinion of Frankfurter, J., joined by Rutledge, J.); *id.,* at 586 (Stone, C.J., concurring, joined by Reed, Murphy, and Burton, JJ.); *id.*, at 590–596 (Douglas, J., dissenting, joined by Black, J.). *See also Massachusetts v. United States,* 435 U.S. 444, 457, and n. 14 (1978) (plurality opinion); *Case v. Bowles,* 327 U.S. 92, 101 (1946).

Even during the heyday of the governmental/proprietary distinction in intergovernmental tax-immunity doctrine the Court never explained the constitutional basis for that distinction.

3. *The consequences of distinguishing public from private activity*. In the following case, *DeShaney v. Winnebago County Dept. of Social Services*, how critical is the distinction between a public and a private frame of reference for the Court's analysis?

E. FRAMING AT THE SUPREME COURT

DESHANEY V. WINNEBAGO COUNTY DEPT. OF SOCIAL SERVICES

No. 87–154
Petition for Certiorari
1987 WL 955329 (July 17, 1987)

QUESTIONS PRESENTED FOR REVIEW

1. Whether reckless, willful and wanton, or grossly negligent misconduct of public officials is enough to trigger the protections of the Due Process Clause.

2. Whether the deliberate refusal of child protection officials to act to protect an identified individual child already under their auspices, and actually known to them to be in extreme danger of death or profound injury, from an identified and known imminent danger, can be sufficiently reckless, willful and wanton, or grossly negligent as to impose liability under 42 U.S.C § 1983.

3. Whether egregious misconduct of public officials, rising to the level of gross negligence or willful and wanton misconduct, leading to massive personal injury to an infant citizen, is excluded from the application of the civil rights laws on the basis that the misconduct was omissive in nature.

As you analyze the following decision (especially the footnotes), and *before* reading the dissents, articulate how a different frame for the case might have compelled the opposite result.

DESHANEY V. WINNEBAGO COUNTY DEPT. OF SOCIAL SERVICES

489 U.S. 189 (1989)

CHIEF JUSTICE REHNQUIST delivered the opinion of the Court. Petitioner is a boy who was beaten and permanently injured by his father, with whom he lived. Respondents are social workers and other local officials who received complaints that petitioner was being abused by his father and had reason to believe that this was the case, but nonetheless did not act to remove petitioner from his father's custody. Petitioner sued respondents claiming that their failure to act deprived him of his liberty in violation of the Due Process Clause of the Fourteenth Amendment to the United States Constitution. We hold that it did not.

I

The facts of this case are undeniably tragic. Petitioner Joshua DeShaney was born in 1979. In 1980, a Wyoming court granted his parents a divorce and awarded custody of Joshua to his father, Randy DeShaney. The father shortly thereafter moved to Neenah, a city located in Winnebago County, Wisconsin, taking the infant Joshua with him. There he entered into a second marriage, which also ended in divorce.

The Winnebago County authorities first learned that Joshua DeShaney might be a victim of child abuse in January 1982, when his father's second wife complained to the police, at the time of their divorce, that he had previously "hit the boy causing marks and [was] a prime case for child abuse." The Winnebago County Department of Social Services (DSS) interviewed the father, but he denied the accusations, and DSS did not pursue them further. In January 1983, Joshua was admitted to a local hospital with multiple bruises and abrasions. The examining physician suspected child abuse and notified DSS, which immediately obtained an order from a Wisconsin juvenile court placing Joshua in the temporary custody of the hospital. Three days later, the county convened an ad hoc "Child Protection Team"—consisting of a pediatrician, a psychologist, a police detective, the county's lawyer, several DSS caseworkers, and various hospital personnel—to consider Joshua's situation. At this meeting, the Team decided that there was insufficient evidence of child abuse to retain Joshua in the custody of the court. The Team did, however, decide to recommend several measures to protect Joshua, including enrolling him in a preschool program, providing his father with certain counseling services, and encouraging his father's girlfriend to move out of the home. Randy DeShaney entered into a voluntary agreement with DSS in which he promised to cooperate with them in accomplishing these goals.

Based on the recommendation of the Child Protection Team, the juvenile court dismissed the child protection case and returned Joshua to the custody of his father. A month later, emergency room personnel called the DSS caseworker handling Joshua's case to report that he had once again been treated for suspicious injuries. The caseworker concluded that there was no basis for action. For the next six months, the caseworker made monthly visits to the DeShaney home, during which she observed a number of suspicious injuries on Joshua's head; she also noticed that he had not been enrolled in school, and that the girlfriend had not moved out. The caseworker dutifully recorded these incidents in her files, along with her continuing suspicions that someone in the DeShaney household was physically abusing Joshua, but she did nothing more. In November 1983, the emergency room notified DSS that Joshua had been treated once again for injuries that they believed to be caused by child abuse. On the caseworker's next two visits to the DeShaney home, she was told that Joshua was too ill to see her. Still DSS took no action.

In March 1984, Randy DeShaney beat 4-year-old Joshua so severely that he fell into a life-threatening coma. Emergency brain surgery revealed a series of hemorrhages caused by traumatic injuries to the head inflicted over a long period of time. Joshua did not die, but he suffered brain damage so severe that he is expected to spend the rest of his life confined to an institution for the profoundly retarded. Randy DeShaney was subsequently tried and convicted of child abuse.

Joshua and his mother brought this action under 42 U.S.C. § 1983 in the United States District Court for the Eastern District of Wisconsin against respondents Winnebago County, DSS, and various individual employees of DSS. The complaint alleged that respondents had deprived Joshua of his liberty without due process of law, in violation of his rights under the Fourteenth Amendment, by failing to intervene to protect him against a risk of violence at his father's hands of which they knew or should have known. The District Court granted summary judgment for respondents.

The Court of Appeals for the Seventh Circuit affirmed, 812 F.2d 298 (1987), holding that petitioners had not made out an actionable § 1983 claim for two alternative reasons. First, the court held that the Due Process Clause of the Fourteenth Amendment does not require a state or local governmental entity to protect its citizens from "private violence, or other mishaps not attributable to the conduct of its employees." In so holding, the court specifically rejected the position endorsed by a divided panel of the Third Circuit in *Estate of Bailey by Oare v. County of York*, 768 F.2d 503, 510–511 (1985), and by dicta in *Jensen v. Conrad,* 747 F.2d 185, 190–194 (CA4 1984), *cert. denied*, 470 U.S. 1052 (1985), that once the State learns that a particular child is in danger of abuse from third parties and actually undertakes to protect him from that danger, a "special relationship" arises between it and the child which imposes an affirmative constitutional duty to provide adequate protection. Second, the court held, in reliance on our decision in *Martinez v. California*, 444 U.S. 277, 285 (1980), that the causal connection between respondents' conduct and Joshua's injuries was too attenuated to establish a deprivation of constitutional rights actionable under § 1983. The court therefore found it unnecessary to reach the question whether respondents' conduct evinced the "state of mind" necessary to make out a due process claim after *Daniels v. Williams*, 474 U.S. 327 (1986), and *Davidson v. Cannon*, 474 U.S. 344 (1986).

Because of the inconsistent approaches taken by the lower courts in determining when, if ever, the failure of a state or local governmental entity or its agents to provide an individual with adequate protective services constitutes a violation of the individual's due process rights, and the importance of the issue to the administration of state and local governments, we granted certiorari. We now affirm.

II

The Due Process Clause of the Fourteenth Amendment provides that "[n]o State shall . . . deprive any person of life, liberty, or property, without due process of law." Petitioners contend that the State[1] deprived Joshua of his liberty interest in "free[dom] from . . . unjustified intrusions on personal security," *see Ingraham v. Wright,* 430 U.S. 651, 673 (1977), by failing to provide him with adequate protection against his father's violence. The claim is one invoking the substantive rather than the procedural component of the Due Process Clause; petitioners do not claim that the State denied Joshua protection without according him appropriate procedural safeguards, but that it was categorically obligated to protect him in these circumstances, *see Youngberg v. Romeo,* 457 U.S. 307 (1982).[2]

But nothing in the language of the Due Process Clause itself requires the State to protect the life, liberty, and property of its citizens against invasion by private actors. The Clause is phrased as a limitation on the State's power to act, not as a guarantee of certain minimal levels of safety and security. It forbids the State itself to deprive individuals of life, liberty, or property without "due process of law," but its language cannot fairly be extended to impose an affirmative obligation on the State to ensure that those interests do not come to harm through other means. Nor does history support such an expansive reading of the constitutional text. Like its counterpart in the Fifth Amendment, the Due Process Clause of the Fourteenth Amendment was intended to prevent government "from abusing [its] power, or employing it as an instrument of oppression," *Davidson v. Cannon, supra,* 474 U.S., at 348; *see also Daniels v. Williams, supra,* 474 U.S., at 331, ("'to secure the individual from the arbitrary exercise of the powers of government,'" and "to prevent governmental power from being 'used for purposes of oppression") (internal citations omitted). Its purpose was to protect the people from the State, not to ensure that the State protected them from each other. The Framers were content

[1] As used here, the term "State" refers generically to state and local governmental entities and their agents.

[2] Petitioners also argue that the Wisconsin child protection statutes gave Joshua an "entitlement" to receive protective services in accordance with the terms of the statute, an entitlement which would enjoy due process protection against state deprivation under our decision in *Board of Regents of State Colleges v. Roth,* 408 U.S. 564 (1972). But this argument is made for the first time in petitioners' brief to this Court: it was not pleaded in the complaint, argued to the Court of Appeals as a ground for reversing the District Court, or raised in the petition for certiorari. We therefore decline to consider it here.

to leave the extent of governmental obligation in the latter area to the democratic political processes.

Consistent with these principles, our cases have recognized that the Due Process Clauses generally confer no affirmative right to governmental aid, even where such aid may be necessary to secure life, liberty, or property interests of which the government itself may not deprive the individual. *See, e.g., Harris v. McRae*, 448 U.S. 297, 317–318 (1980) (no obligation to fund abortions or other medical services) (discussing Due Process Clause of Fifth Amendment); *Lindsey v. Normet,* 405 U.S. 56, 74 (1972) (no obligation to provide adequate housing) (discussing Due Process Clause of Fourteenth Amendment); *see also Youngberg v. Romeo, supra,* 457 U.S., at 317 ("As a general matter, a State is under no constitutional duty to provide substantive services for those within its border"). As we said in *Harris v. McRae:* "Although the liberty protected by the Due Process Clause affords protection against unwarranted *government* interference . . ., it does not confer an entitlement to such [governmental aid] as may be necessary to realize all the advantages of that freedom." If the Due Process Clause does not require the State to provide its citizens with particular protective services, it follows that the State cannot be held liable under the Clause for injuries that could have been averted had it chosen to provide them.[3] As a general matter, then, we conclude that a State's failure to protect an individual against private violence simply does not constitute a violation of the Due Process Clause.

Petitioners contend, however, that even if the Due Process Clause imposes no affirmative obligation on the State to provide the general public with adequate protective services, such a duty may arise out of certain "special relationships" created or assumed by the State with respect to particular individuals. Petitioners argue that such a "special relationship" existed here because the State knew that Joshua faced a special danger of abuse at his father's hands, and specifically proclaimed, by word and by deed, its intention to protect him against that danger. Having actually undertaken to protect Joshua from this danger—which petitioners concede the State played no part in creating—the State acquired an affirmative "duty," enforceable through the Due Process Clause, to do so in a reasonably competent fashion. Its failure to discharge that duty, so the argument goes, was an abuse of governmental power that so "shocks the conscience," *Rochin v. California,* 342 U.S. 165, 172 (1952), as to constitute a substantive due process violation.[4]

---

[3] The State may not, of course, selectively deny its protective services to certain disfavored minorities without violating the Equal Protection Clause. *See Yick Wo v. Hopkins,* 118 U.S. 356 (1886). But no such argument has been made here.

[4] The genesis of this notion appears to lie in a statement in our opinion in *Martinez v. California,* 444 U.S. 277 (1980). In that case, we were asked to decide, *inter alia,* whether state officials could be held liable under the Due Process Clause of the Fourteenth Amendment for the death of a private citizen at the hands of a parolee. Rather than squarely confronting the question presented here—whether the Due Process Clause imposed upon the State an affirmative duty to

We reject this argument. It is true that in certain limited circumstances the Constitution imposes upon the State affirmative duties of care and protection with respect to particular individuals. In *Estelle v. Gamble*, 429 U.S. 97 (1976), we recognized that the Eighth Amendment's prohibition against cruel and unusual punishment, made applicable to the States through the Fourteenth Amendment's Due Process Clause, *Robinson v. California*, 370 U.S. 660 (1962), requires the State to provide adequate medical care to incarcerated prisoners.[5] We reasoned that because the prisoner is unable " 'by reason of the deprivation of his liberty [to] care for himself,' " it is only " 'just' " that the State be required to care for him.

In *Youngberg v. Romeo,* 457 U.S. 307 (1982), we extended this analysis beyond the Eighth Amendment setting, * * * holding that the substantive component of the Fourteenth Amendment's Due Process Clause requires the State to provide involuntarily committed mental patients with such services as are necessary to ensure their "reasonable safety" from themselves and others. * * * As we explained: "If it is cruel and unusual punishment to hold convicted criminals in unsafe conditions, it must be unconstitutional [under the Due Process Clause] to confine the involuntarily committed—who may not be punished at all—in unsafe conditions." * * *

But these cases afford petitioners no help. Taken together, they stand only for the proposition that when the State takes a person into its custody and holds him there against his will, the Constitution imposes upon it a corresponding duty to assume some responsibility for his safety and general well-being. *See Youngberg v. Romeo, supra,* 457 U.S., at 317 ("When a person is institutionalized—and wholly dependent on the State[,] . . . a duty to provide certain services and care does exist"). * * * The

---

protect—we affirmed the dismissal of the claim on the narrower ground that the causal connection between the state officials' decision to release the parolee from prison and the murder was too attenuated to establish a "deprivation" of constitutional rights within the meaning of § 1983. But we went on to say:

> [T]he parole board was not aware that appellants' decedent, as distinguished from the public at large, faced any special danger. We need not and do not decide that a parole officer could never be deemed to 'deprive' someone of life by action taken in connection with the release of a prisoner on parole. But we do hold that at least under the particular circumstances of this parole decision, appellants' decedent's death is too remote a consequence of the parole officers' action to hold them responsible under the federal civil rights law." *Id.,* at 285 (footnote omitted).

Several of the Courts of Appeals have read this language as implying that once the State learns that a third party poses a special danger to an identified victim, and indicates its willingness to protect the victim against that danger, a "special relationship" arises between State and victim, giving rise to an affirmative duty, enforceable through the Due Process Clause, to render adequate protection.

[5] To make out an Eighth Amendment claim based on the failure to provide adequate medical care, a prisoner must show that the state defendants exhibited "deliberate indifference" to his "serious" medical needs; the mere negligent or inadvertent failure to provide adequate care is not enough. *Estelle v. Gamble*, 429 U.S., at 105–106. In *Whitley v. Albers,* 475 U.S. 312 (1986), we suggested that a similar state of mind is required to make out a substantive due process claim in the prison setting.

rationale for this principle is simple enough: when the State by the affirmative exercise of its power so restrains an individual's liberty that it renders him unable to care for himself, and at the same time fails to provide for his basic human needs—*e.g.,* food, clothing, shelter, medical care, and reasonable safety—it transgresses the substantive limits on state action set by the Eighth Amendment and the Due Process Clause. The affirmative duty to protect arises not from the State's knowledge of the individual's predicament or from its expressions of intent to help him, but from the limitation which it has imposed on his freedom to act on his own behalf. * * * In the substantive due process analysis, it is the State's affirmative act of restraining the individual's freedom to act on his own behalf-through incarceration, institutionalization, or other similar restraint of personal liberty-which is the "deprivation of liberty" triggering the protections of the Due Process Clause, not its failure to act to protect his liberty interests against harms inflicted by other means. * * *

The *Estelle-Youngberg* analysis simply has no applicability in the present case. Petitioners concede that the harms Joshua suffered occurred not while he was in the State's custody, but while he was in the custody of his natural father, who was in no sense a state actor.[9] While the State may have been aware of the dangers that Joshua faced in the free world, it played no part in their creation, nor did it do anything to render him any more vulnerable to them. That the State once took temporary custody of Joshua does not alter the analysis, for when it returned him to his father's custody, it placed him in no worse position than that in which he would have been had it not acted at all; the State does not become the permanent guarantor of an individual's safety by having once offered him shelter. Under these circumstances, the State had no constitutional duty to protect Joshua.

It may well be that, by voluntarily undertaking to protect Joshua against a danger it concededly played no part in creating, the State acquired a duty under state tort law to provide him with adequate protection against that danger. *See* RESTATEMENT (SECOND) OF TORTS § 323 (1965) (one who undertakes to render services to another may in some circumstances be held liable for doing so in a negligent fashion); *see generally* W. KEETON, D. DOBBS, R. KEETON, & D. OWEN, PROSSER AND KEETON ON THE LAW OF TORTS § 56 (5th ed. 1984) (discussing "special relationships" which may give rise to affirmative duties to act under the

---

[9] Complaint ¶ 16, App. 6 ("At relevant times to and until March 8, 1984, [the date of the final beating,] Joshua DeShaney was in the custody and control of Defendant Randy DeShaney"). Had the State by the affirmative exercise of its power removed Joshua from free society and placed him in a foster home operated by its agents, we might have a situation sufficiently analogous to incarceration or institutionalization to give rise to an affirmative duty to protect. Indeed, several Courts of Appeals have held, by analogy to *Estelle* and *Youngberg,* that the State may be held liable under the Due Process Clause for failing to protect children in foster homes from mistreatment at the hands of their foster parents. * * * We express no view on the validity of this analogy, however, as it is not before us in the present case.

common law of tort). But the claim here is based on the Due Process Clause of the Fourteenth Amendment, which, as we have said many times, does not transform every tort committed by a state actor into a constitutional violation. A State may, through its courts and legislatures, impose such affirmative duties of care and protection upon its agents as it wishes. But not "all common-law duties owed by government actors were . . . constitutionalized by the Fourteenth Amendment." *Daniels v. Williams*, *supra*, 474 U.S., at 335. Because, as explained above, the State had no constitutional duty to protect Joshua against his father's violence, its failure to do so—though calamitous in hindsight—simply does not constitute a violation of the Due Process Clause. * * *

Judges and lawyers, like other humans, are moved by natural sympathy in a case like this to find a way for Joshua and his mother to receive adequate compensation for the grievous harm inflicted upon them. But before yielding to that impulse, it is well to remember once again that the harm was inflicted not by the State of Wisconsin, but by Joshua's father. The most that can be said of the state functionaries in this case is that they stood by and did nothing when suspicious circumstances dictated a more active role for them. In defense of them it must also be said that had they moved too soon to take custody of the son away from the father, they would likely have been met with charges of improperly intruding into the parent-child relationship, charges based on the same Due Process Clause that forms the basis for the present charge of failure to provide adequate protection.

The people of Wisconsin may well prefer a system of liability which would place upon the State and its officials the responsibility for failure to act in situations such as the present one. They may create such a system, if they do not have it already, by changing the tort law of the State in accordance with the regular lawmaking process. But they should not have it thrust upon them by this Court's expansion of the Due Process Clause of the Fourteenth Amendment. Affirmed.

JUSTICE BRENNAN, with whom JUSTICE MARSHALL and JUSTICE BLACKMUN join, dissenting. "The most that can be said of the state functionaries in this case," the Court today concludes, "is that they stood by and did nothing when suspicious circumstances dictated a more active role for them." Because I believe that this description of respondents' conduct tells only part of the story and that, accordingly, the Constitution itself "dictated a more active role" for respondents in the circumstances presented here, I cannot agree that respondents had no constitutional duty to help Joshua DeShaney.

It may well be, as the Court decides, that the Due Process Clause as construed by our prior cases creates no general right to basic governmental services. That, however, is not the question presented here; indeed, that question was not raised in the complaint, urged on appeal, presented in the petition for certiorari, or addressed in the briefs on the merits. No one, in short, has asked the Court to proclaim that, as a general matter, the Constitution safeguards positive as well as negative liberties.

This is more than a quibble over *dicta*; it is a point about perspective, having substantive ramifications. In a constitutional setting that distinguishes sharply between action and inaction, one's characterization of the misconduct alleged under § 1983 may effectively decide the case. Thus, by leading off with a discussion (and rejection) of the idea that the Constitution imposes on the States an affirmative duty to take basic care of their citizens, the Court foreshadows—perhaps even preordains—its conclusion that no duty existed even on the specific facts before us. This initial discussion establishes the baseline from which the Court assesses the DeShaneys' claim that, when a State has—"by word and by deed"—announced an intention to protect a certain class of citizens and has before it facts that would trigger that protection under the applicable state law, the Constitution imposes upon the State an affirmative duty of protection.

The Court's baseline is the absence of positive rights in the Constitution and a concomitant suspicion of any claim that seems to depend on such rights. From this perspective, the DeShaneys' claim is first and foremost about inaction (the failure, here, of respondents to take steps to protect Joshua), and only tangentially about action (the establishment of a state program specifically designed to help children like Joshua). And from this perspective, holding these Wisconsin officials liable—where the only difference between this case and one involving a general claim to protective services is Wisconsin's establishment and operation of a program to protect children—would seem to punish an effort that we should seek to promote.

I would begin from the opposite direction. I would focus first on the action that Wisconsin *has* taken with respect to Joshua and children like him, rather than on the actions that the State failed to take. Such a method is not new to this Court. Both *Estelle v. Gamble,* 429 U.S. 97 (1976), and *Youngberg v. Romeo,* 457 U.S. 307 (1982), began by emphasizing that the States had confined J.W. Gamble to prison and Nicholas Romeo to a psychiatric hospital. This initial action rendered these people helpless to help themselves or to seek help from persons unconnected to the government. *See Estelle, supra* ("[I]t is but just that the public be required to care for the prisoner, who cannot by reason of the deprivation of his liberty, care for himself"); *Youngberg, supra* ("When a person is institutionalized—and wholly dependent on the State—it is conceded by petitioners that a duty to provide certain services and care does exist"). Cases from the lower courts also recognize that a State's actions can be decisive in assessing the constitutional significance of subsequent inaction. For these purposes, moreover, actual physical restraint is not the only state action that has been considered relevant. *See, e.g., White v. Rochford*, 592

F.2d 381 (CA7 1979) (police officers violated due process when, after arresting the guardian of three young children, they abandoned the children on a busy stretch of highway at night).

Because of the Court's initial fixation on the general principle that the Constitution does not establish positive rights, it is unable to appreciate our recognition in *Estelle* and *Youngberg* that this principle does not hold true in all circumstances. Thus, in the Court's view, *Youngberg* can be explained (and dismissed) in the following way: "In the substantive due process analysis, it is the State's affirmative act of restraining the individual's freedom to act on his own behalf—through incarceration, institutionalization, or other similar restraint of personal liberty—which is the 'deprivation of liberty' triggering the protections of the Due Process Clause, not its failure to act to protect his liberty interests against harms inflicted by other means." This restatement of *Youngberg's* holding should come as a surprise when one recalls our explicit observation in that case that Romeo did not challenge his commitment to the hospital, but instead "argue[d] that he ha[d] a constitutionally protected liberty interest in safety, freedom of movement, and training within the institution; and that petitioners infringed these rights *by failing to provide* constitutionally required conditions of confinement." 457 U.S., at 315 (emphasis added). I do not mean to suggest that "the State's affirmative act of restraining the individual's freedom to act on his own behalf," was irrelevant in *Youngberg;* rather, I emphasize that this conduct would have led to no injury, and consequently no cause of action under § 1983, unless the State then had failed to take steps to protect Romeo from himself and from others. In addition, the Court's exclusive attention to state-imposed restraints of "the individual's freedom to act on his own behalf," suggests that it was the State that rendered Romeo unable to care for himself, whereas in fact—with an I.Q. of between 8 and 10, and the mental capacity of an 18-month-old child—he had been quite incapable of taking care of himself long before the State stepped into his life. Thus, the fact of hospitalization was critical in *Youngberg* not because it rendered Romeo helpless to help himself, but because it separated him from other sources of aid that, we held, the State was obligated to replace. Unlike the Court, therefore, I am unable to see in *Youngberg* a neat and decisive divide between action and inaction.

Moreover, to the Court, the only fact that seems to count as an "affirmative act of restraining the individual's freedom to act on his own behalf" is direct physical control (listing only "incarceration, institutionalization, [and] other similar restraint of personal liberty" in describing relevant "affirmative acts"). I would not, however, give *Youngberg* and *Estelle* such a stingy scope. I would recognize, as the Court apparently cannot, that "the State's knowledge of [an] individual's predicament [and] its expressions of intent to help him" can amount to a "limitation . . . on his freedom to act on his own behalf" or to obtain help from others.

Youngberg and *Estelle* are not alone in sounding this theme. In striking down a filing fee as applied to divorce cases brought by indigents, *see Boddie v. Connecticut,* 401 U.S. 371 (1971), and in deciding that a local government could not entirely foreclose the opportunity to speak in a public forum, we have acknowledged that a State's actions—such as the monopolization of a particular path of relief—may impose upon the State certain positive duties. Similarly, *Shelley v. Kraemer,* 334 U.S. 1 (1948), and *Burton v. Wilmington Parking Authority,* 365 U.S. 715 (1961), suggest that a State may be found complicit in an injury even if it did not create the situation that caused the harm.

Arising as they do from constitutional contexts different from the one involved here, cases like *Boddie* and *Burton* are instructive rather than decisive in the case before us. But they set a tone equally well established in precedent as, and contradictory to, the one the Court sets by situating the DeShaneys' complaint within the class of cases epitomized by the Court's decision in *Harris v. McRae*, 448 U.S. 297 (1980). The cases that I have cited tell us that *Goldberg v. Kelly*, 397 U.S. 254 (1970) (recognizing entitlement to welfare under state law), can stand side by side with *Dandridge v. Williams*, 397 U.S. 471, 484 (1970) (implicitly rejecting idea that welfare is a fundamental right), and that *Goss v. Lopez*, 419 U.S. 565, 573 (1975) (entitlement to public education under state law), is perfectly consistent with *San Antonio Independent School Dist. v. Rodriguez*, 411 U.S. 1, 29–39 (1973) (no fundamental right to education). To put the point more directly, these cases signal that a State's prior actions may be decisive in analyzing the constitutional significance of its inaction. I thus would locate the DeShaneys' claims within the framework of cases like *Youngberg* and *Estelle,* and more generally, *Boddie* and *Schneider,* by considering the actions that Wisconsin took with respect to Joshua.

Wisconsin has established a child-welfare system specifically designed to help children like Joshua. Wisconsin law places upon the local departments of social services such as respondent (DSS or Department) a duty to investigate reported instances of child abuse. While other governmental bodies and private persons are largely responsible for the reporting of possible cases of child abuse, Wisconsin law channels all such reports to the local departments of social services for evaluation and, if necessary, further action. Even when it is the sheriff's office or police department that receives a report of suspected child abuse, that report is referred to local social services departments for action; the only exception to this occurs when the reporter fears for the child's *immediate* safety. In this way, Wisconsin law invites—indeed, directs—citizens and other governmental entities to depend on local departments of social services such as respondent to protect children from abuse.

The specific facts before us bear out this view of Wisconsin's system of protecting children. Each time someone voiced a suspicion that Joshua was being abused, that information was relayed to the Department for investigation and possible action. When Randy DeShaney's second wife told the police that he had "hit the boy causing marks and [was] a prime case for child abuse," the police referred her complaint to DSS. When, on three separate occasions, emergency room personnel noticed suspicious injuries on Joshua's body, they went to DSS with this information. When neighbors informed the police that they had seen or heard Joshua's father or his father's lover beating or otherwise abusing Joshua, the police brought these reports to the attention of DSS. And when respondent Kemmeter, through these reports and through her own observations in the course of nearly 20 visits to the DeShaney home, compiled growing evidence that Joshua was being abused, that information stayed within the Department—chronicled by the social worker in detail that seems almost eerie in light of her failure to act upon it. (As to the extent of the social worker's involvement in, and knowledge of, Joshua's predicament, her reaction to the news of Joshua's last and most devastating injuries is illuminating: "I just knew the phone would ring some day and Joshua would be dead."

Even more telling than these examples is the Department's control over the decision whether to take steps to protect a particular child from suspected abuse. While many different people contributed information and advice to this decision, it was up to the people at DSS to make the ultimate decision (subject to the approval of the local government's Corporation Counsel) whether to disturb the family's current arrangements. When Joshua first appeared at a local hospital with injuries signaling physical abuse, for example, it was DSS that made the decision to take him into temporary custody for the purpose of studying his situation-and it was DSS, acting in conjunction with the corporation counsel, that returned him to his father. Unfortunately for Joshua DeShaney, the buck effectively stopped with the Department.

In these circumstances, a private citizen, or even a person working in a government agency other than DSS, would doubtless feel that her job was done as soon as she had reported her suspicions of child abuse to DSS. Through its child-welfare program, in other words, the State of Wisconsin has relieved ordinary citizens and governmental bodies other than the Department of any sense of obligation to do anything more than report their suspicions of child abuse to DSS. If DSS ignores or dismisses these suspicions, no one will step in to fill the gap. Wisconsin's child-protection program thus effectively confined Joshua DeShaney within the walls of Randy DeShaney's violent home until such time as DSS took action to remove him. Conceivably, then, children like Joshua are made worse off by the existence of this program when the persons and entities charged with carrying it out fail to do their jobs.

It simply belies reality, therefore, to contend that the State "stood by and did nothing" with respect to Joshua. Through its child-protection program, the State actively intervened in Joshua's life and, by virtue of this intervention, acquired ever more certain knowledge that Joshua was in grave danger. These circumstances, in my view, plant this case solidly within the tradition of cases like *Youngberg* and *Estelle*.

It will be meager comfort to Joshua and his mother to know that, if the State had "selectively den[ied] its protective services" to them because they were "disfavored minorities," their § 1983 suit might have stood on sturdier ground. Because of the posture of this case, we do not know why respondents did not take steps to protect Joshua; the Court, however, tells us that their reason is irrelevant so long as their inaction was not the product of invidious discrimination. Presumably, then, if respondents decided not to help Joshua because his name began with a "J," or because he was born in the spring, or because they did not care enough about him even to formulate an intent to discriminate against him based on an arbitrary reason, respondents would not be liable to the DeShaneys because they were not the ones who dealt the blows that destroyed Joshua's life.

I do not suggest that such irrationality was at work in this case; I emphasize only that we do not know whether or not it was. I would allow Joshua and his mother the opportunity to show that respondents' failure to help him arose, not out of the sound exercise of professional judgment that we recognized in *Youngberg* as sufficient to preclude liability, but from the kind of arbitrariness that we have in the past condemned. *See, e.g., Daniels v. Williams*, 474 U.S. 327, 331 (1986) (purpose of Due Process Clause was "to secure the individual from the arbitrary exercise of the powers of government" (citations omitted)); *West Coast Hotel Co. v. Parrish*, 300 U.S. 379, 399 (1937) (to sustain state action, the Court need only decide that it is not "arbitrary or capricious"); *Euclid v. Ambler Realty Co.*, 272 U.S. 365, 389 (1926) (state action invalid where it "passes the bounds of reason and assumes the character of a merely arbitrary fiat," quoting *Purity Extract & Tonic Co. v. Lynch,* 226 U.S. 192, 204 (1912)).

Youngberg's deference to a decisionmaker's professional judgment ensures that once a caseworker has decided, on the basis of her professional training and experience, that one course of protection is preferable for a given child, or even that no special protection is required, she will not be found liable for the harm that follows. (In this way, *Youngberg's* vision of substantive due process serves a purpose similar to that served by adherence to procedural norms, namely, requiring that a state actor stop and think before she acts in a way that may lead to a loss of liberty.) Moreover, that the Due Process Clause is not violated by merely negligent conduct * * * means that a social worker who simply makes a mistake of judgment under what are admittedly complex and difficult conditions will not find herself liable in damages under § 1983.

As the Court today reminds us, "the Due Process Clause of the Fourteenth Amendment was intended to prevent government 'from abusing [its] power, or employing it as an instrument of oppression.' " My disagreement with the Court arises from its failure to see that inaction can be every bit as abusive of power as action, that oppression can result when a State undertakes a vital duty and then ignores it. Today's opinion construes the Due Process Clause to permit a State to displace private sources of protection and then, at the critical moment, to shrug its shoulders and turn away from the harm that it has promised to try to prevent. Because I cannot agree that our Constitution is indifferent to such indifference, I respectfulLY DISSENT.

JUSTICE BLACKMUN, dissenting. Today, the Court purports to be the dispassionate oracle of the law, unmoved by "natural sympathy." But, in this pretense, the Court itself retreats into a sterile formalism which prevents it from recognizing either the facts of the case before it or the legal norms that should apply to those facts. As Justice Brennan demonstrates, the facts here involve not mere passivity, but active state intervention in the life of Joshua DeShaney—intervention that triggered a fundamental duty to aid the boy once the State learned of the severe danger to which he was exposed.

The Court fails to recognize this duty because it attempts to draw a sharp and rigid line between action and inaction. But such formalistic reasoning has no place in the interpretation of the broad and stirring Clauses of the Fourteenth Amendment. Indeed, I submit that these Clauses were designed, at least in part, to undo the formalistic legal reasoning that infected antebellum jurisprudence * * *.

Like the antebellum judges who denied relief to fugitive slaves, the Court today claims that its decision, however harsh, is compelled by existing legal doctrine. On the contrary, the question presented by this case is an open one, and our Fourteenth Amendment precedents may be read more broadly or narrowly depending upon how one chooses to read them. Faced with the choice, I would adopt a "sympathetic" reading, one which comports with dictates of fundamental justice and recognizes that compassion need not be exiled from the province of judging. *Cf.* A. STONE, LAW, PSYCHIATRY, AND MORALITY 262 (1984) ("We will make mistakes if we go forward, but doing nothing can be the worst mistake. What is required of us is moral ambition. Until our composite sketch becomes a true portrait of humanity we must live with our uncertainty; we will grope, we will struggle, and our compassion may be our only guide and comfort").

Poor Joshua! Victim of repeated attacks by an irresponsible, bullying, cowardly, and intemperate father, and abandoned by respondents who placed him in a dangerous predicament and who knew or learned what was going on, and yet did essentially nothing except, as the Court revealingly observes, "dutifully recorded these incidents in [their] files." It is a sad commentary upon American life, and constitutional principles—so full of late of patriotic fervor and proud proclamations about "liberty and justice for all"—that this child, Joshua DeShaney, now is assigned to live out the remainder of his life profoundly retarded. Joshua and his mother, as petitioners here, deserve—but now are denied by this Court—the opportunity to have the facts of their case considered in the light of the constitutional protection that 42 U.S.C. § 1983 is meant to provide.

NOTES AND QUESTIONS

1. *The DeShaney frame(s).* How would you articulate the choice of frames in *DeShaney* that distinguish the majority from the dissents? Does one frame seem more justified to you than another, and, if so, what is your principle of justification?

2. *DeShaney applied.* In May 1999, Ms. Jessica Gonzales, a resident of Castle Rock, Colorado, and the mother of three daughters, was granted a restraining order against her abusive husband, requiring him not to " 'molest or disturb [her] peace or [that] of any child,' and to remain at least 100 yards from the family home at all times." According to her subsequent complaint,

> [A]t about 5 or 5:30 p.m. on Tuesday, June 22, 1999, [her] husband took the three daughters while they were playing outside the family home. No advance arrangements had been made for him to see the daughters that evening. When [she] noticed the children were missing, she suspected her husband had taken them. At about 7:30 p.m., she called the Castle Rock Police Department, which dispatched two officers. The complaint continues: "When [the officers] arrived . . ., she showed them a copy of the [protective order] and requested that it be enforced and the three children be returned to her immediately. [The officers] stated that there was nothing they could do about the [order] and suggested that [she] call the Police Department again if the three children did not return home by 10:00 p.m." * * *
>
> At approximately 8:30 p.m., respondent talked to her husband on his cellular telephone. He told her "he had the three children [at an] amusement park in Denver." She called the police again and asked them to "have someone check for" her husband or his vehicle at the amusement park and "put out an [all points bulletin]" for her husband, but the officer with whom she spoke "refused to do so," again telling her to "wait until 10:00 p.m. and see if" her husband returned the girls.
>
> At approximately 10:10 p.m., respondent called the police and said her children were still missing, but she was now told to wait until

> midnight. She called at midnight and told the dispatcher her children were still missing. She went to her husband's apartment and, finding nobody there, called the police at 12:10 a.m.; she was told to wait for an officer to arrive. When none came, she went to the police station at 12:50 a.m. and submitted an incident report. The officer who took the report "made no reasonable effort to enforce the [protective order] or locate the three children. Instead, he went to dinner."
>
> At approximately 3:20 a.m., respondent's husband arrived at the police station and opened fire with a semiautomatic handgun he had purchased earlier that evening. Police shot back, killing him. Inside the cab of his pickup truck, they found the bodies of all three daughters, whom he had already murdered.

Town of Castle Rock, Colo. v. Gonzales, 545 U.S. 748, 753–54 (2005). Ms. Gonzales filed suit under 42 U.S.C. § 1983 alleging that the town of Castle Rock had violated the Due Process Clause of the Fourteenth Amendment when its police officers, apparently acting pursuant to official policy or custom, failed repeatedly to respond to her reports that her husband had taken their three children in violation of the restraining order against him. An *en banc* majority of the Tenth Circuit ultimately ruled that she had alleged a cognizable due process claim, because, under a Colorado statute requiring police to enforce restraining orders, she had an entitlement to its enforcement, akin to a constitutionally-protected property interest.

The Supreme Court of the United States, *per* Justice Scalia, reversed on the ground *inter alia* that the Due Process Clause "does not protect everything that might be described as a government 'benefit'," especially if government officials have discretion to grant or deny it. Police discretion in the enforcement of restraining orders coexists with mandatory arrest statutes. "The simple distinction between government action that directly affects a citizen's legal rights . . . and action that is directed against a third party and affects the citizen only . . . incidentally, provides a sufficient answer to" cases finding government-provided services to be entitlements," citing *O'Bannon v. Town Court Nursing Center*, 447 U.S. 773, 788 (1980). The Court showed no deference to the determination by the Tenth Circuit Court of Appeals that Colorado law created a protected property interest.

3. *An alternative approach to the distinction between public and private action.* In *Velasquez-Rodriguez v. Honduras*, (Judgment of July 29, 1988) Inter-Am. Ct. H. R. (Ser. C) No. 4 (1988), the Inter-American Court of Human Rights found the government of Honduras liable for the disappearance of certain political opponents, even though there was no direct evidence of government responsibility. The government's liability lay instead in its failure to exercise "due diligence" in the investigation of the disappearances. The case was considered revolutionary at the time because it suggested that a government might be liable if it systematically failed to investigate and prosecute violations of the law in the "private" realm. Addressing the government's obligation under the American Convention of Human rights, the Court said this:

> * * * in principle, any violation of rights recognized by the Convention carried out by an act of public authority or by persons who use their position of authority is imputable to the State. However, this does not define all the circumstances in which a State is obligated to prevent, investigate and punish human rights violations, nor all the cases in which the State might be found responsible for an infringement of those rights. *An illegal act which violates human rights and which is initially not directly imputable to a State (for example, because it is the act of a private person or because the person responsible has not been identified) can lead to international responsibility of the State, not because of the act itself, but because of the lack of due diligence to prevent the violation or to respond to it as required by the Convention.*

Id., at ¶ 172 (emphasis supplied). *See also Osman v. United Kingdom*, in which the European Court of Human Rights held that state authorities have a "positive obligation * * * to take preventive operational measures to protect an individual whose life is at risk from the criminal acts of another individual." 1998-VIII Eur. Ct. H.R. (1998). For example, post-*Velasquez*, a government's systemic failure to prosecute domestic violence and other forms of gender violence would constitute a violation of its obligation to protect the human rights of the victims and survivors. *See* Committee on the Elimination of Discrimination Against Women, *General Recommendation 19*, U.N. Doc. No. A/47/38 (1992). What do these cases suggest about the distinction between public and private action?

Readings

LAURENCE H. TRIBE, *THE CURVATURE OF CONSTITUTIONAL SPACE: WHAT LAWYERS CAN LEARN FROM MODERN PHYSICS*

103 HARV. L. REV. 1 (1989)

I. INTRODUCTION

Although my topic is the constitutional lessons of general relativity and quantum physics, I do not address the subject because I am determined to bring science or mathematics into law. * * * Nor do I wish to suggest that there exists an epistemological hierarchy with the law perched on a lower rung looking up to its superiors for guidance. Rather, my conjecture is that the metaphors and intuitions that guide physicists can enrich our comprehension of social and legal issues. I borrow metaphors from physics tentatively; my purpose is to explore the heuristic ramifications for the law; my criterion of appraisal is whether the concepts we might draw from physics promote illuminating questions and directions. I press forward in this endeavor because I believe that reflection upon certain developments in physics can help us hold on to and refine some of our deeper insights into the pervasive and profound role law plays in shaping our society and our lives.

In the same spirit, I continue to maintain my previous objection to any form of dogmatism that closes down discourse about fundamental values within the law. To search the sciences for authoritative answers to legal questions, or any questions for that matter, is misguided. The formalist philosophy which views science as a "collection" of the "proven" or even of the "provable" is based upon an inappropriate reification. The better vision of science is as a continual and, above all, critical exploration of fruitful insights; the better metaphor is that of a journey. Science is not so much about proving as it is about *im*proving. To look to the natural sciences for authority—that is, for certainty—is to look for what is not there.

This look beyond law in order to understand law is necessary because our formal methods of reasoning about legal problems in general, and constitutional problems in particular, have not always kept pace with widely shared perceptions of what makes sense in thinking and talking about the state, about courts, and about the role of both in society. How we think about these institutions has been fundamentally influenced by new insights into the operation of the physical world. Michel Foucault speaks of "an epistemological space specific to a particular period";[4] he suggests that tacit positive rules of discourse cut across and condition different disciplines in any given period. Interdisciplinary comparison brings greater awareness of preconceptions, and it is the unearthing of such tacit knowledge that often creates the possibility of choice and intellectual progress. Although our intuitive understanding about the relationships among law, the state, and society has evolved, our vocabulary has lagged behind our intuitions: the language in which we still tend to ask legal questions and express legal doctrine has yet to reflect the shift in our perceptions. The result has been to make it easier for courts and lawyers to couch their analyses of many areas in terms that are deeply out of sync with that shift in underlying perceptions.

Thus, while some aspects of Supreme Court jurisprudence, as I will try to show, have become reasonably congruent with this shift, other aspects of that jurisprudence either have never become so or have fallen perceptibly behind our shared insights. In order to illustrate that failure, this essay will discuss some of the work of the Burger and Rehnquist Courts. Beyond this, the essay will argue that the central conceptual shifts represented in modern physics provide useful new ways of thinking and talking about law, legal argument and legal practice.

I am hardly the first to use science to speak of law. Early in our nation's history it was commonplace, for example, to say that the 1787 Constitution was Newtonian in design, with its carefully counterpoised

---

[4] M. FOUCAULT, THE ORDER OF THINGS: AN ARCHAEOLOGY OF HUMAN SCIENCES, at xi (1970).

forces and counterforces, its checks and balances, structured like a "machine that would go of itself" to meet the crises of the future. Later, as the country grew and the pace of social change quickened, and after Darwin's theory of evolution gained acceptance, many thinkers—Justice Holmes, for example, and Woodrow Wilson—saw in the Constitution organic aspects of a living, evolving thing. However interesting these metaphors may be, I want to borrow from science not possible images for describing particular legal institutions from the *outside*, but a language for engaging in legal analysis itself. I hope to shed light not on the nature of the Constitution as a thing but on the character and structure of constitutional analysis as a process.

II. THE CONSTITUTIONAL LESSONS OF MODERN PHYSICS

The Newtonian physics of two centuries ago took the view that objects acted on each other across the expanse of a neutral, undifferentiated space in an objective and knowable manner, according to simple physical laws that seemed to explain observed reality without requiring much further reflection about the basic structure of the universe. As in a game of marbles, objects might collide with one another, but they could not alter the field of play.

Since the 1920's, physics has been guided by two key shifts away from this view. On the grand scale, the general theory of relativity has demonstrated, among other things, that the physical universe, as seen through a telescope, can be explained only by realizing that objects like stars and planets *change* the space around them—they literally "warp" it—so that their effect is both complex and interactive. On the subatomic scale, quantum theory has demonstrated that the universe cannot be observed as though the natural world at the end of the microscope were unaffected by the eye looking into the lens—the very process of observation and analysis can fundamentally alter the things being observed, and can change how they will behave thereafter.

The insights that general relativity and quantum theory have to offer for our purposes require no mastery of technical detail, but do require familiarity with several fairly simple but fundamental concepts. This section offers a brief explication of each of these theories and then examines how their insights might help us arrive at a paradigm[11] of legal reasoning and constitutional analysis to address some of our current difficulties.

---

[11] My approach is obviously inspired to some extent by Thomas Kuhn's vision of paradigmatic discourse found in his seminal work, T. KUHN, THE STRUCTURE OF SCIENTIFIC REVOLUTIONS (2d ed. 1970). I do not, however, rely on the specific structure of Kuhn's "paradigm" paradigm, which has been properly criticized on a number of different levels. * * *

A. General Relativity Theory

1. Curved Physical Space.—In popular culture, the phrase "general relativity" has an almost mystical quality, but as a historical matter its effect was largely demystifying. The theory emerged from an attempt to improve on Newton's theory of gravity. In Newton's theory, gravity is a discrete physical force, in which the greater the mass of an object, the more strongly it "pulls" on other objects. For example, the earth exerts a stronger pull on an object placed on its surface than that which the object experiences on the surface of the moon, which explains why the astronauts get to bounce so high when they are on the moon, and how Alan Shepard managed to set a galactic record in 1971 for driving a golf ball—by his account "miles and miles and miles"—with a six-iron attached to a sampling rod. Although Newton developed a precise formula for calculating this pull, the formula left one huge mystery unexplained: if the sun and planets pull on each other with varying strengths depending on where they happen to be in relation to one another, those bodies must have some way of detecting one another's location. But how? Who or what "tells" the earth where, and how big, the sun is? The only available answers always seemed oddly mystical—as though each atom of the earth were connected to each atom of the sun by an invisible but heavy "rope" of gravity, to each atom of the moon by an equally invisible "string", and to each atom of the distant planets by mere "threads". In this picture, as the planets orbited the sun, the tendrils of this odd "force" called gravity forever shifted; but how such a "force" could act instantaneously and across the vast distances of empty space, between objects that could have no possible "awareness" of one another's existence, or mass, remained a complete puzzle.

General relativity reformulated the theory of gravity from the ground up. In Einstein's view, the planets did not move in reaction to the pull or beckon of some invisible connection to another mass. He posited instead that space itself is bent and shaped by the masses within it, causing masses to move through space and time according to that shape, guided not by invisible forces but by the very curvature of the space around them—much as a marble tossed into a bowl would spin around in accord with the curvature of the bowl itself.

In a curved space the shortest distance between two points is a line that curves along with space itself. In a sense, the planets couldn't care less where the sun is, and aren't connected to it by rope—like gravitational "threads"; they need no marching orders since the paths along which they travel are determined by the geometry of the space around them. So the problem of "action at a distance" is solved by a paradigm-shift—from a paradigm in which space was seen as absolute and uniform, and simply part of the background, to a paradigm in which space is seen as relative and not uniform at all, and just as much a part of the foreground as the objects within it.

2. *Curving Legal "Space".*—Newton's conception of space as empty, unstructured background parallels the legal paradigm in which state power, including judicial power, stands apart from the neutral, "natural" order of things. In the realm of physics, Einstein trenchantly criticized the world view in which

> space as such is assigned a role in the system of physics that distinguishes it from all other elements of physical description. It plays a determining role in all processes, without in its turn being influenced by them. Though such a theory is logically possible, it is on the other hand rather unsatisfactory. Newton had been fully aware of this deficiency, but he had also clearly understood that no other path was open to physics in his time.

In Einstein's view, space is not the neutral "stage" upon which the play is acted, but rather is merely one actor among others, all of whom interact in the unfolding of the story. Einstein's brilliance was to recognize that in comprehending physical reality the "background" could not be abstracted from the "foreground". In the paradigm inspired by Einstein, "[s]pace and time are now dynamic quantities: when a body moves, or a force acts, it affects the *curvature* of space and time—and in turn the structure of space-time affects the way in which bodies move and forces act."

A parallel conception in the legal universe would hold that, just as space cannot extricate itself from the unfolding story of physical reality, so also the law cannot extract itself from social structures; it cannot "step back", establish an "Archimedean" reference point of detached neutrality, and selectively reach in, as though from the outside, to make fine-tuned adjustments to highly particularized conflicts. Each legal decision restructures the law itself, as well as the social setting in which law operates, because, like all human activity, the law is inevitably embroiled in the dialectical process whereby society is constantly recreating itself.

To provide an initial view of how useful the "curve space" metaphor might be in law, we need look no further than two of the most controversial cases that the Supreme Court decided [in 1988].

(a) Child Abuse.—The first case concerns the tragic life of young Joshua DeShaney. Joshua was the infant son of a father who repeatedly beat him severely. Despite the various warnings the social service agencies received about his father's violence, no one came to Joshua's rescue. Joshua now lies in an almost vegetative state, well beyond the powers even of modern science to fully revive. He lies there, forever alone in his own world, because, while the social services authorities of Winnebago County, Wisconsin dutifully recorded the awful things they knew were happening to poor Joshua and kept meticulous, bureaucratically rational records of the child's injuries, they did not lift a finger to help him.

After Joshua was beaten and permanently injured by his father, Joshua's guardian sued the social workers and other local officials who had allowed those terrible beatings to occur, on the theory that their failure to act deprived him of his liberty in violation of the due process clause of the fourteenth amendment, and that Joshua was therefore entitled to recover damages under the civil rights statutes. The Supreme Court held in *DeShaney v. Winnebago County* that there was no violation of the fourteenth amendment, and thus no basis for recovery under the statutes enacted in the wake of the Civil War to enforce that amendment.

The Court spoke movingly of what it called the "undeniably tragic" facts of the case, but proceeded to say:

> nothing in the language of the Due Process Clause . . . requires the State to protect the life, liberty and property of its citizens against invasion by private actors. The Clause is phrased as a limitation on the State's power to act, not as a guarantee of certain minimal levels of safety and security.

Near the close of the majority opinion, written by Chief Justice Rehnquist, the Court paused to note:

> Judges and lawyers, like other humans, are moved by natural sympathy in a case like this to find a way for Joshua and his mother to receive adequate compensation for the grievous harm inflicted upon them. But before yielding to that impulse, it is well to remember once again that the harm was inflicted not by the State of Wisconsin, but by Joshua's father. The most that can be said of the state functionaries in this case is that they stood by and did nothing when suspicious circumstances dictated a more active role for them.

The Court went on to say, in defense of the officials, that

> had they moved too soon to take custody of the son away from the father, they would likely have been met with charges of improperly intruding into the parent-child relationship, charges based on the same Due Process Clause that forms the basis for the present charge of failure to provide adequate protection.

Justice Blackmun, in a bitter dissent, chided the majority for purporting "to be the dispassionate oracle of the law, unmoved by 'natural sympathy.' " He compared the Rehnquist Court to "the antebellum judges who denied relief to fugitive slaves." He had little sympathy for the Court's claim that "its decision, however harsh, is compelled by existing legal doctrine." In his view, the question was "an open one." He argued that the fourteenth amendment precedents could "be read more broadly or narrowly depending upon how one chooses to read them." He wrote that, faced with such a choice, *he* "would adopt a 'sympathetic' reading, one which comports with dictates of fundamental justice and recognizes that compassion need not be exiled from the province of judging."

My purpose here is not to take any position on who has the better of the argument. My distress centers neither on the majority's result, nor on the notion that the majority was too hard-hearted—too unwilling to allow reason to be tempered with mercy. Indeed, I would reject the idea that the majority's mode of analysis really *had* "reason" on its side, or that the dissenters came out where they did principally because they allowed themselves to feel more sympathy for Joshua. My trouble is with the majority's quite primitive vision of the state of Wisconsin as some sort of distinct object, a kind of machine that must be understood to act upon a pre-political, natural order of private life. From the majority's perspective, the state of Wisconsin operates as a thing, its arms exerting force from a safe distance upon a sometimes unpleasant natural world, in which the abuse of children is an unfortunate, yet external, ante-legal and pre-political fact of our society. Courts, as passive and detached observers, may reach in to offer a helping hand only when another arm of the state has reached out and shattered this natural, pre-political order by itself directly harming a young child.

Within the majority's stilted pre-modern paradigm, there is no hint that the hand of the observing state may itself have played a major role in shaping the world it observes. Thus when the Supreme Court majority looked out at one of the most defenseless persons in the universe we know—an abused child—it did not inquire whether the hand of the state may have altered an already political landscape in a way that encouraged such child-beating to go uncorrected. The majority's question in *DeShaney* was simply, "did the State of Wisconsin beat up that child?" and not, "did the law of Wisconsin, taken in its entirety, warp the legal landscape so that it in effect deflected the assistance otherwise available to Joshua DeShaney?"

Only Justice Brennan's dissent bothered to ask whether the state of Wisconsin—by establishing a child welfare system specifically to help children like Joshua, by creating a system for investigating reported instances of child abuse, and by outlawing private intrusions into a home where a child seems imperiled—effectively *channeled* all reports of such abuse, and all actions in response to such reports, to specific agencies. In this way, the state invited citizens and others "to depend on local departments of social services . . . to protect children from abuse." The dissenters, in what I would praise as an admirably post-Newtonian insight, concluded that it belied reality to contend that the state had done *nothing* with respect to Joshua. On the contrary, Wisconsin's child-protection program "actively intervened in Joshua's life" and "effectively confined him within the walls of Randy DeShaney's violent home until such time as DSS took action to remove him." "Conceivably, . . . children like Joshua are made worse off," the dissenters reasoned, "by the existence of this program when the persons and entities charged with carrying it out fail to do their jobs."

Justice Brennan relied heavily on *Youngberg v. Romeo* and *Estelle v. Gamble*—cases holding that the due process clause requires that persons institutionalized by the state be provided with services sufficient to meet basic needs. (In *Youngberg* the institution was a psychiatric hospital; in *Estelle*, it was a prison.) Justice Brennan read these cases "to stand for the . . . generous proposition that, if a State cuts off private sources of aid and then itself refuses to aid, it cannot wash its hands of the harm that results from its inaction." From there he found the *DeShaney* case but a small jump away.

But *Youngberg* and *Estelle* like two will-o'-the-wisps, seem to have lured Justice Brennan away from the perhaps deeper insights offered by *Boddie v. Connecticut*. In *Boddie*, an indigent couple could not obtain a divorce because they could not afford the filing fee. The Court held:

> given the basic position of the marriage relationship in this society's hierarchy of values and the concomitant state monopolization of the means for legally dissolving this relationship, due process does prohibit a State from denying, solely because of inability to pay, access to its courts to individuals who seek judicial dissolution of their marriages.

Of course, Justice Brennan did cite *Boddie*—for the proposition that "the monopolization of a particular path of relief may impose upon the State certain positive duties." He labeled it as "instructive" and included it within a class of cases that "signal that a state's prior actions may be decisive in analyzing the constitutional significance of its inaction." Justice Brennan portrayed *Boddie* as a close parallel to *Youngberg* and *Estelle*: "I . . . would locate the DeShaneys' claims within the framework of cases like *Youngberg* and *Estelle*, and more generally, *Boddie* . . . ."

Yet there is a fundamental distinction to be made between *Youngberg* and *Estelle* on the one hand, and *Boddie* on the other. In both *Youngberg* and *Estelle*, it was the state's institutionalization of a *particular individual* that had isolated that person from alternative means of fulfilling his or her basic needs. In *Boddie*, however, there had been no previous state action directed at the particular individual. It was the legal structure itself—combined, to be sure, with the economic and social circumstances of the individual—that had isolated the person from the fulfillment of an important need.

Boddie, instead of focusing in a Newtonian way on the isolated forces acting on particular individuals, introduced the curved space of a post-Newtonian world in which the focus broadens to encompass the larger geometry of the "space" in which the relevant events and persons interact. If the law creates a state monopoly over the fulfillment of certain needs (dissolution of a failed marriage, protection from a violent parent) and thereby renders some, but not all, individuals particularly vulnerable, can the very act of creating this legal *structure* constitute state action violative of due process? Has the creation of a state monopoly over the fulfillment of a category of needs warped legal space itself in a cognizable fashion? *Boddie* answers "yes," at least where the state's interest in preserving that legal structure in violate is insufficient to "override the interest" of the plaintiff.

Although Justice Brennan stressed *Youngberg* and *Estelle*, the spirit of his argument seems to derive from *Boddie*. From a post-Newtonian perspective, *Boddie* is the more dramatic case and provides the stronger parallel to *DeShaney*. As in *Boddie*, the governmental act in *DeShaney* that isolated Joshua—that is, the establishment of a legal structure that narrowly channeled all information and action in regard to child abuse—was not a force directed at Joshua personally; his isolation was a result of the simple juxtaposition of Wisconsin law and his personal situation. And, again as in *Boddie*, it was the monopoly created by the legal structure in *DeShaney* that made the plaintiff peculiarly vulnerable.

We may all be engulfed by, and dependent upon, the structure of the law, but we are not all rendered equally vulnerable by it. If the special dependence upon the law and its omissions that is experienced by the most vulnerable among us could be dismissed as irrelevant because it was not directly created by any state force targeting such individuals, their heightened dependence might be seen as legally immaterial. But if the systemic vulnerability of some—battered children are perhaps prime examples—is instead regarded as centrally relevant to how the law's shape should be understood, then one is more likely at least to ask whether the legal system's very failure to do more for such persons might not work an unconstitutional deprivation of their rights. The Newtonian judge, viewing those whose fate she determines as though from a removed, objective vantage point, can easily absolve the state of responsibility for their plight. But her post-Newtonian judicial counterpart, viewing the perspectives of those whom her ruling affects as no less legitimate than her own, and asking what social space the body of legal rules helps to define, may find it more difficult to distance the state from the helplessness of the most vulnerable.

The approach I am suggesting here need not lend itself to, nor embrace, an ideology of paternalism. A post-Newtonian heuristic does not force answers upon us; rather, it pushes us to more probing questions. It is not a cry for "all power to the judges," but rather a plea for circumspection and questioning in assessing how the distribution and direction of all public powers—including those of judges—define the legal space through which we all move, and in whose recesses some of us are lost. It may well be that those who are most likely to be lost are those for whom this plea would make the greatest difference. For it is the most vulnerable, the most forgotten, whose perspective is least akin to that of the lawmaker or judge or bureaucrat and whose fate is most forcefully determined by the law's overall design—by its least visible, most deeply embedded gaps and deflections. By another route we arrive at philosopher John Rawls' conclusion that the fundamental fairness of a society is best judged by an examination of its treatment of the least advantaged.

The fact that Justice Brennan's arguments were the impassioned words only of a dissent in *DeShaney* unfortunately reflects the reality that the still-reigning paradigm of constitutional law stands in sharp contrast to most contemporary modes of social thought.

* * *

III. CHANGING LEGAL PARADIGMS

Lawyers and judges have incorporated post-Newtonian insights into some areas of law, but those insights still have a tentative foothold in the culture of accepted legal argument and analysis. As I seek to show in what follows, perhaps the earliest dramatic break with the Newtonian vision of a pre-political and pre-legal background came with the demise of *Lochner v. New York*, [198 U.S. 45 (1905)] in the early twentieth century. Later, in *Shelley v. Kraemer*, [334 U.S. 1 (1948)] and in a series of first amendment cases beginning with *New York Times v. Sullivan,* [376 U.S. 254 (1964)], the Supreme Court extended what might be understood as post-Newtonian conceptions into other areas of the law. However, as the Court's decisions in *Pasadena City Board of Education v. Spangler*, [427 U.S. 424 (1976)], and *Milliken v. Bradley*, [433 U.S. 267 (1977)], suggest, the pre-modern paradigm still reigns in much of legal analysis (notably also in some law and economics scholarship[90] and appears to have undergone a revival under the Burger and Rehnquist Courts.

---

[90] Insights and images traceable to physics may already have played a significant role in shaping law and economics scholarship. Neoclassical economics, upon which much of law and economics draws, assumes, like Newtonian physics, a fixed background: the structure of markets and the motivations of consumers. It then attempts to predict the behavior of markets and consumers without considering how they might fundamentally alter each other in the process of interacting. The neoclassical economic assumption that people are rational optimizers is also akin to the Newtonian postulate that objects in the physical world act on one another according to simple, observable laws.

This parallel is no accident. Economist Phil Mirowski has unearthed a link between neoclassical economics and pre-modern physics. He argues:

> in the final analysis, however coy and ambivalent neoclassicals may appear to be about their physics metaphor, it cannot seriously be repudiated or relinquished, because there is nothing else that can hold the neoclassical research program together. In the absence of the metaphor of utility as nineteenth-century potential energy, there is no alternative theory of value, no heuristic guide to research, no principle upon which to base mathematical formalism.

P. MIROWSKI, MORE HEAT THAN LIGHT 287 (1989) (unpublished manuscript) (on file at the Harvard Law School Library) (emphasis omitted). Mirowski goes on to argue that neoclassical economics borrowed not only its metaphor from nineteenth-century physics, but its legitimacy as well—a dangerous loan, indeed, to the extent that new ways of seeing the physical world can

A. The Delayed Demise of Lochner v. New York

During the early twentieth century, lawyers began to question whether the background of social and economic relations that legislation sought to change might not itself be part of what the law had wrought. Many observers were unpersuaded by the reasoning of judicial decisions from the 1890's to the 1930's that treated "property" and "contract" as categories somehow preexisting the artifice of law. It was the formal rejection of such treatment that finally ended the now infamous *Lochner* era in 1937. The Supreme Court accommodated its doctrine to the growing belief that the "brooding omnipresence" of the common law was not a fact of nature, but an artifact of politics and government and of judge-made rules. In essence, the post-*Lochner* Court acknowledged that the property interests available for people to use as contractual bargaining chips had all along been largely the reflections of prior social choices, expressed through law, about the acquisition and allocation of control over human and material resources, and that a law banning certain employer-employee bargains as unfairly exploitative was therefore no more an affront to the "natural order of things" than were the legal understandings making such one-sided bargains possible in the first place. It is no coincidence that *Erie R.R. Co. v. Tompkins*, [304 U.S. 64 (1938)], which in 1938 ended the *Swift v. Tyson*, [41 U.S. (16 Pet.) 1 (1842),] era in which federal courts had felt free to follow their own views of general common law, was decided within a year of the watershed decision in *West Coast Hotel v. Parrish*, [300 U.S. 379 (1937)], which upheld laws restricting the "liberty of contract" between employers and employees.

In many other areas of law, the Supreme Court has similarly come to recognize that the state cannot be understood as some sort of robot-like thing that one can observe walking about, a machine whose arms—and it's instructive that we still speak of the "arms of the state"—sometimes reach out and grab a Joshua DeShaney, sometimes reach out and perform surgery on an unwilling woman, sometimes interfere with free exchanges between businesses and consumers.

B. The Tentative Emergence of a Post-Newtonian Paradigm

If we are to conduct constitutional discourse through conversation truer to contemporary sensibilities—abandoning the prism of Newtonian

---

subvert the claim that economics has finally become scientific. Once we are aware of underlying analytical presumptions that may have been incorporated into at least some versions of the law and economics method, we can consider alternative metaphors from modern physics that may lead us to ask more fruitful legal questions. * * *

In contrast, some of the best law and economics scholarship, perhaps influenced by post-Newtonian concepts, evokes the warped space notion of general relativity as well as the Heisenbergian view of joint causation and nondeterminism. Whether pre- or post-Newtonian, physics metaphors and concepts have filtered into the development of law and economics but have, thus far, done relatively little to dislodge the persistent notion (reminiscent of neoclassical economics) that the preferences of economic actors are given, rather than shaped by the markets within which those actors' choices are made.

physics and its legal analogies—then we must consistently speak of the state not as a thing but as a set of rules, principles, and conceptions that interact with a background which is in part a product of prior political actions. And we must talk of the events and people involved without pretending they are pre-political; they too are in part shaped by political and legal interactions.

The Supreme Court recognized as much in *Shelley v. Kraemer*, when it held that the common law of Missouri violated the fourteenth amendment insofar as that state's common law made racially restrictive covenants, but not other restraints on the alienation of land, judicially enforceable. Notwithstanding the absence of any racist decision by any particular state actor, what was crucial in *Shelley* was the *geometry* of the state's common law: it drew a line between those restraints on land sales that courts would enforce and those that they would not enforce, and knowingly put racially restrictive covenants on the enforceable side of that line.

A similar understanding of the "geometry" of law was at work in *New York Times v. Sullivan*, [376 U.S. 254 (1964)], in *NAACP v. Claiborne Hardware Co.*, [458 U.S. 886 (1982)], and in *Hustler Magazine v. Falwell*, [485 U.S. 46 (1988)]. In each of those decisions, the Supreme Court held that first amendment principles were violated not by some state official's act of censorship but by the *overall shape* of the state's body of judge-made rules for awarding damages to people allegedly injured by speeches or publications. The fact that the "chilling effect" upon the speech involved in those cases was caused not by any discrete act of a government official, but by the fabric of legal rules developed in a given jurisdiction over time, has not prevented the Supreme Court from perceiving that this fabric of rules might violate the first amendment.

In fact, the Supreme Court's entire development of the "chilling effect" doctrine over the past several decades itself reflects a judicial recognition that widespread private behavior, in the form of self-censorship, can be directly traceable not only to particular enforcement actions by specific state officials but to the very existence of a set of rules or lines that the state stands ready to enforce or to draw. A primitive conception of the state as a mechanism that operates only through exerting direct vectors of force in particular cases could not possibly account for this doctrine. A retreat from the Supreme Court's once vigorous concern with this "chilling" of protected speech might well reflect a partial throwback to a more primitive paradigm.

The paradigm-shift toward a mode of thought that stresses both the geometry of the legal landscape and the interaction between the legal observer and the phenomenon observed thus has deep roots in existing practices and ways of thinking about law. It also accounts for many of the most powerful and salutary insights of contemporary legal analysis. We need not return to the more primitive and simplistic paradigm in which the universe is seen as an empty and apolitical space across whose vast reaches legal actors hurl their thunderbolts of force at distant and discrete objects. * * *

E. Choosing Legal Paradigms

Implicit throughout my discussion of scientific and legal paradigms have been two criteria for choosing among competing paradigms. The first is empirical—which paradigm best explains the available "data"? Although the mathematics needed to work it all out is complex, Einstein's theory is not only simpler in basic conception and more elegant in design than Newton's; it makes better predictions about a number of real-world phenomena[135]—including the degree to which a star's light ray that passes in the sun's vicinity appears to be *deflected* by the sun's mass when visible during a solar eclipse. Similarly, I have tried to suggest that the post-Newtonian legal paradigm fits better our modern intuitions about the state, the courts, and law.

A second criterion for choosing among competing paradigms might be called the "progressivity" of the paradigm—the resilience and usefulness of the paradigm in a new context. A progressive paradigm adapts in a constructive fashion to new "data"—new situations and problems; a "degenerative" paradigm must be revised in an *ad hoc* fashion to handle these new facts or contexts.

Consider Newtonian physics. Its major limitation was that it did not yield a consistent and principled account of events[139]—an explanation that worked independent of the kinds of changes in surrounding conditions that scientists have increasingly agreed should make no difference to the operation of basic physical laws. The most fundamental of the so-called "equivalence principles" that Newton's theories were too primitive to yield is the principle that the basic laws of science should be the same for a body that is undergoing uniform acceleration as they are for a body that is at

[135] As [Stephen] Hawking explains:

For example, very accurate observations of the planet Mercury revealed a small difference between its motion and the predictions of Newton's theory of gravity. Einstein's general theory of relativity predicted a slightly different motion from Newton's theory. The fact that Einstein's predictions matched what was seen, while Newton's did not, was one of the crucial confirmations of the new theory.

[139] As Imre Lakatos explains:

Einstein's theory is not better than Newton's *because* Newton's theory was 'refuted' but Einstein's was not: there are many known 'anomalies' to Einsteinian theory. Einstein's theory is better than—that is, represents progress compared with—Newton's theory *anno 1916* (that is, Newton's laws of dynamics, law of gravitation, the known set of initial conditions; 'minus' the list of known anomalies such as Mercury's perihelion) *because* it explained everything that Newton's theory had successfully explained, and it explained also *to some extent* some known anomalies and, in addition, forbade events like transmission of light along straight lines near large masses about which Newton's theory had said nothing but which had been permitted by other well-corroborated scientific theories of the day; moreover, *at least some* of the unexpected excess Einsteinian content was in fact *corroborated* (for instance, by the eclipse experiments).

rest in a uniform gravitational field. You who feel as though you and anything you happen to drop are being pulled toward the floor by the "force" of gravity, would feel exactly the same "pull" if the entire earth vanished and the building you happened to be occupying were accelerating quite rapidly in the direction you *used* to call "up"—so that the building would be going about 65 miles per hour after the first three seconds, about 130 miles per hour three seconds later, about 200 miles per hour after another three seconds, and so on, and you were in fact continuously being pressed against the floor with a force equal to the earth's gravitational field—one "g," or "gravity."

To understand how much more coherently and consistently Einstein's paradigm can deal with this equivalence between acceleration and gravity, imagine that somebody just outside the room in which you sit as you read this were to shine a laser beam through a small opening located where the wall to your left meets the ceiling, shooting it horizontally across the room. Where would it hit the wall to the right? If the building you occupy were rapidly accelerating in deep space, and if there were a device on the wall to the right to measure it *very* accurately, you would find that the laser beam hits *not* where the wall meets the ceiling, but slightly *below* that point. And if you could trace the path of the laser beam across the room, you would notice it *not* zipping perfectly across the ceiling, but dropping toward the floor in a very slight arc. The reason is clear: as the beam crosses the room, the room continues to speed up, leaving the beam further and further behind as it crosses.

A Newtonian would be satisfied with that discrete explanation. But an Einsteinian would say that the acceleration of the room creates "g" forces that *warp* the space in the room, and the light beam is *bent* by this curved space. Why is that a better explanation? Because with it, an Einsteinian would not be in the least surprised to find, if you performed the laser beam experiment on earth in your room right now, that the beam would drop in an arc in *precisely* the same way. Having said that the earth's mass warps the space in your room exactly as the acceleration of the room in deep space would, she would *expect* the effect on the light beam to be identical.

But the Newtonian would be totally mystified to learn that, even on earth, the laser beam curves downward. To account for the curve, he would probably suggest that the beam should be thought of as a stream of water particles, and he would start making special assumptions about the "weight" of individual "particles" of light that are contained in it, and about how the "gravity" of the earth pulled these particles toward the floor. By contrast, Einstein's approach provides a more consistent explanation for why the physical universe is the way it is, and yields a set of physical laws that would work equally well for earthbound creatures and for astronauts accelerating away from earth. Thus an Einsteinian is spared the fate of being forced to rewrite his laws in an ad hoc way to address each new context. The Einsteinian paradigm is, in this way, more progressive than the Newtonian paradigm.

Back Down on earth, in the constitutional realm, it is equally important to avoid that fate. The most basic substantive principles affecting the kinds of things that government may do in its dealings with people should not depend on accidents of form and appearance—like the accident of whether the government exerts pressure through a single administrative regulation instead of through a series of judicial rulings, or by imposing a fine on those who *do* something instead of offering a benefit only to those who agree *not* to do it.

I believe that, in law just as in physics, the goal of freeing constitutional analysis from such entirely artificial distinctions is best achieved if we think of law, and of governmental action, as changing the social landscape and redirecting the "geometry" of human interactions, instead of regarding government as a physical entity that, through the "forces" exerted by its component parts, tugs and pulls at people who are "out there" in a "state of nature". In this way, the post-Newtonian legal paradigm is more progressive than the Newtonian paradigm. Whether in the child abuse context of *DeShaney*, in the abortion context of *Webster*, in the symbolic speech setting of *Wooley*, or in the resegregation setting of *Spangler*, we are more likely to put better questions if we focus on how collective political action has reconstituted the relevant "social space" than if we simply ask who is laying hands on whom.

IV. CONCLUSION

A corollary of responsible modernism is to admit that we can *see* more than we can do. But this does not mean that we should lie about what we see. Those lies sap the creative tension that fuels progress. Thus, as we consider whether judicial opinions or other governmental measures unconstitutionally tilt the legal landscape in favor of some groups and against others, it is crucial not to ignore the *social meaning* of whatever the state has done.

To understand such meaning in a way that fully acknowledges the interconnectedness of legal events—and to recognize, as modern physics has, the interdependence between the process of observing and what is observed—is to avoid the parochial fallacy of looking at the legal universe only through the eyes of those in power.[146] It requires abandoning any notion that the "objective" picture of the legal universe is the one seen from the vantage point of those who make legal decisions. Difficult as it is to view the world from someone else's perspective, not to make the effort is to

[146] One could interpret John Rawls' "veil of ignorance" as essentially capturing this insight into the nature of justice—that "fairness" requires looking at things from the perspective of those on the bottom of the social ladder. See J. RAWLS, A THEORY OF JUSTICE (1971), at 136–42.

ignore what science learned long ago. How strange that physics should have to reteach the Golden Rule.

Among the consequences of adhering more consistently to this post-Newtonian perspective might well be a reduced tendency to blame the state's victims for the harm done when the state sets them apart—as though their view of what government has done or failed to do is to be discounted in light of their supposedly limited or distorted perspective. The late nineteenth-century Supreme Court did just that in *Plessy v. Ferguson*, [163 U.S. 537 (1896)], when it indicated that forced separation by race merely tracks nature's law; if such separation makes blacks feel stigmatized, it's all in the construction *they* put upon it. Justice O'Connor, in an otherwise sensitive examination of a city's official celebration of a nativity scene at Christmas, fell into a similar trap when she said that no "objective" observer would take that display as an endorsement of Christianity or as a put down of non-Christians.[150]

Discerning the social meaning of a challenged practice—of a legal space shaped by certain acts juxtaposed with certain omissions—entails inquiry into how the practice affects the human geometry of the situation. Such inquiry in turn demands less an effort to uncover the hidden levers, gears or forces that translate governmental actions into objective effects, than an attempt to feel the contours of the world government has built—and to sense what those contours *mean* for those who might be trapped or excluded by them.

So too with discerning the operative effect of an incomplete social welfare program. Just as the path of a beam of starlight passing near the sun is best understood not as responding to a hidden tug but as moving along the shortest distance between two points in a space bent by the sun's very mass, so the citizens who might have come to Joshua DeShaney's aid but for the assumption that the state's elaborate welfare program would do so are best understood not as reacting to a muffled signal or a gentle push but as following the path of least resistance laid out by the very presence and structure of the state's program. And the judicial declaration that Joshua's fate is not the state's fault but the natural result of private action, operates not simply as a passive *observation* about who caused injury to whom, but as an *action* that may entrench all the more deeply the geometry of public indifference that will shape the lives of Joshuas yet unborn.

---

[150] *See Lynch v. Donnelly*, 465 U.S. 668, 692–93 (1984). *But see County of Allegheny v. ACLU Greater Pittsburgh Chapter*, 109 S.Ct. 3086 (1989) (holding that the creche display, when viewed in its overall context, violates the establishment clause since the creche carried a patently Christian message and nothing in the setting detracted from that message); *id.* at 3117–24 (O'Connor, J., concurring).

NOTES AND QUESTIONS

1. *Tribe and paradigms*. Professor Tribe describes his central argument in these terms: "the central conceptual shifts represented in modern physics provide useful new ways of thinking and talking about law, legal argument and legal practice." Is he successful in his effort to use the notion of paradigms as more than a handy metaphor for criticizing the Supreme Court's decision in *DeShaney*? Has he advanced a neutral principle of general applicability, or has he simply hitched the "wagon" of his criticism (and the ideology it reflects) to the "star" of modern physics?

2. *Frame and prevail*. It is a federal crime to "knowingly provid[e] material support or resources to a foreign terrorist organization," 18 U.S.C. § 2339B(a)(1), as designated by the Secretary of State. In *Holder v. Humanitarian Law Project*, 130 S. Ct. 2705 (2010), certain individuals and groups sought pre-enforcement review of the criminal ban in § 2339B, claiming that it was invalid to the extent it prohibited them from training members of the designated groups in the use of international law to resolve disputes peacefully and teaching them how to petition the United Nations and other bodies for relief. The courts below, including the district court and the court of appeals, partially ruled in their favor on the ground that the statute was unconstitutionally vague.

To see the power of framing, consider the competing versions of the question presented. The government's petition for *certiorari*, 2009 WL 1567496, framed the issue in these terms:

> Whether 18 U.S.C. 2339B(a)(1), which prohibits the knowing provision of "any * * * service, * * * training, [or] expert advice or assistance," 18 U.S.C. 2339A(b)(1), to a designated foreign terrorist organization, is unconstitutionally vague.

The cross-petition for *certiorari*, 2009 WL 2197542, is worded quite differently:

> Whether the criminal prohibitions in 18 U.S.C. § 2339B(a)(1) on provision of "expert advice or assistance" "derived from scientific [or] technical * * * knowledge" and "personnel" are unconstitutional with respect to speech that furthers only lawful, nonviolent activities of proscribed organizations.

Strategically, what is the crucial difference between these two formulations?

3. *The veil of ignorance and "the original position."* In one footnote in his essay, Professor Tribe refers to John Rawls' "veil of ignorance," a thought-experiment that appears in Rawls' book, A THEORY OF JUSTICE (1971).[7] The essence of the experiment is to imagine a situation prior to society in which no participant knows what kind of society he or she is about to enter. In Rawls' words,

---

[7] For an example of the veil-of-ignorance frame used well before Professor Rawls' book, *see, e.g.*, J.C. Harsanyi, *Cardinal Utility in Welfare Economics and In the Theory of Risk-Taking*, 61 J. POLIT. ECON. 434 (1953); J.C. Harsanyi, *Cardinal Welfare, Individualistic Ethics, and Interpersonal Comparison of Utility*, 63 J. POLIT. ECON. 309 (1955).

> Among the essential features of this situation is that no one knows his place in society, his class position or social status, nor does any one know his fortune in the distribution of natural assets and abilities, his intelligence, strength and the like. I shall even assume that the parties do not know their conceptions of the good or their special psychological propensities. The principles of justice are chosen behind a veil of ignorance.

One reason for imagining everyone's systematic ignorance of the future—ignorance of themselves and one another and the organization of their society—is to isolate the minimum rules that one would insist upon before willingly and rationally entering into that society. The experiment has been criticized in various ways, but it does offer one "frame" for thinking about a moral society. Assuming that you cannot know what the substantive rules will be, what is the minimal *procedural* rule that you would insist upon in such a situation?

4. *Paradigms at different scales*. So far in this chapter, we have focused on the utility of paradigms within individual cases: framing the case is an adversarial skill that can determine which doctrines apply and control the result in that case. As Thomas Kuhn made clear, paradigms in the scientific world are not case-specific and manipulable in this way. To the contrary, they reflect a community-wide consensus that organizes "normal science" research, determines what evidence is relevant to collect, explains replicable results of experimentation. When paradigms shift, it is because results accumulate which the prevailing paradigm cannot explain.

As the following readings suggest, it is sometimes helpful to think of paradigm-shift-like reconceptualizations in the law generally, and not just as the scaffolding for argument in individual cases. Major doctrines within fields of laws—sometimes entire fields of law—are no less susceptible to paradigm shifts.

W. BRADLEY WENDEL, *EXPLANATION IN LEGAL SCHOLARSHIP: THE INFERENTIAL STRUCTURE OF DOCTRINAL LEGAL ANALYSIS*

96 CORNELL L. REV. 1035, 1036, 1041–43 (2011)

This Essay is aimed at understanding what kind of logical inference underwrites the conclusion that some area of law is "all about" some end or value. It is a contribution to the metatheory of law—that is, it is a theory about what makes theories more or less acceptable. To put it another way, it is an account of explanation in law. * * * [It] draws from the resources of the philosophy of science, in which the methodology of inference to the best explanation (IBE) has been thoroughly analyzed. The analogy with scientific explanation does not depend on a close correspondence with the methods of the empirical sciences. I am not trying to make some kind of

Langdellian claim here that the analytic techniques of legal thought are essentially scientific * * *. Rather, the reason for invoking IBE in science is to suggest that legal scholarship, in its effort to render some area of law intelligible by positing an explanation, tacitly appeals to criteria for inferring to the best explanation. The arguments back and forth about the theoretical justification of some doctrine are actually appeals to these criteria for theory selection. The overall strategy of this analysis is to derive conditions of explanatory adequacy from the answer to the pragmatic question, "what good are explanations?" This Essay aims to begin with this question in law—"what good are legal explanations?"—and proceed from there through some foundational issues in jurisprudence, such as the autonomy of legal reasoning, the objectivity of law, and the role of morality (if any) in the explanation and justification of law and legal authority. * * *

Here are some * * * examples, from various areas of legal scholarship, of the arguments for which an adequate metatheory should be given. I am setting them out as the briefest possible blurb summaries of these theories, which are obviously considerably more complicated and subtle than I make them seem here. I have attempted to select works from different areas of law and with different ambitions (some dealing with one principle or doctrine, others taking on an entire legal subject), in the hopes that readers will be familiar with some of these positions and recognize the inferential structure of the arguments that these theorists offer. The intention here is not to suggest that these scholars are being imprecise, only that these are the types of arguments we are trying to theorize. In fact, the analysis here is quite careful, even if it is not always explicit about the underlying methodological issues.

1. *Beebe on intellectual property.*[18] We tend to think that the purpose of intellectual property law is to promote technological and cultural progress by creating incentives for investing time and energy in creative enterprises.[19] That is a mistake. In fact, the purpose of intellectual property—or, at least, what is coming to be a significant purpose of intellectual property—is to enforce social hierarchy by facilitating the construction of status-based individual and group identities, or at least to preserve the capacity of people to differentiate themselves from others through their patterns of consumption. Intellectual property laws can thus be explained as a means to sustain the possibility of making consumption-based distinctions in status.

---

[18] *See generally* Barton Beebe, *Intellectual Property Law and the Sumptuary Code*, 123 HARV. L. REV. 809 (2010).

[19] *See id.* at 813 ("To be sure, the express purpose and primary effect of intellectual property law remains the prevention of misappropriation and the promotion of technological and cultural progress.").

2. *Underkuffler on the notion of property.*[21] We hold multiple, conflicting ideas about the point of property law. Sometimes we see it as granting stringent protection for individual rights, but in other cases, we permit property-rights claims to yield to other public interests.[22] The variable power of property rights is predictable, and justified, given the structure of property law.[23] The only way to make sense of the idea of property is to see it as encompassing plural values.[24] Any attempt at unifying the underlying values of property law is bound to oversimplify, and thus fail to explain, its subject.

3. *Markovits on contract law.*[25] Contract law scholars generally take an individualistic perspective on the subject, assuming that the purpose of contract law is to promote individual freedom, protect the expectations of other parties, or promote the efficient allocation of resources (and therefore the welfare of both parties).[26] But this misses the point of contracts. Contracts should be understood as establishing relationships of respect and recognition, a kind of community, among those who enter into them.[27] This is true even if the contracting parties have basically self-interested motivations for entering into agreements. Thus, contract law is fundamentally all about collaboration.

4. *Luban on the attorney-client privilege.*[28] The traditional justification for the attorney-client privilege is that, without it, clients will not be forthcoming with their lawyers and thus will receive less effective representation.[29] A better way to understand the rationale behind the privilege, however, is to focus on the cruelty that would result from putting a client in the situation of either revealing an incriminating fact to her lawyer, remaining silent, or lying to the lawyer.[30] Being required to testify against oneself—which is effectively what would happen in the absence of the attorney-client privilege—is a core instance of humiliation and violation of human dignity.[ ] Thus, we should see the attorney-client privilege as aimed at protecting human dignity.

---

21 *See generally* LAURA S. UNDERKUFFLER, THE IDEA OF PROPERTY: ITS MEANING AND POWER (2003)

22 *See id.* at 64 (noting that under the operative conception of property, property law identifies protected individual interests but also recognizes that these interests change as the result of societal needs).

23 *See id.* at 75–84 (setting forth a model that predicts when claimed rights will and should have trumping power).

24 *See id.* at 16–33.

25 *See generally* Daniel Markovits, *Contract and Collaboration*, 113 YALE L.J. 1417 (2004).

26 *See id.* at 1419.

27 *See id.* at 1420.

28 *See* DAVID LUBAN, LEGAL ETHICS AND HUMAN DIGNITY 80–88 (2007).

29 *See id.* at 80.

30 *See id.* at 81.

5. *Siegel on justiciability.*[32] Standing and other justiciability doctrines are a puzzle. Scholars have explained these doctrines as giving litigants a stake in disputes,[33] or giving courts some wiggle room to avoid making socially divisive rulings[34] (as occurred in the *Newdow*[35] case on the Pledge of Allegiance). These explanations are inadequate, however, and a better understanding of justiciability would emphasize its role in ensuring that courts rule only on the legality, as opposed to the wisdom, of actions by other branches of government.[ ]

6. *Coleman on the tort system.*[37] Economic analysis is a bad explanation of tort law.[ ] Economic analysis says that torts is all about welfare-maximization.[39] The negligence standard, for example, indicates which precautions are cost justified and which need not be taken.[40] However, economic analysis fails to explain certain core concepts in tort law, such as duty, wrong, and responsibility. The rival account of corrective justice is a better explanation of tort law because it better accounts for observed features of the law (such as the duty element) and the relationship among the constitutive elements of tort law.[41]

ALAN M. TRAMMELL, DEREK E. BAMBAUER, *PERSONAL JURISDICTION AND THE "INTERWEBS"*

100 CORNELL L. REV. 1129, 1130–35 (2015)

After more than twenty years of silence, the Supreme Court has recently reentered the fray of personal jurisdiction. It has been remarkably active over the last four years, having decided four cases in that span.[2] But the Court has remained conspicuously silent about one of the most vexing and urgent questions in this area: when (if ever) virtual conduct, often through the Internet, can justify the exercise of judicial power.

Most courts are still flummoxed by these questions. They remain tethered to anachronistic approaches that reflect a profound confusion

---

32 *See generally* Jonathan R. Siegel, *A Theory of Justiciability*, 86 TEX. L. REV. 73 (2007).

33 *See id.* at 87.

34 *See id.* at 108.

35 *See generally Newdow v. U.S. Cong.*, 328 F.3d 466 (9th Cir. 2003), *rev'd on other grounds sub nom. Elk Grove Unified Sch. Dist. v. Newdow*, 542 U.S. 1 (2004).

37 [JULES L. COLEMAN, THE PRACTICE OF PRINCIPLE: IN DEFENCE OF A PRAGMATIST APPROACH TO LEGAL THEORY (2001)]. Coleman's book is particularly interesting because he first works through methodological issues with some care and uses what I take to be an IBE methodology to defend his preferred conception of the role of tort law.

39 *See id.* at 16.

40 *See id.* at 14.

41 *See id.* at 21.

2 *See* Walden v. Fiore, 134 S. Ct. 1115 (2014); Daimler AG v. Bauman, 134 S. Ct. 746 (2014); Goodyear Dunlop Tires Operations, S.A. v. Brown, 131 S. Ct. 2846 (2011); J. McIntyre Mach., Ltd. v. Nicastro, 131 S. Ct. 2780 (2011).

about the technology of the medium, deviate from normal civil procedure precedent, bear little relation to the doctrine's underlying principles, and fail to generate consistent results. Current approaches remain stuck in the days of the "Interwebs" and betray the same lack of sophistication that the tongue-in-cheek malapropism captures.

Personal jurisdiction is an elusive concept. Formally, it is rooted in limits on sovereign power and in protections for defendants against the arbitrary assertion of governmental force. While the basis for the doctrine has evolved over time, the theory worked well enough in a world of physicality—where defendants could be found within a forum state, or where their actions had tangible consequences within those borders. However, once personal jurisdiction had to grapple with intangible interests and harms, the doctrine began to go off the rails, and once it had to contend with the borderless information environment of the Internet, it became almost completely unhinged.[3] This Article seeks to return personal jurisdiction to first principles. It identifies the doctrine's core concerns and applies them to the problems of a ubiquitous networked environment. Its arguments will not please everyone. But it offers a consistent and defensible vision of jurisdiction in the context of costless information sharing, and it realigns offline and online jurisdiction in a manner that is theoretically consistent. Courts must stop allowing themselves to be bedazzled and bewitched by the "Interwebs." Like Dorothy in The Wonderful Wizard of Oz, they have always had the power to do so—they need only realize that they never lost it to begin with.[ ]

Since at least the mid-1990s, courts have been aware of the conundrum that the Internet poses to personal jurisdiction analysis. The modern doctrine often turns on the defendant's "contacts"[5] with a particular state and the extent to which those contacts reflect "purposeful" action.[6] In a concurrence in one of the recent Supreme Court cases, Justice Breyer aptly elucidated many of the questions that courts and scholars have confronted over the years. What does it "mean when a company targets the world by selling products from its Web site? And does it matter if, instead of shipping the products directly, a company consigns the products through an intermediary (say, Amazon.com) who then receives and fulfills the orders?"[7] Moreover, should it matter whether the defendant is a small mom-and-pop operation—in Justice Breyer's example, an Appalachian potter who sells cups and saucers—or a large multinational corporation?[8] One can easily add to the litany of questions: How should courts deal with

3 *See* Arthur R. Miller, *Simplified Pleading, Meaningful Days in Court, and Trials on the Merits: Reflections on the Deformation of Federal Procedure*, 88 N.Y.U. L. REV. 286, 350 n.241 (2013) (stating that after Nicastro, "[a]lso left in disarray are personal jurisdiction questions relating to claims arising from a defendant's activities on the Internet"). * * *

5 *See, e.g., Int'l Shoe Co. v. Washington*, 326 U.S. 310, 316, 319 (1945).

6 *See, e.g., World-Wide Volkswagen Corp. v. Woodson*, 444 U.S. 286, 297–98 (1980).

7 *J. McIntyre Mach., Ltd. v. Nicastro*, 131 S. Ct. 2780, 2793 (2011) (Breyer, J., concurring).

8 *See id.*

alleged defamation on the Internet? If a Web site infringes a protected trademark, where exactly has the harm occurred?

In 1997, one district court proposed a way to mold the traditional tests to the new medium. It suggested that a Web site's commercial nature and degree of interactivity essentially can measure contacts and purposefulness.[9] A passive Web site would not be enough to justify jurisdiction. Actually concluding sales on the Internet would be. And between those two extremes, as a Web site evinced greater interactivity, and thus a greater exchange of commercial information with consumers, courts should be increasingly likely to find that Internet activity justifies jurisdiction.[ ] The *Zippo* sliding scale seemed beautifully simple and has proved singularly influential. Most courts to confront the problem of Internet-based jurisdiction have relied favorably on *Zippo*, even though the test's supposed virtues are chimerical. It distorts the doctrine and its guiding principles. It is predicated on a superficial analogy between physical and virtual worlds. And it has proved conspicuously indeterminate. Yet it endures. Legal scholars who study Internet law have struggled with these questions of jurisdiction from the earliest days of the field.[ ] Views of jurisdiction over a defendant by a sovereign state, and of that state's enforcement powers, passed through three eras. In the first, scholars believed (either optimistically or naively) that conventional nation-states had no capability to govern online behavior.[12] So-called Netizens might join together to create new governance structures,[ ] but states, those "weary giants of flesh and steel,"[14] were supposedly impotent in the face of this new communications technology. But Internet censorship in countries such as China and Saudi Arabia quickly demonstrated the fallibility of this view.[ ]

In the second era, legal academics conceded the state's enforcement powers but argued that, as a normative matter, terrestrial governments should withdraw from the field and allow Internet-specific governance to emerge.[16] Those governments rapidly proved unwilling to declare cyberspace a zone of order (or disorder) without law.

Finally, the third era recontextualized the Internet as simply another communications medium, where oversight by law could operate

[9] *See Zippo Mfg. Co. v. Zippo Dot Com*, 952 F. Supp. 1119, 1124 (W.D. Pa. 1997).

[12] *See, e.g.*, Viktor Mayer-Schönberger & Teree E. Foster, *A Regulatory Web: Free Speech and the Global Information Infrastructure*, 3 MICH. TELECOMM. & TECH. L. REV. 45, 55–61 (1997); David G. Post, *Anarchy, State, and the Internet: An Essay on Law-Making in Cyberspace*, 1995 J. ONLINE L. 44, 57–59; Anne Wells Branscomb, *Anonymity, Autonomy, and Accountability: Challenges to the First Amendment in Cyberspace*, 104 YALE L.J. 1639, 1665–70 (1995).

[14] John Perry Barlow, *A Declaration of the Independence of Cyberspace* (Feb. 8, 1996), https://projects.eff.org/~barlow/Declaration-Final.html.

[16] *See, e.g.*, David R. Johnson & David Post, *Law and Borders: The Rise of Law in Cyberspace*, 48 STAN. L. REV. 1367, 1387–92 (1996).

legitimately while taking account of the Net's idiosyncrasies.[17] Jurisdiction by states, under the right circumstances, was not only possible, but desirable.[ ] The progression through these three periods highlights a key issue: whether states should engage in or refrain from adjudication of disputes deriving from online interaction.

Despite intense scholarly interest in this problem at the turn of the century, it remains intractable. Even the best contributions are dated or narrow, or they give insufficient attention to at least one aspect of the problem (that is, either the technology or the procedural nuances). * * * Our contribution charts a new course independent of the cyber-exceptionalists and also those who have argued that courts can readily apply the current doctrine to the Internet world. The Internet is not *sui generis*, but it does present unique challenges that courts should not gloss over.

[In the article from which this brief excerpt is taken, we make] three major contributions to this enduringly unsettled area of law. First, our central argument is that courts have tied themselves in knots over Internet-based contacts because they have failed to appreciate a more significant, overarching dichotomy: the difference between physical harm and intangible harm. Most jurisdictional rules evolved to take account of the ways in which physical harm could present itself. Centuries ago, most harm was localized, and the rules reflected that reality. As society became more mobile, such that a person could cause physical harm far from his home, the jurisdictional rules adapted to that new reality. But the various tests that have developed are still squarely oriented around notions of physical harm—car accidents, defective products, and the like.[ ]

The current tests begin to unravel—both conceptually and pragmatically—when the harm at issue is intangible. For example, in the defamation context, where does one's reputation exist? As courts tried to apply the rules of a physical world to intangible harms, the results were awkward—at times, even incoherent—and laid the path for online follies to come. Thus, the Internet did not create the problem. It did, however, expose and exacerbate a more profound schism between physical and intangible harm.

Second, we argue for a return to personal jurisdiction's underlying principles to figure out how best to craft sensible rules for cases presenting purely intangible harm. To do so, we articulate a tripartite view of personal jurisdiction's deep structure: constitutionally compelled restrictions (imposed by the Due Process Clauses); prudential common law restrictions (crafted by the Supreme Court); and state-specific restrictions (embodied in long-arm statutes). Within each of these layers are limitations on

---

[17] *See, e.g.*, Jack Goldsmith & Tim Wu, Who Controls the Internet?: Illusions of A Borderless World (2006); Joseph H. Sommer, *Against Cyberlaw*, 15 BERKELEY TECH. L.J. 1145, 1205–07 (2000).

judicial authority that derive from different sources and carry different weights. But they share a fundamental concern for fairness and predictability. While personal jurisdiction precedent often interweaves and even conflates various normative rationales,[ ] refocusing the analysis on the overarching goals of fairness and predictability has the potential to extricate the doctrine from unnecessary traps. Moreover, identifying the precise sources of personal jurisdiction demonstrates the latitude that both courts and legislatures have to reorient the doctrine in a more normatively satisfying way.

Finally, we set out three test cases for assessing how Internet-based contacts ought to count in the personal jurisdiction analysis. We discuss how the doctrine should effectuate the goals of fairness and predictability, clearly defined, in the context of those test cases. Specifically, our analysis focuses on private fairness concerns (plaintiffs' and defendants' ability to plan their conduct and vindicate their rights effectively) and society's interest in the efficient use of public resources. In so doing, we develop a proposal to realign courts' approaches to online and offline cases in a way that better effectuates personal jurisdiction's first principles. Put simply, courts should take a narrow approach when dealing with intangible harm, whether that is a traditional harm (such as defamation in print media) or a modern, virtual harm (such as a Web site that infringes a trademark). Courts should no longer indulge the fiction that virtual activity creates physical contact with any particular forum. Dispensing with that fiction undoubtedly will limit the places where a plaintiff can sue for intangible harm, but it will create a more robust, coherent, and workable doctrine. * * *

NOTES AND QUESTIONS

1. *Hunting the paradigm and putting it on display*. How would you articulate the old and the new paradigms being contrasted in each of Professor Rendell's six examples, *supra*? What practical and doctrinal difference does the change make in each example?

2. *Does cyberlaw need its own paradigm?* In what respects is it simply false that "cyberspace" is non-territorial? How should the law handle "mixed" cases that arise *both* territorially and in cyberspace? And for those wrongs that are non-territorial, would a regime of self-help be preferable to a doctrine of legal remedies? What history—if any—offers guidance for non-territorial interactions or goods, like those in cyberspace?

3. *Alternative forms of rational decision-making*. In what sense is the law itself a framing device? What are the principal competing paradigms, and what purpose do they serve?

CHAPTER ELEVEN

STRUCTURES OF LEGAL ARGUMENT (II): REASONING BY DEFAULT: FICTIONS, BURDENS, AND PRESUMPTIONS

■ ■ ■

"A [legal] fiction becomes wholly safe only when it is used with a complete consciousness of its falsity."

— Lon Fuller

"[I]n English law, fiction is a syphilis, which runs in every vein, and carries into every part of the system the principle of rottenness."

— Jeremy Bentham

Orientation

Some arguments in a case—like some babies—start out in life with a distinct head-start. In criminal cases for example, the defense begins with the benefit of a presumption that the defendant is innocent, and the prosecution is put to the burden of proving its case beyond a reasonable doubt. That presumption and that burden of proof operate in tandem as a kind of doctrinal subsidy for the defense, offset to be sure by the prosecution's advantages but placing a thumb on the scale in the defendant's favor at the outset of the case. Or consider corporate counsel, whose practice rests on the legal fiction that corporations are in many respects "persons," entitled to own property, enter into contracts, appear in court, get due process rights, and contribute to political campaigns, among other things. Tort law similarly depends on a variety of fictions, notably the "reasonable person"—that mythical being whose knowledge or discernment or understanding or experience are never fully defined (or definable) but whose judgments are presumptively so ordinary as to be available to every juror in the land. The law is filled with these fictions, presumptions, and burdens. They can define the adversarial contours of virtually any substantive area of law (and indeed virtually any *case*). But what exactly are these default drives in the law? How do they come to be, and what functions do they serve? Why do they sometimes morph or disappear altogether?

This chapter aims to develop the ability to identify, understand, and manage this variety of default artifices used in structuring a legal argument, with special emphasis on fictions, burdens of proof, and presumptions.

A. LEGAL FICTIONS

In his classic analysis,[1] Professor Lon Fuller defined legal fictions as "untruths not intended to deceive." Oddly enough, fictions are not necessarily to be rooted out, as one might think in a profession ostensibly devoted to truth and accountability. To the contrary, they are tools of the trade, often used to update the law by bringing new flexibility or new applications to old doctrines. In this respect, Fuller built on Sir Henry Maine's observation that legal fictions "satisfy the desire for improvement, which is not quite wanting, at the same time that they do not offend the superstitious disrelish for change which is always present."[2] To make this more concrete, consider *United Zinc Co. v. Britt*, 258 U.S. 268 (1922), in which the Supreme Court embraced the fiction that for children, an attractive nuisance has "the legal effect of an invitation" and therefore creates a greater duty of care on the part of landowners than they would otherwise have. Fuller considered the attractive nuisance doctrine "the boldest fiction to be found in the modern law" and used it to demonstrate how an old doctrine—the obligation of landowners to "invitees"—could be improved by extending it to particularly vulnerable *non*-invitees, namely children attracted to things that could hurt them, like an unfenced swimming pool. It was an untruth—the uninvited children were never invitees in fact—but it was not intended to deceive anyone.

At a minimum, without necessarily updating or improving anything, fictions serve substantive law policies. In the criminal law, for example it is a fiction that "each conspirator is an agent of the other" but it means that the "statements of one can therefore be attributable to all." *United States v. Pecora*, 798 F.2d 614, 628 (3d Cir. 1986). That fiction serves the policy of attacking criminal but inchoate conspiracies with rules of evidence that are favorable to the prosecution. Similarly, the location (or *situs*) of an intangible—like a debt or a trademark or a reputation—is necessarily a fiction, but locating it on a map even fictively promotes the policy of certainty in protecting the property and its marketability. The tax code is filled with fictions of statutory origin, and corporate law as noted rests in part on the fiction that corporations are persons. Whenever the law uses

---

1 L. FULLER, LEGAL FICTIONS 21 (1967). For a more contemporary and varied take on the importance of legal fictions, *see generally* MAKSYMILIAN DEL MAR AND WILLIAM TWINING, EDS., LEGAL FICTIONS IN THEORY AND PRACTICE (2015).

2 H. MAINE, ANCIENT LAW 25 (3d ed. 1873). *See also* MORRIS R. COHEN, LAW AND THE SOCIAL ORDER 126 (1933) ("[l]egal fiction is the mask that progress must wear to pass the faithful but blear-eyed watchers of our ancient legal treasures. But though legal fictions are useful in thus mitigating or absorbing the shock of innovation, they work havoc in the form of intellectual confusion.")

the phrase "constructive"—as in a "constructive trust" or "constructive eviction"—it is employing some fiction: a reality within the law that corresponds to no empirical reality outside the law but which serves some substantive purpose.

Of course, not all fictions meet with continuing approval: "fiction" remains one epithet-of-choice, especially in a dissenting opinion, to describe an unacceptable assumption or erroneous conclusion, especially in a majority opinion. And some fictions eventually lose whatever patina of respectability they may at one time have had: in *Johnson v. M'Intosh*, 21 U.S. (8 Wheat.) 543 (1823), for example, the Supreme Court deployed a legal fiction of "discovery" and conquest to guarantee a smooth chain of title from Native Americans to the European colonialists and thereby to dispossess the original nations of full title to their land in U.S. courts.[3] Similarly, for centuries, the common law deployed—and then abandoned—the fiction that the "husband and wife were one person at law (that person, practically speaking, was the husband * * * .)" *United States v. Craft*, 535 U.S. 274, 281 (2002).

Any account of legal fictions must show not only how they can provide a kind of scaffolding for argument in a case, but also how they are created and sometimes fall away.

---

1. THE REASONABLE PERSON

a. The Reasonable "Man" in Torts

In *The Germanic*, 196 U.S. 589, 595–96 (1905), the Supreme Court established the link between the law of negligence and the fiction of the reasonable man, as it was then known. According to Justice Oliver Wendell Homes, Jr.,

> [i]t is quite true that negligence must be determined upon the facts as they appeared at the time and not by a judgment from actual consequences which then were not to be apprehended by a prudent and competent man. This principle nowhere has been more fully recognized than by this court. But it is a mistake to say * * * that if the man on the spot, even an expert, does what his judgment approves, he cannot be found negligent. The standard of conduct, whether left to the jury or laid down by the court, is an external standard, and takes no account of the personal equation of the man concerned.

Id. at 55–96. In other words, "[i]f the typical defendant attempts to avoid liability by asserting and evidencing that he acted consistently with his

---

[3] Jen Camden & Kathryn E. Fort, *"Channeling Thought": The Legacy of Legal Fictions from 1823*, 33 AM. INDIAN L. REV. 77, 79 (2008–2009).

own 'best judgment,' even though a reasonable person would have known better, the effort is almost certain to fail."[4] An English court had anticipated Justice Holmes' test six decades earlier.

VAUGHAN V. MENLOVE

3 Bing. (N.C.) 467, 132 Eng. Rep. 490 (1837)

[The allegations in the case were that Defendant made a hay-stack (or "rick")] near the boundary of his own premises; that the hay was in such a state when put together, as to give rise to discussions on the probability of fire [from spontaneous combustion]: that though there were conflicting opinions on the subject, yet during a period of five weeks, the Defendant was repeatedly warned of his peril; that his stock was insured; and that upon one occasion, being advised to take the rick down to avoid all danger, he said "he would chance it." He made an aperture or chimney through the rick; but in spite, or perhaps in consequence of this precaution, the rick at length burst into flames from the spontaneous heating of its materials; the flames communicated to the Defendant's barn and stables, and thence to the Plaintiff's cottages, which were entirely destroyed. Patteson J. before whom the cause was tried, told the jury that the question for them to consider, was, whether the fire had been occasioned by gross negligence on the part of the Defendant; adding, that he was bound to proceed with such reasonable caution as a prudent man would have exercised under such circumstances. [A verdict was returned in favor of the Plaintiff, and this appeal followed.] * * *

TINDAL C.J. I agree that this is a case [of first impression]; but I feel no difficulty in applying to it the principles of law as laid down in other cases of a similar kind. Undoubtedly this is not a case of contract, such as a bailment or the like where the bailee is responsible in consequence of the remuneration he is to receive: but there is a rule of law which says you must so enjoy your own property as not to injure that of another; and according to that rule the Defendant is liable for the consequence of his own neglect: and though the Defendant did not himself light the fire, yet mediately, he is as much the cause of it as if he had himself put a candle to the rick; for it is well known that hay will ferment and take fire if it be not carefully stacked. It has been decided that if an occupier burns weeds so near the boundary of his own land that damage ensues to the property of his neighbour, he is liable to an action for the amount of injury done, unless the accident were occasioned by a sudden blast which he could not forsee * * *. But put the case of a chemist making experiments with ingredients, singly innocent, but when combined, liable to ignite; if he leaves them

[4] David E. Seidelson, *Reasonable Expectations and Subjective Standards in Negligence Law: The Minor, the Mentally Impaired, and the Mentally Incompetent*, 50 GEO. WASH. L. REV. 17, 19 (1981).

together, and injury is thereby occasioned to the property of his neighbour, can anyone doubt that an action on the case would lie?

It is contended, however, that the learned Judge was wrong in leaving this to the jury as a case of gross negligence, and that the question of negligence was so mixed up with reference to what would be the conduct of a man of ordinary prudence that the jury might have thought the latter the rule by which they were to decide; that such a rule would be too uncertain to act upon; and that the question ought to have been whether the Defendant had acted honestly and bona fide to the best of his own judgment. That, however, would leave so vague a line as to afford no rule at all, the degree of judgment belonging to each individual being infinitely various: and though it has been urged that the care which a prudent man would take, is not an intelligible proposition as a rule of law, yet such has always been the rule adopted in cases of bailment, as laid down in *Coggs. v. Bernard* (2 Ld. Raym. 909). Though in some cases a greater degree of care is exacted than in others, yet in "the second sort of bailment, viz. commodatum or lending *gratis*, the borrower is bound to the strictest care and diligence to keep the goods so as to restore them hack again to the lender; because the bailee has a benefit by the use of them, so as if the bailee be guilty of the least neglect he will be answerable; as if a man should lend another a horse to go westward, or for a month; if the bailee put this horse in his stable, and he were stolen from thence, the bailee shall not be answerable for him: but if he or his servant leave the house or stable doors open and the thieves take the opportunity of that, and steal the horse, he will be chargeable, because the neglect gave the thieves the occasion to steal the horse." The care taken by a prudent man has always been the rule laid down; and as to the supposed difficulty of applying it, a jury has always been able to say, whether, taking that rule as their guide, there has been negligence on the occasion in question.

Instead, therefore, of saying that the liability for negligence should be co-extensive with the judgment of each individual, which would be as variable as the length of the foot of each individual, we ought rather to adhere to the rule which requires in all cases a regard to caution such as a man of ordinary prudence would observe. That was in substance the criterion presented to the jury in this case, and therefore the [decision below is affirmed].

NOTES AND QUESTIONS

1. *One rationale for the fiction of the reasonable person.* One way to begin to appreciate the impact of the reasonable person standard is to articulate the function that it apparently serves. Why does Justice Tindall conclude in *Vaughan* that the law of negligence *must* operate by reference to some fictional reference point like "the man of ordinary prudence?"

2. *What does the reasonable person know?* Over the centuries, writers and jurists have tried to give content to the character of the reasonable person. For example, in *Hall v. Brooklands Auto Racing Club*, 1 K.B. 205, 224 (1933), Lord Justice Greer, citing an unnamed "American author," tried to convey the ordinariness of the character as "the man who takes the magazines at home and in the evening pushes the lawn mower in his shirt sleeves." Multiple English cases refer to the reasonable person as "the man on the Clapham omnibus," a reference to the common passenger on a London bus route. One author, having collected a variety of cases in which the reasonable person standard applied, summarized his findings—replete with case citations—in this way:

> Various judges have assured us that the Reasonable Man knows, among other things the laws of gravity, that fire burns, and "that water drowns." In addition, he knows "the amount of space he occupies," "his ability to lift and carry heavy objects," elementary rules of personal hygiene, that alcohol makes you drunk, and how to keep his balance. He recognizes that some of his unreasonable friends jaywalk on a regular basis, and he drives so as to avoid them. Perhaps the best evidence of his vast knowledge can be found in his knowledge of the law—he knows all of it. He also knows the laws of nature and the qualities and habits of human beings. The Reasonable Man is also quite knowledgeable about the peculiar propensities of small children. He recognizes that children seldom heed advice, often do silly things, and disobey like clockwork. He understands that little boys are naturally mischievous. He knows that children like to climb on everything in sight, that they often wander into the street, that they "do the unexpected, . . . and that they may do the ununderstandable and the unpredictable." He also possesses some rather curious tidbits of knowledge such as the fact that bees do not fly at night. All this may seem rather remarkable, particularly when one considers that the fellow may not even know how to read. * * *
>
> "He invariably looks where he is going and is careful to examine the immediate foreground before he executes a leap or bound." * * * He stacks the chairs properly at Sunday School, never fails to notice and avoid manure on the steps, and always avoids falling down. Occasionally he forgets things, but only with a very good explanation. * * *
>
> He never parks his car on the freeway to scrape his windshield. No one has ever seen him break the law without good reason or throw his television set out the window. * * *.

Randy T. Austin, *Better Off with the Reasonable Man Dead or the Reasonable Man Did the Darndest Things,* 1992 B.Y.U. L. REV. 479, 486–87 (1992) (citations omitted).

Others have tried to characterize the reasonable man, relying not on cases but on parody:

> [The reasonable man] is one who invariably looks where he is going, and is careful to examine the immediate foreground before he executes a leap or bound; who neither star-gazes nor is lost in meditation when approaching trap-doors or the margin of a dock; * * * who never mounts a moving omnibus, and does not alight from any car while the train is in motion; who investigates exhaustively the *bona fides* of every mendicant before distributing alms, and will inform himself of the history and habits of a dog before administering a caress; who believes no gossip, nor repeats it, without firm basis for believing it to be true; who never drives his ball till those in front of him have definitely vacated the putting-green which is his own objective; He never makes an excessive demand upon his wife, his neighbors, his servants, his ox, or his ass; who in the way of business looks only for that narrow margin of profit which twelve men such as himself would reckon to be 'fair', and contemplates his fellow-merchants, their agents, and their goods, with that degree of suspicion and distrust which the law deems admirable; who never swears, gambles or loses his temper. He uses nothing except in moderation.

Sir A.P. Herbert, *Fardell v. Potts, in* MISLEADING CASES IN THE COMMON LAW 10–20 (4th ed. 1937). In short, the reasonable person is extraordinary only in her or his ordinariness.

3. *Saving the fiction from a "category mistake."* The character sketches of the reasonable person in the previous note can distract us from something important if they provoke a shrug of bemusement or indifference. Here after all is a repeat performer in the law—the reasonable person—with a "greater impact on the Anglo-American system of jurisprudence than most of the renowned jurists of the last three centuries,"[5] which makes a ritualized appearance in litigation, but which cannot be defined in advance and which therefore gives no clear notice of what conduct is required. From that perspective, the reasonable person is "law's ghost god," in Lloyd Duhaime's provocative phrase: "Every religion has a God. In law, this is the reasonable person, a mystical, esoteric ethereal being, revered by our high priest and priestess, the judges of our courts of law."[6] A strict legal positivist (*see* Chapter 2) might view the fiction as anti-law: a type of professional nonsense bringing with it the discretion to impose liability for negligence on the basis of some allegedly objective standard that is so abstract as to be content-free.

Criticizing the reasonable person fiction in this way, as though it *should* define precisely the conduct required of people on pain of liability, is what the twentieth-century philosopher Gilbert Ryle described as a "category mistake" or a "category error." GILBERT RYLE, THE CONCEPT OF MIND 16 (1949). Criticizing a ballerina for not throwing more touchdowns in a performance of

---

5 Ronald Collins, *Language, History and the Legal Process: A Profile of the "Reasonable Man,"* 8 RUT.-CAM. L.J. 311 (1977).

6 http://www.duhaime.org/LegalResources/TortPersonalInjury/LawArticle-1378/The-Reasonable-Man-Laws-Ghost-God.aspx (last visited Mar. 6, 2017).

The Nutcracker is a category error: a ballet is not a football game. Insisting that a member of Congress exercise her veto over a law is a category error: no member of the national legislature is the President, who alone has the veto power under the Constitution. Criticizing anything as though it belongs to a particular class of things—or attributing characteristics to it on the basis of that categorization—is a category error, if it turns out that the thing properly understood doesn't belong in that box at all.

Criticizing a legal fiction for not being more like a statute is a category error in that sense. After all, at trial, a judge instructs jurors on the reasonable person standard, generally offering context for their judgment but not particular criteria. In an automobile collision case for example, the judge might instruct the jury as follows: "The duty to keep a proper lookout requires a driver to use ordinary care to look in all directions for vehicles that would affect his [or her] driving, *to see what a reasonable person would have seen*, and *to react as a reasonable person would have acted* to avoid a collision under the circumstances." *See Thomas v. Sweeney*, 2009 WL 7447253 (Va. Cir. Ct. Aug. 31, 2009) (emphasis added). The judge expects the jurors to access some implicit, anthropomorphic amalgam of the community's expectations of human behavior. Those norms admittedly cannot be catalogued or specified in advance, the way a statute defining the elements of the crime of embezzlement might, but that is not what the fiction is designed to do. Instead, the law requires (and privileges) the jurors' conscious judgment-by-consensus in the light of those norms of human behavior. In short, the "reasonable person" defines the plane for argument among the advocates and for judgment among the jurors. It is not a doctrine or a rule that resolves cases, which means that it is a category error to criticize it for not better resembling a statute. Ironically perhaps, this makes the reasonable person instruction work on the basis of other, more basic fictions, namely that the jury is both representative of the community at large and fair (and rational) in its deliberations.

4. *Tolerating popular misconceptions, preserving fictions*. In *United States v. Hall*, 165 F.3d 1095 (7th Cir. 1999), the defendant was convicted of murder in part because the testimony of several eyewitnesses placed him near the location of the crime at relevant times. He appealed on the ground *inter alia* that the trial court had denied his request to introduce expert testimony demonstrating that eyewitness testimony is considerably less reliable than is generally assumed, especially given the difficulties of perception, retention, and recall. The court of appeals affirmed the conviction, holding that the trial court had not abused its discretion in excluding the expert testimony. The court accepted that the proposed testimony qualified as "scientific knowledge" under the Supreme Court's decision in *Daubert v. Merrell Dow Pharmaceuticals, Inc.*, 509 U.S. 579 (1993), but concluded that it would not actually help the jury understand the evidence in the case, as required by Rule 702 of the Federal Rules of Evidence. The *Hall* court said that "[s]uch expert testimony will not aid the jury because it addresses an issue *of which the jury is already generally is [sic] aware*, and it will not contribute to their understanding of the particular dispute." *Hall*, 165 F.3d at 1104 (*quoting United States v. Hudson*, 884 F.2d 1016, 1024 (7th Cir. 1989) (emphasis added)). In effect, the court of appeals

ruled that it is improper to permit an expert to testify regarding facts that people of common understanding can easily comprehend, of which the unreliability of eyewitness testimony is apparently one example. The reasonable juror is allegedly already aware that everybody else—the public studied by the expert—consistently overrates eyewitness testimony.

It might be a challenge to explain *Hall* to your non-lawyer friends. The defendant was trying to dismantle a popular misconception, namely that eyewitness testimony is some kind of gold standard. The law of evidence has no tilt in that direction, and certainly does not privilege eyewitness testimony over other kinds of evidence, so why wasn't Hall allowed to alert the jury to the scientific problems with such testimony? What legal fictions prevailed in the case?

5. *Defining commonality, losing difference.* There are times in the law when the reasonable person—whether considered a fiction or a construct or a metaphor—is either not specific enough or too demanding. What would happen for example if it could be demonstrated that the defendant in *Vaughan* were already well-known to all of his neighbors as uniquely careless or clueless about all things hay-related? Despite their prior knowledge, would they still be able to recover on the theory that *he* had been the unreasonable one? In short, when should the defendant's unique (or subjective) circumstances trump the homogeneous (or objective) benchmark in the reasonable person fiction?

Consider in this regard *Healthcare at Home Limited v. The Common Services Agency*, [2014] UKSC 49, a government contracts case, in which the Supreme Court of the United Kingdom observed that

> The Clapham omnibus has many passengers. The most venerable is the reasonable man, who was born during the reign of Victoria[.] Amongst the other passengers are the right-thinking member of society, [ ] the officious bystander, the reasonable parent, the reasonable landlord, and the fair-minded and informed observer[ ]. They belong to an intellectual tradition of defining a legal standard by reference to a hypothetical person, which stretches back to the creation by Roman jurists of the figure of the *bonus paterfamilias*. * * * In recent times, some additional passengers [ ] have boarded the Clapham omnibus. This appeal is concerned with one of them: the reasonably well-informed and normally diligent tenderer.

Id. at ¶¶ 1–4. "The reasonably well-informed and normally diligent tenderer" is evidently a subcategory of the "reasonable person," suggesting in turn that the overarching fiction is not as monolithic as might at first appear. To the contrary, it can evidently be broken down into special circumstances to serve particular substantive ends. How do the following cases, *Ellison* and *Amore*, demonstrate that the reasonable person standard may insufficiently reflect the differences among people in specific kinds of cases? In each case, what function is served by these specialized avatars of the reasonable person?

---

b. The Reasonable Woman in Employment Law

In *Meritor Savings Bank, FSB v. Vinson*, 477 U.S. 57 (1986), the Supreme Court of the United States ruled that the federal antidiscrimination laws, specifically Title VII of the Civil Rights Act of 1964. 42 U.S.C. § 2000e (1982), are violated whenever a workplace is permeated with "discriminatory intimidation, ridicule, and insult," that is "sufficiently severe or pervasive to alter the conditions of the victim's employment and create an abusive working environment. *Vinson*. 477 U.S. at 65, 67 (citations omitted). To give rise to a sexual harassment claim, "a sexually objectionable environment must be both objectively and subjectively offensive, one that a *reasonable person* would find hostile or abusive, and one that the victim in fact did perceive to be so." *Faragher v. City of Boca Raton*, 524 U.S. 775, 787 (1998) (emphasis added). When it comes to sexual harassment, how is a reasonable person different from a reasonable woman?

ELLISON V. BRADY

924 F.2d 872 (9th Cir. 1991)

Kerry Ellison appeals the district court's order granting summary judgment to the Secretary of the Treasury on her sexual harassment action brought under Title VII of the Civil Rights Act of 1964. 42 U.S.C. § 2000e (1982). This appeal presents two important issues: (1) what test should be applied to determine whether conduct is sufficiently severe or pervasive to alter the conditions of employment and create a hostile working environment, and (2) what remedial actions can shield employers from liability for sexual harassment by co-workers. The district court held that Ellison did not state a prima facie case of hostile environment sexual harassment. We reverse and remand. Both issues require a detailed analysis of the facts, which we consider in the light most favorable to Ellison, the non-moving party. * * * We review summary judgments de novo.

I

Kerry Ellison worked as a revenue agent for the Internal Revenue Service in San Mateo, California. During her initial training in 1984 she met Sterling Gray, another trainee, who was also assigned to the San Mateo office. The two co-workers never became friends, and they did not work closely together. Gray's desk was twenty feet from Ellison's desk, two rows behind and one row over. Revenue agents in the San Mateo office often went to lunch in groups. In June of 1986 when no one else was in the office, Gray asked Ellison to lunch. She accepted. Gray had to pick up his son's forgotten lunch, so they stopped by Gray's house. He gave Ellison a tour of his house.

Ellison alleges that after the June lunch Gray started to pester her with unnecessary questions and hang around her desk. On October 9, 1986, Gray asked Ellison out for a drink after work. She declined, but she suggested that they have lunch the following week. She did not want to have lunch alone with him, and she tried to stay away from the office during lunch time. One day during the following week, Gray uncharacteristically dressed in a three-piece suit and asked Ellison out for lunch. Again, she did not accept.

On October 22, 1986 Gray handed Ellison a note he wrote on a telephone message slip which read:

> I cried over you last night and I'm totally drained today. I have never been in such constant term oil (sic). Thank you for talking with me. I could not stand to feel your hatred for another day.

When Ellison realized that Gray wrote the note, she became shocked and frightened and left the room. Gray followed her into the hallway and demanded that she talk to him, but she left the building.

Ellison later showed the note to Bonnie Miller, who supervised both Ellison and Gray. Miller said "this is sexual harassment." Ellison asked Miller not to do anything about it. She wanted to try to handle it herself. Ellison asked a male co-worker to talk to Gray, to tell him that she was not interested in him and to leave her alone. The next day, Thursday, Gray called in sick.

Ellison did not work on Friday, and on the following Monday, she started four weeks of training in St. Louis, Missouri. Gray mailed her a card and a typed, single-spaced, three-page letter. She describes this letter as "twenty times, a hundred times weirder" than the prior note. Gray wrote, in part:

> I know that you are worth knowing with or without sex. . . . Leaving aside the hassles and disasters of recent weeks. I have enjoyed you so much over these past few months. Watching you. Experiencing you from O so far away. Admiring your style and elan. . . . Don't you think it odd that two people who have never even talked together, alone, are striking off such intense sparks . . . I will [write] another letter in the near future.

Explaining her reaction, Ellison stated: "I just thought he was crazy. I thought he was nuts. I didn't know what he would do next. I was frightened."

She immediately telephoned Miller. Ellison told her supervisor that she was frightened and really upset. She requested that Miller transfer either her or Gray because she would not be comfortable working in the same office with him. Miller asked Ellison to send a copy of the card and letter to San Mateo.

Miller then telephoned her supervisor, Joe Benton, and discussed the problem. That same day she had a counseling session with Gray. She informed him that he was entitled to union representation. During this meeting, she told Gray to leave Ellison alone.

At Benton's request, Miller apprised the labor relations department of the situation. She also reminded Gray many times over the next few weeks that he must not contact Ellison in any way. Gray subsequently transferred to the San Francisco office on November 24, 1986. Ellison returned from St. Louis in late November and did not discuss the matter further with Miller.

After three weeks in San Francisco, Gray filed union grievances requesting a return to the San Mateo office. The IRS and the union settled the grievances in Gray's favor, agreeing to allow him to transfer back to the San Mateo office provided that he spend four more months in San Francisco and promise not to bother Ellison. On January 28, 1987, Ellison first learned of Gray's request in a letter from Miller explaining that Gray would return to the San Mateo office. The letter indicated that management decided to resolve Ellison's problem with a six-month separation, and that it would take additional action if the problem recurred.

After receiving the letter, Ellison was "frantic." She filed a formal complaint alleging sexual harassment on January 30, 1987 with the IRS. She also obtained permission to transfer to San Francisco temporarily when Gray returned. Gray sought joint counseling. He wrote Ellison another letter which still sought to maintain the idea that he and Ellison had some type of relationship.

The IRS employee investigating the allegation agreed with Ellison's supervisor that Gray's conduct constituted sexual harassment. In its final decision, however, the Treasury Department rejected Ellison's complaint because it believed that the complaint did not describe a pattern or practice of sexual harassment covered by the EEOC regulations. After an appeal, the EEOC affirmed the Treasury Department's decision on a different ground. It concluded that the agency took adequate action to prevent the repetition of Gray's conduct.

Ellison filed a complaint in September of 1987 in federal district court. The court granted the government's motion for summary judgment on the ground that Ellison had failed to state a prima facie case of sexual harassment due to a hostile working environment. Ellison appeals.

II

Congress added the word "sex" to Title VII of the Civil Rights Act of 1964 at the last minute on the floor of the House of Representatives. 110 Cong. Rec. 2,577–2,584 (1964). Virtually no legislative history provides guidance to courts interpreting the prohibition of sex discrimination. In *Meritor Savings Bank v. Vinson*, 477 U.S. 57 (1986), the Supreme Court held that sexual harassment constitutes sex discrimination in violation of Title VII.

Courts have recognized different forms of sexual harassment. In "quid pro quo" cases, employers condition employment benefits on sexual favors. In "hostile environment" cases, employees work in offensive or abusive environments. This case, like *Meritor*, involves a hostile environment claim.

The Supreme Court in *Meritor* held that Mechelle Vinson's working conditions constituted a hostile environment in violation of Title VII's prohibition of sex discrimination. Vinson's supervisor made repeated demands for sexual favors, usually at work, both during and after business hours. Vinson initially refused her employer's sexual advances, but eventually acceded because she feared losing her job. They had intercourse over forty times. She additionally testified that he "fondled her in front of other employees, followed her into the women's restroom when she went there alone, exposed himself to her, and even forcibly raped her on several occasions." *Meritor*, 477 U.S. at 60. The Court had no difficulty finding this environment hostile. *Id.* at 67.

Since *Meritor*, we have not often reached the merits of a hostile environment sexual harassment claim. In *Jordan v. Clark*, 847 F.2d 1368, 1373 (9th Cir. 1988), *cert. denied sub nom., Jordan v. Hodel*, 488 U.S. 1006 (1989), we explained that a hostile environment exists when an employee can show (1) that he or she was subjected to sexual advances, requests for sexual favors, or other verbal or physical conduct of a sexual nature, (2) that this conduct was unwelcome, and (3) that the conduct was sufficiently severe or pervasive to alter the conditions of the victim's employment and create an abusive working environment.

In *Jordan*, we reviewed for clear error the district court's determination that an employee was not subjected to particular unwelcome advances. We explained that we will review de novo a district court's final conclusion that conduct is not severe enough or pervasive enough to constitute an abusive environment. Id. at n. 7. We affirmed the district court's judgment in Jordan because we did not find its factual findings clearly erroneous. *Id. See also Vasconcelos v. Meese*, 907 F.2d 111, 112 (9th Cir. 1990) (affirming district court's decision that the working environment was not sexually hostile because the district court's factual findings were not clearly erroneous).

We had another opportunity to examine a hostile working environment claim of sexual harassment in *E.E.O.C. v. Hacienda Hotel*, 881 F.2d 1504 (9th Cir. 1989). In that case the district court found a hostile working environment where the hotel's male chief of engineering frequently made sexual comments and sexual advances to the maids, and where a female supervisor called her female employees "dog[s]" and "whore[s]." Id. at 1508. Upon a de novo review of the facts found by the district court, we agreed that the conduct was sufficiently severe and pervasive to alter the conditions of employment and create a hostile working environment.

III

The parties ask us to determine if Gray's conduct, as alleged by Ellison, was sufficiently severe or pervasive to alter the conditions of Ellison's employment and create an abusive working environment. The district court, with little Ninth Circuit case law to look to for guidance, held that Ellison did not state a prima facie case of sexual harassment due to a hostile working environment. It believed that Gray's conduct was "isolated and genuinely trivial." We disagree.

We begin our analysis of the third part of the framework we set forth in *Jordan* with a closer look at *Meritor*. The Supreme Court in *Meritor* explained that courts may properly look to guidelines issued by the Equal Employment Opportunity Commission (EEOC) for guidance when examining hostile environment claims of sexual harassment. 477 U.S. at 65. The EEOC guidelines describe hostile environment harassment as "conduct [which] has the purpose or effect of unreasonably interfering with an individual's work performance or creating an intimidating, hostile, or offensive working environment." 29 C.F.R. § 1604.11(a)(3). The EEOC, in accord with a substantial body of judicial decisions, has concluded that "Title VII affords employees the right to work in an environment free from discriminatory intimidation, ridicule, and insult." 477 U.S. at 65.

The Supreme Court cautioned, however, that not all harassment affects a "term, condition, or privilege" of employment within the meaning of Title VII. For example, the "mere utterance of an ethnic or racial epithet which engenders offensive feelings in an employee" is not, by itself, actionable under Title VII. Id. at 67. To state a claim under Title VII, sexual harassment "must be sufficiently severe or pervasive to alter the conditions of the victim's employment and create an abusive working environment." *Id.*

The Supreme Court drew its limiting language from *Rogers v. E.E.O.C.*, 454 F.2d 234 (5th Cir. 1971), *cert. denied*, 406 U.S. 957 (1972), the first case to recognize a hostile racial environment claim under Title VII. The *Rogers* phrasing limits hostile environment claims to cases where conduct alters the conditions of employment and creates an abusive working environment. The EEOC guidelines, drawing upon *Rogers* and other decisions, indicate that sexual harassment violates Title VII where conduct creates an intimidating, hostile, or offensive environment or where it unreasonably interferes with work performance. 29 C.F.R. § 1604.11(a)(3).

We do not think that these standards are inconsistent. The Supreme Court used the words "abusive" and "hostile" synonymously in *Meritor*, 477

U.S. at 66. The *Meritor* Court also approved of and paid detailed attention to the EEOC's guidelines, and it implicitly adopted the EEOC's position that sexual harassment which unreasonably interferes with work performance violates Title VII. Similarly, although we only expressly incorporated the limiting language from *Rogers* in the third part of our framework in *Jordan*, that part also encompasses the EEOC's requirements in 29 C.F.R. § 1604.11(a)(3). Conduct which unreasonably interferes with work performance can alter a condition of employment and create an abusive working environment. * * *

Although *Meritor* and our previous cases establish the framework for the resolution of hostile environment cases, they do not dictate the outcome of this case. Gray's conduct falls somewhere between forcible rape and the mere utterance of an epithet. 477 U.S. at 60, 67. His conduct was not as pervasive as the sexual comments and sexual advances in *Hacienda Hotel*, which we held created an unlawfully hostile working environment. 881 F.2d 1504. * * *

We have closely examined *Meritor* and our previous cases, and we believe that Gray's conduct was sufficiently severe and pervasive to alter the conditions of Ellison's employment and create an abusive working environment. We first note that the required showing of severity or seriousness of the harassing conduct varies inversely with the pervasiveness or frequency of the conduct. *See King v. Board of Regents of University of Wisconsin System*, 898 F.2d 533, 537 (7th Cir. 1990) ("[a]lthough a single act can be enough, . . . generally, repeated incidents create a stronger claim of hostile environment, with the strength of the claim depending on the number of incidents and the intensity of each incident.")[.] * * *

Next, we believe that in evaluating the severity and pervasiveness of sexual harassment, we should focus on the perspective of the victim. *King*, 898 F.2d at 537; EEOC Compliance Manual (CCH) § 615, ¶ 3112, C at 3242 (1988) (courts "should consider the victim's perspective and not stereotyped notions of acceptable behavior.") If we only examined whether a reasonable person would engage in allegedly harassing conduct, we would run the risk of reinforcing the prevailing level of discrimination. Harassers could continue to harass merely because a particular discriminatory practice was common, and victims of harassment would have no remedy.

We therefore prefer to analyze harassment from the victim's perspective. A complete understanding of the victim's view requires, among other things, an analysis of the different perspectives of men and women. Conduct that many men consider unobjectionable may offend many women. *See, e.g., Lipsett v. University of Puerto Rico*, 864 F. 2d 881, 898 (1st Cir. 1988) ("A male supervisor might believe, for example, that it is legitimate for him to tell a female subordinate that she has a 'great figure' or 'nice legs.' The female subordinate, however, may find such comments offensive") * * *. *See also* Ehrenreich, *Pluralist Myths and Powerless Men: The Ideology of Reasonableness in Sexual Harassment Law*, 99 YALE L.J. 1177, 1207–1208 (1990) (men tend to view some forms of sexual harassment as "harmless social interactions to which only overly-sensitive women would object"); Abrams, *Gender Discrimination and the Transformation of Workplace Norms*, 42 VAND. L. REV. 1183, 1203 (1989) (the characteristically male view depicts sexual harassment as comparatively harmless amusement).

We realize that there is a broad range of viewpoints among women as a group, but we believe that many women share common concerns which men do not necessarily share. For example, because women are disproportionately victims of rape and sexual assault, women have a stronger incentive to be concerned with sexual behavior. Women who are victims of mild forms of sexual harassment may understandably worry whether a harasser's conduct is merely a prelude to violent sexual assault. Men, who are rarely victims of sexual assault, may view sexual conduct in a vacuum without a full appreciation of the social setting or the underlying threat of violence that a woman may perceive.

In order to shield employers from having to accommodate the idiosyncratic concerns of the rare hyper-sensitive employee, we hold that a female plaintiff states a prima facie case of hostile environment sexual harassment when she alleges conduct which a reasonable woman would consider sufficiently severe or pervasive to alter the conditions of employment and create an abusive working environment. * * *

We adopt the perspective of a reasonable woman primarily because we believe that a sex-blind reasonable person standard tends to be male-biased and tends to systematically ignore the experiences of women. The reasonable woman standard does not establish a higher level of protection for women than men. * * * Instead, a gender-conscious examination of sexual harassment enables women to participate in the workplace on an equal footing with men. By acknowledging and not trivializing the effects of sexual harassment on reasonable women, courts can work towards ensuring that neither men nor women will have to "run a gauntlet of sexual abuse in return for the privilege of being allowed to work and make a living." *Henson v. Dundee*, 682 F.2d 897, 902 (11th Cir. 1982).

We note that the reasonable victim standard we adopt today classifies conduct as unlawful sexual harassment even when harassers do not realize that their conduct creates a hostile working environment. Well-intentioned compliments by co-workers or supervisors can form the basis of a sexual harassment cause of action if a reasonable victim of the same sex as the plaintiff would consider the comments sufficiently severe or pervasive to alter a condition of employment and create an abusive working environment. That is because Title VII is not a fault-based tort scheme. "Title VII is aimed at the consequences or effects of an employment practice and not at the . . . motivation" of co-workers or employers. *Rogers*, 454 F.2d at 239 * * *. To avoid liability under Title VII, employers may have to educate and sensitize their workforce to eliminate conduct which a reasonable victim would consider unlawful sexual harassment. *See* 29 C.F.R. § 1604.11(f) ("Prevention is the best tool for the elimination of sexual harassment.")

The facts of this case illustrate the importance of considering the victim's perspective. Analyzing the facts from the alleged harasser's viewpoint, Gray could be portrayed as a modern-day Cyrano de Bergerac wishing no more than to woo Ellison with his words. There is no evidence that Gray harbored ill will toward Ellison. He even offered in his "love letter" to leave her alone if she wished. Examined in this light, it is not difficult to see why the district court characterized Gray's conduct as isolated and trivial.

Ellison, however, did not consider the acts to be trivial. Gray's first note shocked and frightened her. After receiving the three-page letter, she became really upset and frightened again. She immediately requested that she or Gray be transferred. Her supervisor's prompt response suggests that she too did not consider the conduct trivial. When Ellison learned that Gray arranged to return to San Mateo, she immediately asked to transfer, and she immediately filed an official complaint.

We cannot say as a matter of law that Ellison's reaction was idiosyncratic or hyper-sensitive. We believe that a reasonable woman could have had a similar reaction. After receiving the first bizarre note from Gray, a person she barely knew, Ellison asked a co-worker to tell Gray to leave her alone. Despite her request, Gray sent her a long, passionate, disturbing letter. He told her he had been "watching" and "experiencing" her; he made repeated references to sex; he said he would write again. Ellison had no way of knowing what Gray would do next. A reasonable woman could consider Gray's conduct, as alleged by Ellison, sufficiently severe and pervasive to alter a condition of employment and create an abusive working environment.

Sexual harassment is a major problem in the workplace. Adopting the victim's perspective ensures that courts will not "sustain ingrained notions of reasonable behavior fashioned by the offenders." *Lipsett,* 864 F.2d at 898, *quoting, Rabidue* [*v. Osceola Refining Co.*, 805 F.2d 611 (6th Cir. 1986)] at 626 (Keith, J., dissenting). Congress did not enact Title VII to codify prevailing sexist prejudices. To the contrary, "Congress designed Title VII to prevent the perpetuation of stereotypes and a sense of degradation which serve to close or discourage employment opportunities for women." *Andrews* [*v. City of Philadelphia*, 895 F.2d 1469 (3rd Cir. 1990)], at 1483. We hope that over time both men and women will learn what conduct offends reasonable members of the other sex. When employers and employees internalize the standard of workplace conduct we establish today, the current gap in perception between the sexes will be bridged.

IV

We next must determine what remedial actions by employers shield them from liability under Title VII for sexual harassment by co-workers. * * *

The district court did not reach the issue of the reasonableness of the government's remedy. Given the scant record on appeal, we cannot determine whether a reasonable woman could conclude that Gray's mere presence at San Mateo six months after the alleged harassment would create an abusive environment. Although we are aware of the severity of Gray's conduct (which we do not consider to be as serious as some other forms of harassment), we do not know how often Ellison and Gray would have to interact at San Mateo.

Moreover, it is not clear to us that the six-month cooling-off period was reasonably calculated to end the harassment or assessed proportionately to the seriousness of Gray's conduct. There is evidence in the record which suggests that the government intended to transfer Gray to San Francisco permanently and only allowed Gray to return to San Mateo because he promised to drop some union grievances. We do know that the IRS did not request Ellison's input or even inform her of the proceedings before agreeing to let Gray return to San Mateo. This failure to even attempt to determine what impact Gray's return would have on Ellison shows an insufficient regard for the victim's interest in avoiding a hostile working environment. On remand, the district court should fully explore the facts concerning the government's decision to return Gray to San Mateo.

V

We reverse the district court's decision that Ellison did not allege a prima facie case of sexual harassment due to a hostile working environment, and we remand for further proceedings consistent with this opinion. Although we have considered the evidence in the light most favorable to Ellison because the district court granted the government's motion for summary judgment, we, of course, reserve for the district court the resolution of all factual issues. * * *

---

c. The Reasonable Police Officer in Immunity Cases

AMORE V. NOVARRO

624 F.3d 522 (2d Cir. 2010)

Defendant-Appellant Andrew Novarro, an Ithaca, New York, police officer, appeals from that part of a memorandum decision and order * * * denying his motion for summary judgment on a false arrest claim brought by plaintiff-appellee Joseph Amore under 42 U.S.C. § 1983. The claim is based on Novarro's arrest of Amore pursuant to New York Penal Law § 240.35(3), which, on its face, prohibited loitering in a public place for the purpose of soliciting another person to engage in "deviate" [sic] sexual behavior. Amore alleges that his apprehension constituted a false arrest because the statute, although then officially and unofficially published as currently effective law, had been ruled unconstitutional by the New York Court of Appeals eighteen years before.

The district court concluded that Novarro was not entitled to qualified immunity: Amore had a clearly established constitutional right to be free from unlawful arrest, and it would have been clear to a reasonable officer in Novarro's position that making an arrest under section 240.35(3) after it had been held to be unconstitutional by the New York Court of Appeals in *People v. Uplinger*, 460 N.Y.S.2d 514, 447 N.E.2d 62 (1983) (Mem.), was unlawful.

We disagree. We conclude that Novarro is entitled to qualified immunity under the circumstances of this case. We therefore reverse that part of the district court's order dismissing Novarro's motion for summary judgment on the false arrest claim based on qualified immunity, and remand the cause with instructions to grant the motion. The action against the City of Ithaca may proceed.

BACKGROUND

Plaintiff Joseph Amore encountered defendant Andrew Novarro on October 19, 2001, at around 9:00 p.m. in Stewart Park, a public park in Ithaca, New York. Novarro was there as an undercover police officer, sitting in a parked unmarked car, watching for drug activity. Amore, having been in the park for some while and not knowing who Novarro was or what he was doing there, approached his car, engaged him in conversation, and then offered to perform a sexual act on him.

Novarro identified himself as a police officer and asked Amore for identification, which he produced. Novarro told Amore that he did not have a ticket to write out and would have to call for "backup," which he proceeded to do.

While they waited for another police officer to arrive, Novarro told Amore that he was being charged with "loitering for the purpose of deviant sexual activity." Novarro told Amore that "they were cracking down on this kind of activity in the park." * * *

Some time later, the city prosecutor informed Novarro that Amore had moved to dismiss the charge against him based on *Uplinger*, a 1983 ruling by the New York Court of Appeals holding, in a memorandum decision, that the loitering statute pursuant to which Amore had been arrested, New York Penal Law § 240.35(3), was unconstitutional. The city prosecutor told

Novarro that she therefore could not continue the prosecution. It is undisputed that Novarro was unaware, prior to this conversation, that the statute had been held to be unconstitutional.

* * * [T]he prosecutor moved to dismiss the charge against Amore based on *Uplinger* [ ]. The Ithaca City Court granted the motion on that basis. The court observed that it was "puzzling" that the statute continued to be published in the McKinney's Consolidated Laws of New York Annotated—an annotated compendium of New York statutes that is separate from, and more formal and complete than, the unannotated booklet provided to Novarro and other officers by the police academy—"as if it is still a viable statute." *People v. Amore*, No. 01–36459 (Ithaca City Ct. Nov. 15, 2001). "It is hard to understand why the Legislature would continue this statute on the books, given that it is now close to 20 years since it was determined to be unconstitutional." *Id.*

Some two and one-half years later, [ ] Amore filed a complaint in the United States District Court for the Northern District of New York against Novarro and the City of Ithaca seeking damages pursuant to 42 U.S.C. § 1983. His claims against Novarro were for false arrest, malicious prosecution, abuse of process, and violation of his right to equal protection. His claims against the city were made pursuant to *Monell v. Department of Social Services*, 436 U.S. 658 (1978), for failure to train city employees and for maintaining an improper policy, custom or practice of permitting officers to make arrests under the unconstitutional statute.

The defendants moved to dismiss the complaint. Amore opposed the motion, filing a cross-motion for partial summary judgment on the issue of liability.

On March 28, 2008, the district court denied Amore's cross-motion for summary judgment with respect to all claims, and, treating the defendants' motion as a motion for summary judgment, granted the defendants' motion in part and denied it in part. The district court granted the motion on the malicious prosecution, abuse of process, and equal protection claims against Novarro, and the maintenance of an improper policy or custom claim against the city. * * * None of those claims are at issue on this interlocutory appeal. * * * The district court denied summary judgment on the false arrest claim, however. The court reasoned that Novarro lacked probable cause to arrest Amore under section 240.35(3) because the New York Court of Appeals had declared that statute unconstitutional in *Uplinger*.

The district court acknowledged that such a situation presents a "difficult choice" for a police officer because "[a] common sense reading of [section 240.35(3)] would place [Amore's] actions squarely within the purview of [that provision]." It also recognized that "Novarro would have had to conduct legal research or seek expert advice in order to discover the statute's invalidity." * * * The court concluded nonetheless that Novarro was not entitled to qualified immunity with respect to the false arrest claim because Amore's "right to be free from unlawful arrest under § 240.35(3) was clearly established at the time that he was arrested." In the court's view, in light of *Uplinger*, it was objectively unreasonable for Novarro to believe that the arrest was lawful, because courts "must at least hold [public] officials to a basic standard of awareness where the state's highest court has pronounced a statute facially unconstitutional." * * * The sole question on appeal * * * is whether Novarro is entitled to qualified immunity on the false arrest claim. * * *

II. Qualified Immunity

Qualified immunity is an affirmative defense designed to "protect [ ] the [defendant public] official not just from liability but also from suit . . . thereby sparing him the necessity of defending by submitting to discovery on the merits or undergoing a trial." *X-Men Sec., Inc. v. Pataki*, 196 F.3d 56, 65 (2nd Cir. 1999). In explaining the justification for the provision of qualified immunity to government officers, we have looked to Judge Learned Hand's discussion of absolute immunity in *Gregoire v. Biddle*, 177 F.2d 579 (2nd Cir. 1949), *cert. denied*, 339 U.S. 949 (1950). Judge Hand explained that "to submit all officials, the innocent as well as the guilty, to the burden of a trial and to the inevitable danger of its outcome, would dampen the ardor of all but the most resolute, or the most irresponsible, in the unflinching discharge of their duties. Again and again the public interest calls for action which may turn out to be founded on a mistake. . . ." He emphasized the need to avoid "subject[ing] those who try to do their duty to the constant dread of retaliation." [ ]; *See also Harlow v. Fitzgerald*, 457 U.S. 800, 814 (1982) (quoting *Gregoire* in describing the possible effect of "fear of being sued" on public officials' performance of their duties).

We have since reiterated our concern that for the public benefit, public officials be able to perform their duties unflinchingly and without constant dread of retaliation. *See, e.g., Provost v. City of Newburgh*, 262 F.3d 146, 160 (2nd Cir. 2001) ("Qualified immunity serves important interests in our political system, chief among them to ensure that damages suits do not 'unduly inhibit officials in the discharge of their duties' by saddling individual officers with 'personal monetary liability and harassing litigation.'" (quoting *Anderson v. Creighton*, 483 U.S. 635, 638 (1987))). And the Supreme Court has described the "central purpose" of qualified immunity as preventing threats of liability that would be "'potentially disabling'" to officials. *Elder v. Holloway*, 510 U.S. 510, 514 (1994) (*quoting Harlow*, 457 U.S. at 818).

In light of these considerations, we have developed a standard for determining whether an officer is entitled to qualified immunity that is "forgiving" and "'protects all but the plainly incompetent or those who knowingly violate the law.'" *Provost*, 262 F.3d at 160 (*quoting Malley v. Briggs*, 475 U.S. 335, 341 (1986)). "[Q]ualified immunity . . . is sufficient to shield executive employees from civil liability under § 1983 if either (1) their conduct did not violate clearly established rights of which a reasonable person would have known, or (2) it was objectively reasonable [for them] to believe that their acts did not violate these clearly established rights." *Cornejo v. Bell*, 592 F.3d 121, 128 (2nd Cir. 2010); *see also, e.g., Taravella v. Town of Wolcott*, 599 F.3d 129, 134 (2nd Cir. 2010) ("Even where the law is 'clearly established' and the scope of an official's permissible conduct is 'clearly defined,' the qualified immunity defense also protects an official if it was 'objectively reasonable' for him at the time of the challenged action to believe his acts were lawful." [ ] internal quotation marks omitted)); *Okin v. Village of Cornwall-On-Hudson Police Dep't*, 577 F.3d 415, 433 (2nd Cir. 2009) ("A police officer who has an objectively reasonable belief that his actions are lawful is entitled to qualified immunity.").

"Ordinarily, determining whether official conduct was objectively reasonable requires examination of the information possessed by the officials at that time (without consideration of subjective intent)." *Connecticut ex rel. Blumenthal v. Crotty*, 346 F.3d 84, 106 (2nd Cir. 2003). "In an unlawful arrest action, an officer is . . . subject to suit only if his 'judgment was so flawed that no reasonable officer would have made a similar choice.' " *Provost*, 262 F.3d at 160 (*quoting Lennon v. Miller*, 66 F.3d 416, 425 (2nd Cir. 1995)). "A policeman's lot is not so unhappy that he must choose between being charged with dereliction of duty if he does not arrest when he has probable cause, and being mulcted in damages if he does." *Pierson v. Ray*, 386 U.S. 547, 555 (1967).

III. Novarro's Qualified Immunity

We assume here, not without reason, that when Novarro arrested Amore he violated a constitutional right of Amore not to be arrested for activity made criminal by section 240.35(3), which had been held unconstitutional by the New York Court of Appeals. But the question for purposes of determining Novarro's entitlement to qualified immunity is whether it was objectively reasonable for him to arrest Amore while failing to realize that the statute he was attempting to enforce had been held unconstitutional.

To spare police officers the unenviable choice between failing to enforce the law and risking personal liability for enforcing what they reasonably, but mistakenly, think is the law, we generally extend qualified immunity to an officer for an arrest made pursuant to a statute that is "on the books," so long as the arrest was based on probable cause that the statute was violated. *See Crotty*, 346 F.3d at 105 ("Officials charged with enforcing a statute on the books . . . are generally entitled to rely on the presumption that all relevant legal and constitutional issues have been considered and that the statute is valid."); *see also id.* at 102 ("In order to determine whether [the defendant] may prevail, we consider many factors, but rely primarily on one factor as particularly persuasive: that the challenged conduct involved enforcement of a presumptively valid statute."); *Vives v. City of New York*, 405 F.3d 115, 117 (2nd Cir. 2005) (distinguishing *Crotty* from "case which did not involve state officials acting under the color of a properly-enacted statute."); *Shero v. City of Grove, Okla.*, 510 F.3d 1196, 1204 (10th Cir. 2007) (referring to reliance on statute as "extraordinary circumstance[ ]" that could "so prevent[ ] the official from knowing that his or her actions were unconstitutional that he or she should not be imputed with knowledge of a clearly established right").

We noted some years ago that:

> [I]t has long been clearly established that an arrest without probable cause is a constitutional violation. Nonetheless, the arresting officer is entitled to qualified immunity as a matter of law if the undisputed facts and all permissible inferences favorable to the plaintiff show either (a) that it was objectively reasonable for the officer to believe that probable cause existed, or (b) that officers of reasonable competence could disagree on whether the probable cause test was met.

Robison v. Via, 821 F.2d 913, 921 (2nd Cir. 1987) (citations omitted).

Similarly here, we assume that it is clearly established that an arrest under a statute that has been authoritatively held to be unconstitutional is ordinarily a constitutional violation. And it is clear that Amore was sufficiently detained for him to have been "arrested" for purposes of bringing this false arrest claim, * * * and that the statute under which he was arrested had been held by the New York Court of Appeals to be unconstitutional.

The question is whether it was nonetheless objectively reasonable for Novarro, as the arresting officer, to have believed that the statute in question remained fully in force and that his arrest was therefore not a violation of Amore's constitutional rights.

Section 240.35(3) made it a crime to loiter "in a public place for the purpose of engaging, or soliciting another person to engage, in deviate sexual intercourse or other sexual behavior of a deviate nature." * * * *Uplinger*, 58 N.Y.2d at 937, 460 N.Y.S.2d 514, 447 N.E.2d at 62. In that 1983 decision, the New York Court of Appeals declared the provision unconstitutional. The court explained that "[t]he object of the loitering statute is to punish conduct anticipatory to the act of consensual sodomy. Inasmuch as the conduct ultimately contemplated by the loitering statute may not be deemed criminal, we perceive no basis upon which the State may continue to punish loitering for that purpose." *Id.*, 58 N.Y.2d at 938 * * *.

At the time Novarro arrested Amore—and indeed, until after the issuance of our initial opinion in this appeal—"[d]espite judicial invalidation, the State of New York ha[d] not formally repealed [section 240.35(3)]." *Casale v. Kelly*, 257 F.R.D. 396, 401 (S.D.N.Y. 2009).[15] The Court of Appeals' decision in *Uplinger* notwithstanding, section 240.35(3) continued to be published in official versions of the New York Penal Law. See N.Y. Penal Law § 240.35(3) (2010). WestLaw and Lexis continued to include the text in their services.[16]

Indeed, more than two years after Amore's arrest for violating section 240.35(3), the New York State legislature amended the wording of this very section, thus treating section 240.35(3) as though it were fully in effect despite the holding of the New York Court of Appeals two decades previously that the section was unconstitutional. * * *

In determining whether an officer is entitled to qualified immunity, "[t]he question is not what a lawyer would learn or intuit from researching case law, but what a reasonable person in a defendant's position should know about the constitutionality of the conduct." *Young v. County of Fulton*, 160 F.3d 899, 903 (2nd Cir. 1998); *see also Scarbrough v. Myles*, 245 F.3d 1299, 1303 n. 8 (11th Cir. 2001) ("Police officers are not expected to be lawyers or prosecutors."). It is undisputed that: Novarro did not know that section 240.35(3) was unconstitutional; he had not received instruction or information on the constitutionality of the statute; and he was relying on an accurate, if unannotated, copy of the New York Penal Law when he arrested Amore—indeed, he was literally reading the Penal Law during the course of the arrest.

The plaintiff and *amici* suggest the fact that the statute had been held unconstitutional automatically and necessarily strips the officer of immunity. We disagree.

We accept that it is the unusual case where a police officer's enforcement of an unconstitutional statute will be immune. And there are suggestions from the Supreme Court and our own court that an officer's entitlement to rely on a statute ordinarily expires when a binding court decision declares the statute unconstitutional. *See Michigan v. DeFillippo*, 443 U.S. 31, 38 (1979) (state officials "are charged to enforce laws until and unless they are declared unconstitutional"); *Vives*, 405 F.3d at 117 ("We have held that absent contrary direction, state officials are entitled to rely on a presumptively valid state statute until and unless the statute is declared unconstitutional."); *Crotty*, 346 F.3d at 102 ("[U]ntil judges say

---

[15] New York Governor David Paterson signed a measure repealing section 240.35(3) on July 31, 2010. * * *

[16] To be sure, McKinney's Consolidated Laws of New York Annotated contains a reference to the fact that section 240.35(3) "has been declared unconstitutional." *See* 39 McKinney's Penal Law § 240.35, William C. Donnino, "Practice Commentary" (citing *Uplinger*). WestLaw and Lexis versions of the statute contain similar references. But it is undisputed on this appeal that the copy of the Penal Law provided to Novarro by the police department, published by a professional third-party publisher, contained no such annotation. It is also undisputed that Novarro received no information or instruction regarding the constitutionality of section 240.35(3) prior to the arrest.

otherwise, state officers have the power to carry forward the directives of the state legislature").

There are cases, too, from other circuits where qualified immunity was denied to an officer enforcing a statute that, while still "on the books," had previously been declared unconstitutional in a binding court decision. *See, e.g., Leonard v. Robinson*, 477 F.3d 347, 358–61 (6th Cir. 2007) (denying qualified immunity to a police officer who arrested a citizen for using a "mild profanity while peacefully advocating a political position" at a public assembly, and noting that "it cannot seriously be contended that any reasonable peace officer, or citizen, for that matter, would believe" that such speech constituted a "criminal act," in light of "the prominent position that free political speech has in our jurisprudence and in our society"); *Baribeau v. City of Minneapolis*, 596 F.3d 465, 479 (8th Cir. 2010) (denying qualified immunity to police officers who arrested citizens for "engaging in an artistic protest").

We have no reason to doubt the conclusions of those courts. But the statutes at issue and the circumstances of arrest they were considering differ from the facts presented here. * * * None of these cases, nor any other binding authority of which we are aware, stands for the categorical proposition that if a statute has been held unconstitutional, adherence to it by a law enforcement official is, *ipso facto*, unreasonable for qualified immunity purposes irrespective of the circumstances. We do not think that to be the law. * * *

We ordinarily impute knowledge of the case law to public officials. * * * But, as Judge Hartz of the Tenth Circuit has noted, albeit in dissent, "[t]he statement in *Harlow* that reasonably competent public officials know clearly established law[ ] is a legal fiction." *Lawrence v. Reed*, 406 F.3d 1224, 1237 (10th Cir. 2005) (Hartz, J., dissenting). Qualified immunity is appropriate in "those situations in which the legal fiction does not make sense and applying that fiction would create problems that qualified immunity is intended to avert." *Id.*; *cf. Harlow*, 457 U.S. at 819 ("[I]f the official pleading the [qualified immunity] defense claims extraordinary circumstances and can prove that he neither knew nor should have known of the relevant legal standard, the defense should be sustained.").

While we may not consider an official's subjective intent in determining whether he is entitled to qualified immunity, we do—and must—consider "the particular facts of the case," *Robison*, 821 F.2d at 921, including the objective information before the officer at the time of the arrest. In the case at bar, where the defendant acted deliberately and rationally in seeking to determine the then-valid, applicable and enforceable law before taking the actions for which the plaintiff now seeks to hold him accountable, we cannot say that Novarro's arrest of Amore was objectively unreasonable. His immunity stands. * * *

NOTES AND QUESTIONS

1. *Ellison extended.* The Ninth Circuit has extended *Ellison* from cases involving gender discrimination to cases involving racial discrimination, using an *Ellison*-like formula that balances the importance of an "objective" standard with a heightened sensitivity to the plaintiff's particular circumstances. *See, e.g., McGinest v. GTE Serv. Corp.*, 360 F.3d 1103, 1115 (9th Cir. 2004) ("We now state explicitly what was clear from our holding in *Ellison*, that allegations of a racially hostile workplace must be assessed from the perspective of *a reasonable person belonging to the racial or ethnic group of the plaintiff*.") (emphasis added). The United States Supreme Court has given its apparent imprimatur to this amalgam of objective and subjective factors, adapting the language of the reasonable person test. In *Oncale v. Sundowner Offshore Servs., Inc.*, 523 U.S. 75 (1998), for example, a same-sex hostile work environment case, the Court held that the standard for finding a violation of federal antidiscrimination law is that of "[1] a reasonable person [2] in the plaintiff's position, [3] considering 'all the circumstances.' " *Id.* at 81 (internal citation omitted). What is the effect of adding clauses 2 and 3 to the reasonable person standard?

2. *Amore transposed: reasonable persons interacting with the police.* In *Amore*, Navarro was entitled to immunity because a reasonable police officer may not have known that the law under which the arrest was made had been ruled unconstitutional. (a) On the facts presented, according to the court, who (or what) might be liable if the officer was not? (b) If ignorance of the law is generally no excuse for a citizen charged with a crime, *see, e.g., Cheek v. United States*, 498 U.S. 192 (1991), why is Navarro's ignorance of the law allowable as a basis for his immunity? (c) Suppose Amore, knowing that the law under which the arrest was made had been ruled unconstitutional or repealed, turned and walked away from the arresting officer:

> The test for determining if a police-citizen encounter is consensual depends on whether, under the totality of the circumstances surrounding the encounter, the police conduct would have communicated to a reasonable person that the person was not free to decline the officers' requests or otherwise terminate the encounter. The test is an objective one based upon a reasonable person standard, not the subjective perceptions of the particular individual. The test presumes an innocent reasonable person. In making this determination, the court should consider the sequence of the officer's actions and how a reasonable person would perceive those actions. * * *

State v. Williams, 934 P.2d 282, 285–86 (N.M. App. 1997) (quotations and internal citations omitted). In what ways would an *innocent* reasonable person assess an encounter with the police differently from a *guilty* reasonable person?

3. *Pragmatics*. As noted above, the reasonable person standard may make sense, not as an objective test or standard, but as a plane of argument, a metaphor that guides the arguments of counsel or the deliberations of the jury or the crafting of a judge's opinion. It is, to appropriate Professor Edward Corwin's phrase, "an invitation to struggle" in the course of any litigation in which it appears. *See generally* Douglas Lind, *The Pragmatic Value of Legal Fictions, in* LEGAL FICTIONS IN THEORY AND PRACTICE 83, 93 (Maksymilian Del Mar and William Twining, eds., 2015).

---

2. A "CONSTRUCTIVE" ANYTHING IS FICTIONAL

a. Constructive Evictions

GOTTDIENER V. MAILHOT

179 N.J. Super. 286, 431 A.2d 851 (1981)

The primary question on this appeal is whether defendants, former tenants in plaintiffs' apartment complex, may invoke the remedy of constructive eviction by reason of plaintiffs' claimed failure to take sufficient measures to protect defendants from excessively noisy and unruly neighboring tenants. Plaintiffs sought rent (at the rate of $400 a month) for the months of September, October and November 1979, plus late charges and additional sums to repair and restore defendants' apartment. Defendants denied liability for rent for the months in question principally because plaintiffs' breach of the covenant of quiet enjoyment amounted to a constructive eviction. Defendants also counterclaimed for double the amount of their security deposit, pursuant to [state law].

The matter was tried before Judge Gascoyne, sitting without a jury. The proofs showed that defendants originally became tenants in Oakwood Village, a 516-unit apartment complex, in December 1975, and had renewed their tenancy through January 31, 1980. Defendants experienced no problems during their tenancy until the fall of 1978, when new tenants moved into the apartment immediately beneath defendants. On several occasions in December 1978 and January 1979 defendants complained of "intolerable noise" coming from the downstairs apartment, such as slamming doors, yelling and screaming children, and excessive volume from the television and radio after 10 p. m. Plaintiff Alexander Gottdiener, one of the partners who owned Oakwood Village, expressed sympathy with defendants' plight and made some efforts to effect a resolution of the conflict between defendants and their neighbors. These efforts were not successful and, according to Mr. Mailhot, the neighbors began a campaign of harassment and retaliation. He claimed that in late January 1979 someone from the apartment below had maliciously damaged his vehicle, which he kept in a garage available only to defendants, plaintiffs and the downstairs neighbors.

Defendants brought this incident to the attention of Gottdiener and again requested plaintiffs to take some measures to resolve the problem. Gottdiener responded with a suggestion that defendants and their neighbors amicably settle the dispute, but a subsequent meeting proved fruitless. According to Mailhot, one of the downstairs tenants became very angry and threatened defendants.

Defendants began to look for another place to live in early May, and sometime in June entered into a contract to purchase a home. By letter dated June 29, 1979 they notified plaintiffs that they intended to terminate the tenancy as of August 31. The letter of termination stated that defendants had been "continually harassed and intimidated" by the downstairs tenants and that they believed that plaintiffs' failure to correct the situation constituted a "breach of contract." Gottdiener replied that he still hoped that the matter could be amicably solved, and he suggested that defendants move into another building. Defendants declined the offer and vacated their apartment in late August 1979. Plaintiffs procured another tenant effective December and shortly thereafter notified defendants of the disposition of their security deposit. Plaintiffs then brought this action for rent for the months of September, October and November, and the other charges, minus defendants' security deposit, which plaintiffs retained.

Judge Gascoyne found that, while he initially believed that defendants were "hypersensitive" to noise, his analysis of the proofs convinced him that the conduct of the downstairs neighbors constituted a "substantial interference" with defendants' quiet enjoyment of the premises. He found that one of the downstairs neighbors had vandalized Mailhot's automobile. He reasoned that excessive noise, like flooding or roach infestation, can make rented premises unsuitable for the purpose for which the premises were leased. He also found that defendants had vacated their apartment within a reasonable time. Thus, he held that plaintiffs were not entitled to rent for the months of September, October and November. A judgment was entered dismissing the complaint with prejudice and awarding $548.70 to defendants on their counterclaim. Plaintiffs appeal.

Plaintiffs contend that a landlord has no duty to evict one tenant in order to eliminate a "questionable" disturbance by that tenant of another tenant, and that defendants were not constructively evicted, since the landlord diligently tried to alleviate friction between them and their neighboring co-tenants.

The law of landlord and tenant, including that relating to constructive eviction, has undergone considerable change in recent years. In *Reste Realty Corp. v. Cooper*, 53 N.J. 444, 456–457, 251 A.2d 268 (1969), the court stated that where there is a covenant of quiet enjoyment, whether expressed or implied, which is breached substantially by the landlord, the doctrine of constructive eviction is available as a remedy for the tenant; and that any act or omission of the landlord or anyone acting under his authority which renders the premises substantially unsuitable for the purpose for which they are leased, or which seriously interferes with the beneficial enjoyment of the premises, is a breach of that covenant and constitutes a constructive eviction of the tenant.

In *Millbridge Apartments v. Linden*, 151 N.J. Super. 168, 376 A.2d 611 (Cty. D. Ct. 1977), the court properly held that the *Reste* principle relating to constructive eviction could be applied to a situation similar to that before us. There defendants-tenants frequently complained to their landlord that their neighbors were extremely loud. When the landlord's efforts to correct the problem were unsuccessful, the tenants began withholding their rent. In the landlord's ensuing action for possession based on nonpayment of rent, the tenants contended that the landlord's failure to correct the problem constituted a breach of the covenant of habitability.

Judge Weinberg stated that "repeated loud noise suffered by a residential tenant, which could have been cured by a landlord, can be a defense to a dispossess action under the rubric of the warranty of habitability." 151 N.J. Super. at 170–171, 376 A.2d 611. He said:

> Residential tenants expect to live within reasonable boundaries of quiet. Continual noise of a loud nature infringes upon those expectations and makes one's premises "substantially unsuitable for the purpose for which they are leased," i.e., ordinary residential living. Accordingly, this court holds that noise may constitute a constructive eviction and legally justify a tenant's vacating. [at 171, 376 A.2d 611]

Since noise may constitute a constructive eviction, the court determined that excessive noise could also constitute a breach of the covenant of habitability. * * *

We agree with the reasoning of *Millbridge Apartments v. Linden*. A number of recent cases from other jurisdictions have recognized that a landlord may constructively evict a tenant by failing to prevent other tenants from making excessive amounts of noise. * * *

We hold that in order to justify early termination of the lease, or for that matter an abatement of rent, the tenant must show that the noise or conduct of a cotenant made the premises substantially unsuitable for ordinary residential living and that it was within the landlord's power to abate the nuisance. The test is objective; the noise or disruptive conduct "must be such as truly to render the premises uninhabitable in the eyes of a reasonable person." *Berzito v. Gambino*, 63 N.J. 460, 469, 308 A.2d 17 (1973).

Unquestionably plaintiffs had the power to correct the problem. [Under state law, a] good cause for evicting a residential tenant is that the "person has continued to be, after written notice to cease, so disorderly as to destroy the peace and quiet of the occupants or other tenants living in said house or neighborhood." The landlord may bring a summary dispossess action against such an unruly tenant by giving only three days' notice prior to the institution of the action. In addition, had the downstairs tenant violated any rules and regulations or lease covenants respecting noise, the landlord had the option of bringing a dispossess action [ ].

There is no merit to plaintiffs' argument that the conduct of the downstairs neighbors was not so serious as to constitute a substantial interference with defendants' peaceful enjoyment of the premises, or that plaintiffs did all that reasonably could be expected of them to remedy such conduct. What amounts to a constructive eviction is a question of fact. * * * We find sufficient credible evidence in the record as a whole to support the trial judge's findings and conclusions regarding the nature and extent of the disturbance of defendants' enjoyment of the premises and the constructive eviction of defendants by reason thereof.

Plaintiffs further contend that even assuming that they breached the covenant of quiet enjoyment by not abating the noise, defendants waived their right to terminate the lease and abandon the premises because they failed to take such action within a reasonable time after the right to terminate came into existence. As stated in *Reste Realty Corp. v. Cooper*, *supra*:

> . . . What constitutes a reasonable time depends upon the circumstances of each case. In considering the problem courts must be sympathetic toward the tenant's plight. Vacation of the premises is a drastic course and must be taken at his peril. If he vacates, and it is held at a later time in a suit for rent for the unexpired term that the landlord's course of action did not reach the dimensions of constructive eviction, a substantial liability may be imposed upon him. That risk and the practical inconvenience and difficulties attendant upon finding and moving to suitable quarters counsel caution. [53 N.J. at 461, 251 A.2d 268]

Adequate credible evidence in the record supports the conclusion that defendants waited a reasonable time in order to determine whether plaintiffs would solve the problem, and left only after it was apparent that plaintiffs would not take any further measures. There was thus no waiver of their right to terminate the lease. * * * Affirmed.

---

b. Constructive Trusts

ROWE V. KINGSTON

94 A.D.3d 852, 942 N.Y.S.2d 161 (2012)

In an action to impose a constructive trust upon certain real property, the defendants appeal from a judgment of the Supreme Court, Queens County * * *, entered November 12, 2010, which, upon a decision of the same court dated November 30, 2009, made after a nonjury trial, is in favor of the plaintiff and against them, imposing a constructive trust on the subject property. ORDERED that the judgment is affirmed, with costs.

The plaintiff owned a two-family home and resided in it with the defendants, who are his aunt and uncle. In 1999, the plaintiff transferred title to the two-family home to his aunt for no consideration, with the understanding that she would re-deed the property back to him upon his request. The plaintiff's aunt refinanced the property in her name, although the plaintiff, as per their agreement, continued to collect rent and make the mortgage payments. When the plaintiff allegedly failed to make timely mortgage payments, his aunt assumed direct payment of the mortgage. By then, the plaintiff had moved out of the property. However, his aunt and his uncle continued to live there. The defendants took over paying the utility bills and other maintenance of the property, collected rent from the other tenants, and claimed a tax credit for the mortgage payments. In 2003, the aunt added the uncle to the deed, at which time the defendants refinanced the mortgage on the property, drawing on its equity. Following failed discussions between the parties regarding the return of the property to the plaintiff, the plaintiff commenced this action and, after a nonjury trial before a referee, a constructive trust was imposed in his favor. * * *

A constructive trust is an equitable remedy [ ] and may be imposed "[w]hen property has been acquired in such circumstances that the holder of the legal title may not in good conscience retain the beneficial interest" (*Poupis v. Brown,* 90 A.D.3d 881, 882, 935 N.Y.S.2d 127, *quoting Sharp v. Kosmalski,* 40 N.Y.2d 119, 121, 386 N.Y.S.2d 72, 351 N.E.2d 721 [internal quotation marks omitted]). In general, to impose a constructive trust, four factors must be established: (1) a confidential or fiduciary relationship, (2) a promise, (3) a transfer in reliance thereon, and (4) unjust enrichment * * *. However, as these elements serve only as a guideline, a constructive trust may still be imposed even if all of the elements are not established [ ].

Here, the Supreme Court properly found that the plaintiff satisfied the elements necessary to impose a constructive trust. As familial relatives, the parties shared a confidential relationship * * *. The defendants did not dispute that they promised to re-deed the property back to the plaintiff at a later date, and the record does not support their further contentions that this promise was conditioned on the plaintiff's timely payment of the mortgage or that the plaintiff habitually made late payments on the mortgage. Furthermore, the defendants' argument that, in effect, their investment in the property gave them an ownership interest, is without merit. Although the defendants were responsible for the care and maintenance of the property for eight years, they were living on the premises together with their family, collecting rent, and reaping the tax and home equity benefits associated with owning a home [ ]. The defendants' remaining contention regarding unclean hands is without merit. Accordingly, there is no basis to disturb the Supreme Court's judgment imposing a constructive trust in favor of the plaintiff.

---

c. Constructive Termination from Employment

BRADY V. ELIXIR INDUSTRIES

196 Cal. App. 3d 1299, 242 Cal. Rptr. 324 (1987)

Plaintiff appeals a judgment against her on two causes of action for sexual discrimination and tortious constructive discharge. We reverse, holding [that] the trial court * * * prejudicially erred in instructing that constructive discharge required employer intent to cause the employee to quit.

* * * Plaintiff presented her own testimony and that of several of her superiors who no longer worked for Elixir. This testimony indicated that, because of her sex, plaintiff was not as highly paid as she merited and was otherwise unfairly treated. Two men who were arguably her subordinates received pay substantially equal to or greater than she received. Elixir did present evidence on these issues which contradicted plaintiff's evidence. However, given the substantial character of the evidence plaintiff presented, we must conclude in the words of *Estate of Kime* (1983) 144 Cal. App.3d 246, 260 [193 Cal. Rptr. 718], that had the error not occurred, it is " 'reasonably probable' (though far from certain) that . . . the result would have been different." * * *

On the sole remaining cause of action for tortious constructive discharge, the trial court instructed the jury as follows:

> In order for plaintiff to recover for constructive discharge due to unlawful sexual discrimination, plaintiff must prove by a preponderance of the evidence the following:
>
> 1. There was, in fact, discrimination based on sex,
>
> 2. Which discrimination existed at the time of discharge, and
>
> 3. Which discrimination persisted after the employee protested the same to the employer, and

4. The employer failed to eliminate the discrimination within a reasonable time after notice thereof.

In order for the discrimination to be sufficient to amount to a constructive discharge, it must be such conduct by the employer, made with the intent to cause the employee to resign, and which sex discrimination [*sic*] conduct made working conditions so intolerable that the employee, as a reasonable person, is forced to resign.

We hold that this instruction was prejudicially erroneous. Although none of this state's courts have addressed the issue of what facts and circumstances will constitute a constructive discharge, federal district and appellate courts including the Ninth Circuit, the California Fair Employment and Housing Commission (FEHC), and a number of other state courts have dealt with this issue in statutory as well as common law contexts. All of these authorities agree that a tortious constructive discharge requires proof of a violation of public policy, such as unlawful discrimination, plus circumstances so aggravated or intolerable that a reasonable employee would feel compelled to resign. However, federal and state case and administrative law have taken divergent views as to whether a third element concerning the mental state of the employer must be proved by an employee to establish constructive discharge. The majority does not require a third element, while the minority has required proof of intent, knowledge, or foreseeability on the employer's part that the employee would resign because of those circumstances. * * *

While the majority correctly take the position that requiring intent or actual knowledge is too stringent [ ], not requiring a third element of any kind relating to the employer's knowledge does not adequately insure that a peaceful, on-the-job resolution has been attempted or was futile.

Accordingly, we hold that, to establish a tortious constructive discharge, an employee must show:

(1) the actions and conditions that caused the employee to resign were violative of public policy;

(2) these actions and conditions were so intolerable or aggravated at the time of the employee's resignation that a reasonable person in the employee's position would have resigned; and

(3) facts and circumstances showing that the employer had actual or constructive knowledge of the intolerable actions and conditions and of their impact on the employee and could have remedied the situation.[ ]

Applying this approach to the jury instruction before us, we conclude that the instruction given by the court imposed an unnecessarily heavy burden on the plaintiff. While the four required proofs listed in the first paragraph of that instruction would certainly establish a tortious constructive discharge, points 3 and 4 preclude consideration of facts and circumstances, other than notice to the employer, from which a jury could infer that the employer had actual or constructive knowledge of these conditions and their effect on the employee. The second paragraph of the instruction requires intent by the employer to cause the employee's resignation, rather than the employer's constructive knowledge of the facts and circumstances surrounding the resignation. * * *

NOTES AND QUESTIONS

1. *Common law fictions.* In each of the three principal cases, some requirement for a remedy (or a defense) has been suspended by the court. In each case, the established precondition—an actual trust instrument, an actual eviction from the apartment, an actual termination from the job—has been transformed into a formality, allowing a remedy (or a defense) on the basis of an analogy to the prior line of authority. For example, the landlord in *Gottdiener* did not literally evict anybody, but he did allow noisy and unruly tenants to force other tenants out, and that was sufficiently *like* a literal eviction to trigger a defense to the landlord's action for unpaid rent. The consequence (and perhaps the intent) is that a substantive principle of law—namely, that tenants need not pay rent when the landlord evicts them—has been extended to circumstances to which it literally could not have applied before. The term "eviction" is used constructively, but no actual eviction by the landlord appears anywhere in the picture. The constructive eviction is an untruth not intended to deceive.

This dynamic fits an important and recurring pattern. The ancient system of common law writs required specific factual elements to be pled before a legal action could proceed (or be said to "lie"). Eventually, the rigidity of the writ system made it notoriously unresponsive to new or similar forms of old problems, and the courts decided that the purposes of the old writs were more important than the technical requirements within them. *See* JOHN CHIPMAN GRAY, THE NATURE AND SOURCES OF THE LAW 34 (Roland Gray ed., 2nd ed. 1921) (portraying legal fiction as a way to put "the wine of new law * * * into the bottles of old procedure.") Consider this concrete example:

> The English courts were in the habit of pretending that a chattel, which might in fact have been taken from the plaintiff by force, had been *found* by the defendant. Why? In order to allow an action [under the writ of trover] which otherwise would not have lain. . . . No one believed that the chattel had been found by the defendant simply because the pleadings said so; the fact was known to be otherwise. The deceit, if any, consisted in the concealment by the court of the exercise of legislative power under the guise of this pretense. Or, perhaps more accurately stated—since it is hardly conceivable that

> those living contemporaneously with the development of this fiction could have been unaware that the law was changing—the deceit consisted in the representation that an expansion of the action of trover under this pretense was legitimate. This representation, however, was probably as heartily believed by the authors of the fiction as anyone else.

Lon Fuller, *Legal Fictions*, 25 ILL. L. REV. 363, 367 (1930) (emphasis in original).

If this "exercise of legislative power" by the judges is inappropriate or unconstitutional, is it in principle any different from other common law creations? Is it defensible on the ground that it is essentially incremental and preserves the substance of the prior rule by applying it in new, unforeseen situations? Consider also the possibility that fictions are the product of creative advocacy by lawyers on a case-by-case basis and not the illegitimate pursuit of some reform agenda by judges. From that perspective, the creation of fictions should be traced to the "countless individual lawyers through the centuries, each concerned not with 'the law' as such but with a small immediate predicament of his client." S.F.C. MILSOM, A NATURAL HISTORY OF THE COMMON LAW 27 (2003) ("Only conspiracy theory on a sublime scale could see judges as responsible for fictions. * * * [T]he part of judges in fictional change was essentially passive.").

Consider also the possibility that these fictions gave flexibility to courts of law to do equity or achieve fairness, without seeming to toy with the elements of a legal claim. When courts of equity and courts of law were separate institutions, the fiction might even be seen as way of holding on to a case on grounds that would otherwise take it elsewhere.

2. *Jurisdictional fictions*. One of the most notorious examples of using a fiction to satisfy a writ-based factual requirement that had outlived its usefulness in a particular case is *Mostyn v. Fabrigas*, (1773) 20 St. Tr. 82, [1775] 1 Copp 161, [1775] 98 ER 1021 (1775). In that case, Lord Mansfield decided that the Mediterranean island of Minorca—then a British colony—was in London and specifically "in the parish of St. Mary-le-Bow, in the Ward of Cheap," for the purpose of obtaining jurisdiction in an assault case filed against the governor of the colony. In the absence of that fiction, there would have been no remedy at all—a result Mansfield must have considered unacceptable. Is it equally necessary in the interest of justice and accountability to construct a locational fiction about data stored in cyberspace?

3. *Statutory fictions*. Some fictions are expressed in statutory form. Under the "entry fiction" in immigration law, for example, an "excludable" alien is considered to have been detained at the border, even if he or she is physically within the borders of the United States. 8 U.S.C. § 1182(d)(5). One non-fictional consequence is that the Attorney General has the statutory authority to detain such an alien for a prolonged period without charge. *See Wong Wing v. United States*, 163 U.S. 228, 235 (1896). The federal copyright statute deems an author's employer to be the author of a copyrighted work-for-

hire. *See* 17 U.S.C. § 201(b) (2000). The federal tax code is rife with legislated fictions, including that an individual can be considered the owner of stock actually owned by his or her children and parents, 26 U.S.C. § 318(a)(1)(A), and that a gift made within three years of death was made in contemplation of death, meaning that it is clawed back into the decedent's estate for tax purposes. *See* 26 U.S. C. § 2035. How would you articulate the differences—if any—between these legislative fictions and the adjudicative fictions at work in the principal cases, above? Why would any legislature ever have to resort to a fiction if it is interested in updating or improving the law the way a judge might?

4. *Fictions in the discipline of statutory construction*. In interpreting statutes, judges often indulge in fictions about the legislature and the aggregate behavior and knowledge of its members. For example, when there is ambiguity in a statute, courts routinely turn to a legislative intent to determine the meaning of ambiguous text, but this reconstruction is almost always a fiction. *See* Antonin Scalia, *Judicial Deference to Administrative Interpretations of Law*, 1989 DUKE L.J. 511, 517 (1989) ("any rule adopted in this field [of interpreting agency-administered statutes] represents merely a fictional, presumed intent"). After all, legislators vote for a bill out of a variety of motivations and with a variety of understandings about its meaning and effect, suggesting in turn that there is no single intent except as a fictional construct after the fact. And logically mustn't any collective legislative intent also have to include the understandings and intents of those who voted against the bill? They may have lost the vote, but their understanding of what the law does would be relevant in its subsequent interpretation by reinforcing or refining what was fictively in the minds of the majority. Equally fictional is the legislative history of a statute, generally consisting of committee reports, transcripts of hearings and floor debates or colloquies, documents assembled by legislative staff. It isn't that these things don't exist. They do, but they tend to be assembled after the fact, and they are often consulted to resolve ambiguities in a statute despite the certain knowledge that few if any voting members actually read those materials, understood them, and voted for the bill on the same basis.

One of the most powerful constructs guiding the interpretation of a statute is the "one Congress fiction"—the idea that Congress is permanent, speaks with one voice over time, and enacts all legislation:

> It is not uncommon for judges to justify an interpretation of a disputed statutory provision by looking to a similarly phrased provision in a different statute, drawing inferences from the linguistic similarities, and concluding that Congress must have intended the same meaning in the two statutes. With the full knowledge that the statutes under comparison were passed by different sessions of Congress, arose from different legal and social contexts, and concerned different subject matter, judges using this method nonetheless treat the two statutes as authoritative expressions of a unified Congress.

Note, *Lessons from Abroad: Mathematical, Poetic, and Literary Fictions in the Law*, 115 HARV. L. REV. 2228, 2237 (2002). Relatedly, the members of each Congress are presumed to legislate with full knowledge of existing law, which is ridiculous on its face. Assuming that no one is deceived by this fiction, what value does the fiction bring to the crucial, unavoidable task of statutory construction?

5. *Constitutional fictions*. Consider the argument that a narrative can be morally true even if it is not historically true. That is, a story can point us toward an ideal to which we wish to conform, even if it more resembles fable than fact. In 1835, explaining to a European audience why republican, representative democracy was working in the United States after failing elsewhere, de Tocqueville observed that

> [t]he government of the Union rests almost entirely on legal fictions. The Union is an ideal nation which exists, so to say, only in men's minds and whose extent and limits can only be discerned by the understanding.

ALEXIS DE TOCQUEVILLE, DEMOCRACY IN AMERICA 164 (J. Mayer ed., 1969). In what practical respects does the government of the United States rest on legal fictions, and how do those fictions differ from the common law fictions at work in *Gottdiener*, *Rowe*, and *Brady*?

To get a handle on that question, begin with the recognition that the Supreme Court routinely offers narratives that combine fact and fiction as a way of grounding an interpretation of Constitutional text. *See generally* L.H. LARUE, CONSTITUTIONAL LAW AS FICTION: NARRATIVE IN THE RHETORIC OF AUTHORITY (1995). It might be another category error, *supra*, to criticize these constructions as partial history at best, because they are not used for their historical accuracy. Instead, they are intended to persuade and ultimately to establish a proposition of law to guide future decisions. One standard example is Justice Brandeis's dissent in *Olmstead v. United States*, 277 U.S. 438 (1928):

> The makers of our Constitution undertook to secure conditions favorable to the pursuit of happiness. They recognized the significance of man's spiritual nature, of his feelings and of his intellect. They knew that only a part of the pain, pleasure and satisfactions of life are to be found in material things. They sought to protect Americans in their beliefs, their thoughts, their emotions and their sensations. They conferred, as against the government, the right to be let alone—the most comprehensive of rights and the right most valued by civilized men.

Id. at 478. Of course, this is not literally true: the "right to be let alone" does not appear in the text of the Constitution. But neither is it exactly false. It is a rhetorical device to support an idea that looks like—but is not—a simple retelling of history, and, as an early articulation of the right to privacy, it was used to profound effect in the subsequent contraception and abortion cases. Other famous examples include Justice Black's history of the First Amendment's Establishment Clause in *Everson v. Board of Ed. of Ewing Tp.*,

330 U.S. 1 (1947), which provoked the historian Edward Corwin to observe that "the Court has the right to make history; but it has no right to make it up." EDWARD S. CORWIN, A CONSTITUTION OF POWERS IN A SECULAR STATE 116 (1951). *See generally*, Donald L. Drakeman, Everson v. Board of Education *and the Quest for the Historical Establishment Clause*, 49 AM. J. LEGAL HIST. 119 (2007). In what respect are these historical visions—these constitutional "facts" as found by the Supreme Court—binding on lower courts in subsequent cases?

Are you persuaded by the argument that fictions do or should play less of a role in constitutional cases than in common law cases? Consider this encapsulation of the argument:

> It might be thought that legal fictions ought to play a diminished role in constitutional law, in contrast to their prevalence in common law, for example. For one thing, constitutional law does not lack a text, whereas the common law "professes . . . to develop and apply principles that have never been committed to any authentic form of words," as Frederick Pollock put it. Despite the best efforts of interpretivists, originalists, and self-proclaimed strict constructionists, however, constitutional law as we know it—and as it has been from the start—demonstrates quite clearly that even our written "authentic form of words" requires additional criteria of construction and interpretation."

Aviam Soifer, *Reviewing Legal Fictions*, 20 GA. L. REV. 871, 880 (1986) (quoting F. POLLOCK, A FIRST BOOK OF JURISPRUDENCE 249 (3rd ed. 1911)).

---

3. FICTIONS AS THE SCAFFOLDING FOR UPDATING (OR IMPROVING) THE LAW

BLACK'S LEGAL DICTIONARY defines "legal fiction" as an "assumption that something is true even though it may be untrue, made esp[ecially] in judicial reasoning to alter how a legal rule operates; specif[ically], a device by which a legal rule or institution is diverted from its original purpose to accomplish indirectly some other object."[7] Initially, it may be counter-intuitive to think that fictions enable (and sometimes mask) alterations in the law, so, as you read the following case, identify the preexisting law or doctrine being altered or improved.

---

[7] *See also* Henry S. Maine, ANCIENT LAW 21–22 (17th ed. 1901):

> I * * * employ the expression "Legal Fiction" to signify any assumption which conceals, or affects to conceal, the fact that a rule of law has undergone alteration, its letter remaining unchanged, its operation being modified.

WOOD V. LUCY, LADY DUFF-GORDON

222 N.Y. 88, 118 N.E. 214 (1917)

CARDOZO, J. The defendant styles herself "a creator of fashions." Her favor helps a sale. Manufacturers of dresses, millinery, and like articles are glad to pay for a certificate of her approval. The things which she designs, fabrics, parasols, and what not, have a new value in the public mind when issued in her name. She employed the plaintiff to help her to turn this vogue into money. He was to have the exclusive right, subject always to her approval, to place her indorsements on the designs of others. He was also to have the exclusive right to place her own designs on sale, or to license others to market them. In return she was to have one-half of "all profits and revenues" derived from any contracts he might make. The exclusive right was to last at least one year from April 1, 1915, and thereafter from year to year unless terminated by notice of 90 days. The plaintiff says that he kept the contract on his part, and that the defendant broke it. She placed her indorsement on fabrics, dresses, and millinery without his knowledge, and withheld the profits. He sues her for the damages, and the case comes here on demurrer.

The agreement of employment is signed by both parties. It has a wealth of recitals. The defendant insists, however, that it lacks the elements of a contract. She says that the plaintiff does not bind himself to anything. It is true that he does not promise in so many words that he will use reasonable efforts to place the defendant's indorsements and market her designs. We think, however, that such a promise is fairly to be implied. The law has outgrown its primitive stage of formalism when the precise word was the sovereign talisman, and every slip was fatal. It takes a broader view today. A promise may be lacking, and yet the whole writing may be "instinct with an obligation," imperfectly expressed (Scott, J., in *McCall Co. v. Wright*, 133 App. Div. 62, 117 N. Y. Supp. 775; *Moran v. Standard Oil Co.*, 211 N. Y. 187, 198, 105 N. E. 217). If that is so, there is a contract.

The implication of a promise here finds support in many circumstances. The defendant gave an exclusive privilege. She was to have no right for at least a year to place her own indorsements or market her own designs except through the agency of the plaintiff. The acceptance of the exclusive agency was an assumption of its duties.[ ] We are not to suppose that one party was to be placed at the mercy of the other. [ ] Many other terms of the agreement point the same way. We are told at the outset by way of recital that:

> The said Otis F. Wood possesses a business organization adapted to the placing of such indorsements as the said Lucy, Lady Duff-Gordon, has approved.

The implication is that the plaintiff's business organization will be used for the purpose for which it is adapted. But the terms of the defendant's compensation are even more significant. Her sole compensation for the grant of an exclusive agency is to be one-half of all the profits resulting from the plaintiff's efforts. Unless he gave his efforts, she could never get anything. Without an implied promise, the transaction cannot have such business "efficacy, as both parties must have intended that at all events it should have." Bowen, L.J., in the *Moorcock*, 14 P. D. 64, 68. But the contract does not stop there. The plaintiff goes on to promise that he will account monthly for all moneys received by him, and that he will take out all such patents and copyrights and trade-marks as may in his judgment be necessary to protect the rights and articles affected by the agreement. It is true, of course, as the Appellate Division has said, that if he was under no duty to try to market designs or to place certificates of indorsement, his promise to account for profits or take out copyrights would be valueless. But in determining the intention of the parties the promise has a value. It helps to enforce the conclusion that the plaintiff had some duties. His promise to pay the defendant one-half of the profits and revenues resulting from the exclusive agency and to render accounts monthly was a promise to use reasonable efforts to bring profits and revenues into existence. For this conclusion the authorities are ample. [ ]

The judgment of the Appellate Division should be reversed, and the order of the Special Term affirmed, with costs in the Appellate Division and in this court.

NOTES AND QUESTIONS

1. *Unpacking Lady Duff-Gordon, so to speak.* In this case, Lady Duff-Gordon determined that her exclusive arrangement with Otis Wood interfered with her ability to make more money creating a line of fashion for Sears Roebuck. One way out was to deny that her arrangement with Wood was a contract at all, because the contract did not require him to do anything. To be sure, he had to pass on half "of 'all profits and revenues' derived from any contracts he *might* make," but nothing obliged him to make contracts. By finding an implied promise by Wood "to use reasonable efforts to bring profits and revenues into existence," the court found that there was a contract and that Lady Duff-Gordon had breached it. (a) On what fiction(s) are implied conditions in a contract necessarily based? (b) According to Cardozo, what legal doctrine is being altered by the use of these fictions? (c) In what respect if any has the law been "improved" by this approach? (d) Aviam Soifer has suggested that "[l]ike sunlight, legal fictions affect how growth will tilt." Aviam Soifer, *Reviewing Legal Fictions*, 20 GA. L. REV. 871, 877 (1986). How might you predict contract law would develop in the "sunlight" of this decision and the fictions at its heart? (e) The case was decided 4–3 by the New York Court of Appeals, but there was no separate dissenting opinion. Whether you are

convinced by them or not, what are the strongest arguments for rejecting the majority's analysis?

2. *Change-agent fictions as a feature, not a bug*. Jeremy Bentham's withering attack on legal fictions, *supra*, reminds us that contempt for legal fictions is old and understandable if transparency of principle is fundamental to the rule of law and its legitimacy. *See also* Cass R. Sunstein, *Principles, Not Fictions*, 57 U. CHI. L. REV. 1247, 1256 (1990). But consider Grant Gilmore's suggestion that "the process by which a society accommodates to change without abandoning its fundamental structure is *what we mean by law*." G. GILMORE, THE AGES OF AMERICAN LAW 14 (1977) (emphasis supplied). From that perspective, fictions are simply a microcosm of the law generally. There is in short a direct line to Gilmore's overarching vision of the law from the insight of Fuller and Maine (reflected in BLACK'S LEGAL DICTIONARY), that fictions mediate the conflict between essential continuity and essential change.

3. *Fictions change too*. Some fictions clearly change with society. At one time for example, the "one flesh" fiction of marriage meant that married women could not own property in their own names and suffered other disabilities because their legal identity was fused with that of their husbands. *See* I WILLIAM BLACKSTONE, COMMENTARIES ON THE LAW OF ENGLAND 442 (1765) ("By marriage, the husband and the wife are one person in the law * * * the very being and legal existence of the woman is suspended during the marriage, or at least is incorporated into that of her husband under whose wing [and] protection she performs everything.") Institutionally, should changes in fictions be directed by courts or legislators or something else?

Readings

PETER J. SMITH, *NEW LEGAL FICTIONS*

95 GEO. L.J. 1435 (2007)

* * * As the common law has waned as a source of legal rules, judges have relied on classic legal fictions with less frequency. But even in the age of positive law, judges often fashion new legal rules. And in so doing, they rely, with surprising frequency, on what I call "new legal fictions." A judge deploys a new legal fiction when he relies in crafting a legal rule on a factual premise that is false or inaccurate. Scholars in every area of the law can identify examples of legal rules that are at least ostensibly based on false premises. * * *

Consider the following examples. Ignorance of the law is not a defense because we presume that members of the public in a representative democracy are familiar with the law's requirements.[2] Evidence that is inadmissible at trial for one purpose often is admissible for a different

---

[2] *See, e.g.*, Cheek v. United States, 498 U.S. 192, 199 (1991).

purpose because we presume that jurors can, when ruling at once on the multiple issues in a case, faithfully follow a limiting instruction and simply ignore evidence that they have seen with respect to some questions.[3] *Miranda* rights do not attach in many situations in which police confront and question individuals because we presume that oftentimes when police question individuals, the individuals will feel free to decline to answer or even to leave.[4] Many constitutional questions are answered, even if not exclusively, by referring to historical materials relevant to the Constitution's ratification because we presume that there is—and that it is possible to discern—one fixed, meaningful, singular, original understanding of the Constitution, even with respect to questions that the Framers did not consider at all.[5] We consult dictionaries and canons of construction when we attempt to give meaning to a statute because we presume that Congress was aware of and considered them when it enacted the statute.[6] Eyewitness testimony cannot generally be impeached by expert scientific evidence demonstrating that such testimony often is highly unreliable because we presume that jurors can competently assess the reliability of eyewitness testimony.[7]

These important premises that inform and shape doctrine in diverse areas of the law are all seriously flawed. Even before statutory law and administrative regulations spanned miles of shelf space in libraries, ordinary citizens were unlikely to know precisely what their legal rights and obligations were. Modern psychology tells us that even sophisticated, well-educated jurors cannot ignore for one purpose evidence that is appropriately considered for another. Few citizens—indeed, few lawyers—would truly feel free to leave, regardless of the circumstances, if they were questioned by police officers. Legal realism, public choice theory, and linguistic theory teach that the notion of collective intent is a fiction, even putting aside the obvious problems of attempting to discern it from a fragmented and incomplete historical record for questions (not) considered more than two centuries ago. Members of Congress often do not read the bills on which they are asked to vote, let alone consider the meaning of statutory terms in light of dictionary definitions and canons of construction. Social scientists have demonstrated that eyewitness testimony often is unreliable and that both witnesses and jurors overestimate their abilities to determine its reliability. Of course, for

3 *See, e.g.*, Francis v. Franklin, 471 U.S. 307, 324 n.9 (1985).

4 *See, e.g.*, Stansbury v. California, 511 U.S. 318, 322–25 (1994).

5 *See, e.g.*, Alden v. Maine, 527 U.S. 706, 712–25 (1999) (relying extensively on ratification debates and The Federalist Papers to reach its conclusion that Article I "do[es] not include the power to subject nonconsenting states to private suits for damages in state courts"); Antonin Scalia, *Originalism: The Lesser Evil*, 57 U. CIN. L. REV. 849, 854 (1989).

6 *See, e.g.*, Chan v. Korean Air Lines, Ltd., 490 U.S. 122, 128 (1989) (consulting dictionaries); FAIC Sec., Inc. v. United States, 768 F.2d 352, 363 (D.C. Cir. 1985) (Scalia, J.) (utilizing canons of construction).

7 *See, e.g.*, United States v. Hall, 165 F.3d 1095, 1107 (7th Cir. 1999); State v. Coley, 32 S.W.3d 831, 833–34 (Tenn. 2000).

some—or perhaps all—of these examples, there is room for debate over whether in fact the premises are false. But together the examples suggest a broader, and perhaps more common, phenomenon than we would likely expect to find, and they at least suggest in the aggregate that we often base legal doctrine on false, debatable, or untested premises.

If nothing else, we can identify a new legal fiction only if we have some way to determine the validity of the factual premises on which judges rely in crafting legal rules. Although occasionally general knowledge or conventional wisdom alone can demonstrate a premise's falsity, usually we can confidently say that a premise is false only after measuring it against the results of existing empirical research. There is, to be sure, a lively debate among scholars over the appropriate role of empirical research in the formulation of legal rules. But it is not my intention here to rehash the debate over the appropriate role of social science in legal decision-making. Rather, my principal aim is to demonstrate when and why judges rely on new legal fictions, and to consider when, if ever, the practice is appropriate. Although there are many reasons, I focus here on the six most common and important.

First and most straightforward, sometimes judges' suppositions simply turn out to be inaccurate, and the courts sometimes are open to abandoning the new legal fiction—and generally the legal rule for which it was a premise—when sufficient proof is offered to demonstrate its falsity.[15] In these cases, the new legal fiction is not intended to mask a normative choice but simply is based on a misunderstanding or misreading of empirical reality.

Second, judges often rely on new legal fictions because of the law's general imperviousness to social science and change. Courts have no formal or established mechanism for consideration of empirical research.[16] And even when the lessons of social science penetrate the sphere of judicial decision-making, the mechanisms for correcting legal rules tainted by new legal fictions are cumbersome and institutionally disfavored.

Third, judges' purported factual suppositions sometimes are devices, conscious or not, for concealing the fact that the judges are making normative choices in fashioning legal rules. There are many reasons, of course, why a judge might be reluctant to reveal that he is making such a normative choice—some of which are embraced by the other reasons discussed below that judges rely on new legal fictions. But sometimes judges have no justification for masking the normative choice other than the desire for obfuscation.

---

[15] *See, e.g.,* United States v. Leon, 468 U.S. 897, 928 (1984) (Blackmun, J., concurring).

[16] *See* John Monahan & Laurens Walker, *Social Authority: Obtaining, Evaluating, and Establishing Social Science in Law*, 134 U. PA. L. REV. 477, 485–88 (1986).

Fourth, new legal fictions often are devices for operationalizing legal theories. Proponents of textualism, for example, consult dictionaries, judicial precedent, and canons of construction when they interpret statutes, based on the assumption that members of Congress consult them as well when they draft and vote on proposed legislation. When pressed, textualists generally concede that these assumptions are likely false, but they defend them nevertheless as a way to operationalize a theory of judicial restraint.

Fifth, new legal fictions often serve functional goals and promote administrability in judicial process. For example, although many judges at this point undoubtedly are aware that eyewitness identifications often are unreliable, they continue to exclude expert testimony to that effect because admitting it would risk forcing mini-trials in the countless criminal cases that turn on eyewitness evidence—and would risk undermining a broad range of criminal prosecutions.

Sixth, new legal fictions often serve a legitimating function, and judges may preserve them—even in the face of evidence that they are false—if their abandonment would have delegitimating consequences. What would it mean for public acceptance of the right to a trial by jury, for example, if courts declared that jurors generally are not competent faithfully to follow a judge's instructions about how the law limits their consideration of the evidence? Judges recognize that the law often serves an expressive function, and under certain circumstances they are willing to rely on new legal fictions if they will produce doctrine with positive expressive value. It may be debatable whether in fact the public would view the politico-legal system as any less legitimate if judges abandoned these new legal fictions. But if nothing else, judges' factual assumptions often reflect their aspirations for society and the law, even if those aspirations are unlikely to be realized.

There will of course be times when these justifications for relying on new legal fictions are persuasive. But there are reasons for caution nonetheless. When judges rely on new legal fictions, they generally do not acknowledge the falsity of their premises. Accordingly, unlike classic legal fictions—which, by definition, were not intended to deceive—new legal fictions involve a lack of judicial candor. In the end, we must ask whether these justifications for the reliance on new legal fictions are sufficient. Even assuming that there is virtue in translating legal theory into practice and in harnessing the expressive force of the law, to justify the practice we must conclude that it outweighs the harm worked by the lack of judicial candor and transparency. Here, I tend to share David Shapiro's intuition that "candor is to the judicial process what notice is to fair procedure," and that "the fidelity of judges to law can be fairly measured only if they believe what they say in their opinions and orders."[18] The burden of justification, therefore, is on those who defend the practice of the new legal fiction.

To be sure, some scholars have argued that judicial transparency is not always desirable, some for reasons other than those suggested by the rationales described above for why judges rely on new legal fictions.[19] But I argue that the default preference should be for judicial transparency, which would tend to minimize the frequency of new legal fictions and is more consistent with the general urge to limit unconstrained judicial discretion in light of what Bickel famously called the "counter-majoritarian difficulty."[20] Transparency in this context would require the judge to justify a premise in light of conflicting existing knowledge (whether based on empirical research or some other source), or to ground the legal rule in something other than the false premise. Judicial transparency helps us to determine whether a judicial choice is actually based on the judge's normative preferences or instead is based on the judge's factual suppositions. When judges do in fact craft legal rules based on purely factual suppositions—and are open about it—then we can check and, if necessary, urge change based on the correctness of their empirical conclusions. And when judges make clear that they are instead in fact deciding based upon normative preferences, we can more readily decide whether the normative choice is desirable, and whether it is one that we want judges to have authority to make. * * *

Seventy-five years ago, with legal realism on the rise and the Brandeis Brief a hot topic of discussion, Lon Fuller observed:

> [I]t is not always easy to distinguish between the process of discovering the facts of social life (descriptive science), and the process of establishing rules for the government of society (normative science). Much of what appears to be strictly juristic and normative is in fact an expression, not of a rule for the conduct of human beings, but of an opinion concerning the structure of society. Before one can intelligently determine what *should* be,

---

[18] David L. Shapiro, *In Defense of Judicial Candor*, 100 HARV. L. REV. 731, 750 (1987).

[19] Charles Nesson, for example, has argued that judicial decisions based on probabilities—roughly the equivalent of empirical research in this context—might not be as acceptable as decisions whose grounds are largely hidden from the public. *See* Charles R. Nesson, *Reasonable Doubt and Permissive Inferences: The Value of Complexity*, 92 HARV. L. REV. 1187, 1196 (1979). Guido Calabresi has argued that candor is not always optimal when courts address tragic choices. Meir Dan-Cohen has noted that the lack of "acoustic separation" between decision rules and conduct rules sometimes argues in favor of dispensing with candor. Others have argued that *stare decisis* might in some cases be a countervailing consideration, particularly when the factual assumptions supporting one legal rule have spilled over into other areas of the law. *See, e.g.*, Barefoot v. Estelle, 463 U.S. 880, 896–97 (1983) (rejecting social science research about predictions of future dangerousness in part because of *stare decisis*), *superseded by statute on other grounds*, 28 U.S.C. § 2253 (2000), *as recognized in* Slack v. McDaniel, 529 U.S. 473 (2000) [ ].

[20] ALEXANDER M. BICKEL, THE LEAST DANGEROUS BRANCH 16–17, 207 (2d ed. 1986).

> one must determine what *is*, and in practice the two processes are often inseparably fused.[290]

Fuller's observation remains trenchant today. In his day, of course, the common law legal fiction was the device that judges deployed to mix descriptive and normative judgments. As the common law approach has waned, so has judicial reliance on classic legal fictions. But the judicial urge, or perhaps necessity, to make normative judgments in the creation of legal rules has persisted, as has the judicial desire to obscure the appearance of judicial lawmaking. Today, judges rely less on classic legal fictions than on new legal fictions. But the effect is largely the same.

My point here is not that judges should never be in the business of lawmaking. On the contrary, to properly perform their adjudicative function, judges often must craft legal rules, whether to fill in statutory gaps, interpret ambiguous and general constitutional provisions, or act in a common law fashion. But there is a difference between accepting that judges sometimes must make law, on the one hand, and tolerating unconstrained choice for judges in exercising that power, on the other. Since at least the time of the legal realists, the dirty little secret has been out: judges often make normative choices. Our task is to insist that when they do so, they do so openly, so that we can check, when appropriate, the exercise of their discretion.

We thus must be sensitive to judicial reliance on new legal fictions because new legal fictions more often than not are devices to obscure judges' normative choices. To be sure, there will be times when, on balance, such obfuscation seems preferable to candor. But those times, I think, will be rare. By identifying new legal fictions when we see them, and by focusing discussion on the normative choices obscured by reliance on the device, we can help to limit judicial obfuscation to those rare times when it seems appropriate.

NOTES AND QUESTIONS

1. *The genetic marker of "new" legal fictions.* In Professor Smith's view, what is the difference between the classic fictions and the new ones? Do you think it is true that the new fictions hide normative choices more than the classic ones?

2. *Making the transition to thinking about burdens.* What are the practical and doctrinal consequences of what Professor Smith calls the "burden of justification?" Why does he assign that burden to "those who defend the practice of the new legal fiction?" What exactly is the source of that burden, and how does it differ from the "burden of proof?"

---

290 [LON L. FULLER, LEGAL FICTIONS] 131 [(1967)].

B. BURDENS

Another "tilt" or default in the law structures the arguments in a case by defining and allocating burdens of proof—or more precisely "burdens of persuasion," *infra*—to the parties in a lawsuit. In a criminal case, for example, the prosecution can succeed only by proving *beyond a reasonable doubt* that the defendant is guilty—the most demanding standard in American law, requiring the highest level of confidence in the facts as found by the jury. If there is any reasonable doubt, the defendant is not guilty as a matter of law. By contrast, in a civil case, the plaintiff bears the burden of proving her case by a *preponderance of the evidence*, sometimes articulated as the "balance of probabilities," meaning that her version of the facts is more likely than not. If, in assessing the plaintiff's and the defendant's case the jury finds that the probabilities are exactly balanced, the default inference is that the plaintiff must lose. In these two common examples, the law has assigned the benefit of the doubt to one party and the burden of proof to the other.

In short, burdens are the law's instructions about how to process facts and judgments in a world where little or nothing is known to a certainty and where there are near infinite degrees of uncertainty. In essence, burdens are one way for the law to specify the degree of confidence needed before a legal decision can be reached and justified. That is easiest to see perhaps in a jury's resolution of a criminal or a civil case, especially when reasonable doubt is such a staple of crime shows on television, but the law also articulates the burden in considerably less dramatic (but equally important) settings.

Consider for example the legal headwinds facing those who challenge the action of an administrative agency. Among other specified grounds, the challengers can win if they demonstrate that the "agency action, findings, and conclusions [are] * * * unsupported by *substantial evidence* * * *." 5 U.S.C. § 706(2)(E) (emphasis supplied). That burden on the challenger translates into a powerful doctrine of judicial deference to the agency: so long as there is *merely* substantial evidence in the record supporting the agency's decision, the challengers will lose that part of the argument and have to find some other ground for the challenge. And what qualifies as substantial evidence? The courts have defined is "as more than a 'mere scintilla,' and as 'such relevant evidence as a reasonable mind might accept as adequate to support a conclusion.' " *Selian v. Astrue*, 708 F.3d 409, 417 (2nd Cir. 2013) (internal quotation marks omitted). In a similar vein, one court decided that "substantial evidence is less than a preponderance, but enough that a reasonable mind would find it *adequate* to support the [agency's] decision." *Gonzales v. Barnhart*, 465 F.3d 890, 894 (8th Cir. 2006).

The legally-allowable doubt is also specified for a court's review of a police officer's interaction with a citizen. For example, a police officer need only have a *reasonable suspicion* of illegal activity for a brief investigatory stop, with the understanding that "a suspicion is not reasonable unless officers have based it on 'specific and articulable facts.' " *Terry v. Ohio*, 392 U.S. 1, 21 (1968). A more invasive police encounter—a search or an arrest—must satisfy a more demanding burden, namely *probable cause*. A grand jury indictment also rests on probable cause, which the Supreme Court has explained "is not a high bar: It requires only the "kind of 'fair probability' on which 'reasonable and prudent [people,] not legal technicians, act.' *Florida v. Harris*, 568 U.S. 237, 244 (2013) (*quoting Illinois v. Gates*, 462 U.S. 213, 231, 238 (1983)) * * *."

Burdens are significant enough when they simply lay out requirements for each party in a case: they necessarily channel the advocate's work. But sometimes the standard is itself a matter of argument within a case, as is the party to whom it properly applies. We also know, as suggested in the materials below, that some burdens can shift in the course of litigation, suggesting that burdens can be rigid (or unarguable) guidelines in some cases and the strategic prize in others.

---

1. THE "BURDEN OF PROOF" UNPACKED

DIRECTOR, OFFICE OF WORKERS' COMPENSATION PROGRAMS V. GREENWICH COLLIERIES

512 U.S. 267 (1994)

JUSTICE O'CONNOR delivered the opinion of the Court. * * * [Section] 7(c) of the Administrative Procedure Act (APA) [ ] states that "[e]xcept as otherwise provided by statute, the proponent of a rule or order has the burden of proof." 5 U.S.C. § 556(d). Because the term "burden of proof" is nowhere defined in the APA, our task is to construe it in accord with its ordinary or natural meaning. It is easier to state this task than to accomplish it, for the meaning of words may change over time, and many words have several meanings even at a fixed point in time. Here we must seek to ascertain the ordinary meaning of "burden of proof" in 1946, the year the APA was enacted.

For many years the term "burden of proof" was ambiguous because the term was used to describe two distinct concepts. Burden of proof was frequently used to refer to what we now call the burden of persuasion—the notion that if the evidence is evenly balanced, the party that bears the burden of persuasion must lose. But it was also used to refer to what we now call the burden of production—a party's obligation to come forward with evidence to support its claim. See J. Thayer, Evidence at the Common

Law 355–384 (1898) (detailing various uses of the term "burden of proof" among 19th-century English and American courts).

The Supreme Judicial Court of Massachusetts was the leading proponent of the view that burden of proof should be limited to burden of persuasion. In what became an oft-cited case, Chief Justice Lemuel Shaw attempted to distinguish the burden of proof from the burden of producing evidence. *Powers v. Russell*, 30 Mass. 69 (1833). According to the Massachusetts court, "the party whose case requires the proof of [a] fact, has all along the burden of proof." Though the burden of proving the fact remains where it started, once the party with this burden establishes a *prima facie* case, the burden to "produce evidence" shifts. The only time the burden of proof—as opposed to the burden to produce evidence—might shift is in the case of affirmative defenses. In the century after *Powers*, the Supreme Judicial Court of Massachusetts continued to carefully distinguish between the burden of proof and the burden of production.

Despite the efforts of the Massachusetts court, the dual use of the term continued throughout the late 19th and early 20th centuries. See 4 J. Wigmore, Evidence §§ 2486–2487, pp. 3524–3529 (1905); Thayer, *supra*, at 355; 1 B. Elliott & W. Elliott, Law of Evidence § 129, pp. 184–185 (1904); 2 C. Chamberlayne, Modern Law of Evidence § 936, pp. 1096–1098 (1911). The ambiguity confounded the treatise writers, who despaired over the "lamentable ambiguity of phrase and confusion of terminology under which our law has so long suffered." Wigmore, *supra*, at 3521–3522. The writers praised the "clear-thinking" efforts of courts like the Supreme Judicial Court of Massachusetts, Chamberlayne, *supra*, at 1097, n. 3, and agreed that the legal profession should endeavor to clarify one of its most basic terms. According to Thayer, *supra*, at 384–385, "[i]t seems impossible to approve a continuance of the present state of things, under which such different ideas, of great practical importance and of frequent application, are indicated by this single ambiguous expression." See also Chamberlayne, *supra*, at 1098. To remedy this problem, writers suggested that the term "burden of proof" be limited to the concept of burden of persuasion, while some other term—such as "burden of proceeding" or "burden of evidence"—be used to refer to the concept of burden of production. Chamberlayne, *supra*, § 936; Elliott & Elliott, *supra*, at 185, n. 3. Despite the efforts at clarification, however, a dwindling number of courts continued to obscure the distinction. *See* Annot., 2 A.L.R. 1672 (1919) (noting that some courts still fail to properly distinguish "between the burden of proof and the duty of going forward with the evidence").

This Court tried to eliminate the ambiguity in the term "burden of proof" when it adopted the Massachusetts approach. *Hill v. Smith*, 260 U.S. 592 (1923). Justice Holmes wrote for a unanimous Court that "it will not be necessary to repeat the distinction, familiar in Massachusetts since the time of Chief Justice Shaw, [*Powers*, *supra*], and elaborated in the opinion below, between the burden of proof and the necessity of producing evidence to meet that already produced. The distinction is now very generally accepted, although often blurred by careless speech." *Id.*, at 594.

In the two decades after *Hill*, our opinions consistently distinguished between burden of proof, which we defined as burden of persuasion, and an alternative concept, which we increasingly referred to as the burden of production or the burden of going forward with the evidence. See, e.g., *Brosnan v. Brosnan*, 263 U.S. 345, 349 (1923) (imposition of burden of proof imposes the burden of persuasion, not simply the burden of establishing a *prima facie* case); *Radio Corp. of America v. Radio Engineering Laboratories, Inc.*, 293 U.S. 1, 7–8 (1934) (party who bears the burden of proof "bears a heavy burden of persuasion"); *Commercial Molasses Corp. v. New York Tank Barge Corp.*, 314 U.S. 104, 111 (1941) (party with the burden of proof bears the "burden of persuasion," though the opposing party may bear a burden to "go forward with evidence"); *Webre Steib Co. v. Commissioner*, 324 U.S. 164, 171 (1945) (claimant bears a "burden of going forward with evidence . . . as well as the burden of proof"). During this period the Courts of Appeals also limited the meaning of burden of proof to burden of persuasion, and explicitly distinguished this concept from the burden of production.

The emerging consensus on a definition of burden of proof was reflected in the evidence treatises of the 1930's and 1940's. "The burden of proof is the obligation which rests on one of the parties to an action to persuade the trier of the facts, generally the jury, of the truth of a proposition which he has affirmatively asserted by the pleadings." W. Richardson, EVIDENCE 143 (6th ed. 1944); *see also* 1 B. Jones, LAW OF EVIDENCE IN CIVIL CASES 310 (4th ed. 1938) ("The modern authorities are substantially agreed that, in its strict primary sense, 'burden of proof' signifies the duty or obligation of establishing, in the mind of the trier of facts, conviction on the ultimate issue"); J. McKelvey, EVIDENCE 64 (4th ed. 1932) ("[T]he proper meaning of [burden of proof]" is "the duty of the person alleging the case to prove it," rather than "the duty of the one party or the other to introduce evidence").

We interpret Congress' use of the term "burden of proof" in light of this history, and presume Congress intended the phrase to have the meaning generally accepted in the legal community at the time of enactment. These principles lead us to conclude that the drafters of the APA used the term "burden of proof" to mean the burden of persuasion. As we have explained, though the term had once been ambiguous, that ambiguity had largely been eliminated by the early 20th century. After *Hill*, courts and commentators almost unanimously agreed that the definition was settled. And Congress indicated that it shared this settled understanding, when in the Communications Act of 1934 it explicitly distinguished between the burden of proof and the burden of production. 47 U.S.C. §§ 309(e) and

312(d) (a party has both the "burden of proceeding with the introduction of evidence and the burden of proof"). Accordingly, we conclude that as of 1946 the ordinary meaning of burden of proof was burden of persuasion, and we understand the APA's unadorned reference to "burden of proof" to refer to the burden of persuasion. * * *

---

2. THE "BURDEN OF PROOF" APPLIED

SCHAFFER V. WEAST

546 U.S. 49 (2005)

JUSTICE O'CONNOR delivered the opinion of the Court. The Individuals with Disabilities Education Act (IDEA or Act), as amended, 20 U.S.C. § 1400 *et seq.* (2000 ed. and Supp. V), * * * seeks to ensure that "all children with disabilities have available to them a free appropriate public education". Under IDEA, school districts must create an "individualized education program" (IEP) for each disabled child. § 1414(d). If parents believe their child's IEP is inappropriate, they may request an "impartial due process hearing." § 1415(f). The Act is silent, however, as to which party bears the burden of persuasion at such a hearing. We hold that the burden lies, as it typically does, on the party seeking relief.

I

A

Congress first passed IDEA as part of the Education of the Handicapped Act in 1970 and amended it substantially in the Education for All Handicapped Children Act of 1975. At the time the majority of disabled children in America were "either totally excluded from schools or sitting idly in regular classrooms awaiting the time when they were old enough to 'drop out,' " H.R.Rep. No. 94–332, p. 2 (1975). IDEA was intended to reverse this history of neglect. As of 2003, the Act governed the provision of special education services to nearly 7 million children across the country.

IDEA is "frequently described as a model of 'cooperative federalism.' " *Little Rock School Dist. v. Mauney,* 183 F.3d 816, 830 (C.A. 8 1999). It "leaves to the States the primary responsibility for developing and executing educational programs for handicapped children, [but] imposes significant requirements to be followed in the discharge of that responsibility." *Board of Ed. of Hendrick Hudson Central School Dist., Westchester Cty. v. Rowley,* 458 U.S. 176, 183 (1982). * * *

The core of the statute, however, is the cooperative process that it establishes between parents and schools. *Rowley, supra,* at 205–206 ("Congress placed every bit as much emphasis upon compliance with procedures giving parents and guardians a large measure of participation at every stage of the administrative process, . . . as it did upon the measurement of the resulting IEP against a substantive standard"). The central vehicle for this collaboration is the IEP process. State educational authorities must identify and evaluate disabled children, develop an IEP for each one, and review every IEP at least once a year. Each IEP must include an assessment of the child's current educational performance, must articulate measurable educational goals, and must specify the nature of the special services that the school will provide.

Parents and guardians play a significant role in the IEP process. They must be informed about and consent to evaluations of their child under the Act. Parents are included as members of "IEP teams." They have the right to examine any records relating to their child, and to obtain an "independent educational evaluation of the[ir] child." They must be given written prior notice of any changes in an IEP, and be notified in writing of the procedural safeguards available to them under the Act. If parents believe that an IEP is not appropriate, they may seek an administrative "impartial due process hearing." School districts may also seek such hearings, as Congress clarified in the 2004 amendments. They may do so, for example, if they wish to change an existing IEP but the parents do not consent, or if parents refuse to allow their child to be evaluated. As a practical matter, it appears that most hearing requests come from parents rather than schools.

Although state authorities have limited discretion to determine who conducts the hearings, and responsibility generally for establishing fair hearing procedures, Congress has chosen to legislate the central components of due process hearings. It has imposed minimal pleading standards, requiring parties to file complaints setting forth "a description of the nature of the problem," and "a proposed resolution of the problem to the extent known and available . . . at the time." At the hearing, all parties may be accompanied by counsel, and may "present evidence and confront, cross-examine, and compel the attendance of witnesses." After the hearing, any aggrieved party may bring a civil action in state or federal court. Prevailing parents may also recover attorney's fees. Congress has never explicitly stated, however, which party should bear the burden of proof at IDEA hearings.

B

This case concerns the educational services that were due, under IDEA, to petitioner Brian Schaffer. Brian suffers from learning disabilities and speech-language impairments. From prekindergarten through seventh grade he attended a private school and struggled academically. In 1997, school officials informed Brian's mother that he needed a school that could better accommodate his needs. Brian's parents contacted respondent Montgomery County Public Schools System (MCPS) seeking a placement for him for the following school year.

MCPS evaluated Brian and convened an IEP team. The committee generated an initial IEP offering Brian a place in either of two MCPS middle schools. Brian's parents were not satisfied with the arrangement, believing that Brian needed smaller classes and more intensive services. The Schaffers thus enrolled Brian in another private school, and initiated a due process hearing challenging the IEP and seeking compensation for the cost of Brian's subsequent private education.

In Maryland, IEP hearings are conducted by administrative law judges (ALJs). After a 3-day hearing, the ALJ deemed the evidence close, held that the parents bore the burden of persuasion, and ruled in favor of the school district. The parents brought a civil action challenging the result. The United States District Court for the District of Maryland reversed and remanded, after concluding that the burden of persuasion is on the school district. Around the same time, MCPS offered Brian a placement in a high school with a special learning center. Brian's parents accepted, and Brian was educated in that program until he graduated from high school. The suit remained alive, however, because the parents sought compensation for the private school tuition and related expenses.

Respondents appealed to the United States Court of Appeals for the Fourth Circuit. While the appeal was pending, the ALJ reconsidered the case, deemed the evidence truly in "equipoise," and ruled in favor of the parents. The Fourth Circuit vacated and remanded the appeal so that it could consider the burden of proof issue along with the merits on a later appeal. The District Court reaffirmed its ruling that the school district has the burden of proof. On appeal, a divided panel of the Fourth Circuit reversed. Judge Michael, writing for the majority, concluded that petitioners offered no persuasive reason to "depart from the normal rule of allocating the burden to the party seeking relief." We granted *certiorari* to resolve the following question: At an administrative hearing assessing the appropriateness of an IEP, which party bears the burden of persuasion?

II

A

The term "burden of proof" is one of the "slipperiest member[s] of the family of legal terms." 2 J. Strong, McCormick on Evidence § 342, p. 433 (5th ed. 1999) (hereinafter McCormick). Part of the confusion surrounding the term arises from the fact that historically, the concept encompassed two distinct burdens: the "burden of persuasion," *i.e.,* which party loses if the evidence is closely balanced, and the "burden of production," *i.e.,* which party bears the obligation to come forward with the evidence at different points in the proceeding. *Director, Office of Workers' Compensation Programs v. Greenwich Collieries*, 512 U.S. 267, 272 (1994). We note at the outset that this case concerns only the burden of persuasion, as the parties agree, and when we speak of burden of proof in this opinion, it is this to which we refer.

When we are determining the burden of proof under a statutory cause of action, the touchstone of our inquiry is, of course, the statute. The plain text of IDEA is silent on the allocation of the burden of persuasion. We therefore begin with the ordinary default rule that plaintiffs bear the risk of failing to prove their claims. McCormick § 337, at 412 ("The burdens of pleading and proof with regard to most facts have been and should be assigned to the plaintiff who generally seeks to change the present state of affairs and who therefore naturally should be expected to bear the risk of failure of proof or persuasion"); C. Mueller & L. Kirkpatrick, Evidence § 3.1, p. 104 (3d ed. 2003) ("Perhaps the broadest and most accepted idea is that the person who seeks court action should justify the request, which means that the plaintiffs bear the burdens on the elements in their claims").

Thus, we have usually assumed without comment that plaintiffs bear the burden of persuasion regarding the essential aspects of their claims. For example, Title VII of the Civil Rights Act of 1964, does not directly state that plaintiffs bear the "ultimate" burden of persuasion, but we have so concluded. In numerous other areas, we have presumed or held that the default rule applies. See, *e.g., Lujan v. Defenders of Wildlife*, 504 U.S. 555, 561 (1992) (standing); *Cleveland v. Policy Management Systems Corp.*, 526 U.S. 795, 806 (1999) (Americans with Disabilities Act); *Hunt v. Cromartie*, 526 U.S. 541, 553 (1999) (equal protection); *Wharf (Holdings) Ltd. v. United Int'l Holdings, Inc.*, 532 U.S. 588, 593 (2001) (securities fraud); *Doran v. Salem Inn, Inc.*, 422 U.S. 922, 931 (1975) (preliminary injunctions); *Mt. Healthy City Bd. of Ed. v. Doyle*, 429 U.S. 274, 287 (1977) (First Amendment). Congress also expressed its approval of the general rule when it chose to apply it to administrative proceedings under the Administrative Procedure Act, 5 U.S.C. § 556(d).

The ordinary default rule, of course, admits of exceptions. For example, the burden of persuasion as to certain elements of a plaintiff's claim may be shifted to defendants, when such elements can fairly be characterized as affirmative defenses or exemptions. Under some circumstances this Court has even placed the burden of persuasion over an entire claim on the defendant. But while the normal default rule does not solve all cases, it certainly solves most of them. Decisions that place the *entire* burden of persuasion on the opposing party at the *outset* of a proceeding—as petitioners urge us to do here—are extremely rare. Absent some reason to believe that Congress intended otherwise, therefore, we will conclude that the burden of persuasion lies where it usually falls, upon the party seeking relief.

B

* * * Petitioners [ ] urge that putting the burden of persuasion on school districts will further IDEA's purposes because it will help ensure that children receive a free appropriate public education. In truth,

however, very few cases will be in evidentiary equipoise. Assigning the burden of persuasion to school districts might encourage schools to put more resources into preparing IEPs and presenting their evidence. But IDEA is silent about whether marginal dollars should be allocated to litigation and administrative expenditures or to educational services. Moreover, there is reason to believe that a great deal is already spent on the administration of the Act. Litigating a due process complaint is an expensive affair, costing schools approximately $8,000-to-$12,000 per hearing. Congress has also repeatedly amended the Act in order to reduce its administrative and litigation-related costs. * * *

Petitioners in effect ask this Court to assume that every IEP is invalid until the school district demonstrates that it is not. The Act does not support this conclusion. IDEA relies heavily upon the expertise of school districts to meet its goals. It also includes a so-called "stay-put" provision, which requires a child to remain in his or her "then-current educational placement" during the pendency of an IDEA hearing. Congress could have required that a child be given the educational placement that a parent requested during a dispute, but it did no such thing. Congress appears to have presumed instead that, if the Act's procedural requirements are respected, parents will prevail when they have legitimate grievances. See *Rowley, supra,* at 206 (noting the "legislative conviction that adequate compliance with the procedures prescribed would in most cases assure much if not all of what Congress wished in the way of substantive content in an IEP").

Petitioners' most plausible argument is that "[t]he ordinary rule, based on considerations of fairness, does not place the burden upon a litigant of establishing facts peculiarly within the knowledge of his adversary." *United States v. New York, N.H. & H.R. Co.*, 355 U.S. 253, 256, n. 5 (1957). But this "rule is far from being universal, and has many qualifications upon its application." *Greenleaf's Lessee v. Birth,* 6 Pet. 302, 312 (1832); see also McCormick § 337, at 413 ("Very often one must plead and prove matters as to which his adversary has superior access to the proof"). School districts have a "natural advantage" in information and expertise, but Congress addressed this when it obliged schools to safeguard the procedural rights of parents and to share information with them. As noted above, parents have the right to review all records that the school possesses in relation to their child. They also have the right to an "independent educational evaluation of the[ir] child." The regulations clarify this entitlement by providing that a "parent has the right to an independent educational evaluation at public expense if the parent disagrees with an evaluation obtained by the public agency." 34 CFR § 300.502(b)(1) (2005). IDEA thus ensures parents access to an expert who can evaluate all the materials that the school must make available, and who can give an independent opinion. They are not left to challenge the government without a realistic opportunity to access the necessary evidence, or without an expert with the firepower to match the opposition.

Additionally, in 2004, Congress added provisions requiring school districts to answer the subject matter of a complaint in writing, and to provide parents with the reasoning behind the disputed action, details about the other options considered and rejected by the IEP team, and a description of all evaluations, reports, and other factors that the school used in coming to its decision. Prior to a hearing, the parties must disclose evaluations and recommendations that they intend to rely upon. IDEA hearings are deliberately informal and intended to give ALJs the flexibility that they need to ensure that each side can fairly present its evidence. IDEA, in fact, requires state authorities to organize hearings in a way that guarantees parents and children the procedural protections of the Act. Finally, and perhaps most importantly, parents may recover attorney's fees if they prevail. These protections ensure that the school bears no unique informational advantage.

III

Finally, respondents and several States urge us to decide that States may, if they wish, override the default rule and put the burden always on the school district. Several States have laws or regulations purporting to do so, at least under some circumstances. Because no such law or regulation exists in Maryland, we need not decide this issue today. Justice Breyer [dissenting] contends that the allocation of the burden ought to be left *entirely* up to the States. But neither party made this argument before this Court or the courts below. We therefore decline to address it.

We hold no more than we must to resolve the case at hand: The burden of proof in an administrative hearing challenging an IEP is properly placed upon the party seeking relief. In this case, that party is Brian, as represented by his parents. But the rule applies with equal effect to school districts: If they seek to challenge an IEP, they will in turn bear the burden of persuasion before an ALJ. The judgment of the United States Court of Appeals for the Fourth Circuit is, therefore, affirmed.

JUSTICE GINSBURG, dissenting. When the legislature is silent on the burden of proof, courts ordinarily allocate the burden to the party initiating the proceeding and seeking relief. As the Fourth Circuit recognized, however, "other factors," prime among them "policy considerations, convenience, and fairness," may warrant a different allocation. 377 F.3d 449, 452 (C.A.4 2004) (citing 2 J. Strong, McCormick on Evidence § 337, p. 415 (5th ed.1999) (allocation of proof burden "will depend upon the weight . . . given to any one or more of several factors, including: . . . special policy considerations[,] convenience, [and] fairness")); see also 9 J. Wigmore, Evidence § 2486, p. 291 (J. Chadbourn rev. ed. 1981) (assigning proof burden presents "a question of policy and fairness based on experience in the different situations"). The Court has followed the same counsel. See

Alaska Dept. of Environmental Conservation v. EPA, 540 U.S. 461, 494, n. 17 (2004) ("No 'single principle or rule . . . solve[s] all cases and afford[s] a general test for ascertaining the incidence' of proof burdens." (quoting Wigmore, *supra,* § 2486, p. 288). For reasons well stated by Circuit Judge Luttig, dissenting in the Court of Appeals [in this case], 377 F.3d, at 456–459, I am persuaded that "policy considerations, convenience, and fairness" call for assigning the burden of proof to the school district in this case.

The Individuals with Disabilities Education Act (IDEA) was designed to overcome the pattern of disregard and neglect disabled children historically encountered in seeking access to public education. Under typical civil rights and social welfare legislation, the complaining party must allege and prove discrimination or qualification for statutory benefits. The IDEA is atypical in this respect: It casts an affirmative, beneficiary-specific obligation on providers of public education. School districts are charged with responsibility to offer to each disabled child an individualized education program (IEP) suitable to the child's special needs. The proponent of the IEP, it seems to me, is properly called upon to demonstrate its adequacy.

Familiar with the full range of education facilities in the area, and informed by "their experiences with other, similarly-disabled children," 377 F.3d, at 458 (Luttig, J., dissenting), "the school district is . . . in a far better position to demonstrate that it has fulfilled [its statutory] obligation than the disabled student's parents are in to show that the school district has failed to do so," *id.*, at 457. *Accord Oberti v. Board of Ed. of Borough of Clementon School Dist.*, 995 F.2d 1204, 1219 (C.A.3 1993) ("In practical terms, the school has an advantage when a dispute arises under the Act: the school has better access to relevant information, greater control over the potentially more persuasive witnesses (those who have been directly involved with the child's education), and greater overall educational expertise than the parents."); *Lascari v. Board of Ed. of Ramapo Indian Hills Regional High School Dist.,* 116 N.J. 30, 45–46, 560 A.2d 1180, 1188–1189 (1989) (in view of the school district's "better access to relevant information," parent's obligation "should be merely to place in issue the appropriateness of the IEP. The school board should then bear the burden of proving that the IEP was appropriate. In reaching that result, we have sought to implement the intent of the statutory and regulatory schemes.").

Understandably, school districts striving to balance their budgets, if "[l]eft to [their] own devices," will favor educational options that enable them to conserve resources. *Deal v. Hamilton County Bd. of Ed.,* 392 F.3d 840, 864–865 (C.A.6 2004). Saddled with a proof burden in administrative "due process" hearings, parents are likely to find a district-proposed IEP "resistant to challenge." 377 F.3d, at 459 (Luttig, J., dissenting). Placing the burden on the district to show that its plan measures up to the statutorily mandated "free appropriate public education," 20 U.S.C.

§ 1400(d)(1)(A), will strengthen school officials' resolve to choose a course genuinely tailored to the child's individual needs.

The Court acknowledges that "[a]ssigning the burden of persuasion to school districts might encourage schools to put more resources into preparing IEPs." *Ante,* at 535. Curiously, the Court next suggests that resources spent on developing IEPs rank as "administrative expenditures" not as expenditures for "educational services." *Ibid.* Costs entailed in the preparation of suitable IEPs, however, are the very expenditures necessary to ensure each child covered by the IDEA access to a free appropriate education. These outlays surely relate to "educational services." Indeed, a carefully designed IEP may ward off disputes productive of large administrative or litigation expenses.

This case is illustrative. Not until the District Court ruled that the school district had the burden of persuasion did the school design an IEP that met Brian Schaffer's special educational needs. See *ante,* at 533; Tr. of Oral Arg. 21–22 (Counsel for the Schaffers observed that "Montgomery County . . . gave [Brian] the kind of services he had sought from the beginning . . . once [the school district was] given the burden of proof."). Had the school district, in the first instance, offered Brian a public or private school placement equivalent to the one the district ultimately provided, this entire litigation and its attendant costs could have been avoided.

Notably, nine States, as friends of the Court, have urged that placement of the burden of persuasion on the school district best comports with the IDEA's aim. If allocating the burden to school districts would saddle school systems with inordinate costs, it is doubtful that these States would have filed in favor of petitioners. * * *

One can demur to the Fourth Circuit's observation that courts "do not automatically assign the burden of proof to the side with the bigger guns," for no such reflexive action is at issue here. It bears emphasis that "the vast majority of parents whose children require the benefits and protections provided in the IDEA" lack "knowledg[e] about the educational resources available to their [child]" and the "sophisticat[ion]" to mount an effective case against a district-proposed IEP. In this setting, "the party with the 'bigger guns' also has better access to information, greater expertise, and an affirmative obligation to provide the contested services." 377 F.3d, at 458 (Luttig, J., dissenting). Policy considerations, convenience, and fairness, I think it plain, point in the same direction. Their collective weight warrants a rule requiring a school district, in "due process" hearings, to explain persuasively why its proposed IEP satisfies the IDEA's standards. I would therefore reverse the judgment of the Fourth Circuit.

NOTES AND QUESTIONS

1. *Understanding the general rule and its principled exceptions*. As the principal cases suggest, the burden of persuasion generally falls on those who would change the *status quo*: the proponents of a rule, the plaintiffs in a case, the claimants in a proceeding, the appellants seeking to reverse a lower court's ruling. But when—and on what policy grounds—should the courts make an exception to such a rule?

Consider the decision of the Inter-American Court of Human Rights in the *Velasquez-Rodriguez Case* (Judgment of July 29, 1988), INTER-AM. CT. H. R. (SER. C) NO. 4 (1988). There the family of a man who had been disappeared in Honduras sought compensation from the Honduran government. The Court determined that his disappearance fit a recurrent pattern, with numerous factual consistencies across a variety of cases. The Court ruled that the burden of proof would shift from the claimant to the government once that *prima facie* case was established, not least because "the policy of disappearances, supported or tolerated by the Government, is designed to conceal and destroy evidence of disappearances. *Id.* at ¶ 124. Because the government enjoyed a monopoly over the evidence in such cases, the Court shifted the burden to the government once the claimant made out a *prima facie* case.

In *Immigration and Naturalization Service v. Cardoza-Fonseca*, 480 U.S. 421 (1987), the Supreme Court addressed the Refugee Act of 1980, which established a statutory basis for the granting of asylum in the United States in accordance with international refugee law. For the definition of "refugee" Congress had turned explicitly to the 1951 Convention relating to the Status of Refugees and its 1967 Protocol, to which the United States was a party. At issue in *Cardoza-Fonseca* was the meaning of the term "well-founded fear of persecution," which is used to define "refugee" in the 1951 Convention. The specific question in *Cardoza-Fonseca* was what burden of proof this international definition implied: what must the asylum applicant prove to acquire refugee status under United States law? The government interpreted the "well-founded fear" criterion to require a showing by each individual applicant that persecution was more likely than not. Under this clear probability standard, an individual's fear could be "well-founded" only if the chances for persecution were better than even or amounted to a "realistic likelihood." The Court rejected the government's strict standard, concluding that the international term of art, "well-founded fear of persecution," excuses an asylum applicant from proving that the chances of persecution are more likely than not. The Court evidently concluded that a fear can be well-founded long before the feared event becomes likely: a member of an indigenous group, ten percent of whose members were routinely rounded up and shot, would presumably have a well-founded fear of prosecution, even though the numerical odds of death were "only" one in ten.

From these cases, what general principles can you extract about (a) the proper level of allowable doubt expressed in a burden of proof—*e.g.*, beyond a reasonable doubt, more likely than not, substantial evidence, "well-founded"—and (b) the distribution of the burden of persuasion to one party or another?

2. *Distinguishing types of burdens.* On the strength of the analysis in *Greenwich Collieries*, how would you articulate the difference in theory and in practice between the burden of production and the burden of persuasion? What distinguishes one from the other according to the Court? How does the seemingly abstract distinction between these burdens ground Justice Ginsburg's dissent in *Schaffer v. Weast*?

3. *Judicial solutions to legislative problems.* The allocation of the burden of proof has a substantive effect on the outcome of the litigation. Shouldn't this be a legislative instead of a judicial judgment?

C. PRESUMPTIONS

The law commonly operates through presumptions, *i.e.*, default assumptions about the law or inferences of fact that—when probed—reveal key principles within the legal culture and the hierarchies among those principles. There is for example a presumption at law that federal statutes are constitutional, but the presumption is said to be rebuttable, because in certain, rare circumstances, the statute will be found to be unconstitutional. Similarly, the decisions of administrative agencies are sometimes said to be entitled to a presumption of validity or regularity, which translates into imposing the burden of proving illegality on those challenging the agency's action. Yet another example is the presumption that federal legislation applies only within the territory of the United States, although Congress can explicitly extend its legislative reach abroad, and the courts of the United States will then have to apply the statute extraterritorially.

To these presumptions about the validity or interpretation of statutes we must add a variety of presumptions that infer one legally-significant *fact* from the proof of another. "When one or more things are proved, from which our experience enables us to ascertain that another, not proved, must have happened, we presume that it did happen, as well in criminal as in civil cases." *King v. Burdett*, 1 St. Tr. (N. S.) 111 (1820). Consider, for example, the following statute dealing with the termination of veterans benefits:

> (b) If evidence satisfactory to the Secretary [of Veterans Affairs] is submitted establishing the continued and unexplained absence of any individual from that individual's home and family for seven or more years, and establishing that after diligent search no evidence of that individual's existence after the date of disappearance has been found or received, the death of such individual as of the date of the expiration of such period shall be considered as sufficiently proved.

38 U.S.C. § 108. From certain facts—including an unexplained absence and the passage of seven years—the legally-significant fact of death can be presumed.

In addition to the distinction between presumptions at law and presumptions in fact, the law considers some presumptions conclusive or irrebuttable. The genetic marker of such presumptions is that they cannot be overcome by producing more evidence or argument (*e.g.*, that children under the age of seven are incapable of committing felonies). The absolutism of conclusive presumptions makes them indistinguishable in operation from rules of substantive law. For example, if suspects in police custody make incriminating statements without first receiving notice of their *Miranda* rights to remain silent and to receive the assistance of counsel, their answers are conclusively presumed to be compelled, and as a consequence those answers must be excluded from evidence in the prosecution's case-in-chief at trial. *Oregon v. Elstad*, 470 U.S. 298, 317 (1985). Similarly, an indictment by a federal grand jury is entitled to an irrebuttable presumption that the charges are supported by probable cause. *United States v. Williams*, 504 U.S. 36 (1992). *See also* Niki Kuckes, *The Useful, Dangerous Fiction of Grand Jury Independence*, 41 AM. CRIM. L. REV. 1, 14–15 (2004).

Rebuttable presumptions by contrast operate like burdens of proof. In family law, for example, if a woman is married when she gives birth to a child, there is a rebuttable presumption that her husband is the child's father. The presumption stands as a legal fact unless the challenger can prove by a preponderance of the evidence that it is incorrect. In criminal cases, the presumption of innocence is certainly rebuttable, but it can be overcome only by satisfying the highest burden of proof in the law, namely "beyond a reasonable doubt." Here too the contours and justification of a presumption can be discerned if we first see with a clear eye what it is supposed to do and why it tilts the plane of argument in a particular direction.

VLANDIS V. KLINE

412 U.S. 441 (1973)

MR. JUSTICE STEWART delivered the opinion of the Court. Like many other States, Connecticut requires nonresidents of the State who are enrolled in the state university system to pay tuition and other fees at higher rates than residents of the State who are so enrolled. The constitutional validity of that requirement is not at issue in the case before us. What is at issue here is Connecticut's statutory definition of residents and nonresidents for purposes of the above provision.

Section 126(a)(2) of Public Act No. 5 * * * provides that an unmarried student shall be classified as a nonresident, or "out of state," student if his "legal address for any part of the one-year period immediately prior to his application for admission at a constituent unit of the state system of higher education was outside of Connecticut." With respect to married students, § 126(a)(3) of the Act provides that such a student, if living with his spouse, shall be classified as "out of state" if his "legal address at the time of his application for admission to such a unit was outside of Connecticut." These classifications are permanent and irrebuttable for the whole time that the student remains at the university since § 126(a)(5) of the Act commands that: "The status of a student, as established at the time of his application for admission at a constituent unit of the state system of higher education under the provisions of this section, shall be his status for the entire period of his attendance at such constituent unit." The present case concerns the constitutional validity of this conclusive and unchangeable presumption of nonresident status from the fact that, at the time of application for admission, the student, if married, was then living outside of Connecticut, or, if single, had lived outside the State at some point during the preceding year.

One appellee, Margaret Marsh Kline, is an undergraduate student at the University of Connecticut. In May of 1971, while attending college in California, she became engaged to Peter Kline, a lifelong Connecticut resident. Because the Klines wished to reside in Connecticut after their marriage, Mrs. Kline applied to the University of Connecticut from California. In late May, she was accepted and informed by the University that she would be considered an in-state student. On June 26, 1971, the appellee and Peter Kline were married in California, and soon thereafter took up residence in Storrs, Connecticut, where they have established a permanent home. Mrs. Kline has a Connecticut driver's license, her car is registered in Connecticut, and she is registered as a Connecticut voter. In July 1971, Public Act No. 5 went into effect. Accordingly, the appellant, Director of Admissions at the University of Connecticut, irreversibly classified Mrs. Kline as an out-of-state student, pursuant to § 126(a)(3) of that Act. As a consequence, she was required to pay $150 tuition and a $200 nonresident fee for the first semester, whereas a student classified as a Connecticut resident paid no tuition; and upon registration for the second semester, she was required to pay $425 tuition plus another $200 nonresident fee, while a student classified as a Connecticut resident paid only $175 tuition.

* * * Appellees [ ] brought suit in the District Court pursuant to the Civil Rights Act of 1871, 42 U.S.C. § 1983, contending that they were *bona fide* residents of Connecticut, and that § 126 [ ], under which they were classified as nonresidents for purposes of their tuition and fees, infringed their rights to due process of law and equal protection of the laws, guaranteed by the Fourteenth Amendment to the Constitution. * * *

The appellees do not challenge [ ] the option of the State to classify students as resident and nonresident students, thereby obligating nonresident students to pay higher tuition and fees than do bona fide residents. The State's right to make such a classification is unquestioned here. Rather, the appellees attack Connecticut's irreversible and irrebuttable statutory presumption that because a student's legal address was outside the State at the time of his application for admission or at some point during the preceding year, he remains a non-resident for as long as he is a student there. This conclusive presumption, they say, is invalid in that it allows the State to classify as "out-of-state students" those who are, in fact, bona fide residents of the State. The appellees claim that they have a constitutional right to controvert that presumption of non-residence by presenting evidence that they are bona fide residents of Connecticut. The District Court agreed: "Assuming that it is permissible for the state to impose a heavier burden of tuition and fees on non-resident than on resident students, the state may not classify as 'out of state students' those who do not belong in that class." We affirm the judgment of the District Court.

Statutes creating permanent irrebuttable presumptions have long been disfavored under the Due Process Clauses of the Fifth and Fourteenth Amendments. In *Heiner v. Donnan*, 285 U.S. 312 (1932), the Court was faced with a constitutional challenge to a federal statute that created a conclusive presumption that gifts made within two years prior to the donor's death were made in contemplation of death, thus requiring payment by his estate of a higher tax. In holding that this irrefutable assumption was so arbitrary and unreasonable as to deprive the taxpayer of his property without due process of law, the Court stated that it had "held more than once that a statute creating a presumption which operates to deny a fair opportunity to rebut it violates the due process clause of the Fourteenth Amendment."

The more recent case of *Bell v. Burson*, 402 U.S. 535 90 (1971), involved a Georgia statute which provided that if an uninsured motorist was involved in an accident and could not post security for the amount of damages claimed, his driver's license must be suspended without any hearing on the question of fault or responsibility. The Court held that since the State purported to be concerned with fault in suspending a driver's license, it could not, consistent with procedural due process, conclusively presume fault from the fact that the uninsured motorist was involved in an accident, and could not, therefore, suspend his driver's license without a hearing on that crucial factor.

Likewise, in *Stanley v. Illinois*, 405 U.S. 645 (1972), the Court struck down, as violative of the Due Process Clause of the Fourteenth Amendment, Illinois' irrebuttable statutory presumption that all unmarried fathers are unqualified to raise their children. Because of that presumption, the statute required the State, upon the death of the mother, to take custody of all such illegitimate children, without providing any hearing on the father's parental fitness. It may be, the Court said, "that most unmarried fathers are unsuitable and neglectful parents. * * * But all unmarried fathers are not in this category; some are wholly suited to have custody of their children." Hence, the Court held that the State could not conclusively presume that any individual unmarried father was unfit to raise his children; rather, it was required by the Due Process Clause to provide a hearing on that issue. According to the Court, Illinois "insists on presuming rather than proving Stanley's unfitness solely because it is more convenient to presume than to prove. Under the Due Process Clause that advantage is insufficient to justify refusing a father a hearing . . . ."

The same considerations obtain here. It may be that most applicants to Connecticut's university system who apply from outside the State or within a year of living out of State have no real intention of becoming Connecticut residents and will never do so. But it is clear that not all of the applicants from out of State inevitably fall in this category. Indeed, in the present case, both appellees possess many of the indicia of Connecticut residency, such as year-round Connecticut homes, Connecticut drivers' licenses, car registrations, voter registrations, etc.; and both were found by the District Court to have become bona fide residents of Connecticut before the 1972 spring semester. Yet, under the State's statutory scheme, neither was permitted any opportunity to demonstrate the bona fides of her Connecticut residency for tuition purposes, and neither will ever have such an opportunity in the future so long as she remains a student.

The State proffers three reasons to justify that permanent irrebuttable presumption. The first is that the State has a valid interest in equalizing the cost of public higher education between Connecticut residents and nonresidents, and that by freezing a student's residential status as of the time he applies, the State ensures that its bona fide in-state students will receive their full subsidy. The State's objective of cost equalization between bona fide residents and nonresidents may well be legitimate, but basing the bona fides of residency solely on where a student lived when he applied for admission to the University is using a criterion wholly unrelated to that objective. As is evident from the situation of the appellees, a student may be a bona fide resident of Connecticut even though he applied to the University from out of State. Thus, Connecticut's conclusive presumption of non-residence, instead of ensuring that only its bona fide residents receive their full subsidy, ensures that certain of its *bona fide* residents, such as the appellees, do not receive their full subsidy, and can never do so while they remain students.

Second, the State argues that even if a student who applied to the University from out of State may at some point become a bona fide resident of Connecticut, the State can nonetheless reasonably decide to favor with the lower rates only its established residents, whose past tax contributions to the State have been higher. According to the State, the fact that established residents or their parents have supported the State in the past justifies the conclusion that applicants from out of State—who are presumed not to be such established residents—may be denied the lower rates, even if they have become *bona fide* residents.

Connecticut's statutory scheme, however, makes no distinction on its face between established residents and new residents. Rather, through § 122, the State purports to distinguish, for tuition purposes, between residents and nonresidents by granting the lower rates to the former and denying them to the latter. In these circumstances, the State cannot now seek to justify its classification of certain bona fide residents as nonresidents, on the basis that their Connecticut residency is "new."

Moreover, § 126 would not always operate to effectuate the State's asserted interest. For it is not at all clear that the conclusive presumption required by that section prevents only "new" residents, rather than "established" residents, from obtaining the lower tuition rates. For example, a student whose parents were life-long residents of Connecticut, but who went to college at Harvard, established a legal address there, and applied to the University of Connecticut's graduate school during his senior year, would be permanently classified as an "out of state student," despite his family's status as "established" residents of Connecticut. * * * Thus, even in terms of the State's own asserted interest in favoring established residents over new residents, the provisions of § 126 are so arbitrary as to constitute a denial of due process of law.

The third ground advanced to justify § 126 is that it provides a degree of administrative certainty. The State points to its interest in preventing out-of-state students from coming to Connecticut solely to obtain an education and then claiming Connecticut residence in order to secure the lower tuition and fees. The irrebuttable presumption, the State contends, makes it easier to separate out students who come to the State solely for its educational facilities from true Connecticut residents, by eliminating the need for an individual determination of the bona fides of a person who lived out of State at the time of his application. Such an individual determination, it is said, would not only be an expensive administrative burden, but would also be very difficult to make, since it is hard to evaluate when bona fide residency exists. Without the conclusive presumption, the State argues, it would be almost impossible to prevent out-of-state students from claiming a Connecticut residence merely to obtain the lower rates.

In *Stanley v. Illinois*, *supra*, however, the Court stated that "the Constitution recognizes higher values than speed and efficiency." The State's interest in administrative ease and certainty cannot, in and of itself, save the conclusive presumption from invalidity under the Due Process Clause where there are other reasonable and practicable means of establishing the pertinent facts on which the State's objective is premised. In the situation before us, reasonable alternative means for determining bona fide residence are available. Indeed, one such method has already been adopted by Connecticut; after § 126 was invalidated by the District Court, the State established reasonable criteria for evaluating bona fide residence for purposes of tuition and fees at its university system. These criteria, while perhaps more burdensome to apply than an irrebuttable presumption, are certainly sufficient to prevent abuse of the lower, in-state rates by students who come to Connecticut solely to obtain an education.

In sum, since Connecticut purports to be concerned with residency in allocating the rates for tuition and fees in its university system, it is forbidden by the Due Process Clause to deny an individual the resident rates on the basis of a permanent and irrebuttable presumption of non-residence, when that presumption is not necessarily or universally true, in fact, and when the State has reasonable alternative means of making the crucial determination. Rather, standards of due process require that the State allow such an individual the opportunity to present evidence showing that he is a bona fide resident entitled to the in-state rates. Since § 126 precluded the appellees from ever rebutting the presumption that they were nonresidents of Connecticut, that statute operated to deprive them of a significant amount of their money without due process of law.

We are aware, of course, of the special problems involved in determining the bona fide residence of college students who come from out of State to attend that State's public university. Our holding today should in no wise be taken to mean that Connecticut must classify the students in its university system as residents, for purposes of tuition and fees, just because they go to school there. Nor should our decision be construed to deny a State the right to impose on a student, as one element in demonstrating bona fide residence, a reasonable durational residency requirement, which can be met while in student status. We fully recognize that a State has a legitimate interest in protecting and preserving the quality of its colleges and universities and the right of its own bona fide residents to attend such institutions on a preferential tuition basis.

We hold only that a permanent irrebuttable presumption of non-residence—the means adopted by Connecticut to preserve that legitimate interest—is violative of the Due Process Clause, because it provides no opportunity for students who applied from out of State to demonstrate that they have become bona fide Connecticut residents. The State can establish such reasonable criteria for in-state status as to make virtually certain that students who are not, in fact, bona fide residents of the State, but who have come there solely for educational purposes, cannot take advantage of the in-state rates. * * * Because we hold that the permanent irrebuttable presumption of non-residence created by [the Connecticut statute] violates the Due Process Clause of the Fourteenth Amendment, the judgment of the District Court is affirmed.

SHAW V. MURPHY

532 U.S. 223 (2001)

JUSTICE THOMAS delivered the opinion of the Court. Under our decision in *Turner v. Safley,* 482 U.S. 78 (1987), restrictions on prisoners' communications to other inmates are constitutional if the restrictions are "reasonably related to legitimate penological interests." *Id.* at 89. In this case, we are asked to decide whether prisoners possess a First Amendment right to provide legal assistance that enhances the protections otherwise available under *Turner*. We hold that they do not.

I

While respondent Kevin Murphy was incarcerated at the Montana State Prison, he served as an "inmate law clerk," providing legal assistance to fellow prisoners. Upon learning that inmate Pat Tracy had been charged with assaulting Correctional Officer Glen Galle, Murphy decided to assist Tracy with his defense. Prison rules prohibited Murphy's assignment to the case, but he nonetheless investigated the assault. After discovering that other inmates had complained about Officer Galle's conduct, Murphy sent Tracy a letter, which included the following:

> "I do want to help you with your case against Galle. It wasn't your fault and I know he provoked whatever happened! Don't plead guilty because we can get at least 100 witnesses to testify that Galle is an over zealous guard who has a personal agenda to punish and harrass *[sic]* inmates. He has made homo-sexual *[sic]* advances towards certain inmates and that can be brought up into the record. There are petitions against him and I have tried to get the Unit Manager to do something about what he does in Close II, but all that happened is that I received two writeups from him myself as retaliation. So we must pursue this out of the prison system. I am filing a suit with everyone in Close I and II named against him. So you can use that too!
>
> Another poiont *[sic]* is that he grabbed you from behind. You tell your lawyer to get ahold of me on this. Don't take a plea bargain unless it's for no more time."

In accordance with prison policy, prison officials intercepted the letter, and petitioner Robert Shaw, an officer in the maximum-security unit, reviewed it. Based on the accusations against Officer Galle, Shaw cited Murphy for violations of the prison's rules prohibiting insolence, interference with due process hearings, and conduct that disrupts or interferes with the security and orderly operation of the institution. After a hearing, Murphy was found guilty of violating the first two prohibitions. The hearings officer sanctioned him by imposing a suspended sentence of 10 days' detention and issuing demerits that could affect his custody level.

In response, Murphy brought this action, seeking declaratory and injunctive relief under 42 U.S.C. § 1983. The case was styled as a class action, brought on behalf of himself, other inmate law clerks, and other prisoners. The complaint alleged that the disciplining of Murphy violated due process, the rights of inmates to access the courts, and, as relevant here, Murphy's First Amendment rights, including the right to provide legal assistance to other inmates.

After discovery, the District Court granted petitioners' motion for summary judgment on all of Murphy's claims. * * * The Court of Appeals for the Ninth Circuit reversed. It premised its analysis on the proposition that "inmates have a First Amendment right to assist other inmates with their legal claims." Murphy enjoyed this right of association, the court concluded, because he was providing legal advice that potentially was relevant to Tracy's defense. The Court of Appeals then applied our decision in *Turner,* but it did so only against the backdrop of this First Amendment right, which, the court held, affected the balance of the prisoner's interests against the government's interests. Concluding that the balance tipped in favor of Murphy, the Court of Appeals upheld Murphy's First Amendment claim.

Other Courts of Appeals have rejected similar claims. [ ] To resolve the conflict, we granted *certiorari.*

II

In this case, we are not asked to decide whether prisoners have *any* First Amendment rights when they send legal correspondence to one another. In *Turner,* we held that restrictions on inmate-to-inmate communications pass constitutional muster only if the restrictions are reasonably related to legitimate and neutral governmental objectives. We did not limit our holding to nonlegal correspondence, and petitioners do not ask us to construe it that way. Instead, the question presented here simply asks whether Murphy possesses a First Amendment right to provide legal advice that enhances the protections otherwise available under *Turner.* The effect of such a right, as the Court of Appeals described it, would be that inmate-to-inmate correspondence that includes legal assistance would receive more First Amendment protection than correspondence without any legal assistance. We conclude that there is no such special right.

Traditionally, federal courts did not intervene in the internal affairs of prisons and instead "adopted a broad hands-off attitude toward problems of prison administration." *Procunier v. Martinez,* 416 U.S. 396, 404 (1974). Indeed, for much of this country's history, the prevailing view was that a prisoner was a mere "slave of the State," who "not only forfeited his liberty, but all his personal rights except those which the law in its humanity accords him." *Jones v. North Carolina Prisoners' Labor Union, Inc.*, 433 U.S. 119, 139 (1977) (Marshall, J., dissenting) (quoting *Ruffin v. Commonwealth*, 62 Va. 790, 796 (1871)). In recent decades, however, this Court has determined that incarceration does not divest prisoners of all constitutional protections. Inmates retain, for example, the right to be free from racial discrimination, *Lee v. Washington,* 390 U.S. 333 (1968) *(per curiam),* the right to due process, *Wolff v. McDonnell,* 418 U.S. 539 (1974), and, as relevant here, certain protections of the First Amendment, *Turner, supra.*

We nonetheless have maintained that the constitutional rights that prisoners possess are more limited in scope than the constitutional rights held by individuals in society at large. In the First Amendment context, for instance, some rights are simply inconsistent with the status of a prisoner or "with the legitimate penological objectives of the corrections system," *Pell v. Procunier*, 417 U.S. 817, 822 (1974). We have thus sustained proscriptions of media interviews with individual inmates, prohibitions on the activities of a prisoners' labor union, and restrictions on inmate-to-inmate written correspondence. Moreover, because the "problems of prisons in America are complex and intractable," and because courts are particularly "ill equipped" to deal with these problems, *Martinez, supra*, at 404–405, we generally have deferred to the judgments of prison officials in upholding these regulations against constitutional challenge.

Reflecting this understanding, in *Turner* we adopted a unitary, deferential standard for reviewing prisoners' constitutional claims: "[W]hen a prison regulation impinges on inmates' constitutional rights, the regulation is valid if it is reasonably related to legitimate penological interests." Under this standard, four factors are relevant. First and foremost, "there must be a 'valid, rational connection' between the prison regulation and the legitimate [and neutral] governmental interest put forward to justify it." If the connection between the regulation and the asserted goal is "arbitrary or irrational," then the regulation fails, irrespective of whether the other factors tilt in its favor. In addition, courts should consider three other factors: the existence of "alternative means of exercising the right" available to inmates; "the impact accommodation of the asserted constitutional right will have on guards and other inmates, and on the allocation of prison resources generally"; and "the absence of ready alternatives" available to the prison for achieving the governmental objectives.

Because *Turner* provides the test for evaluating prisoners' First Amendment challenges, the issue before us is whether *Turner* permits an increase in constitutional protection whenever a prisoner's communication includes legal advice. We conclude that it does not. To increase the constitutional protection based upon the content of a communication first requires an assessment of the value of that content. But the *Turner* test, by its terms, simply does not accommodate valuations of content. On the contrary, the *Turner* factors concern only the relationship between the asserted penological interests and the prison regulation.

Moreover, under *Turner* and its predecessors, prison officials are to remain the primary arbiters of the problems that arise in prison management. * * * If courts were permitted to enhance constitutional protection based on their assessments of the content of the particular communications, courts would be in a position to assume a greater role in decisions affecting prison administration. Seeking to avoid " 'unnecessarily perpetuat[ing] the involvement of the federal courts in affairs of prison administration,' " *Turner*, 482 U.S., at 89 (quoting *Martinez*, *supra*, at 407), we reject an alteration of the *Turner* analysis that would entail additional federal-court oversight.

Finally, even if we were to consider giving special protection to particular kinds of speech based upon content, we would not do so for speech that includes legal advice. Augmenting First Amendment protection for inmate legal advice would undermine prison officials' ability to address the "complex and intractable" problems of prison administration. *Turner*, *supra*, at 84, 107 S.Ct. 2254. Although supervised inmate legal assistance programs may serve valuable ends, it is "indisputable" that inmate law clerks "are sometimes a menace to prison discipline" and that prisoners have an "acknowledged propensity . . . to abuse both the giving and the seeking of [legal] assistance." *Johnson v. Avery*, 393 U.S. 483, 488, 490 (1969). Prisoners have used legal correspondence as a means for passing contraband and communicating instructions on how to manufacture drugs or weapons. See Brief for State of Florida et al. as *Amici Curiae* 6–8; see also *Turner*, *supra*, at 93 ("[P]risoners could easily write in jargon or codes to prevent detection of their real messages"). The legal text also could be an excuse for making clearly inappropriate comments, which "may be expected to circulate among prisoners," *Thornburgh v. Abbott*, 490 U.S. 401, 412 (1989), despite prison measures to screen individual inmates or officers from the remarks.

We thus decline to cloak the provision of legal assistance with any First Amendment protection above and beyond the protection normally accorded prisoners' speech. Instead, the proper constitutional test is the one we set forth in *Turner*. Irrespective of whether the correspondence contains legal advice, the constitutional analysis is the same.

III

Under *Turner,* the question remains whether the prison regulations, as applied to Murphy, are "reasonably related to legitimate penological interests." To prevail, Murphy must overcome the presumption that the prison officials acted within their "broad discretion." Petitioners ask us to answer, rather than remand, the question whether Murphy has satisfied this heavy burden. We decline petitioners' request, however, because we granted certiorari only to decide whether inmates possess a special First Amendment right to provide legal assistance to fellow inmates.

NOTES AND QUESTIONS

1. *Understanding Vlandis*. Why exactly did the conclusive presumption in *Vlandis* violate the Due Process Clause of the Constitution? Would making the presumption in that case rebuttable instead of conclusive have made a difference in the result?

2. *Understanding Shaw*. What is the presumption at work in *Shaw*, and what interests does it serve? If you were in a legislature considering the adoption of a *statutory* presumption of agency regularity, what would be the best arguments for and against such an enactment?

3. *Presumptions on matters of fact*. One category of rebuttable presumption allows the inference of a fact by default: in effect, the trier of fact must find the existence of the presumed fact unless evidence is introduced supporting the finding of its nonexistence. Conceived this way, presumptions are typically conceived as a part of the law of evidence, because they allow the inference of a legally-relevant fact from the existence of some other fact. For example, in many jurisdictions, by operation of statute or common law, a man is presumed to be the father of a child if—among other possibilities—he is married to the mother of the child and the child is born during the marriage. The presumption can be overcome by the introduction of evidence showing that someone else is the father, but from the combined facts of marriage and birth during the marriage, the fact of paternity is presumed.

But viewing presumptions as "facts-by-default" misses the role they play as routinized forms of legal reasoning that are at work even before any evidence is brought to bear in a case, indeed that structure the kinds of evidence that is gathered in the first place and then introduced. Over a century ago, James Bradley Thayer wrote that "[p]resumptions are aids to reasoning and argumentation, which assume the truth of certain matters for the purpose of some given inquiry. They may be grounded on general experience, or probability of any kind; or merely on policy and convenience. On whatever basis they rest, *they operate in advance of argument or evidence*, or irrespective of it, by taking something for granted, assuming its existence." JAMES BRADLEY THAYER, A PRELIMINARY TREATISE ON EVIDENCE AT THE COMMON LAW 314 (1898) (emphasis added).

For example, back in the days when people wrote letters to one another on paper and then mailed them in an envelope with a stamp on it, the law embraced a presumption in the form of a default inference of fact that reflected considerable faith in the postal service:

> if a letter properly directed is proved to have been either put into the post office or delivered to the postman, it is presumed, from the known course of business in the post office department, that it reached its destination at the regular time, and was received by the person to whom it was addressed. As was said by Gray, J., "the presumption so arising is not a conclusive presumption of law, but a mere inference of fact founded on the probability that the officers of the government will do their duty and the usual course of business, and when it is opposed by evidence that the letters never were received, must be weighed with all the other circumstances of the case, by the jury in determining the question whether the letters were actually received or not." The presumption that a letter was received is based on such considerations that it is perfectly clear that it applies without regard to the contents of the letter."

Rosenthal v. Walker, 111 U.S. 185, 193–94 (1884) (citations omitted).

Notice that the presumption of mailing defined the field for advocacy in a case, in effect specifying the kinds of evidence and argument that the lawyers had to submit at trial in order to represent their clients successfully. Note specifically which party bore *the risk of non-persuasion* under the presumption. Notice also that the presumption reflected a faith in processes or services completely outside the courtroom. Do you have a similar conviction about the reliability of current technologies for written communication (chat, twitter, texting, e-mail *etc.*)? How would you articulate a new presumption covering such communications?

4. *Presumptions on matters of law.* Presumptions can also structure arguments about pure issues of law, having nothing to do with preferred inferences of fact. Perhaps the most powerful of these is the presumption of constitutionality: (a) a statute is presumed constitutional and (b) cannot be invalidated on constitutional grounds if a constitutional interpretation of the statute is possible. *See, e.g., Hooper v. California*, 155 U.S. 648, 657 (1895) ("The elementary rule is that every reasonable construction must be resorted to, in order to save a statute from unconstitutionality.") *See also Boos v. Barry*, 485 U.S. 312, 330–1 (1988); *Schneider v. Smith*, 390 U.S. 17, 26 (1968). When no "saving construction" is possible, the statute will be struck down. What interests are served by each part of this presumption?

Even if the statute is constitutional, presumptions can guide its interpretation and application. For example, the Supreme Court has long adopted a presumption against the extraterritorial application of U.S. law, rejecting the projection of substantive U.S. regulation into foreign territories and holding that U.S. standards could not govern foreign conduct by foreigners in the absence of a clear congressional directive to the contrary. *See, e.g., Morrison v. National Australia Bank Ltd.* 561 U.S. 247 (2010) (securities regulation); *EEOC v. Arabian Am. Oil Co.*, 499 U.S. 244 (1991) (antidiscrimination law); *F. Hoffmann-La Roche Ltd. v. Empagran S.A.*, 542 U.S. 155 (2004) (antitrust); *Foley Bros. Inc. v. Filardo*, 336 U.S. 281 (1949) (labor law). In other words, the presumption against extraterritoriality is rebuttable: Congress can extend the regulatory reach of U.S. law abroad so long as it makes that intention clear in the statute itself.

There is also a presumption that Congress legislates in conformity with the international obligations of the United States, *unless a contrary intent is unmistakably indicated*. Thus, ambiguous federal statutes will be construed by the courts to conform to the United States' treaty obligations and to the binding but unwritten principles of customary international law. *See* Chapter 14. In the field of refugee law, for example, the Supreme Court conformed US practice to international standards of refugee eligibility in *INS v. Cardoza-Fonseca*, *supra*, interpreting the 1980 Refugee Act in light of the UNHCR HANDBOOK ON PROCEDURES AND CRITERIA FOR DETERMINING REFUGEE STATUS, which, though not binding, offered "significant guidance" to the court.

Notice that each of these presumptions is rebuttable, but only the latter two can be overcome by clear statements in the legislation itself.

5. *One relationship between presumptions and burdens in civil cases.* Federal Rule of Evidence 301, captioned "Presumptions in Civil Actions Generally," provides that

> In a civil case, unless a federal statute or these rules provide otherwise, the party against whom a presumption is directed has the burden of producing evidence to rebut the presumption. But this rule does not shift the burden of persuasion, which remains on the party who had it originally.

Under this provision, the burden of *production* shifts to the party opposing some presumed fact, but the burden of *persuasion* on the presumed facts is unchanged.

To see this rule in operation, consider *Texas Dept. of Community Affairs v. Burdine*, 450 U.S. 248 (1981). In that case, Burdine sued the state Texas Department of Community Affairs (TDCA) under Title VII of the Civil Rights Act of 1964, 42 U.S.C. § 2000e *et seq.*, alleging that she had been terminated from her job at TDCA because of her sex. She had established the *prima facie* case of gender discrimination—meaning that she had alleged sufficient facts to satisfy the elements of the statutory claim if those facts were not rebutted and no affirmative defenses were sustained. "Establishment of the *prima facie* case in effect creates a presumption that the employer unlawfully discriminated against the employee. If the trier of fact believes the plaintiff's evidence, and if the employer is *silent* in the face of the presumption, the court must enter judgment for the plaintiff because no issue of fact remains in the case." *Id.* at 254.

The question presented in the case was "whether, after the plaintiff has proved a *prima facie* case of discriminatory treatment, the burden shifts to the defendant to persuade the court by a preponderance of the evidence that legitimate, nondiscriminatory reasons for the challenged employment action existed." *Id.* at 249–50. The Supreme Court ruled that it did not: the burden of *production* shifted to the employer once the employee made out the *prima facie* case of discrimination, but the ultimate burden of proving discrimination remained with the plaintiff.

6. *One relationship between presumptions and burdens in criminal cases.* The relationship between presumptions and burdens is perhaps easier to see in criminal cases, where the presumption of the defendant's innocence is so powerful that the prosecution bears the heaviest burden of persuasion in U.S. law, that of proving guilt on every element of the offense beyond a reasonable doubt. *In re Winship*, 397 U.S. 358, 364 (1970) ("[T]he Due Process Clause protects the accused against conviction except upon proof beyond a reasonable doubt of every fact necessary to constitute the crime with which he is charged.").

In federal courts, the pattern jury instructions on reasonable doubt read as follows:

> The indictment or formal charge against a Defendant isn't evidence of guilt. The law presumes every Defendant is innocent. The Defendant does not have to prove his innocence or produce any evidence at all. The Government must prove guilt beyond a reasonable doubt. If it fails to do so, you must find the Defendant not guilty. The Government's burden of proof is heavy, but it doesn't have to prove a Defendant's guilt beyond all possible doubt. The Government's proof only has to exclude any reasonable doubt concerning the Defendant's guilt. A "reasonable doubt" is a real doubt based on your reason and common sense after you've carefully and impartially considered all the evidence in the case. "Proof beyond a reasonable doubt" is proof so convincing that you would be willing to rely and act on it without hesitation in the most important of your own affairs. If you are convinced that the Defendant has been proved guilty beyond a reasonable doubt, say so. If you are not convinced, say so.

United States v. Williams, 2017 WL 1208417, at *12 (11th Cir. Apr. 3, 2017). What is the best rationale for deliberately refusing to explain "reasonable doubt" with any greater precision than this?

7. *Presumptions and fictions.* Looking back over the various presumptions explored in this chapter, is every legal presumption based on some legal fiction?

CHAPTER TWELVE

STRUCTURES OF LEGAL ARGUMENT (III): STATUTORY AUTHORITY AND LEGISPRUDENCE

■ ■ ■

"[A]lmost all the perplexed questions, almost all the niceties, intricacies, and delays, (which have sometimes disgraced the English, as well as other courts of justice,) owe their original [*sic*] not to the common law itself, but to innovations that have been made in it by acts of parliament."

— William Blackstone

"Laws, like sausages, cease to inspire respect in proportion as we know how they are made."

— John Godfrey Saxe

"Comparing law-making to sausage-making is offensive to sausage-makers."

— Peter Suderman

Orientation

After an "orgy of statute-making" in the twentieth century,[1] legislation displaced the common law as the dominant form of law in the United States, inverting a pattern that had prevailed since the beginning of the republic. That systemic preference for statutes is in part the result of a perceived "democratic deficit:" the judges, who make common law, are rarely good symbols of representative democracy. They are either unelected or generally obliged to follow the law rather than majority will. And the common law by definition doesn't undergo—let alone survive—the political ordeal laid out in Article I of the Constitution for creating law. The *practical* consequence of the metaphorical orgy is that there is now virtually no area of law that is not affected, if not "controlled," by legislation. Contemporary legal practice is overwhelmingly centered on statutes and the canons of construction used for interpreting them. The *theoretical* consequence is that the art and discipline of interpretation—

---

1 GUIDO CALABRESI, THE COMMON LAW IN THE AGE OF STATUTES 1 (1982).

hermeneutics—have been mainstreamed in contemporary jurisprudence and political theory.

Statutes are sometimes thought to be the antidote to common law doctrines that are insufficiently definite or in excessive flux. The stereotype is that legislation offers coherence and uniformity, while the common law is in a state of near-constant improvisation. The materials in this chapter invite you to challenge that stereotype and to construct the most persuasive way not only of applying and interpreting statutes in practice but also conceptualizing legislation as a theoretical matter, especially the respective roles of the courts and the legislature in a democracy.

The starting point must be that the literal, "plain" or "clear and unambiguous" terms of the statute govern its interpretation, without resorting to other evidence of intent or meaning. "If the statutory language is plain, we must enforce it according to its terms." *King v. Burwell*, 576 U.S. ___, ___, 135 S. Ct. 2480 (2015) (*citing Hardt v. Reliance Standard Life Ins. Co.*, 560 U.S. 242, 251 (2010)). Literalism is the preferred technique in interpreting a statute, because, by convention that best serves the separation of powers, especially the courts' duty of fidelity to the will of the legislature in cases where there is no Constitutional problem. The best evidence of legislative intent is the actual language of the statute, and that trumps whatever the court thinks may have been the legislators' intent. In Justice Holmes' memorable words, "I don't care what their intention was. I only want to know what the words meant."

The essential problem lies not with this literalist impulse in principle but its application in fact. After all, "whether . . . the words of a statute are clear is itself not always clear." *U.S. v. Bonanno Organized Crime Family of La Cosa Nostra*, 879 F.2d 20 (2nd Cir. 1989). What is the proper protocol for identifying ambiguities and then resolving them? It may be useful to conceive of legislation not as inert, finished products awaiting elaboration by the courts, but as a "station" in an on-going conversation between judges and legislators. The legislation is adopted, the courts interpret it, the legislators respond to the court's interpretation with amendatory legislation, the courts interpret that, and the cycle continues. Justice Antonin Scalia offered some ancient examples:

> [T]he statute 1 Edw. VI. c. 12. having enacted that those who are convicted of stealing horses should not have the benefit of clergy, the judges conceived that this did not extend to him that should steal but one horse, and therefore procured a new act for that purpose in the following year. And, to come nearer our own times, by the statute 14 Geo. II. c. 6. stealing sheep, *or other cattle*, was made felony without benefit of clergy. But these general words, "or other cattle," being looked upon as much too loose to create a capital offence, the act was held to extend to nothing but mere sheep. And therefore, in the next sessions, it was found necessary

to make another statute, 15 Geo. II. c. 34. extending the former to bulls, cows, oxen, steers, bullocks, heifers, calves, and lambs by name.

Antonin Scalia, *Assorted Canards of Contemporary Legal Analysis*, 40 CASE W. RES. L. REV. 581 (1990). Others have found it useful to analogize legislation to other texts that require interpretation—literature, lyrics, and sacred texts for example—and for that reason have turned to other disciplines for insights. One intriguing framework for conceptualizing legislation comes from James Boyd White, who acknowledges both the open-endedness of statutes and their "core" meanings by analogizing texts to people: we would never presume to "restate" the character of another human being, but we are nevertheless able to recognize the individual and to know in our conversations generally that are talking about one and the same person.

The following materials are organized around three central and related problems: (i) the logic and the limits of the "plain meaning" approach to statutes, illustrated by two Supreme Court cases with very different applications of the rule; (ii) the meaning and status of the various canons of construction developed by the courts to bring at least the appearance of a discipline to the process of interpretation; and (iii) the paradox that ascertaining legislative intent can be both necessary and impossible. The goal of the chapter is to begin to develop fluency in the recurring tropes and idioms in the language of statutory argumentation.

A. THE "PLAIN MEANING" RULE AND ARGUMENTS FROM ABSURDITY

HOLY TRINITY CHURCH V. UNITED STATES

143 U.S. 457 (1892)

MR. JUSTICE BREWER delivered the opinion of the court. [Holy Trinity Church] is a corporation duly organized and incorporated as a religious society under the laws of the state of New York. E. Walpole Warren was, prior to September, 1887, an alien residing in England. In that month the [Church] made a contract with him, by which he was to remove to the city of New York, and enter into its service as rector and pastor; and, in pursuance of such contract, Warren did so remove and enter upon such service. It is claimed by the United States that this contract on the part of the [Church] was forbidden by chapter 164 [of U.S. immigration laws]; and an action was commenced to recover the penalty prescribed by that act. The circuit court held that the contract was within the prohibition of the statute, and rendered judgment accordingly, and the single question presented for our determination is whether it erred in that conclusion.

The first section [of the relevant legislation] describes the act forbidden, and is in these words:

> * * * it shall be unlawful for any person, company, partnership, or corporation, in any manner whatsoever, to prepay the transportation, or in any way assist or encourage the importation or migration, of any alien or aliens, any foreigner or foreigners, into the United States, its territories, or the District of Columbia, under contract or agreement, parol or special, express or implied, made previous to the importation or migration of such alien or aliens, foreigner or foreigners, to perform labor or service of any kind in the United States, its territories, or the District of Columbia.

It must be conceded that the act of the corporation is within the letter of this section, for the relation of rector to his church is one of service, and implies labor on the one side with compensation on the other. Not only are the general words "labor" and "service" both used, but also, as it were to guard against any narrow interpretation and emphasize a breadth of meaning, to them is added "of any kind;" and, further, as noticed by the circuit judge in his opinion, the fifth section, which makes specific exceptions, among them professional actors, artists, lecturers, singers, and domestic servants, strengthens the idea that every other kind of labor and service was intended to be reached by the first section.

While there is great force to this reasoning, we cannot think congress intended to denounce with penalties a transaction like that in the present case. It is a familiar rule that a thing may be within the letter of the statute and yet not within the statute, because not within its spirit nor within the intention of its makers. * * * This is not the substitution of the will of the judge for that of the legislator; for frequently words of general meaning are used in a statute, words broad enough to include an act in question, and yet a consideration of the whole legislation, or of the circumstances surrounding its enactment, or of the absurd results which follow from giving such broad meaning to the words, makes it unreasonable to believe that the legislator intended to include the particular act. * * *

In *U. S. v. Kirby*, 7 Wall. 482, 486, the defendants were indicted for the violation of an act of congress providing "that if any person shall knowingly and willfully obstruct or retard the passage of the mail, or of any driver or carrier, or of any horse or carriage carrying the same, he shall, upon conviction, for every such offense, pay a fine not exceeding one hundred dollars." The specific charge was that the defendants knowingly and willfully retarded the passage of one Farris, a carrier of the mail, while engaged in the performance of his duty, and also in like manner retarded the steamboat *Gen. Buell*, at that time engaged in carrying the mail. To this indictment the defendants pleaded specially that Farris had been indicted for murder by a court of competent authority in Kentucky; that a bench-warrant had been issued and placed in the hands of the defendant Kirby, the sheriff of the county, commanding him to arrest Farris, and bring him before the court to answer to the indictment; and that, in obedience to this warrant, he and the other defendants, as his posse, entered upon the steamboat *Gen. Buell* and arrested Farris, and used only such force as was necessary to accomplish that arrest. The question as to the sufficiency of this plea was certified to this court, and it was held that the arrest of Farris upon the warrant from the state court was not an obstruction of the mail, or the retarding of the passage of a carrier of the mail, within the meaning of the act. In its opinion the court says:

> All laws should receive a sensible construction. General terms should be so limited in their application as not to lead to injustice, oppression, or an absurd consequence. It will always, therefore, be presumed that the legislature intended exceptions to its language which would avoid results of this character. The reason of the law in such cases should prevail over its letter. The common sense of man approves the judgment mentioned by Puffendorf, that the Bolognian law which enacted "that whoever drew blood in the streets should be punished with the utmost severity," did not extend to the surgeon who opened the vein of a person that fell down in the street in a fit. The same common sense accepts the ruling, cited by Plowden, that the statute of 1 Edw. II., which enacts that a prisoner who breaks prison shall be guilty of felony, does not extend to a prisoner who breaks out when the prison is on fire, "for he is not to be hanged because he would not stay to be burnt." And we think that a like common sense will sanction the ruling we make, that the act of congress which punishes the obstruction or retarding of the passage of the mail, or of its carrier, does not apply to a case of temporary detention of the mail caused by the arrest of the carrier upon an indictment for murder. * * *

Among other things which may be considered in determining the intent of the legislature is the title of the act. We do not mean that it may be used to add to or take from the body of the statute, but it may help to interpret its meaning. In the case of *U. S. v. Fisher*, 2 Cranch 358, 386, Chief Justice Marshall said:

> On the influence which the title ought to have in construing the enacting clauses, much has been said, and yet it is not easy to discern the point of difference between the opposing counsel in this respect. Neither party contends that the title of an act can control plain words in the body of the statute; and neither denies that, taken with other parts, it may assist in removing ambiguities. Where the intent is plain, nothing is left to construction. Where the mind labors to discover the design of the legislature, it seizes everything from which aid can be derived;

> and in such case the title claims a degree of notice, and will have its due share of consideration. * * *

It will be seen that words as general as those used in the first section of this act were by that decision limited, and the intent of congress with respect to the act was gathered partially, at least, from its title. Now, the title of this act is, "An act to prohibit the importation and migration of foreigners and aliens under contract or agreement to perform labor in the United States, its territories, and the District of Columbia." Obviously the thought expressed in this reaches only to the work of the manual laborer, as distinguished from that of the professional man. No one reading such a title would suppose that congress had in its mind any purpose of staying the coming into this country of ministers of the gospel, or, indeed, of any class whose toil is that of the brain. The common understanding of the terms "labor" and "laborers" does not include preaching and preachers, and it is to be assumed that words and phrases are used in their ordinary meaning. So whatever * * * light is thrown upon the statute by the language of the title indicates an exclusion from its penal provisions of all contracts for the employment of ministers, rectors, and pastors.

Again, another guide to the meaning of a statute is found in the evil which it is designed to remedy; and for this the court properly looks at contemporaneous events, the situation as it existed, and as it was pressed upon the attention of the legislative body. The situation which called for this statute was briefly but fully stated by Mr. Justice Brown when, as district judge, he decided the case of *U. S. v. Craig*, 28 Fed. Rep. 795, 798:

> The motives and history of the act are matters of common knowledge. It had become the practice for large capitalists in this country to contract with their agents abroad for the shipment of great numbers of an ignorant and servile class of foreign laborers, under contracts by which the employer agreed, upon the one hand, to prepay their passage, while, upon the other hand, the laborers agreed to work after their arrival for a certain time at a low rate of wages. The effect of this was to break down the labor market, and to reduce other laborers engaged in like occupations to the level of the assisted immigrant. The evil finally became so flagrant that an appeal was made to congress for relief by the passage of the act in question, the design of which was to raise the standard of foreign immigrants, and to discountenance the migration of those who had not sufficient means in their own hands, or those of their friends, to pay their passage.

It appears, also, from the petitions, and in the testimony presented before the committees of congress, that it was this cheap, unskilled labor which was making the trouble, and the influx of which congress sought to prevent. It was never suggested that we had in this country a surplus of brain toilers, and, least of all, that the market for the services of Christian ministers was depressed by foreign competition. Those were matters to which the attention of congress, or of the people, was not directed. So far, then, as the evil which was sought to be remedied interprets the statute, it also guides to an exclusion of this contract from the penalties of the act. * * *

A singular circumstance, throwing light upon the intent of congress, is found in this extract from the report of the senate committee on education and labor, recommending the passage of the bill:

> The general facts and considerations which induce the committee to recommend the passage of this bill are set forth in the report of the committee of the house. The committee report the bill back without amendment, although there are certain features thereof which might well be changed or modified, in the hope that the bill may not fail of passage during the present session. Especially would the committee have otherwise recommended amendments, substituting for the expression, "labor and service," whenever it occurs in the body of the bill, the words "manual labor" or "manual service," as sufficiently broad to accomplish the purposes of the bill, and that such amendments would remove objections which a sharp and perhaps unfriendly criticism may urge to the proposed legislation. The committee, however, believing that the bill in its present form will be construed as including only those whose labor or service is manual in character, and being very desirous that the bill become a law before the adjournment, have reported the bill without change.

And, referring back to the report of the committee of the house, there appears this language:

> It seeks to restrain and prohibit the immigration or importation of laborers who would have never seen our shores but for the inducements and allurements of men whose only object is to obtain labor at the lowest possible rate, regardless of the social and material well-being of our own citizens, and regardless of the evil consequences which result to American laborers from such immigration. This class of immigrants care nothing about our institutions, and in many instances never even heard of them. They are men whose passage is paid by the importers. They come here under contract to labor for a certain number of years. They are ignorant of our social condition, and, that they may remain so, they are isolated and prevented from coming into contact with Americans. They are generally from the lowest social stratum, and live upon the coarsest food, and in hovels of a character before unknown to American workmen. They, as a rule, do not become citizens, and are certainly not a desirable acquisition to the body politic. The inevitable tendency of their presence among us is to

degrade American labor, and to reduce it to the level of the imported pauper labor.

We find, therefore, that the title of the act, the evil which was intended to be remedied, the circumstances surrounding the appeal to congress, the reports of the committee of each house, all concur in affirming that the intent of congress was simply to stay the influx of this cheap, unskilled labor.

But, beyond all these matters, no purpose of action against religion can be imputed to any legislation, state or national, because this is a religious people. This is historically true. From the discovery of this continent to the present hour, there is a single voice making this affirmation. [The Court then cites language invoking God or the grace of God in the commission to Christopher Columbus; the first colonial grant made to Sir Walter Raleigh; the first charter of Virginia granted by King James I and subsequent charters; the Mayflower Compact; the fundamental orders of Connecticut; the charter of privileges granted by William Penn to the province of Pennsylvania; the Declaration of Independence; various state constitutions; and the various oaths of office, *inter alia*].

There is no dissonance in these declarations. There is a universal language pervading them all, having one meaning. They affirm and reaffirm that this is a religious nation. These are not individual sayings, declarations of private persons. They are organic utterances. They speak the voice of the entire people. * * * These, and many other matters which might be noticed, add a volume of unofficial declarations to the mass of organic utterances that this is a Christian nation. In the face of all these, shall it be believed that a congress of the United States intended to make it a misdemeanor for a church of this country to contract for the services of a Christian minister residing in another nation? * * *

[This] is a case where there was presented a definite evil, in view of which the legislature used general terms with the purpose of reaching all phases of that evil; and thereafter, unexpectedly, it is developed that the general language thus employed is broad enough to reach cases and acts which the whole history and life of the country affirm could not have been intentionally legislated against. It is the duty of the courts, under those circumstances, to say that, however broad the language of the statute may be, the act, although within the letter, is not within the intention of the legislature, and therefore cannot be within the statute. * * *

TENNESSEE VALLEY AUTHORITY V. HILL

437 U.S. 153 (1978)

[Section 4 of the Endangered Species Act of 1973 ("Act") authorized the Secretary of the Interior ("Secretary") to declare a biological species "endangered." Section 7 of the Act specified that all

> federal departments and agencies shall, . . . with the assistance of the Secretary, utilize their authorities in furtherance of the purposes of [the] Act by carrying out programs for the conservation of endangered species . . . and by taking such action necessary to insure that actions authorized, funded, or carried out by them do not jeopardize the continued existence of such endangered species and threatened species or result in the destruction or modification of habitat of such species which is determined by the Secretary . . . to be critical.

After the passage of the Act, the Secretary designated a small fish known as the "snail darter" as an endangered species under the Act. The snail darter's only known habitat was a small portion of the Little Tennessee River which would be destroyed by the completion of the Tellico Dam Project of the Tennessee Valley Authority ("TVA"), a federal agency. The Secretary declared that area to be the snail darter's "critical habitat." Despite the near-completion of the multimillion-dollar dam, the Secretary issued a regulation, declaring pursuant to § 7 that "all Federal agencies must take such action as is necessary to ensure that actions authorized, funded, or carried out by them do not result in the destruction or modification of this critical habitat area." A variety of parties, respondents here, brought this suit to enjoin completion of the dam and the "impoundment" of the resulting reservoir, on the ground that that those actions would cause the snail darter's extinction and therefore violate the Act.

After trial, the District Court denied relief and dismissed the complaint. Though finding that the impoundment of the reservoir would probably jeopardize the snail darter's continued existence, the lower court noted that Congress—fully aware of the threat—had nevertheless continued to make appropriations for the Tellico project, and concluded that "[a]t some point in time a federal project becomes so near completion and so incapable of modification that a court of equity should not apply a statute enacted long after inception of the project produce an unreasonable result. . . ."

The Court of Appeals reversed and ordered the District Court to enjoin the completion of the project permanently "until Congress, by appropriate legislation, exempts Tellico from compliance with the Act or the snail darter has been deleted from the list of endangered species or its critical habitat materially redefined." The appellate court held that a *prima facie* violation of § 7 had been demonstrated to the extent that TVA had failed to take necessary action to avoid jeopardizing the snail darter's critical habitat by its "actions." As these cases were proceeding, the TVA repeatedly testified before congressional Appropriations Committees to the effect that the Act did not prohibit completion of the dam project and described the efforts it was undertaking to move the snail darter. The congressional committees consistently recommended appropriations for the dam, and Congress repeatedly approved TVA's general budget, which contained funds for the dam's continued construction. The Supreme Court granted *certiorari* to review the Court of Appeals' decision.]

CHIEF JUSTICE BURGER delivered the opinion of the Court. * * * We begin with the premise that operation of the Tellico Dam will either eradicate the known population of snail darters or destroy their critical habitat. Petitioner does not now seriously dispute this fact. * * * Indeed, no judicial review of the Secretary's determinations has ever been sought and hence the validity of his actions are not open to review in this Court. Starting from the above premise, two questions are presented: (a) Would TVA be in violation of the Act if it completed and operated the Tellico Dam as planned? (b) If TVA's actions would offend the Act, is an injunction the appropriate remedy for the violation? For the reasons stated hereinafter, we hold that both questions must be answered in the affirmative.

(A)

It may seem curious to some that the survival of a relatively small number of three-inch fish among all the countless millions of species extant would require the permanent halting of a virtually completed dam for which Congress has expended more than $100 million. The paradox is not minimized by the fact that Congress continued to appropriate large sums of public money for the project, even after congressional Appropriations Committees were apprised of its apparent impact upon the survival of the snail darter. We conclude, however, that the explicit provisions of the Endangered Species Act require precisely that result.

One would be hard pressed to find a statutory provision whose terms were any plainer than those in § 7 of the Endangered Species Act. Its very words affirmatively command all federal agencies "to *insure* that actions *authorized, funded,* or *carried out* by them do not *jeopardize* the continued existence" of an endangered species or "*result* in the destruction or modification of habitat of such species . . . ." 16 U.S.C. § 1536 (1976 ed.) (emphasis added). This language admits of no exception. Nonetheless, petitioner urges, as do the dissenters, that the Act cannot reasonably be interpreted as applying to a federal project which was well under way when Congress passed the Endangered Species Act of 1973. To sustain that position, however, we would be forced to ignore the ordinary meaning of plain language. It has not been shown, for example, how TVA can close the gates of the Tellico Dam without "carrying out" an action that has been "authorized" and "funded" by a federal agency. Nor can we understand how such action will "*insure*" that the snail darter's habitat is not disrupted. Accepting the Secretary's determinations, as we must, it is clear that TVA's proposed operation of the dam will have precisely the opposite effect, namely the *eradication* of an endangered species.

Concededly, this view of the Act will produce results requiring the sacrifice of the anticipated benefits of the project and of many millions of dollars in public funds. But examination of the language, history, and structure of the legislation under review here indicates beyond doubt that Congress intended endangered species to be afforded the highest of priorities.

When Congress passed the Act in 1973, it was not legislating on a clean slate. The first major congressional concern for the preservation of the endangered species had come with passage of the Endangered Species Act of 1966. In that legislation Congress gave the Secretary power to identify "the names of the species of native fish and wildlife found to be threatened with extinction," as well as authorization to purchase land for the conservation, protection, restoration, and propagation of "selected species" of "native fish and wildlife" threatened with extinction. * * * In 1969 Congress enacted the Endangered Species Conservation Act, which continued the provisions of the 1966 Act while at the same time broadening federal involvement in the preservation of endangered species. Under the 1969 legislation, the Secretary was empowered to list species "threatened with worldwide extinction;" in addition, the importation of any species so recognized into the United States was prohibited. * * *

Despite the fact that the 1966 and 1969 legislation represented "the most comprehensive of its type to be enacted by any nation" up to that time, Congress was soon persuaded that a more expansive approach was needed if the newly declared national policy of preserving endangered species was to be realized. By 1973, when Congress held hearings on what would later become the Endangered Species Act of 1973, it was informed that species were still being lost at the rate of about one per year, 1973 House Hearings 306 (statement of Stephen R. Seater, for Defenders of Wildlife), and "the pace of disappearance of species" appeared to be "accelerating." * * *

That Congress did not view these developments lightly was stressed by one commentator:

> The dominant theme pervading all Congressional discussion of the proposed [Endangered Species Act of 1973] was the overriding need *to devote whatever effort and resources were necessary* to avoid further diminution of national and worldwide wildlife resources. Much of the testimony at the hearings and much debate was devoted to the biological problem of extinction. Senators and Congressmen uniformly deplored the irreplaceable loss to aesthetics, science, ecology, and the national heritage should more

species disappear." Coggins, *Conserving Wildlife Resources: An Overview of the Endangered Species Act of 1973*, 51 N.D.L.REV. 315, 321 (1975). (Emphasis added.)

The legislative proceedings in 1973 are, in fact, replete with expressions of concern over the risk that might lie in the loss of *any* endangered species. * * * Congress was concerned about the *unknown* uses that endangered species might have and about the *unforeseeable* place such creatures may have in the chain of life on this planet.

In shaping legislation to deal with the problem thus presented, Congress started from the finding that "[t]he two major causes of extinction are hunting and destruction of natural habitat." U.S. Code Cong & Admin. News 1973, pp. 2989, 2990. Of these twin threats, Congress was informed that the greatest was destruction of natural habitats; *see* 1973 House Hearings 236 (statement of Associate Deputy Chief for National Forest System, Dept. of Agriculture); *id.,* at 241 (statement of Director of Mich. Dept. of Natural Resources); *id.,* at 306 (statement of Stephen R. Seater, Defenders of Wildlife); * * * Virtually every bill introduced in Congress during the 1973 session responded to this concern by incorporating language similar, if not identical, to that found in the present § 7 of the Act. These provisions were designed, in the words of an administration witness, "for the first time [to] *prohibit* [a] federal agency from taking action which does jeopardize the status of endangered species," Hearings on S. 1592 and S. 1983 before the Subcommittee on Environment of the Senate Committee on Commerce, 93d Cong., 1st Sess., 68 (1973) (statement of Deputy Assistant Secretary of the Interior) (emphasis added); furthermore, the proposed bills would "*direc[t]* all . . . Federal agencies to utilize their authorities for carrying out programs *for the protection* of endangered animals." 1973 House Hearings 205 (statement of Assistant Secretary of the Interior) (emphasis added.)

As it was finally passed, the Endangered Species Act of 1973 represented the most comprehensive legislation for the preservation of endangered species ever enacted by any nation. Its stated purposes were "to provide a means whereby the ecosystems upon which endangered species and threatened species depend may be conserved," and "to provide a program for the conservation of such . . . species . . . ." In furtherance of these goals, Congress expressly stated in § 2(c) that "all Federal departments and agencies *shall* seek *to conserve endangered species* and threatened species . . . ." Lest there be any ambiguity as to the meaning of this statutory directive, the Act specifically defined "conserve" as meaning "to use and the use of *all methods and procedures which are necessary* to bring *any endangered species or threatened species* to the point at which the measures provided pursuant to this chapter are no longer necessary." Aside from § 7, other provisions indicated the seriousness with which Congress viewed this issue: Virtually all dealings with endangered species, including taking, possession, transportation, and sale, were prohibited, except in extremely narrow circumstances. The Secretary was also given extensive power to develop regulations and programs for the preservation of endangered and threatened species. * * *

Section 7 of the Act, which of course is relied upon by respondents in this case, provides a particularly good gauge of congressional intent. [T]his provision had its genesis in the Endangered Species Act of 1966, but that legislation qualified the obligation of federal agencies by stating that they should seek to preserve endangered species only "*insofar as is practicable and consistent with the[ir] primary purposes* . . . ." Likewise, every bill introduced in 1973 contained a qualification similar to that found in the earlier statutes. * * * This type of language did not go unnoticed by those advocating strong endangered species legislation. A representative of the Sierra Club, for example, attacked the use of the phrase "consistent with the primary purpose" in proposed H.R. 4758, cautioning that the qualification "could be construed to be a declaration of congressional policy that other agency purposes are necessarily more important than protection of endangered species and would always prevail if conflict were to occur." 1973 House Hearings 335 (statement of the chairman of the Sierra Club's National Wildlife Committee); see *id.*, at 251 (statement for the National Audubon Society).

What is very significant in this sequence is that the final version of the 1973 Act carefully omitted all of the reservations described above. In the bill which the Senate initially approved (S. 1983), however, the version of the current § 7 merely required federal agencies to "carry out such programs *as are practicable* for the protection of species listed. . . ." S. 1983, § 7(a) (emphasis added.) By way of contrast, the bill that originally passed the House, H.R. 37, contained a provision which was essentially a mirror image of the subsequently passed § 7—indeed all phrases which might have qualified an agency's responsibilities had been omitted from the bill. * * *

Resolution of this difference in statutory language, as well as other variations between the House and Senate bills, was the task of a Conference Committee. The Conference Report, H.R. Conf. Rep. No. 93–740 (1973), basically adopted the Senate bill, S. 1983; but the conferees rejected the Senate version of § 7 and adopted the stringent, mandatory language in H.R. 37. While the Conference Report made no specific reference to this choice of provisions, the House manager of the bill, Representative Dingell, provided an interpretation of what the Conference bill would require, making it clear that the mandatory provisions of § 7 were not casually or inadvertently included * * *.

It is against this legislative background[29] that we must measure TVA's claim that the Act was not intended to stop operation of a project which, like Tellico Dam, was near completion when an endangered species was discovered in its path. While there is no discussion in the legislative history of precisely this problem, the totality of congressional action makes it abundantly clear that the result we reach today is wholly in accord with both the words of the statute and the intent of Congress. The plain intent of Congress in enacting this statute was to halt and reverse the trend toward species extinction, whatever the cost. This is reflected not only in the stated policies of the Act, but in literally every section of the statute. All persons, including federal agencies, are specifically instructed not to "take" endangered species, meaning that no one is "to harass, harm, pursue, hunt, shoot, wound, kill, trap, capture, or collect" such life forms. Agencies in particular are directed by §§ 2(c) and 3(2) of the Act to "use . . . *all methods* and procedures which are necessary" to preserve endangered species. In addition, the legislative history undergirding § 7 reveals an explicit congressional decision to require agencies to afford first priority to the declared national policy of saving endangered species. The pointed omission of the type of qualifying language previously included in endangered species legislation reveals a conscious decision by Congress to give endangered species priority over the "primary missions" of federal agencies.

It is not for us to speculate, much less act, on whether Congress would have altered its stance had the specific events of this case been anticipated. In any event, we discern no hint in the deliberations of Congress relating to the 1973 Act that would compel a different result than we reach here.[31] Indeed, the repeated expressions of congressional concern over what it saw as the potentially enormous danger presented by the eradication of *any* endangered species suggest how the balance would have been struck had the issue been presented to Congress in 1973.

Furthermore, it is clear Congress foresaw that § 7 would, on occasion, require agencies to alter ongoing projects in order to fulfill the goals of the

---

[29] When confronted with a statute which is plain and unambiguous on its face, we ordinarily do not look to legislative history as a guide to its meaning. *Ex parte Collett*, 337 U.S. 55, 61 (1949), and cases cited therein. Here it is not necessary to look beyond the words of the statute. We have undertaken such an analysis only to meet Mr. Justice Powell's suggestion [in the dissent] that the "absurd" result reached in this case is not in accord with congressional intent.

[31] The *only* portion of the legislative history which petitioner cites as being favorable to its position consists of certain statements made by Senator Tunney on the floor of the Senate during debates on S. 1983. Senator Tunney was asked whether the proposed bill would affect the Army Corps of Engineers' decision to build a road through a particular area of Kentucky. Responding to this question, Senator Tunney opined that § 7 of S. 1983 would require consultation among the agencies involved, but that the Corps of Engineers "would not be prohibited from building such a road if they deemed it necessary to do so." 119 CONG.REC. 25689 (1973). Petitioner interprets these remarks to mean that an agency, after balancing the respective interests involved, could decide to take action which would extirpate an endangered species. If that is what Senator Tunney meant, his views are in distinct contrast to every other expression in the legislative history as to the meaning of § 7. * * *

Act.[32] Congressman Dingell's discussion of Air Force practice bombing, for instance, obviously pinpoints a particular activity—intimately related to the national defense—which a major federal department would be obliged to alter in deference to the strictures of § 7. * * *

One might dispute the applicability of these examples to the Tellico Dam by saying that in this case the burden on the public through the loss of millions of unrecoverable dollars would greatly outweigh the loss of the snail darter. But neither the Endangered Species Act nor Art. III of the Constitution provides federal courts with authority to make such fine utilitarian calculations. On the contrary, the plain language of the Act, buttressed by its legislative history, shows clearly that Congress viewed the value of endangered species as "incalculable." Quite obviously, it would be difficult for a court to balance the loss of a sum certain—even $100 million—against a congressionally declared "incalculable" value, even assuming we had the power to engage in such a weighing process, which we emphatically do not.

In passing the Endangered Species Act of 1973, Congress was also aware of certain instances in which exceptions to the statute's broad sweep would be necessary. Thus, § 10 creates a number of limited "hardship exemptions," none of which would even remotely apply to the Tellico Project. In fact, there are no exemptions in the Endangered Species Act for federal agencies, meaning that under the maxim *expressio unius est exclusio alterius*, we must presume that these were the only "hardship cases" Congress intended to exempt. * * *

Notwithstanding Congress' expression of intent in 1973, we are urged to find that the continuing appropriations for Tellico Dam constitute an implied repeal of the 1973 Act, at least insofar as it applies to the Tellico Project. In support of this view, TVA points to the statements found in various House and Senate Appropriations Committees' Reports; * * * those Reports generally reflected the attitude of the *Committees* either that the Act did not apply to Tellico or that the dam should be completed regardless of the provisions of the Act. Since we are unwilling to assume that these latter Committee statements constituted advice to ignore the provisions of a duly enacted law, we assume that these Committees believed that the Act simply was not applicable in this situation. But even under this interpretation of the Committees' actions, we are unable to conclude that the Act has been in any respect amended or repealed.

---

[32] Mr. Justice Powell characterizes the result reached here as giving "retroactive" effect to the Endangered Species Act of 1973. We cannot accept that contention. Our holding merely gives effect to the plain words of the statute, namely, that § 7 affects all projects which remain to be authorized, funded, or carried out. Indeed, under the Act there could be no "retroactive" application since, by definition, any *prior* action of a federal agency which *would* have come under the scope of the Act must have already *resulted* in the destruction of an endangered species or its critical habitat. In that circumstance the species would have already been extirpated or its habitat destroyed; the Act would then have no subject matter to which it might apply.

There is nothing in the appropriations measures, as passed, which states that the Tellico Project was to be completed irrespective of the requirements of the Endangered Species Act. These appropriations, in fact, represented relatively minor components of the lump-sum amounts for the *entire* TVA budget. To find a repeal of the Endangered Species Act under these circumstances would surely do violence to the " 'cardinal rule . . . that repeals by implication are not favored.' " *Morton v. Mancari*, 417 U.S. 535, 549 (1974), quoting *Posadas v. National City Bank*, 296 U.S. 497, 503 (1936). In *Posadas* this Court held, in no uncertain terms, that "the intention of the legislature to repeal must be clear and manifest." *Ibid.* * * * In practical terms, this "cardinal rule" means that "[i]n the absence of some affirmative showing of an intention to repeal, the only permissible justification for a repeal by implication is when the earlier and later statutes are irreconcilable." *Mancari, supra*, 417 U.S., at 550.

The doctrine disfavoring repeals by implication "applies with full vigor when . . . the subsequent legislation is an *appropriations* measure." *Committee for Nuclear Responsibility v. Seaborg*, 463 F.2d 783, 785 (1971) (emphasis added); *Environmental Defense Fund v. Froehlke*, 473 F.2d 346, 355 (CA8 1972). This is perhaps an understatement since it would be more accurate to say that the policy applies with even *greater* force when the claimed repeal rests solely on an Appropriations Act. We recognize that both substantive enactments and appropriations measures are "Acts of Congress," but the latter have the limited and specific purpose of providing funds for authorized programs. When voting on appropriations measures, legislators are entitled to operate under the assumption that the funds will be devoted to purposes which are lawful and not for any purpose forbidden. Without such an assurance, every appropriations measure would be pregnant with prospects of altering substantive legislation, repealing by implication any prior statute which might prohibit the expenditure. Not only would this lead to the absurd result of requiring Members to review exhaustively the background of every authorization before voting on an appropriation, but it would flout the very rules the Congress carefully adopted to avoid this need. House Rule XXI(2), for instance, specifically provides:

> No appropriation shall be reported in any general appropriation bill, or be in order as an amendment thereto, for any expenditure not previously authorized by law, unless in continuation of appropriations for such public works as are already in progress. *Nor shall any provision in any such bill or amendment thereto changing existing law be in order*" (emphasis added.)

See also Standing Rules of the Senate, Rule 16.4. Thus, to sustain petitioner's position, we would be obliged to assume that Congress meant to repeal *pro tanto* § 7 of the Act by means of a procedure expressly prohibited under the rules of Congress. * * *

Quite apart from the foregoing factors, we would still be unable to find that in this case "the earlier and later statutes are irreconcilable," *Mancari*, 417 U.S., at 551; here it is entirely possible "to regard each as effective." *Id.* The starting point in this analysis must be the legislative proceedings leading to the 1977 appropriations since the earlier funding of the dam occurred prior to the listing of the snail darter as an endangered species. In all successive years, TVA confidently reported to the Appropriations Committees that efforts to transplant the snail darter appeared to be successful; this surely gave those Committees some basis for the impression that there was no direct conflict between the Tellico Project and the Endangered Species Act. Indeed, the special appropriation for 1978 of $2 million for transplantation of endangered species supports the view that the Committees saw such relocation as the means whereby collision between Tellico and the Endangered Species Act could be avoided. It should also be noted that the Reports issued by the Senate and House Appropriations Committees in 1976 came within a month of the District Court's decision in this case, which hardly could have given the Members cause for concern over the possible applicability of the Act. This leaves only the 1978 appropriations, the Reports for which issued after the Court of Appeals' decision now before us. At that point very little remained to be accomplished on the project; the Committees understandably advised TVA to cooperate with the Department of the Interior "to relocate the endangered species to another suitable habitat so as to permit the project to proceed as rapidly as possible." H.R.Rep. No. 95–379, p. 11 (1977). It is true that the *Committees* repeated their earlier expressed "view" that the Act did not prevent completion of the Tellico Project. Considering these statements in context, however, it is evident that they " 'represent only the personal views of these legislators,' " and "however explicit, [they] cannot serve to change the legislative intent of Congress expressed before the Act's passage." *Regional Rail Reorganization Act Cases,* 419 U.S. 102, 132 (1974).

(B)

Having determined that there is an irreconcilable conflict between operation of the Tellico Dam and the explicit provisions of § 7 of the Endangered Species Act, we must now consider what remedy, if any, is appropriate. It is correct, of course, that a federal judge sitting as a chancellor is not mechanically obligated to grant an injunction for every violation of law. This Court made plain in *Hecht Co. v. Bowles,* 321 U.S. 321 (1944), that "[a] grant of *jurisdiction* to issue compliance orders hardly suggests an absolute duty to do so under any and all circumstances." As a general matter it may be said that "[s]ince all or almost all equitable remedies are discretionary, the balancing of equities and hardships is appropriate in almost any case as a guide to the chancellor's discretion." D. DOBBS, REMEDIES 52 (1973). Thus, in *Hecht Co.,* the Court refused to grant an injunction when it appeared from the District Court findings that "the issuance of an injunction would have 'no effect by way of insuring better compliance in the future' and would [have been] 'unjust' to [the] petitioner and not 'in the public interest.' "

But these principles take a court only so far. Our system of government is, after all, a tripartite one, with each branch having certain defined functions delegated to it by the Constitution. While "[i]t is emphatically the province and duty of the judicial department to say what the law is," *Marbury v. Madison,* 1 Cranch 137, 177 (1803), it is equally—and emphatically—the exclusive province of the Congress not only to formulate legislative policies and mandate programs and projects, but also to establish their relative priority for the Nation. Once Congress, exercising its delegated powers, has decided the order of priorities in a given area, it is for the Executive to administer the laws and for the courts to enforce them when enforcement is sought.

Here we are urged [by the dissent] to view the Endangered Species Act "reasonably," and hence shape a remedy "that accords with some modicum of common sense and the public weal." But is that our function? We have no expert knowledge on the subject of endangered species, much less do we have a mandate from the people to strike a balance of equities on the side of the Tellico Dam. Congress has spoken in the plainest of words, making it abundantly clear that the balance has been struck in favor of affording endangered species the highest of priorities, thereby adopting a policy which it described as "institutionalized caution."

Our individual appraisal of the wisdom or unwisdom of a particular course consciously selected by the Congress is to be put aside in the process of interpreting a statute. Once the meaning of an enactment is discerned and its constitutionality determined, the judicial process comes to an end. We do not sit as a committee of review, nor are we vested with the power of veto. * * *

We agree with the Court of Appeals that in our constitutional system the commitment to the separation of powers is too fundamental for us to pre-empt congressional action by judicially decreeing what accords with "common sense and the public weal." Our Constitution vests such responsibilities in the political branches.

NOTES AND QUESTIONS

1. *Reconciling the principal cases.* In *Holy Trinity*, the Supreme Court found the literal interpretation of the statute absurd and concluded that the contract in question came within the letter but not the spirit of the statute and therefore exempted the hiring of a foreign pastor from certain restrictive immigration laws. On the other hand, in *Hill*, the Supreme Court found the literal interpretation of the Endangered Species Act compelling, even to the

point of stopping a multi-million dollar dam project already near completion—a project repeatedly funded by Congress *after* the Endangered Species Act had passed. (a) What separately-identifiable principles of statutory interpretation are at work in these two cases? (b) Which of those principles seem in conflict with one another? (c) Which case do you find better reasoned?

2. *The dissent in Hill.* Justice Powell, dissenting in *Hill*, wrote that "[i]t is not our province to rectify policy or political judgments by the Legislative Branch, however egregiously they may disserve the public interest. But where the statutory and legislative history, as in this case, need not be construed to reach such a result, I view it as the duty of this Court to adopt a permissible construction that accords with some modicum of common sense and the public weal." (a) In writing the majority opinion in *Hill*, has Chief Justice Burger pretended that his interpretation is more compelled than it really is? (b) In what sense was the majority's result in *Hill* not "absurd" enough to apply the *Holy Trinity* rule?

3. *The continuing validity of Holy Trinity.* Without overruling *Holy Trinity*, the Supreme Court has said that the rule in that case applies only in "rare and exceptional circumstances. * * * [T]here must be something to make plain the intent of Congress that the letter of the statute is not to prevail." *Crooks v. Harrelson*, 282 U.S. 55, 60 (1930). Justice Scalia once referred to *Holy Trinity* as "that miraculous redeemer of lost causes." *Zuni Public School Dist. No. 89 v. Department of Education*, 550 U.S. 81, 116 (2007) (Scalia, J, dissenting). It is perhaps easy to understand why the courts might now look askance at various parts of *Holy Trinity*, but why do you suppose the Court hasn't explicitly overruled it outright?

In this connection, consider the opinion of Judge Easterbrook in *Jaskolski v. Daniels*, 427 F.3d 456, 462–63 (7th Cir. 2005):

> When an opinion says that courts interpret statutes to avoid absurd results, it is not inviting judges to convert rules into standards. *Church of the Holy Trinity v. United States,* 143 U.S. 457 (1892), which invoked the norm against absurd outcomes to make the law more in line with the Justices' substantive preferences, has no modern traction. Today the anti-absurdity canon is linguistic rather than substantive. It deals with texts that don't scan as written and thus need repair work, rather than with statutes that seem poor fits for the task at hand. In other words, the modern decisions draw a line between poor exposition and benighted substantive choice; the latter is left alone, because what judges deem a "correction" or "fix" is from another perspective a deliberate interference with the legislative power to choose what makes for a good rule. Admit the propriety of "fixing mistakes" and you allow a general power to *identify* "mistakes," which means a privilege to make the real substantive decision. Even when the statute *invites* modification, as the "context clause" in some definitions does, judges are limited to considering the linguistic context rather than trying to "improve" the statute's substantive effect.

> The only recent decision in which the anti-absurdity canon played an important role, *Green v. Bock Laundry Machine Co.,* 490 U.S. 504 (1989), dealt with an incomplete and baffling rule. Other decisions that cite the doctrine, such as *Public Citizen v. Department of Justice,* 491 U.S. 440 (1989), and *United States v. X-Citement Video, Inc.,* 513 U.S. 64 (1994), use it to avoid an unconstitutional reading. The dearth of modern "substantive absurdity" decisions is readily understandable. Scholars as well as judges have recognized that a power to fix statutes substantively would give the Judicial Branch too much leeway to prefer its views about what makes for "good" laws over those of the Legislative Branch. * * * The Supreme Court has been willing to enforce even statutes that seem to set traps for the unwary or unfortunate. *Dodd v. United States,* 545 U.S. 353 (2005), is a good example: The Court held that the statute of limitations for collateral attacks on criminal convictions may expire before the decision supporting the challenge becomes applicable, and it rejected an argument that this linguistically sound reading should be rejected as substantively absurd.

(a) On what separation-of-powers principle must courts accept "absurd" but literally-compelled results when interpreting a statute? (b) What does Judge Easterbrook mean by his distinctions between (i) rules and standards and (ii) between "linguistic" and "substantive" understandings of the anti-absurdity norm?

4. *The "conversation" between courts and Congress.* After the *Hill* decision, work on the Tellico Dam project stopped until 1979, when Congress and President Carter agreed on legislation to exempt the project from the Endangered Species Act.[2] In effect, Congress amended a statute in direct response to the Supreme Court's interpretation of that statute. There are numerous examples of Congress engaging in such "conversations" with the courts. *See* Matthew R. Christiansen & William N. Eskridge, Jr., *Congressional Overrides of Supreme Court Statutory Interpretation Decisions, 1967–2011,* 92 TEXAS L. REV. 1317 (2014) (assembling and analyzing 286 statutory overrides of 275 Supreme Court decisions between 1967 and 2011 that interpreted a federal statute). The number of such legislative overrides has fallen in the twenty-first century, correlating perhaps to a period of greater polarization in Congress, which makes legislative work of all types more difficult; nevertheless, Christiansen and Eskridge found statistically significant correlations between a congressional override of a Supreme Court statutory interpretation decision and multiple variables:

---

[2] For those concerned about the fate of the snail darter after the dam was exempted from the Endangered Species Act, it may be some consolation that other small populations of the fish were discovered in the early 1980s, and an intense program of transplantation was undertaken in other supportive environments in east Tennessee waterways. The status of the species was upgraded from "endangered" to "threatened" in 1984, six years after the Supreme Court's decision in *Hill,* where it remains. As of this writing, the snail darter can still be observed in the wild, if that's your idea of a good time.

- close division (plurality or 5- or 6-Justice majority) among the Justices when deciding the case;
- judicial rejection of the interpretation offered by a federal agency and usually defended by the Solicitor General;
- judicial narrowing of federal regulation, except in tax and intellectual property cases, where regulation-friendly interpretations are often overridden;
- reliance on plain meaning of statutory texts, especially when such reliance depends critically on whole act and whole code arguments or flies in the face of strong legislative history; and
- invitations for Congress to override, issued by majority, concurring, or even dissenting Justices.

Id. at 1321. Why exactly might each of these variables correlate to a congressional override?

What happens to Congress's power to correct the Court's statutory interpretation if that interpretation rests on Constitutional requirements? Congress is not powerless just because the Court has invalidated a statute on constitutional grounds, although its "conversational" options are obviously narrowed when that happens. For example, in *United States v. Alvarez*, 567 U.S. 709 (2012), the Supreme Court used the First Amendment guaranty of free speech to invalidate the Stolen Valor Act, which had prohibited making false claims about military honors. Within months, Congress had revised the Act to criminalize false claims about military honors made for financial gain, fitting the prohibition into an understanding that free speech does not include the power to defraud the marketplace. Similarly, within months after the decision in *United States v. Stevens*, 559 U.S. 460 (2010), which invalidated as overbroad a congressional prohibition on so-called "animal crush videos," Congress limited the prohibition of such videos to those that are legally "obscene" and therefore not protected by the First Amendment. *See generally* Ira C. Lupu, *Statutes Revolving in Constitutional Orbits*, 79 VA. L. REV. 1 (1993).

5. *Making fortresses out of dictionaries. United States v. Kirby*, 74 U.S. (7 Wall.) 482 (1869), cited prominently by Justice Brewer in *Holy Trinity*, interpreted the plain prohibition on obstructing the mail as not applying to a local sheriff's arrest of a mail carrier on a charge of murder: "General terms should be so limited in their application as not to lead to injustice, oppression, or an absurd consequence" *Id.* at 486. *Kirby* and *Holy Trinity* provide modest authority for the so-called "mischief rule," under which interpretation—even of plain language—is guided by answering the question: to what problem is this statute a solution? In *Holy Trinity*, the "mischief" targeted by restrictive immigration laws was not the hiring of foreign pastors. In *Hill*, the "mischief" targeted by the Endangered Species Act was the extinction of natural species, like the snail darter. Similarly, when the Supreme Court sustained the Obama Administration's interpretation of the Affordable Care Act, it specifically conceded that the challenger's plain-meaning arguments were powerful,

distinguishing between tax credits for health insurance purchased on Federal versus State exchanges, but, without invoking the mischief rule by name, the Court went on to observe that

> Congress passed the Affordable Care Act to improve health insurance markets, not to destroy them. If at all possible, we must interpret the Act in a way that is consistent with the former, and avoids the latter. Section 36B [of the Act] can fairly be read consistent with what we see as Congress's plan, and that is the reading we adopt.

King v. Burwell, ___ U.S. ___, 135 S. Ct. 2480, 2496 (2015). Whether you think the mischief rule is perfectly sensible or a judicial power-grab may correlate to whether you are persuaded by Judge Learned Hand's observation that "it is one of the surest indexes of a mature and developed jurisprudence not to make a fortress out of the dictionary; but to remember that statutes always have some purpose or object to accomplish, whose sympathetic and imaginative discovery is the surest guide to their meaning." *Cabell v. Markham*, 148 F.2d 737, 739 (2d Cir. 1945).

6. *The democratic deficit, a.k.a. the counter-majoritarian difficulty*. It is sometimes said that the power to declare or interpret the law *is* the power to create the law. Is it possible to square the court's interpretive function with the ideal of representative democracy? Does democracy require something *other than* fidelity to the majority's will? *See* Jane S. Schacter, *Metademocracy: The Changing Structure of Legitimacy in Statutory Interpretation*, 108 HARV. L. REV. 593, 613–46 (1995) (arguing that the courts should adopt methods of interpretation that advance particular conceptions of democracy).

7. *If the "plain meaning" is so important, does punctuation count?* Punctuation and grammar are designed in part to make a writer's meanings clear (or at least clearer than they would be without the markers). So how much weight should a court give to the punctuation in a statutory provision? The Supreme Court has provided ammunition to both sides of the fight. On one hand, "A statute's plain meaning must be enforced, * * * and the meaning of a statute will typically heed the commands of its punctuation. * * * Statutory interpretation is a holistic endeavor, and, at a minimum, must account for a statute's full text, language *as well as punctuation*, structure, and subject matter." *United States Nat'l Bank of Oregon v. Independent Ins. Agents of Am., Inc.*, 508 U.S. 439, 454–5 (1993) (emphasis supplied). On the other hand, in the very same case, the Supreme Court reserved for itself the power to "disregard the punctuation, or *repunctuate, if need be*, to render the true meaning of the statute." *Id.* at 462 (citation omitted, emphasis supplied). *Cf. Flora v. United States*, 362 U.S. 145, 149 (1960) (noting that a court "does not review congressional enactments as a panel of grammarians"); *United States v. Shreveport Grain & Elevator Co.*, 287 U.S. 77, 82–83 (1932) (daring to disregard a comma); *City of Elizabeth v. 264 First St., LLC*, No. 011716–2014, 2015 WL 1906430, at *15 (N.J. Tax Ct. Apr. 23, 2015) ("Although issues of punctuation will not be dispositive of a statute's apparent meaning, it 'is one of the means for discovering the legislative intent.' [ ] Punctuation is an integral part of any legislation and 'may be considered in the interpretation [ ]

but may not be used to create doubt or to distort or defeat the intention of the legislature. When the intent is uncertain, punctuation, if it affords some indication of the true intention, may be looked to as an aid'" (citations omitted)).

8. *Are statutes like contracts, requiring analogous approaches to interpretation?* From one perspective, both contracts and statutes are the result of (and the expression of) a successful negotiation. (a) In what ways does the interpretation of contracts between private parties resemble the interpretation of statutes? (b) What are the limits of using contract interpretation as a model for statutory interpretation?

B. CANONS OF CONSTRUCTION

UNITED STATES V. DICRISTINA

726 F.3d 92 (2d Cir. 2013)

The United States appeals from an * * * order of the United States District Court for the Eastern District of New York (Jack B. Weinstein, Judge) entering a post-verdict judgment of acquittal in favor of Defendant-Appellee Lawrence DiCristina, setting aside the guilty verdict on one count of violating the Illegal Gambling Business Act (the "IGBA"), 18 U.S.C. § 1955, and one count of conspiring to do so under 18 U.S.C. § 371. The District Court ruled that DiCristina's conviction must be set aside because "Texas Hold'em" poker was not covered by the IGBA. *United States v. Dicristina*, 886 F.Supp.2d 164 (E.D.N.Y. 2012). Because we find that the plain language of the IGBA covers DiCristina's poker business, we reverse the judgment of acquittal and remand to the District Court with instructions to reinstate the jury verdict, enter a judgment of conviction on both counts, and proceed with sentencing DiCristina.

BACKGROUND

The basic facts of this case are not in dispute: between December 2010 and May 2011, DiCristina, along with his co-defendant Stefano Lombardo and others, operated a poker club in the back room of a warehouse in Staten Island, New York, out of which he conducted a legitimate business selling electric bicycles. The poker games,[1] which were generally held twice a week, were advertised by word of mouth and text message. [According to the District Court,] "[t]he club contained two tables at which No Limit Texas Hold'em was played." The dealers collected a five percent "rake" for the house from each pot, twenty-five percent of which they kept as

---

[1] The District Court limited its analysis to Texas Hold'em, which is the variant of poker at issue here. However, we use the term "poker" in this opinion generally to refer to any kind of poker that would be considered gambling under New York State law. For purposes of this opinion, we see no reason to distinguish Texas Hold'em from other variations of poker. * * *

payment. "The remaining funds from the rake were used for expenses relating to the operation of the business and for profits." Other than the operation of these poker games, no unlawful conduct by DiCristina is alleged. * * *

On June 29, 2012, DiCristina moved to dismiss the * * * indictment on the basis that poker is not house-banked[2] or predominated by chance, and thus is not encompassed in the IGBA's enumerated list of illegal types of "gambling." The District Court heard testimony by DiCristina's expert, Dr. Randall Heeb, as to why skill predominates over chance in poker, but reserved decision on the motion to dismiss, and the parties went forward with trial. Over DiCristina's objection, the District Court ruled that the question of whether poker fell within the IGBA was a question of law to be decided by the court, excluded Dr. Heeb's testimony as irrelevant, and instructed the jury that gambling under the IGBA "includes playing poker for money."

The jury found DiCristina guilty on both counts charged in the * * * indictment. DiCristina then renewed his motion to dismiss in the form of a motion for a judgment of acquittal under Federal Rule of Criminal Procedure 29. He argued that (1) in order for conduct to come under the purview of the IGBA, it must be sufficiently similar to the nine games enumerated in § 1955(b)(2); and (2) poker did not fall within the statutory definition of an illegal gambling business because it was neither house-banked nor predominated by chance. The Government argued that subsection (b)(2) did not, by its plain language, restrict the games that constitute unlawful gambling under the IGBA and therefore it was sufficient for purposes of the statute that a gambling activity was illegal under state law, as poker was under New York law in this instance. After considering additional briefing and expert testimony from both sides, the District Court dismissed the * * * indictment and entered a judgment of acquittal.

The District Court determined that both the Government and DiCristina presented plausible readings of the statute, and that the legislative history was not decisive as to whether Congress meant to include poker within the IGBA. Reasoning that the IGBA did not "provide explicit criteria" for defining gambling, and that there were "ambiguities in the federal definition of gambling," the District Court found that the "governing criteria must be derived by determining what common characteristics unif[y] the games listed in § 1955[(b)(2)] into a cohesive group." The District Court found that "dictionary, common law, and other federal definitions of gambling argue in favor of a definition limited to games of chance." It then determined that poker did not constitute

[2] According to the Poker Players' Alliance amicus brief, a house-banked game is one "in which the house competes directly against its customers." (Br. for Amicus Poker Players' Alliance at 23). House-banked games "include blackjack, craps, roulette, bacarrat, *punto banco* (minibaccarat), and the big wheel," as well as "Las Vegas sports betting." *Id.*

"gambling" under the IGBA because poker is predominated by skill rather than chance. This timely appeal followed.

DISCUSSION

I. Applicable Law

* * * When interpreting a statute, we "must begin with the language employed by Congress and the assumption that the ordinary meaning of that language accurately expresses the legislative purpose." *United States v. Kozeny*, 541 F.3d 166, 171 (2nd Cir. 2008) (interpreting 18 U.S.C. § 3292) (*quoting United States v. Albertini*, 472 U.S. 675, 680 (1985)) (internal quotation marks omitted). "Where the statute's language is 'plain, the sole function of the courts is to enforce it according to its terms.' " *Id.* (*quoting United States v. Ron Pair Enters., Inc.*, 489 U.S. 235, 241 (1989)); *see also Conn. Nat'l Bank v. Germain*, 503 U.S. 249, 253–54 (1992) ("We have stated time and again that courts must presume that a legislature says in a statute what it means and means in a statute what it says there.").

Statutory enactments should, moreover, be read so as "to give effect, if possible, to every clause and word of a statute." *Duncan v. Walker*, 533 U.S. 167, 174 (2001) (*quoting United States v. Menasche*, 348 U.S. 528, 538–39 (1955)) (internal quotation marks omitted); *see also United States v. Nordic Vill., Inc.*, 503 U.S. 30, 36 (1992) (noting "the settled rule that a statute must, if possible, be construed in such fashion that every word has some operative effect"); *United States v. Anderson*, 15 F.3d 278, 283 (2nd Cir. 1994) ("[C]ourts will avoid statutory interpretations that render provisions superfluous."). And "[t]he 'whole act' rule of statutory construction exhorts us to read a section of a statute not 'in isolation from the context of the whole Act' but to 'look to the provisions of the whole law, and to its object and policy.' " *United States v. Pacheco*, 225 F.3d 148, 154 (2nd Cir. 2000) (*quoting Richards v. United States*, 369 U.S. 1, 11 (1962)).

In the event that the text of a statute is not clear, a court interpreting the statute may consult the legislative history to discern "the legislative purpose as revealed by the history of the statute." *Concrete Pipe & Prods. of Cal., Inc. v. Constr. Laborers Pension Trust for S. Cal.*, 508 U.S. 602, 627 (1993); *see also United States v. Gayle*, 342 F.3d 89, 93–94 (2nd Cir. 2003) (looking to legislative history where text of statute was ambiguous as to what constitutes a predicate offense under 18 U.S.C. § 922(g)(1)). "Our obligation is to give effect to congressional purpose so long as the congressional language does not itself bar that result." *Johnson v. United States*, 529 U.S. 694, 710 n. 10 (2000). Where Congress provides no definition for a term in a statute, we "consider the ordinary, common-sense meaning of the words." *United States v. Dauray*, 215 F.3d 257, 260 (2nd Cir. 2000).

Finally, we have recognized that "[t]he rule of lenity provides that ambiguities concerning legislative intent in criminal statutes should be resolved in favor of the accused." *United States v. Figueroa*, 165 F.3d 111, 119 (2nd Cir. 1998). The rule of lenity "ensures fair warning by so resolving ambiguity in a criminal statute as to apply it only to conduct clearly covered." *United States v. Lanier*, 520 U.S. 259, 266 (1997). However, "the rule of lenity only applies if, after considering text, structure, history, and purpose, there remains a grievous ambiguity or uncertainty in the statute, such that the Court must simply guess as to what Congress intended." *Barber v. Thomas*, 560 U.S. 474 (2010) (internal citations and quotation marks omitted); *see also Bifulco v. United States*, 447 U.S. 381, 387 (1980) ("[T]he touchstone of the rule of lenity is statutory ambiguity." (internal quotation marks omitted)).

II. Text of the Statute

A. Statutory Scheme

The IGBA provides in relevant part:

Prohibition of illegal gambling businesses

> (a) Whoever conducts, finances, manages, supervises, directs, or owns all or part of an illegal gambling business shall be fined under this title or imprisoned not more than five years, or both.
>
> (b) As used in this section—
>
> (1) "illegal gambling business" means a gambling business which—
>
> > (i) is a violation of the law of a State or political subdivision in which it is conducted;
> >
> > (ii) involves five or more persons who conduct, finance, manage, supervise, direct, or own all or part of such business; and
> >
> > (iii) has been or remains in substantially continuous operation for a period in excess of thirty days or has a gross revenue of $2,000 in any single day.
>
> (2) "gambling" includes but is not limited to pool-selling, bookmaking, maintaining slot machines, roulette wheels or dice tables, and conducting lotteries, policy,[3] bolita[4] or numbers games, or selling chances therein. * * *

[3] Policy is defined as "a daily lottery in which participants bet that certain numbers will be drawn from a lottery wheel." WEBSTER'S THIRD NEW INTERNATIONAL DICTIONARY 1754 (1993).

[4] Bolita is Spanish for "little ball." It is defined as: "1. A game of chance having the character of a lottery in which a bag of small numbered balls is tossed about until only one remains or until one is grasped at random, the ball so selected being considered as bearing the winning number. 2. A numbers game in which one attempts to guess a variously determined 2-digit number." WEBSTER'S THIRD NEW INTERNATIONAL DICTIONARY 248 (1993).

18 U.S.C. § 1955 (emphasis added). Subsection (e) of the IGBA excludes from the statute's scope "any bingo game, lottery, or similar game of chance conducted by" a tax-exempt organization. Id. § 1955(e) (emphasis added).

Pursuant to § 1955(b)(1)(i), we look to state law definitions of gambling. New York law provides that:

> A person engages in gambling when he stakes or risks something of value upon the outcome of a contest of chance or a future contingent event not under his control or influence, upon an agreement or understanding that he will receive something of value in the event of a certain outcome.

N.Y. Penal Law § 225.00(2).

A "contest of chance" is in turn defined under New York law as "any contest, game, gaming scheme or gaming device in which the outcome depends in a material degree upon an element of chance, notwithstanding that skill of the contestants may also be a factor therein." Id. § 225.00(1). The parties do not dispute that poker constitutes gambling under New York State law. *See Dicristina*, 886 F.Supp.2d at 168–69 (noting that DiCristina had waived the argument that poker was not gambling under New York law and explaining that it has no merit).[5]

The Supreme Court has observed that the IGBA "declar[es] that certain gambling activities violate federal as well as state law," thereby "giv[ing] the Federal Government a new substantive weapon" with which to "strike at organized crime's principal source of revenue: illegal gambling." *Iannelli v. United States*, 420 U.S. 770, 788 (1975). In *Sanabria v. United States*, 437 U.S. 54 (1978), the Court noted that:

> Congress did not assimilate state gambling laws per se into the federal penal code, nor did it define discrete acts of gambling as independent federal offenses. The Government need not prove that the defendant himself performed any act of gambling prohibited by state law. It is participation in the gambling business that is a federal offense, and it is only the gambling business that must violate state law.

Id. at 70 (internal citations and footnotes omitted).

B. Requirements of the IGBA

The plain language of § 1955 clearly outlines the activity that it proscribes. It criminalizes the act of running a gambling business that (1) operates in violation of the law of the state in which the business is conducted; (2) is conducted by five people or more; and (3) is either in

[5] As the District Court explained, New York State courts have long held that poker contains a "sufficient element of chance to constitute gambling under that state's laws." Dicristina, 886 F.Supp.2d at 169 (citing Dalton v. Pataki, 11 A.D.3d 62, 780 N.Y.S.2d 47, 64 n. 5 (3d Dep't 2004) (noting that "the term 'game of chance' or 'contest of chance' . . . has been interpreted to include such games as 'stud' poker" (internal citations omitted))* * *.

operation for more than thirty days or earns more than $2,000 in one day. See 18 U.S.C. § 1955(b)(1). The inclusion of elements (2) and (3) demonstrates that the focus of the statute's criminal proscription is not on what game is being played, but on the size of the business and the revenue derived by those who are running it. *See Sanabria*, 437 U.S. at 70 ("It is participation in the gambling business that is a federal offense"). As the District Court noted, "most 'kitchen table' poker games would not satisfy either or both of these requirements." DiCristina's poker business, it is undisputed, satisfied both.

DiCristina contends that the IGBA does not apply to a poker business, however, because poker does not fit within the "definition of gambling" set forth in subsection (b)(2).[6] But unlike subsection (b)(1), which defines "illegal gambling business," or subsection (b)(3), which defines the term "State," subsection (b)(2) is tellingly not prefaced by the verb "means." *See Groman v. Comm'r of Internal Revenue*, 302 U.S. 82, 86 (1937) ("[W]hen an exclusive definition is intended the word 'means' is employed. . . ."). Had Congress intended to create a definition of "gambling" unique to the IGBA, or to confine the reach of the IGBA to businesses involving certain types of gambling, it could have inserted such language.[7] Instead, subsection (b)(2) states that "gambling includes but is not limited to" the nine activities listed. 18 U.S.C. § 1955(b)(2) (emphasis added). It does not include the words "games similar to" or any other such language limiting subsection (b)(2) to include only games analogous to those enumerated.[8] Rather, the

---

[6] We note that DiCristina's argument improperly conflates the important distinction between gambling, which is not prohibited by the IGBA, and operating a gambling business, which is prohibited by the IGBA.

[7] The language of subsection (b)(2) is particularly significant when compared to the earlier version of the IGBA which was not adopted. That version read: "[T]he term 'illegal gambling business' means betting, lottery, or numbers activity which (1) is a violation of the law of a State or political subdivision thereof; (2) involves five or more persons who operate, work in, participate in, or derive revenue from said betting, lottery, or numbers activity; and (3) has been or remains in operation for a period in excess of thirty days or has a gross revenue of $2,000 in any single day." See Illegal Gambling Business Control Act of 1969, S.2022, 91st Cong., 1st Sess. § 201 (April 29, 1969) (emphasis added). Such a statute would be limited to certain types of gambling. However, Congress opted to simply define "illegal gambling business" to mean a business that violates state law, plus the other two elements (five or more persons, and either operation for more than thirty days or gross revenue of $2,000 or more in a single day), and to eliminate the narrow definition of gambling (i.e., applies only to betting, lottery, or numbers activity).

[8] The statutory canon of *ejusdem generis* has no place here because the plain meaning of the statute is apparent. *See* United States v. Turkette, 452 U.S. 576, 581 (1981) (*ejusdem generis* is "an aid to statutory construction problems suggesting that where general words follow a specific enumeration of persons or things, the general words should be limited to persons or things similar to those specifically enumerated"). As the District Court acknowledged, "[t]he rule of *ejusdem generis* . . . comes into play only when there is some uncertainty as to the meaning of a particular clause in a statute." *Dicristina*, 886 F.Supp.2d at 226 (*citing Turkette*, 452 U.S. at 581[ ]. "[C]anons of construction are no more than rules of thumb that help courts determine the meaning of legislation" which do not come into play if the language of the statute is plain. Conn. Nat'l Bank v. Germain, 503 U.S. 249, 253 (1992). Moreover, because we find that subsection (b)(2) is not definitional, we do not need to decide whether poker—or any other type of gambling—is sufficiently like the enumerated games to fall within the IGBA. Rather, the gambling activity must only be prohibited by state law and meet the additional criteria set forth in the IGBA.

phrase "includes but is not limited to" signals a non-exhaustive list of examples of gambling activities.[9]

DiCristina contends that reading the statute in this way renders subsection (b)(2) purposeless. We disagree. Subsection (b)(2) lists acts of running a gambling business—"pool-selling," "bookmaking," "maintaining" gambling devices, and "conducting" games—rather than the games themselves. 18 U.S.C. § 1955(b)(2). It thus serves as an illustration of what may constitute running a gambling operation. As the District Court recognized, this reading of subsection (b)(2) supports the notion that Congress was "concerned with illustrating types of gambling businesses . . . rather than on creating a limiting definition of gambling under federal law."

DiCristina also argues that § 1955(e) "confirms that the unifying characteristic of the prohibited games is that each is a game of chance," because the games that are included by the language of subsection (b)(2) must be the same as those games that are excluded by subsection (e). Subsection (e), it is undisputed, creates an exemption for the activities of charities. It does not make any reference to subsection (b)(2), and does not state that it modifies or applies to that subsection in any way. Had Congress intended to limit the reach of the IGBA to businesses operating games of chance, it could have done so by inserting that language in subsection (b)(2). The District Court's decision to limit the IGBA to games of chance was based on its finding that the statute was ambiguous as to what gambling activities it covered. Because we find no such ambiguity, we decline to limit the statute's reach beyond its plain terms.

Thus, the question of whether skill or chance predominates in poker is inapposite to this appeal. The language of the statute is clear that it contains only three requirements, all set forth in subsection (b)(1), and all of which were met in this case.

Our precedent is consistent with this holding. * * * Indeed, federal courts have repeatedly applied the IGBA to businesses operating games—including poker—that are not enumerated therein, without reading the statute to contain a definition in subsection (b)(2). * * * In sum, courts have overwhelmingly read the IGBA to have only three elements: (1) the gambling business violates the law of the state in which the business is conducted; (2) the business involves five or more persons who conduct, finance, manage, supervise, direct, or own all or part of such business; and (3) the business has been or remains in substantially continuous operation for a period in excess of thirty days or has a gross revenue of $2,000 in any single day. * * * We agree, and today hold that an "illegal gambling

[9] We do not suggest that a statute can never define a term using the verb "includes" or the phrase "includes but is not limited to." Rather, we hold only that § 1955(b)(2) does not define the term "gambling" in light of the specific language of that subsection and the context in which it appears. * * *

business" is one which meets the three elements articulated in subsection (b)(1).

III. Legislative History

Based on the clear text of the IGBA, we could conclude without an examination of Congress's intention in drafting it. Indeed, we look to the legislative history of a statute only where the text itself is not "absolutely clear." *Disabled in Action of Metro. N.Y. v. Hammons*, 202 F.3d 110, 124 (2nd Cir. 2000); *accord Mary Jo C.*, 707 F.3d at 171 ("[H]aving found the relevant provisions of the statute unambiguous, we do not have warrant to [consult the legislative history of the statute]."). We agree with the District Court that there appears to be "something for everybody" in the legislative history, and we review it here briefly only to demonstrate that Congress's unmistakable purpose in enacting the IGBA bolsters our reading of the statute's clear and unambiguous text.

The legislative history is remarkably clear that the passage of this statute was driven by the desire to crack down on organized crime. As the District Court noted, "[t]he debates focused not on prohibiting particular kinds of gambling, but on targeting particular kinds of criminals—*i.e.*, reaching 'those who are engaged in an illicit gambling business of major proportions.' " *Dicristina*, 886 F.Supp.2d at 204 (quoting S. Rep. No. 91–617, at 73 (1969); H.R. Rep. No. 91–1549, at 53 (1970), 1970 U.S.C.C.A.N. 4007). The aim of 18 U.S.C. § 1955 was "to give the Federal Government a new substantive weapon, a weapon which will strike at organized crime's principal source of revenue: illegal gambling." S. Rep. No. 91–617, at 71; see also Senate Judiciary Hr'gs at 449 (Message from the President of the United States Relative to the Fight Against Organized Crime) ("The purpose of this legislation is to bring under federal jurisdiction all large-scale illegal gambling operations which involve or affect interstate commerce."). Thus, the IGBA was driven by concerns about the revenue generated by large scale gambling business rather than the games that were played. *See, e.g.*, S. Rep. No. 91–617, at 71; Senate Judiciary Hr'gs at 158 (statement of Sen. Tydings) ("The greatest single source of revenue for organized crime is its gambling activities, which net an estimated seven (7) to fifty (50) billion dollars a year. . . .").

There was some discussion during the legislative debates of which games organized crime was using toward this end. Various legislators noted the fact that organized crime was involved in "lotteries, dice games, and illegal casinos" in addition to "horse racing and sporting events." 116 Cong. Rec. 590 (Jan. 21, 1970) (statement of Sen. McClellan). "Mafia-run numbers rackets," *Dicristina*, 886 F.Supp.2d at 208, were discussed, as was bookmaking, which many were concerned allowed national crime syndicates to finance their activities, see id. at 208–09 (legislative history reflects concern about money made in bookmaking). As the District Court acknowledged, there is nothing in the legislative history suggesting that whether a game was predominated by chance was relevant to whether a business operating that game constituted an illegal gambling business under the IGBA.

Although poker was not discussed at length, the dialogue about poker that did occur suggests Congress anticipated that poker would be included within the reach of the IGBA as it was ultimately enacted.

> Mr. MIKVA: I would like to yield further but I have more examples of overreach that would even curl the hair of the gentleman from Virginia [Mr. POFF].
>
> I do not know how many of my colleagues engage in a friendly game of poker now and then, but under th[e IGBA's] definition [of gambling] if five or more of them engage in such a game of poker and it lasts past midnight—you do have that safeguard—thus continuing for a period of 2 days, then you have been running an organized gambling business and you can get 20 years, and the Federal Government can grab the pot besides [. . . .]
>
> We have a whole series of new crimes involving gambling and some of them, as I indicated, include even the poker game that goes beyond midnight. Under the bill, it can be an organized gambling game and one can get up to 20 years for having participated in that poker game.

116 CONG. REC. 35204–05 (Oct. 6, 1970).

The concern that the IGBA would criminalize non-commercial private poker games was assuaged by comments mentioning the requirements currently set forth under § 1955(b)(1), and not by comments indicating that poker is a game of skill.

> Mr. POFF: I suggest that the gentleman is in error when he poses his hypothetical statement. I direct his attention to page 11, line 15 and 16 of the bill. There you will find that illegal gambling means a business and has been and remains in substantially continuous operation for a period in excess of 30 days or has a gross revenue in excess of $2,000 in any single day. The poker game which the gentleman has described does not meet that criterion.
>
> Mr. MIKVA: But that is not true because later on there is a presumption that it is an illegal gambling business. That language appears on page 114 and is as follows:
>
>> If five or more persons conduct, finance, manage, supervise, direct, or own all or part of a gambling business and such business operates for 2 or more successive days, then, for the purpose of obtaining warrants for arrests, interceptions, and other searches and seizures, probable cause that the business

> receives gross revenue in excess of $2,000 in any single day shall be deemed to have been established.
>
> Mr. POFF: If they are in the gambling business.
>
> Mr. MIKVA: I suppose it depends on whether you are gambling for profit or pleasure, but I happen to know a lot of people who do enjoy the profit as well as the pleasure, and I would hate to rely on the "nondefinition" of business to protect somebody from a zealous U.S. attorney.

Id. at 35205.

Thus, to the extent that poker was discussed, there was some acknowledgment that some businesses operating poker games would fall within the IGBA, but that the other requirements of the statute would exclude the typical friendly game of poker from the statute's reach.

IV. Rule of Lenity

DiCristina argues that the rule of lenity requires us to construe any ambiguity in the IGBA in his favor. "[T]he rule of lenity only applies if, after considering text, structure, history, and purpose, there remains a grievous ambiguity or uncertainty in the statute." *Barber*, 130 S.Ct. at 2508 (internal quotation marks omitted); *see also United States v. Venturella*, 391 F.3d 120, 133 (2nd Cir. 2004) (noting that this Court applies the rule of lenity as a "last resort"). A statute is not " 'ambiguous' for purposes of lenity merely because it [i]s possible to articulate a construction more narrow than that urged by the Government." *Moskal v. United States*, 498 U.S. 103, 108 (1990). Here, as discussed, the plain language of § 1955 unambiguously indicates that DiCristina's poker business constituted an "illegal gambling business" in violation of the statute. Thus, there is no need to turn to a rule of construction to further divine the meaning of the statute, and the rule of lenity does not apply. * * *

CONCLUSION

Because we find that the plain language of the IGBA includes DiCristina's poker business, we reverse the judgment of acquittal and remand to the District Court to reinstate the jury verdict, enter a judgment of conviction on both counts, and proceed with sentencing DiCristina.

Readings

The following article by Karl Llewellyn is old, and the cases cited in it are considerably older of course, but the dynamic that Llewellyn identified—that canons of statutory construction come in opposing pairs, each with opposing and equally respectable authority behind them—remains current, even if the case citations in a modern version of his argument would be very different. In other words, the footnotes matter in this piece, not because of the specific cases cited there, but because of what the existence of such contrasting authority says about the discipline of statutory interpretation itself.

KARL N. LLEWELLYN, *REMARKS ON THE THEORY OF APPELLATE DECISION AND THE RULES OR CANONS ABOUT HOW STATUTES ARE TO BE CONSTRUED*

3 VAND. L. REV. 395 (1950)

* * * If a statute is to make sense, it must be read in the light of some assumed purpose. A statute merely declaring a rule, with no purpose or objective, is nonsense. If a statute is to be merged into a going system of law, moreover, the court must do the merging, and must in so doing take account of the policy of the statute—or else substitute its own version of such policy. Creative re-shaping of the net result is thus inevitable.

But the policy of a statute is of two wholly different kinds—each kind somewhat limited in effect by the statute's choice of measures, and by the statute's choice of fixed language. On the one hand there are the ideas consciously before the draftsmen, the committee, the legislature: a known evil to be cured, a known goal to be attained, a deliberate choice of one line of approach rather than another. Here talk of "intent" is reasonably realistic; committee reports, legislative debate, historical knowledge of contemporary thinking or campaigning which points up the evil or the goal can have significance.

But on the other hand—and increasingly as a statute gains in age—its language is called upon to deal with circumstances utterly uncontemplated at the time of its passage. Here the quest is not properly for the sense originally intended by the statute, for the sense sought originally to be *put into it,* but rather for the sense which *can be quarried out of it* in the light of the new situation. Broad purposes can indeed reach far beyond details known or knowable at the time of drafting. A "dangerous weapon" statute of 1840 can include tommy guns, tear gas or atomic bombs. "Vehicle," in a statute of 1840, can properly be read, when sense so suggests, to include an automobile, or a hydroplane that lacks wheels. But for all that, the sound quest does not run primarily in terms of historical intent. It runs in terms of what the words can be made to bear, in making sense in the light of the unforeseen. * * *

When it comes to presenting a proposed construction in court, there is an accepted conventional vocabulary. As in argument over points of case-law, the accepted convention still, unhappily requires discussion as if only one single correct meaning could exist. Hence there are two opposing canons on almost every point. An arranged selection is appended. Every lawyer must be familiar with them all: they are still needed tools of argument. At least as early as Fortescue the general picture was clear, on this, to any eye which would see.

Plainly, to make any canon take hold in a particular instance, the construction contended for must be sold, essentially, by means other than the use of the canon: The good sense of the situation and a *simple* construction of the available language to achieve that sense, *by tenable means, out of the statutory language.*

CANONS OF CONSTRUCTION

Statutory interpretation still speaks a diplomatic tongue. Here is some of the technical framework for maneuver:

THRUST	BUT PARRY
1. A statute cannot go beyond its text.[3]	1. To effect its purpose a statute may be implemented beyond its text.[4]
2. Statutes in derogation of the common law will not be extended by construction.[5]	2. Such acts will be liberally construed if their nature is remedial.[6]
3. Statutes are to be read in the light of the common law and a statute affirming a common law rule is to be construed in accordance with the common law.[7]	3. The common law gives way to a statute which is inconsistent with it and when a statute is designed as a revision of a whole body of law applicable to a given subject it supersedes the common law.[8]
4. Where a foreign statute which has received construction has been adopted, previous construction is adopted too.[9]	4. It may be rejected where there is conflict with the obvious meaning of the statute or where the foreign decisions are unsatisfactory in reasoning or where the foreign interpretation is

---

[3] *First National Bank v. DeBerriz*, 87 W. Va. 477, 105 S.E. 900 (1921); SUTHERLAND, STATUTORY CONSTRUCTION § 388 (2d ed. 1904); 59 C.J., Statutes, § 575 (1932).

[4] *Dooley v. Penn. R.R.*, 250 Fed. 142 (D. Minn. 1918); 59 C.J., Statutes § 578 (1932).

[5] *Devers v. City of Scranton*, 308 Pa. 13, 161 Atl. 540 (1932); BLACK, CONSTRUCTION AND INTERPRETATION OF LAWS § 113 (2d ed. 1911); SUTHERLAND, STATUTORY CONSTRUCTION § 573 (2d ed. 1904); 25 R.C.L., Statutes § 281 (1919).

[6] *Becker v. Brown*, 65 Neb. 264, 91 N.W. 178 (1902); BLACK, CONSTRUCTION AND INTERPRETATION OF LAWS § 113 (2d ed. 1911); SUTHERLAND, STATUTORY CONSTRUCTION §§ 573–75 (2d ed. 1904); 59 C.J., Statutes § 657 (1932).

[7] *Bandfield v. Bandfield*, 117 Mich. 80, 75 N.W. 287 (1898); 25 R.C.L., Statutes § 280 (1919).

[8] *Hamilton v. Rathbone*, 175 U.S. 414, 20 Sup. Ct. 155, 44 L. Ed. 219 (1899); State v. Lewis, 142 N.C. 626, 55 S.E. 600 (1906); 25 R.C.L., Statutes §§ 280, 289 (1919).

[9] *Freese v. Tripp*, 70 Ill. 496 (1873); BLACK, CONSTRUCTION AND INTERPRETATION OF LAWS § 176 (2d ed. 1911); 59 C.J., Statutes, §§ 614, 627 (1932); 25 R.C.L., Statutes § 294 (1919).

	not in harmony with the spirit or policy of the laws of the adopting state.[10]
5. Where various states have already adopted the statute, the parent state is followed.[11]	5. Where interpretations of other states are inharmonious, there is no such restraint.[12]
6. Statutes *in pari materia* must be construed together.[13]	6. A statute is not *in pari materia* if its scope and aim are distinct or where a legislative design to depart from the general purpose or policy of previous enactments may be apparent.[14]
7. A statute imposing a new penalty or forfeiture, or a new liability or disability, or creating a new right of action will not be construed as having a retroactive effect.[15]	7. Remedial statutes are to be liberally construed and if a retroactive interpretation will promote the ends of justice, they should receive such construction.[16]
8. Where design has been distinctly stated no place is left for construction.[17]	8. Courts have the power to inquire into real—as distinct from ostensible—purpose.[18]
9. Definitions and rules of construction contained in an interpretation clause are part of the law and binding.[19]	9. Definitions and rules of construction in a statute will not be extended beyond their necessary import nor allowed to

[10] *Bowers v. Smith*, 111 Mo. 45, 20 S.W. 101 (1892); BLACK, CONSTRUCTION AND INTERPRETATION OF LAWS § 176 (2d ed. 1911); SUTHERLAND, STATUTORY CONSTRUCTION § 404 (2d ed. 1904); 59 C.J., Statutes § 628 (1932).

[11] *Burnside v. Wand*, 170 Mo. 531, 71 S.W. 337 (1902).

[12] *State v. Campbell*, 73 Kan. 688, 85 Pac. 784 (1906).

[13] *Milner v. Gibson*, 249 Ky. 594, 61 S.W.2d 273 (1933); BLACK, CONSTRUCTION AND INTERPRETATION OF LAWS § 104 (2d ed. 1911); SUTHERLAND, STATUTORY CONSTRUCTION §§ 443–48 (2d ed. 1904); 25 R.C.L., Statutes § 285 (1919).

[14] *Wheelock v. Myers*, 64 Kan. 47, 67 Pac. 632 (1902); BLACK, CONSTRUCTION AND INTERPRETATION OF LAWS § 104 (2d ed. 1911); SUTHERLAND, STATUTORY CONSTRUCTION § 449 (2d ed. 1904); 59 C.J., Statutes § 620 (1932).

[15] *Keeley v. Great Northern Ry.*, 139 Wis. 448, 121 N.W. 167 (1909); BLACK, CONSTRUCTION AND INTERPRETATION OF LAWS § 119 (2d ed. 1911).

[16] *Falls v. Key*, 278 S.W. 893 (Tex. Civ. App. 1925); BLACK, CONSTRUCTION AND INTERPRETATION OF LAWS § 120 (2d ed. 1911).

[17] *Federoff v. Birks Bros.*, 75 Cal. App. 345, 242 Pac. 885 (1925); SUTHERLAND, STATUTORY CONSTRUCTION § 358 (2d ed. 1904); 59 C.J., Statutes § 570 (1932).

[18] *Coulter v. Pool*, 187 Cal. 181, 201 Pac. 120 (1921); 59 C.J., Statutes § 570 (1932).

[19] *Smith v. State*, 28 Ind. 321 (1867); BLACK, CONSTRUCTION AND INTERPRETATION OF LAWS § 89 (2d ed. 1911); 59 C.J., Statutes § 567 (1932).

	defeat intention otherwise manifested.[20]
10. A statutory provision requiring liberal construction does not mean disregard of unequivocal requirements of the statute.[21]	10. Where a rule of construction is provided within the statute itself the rule should be applied.[22]
11. Titles do not control meaning; preambles do not expand scope; section headings do not change language.[23]	11. The title may be consulted as a guide when there is doubt or obscurity in the body; preambles may be consulted to determine rationale, and thus the true construction of terms; section headings may be looked upon as part of the statute itself.[24]
12. If language is plain and unambiguous it must be given effect.[25]	12. Not when literal interpretation would lead to absurd or mischievous consequences or thwart manifest purpose.[26]
13. Words and phrases which have received judicial construction before enactment are to be	13. Not if the statute clearly requires them to have a different meaning.[28]

[20] *In re Bissell*, 245 App. Div. 395, 282 N.Y. Supp. 983 (4th Dep't 1935); BLACK, CONSTRUCTION AND INTERPRETATION OF LAWS § 89 (2d ed. 1911); 59 C.J., Statutes § 566 (1932).

[21] *Los Angeles County v. Payne*, 82 Cal. App. 210, 255 Pac. 281 (1927); SUTHERLAND, STATUTORY CONSTRUCTION § 360 (2d ed. 1904); 59 C.J., Statutes § 567 (1932).

[22] *State ex rel. Triay v. Burr*, 79 Fla. 290, 84 So. 61 (1920); SUTHERLAND, STATUTORY CONSTRUCTION § 360 (2d ed. 1904); 59 C.J., Statutes § 567 (1932).

[23] *Westbrook v. McDonald*, 184 Ark. 740, 44 S.W. 2d 331 (1931); Huntworth v. Tanner, 87 Wash. 670, 152 Pac. 523 (1915); BLACK, CONSTRUCTION AND INTERPRETATION OF LAWS §§ 83–85 (2d ed. 1911); SUTHERLAND, STATUTORY CONSTRUCTION §§ 339–42 (2d ed. 1904); 59 C.J., Statutes § 599 (1932); 25 R.C.L., Statutes §§ 266–267 (1919).

[24] *Brown v. Robinson*, 275 Mass. 55, 175 N.E. 269 (1931); *Gulley v. Jackson*, 165 Miss. 103, 145 So. 905 (1933); BLACK, CONSTRUCTION AND INTERPRETATION OF LAWS §§ 83–85 (2d ed. 1911); SUTHERLAND, STATUTORY CONSTRUCTION §§ 339–42 (2d ed. 1904); 59 C.J., Statutes §§ 598–99 (1932); 25 R.C.L., Statutes §§ 266, 267 (1919).

[25] *Newhall v. Sanger*, 92 U.S. 761, 23 L. Ed. 769 (1875); BLACK, CONSTRUCTION AND INTERPRETATION OF LAWS § 51 (2d ed. 1911); 59 C.J., Statutes § 569 (1932); 25 R.C.L., Statutes §§ 213, 225 (1919).

[26] *Clark v. Murray*, 141 Kan. 533, 41 P.2d 1042 (1935); SUTHERLAND, STATUTORY CONSTRUCTION § 363 (2d ed. 1904); 59 C.J., Statutes § 573 (1932); 25 R.C.L., Statutes, §§ 214, 257 (1919).

[28] *Dixon v. Robbins*, 246 N.Y. 169, 158 N.E. 63 (1927); BLACK, CONSTRUCTION AND INTERPRETATION OF LAWS § 65 (2d ed. 1911); SUTHERLAND, STATUTORY CONSTRUCTION § 363 (2d ed. 1904).

understood according to that construction.[27]	
14. After enactment, judicial decision upon interpretation of particular terms and phrases controls.[29]	14. Practical construction by executive officers is strong evidence of true meaning.[30]
15. Words are to be taken in their ordinary meaning unless they are technical terms or words of art.[31]	15. Popular words may bear a technical meaning and technical words may have a popular signification and they should be so construed as to agree with evident intention or to make the statute operative.[32]
16. Every word and clause must be given effect.[33]	16. If inadvertently inserted or if repugnant to the rest of the statute, they may be rejected as surplusage.[34]
17. The same language used repeatedly in the same connection is presumed to bear the same meaning throughout the statute.[35]	17. This presumption will be disregarded where it is necessary to assign different meanings to make the statute consistent.[36]

[27] *Scholze v. Sholze*, 2 Tenn. App. 80 (M.S. 1925); BLACK, CONSTRUCTION AND INTERPRETATION OF LAWS § 65 (2d ed. 1911); SUTHERLAND, STATUTORY CONSTRUCTION § 363 (2d ed. 1904).

[29] *Eau Claire National Bank v. Benson*, 106 Wis. 624, 82 N.W. 604 (1900); BLACK, CONSTRUCTION AND INTERPRETATION OF LAWS § 93 (2d ed. 1911).

[30] *State ex rel. Bashford v. Frear*, 138 Wis. 536, 120 N.W. 216 (1909); BLACK, CONSTRUCTION AND INTERPRETATION OF LAWS § 94 (2d ed. 1911); 25 R.C.L., Statutes § 274 (1919).

[31] *Hawley Coal Co. v. Bruce*, 252 Ky. 455, 67 S.W.2d 703 (1934); BLACK, CONSTRUCTION AND INTERPRETATION OF LAWS § 63 (2d ed. 1911; SUTHERLAND, STATUTORY CONSTRUCTION §§ 390, 393 (2d ed. 1904); 59 C.J., Statutes, §§ 577, 578 (1932).

[32] *Robinson v. Varnell*, 16 Tex. 382 (1856); BLACK, CONSTRUCTION AND INTERPRETATION OF LAWS § 63 (2d ed. 1911); SUTHERLAND, STATUTORY CONSTRUCTION § 395 (2d ed. 1904); 59 C.J., Statutes §§ 577, 578 (1932).

[33] *In re Terry's Estate*, 218 N.Y. 218, 112 N.E. 931 (1916); BLACK, CONSTRUCTION AND INTERPRETATION OF LAWS § 60 (2d ed. 1911); SUTHERLAND, STATUTORY CONSTRUCTION § 380 (2d ed. 1904).

[34] *United States v. York*, 131 Fed. 323 (C.C.S.D.N.Y. 1904); BLACK, CONSTRUCTION AND INTERPRETATION OF LAWS § 60 (2d ed. 1911); SUTHERLAND, STATUTORY CONSTRUCTION §§ 384 (2d ed. 1904).

[35] *Spring Canyon Coal Co. v. Industrial Comm'n*, 74 Utah 103, 277 Pac. 206 (1929); BLACK, CONSTRUCTION AND INTERPRETATION OF LAWS § 53 (2d ed. 1911).

[36] *State v. Knowles*, 90 Md. 646, 45 Atl. 877 (1900); BLACK, CONSTRUCTION AND INTERPRETATION OF LAWS § 53 (2d ed. 1911).

18. Words are to be interpreted according to the proper grammatical effect of their arrangement within the statute.[37]	18. Rules of grammar will be disregarded where strict adherence would defeat purpose.[38]
19. Exceptions not made cannot be read.[39]	19. The letter is only the "bark." Whatever is within the reason of the law is within the law itself.[40]
20. Expression of one thing excludes another.[41]	20. The language may fairly comprehend many different cases where some only are expressly mentioned by way of example.[42]
21. General terms are to receive a general construction.[43]	21. They may be limited by specific terms with which they are associated or by the scope and purpose of the statute.[44]
22. It is a general rule of construction that where general words follow an enumeration they are to be held as applying only to persons and things of the same general kind or class specifically mentioned (*ejusdem generis*).[45]	22. General words must operate on something. Further, *ejusdem generis* is only an aid in getting the meaning and does not warrant confining the operations of a statute within narrower limits than were intended.[46]

[37] *Harris v. Commonwealth*, 142 Va. 620, 128 S.E. 578 (1925); BLACK, CONSTRUCTION AND INTERPRETATION OF LAWS § 55 (2d ed. 1911); SUTHERLAND, STATUTORY CONSTRUCTION § 408 (2d ed. 1904).

[38] *Fisher v. Connard*, 100 Pa. 63 (1882); BLACK, CONSTRUCTION AND INTERPRETATION OF LAWS § 55 (2d ed. 1911); SUTHERLAND, STATUTORY CONSTRUCTION § 409 (2d ed. 1904).

[39] *Lima v. Cemetery Ass'n*, 42 Ohio St. 128 (1884); 25 R.C.L., Statutes § 230 (1919).

[40] *Flynn v. Prudential Ins. Co.*, 207 N.Y. 315, 100 N.E. 794 (1913); 59 C.J., Statutes § 573 (1932).

[41] *Detroit v. Redford Twp.*, 253 Mich. 453, 235 N.W. 217 (1931); BLACK, CONSTRUCTION AND INTERPRETATION OF LAWS § 72 (2d ed. 1911); SUTHERLAND, STATUTORY CONSTRUCTION §§ 491–94 (2d ed. 1904).

[42] *Springer v. Philippine Islands*, 277 U.S. 189, 48 Sup. Ct. 480, 72 L. Ed. 845 (1928); BLACK, CONSTRUCTION AND INTERPRETATION OF LAWS § 72 (2d ed. 1911); SUTHERLAND, STATUTORY CONSTRUCTION § 495 (2d ed. 1904).

[43] *De Witt v. San Francisco*, 2 Cal. 289 (1852); BLACK, CONSTRUCTION AND INTERPRETATION OF LAWS § 68 (2d ed. 1911); 59 C.J., Statutes § 580 (1932).

[44] *People ex rel. Krause v. Harrison*, 191 Ill. 257, 61 N.E. 99 (1901); BLACK, CONSTRUCTION AND INTERPRETATION OF LAWS § 69 (1911); SUTHERLAND, STATUTORY CONSTRUCTION § 347 (2d ed. 1904).

[45] *Hull Hospital v. Wheeler*, 216 Iowa 1394, 250 N.W. 637 (1933); BLACK, CONSTRUCTION AND INTERPRETATION OF LAWS § 71 (2d ed. 1911); SUTHERLAND, STATUTORY CONSTRUCTION §§ 422–34 (2d ed. 1904); 59 C.J., Statutes § 581 (1932); 25 R.C.L., Statutes § 240 (1919).

[46] *Texas v. United States*, 292 U.S. 522, 54 Sup. Ct. 819, 78 L. Ed. 1402 (1934); *Grosjean v. American Paint Works*, 160 So. 449 (La. App. 1935); BLACK, CONSTRUCTION AND INTERPRETATION OF LAWS § 71 (2d ed. 1911); SUTHERLAND, STATUTORY CONSTRUCTION §§ 437–41 (2d ed. 1904); 59 C.J., Statutes § 581 (1932); 25 R.C.L., Statutes § 240 (1919).

23. Qualifying or limiting words or clauses are to be referred to the next preceding antecedent.[47]	23. Not when evident sense and meaning require a different construction.[48]
24. Punctuation will govern when a statute is open to two constructions.[49]	24. Punctuation marks will not control the plain and evident meaning of language.[50]
25. It must be assumed that language had been chosen with due regard to grammatical propriety and is not interchangeable on mere conjecture.[51]	25. "And" and "or" may be read interchangeably whenever the change is necessary to give the statute sense and effect.[52]
26. There is a distinction between words of permission and mandatory words.[53]	26. Words imparting permission may be read as mandatory and words imparting command may be read as permissive when such construction is made necessary by evident intention or by the rights of the public.[54]
27. A proviso qualifies the provision immediately preceding.[55]	27. It may clearly be intended to have a wider scope.[56]

[47] *Dunn v. Bryan*, 77 Utah 604, 299 Pac. 253 (1931); BLACK, CONSTRUCTION AND INTERPRETATION OF LAWS § 73 (2d ed. 1911); SUTHERLAND, STATUTORY CONSTRUCTION §§ 420, 421 (2d ed. 1904); 59 CJ., Statutes § 583 (1932).

[48] *Myer v. Ada County*, 50 Idaho 39, 293 Pac. 322 (1930); BLACK, CONSTRUCTION AND INTERPRETATION OF LAWS § 73 (2d ed. 1911); SUTHERLAND, STATUTORY CONSTRUCTION §§ 420, 421 (2d ed. 1904); 59 C.J., Statutes § 583 (1932).

[49] *United States v. Marshall Field & Co.*, 18 C.C.P.A. 228 (1930); BLACK, CONSTRUCTION AND INTERPRETATION OF LAWS § 88 (2d ed. 1911); SUTHERLAND, STATUTORY CONSTRUCTION § 361 (2d ed. 1904); 59 C.J., Statutes § 590 (1932).

[50] *State v. Baird*, 36 Ariz. 531, 288 Pac. 1 (1930); BLACK, CONSTRUCTION AND INTERPRETATION OF LAWS § 87 (2d ed. 1911); SUTHERLAND, STATUTORY CONSTRUCTION § 361 (2d ed. 1904); 59 C.J., Statutes § 590 (1932).

[51] *Hines v. Mills*, 187 Ark. 465, 60 S.W.2d 181 (1933); BLACK, CONSTRUCTION AND INTERPRETATION OF LAWS § 75 (2d ed. 1911).

[52] *Fulghum v. Bleakley*, 177 S.C. 286, 181 S.E. 30 (1935); SUTHERLAND, STATUTORY CONSTRUCTION § 397 (2d ed. 1904); 25 R.C.L., Statutes § 226 (1919).

[53] *Koch & Dryfus v. Bridges*, 45 Miss. 247 (1871); BLACK, CONSTRUCTION AND INTERPRETATION OF LAWS § 150 (2d ed. 1911).

[54] *Jennings v. Suggs*, 180 Ga. 141, 178 S.E. 282 (1935); Ewing v. Union Central Bank, 254 Ky. 623, 72 S.W.2d 4 (1934); BLACK, CONSTRUCTION AND INTERPRETATION OF LAWS § 151 (2d ed. 1911); 59 C.J., Statutes § 631 (1932).

[55] *State ex rel. Higgs v. Summers*, 118 Neb. 189, 223 N.W. 957 (1929); BLACK, CONSTRUCTION AND INTERPRETATION OF LAWS § 130 (2d ed. 1911); SUTHERLAND, STATUTORY CONSTRUCTION § 352 (2d ed. 1904); 59 C.J., Statutes § 640 (1932).

[56] *Reuter v. San Mateo County*, 220 Cal. 314, 30 P.2d 417 (1934); BLACK, CONSTRUCTION AND INTERPRETATION OF LAWS § 130 (2d ed. 1911).

28. When the enacting clause is general, a proviso is construed strictly.[57]	28. Not when it is necessary to ex tend the proviso to persons or cases which come within its equity.[58]

NOTES AND QUESTIONS

1. *"I am shocked, shocked to discover gambling going on in this electric bike shop."* Llewellyn may be right that "statutory interpretation * * * speaks a *diplomatic* tongue," but it is nonetheless a language in which *lawyers* must be fluent. Their fluency may be more difficult to develop if they treat the law as though it consisted of authorities that are either obligatory and controlling or non-binding and irrelevant. After all, canons of statutory construction may merely be "rules of thumb," *Connecticut Nat'l Bank v. Germain*, 503 U.S. 249, 253 (1992), but they made all the difference between Mr. DiCristina's innocence at the district court and his guilt at the court of appeals. Try to identify each of the principles of interpretation considered by the court of appeals in *DiCristina*, including those that either did not apply or did not justify a different result. (Don't forget the footnotes.) (a) How would you describe the legal status of these interpretive guidelines? (b) Picking up on the poker theme, does statutory construction seem more like a game of skill or a game of chance?

2. *Simple contradictions vs. complex guidelines*. According to the Supreme Court, specific canons of statutory construction "are often countered * * * by some maxim pointing in a different direction," exactly as Llewellyn suggested. *Circuit City Stores, Inc. v. Adams*, 532 U.S. 105, 115 (2001). On the other hand, which of Llewellyn's 28 canon-pairs actually contradict each other, and which can be viewed as consistent but contrasting explications of a single complex rule? How many might be viewed for example as "clear statement" rules, which create a rebuttable presumption about how a statute should be interpreted in the absence of a clear statement from the legislature to the contrary?

3. *Varieties of canons of construction (I): the inferential or contextual canons.* You have seen already that the "plain meaning" rule is the first rhetorical step in any case requiring statutory interpretation. The rule is axiomatic and irresistible, but it may be useless in contested cases, because more than one reasonable interpretation fits the "plain" text. Recognizing this reality, the courts have developed a range of canons of construction that allow the court to infer the meaning of the text adopted by the legislature. These are guidelines for determining the meaning of the words in context without regard

---

[57] *Montgomery v. Martin*, 294 Pa. 25, 143 Atl. 505 (1928); BLACK, CONSTRUCTION AND INTERPRETATION OF LAWS § 131 (2d ed. 1911); SUTHERLAND, STATUTORY CONSTRUCTION § 322 (2d ed. 1904).

[58] *Forscht v. Green*, 53 Pa. 138 (1866); BLACK, CONSTRUCTION AND INTERPRETATION OF LAWS § 131 (2d ed. 1911).

to any overarching policy preferences (as explored in the next two notes). Consider the following examples (the Latin phrases are included because the courts routinely refer to the canons that way):

a. *The expression or specification of one is the exclusion of others (expressio unius est exclusio alterius).* The express inclusion of a particular item implies the exclusion of others. For example, if the statute applies explicitly to sheep and goats, and no other animal is listed, the *expressio* canon allows the court to infer that other animals are not covered by the statute. Of course, sometimes a list in a statute is merely illustrative, and there may be some textual signal to that effect; indeed, the list you are now reading is a perfect example of an explicitly illustrative, non-exhaustive list.

b. *Statutes on the same subject matter (in pari materia) should be read in conformity with one another.* Statutes may be enacted at different times but deal with the same subject. When there is ambiguity, statutes *in pari materia* are to be interpreted consistently with one another or in light of one another, because a court may justifiably infer that they address the same problem or share a common goal. *See* canon-pair 6 in Llewellyn's article, *supra.*

c. *Statutes should be read to avoid rendering any term or provision superfluous or redundant.* The courts must give effect, if possible, to every clause and word of a statute so that no provision is superfluous or redundant. *Williams v. Taylor*, 529 U.S. 362, 404 (2000). In *Sprietsma v. Mercury Marine*, 537 U.S. 51, 63 (2003), for example, the Court interpreted the word "law" narrowly because a broad interpretation would have rendered the word "regulation" superfluous in a preemption clause that by its terms applied to a state "law or regulation." *See* canon-pair 16 in Llewellyn's article, *supra.*

d. *Items in a list should be interpreted as belonging to the same class or category (ejusdem generis).* In the Supreme Court's words, "where general words follow an enumeration of specific items, the general words are read as applying *only to other items akin to those specifically enumerated.*" *Harrison v. PPG Industries, Inc.*, 446 U.S. 578, 588 (1980) (emphasis supplied). "This rule is based on the theory that, if the Legislature had intended the general words to be used in their unrestricted sense, it would have made no mention of the particular classes." *In re Bush Terminal Co.*, 93 F.2d 659, 660 (2d Cir. 1938). Suppose for example that a statute refers to "automobiles, motor bikes, 'segways,' and *other motorized vehicles*," and the question arises whether the statute applies to airplanes. Literally airplanes are "motorized vehicles," but a court applying the *ejusdem generis* principle would exclude airplanes on the ground that they do not share some essential characteristics with the listed vehicles. *Compare McBoyle v. United States*, 283 U.S. 25 (1931) (holding that an "airplane" is not a "motor vehicle" for purposes of the National Motor Vehicle Theft Act of 1919). The principle cannot apply if the enumerated categories are too "disparate." *Arcadia v. Ohio Power Co.*, 498 U.S. 73, 78 (1990). *See* canon-pair 22 in Llewellyn's article and footnote 13 in *DiCristina, supra.*

e. *A word is known by the company it keeps* (*noscitur a sociis*). The Supreme Court has declared a corollary to the *ejusdem* principle, namely that "words grouped in a list should be given related meaning." *Dole v. United Steelworkers of America*, 494 U.S. 26, 36 (1990); *Gustafson v. Alloyd Co.*, 513 U.S. 561, 575 (1995) (limiting a statutory definition in light of the first of many groups of words). The *noscitur* principle may also be invoked by a court when it resolves an ambiguity in a word by reference to the rest of the statute. See *Powerex Corp. v. Reliant Energy Servs., Inc.*, 551 U.S. 224, 232 (2007) ("identical words and phrases within the same statute should normally be given the same meaning.") *Cf. General Dynamics Land Systems, Inc. v. Cline*, 540 U.S. 581, 594–599 (2004) (holding that the word "age" means different things in different parts of the Age Discrimination in Employment Act and that the presumption of uniform usage throughout a statute should therefore not apply).

There is an argument that these canons of construction are common sense made solemn through the dark powers of Latin. You might also think of them as labels for conclusions instead of the premises (or guidelines) they purport to be. At a minimum however, the courts have made them markers in cases requiring serious arguments from counsel about statutory text.

Consider, for example, *Lockhart v. United States*, ___ U.S. ___, 136 S. Ct. 958, 962 (2016), in which the Supreme Court had to determine the propriety of a 10-year mandatory minimum term in prison for possession of child pornography. The statute in question imposed the mandatory minimum "if such person has a prior conviction * * * under the laws of any State relating to aggravated sexual abuse, sexual abuse, or abusive sexual conduct *involving a minor or ward.*" 18 U.S.C. § 2252(b)(2). In Justice Sotomayor's words,

> [t]he issue before us is whether the limiting phrase that appears at the end of that list—"involving a minor or ward"—applies to all three predicate crimes preceding it in the list or only the final predicate crime. We hold that "involving a minor or ward" modifies only "abusive sexual conduct," the antecedent immediately preceding it.

136 S. Ct. at 962. The Court applied the "rule of the last antecedent," which provides that "a limiting clause or phrase * * * should ordinarily be read as modifying only the noun or phrase that it immediately follows." *Barnhart v. Thomas*, 540 U.S. 20, 26 (2003). *See also* BLACK'S LAW DICTIONARY 1532–1533 (10th ed. 2014) ("[Q]ualifying words or phrases modify the words or phrases immediately preceding them and not words or phrases more remote, unless the extension is necessary from the context or the spirit of the entire writing"). The Court held that the phrase "involving a minor or ward" modified only "abusive sexual conduct," the antecedent immediately preceding the statutory phrase in question. The practical consequence of applying the rule of the last antecedent

was that the defendant's prior convictions for sexual abuse *involving an adult* qualified as predicate offences triggering the 10-year minimum.

In her dissent, Justice Kagan (joined by Justice Breyer), opened with this homey observation:

> Imagine a friend told you that she hoped to meet "an actor, director, or producer involved with the new Star Wars movie." You would know immediately that she wanted to meet an actor from the Star Wars cast—not an actor in, for example, the latest Zoolander. Suppose a real estate agent promised to find a client "a house, condo, or apartment in New York." Wouldn't the potential buyer be annoyed if the agent sent him information about condos in Maryland or California? And consider a law imposing a penalty for the "violation of any statute, rule, or regulation relating to insider trading." Surely a person would have cause to protest if punished under that provision for violating a traffic statute. The reason in all three cases is the same: Everyone understands that the modifying phrase—"involved with the new Star Wars movie," "in New York," "relating to insider trading"—applies to each term in the preceding list, not just the last. That ordinary understanding of how English works, in speech and writing alike, should decide this case.

136 S. Ct. at 969. The dissenters noted that "the last-antecedent rule does not generally apply to the grammatical construction present here: when '[t]he modifying clause appear[s] . . . at the end of a single, integrated list.' " *Id.* (citing *Jama v. Immigration and Customs Enforcement*, 543 U.S. 335 (2005), at 344, n. 4. Consistent with Llewellyn's observations, *supra*, the "rule of the last antecedent"—invoked by the majority in *Lockhart*—is offset by the "series-qualifier principle" of the dissent.

4. *Varieties of canons of construction (II): the constitutional and quasi-constitutional canons of coherence and institutional respect.* Sometimes the text of the statute will support at least two different interpretations, and the courts will choose between or among them by deploying canons of construction that serve certain constitutional values. These canons not only assure that the separation of powers is respected in the courts' process of interpreting statutes, but they can also promote coherence among the various sources of law in the American legal system. Consider the following examples:

> a. *Construing statutes in conformity with the Constitution.* The courts will generally avoid deciding constitutional issues whenever possible, *Ashwander v. Tenn. Valley Auth.*, 297 U.S. 288, 345–48 (1936) (Brandeis, J., concurring), and the implications for statutory interpretation cases are clear: statutes must be construed so as to avoid constitutional problems. *See, e.g., Pub. Citizen v. U.S. Dep't of Justice*, 491 U.S. 440, 465–66 (1989) ("[i]t has long been an axiom of statutory interpretation that 'where an otherwise acceptable construction of a statute would raise serious constitutional problems, the Court will construe the statute to avoid such problems unless

such construction is plainly contrary to the intent of Congress' " (*quoting Edward J. DeBartolo Corp. v. Fla. Gulf Coast Bldg. & Constr. Trades Council*, 485 U.S. 568, 575 (1988)).

b. *Deferring to agency expertise in the interpretation of statutes.* Executive agencies of government routinely interpret the statutes they are empowered to enforce. The Supreme Court has determined that those agency interpretations are entitled to a measure of deference in the courts. Often—though not exclusively—the analysis derives from *Chevron U.S.A., Inc. v. Natural Res. Def. Council, Inc.*, 467 U.S. 837, 865–66 (1984). Under the *Chevron* framework, the courts ask whether the statute is ambiguous and, if so, whether the agency's interpretation is reasonable. *Id.* at 842–43. This two-step approach "is premised on the theory that a statute's ambiguity constitutes an implicit delegation from Congress to the agency to fill in the statutory gaps." *FDA v. Brown & Williamson Tobacco Corp.*, 529 U. S. 120, 159 (2000).

c. *Construing statutes in conformity with international law.* In *Murray v. The Charming Betsy*, 6 U.S. (2 Cranch) 64 (1804), the Supreme Court declared that "an act of Congress ought never to be construed to violate the law of nations if any other possible construction remains. * * *" In the absence of a clear statement of contrary intent, Congress is presumed to act in conformity with the international obligations of the United States. In consequence, if a court confronts two possible interpretations of a statute—one of which conforms to international law and the other of which violates international law—the *Charming Betsy* principle systematically favors the former. *See, e.g., INS v. Cardoza-Fonseca*, 480 U.S. 421 (1987) (interpreting U.S. asylum law in light of authoritative but non-binding international standards of refugee eligibility).

d. *Avoiding the abrogation of state sovereignty or immunity.* Federalism creates dual sovereigns in the United States and requires the federal courts to allow the States "great latitude under their police powers to legislate as to the protection of the lives, limbs, health, comfort, and quiet of all persons." *Medtronic, Inc. v. Lohr*, 518 U.S. 470, 475 (1996) (*quoting Metropolitan Life Ins. Co. v. Massachusetts*, 471 U.S. 724, 756 (1985)). Subject to constitutional limitations on federal legislative power, the Supremacy Clause of the Constitution gives priority to acts of Congress when they conflict with state law, but those conflicts are to be minimized by interpreting federal legislation in ways that respect state sovereignty. *See, e.g., Gregory v. Ashcroft*, 501 U.S. 452 (1991).

e. *Construing statutes in conformity with the common law.* In a system of legislative supremacy, the common law bends to the will of the legislature, meaning that Congress can by statute override the common law. But, unless Congress does so explicitly, its legislation will be construed consistently with pre-existing common law standards. "[W]here a common law principle is well established, * * * the courts may take it as a given that Congress has legislated with an expectation that the principle will apply except 'when a statutory purpose to the contrary is evident.' " *Astoria Federal Savings & Loan Ass'n v. Solimino*, 501 U.S. 104, 108 (1991) (*quoting Isbrandtsen Co. v. Johnson*, 343 U.S. 779, 783 (1952)). This canon may be especially helpful when the common law provides a definition of words used in the statute and the statute itself does not define the term. A statute regulating certain kinds of contracts for example might not define the term "contract" at all, implicitly incorporating the common law understanding of that legal term of art. *See* canon-pair 3 in Llewellyn's article, *supra*.

f. *Code coherence: the latter-in-time rule, the rule against implicit repeals, and lex specialis*. When one statute unavoidably conflicts with a prior statute, the later statute prevails to the extent of the conflict. *Leges posteriores priores contrarias abrogant* (subsequent laws repeal prior contrary laws.) No session of a legislature can permanently bind the hands of later sessions of the same legislature, meaning that Congress for example can always change its statutory mind. The later-in-time rule is easy enough to apply when the legislature is explicit about the repeal, but there are some critical limitations on that rule. (i) One limitation is the powerful presumption against *implicit* (or *implied*) repeals. In other words, if the legislature has shown no explicit intent to repeal or reject the prior law, courts will try to interpret the later law so as not to conflict with it. *See Morton v. Mancari*, 417 U.S. 535, 550–51 (1974) ("In the absence of some affirmative showing of an intention to repeal, the only permissible justification for a repeal by implication is when the earlier and later statutes are *irreconcilable*. . . . 'The intention of the legislature to repeal must be clear and manifest' " (emphasis supplied, internal citations omitted). (ii) The later-in-time rule may not apply when one of the statutes in conflict is more specific than the other and applies to the case at hand. The general law does not control or undermine the specific law (*generalia specialibus non derogant*). In *Morton v. Mancari*, for example, the Supreme Court held that the Equal Employment Act of 1972 did not supersede the employment preference for Native American employees in the Bureau of Indian Affairs, which had been created pursuant to The Indian Reorganization Act of 1934: "Where there is no clear intention otherwise, a *specific* statute will not be controlled or nullified by a *general* one, regardless of the priority of enactment." *Id.* at 550–1 (emphasis supplied). *See also Nitro-Lift Techs., L.L.C. v. Howard*, 568 U.S. 17 (2012) (*per curiam*). *See generally* ANTONIN SCALIA & BRYAN A. GARNER, READING LAW: THE INTERPRETATION OF LEGAL TEXTS 183–88 (2012).

Drawing on the mischief rule, *supra*, to what problem(s) are these coherence-and-respect canons—separately and in aggregate—a potential solution? *See generally* Amanda L. Tyler, *Continuity, Coherence, and the Canons*, 99 NW. U. L. REV. 1389 (2005).

5. *Varieties of canons of construction (III): the policy canons.* Some canons of construction tilt the interpretation of an ambiguous statute so as to serve certain policy goals that are themselves unrelated to the purposes of the statute itself. Consider the following examples:

a. *The rule of lenity.* "[B]efore a man can be punished as a criminal * * * his case must be plainly and unmistakably within the provisions of some statute." *United States v. Gradwell*, 243 U.S. 476, 485 (1917). In construing a criminal statute therefore, the court should resolve all ambiguities in favor of the defendant. *See McNally v. United States*, 483 U.S. 350 (1987); *cf.*, *Muscarello v. U.S.*, 524 U.S. 125 (1998) (declining to apply the rule of lenity). Why didn't the rule of lenity work in the defendant's favor in *DiCristina* or *Lockhart, supra*?

b. *Resolving ambiguities in favor of Native Americans.* According to the Supreme Court, "statutes are to be construed liberally in favor of the Indians with ambiguous provisions interpreted to their benefit." *Chickasaw Nation v. United States*, 534 U.S. 84, 93–94 (2001); *Montana v. Blackfeet Tribe of Indians*, 471 U.S. 759, 766 (1985). "The canons of construction applicable in Indian law are rooted in the unique trust relationship between the United States and the Indians," *Oneida County v. Oneida Indian Nation*, 470 U.S. 226, 247 (1985). As noted in Chapter 8, *supra*, critical race theory lays out the racist and colonialist structure of this "unique trust relationship," undermining whatever simple meaning of "trust" the canon of construction implies. *See generally* Robert A. Williams Jr., *The Algebra of Federal Indian Law: The Hard Trail of Decolonizing and Americanizing the White Man's Indian Jurisprudence*, [1986] WIS. L. REV. 219.

c. *The presumption against extraterritoriality.* The courts routinely presume that U.S. statutes do not apply outside the territory of the United States unless Congress explicitly directs otherwise. In other words, Congress may legislate extraterritorially, but it must do so explicitly. *See, e.g.*, *Morrison v. National Australia Bank*, 561 U.S. 247 (2010) (securities law); *Boureslan v. Arabian American Oil Co.*, 499 U.S. 244 (1991) (anti-discrimination statute); *Foley Brothers Inc. v. Filardo*, 336 U.S. 281 (1949) (labor law).

d. *The presumption against retroactivity.* The Constitutional prohibition of *ex post facto* laws bars the retroactive application of penal laws, meaning that someone cannot be prosecuted for conduct that was not criminal at the time it occurred. U.S. CONST., Art. I, § 9, cl. 3. There is a parallel canon of construction to the effect that civil statutes presumptively do not apply to events predating enactment, unless Congress clearly directs otherwise. "Requiring clear intent assures that Congress itself has affirmatively considered the potential unfairness of retroactive application and determined that it is an acceptable price to pay for the countervailing benefits." *Landgraf v. USI Film Products*, 511 U.S. 244, 272–73 (1994).

e. *The presumption that action by executive agencies will be reviewable by courts.* The Supreme Court has recognized a "strong presumption that Congress intends judicial review of administrative action." *Bowen v. Michigan Academy of Family Physicians*, 476 U.S. 667, 670 (1986). To some extent, the presumption arises out of the language and structure of the Administrative Procedure Act ("APA"), which provides that "final agency action for which there is no other adequate remedy in a court [is] subject to judicial review," 5 U.S.C. § 704. But the APA also provides that it applies "except to the extent that * * * statutes preclude judicial review," 5 U.S.C. § 701(a). That language clearly leaves Congress the power to shield agency action from review by the courts, but only if it does so explicitly in the statute authorizing the agency to act. *See, e.g., United States v. Fausto*, 484 U.S. 439, 452 (1988) (the text and structure of the Civil Service Reform Act establish congressional intent to preclude judicial review). is clear from the purposes of the, from the entirety of its text, and from the structure of the statutory scheme). For exemplary exemption language, *see, e.g.,* 38 U.S.C. § 511(a):

> The Secretary [of Veterans Affairs] shall decide all questions of law and fact necessary to a decision by the Secretary under a law that affects the provision of benefits by the Secretary to veterans or the dependents or survivors of veterans. Subject to [certain statutory exceptions], the decision of the Secretary as to any such question shall be final and conclusive and may not be reviewed by any other official or by any court, whether by an action in the nature of mandamus or otherwise.

(i) What are the values served by each of these canons? (ii) What is the source of those values? *See also* William N. Eskridge, Jr. and Philip P. Frickey, *Quasi-Constitutional Law: Clear Statement Rules as Constitutional Lawmaking*, 45 VAND. L. REV. 593 (1992).

6. *Ambiguities resolved by context versus ambiguities "created" by context.* It is clear enough that ambiguities in text can be resolved by reference to context, as the courts have held repeatedly. But do not miss the counter-intuitive possibility that context can also expose an ambiguity that isn't obvious on the surface of the plain word or phrase in question. The argument in short is that context can provide the evidence of an ambiguity and not the resources for its resolution, that ambiguity is at least preliminarily the *result* of interpretation. "The meaning—*or ambiguity*—of certain words or phrases may only become evident when placed in context. * * * A court must therefore interpret the statute 'as a symmetrical and coherent regulatory scheme,' *Gustafson v. Alloyd Co.*, 513 U.S. 561, 569 (1995), and 'fit, if possible, all parts into an harmonious whole,' *FTC v. Mandel Brothers, Inc.*, 359 U.S. 385, 389

(1959)." *Food & Drug Admin. v. Brown & Williamson Tobacco Corp.*, 529 U.S. 120, 132–33 (2000) (emphasis supplied). *See also Brown v. Gardner*, 513 U.S. 115, 118 (1994) ("Ambiguity is a creature not of definitional possibilities but of statutory context.") When a court uses context to set up an issue for interpretation, the justification tends to track the obligation "to construe statutes, not isolated provisions." *Graham County Soil and Water Conservation Dist. v. United States ex rel. Wilson*, 559 U. S. 280, 290 (2010).

7. *Canons to induce legislative "conversation," not to discover the legislature's prior preferences.* Canons of construction are sometimes treated as though they were archeological tools, used to unearth the meaning of the legislators' words or to dig up their intent. *See, e.g., Chickasaw Nation v. United States*, 534 U.S. 84, 94 (2001) ("[canons of construction] are designed to help judges determine the Legislature's intent as embodied in particular statutory language.") But it may also be possible to portray the canons not as defaults for estimating the legislature's enacted preferences but as inducements or provocations to some additional legislative reaction when those preferences are uncertain. Einer Elhauge, *Preference-Eliciting Statutory Default Rules*, 102 COLUM. L. REV. 2162, 2192–93 (2002).

Professor Amanda Tyler, among others, has rejected this approach on various grounds: "in gauging current political winds, Elhauge's proposal ignores the legislative deal that brokered the statutory language in question, as well as any background norms against which such language came into being, and usurps the sitting legislature's formal role as the impetus for statutory change." Amanda L. Tyler, *Continuity, Coherence, and the Canons*, 99 NW. U. L. REV. 1389 (2005). Is it realistic to think that Congress can either (a) monitor the constant torrent of judicial interpretations of federal statutes or (b) respond to them coherently?

8. *The derp goes in, the derp comes out. Who can explain it?* Are the orthodox canons of construction any more determinate than the language of the statutes being interpreted? How helpful is it to conclude that the canons of construction "do not aid in ascertaining meaning or deciding cases, but rather serve only to "classify and label results reached by other means." REED DICKERSON, THE INTERPRETATION AND APPLICATION OF STATUTES 234 (1975). On the other hand, perhaps the difficulty arises because the canons give voice to a more fundamental, underlying tension in the ideal judicial role. As noted by Professor (and later Judge) Robert Keeton observed, "[t]he judiciary is * * * on the one hand a guardian of the law's continuity, stability, evenhandedness, and predictability and on the other hand a participant in creative evolution that keeps law contemporary and viable." ROBERT E. KEETON, VENTURING TO DO JUSTICE 24 (1969). In short, the canons are inconclusive or complex or contradictory because they give voice to two opposing but equally vital ideas: the courts' "creative role in improving the law" versus their "guardian role in preserving [the law's] continuity and predictability." *Id.*, at 11.

C. PARADOX ALERT: THE NECESSITY AND THE IMPOSSIBILITY OF RELYING ON LEGISLATIVE HISTORY

STEPHEN BREYER, *ON THE USES OF LEGISLATIVE HISTORY IN INTERPRETING STATUTES*

65 S. CAL. L. REV. 845 (1992)

* * * Until recently an appellate court trying to interpret unclear statutory language would have thought it natural, and often helpful, to refer to the statute's "legislative history." The Judges might have examined congressional floor debates, committee reports, hearing testimony, and presidential messages in an effort to determine what Congress really "meant" by particular statutory language. Should courts refer to legislative history as they try to apply statutes correctly? Is this practice wise, helpful, or proper? Lawyers and judges, teachers and legislators, have begun to reexamine this venerable practice, often with a highly critical eye. Some have urged drastically curtailing, or even totally abandoning, its use. Some argue that courts use legislative history almost arbitrarily. Using legislative history, Judge Leventhal once said, is like "looking over a crowd and picking out your friends." Others maintain that it is constitutionally improper to look beyond a statute's language, or that searching for "congressional intent" is a semi-mystical exercise like hunting the snark.

These and other criticisms are taking their toll. Judge Wald has pointed out that the Supreme Court relied on legislative history in almost every statutory case it decided in 1981. * * * By 1989, the Court decided a significant number of statutory cases (ten out of about sixty-five) without any reference to legislative history at all * * *. Referring to legislative history to resolve even difficult cases may soon be the exception rather than the rule. Although I recognize the possible "rearguard" nature of my task, I should like to defend the classical practice and convince you that those who attack it ought to claim victory once they have made judges more sensitive to problems of the abuse of legislative history; they ought not to condemn its use altogether. They should confine their attack to the outskirts and leave the citadel at peace.

My defense focuses on the "law-declaring function" of federal appellate courts and considers only cases in which statutory language is unclear (for few other cases raise serious problems on appeal). First, I demonstrate that we need to use legislative history of providing examples of its usefulness. Second, I address the major arguments against its use in order to show that these arguments call, not for abandonment of the practice, but at most for its careful use. Finally, I offer some institutional reasons for why any significant change in the extent to which courts look to legislative history would likely prove harmful. * * * Let me begin by providing examples of five circumstances in which courts reasonably use legislative history to help reach correct results in difficult cases. I start with the least controversial examples and end with the kind that most disturbs the critics.

A. AVOIDING AN ABSURD RESULT

Blackstone himself, more than two hundred years ago, pointed out that a court need not follow the literal language of a statute where doing so would produce an absurd result. He said that if "collaterally . . . absurd consequences, manifestly contrary to common reason," arise out of statutes those statutes "are, with regard to those collateral consequences, void." Blackstone further explained:

> Where some collateral matter arises out of the general words [of a statute], and happens to be unreasonable; there the judges are in decency to conclude that this consequence was not foreseen by the parliament, and therefore they are at liberty to expound the statute by equity. . . .[8]

Considering such problematic language in a case, should not a judge examine the history of the statute to see whether the language is, in fact, as absurd as it appears, or whether it may serve a reasonable purpose that did not occur to the parties or to the court?

Courts do just such checking. Consider, for example, the Supreme Court case *Green v. Bock Laundry Machine Co.*[9] A Federal Rule of Evidence, enacted into law as a statute, stated that evidence of a witness's prior convictions was admissible if the "court determines that the probative value of admitting this evidence outweighs its prejudicial effect to the defendant."[11] Why does the Rule use the word "defendant?" Should it not say either "accused," thus limiting the Rule's effect to criminal cases, or "other party?" Suppose the prejudicial effect is not "to the defendant" but to the civil plaintiff. Suppose, for example, that the plaintiff's star witness has a serious but almost irrelevant criminal record. Admission of that record would hurt the plaintiff and help the defendant. Why should anyone wish to distinguish between plaintiffs and defendants in this way in a civil case?

Before concluding that the distinction in a civil case was absurd, that no good reason supported it, and that the courts should read the Rule's instruction as applying only to criminal defendants, the Supreme Court checked the history of the Rule to see if the drafters had some special purpose in mind. Only after the Court found no evidence of any such purpose did it hold that the Rule, despite its language, did not apply to civil defendants. Justice Scalia, a vocal critic of the use of legislative history,

---

[8] 1 WILLIAM BLACKSTONE, COMMENTARIES ON THE LAWS OF ENGLAND (15th ed. 1809).

[9] 490 U.S. 504 (1989).

[11] FED. R. EVID. 609(a)(1) (emphasis added).

wrote that this kind of use was proper. He said that a judge will, and presumably should, consult history "to verify that what seems . . . an unthinkable disposition . . . was indeed unthought-of, and thus to justify a departure from the ordinary meaning of the word[s]" in the statute. This kind of use of legislative history seems uncontroversial.

B. DRAFTING ERROR

Legislative history can also illuminate drafting errors. A statute's language might seem fairly clear. The language might produce a result that does not seem absurd. Yet, legislative history nonetheless might clearly show that the result is wrong because of a drafting error that courts should correct. Consider the following example:

A federal criminal statute says "whoever . . . possesses any false, forged, or counterfeit coin, with intent to defraud any person" is guilty of a crime.[13] The question in a case the First Circuit decided in 1982 was whether the statute covers a person who (with the requisite fraudulent intent) possesses, in the United States, false Krugerrands, gold coins used as currency in South Africa, but not in the United States. Does this particular statutory provision protect against fraudulent use of South Africa's currency in the United States? The language indicates that it does. It refers to "any . . . counterfeit coin," and a false Krugerrand is a counterfeit coin.

The history of this statute, however, shows a narrower meaning. In 1965 Congress reorganized, and slightly rewrote, a set of anti-counterfeiting statutes, of which this particular provision was one. During the 150 years that preceded the reorganization, this provision constituted a small part of a statutory paragraph, most of which prohibited the making of counterfeit coins. This older paragraph contained an important qualifying phrase, indicating clearly that the provision applied to American coins and not to foreign coins. When Congress rewrote the statutes in 1965, it kept the qualifying phrase in the reorganized provision that governs the making of counterfeit coins. That provision now says that "whoever falsely makes . . . any coin . . . in resemblance of" any United States coin or any foreign gold or silver coin that is "current in the United States or in actual use and circulation as money within the United States" is guilty of a crime. But when Congress separated the "possession" provision from the larger paragraph, it did not include the qualifying provision that limited its application to coins "current" as money in the United States.

Now that question seems more difficult. Without this history, one might think that a false Krugerrand obviously falls within the scope of the statute's words "any . . . counterfeit coin." But does it? After all, the word "any" in a statute rarely means "any at all in the universe." It almost

---

13 18 U.S.C. § 485 (1988) (emphasis added). [This example is drawn from *United States v. Falvey,* 676 F.2d 871 (1st Cir. 1982).]

always has some context-implied limitation. Moreover, for 150 years this particular statute explicitly did not apply to ancient coins, Krugerrands, or counterfeits of any other coin not currently used as American currency. Should a court read the provision to continue this limitation, reading the word "any" as so limited, or should it assume that the "possession" statute, unlike its near cousin, the "making" statute, includes false Krugerrands? Either answer seems reasonable.

In answering this question, would you not want to know just what Congress had in mind in 1965 when it reorganized and rewrote the pre-existing statutes? More specifically, would you not want to know why the human being who drafted the new "possession" language left out the qualifying phrase? Was it an accident? Did someone tell the drafter to leave it out? If so, did the legislator who told the drafter to omit the phrase have some policy change in mind? If so, what sort of change?

The 1965 House and Senate Reports on the counterfeiting legislation provide fairly clear answers. They specify that the congressional reenactment of the law, reorganizing it and rewriting some of it, was intended to serve purely organizational objectives. They say that Congress expected, after the changes, that the law would remain what it was before the changes. These reports reveal that the individual staff members who rewrote the law thought that the legislators wanted them to accomplish a purely technical, non-substantive drafting objective. The reports thereby indicate that no one in Congress intended to change substantive law or to rewrite federal counterfeiting law so that it helped protect the currency of all nations, including South Africa, or ancient Greece and Rome.

If a court has such good evidence that no one in Congress intended to change the law substantively, is that not grounds for saying, "Congress did not intend any substantive change?" And is this not grounds for reading the preexisting limitation back into the word "any?" The First Circuit used legislative history to uncover, and then to undo, a drafting error. This use seems to me perfectly appropriate and desirable.

C. SPECIALIZED MEANINGS

Even the strongest critics of the use of legislative history concede that a court should take full account of any special meaning that a statutory word may have. The word "standing," for example, means something quite different in a statute than on a subway poster because the word carries with it a host of technical meanings growing out of context, case law, and history more generally. Presumably the critics see nothing wrong with looking to history to help determine whether a particular word has a specialized meaning and, if so, what sort. But why should that history specifically exclude legislative history?

Consider *Pierce v. Underwood*,[17] a recent Supreme Court opinion authored by Justice Scalia. One of the legal questions in the case concerned the meaning of the phrase "substantially justified," as used in the Equal Access to Justice Act. A private party who wins a suit against the government is entitled to attorneys' fees unless the government's position was "substantially justified." The Court considered whether "substantially justified" means "better than reasonable," or even "less than reasonable."

The Court held that the word "substantial," in effect, means "reasonable." In reaching this conclusion, Justice Scalia made various comparisons with other areas of law, including the following:

> Judicial review of agency action, the field at issue here, regularly proceeds under the rubric of "substantial evidence" set forth in the Administrative Procedure Act, 5 U.S.C. § 706(2)(E). That phrase does not mean a large or considerable amount of evidence but rather "such relevant evidence as a reasonable mind might accept as adequate to support a conclusion." [*citing Consolidated Edison Co. v. NLRB*, 305 U.S. 197, 229 (1938)].

For present purposes, the interesting part of this quotation is the date of the *Consolidated Edison* case, namely 1938. The reason it is interesting is that Justice Scalia uses that case to help explain the somewhat technical meaning of a word in the Administrative Procedure Act, which did not become law until 1946. It is worth asking how Justice Scalia knew that the meaning of the word in the 1946 statute was given in a case decided eight years earlier.

The well-known answer to this question is that the 1946 House and Senate Reports make clear that in the Administrative Procedure Act, Congress intended to enact into law recommendations contained in the Report of the Attorney General's Committee on Administrative Procedure. That report cites the *Consolidated Edison* definition, as does a later report by the Attorney General, which focused specifically on the bill that Congress enacted into law in 1946. This later report appears as an appendix to the Senate Report on the bill, and in the Congressional Record, as an extension of remarks made during floor debate. That is how the administrative law community knows, and is very certain, that the APA's term "substantial evidence" means just what Justice Scalia says it means.

This example demonstrates a fairly common function of legislative history—explaining specialized meanings of terms or phrases in a statute which were previously understood by the community of specialists (or others) particularly interested in the statute's enactment. Justice Scalia's reliance on such materials in *Pierce*, widely accepted like most, represents a fairly noncontroversial use of legislative history.

---

[17] 487 U.S. 552 (1988).

D. IDENTIFYING A "REASONABLE PURPOSE"

A court often needs to know the purpose a particular statutory word or phrase serves within the broader context of a statutory scheme in order to decide properly whether a particular circumstance falls within the scope of that word or phrase. Does the word "persons" in a welfare statute, for example, include a child, the child's mother, a stepfather, or all of them? A clear understanding of the provision's purpose could lead a court to decide that exactly the same word, "persons," appearing three times in the same sentence refers to a different group each time.[24]

How does a court determine the purpose of a statutory phrase? Sometimes it can simply look to the surrounding language in the statute or to the entire statutory scheme and ask, "Given this statutory background, what would a reasonable human being intend this specific language to accomplish?" Often this question has only one good answer, but sometimes the surrounding statutory language and the "reasonable human purpose" test cannot answer the question. In such situations, legislative history may provide a clear and helpful resolution. * * *

E. CHOOSING AMONG REASONABLE INTERPRETATIONS OF A POLITICALLY CONTROVERSIAL STATUTE

Consider as a final example a statute that evoked strong political support and opposition in Congress and was enacted with language that is unclear or silent about an important issue that faces a court. Judicial use of legislative history to determine meaning in this context seems to cause critics the greatest concern, for it is the kind of situation in which courts risk elevating the testimony to the level of a statute. Consider a 1981 case in our court that arose out of the Urban Mass Transportation Act of 1964.[30] That Act provided financial aid for urban mass transit systems, and it foresaw that the states receiving aid would likely acquire privately owned mass transit systems. The Act, in section 13(c), said that if a state received aid the federal Secretary of Labor had to certify that the state had made "fair and equitable arrangements . . . to protect the interests of employees affected" by the transit funding. The Secretary of Labor issued various regulations under section 13(c), the thrust of which was that the Secretary would consider an arrangement "fair and equitable" if the employees and the state employer agreed to them.

The case before us asked whether this provision of federal law, section 13(c), preempted a Massachusetts state statute that instructed its Transit

[24] *See Evans v. Commissioner,* 933 F.2d 1, 6–8 (1st Cir. 1991) (Statutory language permits, and legislative history, supported by agency interpretation, suggests that the use of the term "persons" in a section of the Aid to Families with Dependent Children statute, *42 U.S.C. § 602*(a)(8)(B)(ii) (1988), refers, variously, to all people living in the relevant family or assistance unit, and to only those members of the family or assistance unit who received aid in the previous four months and to whose income the agency considers applying a statutory "disregard.").

[30] *See Local Div. 589 v. Massachusetts,* 666 F.2d 618 (1st Cir. 1981), *cert. denied,* 457 U.S. 1117 (1982).

Authority not to negotiate away its power to insist upon productivity-enhancing work-rule changes whenever it negotiated new contracts with the transit unions. The Authority previously had, in effect, given up this power to the unions and promised not to take it back, not even when the old contracts expired. The federal Secretary of Labor had approved the "arrangement" under which the Authority would never try to take the work-rule change power back. Could Massachusetts, by statute, instruct its Authority to act contrary to this Secretary-approved arrangement? If section 13(c) and regulations promulgated pursuant to it preempted conflicting state law, the answer to this question was "no."

The text of the statute does not answer the preemption question. It simply says that the Secretary must certify that the "arrangements" between employer and employee are "fair and equitable." The legislative history of section 13(c), however, did suggest an answer.

First, the Secretary of Labor, Willard Wirtz, testified about the draft bill that became section 13(c) in the committee hearings that preceded its enactment into law. He said that when the Labor Department drafted the bill it had consulted the Amalgamated Transit Workers' Union and the AFL-CIO, and that section 13(c) would not supersede state law. Second, the preemptive effect of section 13(c) was discussed on the floor of Congress just prior to the bill's enactment. Senators hostile to the entire bill, such as Senator Barry Goldwater, asked whether or not it would preempt state law. Senators favoring the bill, such as Senator Pete Williams and Senator Jacob Javits, replied that section 13(c) would not preempt state law. Secretary Wirtz's testimony, and the floor debate, seemed clear and definite, and they helped our court decide that the provision did not preempt the Massachusetts law.

Were we right to rely upon legislative history in this way? The bill itself, and section 13(c) in particular, were controversial in Congress. But the legislative history with respect to preemption was fairly clear. Of course, the legislators themselves may not have written that history. But suppose that a civil servant actually wrote Secretary Wirtz's testimony after consulting with the unions. Suppose that legislative staff wrote the Goldwater/Williams floor colloquy after consulting with counsels for the Transit Workers' Union, employers groups, and the states. Indeed, suppose that union lawyers, or employer lawyers, wrote the debate word for word. Should that fact make the use of legislative history significantly less legitimate?

Before answering this question "yes," consider, for a moment, how Congress actually works. Congress is no longer (was it ever?) made up of part-time citizen-legislators, extemporaneous orators, who burn the midnight oil as they themselves draft the laws needed to resolve the social and political problems revealed during the day's interchange of spontaneous debate. Rather, Congress is a bureaucratic organization with twenty thousand employees, working full-time, generating legislation through complicated, but organized, processes of interaction with other institutions and groups, including executive branch departments, labor unions, business organizations, and public interest groups. These other institutions and groups (including interest groups) through their representatives (including lobbyists) often initiate legislation; they typically make clear to congressional staff just what they are trying to achieve, and why; they may suggest content and text, not only for statutes, but also for reports or floor statements; they review proposed changes; and they negotiate and compromise with staff, with legislators and with each other. The staff, working with the groups, the legislators, and other staff members, will do the same.

When this process works properly, staff members for each legislator carefully review statutory language, report language, and significant proposed language for floor statements (of the staff member's own, and of other legislators), checking for consistency with the legislator's own objectives and positions, suggesting changes, and negotiating compromises. The staff member flags matters of significant substantive or political controversy, brings them to the legislator's attention, discusses them with the legislator, and obtains instructions from the legislator about how to proceed. On important matters, staff members for legislators who are directly involved will examine with care each word and proposed change, often with representatives of affected interest groups or institutions not only in the language of the statute, but also in each committee report and the many floor statements. Significant matters will again be brought to the attention of the legislators for development of their individual positions, and for them to discuss and resolve with other legislators. The process involves continuous interaction among legislators, staff members, and representatives of those institutions or groups most likely to be affected by the proposed legislation. This process requires each legislator to rely upon staff, in the first instance, to separate the matters that are significant from those that are not; it requires each legislator to make decisions about, and to resolve with other legislators, each significant matter; and it requires each legislator further to rely upon drafters and negotiators to carry out the legislator's decisions.

The process I have just described is an institutional one, in which the legislator relies in part upon the work of staff. In this process, no legislator reads every word of every report or floor statement or proposed statute, which may consist of hundreds of pages of text. However, in this process those words are carefully reviewed by those whom they will likely affect and by the legislator's own employees. Moreover, in this process the legislator makes the significant decisions and takes responsibility for the outcome.

This institutional process, in which the legislator serves as a kind of manager, should seem familiar to those who manage other large institutions such as businesses, labor unions, and government departments. No one expects the top officials in such institutions to have read every document they generate. Yet those top officials typically are held responsible for those documents, and the outside world typically treats those documents as genuine reflections of the institution's position, whether or not the top officials actually read them. Many, if not most, institutions work through downward delegation, with responsibility flowing upward. Of course, the judicial branch, in principle, does not work this way. It is perhaps, then, understandable that law professors, judges and lawyers might hope that the legislative branch would function in a similarly centralized fashion. But, after a little reflection, this hope seems unachievable and perhaps undesirable. The judge's staff is smaller and the judge's involvement in the making of legal decisions is more direct and detailed. Why should the judicial ideal be the model for Congress? Why should the fairly public congressional legislative process, which involves checking with those whom the legislation will most likely affect, and then perhaps publicly adopting and explaining their related points of view, diminish the legitimacy of the resulting legislative history? I shall return to this question later, but, for the moment, emphasize that it is at least plausible to claim legitimacy for that history.

Consider the implications of a rule that forbids the court from examining a statute's history-say, the history of section 13(c) of the Urban Mass Transportation Act. First, how would our court have answered the interpretive question in the transit workers case without its history? Viewed from the perspective of those who worked on the law in 1964, might our answer not seem random? And would a different answer not have had at least one objectionable aspect, namely that it would frustrate the reasonable expectations of those (on both sides) who created the law in Congress?

Second, what would the effect on Congress be if it knew that courts would not consider legislative history? Suppose, in 1964, that the employers, unions, and states had thought that committee testimony, report language, floor statements, and the like could not influence a later judicial interpretation of the law's text. How would the states and employers have obtained the preemption assurance that they sought and that the unions were willing to give? They might have tried to write a statutory provision that embodied appropriate "preemption" language. But, one can easily imagine that time, the complexity and length of the overall bill, and the difficulty of foreseeing future circumstances (including how courts would interpret "anti-preemption" language) might have made it impossible for the groups to agree on statutory language. It was easier, however, for them to agree about floor statements or report language about an "intent." This language is more general in form, and would not bind courts in cases where it would make no sense to do so.

It is possible, then, that if the relevant groups, institutions, and individuals involved in the process did not believe courts would look to legislative history, they might not have agreed on the legislation. Without agreement, perhaps Congress would have enacted no "labor protection" at all, or perhaps it would have failed to pass the Urban Mass Transportation Act. An institutional device that facilitates compromise and helps develop the consensus needed to pass important legislation has at least that much to be said in its favor.

In sum, these five examples identify five different circumstances in which courts might turn to legislative history for help in interpreting a statute: (1) avoiding an absurd result; (2) preventing the law from turning on a drafting error; (3) understanding the meaning of specialized terms; (4) understanding the "reasonable purpose" a provision might serve; and (5) choosing among several possible "reasonable purposes" for language in a politically controversial law. The first three are not very controversial. The last two are controversial. The last two examples suggest, however, how in certain contexts reference to legislative history can promote interpretations that more closely correspond to the expectations of those who helped create the law (and whom the law will likely affect). To that extent, its use seems likely to promote fair and workable results.

III. THE CRITICISMS OF THE USE OF LEGISLATIVE HISTORY

I have tried to group the many different arguments made against the use of legislative history into five categories of criticism. Although many of these criticisms have considerable logical and practical force, the question you should ask is whether they are strong enough to force us to abandon, or significantly to curtail, the often useful practice of looking to legislative history in circumstances such as those I have previously described. Why, of all the many tools judges use to help interpret unclear statutory language (context, tradition, custom, precedent, dictionary meanings, administrability, and so on), should they not use this one?

A. LACK OF UTILITY

The argument most frequently heard against the use of legislative history is that it does not help. Critics quote Justice Jackson's remark that "legislative history here, as usual, is more vague than the statute we are called upon to interpret."[37] Again they will point to Judge Leventhal's comment that searching congressional documents for a statute's legislative history is like "looking over a crowd and picking out your friends." One can

[37] *United States v. Public Utils. Comm'n,* 345 U.S. 295, 320 (1953) (Jackson, J., concurring).

easily find examples of vague or conflicting legislative history. The critics do so, and they cite them.[39]

This kind of argument is strongest when aimed at "misuse" of history. But, how strong a case can it make for abandonment? Logically, the argument is open to the response, "If the history is vague, or seriously conflicting, do not use it." No one claims that history is always useful; only that it sometimes helps. * * *

B. CONSTITUTIONAL ARGUMENTS

Two types of constitutional arguments are made against the use of legislative history. The first concerns the Constitution's requirements for enacting a law. A bill must pass both houses of Congress and obtain the President's signature or a veto override. The result, says the Constitution, is a statute; and that statute, not a floor speech or committee report or testimony or presidential message or congressional "intent," is the law. The use of legislative history, according to this argument, tends to make these other matters—report language and floor speeches—the "law" even though they had received neither a majority vote nor a presidential signature.

Second, the Constitution vests "legislative" power in a Congress made up of elected members. It does not vest legislative power in congressional staff or in lobbyists. Yet these unelected individuals write the floor statements, testimony, reports, and messages that make up legislative history. Indeed, the elected members may not even read these materials. Thus, to use legislative history not only makes "law" out of that which is not law, but also permits the exercise of legislative power by those who do not constitutionally possess it.

These arguments overstate their case. The "statute-is-the-only-law" argument misses the point. No one claims that legislative history is a statute, or even that, in any strong sense, it is "law." Rather, legislative history is helpful in trying to understand the meaning of the words that do make up the statute or the "law." A judge cannot interpret the words of an ambiguous statute without looking beyond its words for the words have simply ceased to provide univocal guidance to decide the case at hand. Can the judge, for example, ignore a dictionary or the historical interpretive practice of the agency that customarily applies some words? Is a dictionary or an historic agency interpretive practice "law?" It is "law" only in a weak sense that does not claim the status of a statute, and in a sense that violates neither the letter nor the spirit of the Constitution.

---

[39] For example, compare *TVA v. Hill,* 437 U.S. 153, 174–93 (1978) (providing that legislative history, particularly the House sponsor's statements, supports the view that § 7 of the Endangered Species Act of 1983 requires a court to enjoin the operation of a virtually completed federal dam that would likely eradicate an endangered species) with *id.* at 207–10 (Powell, J., dissenting) (providing that legislative history, particularly statements of Appropriations Committees of both houses, supports the opposite view). * * *

The delegation argument ("the Senator did not write, or even read, the report") is susceptible to the same type of criticism. After all, no one elected lexicographers or agency civil servants to Congress. The Constitution nowhere grants them legislative power. Yet, judges universally seek their help in resolving interpretive problems.

More importantly, this argument misunderstands how Congress works as an institution. The relevant point here is that nothing in the Constitution seems to prohibit Congress from using staff and relying upon groups and institutions in the way I have described. And, for purposes of establishing the legislator's personal responsibility, that description does not distinguish between different kinds of documents—between committee reports, floor statements, or statutory text. Rather, it holds the legislator personally responsible for the work of staff, and it correlates the legislator's direct personal involvement, not according to the kind of document, but according to the significance of the decision at issue. * * *

C. THE PROBLEM OF CONGRESSIONAL "INTENT"

Critics sometimes argue that the use of legislative history depends upon a mistaken belief that behind every statute lies a congressional "intent." Congressional intent, they say, is a myth; some say that the concept itself lacks intellectual coherence. How can a document written by a committee staffer indicate the inner workings of the mind of even one legislator, let alone the several hundred who voted for the law, perhaps each for different individual reasons? Moreover, a branch of political science, called "public choice" theory, argues that legislation simply reflects the conflicting interactions of interest groups; the resulting law sometimes reflects their private, selfish interests, and sometimes serves no purpose at all.[45] Does it make any sense in such circumstances to ascribe a responsible-sounding purpose to the statute's words?

Conceptually, however, one can ascribe an "intent" to Congress in enacting the words of a statute if one means "intent" in its, here relevant, sense of "purpose," rather than its sense of "motive." One often ascribes "group" purposes to group actions. A law school raises tuition to obtain money for a new library. A basketball team stalls to run out the clock. A tank corps feints to draw the enemy's troops away from the main front. Obviously, one of the best ways to find out the purpose of an action taken by a group is to ask some of the group's members about it. But, this does not necessarily mean that the group's purposes and the members' motives or purposes must be identical. The members of the group participating in the group activity-indeed, whose actions are necessary conditions for its action-may have different, private motives for their own actions; but that

---

[45] *See, e.g.,* David A. Farber & Philip P. Frickey, *Legislative Intent & Public Choice,* 74 VA. L. REV. 423, 426–29 (1988) (discussing skepticism of legislative intent engendered by public choice theory); Frank H. Easterbrook, *Statutes' Domains,* 50 U. CHI. L. REV. 533, 547–48 (1983) (arguing that the discoveries of public choice theory make it clear that legislative bodies cannot have intents, but only outcomes).

fact does not necessarily change the proper characterization of the group's purpose. Perhaps several key members of the faculty voted for the tuition increase, not because they cared about the library, but simply in order to please the Dean. Is a better library any the less the object of the law school's action? Indeed, must it always matter if many, or even most, of the group do not fully understand the group objective of the specific action? Perhaps the basketball team is simply reacting instinctively with long-practiced, set plays, the basic function of which the individual members do not have time to consider, or perhaps have forgotten. Is the purpose of those plays any the less the running of the clock? Perhaps the members of the tank corps do not understand why they head in the direction they take; indeed, perhaps even the commanding general does not understand fully the function of each specific action, the exact purposes of which are spelled out only in a memorandum written by a lowly intelligence officer at brigade headquarters (which officer himself was killed sometime before the attack began). Does this story make any difference at all in respect to the purpose of the individual troop movements?

All this is to say that ascribing purposes to groups and institutions is a complex business, and one that is often difficult to describe abstractly. But that fact does not make such ascriptions improper. In practice, we ascribe purposes to group activities all the time without many practical difficulties.

Of course, the relationship between individual group members' purposes and the group's purpose itself may (depending on the type of group) be particularly complex. It may depend upon the group's internal rules and practices, upon background understandings of the group's role in its social context, and upon the kind of individual purposes or motives at issue, along with the individual statements and actions that reveal those individual purposes. But again, those who understand the group do not ordinarily have trouble properly ascribing purposes to its activities, at least in ordinary cases. A legislator, for example, may vote for language that the legislator believes will extend a statute of limitations solely to obtain campaign contributions, to gain political support, or to defeat the bill on the floor. Those personal motives, however, do not change the purpose of the bill's language, namely, to extend the limitations period. A legislator may vote for technical language that the legislator does not understand, knowing that committee members believe (perhaps because of their faith in the drafting process) that it has a proper function. That fact does not necessarily change its function or its purpose. Professors Hart and Sacks, many years ago, described in detail how knowledge of the institutional workings, internal understandings, and societal role of Congress helps to determine Congress's purpose in enacting a statutory word, a phrase, a section, a title, or an entire statutory scheme. If I am correct in believing that ascribing a purpose to a human institution is an activity related to, but different from, ascribing a purpose to an individual, then I do not see how one can criticize courts that use legislative history on conceptual grounds. To refuse to ascribe a "purpose" to Congress in enacting statutory language simply because one cannot find three or four hundred legislators who have claimed it as a personal purpose, is rather like (to use Professor Ryle's old example) refusing to believe in the existence of Oxford University because one can find only colleges.

The public choice theory arguments against the use of legislative history are more substantial, for they seek to dissolve our belief that ascribing purpose serves any useful descriptive function. Public choice theory describes legislative outcomes in terms of interest-group interaction. The description resembles a psychoanalytic explanation of an individual's actions. Normally such an explanation can coexist with, but not replace, a person's own ordinary purposive account of his behavior. But if an individual's behavior is quite bizarre, if his own long, ordinary-purpose-related accounts of what he is doing do not seem to make much sense, and if the psychoanalytic account is good enough, observers will begin to disregard the individual's own purposive accounts as mere window-dressing, and they will begin to consider the psychoanalytic account as the only (or the most) accurate description and explanation of what is going on. Such is the hope of public choice theorists in respect to their explanation of congressional behavior.

Public choice theory, however, does not yet seem able to explain legislation well enough to warrant abandoning the use of legislative history. Public choice proponents sometimes seem to say that a legislature cannot enact laws in the "public interest" if those laws lack strong private interest group support and face strong private interest group opposition. Empirically, however, this seems wrong. The deregulation movement, for example, began in the airline and trucking industries with virtually no interest-group support. The relevant industries were, in fact, strongly opposed to deregulation and the positions of key labor unions ranged from the unenthusiastic to the adamantly opposed. At other times, the theory's proponents seem to deduce from the fact that legislation was enacted that strong private interest groups supported the legislation. As so used, however, the theory becomes tautological.

Moreover, the experience of those who have worked in legislatures does not confirm many public choice theorists' descriptions of the legislative process. Chief Judge Mikva of the District of Columbia Circuit, a congressman for many years, writes:

> The politicians and other people I have known in public life just do not fit the "rent-seeking" egoist model that the public choice theorists offer. . . . Not even my five terms in the Illinois state legislature-that last vestige of democracy in the "raw"—nor my

five terms in the United States Congress, prepared me for the villains of the public choice literature.[49]

My experience running the staff of the Senate Judiciary Committee led me to conclude that elected officials seriously consider public interest arguments and act upon them far more often than the press, the public choice theorists, or the cynics would lead one to believe.

Finally, one should recall that legislative history is a judicial tool, one judges use to resolve difficult problems of judicial interpretation. It can be justified, at least in part, by its ability to help judges interpret statutes, in a manner that makes sense and that will produce a workable set of laws. If judicial use of legislative history achieves this kind of result, courts might use it as part of their overarching interpretive task of producing a coherent and relatively consistent body of statutory law, even were the "rational member of Congress" a pure fiction, made up out of whole cloth. * * *

E. AVAILABILITY

Critics sometimes argue that the use of legislative history makes planning one's conduct according to law more difficult. The law-abiding citizen, critics assert, must read, not only the statute books, but also all the reports, hearings, and floor debates in order to understand the law properly. Who can take the time, or afford the cost of doing so?

This argument overlooks the fact that courts use history to interpret unclear statutes. The use of legislative history can therefore make it easier, not more difficult, for the law-abiding citizen to plan conduct according to law. Legislative history is not difficult to find, at least not for the lawyer trying to understand an unclear statute. Summaries are available in most libraries and the federal government maintains depository libraries with full texts of relevant documents.

Furthermore, the costs of using history are meaningful only when compared against the benefits of whatever clarity it may bring and with the costs of alternative ways of achieving the same objective. * * * I doubt that reliance upon canons of interpretation as a clarifying device, would be less costly than puzzling statutory language for the ordinary citizen to understand the law.

This discussion of the critics' arguments suggests that no strong theoretical argument militates against the use of legislative history. The legislative history debate is a practical, pragmatic one: Is misuse so common as to warrant radical change? Based on my own experience, I think not. * * *

---

49 Abner J. Mikva, *Foreword,* 74 VA. L. REV. 167, 167 (1988).

Note on Justice Scalia and the use of legislative history. Justice Antonin Scalia's antipathy towards legislative history in statutory interpretation was pronounced. In *Green v. Bock Laundry Mach. Co.*, 490 U.S. 504 (1989), the Court had to determine whether the word "defendant" in Rule 609 of the Federal Rules of Evidence meant only criminal defendants or defendants in civil cases as well. Justice Scalia concurred in the majority's interpretation of the statute but he wrote separately to reject the majority's analysis:

> Approximately four-fifths of [the majority's] substantive analysis is devoted to examining the evolution of Federal Rule of Evidence 609, from the 1942 Model Code of Evidence, to the 1953 Uniform Rules of Evidence, to the 1965 *Luck* case and the 1970 statute overruling it, to the Subcommittee, Committee, and Conference Committee Reports, and to the so-called floor debates on Rule 609 * * *.
>
> I find no reason to believe that any more than a handful of the Members of Congress who enacted Rule 609 were aware of its interesting evolution from the 1942 Model Code; or that any more than a handful of them (if any) voted, with respect to their understanding of the word "defendant" * * *, on the basis of the referenced statements in the Subcommittee, Committee, or Conference Committee Reports, or floor debates—statements so marginally relevant, to such minute details, in such relatively inconsequential legislation. The meaning of terms on the statute books ought to be determined, not on the basis of which meaning can be shown to have been understood by a larger handful of the Members of Congress; but rather on the basis of which meaning is (1) most in accord with context and ordinary usage, and thus most likely to have been understood by the *whole* Congress which voted on the words of the statute (not to mention the citizens subject to it), and (2) most compatible with the surrounding body of law into which the provision must be integrated—a compatibility which, by a benign fiction, we assume Congress always has in mind. I would not permit any of the historical and legislative material discussed by the Court, or all of it combined, to lead me to a result different from the one that these factors suggest.* * * *
>
> I am frankly not sure that, despite its lengthy discussion of ideological evolution and legislative history, the Court's reasons for * * * its decision are much different from mine. I respectfully decline to join that discussion, however, because it is natural for the bar to believe that the juridical importance of such material matches its prominence in our opinions—thus producing a legal culture in which, when counsel arguing before us assert that

> "Congress has said" something, they now frequently mean, by "Congress," a committee report; and in which it was not beyond the pale for a recent brief to say the following: "Unfortunately, the legislative debates are not helpful. Thus, we turn to the other guidepost in this difficult area, statutory language." Brief for Petitioner in *Jett v. Dallas Independent School District,* O.T.1988, No. 87–2084, p. 21.

Id. at 527–530.

In *Zuni Public School Dist. No. 89 v. Department of Education*, 550 U.S. 81 (2007), the Supreme Court complicated the apparent plain meaning of a statutory term, in part by considering the intent of the Congress. In a concurring opinion, Justice Stevens defended the practice, by citing precedent that had been supported by some of the dissenters (notably Chief Justice Rehnquist and Justice Scalia):

> In his oft-cited opinion for the Court in *Griffin v. Oceanic Contractors, Inc.*, 458 U.S. 564, 571 (1982), then-Justice Rehnquist wisely acknowledged that "in rare cases the literal application of a statute will produce a result demonstrably at odds with the intentions of its drafters, and those intentions must be controlling." And in *United States v. Ron Pair Enterprises, Inc.*, 489 U.S. 235, 242 (1989), the Court began its analysis of the question of statutory construction by restating the proposition that "[i]n such cases, the intention of the drafters, rather than the strict language, controls." Justice Scalia provided the decisive fifth vote for the majority in that case.

Justice Scalia's dissent in *Zuni Public School* is pointed and reminiscent of his concurrence in *Green.* After articulating the plain meaning of the statutory phrase in question, he continues:

> How then, if the text is so clear, are respondents [who opposed the plain meaning of the text] managing to win this case? The answer can only be the return of that miraculous redeemer of lost causes, *Church of the Holy Trinity*. In order to contort the statute's language beyond recognition, the Court must believe Congress's intent so crystalline, the spirit of its legislation so glowingly bright, that the statutory text should simply not be read to say what it says. Justice Stevens is quite candid on the point: He is willing to contradict the text. But Justice Stevens' candor should not make his philosophy seem unassuming. He maintains that it is "a correct performance of the judicial function" to "override a strict interpretation of the text" so long as policy-driven interpretation "is faithful to the intent of Congress." But once one departs from "strict interpretation of the text" (by which Justice Stevens means the actual meaning of the text) fidelity to the intent of Congress is a chancy thing. The only thing we know for

certain both Houses of Congress (and the President, if he signed the legislation) agreed upon is the text. Legislative history can never produce a "pellucidly clear" picture of what a law was "intended" to mean, for the simple reason that it is never voted upon—or ordinarily even seen or heard—by the "intending" lawgiving entity, which consists of both Houses of Congress and the President (if he did not veto the bill). *See* U.S. Const., Art. I, §§ 1, 7. Thus, what judges believe Congress "meant" (apart from the text) has a disturbing but entirely unsurprising tendency to be whatever judges think Congress must have meant, *i.e.*, should have meant. In *Church of the Holy Trinity*, every Justice on this Court disregarded the plain language of a statute that forbade the hiring of a clergyman from abroad because, after all (they thought), "this is a Christian nation," 143 U.S., at 471, so Congress could not have meant what it said. Is there any reason to believe that those Justices were lacking that "intellectua[l] honest[y]" that Justice Stevens "presume[s]" all our judges possess? Intellectual honesty does not exclude a blinding intellectual bias. And even if it did, the system of judicial amendatory veto over texts duly adopted by Congress bears no resemblance to the system of lawmaking set forth in our Constitution.

NOTES AND QUESTIONS

1. *Ambivalence about legislative intent and interpretation*. After reading Justice Scalia's critique of legislative history and Professor Llewellyn's acidic collection of opposing canons of construction, *supra*, are you concerned that legislative intent may be the *result* of interpretation instead of its *precondition*? After all, the legislative history of a statute often consists of staff-written reports (sometimes on the basis of text and data submitted by the lobbyists advocating for the legislation), pre-arranged colloquies between two members on the floor of the chamber, transcripts of hearings, excerpts from selected studies or testimony from outside groups. In these circumstances, as Judge Harold Leventhal reportedly observed, "citing legislative history is * * * akin to 'looking over a crowd and picking out your friends.' " Patricia M. Wald, *Some Observations on the Use of Legislative History in the 1981 Supreme Court Term*, 68 IOWA L. REV. 195, 214 (1983) (footnote omitted). It therefore cannot be surprising that determining legislative intent is—and cannot be—as simple as it sounds. *See e.g.*, *United States v. Trans-Missouri Freight Ass'n*, 166 U.S. 290, 318 (1897) ("Looking simply at the history of the bill from the time it was introduced in the Senate until it was finally passed, it would be impossible to say what were the views of a majority of the members of each house in relation to the meaning of the act.") Does this mean that lawyers are required by their professional obligations to make arguments about legislators' intent that are

essentially mythical and that no one with any legislative experience actually believes?

2. *The Breyer-Scalia argument.* Are you persuaded by Justice Breyer's argument, or does he misunderstand the essential position of those most skeptical about the use of legislative intent? Does he identify any rules regarding the legitimate use of legislative history? And what are the essential components of Justice Scalia's position? Do the principles at work in his concurrence in *Green* more closely resemble those in *Holy Trinity* or *Hill*?

3. *Distinguishing a legislator's hopes and expectations.* If the intent behind a piece of legislation is relevant (or crucial) to its interpretation, which is more salient: the legislators' hopes for their statute or their expectations of it? If you are unsure of an answer to that question, or what the justification in principle might be for one or the other, are you necessarily driven away from Justice Breyer's position?

4. *Which legislature's intent?* At first glance, it may seem obvious that the only legislative intent that should matter—if any does—is that of the enacting legislature. *See* Richard A. Posner, *Statutory Interpretation—In the Classroom and in the Courtroom*, 50 U. CHI. L. REV. 800, 810 (1983) (emphasis supplied):

> A court should adhere to the *enacting* legislature's purposes (so far as those purposes can be discerned) even if it is certain that the current legislature has different purposes and will respond by amending the relevant legislation to reverse the court's interpretation. The court's adherence to the initial compromise will not be futile, for the amending legislation will probably be prospective * * *, but judicial interpretations of legislation are retrospective * * *. Thus if the court were to implement the preferences of the current legislature, it would in effect be repealing the statute earlier than the legislature itself would have repealed it.

Consistent with the public choice literature of the law and economics movement, *supra* Chapter 5, one dominant rationale for such a preference might be that the courts are obliged to discover and enforce the deals that made the legislation possible in the first place. *See* William Landes & Richard Posner, *The Independent Judiciary in an Interest-Group Perspective*, 18 J.L. & ECON. 875, 882 (1975). From that perspective, judges are essentially archeologists digging to unearth the canonical understanding of the legislation in question at the very moment that it emerged from the Congressional ooze.

What is the best argument (or series of arguments) that the initial instinct is flawed and that courts need *not* limit their interpretation to the original understanding? In addition to the materials that follow, consider the argument in RONALD DWORKIN, LAW'S EMPIRE 313–54 (1986), *supra*, that statutory interpretation should reflect the court's determination of the "best" construction in light of *current* circumstances, on the ground that the judge in these circumstances is "a partner continuing to develop, in what he believes is the best way, the statutory scheme Congress began." This makes the statute-construing part of the law resemble a serial novel, with different authors for each chapter, each of whom takes the narrative into new territory while trying to keep a coherent story out of what came before. Is that so bad?

D. "DYNAMIC STATUTORY CONSTRUCTION" AND ITS CRITICS

RONALD DWORKIN, LAW'S EMPIRE

313–317 (1986)

[Across his long and distinguished career, the philosopher Ronald Dworkin offered a unique perspective on legal reasoning and especially the proper rubric for deciding hard cases. In LAW'S EMPIRE, he argued that judges should "assume, so far as this is possible that the law is structured by a coherent set of principles about justice and fairness and procedural due process" and "enforce these in the fresh cases that come before them." Acknowledging the difficulty of giving content to these principles, Dworkin created an idealized judge, named "Hercules," with unlimited time and knowledge of the law. Under Dworkin's notion of "law as integrity," Hercules would decide cases according to what best fits and justifies the law as a whole. Fit and justification are separate inquiries of course, but law as integrity requires judges—and not just mythical ones like Hercules—to bring those perspectives to bear in every case. In the following excerpt, Dworkin puts Hercules in the position of deciding *Tennessee Valley Authority v. Hill, supra.*]

One day the snail darter case comes to Hercules' court. He must decide whether the Endangered Species Act gives the secretary of the interior power to halt a vast, almost finished federal power project to save a small and ecologically uninteresting fish, so he must first decide how to read statutes whose meaning is uncertain. * * * Hercules will use much the same techniques of interpretation to read statutes that he uses to decide common-law cases * * *. He will treat Congress as an author earlier than himself in the chain of law, though an author with special powers and responsibilities different from his own, and he will see his own role as fundamentally the creative one of a partner continuing to develop, in what he believes is the best way, the statutory scheme Congress began. He will ask himself which reading of the act—permitting or not permitting the secretary to halt projects almost completed—shows the political history including and surrounding that statute in the better light. His view of how the statute should be read will in part depend on what certain congressmen said when debating it. But it will also depend on the best answer to political questions: how far Congress should defer to public opinion in matters of this sort, for example, and whether it would be absurd as a matter of policy to protect a minor species at so great an expense of funds. He must rely on his own judgment in answering these questions, of course, not because he thinks his opinions are automatically right, but because no one can properly answer any question except by relying at the deepest level on what he himself believes.

Before I develop that general description of how judges should interpret statutes under law as integrity, however, I must first consider an important objection to it * * *. "Hercules' method ignores the important principle, firmly rooted in our legal practice, that statutes should be read, not according to what judges believe would make them best, but according to what the legislators who actually adopted them intended. Suppose Hercules decides, after taking into account everything his interpretive method commends, that the act is a better piece of legislation if it is understood not to give the secretary the power to halt almost completed and very expensive projects. The congressmen who enacted it may have intended to give the secretary exactly that power. In those circumstances our legal practice, supported by democratic principles, insists that Hercules defer to their intention, not to his own different view."

It is true that in American legal practice, judges constantly refer to the various statements congressmen and other legislators make, in committee reports or formal debates, about the purpose of an act. Judges say these statements, taken together, form the "legislative history" of the act, which they must respect. We may, however, take two rather different views of this practice of deferring to legislative history. One is Hercules' view. He treats the various statements that make up the legislative history as political acts that his interpretation of the statute must fit and explain, just as it must fit and explain the text of the statute itself. The other is the view presupposed by the objection I just described. It treats these statements not as events important in themselves, but as evidence of the mental states of the particular legislators who made them, presumed to be representative of the mental states of the majority of legislators whose votes created the statute.

I shall call this the "speaker's meaning" view because it assumes that legislation is an occasion or instance of communication and that judges look to legislative history when a statute is not clear on its face to discover what state of mind the legislators tried to communicate through their votes. * * * The ruling model of this theory is the familiar model of ordinary speech. When a friend says something, we may ask, "What did he mean by that?" and think that our answer to that question describes something about his state of mind when he spoke, some idea he meant to communicate to us in speaking as he did. Wittgenstein and other philosophers warn us against a crude misunderstanding of this picture. Having a thought and choosing words to represent that thought are not two separate activities. Nor are people free to mean anything they like by the words they use, so the question, "What did he mean by those words?" is not purely the question of what he had in mind when he spoke. But the picture serves well enough as a rough description of how we conceive the problem of understanding someone who has spoken ambiguously, and the speaker's meaning theory proposes that we use the same picture for ambiguous or unclear legislation.

If someone accepts the speaker's meaning view, his theory about how to read statutes will have a particular structure. He will present his conclusions as statements about the intention of the statute itself. Is it the purpose or intention of the Endangered Species Act to give the secretary a certain power? But he regards the intention of the statute as a theoretical construction, a compendious statement of the discrete intentions of particular actual people, because only these can actually have conversational intentions of the sort he has in mind. So his theory of statutes must answer the following set of questions. Which historical people count as the legislators? How are their intentions to be discovered? When these intentions differ somewhat from one to another, how are they to be combined in the overall, composite institutional intention? His answers must, moreover, establish a fixed moment when the statute was spoken, when it acquired all the meaning it ever has.

Hercules' view requires no such structure. He understands the idea of a statute's purpose or intention, not as some combination of the purposes or intentions of particular legislators, but as the upshot of integrity, of taking the interpretive attitude toward the political events that include the statute's enactment. He takes note of the statements the legislators made in the process of enacting it, but he treats them as political events important in themselves, not as evidence of any mental state behind them. So he has no need for precise views about which legislators' mental states are in question, or what mental states these are, or how he should combine them into some super-mental state of the statute or institution itself. Nor does he suppose any canonical moment of speech toward which his historical research bends; the history he interprets begins before a statute is enacted and continues to the moment when he must decide what it now declares.

Hercules' methods provide a better interpretation of actual judicial practice than the speaker's meaning theory. The defects of the latter can be cured only by transforming it, in stages, into Hercules' method. The three crucial questions I just mentioned, which must be answered in order to put the speaker's meaning theory into practice, cannot be answered just by probing the root model of communication, just by exploring the internal connections between intention and legislation conceived as a form of speech. They must be answered in political theory, by taking up particular views about controversial issues of political morality. So the speaker's meaning theory cannot make good its presumed claims of political neutrality, its ambition to separate a judge's personal convictions from the way he reads a statute. The most plausible answers to the crucial questions, moreover, push us steadily away from the speaker's meaning theory, as it is commonly understood, toward a different view, one that aims to enforce the most abstract and general political convictions from which legislators act rather than the hopes or expectations or more detailed political opinions they have in mind when voting. This different idea, however, is only a poorly stated and unstable form of Hercules' own method, into which it therefore collapses.

WILLIAM N. ESKRIDGE, JR., *DYNAMIC STATUTORY INTERPRETATION*

135 U. PA. L. REV. 1479 (1987)

Federal judges interpreting the Constitution typically consider not only the constitutional text and its historical background, but also its subsequent interpretational history, related constitutional developments, and current societal facts. Similarly, judges interpreting common law precedents normally consider not only the text of the precedents and their historical context, but also their subsequent history, related legal developments, and current societal context. In light of this, it is odd that many judges and commentators believe judges should consider only the text and historical context when interpreting statutes, the third main source of law. Statutes, however, should—like the Constitution and the common law—be interpreted "dynamically," that is, in light of their present societal, political, and legal context.[1]

Traditional doctrine teaches that statutes should not be interpreted dynamically. Prevailing approaches to statutory interpretation treat statutes as static texts. Thus, the leading treatise states that "[f]or the interpretation of statutes, 'intent of the legislature' is the criterion that is most often cited."[2] This 'intentionalist" approach asks how the legislature originally intended the interpretive question to be answered, or would have intended the question to be answered had it thought about the issue when it passed the statute.[3] A "modified intentionalist" approach uses the

---

1 *Compare* R. DWORKIN, LAW'S EMPIRE 313–54 (1986) (statutes should be interpreted similarly to the common law, with the judicial interpreter determining in each case what is the 'best' application of the statute in light of current circumstances) *with* Brest, *The Misconceived Quest for the Original Understanding*, 60 B.U.L. REV. 204 (1980) (advocating a "nonoriginalist" interpretation of both statutes and the Constitution). Brest's Article is the source for the terminology—"intentionalist," "modified intentionalist," and "originalist"—used in the next paragraph of this Article.

2 2 A. SUTHERLAND, STATUTES AND STATUTORY CONSTRUCTION § 45.05 (4th ed. 1984).

3 For general explanation of the intentionalist approach, *see Lehigh Valley Coal Co. v. Yensavage*, 218 F. 547, 553 (2d Cir. 1914) (L. Hand, J.); R. POSNER, THE FEDERAL COURTS: CRISIS AND REFORM 286–93 (1985); Posner, *Statutory Interpretation—in the Classroom and in the Courtroom*, 50 U. CHI. L. REV. 800, 817–22 (1983) ('The judge should try to think his way as best he can into the minds of the enacting legislators and imagine how they would have wanted the

original purpose of the statute as a surrogate for original intent, especially when the latter is uncertain; the proper interpretation is the one that best furthers the purpose the legislature had in mind when it enacted the statute.[4]

Theoretically, these "originalist" approaches to statutory interpretation assume that the legislature fixes the meaning of a statute on the date the statute is enacted. The implicit claim is that a legislator interpreting the statute at the time of enactment would render the same interpretation as a judge interpreting the same statute fifty years later. This implication seems counterintuitive. Indeed, the legal realists argued this point * * * in the [twentieth] century. For example, gaps and ambiguities exist in all statutes, typically concerning matters as to which there was little legislative deliberation and, hence, no clear intent. As society changes, adapts to the statute, and generates new variations of the problem which gave rise to the statute, the unanticipated gaps and ambiguities proliferate. In such circumstances, it seems sensible that "the quest is not properly for the sense originally intended by the statute, [or] for the sense sought originally to be put into it, but rather for the sense which can be quarried out of it in the light of the new situation."[5] Moreover, as time passes, the legal and constitutional context of the statute may change. Should not an interpreter "ask herself not only what the legislation means abstractly, or even on the basis of legislative history, but also what it ought to mean in terms of the needs and goals of our present day society?"[6]

[My thesis is] that statutes, like the Constitution and the common law, should be interpreted dynamically.[7] * * * [I] accept[ ] the traditional assumptions that a functioning representative democracy exists in our polity, that the legislature is the primary lawmaking body, and that in many cases statutory language will be sufficiently determinate to resolve

---

statute applied to the case at bar.'). A narrower approach emphasizes the statutory text to the exclusion of other contextual factors (such as legislative history). "Textualism" can be defended as the best evidence of what the legislature actually meant when it enacted the statute. *See* Easterbrook, *Statutes' Domains*, 50 U. CHI. L. REV. 533 (1983).

4 *See, e.g.*, H. HART & A. SACKS, THE LEGAL PROCESS: BASIC PROBLEMS IN THE MAKING AND APPLICATION OF LAW 1201 (tent. ed. 1958) (unpublished manuscript); Macey, *Promoting Public-Regarding Legislation through Statutory Interpretation: An Interest Group Model*, 86 COLUM. L. REV. 223 (1986). *See generally* R. DICKERSON, THE INTERPRETATION AND APPLICATION OF STATUTES (1975) (setting forth a coherent modified-intentionalist account of statutory interpretation).

5 K. Llewellyn, *Remarks on the Theory of Appellate Decision and the Rules or Canons about How Statutes Are to Be Construed*, 3 VAND. L. REV. 395, 400 (1950) (emphasis deleted).

6 Phelps, *Factors Influencing Judges in Interpreting Statutes*, 3 VAND. L. REV. 456, 469 (1950).

7 This approach is related to, but stops far short of, the proposal in G. CALABRESI, A COMMON LAW FOR THE AGE OF STATUTES (1982), that courts ought to be able to update statutes by overruling them. Calabresi's thesis has been criticized as inconsistent with traditional assumptions about the role of courts in a representative democracy. *See e.g.*, Posner, *Legal Formalism, Legal Realism, and the Interpretation of Statutes and the Constitution*, 37 CASE W. RES. L. REV. 179, 196–97 (1987).

a given case. Even under these conventional assumptions, however, original legislative expectations should not always control statutory meaning. This is especially true when the statute is old and generally phrased and the societal or legal context of the statute has changed in material ways.

* * * [N]o good reason compels adherence to traditional originalist doctrine. Three major types of arguments have been invoked in favor of statutory intentionalism or modified intentionalism: (1) the formalist argument that the Constitution vests Congress with the exclusive power to create law or policy, leaving courts with no role but to carry out the intent (or purpose) of Congress; (2) the economic argument that statutes are contracts between interest groups and legislatures and as such must be enforced by judges (the "agents" of the legislature) according to their original terms and intent; and (3) the legal process argument that it is illegitimate for nonelected judges to make policy in a majoritarian political system by expanding upon the original meaning of statutes. None of these arguments, however, justifies unexceptioned statutory intentionalism when circumstances have changed and the statutory language is not determinate.

* * * [T]he proposed model of dynamic statutory interpretation [has certain advantages] over other current approaches to statutory interpretation. * * * I only contend that it explains the results of the Supreme Court's cases better and is a more candid analysis of what the Court does. Finally, the Article contrasts my dynamic interpretation model with the more ambitious approach posited by Professor Ronald Dworkin. Dworkin, too, argues for dynamic interpretation, in which statutes change as "law's integrity" develops and changes. My approach is more cautious and conventional than that of Dworkin. He envisions judges performing the truly herculean task of reading magisterial coherence into the law.[10] I envision judges as diplomats, whose ordering authority is severely limited but who must often update their orders to meet changing circumstances.

AMANDA L. TYLER, *CONTINUITY, COHERENCE, AND THE CANONS*

99 NW. U. L. REV. 1389 (2005)

No one can debate seriously the need for some default rules in statutory construction. Indeed, courts consistently are called upon to make sense of ambiguous statutory language and to plug statutory gaps. Congress does not and cannot necessarily contemplate every future application of a statute at the time of its drafting. The real question is what

[10] *See* R. DWORKIN, *supra*, at 239; R. DWORKIN, A MATTER OF PRINCIPLE 316 (1985).

default rules we should have where the formal evidence of congressional purpose—i.e., statutory enactment—leaves us shorthanded. * * *

In pursuing the seemingly elusive goal of choosing a default rule regime that best comports with the constitutional framework for the separation of powers, one truth becomes quickly apparent: whatever one's school of thought—Legal Process, textualist, canonical, dynamic, some combination thereof, or otherwise—in the end, judicial judgment will always creep into the equation in some form. The text will sometimes (if not often) come up short,[77] ascertaining the purpose behind a law may uncover as many questions as it answers, and canons of construction are by their very nature judicially-created guidelines for reading statutes. Dynamic theory fares little better, for its very premise places the courts in the role of updating the legislature's work. Ultimately, Judge Keeton correctly highlighted the unavoidable tension that courts face when interpreting statutes: "[O]ur legal tradition assigns to courts a creative role in improving law, as well as a guardian's role in preserving its continuity and predictability."[79]

In the realm of modern statutory interpretation (that is, where statutes do not clearly delegate a broader lawmaking function to the courts), it is in this guardian's role that the judiciary makes its greatest contribution to the partnership between the judicial and legislative branches by creating and fleshing out the meaning and proper application of statutory law. Dynamic theorists sacrifice this guardian's role in favor of an entirely different conception of the judiciary—namely, one that is charged with engineering legal reform by "updating" statutes to keep them attuned to prevailing political winds or social norms, and in [Professor Einer] Elhauge's case, where this fails, one that should aim to provoke legislative clarification. Elhauge believes that such a framework limits the judiciary's role to that of "honest agent"; likewise, Elhauge contends that his proposal will cabin judicial discretion.

It is not at all clear, however, that the agency—or for that matter democratic—ideal is best served by such an approach to statutory construction. Indeed, quite the opposite seems true: in gauging current political winds, Elhauge's proposal ignores the legislative deal that brokered the statutory language in question, as well as any background norms against which such language came into being, and usurps the sitting legislature's formal role as the impetus for statutory change.[80] The

---

[77] *See* John F. Manning, *The Absurdity Doctrine*, 116 HARV. L. REV. 2387, 2409 (2003) ("[B]ecause all statutory language is at least somewhat open-textured, textualists acknowledge that 'a certain degree of discretion' is inevitable in 'most' judicial decision-making.").

[79] [ROBERT E.] KEETON, [VENTURING TO DO JUSTICE (1969)], at 11. Put another way, "[t]he judiciary is . . . on the one hand a guardian of the law's continuity, stability, evenhandedness, and predictability and on the other hand a participant in creative evolution that keeps law contemporary and viable." *Id.* at 24.

[80] In this vein, Elhauge's proposal falls victim to many of the criticisms of Ronald Dworkin's work in this area, which posits that the judge should view himself as "a partner continuing to

approach likewise denies the contribution that courts make in building a coherent and workable legal framework out of what are often incoherent legislative directives. The added notion that the courts ought to "punt" a substantial number of cases back to the legislature deprives the judiciary in these cases entirely of its ability to act in any meaningful role in fleshing out the meaning and proper application of statutes or developing a coherent framework of statutory law.

This Article promotes as normatively superior the construction of an interpretive regime built on a strong rule of statutory *stare decisis* and consistent application of interpretive guides that advance continuity and coherence. This approach provides a more efficient means of achieving equilibrium and harmony in the legislative-judicial relationship and allows the courts to take up the guardian's role more effectively.[81] By coherence, I refer to the construction of a principled connection between bodies of law. This vision of coherence is not derived so much from metaprinciples of "justice" and "fairness" such as those with which Dworkin's Judge Hercules is concerned when he construes statutes,[82] but more so as shorthand for reconciling and harmonizing linguistic meaning among numerous interpretations over time. Continuity, in turn, embraces the ideal that interpretations should not deviate from the existing statutory baseline absent substantial legislative evidence of a desire for such change. This principle may be understood as viewing statutory change through the lens of incrementalism.

Operating within such a framework, courts build a principled connection between interpretations over time and, in doing so, create a coherent and predictable legal framework within which actors may proceed with some confidence as to the ramifications of their actions. Where Congress takes an issue to the level of enactment, it can predict how its language will be interpreted not only in the situations directly addressed, but also in circumstances unknown and unexpected at the time. Such a framework leaves the role of determining if and when change is appropriate to the most politically accountable body—the legislature.

---

develop, in what he believes is the best way, the statutory scheme Congress began." RONALD DWORKIN, LAW'S EMPIRE 313–54 (1986), at 313.

81 This efficiency will result from a number of things, but mainly from the fact that Congress will have a greater ability *ex ante* (when it has already invested considerable time and attention to the subject matter in play) to predict how its statute will be interpreted versus leaving Congress to police the continuing stream of judicial interpretations handed down over time.

82 I refer here to Dworkin's hypothetical judge who interprets statutory meaning in keeping with such metaprinciples. See Dworkin, *supra*, at 243 (positing that judges should "assume, so far as this is possible that the law is structured by a coherent set of principles about justice and fairness and procedural due process" and "enforce these in the fresh cases that come before them"); *id.* at 313 (noting that Judge Hercules "will use much the same techniques of interpretation to read statutes that he uses to decide common-law cases").

NOTES AND QUESTIONS

1. *"Dynamic" interpretation.* Judging from these brief excerpts, what are the differences between Dworkin's "law as integrity" on one hand and Eskridge's "dynamic interpretation" on the other?

2. *Translating a perspective into an effective practice.* Even if you agree with Professor Eskridge that statutes should "be interpreted 'dynamically,' that is, in light of their present societal, political, and legal context," how would you go about determining what that context is?

3. *Legislation and fidelity to the past.* In stark contrast to the power of precedent in common law reasoning, which is explored in the next chapter, Oliver Wendell Homes thought that law-making by statute can break with the past—without explanation, let alone justification.

> As soon as a legislature is able to imagine abolishing the requirement of a consideration for a simple contract, it is at perfect liberty to abolish it, if it thinks it wise to do so, without the slightest regard to continuity with the past. That continuity simply limits the possibilities of our imagination, and settles the terms in which we shall be compelled to think.

O.W. HOLMES, COLLECTED LEGAL PAPERS 211 (1920). Does your evaluation of the materials in this chapter suggest that there is something missing from this pronouncement? John F. Manning, *Textualism and the Equity of the Statute*, 101 COLUM. L. REV. 1, 29–36 (2001).

CHAPTER THIRTEEN

STRUCTURES OF LEGAL ARGUMENT (IV): THE POWER OF PRECEDENT RECONSIDERED

■ ■ ■

"[I]t is an established rule to abide by former precedents, where the same points come again in litigation: . . . the law in that case being solemnly declared and determined, [and] what before was uncertain . . . is now become a permanent rule, which it is not in the breast of any subsequent judge to alter or vary from, according to his own private sentiments."

— William Blackstone

"PRECEDENT: *n.* In Law, a previous decision, rule or practice which, in the absence of a definite statute, has whatever force and authority a Judge may choose to give it, thereby greatly simplifying his task of doing as he pleases. As there are precedents for everything, he has only to ignore those that make against his interest and accentuate those in the line of his desire."

— Ambrose Bierce

"The lawless science of the law, that codeless myriad of precedent, that wilderness of single instances"

— Alfred, Lord Tennyson

Orientation

The conventional understanding of the common law system is that its doctrines emerge and evolve through individual cases decided over generations of judges, "an infinite number of Grave and Learned Men [and Women]."[1] The notion of "judge-made" law captures this genetic characteristic of the common law and by convention distinguishes it from civil law systems, in which primary authority comes from law enacted and codified by a legislature. But the distinction between the civil law and the common law is easily oversimplified. Even if the common law is quintessentially judge-made, it does not follow that judges are utterly free to make stuff up and call it "law." To the contrary, like a group of novelists,

1 THOMAS HOBBES, A DIALOGUE BETWEEN A PHILOSOPHER AND A STUDENT OF THE COMMON LAW OF ENGLAND 55 (1681) (J. Cropsey ed. 1971).

each of whom writes a separate chapter in a serial novel, a judge is required to keep the story coherent, to deal with what came before, to acknowledge the power of *precedent*. And even in civil law jurisdictions, courts try not to reinvent the wheel in case after case, preferring instead to keep the law coherent over time by respecting prior dispositions in tolerably similar circumstances, even if those prior decisions are not binding.[2]

There are multiple definitions of "precedent" and various histories of its development as one dominant facet of Anglo-American law, but the common theme is that a judge's decision not only resolves the case immediately in front of him or her, it also offers some authority for resolving future cases the same way. For our initial purposes, the Third Circuit Court of Appeals has offered one definition of "precedent" that is as good (and as limited) as any other:

> A judicial precedent attaches a specific legal consequence to a detailed set of facts in an adjudged case or judicial decision, which is then considered as furnishing the rule for the determination of a subsequent case involving identical or similar material facts and arising in the same court or a lower court in the judicial hierarchy.

Allegheny General Hospital v. NLRB, 608 F.2d 965, 969–70 (3rd Cir. 1979). *Compare* BLACK'S LAW DICTIONARY 1280 (8th ed. 2004) (defining "precedent" as "[a] decided case that furnishes a basis for determining later cases involving similar facts or issues.") At its essence, an argument from precedent offers authority for the resolution of a current case on the basis of a previously decided case or a pattern of previously decided cases. Closely aligned with the notion of precedent is *stare decisis* ("let decided matters stand"), a structural admonition that requires lawyers and judges to identify what a prior decision holds and adhere to it in future cases.

It turns out that there is a good philosophical basis for the power of precedent, even if its implementation in actual cases is not always simple. It connects well for example with an intuitive notion of justice—articulated by Aristotle—that like cases should be treated alike and unlike cases should be treated differently. Coherence and uniformity limit the discretion of individual judges, minimizing the possibility of discrimination or arbitrariness in applying the law, and bringing a measure of predictability to human affairs. As the Supreme Court has noted, "*stare decisis* is the preferred course because it promotes the evenhanded, predictable, and consistent development of legal principles, fosters reliance on judicial decisions, and contributes to the actual and perceived integrity of the judicial process."[3] From this perspective, adhering to precedent has moral and practical value that is independent of the content of the rule in the precedent itself: "*Stare decisis* is usually the wise policy, because in most

---

[2] On the essential differences and similarities in the treatment of precedent by civil-law and common-law courts, *see* R. SCHLESINGER *ET AL.*, COMPARATIVE LAW 582–627 (7th ed. 2009).

[3] *Payne v. Tennessee*, 501 U.S. 808, 827 (1991).

matters it is more important that the applicable rule of law be *settled* than that it be settled *right*."[4]

But the theoretical and practical problems of argument by precedent are not trivial. One problem is that you can only determine whether a case is sufficiently "like" another if you already have a standard for assessing them: some prior rule must exist to determine whether cases are alike (or not) and in what relevant ways. And how strictly should precedent be followed? The Supreme Court itself has said that "*stare decisis* is not an inexorable command; rather, it 'is a principle of policy and not a mechanical formula of adherence to the latest decision' "[5] You can also imagine circumstances in which respecting precedent—justice in the form of consistency and uniformity—perpetuates injustice of another sort. Maybe one measure of judges' greatness is their willingness to abandon precedent at the right cultural moment. *See, e.g., Brown v. Board of Education*, 347 U.S. 483 (1954) (unanimously overturning *Plessy v. Ferguson*, 163 U.S. 537 (1896), which had embraced the "separate but equal" treatment of the races and which had served as the legal justification for racial segregation in the United States for nearly sixty years). Besides, there is the inconvenient truth that, in most cases, precedent can be invoked by both sides, or a prior case may stand for multiple ideas simultaneously and its precedential meaning will be a matter of reasoned interpretation in new settings. And sometimes it will be essential to distinguish a court's prior statement as a *holding*, entitled to deference as precedent, from *obiter dicta*—an observation or comment on a legal matter that is not essential to the ruling in the case, and which is entitled to less deference, if any.

Also hidden by any simplistic conception of precedent are the professional techniques for avoiding or limiting its effects. Following precedent and overruling it are only two of the available options: a court may well decide that the case before it is one of "first impression," effectively dismissing the precedents offered by the parties as irrelevant to the issue presented. Or a court may distinguish what precedent exists, offering a principle of distinction or limitation that justifiably treats otherwise like cases differently. Sometimes a prior court will have controlled the precedential value of its decision—and the consequent strictures it lays on itself—by writing an opinion that is explicitly confined to the immediate case in front of it or by declining to publish an opinion at all: often the local rules of procedure in a jurisdiction will provide that an

---

4 *Burnet v. Coronado Oil & Gas Co.*, 285 U.S. 393, 406 (1932) (Brandeis, J., dissenting) (emphasis supplied). For a powerful version of the philosophical argument that respecting precedent is characteristic of the rule of law and legal systems, *see* Anthony T. Kronman, *Precedent and Tradition*, 99 YALE L.J. 1029, 1032 (1990). The early American commitment to precedent as a limit on judges was expressed in THE FEDERALIST, No. 78 at 442 (Alexander Hamilton) (Isaac Kramnick ed., 1987): "To avoid an arbitrary discretion in the courts, it is indispensable that they should be bound down by strict rules and precedents . . . ."

5 *Payne v. Tennessee*, 501 U.S. 808, 828 (1991) (*quoting Helvering v. Hallock*, 309 U.S. 106, 119 (1940)).

unpublished opinion has no precedential value and may not be cited in subsequent cases.[6] At a minimum, the power of precedent may be limited by understanding the "judicial hierarchy" that operates within a jurisdiction, as acknowledged by the Third Circuit in *Allegheny General Hospital, supra*: precedent has a relatively direct application in the *vertical* setting, as when the U.S. Supreme Court resolves a case in a way that binds the lower federal district courts and the intermediate circuit courts of appeals. But what is the precedential value of decisions among courts that are *horizontal* to one another? Suppose for example, that one of the federal circuit courts of appeals in the United States decides a case and a similar case later arises in a different circuit. Technically, the prior decision has no status as precedent in the second proceeding, but on what principle would you as a judge or litigant ignore it altogether? Similarly, the courts of one state are in no sense bound by decisions in other state courts, but a decision from another state's court might have persuasive authority even if it isn't binding, and any successful account of precedent has to deal with that reality as well.

This chapter is designed to assure that the simplistic understanding of precedent gives way to something more valuable, that we become more fluent in the language of arguments through precedent, and that whatever theory of precedent emerges is grounded in the reality of actual practices.

A. PRECEDENT AND ITS LIMITS

The following two decisions from the Supreme Court address similar issues and reach opposing conclusions, even though they were decided only seventeen years apart. As you read them, consider the range of explanations that might account for the fact that *Hardwick* was *not* a controlling or dispositive precedent for the later decision in *Lawrence*.

BOWERS V. HARDWICK

478 U.S. 186 (1986)

JUSTICE WHITE delivered the opinion of the Court. In August 1982, respondent Hardwick (hereafter respondent) was charged with violating the Georgia statute criminalizing sodomy[1] by committing that act with another adult male in the bedroom of respondent's home. After a

---

[6] *See* Richard B. Cappali, *The Common Law's Case Against Non-Precedential Opinions*, 76 S. CAL. L. REV. 755, 761 (2003).

[1] Georgia Code Ann. § 16–6–2 (1984) provides, in pertinent part, as follows:

"(a) A person commits the offense of sodomy when he performs or submits to any sexual act involving the sex organs of one person and the mouth or anus of another. . . .

"(b) A person convicted of the offense of sodomy shall be punished by imprisonment for not less than one nor more than 20 years. . . ."

preliminary hearing, the District Attorney decided not to present the matter to the grand jury unless further evidence developed. Respondent then brought suit in the Federal District Court, challenging the constitutionality of the statute insofar as it criminalized consensual sodomy. He asserted that he was a practicing homosexual, that the Georgia sodomy statute, as administered by the defendants, placed him in imminent danger of arrest, and that the statute for several reasons violates the Federal Constitution. The District Court granted the defendants' motion to dismiss for failure to state a claim, * * * relying on *Doe v. Commonwealth's Attorney for the City of Richmond*, 403 F. Supp. 1199 (E.D. Va.1975), which this Court [had] summarily affirmed.

A divided panel of the Court of Appeals for the Eleventh Circuit reversed. The court first held that, because *Doe* was distinguishable and in any event had been undermined by later decisions, our summary affirmance in that case did not require affirmance of the District Court. Relying on our decisions in *Griswold v. Connecticut*, 381 U.S. 479 (1965); *Eisenstadt v. Baird*, 405 U.S. 438 (1972); *Stanley v. Georgia*, 394 U.S. 557 (1969); and *Roe v. Wade*, 410 U.S. 113 (1973), the court went on to hold that the Georgia statute violated respondent's fundamental rights because his homosexual activity is a private and intimate association that is beyond the reach of state regulation by reason of the Ninth Amendment and the Due Process Clause of the Fourteenth Amendment. The case was remanded for trial, at which, to prevail, the State would have to prove that the statute is supported by a compelling interest and is the most narrowly drawn means of achieving that end. Because other Courts of Appeals have arrived at judgments contrary to that of the Eleventh Circuit in this case, we granted the [Georgia] Attorney General's petition for *certiorari* questioning the holding that the sodomy statute violates the fundamental rights of homosexuals. We agree with petitioner that the Court of Appeals erred, and hence reverse its judgment.

This case does not require a judgment on whether laws against sodomy between consenting adults in general, or between homosexuals in particular, are wise or desirable. It raises no question about the right or propriety of state legislative decisions to repeal their laws that criminalize homosexual sodomy, or of state-court decisions invalidating those laws on state constitutional grounds. The issue presented is whether the Federal Constitution confers a fundamental right upon homosexuals to engage in sodomy and hence invalidates the laws of the many States that still make such conduct illegal and have done so for a very long time. The case also calls for some judgment about the limits of the Court's role in carrying out its constitutional mandate.

We first register our disagreement with the Court of Appeals and with respondent that the Court's prior cases have construed the Constitution to confer a right of privacy that extends to homosexual sodomy and for all intents and purposes have decided this case. The reach of this line of cases was sketched in *Carey v. Population Services International*, 431 U.S. 678, 685 (1977). *Pierce v. Society of Sisters*, 268 U.S. 510 (1925), and *Meyer v. Nebraska*, 262 U.S. 390 (1923), were described as dealing with child rearing and education; *Prince v. Massachusetts*, 321 U.S. 158 (1944), with family relationships; *Skinner v. Oklahoma ex rel. Williamson*, 316 U.S. 535 (1942), with procreation; *Loving v. Virginia*, 388 U.S. 1 (1967), with marriage; *Griswold v. Connecticut*, *supra*, and *Eisenstadt v. Baird*, *supra*, with contraception; and *Roe v. Wade*, 410 U.S. 113 (1973), with abortion. The latter three cases were interpreted as construing the Due Process Clause of the Fourteenth Amendment to confer a fundamental individual right to decide whether or not to beget or bear a child. *Carey v. Population Services International*, *supra*, 431 U.S., at 688–689.

Accepting the decisions in these cases and the above description of them, we think it evident that none of the rights announced in those cases bears any resemblance to the claimed constitutional right of homosexuals to engage in acts of sodomy that is asserted in this case. No connection between family, marriage, or procreation on the one hand and homo-sexual activity on the other has been demonstrated, either by the Court of Appeals or by respondent. Moreover, any claim that these cases nevertheless stand for the proposition that any kind of private sexual conduct between consenting adults is constitutionally insulated from state proscription is unsupportable. Indeed, the Court's opinion in *Carey* twice asserted that the privacy right, which the *Griswold* line of cases found to be one of the protections provided by the Due Process Clause, did not reach so far.

Precedent aside, however, respondent would have us announce, as the Court of Appeals did, a fundamental right to engage in homosexual sodomy. This we are quite unwilling to do. It is true that despite the language of the Due Process Clauses of the Fifth and Fourteenth Amendments, which appears to focus only on the processes by which life, liberty, or property is taken, the cases are legion in which those Clauses have been interpreted to have substantive content, subsuming rights that to a great extent are immune from federal or state regulation or proscription. Among such cases are those recognizing rights that have little or no textual support in the constitutional language. *Meyer*, *Prince*, and *Pierce* fall in this category, as do the privacy cases from *Griswold* to *Carey*.

Striving to assure itself and the public that announcing rights not readily identifiable in the Constitution's text involves much more than the imposition of the Justices' own choice of values on the States and the Federal Government, the Court has sought to identify the nature of the rights qualifying for heightened judicial protection. In *Palko v. Connecticut*, 302 U.S. 319, 325, 326 (1937), it was said that this category includes those fundamental liberties that are "implicit in the concept of ordered liberty," such that "neither liberty nor justice would exist if [they] were sacrificed."

A different description of fundamental liberties appeared in *Moore v. East Cleveland*, 431 U.S. 494, 503 (opinion of Powell, J.), where they are characterized as those liberties that are "deeply rooted in this Nation's history and tradition."

It is obvious to us that neither of these formulations would extend a fundamental right to homosexuals to engage in acts of consensual sodomy. Proscriptions against that conduct have ancient roots. *See generally, Survey on the Constitutional Right to Privacy in the Context of Homosexual Activity*, 40 U. MIAMI L.REV. 521, 525 (1986). Sodomy was a criminal offense at common law and was forbidden by the laws of the original thirteen States when they ratified the Bill of Rights. In 1868, when the Fourteenth Amendment was ratified, all but 5 of the 37 States in the Union had criminal sodomy laws. In fact, until 1961,[7] all 50 States outlawed sodomy, and today, 24 States and the District of Columbia continue to provide criminal penalties for sodomy performed in private and between consenting adults. Against this background, to claim that a right to engage in such conduct is "deeply rooted in this Nation's history and tradition" or "implicit in the concept of ordered liberty" is, at best, facetious.

Nor are we inclined to take a more expansive view of our authority to discover new fundamental rights imbedded in the Due Process Clause. The Court is most vulnerable and comes nearest to illegitimacy when it deals with judge-made constitutional law having little or no cognizable roots in the language or design of the Constitution. That this is so was painfully demonstrated by the face-off between the Executive and the Court in the 1930's, which resulted in the repudiation of much of the substantive gloss that the Court had placed on the Due Process Clauses of the Fifth and Fourteenth Amendments. There should be, therefore, great resistance to expand the substantive reach of those Clauses, particularly if it requires redefining the category of rights deemed to be fundamental. Otherwise, the Judiciary necessarily takes to itself further authority to govern the country without express constitutional authority. The claimed right pressed on us today falls far short of overcoming this resistance.

Respondent, however, asserts that the result should be different where the homosexual conduct occurs in the privacy of the home. He relies on *Stanley v. Georgia*, 394 U.S. 557 (1969), where the Court held that the First Amendment prevents conviction for possessing and reading obscene material in the privacy of one's home: "If the First Amendment means anything, it means that a State has no business telling a man, sitting alone in his house, what books he may read or what films he may watch." *Id.*, at 565.

Stanley did protect conduct that would not have been protected outside the home, and it partially prevented the enforcement of state obscenity

[7] In 1961, Illinois adopted the American Law Institute's Model Penal Code, which decriminalized adult, consensual, private, sexual conduct. * * *

laws; but the decision was firmly grounded in the First Amendment. The right pressed upon us here has no similar support in the text of the Constitution, and it does not qualify for recognition under the prevailing principles for construing the Fourteenth Amendment. Its limits are also difficult to discern. Plainly enough, otherwise illegal conduct is not always immunized whenever it occurs in the home. Victimless crimes, such as the possession and use of illegal drugs, do not escape the law where they are committed at home. *Stanley* itself recognized that its holding offered no protection for the possession in the home of drugs, firearms, or stolen goods. And if respondent's submission is limited to the voluntary sexual conduct between consenting adults, it would be difficult, except by fiat, to limit the claimed right to homosexual conduct while leaving exposed to prosecution adultery, incest, and other sexual crimes even though they are committed in the home. We are unwilling to start down that road.

Even if the conduct at issue here is not a fundamental right, respondent asserts that there must be a rational basis for the law and that there is none in this case other than the presumed belief of a majority of the electorate in Georgia that homosexual sodomy is immoral and unacceptable. This is said to be an inadequate rationale to support the law. The law, however, is constantly based on notions of morality, and if all laws representing essentially moral choices are to be invalidated under the Due Process Clause, the courts will be very busy indeed. Even respondent makes no such claim, but insists that majority sentiments about the morality of homosexuality should be declared inadequate. We do not agree, and are unpersuaded that the sodomy laws of some 25 States should be invalidated on this basis. Accordingly, the judgment of the Court of Appeals is reversed.

CHIEF JUSTICE BURGER, concurring. I join the Court's opinion, but I write separately to underscore my view that in constitutional terms there is no such thing as a fundamental right to commit homosexual sodomy. As the Court notes, the proscriptions against sodomy have very "ancient roots." Decisions of individuals relating to homosexual conduct have been subject to state intervention throughout the history of Western civilization. Condemnation of those practices is firmly rooted in Judeao-Christian moral and ethical standards. Homosexual sodomy was a capital crime under Roman law. During the English Reformation when powers of the ecclesiastical courts were transferred to the King's Courts, the first English statute criminalizing sodomy was passed. 25 Hen. VIII, ch. 6. Blackstone described "the infamous crime against nature" as an offense of "deeper malignity" than rape, a heinous act "the very mention of which is a disgrace to human nature," and "a crime not fit to be named." 4 W. BLACKSTONE, COMMENTARIES *215. The common law of England, including its prohibition of sodomy, became the received law of Georgia and the other Colonies. In 1816 the Georgia Legislature passed the statute at issue here, and that statute has been continuously in force in one form or another since that time. To hold that the act of homosexual sodomy is somehow protected as a fundamental right would be to cast aside millennia of moral teaching. * * *

JUSTICE BLACKMUN, with whom JUSTICE BRENNAN, JUSTICE MARSHALL, and JUSTICE STEVENS join, dissenting. This case is no more about "a fundamental right to engage in homosexual sodomy," as the Court purports to declare, than *Stanley v. Georgia*, 394 U.S. 557 (1969), was about a fundamental right to watch obscene movies, or *Katz v. United States*, 389 U.S. 347 (1967), was about a fundamental right to place interstate bets from a telephone booth. Rather, this case is about "the most comprehensive of rights and the right most valued by civilized men," namely, "the right to be let alone." *Olmstead v. United States*, 277 U.S. 438, 478 (1928) (Brandeis, J., dissenting).

The statute at issue denies individuals the right to decide for themselves whether to engage in particular forms of private, consensual sexual activity. The Court concludes that [the statute] is valid essentially because "the laws of . . . many States . . . still make such conduct illegal and have done so for a very long time." But the fact that the moral judgments expressed by statutes like [the statute] may be " 'natural and familiar . . . ought not to conclude our judgment upon the question whether statutes embodying them conflict with the Constitution of the United States.' " *Roe v. Wade*, 410 U.S. 113 (1973), *quoting Lochner v. New York*, 198 U.S. 45, 76 (1905) (Holmes, J., dissenting). Like Justice Holmes, I believe that "[i]t is revolting to have no better reason for a rule of law than that so it was laid down in the time of Henry IV. It is still more revolting if the grounds upon which it was laid down have vanished long since, and the rule simply persists from blind imitation of the past." Holmes, *The Path of the Law*, 10 HARV. L. REV. 457, 469 (1897). I believe we must analyze Hardwick's claim in the light of the values that underlie the constitutional right to privacy. If that right means anything, it means that, before Georgia can prosecute its citizens for making choices about the most intimate aspects of their lives, it must do more than assert that the choice they have made is an " 'abominable crime not fit to be named among Christians.' " *Herring v. State*, 119 Ga. 709, 721, 46 S.E. 876, 882 (1904). * * *

Only the most willful blindness could obscure the fact that sexual intimacy is "a sensitive, key relationship of human existence, central to family life, community welfare, and the development of human personality," *Paris Adult Theatre I v. Slaton*, 413 U.S. 49, 63 (1973); *see also Carey v. Population Services International*, 431 U.S. 678, 685 (1977). The fact that individuals define themselves in a significant way through their intimate sexual relationships with others suggests, in a Nation as diverse as ours, that there may be many "right" ways of conducting those relationships, and that much of the richness of a relationship will come from the freedom an individual has to choose the form and nature of these intensely personal bonds.

[The separate opinion of Justice Stevens, dissenting, is omitted.]

LAWRENCE V. TEXAS

539 U.S. 558 (2003)

JUSTICE KENNEDY delivered the opinion of the Court. * * * The question before the Court is the validity of a Texas statute making it a crime for two persons of the same sex to engage in certain intimate sexual conduct. In Houston, Texas, officers of the Harris County Police Department were dispatched to a private residence in response to a reported weapons disturbance. They entered an apartment where one of the petitioners, John Geddes Lawrence, resided. The right of the police to enter does not seem to have been questioned. The officers observed Lawrence and another man, Tyron Garner, engaging in a sexual act. The two petitioners were arrested, held in custody overnight, and charged and convicted before a Justice of the Peace. The complaints described their crime as "deviate sexual intercourse, namely anal sex, with a member of the same sex (man)." The applicable state law is Tex. Penal Code Ann. § 21.06(a) (2003). It provides: "A person commits an offense if he engages in deviate sexual intercourse with another individual of the same sex." The statute defines "[d]eviate sexual intercourse" as follows:

> "(A) any contact between any part of the genitals of one person and the mouth or anus of another person; or
>
> "(B) the penetration of the genitals or the anus of another person with an object." § 21.01(1).

The petitioners exercised their right to a trial *de novo* in Harris County Criminal Court. They challenged the statute as a violation of the Equal Protection Clause of the Fourteenth Amendment and of a like provision of the Texas Constitution. Tex. Const., Art. 1, § 3a. Those contentions were rejected. The petitioners, having entered a plea of *nolo contendere*, were each fined $200 and assessed court costs of $141.25.

The Court of Appeals for the Texas Fourteenth District considered the petitioners' federal constitutional arguments under both the Equal Protection and Due Process Clauses of the Fourteenth Amendment. After hearing the case *en banc* the court, in a divided opinion, rejected the constitutional arguments and affirmed the convictions. The majority opinion indicates that the Court of Appeals considered our decision in *Bowers v. Hardwick*, 478 U.S. 186 (1986), to be controlling on the federal due process aspect of the case. *Bowers* then being authoritative, this was proper. We granted *certiorari* to consider [among other things] whether *Bowers v. Hardwick* should be overruled. * * *

We conclude the case should be resolved by determining whether the petitioners were free as adults to engage in the private conduct in the exercise of their liberty under the Due Process Clause of the Fourteenth Amendment to the Constitution. For this inquiry we deem it necessary to reconsider the Court's holding in *Bowers*.

There are broad statements of the substantive reach of liberty under the Due Process Clause in earlier cases, including *Pierce v. Society of Sisters*, 268 U.S. 510 (1925), and *Meyer v. Nebraska*, 262 U.S. 390 (1923); but the most pertinent beginning point is our decision in *Griswold v. Connecticut*, 381 U.S. 479 (1965).

In *Griswold* the Court invalidated a state law prohibiting the use of drugs or devices of contraception and counseling or aiding and abetting the use of contraceptives. The Court described the protected interest as a right to privacy and placed emphasis on the marriage relation and the protected space of the marital bedroom. After *Griswold* it was established that the right to make certain decisions regarding sexual conduct extends beyond the marital relationship. In *Eisenstadt v. Baird*, 405 U.S. 438 (1972), the Court invalidated a law prohibiting the distribution of contraceptives to unmarried persons. The case was decided under the Equal Protection Clause, but with respect to unmarried persons, the Court went on to state the fundamental proposition that the law impaired the exercise of their personal rights. It quoted from the statement of the Court of Appeals finding the law to be in conflict with fundamental human rights, and it followed with this statement of its own:

> It is true that in *Griswold* the right of privacy in question inhered in the marital relationship. . . . If the right of privacy means anything, it is the right of the individual, married or single, to be free from unwarranted governmental intrusion into matters so fundamentally affecting a person as the decision whether to bear or beget a child.

Id., at 453.

The opinions in *Griswold* and *Eisenstadt* were part of the background for the decision in *Roe v. Wade*, 410 U.S. 113 (1973). As is well known, the case involved a challenge to the Texas law prohibiting abortions, but the laws of other States were affected as well. Although the Court held the woman's rights were not absolute, her right to elect an abortion did have real and substantial protection as an exercise of her liberty under the Due Process Clause. * * * *Roe* recognized the right of a woman to make certain fundamental decisions affecting her destiny and confirmed once more that the protection of liberty under the Due Process Clause has a substantive dimension of fundamental significance in defining the rights of the person.

In *Carey v. Population Services Int'l*, 431 U.S. 678 (1977), the Court confronted a New York law forbidding sale or distribution of contraceptive devices to persons under 16 years of age. Although there was no single opinion for the Court, the law was invalidated. Both *Eisenstadt* and *Carey*, as well as the holding and rationale in *Roe*, confirmed that the reasoning of *Griswold* could not be confined to the protection of rights of married adults. This was the state of the law with respect to some of the most relevant cases when the Court considered *Bowers v. Hardwick*.

The facts in *Bowers* had some similarities to the instant case. A police officer, whose right to enter seems not to have been in question, observed Hardwick, in his own bedroom, engaging in intimate sexual conduct with another adult male. The conduct was in violation of a Georgia statute making it a criminal offense to engage in sodomy. One difference between the two cases is that the Georgia statute prohibited the conduct whether or not the participants were of the same sex, while the Texas statute, as we have seen, applies only to participants of the same sex. Hardwick was not prosecuted, but he brought an action in federal court to declare the state statute invalid. He alleged he was a practicing homosexual and that the criminal prohibition violated rights guaranteed to him by the Constitution. The Court, in an opinion by Justice White, sustained the Georgia law. Chief Justice Burger and Justice Powell joined the opinion of the Court and filed separate, concurring opinions. Four Justices dissented.

The Court began its substantive discussion in *Bowers* as follows: "The issue presented is whether the Federal Constitution confers a fundamental right upon homosexuals to engage in sodomy and hence invalidates the laws of the many States that still make such conduct illegal and have done so for a very long time." That statement, we now conclude, discloses the Court's own failure to appreciate the extent of the liberty at stake. To say that the issue in *Bowers* was simply the right to engage in certain sexual conduct demeans the claim the individual put forward, just as it would demean a married couple were it to be said marriage is simply about the right to have sexual intercourse. The laws involved in *Bowers* and here are, to be sure, statutes that purport to do no more than prohibit a particular sexual act. Their penalties and purposes, though, have more far-reaching consequences, touching upon the most private human conduct, sexual behavior, and in the most private of places, the home. The statutes do seek to control a personal relationship that, whether or not entitled to formal recognition in the law, is within the liberty of persons to choose without being punished as criminals. * * *

Having misapprehended the claim of liberty there presented to it, and thus stating the claim to be whether there is a fundamental right to engage in consensual sodomy, the *Bowers* Court said: "Proscriptions against that conduct have ancient roots." In academic writings, and in many of the scholarly *amicus* briefs filed to assist the Court in this case, there are fundamental criticisms of the historical premises relied upon by the majority and concurring opinions in *Bowers*. We need not enter this debate in the attempt to reach a definitive historical judgment, but the following considerations counsel against adopting the definitive conclusions upon which *Bowers* placed such reliance.

At the outset it should be noted that there is no longstanding history in this country of laws directed at homosexual conduct as a distinct matter. Beginning in colonial times there were prohibitions of sodomy derived from the English criminal laws passed in the first instance by the Reformation Parliament of 1533. The English prohibition was understood to include relations between men and women as well as relations between men and men. Nineteenth-century commentators similarly read American sodomy, buggery, and crime-against-nature statutes as criminalizing certain relations between men and women and between men and men. The absence of legal prohibitions focusing on homosexual conduct may be explained in part by noting that according to some scholars the concept of the homosexual as a distinct category of person did not emerge until the late 19th century. Thus early American sodomy laws were not directed at homosexuals as such but instead sought to prohibit non-procreative sexual activity more generally. * * *

Laws prohibiting sodomy do not seem to have been enforced against consenting adults acting in private. * * * To the extent that there were any prosecutions for the acts in question, 19th-century evidence rules imposed a burden that would make a conviction more difficult to obtain even taking into account the problems always inherent in prosecuting consensual acts committed in private. Under then-prevailing standards, a man could not be convicted of sodomy based upon testimony of a consenting partner, because the partner was considered an accomplice. A partner's testimony, however, was admissible if he or she had not consented to the act or was a minor, and therefore incapable of consent. The rule may explain in part the infrequency of these prosecutions. In all events that infrequency makes it difficult to say that society approved of a rigorous and systematic punishment of the consensual acts committed in private and by adults. The longstanding criminal prohibition of homosexual sodomy upon which the *Bowers* decision placed such reliance is as consistent with a general condemnation of non-procreative sex as it is with an established tradition of prosecuting acts because of their homosexual character. * * *

It was not until the 1970's that any State singled out same-sex relations for criminal prosecution, and only nine States have done so. * * *

In summary, the historical grounds relied upon in *Bowers* are more complex than the majority opinion and the concurring opinion by Chief Justice Burger indicate. Their historical premises are not without doubt and, at the very least, are overstated.

It must be acknowledged, of course, that the Court in *Bowers* was making the broader point that for centuries there have been powerful voices to condemn homosexual conduct as immoral. The condemnation has been shaped by religious beliefs, conceptions of right and acceptable behavior, and respect for the traditional family. For many persons these are not trivial concerns but profound and deep convictions accepted as ethical and moral principles to which they aspire and which thus determine the course of their lives. These considerations do not answer the question before us, however. The issue is whether the majority may use the power of the State to enforce these views on the whole society through operation of the criminal law. "Our obligation is to define the liberty of all, not to mandate our own moral code." *Planned Parenthood of Southeastern Pa. v. Casey*, 505 U.S. 833, 850 (1992).

Chief Justice Burger joined the opinion for the Court in *Bowers* and further explained his views as follows: "Decisions of individuals relating to homosexual conduct have been subject to state intervention throughout the history of Western civilization. Condemnation of those practices is firmly rooted in Judeao-Christian moral and ethical standards." As with Justice White's assumptions about history, scholarship casts some doubt on the sweeping nature of the statement by Chief Justice Burger as it pertains to private homosexual conduct between consenting adults. *See, e.g.,* Eskridge, *Hardwick and Historiography*, 1999 U. ILL. L.REV. 631, 656. In all events we think that our laws and traditions in the past half century are of most relevance here. These references show an emerging awareness that liberty gives substantial protection to adult persons in deciding how to conduct their private lives in matters pertaining to sex. * * *

This emerging recognition should have been apparent when *Bowers* was decided. In 1955 the American Law Institute promulgated the Model Penal Code and made clear that it did not recommend or provide for "criminal penalties for consensual sexual relations conducted in private." ALI, Model Penal Code § 213.2, Comment 2, p. 372 (1980). It justified its decision on three grounds: (1) The prohibitions undermined respect for the law by penalizing conduct many people engaged in; (2) the statutes regulated private conduct not harmful to others; and (3) the laws were arbitrarily enforced and thus invited the danger of blackmail. ALI, Model Penal Code, Commentary 277–280 (Tent. Draft No. 4, 1955). In 1961 Illinois changed its laws to conform to the Model Penal Code. Other States soon followed. * * *

The sweeping references by Chief Justice Burger to the history of Western civilization and to Judeo-Christian moral and ethical standards did not take account of other authorities pointing in an opposite direction. A committee advising the British Parliament recommended in 1957 repeal of laws punishing homosexual conduct. THE WOLFENDEN REPORT: REPORT OF THE COMMITTEE ON HOMOSEXUAL OFFENSES AND PROSTITUTION (1963).

Parliament enacted the substance of those recommendations 10 years later. Sexual Offences Act 1967, § 1.

Of even more importance, almost five years before *Bowers* was decided the European Court of Human Rights considered a case with parallels to *Bowers* and to today's case. An adult male resident in Northern Ireland alleged he was a practicing homosexual who desired to engage in consensual homosexual conduct. The laws of Northern Ireland forbade him that right. He alleged that he had been questioned, his home had been searched, and he feared criminal prosecution. The court held that the laws proscribing the conduct were invalid under the European Convention on Human Rights. *Dudgeon v. United Kingdom*, 45 Eur. Ct. H.R. (1981) & ¶ 52. Authoritative in all countries that are members of the Council of Europe (21 nations then, 45 nations now), the decision is at odds with the premise in *Bowers* that the claim put forward was insubstantial in our Western civilization.

In our own constitutional system the deficiencies in *Bowers* became even more apparent in the years following its announcement. The 25 States with laws prohibiting the relevant conduct referenced in the *Bowers* decision are reduced now to 13, of which 4 enforce their laws only against homosexual conduct. In those States where sodomy is still proscribed, whether for same-sex or heterosexual conduct, there is a pattern of non-enforcement with respect to consenting adults acting in private. The State of Texas admitted in 1994 that as of that date it had not prosecuted anyone under those circumstances.

Two principal cases decided after *Bowers* cast its holding into even more doubt. In *Planned Parenthood of Southeastern Pa. v. Casey*, 505 U.S. 833 (1992), the Court reaffirmed the substantive force of the liberty protected by the Due Process Clause. The *Casey* decision again confirmed that our laws and tradition afford constitutional protection to personal decisions relating to marriage, procreation, contraception, family relationships, child rearing, and education. In explaining the respect the Constitution demands for the autonomy of the person in making these choices, we stated as follows:

> These matters, involving the most intimate and personal choices a person may make in a lifetime, choices central to personal dignity and autonomy, are central to the liberty protected by the Fourteenth Amendment. At the heart of liberty is the right to define one's own concept of existence, of meaning, of the universe, and of the mystery of human life. Beliefs about these matters could not define the at-tributes of personhood were they formed under compulsion of the State.

Persons in a homosexual relationship may seek autonomy for these purposes, just as heterosexual persons do. The decision in *Bowers* would deny them this right.

The second post-*Bowers* case of principal relevance is *Romer v. Evans*, 517 U.S. 620 (1996). There the Court struck down class-based legislation directed at homosexuals as a violation of the Equal Protection Clause. *Romer* invalidated an amendment to Colorado's Constitution which named as a solitary class persons who were homosexuals, lesbians, or bisexual either by "orientation, conduct, practices or relationships," *id.*, at 624 (internal quotation marks omitted), and deprived them of protection under state antidiscrimination laws. We concluded that the provision was "born of animosity toward the class of persons affected" and further that it had no rational relation to a legitimate governmental purpose. * * *

The stigma this criminal statute imposes, moreover, is not trivial. The offense, to be sure, is but a class C misdemeanor, a minor offense in the Texas legal system. Still, it remains a criminal offense with all that imports for the dignity of the persons charged. The petitioners will bear on their record the history of their criminal convictions. * * * This underscores the consequential nature of the punishment and the state-sponsored condemnation attendant to the criminal prohibition. Furthermore, the Texas criminal conviction carries with it the other collateral consequences always following a conviction, such as notations on job application forms, to mention but one example.

The foundations of *Bowers* have sustained serious erosion from our recent decisions in *Casey* and *Romer*. When our precedent has been thus weakened, criticism from other sources is of greater significance. In the United States criticism of *Bowers* has been substantial and continuing, disapproving of its reasoning in all respects, not just as to its historical assumptions. *See, e.g.*, C. FRIED, ORDER AND LAW: ARGUING THE REAGAN REVOLUTION—A FIRSTHAND ACCOUNT 81–84 (1991); R. POSNER, SEX AND REASON 341–350 (1992). The courts of five different States have declined to follow it in interpreting provisions in their own state constitutions parallel to the Due Process Clause of the Fourteenth Amendment.

To the extent *Bowers* relied on values we share with a wider civilization, it should be noted that the reasoning and holding in *Bowers* have been rejected elsewhere. The European Court of Human Rights has followed not *Bowers* but its own decision in *Dudgeon v. United Kingdom*. *See P.G. & J.H. v. United Kingdom*, App. No. 00044787/98, & ¶ 56 (Eur.Ct.H. R., Sept. 25, 2001); *Modinos v. Cyprus*, 259 Eur. Ct. H.R. (1993); *Norris v. Ireland*, 142 Eur. Ct. H.R. (1988). Other nations, too, have taken action consistent with an affirmation of the protected right of homosexual adults to engage in intimate, consensual conduct. *See* Brief for Mary Robinson et al. as Amici Curiae 11–12. The right the petitioners seek in this case has been accepted as an integral part of human freedom in many other countries. There has been no showing that in this country the governmental interest in circumscribing personal choice is somehow more legitimate or urgent.

The doctrine of *stare decisis* is essential to the respect accorded to the judgments of the Court and to the stability of the law. It is not, however, an inexorable command. * * * In *Casey* we noted that when a court is asked to overrule a precedent recognizing a constitutional liberty interest, individual or societal reliance on the existence of that liberty cautions with particular strength against reversing course. 505 U.S., at 855–856 ("Liberty finds no refuge in a jurisprudence of doubt"). The holding in *Bowers*, however, has not induced detrimental reliance comparable to some instances where recognized individual rights are involved. Indeed, there has been no individual or societal reliance on *Bowers* of the sort that could counsel against overturning its holding once there are compelling reasons to do so. *Bowers* itself causes uncertainty, for the precedents before and after its issuance contradict its central holding.

The rationale of *Bowers* does not withstand careful analysis. In his dissenting opinion in Bowers Justice Stevens came to these conclusions:

> Our prior cases make two propositions abundantly clear. First, the fact that the governing majority in a State has traditionally viewed a particular practice as immoral is not a sufficient reason for upholding a law prohibiting the practice; neither history nor tradition could save a law prohibiting miscegenation from constitutional attack. Second, individual decisions by married persons, concerning the intimacies of their physical relationship, even when not intended to produce offspring, are a form of 'liberty' protected by the Due Process Clause of the Fourteenth Amendment. Moreover, this protection extends to intimate choices by unmarried as well as married persons.

478 U.S., at 216 (footnotes and citations omitted). Justice Stevens' analysis, in our view, should have been controlling in *Bowers* and should control here. *Bowers* was not correct when it was decided, and it is not correct today. It ought not to remain binding precedent. *Bowers v. Hardwick* should be and now is overruled.

The present case does not involve minors. It does not involve persons who might be injured or coerced or who are situated in relationships where consent might not easily be refused. It does not involve public conduct or prostitution. It does not involve whether the government must give formal recognition to any relationship that homosexual persons seek to enter. The case does involve two adults who, with full and mutual consent from each other, engaged in sexual practices common to a homosexual lifestyle. The petitioners are entitled to respect for their private lives. The State cannot demean their existence or control their destiny by making their private sexual conduct a crime. Their right to liberty under the Due Process Clause gives them the full right to engage in their conduct without intervention of the government. * * * The Texas statute furthers no legitimate state interest which can justify its intrusion into the personal and private life of the individual.

Had those who drew and ratified the Due Process Clauses of the Fifth Amendment or the Fourteenth Amendment known the components of liberty in its manifold possibilities, they might have been more specific. They did not presume to have this insight. They knew times can blind us to certain truths and later generations can see that laws once thought necessary and proper in fact serve only to oppress. As the Constitution endures, persons in every generation can invoke its principles in their own search for greater freedom.

The judgment of the Court of Appeals for the Texas Fourteenth District is reversed, and the case is remanded for further proceedings not inconsistent with this opinion.

NOTES AND QUESTIONS

1. *Strictly a matter of personnel?* Why exactly didn't *Bowers* qualify as binding precedent for the *Lawrence* decision? Other than the composition of the Court,[7] what changed between 1986 (when *Bowers* was decided) and 2003 (when *Lawrence* was decided) that would account for the difference between these two cases?

2. *A precedent's use of precedent. Bowers* and *Lawrence* deal with several precedents in common. In both cases, the majority felt compelled to address prior cases like *Griswold, Eisenstadt, Carey,* and *Roe v. Wade*, among others. Consider first how each of these prior cases was interpreted differently in *Bowers* and in *Lawrence*. Can you explain how these precedents might be cited by the majorities in both of the principal cases to reach opposite conclusions?

3. *A sliding scale for the "weight" of a precedent*. Should the deference shown to precedent vary with the type of case? For example, what are the best arguments for giving *less* deference to prior courts' interpretation of the Constitution—as in *Bowers* and *Lawrence*—than to their interpretation of a statute or some common law doctrine? Is there an argument that the one place deference to precedent should *never* be required is (a) in the Supreme Court (b) on Constitutional issues?

Consider in this connection that a Constitutional mistake by the Court can only be fixed by amendment, a highly cumbersome and rare procedure, whereas a mistake in the court's interpretation of a statute can always be fixed by Congress. What is the best argument that this difference in fixing mistakes translates into a policy of respecting *stare decisis* more in the statutory cases

---

[7] In 1986, the Supreme Court consisted of Justices Blackmun, Brennan, Burger, Marshall, O'Connor, Powell, Stevens, Rehnquist, and White. By 2003, six of these justices—three "liberal-moderates" (Blackmun, Brennan, and Marshall) and three "conservative-moderates" (Burger, Powell, and White)—had been replaced, and the Court consisted of Justices Breyer, Ginsburg, Kennedy, O'Connor, Rehnquist, Scalia, Souter, Stevens, and Thomas.

than in the constitutional cases? *Compare Smith v. Allwright*, 321 U.S. 649, 665 (1944) ("In constitutional questions, where correction depends upon amendment and not upon legislative action this Court throughout its history has freely exercised its power to reexamine the basis of its constitutional decisions") *with Neal v. United States*, 516 U.S. 284, 295 (1996) (Kennedy, J.) ("One reason that we give great weight to *stare decisis* in the area of statutory construction is that 'Congress is free to change this Court's interpretation of its legislation' " (*quoting Illinois Brick Co. v. Illinois*, 431 U.S. 720, 736 (1977)). What are the counter-arguments? *See generally*, Rafael Gely, *Of Sinking and Escalating: A (Somewhat) New Look at Stare Decisis*, 60 U. PITT. L. REV. 89, 109 (1998) ("common law precedents enjoy a presumption of correctness stronger than that applied to constitutional cases, but not as constraining as that enjoyed by statutory precedents").

Consider another possible factor that might affect the weight to be given precedent within the common law, namely the importance of reliance and doctrinal stability within particular fields of law. When planning is at a premium, as for example when people enter into contracts or plan their wills, they direct their affairs in light of existing law and rely on the law to remain fairly stable. The law in those areas directly affects their out-of-court behavior. Tort law, by contrast, to the extent that it deals with accidents and negligence, is not generally on the minds of tortfeasors at the time of their legally-relevant conduct outside of court. Does that difference translate into a principle of giving greater weight to precedent in commercial or mercantile law (or the law of wills and estates) than to precedent setting the standard for, say, the intentional infliction of emotional distress?

4. *Precedent, "super-precedent," "super-duper precedent," and "mind-blowing" or "cosmic" precedent.* In 2000, Judge J. Michael Luttig, writing for the Fourth Circuit Court of Appeals, invalidated a Virginia statute that prohibited what the law's proponents called "partial birth abortions." In Judge Luttig's words, "I understand the Supreme Court to have intended its decision in *Planned Parenthood v. Casey* [also cited in *Lawrence, supra*] to be a decision of super-*stare decisis* with respect to a woman's fundamental right to choose whether or not to proceed with a pregnancy." *Richmond Medical Center for Women v. Gilmore,* 219 F.3d 376, 377 (4th Cir. 2000). Five years later, at his confirmation hearing, Judge John Roberts—later Chief Justice of the United States—was asked by Senator Arlen Specter, "Would you think that *Roe [v. Wade]* might be a super-duper precedent?"

Perhaps inadvertently, both Senator Specter and Judge Luttig were echoing the argument of Professors Landes and Posner in 1976 that some cases qualify as "super-precedents," a status they attempted to prove in part by counting the number of times that a particular case was cited in subsequent decisions. Of course, counting citations could be badly misleading: a decision could qualify as a "super-precedent" if it were

> so effective in defining the requirements of the law that it prevents legal disputes from arising in the first place, or, if they do arise, induces them to be settled without litigation. In the limit, such a

> "super-precedent" might never be cited in an appellate opinion yet have greater precedential significance than most frequently cited cases.

William Landes & Richard Posner, *Legal Precedent: A Theoretical and Empirical Analysis*, 19 J. LAW & ECON. 249, 251 (1976). The idea of super-precedent raises a number of questions:

> (a) *The criteria in principle*. What must a case be (or do, or have, or reflect) in order to qualify as "super-precedent?" And what are the practical consequences of such a designation? Must the decision be unanimous? Would you distinguish between cases that had been repeatedly upheld over various challenges or simply cited without question? If there had been multiple failed attempts to overturn or restrict the case by legislation, would that undermine or support the precedential value of the decision? *See generally* Daniel A. Farber, *The Rule of Law and the Law of Precedents*, 90 MINN. L. REV. 1173 (2006).
>
> (b) *Generalizing from particulars*. Try to identify a few cases that might qualify as super-precedents (if anything would) and then decide what they have in common with one another that distinguishes them from other cases. Potential nominees might include: *Marbury v. Madison*, 1 Cranch 137, 5 U.S. 137 (1803), for the proposition that the federal courts of the United States have the inherent authority to determine the constitutionality of statutes enacted by Congress, and *Hadley v. Baxendale*, 156 Eng. Rep 145 (1854) (Court of Exch.), which laid down certain principles by which a jury ought to be guided in determining the damages arising from a breach of contract.
>
> (c) *Implying the opposite*. Does the idea of "super-precedent" imply the existence of its opposite, something like "pseudo-precedent" or "wussy precedent" or "measly precedent"? Consider *Korematsu v. United States*, 323 U.S. 224 (1944), a decision from the World War II era, which upheld the constitutionality of the U.S. government detaining Japanese-Americans in concentration camps. *Korematsu* has never been explicitly overturned, it has never been applied to justify the internment of U.S. citizens, and Congress declared that the decision had been "overruled in the court of history" and eventually authorized the payment of compensation to those who had been interned. In 1998, President Clinton awarded the Presidential Medal of Freedom to Mr. Korematsu. It would be folly bordering on malpractice to cite *Korematsu* favorably; indeed, in 2011, the Acting Solicitor General of the United States acknowledged the error of that office and of the court in reaching that decision in 1944.

5. *Non-precedential authority*. Note that Justice Kennedy—writing the opinion for the Court in *Lawrence*—refers to certain international or foreign authorities, including decisions of the European Court of Human Rights. What

role do these contemporary authorities play in the decision, and why should they have any weight whatsoever? Are they more or less relevant than Chief Justice Burger's citation in *Bowers* of an English statute from the time of King Henry VIII?

6. *Logical objections to reasoning by precedent.* How do you respond to the criticism that precedent is a particularly inefficient and illogical way to discern what the law is? After all, a case with all its particularities and factual idiosyncracies might contain multiple ideas or doctrines simultaneously. Logicians would object that it is fallacious in any event to draw a generalization from so particular a data point, what Tennyson, *supra*, captured in his image of a "wilderness of single instances." *See* Felix Cohen, *The Ethical Basis for Legal Criticism*, 41 YALE L. J. 201 (1931) ("The periodic attempts of students of the common law to put forward logical formulae for discovering 'the rule of a case' all betray an elementary ignorance of the fact that no particular proposition can imply a general proposition.")

7. *Moral objections to reasoning by precedent.* Consider this observation by Oliver Wendell Holmes, Jr., in *The Path of the Law*, 10 HARV. L. REV. 457, 469, 472 (1897):

> It is revolting to have no better reason for a rule of law than that so it was laid down in the time of Henry IV. It is still more revolting if the grounds upon which it was laid down have vanished long since, and the rule simply persists from blind imitation of the past. . . . Everywhere the basis of principle is tradition, to such an extent that we even are in danger of making the role of history more important than it is.

Without denying the importance of precedent, Holmes is appalled by the possibility that an injustice might be perpetuated, even fetishized, in the name of precedent, solely because it made sense at some other time, in some other setting. In the trade-off between stability and innovation, precedent obviously stacks the deck against reform.

Quite apart from the problem of perpetuating injustice by privileging precedent, consider the moral problem of notice. Jeremy Bentham once observed that "[for] a law [to] be obeyed, it is necessary that it should be known." THE WORKS OF JEREMY BENTHAM: OF PROMULGATION OF THE LAW 157 (Bowring ed. 1859). But of course there is no precedent until a case announcing it is decided—a fact that led to Bentham's unflattering characterization of the common law-making process:

> Do you know how they make [common law]? Just as a man makes laws for his dog. When your dog does anything you want to break him of, you wait till he does it, and then beat him for it. This is the way you make laws for your dog: and this is the way the judges make law for you and me.

Id., at 235. Bentham's portrayal may be funny, but is it accurate? Is the common law essentially unknowable?

8. *Another example of precedent lost or regained: corporate political speech.* In *Austin v. Michigan State Chamber of Commerce*, 494 U.S. 652 (1990), a business organization challenged a Michigan statute that prohibited corporations from contributing to or against political candidates in elections for state office. Prior cases had suggested that corporate speech was protected by the First Amendment. *See, e.g., Buckley v. Valeo*, 424 U.S. 1 (1976); *First Nat'l Bank of Boston v. Bellotti*, 435 U.S. 765 (1978). In *Austin*, however, the Supreme Court found that the Michigan statute survived strict scrutiny. First, the Court found a compelling state interest in preventing "the corrosive and distorting effects of immense aggregations of [corporate] wealth . . . that have little or no correlation to the public's support for the corporation's political ideas." 494 U.S., at 660. Second, the Court ruled that the statute was narrowly tailored to achieve that goal: "[w]e find that the Act is precisely targeted to eliminate the distortion caused by corporate spending while also allowing corporations to express their political views." Id. at 660.

Twenty years later, the Supreme Court expressly overruled *Austin* in *Citizens United v. Federal Election Commission*, 558 U.S. 310 (2010). Under *Citizens United,* the government violates the First Amendment when it suppresses political speech by corporations or bars independent corporate expenditures for election-related communications:

> Our precedent is to be respected unless the most convincing of reasons demonstrates that adherence to it puts us on a course that is sure error. "Beyond workability, the relevant factors in deciding whether to adhere to the principle of *stare decisis* include the antiquity of the precedent, the reliance interests at stake, and of course whether the decision was well reasoned." *Montejo v. Louisiana*, 556 U.S. 778 (2009) (overruling *Michigan v. Jackson*, 475 U.S. 625 (1986)). We have also examined whether "experience has pointed up the precedent's shortcomings." *Pearson v. Callahan*, 555 U.S. 223 (2009) (overruling *Saucier v. Katz*, 533 U.S. 194 (2001)).

Applying those standards, the majority in *Citizens United*—some of whom had dissented in *Austin*—determined that the prior case was not well-reasoned, that *Austin* had itself been inconsistent with precedent like *Buckley* and *Bellotti,* and that whatever reliance interests had been created by *Austin* were insignificant. What about the reliance interests of state legislatures that had enacted limits on corporate spending in elections, concluding after *Austin* that such statutes would be sustained?

9. *Reliance interests as a brake on overturning precedent.* One of the Supreme Court's most explicit, extended exchanges on the nature of precedent occurs in *Planned Parenthood v. Casey*, 505 U.S. 833 (1992), in which a fractured Court reaffirmed *Roe v. Wade*'s essential holding that women have a Constitutional right to choose an abortion before fetal viability. Justice O'Connor, writing for herself and Justices Kennedy and Souter, said:

> [The] Court must take care to speak and act in ways that allow people to accept its decisions on the terms the Court claims for them, as

> grounded truly in principle, not as compromises with social and political pressures having, as such, no bearing on the principled choices that the Court is obliged to make. . . . [T]he Court's legitimacy depends on making legally principled decisions under circumstances in which their principled character is sufficiently plausible to be accepted by the Nation. . . .
>
> Where, in the performance of its judicial duties, the Court decides a case in such a way as to resolve the sort of intensely divisive controversy reflected in *Roe* and those rare, comparable cases, its decision has a dimension that the resolution of the normal case does not carry. It is the dimension present whenever the Court's interpretation of the Constitution calls the contending sides of a national controversy to end their national division by accepting a common mandate rooted in the Constitution. . . . [T]o overrule under fire in the absence of the most compelling reason to reexamine a watershed decision" would appear simply to be "a surrender to political pressure, and an unjustified repudiation of the principle on which the Court staked its authority in the first instance."

505 U.S., at 865–67 (internal citations omitted).

The essential reaffirmation of *Roe* on grounds of *stare decisis* is clear from the separate concurring opinions of Justices Stevens and Blackmun. In his concurrence, Justice Stevens noted that

> The Court is unquestionably correct in concluding that the doctrine of *stare decisis* has controlling significance in a case of this kind, notwithstanding an individual Justice's concerns about the merits. The central holding of *Roe v. Wade* has been a "part of our law" for almost two decades. It was a natural sequel to the protection of individual liberty established in *Griswold v. Connecticut*, 381 U.S. 479 (1965). The societal costs of overruling *Roe* at this late date would be enormous. *Roe* is an integral part of a correct understanding of both the concept of liberty and the basic equality of men and women.

Id. at 912.

Justice Blackmun in his concurrence observed that

> Make no mistake, the joint opinion of Justices O'Connor, Kennedy, and Souter is an act of personal courage and constitutional principle. In contrast to previous decisions in which Justices O'Connor and Kennedy postponed reconsideration of *Roe v. Wade*, the authors of the joint opinion today join Justice Stevens and me in concluding that "the essential holding of Roe v. Wade should be retained and once again reaffirmed." In brief, five Members of this Court today recognize that "the Constitution protects a woman's right to terminate her pregnancy in its early stages."

Id. at 923.

By contrast, the dissent in *Casey*—written by Chief Justice Rehnquist and joined by Justices White, Scalia and Thomas—is a textbook example of the arguments against precedent for its own sake, especially on questions of Constitutional law:

> The joint opinion [of Justices O'Connor, Kennedy, and Souter], following its newly minted variation on *stare decisis*, retains the outer shell of *Roe v. Wade*, but beats a wholesale retreat from the substance of that case[, endorsing an undue burden test instead of the trimester test in *Roe*]. We believe that *Roe* was wrongly decided, and that it can and should be overruled consistently with our traditional approach to *stare decisis* in constitutional cases. . . . The joint opinion . . . points to the reliance interests involved in this context in its effort to explain why precedent must be followed for precedent's sake. Certainly it is true that where reliance is truly at issue, as in the case of judicial decisions that have formed the basis for private decisions, "[c]onsiderations in favor of *stare decisis* are at their acme." *Payne v. Tennessee*, 501 U.S., at 828. But, as the joint opinion apparently agrees, any traditional notion of reliance is not applicable here. The Court today cuts back on the protection afforded by *Roe*, and no one claims that this action defeats any reliance interest in the disavowed trimester framework. Similarly, reliance interests would not be diminished were the Court to go further and acknowledge the full error of *Roe*, as "reproductive planning could take virtually immediate account of" this action.

Id. at 956.

On the basis of these short extracts from the joint opinion and the dissent in *Casey*:

(a) How would you articulate and assess the competing arguments among the Justices about maintaining the Court's "legitimacy"? (b) What kind of evidence should the Court consider when it determines whether reliance interests based on a prior decision strengthen the gravitational pull of *stare decisis* or not?

10. *Getting it right versus getting it settled*. Justice Louis Brandeis once observed that it is generally "more important that the applicable rule of law be settled than that it be settled right." *Burnet v. Coronado Oil & Gas Co.*, 285 U.S. 393, 406 (1932) (Brandeis, J., dissenting). Can you think of an issue either so morally balanced or so routine (or trivial) that it doesn't matter which way it's resolved so long as it's resolved consistently? For every issue you find that fits this description, would it matter to you that the resolution was crafted by judges instead of elected legislators?

11. *Res judicata and law of the case distinguished from precedent*. The law has multiple doctrines, including *stare decisis*, for avoiding the relitigation of decided issues, but these doctrines may apply in different settings, serve different functions, and have different effects.

(a) Consider for example the doctrine of *res judicata* and collateral estoppel. In *Allen v. McCurry*, 449 U.S. 90 (1980), the Supreme Court observed:

> The federal courts have traditionally adhered to the related doctrines of *res judicata* and collateral estoppel. Under *res judicata*, a final judgment on the merits of an action precludes the parties or their privies from relitigating issues that were or could have been raised in that action. Under collateral estoppel, once a court has decided an issue of fact or law necessary to its judgment, that decision may preclude relitigation of the issue in a suit on a different cause of action involving a party to the first case. As this Court and other courts have often recognized, *res judicata* and collateral estoppel relieve parties of the cost and vexation of multiple lawsuits, conserve judicial resources, and, by preventing inconsistent decisions, encourage reliance on adjudication.

Id. at 94 (citations omitted). On the basis of this description, what are the primary differences among *res judicata*, collateral estoppel, and *stare decisis*?

(b) Consider also the "law of the case" doctrine, under which "courts will not review former decisions made by the same court, in the same cause, and on the same facts." *The People's Savings Bank v. Eberts*, 96 Mich. 396, 398, 55 N.W. 996 (1893). So for example, "rulings made by a trial court and not challenged on appeal become the law of the case" for that litigation. *Hughes v. State*, 490 A.2d 1034,1048 (Del. 1985). The Sixth Circuit has described the doctrine somewhat more systematically:

> The "law of the case" doctrine precludes a court from "reconsideration of identical issues." Issues decided at an early stage of the litigation, either explicitly or by necessary inference from the disposition, constitute the law of the case." As we have held, however, this "law of the case" doctrine is "directed to a court's common sense" and is not an "inexorable command." We previously have stated three reasons to reconsider a ruling: (1) where substantially different evidence is raised on subsequent trial; (2) where a subsequent contrary view of the law is decided by the controlling authority; or (3) where a decision is clearly erroneous and would work a manifest injustice.

Hanover Ins. Co. v. American Engineering Co., 105 F.3d 306, 312 (6th Cir. 1997) (citations omitted). Compare the pithier view of Justice Oliver Wendell Holmes, Jr., in *Messinger v. Anderson*, 225 U.S. 436, 444 (1912): "In the absence of statute, the phrase, 'law of the case,' as applied to the effect of previous orders on the later action of the court rendering them in the same case, merely expresses the practice of courts generally to refuse to reopen what has been decided, not a limit to their power." On the basis of this description, how does the "law of the case" doctrine differ from precedent?

B. PRECEDENT IN LIMBO

In the following case, consider how the lawyers for the winning side characterized the applicable precedent as "implicitly overruled?" How would they know, or how could they prove, that the court that had decided the precedent had abandoned it?

SYSCOMM INTERN. CORP. V. SYNOPTICS COMMUNICATIONS, INC.

856 F.Supp. 135 (E.D.N.Y. 1994)

[In the course of a commercial arbitration that arose out of a breach of contract, Syscomm International, one party to the arbitration, discovered that other parties, including Synoptics Communications, had apparently violated the antitrust laws of the United States, which among other things prevent monopolization of markets, price-fixing, and other illegal restraints of trade, *inter alia*. Syscomm then sued SynOptics for those violations and requested a stay of the ongoing arbitration while the litigation proceeded. SynOptics opposed the motion and requested the district court to exercise its power under federal statute to compel arbitration of the statutory antitrust claims in addition to the original commercial claims.]

[T]he issue presented is whether antitrust claims arising from domestic transactions are arbitrable where the parties have agreed to arbitrate them. While, at one time, the answer to this question in the Second Circuit would have been that such claims are nonarbitrable, *see American Safety Equipment Corp. v. J.P. Maguire & Co.*, 391 F.2d 821 (2nd Cir.1968), this Court believes that the Second Circuit and the Supreme Court, if faced with this issue, would conclude that antitrust claims arising from domestic transactions are arbitrable.

Syscomm argues that the Second Circuit's decision in *American Safety*, which held that domestic antitrust claims are nonarbitrable, controls the decision in this case. SynOptics, on the other hand, argues that the *American Safety* doctrine has been implicitly overruled by recent Supreme Court decisions upholding the enforceability of agreements to arbitrate international antitrust disputes, see *Mitsubishi Motors Corp. v. Soler Chrysler-Plymouth, Inc.*, 473 U.S. 614 (1985), and agreements to arbitrate domestic securities law claims and RICO claims, see *Rodriguez de Quijas v. Shearson/American Express, Inc.*, 490 U.S. 477 (1989) (holding that claims under the Securities Act of 1933 are arbitrable); *Shearson/American Express, Inc. v. McMahon*, 482 U.S. 220 (1987) (holding that claims under the Securities Act of 1934 and RICO claims are arbitrable). Because this Court agrees that the Second Circuit would no longer adhere to the *American Safety* doctrine, this Court grants

SynOptics' request to compel arbitration and denies Syscomm's request for a stay of the pending Arbitration Proceeding.

In *Mitsubishi*, the Supreme Court upheld the enforceability of an agreement to resolve antitrust claims by arbitration when the agreement arises from an international commercial transaction. Although the Mitsubishi court found it "unnecessary to assess the legitimacy of the *American Safety* doctrine as applied to agreements to arbitrate arising from domestic transactions," it "confess[ed] to some skepticism of certain aspects of the *American Safety* doctrine." *Mitsubishi*, 473 U.S. at 629, 632. Upon identifying four ingredients or concerns of the *American Safety* doctrine, the Court first rejected as unjustified the concern that there is a "strong possibility that contracts which generate antitrust disputes may be contracts of adhesion." Rather, the Court observed that a party resisting arbitration may attack directly the validity of the agreement or make a showing that would warrant setting aside the forum-selection clause. The Court then determined that the "potential complexity [of antitrust issues] should not suffice to ward off arbitration," thereby rejecting the concern that antitrust issues are "ill-adapted to the arbitral process." In this respect the Court noted, in particular, that "adaptability and access to expertise are hallmarks of arbitration," and that "even the courts following *American Safety* . . . have agreed that an undertaking to arbitrate antitrust claims entered into after the dispute arises is acceptable." *Id.* at 633 (emphasis in original). Next, the Court rejected, as another concern of the *American Safety* doctrine, the "proposition that an arbitration panel will pose too great a danger of innate hostility to the constraints on business conduct that antitrust law imposes." *Id.* at 634. Lastly, the Court addressed the ingredient it considered the "core of the *American Safety* doctrine—the fundamental importance to American democratic capitalism of the regime of the antitrust laws." *Id.* After noting that the private cause of action, designed to afford compensation to injured competitors and to pose a deterrent to potential violators, plays a central role in enforcing this regime, and finding no reason to assume at the outset of the dispute that international arbitration will not provide an adequate mechanism, the Court concluded that "so long as the prospective litigant effectively may vindicate its statutory cause of action in the arbitral forum, the statute will continue to serve both its remedial and deterrent function." *Id.* at 636–37. Thus, the Court found none of the four ingredients or concerns of the *American Safety* doctrine justified denying enforcement of an agreement to arbitrate antitrust claims arising from an international commercial transaction.

Syscomm contends that the *American Safety* doctrine is "still good law and has not been overturned by the United States Supreme Court or any other decision." In support of its position, Syscomm relies on *Stendig International, Inc. v. B. & B. Italia, S.p.A.*, 633 F. Supp. 27 (S.D.N.Y.1986), a 1986 district court decision, which held that because *Mitsubishi* did not overrule *American Safety*, *American Safety* was still binding on the court. The *Stendig* court therefore refused to compel arbitration of an antitrust claim arising from a domestic transaction. However, *Stendig* was decided prior to the Supreme Court's decisions in *Rodriguez de Quijas* and *McMahon*, and more recent lower court cases have held that *American Safety* would no longer be followed by the Second Circuit, *see, e.g., Hough v. Merrill, Lynch, Pierce, Fenner & Smith, Inc.*, 757 F. Supp. 283, 286 (S.D.N.Y.), *aff'd without opinion*, 946 F.2d 883 (2d Cir.1991); *Gemco Latinoamerica, Inc. v. Seiko Time Corp.*, 671 F. Supp. 972, 978–80 (S.D.N.Y.1987), *adhered to in part and dismissed in part on reconsideration*, 685 F. Supp. 400 (S.D.N.Y.1988); *see also GKG Caribe, Inc. v. Nokia-Mobira, Inc.*, 725 F. Supp. 109, 111–13 (D.P.R.1989) (concluding that the Supreme Court "would most certainly discard [the *American Safety*] doctrine"). * * *

While *American Safety* has not been explicitly overruled, this Court believes that in light of the federal policy favoring arbitration agreements that has fueled the expansion of the types of federal statutory claims that may be arbitrated, the Second Circuit would now hold that the principle of *Mitsubishi* is not limited to antitrust claims arising in international transactions, and that domestic antitrust claims are arbitrable. *See Hough*, 757 F.Supp. at 286; *see also Gemco*, 671 F.Supp. at 980 ("[W]e find that none of the justifications for the *American Safety* doctrine retain their vigor and that our Court of Appeals would now hold that domestic antitrust claims are subject to arbitration."); *cf. Bird*, 926 F.2d at 118–22 (agreement to arbitrate statutory ERISA claims held enforceable).

Because Syscomm's antitrust claims fall within the Agreement's arbitration clause, and because those claims are arbitrable, SynOptics' request to compel arbitration is granted and Syscomm's motion for a stay of the pending Arbitration Proceeding is denied. Consequently, Syscomm must submit its antitrust claims against SynOptics to arbitration in accordance with the Agreement.

NOTES AND QUESTIONS

1. *Forget the prior narrow holding, forget the judicial hierarchy: undermine the reasoning, and cripple the precedent.* In *Syscomm*, the district court identified the essential issue as whether antitrust claims in domestic transactions are arbitrable or not. From one perspective, the case was easy, should never have been litigated, and should have come out the other way in any event: that very issue had been clearly resolved in the negative by the relevant court of appeals in *American Safety*. From that perspective, perhaps the judge in *Syscomm* committed reversible error, setting up an appeal that would have allowed the Second Circuit to decide in the first instance and for itself whether it wished to reconsider *American Safety*. On the other hand, a

few Supreme Court cases had arguably undermined the reasoning in *American Safety*, especially *Mitsubishi*, at least with respect to antitrust claims in *international* transactions. But *American Safety* had never been reversed by the Supreme Court, nor had it been modified—let alone overturned—by the Second Circuit itself.

So, without any direct abandonment of *American Safety* by any court higher in the vertical hierarchy, the district court in *Syscomm* asked and answered a hypothetical: what would the court of appeals do *if* it were asked to reconsider *American Safety* in light of *Mitsubishi*? And the court concluded that "the Second Circuit would no longer adhere to the *American Safety* doctrine, [and] therefore this Court grants SynOptics' request to compel arbitration. . . ."

As you think about the *Syscomm* court's approach to precedent, what does the decision stand for *other than* the arbitrability of antitrust claims in domestic transactions? *Cf. In re Methyl Tertiary Butyl Ether Prods. Liab.*, No. 1:00–1898, MDL 1358 (SAS), 2005 WL 106936, at *4 (S.D.N.Y. Jan. 18, 2005) (emphasis supplied):

> It is well established that lower courts are *bound not only by the specific holding of a Supreme Court opinion but also its reasoning.* Thus, as the Second Circuit and other circuits have recognized, when there is an intervening Supreme Court decision that casts doubt on [the Second Circuit's] controlling precedent that precedent may no longer be binding.

See also the observation of Lord Mansfield that "[t]he *reason and spirit* of cases make law, not the letter of particular precedents." *Fisher v. Prince*, 3 Burr. 1364 (1763) (emphasis supplied). *See also* 1 WILLIAM BLACKSTONE, COMMENTARIES *70–1 (1765) ("the 'law,' and the 'opinion of the judge' are not . . . one and the same thing; since it sometimes may happen that the judge may mistake the law.") SIR MATTHEW HALE, THE HISTORY OF THE COMMON LAW OF ENGLAND 68 (1739) (judicial decisions "do not make a Law properly so-called," but "they have a great Weight and Authority in Expounding, Declaring, and Publishing what the Law of this Kingdom is, [and] are a greater Evidence [of a law] than the Opinion of any private Persons, as such, whatsoever.")

In principle, given these authorities, what is it exactly in a prior case that deserves respect as precedent? What would the Legal Realists (described in Chapter 3, *supra*) say about these eighteenth-century depictions of precedent and law?

2. *"Horizontal" precedent.* Near the end of its opinion, the district court in *Syscomm* refers to decisions not of superior courts, like the court of appeals or the Supreme Court, but of other district courts—two within the Second Circuit, and one from a completely different circuit. What is the value of these decisions? In what sense if any are they "precedents" for *Syscomm*?

3. *Unpublished opinions and precedential limbo.* A high percentage of federal court decisions are not published, which generally deprives them of

precedential value under the local rules of procedure. For example, Local Rule 28A(i) of the Eighth Circuit Court of Appeals provides that

> Unpublished opinions are not precedent and parties generally should not cite them. When relevant to establishing the doctrines of *res judicata*, collateral estoppel, or the law of the case, however, the parties may cite any unpublished opinion.

What accounts for the fact that unpublished opinions can be cited for purposes of applying *res judicata* or the law of the case doctrine, but not *stare decisis*? *See* Note 10, *supra*. Thinking more abstractly, is it appropriate (even inevitable) that courts should be able to control the precedential effect of their decisions in this way? On the other hand, is there an argument that these rules are unconstitutional—as a violation of the common law understanding of the "Judicial Power" conferred in Article III? And quite apart from constitutional arguments, what are the potential costs of giving courts broad authority to deny their decisions precedential effect?

The issue has been litigated in the courts and debated in the academic journals.[8] *See Anastasoff v. United States*, 223 F.3d 898 (8th Cir. 2000) (deciding that Local Rule 28A(i) is unconstitutional "insofar as it would allow us to avoid the precedential effect of our prior decisions [or] purports to expand the judicial power beyond the bounds of Article III"), *vacated as moot en banc*, 235 F.3d 1054, 1056 (8th Cir. 2000) ("The constitutionality of that portion of Rule 28A(i) which says that unpublished opinions have no precedential effect remains an open question in this Circuit."). *Cf. Hart v. Massanari*, 266 F.3d 1155, 1160 (9th Cir. 2001) ("Rules that empower courts of appeals to issue non-precedential decisions do not cut those courts free from all legal rules and precedents; if they did, we might find cause for alarm. But such rules have a much more limited effect: They allow panels of the courts of appeals to determine whether future panels, as well as judges of the inferior courts of the circuit, will be bound by particular rulings. This is hardly the same as turning our back on all precedents, or on the concept of precedent altogether.").

C. DISTINGUISHING A PRECEDENT'S HOLDING FROM ITS REASONING AND ITS DICTA

One conventional account of precedent is that it requires the faithful application of a rule or principle articulated by the court in a previous case. Typically, the requirement of fidelity is limited to what the prior court *actually* and *necessarily* decided with respect to the issues litigated by the parties. In the simplified world that this description fits, a decision would

---

[8] *See e.g.*, Richard S. Arnold, *Unpublished Opinions: A Comment*, 1 J.APP. PRAC. & PROCESS 219 (1999); Coleen M. Barger, *Anastasoff, Unpublished Opinions, and "No-Citation" Rules*, 3 J.APP. PRAC. & PROCESS 169 (2001); Stephen R. Barnett, *No-Citation Rules Under Siege: A Battlefield Report and Analysis*, 5 J. App. Prac. & Process 473 (2003); Jessie Allen, *Just Words? The Effects of No-Citation Rules in Federal Courts of Appeals*, 29 VERMONT. L. REV. 555 (2005).

stand for one clear thing that was litigated and resolved, and a long line of judges would subsequently interpret that decision in exactly the same way. In that world, a law professor, asking a student to state the "holding" in some case, would be asking in essence for something like a fact—a relic that could be unearthed and understood through a process resembling archeology: dig in the right place, extract the artifact, clean away the dirt, analyze the piece, catalogue it, check its relationship to other known artifacts, put it on display for future use, and develop a professional consensus about its origins and meaning. Perhaps there are cases that fit that simplified model, although litigants rarely take on the costs of a lawsuit if the result is obvious or compelled, which means in turn that those cases would almost never be brought, fought, decided, or reported.

In *Hadley v. Baxendale*,[9] for example, one of the chestnuts of first-year contract law, the court famously laid out certain principles to guide a jury in the assessment of damages for a breach of contract and decided that damages that were not reasonably foreseeable from a breach were not recoverable:

> [1] Where two parties have made a contract which one of them has broken, the damages which the other party ought to receive in respect of such breach of contract should be such as may fairly and reasonably be considered either [a] arising naturally, *i.e.*, according to the usual course of things, from such breach of contract itself, or [b] such as may reasonably be supposed to have been in the contemplation of both parties, at the time they made the contract, as the probable result of the breach of it.

On the facts of the case, the lost profits for which plaintiff sought recovery did not "aris[e] naturally" from the defendant's failure to deliver a mill shaft on time (perhaps, as far as the defendant knew at the time of the contract, the plaintiffs might have had a useable spare in the "usual course of things" or could pursue other profitable work while the shaft was being delivered). Nor could the plaintiffs recover under the second part of the rule, because there was no indication that both parties "contemplate[ed]" that profits would be lost if performance were delayed.

The opinion in *Hadley v. Baxendale* might have ended there, but the court also acknowledged that different facts might justify a different result and addressed the principles that would apply in that hypothetical situation:

> [2] Now, if the special circumstances under which the contract was actually made were communicated by the plaintiffs to the defendants, and thus known to both parties, the damages resulting from the breach of such a contract, which they would reasonably contemplate, would be the amount of injury which

[9] 156 Eng. Rep. 145, 152 (1854) (Court of Exch.).

> would ordinarily follow from a breach of contract under these special circumstances so known and communicated. [3] But, on the other hand, if these special circumstances were wholly unknown to the party breaking the contract, he, at the most, could only be supposed to have had in his contemplation the amount of injury which would arise generally, and in the great multitude of cases not affected by any special circumstances, from such a breach of contract. For, had the special circumstances been known, the parties might have specially provided for the breach of contract by special terms as to the damages in that case, and of this advantage it would be very unjust to deprive them.

The court seemed entirely conscious that it was not simply justifying its resolution of the case before it: in language that might equally appear in the legislative history of a statute on the subject of contract damages, the court observed:

> [4] Now the above principles are those by which we think the jury ought to be guided in estimating the damages arising out of any breach of contract. . .

Finally, the court applied its rule to the facts of the case:

> [5] [I]t is obvious that, in the great multitude of cases of millers sending off broken shafts to third persons by a carrier under ordinary circumstances, such consequences would not, in all probability, have occurred, and these special circumstances were here never communicated by the plaintiffs to the defendants. [6] It follows, therefore, that the loss of profits here cannot reasonably be considered such a consequence of the breach of contract as could have been fairly and reasonably contemplated by both the parties when they made this contract.

156 Eng. Rep. 145, 152 (1854) (numbers added for reference). One measure of the importance (and the extended shelf-life) of this approach to contract damages is that, a century after the decision, the drafters of the Restatement (Second) of Contracts adopted the multi-layered rule in *Hadley*,[10] and the case continues to be cited routinely. *See, e.g., Sunnyland*

---

[10] AMERICAN LAW INSTITUTE, RESTATEMENT (SECOND) OF CONTRACTS § 351 (1981) (*Unforeseeability and Related Limitations on Damages)*:

> (1) Damages are not recoverable for loss that the party in breach did not have reason to foresee as a probable result of the breach when the contract was made.
>
> (2) Loss may be foreseeable as a probably result of a breach because it follows from the breach
>
> (a) in the ordinary course of events, or
>
> (b) as a result of special circumstances, beyond the ordinary course of events, that the party in breach had reason to know.
>
> (3) A court may limit damages for foreseeable loss by excluding recovery for loss of profits, by allowing recovery only for loss incurred in reliance, or otherwise if it concludes that in circumstances justice so requires in order to avoid disproportionate compensation.

Farms, Inc. v. Central New Mexico Elec. Co-op., Inc., 301 P.3d 387 (New Mexico, 2013). Does *Hadley v. Baxendale*, a case cited repeatedly for generations, actually fit the simple model of precedent described above? Is it in essence an archeological artifact?

Decided, litigated, and necessary. The quoted text from *Hadley v. Baxendale* is evidence that the court addressed and resolved each of the issues in the statements we have numbered (1)–(6). And you could consult the briefs of the parties, the transcript of the oral arguments, or some summary of the parties' submissions to determine whether there was an adversarial presentation of—and engagement on—the issue as articulated and resolved by the court. But how would you go about determining whether each statement was also *necessary* to the ruling?

One classic approach to that problem is to reverse each of the court's statements, one at a time, and see if that would compel the opposite result. For example, the standards articulated in statements (2) and (3)—dealing with "special circumstances" not factually present in *Hadley*—could be exactly reversed without changing the result in the case. Similarly, suppose that the *Hadley* court had said the direct opposite of statement (4), declaring that the principles it had just articulated were solely for application in this particular case and should not be taken as guiding principles for future cases. That would not change the result in *Hadley* at all, so it is not a necessary part of the analysis. By contrast, statements (5) and (6) refer to the facts of the particular case—note the court's use of the word "here"—and statement (1) lays out a principle that resolves the case, so none of these could be reversed without changing the result fundamentally.

A court's statements that are not considered necessary to the result are sometimes described as *dicta* (or in the singular *dictum*). In the words of one respected contemporary jurist, "[a] *dictum* is an assertion in a court's opinion of a proposition of law which does not explain why the court's judgment goes in favor of the winner."[11] The orthodox assumption is that the *dicta* in prior cases are not entitled to precedential status. Chief Justice John Marshall offered the classic articulation of this principle in his opinion for a unanimous court in *Cohens v. Virginia*, 19 U.S. (6 Wheat.) 264 (1821):

> It is a maxim, not to be disregarded, that general expressions, in every opinion, are to be taken in connection with the case in which those expressions are used. If they go beyond the case, they may be respected, but ought not to control the judgment in a subsequent suit, when the very point is presented for decision. The reason of this maxim is obvious. The question actually before the court is investigated with care, and considered in its full

[11] Pierre N. Leval, *Judging Under the Constitution: Dicta About Dicta,* 81 N.Y.U. L. Rev. 1249, 1256 (2006).

> extent. Other principles which may serve to illustrate it, are considered in their relation to the case decided, but their possible bearing on all other cases is seldom completely investigated.

Id., at 399–400.[12] Apparently, courts are more careful about holdings and more cavalier about *dicta*, and so, as a matter of quality control in judicial law-making, attorneys and courts should honor holdings and respect *dicta* (but not too much).

Chief Justice Marshall's "maxim" may be basic, but it only defines the stakes of the game: the lawyer who successfully characterizes a statement in a prior case as a holding gets to claim it as precedent. On the other hand, the lawyer trying to minimize the effect of that statement and who successfully argues that it was mere *dicta*, and not a holding at all, prevails. In short, the maxim identifies the prize but offers no hint of a technique for winning it. Worse, it presumes a definitive line between holding and *dicta* that exists only in the abstract. After all, a case typically stands for multiple ideas simultaneously, or there may be alternate holdings for the result, or the judge's opinion may not make the analysis transparent enough to distinguish holdings from *dicta*. *See United States v. Ronder, infra*. In addition, a contemporary empirical analysis suggests that the *Cohens* maxim is radically oversimplified. *See e.g., Peterson v. Martinez*, 707 F.3d 1197, 1210 (10th Cir. 2013) (lower courts "are bound by Supreme Court *dicta* almost as firmly as by the Court's outright holdings, particularly when the *dicta* is recent and not enfeebled by later statements.") *See generally* Michael Abramowicz & Maxwell Stearns, *Defining Dicta*, 57 STAN. L. REV. 953 (2005).

Complicating the entire apparatus is the traditional tendency of courts to distinguish between types or categories of *dicta*, entitled to varying degrees of deference:

> "Dictum" is of two kinds, "*obiter*" and "judicial." "*Obiter dictum*" is an expression of opinion by the court or judge on a collateral question not directly involved or mere argument or illustration originating with him [or her], while "judicial dictum" is an expression of opinion on a question directly involved, argued by counsel, and deliberately passed on by the court, though not necessary to a decision. While neither is binding as a decision, judicial dictum is entitled to much greater weight than the other and should not be lightly disregarded.

---

[12] *See also Grigsby v. Reib*, 105 Tex. 597, 602, 153 S.W. 1124, 1126 (Tex.1913):

"*Dictum*" is defined to be: "An opinion expressed by a court, but which, not being necessarily involved in the case, lacks the force of an adjudication; an opinion expressed by a judge on a point not necessarily arising in a case; an opinion of a judge which does not embody the resolution or determination of the court, and made without argument, or full consideration of the point; not the professed deliberate determination of the judge himself [or herself]."

Application of Sherretz, 1952 WL 7368, 4 (Hawai'i Terr.) (Haw. Terr. 1952). This puts a burden on advocates and courts alike not only to distinguish holdings from dicta (which can be difficult enough), but also to categorize the dicta themselves as either judicial dicta, which are not to be "lightly disregarded," or mere *obiter dicta*, which can apparently be treated like some more-or-less interesting judicial noise. Passages in an opinion rarely arrive with a little sign around their necks identifying them as *dicta* on one side of the line or the other, so it falls to the advocates in a particular proceeding to characterize precedential language in ways that advance their theory of the case.

Ratio decendendi. Once the *dicta* are identified and segregated, it becomes necessary to identify what *is* precedential about a case, and for those purposes it is necessary to revisit the operative assumption that holdings are what bind future courts. It is sometimes said that the reason for the court's decision—the *ratio decidendi*—is what constitutes the "precedent" and not the specific holding as between the litigants. Lord Mansfield famously captured that understanding in *Fisher v. Prince*, *supra*, when he wrote that "[t]he *reason and spirit* of cases make law, not the letter of particular precedents." Equally dogmatic versions of the argument that the reasoning is the binding part of a precedent appear two centuries later, and they persist. *See, e.g., Harkless v. Sweeny Ind. School Dist.*, 427 F.2d 319, 321 (5th Cir.1970) (holding that "under our system of law, a decision of a higher court is binding as a precedent to the extent of the *ratio decidendi* of the case").

> It may be laid down as a general rule that that part *alone* of a decision of a court of law is binding upon courts of coordinate jurisdiction and inferior courts which consists of the *enunciation of the reason or principle* upon which the question before the court has really been determined. This underlying principle which forms the only authoritative element of a precedent is often termed the *ratio decidendi*.[13]
>
> A precedent, therefore, is a judicial decision which contains in itself a principle. The underlying principle which thus forms its authoritative element is often termed the *ratio decidendi*. The concrete decision is binding between the parties to it, but *it is the abstract ratio decidendi which alone has the force of law as regards the world at large*.[14]
>
> Through the principle of *stare decisis*, *ratio decidendi* . . . constitutes binding precedent on lower courts.[15]

[13] 18 HALSBURY'S LAWS OF ENGLAND 210 (1911) (emphasis supplied).

[14] SIR JOHN SALMOND, JURISPRUDENCE 201 (7th ed. 1924) (emphasis supplied).

[15] Arthur L. Goodhart, *Determining the Ratio Decidendi of a Case*, 40 YALE L. J. 161, 164 (1930).

The central problem with this apparently crucial exercise is that the labels—*dicta* and *ratio decidendi*—tend to encapsulate an adversarial conclusion, rather than constrain the argument: "The rule is quite simple, if you agree with the other bloke you say it is part of the *ratio*; if you don't you say it is *obiter dictum*, with the implication that he is a congenital idiot." RUPERT CROSS, PRECEDENT IN ENGLISH LAW 45 (1961).

To illustrate the adversarial process of articulating the *ratio*, consider again *Hadley v. Baxendale* and identify its holding and its rationale—conscious always that there are innumerable ways to do this successfully. One version of the holding for example might be that this plaintiff was unable to recover lost profits from a delay in this defendant's performance because damages of that sort were not fairly and reasonably foreseeable at the time of this contract, and plaintiff had not communicated any special circumstances to the defendant regarding the timing of delivery. The principled explanation of that specific holding appears once the court identifies the applicable standard for determining when lost-profit damages really are foreseeable: to quote Statement (1) above, those damages are only recoverable to the extent that they "aris[e] naturally, *i.e.*, according to the usual course of things, from such breach of contract itself, or [are] such as may reasonably be supposed to have been in the contemplation of both parties, at the time they made the contract, as the probable result of the breach of it."

Without simply quoting the opinion, the *ratio* might be articulated differently and more abstractly: in a contracts case, lost profits should not be included in the calculation of recoverable damages where they could not reasonably be considered a foreseeable consequence of the breach. Or perhaps: the damages that are recoverable from a breach of contract include only what the parties might reasonably have contemplated them to be. Or perhaps: a party injured by a breach of contract may recover only those damages reasonably considered to arise naturally from the breach or those damages within the reasonable contemplation of the parties at the time of contracting. These formulations vary and stress different parts of the *Hadley* principle. The essential point here is that the particular holding of a case becomes generalizable and meaningful for future argument and decision only once the court's *ratio* is isolated and characterized.

Note too that the *principle* of the decision for these purposes is different from whatever *policy* reasons might support the rule. That is, a legislator considering a statute that adopted the *Hadley* rule may conclude that the commercial balance between buyers and sellers would be thrown off if the latter were responsible for damages it could not reasonably have foreseen at the time of the contract and which were not communicated at the time. That might turn sellers into guarantors without notice or consent. By contrast, a *Hadley* statute would efficiently reward explicit bargaining in ways that our hypothetical legislator might consider valuable to society at large. Articulating—and choosing among—those policy rationales are legislative prerogatives, and in the abstract they are distinct from the judicial prerogative to articulate—and choose among—the legal principles that are available to ground the *ratio* of a decision.[16]

Subsequent judicial treatment. It is a little hard to imagine Judge Alderson, who wrote the opinion in *Hadley*, settling into a comfy chair at his wood-paneled club later that evening and reflecting over port on what a terrific precedent for the ages he had set that day. He almost certainly would not have said that he had consulted some oracle and come up with a new rule on his own to govern a huge swath of common law cases. To the contrary, although he cited not a single case governing damages in his opinion, there were prior authorities adopting a foreseeability rule to govern recoverable damages in breach-of-contract cases.[17] Whatever may have been in Judge Alderson's mind at the time, a century later Grant Gilmore could declare that *Hadley v. Baxendale* was "a fixed star in the jurisprudential firmament."[18]

The precedential effect and meaning of a case is ultimately a function of history, not intent, and can be seen more clearly in the rearview mirror than through the windshield. In short, a case evolves towards a meaning and a status that are not always (or typically) predictable at the time of the decision and that do not necessarily remain stable over time. That suggests in turn that arguments about a precedent are often filtered through a variety of subsequent cases, refracting the light of the original case in ways that lawyers ignore at their peril. Indeed, despite its presence in virtually every first-year contract course, the *Hadley* test for the remoteness of contractual damages was qualified in 2008 by a decision of the House of Lords in *The Achilleas*, [2008] UKHL 48, requiring that a defaulting party not only "contemplated" the damage resulting from its breach of contract but also assumed responsibility for it. A subsequent decision by the English High Court, *Sylvia Shipping Co. Ltd. v Progress Bulk Carriers Ltd.*, [2010] EWHC 542, appeared in turn to define and limit *The Achilleas* "assumption of responsibility" test. Should these changes in the doctrine of recoverable damages, announced by the courts that originally decided *Hadley*, affect the interpretation of that case in U.S. courts or its inclusion in the first-year curriculum in U.S. law schools? Does consistency with precedent require courts to take these changes into account?

---

[16] In the post-Legal Realist world, the formalist distinction between principle and policy—and the arch-fiction that judges do not make policy choices in reaching their decisions—may be unacceptably naïve, even if it does undoubtedly frame advocates' arguments. *See* Chapter 3, *supra*. For an effort to determine the empirical effects of ideology and *stare decisis* on the decisions of individual justices of the Supreme Court, *see* Jeffrey Segal & Harold Spaeth, *The Influence of Stare Decisis on the Votes of the United States Supreme Court Justices*, in COURT, JUDGES, AND POLITICS: AN INTRODUCTION TO THE JUDICIAL PROCESS (Walter Murphy *et al.* eds., 2006).

[17] *See generally* Florian Faust, *Hadley v. Baxendale: An Understandable Miscarriage of Justice,* 15 J. LEGAL HIST. 41 (1994).

[18] GRANT GILMORE, THE DEATH OF CONTRACT 83 (1974).

Rules and standards. Another weapon in the adversarial arsenal when arguing about precedent is the distinction between holdings as *rules* and holdings as *standards.* As suggested in the readings below, this is a specialized version of a jurisprudential debate about the very nature of law and the interpretive power of courts, but it has a deeply pragmatic payoff when building arguments from precedent. Those arguments invariably require lawyers to argue about the scope of a holding and the room that it leaves for maneuver in future cases. Like a statute, a holding can be expressed in a highly specific form—analogous to a speed limit or some other rule of the road with minimal room for interpretation—or it can lay out a general standard and effectively delegate the job of interpreting and applying it to some other decision-maker at some later date. For example, an argument about the holding in *Hadley v. Baxendale* might turn on one characterization focusing on the "rule" side, which links recoverable damages to foreseeability, the way a legislature might have directed. On the other hand, if the holding were characterized as a standard, the determinative finding of foreseeability would be left to future courts dealing with the facts of particular disputes, including what each party knew about the other's circumstances. In broad terms, the distinction between rules and standards can be a useful heuristic and rhetorical device, and your view of which predominates in the law helps in finding your place on the spectrum between legal positivism and legal realism and their offshoots. But this distinction also has limits: over time, standards—in either legislative or precedential form—can evolve into something more determinate, as decisions applying the standard accumulate and coalesce around something more rule-like. Sometimes those decisions will be later distilled into legislation or collected into a Restatement.

In the following case, how might the distinction between rules and standards—or between *dicta* and holding—affect a later courts' interpretation of the decision?

UNITED STATES V. RONDER

639 F.2d 931 (2d Cir. 1981)

The primary issue on this appeal concerns the procedure for handling inquiries from a jury during deliberations. Charles S. Ronder appeals from a judgment of the District Court for the Northern District of New York (James T. Foley, Judge), convicting him after a jury trial of conspiracy to make and file false corporate income tax returns for the years 1971–1973, in violation of 18 U.S.C. § 371 (1976), and of the substantive offense of aiding and assisting in the filing of a false corporate income tax return for the year 1973, in violation of 26 U.S.C.§ 7206(2) (1976). Appellant's claim is that the District Judge failed to afford defense counsel a timely opportunity to see and suggest responses to inquiries submitted by the jury during deliberations. Because we agree that the procedure followed was erroneous and because we are unable to conclude that the error may not have contributed to the jury's verdict, we reverse the conviction and remand for a new trial.

Assessment of appellant's claim requires some consideration of the factual issues facing the jury. Ronder is a certified public accountant and a lawyer. The Government's evidence tended to prove that he knowingly participated in a scheme to reduce the tax liability of one of his corporate clients, Ulster Electric Supply Co. (Ulster). The scheme was originated by Gerald Gruberg, Ulster's President. It involved the addition of false amounts to Ulster's purchases in order to reduce profits and consequent tax liabilities.

Three witnesses testified to Ronder's knowing complicity in the scheme. Gruberg testified that he told Ronder that the purchase figures were to be falsely inflated. Gruberg also said that in each of the three years of the scheme Ronder calculated the amount of false purchases necessary to reduce Ulster's tax liability to the level specified by Gruberg. Ulster's bookkeeper testified that Ronder discussed aspects of the scheme with her, instructing her how to enter the false items. A third witness was an attorney in a law firm to which Gruberg turned for advice after the Internal Revenue Service began its inquiry. The attorney testified that Ronder admitted having knowledge of the scheme during its existence. Ronder signed the 1973 return as the preparer.

The defense disputed Ronder's complicity in three ways. Ronder denied any participation in the scheme or in the incriminating conversations alleged by prosecution witnesses. A witness who was present at some of the meetings in which Gruberg and Ronder were alleged to have discussed execution of the scheme denied that the conversations implicating Ronder had occurred. Finally, the defense suggested that each of the three prosecution witnesses had motives to implicate Ronder in order to curry favor with the prosecution. Gruberg had been permitted to plead guilty to a single count; the bookkeeper had been granted immunity; and the new lawyer for Ulster, according to Ronder, was motivated to accuse Ronder in order to deflect Government attention from his firm's role in the preparation of Ulster's 1974 return, which Ronder alleges was a false return.

With the evidence thus sharply disputed, the jury experienced considerable difficulty in reaching a verdict. The jury received the case for deliberation at 11 a.m. At 1:30 p.m. the jury requested a rereading of the charge concerning the credibility of the Government's witnesses. At 4:15 p.m. the jury sent a note indicating a possible deadlock:

> Judge Foley, We have debated and there are several of us that refuse to believe the most important evidence is truthful. Further discussions seem fruitless. What is your advice?

After reading the note to counsel and engaging in a brief colloquy with them, Judge Foley told the jury to recess for the evening and return the next day. He also gave some mild instructions concerning the desirability of reaching a verdict.

On the third and final day of deliberations there occurred the episodes giving rise to this appeal. At 1:45 p.m. the jury sent a note firmly reporting a deadlock: "We cannot reach a verdict on either charge." The trial judge did not disclose the note to counsel before responding nor elicit their views as to an appropriate response. He recalled the jury to the courtroom and gave them a modified *Allen*[2] charge. Though endeavoring to give a balanced charge and avoid coercion, the judge chose language that may not have successfully achieved his objectives. First, he dealt with each side's interest in avoiding a deadlock:

> It is important to the government to have a verdict because the government is anxious to see the law enforced. It is important to this defendant, Mr. Ronder on trial. He has gone through a long trial, and it is an ordeal in some respects, as you know. He is entitled to have the verdict. So you have that situation.

These words, as defense counsel observed after hearing them, might have given the jury the impression that the Government's interest in a verdict was more meritorious that the purely personal concerns of the defendant. The Government's interest in having the law enforced would more appropriately have been balanced by mention of the defendant's interest in being exonerated if he is innocent. Second, the trial judge eschewed the familiar and approved cautions, variously expressed,[3] that no juror should abandon a conscientiously held view of the evidence simply to enable a verdict to be returned. Instead, the judge made the somewhat less forceful statement, "You have a right, as I told you, to stand on your own independent conviction."

Later the same afternoon, while the jury was continuing to deliberate, the trial judge met with counsel in chambers to hear defense counsel's motion for a mistrial because of the previously reported jury deadlock. Prior to this conference the judge had received a second note from the jury.

---

[2] *Allen v. United States*, 164 U.S. 492, 501–02 (1896). [Editors' note: In the federal courts, and with considerable local variations, an "Allen charge" is a judge's instruction to a deadlocked jury, instructing it to continue deliberation, directing both majority and minority jurors to reconsider their positions, and cautioning them not to surrender their personal convictions merely to achieve consensus.]

[3] *E. g.,* a juror "should never surrender your honest conviction as to the weight or effect of evidence solely because of the opinion of other jurors or for the mere purpose of returning a verdict," *United States v. Barash*, 412 F.2d 26, 31 n.9 (2d Cir.), *cert. denied*, 396 U.S. 832 (1969); no juror should violate "a conviction which he conscientiously holds predicated upon the weight and effect of the evidence," *United States v. Miller*, 478 F.2d 1315, 1320 (2d Cir.), *cert. denied*, 414 U.S. 851 (1973); jurors should vote "finally according to your conscientious judgment," *United States v. Hynes*, 424 F.2d 754, 756 n.2 (2d Cir.), *cert. denied*, 399 U.S. 933 (1970); jurors should try to reach unanimity "without any juror yielding a conscientious conviction," *United States v. Rao*, 394 F.2d 354, 355 (2d Cir.), *cert. denied*, 393 U.S. 845 (1968).

Disclosing the existence of this note, the judge told counsel that "it says that they have made some progress" and that "there is one juror who refuses to discuss the issues." However, he declined to read the text of the note when specifically asked to do so by Government counsel. The note read as follows:

> Judge Foley, We have made progress yet there is one juror who refuses to discuss the issues. That person complains of a headache. Could you talk to us and explain again what our duties are in the jury room, that it is important to open our minds. That one person feels that he or she is being badgered because we ask for evidence on their position to discuss.

Judge Foley denied the defendant's motion for a mistrial, whereupon the prosecutor asked the judge to give an *Allen* charge. Court was then reconvened and the jury recalled.

In addressing the jury on this occasion, Judge Foley mentioned the existence of a third note, apparently received by him shortly after the report of the jury's progress. The third note read as follows:

> Is it possible to bring a verdict of guilty to charge 1 (the conspiracy offense) and not guilty to charge 3 (the substantive offense)? Some of us feel that the two charges are tied together and that the same verdict has to be reached for both. Maybe if you would redefine both charges for us and explain how much involvement constitutes guilt.

Counsel did not know of the content or even of the existence of this third note.

Dealing with the note he had mentioned to counsel, Judge Foley gave a carefully worded *Allen* charge. The prior reference to the Government's interest in enforcing the law was omitted, and each juror was told not to "surrender an honest conviction solely because of the opinion of a fellow juror, or for the mere purpose of reaching a verdict." Turning next to the inquiry in the third note, Judge Foley responded by pointing out that the two charges against Ronder were "separate" and by reviewing the elements of both the conspiracy and the substantive offenses. He gave special attention to the element of the substantive offense that required falsity as to at least one material matter, suggesting to the jurors that this element "is the one that you may have had some difficulty about."

After the jury retired to resume deliberations, defense counsel urged a fuller explanation of the terms "willfully" and "knowingly," which he asserted was "really the issue." Judge Foley declined further elaboration and at that point afforded counsel their first opportunity to inspect the second and third notes. After reading the notes, neither counsel requested further instructions. Approximately one-half hour later, the jury returned verdicts of guilty on both counts.

It is settled law that messages from a jury should be disclosed to counsel and that counsel should be afforded an opportunity to be heard before the trial judge responds. *Rogers v. United States*, 422 U.S. 35, 39 (1975); *United States v. Robinson*, 560 F.2d 507, 516 (2d Cir. 1977) (en banc), *cert. denied*, 435 U.S. 905 (1978) [citations omitted]. *See United States v. Schor*, 418 F.2d 26 (2d Cir. 1969).

The proper practice should include these steps. (1) The jury's inquiry should be submitted in writing. This is the surest way of affording the court and counsel an appropriate opportunity to confer about a response. (2) Before the jury is recalled, the note should be marked as a court exhibit and be read into the record in the presence of counsel and the defendant. This avoids any later claim by the defendant that he remained unaware of the note's content, despite his counsel's knowledge of it. (3) Counsel should be afforded an opportunity to suggest appropriate responses. During this colloquy, it is also helpful for the judge to inform counsel of the substance of his proposed response, or even to furnish a written text of it, if available. *Cf.* FED. R. CRIM. P. 30, requiring the trial judge to inform counsel of the disposition of proposed requests to charge prior to summations. (4) After the jury is recalled, the trial judge should generally precede his response by reading into the record in their presence the content of any note concerning substantive inquiries. This assures that all jurors appreciate the question to which the response is directed, in the event the note was not discussed among all the jurors. It also provides an opportunity to correct any failure by the foreman to convey accurately the inquiry of one or more of the jurors, in the event the foreman has undertaken to author all substantive notes. On occasion the personal nature of a note or the risk of exacerbating tensions among jurors may make it appropriate to forgo reading the text of the note to the entire jury; in that event it may be appropriate to disclose the note to counsel in camera or even to make some redaction. *See United States v. Robinson, supra*, 560 F.2d at 516–17 (juror's name). Recalling the jury may be unnecessary when the inquiry concerns routine housekeeping details. Of course, the emergency nature of a communication may require even more expeditious handling.

In this case, it is undisputed that none of the three notes submitted by the jury on the third and final day of deliberations was disclosed to counsel before the trial judge responded. Appellant challenges both this procedural error and the substantive content of the supplemental instructions, contending that the instructions were coercive and insufficient to respond to the jury's inquiries. The Government contends that the responses were substantively adequate and that the procedural error was not prejudicial because defense counsel suggested no additional or corrective instructions after seeing the content of the notes.

Though the issue is close, we are persuaded that, in the circumstances of this case, the procedural error requires a new trial. The crucial evidence against the accused was sharply disputed, and, more significantly, the jury was experiencing considerable difficulty in resolving the dispute, twice reporting a deadlock. In such circumstances the wording of the trial judge's responses to the jury's inquiries assumed even added significance to that normally attending this critical stage of a criminal trial. Had the first note been discussed with counsel, the phrases in the response concerning the Government's view of the importance of the case might well have been avoided, and the traditional cautionary language concerning not abandoning a conscientiously held view merely to return a verdict might well have been included. Disclosure of the second note might well have prompted counsel to suggest a response appropriately tailored to the circumstances of the juror who felt badgered, and surely would have permitted more focused argument in support of the motion for a mistrial. Disclosure of the third note would have afforded counsel an opportunity to suggest a specific response to the jury's significant request for an explanation of "how much involvement constitutes guilt." While we do not decide that the judge's review of the elements of the two offenses was an erroneous response to the inquiry, his emphasis on materiality, which was not disputed, and the lack of specific discussion of participation, which was a significant point of the inquiry, resulted in a supplemental instruction less favorable to the accused than would probably have resulted if counsel had been consulted.

We do not think the procedural error can be ignored because of defense counsel's failure to suggest further instructions after seeing the contents of the notes. In the first place, counsel may reasonably have thought it unlikely that a jury in the midst of deliberations would be recalled simply to accommodate his preference for particular wording of a supplemental instruction.[4] Yet at this critical stage of the trial the wording may be as significant as the substance of the response. Moreover, defense counsel did note his objection to the wording of the first modified Allen charge, and, following the judge's response to the third note, did begin to complain about that instruction as well. At that point the judge made reasonably clear that the supplemental instructions were not going to be revised.

In sum, we cannot say "with fair assurance," *United States v. Schor*, *supra*, 418 F.2d at 30, that the procedural error in the handling of the jury's inquiries did not affect the verdict. Accordingly, we reverse and remand for a new trial.

---

[4] The context differs from the circumstances at the conclusion of the initial charge to the jury, at which point counsel's obligation to object is clear. FED.R.CRIM.P. 30. At that point the jury has not yet begun deliberations, normally being told to await an indication that deliberations may begin. In some districts this is accomplished by sending to the jury room the indictment and the exhibits, only after exceptions to the charge have been considered and supplemental instructions given, if needed. Of course, even after supplemental instructions in response to a jury's inquiry, counsel is well advised to specify to the trial judge any objection while the opportunity to make a correction still exists.

NOTES AND QUESTIONS

1. *Distinguishing holding from dicta in Ronder.* Reconsider the paragraph in *Ronder* beginning with the sentence, "The proper practice should include these steps." Is that paragraph a holding in the case, or is it *dicta*? And what are the best arguments on both sides of that question? Is the "decided, litigated, and necessary" formula helpful is determining the precedential value of that paragraph? Perhaps another way to approach the question of what is holding and what is *dicta* in *Ronder* is to ask whether, after the decision, trial courts in the Second Circuit were free to disregard that paragraph (or parts of it) when dealing with notes from juries. How helpful is it to know that the Second Circuit subsequently found (a) that district courts' deviation from these practices constituted error and (b) that the error could be "harmless" and therefore not require reversal? *See, e.g.*, *United States v. Johnpoll*, 739 F.2d 702, 710–11 (2d Cir. 1984); *United States v. Blackmon*, 839 F.2d 900, 915 (2d Cir. 1988); *United States v. Ruggiero*, 928 F.2d 1289, 1300 (2d Cir. 1991); *United States v. Leung*, 40 F.3d 577, 584 (2d Cir. 1994).

2. *Headnotes.* In the Westlaw version of *Ronder*, readers will discover that there are three headnotes for the *Ronder* case, all under the rubric "Criminal Law." These headnotes are written not by the judges but by editors at West on the basis of the opinion. In *Ronder*, the headnotes are:

> 1. Messages from jury should be disclosed to counsel and counsel should be afforded an opportunity to be heard before trial judge responds.
>
> 2. Jury's inquiry to trial court should be submitted in writing, and before jury is recalled, the note should be marked as an "exhibit" and be read into record in presence of counsel and defendant; counsel should be afforded opportunity to suggest appropriate response, and after jury is recalled, trial judge should generally precede his response by reading into record in their presence the content of any note concerning substantive inquiries.
>
> 3. In prosecution for filing false corporate income tax returns and conspiracy, trial court committed reversible error in failing to disclose to counsel written inquiries from jury before responding to such inquiries, since crucial evidence against accused was sharply disputed and jury had experienced considerable difficulty in resolving the dispute.

Can you identify any other propositions of law for which *Ronder* (a) is precedent or (b) offers authority?

3. *Precedent, judicial law-making, and legitimacy.* Assume that the *Ronder* court thought that it was laying down a rule of four "practices" to govern the treatment of notes from a jury and that failing to abide by any one of those practices would constitute reversible error, subject to the harmless

error rule. By what inherent authority, if any, would an appeals court—as distinct from Congress or the Supreme Court of the United States—adopt such a rule and enforce it? Would Congress's statutory authorization allowing the courts to make rules of procedure or "rules of court" cover the *Ronder* rules? *See* 28 U.S.C.A. § 2071(a): "The Supreme Court and all courts established by Act of Congress may from time to time prescribe rules for the conduct of their business. Such rules shall be consistent with Acts of Congress and rules of practice and procedure prescribed under section 2072 of this title." Those rules in turn "shall not abridge, enlarge or modify any substantive right." *Id.*, at § 2702. In your view, do the *Ronder* rules "abridge, modify, or enlarge" any substantive right?

4. *Hadley v. Baxendale reassessed.* For the argument that *Hadley v. Baxendale* is seriously overrated, motivated by the judges' unacknowledged commercial interests or their ongoing battle with the discretion of juries, *see* Florian Faust, *Hadley v. Baxendale: An Understandable Miscarriage of Justice*, 15 J. LEGAL HIST. 41 (1994). *Compare* Grant Gilmore's summary:

> [W]hy such an essentially uninteresting case, decided in a not overly good opinion by a judge otherwise unknown to fame, should immediately have become celebrated on both sides of the Atlantic is one of the mysteries of legal history.

GRANT GILMORE, THE DEATH OF CONTRACT 49 (1974).

5. *Resisting the assumption that dicta are always less important than holdings.* For an example of a case in which the dicta are ultimately more important than the holding, *see, e.g., Hilton v. Guyot,* 159 U.S. 113 (1895), holding that a French court's judgment would not be recognized or enforced in the United States in the absence of reciprocity, that is, proof that a French court would enforce a U.S. judgment if the circumstances were reversed. But the Court also indicated in dicta that it might give the French judgment a presumptive validity in certain circumstances:

> [1] where there has been opportunity for a full and fair trial abroad [2] before a court of competent jurisdiction, [3] conducting the trial upon regular proceedings, [4] after due citation or voluntary appearance of the defendant, and [5] under a system of jurisprudence likely to secure an impartial administration of justice between the citizens of its own country and those of other countries, and [6] there is nothing to show either prejudice in the court, or [7] in the system of laws under which it was sitting, or [8] fraud in procuring the judgment, or [9] any other special reason why the comity of this nation should not allow it full effect, the merits of the case should not, in an action brought in this country upon the judgment, be tried afresh. . . .

Id., at 202–3. Over time, these dicta have had more staying power than the reciprocity requirement at the heart of *Hilton*'s 5–4 holding. Though reciprocity has not entirely disappeared as a factor in the recognition and enforcement of foreign judgments at the state level, reciprocity as endorsed by the *Hilton* court "is no longer an element of the federal law of enforcement of foreign judgments." *McCord v. Jet Spray International Corp.*, 874 F. Supp. 436 (D. Mass. 1994) (*quoting Tahan v. Hodgson*, 662 F.2d 862, 867 & n. 21 (D.C. Cir. 1981)). The continuing vitality of *Hilton* rests instead on its specification of the defenses to recognition and enforcement and its endorsement of comity as the essence of U.S. courts' approach to foreign judgments, at least in the absence of a controlling statute or treaty.

Readings

H.L.A. HART, THE CONCEPT OF LAW

121–23 (1962)

In any large group general rules, standards, and principles must be the main instrument of social control, and not particular directions given to each individual separately. If it were not possible to communicate general standards of conduct, which multitudes of individuals could understand, without further direction, as requiring from them certain conduct when occasion arose, nothing that we now recognize as law could exist. Hence the law must predominantly, but by no means exclusively, refer to classes of person, and to classes of acts, things, and circumstances; and its successful operation over vast areas of social life depends on a widely diffused capacity to recognize particular acts, things, and circumstances as instances of the general classifications which the law makes.

Two principal devices, at first sight very different from each other, have been used for the communication of such general standards of conduct in advance of the successive occasions on which they are to be applied. One of them makes a maximal and the other a minimal use of general classifying words. The first is typified by what we call legislation and the second by precedent. We can see the distinguishing features of these in the following simple non-legal cases. One father before going to church says to his son, "Every man and boy must take off his hat on entering a church." Another baring his head as he enters the church says, "Look: this is the right way to behave on such occasions."

The communication or teaching of standards of conduct by example may take different forms, far more sophisticated than our simple case. Our case would more closely resemble the legal use of precedent, if instead of the child being told on the particular occasion to regard what his father did on entering the church as an example of the right thing to do, the father assumed that the child would regard him as an authority on proper behaviour, and would watch him in order to learn the way to behave. To approach further the legal use of precedent, we must suppose that the father is conceived by himself and others to subscribe to traditional standards of behaviour and not to be introducing new ones.

Communication by example in all its forms, though accompanied by some general verbal directions such as "Do as I do", may leave open ranges of possibilities, and hence of doubt, as to what is intended even as to matters which the person seeking to communicate has himself clearly envisaged. How much of the performance must be imitated? Does it matter if the left hand is used, instead of the right, to, remove the hat? That it is done slowly or smartly? That the hat is put under the seat? That it is not replaced on the head inside the church? These are all variants of general questions which the child might ask himself: "In what ways must my conduct resemble his to be right?" "What precisely is it about his conduct that is to be my guide?" In understanding the example, the child attends to some of its aspects rather than others. In so doing he is guided by common sense and knowledge of the general kind of things and purposes which adults think important, and by his appreciation of the general character of the occasion (going to church) and the kind of behaviour appropriate to it.

In contrast with the indeterminacies of examples, the communication of general standards by explicit general forms of language ("Every man must take off his hat on entering a church") seems clear, dependable, and certain. The features to be taken as general guides to conduct are here identified in words; they are verbally extricated, not left embedded with others in a concrete example. In order to know what to do on other occasions the child has no longer to guess what is intended, or what will be approved; he is not left to speculate as to the way in which his conduct must resemble the example if it is to be right. Instead, he has a verbal description which he can use to pick out what he must do in future and when he must do it. He has only to recognize instances of clear verbal terms, to "subsume" particular facts under general classificatory heads and draw a simple syllogistic conclusion. He is not faced with the alternative of choosing at his peril or seeking further authoritative guidance. He has a rule which he can apply by himself to himself.

Much of the jurisprudence of this century has consisted of the progressive realization (and sometimes the exaggeration) of the important fact that the distinction between the uncertainties of communication by authoritative example (precedent), and the certainties of communication by authoritative general language (legislation) is far less firm than this naïve contrast suggests. Even when verbally formulated general rules are used, uncertainties as to the form of behaviour required by them may break out in particular concrete cases. Particular fact-situations do not await us already marked off from each other, and labelled as instances of the general rule, the application of which is in question; nor can the rule itself step forward to claim its own instances. In all fields of experience, not only that of rules, there is a limit, inherent in the nature of language, to the guidance which general language can provide. * * *

FREDERICK SCHAUER, *PRECEDENT*

39 STAN. L. REV. 571, 595–602 (1987)

What does it mean for a past event to be precedent for a current decision? And how does something we do today establish a precedent for the future? Can decisions really be controlled by the past and responsible to the future, or are appeals to precedent just so much window dressing, masking what is in reality a decision made for today only? And even if precedent can constrain decision-makers, why should a procedure for decision-making impose such a constraint? Why should the best decision for now be distorted or thwarted by obeisance to a dead past, or by obligation to an uncertain and dimly perceived future? Equally important is the question of weight. When precedent matters, just how much should it matter? If we are to be shackled to the past and beholden to the future, just how tight are those bonds, and what should it take to loose them?

An appeal to precedent is a form of argument, and a form of justification, that is often as persuasive as it is pervasive. The bare skeleton of an appeal to precedent is easily stated: The previous treatment of occurrence X in manner Y constitutes, solely because of its historical pedigree, a reason for treating X in manner Y if and when X again occurs.[3]

THE VIRTUES OF PRECEDENTIAL CONSTRAINT

* * * Why should a decision-making mechanism incorporate substantial precedential constraints within it? Why should a decision in Case 1 constrain a decision-maker in Case 2 and itself be constrained by the knowledge of this secondary impact?

A. The Argument from Fairness

Among the most common justifications for treating precedent as relevant is the argument from fairness, sometimes couched as an argument from justice. The argument is most commonly expressed in terms of the simple stricture, "Treat like case alike."[49] To fail to treat similar cases similarly, it is argued, is arbitrary, and consequently unjust or unfair. We achieve fairness by decision-making rules designed to achieve consistency

---

[3] Standard treatments are found in R.W.M. DIAS, JURISPRUDENCE 162–217 (4th ed. 1976): G. W. PATON, A TEXT-BOOK OF JURISPRUDENCE 179–95 (D. Derham 3rd ed. 1964); P. FITZGERALD, SALMOND ON JURISPRUDENCE 141–87 (12th ed. 1966). . . .

[49] *See, e.g.*, Goodhart, *Precedent in English and Continental Law*, 50 LAW Q. REV. 40, 56–58 (1934); Wade, *The Concept of Legal Certainty: A Preliminary Skirmish*, 4 MOD. L. REV. 183 (1940–1941). Useful deconstructions of the idea, partly consistent with what I argue here, include Westen, *The Empty Idea of Equality*, 95 HARV. L. REV. 537 (1982); Winston, *On Treating Like Cases Alike*, 62 CALIF. L. REV. 1 (1974).

across a range of decisions. Where the consistency is among individuals at the same time, we express this decisional rule as "equality." Where the consistency among decisions takes place over time, we call our decisional rule "precedent." Equality and precedent are thus, respectively, the spatial and temporal branches of the same larger normative principle of consistency.

The idea of fairness as consistency forms the bedrock of a great deal of thinking about morality. Whether expressed as Kantian universalizability,[50] as the decisions that people would make if cloaked in a Rawlsian veil of ignorance about their own circumstances,[51] or simply as The Golden Rule, the principle emerges that decisions that are not consistent are, for that reason, unfair, unjust, or simply wrong.

How can we apply this broad principle of fairness more specifically as a potential justification for adopting a decision procedure in which precedent matters? Initially, the principle that like cases should be decided alike would seem to make an unassailable argument for precedent. But the difficulty of denying that like cases should be decided alike is precisely the problem. The statement is so broad as to be almost meaningless. The hard question is what we mean by "alike." . . . [T]he question is whether the categories of likeness should be large or small. If the categories of likeness, of assimilation, are so small as to enable a decision-maker to take into account virtually every variation between separate events, then like cases are indeed being decided alike, yet the norm of precedent scarcely constrains. But if relatively large categories act to group many slightly different particular cases under general headings of likeness, then the stricture of deciding like cases alike makes reliance on precedent a substantial constraint.

The issue is thus not the sterile question of treating like cases alike. It is instead the more difficult question of whether we should base our decision-making norm on relatively large categories of likeness, or by contrast leave a decision-maker more or less at liberty to consider any possible way in which this particular array of facts might be unique. The purely formal constraint of treating like cases alike does not speak to this question. Yet the first of these alternatives describes a system of precedent; the second describes a system in which the constraint of precedent is for all practical purposes absent.

Alone, therefore, the argument from fairness, the prescription to treat like cases alike, does not help us choose between a decisional system with a strong precedential constraint and one with virtually no precedential constraint. If we are to find arguments directly addressing the question of

---

[50] *See* R.M. HARE, FREEDOM AND REASON (1963).

[51] *See* J. RAWLS, A THEORY OF JUSTICE 136–42 (1973).

precedent, we must look for substantive reasons to choose larger rather than smaller categories of decision.

B. The Argument from Predictability

The most commonly offered of the substantive reasons for choosing strong over weak precedential constraint is the principle of predictability. When a decision-maker must decide this case in the same way as the last, parties will be better able to anticipate the future. The ability to predict what a decision-maker will do helps us plan our lives, have some degree of repose, and avoid the paralysis of foreseeing only the unknown.

As a value, predictability is neither transcendent nor free from conflict with other values. Yet predictability plainly is, ceteris paribus, desirable. We attain predictability, however, only by diminishing our ability to adapt to a changing future. In the language of precedent, following a precedent at a particular time may produce a decision other than the decision deemed optimal on the facts of the particular instance. Where this divergence is absent, the effect of precedent is minimal. But if following precedent will produce a result different from that which would be produced without the constraint of the rule of precedent, then we have identified a case in which precedent matters. And thus we can rephrase the question: To what extent is a decision-making environment willing to tolerate suboptimal results in order that people may plan their lives according to decisions previously made?

When we reformulate the question in this way, it becomes clear that the force of the argument from predictability, even if persuasive in the abstract, will vary with numerous factors whose weight cannot be generalized across all decisional environments. For example, how often will the use of large generalizations prevent making decisions on the basis of unique facts that would be dispositive in a particular case? To answer this question requires delving into a panoply of factors relating to the kinds of decisions that are to be made in a given decision-making environment. These factors may include the size of the relevant categories, the likelihood of significant factual variation, and many others that vary from environment to environment. I thus merely note, without intending to resolve, that one important issue is the expected frequency of suboptimal results.

The consequences of such a suboptimal decision provide a closely related concern, one touched on earlier. Once we realize that maintaining a serious regime of precedential constraint entails some number of suboptimal decisions, we see that we can express the price we pay for predictability in terms of some number of decisions in which the predicted result, and therefore the actual result if precedent is followed, is not in fact the best result. But the relationship of these costs to the possible benefits of predictability will vary across different kinds of decisions. When Justice Brandeis noted that "in most matters it is more important that the applicable rule of law be settled than that it be settled right," he was reminding us of one side of this question. The other side, of course, is that sometimes it is more important that things be settled correctly than that they be settled for the sake of settlement. To take an extreme example, making all capital punishment decisions under a strict precedential rule would satisfy desires for predictability but would also entail putting to death some people who would live if their individual cases were scrutinized carefully. And, at the other extreme, many decisions involving the formalities of contracts or real estate transactions are decisions in which sacrificing optimality for predictability would involve negative consequences that are far from catastrophic.

Finally, it is worthwhile adding to the equation some variability in the value of predictability. Much of what we value about predictability is psychological. I feel better knowing that the letter carrier will come at the same time every day, that faculty meetings will not be scheduled on short notice, and that April brings the opening of the baseball season. Predictability thus often has value even when we cannot quantify it.

Thus, the value of predictability is really a question of balancing expected gain against expected loss. We ask how important predictability is for those affected by the decisions, and we then ask whether that amount of predictability is worth the price of the frequency of suboptimal results multiplied by the costs of those suboptimal results. But there is no best answer to this calculation, for the answer will vary with the kinds of decisions that given decision-makers are expected to make.

C. The Argument from Strengthened Decision-making

1. Decision-making efficiency.

When a precedent has no decisional significance as a precedent, the conscientious decision-maker must look at each case in its own fullness. But when a rule external to the decision-maker compels reliance on the decisions of others, it frees the decision-maker from these responsibilities. Although a decision-maker in a precedential system may in every case consider whether to disregard those constraints,[57] this does not deny that a decision-maker may choose to follow precedent, nor that a decision-maker who chooses to rely on precedent is in most cases operating within the norms of the system. Thus, a decision-maker choosing to rely on precedent may justifiably "relax," in the sense of engaging in less scrutiny of the case, where that decision-maker chooses to rely on a precedent. And where a rule of precedent urges a decision-maker to relax in this sense, the net product will be a substantial reduction in decision-making effort.

In this respect, efficiency may justify a rule of precedent. This argument properly relies on the fact that a regime of precedent allows less reconsideration of questions already considered than a system containing

[57] *See* Kennedy, *Legal Formality*, 2 J. LEGAL STUD. 351 (1973).

no rule of precedent. If we wish to conserve the decisional resources of the decision-makers, therefore, we have an independent argument for a system of precedent. . . .

2. Strengthening the decision-making institution.

But now let us abandon the assumption of similarity among decision-makers. If we retain the assumption of assimilability of events, more than mere decisional efficiency must be at work. The system of precedent must operate to dampen the variability that would otherwise result from dissimilar decision-makers. Why should we encourage this process? One possibility is that it might be thought important to create the aura of similarity among decision-makers even where none may exist. Using a system of precedent to standardize decisions subordinates dissimilarity among decision-makers, both in appearance and in practice.

Even more substantially, this subordination of decisional and decision-maker variance is likely in practice to increase the power of the decision-making institution. If internal consistency strengthens external credibility, then minimizing internal inconsistency by standardizing decisions within a decision-making environment may generally strengthen that decision-making environment as an institution.[59]

The considerations surrounding the argument from decision-making efficiency rest upon a broad notion about the value of stability in decision-making distinct from anything about the actual decisions made. It is also apparent that any attempt to stabilize decision-making in an unstable world is likely to produce some suboptimal results. The argument from enhanced decision-making, then, suggests that the efficiency advantages may justify putting on blinders to the full richness of human experience. This is by no means an implausible argument, but its strength with depend upon many of the same factors discussed in the context of the argument from predictability. Likewise, whether this strength is sufficient to outweigh its costs will vary with those same factors. Once it becomes clear that no argument from invariable principle supports either the argument from predictability or the argument from enhanced decision-making, the evaluation of these alternatives turns into a weighing of costs and benefits that varies with different decision-making settings. Further elaboration must be relegated to discussions of the goals to be served and the characteristics of decision-making in various decision-making settings.

D. Precedent and Stability

Although the various arguments for incorporating a rule of precedent into a particular decisional environment each retains its own irreducible

---

[59] *See* Shapiro, *Toward a Theory of Stare Decisis*, 1 J. LEGAL STUD. 125 (1972). It is worthwhile to note that this perspective could explain why the Supreme Court should be constrained by precedent, and, more cynically, why the Court purports to be constrained by precedent even when it is not. . . .

core of justification, in some sense these arguments coalesce. Arguments premised on the values of reliance, predictability, and decisional efficiency all share a focus on stability for stability's sake. The extent to which stability will be promoted is largely a function of the size of the groupings employed within a decisional domain. We must ask whether, at the extremes, large numbers of differences between instances will be suppressed, thus generating comparatively few large categories, or whether all variation will be taken into account, thus generating many smaller categories. Naturally there are gradations between these extremes. But by viewing the issue this way, we see that the various abstract and formal justifications for precedent all rest on conclusions about what ranges of events we wish to treat in like manner.

At times these size-determining factors may be based on substantive value choices. We may broadly draw the category of "person" in many contexts precisely because we believe it substantively evil to distinguish among people on the basis of race, gender, national origin, or even height. At other times the size of the categories will be controlled by the size of the categories at large in the world. Our language and its accompanying conceptual apparatus often inhibit attempts by decision-makers to draw fine distinctions among the particulars that inhabit the larger categories of our existence. No amount of stress on particularization, for example, could completely prevent categories like "people," "dwellings," or "vehicles" from hindering a decision-maker's efforts to see differences among people, dwellings, or vehicles. Finally, and perhaps most importantly, the size of the categories of assimilation may be a function of what we expect to accomplish in a decision-making setting. This is particularly germane here, for it links the principle of stability, hovering around all of the separate justifications for precedent, to the particular system actually generated.

Some decision-making environments emphasize today—the richness and uniqueness of immediate experience. In those environments we seek the freedom to explore every possible argument or fact that might bear on making the best decision for this case, for it is precisely the thisness of the case that is most vital. At its extreme, such a system might, and arguably should, deny the relevance of precedent entirely. The virtues of stability would bow to the desire 'to get it just right,' and in such a framework a past decision would have little if any precedential force. More realistically, perhaps, such a system might still acknowledge precedent, but in small units. For if we see precedents as small units, full of rarely duplicated particulars, we are likely to find few cases in which the current small unit is like some small unit of the past.

By contrast, other decisional environments focus on yesterday and tomorrow, emphasizing the recurrent rather than the unique elements of the human condition. Here precedent has its greatest role to play, generating a format for decision-making that channels decisions toward consideration of a comparatively limited number of factors likely to be repeated over time. In the context of this essay, this would translate into the use of larger categories of assimilation, gathering many conceivably distinguishable particulars within the embrace of the larger categories.

Without a universal answer to the question of whether stability is a good thing, we cannot decide whether decision according to precedent is a good thing. Stability may be unimpeachable in the abstract, but in reality stability comes only by giving up some of our flexibility to explore fully the deepest corners of the events now before us. Whether this price is worth paying will vary with the purposes to be served within a decisional domain, and we get no closer to knowing those purposes by understanding the relationship between stability and categorial size. Still, focusing on this relationship is valuable, because it enables us to see more clearly just how stability is achieved and just what kind of price we must pay to obtain it.

[JUDGE] PIERRE N. LEVAL, *JUDGING UNDER THE CONSTITUTION: DICTA ABOUT DICTA*

81 N.Y.U. L. REV. 1249 (2006)

* * * In the quaint language of eighteenth-century England, when judges elevated their status and authority by conducting their business in Latin, it was known as "*obiter dictum*"—in the plural, "dicta." This referred to a judge's insignificant aside remark—something to be treated lightly, or frankly, ignored. Cardozo in his time expressed amazement that judges, of all people, might "put their faith in dicta."[3] * * * The problem is that dicta no longer have the insignificance they deserve. They are no longer ignored. Judges do more than put faith in them; they are often treated as binding law. The distinction between dictum and holding is more and more frequently disregarded. Although I think most agree in the abstract with the proposition that dictum does not establish binding law, this rule is now honored in the breach with alarming frequency. Today more and more, dicta flex muscle to which, I submit, they are not entitled by constitutional right.

We judges regularly undertake to promulgate law through utterance of dictum made to look like a holding—in disguise, so to speak. When we do so, we seek to exercise a lawmaking power that we do not rightfully possess. Also, we accept dictum uttered in a previous opinion as if it were binding law, which governs our subsequent adjudication. When we do so, we fail to discharge our responsibility to deliberate on and decide the question which needs to be decided. * * * Consider two representative recent instances exemplifying two facets of the problem.

---

[3] BENJAMIN N. CARDOZO, THE NATURE OF THE JUDICIAL PROCESS 29 (1921).

1. *Barapind v. Enomoto.*[4] Recently, one of the circuit courts of appeals convened *en banc* to review an order to extradite a Sikh militant to India to answer murder charges. In an earlier extradition case involving an Irishman, Quinn, a panel of the same circuit, in dictum, had expressed views on one issue while deciding the case on a different basis.[6] The lower court judge in the Sikh's case disagreed with the *Quinn* panel's dictum and declined to follow it, as dictum is not binding.[7] The court of appeals chastised the judge for failing to follow its earlier dictum. "The [lower] court operated under a mistaken understanding of what constitutes circuit law.... [O]ur articulation [in *Quinn*] ... became law of the circuit, regardless of whether it was in some technical sense 'necessary'[8] to our disposition of the case. The [lower court was] ... required to follow [it]."[9] According to this view, a court has the power to make binding law, at least on an issue argued by the parties, simply by announcing a rule, irrespective of whether the rule plays any functional role in the court's decision of the case—a very considerable power, and without constitutional justification.

2. *Myers v. Loudoun County Public Schools.*[10] Also recently, another circuit decided (or should I say, "failed to decide") a constitutional challenge to the Pledge of Allegiance. The plaintiff Myers, the father of a child in public school, contended that school recitation of the Pledge of Allegiance, with its invocation of God, violates the Establishment of Religion Clause of the First Amendment. The Supreme Court had considered a similar attack just the previous term in *Elk Grove v. Newdow.*[13] In *Newdow*, the Supreme Court had dodged the divisive issue and dismissed the suit on the ground that the plaintiff, the divorced noncustodial parent of the affected schoolchild, lacked standing to challenge the practice. Notwithstanding that the Supreme Court had expressly left open the constitutional question, the majority of the circuit panel in *Myers* reasoned that it was compelled

[4] 400 F.3d 744 (9th Cir. 2005) (*en banc*).

[6] *See Quinn v. Robinson*, 783 F.2d 776, 810–14 (9th Cir. 1986). The *Quinn* opinion rejected Quinn's defense to extradition because he had failed to show the existence of an "uprising." The court also digressed in a lengthy discussion of when criminal conduct can be deemed "incidental" to an uprising, which discussion had no effect on the court's decision and was therefore dictum.

[7] *In re Extradition of Singh*, 170 F. Supp. 2d 982, 998 (E.D. Cal. 2001) ("The portion of *Quinn* that addresses the 'incidental to' prong is dicta and is only persuasive, non-binding authority.").

[8] Had the court's discussion of the meaning of "incidental" supported its judgment, this position would have been reasonable, even if the discussion was not strictly "necessary" to the *Quinn* decision. However, the *Quinn* court's articulation of the meaning of "incidental" was not only not "necessary" to its disposition; in fact, it played no role whatsoever in supporting the decision. Quinn would have defeated extradition if he had shown that his crime was "incidental" to an "uprising" and therefore a "political offense." As noted, the court ruled against him on the ground that there was no uprising. The court's additional discussion of the meaning of "incidental" did not give additional support for the judgment. To the contrary, this discussion supported Quinn, expressing the view that, had there been an uprising, his crime would have been "incidental" to it. The district judge in *Barapind* was correct in regarding this discussion as dictum and therefore not binding law.

[9] *Barapind*, 400 F.3d at 750–51 (citations omitted).

[10] 418 F.3d 395 (4th Cir. 2005).

[13] *Elk Grove Unified School Dist. v. Newdow*, 542 U.S. 1 (2004).

by prior Supreme Court opinions to uphold the Pledge—not by Supreme Court holdings, but by Supreme Court dicta. One judge even made clear that, were it not for the binding force of the dicta, the judge would find the question very difficult because the Supreme Court's holdings were in conflict.

I express no views about the merits of that case. My point is simply that the court had a duty to decide the case in accordance with law. If established law governed the question, the court was bound to follow the established precedent. If the established law was inconclusive, the court was obligated in the discharge of its constitutional duties to adjudicate the question—to wrestle with the issue and reach its own conclusion. It did neither. * * *

It is difficult to make the point I advocate without being misunderstood as opposing the use of dictum. Let me make as clear as I can that I do not in the least oppose the careful use of dictum in judicial opinions. To the contrary, I believe that dicta often serve extremely valuable purposes. They can help clarify a complicated subject. They can assist future courts to reach sensible, well-reasoned results. They can help lawyers and society to predict the future course of the court's rulings. They can guide future courts to adopt fair and efficient procedures. What is problematic is not the utterance of dicta, but the failure to distinguish between holding and dictum. . . .

You might well ask, "So what? Are you wasting our time, Judge Leval, carping about technicalities? What does it matter whether a proposition becomes established as law when it is first uttered in a court's dictum, or later when it is uttered as a holding justifying the court's ruling?" The distinction is not a mere technicality. It is by no means inevitable that rules initially expressed in gratuitous, nonbinding dictum would be ultimately adopted when it came time for the court to decide the issue. An important aspect of my point is that courts are more likely to exercise flawed, ill-considered judgment, more likely to overlook salutary cautions and contraindications, more likely to pronounce flawed rules, when uttering dicta than when deciding their cases. The practices I discuss impair the quality and reliability of our performance. *Giving dictum the force of law increases the likelihood that the law we produce will be bad law.*[18]

---

[18] [Emphasis supplied]. In *Cohens v. Virginia*, 19 U.S. (6 Wheat.) 264 (1821), the Supreme Court wrote:

> It is a maxim not to be disregarded, that general expressions, in every opinion, are to be taken in connection with the case in which those expressions are used. If they go beyond the case, they may be respected, but ought not to control the judgment in a subsequent suit when the very point is presented for decision. The reason of this maxim is obvious. The question actually before the Court is investigated with care, and considered in its full extent. Other principles which may serve to illustrate it, are considered in their relation to the case decided, but their possible bearing on all other cases is seldom completely investigated.

Id. at 399–400.

My criticism is directed no less against myself than others. Insufficient attention to the distinction between holding and dictum and to the importance of the distinction has become endemic. This comes perhaps in part from a gradual change in the self-image of courts. Once, the perception of the judicial function was relatively modest—to settle disputes under an existing body of rules; judges were not seen as making law through their opinions, but rather as finding the common law, which existed already, waiting only to be discovered.[19] Gradually, first with the advent of *stare decisis*, and with the central role courts have increasingly played in resolving important social questions, we have come to see ourselves as something considerably grander—as lawgivers, teachers, fonts of wisdom, even keepers of the national conscience. This change of image has helped transform dicta from trivia into a force. The second aspect of the problem—the acceptance of prior dictum as if it were binding law—results in some part from time pressures on an overworked judiciary, the ever-increasing length of judicial opinions, and the precision-guided weaponry of computer research—all of which contribute to our taking previously uttered statements out of context, without a careful reading to ascertain the role they played in the opinion.

Definition. I should pause to make sure we are on the same page as to the meaning of "dictum." A dictum is an assertion in a court's opinion of a proposition of law which does not explain why the court's judgment goes in favor of the winner. If the court's judgment and the reasoning which supports it would remain unchanged, regardless of the proposition in question, that proposition plays no role in explaining why the judgment goes for the winner. It is superfluous to the decision and is dictum. The dictum consists essentially of a comment on how the court would decide some other, different case, and has no effect on its decision of the case before it. If the court's function is to decide the case in accordance with the rules of law, explaining what are the rules that govern the decision, and explaining the interaction between those rules and the facts of the case, the utterance of such dictum is superfluous to the court's performance of its function.

To identify dictum, it is useful to turn the questioned proposition around to assert its opposite, or to assert whatever alternative proposition the court rejected in its favor. If the insertion of the rejected proposition into the court's reasoning, in place of the one adopted, would not require a change in either the court's judgment or the reasoning that supports it,

---

19 *See, e.g., Willis v. Baddeley*, (1892) 2 Eng. Rep. 324, 326 (Q.B.D.) ("There is in fact no such thing as judge-made law, for the judges do not make the law, though they frequently have to apply existing law to circumstances as to which it has not previously been authoritatively laid down that such law is applicable."); R.W.M. DIAS, JURISPRUDENCE 151 (5th ed. 1985) ("The orthodox Blackstonian view . . . is that judges do not make law, but only declare what has always been the law."). . . .

then the proposition is dictum. It is superfluous. It had no functional role in compelling the judgment. * * *

To say that a court's statement is a dictum is to say that the statement is not the holding. Holding and dictum are generally thought of as mutually exclusive categories. However, it is not always immediately apparent at a glance whether a pronouncement of law is holding or dictum. One cannot tell by reading the statement in isolation, without reference to the overall discussion. The distinction requires recognition of what was the question before the court upon which the judgment depended, how (and by what reasoning) the court resolved the question, and what role, if any, the proposition played in the reasoning that led to the judgment. A dictum is not converted into holding by forceful utterance, or by preceding it with the words "We hold that . . . ."[21] Judge Friendly cautioned, "A judge's power to bind is limited to the issue that is before him; he cannot transmute dictum into decision by waving a wand and uttering the word 'hold.' "[22]

I do not mean to imply that in all cases it is easy, or even possible, to reach a confident conclusion whether a statement should be considered dictum or holding. At times a proposition advanced by the court will support the court's decision to grant judgment to the plaintiff or defendant, but indirectly or remotely. There is no line demarcating a clear boundary between holding and dictum. What separates holding from dictum is better seen as a zone, within which no confident determination can be made whether the proposition should be considered holding or dictum.

Nonetheless, to say that the distinction between holding and dictum is sometimes murky does not mean that it is always murky. In many instances there can be no doubt that the proposition in question played no role in the court's justification of its judgment. Court opinions today are crammed full of such superfluous declarations of law. * * *

Why Does This Matter? Why do we care whether a rule announced by a court is dictum? The distinction between holding and dictum was always important to the common law tradition of fidelity to prior holdings. It took on a heightened importance with the adoption of the prudential rule known by the Latin phrase "*stare decisis*" (meaning "to remain decided"). This rule requires that once a court has decided a case based on a proposition of law, the court must thereafter adhere to that proposition of law, deciding like cases in like manner (unless it takes the rare step of disavowing and overruling the proposition).

---

21 Nor can the classification of a pronouncement of law be determined based on whether a subsequent court has described it as holding or dictum. The words, "In Smith v. Jones, the court held. . ." are often written without the slightest attention to whether the proposition was a holding or dictum. Frequently, it means no more than "the court wrote. . . ." And a subsequent court's description of an earlier proposition as dictum is often attributable to a motivation to diminish the status of the prior pronouncement, rather than to a reasoned justification.

22 *United States v. Rubin*, 609 F.2d 51, 69 (2d Cir. 1979) (Friendly, J., concurring).

Stare decisis inevitably results in courts having some lawmaking power. If the court is obliged to adhere to its prior decisions, every decision becomes a part of binding law. But it was not the purpose of *stare decisis* to increase court power. To the contrary, the rule was intended as a limitation on the courts. It was designed to keep courts principled and consistent—to prevent courts from acting arbitrarily or capriciously, deciding the same facts one way in Jones's case and another way in Smith's case. The idea behind it was that courts would better perform their assigned function of deciding cases if compelled to decide them consistently.

Stare decisis requires a court to adhere only to its decisions—its holdings—not to any utterance the court may make. It thus becomes of great importance to distinguish between a court's holdings, which become binding law for the future, and its dicta, which at least in theory do not.

Questions. I pose two questions. First: Is judicial lawmaking through dictum consistent with the powers and duties of courts prescribed by the Constitution? Second: Is the treatment of dictum as established, binding law consistent with common sense and sound judicial practice? I believe the answer to both questions is "No."

II

The Constitution

What does the Constitution have to say that bears on making law by dictum? It does not address the subject directly. Nonetheless, the Constitution's message is forceful, if oblique and terse. The only role granted to the federal courts in Article III was to exercise "the judicial power" in "Cases" and "Controversies."[24] What does this mean? The constitutional function of the courts is to adjudicate—to decide cases. The Constitution does not explicitly grant to courts the power to make law. The power to make law generally is encompassed in the words, "All legislative powers," and was vested by Article I, Section 1, in the Congress.

Needless to say, courts do legitimately make law under the Constitution. But they do so not because the Constitution conferred lawmaking power on them. It didn't. They do so only because the rule of *stare decisis* evolved to require that courts judge consistently. Given that the court's sole constitutional authority is to decide cases, what should we make of the constitutional legitimacy of lawmaking through proclamation of dicta? It is simply without justification. Courts make law only as a consequence of the performance of their constitutional duty to decide cases. They have no constitutional authority to establish law otherwise.

What if we in the Second Circuit, without any filed dispute between parties, were to publish a tract entitled In re Securities Litigation, in which

---

[24] U.S. CONST. art. III, § 1.

we promulgated a compendium of rules to govern securities cases? I think all would agree that we lack constitutional authority to establish binding law in this fashion. Then what if, when a securities dispute comes before us, after giving judgment on the disputed issue, we go on to say, "Having focused our attention on the subject of securities litigation, we will go beyond the particular issue in dispute and proclaim a set of rules to be followed." Is this meaningfully different from the previous example? The ordinary instance of courts making law through dictum is less blatant—better disguised, more interwoven with the issues in dispute—but essentially not different. It is beyond our authority. * * *

I turn now to practical considerations, which reinforce the wisdom of this constitutional structure. How well do courts do their job when dictum is treated as holding? In their structure and manner of operation, courts are poorly equipped to promulgate law, and even more poorly equipped to do so in dictum. When they make law in dictum, the likelihood is high that it will be bad law.

A. *Structure of Courts As Lawmakers.*

Brandeis observed that "[c]ourts are ill-equipped to make the investigations which should precede" legislation.[27] Think what a lawmaking body should do before promulgating laws. By their structure and manner of operation, courts lack the ability to perform those tasks. If we were designing an ideal body to promulgate laws for society, it would not look at all like a federal court.

The ideal lawmaking body would be designed to undertake a broad, integrated study of the area requiring attention. It would issue public notices so that affected persons could make submissions and participate in hearings. It would seek advice from experts. It would employ a staff to make a detailed, independent study. It would deliberate and wait as long as it considered useful before promulgating a new rule. A court functions very differently. It focuses on whatever fragmentary portion of an area of law the case of the moment happens to place before it. Usually, the only input the court receives is from the litigants. The court is barred from researching the facts privately on its own. It rarely employs neutral experts. It works with a tiny staff, whose attention is spread over the multitude of cases and areas on which the court will need to rule. And the court is under pressure to make its adjudication promptly after the submission of the case.

The poor design of courts for the task of lawmaking suggests that lawmaking by courts is best limited to where the lawmaking inescapably results from the court's performance of its duty to decide the case. This is never true when law is made by dictum, which is always—by definition—superfluous to the court's performance of its job.

---

[27] *Int'l News Serv. v. Associated Press*, 248 U.S. 215, 267 (1918) (Brandeis, J., dissenting).

B. *Structure with Regard to Dictum.*

However poorly courts are designed for lawmaking generally, their structural limitations particularly disfavor lawmaking through dictum. Why? A number of reasons:

1. *Absence of Briefing and Adversity.* Our readiness to trust a court's rulings of law depends on the assumption that the adverse parties will each vigorously assert the best defense of its positions. The court reaches its decision only after confronting conflicting arguments powerfully advanced by both sides. When, however, the court asserts rules outside the scope of its judgment, that salutary adversity is often absent. In many instances the court will have no briefing whatsoever on the issue, because the parties usually have no interest in a question whose resolution will not affect the result of their case.

2. *Concreteness.* Conditions that best favor lawmaking by courts are those where the dispute is framed by concrete facts. Two of the most difficult challenges in lawmaking are understanding the facts that call for regulation and understanding what effect the imposition of any rule will have on those facts. When the assertion of a proposition of law determines a case's outcome, the court necessarily sees how that proposition functions in at least one factual context, at least with respect to the immediate result. In contrast, when a court asserts a rule of law in dictum, the court will often not have before it any facts affected by that rule. In addition, the lack of concrete facts increases the likelihood that readers will misunderstand the scope of the rule the court had in mind.

3. *The Lack of Appeal.* Another weakness of law made through dicta is that there is no available correction mechanism. No appeal may be taken from the assertion of an erroneous legal rule in dictum. Frequently, what's more, no party has a motive to try to get the bad proposition corrected. No party will even ask the court to reconsider its unfortunate dicta.

4. *Insufficient Judicial Scrutiny.* My experience as a judge has shown me that assertions made in dictum are less likely to receive careful scrutiny, both in the writing chambers and in the concurring chambers. When a panel of judges confers on a case, the judges generally focus on the outcome and on the reasoning upon which the outcome depends. Judges work under great time pressure. When the concurring chambers receive the writing judge's draft for their review, they are likely to look primarily at whether the opinion fulfills their expectations as to the judgment and the reasoning given in support. There is a high likelihood that peripheral observations, alternative explanations, and dicta will receive scant attention.

Of cardinal importance to this point is Leval's rule of restaurant selection: If a restaurant's location assures that customers will come whether the food is good or bad, it will be bad. This is a corollary of a broader rule: Stuff you get for free ain't worth more than you paid for it. The rule applies loosely to dicta.

When a court justifies a judgment in favor of the plaintiff or the defendant, the court necessarily confronts the cautionary realization that the rule relied upon determines the outcome of the litigation. The court metaphorically "pays the price" of the rule it has declared. When a rule is uttered in dictum, the court pays no price; the statement comes free, as it has no consequence for the case. In my experience, when courts declare rules that have no consequence for the case, their cautionary mechanism is often not engaged. They are far more likely in these circumstances to fashion defective rules, and to assert misguided propositions, which have not been fully thought through.

I cannot tell you how many times I have read briefs asserting an improbable proposition of law and citing a case as authority. The proposition sounds so dubious that I immediately look it up to see if the cited court can really have made this ruling. So often I find the proposition is indeed there, but was uttered in dictum—where the court paid no price, and consequently paid little attention.

IV

Where Dicta Are Found

We will now explore briefly where abuses of dictum are commonly found—and why.

A. *Question Beyond the Case*

Among the most common manifestations of disguised dictum occurs where the court ventures beyond the issue in controversy to declare the solution to a further problem—one that will arise in another case, or in a later phase of the same case. Why do we judges do this? Don't we have enough work deciding the controversies before us? The reasons are numerous and grow in part out of our human frailties. (1) At times our exuberance for a point of view gets out of hand. (2) At times we may devise a strategic gambit in ideological warfare. We may reach beyond the case in order to preempt colleagues who might later decide a further issue in a manner not to our liking. (3) You will surely be amazed at the further suggestion that judges may at times be prey to vanity. Like professors, we have not been encouraged to view ourselves modestly. * * * A judge tends to think, "I've looked at this stuff closely and I understand it. It will come out better if I cover these questions now, rather than leaving them to whatever (perhaps less thoughtful) judge comes along next." (4) We are tempted also by the seductive lure of establishing the landmark precedent, which, like the great opinions of Hand and Friendly, will be repeatedly cited as the authoritative guidepost for the area. We think the further we venture in the opinion, the more likely it is to achieve landmark status. We fail to recognize how likely we are to make mistakes when addressing issues beyond the scope of the decision. * * *

B. The Counterfactual Hypothesis

Another version is the contrary-to-fact hypothetical. While explaining a ruling in favor of the winner, courts often add that if the facts had been otherwise, the court would have ruled the other way. At times, judges seem to be motivated by an emotional need to demonstrate that they are not biased against such claims; had the facts only been slightly different, the ruling would have been for the adversary. This is a dangerous practice, which can easily engender bad law.

An interesting example is *Sony Corp. of America v. Universal City Studios, Inc.*[42] In determining whether the emerging technology for videotaping television transmissions should be considered a contributory infringement of copyrighted programs, the Supreme Court considered whether fair use would protect a family's recording of a program, so as to permit the family to watch it at a more convenient hour. Emphasizing that such copying would be done without commercial exploitation, the Court concluded it would not be considered infringing. It added unnecessarily that "every commercial use of copyrighted material is presumptively an unfair exploitation of the [copyright] privilege."[45]

This last observation was pure dictum and involved all of dictum's weaknesses. It sounded good, but it seriously misunderstood the law. The vast majority of publications are commercial. Whether commercial copying of copyrighted material infringes or is a fair use depends on context. Newspapers, book reviews, biographies, histories—they are all published commercially for profit. They regularly quote from protected material in such manner that the quoting work does not compete in the original work's market and receives fair use protection.

This unfortunate dictum in *Sony*—stated as if the Supreme Court were proclaiming a rule of law—introduced confusion which plagued the understanding of copyright doctrine for ten years, until the Court finally mopped up the mess in *Campbell v. Acuff-Rose Music, Inc.*[46]

Without doubt, in some circumstances there can be good reason for suggesting the limitations of the rule that compels the particular judgment—to lessen the risk that the holding will be read too broadly. While the practice is surely useful, it carries the risks I have described of inadequate consideration. The court should make clear that its

---

42 464 U.S. 417 (1984).

45 *Id.* [at 451] (emphasis added) ("Thus, although every commercial use of a copyrighted material is presumptively an unfair exploitation of the monopoly privilege that belongs to the owner of the copyright, noncommercial uses are a different matter.").

46 510 U.S. 569, 583–85 (1994). * * *

specification of the limits of the doctrine is dictum, and thus open for rethinking.

C. Erudite Opinions and Gratuitous Statement of Standards

Another pernicious stimulus for making law through dictum lies in the desire of us judges to appear erudite and to demonstrate our subservience to law by copious recitation of legal rules. Rather than focus simply on the identification of what is in dispute and the explanation of our decision, buttressed by citation of supporting authority, we engage in unnecessary, discursive, scholarly discussions of doctrine; we gratuitously recite standards of law that are not in dispute and have no effect on the judgment.

As a tiny, but recurring example, for every issue considered in courts of appeals, we pronounce ritualistically that our review is "de novo," or "for abuse of discretion," even where it makes no difference in the case because we conclude there was no error of any sort. It is the fashion in appellate decisions today to proclaim the standard that governs the type of questions, even when the particular standard announced will have no bearing on the resolution of the dispute. Characteristically, a statement of a standard will be lifted without examination from a prior opinion. We think this practice is harmless. After all, we are doing nothing more than correctly stating a rule of law.

If these superfluous pronouncements were indeed always correct, there would be no problem. Unfortunately, however, law is endlessly complex and subtle. * * * When we thoughtlessly copy a statement of law from a prior opinion in a manner that determines nothing in the case before us, we risk misunderstanding the context and getting it wrong, introducing confusion and error.

Particularly to be feared is the scholarly, treatise-type opinion, which for no good reason lectures on the nature and origins of the doctrine, making pronouncements that have no consequence for the dispute. Although the court generally believes it is correctly explaining non-controversial matters, the practice is risky.

D. Other Non-Dispositive Determinations

The dangers of dictum uttered without "paying the price" are also present in two other common circumstances: first, when an appellate court asserts that a ruling below was error, but goes on to affirm because the error was harmless; and second, when the court asserts there was no error as to some of the claims on appeal, but ultimately goes on to reverse on another basis. None of the original assertions affects the judgment. They come for free. Because they have no consequences for the judgment, such pronouncements are often glibly uttered, without careful scrutiny, and are therefore often mistaken.

Courts should recognize these types of statements as dictum and so label them. Indeed in some cases, unless the court is confident that what was done below was error, it might in some circumstances be best to hedge the assertion of error, or omit it. * * *

VI

Supreme Court Dicta

What about Supreme Court dicta? Some who would agree with my point as applied to the inferior courts would assert that things are different when it comes to the Supreme Court. It is sometimes argued that the lower courts must treat the dicta of the Supreme Court as controlling.[76] Various reasons are given: Great respect is owed to the Supreme Court; it always sits *en banc*, assuring that all of its Justices have participated in whatever it decides; its small docket means it will not likely hear enough cases to cover any area of law by its holdings.

I certainly agree that great respect is owed to the Supreme Court. It is indisputably supreme among courts. By the same token, however, it is but a court. It may make law only in the ways in which a court may make law. Its constitutional function is to adjudicate. Its holdings are without doubt the law of the land. Its dicta? Anything the Supreme Court says should be considered with care; nonetheless, there is a significant difference between statements about the law, which courts should consider with care and respect, and utterances which have the force of binding law. The Supreme Court's dicta are not law. The issues so addressed remain unadjudicated. When an inferior court has such an issue before it, it may not treat the Supreme Court's dictum as dispositive. It must adjudicate.[78]

I am not counseling disrespect for a higher court, least of all the Supreme Court. I am saying only that a lower court has a constitutional responsibility to decide the case in accordance with law. Dictum is not law. The court must decide a previously undecided question. * * *

---

[76] *See, e.g., McCoy v. M.I.T.*, 950 F.2d 13, 19 (1st Cir. 1991) (finding itself "both unable . . . and unwilling" to ignore "considered" Supreme Court dictum); *Faheem-El v. Klincar*, 841 F.2d 712, 731 (7th Cir. 1988) (Easterbrook, J., concurring) (finding Supreme Court discussion—"wise or not"—to be authoritative). * * *

[78] Congress is also entitled to respect. If all the members of the Congress were to subscribe to a resolution, not following the procedures necessary to enact statutory law, the resolution would not be law because it was not promulgated in the manner in which Congress is permitted to make law. The same should be true when the Supreme Court or any other court makes pronouncements in a manner that is not within its constitutional power to make law.

If the lower courts treat the Supreme Court's dicta as binding law, as in the Pledge of Allegiance case mentioned above, the functioning of our legal system is undermined. Under the design of the system, the lower courts are expected to grapple with the issues that arise in their cases. The Supreme Court, with the issues illuminated by the efforts of the lower courts, reviews their efforts and renders the ultimate determinative judgment. If, however, the lower courts, instead of making their own effort to decide the issues, have merely regurgitated the Supreme Court's dicta, the Supreme Court receives no benefit from lower court consideration. The judicial system is impaired.

CONCLUSION

If any of what I have said makes sense, what course does this suggest for professors, students, practitioners, and judges?

To professors I would say: You have a responsibility to make sure your students understand and are alert to the distinction between holding and dictum—and its importance. It is not something to be discussed only in a brief, first-year intro-to-law lecture. Students who graduate without a grasp of it are not well trained for the profession.

To students and practitioners I would say that, in arguing to courts, you will need to be keenly aware what is holding and what is dictum. It is often the best way to undermine unfavorable language in a prior opinion. By the same token, it can alert you that your argument is built on a house of cards.

To myself and other judges I would say three things: First, dictum can serve useful purposes. We have no need to purge dictum from our opinions and we shouldn't be embarrassed by its presence. We must only remember that it is not law. To avoid trespassing beyond the territory confided to us by the Constitution, to avoid creating law in circumstances likely to produce bad law, and to avoid creating confusion, we should not disguise dictum, but should forthrightly label it as what it is. Second, rather than reciting rules of law, which are not in dispute in the case, we should focus sharply on exactly what is in dispute and set forth rules in our opinions only as rulings on the disputed questions. Third, before relying on a formulation of law in a prior opinion, we must determine whether it was holding or dictum. We must make that inquiry even when the prior court was the Supreme Court. If a rule was declared only in dictum, the question remains undecided, and we have a constitutional duty to make our own determination of the answer. Unless we do, we have not done our job. * * *

NOTES AND QUESTIONS

1. *Realpolitik*. Does the rule of *stare decisis* increase or decrease judicial power?

2. *Information and value*. Professor Anthony Kronman has argued that "the past is, for lawyers and judges, a repository not just of information but of value, with the power to confer legitimacy on actions in the present. . . ." Anthony T. Kronman, *Precedent and Tradition*, 99 YALE L.J. 1029, 1032–33 (1990). What in the excerpts from Hart and Schauer demonstrates the accuracy of Kronman's insight?

3. *Means and ends*. Professor Max Radin once observed that "the rule of precedent, or *stare decisis*, is a means and not an end." Max Radin, *The Trail of the Calf*, 32 CORNELL L. Q. 137, 159 (1946). On the basis of what you have

read in this chapter, especially Professor Schauer's analysis of the debatable virtues of precedent, what did Radin mean, and what is the current practical value of his insight?

The evocative title of Professor Radin's article—*the Trail of the Calf*—comes from the following poem, which may say more in its way about precedent in fewer words than anything else in this chapter:

> One day through the primeval wood
>
> A calf walked home as good calves should;
>
> But made a trail all bent askew,
>
> A crooked trail as all calves do. . . . .
>
> And men two centuries and a half
>
> Trod in the footsteps of that calf. . . . .
>
> They followed still his crooked way,
>
> And lost one hundred years a day;
>
> For thus such reverence is lent
>
> To well-established precedent.

Sam Walter Foss, *The Calf-Path*, in WHIFFS FROM WILD MEADOWS 77, 77–79 (1895).

4. *Precedent and the professional responsibility of candor.* Precedent may be more judicial policy than inexorable command, but it is still a violation of professional ethics for a lawyer to ignore "controlling precedent" that is directly contrary to his or her client's position. *See, e.g., Schoofield v. Barnhart*, 220 F.Supp.2d 512, 522 (D. Md. 2002) (applying the Maryland Rules of Professional Conduct). Is "controlling precedent" a thing? On the other hand, would you be willing to risk your professional license by arguing that no precedent is truly controlling in the end?

5. *Precedent and fashion.* Consider the possibility that the effectiveness of arguments from precedent may be cyclical, like fashion, and that eras in the law can be distinguished by their overall orientation to precedent. *See* Thomas R. Lee, *Stare Decisis in Historical Perspective: From the Founding Era to the Rehnquist Court*, 52 VAND. L. REV. 647 (1999). Frederick G. Kempin, Jr., *Precedent and Stare Decisis: The Critical Years 1800–1850*, 3 AM. J. LEGAL HIST. 28 (1959).

6. *Are parents and Presidents bound by precedent too?* One mark of the instinctive appeal of arguments from precedent is that courts are not the only forum where such arguments can predominate and prevail. To the contrary, Professor Schauer has observed that

> [f]orms of argument that may be concentrated in the legal system are rarely isolated there, and the argument from precedent is a prime example of the nonexclusivity of what used to be called "legal reasoning." Think of the child who insists that he should not have to

> wear short pants to school because his older brother was allowed to wear long pants when he was seven. Or think of the bureaucrat who responds to the supplicant for special consideration by saying that "we've never done it that way before." In countless instances, out of law as well as in, the fact that something was done before provides, by itself, a reason for doing it that way again. Reliance on precedent is part of life in general.

Frederick Schauer, *Precedent*, 39 STAN. L. REV. 571, 572 (1987). In administrative law for example, executive agencies are subject to a requirement of reasoned consistency, which does not mean that an agency may never change its mind or deviate from its original practice or policy position, but only that any change from its established pattern of conduct must be explained. *See* Thomas Merrill, *Judicial Opinions as Binding Law and as Explanations for Judgments*, 15 CARDOZO L. REV. 43 (1993).

7. *Alternative explanations for the emergence of the law of precedents*. Consider the possibility that the doctrine of *stare decisis* depended fundamentally on the technology of reporting and printing prior decisions, not to mention the reconciliation of different court systems into a relatively coherent hierarchy:

> Various scholars of legal history allege the doctrine of *stare decisis* was brought into being by the influence of: (1) The invention of the printing press; (2) The development of court hierarchy by the 19th century; and (3) The efforts of entrepreneurial printers and publishers. Sir William Holdsworth, in his multi-volume treatise on the history of English law, claimed that the invention and application of the printing press influenced the rise of *stare decisis*, arguing "it could be attributed to the fact that reports of judicial opinions were by that time not only officially reported in writing, but printed and published." Others have repeated the claim that the technology of the printing press may have influenced the rise of *stare decisis*. Traditional legal scholars have argued that the rise of *stare decisis* was due to the hierarchy of courts that emerged in the early 19th century. Still others attribute the rise of *stare decisis* to the efforts of individual entrepreneurs in the printing and publishing world who stood to make profits from the requirements of large book purchases by lawyers across the country.

R.W.M. DIAS, JURISPRUDENCE 30–31 (2nd ed.1964) (citations omitted). Prior to these technological and institutional developments, what do you think were the dominant sources of common law? According to the Ninth Circuit Court of Appeals:

> For centuries, the most important sources of law were not judicial opinions themselves, but treatises that restated the law, such as the commentaries of Coke and Blackstone. Because published opinions were relatively few, lawyers and judges relied on commentators' synthesis of decisions rather than the verbatim text of opinions. . . .

> In the first century of American jurisprudence, Blackstone's "Commentaries were not merely an approach to the study of law; for most lawyers they constituted all there was of the law."

Hart v. Massanari, 266 F.3d 1155, 1165–1166 (9th Cir. 2001) (*quoting* DANIEL J. BOORSTIN, THE MYSTERIOUS SCIENCE OF THE LAW 3 (1941).

8. *Competing philosophies of law, competing accounts of precedent.* In Part I of this book, you were introduced to various schools of jurisprudence, including natural law, positivism, legal realism, legal process, law and economics, and critical legal studies, feminist jurisprudence, and critical race theory. What spin do you think each of these philosophies of law would put on the doctrine of *stare decisis*? More precisely, how might each school articulate the justifications for, and the limits on, the power of precedent?

9. *Non-precedential forms of justice.* Can you imagine a way of thinking about justice that is neutral or hostile towards precedent altogether? What would a conception of justice look like that actively rejected the conventional morality of precedent? Obviously, revolutionary justice has no place for precedent, and Confucius thought that precedent was a snare—a legalistic distraction from the virtuous and current consciousness of the elders. *See* 2 JOSEPH NEEDHAM, SCIENCE AND CIVILISATION IN CHINA 522 (1956). Justice is obviously possible in civil law countries, like those in Continental Europe, which do not consider precedent a source of law. The Statute of the International Court of Justice explicitly relieves the Court from any constraint imposed by *stare decisis*, without suggesting at all that its decisions are for that reason free from considerations of justice or more likely to be unjust. *See* ICJ STAT., art. 59 ("The decision of the Court has no binding force except between the parties and in respect of that particular case"). One entry point for thinking about this question is to recall Professor Schauer's observation that "a decision-maker choosing to rely on precedent may justifiably 'relax,' in the sense of engaging in less scrutiny of the case, where that decision-maker chooses to rely on a precedent." Acknowledging the rhetorical power of arguments from precedent, what moral or analytical muscle is being relaxed when such arguments are at work?

PART III

PERSPECTIVES TESTED

■ ■ ■

CHAPTER FOURTEEN

THEORIES OF LAW TESTED: IS INTERNATIONAL LAW REALLY "LAW?"

■ ■ ■

"[International law] . . . is the vanishing point of jurisprudence."

—Thomas Erskine Holland

"It is probably the case that almost all nations observe almost all principles of international law and almost all of their obligations almost all of the time."

— Louis Henkin

"The surprising thing about international law is that nations *ever* obey its strictures or carry out its mandates. . . . Why should rules, unsupported by an effective structure of coercion comparable to a national police force, nevertheless elicit so much compliance, even against perceived self-interest, on the part of sovereign states?"

— Thomas M. Franck

Orientation

For centuries, the organizing principle behind international law—the idea that has given international law its essential structure and character—has been that it is in some sense "horizontal." The legal order, such as it is, rests on the will of co-equal states, who make the rules for themselves to regulate their relationships with one another.[1] There is no legislature with global authority to pass laws for the governments and peoples of the world. There is no centralized police force or executive body to enforce the law. Whatever international judiciary exists for enforcing international law against states operates only when governments consent to its jurisdiction. There is in short no sovereign over sovereigns.

---

1 According to the Permanent Court of International Justice (predecessor to the International Court of Justice at The Hague):

> International law governs relations between independent States. The rules of law binding upon States therefore emanate from their own free will as expressed in conventions or by usages generally accepted as expressing principles of law and established in order to regulate the relations between these coexisting independent communities or with a view to the achievement of common aims.

Case of the S.S. Lotus, [1927] P.C.I.J., ser. A, No. 10, at 18.

Admittedly, some states are extremely powerful and others are not, so there is something vaguely hallucinatory about the assumption that international law is made by co-equal states. But, if anything, that element of *realpolitik* simply reinforces the difference between international law and "real" law, like domestic criminal law, which fits the "vertical" form: a law is in effect "handed down" from sovereign to subject. True, in a representative democracy, the legislature presumably responds to the will of the people. But that is something of a political abstraction, and even our daily language has citizens living "under" the rule of law or "under" a system of legislative supremacy—language that reinforces the idea that legal systems are at least figuratively vertical.

When skeptics observe that international law is not really law at all, they generally mean that it has none of the coercive characteristics that define more familiar forms of law. The objection is that international law is unenforced and unenforceable, that violators routinely go unpunished, that no state will obey international law if that goes against their immediate self-interest. Certainly one of the consequences of the "horizontality" of international law is that it is better at stating norms (or authoritative expectations) than it is at imposing punishments for non-compliance. Another is that it preserves more state power than it constrains. That is, the law defines and protects a zone of freedom and discretion within which governments can act as they choose, beyond international scrutiny. Throughout much of its existence, international law has been primarily a matter of jurisdictional line-drawing, "a negative code of rules of abstentions"[2] and immunities. The essence of the law was that it confirmed the power of states to be left alone. In effect, the law built and policed *fences* between states and gave them the legal right to be left alone.

But increasingly international law is less about fences and more about *bridges*. Topics or conduct that may lie within a state's exclusive domestic jurisdiction have changed radically over time, suggesting that something within a state's discretion may not always stay there, especially when governments come to see some communal benefit in a harmonized approach. In short, international law has been transformed from a "negative code" into a more affirmative code of obligations of states to cooperate in the solution of problems perceived to be communal. Consider for example the rise of intergovernmental institutions to address issues of common concern by promoting international communication, protecting world health, and fighting international crimes. One prime example of the transformation from fences to bridges is international law of human rights—the twin ideas that individuals have certain rights simply by virtue of being human and that states are obliged to protect those rights in certain ways.

---

[2] WOLFGANG FRIEDMANN, THE CHANGING STRUCTURE OF INTERNATIONAL LAW 62 (1964).

We are of course confronted daily with evidence that the human rights project is a failure, that human rights abuses are common and that some of the most powerful countries in the world are serial violators of human rights standards. But we shouldn't lose the sense of surprise that human rights by historical standards received unprecedented protection yesterday. Torture has gone from being a lawful commonplace, defined without shame as a public punishment for crimes real or imagined, to an unlawful though not eradicated scourge, so shameful as to require denial, cover ups, strategic redefinition, as well as investigation and sanction. It is the violations—the aberrations in short—that come into and dominate our consciousness.

Imagine a pathetic but articulate observer who happens to live in a hospital emergency room. This hypothetical observer gets daily confirmation of all the bad things that happen to people: assaults, murders, accidents, disease. And if this hypothetical observer were to construct his version of reality outside the emergency room, it would look like something out of *War of the Worlds*: chaotic, violent, cruel, random, hateful. But, from an outside perspective, we know that this is a pathological view of reality based on the very real, very hard, and very limited perspective of an emergency room denizen.

It is certainly true that violations of international human rights norms are an everyday occurrence. But it is also true that murder occurs daily, and domestic violence and antitrust violations are commonplace, but few argue that these violations prove that criminal law or antitrust law are not really law after all. Instead, those acts are assumed to be wrong and that in principle whoever commits those wrongs will be liable for damages or face some other legitimate sanction.

One right question is whether there is something similarly pathological about concluding on the basis of high-profile violations that there is something congenitally anti-law about international norms? Virtually every international border remained stable last night, and yet there are no headlines about it. Somehow, for yet another day, international organizations did their work within a framework of law for the protection of people's health or cross-boundary administrative harmonization or economic development, but the headlines focus on what violations there were, suggesting just how much we have come to expect of governments. In other words, one might look at the inkblot of state practices with respect to human rights for example and say with the skeptic that it only confirms the worst suspicions about states. Or one might consider the dog that didn't bark, and find it remarkable that international law received as much respect as it did. Without minimizing the very real problem of under- or non-enforcement, we are perhaps especially attuned to the notorious violations of international legal standards, and rather less attuned to the routinization of compliance.

It turns out that one dominant, largely under-theorized means of enforcing international law is this process of internalization or bureaucratization by governments. For one analogy, think about how drivers stop (or at least move their foot instinctively towards the brake) when they drive up to a stop sign, even if there is no traffic and no police officer is in sight. And if they do not stop, they probably would not bother to argue that the stop sign imposes no legal obligation or that what they did was lawful.

The materials in this chapter invite you to confront both the skepticism and the idealism that lie at the heart of opposing conceptions of international law *as law*. Each of the jurisprudential traditions identified in Part I of this book offers perspectives on international law, as illustrated by the readings below. But cases involving the litigation of international law also shed light on the power and limits of those schools. It exposes our sometimes hidden conceptions and value judgments about law more generally: is enforceability a precondition for the existence of law, or do we need to expand our working notion of what enforceability actually is? Based on what you have already studied, how would you go about arguing or proving that international law really is "law?"

Traditionally, international law is derived from multiple sources, and they catalogued in the instrument that created the International Court of Justice—the principal judicial organ of the United Nations:

Statute of the International Court of Justice

Article 38

33 U.N.T.S. 993

(1) The Court, whose function is to decide in accordance with international law such disputes as are submitted to it, shall apply:

a. international conventions, whether general or particular, establishing rules expressly recognized by the contesting states;

b. international custom, as evidence of a general practice accepted as law;

c. the general principles of law recognized by civilized nations;

d. * * * judicial decisions and the teachings of the most highly qualified publicists of the various nations, as subsidiary means for the determination of rules of law.

(2) This provision shall not prejudice the power of the Court to decide a case *ex aequo et bono*, if the parties agree thereto.

At a minimum, this provision suggests that international law comprises both *contractual* forms of obligations, corresponding to treaties (Art. 38(1)(a)), and *behavioral* forms of obligation, corresponding to so-called "customary international law" or, as it was once known, the "law of nations" (Art. 38(1)(b)). The specific formulation for the latter—"a general practice accepted as law"—suggests two criteria for customary international law: (i) a general practice among states, meaning that states conform in fact to a standard of behavior or that their conduct follows a consistent, empirical pattern, and (ii) a sense of legal obligation or *opinio juris*, meaning that states behave in these patterned ways not out of ideology or public relations but out of the conviction that the behavior is required by law. At first blush, these two traditional forms of international law seem to derive from two quite separate processes: a dynamic of *ad hoc* consent leading to obligations binding upon the parties to the written agreement versus a dynamic of habitual usage observed by nations as law and binding upon each of them. As suggested below however, contemporary international law has witnessed the proliferation of normative types that do not fit into the either/or world of treaties and custom and which blur any simple-minded distinction between them.

Article 38(1)(c) also lists "the general principles of law recognized by civilized nations" as a potential source of international law norms. Ignoring for the moment the difficulty of identifying "civilized nations," the core of this category is that some principles of law seem valid across virtually all human societies or seem basic to the very idea of a legal system generally. International law can arise out of the comparative exercise of finding general principles in the various municipal systems of law in the world and applying them at the international plane. For example, virtually all domestic legal systems have some principle like "a party cannot take advantage of its own wrong" or "every violation of a promise or a duty triggers an obligation to make reparation." Although there is nothing distinctly international about these principles by their terms, states have reasoned that these principles—in spite of their domestic pedigree—may operate at the international and apply to states. There can in short be a comparative element to international obligations.

Article 38(1)(d) of the ICJ Statute identifies "as subsidiary means for the determination of rules of law," judicial decisions and the teachings of the most highly qualified publicists of the various nations. Though international law includes no formal notion of precedent or *stare decisis*, the decisions of national courts may nonetheless be relevant in giving content to international law, and the International Court of Justice routinely refers to its own prior decisions on the obvious principle that similar cases should be resolved similarly. The ICJ's determination in one case that a norm had become customary law would be considered virtually conclusive evidence in other settings. Scholarly writing—"the teachings of the most highly qualified publicists of the various nations"—may also exert considerable influence, not because scholars have or claim some authority to make law but because the collection and evaluation of state practice plays a critical evidentiary role in determining what the law is.

Consider how these four traditional sources of international law—treaties, customary international law, general principles, and the "subsidiary" combination of judicial decisions of the various nations and teachings of publicists—are used to find a rule of decision in the following cases.

A. INTERNATIONAL LAW IN INTERNATIONAL COURTS

VELÁSQUEZ-RODRÍGUEZ CASE (JUDGMENT OF JULY 29, 1988)

INTER-AM. CT. H. R. (Ser. C) No. 4 (1988)

1. The Inter-American Commission on Human Rights (hereinafter "the Commission") submitted the instant case to the Inter-American Court of Human Rights (hereinafter the "Court") on April 24, 1986. It originated in a petition against the State of Honduras (hereinafter "Honduras" or "the Government"), which the Secretariat of the Commission received on October 7, 1981.

2. In submitting the case, the Commission invoked Articles 50 and 51 of the American Convention on Human Rights (hereinafter "the Convention" or "the American Convention") and requested that the Court determine whether the State in question had violated Articles 4 (Right to Life), 5 (Right to Humane Treatment) and 7 (Right to Personal Liberty) of the Convention in the case of Angel Manfredo Velásquez Rodríguez (also known as Manfredo Velásquez). In addition, the Commission asked the Court to rule that "the consequences of the situation that constituted the breach of such right or freedom be remedied and that fair compensation be paid to the injured party or parties."

3. According to the petition filed with the Commission, and the supplementary information received subsequently, Manfredo Velasquez, a student at the National Autonomous University of Honduras, "was violently detained without a warrant for his arrest by members of the National Office of Investigations (DNI) and G-2 of the Armed Forces of Honduras." The detention took place in Tegucigalpa on the afternoon of September 12, 1981. According to the petitioners, several eyewitnesses reported that Manfredo Velasquez and others were detained and taken to the cells of Public Security Forces Station No. 2 located in the Barrio E1 Manchen of Tegucigalpa, where he was "accused of alleged political crimes

and subjected to harsh interrogation and cruel torture." The petition added that on September 17, 1981, Manfredo Velásquez was moved to the First Infantry Battalion, where the interrogation continued, but that the police and security forces denied that he had been detained. * * *

95. The Court received testimony which indicated that somewhere between 112 and 130 individuals were disappeared from 1981 to 1984. A former member of the Armed Forces testified that, according to a list in the files of Battalion 316, the number might be 140 or 150 * * *.

99. According to testimony on the *modus operandi* of the practice of disappearances, the kidnappers followed a pattern: they used automobiles with tinted glass (which requires a special permit from the Traffic Division), without license plates or with false plates, and sometimes used special disguises, such as wigs, false mustaches, masks, *etc.* The kidnappings were selective. The victims were first placed under surveillance, then the kidnapping was planned. Microbuses or vans were used. Some victims were taken from their homes; others were picked up in public streets. On one occasion, when a patrol car intervened, the kidnappers identified themselves as members of a special group of the Armed Forces and were permitted to leave with the victim * * *.

100. A former member of the Armed Forces, who said that he belonged to Battalion 316 (the group charged with carrying out the kidnappings) and that he had participated in some kidnappings, testified that the starting point was an order given by the chief of the unit to investigate an individual and place him under surveillance. According to this witness, if a decision was made to take further steps, the kidnapping was carried out by persons in civilian clothes using pseudonyms and disguises and carrying arms. The unit had four double-cabin Toyota pick-up trucks without police markings for use in kidnappings. Two of the pickups had tinted glass[.] * * *

103. The former member of the Armed Forces confirmed the existence of secret jails and of specially chosen places for the burial of those executed. He also related that there was a torture group and an interrogation group in his unit, and that he belonged to the latter. The torture group used electric shock, the water barrel and the "capucha." They kept the victims nude, without food, and threw cold water on them. He added that those selected for execution were handed over to a group of former prisoners, released from jail for carrying out executions, who used firearms at first and then knives and machetes * * *.

104. The current Director of Intelligence denied that the Armed Forces had secret jails, stating that it was not its *modus operandi*. He claimed that it was subversive elements who do have such jails, which they call "the peoples' prisons." He added that the function of an intelligence service is not to eliminate or disappear people, but rather to obtain and process information to allow the highest levels of government to make informed decisions * * *.

105. A Honduran officer, called as a witness by the Court, testified that the use of violence or psychological means to force a detainee to give information is prohibited * * *.

107. According to the testimony of his sister, eyewitnesses to the kidnapping of Manfredo Velásquez told her that he was detained on September 12, 1981, between 4:30 and 5:00 p.m., in a parking lot in downtown Tegucigalpa by seven heavily-armed men dressed in civilian clothes * * *.

108. This witness informed the Court that Col. Leonidas Torres Arias, who had been head of Honduran military intelligence, announced in a press conference in Mexico City that Manfredo Velásquez was kidnapped by a special squadron commanded by Capt. Alexander Hernández, who was carrying out the direct orders of General Gustavo Alvarez Martínez * * *.

109. Lt. Col. Hernández testified that he never received any order to detain Manfredo Velásquez and had never worked in police operations[.] * * *

113. The former member of the Armed Forces who claimed to have belonged to the group that carried out kidnappings told the Court that, although he did not take part in the kidnapping of Manfredo Velásquez, Lt. Flores Murillo had told him what had happened. According to this testimony, Manfredo Velásquez was kidnapped in downtown Tegucigalpa in an operation in which Sgt. José Isaías Vilorio, men using the pseudonyms Ezequiel and Titanio, and Lt. Flores Murillo himself, took part. The Lieutenant told him that during the struggle Ezequiel's gun went off and wounded Manfredo in the leg. They took the victim to INDUMIL (Military Industries) where they tortured him. They then turned him over to those in charge of carrying out executions who, at the orders of General Alvarez, Chief of the Armed Forces, took him out of Tegucigalpa and killed him with a knife and machete. They dismembered his body and buried the remains in different places[.]* * *

122. Before weighing the evidence, the Court must address some questions regarding the burden of proof and the general criteria considered in its evaluation and finding of the facts in the instant proceeding.

123. Because the Commission is accusing the Government of the disappearance of Manfredo Velásquez, it, in principle, should bear the burden of proving the facts underlying its petition.

124. The Commission's argument relies upon the proposition that the policy of disappearances, supported or tolerated by the Government, is designed to conceal and destroy evidence of disappearances. When the existence of such a policy or practice has been shown, the disappearance of a particular individual may be proved through circumstantial or indirect evidence or by logical inference. Otherwise, it would be impossible to prove that an individual has been disappeared.

125. The Government did not object to the Commission's approach. Nevertheless, it argued that neither the existence of a practice of disappearances in Honduras nor the participation of Honduran officials in the alleged disappearance of Manfredo Velásquez had been proven.

126. The Court finds no reason to consider the Commission's argument inadmissible. If it can be shown that there was an official practice of disappearances in Honduras, carried out by the Government or at least tolerated by it, and if the disappearance of Manfredo Velásquez can be linked to that practice, the Commission's allegations will have been proven to the Court's satisfaction, so long as the evidence presented on both points meets the standard of proof required in cases such as this. * * *

130. [The practice of international and domestic courts] shows that direct evidence, whether testimonial or documentary, is not the only type of evidence that may be legitimately considered in reaching a decision. Circumstantial evidence, indicia, and presumptions may be considered, so long as they lead to conclusions consistent with the facts.

131. Circumstantial or presumptive evidence is especially important in allegations of disappearances, because this type of repression is characterized by an attempt to suppress all information about the kidnapping or the whereabouts and fate of the victim. * * *

133. The above principle is generally valid in international proceedings, but is particularly applicable in human rights cases.

134. The international protection of human rights should not be confused with criminal justice. States do not appear before the Court as defendants in a criminal action. The objective of international human rights law is not to punish those individuals who are guilty of violations, but rather to protect the victims and to provide for the reparation of damages resulting from the acts of the States responsible.

135. In contrast to domestic criminal law, in proceedings to determine human rights violations the State cannot rely on the defense that the complainant has failed to present evidence when it cannot be obtained without the State's cooperation.

136. The State controls the means to verify acts occurring within its territory. Although the Commission has investigatory powers, it cannot exercise them within a State's jurisdiction unless it has the cooperation of that State.

137. Since the Government only offered some documentary evidence in support of its preliminary objections, but none on the merits, the Court must reach its decision without the valuable assistance of a more active participation by Honduras, which might otherwise have resulted in a more adequate presentation of its case.

138. The manner in which the Government conducted its defense would have sufficed to prove many of the Commission's allegations by virtue of the principle that the silence of the accused or elusive or ambiguous answers on its part may be interpreted as an acknowledgment of the truth of the allegations, so long as the contrary is not indicated by the record or is not compelled as a matter of law. This result would not hold under criminal law, which does not apply in the instant case (supra 134 and 135). The Court tried to compensate for this procedural principle by admitting all the evidence offered, even if it was untimely, and by ordering the presentation of additional evidence. This was done, of course, without prejudice to its discretion to consider the silence or inaction of Honduras or to its duty to evaluate the evidence as a whole. * * *

147. The Court now turns to the relevant facts that it finds to have been proven. They are as follows:

> "a. During the period 1981 to 1984, 100 to 150 persons disappeared in the Republic of Honduras, and many were never heard from again * * *;
>
> b. Those disappearances followed a similar pattern, beginning with the kidnapping of the victims by force, often in broad daylight and in public places, by armed men in civilian clothes and disguises, who acted with apparent impunity and who used vehicles without any official identification, with tinted windows and with false license plates or no plates * * *;
>
> c. It was public and notorious knowledge in Honduras that the kidnappings were carried out by military personnel or the police, or persons acting under their orders * * *;
>
> d. The disappearances were carried out in a systematic manner, regarding which the Court considers the following circumstances particularly relevant:
>
> > i. The victims were usually persons whom Honduran officials considered dangerous to State security * * *:
> >
> > ii. The arms employed were reserved for the official use of the military and police, and the vehicles used had tinted glass, which requires special official authorization. In some cases, Government agents carried out the detentions openly and without any pretense or disguise; in others, government agents had cleared the areas where the kidnappings were to take place and, on at least one occasion, when government agents stopped the kidnappers they were allowed to continue freely on their way after showing their identification * * *;
> >
> > iii. The kidnappers blindfolded the victims, took them to secret, unofficial detention centers and moved them from one

center to another. They interrogated the victims and subjected them to cruel and humiliating treatment and torture. Some were ultimately murdered and their bodies were buried in clandestine cemeteries * * *;

iv. When queried by relatives, lawyers and persons or entities interested in the protection of human rights, or by judges charged with executing writs of habeas corpus, the authorities systematically denied any knowledge of the detentions or the whereabouts or fate of the victims. That attitude was seen even in the cases of persons who later reappeared in the hands of the same authorities who had systematically denied holding them or knowing their fate * * *;

v. Military and police officials as well as those from the Executive and Judicial Branches either denied the disappearances or were incapable of preventing or investigating them, punishing those responsible, or helping those interested discover the whereabouts and fate of the victims or the location of their remains. The investigative committees created by the Government and the Armed Forces did not produce any results. The judicial proceedings brought were processed slowly with a clear lack of interest and some were ultimately dismissed * * *;

e. On September 12, 1981, between 4:30 and 5:00 p.m., several heavily-armed men in civilian clothes driving a white Ford without license plates kidnapped Manfredo Velásquez from a parking lot in downtown Tegucigalpa. Today, nearly seven years later, he remains disappeared, which creates a reasonable presumption that he is dead * * *;

f. Persons connected with the Armed Forces or under its direction carried out that kidnapping * * *;

g. The kidnapping and disappearance of Manfredo Velásquez falls within the systematic practice of disappearances referred to by the facts deemed proved in paragraphs a-d. To wit:

i. Manfredo Velásquez was a student who was involved in activities the authorities considered "dangerous" to national security * * *;

ii. The kidnapping of Manfredo Velásquez was carried out in broad daylight by men in civilian clothes who used a vehicle without license plates* * *;

iii. In the case of Manfredo Velásquez, there were the same type of denials by his captors and the Armed Forces, the same omissions of the latter and of the Government in investigating and revealing his whereabouts, and the same ineffectiveness of the courts where three writs of habeas corpus and two criminal complaints were brought * * *;

h. There is no evidence in the record that Manfredo Velásquez had disappeared in order to join subversive groups, other than a letter from the Mayor of Langue, which contained rumors to that effect. The letter itself shows that the Government associated him with activities it considered a threat to national security. However, the Government did not corroborate the view expressed in the letter with any other evidence. Nor is there any evidence that he was kidnapped by common criminals or other persons unrelated to the practice of disappearances existing at that time."

148. Based upon the above, the Court finds that the following facts have been proven in this proceeding: (1) a practice of disappearances carried out or tolerated by Honduran officials existed between 1981 and 1984; (2) Manfredo Velásquez disappeared at the hands of or with the acquiescence of those officials within the framework of that practice; and (3) the Government of Honduras failed to guarantee the human rights affected by that practice.

149. Disappearances are not new in the history of human rights violations. However, their systematic and repeated nature and their use not only for causing certain individuals to disappear, either briefly or permanently, but also as a means of creating a general state of anguish, insecurity and fear, is a recent phenomenon. Although this practice exists virtually worldwide, it has occurred with exceptional intensity in Latin America in the last few years.

150. The phenomenon of disappearances is a complex form of human rights violation that must be understood and confronted in an integral fashion.

151. The establishment of a Working Group on Enforced or Involuntary Disappearances of the United Nations Commission on Human Rights, by Resolution 20 (XXXVI) of February 29, 1980, is a clear demonstration of general censure and repudiation of the practice of disappearances, which had already received world attention at the UN General Assembly (Resolution 33/173 of December 20, 1978), the Economic and Social Council (Resolution 1979/38 of May 10, 1979) and the Subcommission for the Prevention of Discrimination and Protection of Minorities (Resolution 5B (XXXII) of September 5, 1979). The reports of the rapporteurs or special envoys of the Commission on Human Rights show concern that the practice of disappearances be stopped, the victims reappear and that those responsible be punished.

152. Within the inter-American system, the General Assembly of the Organization of American States (OAS) and the Commission have repeatedly referred to the practice of disappearances and have urged that disappearances be investigated and that the practice be stopped * * *.

153. International practice and doctrine have often categorized disappearances as a crime against humanity, although there is no treaty in force which is applicable to the States Parties to the Convention and which uses this terminology (Inter-American Yearbook on Human Rights, 1985, pp. 368, 686 and 1102). The General Assembly of the OAS has resolved that it "is an affront to the conscience of the hemisphere and constitutes a crime against humanity" (AG/RES.666, *supra*) and that "this practice is cruel and inhuman, mocks the rule of law, and undermines those norms which guarantee protection against arbitrary detention and the right to personal security and safety" (AG/RES.742, *supra*).

154. Without question, the State has the right and duty to guarantee its security. It is also indisputable that all societies suffer some deficiencies in their legal orders. However, regardless of the seriousness of certain actions and the culpability of the perpetrators of certain crimes, the power of the State is not unlimited, nor may the State resort to any means to attain its ends. The State is subject to law and morality. Disrespect for human dignity cannot serve as the basis for any State action.

155. The forced disappearance of human beings is a multiple and continuous violation of many rights under the Convention that the States Parties are obligated to respect and guarantee. The kidnapping of a person is an arbitrary deprivation of liberty, an infringement of a detainee's right to be taken without delay before a judge and to invoke the appropriate procedures to review the legality of the arrest, all in violation of Article 7 of the Convention * * *.

156. Moreover, prolonged isolation and deprivation of communication are in themselves cruel and inhuman treatment, harmful to the psychological and moral integrity of the person and a violation of the right of any detainee to respect for his inherent dignity as a human being. Such treatment, therefore, violates Article 5 of the Convention, which recognizes the right to the integrity of the person * * *.

157. The practice of disappearances often involves secret execution without trial, followed by concealment of the body to eliminate any material evidence of the crime and to ensure the impunity of those responsible. This is a flagrant violation of the right to life, recognized in Article 4 of the Convention * * *.

158. The practice of disappearances, in addition to directly violating many provisions of the Convention, such as those noted above, constitutes a radical breach of the treaty in that it shows a crass abandonment of the values which emanate from the concept of human dignity and of the most

basic principles of the inter-American system and the Convention. The existence of this practice, more over, evinces a disregard of the duty to organize the State in such a manner as to guarantee the rights recognized in the Convention, as set out below.

159. The Commission has asked the Court to find that Honduras has violated the rights guaranteed to Manfredo Velasquez by Articles 4, 5 and 7 of the Convention. The Government has denied the charges and seeks to be absolved.

160. This requires the Court to examine the conditions under which a particular act, which violates one of the rights recognized by the Convention, can be imputed to a State Party thereby establishing its international responsibility.

161. Article 1(1) of the Convention provides:

> Article 1. Obligation to Respect Rights. The States Parties to this Convention undertake to respect the rights and freedoms recognized herein and to ensure to all persons subject to their jurisdiction the free and full exercise of those rights and freedoms, without any discrimination for reasons of race, color, sex, language, religion, political or other opinion, national or social origin, economic status, birth, or any other social condition.

162. This article specifies the obligation assumed by the States Parties in relation to each of the rights protected. Each claim alleging that one of those rights has been infringed necessarily implies that Article 1(1) of the Convention has also been violated. * * *

164. Article 1(1) is essential in determining whether a violation of the human rights recognized by the Convention can be imputed to a State Party. In effect, that article charges the States Parties with the fundamental duty to respect and guarantee the rights recognized in the Convention. Any impairment of those rights which can be attributed under the rules of international law to the action or omission of any public authority constitutes an act imputable to the State, which assumes responsibility in the terms provided by the Convention.

165. The first obligation assumed by the States Parties under Article 1(1) is "to respect the rights and freedoms" recognized by the Convention. The exercise of public authority has certain limits which derive from the fact that human rights are inherent attributes of human dignity and are, therefore, superior to the power of the State* * *.

166. The second obligation of the States Parties is to "ensure" the free and full exercise of the rights recognized by the Convention to every person subject to its jurisdiction. This obligation implies the duty of the States Parties to organize the governmental apparatus and, in general, all the structures through which public power is exercised, so that they are

capable of juridically ensuring the free and full enjoyment of human rights. As a consequence of this obligation, the States must prevent, investigate and punish any violation of the rights recognized by the Convention and, moreover, if possible attempt to restore the right violated and provide compensation as warranted for damages resulting from the violation.

167. The obligation to ensure the free and full exercise of human rights is not fulfilled by the existence of a legal system designed to make it possible to comply with this obligation—it also requires the government to conduct itself so as to effectively ensure the free and full exercise of human rights. * * *

169. According to Article 1(1), any exercise of public power that violates the rights recognized by the Convention is illegal. Whenever a State organ, official or public entity violates one of those rights, this constitutes a failure of the duty to respect the rights and freedoms set forth in the Convention.

170. This conclusion is independent of whether the organ or official has contravened provisions of internal law or overstepped the limits of his authority: under international law a State is responsible for the acts of its agents undertaken in their official capacity and for their omissions, even when those agents act outside the sphere of their authority or violate internal law.

171. This principle suits perfectly the nature of the Convention, which is violated whenever public power is used to infringe the rights recognized therein. If acts of public power that exceed the State's authority or are illegal under its own laws were not considered to compromise that State's obligation under the treaty, the system of protection provided for in the Convention would be illusory.

172. *Thus, in principle, any violation of rights recognized by the Convention carried out by an act of public authority or by persons who use their position of authority is imputable to the State. However, this does not define all the circumstances in which a State is obligated to prevent, investigate and punish human rights violations, nor all the cases in which the State might be found responsible for an infringement of those rights. An illegal act which violates human rights and which is initially not directly imputable to a State (for example, because it is the act of a private person or because the person responsible has not been identified) can lead to international responsibility of the State, not because of the act itself, but because of the lack of due diligence to prevent the violation or to respond to it as required by the Convention.*

173. Violations of the Convention cannot be founded upon rules that take psychological factors into account in establishing individual culpability. For the purposes of analysis, the intent or motivation of the agent who has violated the rights recognized by the Convention is

irrelevant—the violation can be established even if the identity of the individual perpetrator is unknown. What is decisive is whether a violation of the rights recognized by the Convention has occurred with the support or the acquiescence of the government, or whether the State has allowed the act to take place without taking measures to prevent it or to punish those responsible. Thus, the Court's task is to determine whether the violation is the result of a State's failure to fulfill its duty to respect and guarantee those rights, as required by Article 1(1) of the Convention.

174. The State has a legal duty to take reasonable steps to prevent human rights violations and to use the means at its disposal to carry out a serious investigation of violations committed within its jurisdiction, to identify those responsible, to impose the appropriate punishment and to ensure the victim adequate compensation.

175. This duty to prevent includes all those means of a legal, political, administrative and cultural nature that promote the protection of human rights and ensure that any violations are considered and treated as illegal acts, which, as such, may lead to the punishment of those responsible and the obligation to indemnify the victims for damages. It is not possible to make a detailed list of all such measures, since they vary with the law and the conditions of each State Party. Of course, while the State is obligated to prevent human rights abuses, the existence of a particular violation does not, in itself, prove the failure to take preventive measures. On the other hand, subjecting a person to official, repressive bodies that practice torture and assassination with impunity is itself a breach of the duty to prevent violations of the rights to life and physical integrity of the person, even if that particular person is not tortured or assassinated, or if those facts cannot be proven in a concrete case.

176. The State is obligated to investigate every situation involving a violation of the rights protected by the Convention. If the State apparatus acts in such a way that the violation goes unpunished and the victim's full enjoyment of such rights is not restored as soon as possible, the State has failed to comply with its duty to ensure the free and full exercise of those rights to the persons within its jurisdiction. The same is true when the State allows private persons or groups to act freely and with impunity to the detriment of the rights recognized by the Convention.

177. In certain circumstances, it may be difficult to investigate acts that violate an individual's rights. The duty to investigate, like the duty to prevent, is not breached merely because the investigation does not produce a satisfactory result. Nevertheless, it must be undertaken in a serious manner and not as a mere formality preordained to be ineffective. An investigation must have an objective and be assumed by the State as its own legal duty, not as a step taken by private interests that depends upon the initiative of the victim or his family or upon their offer of proof, without an effective search for the truth by the government. This is true regardless

of what agent is eventually found responsible for the violation. Where the acts of private parties that violate the Convention are not seriously investigated, those parties are aided in a sense by the government, thereby making the State responsible on the international plane.

178. In the instant case, the evidence shows a complete inability of the procedures of the State of Honduras, which were theoretically adequate, to carry out an investigation into the disappearance of Manfredo Velásquez, and of the fulfillment of its duties to pay compensation and punish those responsible, as set out in Article 1(1) of the Convention.

179. As the Court has verified above, the failure of the judicial system to act upon the writs brought before various tribunals in the instant case has been proven. Not one writ of habeas corpus was processed. No judge had access to the places where Manfredo Velasquez might have been detained. The criminal complaint was dismissed.

180. Nor did the organs of the Executive Branch carry out a serious investigation to establish the fate of Manfredo Velasquez. There was no investigation of public allegations of a practice of disappearances nor a determination of whether Manfredo Velásquez had been a victim of that practice. The Commission's requests for information were ignored to the point that the Commission had to presume, under Article 42 of its Regulations, that the allegations were true. The offer of an investigation in accord with Resolution 30/83 of the Commission resulted in an investigation by the Armed Forces, the same body accused of direct responsibility for the disappearances. This raises grave questions regarding the seriousness of the investigation. The Government often resorted to asking relatives of the victims to present conclusive proof of their allegations even though those allegations, because they involved crimes against the person, should have been investigated on the Government's own initiative in fulfillment of the State's duty to ensure public order. This is especially true when the allegations refer to a practice carried out within the Armed Forces, which, because of its nature, is not subject to private investigations. No proceeding was initiated to establish responsibility for the disappearance of Manfredo Velásquez and apply punishment under internal law. All of the above leads to the conclusion that the Honduran authorities did not take effective action to ensure respect for human rights within the jurisdiction of that State as required by Article 1(1) of the Convention.

181. The duty to investigate facts of this type continues as long as there is uncertainty about the fate of the person who has disappeared. Even in the hypothetical case that those individually responsible for crimes of this type cannot be legally punished under certain circumstances, the State is obligated to use the means at its disposal to inform the relatives of the fate of the victims and, if they have been killed, the location of their remains.

182. The Court is convinced, and has so found, that the disappearance of Manfredo Velásquez was carried out by agents who acted under cover of public authority. However, even had that fact not been proven, the failure of the State apparatus to act, which is clearly proven, is a failure on the part of Honduras to fulfill the duties it assumed under Article 1(1) of the Convention, which obligated it to ensure Manfredo Velásquez the free and full exercise of his human rights.

183. The Court notes that the legal order of Honduras does not authorize such acts and that internal law defines them as crimes. The Court also recognizes that not all levels of the Government of Honduras were necessarily aware of those acts, nor is there any evidence that such acts were the result of official orders. Nevertheless, those circumstances are irrelevant for the purposes of establishing whether Honduras is responsible under international law for the violations of human rights perpetrated within the practice of disappearances.

184. According to the principle of the continuity of the State in international law, responsibility exists both independently of changes of government over a period of time and continuously from the time of the act that creates responsibility to the time when the act is declared illegal. The foregoing is also valid in the area of human rights although, from an ethical or political point of view, the attitude of the new government may be much more respectful of those rights than that of the government in power when the violations occurred.

185. The Court, therefore, concludes that the facts found in this proceeding show that the State of Honduras is responsible for the involuntary disappearance of Angel Manfredo Velásquez Rodríguez. Thus, Honduras has violated Articles 7, 5 and 4 of the Convention.

NOTES AND QUESTIONS

1. *Is sovereignty necessarily lawless?* The *Lotus* Case, cited in the introduction to this chapter, involved a deadly accident on the high seas involving a French-flagged ship, the *Lotus*, and a Turkish-flagged ship, the *Boz-Kourt*. Over the French government's protest, Turkey prosecuted the French officer-of-the-watch under Turkish law for criminal negligence. The case wended its way to the Permanent Court of International Justice ("PCIJ"), the judicial arm of the League of Nations, which had to decide whether Turkey's actions violated principles of international law.

The Court ruled that Turkey did not have to find permission at international law to apply its law to these extraterritorial actions. Restrictions on sovereignty cannot be presumed, and, the prosecution had to be considered legal unless France could find an international prohibition on Turkey's actions.

Although there had been few prosecutions in these circumstances over the centuries, the Court found no customary prohibition on them:

> Even if the rarity of the judicial decisions to be found among the reported cases were sufficient to prove the circumstance alleged by the French government, it would merely show that States had often, in practice, abstained from instituting criminal proceedings, and not that they recognized themselves as being obliged to do so; *for only if such abstention were based on their being conscious of a duty to abstain would it be possible to speak of an international custom*. The alleged fact does not allow one to infer that states have been conscious of having such a duty. * * *

Case of the S.S. Lotus, [1927] P.C.I.J., ser. A, No. 10, at 28 (emphasis added).

International law understood this way preserves power and discretion for governments: those who object to a government's action under international law must find a prohibitory rule there. France found no such prohibition in international law, and so Turkey was allowed to criminalize the French officer's conduct on a French-flag vessel on the high seas. The *Lotus* case illustrates the difficulties of such a showing, especially the proof of *opinio juris*—in this case states behaving in a patterned way while "being conscious of a duty" to do so.

Significant as that is standing alone, the case also illustrates the use of an international judiciary to settle disputes between sovereigns who consent to its jurisdiction and respect its judgments. And considered in light of the subsequent evolution of flag-state jurisdiction, *Lotus* establishes that one incident of sovereignty is the power to give it away by treaty; indeed, although France lost its argument that only the flag state has jurisdiction over crimes committed on board its vessels, that very principle was later codified in the Convention on the High Seas, Apr. 29, 1958, 13 U.S.T. 2312, 450 U.N.T.S. 11, at Art. 11(1), and the Law of the Sea Convention, Dec. 10, 1982, 1833 U.N.T.S. 3, at Art. 97.

Since 1927, states have broadly exercised their sovereignty by constraining it, *i.e.*, by finding common ground in a range of areas and declared their mutual self-interest through treaties. Today, there is virtually no area of legal practice that remains untouched by treaties: private investment abroad; intellectual and cultural property; the rights of workers and prisoners; international crimes; environmental protection; arms control and the use of force; borders; gender and race discrimination. Treaties set the conditions for international trade and telecommunications, establish uniform rules for wills and trusts and bankruptcy proceedings, limit the testing of nuclear weapons, provide for the transnational service of process, and establish the basis for the international air transportation industry. Treaties are not self-enforcing of course, and there is always a question how treaty violations will be handled, but, taken as a whole, sovereignty routinely subjects itself to law. That these limits are not exclusively in contractual or treaty form is clear from the *Filártiga* case below.

2. *A "reverse Nuremberg" and the rise of states' due diligence requirement.* After World War II, the International Military Tribunal at Nuremberg declared that international wrongs are committed by individual people—criminals—and not by abstractions like the "state." But the Inter-American Court of Human Rights, like other regional human rights courts in Europe and Africa, was established to hold *governments* accountable for violations of international law. *Velásquez-Rodríguez* is significant because it found Honduras responsible for the disappearance at issue, even in the absence of any direct evidence implicating the Honduran government. Instead, the government's responsibility lay in its failure to exercise due diligence in the investigation of the allegations that persons acting under color of its authority had kidnapped and killed Velasquez. *See* ¶ 172, *supra.* The case was considered revolutionary at the time because it suggested that a government might be liable if it systematically failed to investigate and prosecute violations of the law in the "private" realm. *See also Osman v. United Kingdom*, in which the European Court of Human Rights held that state authorities have a "positive obligation * * * to take preventive operational measures to protect an individual whose life is at risk from the criminal acts of another individual." 1998-VIII Eur. Ct. H.R. (1998).

For example, post-*Velásquez*, a government's systemic failure to prosecute domestic violence and other forms of gender violence would constitute a violation of its obligation to protect the human rights of the victims and survivors. *See* Committee on the Elimination of Discrimination Against Women, *General Recommendation 19*, U.N. Doc. No. A/47/38 (1992). What were the Court's analytical steps, especially with respect to the definition of the wrong and the burdens of proof? Equally important, where did the Court find the textual basis for its holding? More abstractly but perhaps most important, how does the decision suggest that state sovereignty—the legal right to be left alone—is not now what it once was?

3. *A little skepticism about skepticism.* One view of international law is that governments obey international law only when it is in their self-interest to do so. In short, there are no non-instrumental reasons for complying with international norms. *See, e.g.*, JACK GOLDSMITH & ERIC POSNER, THE LIMITS OF INTERNATIONAL LAW (2005). Especially with respect to the asserted legal limits on the international use of force,[3] the law may look like some utopian hallucination. But of course, international law takes many forms, not just purported limits on the use of military force, and, if the skepticism were fully justified or entirely persuasive, much of modern international life would be completely inexplicable. For example, the government of Honduras ultimately complied with the judgment in *Velásquez-Rodríguez* and paid compensation to the family. If the "non-instrumental reasons" for doing so include good public relations or better international relations with the other members of the Organization of American States, or rough humanitarianism, or even some

[3] *See, e.g.*, Article 2(4) of the United Nations Charter: "All Members [of the United Nations] shall refrain in their international relations from the threat or use of force against the territorial integrity or political independence of any state, or in any other manner inconsistent with the Purposes of the United Nations."

politically-motivated respect for the rule of law, then the very notion of self-interest may have become so elastic as to lose its exclusively Machiavellian meanings. And why would Honduras—or any country—sign on to the American Convention on Human Rights—or any human rights treaty—in the first place? How might the hypocrisy of governments actually be a useful, even an essential, thing for human rights activists?

B. CUSTOMARY INTERNATIONAL LAW IN DOMESTIC COURTS

FILÁRTIGA V. PENA-IRALA

630 F.2d 876 (2d Cir. 1980)

KAUFMAN, J. Upon ratification of the Constitution, the thirteen former colonies were fused into a single nation, one which, in its relations with foreign states, is bound both to observe and construe the accepted norms of international law, formerly known as the law of nations. Under the Articles of Confederation, the several states had interpreted and applied this body of doctrine as a part of their common law, but with the founding of the "more perfect Union" of 1789, the law of nations became preeminently a federal concern.

Implementing the constitutional mandate for national control over foreign relations, the First Congress established original district court jurisdiction over "all causes where an alien sues for a tort only [committed] in violation of the law of nations." Judiciary Act of 1789, * * * codified at 28 U.S.C. § 1350. Construing this rarely invoked provision, we hold that deliberate torture perpetrated under color of official authority violates universally accepted norms of the international law of human rights, regardless of the nationality of the parties. Thus, whenever an alleged torturer is found and served with process by an alien within our borders, § 1350 provides federal jurisdiction. Accordingly, we reverse the judgment of the district court dismissing the complaint for want of federal jurisdiction.

I

The appellants, plaintiffs below, are citizens of the Republic of Paraguay. Dr. Joel Filártiga, a physician, describes himself as a longstanding opponent of the government of President Alfredo Stroessner, which has held power in Paraguay since 1954. His daughter, Dolly Filártiga, arrived in the United States in 1978 under a visitor's visa, and has since applied for permanent political asylum. The Filártigas brought this action in the Eastern District of New York against Americo Norberto Pena-Irala (Pena), also a citizen of Paraguay, for wrongfully causing the death of Dr. Filártiga's seventeen-year old son, Joelito. Because the district court dismissed the action for want of subject matter jurisdiction, we must accept as true the allegations contained in the Filártigas' complaint and affidavits for purposes of this appeal.

The appellants contend that on March 29, 1976, Joelito Filártiga was kidnapped and tortured to death by Pena, who was then Inspector General of Police in Asuncion, Paraguay. Later that day, the police brought Dolly Filártiga to Pena's home where she was confronted with the body of her brother, which evidenced marks of severe torture. As she fled, horrified, from the house, Pena followed after her shouting, "Here you have what you have been looking for for so long and what you deserve. Now shut up." The Filártigas claim that Joelito was tortured and killed in retaliation for his father's political activities and beliefs.

Shortly thereafter, Dr. Filártiga commenced a criminal action in the Paraguayan courts against Pena and the police for the murder of his son. As a result, Dr. Filártiga's attorney was arrested and brought to police headquarters where, shackled to a wall, Pena threatened him with death. This attorney, it is alleged, has since been disbarred without just cause.

During the course of the Paraguayan criminal proceeding, which is apparently still pending after four years, another man, Hugo Duarte, confessed to the murder. Duarte, who was a member of the Pena household, claimed that he had discovered his wife and Joelito *in flagrante delicto*, and that the crime was one of passion. The Filártigas have submitted a photograph of Joelito's corpse showing injuries they believe refute this claim. Dolly Filártiga, moreover, has stated that she will offer evidence of three independent autopsies demonstrating that her brother's death "was the result of professional methods of torture." Despite his confession, Duarte, we are told, has never been convicted or sentenced in connection with the crime.

In July of 1978, Pena * * * entered the United States under a visitor's visa. He was accompanied by Juana Bautista Fernandez Villalba, who had lived with him in Paraguay. The couple remained in the United States beyond the term of their visas, and were living in Brooklyn, New York, when Dolly Filártiga, who was then living in Washington, D. C., learned of their presence. Acting on information provided by Dolly the Immigration and Naturalization Service arrested Pena and his companion, both of whom were subsequently ordered deported . . . following a hearing. They had then resided in the United States for more than nine months.

Almost immediately, Dolly caused Pena to be served with a summons and civil complaint at the Brooklyn Navy Yard, where he was being held pending deportation. The complaint alleged that Pena had wrongfully caused Joelito's death by torture and sought compensatory and punitive damages of $10,000,000. The Filártigas also sought to enjoin Pena's deportation to ensure his availability for testimony at trial. The cause of action is stated as arising under "wrongful death statutes; the U. N.

Charter; the Universal Declaration on Human Rights; the U.N. Declaration Against Torture; the American Declaration of the Rights and Duties of Man; and other pertinent declarations, documents and practices constituting the customary international law of human rights and the law of nations," as well as 28 U.S.C. § 1350, Article II, sec. 2, and the Supremacy Clause of the U.S. Constitution. Jurisdiction is claimed under the general federal question provision, 28 U.S.C. § 1331 and, principally on this appeal, under the Alien Tort Statute, 28 U.S.C. § 1350.

Judge Nickerson stayed the order of deportation, and Pena immediately moved to dismiss the complaint on the grounds that subject matter jurisdiction was absent and for *forum non conveniens*. On the jurisdictional issue, there has been no suggestion that Pena claims diplomatic immunity from suit. The Filártigas submitted the affidavits of a number of distinguished international legal scholars, who stated unanimously that the law of nations prohibits absolutely the use of torture as alleged in the complaint.[4] Pena, in support of his motion to dismiss on the ground of *forum non conveniens*, submitted the affidavit of his Paraguayan counsel, * * * who averred that Paraguayan law provides a full and adequate civil remedy for the wrong alleged. Dr. Filártiga has not commenced such an action, however, believing that further resort to the courts of his own country would be futile.

Judge Nickerson heard argument on the motion to dismiss . . ., and . . . dismissed the complaint on jurisdictional grounds. The district judge recognized the strength of appellants' argument that official torture violates an emerging norm of customary international law. Nonetheless, he felt constrained by dicta contained in two recent opinions of this Court, *Dreyfus v. von Finck,* 534 F.2d 24 (2d Cir.), *cert. denied*, 429 U.S. 835 (1976); *IIT v. Vencap, Ltd.,* 519 F.2d 1001 (2d Cir. 1975), to construe narrowly "the law of nations," as employed in § 1350, as excluding that law which governs a state's treatment of its own citizens. * * * Shortly thereafter, Pena and his companion returned to Paraguay.

II

Appellants rest their principal argument in support of federal jurisdiction upon the Alien Tort Statute, 28 U.S.C. § 1350, which provides:

---

[4] Richard Falk, the Albert G. Milbank Professor of International Law and Practice at Princeton University, and a former Vice President of the American Society of International Law, avers that, in his judgment, "it is now beyond reasonable doubt that torture of a person held in detention that results in severe harm or death is a violation of the law of nations." Thomas Franck, professor of international law at New York University and Director of the New York University Center for International Studies offers his opinion that torture has now been rejected by virtually all nations, although it was once commonly used to extract confessions. Richard Lillich, the Howard W. Smith Professor of Law at the University of Virginia School of Law, concludes, after a lengthy review of the authorities, that officially perpetrated torture is "a violation of international law (formerly called the law of nations)." Finally, Myres MacDougal, a former Sterling Professor of Law at the Yale Law School, and a past President of the American Society of International Law, states that torture is an offense against the law of nations, and that "it has long been recognized that such offenses vitally affect relations between states."

"The district courts shall have original jurisdiction of any civil action by an alien for a tort only, committed in violation of the law of nations or a treaty of the United States." Since appellants do not contend that their action arises directly under a treaty of the United States, a threshold question on the jurisdictional issue is whether the conduct alleged violates the law of nations. In light of the universal condemnation of torture in numerous international agreements, and the renunciation of torture as an instrument of official policy by virtually all of the nations of the world (in principle if not in practice), we find that an act of torture committed by a state official against one held in detention violates established norms of the international law of human rights, and hence the law of nations.

The Supreme Court has enumerated the appropriate sources of international law. The law of nations "may be ascertained by consulting the works of jurists, writing professedly on public law; or by the general usage and practice of nations; or by judicial decisions recognizing and enforcing that law." *United States v. Smith,* 18 U.S. (5 Wheat.) 153, 160–61 (1820). * * * In *Smith*, a statute proscribing "the crime of piracy [on the high seas] as defined by the law of nations," was held sufficiently determinate in meaning to afford the basis for a death sentence. The *Smith* Court discovered among the works of Lord Bacon, Grotius, Bochard and other commentators a genuine consensus that rendered the crime "sufficiently and constitutionally defined."

The Paquete Habana, 175 U.S. 677 (1900), reaffirmed that

> where there is no treaty, and no controlling executive or legislative act or judicial decision, resort must be had to the customs and usages of civilized nations; and, as evidence of these, to the works of jurists and commentators, who by years of labor, research and experience, have made themselves peculiarly well acquainted with the subjects of which they treat. Such works are resorted to by judicial tribunals, not for the speculations of their authors concerning what the law ought to be, but for trustworthy evidence of what the law really is.

Id. at 700. Modern international sources confirm the propriety of this approach [citing the Statute of the International Court of Justice, art. 38, *supra*].

Habana is particularly instructive for present purposes, for it held that the traditional prohibition against seizure of an enemy's coastal fishing vessels during wartime, a standard that began as one of comity only, had ripened over the preceding century into "a settled rule of international law" by "the general assent of civilized nations." Thus it is clear that courts must interpret international law not as it was in 1789, but as it has evolved and exists among the nations of the world today.

The requirement that a rule command the "general assent of civilized nations" to become binding upon them all is a stringent one. Were this not so, the courts of one nation might feel free to impose idiosyncratic legal rules upon others, in the name of applying international law. Thus, in *Banco Nacional de Cuba v. Sabbatino,* 376 U.S. 398 (1964), the Court declined to pass on the validity of the Cuban government's expropriation of a foreign-owned corporation's assets, noting the sharply conflicting views on the issue propounded by the capital-exporting, capital-importing, socialist and capitalist nations.

The case at bar presents us with a situation diametrically opposed to the conflicted state of law that confronted the *Sabbatino* Court. Indeed, to paraphrase that Court's statement, *id.* at 428, there are few, if any, issues in international law today on which opinion seems to be so united as the limitations on a state's power to torture persons held in its custody.

The United Nations Charter (a treaty of the United States) makes it clear that in this modern age a state's treatment of its own citizens is a matter of international concern. It provides:

> With a view to the creation of conditions of stability and wellbeing which are necessary for peaceful and friendly relations among nations . . . the United Nations shall promote . . . universal respect for, and observance of, human rights and fundamental freedoms for all without distinctions as to race, sex, language or religion.

Id., Art. 55. And further:

> All members pledge themselves to take joint and separate action in cooperation with the Organization for the achievement of the purposes set forth in Article 55.

Id., Art. 56.

* * * While this broad mandate has been held not to be wholly self-executing, *Hitai v. Immigration and Naturalization Service,* 343 F.2d 466, 468 (2d Cir. 1965), this observation alone does not end our inquiry.[9] For although there is no universal agreement as to the precise extent of the "human rights and fundamental freedoms" guaranteed to all by the Charter, there is at present no dissent from the view that the guaranties include, at a bare minimum, the right to be free from torture. This prohibition has become part of customary international law, as evidenced and defined by the Universal Declaration of Human Rights, General

[9] We observe that this Court has previously utilized the U.N. Charter and the Charter of the Organization of American States, another non-self-executing agreement, as evidence of binding principles of international law. *See United States v. Toscanino,* 500 F.2d 267 (2d Cir. 1974). In that case, our government's duty under international law to refrain from kidnapping a criminal defendant from within the borders of another nation, where formal extradition procedures existed, infringed the personal rights of the defendant, whose international law claims were thereupon remanded for a hearing in the district court.

Assembly Resolution 217 (III)(A) (Dec. 10, 1948) which states, in the plainest of terms, "no one shall be subjected to torture."[10] The General Assembly has declared that the Charter precepts embodied in this Universal Declaration "constitute basic principles of international law." G.A.Res. 2625 (XXV) (Oct. 24, 1970).

Particularly relevant is the Declaration on the Protection of All Persons from Being Subjected to Torture, General Assembly Resolution 3452, 30 U.N. GAOR Supp. (No. 34) 91, U.N.Doc. A/1034 (1975). * * * The Declaration expressly prohibits any state from permitting the dastardly and totally inhuman act of torture. Torture, in turn, is defined as "any act by which severe pain and suffering, whether physical or mental, is intentionally inflicted by or at the instigation of a public official on a person for such purposes as ... intimidating him or other persons." The Declaration goes on to provide that "[w]here it is proved that an act of torture or other cruel, inhuman or degrading treatment or punishment has been committed by or at the instigation of a public official, the victim shall be afforded redress and compensation, in accordance with national law." This Declaration, like the Declaration of Human Rights before it, was adopted without dissent by the General Assembly. * * *

These U.N. declarations are significant because they specify with great precision the obligations of member nations under the Charter. Since their adoption, "[m]embers can no longer contend that they do not know what human rights they promised in the Charter to promote." * * * Sohn, "A Short History of United Nations Documents on Human Rights," in THE UNITED NATIONS AND HUMAN RIGHTS, 18th Report of the Commission (Commission to Study the Organization of Peace ed. 1968). Moreover, a U.N. Declaration is, according to one authoritative definition, "a formal and solemn instrument, suitable for rare occasions when principles of great and lasting importance are being enunciated." 34 U.N. ESCOR, Supp. (No. 8) 15, U.N. Doc. E/cn.4/1/610 (1962) (memorandum of Office of Legal Affairs, U.N. Secretariat). Accordingly, it has been observed that the Universal Declaration of Human Rights "no longer fits into the dichotomy of 'binding treaty' against 'nonbinding pronouncement,' but is rather an authoritative statement of the international community." E. SCHWELB, HUMAN RIGHTS AND THE INTERNATIONAL COMMUNITY 70 (1964). Thus, a Declaration creates an expectation of adherence, and "insofar as the expectation is gradually justified by State practice, a declaration may by custom become recognized as laying down rules binding upon the States." 34 U.N. ESCOR, *supra*. Indeed, several commentators have concluded that the Universal Declaration has become, *in toto*, a part of binding, customary international law. * * *

---

[10] Eighteen nations have incorporated the Universal Declaration into their own constitutions. 48 REVUE INTERNATIONALE DE DROIT PENAL Nos. 3 & 4, at 211 (1977).

Turning to the act of torture, we have little difficulty discerning its universal renunciation in the modern usage and practice of nations. The international consensus surrounding torture has found expression in numerous international treaties and accords [*citing* the American Convention on Human Rights, Art. 5, ("No one shall be subjected to torture or to cruel, inhuman or degrading punishment or treatment"); the International Covenant on Civil and Political Rights, (identical language); the European Convention for the Protection of Human Rights and Fundamental Freedoms, Art. 3, (*semble*)]. The substance of these international agreements is reflected in modern municipal, *i.e.*, national law as well. Although torture was once a routine concomitant of criminal interrogations in many nations, during the modern and hopefully more enlightened era it has been universally renounced. According to one survey, torture is prohibited, expressly or implicitly, by the constitutions of over fifty-five nations, including both the United States and Paraguay. Our State Department reports a general recognition of this principle:

> There now exists an international consensus that recognizes basic human rights and obligations owed by all governments to their citizens. . . . There is no doubt that these rights are often violated; but virtually all governments acknowledge their validity.

Department of State, COUNTRY REPORTS ON HUMAN RIGHTS FOR 1979, at 1. We have been directed to no assertion by any contemporary state of a right to torture its own or another nation's citizens. Indeed, United States diplomatic contacts confirm the universal abhorrence with which torture is viewed:

> In exchanges between United States embassies and all foreign states with which the United States maintains relations, it has been the Department of State's general experience that no government has asserted a right to torture its own nationals. Where reports of torture elicit some credence, a state usually responds by denial or, less frequently, by asserting that the conduct was unauthorized or constituted rough treatment short of torture.[15]

Memorandum of the United States as Amicus Curiae at 16.

Having examined the sources from which customary international law is derived, the usage of nations, judicial opinions and the works of jurists,[16]

---

15 The fact that the prohibition of torture is often honored in the breach does not diminish its binding effect as a norm of international law. As one commentator has put it, "The best evidence for the existence of international law is that every actual State recognizes that it does exist and that it is itself under an obligation to observe it. States often violate international law, just as individuals often violate municipal law; but no more than individuals do States defend their violations by claiming that they are above the law." J. BRIERLY, THE OUTLOOK FOR INTERNATIONAL LAW 45 (Oxford 1944).

16 *See* note 4, *supra*: *see also Ireland v. United Kingdom*, Judgment of Jan. 18, 1978 (European Court of Human Rights) (holding that Britain's subjection of prisoners to sleep deprivation, hooding, exposure to hissing noise, reduced diet and standing against a wall for hours

we conclude that official torture is now prohibited by the law of nations. The prohibition is clear and unambiguous, and admits of no distinction between treatment of aliens and citizens. Accordingly, we must conclude that the dictum in *Dreyfus v. von Finck, supra,* * * * to the effect that "violations of international law do not occur when the aggrieved parties are nationals of the acting state," is clearly out of tune with the current usage and practice of international law. The treaties and accords cited above, as well as the express foreign policy of our own government,[17] all make it clear that international law confers fundamental rights upon all people *vis-a-vis* their own governments. While the ultimate scope of those rights will be a subject for continuing refinement and elaboration, we hold that the right to be free from torture is now among them. We therefore turn to the question whether the other requirements for jurisdiction are met.

III

Appellee submits that even if the tort alleged is a violation of modern international law, federal jurisdiction may not be exercised consistent with the dictates of Article III of the Constitution. The claim is without merit. Common law courts of general jurisdiction regularly adjudicate transitory tort claims between individuals over whom they exercise personal jurisdiction, wherever the tort occurred. Moreover, as part of an articulated scheme of federal control over external affairs, Congress provided, in the first Judiciary Act, § 9(b), * * * for federal jurisdiction over suits by aliens where principles of international law are in issue. The constitutional basis for the Alien Tort Statute is the law of nations, which has always been part of the federal common law.

It is not extraordinary for a court to adjudicate a tort claim arising outside of its territorial jurisdiction. A state or nation has a legitimate interest in the orderly resolution of disputes among those within its borders, and where the *lex loci delicti commissi* [the law of the place where the wrong was committed] is applied, it is an expression of comity to give effect to the laws of the state where the wrong occurred. Thus, Lord Mansfield in *Mostyn v. Fabrigas, 1 Cowp.* 161 (1774), *quoted in McKenna v. Fisk,* 42 U.S. (1 How.) 241, 248 (1843), said:

> If A becomes indebted to B, or commits a tort upon his person or upon his personal property in Paris, an action in either case may be maintained against A in England, if he is there found. . . . As

was "inhuman and degrading," but not "torture" within meaning of European Convention on Human Rights).

[17] *E.g.*, 22 U.S.C. § 2304(a)(2) ("Except under circumstances specified in this section, no security assistance may be provided to any country the government of which engages in a consistent pattern of gross violations of internationally recognized human rights."); 22 U.S.C. § 2151(a). ("The Congress finds that fundamental political, economic, and technological changes have resulted in the interdependence of nations. The Congress declares that the individual liberties, economic prosperity, and security of the people of the United States are best sustained and enhanced in a community of nations which respect individual civil and economic rights and freedoms.").

> to transitory actions, there is not a colour of doubt but that any action which is transitory may be laid in any county in England, though the matter arises beyond the seas.

Mostyn came into our law as the original basis for state court jurisdiction over out-of-state torts, *McKenna v. Fisk, supra,* (personal injury suits held transitory); *Dennick v. Railroad Co.,* 103 U.S. 11 (1880) (wrongful death action held transitory), and it has not lost its force in suits to recover for a wrongful death occurring upon foreign soil, *Slater v. Mexican National Railroad Co.,* 194 U.S. 120 (1904), as long as the conduct complained of was unlawful where performed. Here, where *in personam* jurisdiction has been obtained over the defendant, the parties agree that the acts alleged would violate Paraguayan law, and the policies of the forum are consistent with the foreign law, state court jurisdiction would be proper. Indeed, appellees conceded as much at oral argument.

Recalling that *Mostyn* was freshly decided at the time the Constitution was ratified, we proceed to consider whether the First Congress acted constitutionally in vesting jurisdiction over "foreign suits," *Slater, supra,* * * * alleging torts committed in violation of the law of nations. A case properly "aris[es] under the . . . laws of the United States" for Article III purposes if grounded upon statutes enacted by Congress or upon the common law of the United States. *See Illinois v. City of Milwaukee,* 406 U.S. 91, 99–100 (1972); *Ivy Broadcasting Co., Inc. v. American Tel. & Tel. Co.,* 391 F.2d 486, 492 (2d Cir. 1968). The law of nations forms an integral part of the common law, and a review of the history surrounding the adoption of the Constitution demonstrates that it became a part of the common law of the United States upon the adoption of the Constitution. Therefore, the enactment of the Alien Tort Statute was authorized by Article III.

During the eighteenth century, it was taken for granted on both sides of the Atlantic that the law of nations forms a part of the common law. Under the Articles of Confederation, the Pennsylvania Court of Oyer and Terminer at Philadelphia, per McKean, Chief Justice, applied the law of nations to the criminal prosecution of the Chevalier de Longchamps for his assault upon the person of the French Consul-General to the United States, noting that "[t]his law, in its full extent, is a part of the law of this state. . . ." *Respublica v. DeLongchamps,* 1 U.S. (1 Dall.) 113, 119 (1784). Thus, a leading commentator has written:

> It is an ancient and a salutary feature of the Anglo-American legal tradition that the Law of Nations is a part of the law of the land to be ascertained and administered, like any other, in the appropriate case. This doctrine was originally conceived and formulated in England in response to the demands of an expanding commerce and under the influence of theories widely accepted in the late sixteenth, the seventeenth and the eighteenth

> centuries. It was brought to America in the colonial years as part of the legal heritage from England. It was well understood by men of legal learning in America in the eighteenth century when the United Colonies broke away from England to unite effectively, a little later, in the United States of America.

Dickenson, "The Law of Nations as Part of the National Law of the United States," 101 U.PA.L.REV. 26, 27 (1952).

Indeed, Dickenson goes on to demonstrate, that one of the principal defects of the Confederation that our Constitution was intended to remedy was the central government's inability to "cause infractions of treaties or of the law of nations, to be punished." 1 FARRAND, RECORDS OF THE FEDERAL CONVENTION 19 (Rev. ed. 1937) (Notes of James Madison). And, in Jefferson's words, the very purpose of the proposed Union was "to make us one nation as to foreign concerns, and keep us distinct in domestic ones." Dickenson, *supra.*

As ratified, the judiciary article contained no express reference to cases arising under the law of nations. Indeed, the only express reference to that body of law is contained in Article I, sec. 8, cl. 10, which grants to the Congress the power to "define and punish . . . offenses against the law of nations." Appellees seize upon this circumstance and advance the proposition that the law of nations forms a part of the laws of the United States only to the extent that Congress has acted to define it. This extravagant claim is amply refuted by the numerous decisions applying rules of international law uncodified in any act of Congress. *E.g., Ware v. Hylton,* 3 U.S. (3 Dall.) 199 (1796); *The Paquete Habana, supra*; *Sabbatino, supra.* A similar argument was offered to and rejected by the Supreme Court in *United States v. Smith, supra,* and we reject it today. As John Jay wrote in *The Federalist* No. 3, at 22 (1 Bourne ed. 1901), "Under the national government, treaties and articles of treaties, as well as the laws of nations, will always be expounded in one sense and executed in the same manner, whereas adjudications on the same points and questions in the thirteen states will not always accord or be consistent." Federal jurisdiction over cases involving international law is clear.

Thus, it was hardly a radical initiative for Chief Justice Marshall to state in *The Nereide,* 13 U.S. (9 Cranch) 388, 422 (1815), that in the absence of a congressional enactment,[20] United States courts are "bound by the law of nations, which is a part of the law of the land." These words were echoed in *The Paquete Habana, supra:* "international law is part of our law, and must be ascertained and administered by the courts of justice of

[20] The plainest evidence that international law has an existence in the federal courts independent of acts of Congress is the longstanding rule of construction first enunciated by Chief Justice Marshall: "an act of congress ought never to be construed to violate the law of nations, if any other possible construction remains . . . ." *The Charming Betsy,* 6 U.S. (2 Cranch) 64, 67 (1804), quoted in *Lauritzen v. Larsen,* 345 U.S. 571, 578 (1953).

appropriate jurisdiction, as often as questions of right depending upon it are duly presented for their determination." * * *

The Filártigas urge that 28 U.S.C. § 1350 be treated as an exercise of Congress's power to define offenses against the law of nations. While such a reading is possible, * * * we believe it is sufficient here to construe the Alien Tort Statute, not as granting new rights to aliens, but simply as opening the federal courts for adjudication of the rights already recognized by international law. The statute nonetheless does inform our analysis of Article III, for we recognize that questions of jurisdiction "must be considered part of an organic growth, part of an evolutionary process," and that the history of the judiciary article gives meaning to its pithy phrases. *Romero v. International Terminal Operating Co.,* 358 U.S. 354, 360 (1959). The Framers' overarching concern that control over international affairs be vested in the new national government to safeguard the standing of the United States among the nations of the world therefore reinforces the result we reach today.

Although the Alien Tort Statute has rarely been the basis for jurisdiction during its long history,[21] in light of the foregoing discussion, there can be little doubt that this action is properly brought in federal court. This is undeniably an action by an alien, for a tort only, committed in violation of the law of nations. The paucity of suits successfully maintained under the section is readily attributable to the statute's requirement of alleging a "*violation* of the law of nations" (emphasis supplied) at the jurisdictional threshold. Courts have, accordingly, engaged in a more searching preliminary review of the merits than is required, for example, under the more flexible "arising under" formulation. Thus, the narrowing construction that the Alien Tort Statute has previously received reflects the fact that earlier cases did not involve such well-established, universally recognized norms of international law that are here at issue.

For example, the statute does not confer jurisdiction over an action by a Luxembourgeois international investment trust's suit for fraud, conversion and corporate waste. *IIT v. Vencap,* 519 F.2d 1001, 1015 (1975). In *IIT*, Judge Friendly astutely noted that the mere fact that every nation's municipal law may prohibit theft does not incorporate "the Eighth Commandment, 'Thou Shalt not steal' . . . [into] the law of nations." It is only where the nations of the world have demonstrated that the wrong is of mutual, and not merely several, concern, by means of express international accords, that a wrong generally recognized becomes an

[21] Section 1350 afforded the basis for jurisdiction over a child custody suit between aliens in *Adra v. Clift,* 195 F. Supp. 857 (D.Md.1961), with a falsified passport supplying the requisite international law violation. In *Bolchos v. Darrel*, 3 Fed. Cas. 810 (D.S.C.1795), the Alien Tort Statute provided an alternative basis of jurisdiction over a suit to determine title to slaves on board an enemy vessel taken on the high seas.

international law violation within the meaning of the statute. Other recent § 1350 cases are similarly distinguishable.[23]

IIT adopted a dictum from *Lopes v. Reederei Richard Schroder,* 225 F. Supp. 292 (E.D.Pa.1963), to the effect that "a violation of the law of nations arises only when there has been 'a violation by one or more individuals of those standards, rules or customs (a) affecting the relationship between states or between an individual and a foreign state and (b) used by those states for their common good and/or in dealings inter se.' " We have no quarrel with this formulation so long as it be understood that the courts are not to prejudge the scope of the issues that the nations of the world may deem important to their interrelationships, and thus to their common good. As one commentator has noted:

> the sphere of domestic jurisdiction is not an irreducible sphere of rights which are somehow inherent, natural, or fundamental. It does not create an impenetrable barrier to the development of international law. Matters of domestic jurisdiction are not those which are unregulated by international law, but those which are left by international law for regulation by States. There are, therefore, no matters which are domestic by their "nature." All are susceptible of international legal regulation and may become the subjects of new rules of customary law of treaty obligations.

Preuss, "Article 2, Paragraph 7 of the Charter of the United Nations and Matters of Domestic Jurisdiction," HAGUE RECEUIL (Extract, 149) at 8, *reprinted in* H. Briggs, THE LAW OF NATIONS 24 (1952). Here, the nations have made it their business, both through international accords and unilateral action, to be concerned with domestic human rights violations of this magnitude. The case before us therefore falls within the *Lopes/IIT* rule.

Since federal jurisdiction may properly be exercised over the Filártigas' claim, the action must be remanded for further proceedings.

---

[23] *Dreyfus v. von Finck,* 534 F.2d 24 (2d Cir.), *cert. denied,* 429 U.S. 835 (1976), concerned a forced sale of property, and thus sought to invoke international law in an area in which no consensus view existed. *See Sabbatino, supra,* 376 U.S. at 428. Similarly, *Benjamins v. British European Airways,* 572 F.2d 913 (2d Cir. 1978), *cert. denied,* 439 U.S. 1114 (1979), held only that an air disaster, even if caused by "wilful" negligence, does not constitute a law of nations violation. *Id.* at 916. In *Khedivial Line, S.A E. v. Seafarers' International Union,* 278 F.2d 49 (2d Cir. 1960), we found that the "right" to free access to the ports of a foreign nation was at best a rule of comity, and not a binding rule of international law.

The cases from other circuits are distinguishable in like manner. The court in *Huynh Thi Anh v. Levi,* 586 F.2d 625 (6th Cir. 1978), was unable to discern from the traditional sources of the law of nations "a universal or generally accepted substantive rule or principle" governing child custody, *id. at 629,* and therefore held jurisdiction to be lacking. *Cf. Nguyen Da Yen v. Kissinger,* 528 F.2d 1194, 1201 n.13 (9th Cir. 1975) ("the illegal seizure, removal and detention of an alien against his will in a foreign country would appear to be a tort . . . and it may well be a tort in violation of the 'law of nations' ") (§ 1350 question not reached due to inadequate briefing). Finally, the district court in *Lopes v. Reederei Richard Schroder,* 225 F. Supp. 292 (E. D. Pa. 1963) simply found that the doctrine of seaworthiness, upon which the plaintiff relied, was a uniquely American concept, and therefore not a part of the law of nations.

Appellee Pena, however, advances several additional points that lie beyond the scope of our holding on jurisdiction. Both to emphasize the boundaries of our holding, and to clarify some of the issues reserved for the district court on remand, we will address these contentions briefly.

IV

Pena argues that the customary law of nations, as reflected in treaties and declarations that are not self-executing, should not be applied as rules of decision in this case. In doing so, he confuses the question of federal jurisdiction under the Alien Tort Statute, which requires consideration of the law of nations, with the issue of the choice of law to be applied, which will be addressed at a later stage in the proceedings. The two issues are distinct. Our holding on subject matter jurisdiction decides only whether Congress intended to confer judicial power, and whether it is authorized to do so by Article III. The choice of law inquiry is a much broader one, primarily concerned with fairness; consequently, it looks to wholly different considerations. *See Lauritzen v. Larsen,* 345 U.S. 571 (1954). Should the district court decide that the *Lauritzen* analysis requires it to apply Paraguayan law, our courts will not have occasion to consider what law would govern a suit under the Alien Tort Statute where the challenged conduct is actionable under the law of the forum and the law of nations, but not the law of the jurisdiction in which the tort occurred.[25]

Pena also argues that "if the conduct complained of is alleged to be the act of the Paraguayan government, the suit is barred by the Act of State doctrine." This argument was not advanced below, and is therefore not before us on this appeal. We note in passing, however, that we doubt whether action by a state official in violation of the Constitution and laws of the Republic of Paraguay, and wholly unratified by that nation's government, could properly be characterized as an act of state. *See Banco Nacionale de Cuba v. Sabbatino, supra*; *Underhill v. Hernandez*, 168 U.S. 250 (1897). Paraguay's renunciation of torture as a legitimate instrument of state policy, however, does not strip the tort of its character as an international law violation, if it in fact occurred under color of government authority. *See* Declaration on the Protection of All Persons from Being Subjected to Torture, *supra* * * *; *cf. Ex parte Young*, 209 U.S. 123 (1908)

---

[25] In taking that broad range of factors into account, the district court may well decide that fairness requires it to apply Paraguayan law to the instant case. *See Slater v. Mexican National Railway Co.,* 194 U.S. 120 (1904). Such a decision would not retroactively oust the federal court of subject matter jurisdiction, even though plaintiff's cause of action would no longer properly be "created" by a law of the United States. *See American Well Works Co. v. Layne & Bowler Co.*, 241 U.S. 257, 260 (1916) (Holmes, J.). Once federal jurisdiction is established by a colorable claim under federal law at a preliminary stage of the proceeding, subsequent dismissal of that claim (here, the claim under the general international proscription of torture) does not deprive the court of jurisdiction previously established. *See Hagans v. Lavine*, 415 U.S. 528 (1974); *Romero v. International Terminal Operating Co.*, 358 U.S. 354 (1959); *Bell v. Hood*, 327 U.S. 678 (1946). *Cf. Huynh Thi Ahn, supra*, 586 F.2d at 633 (choice of municipal law ousts § 1350 jurisdiction when no international norms exist).

(state official subject to suit for constitutional violations despite immunity of state.).

Finally, we have already stated that we do not reach the critical question of *forum non conveniens*, since it was not considered below. In closing, however, we note that the foreign relations implications of this and other issues the district court will be required to adjudicate on remand underscores the wisdom of the First Congress in vesting jurisdiction over such claims in the federal district courts through the Alien Tort Statute. Questions of this nature are fraught with implications for the nation as a whole, and therefore should not be left to the potentially varying adjudications of the courts of the fifty states.

In the twentieth century the international community has come to recognize the common danger posed by the flagrant disregard of basic human rights and particularly the right to be free of torture. Spurred first by the Great War, and then the Second, civilized nations have banded together to prescribe acceptable norms of international behavior. From the ashes of the Second World War arose the United Nations Organization, amid hopes that an era of peace and cooperation had at last begun. Though many of these aspirations have remained elusive goals, that circumstance cannot diminish the true progress that has been made. In the modern age, humanitarian and practical considerations have combined to lead the nations of the world to recognize that respect for fundamental human rights is in their individual and collective interest. Among the rights universally proclaimed by all nations, as we have noted, is the right to be free of physical torture. Indeed, for purposes of civil liability, the torturer has become like the pirate and slave trader before him *hostis humani generis*, an enemy of all mankind. Our holding today, giving effect to a jurisdictional provision enacted by our First Congress, is a small but important step in the fulfillment of the ageless dream to free all people from brutal violence.

NOTES AND QUESTIONS

1. *Filártiga and its aftermath*. The *Filártiga* decision denied the defendant's pre-trial motion to dismiss. It was not a finding of liability, and, on remand from the Court of Appeals, the district court avoided a narrow interpretation of the Alien Tort Claims Act (sometimes also known as the Alien Tort Statute or ATS):

> The international law prohibiting torture established the standard and referred to the national states the task of enforcing it. By enacting Section 1350 Congress entrusted the task to the federal courts and gave them power to choose and develop federal remedies to effectuate the purposes of the international law incorporated into United States common law. In order to take the international

> condemnation of torture seriously this court must adopt a remedy appropriate to the ends and reflective of the nature of the condemnation. * * * If the courts of the United States are to adhere to the consensus of the community of humankind, any remedy they fashion must recognize that this case concerns an act so monstrous as to make its perpetrator an outlaw around the globe. * * * [The court went on to award $10,385,364 to the plaintiff in compensatory and punitive damages *inter alia*.]

Filártiga v. Pena-Irala, 577 F. Supp. 860, 867–68 (E.D.N.Y. 1984). The *Filártiga* decision received the imprimatur of Congress in 1992, with the enactment of the Torture Victim Protection Act, extending *Filártiga*-like jurisdiction to U.S. citizens who are tortured by a foreign government.

Since 1980, scores of cases have been filed under the ATS, and the Supreme Court cited *Filártiga* with approval in *Sosa v. Alvarez-Machain*, 542 U.S. 692 (2004). The class of actionable wrongs has evolved beyond torture to include genocide, slavery, war crimes, crimes against humanity, disappearances, extrajudicial killings, prolonged arbitrary detention, and violations of other norms that are similarly "specific, universal, and obligatory." *In re Estate of Ferdinand Marcos Human Rights Litigation*, 25 F.3d 1467, 1475 (9th Cir. 1994). By contrast, ordinary business torts, brief detention in excess of lawful authority, defamation, and international environmental claims have generally been rejected under the ATS. *See, e.g., Flores v. S. Peru Copper Corp.*, 414 F.3d 233, 251 (2d Cir. 2003). The defendants-of-choice have also evolved from the individual who physically committed the violation, to those who ordered or tolerated it, including former heads-of-state, cabinet ministers, and military commanders. More recently, the question has arisen whether "private" actors, like corporations, can be defendants under the ATS or are immune from liability under international law, a question before the Supreme Court as of this writing. *Jesner, et al. v. Arab Bank PLC*, No. 16–499.

Is it fair or persuasive to argue that international law *must* qualify as law if it can provide the rule of decision in a domestic court?

2. *A doctrinal firebreak between international and domestic law?* The *Filártiga* decision suggests that there is no absolute (or stable) boundary line between international and domestic law. Domestic laws and practices can qualify as general principles or as the state practice component of customary international law. International law is also "part of our law," as the Supreme Court noted in *Paquete Habana*, cited prominently in *Filártiga*. *See also The Nereide,* 13 U.S. (9 Cranch) 388, 423 (1815) ("the Court is bound by the law of nations which is part of the law of the land.") In addition, international law in the form of treaties qualifies as "the Supreme Law of the Land," under the Supremacy Clause of the U.S. Constitution, *infra*. In these circumstances, why would international law provoke such profound and intergenerational skepticism? Is it any more or less law-like than other fields of law you have encountered?

3. *Proving the content of customary international law.* As noted above, states recognize the existence of customary international law, arising not out of an explicit agreement to some authoritative text—as with a treaty or convention—but out of a "general practice accepted as law." Advocates attempting to prove the existence and meaning of a customary international norm must be prepared to demonstrate both the *empirical* element, namely that states behave in certain patterned ways, as well as the *motivational* element, namely that states conform to the pattern from a sense of legal obligation (*opinio juris*), and not out of grace or humanitarianism or public relations. Both the empirical and the motivational elements can be difficult to establish, and, unlike a treaty or a statute that has an effective date, there is no magic moment when customary international law suddenly springs into existence. So consider the evidence used by the *Filártiga* court to determine that torture was a violation of the law of nations.

A. *Resolutions and declarations of the United Nations.* The Charter of the United Nations does not make the organization an international legislature, and resolutions and declarations are not equivalent to binding legislation. What role do these instruments play in the Second Circuit's opinion?

B. *Treaties in consistent form.* The *Filártiga* court referred to various treaties condemning torture, but the United States was not a party to these treaties at the time of the decision. Does that matter? Of what relevance is the fact that the Torture Convention was at the time of the decision in draft form?

C. *Constitutions and laws of the various nations.* What is the Second Circuit's response to the argument that the written laws around the world that prohibit torture are meaningless when states commonly practice torture in violation of their own law? How can the state practice and *opinio juris* requirements of customary international law be satisfied if, at the time of the *Filártiga* decision, torture was practiced to some extent on virtually every continent? Would it matter if some states considered flogging or whipping a form of torture and others did not?

D. *Executive branch submissions.* The *Filártiga* court relied in part on a brief submitted by the government of the United States, establishing that a state's torture of its own citizens is a violation of the law of nations and arguing that the lower court's decision should be reversed. What is the best argument that it is improper for the courts to defer to the executive branch's interpretation of a purely jurisdictional statute? Is there a reason to defer more to the executive branch in cases under the Alien Tort Statute than in cases controlled by other jurisdictional statutes—like those establishing diversity jurisdiction or federal question jurisdiction?

E. *Scholarly writings.* Is there reason to think that the writings of scholars and publicists are more relevant in international cases than in domestic cases? What are the best rationales for that difference in treatment?

Taken separately, each of these evidentiary sources might seem less than compelling, and yet the *Filártiga* court apparently found the evidentiary whole greater than the sum of its parts. Certainly no state objected to the Second Circuit's conclusion that torture is a violation of the law of nations. If customary international law can be seen as the result of a continuous feedback loop—with each conforming example of state practice reinforcing the status and meaning of a norm—the decision might be understood as contributing to the very norm that it was applying. The decision could in short be used in subsequent cases to show how states interpret and apply the customary norm against torture.

4. *Foreign affairs implications*. From one political perspective, *Filártiga* might be puzzling, because it allowed a human rights suit to go forward against an official from a nation with which the United States had good diplomatic relations. But in the U.S. government's *amicus* brief, the Department of State joined the Department of Justice in urging the Second Circuit to rule in the Filártigas' favor. That may in turn suggest that it might have been more embarrassing politically to find torture lawful—or to give safe haven to an alleged torturer—than it would be to adjudicate the case.

The courts retain the power to find certain issues non-justiciable under the political question doctrine, but that doctrine covers political *questions*, not political *cases*. *Baker v. Carr*, 369 U.S. 186, 217 (1962), and "it is error to suppose that every case or controversy which touches foreign relations lies beyond judicial cognizance." *Id.* at 212. Where there is law to apply—what the *Baker* court denominated "judicially-manageable standards"—the court should not find the case non-justiciable just because it is politically charged. *See e.g.*, *Zivotofsky ex rel. Zivotofsky v. Clinton*, 132 S. Ct. 1421 (2012) (rejecting the application of the political question doctrine in a case that involved the high politics of the Israeli-Palestinian conflict). As a consequence, in establishing a tort "in violation of the law of nations" at the jurisdictional stage, successful plaintiffs would simultaneously undermine the application of the political question doctrine.

There is a foreign affairs analogue to the political question doctrine, called the "act of state doctrine," which precludes U.S. courts "from inquiring into the validity of the public acts of a recognized foreign sovereign power committed within its own territory * * *." *Banco Nacional de Cuba v. Sabbatino*, 376 U.S. 398, 421 (1964). But here too there is reason to conclude that the act of torture in *Filártiga* would not qualify as a non-justiciable act of state. The Supreme Court has held that the act of state doctrine only applies "in the absence of a treaty or other unambiguous agreement regarding controlling legal principles * * *. [T]he greater the degree of codification or consensus concerning a particular area of international law, the more appropriate it is for the judiciary to render decisions regarding it." *Sabbatino*, 376 U.S., at 428. Moreover, the possibility of embarrassment is not enough to trigger the doctrine: "The act of state doctrine does not establish an exception for cases and controversies that may embarrass foreign governments * * *." *W.S. Kirkpatrick & Co., Inc. v. Environmental Tectonics Corp.*, 493 U.S. 400, 405 (1990).

How would a skeptic about the "law-ness" of international law account for these justiciability doctrines, which force advocates and judges to distinguish *case-by-case* between law and politics?

C. TREATIES IN DOMESTIC COURTS

UNITED STATES V. ALVAREZ-MACHAIN

504 U.S. 655 (1992)

CHIEF JUSTICE REHNQUIST delivered the opinion of the Court. The issue in this case is whether a criminal defendant, abducted to the United States from a nation with which it has an extradition treaty, thereby acquires a defense to the jurisdiction of this country's courts. We hold that he does not, and that he may be tried in federal district court for violations of the criminal law of the United States.

Respondent, Humberto Alvarez-Machain, is a citizen and resident of Mexico. He was indicted for participating in the kidnap and murder of United States Drug Enforcement Administration (DEA) special agent Enrique Camarena-Salazar and a Mexican pilot working with Camarena, Alfredo Zavala-Avelar. The DEA believes that respondent, a medical doctor, participated in the murder by prolonging Agent Camarena's life so that others could further torture and interrogate him. On April 2, 1990, respondent was forcibly kidnapped from his medical office in Guadalajara, Mexico, to be flown by private plane to El Paso, Texas, where he was arrested by DEA officials. The District Court concluded that DEA agents were responsible for respondent's abduction, although they were not personally involved in it. *United States v. Caro-Quintero*, 745 F.Supp. 599, 602–604, 609 (CD Cal.1990).[2]

Respondent moved to dismiss the indictment, claiming that his abduction constituted outrageous governmental conduct, and that the District Court lacked jurisdiction to try him because he was abducted in violation of the extradition treaty between the United States and Mexico. Extradition Treaty, May 4, 1978, [1979] United States-United Mexican States, 31 U.S.T. 5059, T.I.A.S. No. 9656 (Extradition Treaty or Treaty). The District Court rejected the outrageous governmental conduct claim, but held that it lacked jurisdiction to try respondent because his abduction

---

[2] Apparently, DEA officials had attempted to gain respondent's presence in the United States through informal negotiations with Mexican officials, but were unsuccessful. DEA officials then, through a contact in Mexico, offered to pay a reward and expenses in return for the delivery of respondent to the United States.

violated the Extradition Treaty. The District Court discharged respondent and ordered that he be repatriated to Mexico.

The Court of Appeals affirmed the dismissal of the indictment and the repatriation of respondent, relying on its decision in *United States v. Verdugo-Urquidez*, 939 F.2d 1341 (CA9 1991), *cert. pending*, No. 91–670, 946 F.2d 1466 (1991). In *Verdugo*, the Court of Appeals held that the forcible abduction of a Mexican national with the authorization or participation of the United States violated the Extradition Treaty between the United States and Mexico. Although the Treaty does not expressly prohibit such abductions, the Court of Appeals held that the "purpose" of the Treaty was violated by a forcible abduction, which, along with a formal protest by the offended nation, would give a defendant the right to invoke the Treaty violation to defeat jurisdiction of the District Court to try him. The Court of Appeals further held that the proper remedy for such a violation would be dismissal of the indictment and repatriation of the defendant to Mexico.

In the instant case, the Court of Appeals affirmed the District Court's finding that the United States had authorized the abduction of respondent, and that letters from the Mexican Government to the United States Government served as an official protest of the Treaty violation. Therefore, the Court of Appeals ordered that the indictment against respondent be dismissed and that respondent be repatriated to Mexico. We granted certiorari, and now reverse.

Although we have never before addressed the precise issue raised in the present case, we have previously considered proceedings in claimed violation of an extradition treaty and proceedings against a defendant brought before a court by means of a forcible abduction. We addressed the former issue in *United States v. Rauscher*, 119 U.S. 407 (1886); more precisely, the issue whether the Webster-Ashburton Treaty of 1842, 8 Stat. 572, 576, which governed extraditions between England and the United States, prohibited the prosecution of defendant Rauscher for a crime other than the crime for which he had been extradited. Whether this prohibition, known as the doctrine of specialty, was an intended part of the treaty had been disputed between the two nations for some time. Justice Miller delivered the opinion of the Court, which carefully examined the terms and history of the treaty; the practice of nations in regards to extradition treaties; the case law from the States; and the writings of commentators, and reached the following conclusion:

> [A] person who has been brought within the jurisdiction of the court by virtue of proceedings under an extradition treaty, can only be tried for one of the offences described in that treaty, and for the offence with which he is charged in the proceedings for his extradition, until a reasonable time and opportunity have been given him, after his release or trial upon such charge, to return to

> the country from whose asylum he had been forcibly taken under those proceedings. *Id.*, at 430.

In addition, Justice Miller's opinion noted that any doubt as to this interpretation was put to rest by two federal statutes which imposed the doctrine of specialty upon extradition treaties to which the United States was a party. Unlike the case before us today, the defendant in *Rauscher* had been brought to the United States by way of an extradition treaty; there was no issue of a forcible abduction.

In *Ker v. Illinois*, 119 U.S. 436 (1886), also written by Justice Miller and decided the same day as *Rauscher*, we addressed the issue of a defendant brought before the court by way of a forcible abduction. Frederick Ker had been tried and convicted in an Illinois court for larceny; his presence before the court was procured by means of forcible abduction from Peru. A messenger was sent to Lima with the proper warrant to demand Ker by virtue of the extradition treaty between Peru and the United States. The messenger, however, disdained reliance on the treaty processes, and instead forcibly kidnapped Ker and brought him to the United States.[6] We distinguished Ker's case from *Rauscher*, on the basis that Ker was not brought into the United States by virtue of the extradition treaty between the United States and Peru, and rejected Ker's argument that he had a right under the extradition treaty to be returned to this country only in accordance with its terms.[7] We rejected Ker's due process argument more broadly, holding in line with "the highest authorities" that "such forcible abduction is no sufficient reason why the party should not answer when brought within the jurisdiction of the court which has the right to try him for such an offence, and presents no valid objection to his trial in such court." *Ker*, *supra*, at 444.

Two cases decided during the Prohibition Era in this country have dealt with seizures claimed to have been in violation of a treaty entered into between the United States and Great Britain to assist the United States in offshore enforcement of its prohibition laws, and to allow British passenger ships to carry liquor while in the waters of the United States. The history of the negotiations leading to the treaty is set forth in *Cook v. United States*, 288 U.S. 102, 111–118 (1933). In that case we held that the treaty provision for seizure of British vessels operating beyond the 3-mile limit was intended to be exclusive, and that therefore liquor seized from a

---

[6] Although the opinion does not explain why the messenger failed to present the warrant to the proper authorities, commentators have suggested that the seizure of Ker in the aftermath of a revolution in Peru provided the messenger with no "proper authorities" to whom the warrant could be presented. See Kester, *Some Myths of United States Extradition Law*, 76 GEO.L.J. 1441, 1451 (1988).

[7] In the words of Justice Miller, the "treaty was not called into operation, was not relied upon, was not made the pretext of arrest, and the facts show that it was a clear case of kidnapping within the dominions of Peru, without any pretence of authority under the treaty or from the government of the United States." *Ker v. Illinois*, 119 U.S., at 443.

British vessel in violation of the treaty could not form the basis of a conviction.

In *Ford v. United States*, 273 U.S. 593 (1927), the argument as to personal jurisdiction was deemed to have been waived.

In *Frisbie v. Collins*, 342 U.S. 519, *rehearing denied*, 343 U.S. 937 (1952), we applied the rule in *Ker* to a case in which the defendant had been kidnapped in Chicago by Michigan officers and brought to trial in Michigan. We upheld the conviction over objections based on the Due Process Clause and the federal Kidnapping Act and stated:

> This Court has never departed from the rule announced in [*Ker*] that the power of a court to try a person for crime is not impaired by the fact that he had been brought within the court's jurisdiction by reason of a 'forcible abduction.' No persuasive reasons are now presented to justify overruling this line of cases. They rest on the sound basis that due process of law is satisfied when one present in court is convicted of crime after having been fairly apprized of the charges against him and after a fair trial in accordance with constitutional procedural safeguards. There is nothing in the Constitution that requires a court to permit a guilty person rightfully convicted to escape justice because he was brought to trial against his will. *Frisbie*, *supra*, at 522.

The only differences between *Ker* and the present case are that *Ker* was decided on the premise that there was no governmental involvement in the abduction, 119 U.S., at 443; and Peru, from which Ker was abducted, did not object to his prosecution.[9] Respondent finds these differences to be dispositive, as did the Court of Appeals in *Verdugo*, contending that they show that respondent's prosecution, like the prosecution of Rauscher, violates the implied terms of a valid extradition treaty. The Government, on the other hand, argues that *Rauscher* stands as an "exception" to the rule in *Ker* only when an extradition treaty is invoked, and the terms of the treaty provide that its breach will limit the jurisdiction of a court. Therefore, our first inquiry must be whether the abduction of respondent from Mexico violated the Extradition Treaty between the United States and Mexico. If we conclude that the Treaty does not prohibit respondent's abduction, the rule in *Ker* applies, and the court need not inquire as to how respondent came before it.

In construing a treaty, as in construing a statute, we first look to its terms to determine its meaning. The Treaty says nothing about the obligations of the United States and Mexico to refrain from forcible abductions of people from the territory of the other nation, or the consequences under the Treaty if such an abduction occurs. Respondent

---

[9] Ker also was not a national of Peru, whereas respondent is a national of the country from which he was abducted. Respondent finds this difference to be immaterial. Tr. of Oral Arg. 26.

submits that Article 22(1) of the Treaty, which states that it "shall apply to offenses specified in Article 2 [including murder] committed before and after this Treaty enters into force," evidences an intent to make application of the Treaty mandatory for those offenses. However, the more natural conclusion is that Article 22 was included to ensure that the Treaty was applied to extraditions requested after the Treaty went into force, regardless of when the crime of extradition occurred.

More critical to respondent's argument is Article 9 of the Treaty, which provides:

> 1. Neither Contracting Party shall be bound to deliver up its own nationals, but the executive authority of the requested Party shall, if not prevented by the laws of that Party, have the power to deliver them up if, in its discretion, it be deemed proper to do so.
>
> 2. If extradition is not granted pursuant to paragraph 1 of this Article, the requested Party shall submit the case to its competent authorities for the purpose of prosecution, provided that Party has jurisdiction over the offense."

According to respondent, Article 9 embodies the terms of the bargain which the United States struck: If the United States wishes to prosecute a Mexican national, it may request that individual's extradition. Upon a request from the United States, Mexico may either extradite the individual or submit the case to the proper authorities for prosecution in Mexico. In this way, respondent reasons, each nation preserved its right to choose whether its nationals would be tried in its own courts or by the courts of the other nation. This preservation of rights would be frustrated if either nation were free to abduct nationals of the other nation for the purposes of prosecution. More broadly, respondent reasons, as did the Court of Appeals, that all the processes and restrictions on the obligation to extradite established by the Treaty would make no sense if either nation were free to resort to forcible kidnapping to gain the presence of an individual for prosecution in a manner not contemplated by the Treaty.

We do not read the Treaty in such a fashion. Article 9 does not purport to specify the only way in which one country may gain custody of a national of the other country for the purposes of prosecution. In the absence of an extradition treaty, nations are under no obligation to surrender those in their country to foreign authorities for prosecution. *Rauscher*, 119 U.S., at 411–412. Extradition treaties exist so as to impose mutual obligations to surrender individuals in certain defined sets of circumstances, following established procedures. The Treaty thus provides a mechanism which would not otherwise exist, requiring, under certain circumstances, the United States and Mexico to extradite individuals to the other country, and establishing the procedures to be followed when the Treaty is invoked.

The history of negotiation and practice under the Treaty also fails to show that abductions outside of the Treaty constitute a violation of the Treaty. As the Solicitor General notes, the Mexican Government was made aware, as early as 1906, of the *Ker* doctrine, and the United States' position that it applied to forcible abductions made outside of the terms of the United States-Mexico Extradition Treaty.[11] Nonetheless, the current version of the Treaty, signed in 1978, does not attempt to establish a rule that would in any way curtail the effect of *Ker*. Moreover, although language which would grant individuals exactly the right sought by respondent had been considered and drafted as early as 1935 by a prominent group of legal scholars sponsored by the faculty of Harvard Law School, no such clause appears in the current Treaty.

Thus, the language of the Treaty, in the context of its history, does not support the proposition that the Treaty prohibits abductions outside of its terms. The remaining question, therefore, is whether the Treaty should be interpreted so as to include an implied term prohibiting prosecution where the defendant's presence is obtained by means other than those established by the Treaty. *See Valentine*, 299 U.S., at 17 ("Strictly the question is not whether there had been a uniform practical construction denying the power, but whether the power had been so clearly recognized that the grant should be implied").

Respondent contends that the Treaty must be interpreted against the backdrop of customary international law, and that international abductions are "so clearly prohibited in international law" that there was no reason to include such a clause in the Treaty itself. The international censure of international abductions is further evidenced, according to respondent, by the United Nations Charter and the Charter of the Organization of American States. Respondent does not argue that these sources of international law provide an independent basis for the right respondent asserts not to be tried in the United States, but rather that they should inform the interpretation of the Treaty terms.

---

[11] In correspondence between the United States and Mexico growing out of the 1905 Martinez incident, in which a Mexican national was abducted from Mexico and brought to the United States for trial, the Mexican Chargé wrote to the Secretary of State protesting that as Martinez' arrest was made outside of the procedures established in the extradition treaty, "the action pending against the man can not rest [on] any legal foundation." Letter of Balbino Davalos to Secretary of State, *reprinted in* Papers Relating to the Foreign Relations of the United States, H.R.Doc. No. 1, 59th Cong., 2d Sess., pt. 2, p. 1121 (1906). The Secretary of State responded that the exact issue raised by the Martinez incident had been decided by *Ker*, and that the remedy open to the Mexican Government, namely, a request to the United States for extradition of Martinez' abductor, had been granted by the United States. Letter of Robert Bacon to Mexican Chargé, reprinted in Papers Relating to the Foreign Relations of the United States, H.R.Doc. No. 1, supra, at 1121–1122.

Respondent and the Court of Appeals stress a statement made in 1881 by Secretary of State James Blaine to the Governor of Texas to the effect that the extradition treaty in its form at that time did not authorize unconsented to abductions from Mexico. This misses the mark, however, for the Government's argument is not that the Treaty authorizes the abduction of respondent, but that the Treaty does not prohibit the abduction.

The Court of Appeals deemed it essential, in order for the individual defendant to assert a right under the Treaty, that the affected foreign government had registered a protest. *Verdugo*, 939 F.2d, at 1357 ("[I]n the kidnapping case there must be a formal protest from the offended government after the kidnapping"). Respondent agrees that the right exercised by the individual is derivative of the nation's right under the Treaty, since nations are authorized, notwithstanding the terms of an extradition treaty, to voluntarily render an individual to the other country on terms completely outside of those provided in the treaty. The formal protest, therefore, ensures that the "offended" nation actually objects to the abduction and has not in some way voluntarily rendered the individual for prosecution. Thus the Extradition Treaty only prohibits gaining the defendant's presence by means other than those set forth in the Treaty when the nation from which the defendant was abducted objects.

This argument seems to us inconsistent with the remainder of respondent's argument. The Extradition Treaty has the force of law, and if, as respondent asserts, it is self-executing, it would appear that a court must enforce it on behalf of an individual regardless of the offensiveness of the practice of one nation to the other nation. In *Rauscher*, the Court noted that Great Britain had taken the position in other cases that the Webster-Ashburton Treaty included the doctrine of specialty, but no importance was attached to whether or not Great Britain had protested the prosecution of Rauscher for the crime of cruel and unusual punishment as opposed to murder.

More fundamentally, the difficulty with the support respondent garners from international law is that none of it relates to the practice of nations in relation to extradition treaties. In *Rauscher*, we implied a term in the Webster-Ashburton Treaty because of the practice of nations with regard to extradition treaties. In the instant case, respondent would imply terms in the Extradition Treaty from the practice of nations with regards to international law more generally.[14] Respondent would have us find that the Treaty acts as a prohibition against a violation of the general principle of international law that one government may not "exercise its police power in the territory of another state." Brief for Respondent 16. There are many actions which could be taken by a nation that would violate this principle, including waging war, but it cannot seriously be contended that an

---

[14] Similarly, the Court of Appeals in *Verdugo* reasoned that international abductions violate the "purpose" of the Treaty, stating that "[t]he requirements extradition treaties impose constitute a means of safeguarding the sovereignty of the signatory nations, as well as ensuring the fair treatment of individuals." 939 F.2d, at 1350. The ambitious purpose ascribed to the Treaty by the Court of Appeals, we believe, places a greater burden on its language and history than they can logically bear. In a broad sense, most international agreements have the common purpose of safeguarding the sovereignty of signatory nations, in that they seek to further peaceful relations between nations. This, however, does not mean that the violation of any principle of international law constitutes a violation of this particular treaty.

invasion of the United States by Mexico would violate the terms of the Extradition Treaty between the two nations.

In sum, to infer from this Treaty and its terms that it prohibits all means of gaining the presence of an individual outside of its terms goes beyond established precedent and practice. In *Rauscher*, the implication of a doctrine of specialty into the terms of the Webster-Ashburton Treaty, which, by its terms, required the presentation of evidence establishing probable cause of the crime of extradition before extradition was required, was a small step to take. By contrast, to imply from the terms of this Treaty that it prohibits obtaining the presence of an individual by means outside of the procedures the Treaty establishes requires a much larger inferential leap, with only the most general of international law principles to support it. The general principles cited by respondent simply fail to persuade us that we should imply in the United States-Mexico Extradition Treaty a term prohibiting international abductions.

Respondent and his *amici* may be correct that respondent's abduction was "shocking," and that it may be in violation of general international law principles. Mexico has protested the abduction of respondent through diplomatic notes, and the decision of whether respondent should be returned to Mexico, as a matter outside of the Treaty, is a matter for the Executive Branch. We conclude, however, that respondent's abduction was not in violation of the Extradition Treaty between the United States and Mexico, and therefore the rule of *Ker v. Illinois* is fully applicable to this case. The fact of respondent's forcible abduction does not therefore prohibit his trial in a court in the United States for violations of the criminal laws of the United States. * * * The judgment of the Court of Appeals is therefore reversed, and the case is remanded for further proceedings consistent with this opinion.

JUSTICE STEVENS, with whom JUSTICE BLACKMUN and JUSTICE O'CONNOR join, dissenting. The Court correctly observes that this case raises a question of first impression. The case is unique for several reasons. It does not involve an ordinary abduction by a private kidnaper, or bounty hunter, as in *Ker v. Illinois*; nor does it involve the apprehension of an American fugitive who committed a crime in one State and sought asylum in another, as in *Frisbie v. Collins*. Rather, it involves this country's abduction of another country's citizen; it also involves a violation of the territorial integrity of that other country, with which this country has signed an extradition treaty.

Mexican citizen was kidnapped in Mexico and charged with a crime committed in Mexico; his offense allegedly violated both Mexican and American law. Mexico has formally demanded on at least two separate occasions[1] that he be returned to Mexico and has represented that he will

1 The abduction of respondent occurred on April 2, 1990. Mexico responded quickly and unequivocally. On April 18, 1990, Mexico requested an official report on the role of the United

be prosecuted and, if convicted, punished for his offense.[2] It is clear that Mexico's demand must be honored if this official abduction violated the 1978 Extradition Treaty between the United States and Mexico. In my opinion, a fair reading of the treaty in light of our decision in *United States v. Rauscher* and applicable principles of international law, leads inexorably to the conclusion that the District Court, and the Court of Appeals for the Ninth Circuit correctly construed that instrument.

I

The extradition treaty with Mexico is a comprehensive document containing 23 articles and an appendix listing the extraditable offenses covered by the agreement. The parties announced their purpose in the preamble: The two governments desire "to cooperate more closely in the fight against crime and, to this end, to mutually render better assistance in matters of extradition."[4] From the preamble, through the description of the parties' obligations with respect to offenses committed within as well as beyond the territory of a requesting party, the delineation of the procedures and evidentiary requirements for extradition, the special provisions for political offenses and capital punishment, and other details, the Treaty appears to have been designed to cover the entire subject of extradition. Thus, Article 22, entitled "Scope of Application," states that the "Treaty shall apply to offenses specified in Article 2 committed before and after this Treaty enters into force," and Article 2 directs that "[e]xtradition shall take place, subject to this Treaty, for willful acts which fall within any of [the extraditable offenses listed in] the clauses of the Appendix." Moreover, as noted by the Court, Article 9 expressly provides that neither contracting party is bound to deliver up its own nationals, although it may do so in its discretion, but if it does not do so, it "shall submit the case to its competent authorities for purposes of prosecution."

Extradition treaties prevent international conflict by providing agreed-upon standards so that the parties may cooperate and avoid retaliatory invasions of territorial sovereignty. * * * The object of reducing conflict by promoting cooperation explains why extradition treaties do not

States in the abduction, and on May 16, 1990, and July 19, 1990, it sent diplomatic notes of protest from the Embassy of Mexico to the United States Department of State. In the May 16th note, Mexico said that it believed that the abduction was "carried out with the knowledge of persons working for the U.S. government, in violation of the procedure established in the extradition treaty in force between the two countries," and in the July 19th note, it requested the provisional arrest and extradition of the law enforcement agents allegedly involved in the abduction.

2 Mexico has already tried a number of members involved in the conspiracy that resulted in the murder of the Drug Enforcement Administration agent. For example, Rafael Caro-Quintero, a coconspirator of Alvarez-Machain in this case, has already been imprisoned in Mexico on a 40-year sentence.

4 *Id.*, at 5061. In construing a treaty, the Court has the "responsibility to give the specific words of the treaty a meaning consistent with the shared expectations of the contracting parties." *Air France v. Saks*, 470 U.S. 392, 399 (1985). It is difficult to see how an interpretation that encourages unilateral action could foster cooperation and mutual assistance—the stated goals of the Treaty. See also Presidential Letter of Transmittal attached to Senate Advice and Consent 3 (Treaty would "make a significant contribution to international cooperation in law enforcement").

prohibit informal consensual delivery of fugitives, but why they do prohibit state-sponsored abductions. *See* RESTATEMENT (THIRD) OF FOREIGN RELATIONS (RESTATEMENT) § 432, and Comments a–c (1987).

The Government's claim that the Treaty is not exclusive, but permits forcible governmental kidnapping, would transform these, and other, provisions into little more than verbiage. For example, provisions requiring "sufficient" evidence to grant extradition (Art. 3), withholding extradition for political or military offenses (Art. 5), withholding extradition when the person sought has already been tried (Art. 6), withholding extradition when the statute of limitations for the crime has lapsed (Art. 7), and granting the requested Country discretion to refuse to extradite an individual who would face the death penalty in the requesting country (Art. 8), would serve little purpose if the requesting country could simply kidnap the person. As the Court of Appeals for the Ninth Circuit recognized in a related case, "[e]ach of these provisions would be utterly frustrated if a kidnapping were held to be a permissible course of governmental conduct." *United States v. Verdugo-Urquidez*, 939 F.2d 1341, 1349 (1991). In addition, all of these provisions "only make sense if they are understood as requiring each treaty signatory to comply with those procedures whenever it wishes to obtain jurisdiction over an individual who is located in another treaty nation." *Id.*, at 1351.

It is true, as the Court notes, that there is no express promise by either party to refrain from forcible abductions in the territory of the other nation. Relying on that omission,[10] the Court, in effect, concludes that the Treaty merely creates an optional method of obtaining jurisdiction over alleged offenders, and that the parties silently reserved the right to resort to self-help whenever they deem force more expeditious than legal process.[11] If the United States, for example, thought it more expedient to torture or simply to execute a person rather than to attempt extradition, these options would be equally available because they, too, were not explicitly prohibited by the Treaty.[12] That, however, is a highly improbable

[10] The Court resorts to the same method of analysis as did the dissent in *United States v. Rauscher*, 119 U.S. 407 (1886). Chief Justice Waite would only recognize an explicit provision, and in the absence of one, he concluded that the treaty did not require that a person be tried only for the offense for which he had been extradited: "The treaty requires a delivery up to justice, on demand, of those accused of certain crimes, but says nothing about what shall be done with them after the delivery has been made. It might have provided that they should not be tried for any other offences than those for which they were surrendered, but it has not." *Id.*, at 434. That approach was rejected by the Court in *Rauscher* and should also be rejected by the Court here.

[11] To make the point more starkly, the Court has, in effect, written into Article 9 a new provision, which says: "Notwithstanding paragraphs 1 and 2 of this Article, either Contracting Party can, without the consent of the other, abduct nationals from the territory of one Party to be tried in the territory of the other."

[12] It is ironic that the United States has attempted to justify its unilateral action based on the kidnapping, torture, and murder of a federal agent by authorizing the kidnapping of respondent, for which the American law enforcement agents who participated have now been charged by Mexico. This goes to my earlier point * * * that extradition treaties promote harmonious relations by providing for the orderly surrender of a person by one state to another, and without such treaties, resort to force often followed.

interpretation of a consensual agreement,[13] which on its face appears to have been intended to set forth comprehensive and exclusive rules concerning the subject of extradition.[14] In my opinion, "the manifest scope and object of the treaty itself," *Rauscher*, 119 U.S., at 422, plainly imply a mutual undertaking to respect the territorial integrity of the other contracting party. That opinion is confirmed by a consideration of the "legal context" in which the Treaty was negotiated.[15] *Cannon v. University of Chicago*, 441 U.S. 677, 699 (1979). * * *

Commenting on the precise issue raised by this case, the chief reporter for the American Law Institute's Restatement of Foreign Relations used language reminiscent of Justice Story's characterization of an official seizure in a foreign jurisdiction as "monstrous":

> When done without consent of the foreign government, abducting a person from a foreign country is a gross violation of international law and gross disrespect for a norm high in the opinion of mankind. It is a blatant violation of the territorial integrity of another state; it eviscerates the extradition system (established by a comprehensive network of treaties involving virtually all states).[24]

In the *Rauscher* case, the legal background that supported the decision to imply a covenant not to prosecute for an offense different from that for which extradition had been granted was far less clear than the rule against invading the territorial integrity of a treaty partner that supports Mexico's position in this case.[25] If *Rauscher* was correctly decided—and I am

---

[13] This Court has previously described a treaty as generally "in its nature a contract between two nations," *Foster v. Neilson*, 2 Pet. 253, 314 (1829); see *Rauscher*, 119 U.S., at 418; it is also in this country the law of the land. 2 Pet., at 314.

[14] Mexico's understanding is that "[t]he extradition treaty governs comprehensively the delivery of all persons for trial in the requesting state 'for an offense committed outside the territory of the requesting Party.' " *Brief for United Mexican States as Amicus Curiae*, O.T.1991, No. 91670, p. 6. And Canada, with whom the United States also shares a large border and with whom the United States also has an extradition treaty, understands the treaty to be "the exclusive means for a requesting government to obtain . . . a removal" of a person from its territory, unless a nation otherwise gives its consent. *Brief for Government of Canada as Amicus Curiae* 4.

[15] The United States has offered no evidence from the negotiating record, ratification process, or later communications with Mexico to support the suggestion that a different understanding with Mexico was reached. *See* BASSIOUNI, INTERNATIONAL EXTRADITION: UNITED STATES LAW AND PRACTICE, ch. 2, § 4.3, at 82 ("Negotiations, preparatory works, and diplomatic correspondence are an integral part of th[e] surrounding circumstances, and [are] often relied on by courts in ascertaining the intentions of the parties") (footnote omitted).

[24] Henkin, *A Decent Respect to the Opinions of Mankind*, 25 JOHN MARSHALL L. REV. 215, 231 (1992) (footnote omitted).

[25] Thus, the RESTATEMENT states in part:

(2) A state's law enforcement officers may exercise their functions in the territory of another state only with the consent of the other state, given by duly authorized officials of that state. * * *

"c. Consequences of violation of territorial limits of law enforcement. If a state's law enforcement officials exercise their functions in the territory of another state without the latter's consent, that state is entitled to protest and, in appropriate cases, to receive reparation from the offending state. If the unauthorized action includes abduction of a

convinced that it was—its rationale clearly dictates a comparable result in this case. * * *

III

* * * A critical flaw pervades the Court's entire opinion. It fails to differentiate between the conduct of private citizens, which does not violate any treaty obligation, and conduct expressly authorized by the Executive Branch of the Government, which unquestionably constitutes a flagrant violation of international law, and in my opinion, also constitutes a breach of our treaty obligations. Thus, at the outset of its opinion, the Court states the issue as "whether a criminal defendant, abducted to the United States from a nation with which it has an extradition treaty, thereby acquires a defense to the jurisdiction of this country's courts." That, of course, is the question decided in *Ker v. Illinois*, 119 U.S. 436 (1886); it is not, however, the question presented for decision today. * * *

IV

As the Court observes at the outset of its opinion, there is reason to believe that respondent participated in an especially brutal murder of an American law enforcement agent. That fact, if true, may explain the Executive's intense interest in punishing respondent in our courts. Such an explanation, however, provides no justification for disregarding the Rule of Law that this Court has a duty to uphold.[33] That the Executive may wish to reinterpret[34] the Treaty to allow for an action that the Treaty in no way authorizes should not influence this Court's interpretation. Indeed, the desire for revenge exerts "a kind of hydraulic pressure . . . before which even well settled principles of law will bend," *Northern Securities Co. v.*

> person, the state from which the person was abducted may demand return of the person, and international law requires that he be returned. If the state from which the person was abducted does not demand his return, under the prevailing view the abducting state may proceed to prosecute him under its laws."

§ 432, and Comment c.

[33] As Justice Brandeis so wisely urged:

> In a government of laws, existence of the government will be imperilled if it fails to observe the law scrupulously. Our Government is the potent, the omnipresent teacher. For good or for ill, it teaches the whole people by its example. Crime is contagious. If the Government becomes a lawbreaker, it breeds contempt for law; it invites every man to become a law unto himself; it invites anarchy. To declare that in the administration of the criminal law the end justifies the means—to declare that the Government may commit crimes in order to secure the conviction of a private criminal—would bring terrible retribution. Against that pernicious doctrine this Court should resolutely set its face.

Olmstead v. United States, 277 U.S. 438, 485 (1928) (dissenting opinion).

[34] Certainly, the Executive's view has changed over time. At one point, the Office of Legal Counsel advised the administration that such seizures were contrary to international law because they compromised the territorial integrity of the other nation and were only to be undertaken with the consent of that nation. 4B Op. Off. Legal Counsel 549, 556 (1980). More recently, that opinion was revised, and the new opinion concluded that the President did have the authority to override customary international law. *Hearing before the Subcommittee on Civil and Constitutional Rights of the House Committee on the Judiciary*, 101st Cong., 1st Sess., 45 (1989) (statement of William P. Barr, Assistant Attorney General, Office of Legal Counsel, U.S. Department of Justice).

United States, 193 U.S. 197 (1904) (Holmes, J., dissenting), but it is precisely at such moments that we should remember and be guided by our duty "to render judgment evenly and dispassionately according to law, as each is given understanding to ascertain and apply it." *United States v. Mine Workers*, 330 U.S. 258, 342 (1947) (Rutledge, J., dissenting). The way that we perform that duty in a case of this kind sets an example that other tribunals in other countries are sure to emulate.

The significance of this Court's precedents is illustrated by a recent decision of the Court of Appeal of the Republic of South Africa. Based largely on its understanding of the import of this Court's cases—including our decision in Ker—that court held that the prosecution of a defendant kidnapped by agents of South Africa in another country must be dismissed. *S v. Ebrahim*, S. Afr. L. Rep. (Apr.–June 1991).[36] The Court of Appeal of South Africa—indeed, I suspect most courts throughout the civilized world—will be deeply disturbed by the "monstrous" decision the Court announces today. For every nation that has an interest in preserving the Rule of Law is affected, directly or indirectly, by a decision of this character. As Thomas Paine warned, an "avidity to punish is always dangerous to liberty" because it leads a nation "to stretch, to misinterpret, and to misapply even the best of laws."[38] To counter that tendency, he reminds us: "He that would make his own liberty secure must guard even his enemy from oppression; for if he violates this duty he establishes a precedent that will reach to himself."[39] I respectfully dissent.

NOTES AND QUESTIONS

1. *Treaties as law of the United States*. The place of treaties in the legal system of the United States is defined by the Supremacy Clause of the Constitution:

> This Constitution and the laws of the United States which shall be made in Pursuance thereof; and all treaties made, or which shall be made, under the Authority of the United States, shall be the supreme law of the land; and the judges in every state shall be bound thereby, anything in the constitution or laws of any state to the contrary notwithstanding.

U.S. CONST., Art. VI, § 2. At a minimum, this language places treaties on an equal footing with federal statutes. From the beginning of the Republic, treaties have provided a rule of decision in domestic cases to which the treaties

---

[36] The South African court agreed with appellant that an "abduction represents a violation of the applicable rules of international law, that these rules are part of [South African] law, and that this violation of the law deprives the Court . . . of its competence to hear [appellant's] case. . . ." S.Afr.L.Rep., at 89.

[38] 2 THE COMPLETE WRITINGS OF THOMAS PAINE 588 (P. Foner ed. 1945).

[39] *Ibid.*

apply. *Ware v. Hylton*, 3 U.S. (3 Dall.) 199 (1796). Determining whether a treaty applies in the first place is itself sometimes contested, as in *Alvarez-Machain*. *See also Bond v. United States*, ___ U.S. ___, 134 S. Ct. 2077 (2014) (holding that a minor assault with a chemical irritant does not fall within the Chemical Weapons treaty, which had been adopted after the horrific use of chemical weapons in World War I.) There are also domestic rules of law that can block or qualify the enforcement of a treaty, including the political question doctrine, principles of federalism, and the self-executing treaty doctrine. In short, a treaty *can* provide the rule of decision in a domestic case, consistent with the Supremacy Clause, but it is not necessarily a simple or straight-forward matter.

2. *Literalism and treaty interpretation*. The courts of the United States have frequently declared that they are unqualified to "make" treaties and have rejected any construction of a treaty that was so detached from the text or the intent of the parties or the negotiating history as to create, rather than construe, the agreement in question. "Judicial treaty-making" is the epithet of choice for those interpretations of a treaty which are considered excessively creative. The epithet works because it is shorthand for an implied and generalized incapacity that perpetuates the distinction between "making" and "finding" the law. In this view, courts perform their proper function in finding or declaring what the law is, including the obligation of a treaty, and they usurp some political function when their interpretation starts to resemble legislation.

The need to keep interpretation to a minimum has led to the "plain meaning" rule of treaty interpretation, which means that the literal text governs every case, except in the extraordinary case in which "application of the words of the treaty according to their obvious meaning effects a result inconsistent with the intent or expectations of its signatories." *Maximov v. United States*, 373 U.S. 49, 54 (1963); *The Amiable Isabella*, 19 U.S. (6 Wheat.) 1, 72 (1821).

In practice, the illegitimacy of "judicial treaty-making" not only favors literal interpretations of treaties, it favors in particular the literalist conclusions of the executive branch. The President, through the Solicitor General and the Legal Advisor to the Department of State, routinely submits briefs and other material to the courts, articulating the executive's position on treaty matters as they may affect a contested case. On a number of specific issues, the president's views are presumptively preferred and frequently decisive, as for example, when the court must identify an authoritative text, or determine the "obvious" meaning of the words in the treaty, or assess the mutual understanding of the parties, or determine the very existence of an inconsistency between the obvious meaning and the parties' intentions. The practice of deferring to the executive is thus a powerful corollary to the ideal of "plain meaning" interpretations.

Is it fair to say that the majority in *Alvarez-Machain* concluded that state-sponsored kidnapping is not a violation of the Extradition Treaty because nothing in the treaty explicitly forbids it? If so, is that an example of positivist reasoning, grounded in literalism? Keeping in mind the obligation to interpret a treaty so as to render none of its provisions superfluous, does the dissent have an equally literal or text-based argument?

3. *The virtue and the vice of literalism.* (a) Assume that you are playing a game of Monopoly™, and one of your opponents simply robs the bank. She points out in her defense that the written rules of the game do not explicitly prohibit players from robbing the bank. (b) The story is told of an admiral in ancient times who agreed to return half of the enemy's captured fleet if the other side would agree to a truce. The other side did agree, and the admiral—true to his literal word—neatly sawed each ship in half and returned that useless hulk to his enemy.

Literally, your opponent and the admiral are right. So what is the source and content of the implicit conditions in the rules that have been broken? Should some similar rule(s) have applied in *Alvarez-Machain*?

4. *Looking beyond the text.* What kind of authorities might be relevant to the question of what the Extradition Treaty "means" with respect to the legality of state-sponsored abduction? (a) Suppose for example, you could ask the members of the Senate who gave their advice and consent to the ratification of the treaty whether they would approve a treaty that allows transboundary abduction. (b) Would it matter if the other party to the Extradition Treaty submitted its interpretation of the agreement, which was directly contrary to the position of the U.S. Executive Branch in the case? (c) Suppose it could be demonstrated that "the first and foremost restriction imposed by international law upon a State is that—failing the existence of a permissive rule to the contrary—*it may not exercise its powers in any form in the territory of another State.*" *S.S. Lotus (Turkey v. France)*, [1927] P.C.I.J. (ser. A.) No. 10 at 18 (emphasis added). Is that customary principle useful in the interpretation of the treaty?

5. *On the merits.* After the Supreme Court's decision, Alvarez-Machain went on trial in Los Angeles for the abduction and killing of Enrique Camarena and his pilot, Alfredo Zavala Avelar. After the prosecution rested its case, the district judge—a former prosecutor—granted a motion for acquittal, finding that the prosecution's case was based on mere "speculation" and "wild hunches" and not on sufficient evidence to submit the case to a jury. Alvarez-Machain was returned to Mexico soon thereafter.

6. *The philosophical payoff.* At the end of the day, does the action of the U.S. government and the decision of the Supreme Court in *Alvarez-Machain* suggest that international law in either treaty or customary form is irreducibly optional and therefore not really law at all? Is there a less sweeping interpretation of the case?

Readings

1. INTERNATIONAL LAW AND POSITIVISM

JOHN AUSTIN, THE PROVINCE OF JURISPRUDENCE DETERMINED (1832)

133, 201 (1954 ed.)

Laws properly so called are a species of commands. But, being a command, every law properly so called flows from a determinate source. * * * [W]henever a command is expressed or intimated, one party signifies a wish that another shall do or forbear: and the latter is obnoxious to an evil which the former intends to inflict in case the wish be disregarded. * * *

And hence it inevitably follows, that the law obtaining between nations is not positive law: for every positive law is set by a given sovereign to a person or persons in a state of subjection to its author. * * * [T]he law obtaining between nations is law (improperly so called) set by general opinion. The duties which it imposes are enforced by moral sanctions: by fear on the part of nations, or by fear on the part of sovereigns, of provoking general hostility, and incurring its probable evils, in case they shall violate maxims generally received and respected.

H. L. A. HART, THE CONCEPT OF LAW

209 (1961)

[T]hough it is consistent with the usage of the last 150 years to use the expression "law" [with respect to international "law"], the absence of an international legislature, courts with compulsory jurisdiction, and centrally organized sanctions have inspired misgivings, at any rate in the breasts of legal theorists. The absence of these institutions means that the rules for states resemble the simple form of social structure, consisting only of primary rules of obligation, which, when we find it among societies of individuals, we are accustomed to contrast with a developed legal system. It is indeed arguable, as we shall show, that international law not only lacks the secondary rules of change and adjudication which provide for legislatures and courts, but also a unifying rule of recognition specifying "sources" of law and providing general criteria for the identification of its rules. These differences are indeed striking and the question "Is international law really law?" can hardly be put aside.

HANS KELSEN, *THE PURE THEORY OF LAW AND ANALYTICAL JURISPRUDENCE*

55 HARV. L. REV. 44–45, 66–70 (1941)

The pure theory of law is a theory of positive law; a general theory of law, not a presentation or interpretation of a special legal order. From a comparison of all the phenomena which go under the name of law, it seeks to discover the nature of law itself, to determine its structure and its typical forms, independent of the changing content which it exhibits at different times and among different peoples. In this manner it derives the fundamental principles by means of which any legal order can be comprehended. As a theory, its sole purpose is to know its subject. It answers the question of what the law is, not what it ought to be. The latter question is one of politics, while the pure theory of law is science.

It is called "pure" because it seeks to preclude from the cognition of positive law all elements foreign thereto. The limits of this subject and its cognition must be clearly fixed in two directions: the specific science of law, the discipline usually called jurisprudence, must be distinguished from the philosophy of justice, on the one hand, and from sociology, or cognition of social reality, on the other.

To free the concept of law from the idea of justice is difficult, because they are constantly confused both in political thought and in general speech, and because this confusion corresponds to the tendency to let positive law appear as just. In view of this tendency, the effort to deal with law and justice as two different problems falls under the suspicion of dismissing the requirement that positive law should be just. But the pure theory of law simply declares itself incompetent to answer either the question whether a given law is just or not, or the more fundamental question of what constitutes justice. The pure theory of law—a science—cannot answer these questions because they cannot be answered scientifically at all. * * *

International and National Law

If there is a legal order superior to the national legal orders, it must be international law. Whether it is really law in the same sense as national law, and whether, as a legal order, it stands above the national legal orders, are the two decisive questions. Austin answers both negatively, admitting the validity of international law only as "positive international morality." Therefore the theory of international law, like the theory of the state, is eliminated from the province of Austin's jurisprudence. The pure theory of law, on the other hand, shows that it is quite possible to consider international law as real law, since it contains all the essential elements of a legal order. It is a coercive order in the same sense as national law: it obligates states to definite mutual behavior, in that it provides sanctions against contrary conduct. The sanctions provided by international law are reprisals and war. The pure theory of law attempts to prove that according to international law not only reprisals but war, as well, is permissible only as a reaction against a wrong that has been suffered. The pure theory of law shows that the principle of [the just war] is a principle of positive international law. International law is real law, but it is primitive law. This is so especially because the reaction against the delict, the execution of the sanction, is left to the state itself, the very subject whose rights are infringed, instead of being delegated to a central organ as is the case in the national legal order. Thus the international legal order is radically decentralized, and for this very reason the international community constituted by international law is not a state, but only a union of states. A certain degree of centralization is essential to the state. Similarly the completely decentralized community of a primitive tribe is not a state, although there is no doubt that the order constituting it is a legal order.

There are today two opposing views in regard to the relation between national and international law, the one dualistic and the other monistic. The former maintains that national law and international law are two completely distinct and mutually independent systems of norms, like positive law and morality, for instance. The pure theory of law shows that such a dualistic concept of the relation between national and international law is logically impossible, and that none of the followers of the dualistic theory is able to maintain his point of view consistently. If one assumes that two systems of norms are considered as valid simultaneously from the same point of view, one must also assume a normative relation between them; one must assume the existence of a norm or order that regulates their mutual relations. Otherwise insoluble contradictions between the norms of each system are unavoidable, and the logical principle that excludes contradictions holds for the cognition of norms as much as for the cognition of natural reality. When positive law and morality are asserted to be two distinct mutually independent systems of norms, this means only that the jurist, in determining what is legal, does not take into consideration morality, and the moralist, in determining what is moral, pays no heed to the prescriptions of positive law. Positive law and morality can be regarded as two distinct and mutually independent systems of norms, because and to the extent that they are not conceived to be simultaneously valid from the same point of view. But once it is conceded that national and international law are both positive law, it is obvious that both must be considered as valid simultaneously from the same juristic point of view. For this reason, they must belong to the same system of norms, they must in some way supplement each other.

The monistic theory meets this logical requirement. It regards national and international law as one system of norms, as a unity. Opinions differ, however, as to how this whole is constructed. Some assert international law to be a part of national law, those norms of national law that regulate the relation of the state to other states. The rules admitted to be international law can bind the individual state only when the latter recognizes them and thereby takes them over into its own legal order. This is the theory of the primacy of national law, obviously proceeding from the idea that the state is sovereign, that is, that the national legal order is an order of the highest rank, above which no other order can be deemed valid. As this is true for each of the many national legal orders, there is, according to this theory, not one international law, but as many as there are national legal orders. In truth, there is no international law at all as such, but only national law. The relationship between the different national legal orders can be established only from the point of view of one given order, whose norms alone determine its relations to the other orders. From such a point of view, that is, from the standpoint of a definite national legal order, all other orders appear not as sovereign, but rather as delegated orders. They are systems of valid norms only to the extent that they are recognized as such by the state whose legal order constitutes the point of departure.

The pure theory of law shows that this monistic theory is indeed logically possible, but that it is not consonant with the idea that all states or national legal orders are of the same rank. The primacy of national law means the primacy of one national legal order not only in regard to international law, but in regard to all the other national legal orders as well. The idea quite generally held, that all states form a community in which they stand side by side on a footing of equality, is possible only on the assumption that above the states, or above the national legal orders, there is a legal order that makes them equal by defining their mutual spheres of validity. This order can be only international law. The pure theory of law shows by an analysis of positive international law that it actually does perform the function just mentioned, and hence can be regarded, if one foregoes the assumption of the sovereignty of the individual states, as a system of norms standing above the national legal orders, according them equal rank, and binding them together into a universal legal order. This is the theory of the primacy of international law, the theoretic basis for which was revealed for the first time by the pure theory of law.

There is nothing to prevent this interpretation of the legal material except the idea of the sovereignty of the state. One of the most important results of the pure theory of law is that sovereignty, in the specific sense which this idea has in a theory of law, is not a real characteristic of a real thing. Sovereignty is a judgment of value and as such it is an assumption. The individualistic philosophy of the 18th and 19th centuries proceeded from the idea that the human individual was sovereign, *i.e.*, of the highest value. From this it was concluded that a social order can be binding on the individual only when it is recognized by the individual as binding. From this came the doctrine of the social contract, which still has its exponents; but today the inclination is rather to a universalistic philosophy of values according to which the community is superior to the individual.

In the sphere of international relations the view that the state is essentially sovereign is an individualistic philosophy, based on the individuality of the state. The dogma of sovereignty is not the result of scientific analysis of the phenomenon of the state, but the assumption of a philosophy of values. Consequently it cannot be contradicted scientifically. One can only show that an interpretation which proceeds from another assumption—namely, from that of the sovereignty of the international legal community—is just as possible, and that positive international law itself, so far as its validity is admitted, requires this interpretation.

The analysis of positive international law made by the pure theory of law shows that its norms are incomplete norms, which need supplementing by the norms of the national legal orders. The generally accepted proposition that international law obligates only states means not that international law does not obligate individuals, but rather that while, like every law, it obligates individuals, it does so indirectly, through the medium of national legal orders. To say that international law obligates a state to certain conduct means that international law obligates an individual as an organ of this state to such conduct, but that international law determines directly only the conduct, leaving the national legal order to determine the individual whose conduct forms the content of the international obligation. Thus international law presupposes the simultaneous validity of national legal orders within one and the same system of legal norms that embraces international law as well.

A generally recognized principle of international law, formulated in the usual manner, reads as follows: if a power is established anywhere, in any manner, which is able to ensure permanent obedience to its coercive order among the individuals whose behavior this order regulates, then the community constituted by this coercive order is a state in the sense of international law. The sphere in which this coercive order is permanently effective is the territory of the state; the individuals who live in the territory are the people of the state in the sense of positive international law. This is the principle of effectiveness, so important throughout international law. By this legal principle, international law defines the territorial and personal spheres of validity of the national legal orders, spheres which each state is bound to respect. By it also is determined the validity of the national orders. These are valid, in the sense of international law, because and to the extent that they satisfy the requirement of effectiveness. If jurisprudence, as we have shown, considers a legal norm as valid only when it belongs to a legal order which is in the main effective, it is using a principle of positive law itself, a principle of international law.

Since the national legal orders find the reason for their validity in the international legal order, which at the same time defines their spheres of validity, the international legal order must be superior to each national order. Thus it forms, together with them, one uniform universal legal system.

As it is the task of natural science to describe its object—reality—in one system of natural laws, so it is the task of jurisprudence to comprehend all human law in one system of norms. This task Austin's jurisprudence did not see; the pure theory of law, imperfect and inaccurate though it may be in detail, has gone a measurable distance toward its accomplishment.

NOTES AND QUESTIONS

1. *Three different positivists, three different positivist approaches to international law.* Austin, Hart, and Kelsen are all generally considered positivists, but their assessments of international law *as law* are strikingly different. (a) Based on these excerpts, what are the differences, and more importantly, what accounts for those differences? (b) How should we refine our core notion of what qualifies as "positivism?" (c) What both ties these otherwise disparate jurists together and also distinguishes them from other schools of jurisprudence?

2. *One potentially clarifying perspective.* Two highly-respected scholars have condensed the positivist account of international law as follows:

> Positivism summarizes a range of theories that focus upon describing the law as it is, backed up by effective sanctions, with reference to formal criteria, independently of moral or ethical considerations. For positivists, international law is no more or less than the rules to which states have agreed through treaties, custom, and perhaps other forms of consent. In the absence of such evidence of the will of states, positivists will assume that states remain at liberty to undertake whatever actions they please. Positivism also tends to view states as the only subjects of international law, thereby discounting the role of non-state actors.

Steven R. Ratner & Anne-Marie Slaughter, *Appraising the Methods of International Law: A Prospectus for Readers*, 93 AM. J. INT'L L. 291, 293 (1999). Taking this summary as broadly accurate, consider the three principal cases in this chapter—*Velásquez-Rodríguez, Filártiga*, and *Alvarez-Machain*—and try to identify elements of contemporary international law that seem (a) to fit and (b) not fit the positivist mold.

---

2. INTERNATIONAL LAW AND NATURAL LAW

MARY ELLEN O'CONNELL, THE POWER AND PURPOSE OF INTERNATIONAL LAW: INSIGHTS FROM THE THEORY AND PRACTICE OF ENFORCEMENT

9–14 (2008)

* * * [T]here is much about international law that transcends the material, positive acts such as consent. International law's claim to be law is based ultimately on belief. It contains peremptory norms, *jus cogens* principles, that cannot be altered by positive acts, including the norms against genocide, apartheid, extra-judicial killing, slavery, and torture. The third primary source of international law rules after customary international law and treaties is the general principles of law—which have counterparts in principles articulated by the great jurists of classical Roman law. They understood them as requirements or implications of reason, inspired by the natural order of things. General principles from this category, such as necessity, proportionality, and good faith, play an important role in regulating enforcement measures. While most of international law is based on positive acts of consent, ultimately the ontology and legitimacy of international law is based on more than consent, just as it is more than sanctions.

Nevertheless, consent and sanctions are vital aspects of international law, providing important evidence that the community believes in the system. Although it is true that "[t]he essence of a legal system is the inherent fact, based on various psychological factors, that law is accepted by the community as a whole as binding, and the element of sanction is not an essential, or perhaps even an important, element in the functioning of the system,"[42] one of the ways that the international community demonstrates acceptance or belief that international law is law is through the system for sanctioning violations.

The violation of any rule of international law may be subject to a coercive sanction. These sanctions do not ensure complete compliance with the law, as some would like, but they do play at least three other significant roles in the establishment of international law as real law: they play a formal role in identifying legally binding rules; they coerce at least some violators into compliance; and, because of the first two roles, sanctions play a role in "internalizing" respect for international legal rules, thereby decreasing the need for coercive enforcement. Thus, sanctions are an essential part of international law, like any legal system, but not in the unsophisticated manner of simple police enforcement.

A community-created right to sanction noncompliance through forceful means is a key indicator that a rule is regarded as a legal rule and

---

[42] M.D.A. FREEMAN, LLOYD'S INTRODUCTION TO JURISPRUDENCE 215 (7th ed. 2001).

not a moral, social, or other type of rule. To allow coercive enforcement of anything short of a legal rule would be to allow the use of force outside the confines of law. It is to prevent just such unconstrained uses of force that law came to be instituted in human communities.

In addition to signaling that a rule is a legal rule, the very fact of the sanction imparts authority to international law rules, generating respect without the need for the application of the sanction. As Harold Koh of Yale University has written, international law compliance is the product of rule internalization, too.[46] He suggests that this happens if international law rules are implemented in domestic law, enforced by domestic courts, and administered by government agencies. In addition to all of these things, which happen in every country in the world, international law will share in a community's respect for law generally. It is, after all, international "law," and in many countries there is a tradition of respect for international law. Certainly that is the case of the United States.[47] Some empirical work supports the linkage between an enforcement system and the seriousness with which international law rules are regarded. * * *

Further, and related to the first two points, some international law violators will in fact be sanctioned. This actual application of the sanction will coerce some violators into compliance or into providing a remedy for noncompliance. The application of sanctions reminds others that sanctions exist, which in turn, supports more voluntary law compliance. Thus, sanctions, in a variety of ways help to ensure that international law compliance is occurring on a level sufficient to consider it effective law. Penalties or sanctions are:

> required not as the normal motive for obedience, but as the guarantee that those who would voluntarily obey shall not be sacrificed to those who would not. To obey, without this, would be to risk going to the wall. Given this standing danger, what reason demands is voluntary co-operation in a coercive system.[50]

The majority in society must voluntarily comply with the rules for a legal system to be maintained. Without this majority compliance, it would not be possible to claim that the community believes in the authority of the law.[51]

Thus, general compliance, which is connected to the existence of sanctions for law violation, is important evidence that international law is accepted as law. Further evidence is found in the formal processes of law making, which, again, are related to the existence of sanctions. As mentioned above, the sources of international law are positivist—treaty,

---

[46] Harold Hongju Koh, *Why Do Nations Obey?*, 106 YALE L.J. 2599 (1997).

[47] *See, e.g.*, MARK WESTON JANIS, THE AMERICAN TRADITION OF INTERNATIONAL LAW: GREAT EXPECTATIONS 1789–1974 (2004).

[50] H.L.A. HART, THE CONCEPT OF LAW 193 (1961).

[51] *Id.* at 196.

customary international law, and to some extent general principles, but some general principles are grounded in natural law sources as are the peremptory norms. Rules emanating from these sources are binding and law violators may be sanctioned for noncompliance. Nonbinding principles are sometimes called "soft law" to indicate the expectation of compliance but no right of sanction. The term is perhaps misleading in that without the sanction, principles are not "law" at all, soft or otherwise.

Because some aspects of international law are best explained using natural law theory, courts and tribunals play an important role in interpreting these aspects, but courts are, arguably, just as vital in interpreting and applying the rules emerging from the positive sources. Some form of adjudicative process has been part of international law since it began with the end of the Thirty Year' War in Europe in 1648. The treaties that ended that war, the Peace of Westphalia, contained elements that still comprise fundamental components of the international legal system, including the obligation to settle disputes through legal discourse not armed conflict. Grotius extolled the use of arbitration as an alternative to armed conflict in his 1625 book, ON THE LAW OF WAR AND PEACE. Several of the Spanish Scholastics, Grotius's predecessors, had suggested arbitration as a process to fill the gap in intercommunal relations left by the declining earthly authority of the Pope and Holy Roman Emperor. From these early ideas, courts have grown steadily in importance in both the theory and practice of international law. Not only do courts today adjudicate the existence and meaning of rules, they are playing a larger role in the proper application of sanctions. For sanctions to be legal sanctions, not just self-help actions of reprisal or revenge, Kelsen and Lauterpacht explained the importance of courts in adjudicating both the wrong and the remedy.[55] In addition to courts resolving disputes among states, Kelsen was an early advocate of courts for the purpose of holding individuals accountable for violations of international law. Individual accountability was in line with his view that states are led by real people, and people exercise their will, not the state itself.[56]

Today, courts are generally available for both the interstate resolution of disputes and individual accountability. Thanks in particular to the World Trade Organization's (WTO's) Dispute Settlement Understanding (DSU), ever more sophisticated principles for the application of sanctions are being developed and applied. International criminal courts are now active in several places in the world. * * *

International law has deficits, yet it persists as the single, generally accepted means to solve the world's problems.[60] It is not religion or ideology

---

[55] HERSCH LAUTERPACHT, THE FUNCTION OF LAW IN THE INTERNATIONAL COMMUNITY 424 (1933).

[56] HANS KELSEN, PEACE THROUGH LAW 84–85 (1944).

[60] C.G. WEERAMANTRY, UNIVERSALIZING INTERNATIONAL LAW 1–3 (2004).

that the world has in common, but international law. Through international law, diverse cultures can reach consensus about the moral norms that we will commonly live by. As a result, international law is uniquely suited to mitigate the problems of armed conflict, terrorism, human rights abuse, poverty, disease, and the destruction of the natural environment. It is the closest thing we have to a neutral vehicle for taking on the world's most complex issues and pressing problems.

NOTES AND QUESTIONS

1. *The contested natural law origins of international law.* One orthodox assessment of international law is that it assumed its contemporary form only after the Peace of Westphalia (1648), which both reflected and preserved an emerging system of state sovereignty in central Europe. "International law as a law between sovereign and equal states based on the common consent of those states is a product of modern Christian civilization, and may be said to be about four hundred years old." HERSCH LAUTERPACHT, ED., OPPENHEIM'S INTERNATIONAL LAW: A TREATISE 68 (1948). A separate but compatible orthodoxy traces certain elements of international law to the non-Christian ancients, especially norms governing diplomacy, treaty-making and warfare, and looks beyond Europe. DAVID J. BEDERMAN, INTERNATIONAL LAW IN ANTIQUITY (2001). From that perspective, for most of its existence, the law of nations was viewed as a species of natural law until the rise of legal positivism in the nineteenth century. "With regard to International Law, * * * all authorities down to the end of the eighteenth century, and almost all outside England to this day, have treated it as a body of doctrine *derived from and justified* by the Law of Nature." SIR FREDERICK POLLOCK, ESSAYS IN LAW 63 (1922) (emphasis added).

To be specific, one category of law in ancient Rome was the *jus* (or *ius*) *gentium*, the precursor to what the 18th-century lawyers called "the law of nations," and it consisted of general principles common among civilized communities, Roman and non-Roman alike. This was the body of law—generally covering what are now considered torts or contracts or other branches of private law—that Roman magistrates would apply in resolving "transnational" cases involving non-Romans. The *jus gentium* ("the law among peoples or nations") was not codified by statute, and that reality combined with its claims to universality and its basis in reason suggest its relationship to natural law generally. In words generally attributed to Justinian, "the law that natural reason has established among all persons, that law is observed uniformly among all, and is called the law of peoples." AARON X. FELLMETH & MAURICE HORWITZ, GUIDE TO LATIN IN INTERNATIONAL LAW 244 (2009).

2. *Natural law constructs in contemporary international law.* In ancient Roman law, *jus cogens* referred to unwritten but peremptory standards that limited what private parties could accomplish by contract. These natural law norms reflected baseline, communitarian values that could not be subverted

by contract: they were beyond the power of the parties' consent. For example, a contract in which the parties agreed to commit a crime or to suspend the duty of good faith in all of their other contracts would be unenforceable as a violation of *jus cogens*.

In contemporary international law, a treaty can in some circumstances be analogized to a contract, and a treaty in violation of *jus cogens* is similarly void. Consider the following provisions of the Vienna Convention on the Law of Treaties, *opened for signature* May 23, 1969, 1155 U.N.T.S. 331:

> Article 53. *Treaties Conflicting with a Peremptory Norm of General international Law ("Jus Cogens")*. A treaty is void if, at the time of its conclusion, it conflicts with a peremptory norm of general international law. For the purposes of the present Convention, a peremptory norm of general international law is a norm accepted and recognized by the international community of States as a whole as a norm from which no derogation is permitted and which can be modified only by a subsequent norm of general international law having the same character.
>
> Article 64. *Emergence of a New peremptory Norm of general International Law ("Jus Cogens")*. If a new peremptory norm of general international law emerges, any existing treaty which is in conflict with that norm becomes void and terminates.

As with other natural law constructs, it can be difficult to determine the source and content of *jus cogens* norms, and no conclusive, authoritative catalogue of such norms has ever been concluded. One recurring difficulty is drawing the line between customary international law on one hand, which can be made and unmade by the practice of states acting out of a sense of legal obligation, and *jus cogens* on the other, which is an elite set of norms apparently invulnerable to treaties. Despite these difficulties, governments have adopted the Vienna Convention on the Law of Treaties with its provisions on *jus cogens*, suggesting that questions about the status and content of *jus cogens* norms are not fatal to the concept. In addition, there seems to be general consensus that a hypothetical treaty in which the parties agreed to invade some third country and commit genocide there would be void and unenforceable as a violation of the *jus cogens* norm against genocide. A treaty suspending the operation of good faith in all other treaty relations would be similarly treated as a violation of the *jus cogens* norm that treaties must be performed in good faith.

Can the pure consent theory of international legal obligations—that a state can have only those obligations to which it gives its continuing consent—account for these norms that are essentially *beyond* consent? *Must* a positivist account of international law dismiss or disparage these norms?

3. *Deciding cases "ex aequo et bono."* Article 38(2) of the ICJ Statute, *supra*, preserves "the power of the Court to decide a case *ex aequo et bono*, if the parties agree thereto." As generally understood, the power to resolve a case *ex aequo et bono* (*i.e.*, from considerations of fairness and good) frees the court

to go beyond the strict requirements of the law and to consider instead what is just. One interpretation of this authority is that it imports considerations of justice that are better captured in the natural law tradition than in any of its jurisprudential competitors. (a) Why do you suppose the International Court of Justice can only turn to such principles "when the parties agree thereto?" (b) What does that limited authority in Article 38(2) to apply principles of fairness say, if anything, about the four sources of international law listed in Article 38(1)?

---

3. INTERNATIONAL LAW AND LEGAL REALISM

JACK GOLDSMITH & ERIC POSNER, *THE NEW INTERNATIONAL LAW SCHOLARSHIP*

34 GA. J. INT'L & COMP. L. 463 (2006)

[Our book,] THE LIMITS OF INTERNATIONAL LAW sets forth a general theory of international law. The book rejects the traditional explanations of international law based on legality, morality, *opinio juris*, and related non-instrumental concepts. Using simple rational choice tools, the book seeks instead to provide an instrumental account of when and why nations use international law, when and why they comply with it, and when and why international law changes. The basic descriptive story is that international law emerges from and is sustained by nations acting rationally to maximize their interests (*i.e.,* their preferences over international relations outcomes), given their perception of the interests of other states, and the distribution of state power. LIMITS also makes two normative arguments: nations have no moral obligation to comply with international law, and liberal democratic nations have no duty to engage in the strong cosmopolitan actions so often demanded of them. * * *

The primary intellectual target of LIMITS is the claim—widespread in earlier generations of international law scholarship, and still dominant today—that nations comply with international law for non-instrumental reasons. Non-instrumental explanations for compliance can include a sense of obligation to comply (*opinio juris*), or international law's normative pull, or the absorption of international law into a nation's internal value set. * * *

Our essential claims are as follows. International law provides a focal point for coordination, and establishes what counts as cooperation in a prisoner's dilemma. Such patterns of behavior can arise in a decentralized fashion, in which case they are identified as rules of customary international law (CIL). But CIL rules tend to be relatively unclear, making cooperation and coordination by custom relatively fragile. Through communication, negotiation, and drafting common documents, nations can clarify their expectations about the opportunities for the joint gains that can be achieved by coordination and cooperation. In a repeated prisoner's dilemma, a clear rule of cooperation can reduce both opportunism and unintended defections from the cooperative game. In a coordination situation, a clear rule reduces the likelihood of an unintended failure of coordination.

Once the rule of cooperation or focal point for coordination is established by custom or treaty, nations comply for one of three general (and not mutually exclusive) reasons. The first is fear of retaliation in a prisoner's dilemma. Each state complies with the rule because it fears retaliation, and a loss of the cooperative surplus, if it does not. The second is fear of a failure of coordination. A CIL rule or treaty works by aligning the relevant expectations and helping parties to avoid the costs of failing to coordinate. A third and quite different reason is fear of reputational loss from failing to comply with the rule.

Under this theory, international law does not pull states toward compliance contrary to their interests. International law emerges from states pursuing their interests to achieve mutually beneficial outcomes, and it is sustained to the degree to which it continues to serve those interests. When international law changes, as it often does, it does so because state interests (again, state preferences over international relations outcomes) change due (for example) to changes in technology, or in relative wealth, or in domestic government. The transition from the old to new rule of international law is not always smooth, for the world lacks stable international institutions—legislatures, regulatory agencies, effective courts-to facilitate the change. Instead, we often see violation, rhetorical clashes, retaliation, and sometimes war as the international order shifts from an old to a new equilibrium.

With this background, it should be clear that we do not * * * think international law is irrelevant or unimportant. It is very important, and indeed often crucial, in helping nations to reap gains from (and avoid losses from) interaction. Nor do we think that international law is inconsequential. The terms of a treaty matter to the gains each state receives from the treaty through cooperation or coordination. That is why states negotiate so intensely over treaty terms. We even accept that international law "constrains" states, as long as one is careful to understand "constraint" to mean that when international law establishes a focal point for coordination or the cooperative solution in a prisoner's dilemma, nations wanting to reap the benefits of coordination or cooperation will be constrained to abide by the coordinating or cooperating solution.

We do, however, think it is generally wrong and theoretically unhelpful to view international law as an exogenous force on state behavior. In that sense, and that sense primarily, our theory does not give international law the same type of importance attributed to it by traditional international law scholars. In addition, we show throughout the book that the evidence traditional scholars have used to show the exogenous force of international law is susceptible to multiple plausible interpretations, including the very simple interpretation that states are acting consistently with the law because the law does not require that they deviate from their private interest (the "coincidence of interest" paradigm). Perhaps some scholars mistake the last claim to be an argument that international law does nothing at all—a claim associated with some "realists" in political science—but that is a serious misreading of our book.

It is true that our book emphasizes the "Limits" of international law, and that we are more skeptical than most scholars about what international law might accomplish. But it is important to understand why, in our view, international law is so limited. International law is limited because it is a product of, and is bounded by, state interests and the distribution of power. Given the multiple conflicting interests of states on various issues, and the particular distribution of state power with respect to those issues, many global problems are unsolvable. To recognize this point is not to reject international law.

Indeed, the view to the contrary implicitly adopts a kind of "Whig" theory of the development of international law, analogous to the long discredited Whig theory of history, which holds that history is a story of constant improvement toward some ideal end. International law scholars recognize the current imperfection of international law, but, lacking a theory of the limits of international law, see no reason why this imperfection should be tolerated. Thus, they are drawn to the conclusion that international law can only get better, and all that stands in the way of its improvement is error or ideological rigidity. This is not a plausible view of either international law or history. * * *

ROGER FISHER, *BRINGING LAW TO BEAR ON GOVERNMENTS*

74 HARV. L. REV. 1130, 1130–35 (1961)

Most lawyers hold in common a view of international law which runs somewhat as follows: There is a great difference between positive law—law with a policeman behind it—and so-called international law. International law is a body of vague rules for the attention of the political scientist and the amusement of the law student not much interested in law. It should not be confused with real law, which, as Mr. Justice Holmes pointed out, is "the articulate voice of some sovereign or quasi-sovereign that can be identified,"[3] and "does not exist without some definite authority behind it."[4] Law is the command of a sovereign backed by force. And however much it is hoped that nations will abide by acknowledged rules some day, they do not now; nor can they ever be compelled to do so, at least in the absence of world government. Only woolly thinking would confuse positive law enforced by our courts—our Constitution, our civil and criminal laws—with the moral directives which go by the name of international law. * * *

The command theory of law, which was used to distinguish the law that is from the law that ought to be, was evidently developed out of an examination of the typical private action for a tort or on a contract. If a court declared that Doe must pay Roe a stated amount, the sheriff and the marshall stood ready to enforce the judgment with the full power of the state. This was the situation envisioned by Austin when he spoke of laws as commands. His definition of law did not apply to rules restraining the behavior of the state itself which Austin referred to as rules of "positive morality." The "power of the government," he said, "is incapable of legal limitation." It followed that a government had neither legal rights nor legal duties. * * *

Within such a theory, international law is clearly no more than positive morality. But much of the modern law school curriculum besides international law would have to be similarly characterized. Courses in constitutional law, administrative law, and tax law, to name only a few, deal in large part with limitations on governmental action or involve the Government as a party to a dispute in courts deriving jurisdiction from itself. * * *

Whether or not we are content to call all these areas of law "positive morality," the fact remains that a large part of our courts' work lies in these very areas. Whether or not governments are theoretically capable of legal limitation, they do regularly submit to adverse court decisions. I suggest that we lawyers, in uncritically accepting the command theory and applying it to international law have ourselves been guilty of woolly thinking. I suggest that in denying the status of international law because there is no apparent sovereign issuing the commands, we show a limited understanding of how a court system operates in its relations with a government. In blandly assuming that all law rests on superior force, we have ignored the cases in which the government loses a judgment and honors it.

Is organized force essential to such compliance? Clearly it is not. When a judgment is entered against the United States in the Court of Claims, no superior sovereign compels Congress to vote an appropriation. The judgment is paid because that is the law; but the law is not the articulate

---

3 *Southern Pac. Co. v. Jensen*, 244 U.S. 205, 222 (1917) (dissenting opinion).

4 *Black & White Taxicab & Transfer Co. v. Brown & Yellow Taxicab & Transfer Co.*, 276 U.S. 518, 533 (1928) (dissenting opinion).

voice of a superior sovereign. When, in [*Youngstown Sheet & Tube Co. v. Sawyer*, 343 U.S. 579 (1952)], the Supreme Court ordered the Secretary of Commerce to return the steel mills which the President had ordered him to seize, the Court had no regiments at its command. But despite the fact that the Supreme Court sitting in Washington had no greater force at its command vis-à-vis the Government than does the International Court of Justice sitting at the Hague, the steel mills were returned.

The more closely one examines law within this country and within others, the less significant seems the element of force. Even such hard, positive laws as the criminal and tax laws depend ultimately on compliance with them by the Government, and the general pattern is one of compliance. * * * This record, even if less than perfect, demonstrates that a pattern of governmental compliance can be secured without a supra-governmental police force. * * *

If it is not the threat of force which induces governmental compliance with domestic law, it is not the absence of force which explains why our Government feels less strongly bound by international law than, for example, by the Constitution. Nor does an explanation lie in the fact that international rules are generically more vague than constitutional rules. They are not. Nor can we look for an answer in our Government's denying the binding nature of international law. It does not. Nor is an answer to be found in the assumption that the Government will comply more readily with rules benefiting citizens than with those benefiting foreigners. The due process clause protects citizen and alien alike.

What is the difference, then, between a judgment of the Court of Claims and a judgment of the International Court? Is it merely that the United States accepted the jurisdiction of the former one hundred years ago and has not yet really accepted the jurisdiction of the latter? The question is worth exploring. An understanding of the factors inducing governmental obedience to domestic law may shed light on the problem of securing obedience to international law. We should not expect to find factors that guarantee obedience. Governments do not always obey rules. In a given case, what are considered vital interests may lead a government to break the law just as they may persuade an individual to steal. The question, rather, is: What are the forces which tend to induce obedience, the elements which impart strength to the law? Knowing that these elements are in fact strong enough to bring about general governmental compliance with domestic law, we will want to appraise their ability to bring about governmental compliance with international law.

In considering whether to respect a rule, one factor which a government takes into account is the danger of external consequences should it not respect the rule. Even where there is no organized superior sovereign power to compel obedience, a government is not free to ignore the conduct and attitudes of those with whom it must deal. The United States

Government, considered as an entity, respects the Constitution partly because it fears the retaliatory action which might be taken by the citizens if it did not. A focal point for such retaliation might be the polls. And the Government respects the right to vote, influenced in part, perhaps, by fear of more violent action if it were denied.

NOTES AND QUESTIONS

1. *Legal realism and international law.* Chapter 3, *supra*, is devoted to an exploration of American legal realism and especially its core descriptive claim about the nature of adjudication: judicial reasoning reflects a conventional, formalistic process that hides the open texture of rules and minimizes the appearance of the judges' agency in deciding cases by hunches, instincts, and biases. The legal realists' insight might seem especially potent in international law, because their skepticism about adjudication gets transformed into a broad-gauged skepticism about the effectiveness of rules for governments. Even those who may find legal realism reductionistic as a general account of domestic legal practice may be attracted to the idea that international law rules cannot exist if they are essentially optional, with no predictable or effective sanction for disobedience.

Considering only the cases excerpted above—*Velásquez-Rodríguez*, *Filártiga*, and *Alvarez-Machain*—and the observations of Professors Goldsmith, Posner, and Fisher, *supra*, what is there—if anything—about the conventional, Austinian understanding of the concept of sanctions that deserves rethinking when it comes to international law?

2. *Multiple meanings of "realism."* One of the most virulent attacks on international law *as law* came not from lawyers or legal philosophers but from international relations ("IR") theorists. They have had their own varieties of "realism," with differences profound and subtle among them, but the unifying thesis was that the international system is essentially anarchical (though without connotations of chaos or irrationality), driven by self-interest and the various sorts of power that exist to advance it. *See* KENNETH WALTZ, THEORY OF INTERNATIONAL POLITICS (1979); Jack Donnelly, *The Discourse of Anarchy in IR*, 7 INTERNATIONAL THEORY 393 (2015).

The scholarly literature in this tradition can be traced back centuries to Thucydides and Machiavelli, and it is too vast to summarize here, but it does have one significant consequence for our purposes: it concluded that international law is impotent in the face of power, indeed that it is just another manifestation of power and not some exogenous constraint on state decision-making. In short, states do what is in their interest, and, when they comply with international norms, they do so because it is in their interest and not because they are in any sense obligated to do so. If they are powerful enough, no meaningful sanction will follow their noncompliance, and it is dangerous and naïve to assume otherwise. EDWARD H. CARR, THE TWENTY YEARS CRISIS,

1919–1939 (1939); MICHAEL BYERS, THE ROLE OF LAW IN INTERNATIONAL POLITICS: ESSAYS IN INTERNATIONAL POLITICS (2000).

Some international lawyers and academics have responded to the IR realists' insights and their methods, sometimes by incorporating them into an interdisciplinary approach to international norm creation and compliance. *See, e.g.*, Anne-Marie Slaughter, Andrew S. Tulumello, and Stephan Wood, *International Law and International Relations Theory: A New Generation of Interdisciplinary Scholarship*, 92 AMER. J. INT'L L. 367 (1998); Kenneth W. Abbott, *Modern International Relations Theory: A Prospectus for International Lawyers*, 14 YALE J. INT'L L. 335 (1989). Over the last twenty years, the discourses of international law on one hand and international relations on the other have come to influence each other in a reciprocal process of adjustment, response, incorporation, evolution, and refinement. *See, e.g.*, ADRIANA SINCLAIR, INTERNATIONAL RELATIONS THEORY AND INTERNATIONAL LAW: A CRITICAL APPROACH (2010); ROBERT J. BECK, ED., LAW AND DISCIPLINARITY: THINKING BEYOND BORDERS (2013).

3. *How realistic are the descriptive claims of realism?* Both excerpts above—from Goldsmith & Posner and from Fisher—purport to be grounded in a realistic assessment of the way international law works (or doesn't). How would you articulate the differences between these two realisms, and which seems more realistic to you?

---

4. INTERNATIONAL LAW AND THE LEGAL PROCESS SCHOOL

ABRAM CHAYES, THOMAS EHRLICH, & ANDREAS F. LOWENFELD, INTERNATIONAL LEGAL PROCESS: MATERIALS FOR AN INTRODUCTORY COURSE XIII–IV

(1968)

The international system does not approach developed domestic systems in cohesion or articulation or in the existence of an authoritatively ascertainable body of rules. Still, it is a functioning system comprising innumerable arrangements for ordering affairs across state borders. All but a tiny fraction of these matters are handled according to the prescription of the system, and without conflict, let alone newspaper headlines. * * *

Between states, however, as between individuals, there are areas of sharply conflicting interest. Many of these involve law—either because the applicable law is itself at issue, or because the law and legal institutions enter into the settlement process. The most striking difference between international and domestic law is that internationally, at least when states are parties, there is only rarely an established institution with power to make an authoritative disposition. Some international agreements provide in advance for arbitral settlements, and in some cases states agree to adjudication of a dispute after it arises. But for the most part, international disputes are not subject to authoritative third-party decision. They are resolved by the parties, under pressure generated by other kinds of settlement institutions. Often, they are simply outlived.

If these characteristics mark important differences between international and municipal legal systems, the differences are in of degree and not of kind. The domestic system is by no means wholly coherent, for ambiguity inevitably intrudes into the effort to subject unique events to abstract general rules. Most domestic controversies, like international ones, are resolved without the benefit of adjudication. Beyond this, there are immense areas of domestic activity, as there are of international activity, that are not subject to any legal regulation, judicial or otherwise.

HAROLD KOH, *TRANSNATIONAL LEGAL PROCESS*

75 NEB. L. REV. 181 (1996)

Transnational legal process describes the theory and practice of how public and private actors—nation-states, international organizations, multinational enterprises, non-governmental organizations, and private individuals—interact in a variety of public and private, domestic and international fora to make, interpret, enforce, and ultimately, internalize rules of transnational law.

Transnational legal process has four distinctive features. First, it is nontraditional: it breaks down two traditional dichotomies that have historically dominated the study of international law: between domestic and international, public and private. Second, it is non-statist: the actors in this process are not just, or even primarily, nation-states, but include non-state actors as well. Third, transnational legal process is dynamic, not static. Transnational law transforms, mutates, and percolates up and down, from the public to the private, from the domestic to the international level and back down again. Fourth and finally, it is normative. From this process of interaction, new rules of law emerge, which are interpreted, internalized, and enforced, thus beginning the process all over again. Thus, the concept embraces not just the descriptive workings of a process, but the normativity of that process. It focuses not simply upon how international interaction among transnational actors shapes law, but also on how law shapes and guides future interactions: in short, how law influences why nations obey.

To see these four features, consider the case of a California engineering firm called Dames & Moore.[7] In the late 1960s, the firm signed a contract

[7] *See Dames & Moore v. Regan*, 453 U.S. 654 (1981).

to conduct a nuclear power plant site study. By most measures such a contract would constitute the classic "private domestic business deal," except that it was struck not with Pacific Gas and Electric, but with the Atomic Energy Organization of Iran. Moreover, this agreement was negotiated against a "public" backdrop not just of Iranian and United States domestic law, but of numerous bilateral and multilateral treaty commitments between the Iranian and United States governments. In 1979, a cataclysmic public event—the ouster of the Shah, his flight to the United States, and the seizure of 52 American hostages—triggered a surge of emergency host and home-country regulations that dramatically affected these preexisting "private" deals.[8] The Atomic Energy Organization cancelled the contract, leading Dames & Moore to sue Iran and its instrumentalities in United States district court. When the court vacated Dames & Moore's judicial attachment of Iranian bank property based on the January 1981 executive orders implementing the United States-Iran executive agreement that freed the hostages, Dames & Moore filed a new district court complaint against the United States, seeking to enjoin enforcement of those executive orders. That suit ultimately resulted in a historic loss in the United States Supreme Court a few months later. As a last resort, Dames & Moore proceeded to the Iran-United States Claims Tribunal, which excluded it from the Tribunal's jurisdiction, citing to an Iranian forum-selection clause in its original contract.[9]

The Iranian Hostages crisis illustrates each of the features of transnational legal process mentioned above. First, it does not fit traditional categories. It cannot be neatly cabined within "domestic law"—traditionally thought to govern conduct within borders—or "international" law, which has been thought to govern conduct across borders. Nor can it be characterized as "public" international law—the law among nation-states, which encompasses what nations do to or with each other[10]—or "private" international law, classically thought of as cross-border law among non-state actors. Second, the process was dynamic, not static. An ostensibly "private business deal" entered between a United States multinational and a developing-country government dissolved into a domestic legal dispute, then percolated upward into a public international dispute, which was ultimately resolved by sovereign governments by an agreement based on public international and domestic public law in a

8 These regulations took the form of Iranian expropriatory actions and retaliatory United States government sanctions, including a trade embargo, an extraterritorial assets freeze, and, ultimately, an executive agreement that nullified judicial attachments on frozen Iranian assets, suspended private claims against Iran, and transferred them to arbitration before the newly created Iran-United States Claims Tribunal.

9 *See Dames & Moore v. Iran*, Award No. 97–54–3, Dec. 20, 1983, IRANIAN ASSETS LIT. REP. 7,727 (Jan. 13, 1984); Dissenting Opinion of Judge Mosk, Dec. 21, 1983, IRANIAN ASSETS LIT. REP. at 7,738 (Jan. 13, 1984).

10 *E.g.*, making war and peace; forming international agreements; allocating rights to air, sea, and space; state responsibility; international organizations; and such topics as jurisdiction, immunities, and diplomatic relations.

manner that triggered both domestic constitutional claims by a multinational corporation against its own government in its own domestic courts and international expropriation and breach of contract claims against a foreign government in a newly-minted international forum.[11]

Third, the key actors in this process were not just nation-states, but also the International Monetary Fund, various multinational enterprises (particularly the large banks who participated in freezing and transferring the assets), and the individual hostages whose human rights were at stake. Fourth and finally, the interaction among these transnational players was what Robert Cover calls "jurisgenerative."[12] It not only generated law—the domestic private law of letters of credit, the domestic public law of executive power, the international private law of dispute-resolution, and the public international law of diplomatic relations law—but generated new interpretations of those rules and internalized them into domestic law that now guides and channels those actors' future conduct.

NOTES AND QUESTIONS

1. *The Legal Process School opens an international branch*. Chapter 4, *supra*, identified certain recurring elements of the Legal Process School as a pragmatic account of American legal practice, including: (i) "institutional settlement" of disputes and public policy debates. (ii) the power of "reasoned elaboration" by the courts acting within a restricted zone of competence; (iii) the distinction between—and the relation between—public and private institutions; and (iv) law as a purposive enterprise, with social improvement as its object. In the summary of two leading scholars, international legal process "has seen the key locus of inquiry of international law as the role of law in constraining decision makers and affecting the course of international affairs." Steven R. Ratner & Anne-Marie Slaughter, *Appraising the Methods of International Law: A Prospectus for Readers*, 93 AM. J. INT'L L. 291, 294 (1999).

Considering again the cases excerpted above—*Velásquez-Rodríguez*, *Filártiga*, and *Alvarez-Machain*, as well as the brief excerpts from the Chayes, Ehrlich, & Lowenfeld casebook and Professor Koh's article—what echoes of the Legal Process School can you find in its international version?

---

[11] For a similar process of mutation, witness transnational contract law, which began as customary international law—the law merchant or lex mercatoria—but transformed into English common law when England became the world's leading commercial power. Upon the founding of the United States, that English common law migrated to the United States as federal general common law. *See Swift v. Tyson*, 41 U.S. (16 Pet.) 1 (1842). Such contract law then became the subject of state codification in the Uniform Commercial Code until, in 1988, the United States became a party to the U.N. Convention for Contracts for the International Sale of Goods, an act that re-elevated transnational contract questions to positive international treaty law.

[12] Robert M. Cover, *The Supreme Court, 1982 Term—Foreword, Nomos and Narrative*, 97 HARV. L. REV. 4 (1983).

2. *Unmasking the normative orientation in something that describes itself as process-oriented.* As noted in chapter 4, the Legal Process School

> rested on the complacent, simplistic assumption that American society consisted of happy, private actors maximizing their valid human wants while sharing their profound belief in institutional competencies. That may have reflected the mind-set of many in the 1950s, but by the end of the 1960s it seemed oddly out of touch with reality.

Elizabeth Mensch, *Mainstream Legal Thought*, *in* THE POLITICS OF LAW: A PROGRESSIVE CRITIQUE (David Kairys ed., 1982), at 30. What implicit or explicit normative values can you find in Professor Koh's account of international legal process?

3. *Law school pedagogy and the Legal Process School.* One of the peculiarities of the Legal Process School is that it emerged from a famous casebook that remained unpublished for nearly forty years. HENRY M. HART & ALBERT SACKS, THE LEGAL PROCESS: BASIC PROBLEMS IN THE MAKING AND APPLICATION OF LAW (tent. ed. 1958). *See* WILLIAM ESKRIDGE AND PHILIP FRICKEY, EDS., HART AND SACKS' THE LEGAL PROCESS: BASIC PROBLEMS IN THE MAKING AND APPLICATION OF LAW (1994). International Legal Process also emerged from a casebook by the same name, very much influenced by the methods and insights of the Hart and Sacks manuscript. ABRAM CHAYES, THOMAS EHRLICH & ANDREAS LOWENFELD, INTERNATIONAL LEGAL PROCESS: MATERIALS FOR AN INTRODUCTORY COURSE xxi (1968) ("To Professors Henry M. Hart, Jr. and Albert M. Sacks, we owe much more than just our title.") What is it about the process schools that (a) lends itself to law school teaching and (b) resists philosophical treatments?

---

5. INTERNATIONAL LAW AND ECONOMICS

JOEL P. TRACHTMAN, THE ECONOMIC STRUCTURE OF INTERNATIONAL LAW

2, 4–7, 10–11, 15–16 (2008)

Economic analysis holds great promise for international law. This promise lies in the ability of economic analysis to suggest useful methods for analyzing the actual or potential consequences of particular legal rules. * * * Economic models begin with price theory, which assumes that, all things being equal, people prefer cheaper goods and services, as well as more efficient means of achieving their nonconsumption goals. * * * An additional level of complexity is added by transaction costs analysis, which simply recognizes, within price theory, that there are costs to engaging in transactions, and that those costs may prevent otherwise efficient transactions or may account for institutional structures. A third level of complexity is added by game theory, which recognizes that the strategic position of states may prevent or add costs to otherwise efficient arguments. * * *

I will now provide some examples of the application of price theory, transaction costs analysis, [and] game theory * * * in international law. * * *

Price theory is the basis for cost-benefit analysis: in seeking to achieve our preferences, we seek to maximize benefits and minimize costs (benefits and costs are measured in terms of the achievement of our preferences, which are not necessarily monetized or monetizable.) Therefore, if my preferences include engagement in ethnic cleansing, I would examine the costs of weapons, of retaliation by my target, or of my reputation. If there exists an international legal rule against ethnic cleansing that is enforced and could result in my punishment. The discount factor would relate to the likelihood of my apprehension and punishment, and the delay until my apprehension and punishment. Therefore, based on the price theory model, we would hypothesize that *mutatis mutandis*, a reliably enforceable legal rule with substantial punishment would reduce the likelihood of ethnic cleansing. * * *

Transaction cost economics addresses the difficulty of identifying partners for the exchanges of goods, services, or promises; negotiating exchange; and enforcing terms of exchange. In international law, we might consider the difficulty of establishing treaties dealing with specific (as opposed to more general) environmental problems. Thus, there may be a smelter in Canada that causes air pollution that, due to prevailing winds, travels to the United States. While it may be useful to deal with some larger environmental issues between the United States and Canada, this particular issue may be too small to merit the devotion of diplomatic energy. Absent transaction costs, this cross-border issue might be resolved, but given transaction costs it goes unresolved. In this case, the cost of the injury would remain with the injured person in the United States. This may be efficient: transaction costs are real costs. However, there may be ways to reduce transaction costs to establish a rule of liability, such as *sic utere tuo*, to the effect that the polluter is responsible for damage to others. Given a rule such as *sic utere tuo*, it may be easier for the parties to negotiate a solution that minimizes the joint costs.

Game theory can help us understand possible solutions to problems of international cooperation. * * * The prisoner's exchange dilemma[4] * * * provides a way of understanding the problem of cooperation in circumstances where each individual can do better by violating a customary international rule or treaty, but both sides will do worse if both violate the rule or treaty. The bilateral prisoner's dilemma, resulting in inefficient violation by both sides, may be escaped by repetition. If you

4 [Editor's note: See chapter 5, *supra*.]

violate the first time, I can retaliate later. If you understand this and value the future sufficiently (*i.e.*, are sufficiently patient), you may determine not to violate the first time. The shadow of the future provides incentives for cooperation. The development of customary international law may be understood in this way. * * *

[A]ccording to the economic perspective, the international system, like economic markets, is formed by the interaction of self-regarding units—largely, but not exclusively, states. These utilitarian states interact to "overcome the deficiencies that make it impossible to consummate . . . mutually beneficial agreements. Actors in each system are willing—to some extent—to relinquish autonomy in order to obtain certain benefits. * * *

The assets traded in this international "market" are not goods or services *per se*, but assets peculiar to states: components of power, or jurisdiction. "Jurisdiction" is the word lawyers use for allocation of authority: the institutionalized exercise of power. In a legal context, power is effective jurisdiction, including jurisdiction to prescribe, jurisdiction to adjudicate, and jurisdiction to enforce. In international society, the equivalent of the market is simply the place where states interact to cooperate on particular issues—to trade in power—in order to maximize their baskets of preferences. * * * Thus, the transaction in jurisdiction is the fundamental unit of analysis. * * *

The central theory suggested by the economic approach to international law is that states use and design international transactions (including all rules of international law) or institutions to maximize the participants' net gains, which equal the excess of transaction gains from engaging in intergovernmental transactions, over the sum of transaction losses from engaging in intergovernmental and transaction costs of intergovernmental transactions (including transaction costs of international agreement or of not creating and running institutions). Most, if not all, international law may be characterized as involving transactions in jurisdiction, either horizontal or vertical, with this purpose in mind. * * *

It may be useful to have in mind a couple of examples. An international legal rule prohibiting the acquisition of territory by use of force may be seen as maximizing net benefits by virtue of the greater security that states enjoy, allowing individual states to spend less on self-defense. They may spend less on self-defense because the threat of aggression is reduced by the virtue of the fact that the rewards of aggression are reduced insofar as aggression cannot be the basis for the acquisition of territory. Absent this legal prohibition, each state has the authority to acquire territory by force, but by entering into this rule, each transfers this authority away. It is a transaction in authority.

Similarly, international human rights treaties may be understood as transactions in authority. Although it is sometimes difficult to see the externality when one state abuses the human rights of its own citizens, these externalities may arise in the form of instability, refugees, competitive externalities, or simply feelings of concern. When states enter into these treaties, they are implicitly bartering autonomy to commit human rights abuses. This is also a transaction in authority. Of course, it may be necessary to provide other inducement or side payments in particular cases. But the main point is that we can understand these transactions as transactions in authority. Another word for authority in our context is jurisdiction.

MOHAMMED BEDJAOUI, TOWARDS A NEW INTERNATIONAL ECONOMIC ORDER

49–50, 62–63 (1979)

Traditional international law is derived from the laws of the capitalist economy and the liberal political system. From these two sources it derives the elements and factors of a certain consistency to be found in its theoretical construction and in the terms of its actual rules.

The [legal] order set up by the former international society gave the impression of neutrality or indifference. But the laissez-faire and easy-going attitude which it thus sanctioned led in reality to * * * the seizure of the wealth and possessions of weaker peoples. Classic international law in its apparent indifference was ipso facto permissive. It recognized and enforced a "right of dominion" for the benefit of the "civilized nations". This was a colonial and imperial right, institutionalized at the 1885 Berlin Conference on the Congo.

In addition to ratifying the European countries' right to conquer and occupy the territories concerned, international law recognized the validity of "unequal treaties", essentially leonine, whereby the weaker people for a long time delivered up their natural wealth on terms imposed on them by the stronger States. Neutral or indifferent, international law was thus also a formalistic law, attached to the semblance of equality which barely hid the flagrant inequalities of the relationships expressed in these leonine treaties.

It was also a law eminently suited to the protection of the "civilized countries" privileges, through the interests of their nationals. By virtue of diplomatic protection and intervention, the law enabled the nationals of the countries concerned to obtain, in certain States, advantages which were not even awarded to the citizens of those States.

International law made use of a series of justifications and excuses to create legitimacy for the subjugation and pillaging of the Third World, which was pronounced uncivilized. * * * However, the consistency of the system required that the freedom of action allotted by international law to a "civilized" State should be matched by the same freedom for any other civilized State. This accepted international law was thus obliged to assume the essential function of reconciling the freedom of every State belonging to the family of "civilized nations" with the freedom of all other States in the same family.

To keep in line with the predatory economic order, this international law was thus obliged simultaneously to assume the guise of: (a) an oligarchic law governing the relations between civilized States members of an exclusive club; (b) a plutocratic law allowing these States to exploit weaker peoples; (c) a non-interventionist law (to the greatest possible extent), carefully drafted to allow a wide margin of laissez-faire and indulgence to the leading States in the club, while at the same time making [it] possible to reconcile the total freedom allowed to each of them. However, this matter of controlling rival appetites was not taken very far.

Until the League of Nations came into being, this international law was simply a European law, arising from the combination of regional fact with material power, and transposed as a law dominating all international relations. The European States thus projected their power and their law on to the world as a whole. Here we come to the real nature of the so-called "international" law, to its substance and even to the reality of its existence. As it had been formed historically on the basis of regional acts of force, it could not be an international law established by common accord, but an international law given to the whole world by one or two dominant groups. This is how it was able to serve as a legal basis for the various political and economic aspects of imperialism.

This classic international law thus consisted of a set of rules with a geographical basis (it was a European law), a religious-ethical inspiration (it was a Christian law), an economic motivation (it was a mercantilist law) and political aims (it was an imperialist law).

Until the recent period of successive decolonizations, there was no perceptible change in this law as a backing for imperialism, apart from the fact that the emergence of the two super-great powers eclipsed the European influence and provoked a large-scale revision of the boundaries of spheres of influence in the world. * * * Traditional international law has always lagged behind emerging trends, set fast in its function of conserving a status quo which takes little account of the changes in the international community and the needs it expresses.

* * * Like a mastodon crushing the interests of the Third World countries, while the latter attempt with great difficulty to shift it, traditional international law "is, as a whole, the embodiment of situations of predominance of the strong over the weak". * * *

But it is mainly in the economic sphere that the dichotomy between law and reality appears most clearly. This may be seen, for example, in connection with the activities of the multinational firms. Although they dominate the world economy and cause incalculable prejudice to the underdeveloped countries, these enterprises, which snap their fingers at all legal or moral standards, have so far not once been called to order or taken to task by international law. They are to economic domination what the colonial companies of the nineteenth century were to political domination. Although they are the ones who determine international relationships, these giant enterprises are left untouched by international law.

This historical retrospect revealing the origins of the disastrous economic situation from which the world now suffers, enables the true nature of international law to be perceived. Under cover of neutrality and the refusal of any political affiliation, it has permitted colonization, the exploitation of man by man, and racial discrimination. Through formal, abstract regulations, it has facilitated and legalized the enrichment of the affluent countries through the impoverishment of the poor countries.

But this law, which has done nothing to help poor countries, may nevertheless be improved thanks to them. This is the task which the developing countries have undertaken, being resolve to free international law from its paralysing formalism and its heavy armour of hypocrisy, and to steer it towards a nobler, more humane and more essential goal—the promise of development.

NOTES AND QUESTIONS

1. *One law and economics approach to international law*. Professor Trachtman demonstrates the power of rational-choice and game-theoretical approaches to various fields in international law. In his larger work (and that of like-minded scholars), the economic approach to international law predicts and regulates or incentivizes traditional economic behavior, as in trade and commercial relations, but in other fields as well, including international humanitarian law (or the law of war). *See, e.g.*, Jeffrey L. Dunoff & Joel P. Trachtman, *The Law and Economics of Humanitarian Law Violations in Internal Conflict*, 93 AMER. J. INT'L L. 394 (1999). In part, this analysis rests on the creation of a fictive or metaphorical market: "In international society, the equivalent of the market is simply the place where states interact to cooperate on particular issues—to trade in power—in order to maximize their baskets of preferences. * * * Thus, the transaction in jurisdiction is the fundamental unit of analysis." Can you translate the doctrine and analysis in the principal cases in this chapter—*Velásquez-Rodríguez*, *Filártiga*, and *Alvarez-Machain*—into this language?

2. *A different law and economics approach to international law: TWAIL.* In the excerpt above, Mohammed Bedjaoui offers a blistering assessment of the economic effects of international law as conventionally conceived and practiced: "Like a mastodon crushing the interests of the Third World countries, while the latter attempt with great difficulty to shift it, traditional international law 'is, as a whole, the embodiment of situations of predominance of the strong over the weak'." He was an early voice in a scholarly movement that became known as Third World Aspects of International Law ("TWAIL"). TWAIL scholars tracked out the economic consequences of seemingly neutral principles of international law, demonstrating how they typically worked to the systematic disadvantage of people in less developed countries:

> For TWAIL scholars, international law makes sense only in the context of the lived history of the peoples of the Third World. Two important characteristics of TWAIL thinking emerge from this. First, the experience of colonialism and neo-colonialism has made Third World peoples acutely sensitive to power relations among states and to the ways in which any proposed international rule or institution will actually affect the distribution of power between states and peoples. Second, it is the actualized experience of these peoples and not merely that of states which represent them in international fora, that is the interpretive prism through which rules of international law are to be evaluated. This is because, for reasons detailed below, Third World states often act in ways which are against the interests of their peoples. For us, then, Third World peoples' resistance to, or acceptance of, international rules and practices which affect their lives offers strong evidence of the justice or injustice of those rules and practices.

Antony Anghie & B.S. Chimni, *Third World Approaches to International Law and Individual Responsibility in Internal Conflicts*, [2003] CHIN. J. INT'L L. 77, 78. *See also* B.S. Chimni, *Third World Approaches to International Law: A Manifesto*, 8 INT'L COMM. L. REV. 3 (2006) ("International law is playing a crucial role in helping legitimize and sustain the unequal structures and processes that manifest themselves in the growing north-south divide. Indeed, international law is the principal language in which domination is coming to be expressed in the era of globalization.")

Is it fair to say that TWAIL is more forthright in articulating its normative commitments than is the dominant law and economics approach?

---

6. INTERNATIONAL LAW AND CRITICAL LEGAL STUDIES (a.k.a. "NEW STREAM SCHOLARSHIP")

MARTII KOSKENNIEMI, FROM APOLOGY TO UTOPIA: THE STRUCTURE OF INTERNATIONAL LAW ARGUMENT

1, 3–4, 6, 11–13 (2005)

This is not only a book in international law. It is also an exercise in social theory and social philosophy. One of the principal theses of the book is that it is neither useful nor ultimately possible to work with international law in abstraction from descriptive theories about the character of social life among States and normative views about the principles of justice which should govern international conduct. * * *

The modern international lawyer has assumed that frustration about theory can be overcome by becoming doctrinal, or technical. But it is doubtful whether this strategy has ever worked out very well. For the lawyer is constantly faced with two disappointing experiences. In the first place, the doctrinal outcomes often seem irrelevant. In the practice of States and international organizations these are every day overridden by informal, political practices, agreements, and understandings. If they are not overridden, this seems to be more a matter of compliance being politically useful than a result of the "legal" character of the outcomes or the methods whereby they were received. To explain that despite this experience, international law is in some sense "relevant" will, however, demand a "theoretical" discussion about how to disentangle law from other aspects of social life among States. And this would seem to involve precisely the sort of conceptual analysis from which will emerge the indeterminate classic controversies about the "nature" of law. In the second place, most doctrinal outcomes remain controversial. Anyone with some experience in doctrinal argument will soon develop a feeling of *déjá-vu* towards that argument. In crucial doctrinal areas, treaties, customary law, general principles, *jus cogens,* and so on conflicting views are constantly presented as "correct" normative outcomes. Each general principle seems capable of being opposed with an equally valid counter-principle. Moreover, these conflicting views and principles are very familiar and attempts to overcome the conflicts they entail seem to require returning to "theory" which, however, merely reproduces the conflicts at a higher level of abstraction. There is this dilemma: In order to avoid the problems of theory, the lawyer has retreated into doctrine. But doctrine constantly reproduces problems which seem capable of resolution only if one takes a theoretical position. * * *

The approach followed here is one of "regressive analysis." I shall attempt to investigate discourse about international law by arguing back to the existence of certain conditions without which the discourse could not possess the kind of self-evidence for professional lawyers which it has. In other words, I shall argue, as it were, "backwards" from explicit arguments to their "deep structure," the assumptions within which the problems which modern lawyers face, either in theory or practice, are constituted. This approach could also be labelled "deconstructive." * * *

I shall argue that express arguments and doctrines about international law are only a contingent surface of a socially shared manner of envisaging international relations. * * * [International law] conveys to us a certain interpretation of the social reality to which it is addressed, under the veil of objectivity, or naturalness. Deconstruction seeks to bring out the conventional character of this interpretation and its dependence on certain contestable assumptions. It becomes critical as it shows that legal argument cannot produce the kinds of objective resolutions it claims to produce—indeed, the production of which it assumes for its principal justification. Thus it opens up the possibility for alternative descriptive—and simultaneously normative—characterizations of the world in which States live.

By providing an "insider's view" to legal discourse, such an approach might produce a therapeutic effect on lawyers frustrated with their inability to cope with the indeterminacy of theory and the irrelevance of doctrine. It will indicate that legal discourse cannot permanently solve the lawyer's problems for him. The line drawn in the midst of the universe of normative statements which has separated the "subjective" politics from "objective" law will appear without foundation. By thus "politicizing" law (but equally "legalizing" politics) an analysis of its structure might point a way towards an alternative way of understanding the relationship between law and its neighboring discourses, social description and political prescription.

NOTES AND QUESTIONS

1. *Internationalizing the divide between natural law and positivist theories.* One way to think of critical legal studies is as a plague on both houses of traditional jurisprudence: natural law and positivism. Generations of conflict between the two camps centered around the failure of each school to recognize its own explanatory or normative weaknesses and the strengths of the other. Positivism seemed excessively fixed on history and rule-worship, which bore little relation to the way legal actors reached decisions. Natural law theories at least confronted the normative and social values at work in the law but offered no authoritative way to resolve or accommodate them. Professor Koskenniemi refers to the gap between them as reflecting "the distinction between (material but subjective) morality and (formal but objective) law." MARTII KOSKENNIEMI, FROM APOLOGY TO UTOPIA: THE STRUCTURE OF INTERNATIONAL LEGAL ARGUMENT 6 (1989). But critical legal studies was also a sustained attack on what it considered an unproductive pragmatism that

emerged from the failure of the old schools. In international law, pragmatism took the form of the international legal process school developed by Chayes et al., *supra*, and to some extent the New Haven School, *infra*.

In the end, the CLS's analysis of international law, like its analysis of domestic law, is that it largely incoherent and indeterminate but that it also

> seems to have some experiential authority. Its authority operates on two levels. On the most basic level, sovereigns seem to take for granted the propriety of engaging in international legal discourse (instead of some other type of discourse) when they seek to resolve international issues. Moreover, international law operates as though it makes a difference. Sovereigns seem to debate international legal principles as though they were determinate and coherent. On occasion, states seem to act if they actually were "complying" with international law. Sovereign acceptance of the rule of law as the appropriate mechanism for structuring intentional state life represents the second source of international law's authority.

Nigel Purvis, *Critical Legal Studies in Public International Law*, 32 HARV. INT'L L.J. 81, 109–10 (1991). How, if at all, does this expand your notion of what counts as law?

2. *Politicizing law, legalizing politics*. Near the end of the quoted excerpt, Professor Koskenniemi refers to " 'politicizing' law (but equally 'legalizing' politics)." Assuming that this is not just about adjusting the theoretical boundaries between the disciplines of law and political science, what might be the practical benefits of embracing this line-blurring for international lawyers? *See* David Kennedy, *A New Stream of International Law Scholarship*, 7 WIS. INT'L L.J. 1 (1988); James Boyle, *Ideals and Things: International Legal Scholarship and the Prison House of Language*, 26 HARV. INT'L L.J. 327 (1985).

3. *Maybe grand unitary theories are the problem*. Is theorizing about international law ultimately futile because it is not a single thing? Consider the observation of Professor Philip Trimble: "Instead of being seen as a single, unitary system applicable across the 'world community,' public international law should be imagined as a series of parallel systems, more or less convergent depending on the subject, separately applicable within the various nations of the world."). Philip Trimble, "International Law, World Order, and Critical Legal Studies," 42 STAN. L. REV. 811, 835 (1990).

4. *Semantics only?* How would an adherent to the international law version of CLS respond to the observation that, whether international law is really "law" or not is largely and merely a semantic debate. *See* Glanville L. Williams, *International Law and the Controversy Concerning the Word "Law,"* 22 BRIT. Y.B. INT'L L. 146, 158–62 (1945).]

---

7. INTERNATIONAL LAW AND FEMINIST JURISPRUDENCE

HILARY CHARLESWORTH, CHRISTINE CHINKIN, & SHELLEY WRIGHT, *FEMINIST APPROACHES TO INTERNATIONAL LAW*

85 AMER. J. INT'L L. 613 (1991)

The development of feminist jurisprudence in recent years has made a rich and fruitful contribution to legal theory. Few areas of domestic law have avoided the scrutiny of feminist writers, who have exposed the gender bias of apparently neutral systems of rules. A central feature of many western theories about law is that the law is an autonomous entity, distinct from the society it regulates. A legal system is regarded as different from a political or economic system, for example, because it operates on the basis of abstract rationality, and is thus universally applicable and capable of achieving neutrality and objectivity. These attributes are held to give the law its special authority. More radical theories have challenged this abstract rationalism, arguing that legal analysis cannot be separated from the political, economic, historical and cultural context in which people live. Some theorists argue that the law functions as a system of beliefs that make social, political and economic inequalities appear natural. Feminist jurisprudence builds on certain aspects of this critical strain in legal thought. It is much more focused and concrete, however, and derives its theoretical force from immediate experience of the role of the legal system in creating and perpetuating the unequal position of women.

There is no single school of feminist jurisprudence. Most feminists would agree that a diversity of voices is not only valuable, but essential, and that the search for, or belief in, one view, one voice is unlikely to capture the reality of women's experience or gender inequality. * * *

International law has thus far largely resisted feminist analysis. The concerns of public international law do not, at first sight, have any particular impact on women: issues of sovereignty, territory, use of force and state responsibility, for example, appear gender free in their application to the abstract entities of states. Only where international law is considered directly relevant to individuals, as with human rights law, have some specifically feminist perspectives on international law begun to be developed.

* * * [W]e question the immunity of international law to feminist analysis—why has gender not been an issue in this discipline?—and indicate the possibilities of feminist scholarship in international law. * * *

Why is it significant that all the major institutions of the international legal order are peopled by men? Long-term domination of all bodies wielding political power nationally and internationally means that issues traditionally of concern to men become seen as general human concerns, while "women's concerns" are relegated to a special, limited category. Because men generally are not the victims of sex discrimination, domestic violence, and sexual degradation and violence, for example, these matters can be consigned to a separate sphere and tend to be ignored. The orthodox face of international law and politics would change dramatically if their institutions were truly human in composition: their horizons would widen to include issues previously regarded as domestic-in the two senses of the word. Balanced representation in international organizations of nations of differing economic structures and power has been a prominent theme in the United Nations since the era of decolonization in the 1960s. The importance of accommodating interests of developed, developing and socialist nations and of various regional and ideological groups is recognized in all aspects of the UN structure and work. This sensitivity should be extended much further to include the gender of chosen representatives.

The Normative Structure of International Law

Since the primary subjects of international law are states, it is sometimes assumed that the impact of international law falls on the state and not directly on individuals. In fact, the application of international law does affect individuals, which has been recognized by the International Court [of Justice] in several cases.[71] International jurisprudence assumes that international law norms directed at individuals within states are universally applicable and neutral. It is not recognized, however, that such principles may impinge differently on men and women; consequently, women's experiences of the operation of these laws tend to be silenced or discounted.

The normative structure of international law has allowed issues of particular concern to women to be either ignored or undermined. For example, modern international law rests on and reproduces various dichotomies between the public and private spheres, and the "public" sphere is regarded as the province of international law. One such distinction is between public international law, the law governing the relations between nation-states, and private international law, the rules about conflicts between national legal systems. Another is the distinction between matters of international "public" concern and matters "private" to states that are considered within their domestic jurisdiction, in which the international community has no recognized legal interest. Yet another is

---

[71] *See, e.g., Legal Consequences for States of the Continued Presence of South Africa in Namibia (South West Africa) notwithstanding Security Council Resolution 276* (1970), 1971 ICJ Rep. 16, 56, para. 125 (Advisory Opinion of June 21), where it was stated that the non-recognition of South Africa's administration in South West Africa should not be allowed to have an adverse impact on the people of Namibia. In the *Anglo-Norwegian Fisheries case (UK v. Nor.)*, 1951 ICJ Rep. 116 (Judgment of Dec. 18), and *Fisheries Jurisdiction (UK v. Ice.)*, Merits, 1974 ICJ Rep. 3 (Judgment of July 25), the impact of changed fishing zones on the livelihood of people in the various states who engaged in fishing was taken into account by the Court.

the line drawn between law and other forms of "private" knowledge such as morality.[73]

At a deeper level one finds a public/private dichotomy based on gender. One explanation feminist scholars offer for the dominance of men and the male voice in all areas of power and authority in the western liberal tradition is that a dichotomy is drawn between the public sphere and the private or domestic one. The public realm of the work place, the law, economics, politics and intellectual and cultural life, where power and authority are exercised, is regarded as the natural province of men; while the private world of the home, the hearth and children is seen as the appropriate domain of women. The public/private distinction has a normative, as well as a descriptive, dimension. Traditionally, the two spheres are accorded asymmetrical value: greater significance is attached to the public, male world than to the private, female one. The distinction drawn between the public and the private thus vindicates and makes natural the division of labor and allocation of rewards between the sexes. Its reproduction and acceptance in all areas of knowledge have conferred primacy on the male world and supported the dominance of men.

Feminist concern with the public/private distinction derives from its centrality to liberal theory. Explanations for the universal attribution of lesser value to women and their activities have sometimes proposed a variation of the public/private dichotomy: women are identified with nature, which is regarded as lower in status than culture-the province of men. As Carole Pateman has pointed out, however, this universal explanation for the male domination of women does not recognize that the concept of "nature" may vary widely among different societies. Such an analysis can be reduced easily to a simple biological explanation and does not explain particular social, historical or cultural situations.[77] Women are not always opposed to men in the same ways: what is considered "public" in one society may well be seen as "private" in another. But a universal pattern of identifying women's activities as private, and thus of lesser value, can be detected.

How is the western liberal version of the public/private distinction maintained? Its naturalness rests on deeply held beliefs about gender. Traditional social psychology taught that the bench marks of "normal" behavior for men, on the one hand, and women, on the other, were entirely different. For men, normal and natural behavior was essentially active: it involved tenacity, aggression, curiosity, ambition, responsibility and

---

[73] *E.g., South West Africa, Second Phase*, 1966 ICJ Rep. 6 (Judgment of July 18). *Cf. Western Sahara Case*, 1975 ICJ Rep. 12, 77 (Advisory Opinion of Oct. 16): "economics, sociology and human geography are not law" (Gros, J., sep. op.).

[77] Pateman, [*Feminist Critiques of the Public/Private Dichotomy*, in PUBLIC AND PRIVATE IN SOCIAL LIFE (S. I. Benn & G. F. Gaus eds. 1983)], at 288. *See also* Rosaldo, "The Use and Abuse of Anthropology: Reflections on Feminism and Cross-Cultural Understanding," 5 *Signs* 409 (1980); Goodall, "Public and Private" in "Legal Debate," 18 INT'L J. SOC. L. 445 (1990).

competition-all attributes suited to participation in the public world. "Normal" behavior for women, by contrast, was reactive and passive: affectionate, emotional, obedient and responsive to approval.

Although the scientific basis of the public/private distinction has been thoroughly attacked and exposed as a culturally constructed ideology, it continues to have a strong grip on legal thinking. The language of the public/private distinction is built into the language of the law itself: law lays claim to rationality, culture, power, objectivity—all terms associated with the public or male realm. It is defined in opposition to the attributes associated with the domestic, private, female sphere: feeling, emotion, passivity, subjectivity. Moreover, the law has always operated primarily within the public domain; it is considered appropriate to regulate the work place, the economy and the distribution of political power, while direct state intervention in the family and the home has long been regarded as inappropriate. Violence within the home, for example, has generally been given different legal significance from violence outside it; the injuries recognized as legally compensable are those which occur outside the home. Damages in civil actions are typically assessed in terms of ability to participate in the public sphere. Women have difficulty convincing law enforcement officials that violent acts within the home are criminal.

In one sense, the public/private distinction is the fundamental basis of the modern state's function of separating and concentrating juridical forms of power that emanate from the state. The distinction implies that the private world is uncontrolled. In fact, the regulation of taxation, social security, education, health and welfare has immediate effects on the private sphere. The myth that state power is not exercised in the "private" realm allocated to women masks its control.

What force does the feminist critique of the public/private dichotomy in the foundation of domestic legal systems have for the international legal order? Traditionally, of course, international law was regarded as operating only in the most public of public spheres: the relations between nation-states. We argue, however, that the definition of certain principles of international law rests on and reproduces the public/private distinction. It thus privileges the male world view and supports male dominance in the international legal order.

The grip that the public/private distinction has on international law, and the consequent banishment of women's voices and concerns from the discipline, can be seen in the international prohibition on torture. The right to freedom from torture and other forms of cruel, inhuman or degrading treatment is generally accepted as a paradigmatic civil and political right. It is included in all international catalogs of civil and political rights[85] and

---

[85] *E.g.*, International Covenant on Civil and Political Rights, Dec. 16, 1966, Art. 7, 999 UNTS 171; European Convention for the Protection of Human Rights and Fundamental Freedoms, Nov. 4, 1950, Art. 3, 213 UNTS 221 [hereinafter European Convention]; American Convention on

is the focus of specialized United Nations and regional treaties.[86] The right to be free from torture is also regarded as a norm of customary international law-indeed, like the prohibition on slavery, as a norm of *jus cogens*.[87]

The basis for the right is traced to "the inherent dignity of the human person."[88] Behavior constituting torture is defined in [Article 1(1) of] the Convention against Torture as

> any act by which severe pain or suffering, whether physical or mental, is intentionally inflicted on a person for such purposes as obtaining from him or a third person information or a confession, punishing him for an act he or a third person has committed or is suspected of having committed, or intimidating or coercing him or a third person, or for any reason based on discrimination of any kind, when such pain or suffering is inflicted by or at the instigation of or with the consent or acquiescence of a public official or other person acting in an official capacity.

This definition has been considered broad because it covers mental suffering and behavior "at the instigation of" a public official." However, despite the use of the term "human person" in the Preamble, the use of the masculine pronoun alone in the definition of the proscribed behavior immediately gives the definition a male, rather than a truly human, context. More importantly, the description of the prohibited conduct relies on a distinction between public and private actions that obscures injuries to their dignity typically sustained by women. The traditional canon of human rights law does not deal in categories that fit the experiences of women. It is cast in terms of discrete violations of rights and offers little redress in cases where there is a pervasive, structural denial of rights.

The international definition of torture requires not only the intention to inflict suffering, but also the secondary intention that the infliction of suffering will fulfill a purpose. Recent evidence suggests that women and children, in particular, are victims of widespread and apparently random terror campaigns by both governmental and guerrilla groups in times of civil unrest or armed conflict. Such suffering is not clearly included in the international definition of torture.

Human Rights, Nov. 22, 1969, Art. 5, reprinted in ORGANIZATION OF AMERICAN STATES, HANDBOOK OF EXISTING RULES PERTAINING TO HUMAN RIGHTS IN THE INTER-AMERICAN SYSTEM, OEA/Ser.L/V/II.65, doc. 6, at 103 (1985).

[86] United Nations Convention against Torture and Other Cruel, Inhuman or Degrading Treatment or Punishment, GA Res. 39/46 (Dec. 10, 1984), draft reprinted in 23 ILM 1027 (1984), substantive changes noted in 24 ILM 535 (1985) [hereinafter Torture Convention]; Inter-American Convention to Prevent and Punish Torture, Dec. 9, 1985, *reprinted in* 25 ILM 519 (1986); European Convention for the Prevention of Torture and Inhuman or Degrading Treatment or Punishment, Nov. 26, 1987, Council of Europe Doc. H (87) 4, *reprinted in* 27 ILM 1152 (1988).

[87] *See Filartiga v. Pena-Irala*, 630 F.2d 876 (2d Cir. 1980).

[88] Torture Convention, *supra*, Preamble.

A crucial aspect of torture and cruel, inhuman or degrading conduct, as defined, is that they take place in the public realm: a public official or a person acting officially must be implicated in the pain and suffering. The rationale for this limitation is that "private acts (of brutality) would usually be ordinary criminal offenses which national law enforcement is expected to repress. International concern with torture arises only when the State itself abandons its function of protecting its citizenry by sanctioning criminal action by law enforcement personnel."[93] Many women suffer from torture in this limited sense.[94] The international jurisprudence on the notion of torture arguably extends to sexual violence and psychological coercion if the perpetrator has official standing. However, severe pain and suffering that is inflicted outside the most public context of the state-for example, within the home or by private persons, which is the most pervasive and significant violence sustained by women-does not qualify as torture despite its impact on the inherent dignity of the human person. Indeed, some forms of violence are attributed to cultural tradition. The message of violence against women, argues Charlotte Bunch, is domination:

> [S]tay in your place or be afraid. Contrary to the argument that such violence is only personal or cultural, it is profoundly political. It results from the structural relationships of power, domination, and privilege between men and women in society. Violence against women is central to maintaining those political relations at home, at work, and in all public spheres.[96]

States are held responsible for torture only when their designated agents have direct responsibility for such acts and that responsibility is imputed to the state. States are not considered responsible if they have maintained a legal and social system in which violations of physical and mental integrity are endemic. * * * A feminist perspective on human rights would require a rethinking of the notions of imputability and state responsibility and in this sense would challenge the most basic assumptions of international law. If violence against women were considered by the international legal system to be as shocking as violence against people for their political ideas, women would have considerable support in their struggle.

The assumption that underlies all law, including international human rights law, is that the public/private distinction is real: human society, human lives can be separated into two distinct spheres. This division,

---

93 Rodley, *The Evolution of the International Prohibition of Torture*, in AMNESTY INTERNATIONAL, THE UNIVERSAL DECLARATION OF HUMAN RIGHTS 1948–1988: HUMAN RIGHTS, THE UNITED NATIONS AND AMNESTY INTERNATIONAL 55, 63 (1988).

94 *See* Amnesty International, [WOMEN IN THE FRONT LINE: HUMAN RIGHTS VIOLATIONS AGAINST WOMEN 45–46 (1991), *passim*.

96 Bunch, ["Women's Rights as Human Rights: Toward a Re-vision of Human Rights," 12 HUM. RTS. Q. 486 (1990)], at 490–91.

however, is an ideological construct rationalizing the exclusion of women from the sources of power. It also makes it possible to maintain repressive systems of control over women without interference from human rights guarantees, which operate in the public sphere. By extending our vision beyond the public/private ideologies that rationalize limiting our analysis of power, human rights language as it currently exists can be used to describe serious forms of repression that go far beyond the juridically narrow vision of international law. For example, coercive population control techniques, such as forced sterilization, may amount to punishment or coercion by the state to achieve national goals. * * *

Modern international law is not only androcentric, but also Euro-centered in its origins, and has assimilated many assumptions about law and the place of law in society from western legal thinking. These include essentially patriarchal legal institutions, the assumption that law is objective, gender neutral and universally applicable, and the societal division into public and private spheres, which relegates many matters of concern to women to the private area regarded as inappropriate for legal regulation. Research is needed to question the assumptions of neutrality and universal applicability of norms of international law and to expose the invisibility of women and their experiences in discussions about the law. A feminist perspective, with its concern for gender as a category of analysis and its commitment to genuine equality between the sexes, could illuminate many areas of international law; for example, state responsibility, refugee law, use of force and the humanitarian law of war, human rights, population control and international environmental law. Feminist research holds the promise of a fundamental restructuring of traditional international law discourse and methodology to accommodate alternative world views. As Elizabeth Gross points out, this restructuring will not amount to the replacement of one set of "truths" with another: "feminist theory aims to render patriarchal systems, methods and presumptions unable to function, unable to retain their dominance and power. It aims to make clear how such a dominance has been possible; and to make it no longer viable."[202]

The centrality of the state in international law means that many of the structures of international law reflect its patriarchal forms. Paradoxically, however, international law may be more open to feminist analysis than other areas of law. The distinction between law and politics, so central to the preservation of the neutrality and objectivity of law in the domestic sphere, does not have quite the same force in international law. So, too, the western domestic model of legal process as ultimately coercive is not echoed in the international sphere: the process of international law is consensual and peaceful coexistence is its goal. Finally, the sustained Third World

[202] Gross, ["What is Feminist Theory?," in FEMINIST CHALLENGES: SOCIAL AND POLITICAL THEORY 190, 196–97 (C. Pateman & E. Gross eds. 1986)], at 197.

critique of international law and insistence on diversity may well have prepared the philosophical ground for feminist critiques.

A feminist transformation of international law would involve more than simply refining or reforming existing law. It could lead to the creation of international regimes that focus on structural abuse and the revision of our notions of state responsibility. It could also lead to a challenge to the centrality of the state in international law and to the traditional sources of international law. * * *

NOTES AND QUESTIONS

1. *CEDAW.* In 1979, The Convention on the Elimination of All Forms of Discrimination Against Women (CEDAW) was opened for signature. It is now one of the most widely ratified treaties in the world, although it is also subject to the widest range of reservations. Among other things, CEDAW requires parties "to modify social and cultural practices," to condemn discrimination and "not to invoke custom, tradition or religious considerations" to avoid obligations to eliminate discrimination. How might a state actually go about "modify[ing] social and cultural practices?" Specifically, what tools does the state have its disposal to induce the obligatory cultural shifts? And how successful has this project been?

2. *Violence against women.* From the starting point that only states can violate human rights, what are the analytical steps necessary to conceive of domestic violence as a human rights violation (especially as a form of discrimination), and how might the government's "due diligence" obligation—derived perhaps from *Velásquez-Rodríguez, supra*—be used to combat it? It is now well-established that violence against women in all its forms is a violation of international law, enforceable in international criminal courts and in regional and specialized human rights bodies.

3. *Finding the patriarchy in contemporary international law.* Although there are now more intergovernmental institutions and instruments addressing the rights and concerns of women than there were when Professors Charlesworth, Chinkin, and Wright published their foundational piece, issues remain for both normative development and enforcement, including women's reproductive rights, freedom of religion, right to property and education, gender identity, equal opportunity, and the particular situation of women and girls in armed conflict, among many others.

4. *The receptivity of international law to feminist jurisprudence.* What do Professors Charlesworth, Chinkin, and Wright mean when they say that "international law may be more open to feminist analysis than other areas of law"?

---

8. INTERNATIONAL LAW AND CRITICAL RACE THEORY

MAKAU MUTUA, *CRITICAL RACE THEORY AND INTERNATIONAL LAW: CONVERGENCE AND DIVERGENCE*

45 VILL. L. REV. 841–45, 848–51 (2000)

* * * A casual examination of CRT and international law deceptively indicates two contradictory, if convergent, thrusts. At first blush, CRT is located in a particular cultural and political space. It is born out of the American saga of racist and sexist subordination and resistance. As an intellectual movement, it is steeped in European-American postmodernism. A cursory survey of CRT denies its universality and reveals a myopia in terms of its origins, concerns, purposes and subjects. In fact, CRT is so site and context specific that it does not immediately make any universal claims of itself.

On the face of it, therefore, CRT has thus far only concerned itself with the struggles of various minority groups in the United States. One area of particular focus for CRT has been the black experience in the United States. This focus seems to be very narrowly defined and would appear to be of no immediate utility to a global population of some six billion people, three quarters of whom live in the developing or so-called 'Third World.' But CRT has also developed a theoretical methodology that is useful in studying the struggles of other subordinated groups. Sexual minorities, for example, have deployed this methodology in their struggle for social justice. Two of these key innovations by CRT—multidimensionality[9] and intersectionality[10]—are tools that debunk essentialist constructions and allow for a more nuanced understanding of the use of identities as social and legal phenomena. They help unpack various oppressions and assist in the forging of new and multidimensional sites of resistance.

International law, on the other hand, is by definition 'universal,' even though its authors have no doubt about its Christian and European origin. Unlike CRT, which is an idiom of resistance and liberation, international law has been a medium of conquest and domination. The most critical phases in the development of international law took place during the Age of the Empire, when most non-European peoples were subjected to European domination and colonialism. By the end of the nineteenth century, any doubts about the 'universality' of international law were erased by the European imperial conquest and the forcible embrace of all

---

[9] Multiplicity recognizes that any one individual simultaneously carries a basket of identities, some of which may be contradictory.

[10] Intersectionality is a further development of multidimensionality and points to the cross-cutting, intersecting and interacting identities that produce multilayered, multidimensional social hierarchies and situations.

states—in Africa, Asia, the Americas and the Pacific—by this new legal code of international governance. International law is, therefore, Eurocentric in that it issues from European thought, culture and experiences. This specificity denies international law universality.

Today, however, international law is universal in its geographic scope and application. Its guardians present it as a coherent and reasonable body of rules which are universally applicable to all humanity, without regard to nationality, culture, religion and philosophy. Unlike CRT, international law explicitly holds itself out as universally human and thus, it automatically and forcibly embraces all human societies. Underlying this assumption is a feeling of inevitability. Who, for example, can imagine an 'international community' without law, a predictable set of norms that govern the relationships between states? In fact, international law is so ubiquitous today that most of the same non-European states and peoples who have been its principal victims claim it as a shield and medium of international exchange.

Like all discourses and paradigms that rest on the mantle of universality, international law claims for itself a higher moral plane in which good and eternal truths can be realized. In this case, order and stability can be assured on a global scale. Implicit in international law is the warning that no group, nation, state or people can achieve progress without membership in the 'society' of nations, in essence 'international society." Put differently, assimilation in international law is a *sine qua non* for civilization. International 'reality' suggests that to step out of international law is to in effect opt out of 'civilized' society and to become a 'rogue' or 'pariah' nation, state or society.

These two basic assumptions, the particularity and specificity of CRT, and the universality and internationality of international law, are the focal points of my interrogation. Are these assumptions correct, and if so, to what extent? I want to argue that the reverse is most likely true. While CRT has an enormous emancipatory potential universally, international law has largely been developed and deployed as a vehicle for advancing particular interests, for the benefit of specific peoples, cultures and regions and, as a consequence, for the detriment of particular interests, peoples, cultures and regions.

This [essay] makes the point that international law has largely been an instrument for fostering 'unfreedom' and for enhancing and aggravating human suffering, not for alleviating it. But it also contends that international law need not be an instrument for exclusion and exploitation, and asserts that it can and should speak to more noble ideals. I want to suggest that CRT has a large emancipatory potential at the global level, a potential that can be tapped and deployed as part of the project for the reconstruction of international law. * * *

As I understand it, CRT is a project of outsider jurisprudence. It concerns itself with social justice for 'outsider' groups, that is, groups that have traditionally been subordinated in the United States. Heavily influenced by elite black women—who come from one of the most subordinated groups in American society—CRT has primarily dedicated itself to anti-racist and anti-sexist struggles, and has served mainly to express the short comings of civil rights and social reforms that signify formal, but not substantive change. It is therefore a very specific form of scholarship.

CRT is driven primarily by anti-subordination and employs multidimensionality and intersectionality to free analysis from the strictures and blindness of single category/identity analysis. Thus, CRT is currently an inclusive method. It seeks to take into account many of the variables that create powerlessness, marginalization, debilitating and degrading social hierarchies and exclusion. In effect, what it does is to universalize and globalize—by its holistic method—the struggles against subordination. Its specific location belies the universal tools of analysis that it has contributed to the disaggregation of complex social and legal phenomena.

The universalization that I refer to here is not, of course, geographical. It rather refers to CRT's ability to acknowledge and account for many of the indicia of subordination in the struggle against powerlessness. Thus, while the origin and purpose of CRT are particular, its instincts and goals are universal in that they aim to universally advance and protect human dignity without regard to the category/identity under attack. CRT says that no category/identity should be left out in understanding or fighting against exploitation and subordination. This method knows no geographic, spatial or cultural boundaries. Because many of these categories exist in societies outside the United States, it would be useful for social, political and legal scholars and activists elsewhere to study the CRT method and explore what aspects of it might inform or advance their own struggles.

Herein lies the emancipatory potential for CRT to shed some light on the reconceptualization of international law. This is a method which can be particularly useful in understanding the many multi-faceted and layered injustices and oppressions that the international legal, political, cultural and economic orders impose on societies all over the world and, particularly, in the Third World. * * *

In contrast to CRT, international law is the system, the jurisprudence of 'insider' groups and dominant global interests. It is the normative center and the legitimating code of conduct for international society. Rooted in a deep-seated sense of European and global predestination, international law is founded on European biases that treat the universe as a theater for European and North American military, political, economic and cultural interests. This global, white European supremacy over non-European peoples is premised on Europe as the center, Christianity as the fountain of civilization, the innateness of capitalist economics, and political imperialism as a necessity.

In this scheme of international law, Europe is the geographical center of the world, the point of reference; every other country or region is described as 'remote'—the 'Far East' or the 'Middle East'—all relationships to their location to Europe. Christianity is the moral and naturalist foundation of civilization, and the reason without which full humanity is unattainable; thus, the coupling of Christianity to the colonial project and the fusion of church, state and empire are achieved. Capitalism is constructed as innate in humans, and, therefore, the basis for the regimes of the ownership, protection and distribution of global resources. Finally, political imperialism is an indispensable paradigm in the ordering of the relationship between Europeans and non-Europeans, with the manifest duty of the European to convey the gifts of civilization to backward and uncivilized races.

International law orders the world into the European and the non-European, and gives primacy to the former. This is done by creating the notion of the hierarchy of cultures and peoples. The fundamental principles of international law evidence this inflexible view of the discipline. Sovereignty and statehood are defined in such a way as to exclude or subordinate non-European societies. Membership in international society is a prerogative of European powers, which alone decides who belongs to this international society and can therefore enjoy the privileges of international law. The creation and re-creation of states, as well as their recognition, has largely been a prerogative of the American-European alliance. In 1967, for example, the 'international community' refused to recognize Biafra, the Ibo-dominated state, which broke off from the Nigerian post-colonial state, even though Tanzania and several other African states made a strong case for secession. In contrast, no hurdles prevented European states in the early 1990s from recognizing the states resulting from the fall of the Soviet Union and the collapse of Yugoslavia.

What the world has witnessed in the last five centuries is the universalization of an international law that is particular to Europe and seeks not universal justice, but an international legal order that erects, preserves and embraces European and American domination of the globe. It is impossible to provide any other reading for the racialization of international law by its chief authors, the Europeans and the Americans.

Even the international law of human rights, arguably the most benign of all the areas of international law, seeks the universalization of Eurocentrism. The human rights corpus is driven by what I have called the savage-victim-savior metaphor, in which human rights is a grand narrative of an epochal contest that pits savages against victims and saviors. In this script of human rights, democracy and western liberalism are internationalized to save savage non-Western cultures from themselves and to 'alleviate' the suffering of victims, who are generally non-Western and non-European.

In the human rights idiom, the European West becomes the savior of hapless victims whose salvation lies only in the transformation of their savage cultures through the imposition of human rights. Attempts to craft a truly universal regime of rights, one that reflects the complexity and the diversity of all cultures, have generally been viewed with indifference or hostility by the official guardians of human rights. * * *

NOTES AND QUESTIONS

1. *Critical race theory and international law.* CRT has often been tied to the tradition of racial inequality in the United States, and its explanatory power in international law has rarely been assessed. How does Professor Matua demonstrate that CRT is not limited to the experience of African Americans and offers insights into other countries, with their own histories of racism and discrimination?

2. *Self-determination.* Self-determination has made for itself a history as a dysfunctional norm that parallels the history of antidiscrimination law in the United States. Just as Professor Crenshaw and many others have demonstrated that domestic law designed to rectify racial inequality cannot address the current race-based manifestations of unfairness and has become counterproductive in that effort, so too, any persuasive account of the right to self-determination must confront the paradox that self-determination can work against itself, generating—indeed inviting—claims the community as a whole is not prepared to accept.

The fact is that we live in an era in which the discourse about self-determination has become highly ritualized. One dominant orthodoxy portrays the self-determination of peoples as *jus cogens*, *i.e.* one of the preferred, even elite norms of general international law from which no derogation is permitted. In this view, self-determination—the process and the justification of decolonialization in the post-war world—has become the genetic marker of a system now irrevocably committed to collective and individual rights. The International Law Commission has adopted such a conclusion, having designated the obstruction of a people's right to self-determination as one of a handful of state crimes, and it is now meaningful to speak of an international right to participatory forms of government as the widely-accepted corollary to self-determination doctrine, if not its preferred denotation. But there is an equal and opposite orthodoxy that "self-determination" names no meaningful, binding norm of law at all, especially now that the formalities of de-colonialization have been completed. The skepticism rests on the observation that the history of self-determination is one of periodic transformation and perversion: a doctrine traceable to the liberationist ideology of the

Enlightenment and designed to free peoples from colonial domination has evolved instead into a doctrine for the protection of states' prerogatives, specifically the right of a state to be left alone and to protect its territorial integrity. And, throughout the past century, the right of self-determination has provided a pretextual basis for expansionism, ethnic exclusiveness, and repression.

---

9. THE NEW HAVEN SCHOOL: A POLICY-ORIENTED JURISPRUDENCE

From the mid- to late-twentieth century, Yale Professors Myres McDougal, Harold Lasswell, Michael Reisman (and others) developed a "policy-oriented approach" to jurisprudence and international law, rejecting the conception of law as rules backed by sanctions and treating international law as more than a matter of sovereigns' consent and power.[5] Instead, the New Haven School ("NHS"), as it came to be known, conceived international law as a "world constitutive process" that a variety of actors in the global community treat as an authoritative framework for articulating, protecting, and implementing their common interests.[6]

The New Haven School resists easy summarization and classification, because it combined the insights of many different schools of jurisprudence and international relations theory. For example, it relied in part on the international relations realists' empiricism, focusing on what international actors actually do and how their authoritative assertions of control could create and stabilize patterns of behavior by both state and non-state actors. But it also rested in part on the natural law theorists' normative commitments without adopting their theology or their metaphysics; indeed, some NHS adherents describe certain recurring values as universal, rationally deducible, and reflecting justice (or what they called a "world public order of human dignity"), which clearly echoes the natural law argument. These shared community values included wealth, enlightenment, skill, well-being, affection, respect, and rectitude, and they were spelled out in a specialized and systematic vocabulary, which was not always easily accessible to those not already part of the school.[7]

---

[5] *See, e.g.*, MYRES S. MCDOUGAL & W. MICHAEL REISMAN, INTERNATIONAL LAW IN CONTEMPORARY PERSPECTIVE: THE PUBLIC ORDER OF THE WORLD COMMUNITY (1981); MYRES S. MCDOUGAL, HAROLD D. LASSWELL, & LUNG-CHU CHEN, HUMAN RIGHTS AND WORLD PUBLIC ORDER (1980); HAROLD D. LASSWELL & MYRES S. MCDOUGAL, JURISPRUDENCE FOR A FREE SOCIETY: STUDIES IN LAW, SCIENCE AND POLICY (1992).

[6] *See, e.g.*, Myres S. McDougal et al., *The World Constitutive Process of Authoritative Decision*, 19 J. LEGAL EDUC. 253 (1967); Myres S. McDougal & W. Michael Reisman, *The Prescribing Function in the World Constitutive Process: How International Law Is Made*, *in* INTERNATIONAL LAW ESSAYS 355, 377 (Myres S. McDougal & W. Michael Reisman eds., 1981).

[7] In one typical critique, Gerald Fitzmaurice identified the "highly esoteric private language" at the heart of the NHS. Gerald Fitzmaurice, *Vae Victis, Or Woe to the Negotiators! Your Treaty or Our 'Interpretation' of It?*, 65 AM. J. INT'L L. 358, 360 (1971). Others were less polite.

The NHS responded to American legal realism by accepting a version of its strict rule skepticism:

> To ask, however tentatively, "what are rules?" is unwittingly to endow them with a kind of reality or existence * * * which is illusory. Rules of law do not "exist" in the sense in which a tree or a stone or the planet Mars might be said to exist. True, they may be articulated and put on paper and in that form they exist, but, whatever their form, they are expressed in words which are merely signs mediating human subjectivities.

Hardy Dillard, *The Policy-Oriented Approach to Law*, 40 VA. Q. REV. 626, 629 (1964). But, in a profound break with the realists, the NHS found in rules something of sociological or behavioral value, and thus a proper subject for what they considered scientific study:

> [Rules of law] represent and arouse expectations which are capable of being explored scientifically. The "law" is thus not a "something" impelling obedience; it is a constantly evolving process of decision making and the way it evolves will depend on the knowledge and insights of the decision makers. So viewed, norms of laws should be considered less as compulsive commands than as tools of thought or instruments of analysis.

Id. Like the realists, some of whom were architects of the New Deal, the NHS pursued an avowedly reformist agenda, specifically to create a minimum world public order in which shared values and "community value processes"—including global institutions—might thrive. These ambitions arose not out of idealism alone but out of the pragmatism that sometimes rises from a cataclysm survived, in this case World War II and the nuclear-armed ideological confrontation called the Cold War.

That attention to the workings within, and the relationships among, authoritative decision-making institutions also connects the NHS to the domestic Legal Process School, discussed above. And, as with the Legal Process School, the subsequent critical jurisprudence exposed its implicit values:

> [T]he implicit assumption of the Policy-approach was that the abstract goal of human dignity could be made concrete and given meaning without losing its universal appeal. Yet, as Policy-approach scholars sought to elaborate the principle of human dignity, their own idiosyncratic and subjective normative hierarchy became apparent. To McDougal, for example, human dignity seemed entirely equivalent to the constitutional liberalism

---

"[The NHS] is currently the jurisprudential counterpart of L.S.D.: its effects on individuals vary from exhilaration, to deep depression, to indifference and nobody is quite sure to what extent it is habit-forming. There are some who would make it the basis of a religion." W. L. TWINING, PERICLES AND THE PLUMBER 25 (1967).

> of the United States. Once reduced to contextual terms, the Policy-approach could not achieve universality. Absent a consensus on the nature of human dignity, any substantive theory based on the Policy-approach necessarily became vulnerable to the same criticisms as naturalism.

Nigel Purvis, *Critical Legal Studies in Public International Law*, 32 HARV. INT'L L.J. 81, 85–86 (1991).

W. MICHAEL REISMAN, SIEGFRIED WIESSNER & ANDREW R. WILLARD, *THE NEW HAVEN SCHOOL: A BRIEF INTRODUCTION*

32 YALE JOURNAL OF INTERNATIONAL LAW 575 (2007)

The New Haven School defines law as a process of decision that is both authoritative and controlling; it places past such decisions in the illuminating light of their conditioning factors, both environmental and predispositional, and appraises decision trends for their compatibility with clarified goals; it forecasts, to the extent possible, alternative future decisions and their consequences; and it provides conceptual tools for those using it to invent and appraise alternative decisions, constitutive arrangements, and courses of action using the guiding light of a preferred future world public order of human dignity. To achieve these goals, the New Haven School adapts focal lenses from the social sciences, a mode of organizing data about various social processes though cultural anthropology's modality of phase analysis and an analytical break-down of the actual components of a decision. To facilitate actual decision-making, it proposes a praxis of five intellectual tasks: goal formulation, trend description, factor analysis, projection of future decisions, and the invention of alternatives. A public order of human dignity is defined as one which approximates the optimum access by all human beings to all things they cherish: power, wealth, enlightenment, skill, well-being, affection, respect, and rectitude. This, in a nutshell, characterizes the contribution the New Haven School has made to the law's academic and policy enterprise. * * *

[T]he New Haven School can be especially empowering for individuals not associated with the state, a class that classical international law all but disenfranchised. In the past, the international lawyer's client was, for the most part, the Prince or, put in more prosaic terms, governments, however they were organized. That is no longer the case. Equipped with an appropriate jurisprudential frame, each and every person can now participate, whether directly or through the mediation of groups, in the processes of decision that affect their lives. To that extent, we all have the potential to function as the Prince or as Austin's "political superior." The constant formation and reformation of interest groups on a planet in which economical, electronic simultaneity permits effective coordination without face-to-face contact means that the possibility of meaningful participation in key functions of international decision is within the reach of more and more people who are not affiliated with governments. But only if they know how.

For all these actors, the New Haven School assembles a set of tools for enhancing the understanding and more effective influencing of these international processes. It is a truism that law is policy, but this is an approach that is policy-oriented in a much broader sense. With respect to particular problems, the School seeks not only to map decision processes, assess the often contradictory trends and the factors conditioning them, predict the range of probable outcomes, and enhance the skills necessary for influencing the decision processes of concern so that preferred outcomes ensue. It also undertakes to improve the performance of decision processes themselves and enhance their capacity to achieve outcomes more consonant with human dignity. This necessarily involves a careful assessment and critique of current processes, institutions and practices.

Now it is clear that, given the characteristics of the international political process, a way of mapping the processes that lawyers try to influence, and which are influencing lawyers, requires a different set of analytical tools. A "conventional" analysis in terms of government organs and of the technical doctrines employed by officials, an effective technique for certain problems, is inappropriate for the study of international decision. Conventional usage must here yield to "functional" analysis, because no dependable relationship exists between formal structures and the facts of authority and control on the global scale. It is far from unusual to discover, for example, that the authority formally provided in a written constitution may be ignored or totally redefined by unwritten practice; there, too, myth system must be distinguished from operational code, the law-in-the-books from the law-in-action. * * *

The comprehensive, analytic framework required must, accordingly, include a conceptual technique for mapping the relevant processes. The New Haven School has adapted, with a number of adjustments, a scheme of cultural anthropology, in which any social process is described systematically in terms of those who engage in it (the participants); the subjective dimensions that animate them (their perspectives); the situations in which they interact; the resources upon which they draw (bases of power); the ways they manipulate those resources (strategies); and the aggregate outcomes of the process of interaction, which are conceived in terms of a comprehensive set of values.

The participants in any decision process include those formally endowed with decision competence, such as executives, legislators and judges, and all those other actors who, though not endowed with formal competence, may nonetheless play important roles in influencing decision outcomes. In international decision, this means examining, in addition to formal international organizations, state officials, non-governmental organizations, pressure groups, interest groups, gangs, and individuals, who act on behalf of other participants and on their own.

By the same token, the inventory will not be of much use if it does not take account of the perspectives of these actors. These perspectives include their specific patterns of identification and disidentification, their matter-of-fact expectations of past and future, and the value demands they project. It is clear that in a complex arena, such as international politics, the perspectives of the various participants actually playing a role in decision often diverge greatly in critical ways.

Situations, as the New Haven School uses the term, refers generally to where decisions are made and the distinctive properties of that "where." Conventional legal analysis generally looks to courts, secondarily examining the work of executive branches and legislatures. The New Haven School adopts a more functional approach in which it focuses on the range of centralized and decentralized settings in which decisions are actually taken, their varying degree of organization and formality, the extent to which they are specialized or not specialized, and the extent to which they are continuous or episodic. We also consider it important to examine the extent to which participants in a particular situation perceive themselves to be in a state of crisis in which critical values are deemed to be at stake.

The resources on which participants draw—their "bases of power"—incorporate both effective power and symbols of authority. The New Haven School considers it appropriate for the jurist to correlate the extent to which control of power is available to support particular formulations that are presented as law.

The ways in which resources (material and symbolic) are manipulated, or the strategies used by different participants, involve the management of resources aimed at optimizing preferred outcomes. Strategic modes are considered along a persuasive-coercive continuum. They include diplomatic, propagandistic, economic, and military techniques in varying ensembles.

The outcomes of interaction are tracked on a continuing basis and in terms of the five previously identified phases or features of a context.

The mapping of social and decisional contexts permits the observer or the person trying to influence decision to orient himself or herself contextually in the relevant processes. It is clear that there can be no single one-size-fits-all map for every problem. Contexts vary enormously. Thus the participants who will be relevant for a problem involving international security will include the major powers, those who can support or work against them, including major antagonists, international organizations or other institutions which may be relevant for some of the decision functions. For example, for a problem involving international investment law in a particular context, the critical participants are likely to be the states concerned, the multinational enterprises involved in a particular investment, civil society, and institutions specialized in the transnational wealth process. The point of emphasis is that a functional approach, using a mapping procedure that is designed to minimize the chances of overlooking pertinent factors and relationships, enables the lawyer and policy-scientist to operate with a realistic sense of the relevant processes. * * *

One component of the most comprehensive process, as of all the lesser community processes, is a process of effective power in the sense that decisions are in fact taken and enforced, by severe deprivations or high indulgences, which are inclusive in their effects. The experience of those who use the jurisprudence of the New Haven School shows that full and realistic description of such effective power processes—in terms that include all important participants, perspectives, arenas, bases of power, strategies, and outcomes—is necessary, both for understanding and influencing.

The New Haven School also provides a way of organizing thought and action with respect to any decision process. The School identifies seven decision functions, each of which is engaged in every decision process. The functions that compose decision processes include intelligence, promotion, prescription, invocation, application, termination, and appraisal. The fact that each function is always in operation does not mean that it is being performed well. Accordingly, the New Haven School offers criteria for appraising the performance of each function, and by bringing each function into clear view, the School provides a nuanced and realistic way to improve decision.

Starting from the premise that law should serve human beings, the New Haven School anchors its policy-oriented search for a world public order of human dignity in the universe of human aspirations, which are expressed empirically in its characterization of eight values, *i.e.*, power, enlightenment, wealth, well-being, skill, affection, respect, and rectitude. The jurisprudence of the School allows for goal-setting beyond what has been achieved in the past, and for intellectual preparation for leadership in the face of ever-new problems in an ever-changing world. * * *

NOTES AND QUESTIONS

1. *A functional approach*. As Professors Reisman, Wiessner and Willard show, NHS adherents sometimes describe the approach as "functional." As

opposed to what exactly? And what makes the New Haven School "functional" in the first place? What exactly is the significance of the word "empirically" in their encapsulation of the NHS as advancing a "world public order of human dignity in the universe of human aspirations, which are expressed empirically in its characterization of eight values, *i.e.*, power, enlightenment, wealth, well-being, skill, affection, respect, and rectitude"? *See generally* Hengameh Saberi, *Yale's Policy Science and International Law: Between Legal Formalism and the Policy Conceptualism*, in F. Hoffmann, & A. Orford (Eds.). OXFORD HANDBOOK OF INTERNATIONAL LEGAL THEORY (2016).

2. *The New Haven School as an improvement over its contemporaries.* Professor Paul Schiff Berman has offered a clear-eyed assessment of the NHS as a useful alternative to its jurisprudential competitors:

> The New Haven School of International Law offered a significant, process-based rejoinder to the realism and positivism that had dominated international relations theory in the United States since the close of World War II. Whereas international relations realists viewed international law as merely a product of state power relations, and positivists dismissed international law entirely because it lacked both sovereign commands and a rule of recognition, scholars of the New Haven School studied law as a social process of authoritative decision-making. Such a study necessarily expanded the state-focused perspective of both the realists and positivists by drawing attention to ongoing interactions among variously situated bureaucratic and institutional actors.

Paul Schiff Berman, *A Pluralist Approach to International Law*, 32 YALE J. INT'L L. 301, 301–02 (2007). From this perspective, why might the rise of the NHS and the rise of international human rights law, as described in *Filártiga*, *supra*, be related?

3. *One final act of synthesis.* Of all the theoretical approaches to international law, described in this chapter, which seems the least inadequate?

INDEX

References are to Pages

A

B

C

D

E

F

G

H

I

J

K

L

Q

R

S

T

U

V

W

Y